W9-AQN-992

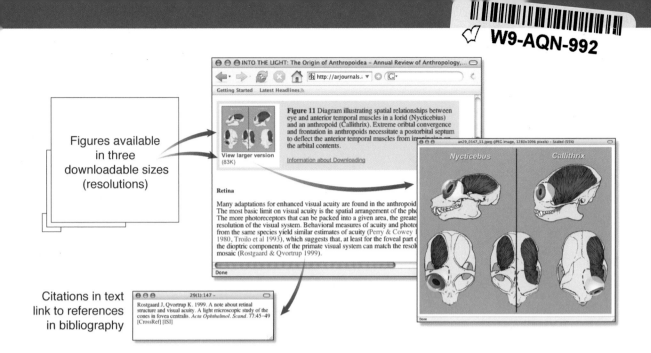

Figures available in three downloadable sizes (resolutions)

Citations in text link to references in bibliography

References in Annual Reviews chapter bibliography link out to sources of cited articles online

Annual Review of
Anthropology

NOV 2006
Received
Ohio Dominican

Editorial Committee (2006)

Cynthia M. Beall, Case Western Reserve University
John R. Bowen, Washington University
Donald Brenneis, University of California, Santa Cruz
William H. Durham, Stanford University
Susan Greenhalgh, University of California, Irvine
Jane Hill, University of Arizona, Tucson
Carla M. Sinopoli, University of Michigan, Ann Arbor
Greg Urban, University of Pennsylvania

Responsible for the Organization of Volume 35
(Editorial Committee, 2004)

Ana Alonso
Jean Comaroff
William H. Durham
Peter T. Ellison
Susan Greenhalgh
Jane Hill
Carla M. Sinopoli
Greg Urban
William Balée (Guest)
Victoria R. Bricker (Guest)
Meredith Dudley (Guest)
James Welch (Guest)

International Correspondents

Nick Enfield
Thomas H. Eriksen
María Teresa Sierra

Production Editor: Jennifer E. Mann
Bibliographic Quality Control: Mary A. Glass
Electronic Content Coordinator: Suzanne K. Moses
Illustration Editor: Douglas Beckner
Subject Indexer: Suzanne Copenhagen

OCT 2007
Received
Ohio Dominican

Annual Review of Anthropology

Volume 35, 2006

William H. Durham, *Editor*
Stanford University

Jane Hill, *Associate Editor*
University of Arizona, Tucson

www.annualreviews.org • science@annualreviews.org • 650-493-4400

Annual Reviews
4139 El Camino Way • P.O. Box 10139 • Palo Alto, California 94303-0139

301.2 A615a v.35 2006

Annual review of
anthropology

Ⱥℝ Annual Reviews
Palo Alto, California, USA

COPYRIGHT © 2006 BY ANNUAL REVIEWS, PALO ALTO, CALIFORNIA, USA. ALL RIGHTS RESERVED. The appearance of the code at the bottom of the first page of an article in this serial indicates the copyright owner's consent that copies of the article may be made for personal or internal use, or for the personal or internal use of specific clients. This consent is given on the condition that the copier pay the stated per-copy fee of $20.00 per article through the Copyright Clearance Center, Inc. (222 Rosewood Drive, Danvers, MA 01923) for copying beyond that permitted by Section 107 or 108 of the U.S. Copyright Law. The per-copy fee of $20.00 per article also applies to the copying, under the stated conditions, of articles published in any *Annual Review* serial before January 1, 1978. Individual readers, and nonprofit libraries acting for them, are permitted to make a single copy of an article without charge for use in research or teaching. This consent does not extend to other kinds of copying, such as copying for general distribution, for advertising or promotional purposes, for creating new collective works, or for resale. For such uses, written permission is required. Write to Permissions Dept., Annual Reviews, 4139 El Camino Way, P.O. Box 10139, Palo Alto, CA 94303-0139 USA.

International Standard Serial Number: 0084-6570
International Standard Book Number: 0-8243-1935-4
Library of Congress Catalog Card Number: 72-821360

All Annual Reviews and publication titles are registered trademarks of Annual Reviews.

⊗ The paper used in this publication meets the minimum requirements of American National Standards for Information Sciences—Permanence of Paper for Printed Library Materials, ANSI Z39.48-1992.

Annual Reviews and the Editors of its publications assume no responsibility for the statements expressed by the contributors to this *Annual Review*.

TYPESET BY TECHBOOKS, FALLS CHURCH, VIRGINIA
PRINTED AND BOUND BY MALLOY INCORPORATED, ANN ARBOR, MICHIGAN

Preface: The Great Theme Experiment

The publication of the volume before you marks the twelfth year that we have included an annual theme section in the *Annual Review of Anthropology (ARA)*. Theme sections are a deliberate effort by the Editorial Committee to solicit a small collection of chapters by different authors related to the same general topic. In this volume, for example, we have assembled seven chapters apiece on anthropological aspects of "Environmental Conservation" (Theme I) and "Food" (Theme II). In each case, the letter of invitation is sent to prospective authors explaining the theme we propose and suggesting a title for the author's related contribution. When authors accept, they are given the names and chapter titles for other contributors to the theme and urged to communicate with one another as warranted to promote synergism and prevent overlap.

When I proposed years ago (in the context of preparations for Vol. 24 in 1995) that the *ARA* experiment with themes, I had two related objectives in mind. First, I wanted to see if themes would provide a venue for covering topics in the *ARA* that seemed just too extensive to be thoughtfully reviewed in a single chapter by a single author or set of coauthors. Border issues, for example, loomed large in those days (not that they have diminished in the meantime), and their various dimensions and complexities (political, social, cultural, linguistic, economic, etc.) seemed to beg for attention by a number of scholars at the same time. Second, I wanted to see if themes would help increase the intellectual exchange and cross talk among the various subfields of anthropology. If we chose themes with adequate breadth, then all or most of the subfields of anthropology would have worthy material for review on a given theme. Including many subfields, then, would enliven our Editorial Committee meetings, challenging members to come up with diverse subfield contributions on a given theme, and the eventual published volume would make it possible, indeed enticing, for scholars to read and think across our own internal borders within anthropology. The Editorial Committee seemed to like the idea and even suggested that enhanced classroom usage of the *ARA* was a third objective that might be achieved through timely and broad-ranging theme sections.

So now, after a dozen years of themes, it is time we asked, how well has the experiment been working? Here follows a list of the themes we have featured from the beginning, together with the number of pertinent chapters published in the hardcopy volume (Table 1). Note that this list contains only those chapters published in the theme year and volume; in some few cases authors requested and were granted deferrals for a theme chapter to appear in a subsequent volume.

Table 1 List of *ARA* themes since 1995

Year (Volume)	Theme I (number of chapters)	Theme II (number of chapters)
1996 (Vol. 25)	Environmental Issues (3)	Childhood (2)
1997 (Vol. 26)	Governmentality (6)	Religion (3)
1998 (Vol. 27)	Demographic Anthropology (3)	Human Genetic Diversity (4)
1999 (Vol. 28)	Millennium (3)	Empire and its Aftermath (2)
2000 (Vol. 29)	Capitalism and Anthropology* (4)	Anthropological Evidence (4)
2001 (Vol. 30)	HIV/AIDS (3)	Diasporas (3)
2002 (Vol. 31)	Childhood (3)	Everyday Life (6)
2003 (Vol. 32)	Urban Worlds (4)	Inequality (2)
2004 (Vol. 33)	The Body as a Public Surface (6)	Technologies of Communication (5)
2005 (Vol. 34)	Race and Racism (5)	Indigenous Peoples (11)
2006 (Vol. 35)	Environmental Conservation (7)	Food (7)

*Theme title shortened for the table from "Capitalism and the Reinvention of Anthropology"

One must refrain from a tendency to overanalyze such small-sample data, especially because the Editorial Committee—which initially aimed to invite 6 chapters per year—did not always solicit an equal number of chapters from topic to topic and from year to year. Still, it is surprising that some topics such as "Gender," "Environmental Issues," and "Inequality" produced so few review chapters by our annual deadlines. In the case of "Childhood," the Committee felt that the first low turnout (1996: 2 chapters) might have been a fluke, and thus tried again (2002) picking up only three chapters. We were all surprised when "Millennium" and "Empire and its Aftermath" came in with only five chapters between them on the eve of the new millennium. Of course, there are many hypotheses to explain the variation—some topics are "hotter" and more ready for review than others are, for example—but we have also become more variable in recent years in the number of our invitations. So it remains difficult to draw firm conclusions.

However, this is an area where our readers can help. In the interest of evaluating *ARA* theme sections for the future, we would dearly love to hear from readers on this topic, er, theme. How could we make the theme sections more useful? Do you find it handy to have them published in print and online in the same year, or do search engine capabilities make that restriction unnecessary? Are there important theme topics that we have been missing? Please send us your comments and suggestions to the email address below, and we will take them up at our next Editorial Committee meeting.

In the meantime, there are two very recent, discussion-worthy aspects of the theme experiment. First, in 2005, as we met to plan the 2007 volume, I was surprised to find that the consensus of the Editorial Committee was to "take a year off" from themes. There was a sense that themes had been so successful, with 5 or more chapters per theme since 2004, that we were accumulating many non-theme topics in the various subfields that needed to be reviewed. More than surprised, I was actually a bit downcast. Just when authors seemed to be voting one way with their pens (or keyboards, as the case may be), the Committee was voting the other. But I waited a year to see what would happen, and I am glad I did. The Committee came roaring back to our most recent meeting (for planning the 2008 volume) with enough suggestions to fill the next volume completely with two nicely related themes: "Evolution in Anthropology" and "Reproduction." So now I can say in all honesty that the theme experiment remains in full swing. Do let us hear from you as we continue the experiment!

As Volume 35 heads to press, it gives me another opportunity to thank Jennifer Mann for her uncommon efficiency and good cheer as Production Editor. Our very special thanks and well wishes also go to Jane Hill who, with this volume, rotates off her position as Associate Editor. For two different stints during my years as Editor, Jane has served the Board with the special diligence and insight of a scholar who cares deeply about the whole discipline of anthropology. The full Committee joins me in thanks to Jane for her many thoughtful contributions to, and her steadfast support of, the *ARA*.

William H. Durham
Editor
eb.whd@stanford.edu

A|R

Annual Review of
Anthropology

Volume 35, 2006

Contents

Evolution of the Size and Functional Areas of the Human Brain

Linguistics and Communicative Practices

Mayan Historical Linguistics and Epigraphy: A New Synthesis

Environmental Discourses

Old Wine, New Ethnographic Lexicography

International Anthropology and Regional Studies

The Ethnography of Finland

Sociocultural Anthropology

The Anthropology of Money

Food and Globalization

The Research Program of Historical Ecology

Anthropology and International Law

Institutional Failure in Resource Management

Indigenous People and Environmental Politics

Parks and Peoples: The Social Impact of Protected Areas

Sovereignty Revisited

Local Knowledge and Memory in Biodiversity Conservation

Theme 1: Environmental Conservation

Theme 2: Food

Indexes

Errata

An online log of corrections to *Annual Review of Anthropology* chapters (if any, 1997 to
the present) may be found at http://anthro.annualreviews.org/errata.shtml

Related Articles

From the *Annual Review of Nutrition*, Volume 26 (2006)

From the *Annual Review of Political Science*, Volume 9 (2006)

From the *Annual Review of Psychology*, Volume 57 (2006)

From the *Annual Review of Sociology*, Volume 32 (2006)

Annual Reviews is a nonprofit scientific publisher established to promote the advancement of the sciences. Beginning in 1932 with the *Annual Review of Biochemistry*, the Company has pursued as its principal function the publication of high-quality, reasonably priced *Annual Review* volumes. The volumes are organized by Editors and Editorial Committees who invite qualified authors to contribute critical articles reviewing significant developments within each major discipline. The Editor-in-Chief invites those interested in serving as future Editorial Committee members to communicate directly with him. Annual Reviews is administered by a Board of Directors, whose members serve without compensation.

2006 Board of Directors, Annual Reviews

Richard N. Zare, *Chairman of Annual Reviews, Marguerite Blake Wilbur Professor of Chemistry, Stanford University*

John I. Brauman, *J.G. Jackson–C.J. Wood Professor of Chemistry, Stanford University*

Peter F. Carpenter, *Founder, Mission and Values Institute, Atherton, California*

Sandra M. Faber, *Professor of Astronomy and Astronomer at Lick Observatory, University of California at Santa Cruz*

Susan T. Fiske, *Professor of Psychology, Princeton University*

Eugene Garfield, *Publisher,* The Scientist

Samuel Gubins, *President and Editor-in-Chief, Annual Reviews*

Steven E. Hyman, *Provost, Harvard University*

Daniel E. Koshland Jr., *Professor of Biochemistry, University of California at Berkeley*

Joshua Lederberg, *University Professor, The Rockefeller University*

Sharon R. Long, *Professor of Biological Sciences, Stanford University*

J. Boyce Nute, *Palo Alto, California*

Michael E. Peskin, *Professor of Theoretical Physics, Stanford Linear Accelerator Center*

Harriet A. Zuckerman, *Vice President, The Andrew W. Mellon Foundation*

Management of Annual Reviews

Samuel Gubins, President and Editor-in-Chief
Richard L. Burke, Director for Production
Paul J. Calvi Jr., Director of Information Technology
Steven J. Castro, Chief Financial Officer and Director of Marketing & Sales
Jeanne M. Kunz, Human Resources Manager and Secretary to the Board

Annual Reviews of

Anthropology	Fluid Mechanics	Pharmacology and Toxicology
Astronomy and Astrophysics	Genetics	Physical Chemistry
Biochemistry	Genomics and Human Genetics	Physiology
Biomedical Engineering	Immunology	Phytopathology
Biophysics and Biomolecular Structure	Law and Social Science	Plant Biology
	Materials Research	Political Science
Cell and Developmental Biology	Medicine	Psychology
Clinical Psychology	Microbiology	Public Health
Earth and Planetary Sciences	Neuroscience	Sociology
Ecology, Evolution, and Systematics	Nuclear and Particle Science	
	Nutrition	SPECIAL PUBLICATIONS
Entomology	Pathology: Mechanisms of Disease	Excitement and Fascination of Science, Vols. 1, 2, 3, and 4
Environment and Resources		

Kent V. Flannery

On the Resilience of Anthropological Archaeology

Kent V. Flannery

Museum of Anthropology, University of Michigan, Ann Arbor, Michigan 48109-1079

Annu. Rev. Anthropol. 2006. 35:1–13

The *Annual Review of Anthropology* is online at anthro.annualreviews.org

This article's doi: 10.1146/annurev.anthro.35.081705.123304

Copyright © 2006 by Annual Reviews. All rights reserved

0084-6570/06/1021-0001$20.00

Key Words

New Archaeology, scientific archaeology, postmodern archaeology, fruity humanistic drivel

Abstract

I have now lived through eras when anthropological archaeology was (*a*) mainly culture history; (*b*) part of four-field anthropology; (*c*) hypothetico-deductive science; (*d*) under attack from postmodernism, postcolonialism, and feminism; and (*e*) saved from extinction by its own resilience. In this never-before-published interview, I reveal its likely future direction. (Drum roll, please.)

When the *Annual Review* asked me to contribute this retrospective, I knew it would be hard to come up with something new. So I've submitted an abridged version of the interview I once gave a famous journalist, who I'll simply call "Barbara W." The interview occurred as a result of our both having been stranded for hours in the departure lounge at Chicago's O'Hare airport. (Initially flattered by her having chosen me The Most Intriguing Person in the Lounge, I later realized that we were the only two people there.) Because I kept no notes, my version of the interview will have to be considered "novelized."

Barbara and I talked about archaeology's place in traditional four-field anthropology; about the era, prior to 1960, when archaeology was mostly culture history; about the tumultuous rise of the New Archaeology; about the efforts to derail hypothetico-deductive archaeology during the 1980s; and finally, about the rejuvenation of scientific archaeology and the decline of postmodernism.

Aside from these five main discussion topics, we touched on some of my personal anecdotes as well.

BW: Let's begin with your choice of career. I notice that when the Walter Jeffords estate was auctioned at Sotheby's recently, several of your father's paintings were included. Did you ever consider becoming an artist?

KVF: Not after one of his clients bent down, shook my tiny hand, and whispered, "Don't go into art, my boy, because you'll always be compared to your father."

BW: How did you become interested in archaeology?

KVF: Through an accident, one whose lasting effect I realized only years later. Whenever my mother left our farm to buy groceries, she dumped me in my father's studio. He was a patient man, but having a six-year-old poking into his Burnt Sienna and Raw Umber had to be annoying. One day he hit upon a solution. He asked me, "Would you like to be a cave man for a while?" and I said, "Sure."

Halfway up the wall of his studio was a small loft where he stored drying canvases and gesso panels. He lifted me up to the loft with a sketch pad, thumbtacks, and a set of pastels. Recalling his courses at the Chicago Art Institute, he explained, "Stone Age men covered the walls of their caves with paintings of woolly mammoths, red deer, and hunters with bows and arrows." Doing Lascaux-style drawings for the wall of the loft became my quality time with him.

It was only decades later, as a graduate student working in Iran, that I realized the full impact of that time. Frank Hole and I were testing a small cave in the Sar-i-Pul Valley. The deposits were shallow and the flint tools were Zagros Mousterian. We had backfilled, but for some reason I felt reluctant to leave the site. Suddenly, in a moment of epiphany, I realized that the cave was similar in size to the loft in my father's studio and that I was subconsciously waiting for him to lift me back down to the floor. My career choice made sense once I understood that my father had made cave men the most interesting friends a boy could have.

BW: Was that his main influence on your career?

KVF: Not at all. I also watched him do empirical research before every painting. I saw him walk around the subject, take notes and photographs, and make preliminary sketches. I watched him begin the picture with an egg-tempera layout in white, black, and gray, adding the oil colors only after the tempera had dried. "If you don't start with a good design," he said, "all the color in the world won't save it." It's just as true in archaeological research.

And there is one more thing: He used to sneak into exhibits of his own paintings without wearing a name tag, eavesdropping on the crowd. He was greatly amused by how inaccurate some critics' versions could be of "what the artist was trying to communicate." "If they can't even understand an artist from their own country," my father said, "what hope do they have of understanding artists from other countries?" Believe me, I remember that when I read what some of my colleagues write about Precolumbian art.

BW: How did you come to choose the University of Chicago?

KVF: I did not. I had no say in the matter. One day in the spring of my sophomore year of high school, my parents announced that I would soon be taking the entrance exam for Chicago. I knew that my father was a fan of their former chancellor, Robert Maynard Hutchins. What I didn't know was that Hutchins had established an early-entrant program for high school sophomores and juniors.

Seeing how much it meant to my parents, I took the exam, passed, and later that year found myself in Burton-Judson Courts, the Gothic fortress of a dormitory on 60th Street. There, we were all given placement tests. I tested out of four courses, enabling me to graduate in three years. It all happened much too fast.

BW: Did you feel that your parents were pushing you too hard?

KVF: It was not until years after my father's death that I found out why. My mother finally explained that Chicago had been his first choice for college, but they had turned him down. He vowed at that time that if he ever had a child, he would do whatever it took to get him or her into Chicago.

BW: It must have been a difficult adjustment for a teenager.

KVF: The culture change was greater than the academic stress. I had gone from a farm on the Susquehanna River to densely urban Chicago. I had gone from a private boarding school, filled with the sons of Republican businessmen, to a dorm filled with descendants of the International Workers of the World. I had grown up on country ham cured in my family's own smokehouse; my roommate arrived from the Bronx with a jar of his Mom's homemade gefilte fish.

One night I watched a candlelight procession make its way across the darkened Midway Plaisance. As the robed marchers neared us, I asked an older student the reason for the procession. His look told me that I still had lots to learn. "It's Trotsky's birthday, dickhead," he explained.

BW: What sustained you through those years?

KVF: My classmates. Hundreds of early entrants were in the same boat. Three of them went on to be archaeologists: Les Freeman at Chicago, Jim Brown at Northwestern, and Jim Schoenwetter at Arizona State. And there was this kid from Rahway, New Jersey, named Carl Sagan, who wanted to be an astronomer (**Figure 1**).

BW: I understand that you actually had food fights with Sagan in the Burton-Judson cafeteria.

KVF: Already at 16, Carl had mastered the skills necessary to land an object on the moon. Using a soup spoon and an overturned salt shaker as a catapult, he could deliver a soybean veggie cutlet into anyone's lap at any table.

BW: What did you do after graduation?

KVF: Thanks to my inspiring high-school biology teacher, I was more interested in evolution than anything else. I went into zoology, which was one of Chicago's strongest graduate programs. They had ecologists such as W.C. Allee, population biologists such as Thomas Park, systematists such as Hewson Swift, and geneticists such as Sewall Wright. I was taken on fabulous field trips by my advisor, Alfred E. Emerson, the expert on social insects before there was an E.O. Wilson.

BW: How did you wind up in anthropology?

KVF: I went to Mexico to collect Salticid spiders for a Master's thesis in zoology. While there, I got a chance to excavate the ruins of Yagul, Oaxaca, with the University of the Americas. John Paddock, the professor leading the dig, thought there might be a "big unfilled niche" for an archaeologist with a background in zoology: I could identify animal bones and reconstruct paleoenvironments.

On my return to Chicago, I started taking human paleontology courses with F. Clark Howell, and he recommended me to

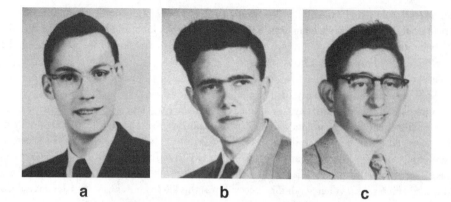

Figure 1

These five teenagers survived the leap from high-school sophomore to early entrant at the University of Chicago. For extra credit, identify the one who did not become an archaeologist. *a*, Leslie G. Freeman. *b*, James A. Brown. *c*, James Schoenwetter. *d*, Carl Sagan. *e*, Kent V. Flannery.

Robert Braidwood, who was working on early plant and animal domestication. I wound up doing an anthropological Master's thesis on how to distinguish wild and domestic pigs.

BW: What was Chicago's anthropology department like in those days?

KVF: Every bit as elite as the zoology program. In addition to Braidwood and Howell, there were Robert McC. Adams, Fred Eggan, McKim Marriott, Milton Singer, Sol Tax, Manning Nash, Lloyd Fallers, David Schneider, Norman McQuown, and a host of other luminaries.

BW: What was the atmosphere like for students?

KVF: There was no grade inflation, no coddling, and no nurturing. They threw you into the deep end of the pool without a life jacket,

and you either learned to swim or drowned. I mentioned this to one of my former professors years later, and he smiled in agreement. "Students," he said, "were the flesh-colored stuff between the cleats of our hobnailed boots." It was supposed to make you tough and self-reliant.

BW: Did you adopt that approach for your students at Michigan?

KVF: No. Three archaeologists on the Michigan faculty—Bob Whallon, Henry Wright, and I—went through the Chicago system, and we all agreed to do the opposite at Michigan. We put our students in the shallow end of the pool and give them immediate CPR if they stumble.

BW: The so-called New Archaeology arose at Chicago. Tell me a little about that.

KVF: In the spring of 1961, Lew Binford interviewed for a position at Chicago. His job talk was a mesmerizing account of prehistoric strategies in piedmont and tidewater Virginia. He was given a three-year contract, at the end of which he was "terminated with prejudice."

BW: Were they turbulent years?

KVF: Binford was a charismatic southerner who had mastered the fire-and-brimstone style of a revival meeting. He opened his first class by announcing, "My name is Lewis R. Binford, and the name of this course is Revelations!" By the end of that class, half the students were speaking in tongues.

Then Chicago made the mistake of teaming Binford with Braidwood in a course on world prehistory. It was Counter Culture vs. the Establishment. At one point Braidwood, introducing the Ubaid period in Mesopotamia, opined that "this was the first moment in the Near East when Established Village Farming so freed man from the eternal food quest that he had leisure time to elaborate his culture." Binford leapt to his feet, his voice an octave higher in protest, and replied, "Dr. Braidwood, studies show that no one on Earth had more leisure time than precontact hunters and gatherers. And most of them just spent it subincising themselves, whirling churingas, and engaging in bizarre sex practices." Had there been a mosh pit available, Binford would have been carried around on the adoring students' shoulders.

The Revolution was underway. The Establishment would be overthrown. Old-fashioned culture history would be replaced by hypothetico-deductive archaeology, with rigorous testing of hypotheses, sampling techniques, measures of significance, and other approaches seductive to people under the age of 30.

Every revolution has its nerve center, its Left Bank café where the conspirators meet. The nerve center for the fledgling New Archaeology was Stuart Struever's kitchen in the Beechwood Apartments, 1223 E. 57th, between Woodlawn and Kimbark (**Figure 2**). There, a lively roundtable was hosted by Struever, Binford's sometime teaching fellow, and his wife Alice, whose mugs of "deadly Java" could generate hypotheses all by themselves. Binford dropped by after dinner to find students like Howard Winters, Bill Longacre, Jim Hill, Jim Brown, Les Freeman, and myself already overcaffeinated.

My presence at this ongoing seminar was serendipitous: I lived in a one-room apartment on the third floor of the Beechwood, a floor to which the building's heat did not ascend. The warmest place in my room was in the center of my fist as I broke the ice on my soup. Coming down to Struever's kitchen thawed me out, and the arguments were so lively that I could not tear myself away. It's a shame the Beechwood went condo before we could put a bronze plaque on the kitchen wall.

In those days, Chicago advocated a four-field anthropology, with ethnology, linguistics, archaeology, and biological anthropology as equal partners. We were never convinced, however, that the ethnologists felt they needed us the way we needed them. Most ethnology students believed E. Adamson Hoebel's famous observation that "archaeology is forever doomed to be the lesser part of anthropology." We, on the other hand, felt that the only conceivable purpose for ethnology was to provide archaeologists with descriptions of living cultures, helping them to interpret the evidence of the past.

I was friends with most of the ethnology students—even the teaching fellow for Sol Tax's History of Anthropology course, who wrote on my term paper, "You may want to consider an alternative career." I did not know at the time, of course, that some of the ethnology students were predestined to contribute to the postmodernist, postcolonialist, and feminist critiques of the 1980s. A few of the brightest stand out in my memory. There was Herman Newtick, with whom I spent many evenings at Jimmy's Tavern on 55th Street. And of course, Eileen Farr. Since her marriage to a fellow Hyde Park radical, her colleagues know her better as Eileen Farr-Tudaleft.

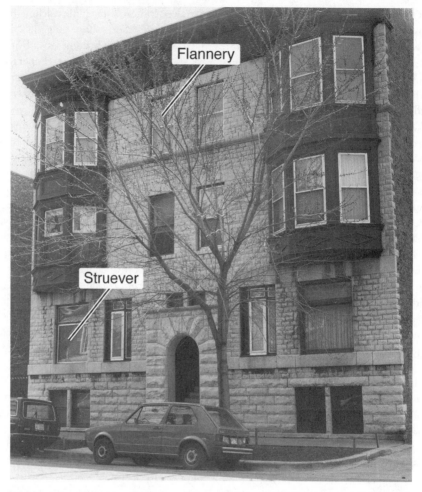

Figure 2

The Beechwood Apartments on 57th Street in Hyde Park, Chicago. In a first-floor kitchen of this building, Lewis R. Binford and his students met from 1961 to 1964 to foment the New Archaeology (photo courtesy of James Phillips).

Herman, like many of my classmates, was a Marxist. His deepest conviction was that Western Civilization was the world's most loathsome evil, and he had decided to fight it by refusing to bathe. Eileen was a Maoist and regarded Marxists like Herman to be pathetic revisionists. Every civil rights movement received her passionate support. Eileen strode proudly through Hyde Park with her T-shirt emblazoned in capital letters: "THERE'S NO EXCUSE FOR VIOLENCE AGAINST WOMEN" (and below

it, in fine print, "Against men, that's a different story").

BW: How did archaeology students in those days prepare themselves to run their own big interdisciplinary projects?

KVF: By doing fieldwork on imaginative projects run by senior role models. To this day, I marvel at the opportunities I was given between 1960 and 1964. I was continuously in the field, usually on projects related to the origins of agriculture and village life, and I worked with some real heavyweights.

It began with six months in Iran under Braidwood, digging sites called Sarab and Asiab. That summer I dug in South Dakota with Warren Caldwell and Charlie McNutt. The next summer found me digging Maya sites in Chiapas with Bob Adams. He recommended me to Michael Coe, with whom I dug Salinas La Blanca on the Guatemalan coast. Coe, in turn, recommended me to Scotty MacNeish, who was working on the origins of agriculture in Mexico's Tehuacán Valley. From there I went back to Iran to dig Ali Kosh with Frank Hole and Jim Neely. The reason most of these people hired me was because of my background in zoology and ecology. They needed someone to create comparative skeletal collections of modern animals, use them to identify ancient fauna, and reconstruct past environments.

BW: What should one do when he has such great opportunities?

KVF: Observe one or two qualities of each project director and emulate them. From Braidwood I learned that you should assemble the best interdisciplinary staff you can. From MacNeish I learned how to set goals and pursue them relentlessly. From Hole I learned efficiency: how to set deadlines and meet them. From Coe I learned how to define pottery types and use them to establish a regional chronology. From Caldwell and McNutt I learned how to find postmolds and ephemeral earthen floors. From Adams I learned to think big and to never, ever sweat the small stuff.

I wrote a thesis and started looking for a job. Caldwell recommended me for a post with the Nebraska State Historical Society, but its director, Marvin F. "Gus" Kivett, decided that I had "a limited future in archaeology." Several universities felt that I was "just a faunal analyst," not the "generalist" they were looking for.

Then came a ray of sunshine. A curatorship in Mesoamerican archaeology opened up at the Smithsonian, and Coe's and MacNeish's letters convinced Clifford Evans to give me a try. Evans made it clear what was expected of me: "Start a research project in Mexico, boy, and the sooner the better."

Building on what I already knew, I headed off to Oaxaca, looking for a dry cave and a couple of early villages. I knew I would be working with plants and animals, pollen samples, nets, baskets, and chipped stone tools. The last thing I expected was that my horizon would one day be expanded to include religion, iconography, Precolumbian writing, and the rise of the state. Nor could I have anticipated that within 20 years, the whole notion of scientific archaeology would be attacked as "decadent colonialism."

I loved the Smithsonian, but in 1967 James B. Griffin lured me to Michigan with the promise of letting me train the next generation of archaeologists. For the third time in my life I was surrounded by stimulating professors, this time with names like Leslie White, Marshall Sahlins, Eric Wolf, Elman Service, Mervyn Meggitt, Robbins Burling, and new arrivals like Roy Rappaport, Ray Kelly, Conrad Kottak, and Aram Yengoyan.

BW: Exactly when did you team up with Joyce Marcus?

KVF: By the 1970s, my Michigan excavation team was creeping up on the transition from chiefdom to state in Oaxaca. Meanwhile, a survey team, made up of colleagues from Purdue, Georgia, Wisconsin, and McMaster, was collecting complementary data on the early Zapotec state. A third body of evidence, however, lay fallow: hundreds of stone monuments and texts in Zapotec hieroglyphs, whose study had not progressed much since the time of Alfonso Caso. Maya inscriptions had begun to yield their secrets by 1972; surely the Zapotec texts could too.

Michael Coe told me of a young epigrapher at Harvard who was "doing unprecedented things" with Maya glyphs; she was "the first student Tatiana Proskouriakoff had ever volunteered to work with." Could she be persuaded to look at Zapotec texts? I got my answer when Stephen Williams invited me to speak to his class at Harvard.

The students from Williams' class filed past me before dinner at the Harvard Faculty Club. As we shook hands, one young woman after another described her thesis topic and joked about her past as a field hockey player for some girls' prep school in New England. Suddenly I came face to face with my epigrapher.

"I'm guessing that you *didn't* play field hockey in New England," I observed.

"Right," she said. "I'm Joyce Marcus, and I played beach volleyball in California. We didn't play in those little plaid skirts, either. We played in bikinis."

Suddenly everyone else in the Harvard Faculty Club had become invisible.

Joyce came to Oaxaca in 1972, and by 1973 she had already assigned the Zapotec texts to three eras: a period of militarism and conquest, bracketing state formation; a period of diplomacy, as the Zapotec achieved détente with Teotihuacan; and a phase of preoccupation with noble genealogies, as the early state broke up into balkanized principalities. Soon Joyce had teased out word order, grammar, verbs, ordinal numbers, puns, two calendars, and a series of place glyphs for territories claimed. She did it during her time off between finding postmolds (as she had done in Nevada for Robert Heizer) and excavating masonry buildings (as she had done in the Maya lowlands).

There are times in your life when you realize that you are a jigsaw puzzle with one big piece missing, and someone else is the missing piece. Joyce came from a very different academic tradition, bringing with her a background in cosmology, ideology, religion, iconography, and political anthropology, which complemented my training in biology, ecology, and evolution. When you combine them all, you get a more holistic anthropological archaeology. And so in the spring of 1973, with catering provided by Tippy's Taco House near Dumbarton Oaks, we combined them permanently. There is, after all, no better advice than that given to Nausicaa by Odysseus centuries ago, namely that

there is nothing mightier or nobler than when two people who see eye to eye keep house as man and wife, confounding their enemies and delighting their friends. (The Odyssey, Book VI, lines 182–85 in the original Greek; see Tebben 1994)

BW: I'm guessing that this was a career turning point for both of you.

KVF: Yes. It allowed us to generate a more holistic model of the past, one previewed in our coauthored essay "Formative Oaxaca and the Zapotec cosmos" (Flannery & Marcus 1976). By then it was clear to us that even as basic a subsistence activity as agricultural water use could not be explained with the usual ecological models. The Zapotec understanding of where water came from did not match that of agronomists. With ancestors acting as intermediaries, an offering of one's own blood could induce Lightning to split the clouds and bring rain; only after the water reached Earth could the indigenous engineering of wells and canals take place.

Ecological archaeologists had always considered hydroagriculture to be the infrastructure that supported the cognitive superstructure of the Zapotec. They cared about the canals and the carbonized corncobs, but not about the bloodletting tools, the sacrificed quail, and the temples oriented to the sun's path at equinox. That was for humanists to speculate on. But when we combined native cosmology and ritual with a Western understanding of soil and water, it became possible to provide a single model that explained both. It even raised the possibility that the real infrastructure might lie in the Zapotec mind.

We met real resistance from most cultural ecologists on this idea. "Fruity humanistic drivel" was a typical comment. But we persisted, and eventually other archaeologists joined us. (Unfortunately, some archaeologists began to ignore environment and subsistence altogether, and as a result, a few really did produce fruity humanistic drivel. But that's another story.)

BW: You were trying to do holistic anthropological archaeology, basing your interpretations on what was known of living societies and establishing a kind of dialogue between the archaeological data and the ethnographic record. It must have struck you as strange when ethnologists started saying, "Oh, stop reading those classic ethnographies. They were written by people who were tools of a colonial power."

KVF: Yes, especially since our archaeological data so often reinforce the models advanced by the best ethnologists. For example, our discovery that the first segmentary societies in Oaxaca built defensive palisades confirms Kelly's (2000) model for the origins of war. Our data on the subsequent emergence of hereditary rank in those same societies resonate with Leach's (1954) and Friedman's (1979) descriptions of the same phenomenon in Southeast Asia. Still later in the Oaxaca sequence, we have evidence for warring chiefdoms whose behavior matches ethnohistorically documented societies in Colombia (Carneiro 1991) and New Zealand (Buck 1949). Additionally, the Oaxaca data show that the Zapotec state formed in the context of rival chiefdoms, when one of those societies gained advantage over its rivals and reduced them to provinces in a larger polity. This is very much the way Cohen (1978) sees it happening, and it is clearly similar to the way historically documented states formed among the Zulu, Ashanti, Hunza, and Hawaiians (Flannery 1999).

In other words, we felt we were using anthropological archaeology to create a dialogue among ethnologists, ethnohistorians, and archaeologists. We did not anticipate that it would be the ethnologists who dropped out first.

BW: Did you think that postmodernism was a new direction or only a phase through which anthropology was passing?

KVF: Definitely the latter. Anthropology tends to pass through phases that last about 20 years (Ortner 1984). And as for "postprocessualism"—the archaeological version of postmodernism—I expected it to be even less enduring. After all, the difference between anthropological archaeology and postprocessual archaeology is like the difference between reality and "reality TV."

BW: When did the pendulum begin to swing away from postmodernism?

KVF: For social anthropology, there were plenty of indications during the 1990s: Windschuttle's (1996) *The Killing of History*, Kuznar's (1997) *Reclaiming a Scientific Anthropology*, and Lewis's (1998) "The misrepresentation of anthropology and its consequences."

For archaeology, one of the most thoughtful critiques was Bintliff's (1993) paper, "Why Indiana Jones is Smarter than the Postprocessualists." His title refers to a moment in the movie *Indiana Jones and the Last Crusade* when Harrison Ford says, "Archaeology is about facts; if you want Truth, go next door to the philosophy department." Bintliff feels that "processual versus postprocessual" is just one more stage in the centuries-old debate between positivism and idealism. He reveals that postprocessualism's influence is already

> waning in Britain, linked to the decline of its parent Post-Modernism. Both lost credibility through attempting to dominate discourse, and their negative implications for human rights. (Bintliff 1993, p. 91)

In the case of postprocessualism, of course, there was another reason it drew fire: its naïve attempt to adopt postmodern buzzwords like "identity," "memory," and "legitimacy" and transfer them wholesale to dirt archaeology. It is one thing to present evidence for those phenomena when you have living informants or really good written documents. It is quite another thing to claim that you've recovered evidence for them while digging a Natufian cave terrace or an Early Woodland midden. You can only proclaim such "insights" a couple of times before your colleagues start asking what mesh size of screen you need to recover "memory."

BW: Wasn't there also an anti-Western, antiscience undercurrent to some critiques of anthropology and scientific archaeology?

KV: There was indeed. Windschuttle (1996) attributes at least some of it to the fall of the Berlin Wall, which necessitated a change in anti-Western rhetoric.

BW: Was that the case with your friend Herman Newtick?

KVF: Actually, Herman went into paradigm shock. As Windschuttle (1996, p. 181) puts it, "not only had communism been consigned to the dustbin of history but with it had gone the prospect of replacing capitalism with any kind of revolutionary regime based on socialism." But then Herman discovered Foucault and Bourdieu and Giddens and realized that he still had a reason to hate the West. Suddenly all Western science, including anthropology, could be seen as a plot to create an "asymmetry of power" vis-à-vis native peoples.

As a student, Herman had embraced social evolutionism because it reminded him of the Marxist stages of Primitive Herd-Matriarchy-Patriarchy, and so on. Now, alas, to be an evolutionist meant that you might be someone who considered inequality and exploitation to be the natural state of affairs in human society. And even if that turned out to be part of our natural state, it would not be politically correct to say so. People could be subjected to witch hunts by the American Anthropological Association (AAA) for expressing ideas like that.

Herman burned every ethnography in his library that had been written in the era of colonialism. "We shouldn't do any new ethnographies," he told me. "Our duty is to deconstruct the old." Herman also felt that no term should ever be applied to a society if it implied a status below that of a United Nations–recognized nation. Hunting-gathering bands were to be called "agriculturally challenged societies." Chiefdoms were simply "bureaucratically challenged states." Herman referred frequently to "the Cro-Magnon Nation," not wanting to hurt their feelings.

"I cannot believe," he told me, "that you continue to use Western, hypothetico-deductive, logical-positivist science to study Neolithic villages. You need polyvocality. You need to hear the voices of the Neolithic villagers, instead of simply pigeonholing them."

"I think I hear their voices," I replied. "They're telling me that you're about two fries short of a Happy Meal."

BW: But wasn't Herman's rejection of Western science typical of the "social science wars" described by Hochschild (2004)?

KVF: Yes. And it continued until he discovered one day that he had cancer.

Did he go to a non-Western healer? A Huichol shaman, a New Age priestess, or an expert in healing with crystals? No, he headed right for Cedars-Sinai and had radiation treatments followed by chemotherapy.

"I thought that you felt Western science was a fraud, an 'asymmetry of power' to be soundly rejected," I reminded him.

"Hey," he said. "This is my health we're talking about."

"So Western science is okay for your health, but not for your profession?"

"That's right," said Herman. "For my health I want something whose reliability I can trust, because it's been subjected to years of objective research, tested by multiple investigators, and based on an underlying universal theory that has survived repeated attempts to falsify it."

"And for your profession?"

"For my profession," he explained, "I want something politically correct, that admits to no universal regularities in human culture, and is so personal, intuitive, interpretive, and humanistic that it cannot be tested, weighed, counted, measured, or compared with anything else."

"Like the idea that illness exists only in the mind of the patient, and that no one from another ethnic group could even imagine, let alone cure, that patient's malady?"

"Exactly."

"Were you aware," I asked him, "that your radiologist was Vietnamese?"

That was the last time I saw Herman. He's cured, but now he's suing Cedars-Sinai for testing a new type of chemotherapy on him, in violation of the AAA's Human Subjects Guidelines.

I still send Herman books from time to time, such as Harris's (1999) *Theories of Culture in Postmodern Times*. But that is just to tease him. Herman's basically a good guy; he just got deconstructed by some French philosophers.

BW: Surely not all your ethnographic colleagues were as deeply affected as Herman by the collapse of world socialism.

KVF: One who remained singularly unaffected was my friend Eileen Farr-Tudaleft. It did not matter that Western capitalism had survived; there were fellow anthropologists who needed punishing even more. Her list of unacceptable research was very long. Anyone who considered the smallest percentage of human behavior to have a genetic basis was "racist." Anyone who drew blood samples from subjects was "engaged in genocide." Anyone who asked informants a question, however innocent, that they didn't want to answer "should be censured by the Ethics Committee."

Eventually, Eileen concluded that she had been put on this earth to free Third World peoples from undemocratic governments. It was not enough to study a village in Brunei; you had to bring down the Sultan. It was not enough to study poverty in Somalia; you had to depose at least one warlord.

Joyce and I bought Eileen dinner and drove her to the airport on the night she left for the Sudan. She was as happy and excited as I had ever seen her. After months of negotiation, she had received permission to study a community filled with the most downtrodden ethnic minorities in the region. "I'm going in barefoot," she said, "I'm going to be an 'engaged anthropologist.'"

I never found out how much actual ethnographic data Eileen was able to collect. Three months later, however, I did learn from CNN

that she had succeeded in inciting a peasant uprising that claimed 30,000 lives.

BW: I'm guessing that some of her favorite causes lost support during her absence.

KVF: Yes. And by the year 2000, a lot of serious, empirically grounded archeologists were getting tired of seeing fairly limited, sometimes even mediocre, field data "enhanced" by the addition of postmodern phrases. We had seen half a dozen spindle whorls used as evidence that Prehispanic women were "resisting male domination." We had seen a mute, 600-year-old skeleton described as "biologically a robust male, but gender female." We had even heard archaeologists claim to have tapped into the "memory" of villagers who had been dead for 8000 years. Forgive my skepticism.

"I don't know where all this jargon has gotten us," said one of my most recalcitrant colleagues, a "hardwired behaviorist" named Dieter Ministic. "For the postmodernists, nobody 'achieves' or 'inherits' status any more; they just 'negotiate' it. ('What'll you take to let me be king next year?' 'Make me an offer.') And another of their favorite terms is 'power relations.' Speaking of which, didn't 'power' used to be the ability to force other people to do something they did not want to do? Yesterday I heard one colleague say that she had been 'empowered' by taking a course in Pilates. I told her, 'Good, then you'll have no trouble forcing North Korea to give up its nuclear weapons.'"

"Finish your beer, Dieter," I told him. "The world has passed you by."

"Just once," he said, "I'd like to see somebody say, right in the *American Anthropologist*, 'Enough already. We're tired of just spinning our wheels. We want to get back to empirical research.'"

"It'll never happen," I assured him.

But I was wrong. One day in 2004 I opened the *Anthropologist*, and a group of five authors had said just that. After acknowledging the problems identified by postmodernist, postcolonialist, and feminist critiques over the previous 20 years, Bashkow et al. (2004) decided that "work in the wake of these critiques has had no more success in 'solving' such problems than the theoretical traditions it seeks to supplant." They went on to say that

> [m]any, we think, have been too quick to reject, in wholesale fashion, the anthropological past—too indiscriminate in their characterization of all anthropological epistemologies as positivistic, all anthropological politics as complicit in imperialism. (p. 433)

For these statements to appear in the flagship journal of what had been, for at least 20 years, the most politicized and antiscientific organization in the social sciences meant that another sea change could be in the works. Perhaps somewhere—in a 2004 version of Struever's kitchen—a new group of anthropological archaeologists was telling each other that generalizing archaeology, committed to empirical data and aimed at discovering regularities in prehistoric behavior, was resilient enough to survive any critique. It even seemed likely that the archaeology of the future would involve science more deeply, reaching down to the molecular level through phytoliths, bone chemistry, isotopic analysis, and DNA (Jones 2001).

BW: Have you told this to your students?

KVF: I long ago advised them not to jump on the postmodern bandwagon. Science, Barbara, is an unstoppable express train. Postmodernism was just an idealistic siding that led nowhere. Most archaeologists believe that the world's fascinating past will only surrender its secrets to research that is as objective as we can make it. You certainly can't get at them through political correctness. We are tired of hearing—to borrow a phrase from Tooby & Cosmides (1992)—that we are all "racist, sexist, or crazy" unless we distort the data of prehistory to fit someone's political agenda.

BW: Since I think I just heard my flight announced at last, I'll ask you my standard final question: If you could be a tree, what kind would you be?

KVF: A bristlecone pine.

BW: What a strange choice.

KVF: Not at all. Bristlecones are not the handsomest pines—they're actually kind of gnarly—but some live more than 4000 years, which means that they witness more sociocultural change than any other tree. And even after they die, they are useful: Their thousands of rings can be used to dendrocalibrate radiocarbon dates.

BW: And what would you like on your tombstone?

KVF: That's easy: "He hated to leave while the party was still going on."

LITERATURE CITED

Bashkow I, Bunzl M, Hander R, Orta A, Rosenblatt D. 2004. A new Boasian anthropology: theory for the 21st century (Introduction). *Am. Anthropol.* 106:433–34

Bintliff J. 1993. Why Indiana Jones is smarter than the postprocessualists. *Norw. Archaeol. Rev.* 26:91–100

Buck PH. 1949. *The Coming of the Maori*. Wellington, NZ: Whitcombe and Tombs

Carneiro RL. 1991. The nature of the chiefdom as revealed by evidence from the Cauca Valley of Colombia. In *Profiles in Cultural Evolution*, ed. A. Rambo, K. Gillogly, pp. 167–90. *Anthropol. Pap.* 85. Ann Arbor: Univ. Mich. Mus. Anthropol.

Cohen R. 1978. State origins: a reappraisal. In *The Early State*, ed. HJM Claessen, P Skalník, pp. 31–75. The Hague, The Neth.: Mouton

Flannery KV. 1999. Process and agency in early state formation. *Cambridge Archaeol. J.* 9:3–21

Flannery KV, Marcus J. 1976. Formative Oaxaca and the Zapotec cosmos. *Am. Sci.* 64(4):374–83

Friedman J. 1979. *System, Structure, and Contradiction. The Evolution of "Asiatic" Social Formations*. Copenhagen: Natl. Mus. Denmark

Harris M. 1999. *Theories of Culture in Postmodern Times*. Walnut Creek, CA: AltaMira

Hochschild J. 2004. On the social science wars. *Daedalus* 133:91–94

Jones M. 2001. *The Molecule Hunt. Anthropology and the Search for Ancient DNA*. New York: Arcade

Kelly RC. 2000. *Warless Societies and the Origin of War*. Ann Arbor: Univ. Mich. Press

Kuznar LA. 1997. *Reclaiming a Scientific Anthropology*. Walnut Creek, CA: AltaMira

Leach ER. 1954. *Political Systems of Highland Burma. A Study of Kachin Social Structure*. Norwich, UK: Fletcher

Lewis HS. 1998. The misrepresentation of anthropology and its consequences. *Am. Anthropol.* 100:716–31

Ortner SB. 1984. Theory in anthropology since the sixties. *Comp. Stud. Soc. Hist.* 26:126–66

Tebben JR. 1994. *Concordantia Homerica. A Computer Concordance to the Van Thiel Edition of Homer's Odyssey*. Hildesheim, Germ.: Olms-Weidmann

Tooby J, Cosmides L. 1992. The psychological foundations of culture. In *The Adapted Mind. Evolutionary Psychology and the Generation of Culture*, ed. JH. Barkow, L. Cosmides, J. Tooby, pp. 19–136. New York: Oxford Univ. Press

Windschuttle K. 1996. *The Killing of History. How Literary Critics and Social Theorists Are Murdering our Past*. San Francisco: Encounter

The Anthropology of Money

Bill Maurer

Department of Anthropology, University of California, Irvine, California 92697–5100;
email: wmmaurer@uci.edu

Annu. Rev. Anthropol. 2006. 35:15–36

First published online as a Review in
Advance on July 6, 2006

The *Annual Review of Anthropology* is
online at anthro.annualreviews.org

This article's doi:
10.1146/annurev.anthro.35.081705.123127

Copyright © 2006 by Annual Reviews.
All rights reserved

0084-6570/06/1021-0015$20.00

Key Words

abstraction, commensuration, currency, finance, number,
quantification

Abstract

This review surveys anthropological and other social research on
money and finance. It emphasizes money's social roles and meanings
as well as its pragmatics in different modalities of exchange and circulation. It reviews scholarly emphasis on modern money's distinctive
qualities of commensuration, abstraction, quantification, and reification. It also addresses recent work that seeks to understand the
social, semiotic, and performative dimensions of finance. Although
anthropology has contributed finely grained, historicized accounts
of the impact of modern money, it too often repeats the same story of
the "great transformation" from socially embedded to disembedded
and abstracted economic forms. This review speculates about why
money's fictions continue to surprise.

INTRODUCTION: THE COIN'S MANY SIDES

A special difficulty arises when reviewing the anthropology of money. It concerns the form of the review itself. Review articles gather diverse exemplars and perspectives to provide an ordered and, at least momentarily, stable account of the topic at hand. They are supposed to provide a unifying framework and a rubric against which to calibrate and evaluate specific works in relation to wider bodies of scholarship. By definition they oscillate between the general and the specific to generate intellectual value. In so doing, review articles function something like modern money, and something like anthropology. Modern money, at least as it is described in the classical accounts of Marx, Weber, and Simmel, provides a universal yardstick against which to measure and evaluate the universe of objects, relations, services, and persons. It "commensurates incommensurabilities" (Carruthers & Espeland 1998, p. 1400) and "makes impossibilities fraternize" (Marx 1844, p. 110) by bringing things under a common rubric. Anthropology, at least as it has been practiced since the disciplinary stabilization of academic knowledge, provides generalizations about social and cultural life using detailed descriptions of particular incommensurate worlds. It makes the strange familiar. This, like money, is a fantastical endeavor (see Strathern 2005, p. vii). The chapter before you, therefore, necessarily operates as if in a hall of mirrors because the terms it would bring under the prescriptions of the review format exist in an awkward relationship of doubling with each other and with the review form. In assessing the classical account of money against recent scholarship in the human sciences, this review finds considerable openness and paradox, and it does not work to "solve" so much as to prod and to irritate. In this it may thus be more true to the character of modern money (and contemporary anthropology) than the classical accounts would have it.

The difficulty in reviewing the anthropology of money is compounded by the reliance of much anthropological research on theories of meaning and symbol that derived analytical precision through monetary metaphors. Thus, Saussure's structuralist semiotics, on the notion of linguistic value as a function of relations of difference, borrowed from Swiss colleague Vilfredo Pareto's marginalist economics of price (see Maurer 2005b, pp. 159–60):

> To determine what a five-franc piece is worth one must therefore know: (1) that it can be exchanged for a fixed quantity of a different thing, e.g., bread; and (2) that it can be compared with a similar value of the same system, e.g., a one-franc piece, or with coins of another system (a dollar, etc.). In the same way a word can be exchanged for something dissimilar, an idea; besides, it can be compared with something of the same nature, another word. (Saussure 1966, p. 115)

Goux (1973) sees in Saussurian linguistics an isomorphism and psychic homology between economic exchange and linguistic exchange, both animated by the lack of a transcendental signified (the general equivalent in Marx, the murdered father in Freud, the phallus in Lacan). "Between money and language," he writes, "one finds in the history of Western philosophy the insistence of a comparison that is not exterior...but is the local, fragmentary perception of a real, historical-social coherence" (Goux 1973, p. 183; see Maurer 2005b, p. 162). If the language is interior to the money form, and vice versa, it is difficult to say anything meaningful about money at all that is not immediately and already part of money itself (Sohn-Rethel 1978). And this review could end here.

I am not particularly taken by the logic of interiors and exteriors, and as this review should make evident, I am much more concerned with money's pragmatics than its semiotics, at least in the structuralist sense. I am also, however, deeply interested in anthropology's pragmatic contribution to money and scholarly discussions about it. The emerging social studies of finance literature that brings together scholars from anthropology, geography, sociology, international political economy, and science studies has spotlighted academic theories' constitutive relationships to their objects of study (de Goede 2005a). Given the wide dissemination of older anthropological assessments of money, value, and exchange, it would be surprising not to find anthropology's performative effects on money itself, if only we would look.

In a recent review, Gilbert (2005) argues persuasively for "drawing out the paradoxes of money as always a symbolic referent, a social system, *and* a material practice" (p. 361, emphasis in original). None of these three characteristics, she asserts, can be separated from the others. The anthropology of money occupies a familiar place in her review. First, it provides a narrative foil: the anthropology of money reinforces the conventional evolutionary account of the transition from barter to special purpose, socially embedded moneys to general purpose, disembedded, and depersonalized moneys (Weatherford 1998), which Gilbert rightly criticizes (and which recent anthropological research on the "return" of barter in postsocialist states seriously challenges) (Humphrey 2002). Second, anthropology contributes methodological rigor and empirical specificity. It provides ethnographic studies of monetary practices on the ground, which, in demonstrating the social embeddedness of nonmodern money, provides methodological suggestions for investigating the embeddedness of modern money, too.

Yet why is the anthropology of money still so often a retelling of the "great transformation" postulated by Polanyi (1944), a compendium of exotica coupled with a morality tale about the world that "we" have lost? In part, at least, this is a fault of our fidelity. One might just as well ask why we keep teaching Mauss (1954), Bohannan (1959), and Taussig (1980). We are remarkably faithful to that

which we still claim as our unique contribution to knowledge: "the ethnographic record," and the manner in which it makes us "think different" about our own situation.

I do not want to deny the great transformation: It is a good story, and it works pedagogical wonders in our classrooms and can still stop some economists and sociologists in their tracks. Still, anthropologists and other social scientists have been remarkably adept at reinventing the wheel where the study of money is concerned. We have also been good at containing our more exciting insights about money (conveyed in several exemplary edited collections, e.g., Akin & Robbins 1999, Guyer 1995b, Parry & Bloch 1989), while presenting to the outside world the comforting plotline we are always expected to relate, about the impact of money on "traditional" societies and the dehumanizing and homogenizing effects of monetary incursion on all aspects of life in our own society. We do this even as we rediscover the moral, embedded, and special-purpose functions of our "own" money and the calculative and rational dimensions of nonmodern money (Appadurai 1986). I wonder whether the repetition compulsion to circle back to the classical account of the invention and impact of modern money is a crucial component of that money form itself. Social inquiry provides both an analysis and a folk theory about money in the capitalist West. And that folk theory has effects: The telling of the tale and the criticisms of the tale—for neglecting the embeddedness of the economy (Granovetter 1985), for overlooking money's earmarking for special purposes (Zelizer 1994), for obviating the diverse and multiple monetary repertoires with which people engage and create spaces and times of value (Guyer 2004)—may in fact constitute money today, its indeterminacy, its openness.

This is not to put wholly to one side the claim that the state of anthropological and indeed broader social scientific discussion about money is at an impasse. The notion of spheres of exchange continues to be reformed (Hutchinson 1992, Piot 1991,

Strathern & Stewart 1999). The relative weight of money's different "functions" continues to be debated, with some scholars emphasizing its function as a means of exchange (Robbins & Akin 1999), others stressing its function as a unit of account (Ingham 2004, after Grierson 1977), and others refining the Marxist tradition on money as the ur-commodity (Lapavitsas 2005; compare LiPuma 1999). One could easily argue that not much has happened since Bloch & Parry's (1989) signal intervention, which sought to unseat the old distinctions between primitive and modern, special-purpose and general-purpose moneys by redirecting analytical attention to the different time scales according to which transactions take place (discussed further below). And even Bloch & Parry's contribution has not been fully absorbed (but see Gamburd 2004, Znoj 1998).

Recent years have seen new attention to money, however, even more than in the heyday of the debate in economic anthropology between the formalists and substantivists. Perhaps this is because the past three decades have witnessed the advent of what Gregory (1997) calls "savage money": money increasingly detached from political control as well as from the material goods and labor that supposedly provide its backing. In the early 1970s, the international monetary regime created through the Bretton Woods agreements ended. In 1971, U.S. President Richard Nixon "closed the gold window," halting the U.S. dollar's fixed relationship to that precious metal and ushering in an era of flexible exchange rates. Deregulation in banking and finance permitted an explosion of new financial products and relationships; post-Fordist, just-in-time, and flexible production strategies required speedy movements of capital and new extensions of credit and debt to the point at which credit, exchange, and circulation displaced production, at least in the social imaginary (and in cultural theory) (Spivak 1988). Offshore finance blossomed (Hampton & Christensen 2002; Hudson 2000; Maurer 2001; Palan 2003; Rawlings 2005a,b; Roberts 1994). Financial

derivatives hit the headlines, mainly in scandal (Pryke & Allen 2000, Tickell 2000), and scholars started paying serious attention to the new culture of risk in financial markets (Garsten & Hasselström 2003, Green 2000). A vast literature exists in geography and international political economy on the rise and fall of Bretton Woods (see Cohen 1998, Corbridge & Thrift 1994, Helleiner 1994, Leyshon & Thrift 1997, Strange 1998, Tickell 2003).

Perhaps anthropologists are now fascinated again with money because it is their new exotic. Most living anthropologists today have grown up and were trained during or immediately after the Bretton Woods era. The end of that era has made a direct impact on our lives as academic employees and citizens of nation-states. We are increasingly called on to "enterprise up" our contributions to knowledge and demonstrate the value-added of anthropological research in the corporatizing university (Poovey 2001, Strathern 2004). And we are increasingly made responsible not only for accounts-keeping at work but also for portfolio management at home, as the possibility of retirement hinges on our financial investments, not our affective attachments to a lifetime employer or a national welfare state.

If in his Malinowski lecture Hart (1986) could put forward an analysis of money's two sides—heads, the creation of value by state fiat, and tails, the marking of value to the market—the world today seems ever more determined by markets outside the control of any state or, indeed, any human agents at all. Finance's formulae, once unleashed in distributed calculative networks of human and technological agents (Callon & Muniesa 2005), seem to work all by themselves and rework the world. The fictions of finance, the "economy of appearances" (Tsing 2000), the "cultures of circulation" (LiPuma & Lee 2004; compare Eiss 2002), wizard worlds at once abstract, distant and mesmerizing. Ethnographic inquiry founders when it attempts to capture these fantastic fictions; our attachment to certain forms of empiricism encourages skepticism (Moore

1999). Yet ethnography meanwhile discovers traces of these financial confabulations in the worldwide resurgence of occult economies of witchcraft (Geschiere 1997), zombie stories, and the interplay of transparency and conspiracy (Comaroff & Comaroff 1999, 2000; West & Sanders 2003). Where anthropology once contributed reports of special-purpose moneys that were grounded in social relations of rank and prestige, it now records the responses of people on the ground to the abstractions of finance circulating over their heads. In both sets of accounts, however, money and the violence of its abstractions erode the sociability subtending human existence, and the very idea of society itself. Money's baaaaaaaaaad.

It was precisely this emphasis on the amoral or actively immoral aspects of modern money that Bloch & Parry (1989) sought to correct. They attempted to refocus anthropological attention away from Western folk theories of monetary transformation (the root of all evil, the camel through the eye of the needle. . .) embodied in influential accounts from Aristotle to Marx, Weber, and Simmel. Instead of money changing everything, they suggested, existing world views give "rise to particular ways of representing money" (p. 19). This was not, strictly speaking, a relativizing gesture: Once the focus is shifted to "whole transactional systems" Bloch & Parry found "significant regularities which strongly qualify the highly relativistic conclusions" brought about by a consideration of money's meanings in isolation (p. 23). These regularities concern the time scale of monetary transactions: Short-term gain is generally morally permissible so long as it does not interfere with the long-term stability of an "enduring social and cosmic order" (p. 28). Money determines the morality of exchange only insofar as previously existing moral orders maintain, in the long run, their durability in the face of short-term individual competition.

Hart's (1999) "memory bank" of the history of monetary ideas and practices contains within it a certain hope for a new money that would reground economic exchange and value creation and storage in moral and social relationships and nurture a long-term cosmological order based on trust and justice. I am not interested in the normative, prescriptive aspects of Hart's work except in so far as they serve as an exemplar of discussions about socially embedded and embedding moneys in other domains. It is no coincidence that alternative currencies and local exchange and trading systems (LETS) have emerged—and sparked intense intellectual interest—in the same historical moment as the rise of high finance and the increasing mathematical abstraction and complexity of international monetary transactions. Attention to dominant forms of money had led to a neglect of "subalternate" moneys (Gregory 1997). But why is it seen as an unqualified good that money should be regrounded in sociality, community, and regard? What can such moral moneys like LETS (see Helleiner 2000, Karatani 2003, Lee 1996, North 1999) tell us about the state of money itself as well as the state of the academic and popular imagination about money? Bloch & Parry (1989) identified money's depersonalizing effects as a Western folk theory of money; money's role in commensuration, abstraction, and quantification is also a Western folk theory, even if it is instantiated (performed, if you will) in monetary practices.

GREAT TRANSFORMATIONS? ABSTRACTION AND COMMENSURATION

In Simmel's (1907) account, money's abstraction and anonymity liberated humans from age-old distinctions of status and fostered a double-edged egalitarianism: Money freed people from corporate statuses but left them with nothing but money itself with which to evaluate and judge the social and natural worlds around them (Turner 1986). It is cause and consequence of the transformation from gemeinschaft to gesellschaft (Keister 2002, p. 40), the disembedding of the economy from society that sparked the "great transformation."

It was from Polanyi that Bohannan (1959) introduced to anthropology the concepts of general-purpose and special-purpose money. General-purpose money serves three (or four, or five, depending on who is consulted) functions: means of exchange, method of payment, standard of value (and store of wealth, and unit of account). Special-purpose moneys serve only one or two of these functions, and, in Bohannan's exposition of the Tiv economy, only within specific spheres of exchange. Morally neutral "conveyances" occurred within the spheres of exchange and morally charged "conversions" occurred between them (p. 496). With the introduction of Western, general-purpose money, the brass rods used in the prestige sphere increasingly came to assume the other functions. General-purpose money allowed conversions between the spheres. The increasing access to and circulation of general-purpose money sparked inflationary pressure on bridewealth because the amount of general-purpose money increased while the number of marriageable women remained constant (p. 502; see Strathern 2005, p. 124). Those with access to general-purpose money could thus thwart the older distinctions of rank. Such inflation has been widely reported in the anthropological literature on the interaction between special-purpose moneys like wampum, cowries and coppers, and colonial currencies (Dalton 1965, pp. 60–61; Graeber 2001; Hogendorn & Johnson 1986; Law 1995; see also the contributions to Guyer 1995b), even as colonial and postcolonial peoples often actively resisted the adoption of colonial currencies (Saul 2004). Meanwhile, what came to be called the currency revolution in Africa was variously taken up (Hopkins 1966, Ofonagoro 1979) and criticized for being insufficiently attentive to history and regional trading networks (Dalton 1999, Dorward 1976, Guyer 1995a, Guyer 2004). Those brass rods, after all, were imported from Europe.

The Polanyist position was carried forward by substantivist economic anthropologists like Dalton (1965). Dalton faulted Malinowski and Firth for basing their models of money on their own general-purpose kind. They therefore found that the Trobrianders and others lacked money because their tokens of wealth and strings of shell disks did not serve all the functions of money. Dalton argued that because our own economy uses the same stuff for commercial and noncommercial exchanges, Malinowski and Firth did not understand "primitive" special-purpose moneys used for noncommercial exchanges to be "money." For Dalton, the key variable in understanding "primitive money" is the degree of a society's integration into the commercial market. This places some moneys in a new light: Dalton's reanalysis of Rossel Island shell money hinged on the fact that the shells were not media of commercial exchange, but were ranked into a hierarchy for the purposes of noncommercial exchange. They thus did not have to possess some of the qualities generally associated with money, such as divisibility and portability. Now, when Western moneys started being used for noncommercial payments like bridewealth, Dalton argued, they constituted a "structural link. . .between spheres of exchange" with "inevitable repercussions on traditional social organization and practice" (Dalton 1965, p. 61).

Classic anthropological accounts of money thus stressed its peculiarity among exchangeable objects, a peculiarity brought into sharp relief when modern, capitalist, state-backed moneys began to circulate in the nonmonetized economies of so-called primitive societies. According to Marx, Simmel, and Weber, capitalist moneys render everything quantifiable according to one scale of value and permit previously unthinkable comparisons among objects, persons, and activities. Uniscalar valuation (Kelly 1992) and universal commodification (Taussig 1980) were seen as the hallmarks of modern, capitalist money, and as eroding other societies' systems of value, flattening the dense and complex networks of value formation that had previously been built on distinctions of gender, rank, age, and status. Money makes inanimate things reproduce and confounds categories among human, spirit, and natural worlds, and so "primitive" and peasant societies encountering money in the colonial transformation of labor experienced it as Aristotle did at the time of the ascendance of the Greek democratic polis against the symposia of hierarchical elites (Kurke 1999, Taussig 1980).

As anthropologists delved more deeply into the impact of money on subsistence economies, and as the societies' anthropologists studied themselves transformed under the impact of capitalist money, scholars became less certain that money's homogenizing effects were as complete as once believed. Melanesianists and Africanists provide important correctives to Bohannan's model. They note its emphasis on objects as "things in themselves" (Hutchinson 1996, p. 90) as opposed to social relationships (Piot 1991; Robbins & Akin 1999, p. 9). They also have insisted on identifying different modalities of exchange, including, in Melanesia, the exchange of "exact equivalents" (Robbins & Akin 1999, p. 9), as well as more familiar modalities of sharing, buying, and delayed-return exchange. In certain cases introduced moneys become associated with the foreign, but money can be either feared or, contra Simmel, incorporated, encompassed, and re-localized (Rutherford 2001) or sacralized (Eiss 2002). In some cases, introduced moneys become associated with exploitation (through wage labor or trade in imported goods, for example) while local moneys are taken anew to index "culture" or heritage (Akin 1999). Arno (2005) provides an interesting ethnography of "cultural currencies"—"performative expenditures," not money per se—that are deployed in the service of sentiment.

In an ample number of documented cases the introduction of modern money is met with a shrug, or at least with little of the anxiety the great transformation narrative would predict; modern moneys are often simply welcomed because they are, well, "modern" (Robbins 1999). Purportedly distinctive aspects of commodity exchange, such as the individualist concern with getting ahead at the expense of others, sometimes "resonates with aspects of the indigenous social system" (Brison 1999, p. 153). In "societies where individuals are preadapted to wanting to expand their material base in order to gain influence," such supposedly capitalist orientations to material gain can "catch on" quite quickly (Brison 1999, p. 152; Foster 1995a). In such situations, people are less likely to be concerned with the medium of exchange so much as with the dynamics of its blockage and flow (Foster 1999). Shifting the optic from exchange to flow or circulation also returns the objects of exchange to "the space and time of their genesis" (Eiss 2002, p. 293; Gilbert 2005; Keane 2001), revealing relationships missed by the reification of subjects and objects that is sometimes presumed by the analytical category of exchange. Anthropologists found that although money is powerful, its introduction is met with appreciation, fear, and even ennui [note that Robbins & Akin's (1999, p. 35) comment that "bitter money" (Shipton 1989) has "made few appearances in Melanesia"]. It has not always and everywhere displaced traditional currencies. It does not always gather to itself exclusively the functions social scientists have ascribed to it, as a means of exchange, store of wealth, measure of value, method of payment, or unit of account.

Similarly, in complicating the picture of the great transformation in the capitalist West, sociologists found instances during which money and finance seemed more dependent on their re-embedding in social relations than on their depersonalized abstraction (Keister 2002). It is not clear that money always flattens social relations, rather than creating new ones just as complex. Extensions and reformulations of the classic accounts of money's effects revolved around the reach of money's abstractions and the social dynamics of commensuration itself (Espeland & Stevens 1998). Sociologists note that modern money can be just as socially embedded and special purpose as so-called primitive money (Zelizer 1994, 1998).

None of this should be news, however. Writing in *American Anthropologist*, Melitz (1970) challenged the Polanyist paradigm by pointing out the ways in which general-purpose money is often rejected for some purposes (we do not indiscriminately accept just anyone's checks; we shun the receipt of pocketfuls of coin). He also noted that we engage in "baby-sitter exchanges, car pools, trade-ins, exchanges of free services within professions" and hold nonmonetized relationships of "allegiance, and good-will" that are convertible into goods without the intervention of money (Melitz 1970, p. 72). Although Melitz concluded with an economist's analysis of money as reducing transaction costs, he pointed to the social significance and differentiation of modern money and the fuzzy boundary between "primitive" and "modern," long before Appadurai stressed the calculative dimension of gift societies and the moral dimension of commodity societies or Zelizer drew attention to the social meanings and uses of modern money.

Part of the problem, as Bloch & Parry (1989) noted, is that monetary meanings and uses were often treated in isolation from wider transactional orders. Guyer's brilliant reformulation of Bohannan is based precisely on the wider view, both spatially and temporally. "One can simply lift off the boundedness of the model [of spheres of exchange] and connect each sphere to its regional trading networks," she writes (2004, p. 28). One then sees "not barriers [between spheres] but institutions that facilitated asymmetrical exchanges across value registers" (p. 28). A further difficulty arises, however, when we are confronted with "societies" in which the very question of "the larger social order...is itself highly and openly contested" (Robbins & Akin 1999, p. 35). Robbins & Akin (1999) are referring

to Melanesia, but we might just as well consider postwelfare state Euro-American worlds in which, as Margaret Thatcher put it, there is no such thing as society, only individual men and women, and families. How are relationships objectified, indigenously and analytically, and what should the anthropologist do when indigenous and analytical objectifications converge (Riles 2000)?

Another part of the problem is we are dazzled by the act of commensuration that seems so central to modern money and the process of abstraction on which it depends. Popular and scholarly accounts of commensuration and abstraction express a fascination with boundary objects whose commodification and entry into the monetary calculus is often morally fraught, such as children, body parts, sex, ideas, and so-called cultural properties. How can such things be placed on one scale of value, the same scale of value as subsistence, labor, luxuries, or anything else? As Strathern argued, and I have discussed elsewhere in a different context (Maurer 2003), comparison demands the creation of numerical ratios between different goods to commensurate differences in value. Other operations, such as the exact substitution involved in some Melanesian exchange, create analogies rather than ratios. Thus finding equivalencies between objects in the exchange of gifts "will always (can only) appear as a matching of units" understood as analogues of one another (Strathern 1992, p. 171), not as a comparison of ratios. So, gift exchange does not depend on "how many ones make up 20 or 30" in an exchange of pig for sago, but "how many ones make up the right one" (p. 187, parentheses omitted). If we are dazzled by the counting in gift exchange, we are utterly blinded by the mathematics of monetary commensuration in "modern" societies, for we persist in viewing money as the "most quantifiable expression of the commodity," as the "expression, index, and measure of...commensurability" (LiPuma 1999, p. 198). It is, and it isn't. This paradox deserves scrutiny.

NUMBER AND QUANTIFICATION

Closely related to the question of commensuration and abstraction is the problem of money's mathematics—the kinds of calculation and equivalence it encourages. Helen Codere (1968) created a classification of money systems and monetary semiotics based on the extent and magnitude of the numbers involved. Her account interested Melitz because it seemed to "contrast abstract numerical manipulation with practical numerical application" (Melitz 1970, p. 1035). It was notable for its attempt to categorize moneys on the basis of the interrelationships among symbol, number, and use. Although earlier work such as this found a direct relationship between quantification, commensuration, and the "great transformation," money does not always divide up the world into quantifiable bits without remainder. Money may render everything calculable, but the systems of calculation and quantification on which it depends are not always as straightforwardly algebraic as one might imagine. Number, like money, is representationally complex (Foster 1999). Numbers do not always point to enumerable objects in the world (Rotman 1997) but can, for example, also signify the divine, the transcendent, the ineffable (Maurer 2002). And even where calculation seems dominant, it can be put to new uses and effects, as when people use the mathematics of money outside the sphere of the economy proper, to make sense of their lives, loves, and longings in other domains (Miyazaki 2003).

Consider Crump's (1978) analysis of money, number, and market relations in the state of Chiapas in southern Mexico in the 1970s. Market transactions using money, he argued, introduced notions of number and classification that were alien to Tzotzil counting and linguistic classifier systems. Money and number were thus the leading edge of linguistic conversion and cultural assimilation. As he put it, "the equivalence property of money…converts two unlike things into each other, and so money, in its own terms, effaces the distinctions inherent in any system of classification, so you can mix chalk with cheese" (p. 507). This echoes the common idea in the sociology of money, via Marx and Simmel, that money commensurates, flattens, and homogenizes.

A number of other case studies reach similar conclusions. Ferreira's study of counting among some Brazilian indigenous groups finds that monetized market transactions reshape number so that money and number together become the chief means of quantitative comparison, measurement, and evaluation and create a "conflict with other value systems" (Ferreira 1997, p. 135). Hutchinson's study of the Nuer demonstrates how money's commensuration of values increasingly flattens relationships and simultaneously invests personal possessions with deeper importance and meaning.

> If modern man is free—free because he can sell everything, and free because he can buy everything—then he now seeks…in the objects themselves that vigor, stability, and inner unity which he has lost because of the changed money-conditioned relationships that he has with them. (Simmel, quoted in Hutchinson 1992, p. 294).

When monetary exchange is anonymous and anonymizing, the social identities of transacting parties are irrelevant to the value of the objects mediated by money (Graeber 1996, p. 6), and so the things take on the powers of the fetish described by Marx and the object of desire discussed by Lacan, Žižek, and others.

This does not mean that numbers always do what we think they do, or that numbers really are abstract and disembodied entities from a realm of pure form (Rotman 1997). We should aim to develop richer vocabularies of numerical scale and quantification techniques and procedures, even borrowing such vocabularies from the realm of statistics and mathematics themselves. We should also examine the interaction of the different scales, for example, of time and money in wage labor and the new disciplines of loan repayments in colonial and postcolonial contexts (Berry 1995; Elyachar 2002; Falola 1995; Stiansen & Guyer 1999, p. 10). And we might want to leave Marx to one side while we do this. As Guyer writes in the conclusion to her study of monetary repertoires in West Africa, "we need to increasingly incorporate attention to thought [i.e., processes of abstraction and analysis common to economic practice and to social description and explanation] and calculation.... [O]ne needs to 'think other' precisely about number, measurement, and money in the awkward and dangerous present because they are such powerful constructions in a quantified and insurgently commercial world" (Guyer 2004, pp. 174–75).

I part with Guyer only on the last phrase. Here Guyer, like many others, indicates a concern that the quantitative function of money "downplays, or even ignores those aspects of value that cannot be reduced to a single number" (Carruthers & Espeland 1998, p. 1401). We should not fear numbers simply because they are numbers and we think we know what numbers do, always and everywhere. I have written elsewhere that the anxiety about number is based on a bringing together of the equivalence function of modern money with the Simmelian money-as-acid hypothesis, and the folk theory that presumes that whenever we see numbers and math we see something that counts, calculates, equates, desacralizes, and rationalizes (Maurer 2005). The anthropology of number and counting belies the common sense of calculation (Mimica 1988, Urton 1997, Verran 2001). Does number actually always permit "a generalized abstraction of value across otherwise incommensurable domains" (Maurer 2005b, p. 104)? This is a research question. When does it do so, and when does it do something else?

In numerous instances, quantification and money, together, resacralize exchanges and conversions, although this is rarely drawn

out in the literature with the detail one would like: with the dead, for example, in the burning of ghost moneys (which have taken on special significance in the wake of economic transition in China and Vietnam; see Jones 2003; Kwon 2006; Yang 2000; see also Feuchtwang 1992), in prosperity cults (Jackson 1999), in rotating credit associations (Kurtz & Showman 1978), and in a host of other religious practices (Belk & Wallendorf 1990, Werner & Bell 2004). One suspects that moral assessments of certain adjectivally marked moneys—dirty money, hot money (Znoj 1998), bitter money (Shipton 1989), money that burns like oil (Gamburd 2004), "liquid" money (literally, Rogers 2005; and figuratively, Ho 2005)—derive from those moneys' positions as hinges between short-term and long-term transactional orders (Bloch & Parry 1989). Guyer provides an analytical vocabulary that can help anthropologists begin to flesh out their analyses of the relationship between morally marked moneys, transactional orders, and different numerical scales. Even specifying whether we are dealing with nominal, ordinal, interval, or ratio scales when we see money's numbers in specific exchange modalities would go far toward moving the discussion of calculation away from the money-as-acid hypothesis (see Guyer 2004, p. 49).

What interests me most about anxiety about quantification is the way the folk theory works. It is exemplified in the title of Crump's (1978) essay, "Money and Number: The Trojan Horse of Language." Counting money, an abstract scale for measuring value, spills over into other domains of enumeration because money itself brings ever more objects, entities, or activities from those domains into its calculus. The use of the sign of money outside the domain of the limited market for subsistence goods—in Crump's case—feeds back to warrant the whole sign-game of the economy itself.

The problem here concerns the theory of the sign. Guyer (2004) and Munn (1986) can help us see that the assumption that money enforces a kind of colonizing quantification misses that quantity is simultaneously a quality of things. Guyer argues that, in "Atlantic Africa," "number and kind were both scales, among others; none were anchored in a foundational invariant; all were at play" (2004, p. 12). Furthermore, the set of scales did "not constitute a cognitive map" but rather a "repertoire, the elements pegged to each other in performance" (p. 60). Guyer thus adopts a performative and pragmatic approach to number that has far-reaching implications for assessing the relationship between numeration and money.

In her deconstruction of cognitivist accounts of mathematics via Californians' comparisons of quantity and value in the supermarket, Lave argued that anthropologists and psychologists held a functionalist theory of knowledge. Knowledge was presumed to be "context-free, value-free, body-free and factual" (Lave 1988, p. 88); and cultural knowledge mirrored the academic "(professional) mind" in arranging knowledge in discrete and hierarchically nested domains (Lave 1988, p. 88). Her point was not simply that one needed to add the contexts and the bodies to come to a better appreciation of the facts. More centrally, she argued that problem solving is not a cognitive operation but an ongoing activity involving "other kinds of concerns" beyond the math problem per se; "relations of quantity are merged (or submerged) into ongoing activity" (p. 120). "What motivates problem-solving activity in everyday situations appears to be dilemmas that require resolution," not problems requiring definitive solutions (p. 139).

MATERIALITY AND THE FICTIONS OF FINANCE

Renewed attention is being given to quantification because of the highly complex and abstract mathematical operations of modern finance in the post–Bretton Woods world. The contrast between Crump on the one hand and Guyer and Lave on the other hand is replicated in the finance literature in the contrast between, say, LiPuma & Lee (2004), and Callon (1998) and MacKenzie (2001). LiPuma & Lee (2004) suggest that the ascendance of specific quantitative principles in contemporary capitalism is ipso facto transforming social imaginaries. "[N]ew financial instruments assume that particular forms of risk...can be aggregated as an abstract form, determinable by mathematical calculation" (p. 208). Taking to a new level the social statistics of nineteenth-century forms of knowledge and power—beyond the nation-bound form of such statistics and toward a vision of a global totality—the "contemporary objectification, calculation, and distribution of risk rely on larger and more accurate data sets and increased computer power, all driven by competition among mathematically sophisticated quantitative experts" (LiPuma & Lee 2004, p. 209).

Similarly, Poovey (2001) explicitly contrasts quantification with humanism, arguing in the case of university financing that the penetration of market values "erodes" humanity by disallowing "goods that are goods in themselves—that defy market evaluation because they are not quantifiable, thus not subject to commodification" (pp. 11–12). In making this contrast Poovey echoes Simmel, of course. In taking as its content only "the most objective practices, the most logical, purely mathematical norms," money also bequeaths "the absolute freedom from everything personal" (Simmel 1907, p. 128). This is a tale of the infinite extendibility of calculative abstraction. As with the Trojan horse of language and the transformation of the social imaginary caused by the extension of abstract quantification, that extendibility is presumed to just happen. Once the calculative agencies are unleashed, they cover the world and make all meanings of the same species, from sign to meaning to matter. There can be no going back.

Now, as Callon & Muniesa (2005) write, "economic calculation is not an anthropological fiction"; it is out there in the world and demands critical attention. But it is not the preserve of a set of technical experts bent on world domination. Rather, it is "distributed among human actors and material devices," and because of its distributed character across human and nonhuman agents, there are always "several ways of calculating values and reaching compromises" (p. 1254). This demands attention to how calculative agencies produce their effects, without assuming in advance what those effects might be. The approach is less semiotic and more pragmatic or performative; it stresses feedback loops between the worlds modeled and instantiated by finance theory. MacKenzie (2001) shows how even the activities of those who disbelieve the efficient markets hypothesis help make the market more efficient by seeking out and closing off arbitrage opportunities (p. 129), creating a world in the image of the mathematical models of finance (see also MacKenzie & Millo 2003). Over time, the effect has been to make "the typical assumptions of finance theory...empirically more realistic" (p. 132). Such feedback loops are "performative" and depend on their enactments and iterations rather than on their meanings (but see Miller 2002, Neiburg 2006; see also de Goede 2005a). There is surprisingly little research, however, on the impact of anthropological theories on their objects of study, although the recent turn toward ethnography among some financial and other professionals outside of academia may begin to generate anthropological interest (Holmes & Marcus 2005).

As Miyazaki (2005) points out, the performative approach derived from Callon (1998) holds fast to the assumption that quantification materializes an economy, rather than being open to the possibility that quantification makes other effects. He and Zaloom (2003) both demonstrate how the numbers and the calculations do not always refer to the commodities and contracts behind them, and they are not undertaken solely for the purposes of financial risk management or profit making. Zaloom finds among Chicago and London futures traders a corporeal investment in numbers, not just rational calculation. She documents the bodily practices traders develop around their work with numbers and how they develop affective relationships or a feel for them rather than seeing them entirely as a rational calculus. Indeed, for some, "the first step" of becoming a successful trader "is learning *not* to calculate" (Zaloom 2003, p. 264; see also Knorr-Cetina & Bruegger 2002). Miyazaki finds that among Japanese arbitrageurs, who exploit and in the process close off temporal gaps in global prices, the multiple and incongruous temporalities with which traders are involved also constitute their life trajectories; the numbers redound into their self-perceptions. Arbitrageurs come to view not only their careers but also their life course itself as a process of arbitrage and even plot out other domains of their lives on the model of the numerical spreadsheet (Miyazaki 2003). Here is a case in which the mathematical models of economics and finance create not only "the economy" but also traders' personal biographies.

I have reviewed the anthropology of finance at length elsewhere and do not repeat that work here (Maurer 2005a). However, new social scientific research on finance, such as Miyazaki's (2005) and Riles's (2004), is redirecting attention away from the obvious fictions of finance and toward its material instantiations in lives, documents, and worlds. The financialization of the world economy since the 1970s and the end of Bretton Woods era have made even professionals—bankers, financiers, lawyers—acutely aware of money's fictional qualities, its imaginative economies, and its ability to literalize its metaphorical possibilities. The anthropology of finance is illuminating the worlds of the stock market trading floors and of the financial engineers who seek to create new products, and new moneys, for a changing world (Garsten & Hasselström 2003, Hertz 1998, Ho 2005, Miyazaki 2003, Riles 2004, Zaloom 2003). It is doing so in conversation with sociologists (Knorr Cetina & Preda 2005), geographers (Clark Thrift & Tickell 2004), international political economy (de Goede 2005b), and scholars working in science and technology studies (MacKenzie and Millo 2003). Although there are some distinct disciplinary differences here (see de Goede 2005a; Maurer 2005a) the cross-fertilization between fields has been quite generative.

Money's materiality—the stuff of which it is made—has always been a source of fascination for those exposed to it anew and for social theorists. Against Plato's contention that money was a mere token, Aristotle and Locke argued that money had to possess certain substantive attributes (durability, transportability, as well as inherent value; compare Robbins & Akin 1999) to become a medium of exchange and payment. The history of these contending viewpoints is, in many respects, the history of the development of Western moneys themselves, from specie to specie marked with the stamp of the sovereign to specie-backed paper to notional ledger-ticks, electronic or otherwise. Between the electrum of ancient Lydian coins to the electronic currencies of the present day, money has been a metaphor for and exemplar of the problem of the relationship between sign and substance, thought and matter, abstract value and its instantiation in physical and mental labors and products (Shell 1982, 1995). This problem is at the center of much of the recent work on finance.

Anthropologists and other social theorists have long queried money's relation to political entities and to markets, the "two sides of the coin" around which Hart (1986) reoriented much discussion of money in the 1980s—a token backed by the state, commodity set in motion by the market. On the one hand, Hart's intervention directed anthropologists to the relationship between "market-mediated and state-regulated" monetary transactions (Guyer 1999, p. 245). The state side of the coin reflected hierarchical relationships of political authority; the market side reflected the putatively equal and horizontal relationships of the parties to market exchange. Hart postulated a historical process of oscillation between the two. As Guyer (1999) points out, Africanist studies of monetary transformations tended to take their lead from Hart, rather than from Bloch & Parry (1989). This may be because the emphasis on the state and political economy fit better with West African histories of social payments among unequals and the imposition of colonial currencies through state payments such as taxes as well as the oscillation between state payments and wider regional market networks.

The two sides of Hart's coin—state/market or token/commodity—map neatly onto the word/substance distinction central to long-standing Western monetary imaginaries (Shell 1982), if states create value by the strength of their word and markets create value through substantial exchange. Studies of monetary iconography (Gilbert 1998; Hewitt 1994, 1995) and money's symbolism have sought to understand how money comes to signify national identity, or how money is used in national projects to stitch together national sentiment and solidarity (Helleiner 1998, 1999, 2003).

Just as it is not news to anthropology that money is a social relation, a symbolic system, and a material reality, so too it is not news to other scholars of money that people freak out when the apparent hegemony of money's fictionality and abstraction is newly revealed. There are strong resonances between the contemporary discussions of money's increasing abstraction and finance's fantasies and that of postbellum arguments in the United States among Greenbackers, goldbugs, and bimetallists. Sociologists Carruthers & Babb (1996) argue that the contemporary discussion of money is far more muted than that of the nineteenth century—"family values," they write, "loom larger in the political consciousness than specie values" (p. 1582). Given all the attention to finance in the past ten years, the East Asian and Argentine currency crises, Enron, Barings Bank, the Orange County bankruptcy, the emerging U.S. pension crisis, etc., I am not so sure. Regardless, Carruthers

& Babb argue that when money's value becomes uncertain and exchange more difficult, its social construction is no longer hidden, its "naturalness" can no longer be taken for granted, and the "potential for a radical reconstruction becomes greater" (p. 1580; see Dominguez 1988 and Pedersen 2002).

Besides redefining the nature of the republic, Reconstruction aimed to redefine the nature of money. The debate over money culminated in the antimonopolist movement and the popularization of what was then termed the movement for free coinage of silver. This movement grew from farmer discontent in the American midwest with the coming of the railroads, which charged exorbitant rates for the transport of farm produce (Ritter 1997). Historian O'Malley (1994) argues that notions of natural kinds animated by the Darwinian species concept interdigitated with debates over monetary specie. The money question was "viewed in light of anxieties about value and identity in Victorian American male culture" brought to the fore in American racial formation after Emancipation (p. 395). This was at a time when seemingly insubstantial paper money, printed to fund the war effort, circulated just as the newly emancipated slaves entered the labor market. This populist movement culminated in William Jennings Bryan's run for the presidency in 1896. The latter third of the nineteenth century, thus, witnessed intense debate among the rank and file about the nature of money, the signifier of race, the value of (free) labor, the power of conglomerates, and the American financial system. L. Frank Baum, one of Bryan's compatriots, imagined a city where everyone wears green-tinted glasses and, as the Wizard tells Dorothy, "everyone must pay for everything he gets" (Baum 1900, p. 130). A little girl from Kansas, the populist midwest, unmasks the Wizard's deceptions, skipping in silver slippers down a road paved with gold, a symbol of bimetallism that any contemporary reader would have recognized.

Late Victorians and early twentieth-century modernists certainly thought that modern money, freed from the constraints of rank, reputation, and material reality in specie, was destroying social solidarity and epistemological certainty. Literary critics and historians have long noted that the monetary allegories of figures like Poe, Gide, and Baudelaire revolved around questions of identity, trust, and faith in the stability of that which is evident to the senses, questions raised by a money seemingly backed by nothing at all (Derrida 1992, Goux 1984, Michaels 1987, Shell 1978). And even earlier than the nineteenth century, Ingrassia (1998) documents the historical coemergence in the seventeenth century of finance and fiction writing and the gendering of each activity as female. Only women and feminized stock-jobbers could be seen as credulous enough to believe in the structurally similar and sociologically interconnected speculative follies of finance and fiction writing. If fictional accounts of riches in Argentina could spur frenzied trading, written stories about nonexistent people could generate income for authors in the new genre. The argument bears on the interconnected fictions of state: Brantlinger (1996) examines the literary, historical, and political history of the relationship between public credit and state authority from the late seventeenth century to the twentieth.

How should one think about this history repeating itself? Carruthers & Babb's (1996) argument would seem to hold: These are all moments when the link between the representation and reality of money and finance break down, denaturalizing the taken-for-granted monetary order, and place value in question. This idea certainly resonates with some of the Melanesian literature in which money's value derives not from its publicity but from its hidden qualities, where money reflects forms of social power like magic and sorcery (Graeber 1996; Mosko 1999; Robbins & Akin 1999, p. 28). When the not-seen is suddenly thrust into light, the agencies animating value can receive new social scrutiny.

On the one hand, anthropology and social studies of finance have been contributing needed research on the socio-technical arrangements that produce financial representations and their effects, on the trading floor and through new communications and visualization technologies (Buenza & Muniesa 2005; Buenza & Stark 2004; Knorr Cetina & Bruegger 2002, 2000; Zaloom 2003). On the other hand, however, there is risk that documenting the relationship between the techniques of representation in markets and the social imaginaries of money will result in either "the bottomless problem of the ontological status of particular practices or concepts" (Roitman 2005, p. 8) or in the replication of evolutionary stories of transition in the form of "a series of representations of the foundations of wealth that have been replaced, over time, by novel or radically transformed ones" (Roitman 2005, p. 202), as Roitman has argued regarding emergent forms of value and regulation in Cameroon and more generally.

"Seeing" may be a deconstructive, denaturalizing move (remember Dorothy, Toto, and the man behind the curtain), but seeing also depends on the relative stability of the empiricist gesture to know based on the evidence of the senses. Buenza & Muniesa (2005) discuss the crisis of figurative finance that has been taking place in financial domains and in social studies of finance, which have shifted from an emphasis on informal networks and gossip to the traders' and analysts' visual representations of financial markets. Those visual representations, however, are themselves the product of mathematical abstractions such as market indexes and do not unproblematically refer to anything backing them. So, although we "see" something in the spread plot, we are also engaging in a nonempirical modality of knowledge founded in "tricks of transparency" (p. 633). Still, that nonempirical modality is an effort for financial actors themselves to "see" and to shape value. Making visible does not denaturalize but contributes to a "staging [of] one of the more ferocious crises of representation since Shakespearian times: that of what things are worth" (p. 633).

CONCLUSION

Whether we look to the emergence of modern stock markets in northwestern Europe in the seventeenth century, or to postbellum greenbacks, or to the closing of the gold window in 1971 and the breakdown of the Bretton Woods agreements that lent an aura of stability to money through the middle of the twentieth century, we find similar debates about the relationship between "real" economic value and "insubstantial" fictions of fiat currencies and finance and a concern about the effects of the transition from "true" money to the promissory kind on the fabric of society itself. Anthropologists found the same sort of debates in the colonial imposition of capitalist currencies through wage labor, taxes, land rents, and commodity markets. One could argue that the differences among the assessments of money and finance in the seventeenth, nineteenth, and twenty-first centuries lie in their specific manifestations: from feminized, passionate frenzy, to the irreality of a world untethered from comfortable essentialisms of species and specie, to occult economies and conspiracies of abstraction. I would suggest that the new anthropology of money is taking a different tack. The continual "discovery" and then subsequent decomposition of money's supposedly unique attributes are themselves integral to money, to its own analytical abstractions, and to those social scientists trying to catch up behind it.

We will, however, continue to run in circles if we do not at least momentarily abandon the semiotic ideology that founds much of the history of reflection on money. This is the notion of the sign that posits that "signification offers the subject an escape from materiality" (Keane 2001, p. 87) and that denies an escape from "the ontological division of the world into 'spirit' and 'matter'" (Keane 2003, p. 409), or, one could add, word and substance, (state) fiat and (market) commodity, etc. Money can, after all, retain "indexical links to its sources and owners" (Keane 2001, p. 77), and not just in places like Sumba. After surveying the nineteenth-century American monetary debate, Foster concludes that Melanesians receive new national moneys in a manner that "exceeds the limits" of representation and abstraction, for "money can never represent or stand for anything else 'truly,' that is, fully and finally....[T]he issue is no longer one of representation's arbitrariness, but rather its ultimate failure. In other words, money is always representationally flawed" (Foster 1999, pp. 230–31). Keane, Foster, Roitman, and Guyer help reorient the anthropology of money from meanings to repertoires, pragmatics, and indexicality.

Representational flaw does not mean representational failure, either for money or for anthropological accounts of it. Money "works" because of its failures. Analytically, this suggests a fidelity to the gaps between representation and reality and sign and substance, and their "unresolved antagonisms" (Žižek 2004, p. 134, writing on Karatani 2003). It is this kind of fidelity the anthropology of money is getting good at.

LITERATURE CITED

Akin D. 1999. Cash and shell money in Kwaio, Solomon Islands. See Akin & Robbins 1999, pp. 103–30

Akin D, Robbins J, eds. 1999. *Money and Modernity: State and Local Currencies in Melanesia*. Pittsburgh, PA: Univ. Pittsburgh Press

Appadurai A. 1986. Introduction: commodities and the politics of value. In *The Social Life of Things: Commodities in Cultural Perspective*, ed. A Appadurai, pp. 3–63. Cambridge, UK: Cambridge Univ. Press

Arno A. 2005. *Cobo* and *tabua* in Fiji: two forms of cultural currency in an economy of sentiment. *Am. Ethnol.* 32(1):46–62

Baum LF. 1997 [1900]. *The Wonderful Wizard of Oz*. Oxford, UK: Oxford Univ. Press

Belk RW, Wallendorf M. 1990. The sacred meanings of money. *J. Econ. Psychol.* 11:35–67

Berry S. 1995. Stable prices, unstable values: some thoughts on monetization and the meaning of transactions in West African economies. In *Money Matters: Instability, Values and Social Payments in the Modern History of West African Communities*, ed. J Guyer, pp. 299–313. Portsmouth, NH: Heinemann

Bloch M, Parry J. 1989. Introduction: money and the morality of exchange. In *Money and the Morality of Exchange*, ed. P Barry, M Bloch, pp. 1–32. Cambridge, UK: Cambridge Univ. Press

Bohannan P. 1959. The impact of money on an African subsistence economy. *J. Econ. Hist.* 19:491–503

Brantlinger P. 1996. *Fictions of State: Culture and Credit in Britain, 1694–1994*. Ithaca, NY: Cornell Univ. Press

Brison K. 1999. Money and the morality of exchange among the Kwanga, East Sepik Province, Papua New Guinea. See Akin & Robbins 1999, pp. 151–63

Buenza D, Muniesa F. 2005. Listening to the spread plot. In *Making Things Public*, ed. B Latour, P Weibel, pp. 628–33. Cambridge, MA: MIT Press

Buenza D, Stark D. 2004. Tools of the trade: the socio-technology of arbitrage in a Wall Street trading room. *Industr. Corp. Change* 13(2):369–400

Callon M. 1998. The embeddedness of economics markets in economics. In *The Laws of the Markets*, ed. M. Callon, pp.1–57. Oxford, UK: Blackwell

Callon M, Muniesa F. 2005. Economic markets as calculative collective devices. *Org. Stud.* 26(8):1229–50

Carruthers BG, Babb S. 1996. The color of money and the nature of value: greenbacks and gold in postbellum America. *Am. J. Soc.* 101(6):1556–91

Carruthers BG, Espeland WE. 1998. Money, meaning, and morality. *Am. Behav. Sci.* 41(10):1384–408

Clark GL, Thrift N, Tickell A. 2004. Performing finance: the industry, the media and its image. *Rev. Int. Polit. Econ.* 11(2):289–310

Codere H. 1968. Money-exchange systems and a theory of money. *Man* 3:557–77

Cohen BJ. 1998. Phoenix risen: the resurrection of global finance. *World Politics* 48:268–96

Comaroff J, Comaroff J. 1999. Occult economies and the violence of abstraction: notes from the South African postcolony. *Am. Ethnol.* 26(2):279–303

Comaroff J, Comaroff J. 2000. Millennial capitalism: first thoughts on a second coming. *Public Cult.* 12(2):291–343

Corbridge S, Thrift N. 1994. Money, power and space: introduction and overview. In *Money, Power and Space*, ed. S Corbridge, R Martin, N Thrift, pp. 1–25. Oxford: Basil Blackwell

Crump T. 1978. Money and number: the Trojan horse of language. *Man* 13(4):503–18

Dalton D. 1999. Meaning, contingency, and colonialism: reflections on a Papua New Guinea shell gift. See Akin & Robbins 1999, pp. 62–81

Dalton G. 1965. Primitive money. *Am. Anthropol.* 61(1):44–65

De Goede M. 2005a. Resocialising and repoliticising financial markets: contours of social studies of finance. *Econ. Soc. Newsletter* May:19–28

De Goede M. 2005b. *Virtue, Fortune and Faith: A Genealogy of Finance*. Minneapolis: Univ. Minn. Press

Derrida J. 1992. *Given Time I: Counterfeit Money*. Trans. Peggy Kamuf. Chicago: Univ. Chicago Press

Dominguez V. 1990. Representing value and the value of representation: a different look at money. *Cult. Anthropol.* 5(1):16–44

Dorward DC. 1976. Precolonial Tiv trade and cloth currency. *Int. J. Afr. Hist. Stud.* 9:576–91

Eiss PK. 2002. Hunting for the Virgin: meat, money, and memory in Tetiz, Yucatan. *Cult. Anthropol.* 17(3):291–330

Elyachar J. 2002. Empowerment money: the World Bank, nongovernmental organizations, and the value of culture in Egypt. *Pub. Cult.* 14(3):493–513

Espeland WN, Stevens ML. 1998. Commensuration as a social process. *Am. Rev. Sociol.* 24:313–43

Falola T. 1995. Money and informal credit institutions in colonial Western Nigeria. In *Money Matters: Instability, Values and Social Payments in the Modern History of West African Communities*, ed. J Guyer, pp. 162–87. Portsmouth, NH: Heinemann

Ferreira MKL. 1997. When 1+1 ≠ 2: making mathematics in central Brazil. *Am. Ethnol.* 24(1):132–47

Feuchtwang S. 1992. *The Imperial Metaphor: Popular Religion in China*. London: Routledge

Foster R. 1995. *Social Reproduction and History in Melanesia: Mortuary Ritual, Gift Exchange, and Custom in the Tanga Islands*. Cambridge, UK: Cambridge Univ. Press

Foster R. 1999. In God We Trust? The legitimacy of Melanesian currencies. See Akin & Robbins 1999, pp. 214–31

Gamburd MR. 2004. Money that burns like oil: a Sri Lankan cultural logic of morality and agency. *Ethnology* 43(2):167–84

Garsten C, Hasselström A. 2003. Risky business: discourses of risk and (ir)responsibility in globalizing markets. *Ethnos* 68(2):249–70

Geschiere P. 1997. *The Modernity of Witchcraft: Politics and the Occult in Postcolonial Africa.* Charlottesville: Univ. Va. Press

Gilbert E. 1998. "Ornamenting the façade of Hell": iconographies of nineteenth-century Canadian paper money. *Environ. Plan. D: Soc. Space* 16:57–80

Gilbert E. 2005. Common cents: situating money in time and place. *Econ. Soc.* 34(3):357–88

Goux JJ. 1973. *Economie et Symbolique: Marx, Freud.* Paris: Seuil

Goux JJ. 1984. *The Coiners of Language.* Trans. JC Gage. Norman: Univ. Okla. Press

Graeber D. 1996. Beads and money: notes toward a theory of wealth and power. *Am. Ethnol.* 23:4–24

Graeber D. 2001. *Toward an Anthropological Theory of Value: The False Coin of Our Own Dreams.* New York: Palgrave

Granovetter M. 1985. Economic action and social structure: the problem of embeddedness. *Am. J. Soc.* 91:481–510

Green S. 2000. Negotiating with the future: the culture of modern risk in global financial markets. *Env. Plan. D: Soc. Space* 18:77–89

Gregory CA. 1997. *Savage Money: The Anthropology and Politics of Commodity Exchange.* Amsterdam: Harwood Acad. Publ.

Grierson P. 1977. *The Origins of Money.* London: Althone

Guyer J, ed. 1995a. Introduction: the currency interface and its dynamics. In *Money Matters: Instability, Values and Social Payments in the Modern History of West African Communities,* ed. J Guyer, pp. 1–37. Portsmouth, NH: Heinemann

Guyer J, ed. 1995b. *Money Matters: Instability, Values and Social Payments in the Modern History of West African Communities.* Portsmouth, NH: Heinemann

Guyer J, ed. 1999. Comparisons and equivalencies in Africa and Melanesia. See Akin & Robbins 1999, pp. 232–45

Guyer J. 2004. *Marginal Gains: Monetary Transactions in Atlantic Africa.* Chicago: Univ. Chicago Press

Hampton MP, Christensen J. 2002. Offshore pariahs? Small island economies, tax havens, and the reconfiguration of global finance. *World Dev.* 39(9):1657–73

Hart K. 1986. Heads or tails? Two sides of the coin. *Man* 21(4):637–56

Hart K. 1999. *The Memory Bank: Money in an Unequal World.* London: Profile Books

Helleiner E. 1994. *States and the Reemergence of Global Finance: From Bretton Woods to the 1990s.* Ithaca: Cornell Univ. Press

Helleiner E. 1998. National currencies and national identities. *Am. Behav. Sci.* 41(10):1409–36

Helleiner E. 1999. Historicizing territorial currencies: monetary space and the nation-state in North America. *Pol. Geogr.* 18:309–39

Helleiner E. 2000. Think globally, transact locally: green political economy and the local currency movement. *Glob. Soc.* 14(1):35–51

Helleiner E. 2003. *The Making of National Money: Territorial Currencies in Historical Perspective.* Ithaca, NY: Cornell Univ. Press

Hertz E. 1998. *The Trading Crowd: An Ethnography of the Shanghai Stock Market.* Cambridge, UK: Cambridge Univ. Press

Hewitt V. 1994. *Beauty and the Banknote: Images of Women on Paper Money.* London: Br. Mus.

Hewitt V, ed. 1995. *The Banker's Art: Studies in Paper Money.* London: Br. Mus.

Ho K. 2005. Situating global capitalisms: a view from Wall Street investment banks. *Cult. Anthropol.* 20(1):68–96

Hogendorn J, Johnson M. 1986. *The Shell Money of the Slave Trade.* Cambridge, UK: Cambridge Univ. Press

Holmes D, Marcus G. 2005. Cultures of expertise and the management of globalization: toward the refunctioning of ethnography. In *Global Assemblages: Technology, Politics, and Ethics as Anthropological Problems*, ed. A Ong, SJ Collier, pp. 235–52. Oxford: Blackwell

Hopkins AG. 1966. The currency revolution in south-west Nigeria in the late nineteenth century. *J. Hist. Soc. Nigeria* 3:471–83

Hudson A. 2000. Offshoreness, globalization and sovereignty: a postmodern geo-political economy? *Trans. Inst. Br. Geogr.* 25:269–83

Humphrey C. 2002. *The Unmaking of Soviet Life: Everyday Economies after Socialism*. Ithaca, NY: Cornell Univ. Press

Hutchinson S. 1992. The cattle of money and the cattle of girls among the Nuer, 1930–83. *Am. Ethnol.* 19(2):294–316

Hutchinson S. 1996. *Nuer Dilemmas: Coping with War, Money and the State*. Berkeley: Univ. Calif. Press

Ingham G. 2004. *The Nature of Money*. Cambridge, UK: Polity

Ingrassia C. 1998. *Authorship, Commerce, and Gender in Early Eighteenth-Century England: A Culture of Paper Credit*. Cambridge, UK: Cambridge Univ. Press

Jackson PA. 1999. Royal spirits, Chinese gods, and magic monks: Thailand's boom-time religions of prosperity. *S. East Asia Res.* 7(3):245–320

Jones CB. 2003. Religion in Taiwan at the end of the Japanese colonial period. In *Religion in Modern Taiwan: Tradition and Innovation in a Changing Society*, ed. P Clart, CB Jones, pp. 10–35. Honolulu: Univ. Hawaii Press

Karatani K. 2003. *TransCritique: On Kant and Marx*. Trans. Sabu Kohso. Cambridge, MA: MIT Press

Keane W. 2001. Money is no object: materiality, desire, and modernity in an Indonesian society. In *The Empire of Things: Regimes of Value and Material Culture*, ed. FR Myers, pp. 65–90. Santa Fe, NM: SAR Press

Keane W. 2003. Semiotics and the social analysis of material things. *Lang. Commun.* 23:409–25

Keister LA. 2002. Financial markets, money, and banking. *Annu. Rev. Sociol.* 28:39–61

Kelly JD. 1992. Fiji Indians and "commoditization of labor." *Am. Ethnol.* 19(1):97–120

Knorr Cetina K, Bruegger U. 2000. The market as an object of attachment: exploring postsocial relations in financial markets. *Can. J. Soc.* 25(2):141–68

Knorr Cetina K, Bruegger U. 2002. Global microstructures: the virtual societies of financial markets. *Am. J. Soc.* 107(4):905–50

Knorr Cetina K, Preda A, eds. 2005. *The Sociology of Financial Markets*. Oxford, UK: Oxford Univ. Press

Kurke L. 1999. *Coins, Bodies, Games, and Gold: The Politics of Meaning in Archaic Greece*. Princeton, NJ: Princeton Univ. Press

Kurtz DV, Showman M. 1978. The tanda: a rotating credit association in Mexico. *Ethnology* 17:65–74

Kwon H. 2006. The dollarisation of Vietnamese ghost money. *J. R. Anthropol. Inst.* In press

Lapavitsas C. 2005. The social relations of money as a universal equivalent: a response to Ingham. *Econ. Soc.* 34(3):389–403

Lave J. 1988. *Cognition in Practice*. Cambridge, UK: Cambridge Univ. Press

Law R. 1995. Cowries, gold and dollars: exchange rate instability and domestic price inflation in Dahomey in the eighteenth and nineteenth centuries. In *Money Matters: Instability, Values and Social Payments in the Modern History of West African Communities*, ed. JI Guyer, pp. 53–73. Portsmouth, NH: Heinemann

Lee R. 1996. Moral money? LETS and the social construction of local economic geographies in Southeast England. *Environ. Plan. A* 28:1377–94

Leyshon A, Thrift T. 1997. *Money/Space: Geographies of Monetary Transformation*. London: Routledge

LiPuma E. 1999. The meaning of money in the age of modernity. See Akin & Robbins 1999, pp. 192–213

LiPuma E, Lee B. 2004. *Financial Derivatives and the Globalization of Risk*. Durham, NC: Duke Univ. Press

MacKenzie D. 2001. Physics and finance: S-terms and modern finance as a topic for science studies. *Sci. Technol. Hum. Val.* 26(2):115–44

MacKenzie D, Millo Y. 2003. Constructing a market, performing theory: the historical sociology of a financial derivatives exchange. *Am. J. Sociol.* 109(1):107–45

Marx K. 1977 [1844]. Economic and philosophic manuscripts. In *Karl Marx, Selected Writings*, ed. D McLellan, pp. 75–112. Oxford, UK: Oxford Univ. Press

Maurer B. 2005a. Finance. In *Handbook of Economic Anthropology*, ed. J Carrier, pp. 176–93. Cheltenham, UK: Edward Elgar

Maurer B. 2005b. *Mutual Life, Limited: Islamic Banking, Alternative Currencies, Lateral Reason*. Princeton, NJ: Princeton Univ. Press

Maurer B. 2001. Islands in the net: rewiring technological and financial circuits in the 'offshore' Caribbean. *Comp. Stud. Soc. Hist.* 43(3):467–501

Maurer B. 2002. Repressed futures: financial derivatives theological unconscious. *Econ. Soc.* 31(1):15–36

Maurer B. 2003. Got language? Law, property and the anthropological imagination. *Am. Anthropol.* 105(4):775–81

Mauss M. 1954. *The Gift*. New York: Norton

Melitz J. 1970. The Polanyi school of anthropology of money: an economist's view. *Am. Anthropol.* 72(5):1020–40

Michaels WB. 1987. *The Gold Standard and the Logic of Naturalism*. Berkeley: Univ. Calif. Press

Miller D. 2002. Turning Callon the right way up. *Econ. Soc.* 32(2):28–33

Mimica J. 1988. *Intimations of Infinity: The Mythopoeia of the Iqwaye Counting System and Number*. Oxford, UK: Berg

Miyazaki H. 2003. The temporalities of the market. *Am. Anthropol.* 105(2):255–65

Miyazaki H. 2005. The materiality of finance theory. In *Materiality*, ed. D Miller, pp. 165–81. Durham, NC: Duke Univ. Press

Moore SF. 1999. Reflections on the Comaroff lecture. *Am. Ethnol.* 26(2):304–6

Mosko M. 1999. Magical money: commoditization and the linkage of *maketsi* ("market") and *kangakanga* ("custom") in contemporary North Mekeo. See Akin & Robbins 1999, pp. 41–61

Munn N. 1986. *The Fame of Gawa: A Symbolic Study of Value Transformation in a Massim (Papua New Guinea) Society*. Cambridge, UK: Cambridge Univ. Press

Neiburg F. 2006. Inflation: economists and economic cultures in Brazil and Argentina. *Comp. Stud. Soc. Hist.* 48(3): In press

North P. 1999. Explorations in heterotopia: LETS and the micropolitics of money and livelihood. *Environ. Plan. D: Soc. Space* 17(1):69–86

Ofonagoro WI. 1979. From traditional to British currency in southern Nigeria: analysis of a currency revolution 1880–1948. *J. Econ. Hist.* 39:623–54

O'Malley M. 1994. Specie and species: race and the money question in nineteenth-century America. *Am. Hist. Rev.* 99(2):369–95

Palan R. 2003. *The Offshore World: Sovereign Markets, Virtual Places and Nomad Millionaires*. Ithaca, NY: Cornell Univ. Press

Parry J, Bloch M, eds. 1989. *Money and the Morality of Exchange*. Cambridge, UK: Cambridge Univ. Press

Pedersen D. 2002. The storm we call dollars: determining value and belief in El Salvador and the United States. *Cult. Anthropol.* 17(3):431–59

Piot C. 1991. Of persons and things: some reflections on African spheres of exchange. *Man* 26:405–24

Polanyi K. 1944. *The Great Transformation*. Boston: Beacon

Poovey M. 2001. The twenty-first-century university and the market: what price economic viability? *Differences* 12(1):1–16

Pryke M, Allen J. 2000. Monetized time-space: derivatives—money's 'new imaginary'? *Econ. Soc.* 29(2):264–84

Rawlings G. 2004. Laws, liquidity and Eurobonds: the making of the Vanuatu tax haven. *J. Pac. Hist.* 39(3):325–41

Rawlings G. 2005. Mobile people, mobile capital and tax neutrality: sustaining a market for offshore finance centers. *Account. Forum* 29:289–310

Riles A. 2000. *The Network Inside-Out*. Ann Arbor: Univ. Mich. Press

Riles A. 2004. Real time: governing the market after the failure of knowledge. *Am. Ethnol.* 31(3):1–14

Ritter G. 1997. *Goldbugs and Greenbacks: The Antimonopoly Tradition and the Politics of Finance in America, 1865–1896*. Cambridge, UK: Cambridge Univ. Press

Robbins J. 1999. This is our money: modernism, regionalism, and dual currencies in Urapmin. See Akin & Robbins 1999, pp. 82–102

Robbins J, Akin D. 1999. An introduction to Melanesian currencies: agency, identity, and social reproduction. See Akin & Robbins 1999, pp. 1–40

Roberts S. 1994. Fictitious capital, fictitious spaces: the geography of offshore financial flows. In *Money, Power and Space*, ed. S Corbridge, R Martin, N Thrift, pp. 91–115. Oxford: Basil Blackwell

Rogers D. 2005. Moonshine, money, and the politics of liquidity in rural Russia. *Am. Ethnol.* 32(1):63–81

Roitman J. 2005. *Fiscal Disobedience: An Anthropology of Economic Regulation in Central Africa*. Princeton, NJ: Princeton Univ. Press

Rotman B. 1997. The truth about counting. *Sciences* Nov/Dec:34–39

Rutherford D. 2001. Intimacy and alienation: money and the foreign in Biak. *Pub. Cult.* 13(2):299–324

Saul M. 2004. Money in colonial transition: cowries and francs in West Africa. *Am. Anthropol.* 106(1):71–84

Saussure F. 1966. *Course in General Linguistics*. New York: McGraw Hill

Shell M. 1995. *Art and Money*. Chicago: Univ. Chicago Press

Shell M. 1978. *The Economy of Literature*. Baltimore, MD: Johns Hopkins Univ. Press

Shell M. 1982. *Money, Language, and Thought*. Baltimore, MD: Johns Hopkins Univ. Press

Shipton P. 1989. *Bitter Money: Cultural Economy and Some African Meanings of Forbidden Commodities*. Am. Ethnol. Soc. Monogr. Ser. No. 1. Washington, DC: Am. Anthropol. Assoc.

Simmel G. 1990 [1907]. *Philosophy of Money*. London: Routledge

Sohn-Rethel A. 1978. *Intellectual and Manual Labour: A Critique of Epistemology*. Highlands, NJ: Humanities

Spivak G. 1988. Scattered speculations on the question of value. In *In Other Worlds: Essays in Cultural Politics*, ed. G Spivak, pp. 154–78. New York: Routledge

Stiansen E, Guyer J, eds. 1999. *Credit, Currencies and Culture: African Financial Institutions in Historical Perspective*. Stockholm: Nordiska Afrikainstitutet

Strange S. 1998. *Mad Money: When Markets Outgrow Governments*. Ann Arbor: Univ. Mich. Press

Strathern A, Stewart PJ. 1999. Objects, relationships, and meanings: historical switches in currencies in Mount Hagen, Papua New Guinea. See Akin & Robbins 1999, pp. 164–91

Strathern M. 1992. Qualified value: the perspective of gift exchange. In *Barter, Exchange and Value: An Anthropological Approach*, ed. C Humphrey, S Hugh-Jones, pp. 169–91. Cambridge, UK: Cambridge Univ. Press

Strathern M. 2004. *Commons and Borderlands: Working Papers on Interdisciplinarity, Accountability and the Flow of Knowledge*. Oxon, UK: Sean Kingston

Strathern M. 2005. *Kinship, Law and the Unexpected: Relatives Are Always a Surprise*. Cambridge, UK: Cambridge Univ. Press

Taussig M. 1980. *The Devil and Commodity Fetishism in South America*. Chapel Hill: Univ. N.C. Press

Tickell A. 2000. Dangerous derivatives: controlling and creating risks in international money. *Geoforum* 31:87–99

Tickell A. 2003. Cultures of money. In *The Handbook of Cultural Geography*, ed. K Anderson, M Domosh, S Pile, N Thrift, pp. 116–30. London: Sage

Tsing A. 2000. Inside the economy of appearances. *Public Cult.* 12(1):115–44

Turner B. 1986. Simmel, rationalization, and the sociology of money. *Sociol. Rev.* 34:93–114

Urton G. 1997. *The Social Life of Numbers: A Quecha Philosophy of Numbers and Philosophy of Arithmetic*. Austin: Univ. Tex. Press

Verran H. 2001. *Science and an African Logic*. Chicago: Univ. Chicago Press

Weatherford J. 1998. *The History of Money*. New York: Crown

Werner C, Bell D, eds. 2004. *Values and Valuables: From the Sacred to the Symbolic*. Soc. Econ. Anthropol. Monogr. Lanham, MD: Altamira

West H, Sanders T, eds. 2003. *Transparency and Conspiracy: Ethnographies of Suspicion in the New World Order*. Durham, NC: Duke Univ. Press

Yang M. 2000. Putting global capitalism in its place: economic hybridity, Bataille, and ritual expenditure. *Curr. Anthropol.* 41(4):477–509

Zaloom C. 2003. Ambiguous numbers: trading technologies and interpretation in financial markets. *Am. Ethnol.* 30(2):258–72

Zelizer VA. 1994. *The Social Meaning of Money*. New York: Basic Books

Zelizer VA. 1998. How people talk about money. *Am. Behav. Sci.* 41(10):1373–83

Zelizer VA. 2000. Fine tuning the Zelizer view. *Econ. Soc.* 29(3):383–89

Žižek S. 2004. The parallax view. *New Left Rev.* Jan./Feb.:121–34

Znoj H. 1998. Hot money and war debts: transactional regimes in southwestern Sumatra. *Comp. Stud. Soc. Hist.* 40(2):193–222

Food and Globalization

Lynne Phillips

Department of Sociology and Anthropology, University of Windsor, 401 Sunset Ave., Windsor, Ontario, Canada N9B 3P4; email: lynnep@uwindsor.ca

Annu. Rev. Anthropol. 2006. 35:37–57

The *Annual Review of Anthropology* is online at anthro.annualreviews.org

This article's doi: 10.1146/annurev.anthro.35.081705.123214

Copyright © 2006 by Annual Reviews. All rights reserved

0084-6570/06/1021-0037$20.00

Key Words

agriculture, trade, global governance, consumption, hunger, policy, politics

Abstract

This review takes two key approaches for exploring the theme of food and globalization: first, how food has been mobilized as a commodity in global production and trade systems and governed through global institutions; and second, how the idea of globalization has been nourished through food, particularly with the mobility of people and of ideas about cuisine and nutrition. Stark global inequalities are also noted, and the review calls for attention to policy-based research and to the analytical connections between governance, food politics, and food citizenship in future studies.

INTRODUCTION

"If you ate today thank a farmer." Passing this message on my way to work everyday, I think about what I've just eaten for breakfast—all ingredients purchased at the local supermarket—and wonder how one might best do that. To thank local farmers, most of whom grow feed corn, which will travel somewhere far away, seems no more appropriate than thanking the grocer and telling him to pass it on. The conundrum reveals something of the crooked pathways of globalization and suggests that tracing the trajectories of food might be a fruitful way to investigate the processes that we now commonly consider "global." But, as Barndt (2002) discovers in her study of the tomato, the roots and routes of food in the world today are tangled and slippery. Moreover, as the following review indicates, the approaches taken are varied, each one illuminating a slightly different story about this increasingly important area of study. I review these contributions with an eye to opening up new lines of inquiry for the place of food in nurturing our thinking about theory, policy, and politics in a globalizing world.

The exchange of food across regions, nations, and continents has occurred for centuries, although the study of the relationship between food and globalization is relatively new to anthropology. Anthropologists have long been interested in food and its production, consumption, and exchange (see Miller 1995, Mintz & Du Bois 2002 for important reviews), but food issues have largely been examined within the context of relatively closed systems of production—in households, in local communities, and in ethnic groups. The focus, historically, was on how food may reinforce, and at times create, distinct cultural worlds. Not until the 1970s and 1980s were there hints of the global processes at work within local and regional agricultural systems, especially with the anthropological focus on subsistence production in the developing world. A turning point can be identified with

Mintz's (1985) examination of sugar, a book that burst the seams of what anthropologists had until that time considered the "field." In tracing the evolution of the rise of sugar through global systems of production, consumption, sociality, and identity, Mintz offered a unique analytical framework for exploring the nexus of food and globalization. Yet, Mintz's book appeared before the virtual explosion of literature on globalization and culture (Appadurai 1996, 2001; Friedman 1994; Inda & Rosaldo 2002; Jameson & Miyoshi 1998; Tomlinson 1999, to name just a few), a literature that, interestingly, seldom investigates food. The time seems ripe therefore for interrogating ideas about food through the lens of globalization, and globalization through the lens of food.

I begin this review by asking how food has been mobilized on global scales. Here I consider globalization in terms of three distinct, although often interrelated, analytical paths to understanding projects of globality (Tsing 2000)—the international circulation of food products as commodities, the transnational expansion of food-based corporations, and the global governance of food and food issues. In the subsequent section, I examine how food "feeds" globalization as an imagined construct and discuss how the mobilization of ideas and people help shape a global imaginary. Twinning the ideas of globalizing food and feeding globalization challenges common binaries that pervade much of the literature. In the concluding section I consider future directions for research on food and globalization, raising some questions about how anthropologists might "think through food" to offer alternative perspectives on the changing relationships between global processes, food identities, and food politics.

GLOBALIZING FOOD

Commodities

Researchers began to focus systematically on the expansion of commodity relations beyond national borders in the 1990s (Bonanno et al. 1994, Goodman & Watts 1997, McMichael 1994), replacing nation-based concerns about agrarian structures with an examination of emerging models of international trade (such as the promotion of nontraditional exports and free trade agreements) and their implications for agri-food systems in developing and developed nations. Although scholars have debated how to conceptualize these changes—are they best labeled postfordist or a new regime of private global regulation? (Bonanno 1998; Friedmann & McMichael 1989)—there is considerable agreement that a new era in the global regulation of food has been in the making, marked by a shift to more flexible systems of production, the corporate search for higher profits in new and multiple territories, and a new approach to international trade to permit a freer flow of goods across national borders. For some, the emergence of this new era was a "quiet revolution" (Schertz & Daft 1994); for many it was a threat (Magdoff et al. 2000) or outright piracy (Shiva 1997).

Friedmann's (1982) research on world food regimes proved useful for mapping important trends in these new commodity production and distribution processes. The concept of a global food regime has helped explain the adoption of standardized planting, picking, and packing practices in agriculture around the world (Barndt 1999, McCann 2001, Pritchard & Burch 2003). The concept also sheds light on increased global sourcing for and distribution of fresh fruit and vegetable systems (Friedland 1994); the standardization of production systems in the chicken, hog, and livestock industries (Boyd & Watts 1997, Bonanno & Constance 2001, Sanderson 1986); and the mobility of the tuna industry to avoid restrictive legislation (Bonanno & Constance 1996).

Other analysts have highlighted the global shift to more flexible labor relations to produce food for export (Collins & Krippner 1999, Kritzinger et al. 2004, Ortiz 2002).

Barnet & Cavanagh (1996) refer to this shift as the "feminization" of labor to foreground the temporary nature of labor contracts and increased labor vulnerability. By following women's work in the tomato industry from Mexico to Canada, Barndt (1999) effectively demonstrates the variations in what flexibility means to transnational corporations and to women workers as packers, food processors, supermarket cashiers, and food service providers. As also evidenced in prawn production for export in Bangladesh (Ito 2002), demands for flexibility in food production usually signal the intensification of women's labor. The overall costs of orienting local economies to world food regimes are usefully outlined by Murray (2001) and include the destruction of the domestic food base, the loss of plant diversity through monoculture, and increased food insecurities for rural populations.

Researchers have noted concerns about the inability of a food regime approach to explain the diverse and specific circumstances of food production in local-national-global relations (Araghi 2003, Goodman & Dupuis 2002, Goodman & Watts 1997, Moran et al. 1996). Alternative approaches emphasize varied cultural and historical trajectories (Freidberg 2003, Gupta 2003, Hollander 1995, Ohnuki-Tierney 1999, Warman 2003) and the importance of networks and local/actor agencies rather than structures (Arce 1993, Jarosz 2000, Marsden 2000, Marsden Cavalcanti & Irmão 1996) in the globalization of specific commodities. For example, Sonnenfeld et al. (1998), employing a version of the network approach, show that local growers in Washington State have long been actively involved in globalizing the apple industry but primarily in the distribution of the commodity rather than in the vertical integration of its production. Rosset et al. (1999) challenge the parallels being drawn between the globalization of the agro-food industry and that of other industries (electronics and automobiles) by critically assessing the variations involved in the case of the world tomato. Through investigating the uneven local responses to global demands for fresh fruit and vegetables, Arce (1993) argues that rather than leading farming in Latin America into uniform patterns, the new globalization processes may play a role in reproducing distinct rural localities (p. 49).

Anthropologists most often enter discussions about the globalization of food commodities by insisting that the discussions be placed in their cultural and historical contexts. Commodities are not just products flowing through economic channels; they have social lives (Appadurai 1986). Thus, the symbolic value attached to the production and consumption of tortillas depends on the exchange context in which they are circulated (Lind & Barham 2004). The cultural and class-based status associated with healthy eating is central to the success of the Chilean fresh fruit trade (Goldfrank 2005). Emphasizing what past global projects may have to teach us, Gupta (2003) follows the spice trade in Asia and elsewhere before and after the fifteenth century to hint at an alternative globalization at work, one that tends to be eclipsed by the western European–based view of the sugar trade. Like Gupta, Ohnuki-Tierney (1999) subtly challenges the "temporally shallow frame" (Gupta 2003, p. 2) of current globalization theory by showing how the local-global interplay of rice and meat have long played a role in constituting Japanese identity. A fascinating examination of the uncoordinated and fractured globalization of shea butter, as it moves from a preindustrial to a postindustrial commodity, is provided by Chalfin (2004), who demonstrates the key role played by the domestic market in Ghana over time and by a multiplicity of gendered actors. The argument that commodities cannot be understood outside the networks of meaning and power in which they are circulated opens up lines of inquiry that challenge the idea of globalization as a predominantly economic, hegemonic, or singular process.

Corporations

A different, although clearly related, approach to food and globalization takes the growth and operations of food-related transnational corporations (TNCs) as its starting point. Heffernan & Constance (1994) argue that "if the research question is, 'What is the driving force behind the restructuring of the global food system?' the unit of analysis has to be the TNC" (p. 29). Food-related TNCs share the characteristic of having global investments in the food industry and controlling much of how food is grown, processed, distributed, and/or purchased. The literature on food-related TNCs considers both their increased expansion into new territories for cheaper labor and new markets (Bonanno 2004; Kneen 1995, 1997; Rosset et al. 1999; Van Esterik 1989) and their remarkable consolidation and concentration in North America and elsewhere (Banaji 1997, Garcia Martinez & Salas 1999, Lyson & Raymer 2000, Paul & Steinbrecher 2003). Llambí (1993) helpfully distinguishes four generations of food-related TNCs, with the latest and current generation being "constituted by extremely flexible and decentralized forms of organization" (p. 22). It may be useful to distinguish food-related TNCs, as does Friedland (1994), in terms of those companies involved primarily in how food is produced (e.g., agri-business and food processors), those that distribute and trade food, and those that market food (wholesalers, retailers, and food services), but it is very clear that operations are often intertwined in practice (McKenna Roche & LeHeron 1999, p. 38). Indeed, a company may radically change its specialization over time, as Lyson & Raymer (2000) show for the case of Green Giant foods.

For most studies, the global corporation model is an ideal type (Pritchard & Fagan 1999), as closer scrutiny reveals inevitable variations in corporate strategies. Although global sourcing and just-in-time requirements encourage the development of standardized yet flexible production systems, such development takes place with considerable variability in different locales. In their research on Nestlé, Pritchard & Fagan (1999) refer to the company's different "geographies of accumulation" to highlight these variations. Kneen (1999) explores how the corporate strategies of Monsanto and Cargill differ. Yenal (1999) argues that the local context (Turkey) makes a difference for how Unilever and Nestlé operate. Friedland (1994) reveals important differences between Chiquita and Dole in the fresh fruit industry, and McKenna et al. (1999) note a complex "fluidity" in the relationships between Heinz and growers in New Zealand. Excellent case studies of how agribusinesses have changed in response to criticisms, including becoming "green" themselves, can be found in Jansen & Vellema (2004).

How food is globally traded and marketed can also be highly variable and culturally framed. Arce's (2000) research with international food traders in Chile reveals how, despite working with a dazzling display of technology, traders still find that "it is essential to know the other person well[;] otherwise you lack the element of trust" (p. 42) for food trade negotiations. Applbaum's (2004) unique investigation into the cultural logic of global marketing in itself indicates how reference (and at times deference) to cultural contexts is central to the success of food-related TNCs. These studies help remind us that what we see today as global corporate power in the food industry is not a given, but is instead a product of actions taken by a whole series of actors, including laborers, growers, traders, professional marketers, investors, financial advisors, and grocers.

One important debate in studies of the impact of food-related TNCs on food consumption focuses on the cultural impact of the global outreach of TNCs. Whereas Ritzer (1993) promotes the view that the global proliferation of McDonald's and Kentucky Fried Chicken (KFC) constitutes a form of cultural imperialism, others (primarily anthropologists) challenge this position by an-

alytically placing consumption in its cultural context. In his edited book on McDonald's, Watson (1997) has taken a leading role in investigating what is referred to as the "localizing" practices of food-related TNCs, examining how their influence on eating patterns, taste preferences, and family life has not been what one might presume. Lozada (2000), examining KFC in China, similarly argues that the corporation's success is related to "its ability to become local" (p. 134) and shows how, despite the appearance of increasing cultural homogenization, studies of the consumption process reveal an expansion of cultural specificities and diversities. Watson & Caldwell's (2005) new reader brings together published work that explores this area of study, including the important work of Miller (1998) and Roseberry (1996) on drink (Coca-Cola and gourmet coffee, respectively).

The expansion of food-related TNCs into developing countries generally involves negative effects on nutrition, as imported food replaces local diets (Beardsworth & Keil 1997, Lentz 1999). Weismantel's (1988, 1999) research highlights how imported foods may culturally introduce "bitter gifts" to indigenous economies. Some evidence shows that developing countries are experiencing increased obesity as a result (Evans et al. 2003; Sobal 1999, 2001; WHO 1998). Concerns about globalizing the "modern" food system have become more acute with North America's increasing obsession about obesity and other health costs of fast food and highly industrialized diets (Brownell 2004, Culhane 2004, Nestle 2002, Tillotson 2004).

Research is sparse on the role of supermarkets, as corporate retail outlets, in reshaping food production and consumption. Although it appears that the emergence of supermarkets in developing countries supports greater dietary choice for those who can afford it, the significant role of supermarkets in deepening the vertical integration of the production process has implied more vulnerability for small farmers (Dugger 2004, Guptill & Wilkins 2002, Konefal et al. 2005,

Myers 2004) and street vendors (Tinker 1999). Guptill & Wilkins (2002), looking at the U.S. situation, show that food retailing has actually moved away from providing standardized food and is including foods from the local economy in its strategy to diversify. The authors argue that this strategy may in fact "weaken the capacity of local food flows to empower regular citizens to shape the local economy" (p. 49). More research on the power of retail outlets to control food availability and choice is required to assess further the implications for both farmers and consumers.

Global Governance

A third approach to the study of the globalization of food considers how international organizations and institutions may mobilize and govern food within and beyond nation-states. Studies have focused on how agricultural production has been shaped by multilateral financial aid and lending institutions such as the World Bank and the International Monetary Fund (IMF) (Escobar 1995, Li 2004, Raynolds 1994) and international trade agreements such as the General Agreement on Tariffs and Trade (GATT) and the World Trade Organization (Anderson 2000, Desta 2001, McMichael 2000, Myers 2004, Raffer 1997). Some analysts understand these institutions to be little more than the handmaidens of TNCs, which demand stable yet flexible arrangements for trade and investment to establish a new global order (McMichael 1999). Yet detailed examination of these agencies shows that their operations are not merely a reflection of TNC requirements.

The United Nations (UN), created with a mandate to develop a new era of international cooperation after World War II, remains relatively understudied from the perspective of food and its globalization. Research into the central role historically played by the UN's Food and Agricultural Organization (FAO) in the global management of food challenges the commonly held view that it was only in the 1990s that nation-states were restricted in the regulation of their own food systems (Ilcan & Phillips 2003, Phillips & Ilcan 2003). Sending food experts and agricultural scientists to countries throughout the world from the 1940s onward, the FAO actively intervened in regional and national agricultural systems and dietary patterns and undertook extensive training of populations to carry on the work of producing "modern" farmers and consumers. The part played by the World Health Organization in promoting a scientific approach to infant feeding in developing countries is also noteworthy from this perspective (Gottschang 2000).

Studies link the global expansion of food exports to the lowering of trade barriers through the Uruguay Round of GATT in the 1980s and the establishment of the World Trade Organization (WTO) in 1995 (Anderson & Josling 2005, Ingco & Nash 2004). Today trade arrangements have come to involve much more than trade tariffs, expanding into food quality and safety standards, patents, and intellectual property rights (Madeley 2000). These agreements raise questions about the future availability of land for local food production as more land is devoted to export agriculture and about the social and economic consequences of standardizing agricultural practices and food products (McKenna & Campbell 2002). The price for local economies is outlined by Myers (2004) who focuses on the impact on Caribbean societies of new trade agreements in bananas.

The issue of how standards should be set and who should set them have troubled farmers, governments, and consumers alike. Putting the Codex Alimentarius in charge of a wide range of responsibilities in these matters (Schaeffer 1993) reinforces the historical preference of international organizations for depoliticizing issues of global food standardization through expertise (Ilcan & Phillips 2006). The current effort from many camps within the UN to help countries meet the WTO sanitary measures alerts us to an increasing convergence of global institutions around neoliberal models of food governance (Phillips &

Ilcan 2004) and is an issue that requires more research.

The ultimate success of the WTO in governing food and agriculture remains a question. Research focusing on the negotiating process fails to produce a consistent "winner" and reminds us that global trade agreements are not a given, but a product of political struggles and negotiations (Curtis 2001, Schaeffer 1993). In this vein, Llambí (1993) usefully follows the political struggles between the United States, Europe, and Japan over their respective agricultural policies, highlights their agency in pursuing loopholes in GATT rules, and documents the persistent challenges to a U.S. hegemony over the agrofood system. National food boards can also be important for trade outcomes, as has been argued for the case of New Zealand (Curtis 2001, McKenna Le Heron & Roche 2001). A promising area is the development of alternative trade agreements such as fair trade. Although researchers are wise enough not to point to fair trade as a panacea, there are glimmerings of hope that these efforts raise incomes for producers and improve the quality of their environment (McKenna & Campbell 2002; Murray & Raynolds 2000; Raynolds & Murray 1998; Raynolds 2000, 2002; Renard 1999). Some analysts have also considered the potential of LETS (local exchange and trading systems) to "relocalize" rural areas that have been negatively affected by the uneven globalization of food (Pacione 1997). Thus, although intergovernmental organizations have emerged as key figures in debates about global governance, much skepticism remains about their ability to develop sustainable global arrangements for food provisioning. Given the unique perspectives on globalization that anthropologists have been able to offer as they document the interfaces between different kinds of knowledges (Long & Long 1992; Hobart 1993; Inda & Rosaldo 2002), these and other international institutions should be investigated further through an anthropological lens.

FEEDING GLOBALIZATION

A full examination of what might be called the production of globalization through food also introduces questions about food producers and consumers as mobilized subjects. By which mechanisms do people and ideas associated with food systems help create, reinforce, and challenge processes of globalization? Supported by literature that interrogates globalization as flows of ideas and people across institutionalized (e.g., national) borders (Appadurai 1996, 2001; Gupta & Ferguson 1997), one can ask how projects of globality are fed by the imagination and practices of mobile and mobilized populations.

Feeding the Global Imaginary

Food has been, and continues to be, central to the production of a global imaginary. Throughout much of the past century, the world was imagined as food—scarce and, indeed, in urgent need of more food for the malnourished, the vulnerable, the victims of famine. The concept of a "modern" globe has been and is still tied to the consumption of particular kinds of foods, the adoption of particular food production regimes (e.g., industrial agriculture), and the acceptance of particular kinds of food knowledge (Escobar 1995). Flows of scientific knowledge have been central to imagining the possibilities of a global modern agriculture (Goodman & Watts 1997, Goodman & Redclift 1991, Gupta 1998, Phillips & Ilcan 2003, Scott 1998) and planet-wide modern nutrition and diet (Gottschang 2000, Jing 2000, Weismantel 1988). Food can play an important role in imagining nations (Appadurai 1988, Caldwell 2002) at the same time that it may problematize the "national." In this sense, food forms part of what Tsing (2000) refers to as the politics of scale-making.

Both the idea of the farmer who produces food for the world and the idea of the consumer who eats food of (and sometimes for) the world play a role in the production of a global imaginary. An awareness of this process raises the question of how farmers and consumers are positioned as global subjects and how they, in turn, may nurture multiple ideas about globality—including those related to the environment, to politics, and to citizenship. The international expansion of neoliberal policies has altered farmers' relationships to the global market; farmers have been made responsible for their economic futures (Hall 1998a) and compelled to respond to restructuring only in a limited number of ways (Bonanno & Lyman 1999, Crabtree 2002, Murray 2002, Preibisch et al. 2002). At the same time, international agricultural institutions disseminate the idea of the successful farmer as a "globalizer" who is responsive to the market, technologically savvy, and flexible about knowledge acquisition (Bruinsma 2003). Science and technology play a large role in discursively and materially positioning farmers to relate to the world in its global dimensions (Marglin 1996). Extensively partnered organizations such as CGIAR (Consultative Group on International Agricultural Research) explicitly circulate science-based, growth-oriented models of production as politically neutral solutions to agricultural problems (CGIAR 1998). The argument that genetically modified crops will feed the world by 2030 (McMichael 2000; see also Pinstrup-Andersen & Schioler 2000) is a compelling one that positions farmers in the global imaginary with contradictory consequences for their agency. Indeed much of the biotechnology literature could be usefully reread in these terms.

How gender figures in this portrayal of a global food imaginary is a question not often raised. Women remain invisible as food production/processing innovators within the dominant narrative of science as progress (Ferguson 1994), a fact that is not surprising given the gender biases found in research on scientific knowledge and agricultural economics (Elson 2002, Haraway 1991, Harding 1991, Waring 1988). Women often experience food security issues more severely, as

their subsistence base is eroded (Gladwin et al. 2001, Nash 1994, Weismantel 1999) and as men migrate in search of more stable employment (Messer & Shipton 2002). Even alternative forms of agricultural production such as organic farming, which often recognize the importance of women's activities, are co-opted by industrial agriculture in ways that continue to marginalize the work of women (Bellows & Hamm 2001, Hall 1998b, Trauger 2004). An investigation of the global farmer discourse hints at a highly masculinized picture. One analytical way to reconnect women's activities to globalization processes is to challenge the association of men with things global and women with things local. A useful starting point for this project is provided by Freeman (2001) who demonstrates how the mobility of Caribbean higglers shapes the dynamics of globalization. The study of efforts by international organizations to govern gender and food on global scales (Phillips 2005) complements this approach, as does research that highlights women's activism and struggles for survival in the face of structural adjustment and neoliberal policies (Beneria 2003, DeKoven 2001, Frank 2005, Peltre-Wurtz 2004, Razavi 2002, Walton & Seddon 1994).

Work written for the general public more than 30 years ago forced North Americans and Europeans to "think globally" about adjusting their diets to a "small planet" (Lappé 1973) and making connections to "how the other half dies" (George 1977). Recent panics around food risks and food safety have helped reintroduce food as global news (Gee 2002, Lien & Nerlich 2004), as has the "discovery" of its genetic health benefits in genome projects (see *Newsweek*, Jan. 17, 2005, pp. 40–48). Tourism has also played an important role in the global circulation of knowledge about culinary cultures. Today, engagement with good food (whether haute cuisine, fusion, or slow food) reinforces ideas about lifestyle and class within a new world of political associations and choices (Fantasia 1995, Miele & Murdoch 2002, Roseberry 1996). On the one hand, media and product advertising have been a crucial technical component to how the global imagination regarding consumption practices has been fed (Applbaum 2004). On the other hand, as images of famine victims and malnourished children are regularly circulated for aid and sponsorship efforts, hunger has also formed a central part of the global imaginary (Messer & Shipton 2002). Ironically, even literature that stresses a return to locality contributes to a global imaginary by posing a global "consumer monoculture" as the backdrop for its arguments (Norberg-Hodge 2003, Norberg-Hodge et al. 2002).

Mobile and Gated Bodies

Global imaginaries are realized, and challenged, as people act and move. Traveling itself involves a way of thinking (Clifford 1997), and migrant laborers, refugees and resettled populations, immigrants, students, business consultants, nutritionists, agronomists, tourists, and other travelers all play a role in the reproduction and expansion of ideas about food and food systems, although not all to the same extent or in the same manner. Cunningham's (2004) concept of the "gated globe" (referring to greater obstacles to movement for some and not others) is worth noting in this respect, as is Friedman's (2001, p. 68) observation that some travelers have more "pretensions about reorganizing the world" than do others.

Still, research points to the significance of migration to the development of international agriculture (Basok 2002; Kearney 1986, 1996; Sanderson 1985; Smart 1997) and to the production of diasporic food memories (Mankekar 2005). Immigrants, often finding the restaurant business to be their only viable source of revenue, bring their kitchen histories with them but do not impose them exactly as they please (Smart 2003). One of Smart's case studies, who had lengthy experience in food catering in Hong Kong before coming to Canada, had to learn how to cook Canadianized Chinese food (i.e., "deep fried and topped with lots of sweet thick sauce" (2003, p. 332) to make a profit. Strategic transborder migration and flexible culinary expertise are central to the entrepreneurial success of Chinese immigrants in the food business.

Studies of nontravelers and their potential contributions to globalization are more rare. Given evidence of international efforts to produce globally astute farmers, it would seem imperative to investigate how farmers and farm workers who are not crossing national and international borders are engaging with such projects. More research is needed on how farmers and farm workers are making ends meet (Hellin & Higman 2003), how their health and environment may or may not be compromised by the global farmer model (Andreatta 1998, Hollander 1995), how new food technologies are being acted on, and how the household has been transformed as a site of production, distribution, and consumption (Preibisch et al. 2002). In short, how are the demands of new food-related processes being reinscribed by nonmigrating people in the current context? One wonders whether the interrelationships between food and globalization would be theorized differently if we balanced studies of globalization and mobility with studies of this kind.

This discussion of food and the global imaginary has highlighted how constructions of the local and the global "nourish each other" (Ohnuki-Tierney 1999, p. 260). Anthropological studies that stay attuned to the role of food in localizing processes can register a "traffic in meaning" (Inda & Rosaldo 2002, p. 11): Foodways may be "deterritorialized" by global projects, but at the same time re-embedded in some place, as changing ideas about food and the world are reinscribed by people. The lesson here is to attend analytically both to how people are being mobilized in new ways through globalization processes and how they produce new meanings as they undertake their food-related practices. In the concluding section, this lesson inhabits my discussion of potential future directions for the theory, policy, and politics of food.

CREATING FOOD FUTURES?

A theoretical shift in the discipline can be noted over the past decade from an emphasis on issues of food production (e.g., how peasant farmers have been marginalized by the global economy) to questions of food consumption (e.g., does the proliferation of fast-food outlets signify the emergence of a global consumer?). Balancing earlier work developed within political economic frameworks, this recent shift attends to the important process of culture-making as a central component of globalization. Yet the heavier emphasis on consumption practices in the current period seems to reflect a bias toward privileged subjects, toward those consumers who can really afford to consume. As particular theoretical orientations rise and fall, it is worth reminding ourselves that food production and food consumption are always two sides of the same coin. As Miller (1995) and Mintz (1996) have reminded us, from quite different perspectives, concepts of commodities are linked to concepts of persons. This insight signals a way forward for addressing the economic/cultural analytical divide that continues to pervade the study of food and raises the following question: If the ideas and practices of food mark human difference, what do current projects of food and globality tell us about who we are? Specifically, what kinds of markers of food exclusion and inclusion are being created in the current situation, how are these markers maintained by global projects, and what do they imply for developing sustainable places to live? This question, which can be explored in a number of ways, is linked to the larger problem of how to create alternative food futures (Le Heron 2003).

One route suggested by the reviewed literature is to document the "lives" of edible commodities in people's lives. Ethnographic studies of how commodity markets, food-based corporations, and international organizations contribute to the identities and practices of the communities in which they are embedded may provide a fruitful path to understanding this process. Dupuis's (2002) research on milk as America's drink, Cook's (2004) investigation of the papaya, and Selfa & Qazi's (2005) analysis of farmer and consumer notions of "local" and "sustainable" take useful steps in this direction. Such work advances understanding of the multiple connections between food governance and food identities, and potentially facilitates the development of a broader politics of food.

An alternative route for addressing this question might be through a consideration of the body: How are bodies going global along with food? To what extent are (gendered) concepts of the body becoming standardized and governed, and how does food figure into this process? During a recent trip to Ecuador—a country with its fair share of hungry people—I was amazed to discover a *Curves* fitness center. What does this center, located in the nation's capital, say about the production of bodies through national and global associations? The current anthropological interest in fat (Kulick & Meneley 2005, Papenoe 2004), placed within an understanding of globalization processes, may provide insight into the connections between the circulation of industrial diets and the commodification and changing aesthetics of human bodies to offer a unique view on food and globalization.

A third avenue for exploring this question is to examine the relationships between scale-making projects (local, regional, national, global, etc.) and the emergence of new landscapes of food accessibility and scarcity. Focusing on scale-making projects helps to make visible the changing relationships between space and place (Dirlik 2001, Friedman 2001, Gupta & Ferguson 1997) and their implications for crafting sustainable food systems. For example, we may ask how the relationships between people, food, and space have been altered by global projects to create or displace specific ideas of home, community, and region. How may localizing practices for securing food undermine or be undermined by global projects and, alternatively, how may they be supported by such projects (Bellows & Hamm 2001, Feenstra 2002, Koc et al. 1999, Haan 2000, Hendrickson & Heffernan 2002, Hinrichs 2003)? These research possibilities hint at the tension between sustainable, food-enhanced places and unsustainable and food-deprived places, the boundaries of which are neither static nor always easily discernible (Riches 1997; see *Anthropology News*, Oct. 2004, p. 55).

It is interesting that the study of hunger, and its links to food-deprived places, is dominated by international organizations (FAO 2002, Pinstrup-Andersen & Pandya-Lorch 2001). Important anthropological exceptions are Messer & Shipton (2002), Scheper-Hughes (1992), and Shipton (1990). Not only do these authors examine how food policies produce new borderlands of exclusion (within, as well as between, nations), but they also hint at how little anyone cares about such exclusions until they are shown to interfere with economic or social requirements. In explaining why poor people in northeast Brazil purchase medication instead of food to survive, Scheper-Hughes (1992) argues that health claims are given more attention than are claims of hunger. This point might well be applied to the discipline of anthropology itself. Why do we generally choose to theorize through consumption and health rather than through hunger? A related question is the impact that such theoretical biases may have on policy and politics: Does a focus on consumption politics indirectly contribute to inappropriate policies of intervention, or to a general politics of indifference to food insecurities?

This quandary leads to an obvious, policy-based question: Once we find that global projects create new exclusions through food, what proposals should be put forward to do something about it? What is to be done, for example, about the shifting borderlands of malnutrition and hunger? Messer & Shipton (2002) note that the growing response to this question in the case of Africa—that famines and hunger are "very complicated"—only feeds paralysis, which is an untenable position in the current context. Sustainable farming practices can be encouraged, better trade agreements can be developed, and the production of adequate and healthy food can be promoted. All these policy decisions could be more easily developed if anthropologists undertook research to support them. Scholars widely recognize that anthropological contributions to policy development are needed (Okongwu 2000, Webb et al. 1998). Because, as anthropologists, we understand food as a marker of difference, we can make important contributions to policy by demonstrating how, in different ethnographic contexts, notions of gender, ethnicity, race, age, class, and nation are drawn into service for new border-making projects that systematically exclude some people, and not others, from healthy food.

A more general policy question that needs to be considered is, how might we all eat and produce food differently—more sustainably and less hierarchically—in a globalizing world? Much of the literature points to the need for consumers to create and choose alternatives to corporately produced and corporation-traded food by growing and eating organic food, by supporting social movements (the Green movement, the Terra Madre movement, and the Community-Shared Agriculture movement), and by participating in alternative trade and other networks (Barrientos 2000, Cone & Myhre 2001, Guthman 2000, Heller & Escobar 2003, Hendrickson & Heffernan 2002, Miele & Murdoch 2002, Murray & Raynolds 2000, Raynolds 2000, Wallace 2005, Whatmore & Thorne 1997). Although writers such as Vandana Shiva (2000) and Frances Moore Lappé (1973, 1980, 2002) have been influential in giving food alternatives a high public profile, anthropologists have tended to shy away from public-policy debates on food. This has left much room for those with different interests to define the problem of food security and to set the agenda for its resolution. Most anthropologists know, for example, that the global food security problem is not to be solved through more education, more science, and more modeling (compare Runge et al. 2003), but their invisibility in policy circles leaves such approaches unchallenged. Moreover, because anthropologists are well aware of how capital and more powerful others can absorb alternatives when these alternatives begin to look like competitors (Paley 2002; Edelman 1999), the public would be well served if the discipline systematically took on the (admittedly, mammoth) task of identifying the barriers to and possibilities for successful projects pursuing healthy and sustainable food alternatives.

Many analysts, not content to depend on policy for social change, have pointed to the expansion of political struggles around food consumption issues as an opportunity for moving forward (Canclini 2001, Goodman & Redclift 1991, Lien & Nerlich 2004). Others call for an analytical return to an emphasis on the industrial appropriation of food, and thus a politics embedded in the production of food (Buttel 2000, Carrier & Heyman 1997). Guptill & Wilkins (2002) suggest a resolution by replacing the concept of the food consumer and food producer with the idea of the food citizen. Although the idea fuels the legalistic framework that considers food a right, the notion of all of us being food citizens does help to encourage alliances, between producers and consumers and across borders, to build potential policy and political coalitions around food. It is perhaps as food citizens that we can begin to become more analytically and politically engaged with projects centered on producing sustainable places that attend to food issues, rather than presume them as a backdrop.

Everyone is becoming responsible for making better food decisions today, a process linked to global governance in ways that should make wary social movements organized around food concerns (Hassanein 2003, Le Heron 2003). The contradiction of making responsible consumption decisions in the context of questionable production and distribution practices is already revealing itself, as Johnston's (2001) attention to the problems of "consuming social justice" makes clear. A politics of food citizenship challenges us to make it our global responsibility to be aware of the convoluted paths that currently prevent many consumers from giving appropriate thanks for the food system that keeps them alive and well. Because this food system at the same time keeps others barely fed, our responsibility extends to challenging the ways in which the food world is currently structured and reproduced. In this review I argue that such a challenge requires both an interrogation of multiple arenas of global governance and a recognition of the important role played by imagination and agency in galvanizing the outcomes of the processes we refer to as globalization. Although it is clear that our practices in and visions of food worlds may either reinforce or undermine exclusionary and inequitable food systems, what is not as apparent is how food citizenship may be developed as a sustainable politics to include everyone, not just the privileged. This next step requires both reflexivity and commitment and is crucial in the continuing search for resolutions to these pressing issues.

ACKNOWLEDGMENTS

I extend appreciation to Sally Cole, Ellen Judd, Alan Smart, and Josie Smart for their useful suggestions and to Akhil Gupta and James Watson for their help. Many thanks are also due to Karina Schneider for her able research assistance for this project.

LITERATURE CITED

Anderson K, Josling T, eds. 2005. *The WTO and Agriculture*, Vol. 1. Cheltenham, UK/Northampton, MA: Elgar

Anderson S, ed. 2000. *Views from the South: The Effects of Globalization and the WTO on Third World Countries*. Chicago: Food First Books and the Int. Forum on Glob.

Andreatta SL. 1998. Agrochemical exposure and farmworker health in the Caribbean: a local/global perspective. *Hum. Organ.* 57:350–58

Appadurai A, ed. 1986. *The Social Life of Things: Commodities in Cultural Perspective*. Cambridge, UK: Cambridge Univ. Press

Appadurai A. 1988. How to make a national cuisine: cookbooks in contemporary India. *Comp. Stud. Soc. His.* 30(1):3–24

Appadurai A. 1996. *Modernity at Large*. Minneapolis: Univ. Minn. Press

Appadurai A. 2001. *Globalization*. Durham, NC/London: Duke Univ. Press

Applbaum K. 2004. *The Marketing Era: From Professional Practice to Global Provisioning*. New York/London: Routledge

Araghi F. 2003. Food regimes and the production of value: some methodological issues. *J. Peasant Stud.* 30(2):41–70

Arce A. 1993. New tastes in industrialized countries and transformations in the Latin-American countryside: an introduction to the local cases of Mexico and Chile. *Int. J. Sociol. Agric. Food* 3:48–70

Arce A. 2000. Creating or regulating development: representing modernities through language and discourse. In *Anthropology, Development and Modernities*, ed. A Arce, N Long, pp. 32–51. London/New York: Routledge

Banaji J. 1997. Globalization and restructuring in the Indian food industry. *J. Peasant Stud.* 24:191–210

Barndt D, ed. 1999. *Women Working the NAFTA Food Chain: Women, Food & Globalization*. Toronto: Second Story Press

Barndt D. 2002. *Tangled Routes: Women, Work, and Globalization on the Tomato Trail*. Lanham, UK: Rowman & Littlefield

Barnet R, Cavanagh J. 1996. *Global Dreams: Imperial Corporations and the New World Order*. New York: Simon & Shuster

Barrientos S. 2000. Globalization and ethical trade: assessing the implications for development. *J. Int. Dev.* 12:559–70

Basok T. 2002. *Tortillas and Tomatoes*. Montreal: McGill-Queen's Univ. Press

Beardsworth A, Keil T. 1997. *Sociology on the Menu: An Invitation to the Study of Food and Society*. London/New York: Routlege

Bellows AC, Hamm MW. 2001. Local autonomy and sustainable development: testing import substitution in localizing food systems. *Agric. Hum. Val.* 18:271–84

Beneria L. 2003. *Gender, Development, and Globalization: Economics as if All People Mattered*. New York/London: Routledge

Bonanno A. 1998. Liberal democracy in the global era: implications for the agro-food sector. *Agric. Hum. Val.* 15:223–42

Bonanno A. 2004. Globalization, transnational corporations, the state and democracy. *Int. J. Sociol. Agric. Food* 12(1):37–48

Bonanno A, Busch L, Friedland W, Gouveia L, Mingoine E, eds. 1994. *From Columbus to ConAgra: The Globalization of Agriculture and Food*. Lawrence: Univ. Press Kansas

Bonanno A, Constance DH. 1996. *Caught in the Net: The Global Tuna Industry, Environmentalism and the State*. Lawrence: Univ. Press Kansas

Bonanno A, Constance DH. 2001. Corporate strategies in the global era: the case of mega-hog farmers in the Texas Panhandle region. *Int. J. Sociol. Agric. Food* 9:5–28

Bonanno A, Lyman K. 1999. The introduction of capitalism in Russian agriculture: popular response to neoliberal reforms. *Rural Sociol.* 64(1):113–32

Boyd W, Watts M. 1997. Agro-industrial just-in-time: the chicken industry and post-war American capitalism. In *Globalizing Food: Agrarian Questions and Global Restructuring*, ed. D Goodman, M Watts. London/New York: Routledge

Brownell K. 2004. *Food Fight*. New York: McGraw Hill

Bruinsma J, ed. 2003. *World Agriculture: Towards 2015./2030.—An FAO Perspective*. London: Earthscan

Buttel FH. 2000. The recombinant BGH controversy in the United States: toward a new consumption politics of food. *Agric. Hum. Val.* 17:5–20

Caldwell M. 2002. The taste of nationalism: food politics in postsocialist Moscow. *Ethnos* 67(3):295–319

Canclini NG. 2001. *Consumers and Citizens: Globalization and Multicultural Conflicts*. Minneapolis: Univ. Minn. Press

Carrier JG, Heyman J. 1997. Consumption and political economy. *J. R. Anthropol. Inst.* 3(2):355–73

Chalfin B. 2004. *Shea Butter Republic: State Power, Global Markets, and the Making of an Indigenous Commodity*. New York: Routledge

Clark RP. 2000. *Global Life Systems: Population, Food, and Disease in the Process of Globalization*. Lanham, UK: Rowman & Littlefield

Clifford J. 1997. *Routes: Travel and Translation in the Late Twentieth Century*. Cambridge, MA: Harvard Univ. Press

Collins JL, Krippner GR. 1999. Permanent labor contracts in agriculture: flexibility and subordination in a new export crop. *Comp. Study Soc. His.* 41(3):510–34

Cone C, Myhre A. 2001. Community-supported agriculture: a sustainable alternative to industrial agriculture? *Hum. Organ.* 59:187–97

Consult. Group Int. Agric. Res. (CGIAR). 1998. Mobilizing science for global food security: fourth external review of CIMMYT. *Tech. Advisory Comm.*, CGIAR (FAO electronic document accessed Feb. 2, 2003)

Cook I. 2004. Follow the thing: papaya. *Antipode* 36(4):642–64

Crabtree J. 2002. The impact of neo-liberal economics on Peruvian peasant agriculture in the 1990s. *J. Peasant Stud.* 29(3–4):131–61

Culhane C. 2004. Super size me. *Food Can.* 64(5):30–35

Cunningham H. 2004. Nations rebound? Crossing borders in a gated globe. *Identities* 11(3):329–50

Curtis BM. 2001. Reforming New Zealand agriculture: the WTO way or farmer control? *Int. J. Sociol. Agric. Food* 9(1):29–42

DeKoven M, ed. 2001. *Feminist Locations: Global/Local/Theory/Practice in the Twenty-First Century*. New Brunswick, NJ: Rutgers Univ. Press

Desta MG. 2001. Food security and international trade law: an appraisal of the World Trade Organization approach. *J. World Trade* 35(3):449–68

Dirlik A. 2001. Place-based imagination: globalism and the politics of place. In *Places and Politics in an Age of Globalization*, ed. R Przniak, A Dirlik, pp. 15–51. Lanham, UK/Boulder, CO/New York/Oxford, UK: Rowman & Littlefield

Dugger CW. 2004. Supermarket giants crush Central American farmers. *NY Times* Dec. 8

Dupuis EM. 2002. *Nature's Perfect Food: How Milk Became America's Drink*. New York: New York Univ. Press

Edelman M. 1999. *Peasants Against Globalization: Rural Social Movements in Costa Rica*. Stanford, CA: Stanford Univ. Press

Elson D. 2002. Gender justice, human rights, and neo-liberal economic policies. In *Gender Justice, Development, and Rights*, ed. M Molyneux, S Razavi, pp. 78–114. Oxford, UK: Oxford Univ. Press

Escobar A. 1995. *Encountering Development: The Making and Unmaking of the Third World*. Princeton, NJ: Princeton Univ. Press

Evans M, Sinclair R, Fusimalohi C, Laiva'a V, Freeman M. 2003. Consumption of traditional versus imported foods in Tonga: implications for programs designed to reduce diet-related non-communicable diseases in developing countries. *Ecol. Food Nutr.* 42:153–76

Fantasia R. 1995. Fast food in France. *Theory Soc.* 24(2):201–43

Feenstra G. 2002. Creating space for sustainable food systems: lessons from the field. *Agric. Hum. Val.* 19:99–106

Ferguson AE. 1994. Gendered science: a critique of agricultural development. *Am. Anthropol.* 96(3):540–52

Food and Agric. Organ. (FAO). 2002. *Anti-Hunger Programme: Reducing hunger Through Sustainable Agricultural and Rural Development and Wider Access to Food*. 2nd draft. Rome: FAO

Frank D. 2005. *Bananeras: Women Transforming the Banana Unions of Latin America*. Cambridge, MA: South End Press

Freeman C. 2001. Is local: global as feminine: masculine? Rethinking the gender of globalization. *Signs* 26(4):1007–37

Freidberg SE. 2003. Culture, conventions and colonial constructs of rurality in south-north horticultural trades. *J. Rural Stud.* 19:97–109

Friedland WH. 1994. The global fresh fruit and vegetable system: an industrial organization analysis. See McMichael 1994, pp. 173–89

Friedman J. 1994. *Cultural Identity and Global Process*. London: Sage

Friedman J. 2001. Indigenous struggles and the discreet charm of the bourgeoisie. In *Places and Politics in an Age of Globalization*, ed. R Prazniak, A Dirlik, pp. 53–69. Lanham, UK/Boulder, CO/New York/Oxford, UK: Rowman & Littlefield

Friedmann H. 1982. The political economy of food: the rise and fall of the postwar international food order. *Am. J. Sociol.* 88(Suppl.):S248–86

Friedmann H, McMichael P. 1989. Agriculture and the state system: the rise and decline of national agricultures, 1870 to the present. *Sociologia Ruralis* 29:93–117

Garcia LAH, Martinez EB, Sala HQ. 1999. The role of national and transnational corporations in the globalization of dairying in La Laguna, Mexico. *Int. J. Sociol. Agric. Food* 8:52–70

Gee H. 2002. Food and the future. *Nature* 418(6898):1–3

George S. 1977. *How the Other Half Dies: The Real Reasons for World Hunger*. Montclair, NJ: Allenheld, Osman and Co.

Gladwin C, Thomson A, Peterson J, Anderson A. 2001. Addressing food security in Africa via multiple livelihood strategies of women farmers. *Food Policy* 26:177–207

Goldfrank W. 2005. Fresh demand: the consumption of Chilean produce in the United States. See Watson & Caldwell 2005, pp. 42–53

Goodman D, Depuis EM. 2002. Knowing food and growing food: beyond the production-consumption debate in sociology of agriculture. *Sociologia Ruralis* 42(1):5–22

Goodman D, Redclift M. 1991. *Refashioning Nature: Food, Ecology and Culture*. London: Routledge

Goodman D, Watts M, ed. 1997. *Globalizing Food: Agrarian Questions and Global Restructuring*. London: Routledge

Gottschang SK. 2000. A baby-friendly hospital and the science of infant feeding. See Jing 2000, pp. 160–84

Gupta A. 1998. *Postcolonial Developments: Agriculture in the Making of Modern India.* Durham, NC: Duke Univ. Press

Gupta A. 2003. *Global movements of crops since the 'Age of Discovery' and changing culinary cultures.* Sirindhorn Anthropology Lecture, Princess Maha Chaki Sirindhorn Anthropology Centre, Bangkok, March 26

Gupta A, Ferguson J, eds. 1997. *Culture, Power, Place: Explorations in Critical Anthropology.* Durham, NC: Duke Univ. Press

Guptill A, Wilkins JL. 2002. Buying into the food system: trends in food retailing in the US and implications for local foods. *Agric. Hum. Val.* 19:39–51

Guthman J. 2000. Raising organic: an agro-ecological assessment of grower practice in California. *Agric. Hum. Val.* 17:257–66

Haan de LJ. 2000. Globalization, localization and sustainable livelihood. *Sociologia Ruralis* 40(3):339–65

Hall A. 1998a. Pesticide reforms and the challenges of globalization: making the farmers responsible. *Can. J. Law Soc.* 13(1):187–213

Hall A. 1998b. Sustainable agriculture: implications for gender and the family farm. In *Transgressing Borders: Critical Perspectives on Gender, Household, and Culture*, ed. S Ilcan, L Phillips, pp. 209–25. Westport, CT: Bergin & Garvey

Haraway D. 1991. *Simians, Cyborgs and Women: The Reinvention of Nature.* New York: Routledge

Harding S. 1991. *Whose Science? Whose Knowledge?: Thinking from Women's Lives.* Ithaca, NY: Cornell Univ. Press

Hassanein N. 2003. Practicing food democracy: a pragmatic politics of transformation. *J. Rural Stud.* 19:77–86

Heffernan W, Constance D. 1994. Transnational corporations and the globalization of the food system. In *From Columbus to ConAgra: The Globalization of Agriculture and Food*, ed. A Bonanno, L Busch, W Friedland, L Gouveia, E Mingoine, pp. 29–51. Lawrence: Univ. Press Kansas

Heller C, Escobar A. 2003. From pure genes to GMOS: transnationalized gender landscapes in the biodiversity and transgenic food networks. In *Genetic Nature/Culture: Anthropology and Science beyond the Two-Culture Divide*, ed. A Goodman, D Heath, MS Lindee, pp. 155–75. Berkeley/London: Univ. Calif. Press

Hellin J, Higman S. 2003. *Feeding the Market: South American Farmers, Trade and Globalization.* Bloomfield, CT: Kumarian

Hendrickson MK, Heffernan WD. 2002. Opening spaces through relocalization: locating potential resistance in the weaknesses of the global food system. *Sociologia Ruralis* 42(4):347–69

Hinrichs CC. 2003. The practice and politics of food system localization. *J. Rural Stud.* 19:33–45

Hobart M, ed. 1993. *An Anthropological Critique of Development.* London: Routledge

Hollander GM. 1995. Agroenvironmental conflict and world food system theory: sugarcane in the Everglades agricultural area. *J. Rural Stud.* 11(3):309–18

Ilcan S, Phillips L. 2003. Making food count: expert knowledge and global technologies of government. *Can. Rev. Sociol. Anthropol.* 40(4):441–62

Ilcan S, Phillips L. 2006. Circulations of insecurity: globalizing food standards in historical perspective. In *Agricultural Standards: The Shape of the Global Food and Fiber System*, ed. J Bingen, L Bush, pp. 51–72. Dordrecht, The Neth.: Springer

Inda J, Rosaldo R, eds. 2002. *The Anthropology of Globalization*: Oxford, UK: Blackwell

Ingco MD, Nash JD. 2004. *Agriculture and the WTO: Creating a Trading System for Development.* Washington, DC: World Bank/Oxford Univ. Press

Ito S. 2002. From rice to prawns: economic transformation and agrarian structure in rural Bangladesh. *J. Peasant Stud.* 29(2):47–70

Jameson F, Miyoshi M. 1998. *The Cultures of Globalization.* Durham, NC: Duke Univ. Press

Jansen K, Vellema S, eds. 2004. *Agribusiness and Society: Corporate Responses to Environmentalism, Market Opportunities, and Public Regulation.* London/New York: Zed

Jarosz L. 2000. Understanding agri-food networks as social relations. *Agric. Hum. Val.* 17:279–83

Jing J, ed. 2000. *Feeding China's Little Emperors: Food, Children and Social Change.* Stanford, CA: Stanford Univ. Press

Jing J. 2000. Food, nutrition, and cultural authority in a Gansu village. See Jing 2000, pp. 135–59

Johnston J. 2001. Consuming social justice. *Arena* (Electronic document accessed Feb. 7, 2005)

Kearney M. 1986. From the invisible hand to visible feet: anthropological studies of migration and development. *Annu. Rev. Anthropol.* 15:331–61

Kearney M. 1996. *Reconceptualizing the Peasantry: Anthropology in Global Perspective.* Boulder, CO: Westview

Kneen B. 1995. *Invisible Giant: Cargill and its Transnational Strategies.* London: Pluto

Kneen B. 1999. Restructuring food for corporate profit: the corporate genetics of Cargill and Monsanto. *Agric. Hum. Val.* 16:161–67

Koc M, MacRae R, Mougeot L, Welsh J, eds. 1999. *For Hunger-Proof Cities: Sustainable Urban Food Systems.* Ottawa: Int. Dev. Res. Cent.

Konefal J, Mascarenhas M, Hatanaka M. 2005. Governance in the global agro-food system: backlighting the role of transnational supermarket chains. *Agric. Hum. Val.* 22:291–302

Kritzinger A, Barrientos S, Rossouw H. 2004. Global production and flexible employment in South African horticulture: experiences of contract workers in fruit exports. *Sociologia Ruralis* 44(1):17–39

Kulick D, Meneley A. 2005. *Fat: The Anthropology of an Obsession.* New York: Tarcher/Penguin

Lappé FM. 1973. *Diet for a Small Planet.* New York: Ballentine

Lappé FM, Collins J. 1980. *World Hunger: Ten Myths.* Grove Press, NY: Food First

Lappé FM, Lappé A. 2002. *Hope's Edge: The Next Diet for a Small Planet.* New York: J.P.Tarcher/Putnam

Le Heron R. 2003. Creating food futures: reflections on food governance issues in New Zealand's agri-food sector. *J. Rural Stud.* 19(1):111–25

Lentz C, ed. 1999. *Changing Food Habits: Case Studies from Africa, South America and Europe.* Amsterdam: Harwood Academic

Li T. 2004. *Government through community at the World Bank.* Presented at Annu. Meet. Can. Anthropol. Soc./Soc. Can. Anthropol. (CASCA), May 6, London

Lien MF, Nerlich B, eds. 2004. *The Politics of Food.* Oxford, UK: Berg

Lind D, Barham E. 2004. The social life of the tortilla: food, cultural politics, and contested commodification. *Agric. Hum. Val.* 21:47–60

Llambí L. 1993. Global agro-food restructuring: the role of transnational corporations and nation-States. *Int. J. Sociol. Agric. Food* 3:19–38

Long N, Long A, eds. 1992. *The Battlefields of Knowledge: The Interlocking of Theory and Practice in Social Research and Development.* London/New York: Routledge

Lozada EP Jr. 2000. Globalized childhood? Kentucky Fried Chicken in Beijing. See Jing 2000, pp. 114–34

Lyson TA, Raymer AL. 2000. Stalking the Wily Multinational: power and control in the US food system. *Agric. Hum. Val.* 17:199–208

Madeley J. 2000. *Hungry for Trade: How the Poor Pay for Free Trade.* London: Zed

Magdoff F, Foster JM, Buttel F, ed. 2000. *Hungry for Profit: The Agribusiness Threat to Farmers, Food, and the Environment.* New York: Monthly Rev. Press

Mankekar P. 2005. 'India Shopping': Indian grocery stores and transnational configurations of belonging. See Watson & Caldwell 2005, pp. 197–214

Marglin S. 1996. Farmers, seedsmen, and scientists: systems of agriculture and systems of knowledge. In *Decolonizing Knowledge: From Development to Dialogue,* ed. F Apfel-Marglin, S. Marglin, pp. 198–248. Oxford, UK: Clarendon

Marsden T. 2000. Food matters and the matter of food: towards a new food governance? *Sociologia Ruralis* 40(1):20–29

Marsden T, Cavalcanti JSB, Irmão JF. 1996. Globalisation, regionalisation and quality: the socio-economic reconstitution of food in the San Francisco Valley, Brazil. *Int. J. Sociol. Agric. Food* 5:85–114

McCann J. 2001. Maize and grace: history, corn, and Africa's new landscapes, 1500–1999. *Comp. Study Soc. His.* 43(2):246–72

McKenna M, Campbell H. 2002. It's not easy being green: the development of 'food safety' practices in New Zealand's apple industry. *Int. J. Sociol. Agric. Food* 10(2):45–55

McKenna M, Roche M, Le Heron R. 1999. H. J. Heinz and global gardens: creating quality, leveraging localities. *Int. J. Sociol. Agric. Food* 8:35–51

McKenna M, Le Heron R, Roche M. 2001. Living local, growing global: renegotiating the export production regime in New Zealand's pipfruit sector. *Geoforum* 32:157–66

McMichael P, ed. 1994. *The Global Restructuring of Agro-Food Systems.* Ithaca, NY: Cornell Univ. Press

McMichael P. 1999. Virtual capitalism and agri-food restructuring. In *Restructuring Global and Regional Agricultures,* ed. D Burch, J Goss, G Lawrence, pp. 3–22. Aldershot, UK: Ashgate

McMichael P. 2000. The power of food. *Agric. Hum. Val.* 17:21–33

Messer E, Shipton P. 2002. Hunger in Africa: untangling its human roots. In *Exotic No More: Anthropology on the Front Lines,* ed. J MacClancey, pp. 227–50. Chicago: Univ. Chicago Press

Miele M, Murdoch J. 2002. The practical aesthetics of traditional cuisines: slow food in Tuscany. *Sociologia Ruralis* 42(4):312–28

Miller D. 1995. Consumption and commodities. *Annu. Rev. Anthropol.* 24:141–61

Miller D. 1998. Coca-Cola: a black sweet drink from Trinidad. In *Material Cultures: Why Some Things Matter,* ed. D Miller, Chicago: Univ. Chicago Press

Mintz SW. 1985. *Sweetness and Power: The Place of Sugar in Modern History.* New York: Penguin

Mintz SW. 1996. *Tasting Food, Tasting Freedom.* Boston: Beacon

Mintz SW, Du Bois CM. 2002. The anthropology of food and eating. *Annu. Rev. Anthropol.* 31:99–119

Moran W, Blunden G, Workman M, Bradley A. 1996. Family farmers, real regulation and the experience of food regimes. *J. Peasant Stud.* 12(3):245–58

Murray W. 2001. The second wave of globalization and agrarian change in the Pacific Islands. *J. Rural Stud.* 17:135–48

Murray W. 2002. From dependency to reform and back again: the Chilean peasantry during the twentieth century. *J. Peasant Stud.* 29(3–4):190–227

Murray DL, Raynolds LT. 2000. Alternative trade in bananas: obstacles and opportunities for progressive social change in the global economy. *Agric. Hum. Val.* 17:65–74

Myers G. 2004. *Banana Wars: The Price of Free Trade*. London/New York: Zed

Nash J. 1994. Global integration and subsistence insecurity. *Am. Anthropol.* 96(1):7–30

Nestle M. 2002. *Food Politics: How the Food Industry Influences Nutrition and Health*. Berkeley: Univ. Calif. Press

Norberg-Hodge H. 2003. The consumer monoculture. *Int. J. Consum. Stud.* 27(4):258–61

Norberg-Hodge H, Merrifield T, Gorelick S. 2002. *Bringing the Food Economy Home: Local Alternatives to Global Agribusiness*. London: Zed Books

Ohnuki-Tierney E. 1999. We eat each other's food to nourish our body: the global and local as mutually constituent forces. In *Food in Global History*, ed. R Grew, pp. 240–72. Boulder, CO: Westview

Okongwu AF. 2000. The anthropology of public policy. *Annu. Rev. Anthropol.* 29:107–24

Ortiz S. 2002. Laboring in the factories and in the fields. *Annu. Rev. Anthropol.* 31:395–417

Pacione M. 1997. Local exchange trading systems—a rural response to the globalization of capitalism? *J. Rural Stud.* 13(4):415–27

Paley J. 2002. Toward an anthropology of democracy. *Annu. Rev. Anthropol.* 31:469–96

Papenoe R. 2004. *Feeding Desire: Fatness, Beauty, and Sexuality Among a Saharan people*. London/New York: Routledge

Paul H, Steinbrecher R. 2003. *Transnational Biotech Companies Colonize the Food Chain*. London/New York: Zed

Peltre-Wurtz J. 2004. Luchar para Comer: estrategias familiares para la alimentación en sectores populares. Quito, Ecuador: CEDIME, IRD, Abya-Yala

Phillips L. 2005. Gender mainstreaming: the global governance of women? *Can. J. Dev. Stud.* 26:651–63

Phillips L, Ilcan S. 2003. A world free from hunger: global imagination and governance in the age of scientific management. *Sociologia Ruralis* 43(4):434–53

Phillips L, Ilcan S. 2004. Capacity-building: the neoliberal governance of development. *Can. J. Dev. Stud.* 15(3):393–409

Pinstrup-Andersen P, Pandya-Lorch R. 2001. *The Unfinished Agenda: Perspectives on Overcoming Hunger, Poverty, and Environmental Degradation*. Washington, DC: IPRI

Pinstrup-Andersen P, Schioler E. 2000. *Seeds of Contention: World Hunger and the Global Controversy over GM Crops*. Baltimore/London: John Hopkins Univ.

Preibisch K, Rivera Herrejon G, Wiggins S. 2002. Defending food security in a free-market economy: the gendered dimensions of restructuring in rural Mexico. *Hum. Org.* 61(1):68–79

Pritchard B, Burch D. 2003. *Agri-Food Globalization in Perspective: International Restructuring in the Processing Tomato Industry*. Aldershot, UK: Ashgate

Pritchard B, Fagan R. 1999. Circuits of capital and transnational corporate spatial behaviour: Nestlé in Southeast Asia. *Int. J. Sociol. Agric. Food* 8:3–20

Raffer K. 1997. Helping southern net food importers after the Uruguay Round: a proposal. *World Development* 25(11):1901–7

Raynolds LT. 1994. The restructuring of third world agro-exports: changing production relations in the Dominican Republic. See McMichael 1994, pp. 214–37

Raynolds LT. 2000. Re-embedding global agriculture: the international organic and fair trade movements. *Agric. Hum. Val.* 17:297–309

Raynolds LT. 2002. Consumer/producer links in fair trade coffee networks. *Sociologia Ruralis* 42(4):404–24

Raynolds LT, Murray D. 1998. Yes, we have no bananas: reregulating global and regional trade. *Int. J. Sociol. Agric. Food* 7:7–44

Razavi S, ed. 2002. *Shifting Burdens: Gender and Agrarian Change Under Neoliberalism*. Bloom-field, CT: Kumarian

Renard MC. 1999. The interstices of globalization: the example of fair coffee. *Sociologia Ruralis* 39:484–500

Riches G, ed. 1997. *First World Hunger: Food Security and Welfare Politics*. New York: St. Martin's

Ritzer G. 1993. *The McDonaldization of Society*. Thousand Oaks, CA: Pine Forge Press

Rocheleau D, Thomas-Slater B, Wangari E, eds. 1996. *Feminist Political Ecology: Global Perspectives and Local Insights*. London/New York: Routledge

Roseberry W. 1996. The rise of the yuppie coffees and the reimagination of class in the United States. *Am. Anthropol.* 98(4):762–75

Rosset P, Rice R, Watts M. 1999. Thailand and the World Tomato: globalization, new agricultural countries (NACs) and the agrarian question. *Int. J. Sociol. Agric. Food* 8:71–85

Runge CF, Senauer B, Pardey PG, Rosegrant M. 2003. *Ending Hunger in our Lifetime: Food Security and Globalization*. Published for IFPRI (Int. Food Policy Res. Inst.). Baltimore/London: John Hopkins Univ. Press

Sanderson S, ed. 1985. *The Americas in the New International Division of Labor*. New York: Holmes and Meier

Sanderson S. 1986. The emergence of the 'world steer': internationalization and foreign domination in Latin American cattle production. In *Food, the State and International Political Economy*, ed. FL Tullis, WL Hollist, pp. 123–48. Lincoln: Univ. Neb. Press

Schaeffer R. 1993. Standardization, GATT and fresh food. *Int. J. Sociol. Agric. Food* 3:71–81

Scheper-Hughes N. 1992. *Death Without Weeping: The Violence of Everyday Life in Brazil*. Berkeley/Los Angeles: Univ. Calif. Press

Schertz LP, Daft LM, ed. 1994. *Food and Agriculture Markets: The Quiet Revolution*. Washington, DC: Econ. Res. Serv. U.S. Dep. Agric., Food and Agric. Comm. Natl. Plan. Assoc.

Scott J. 1998. *Seeing like a State: How Certain Schemes to Improve the Human Condition Have Failed*. New Haven, CT/London: Yale Univ. Press

Selfa T, Qazi J. 2005. Place, taste, or face-to-face? Understanding producer-consumer networks in 'local' food systems in Washington State. *Agric. Hum. Val.* 22(4):451–64

Shipton P. 1990. African famines and food security: anthropological perspectives. *Annu. Rev. Anthropol.* 19:353–94

Shiva V. 1997. *Biopiracy: The Plunder of Nature and Knowledge*. Cambridge, MA: South End

Shiva V. 2000. *Stolen Harvest: The Highjacking of the Global Food Supply*. Cambridge, MA: South End

Smart J. 1997. Borrowed men on borrowed time: globalization, labor migration, and local economies in Alberta. *Can. J. Region. Sci.* 20(1–2):141–56

Smart J. 2003. Ethnic entrepreneurship, transmigration, and social integration: an ethnographic study of Chinese restaurant owners in rural western Canada. *Urban Anthropol.* 32(3–4):311–42

Sobal J. 1999. Food system globalization, eating transformations, and nutrition transitions. In *Food in Global History*, ed. R Grew, pp. 171–93. Boulder, CO: Westview

Sobal J. 2001. Commentary: globalization and the epidemiology of obesity. *Int. J. Epidemiol.* 30:1136–37

Sonnenfeld D, Schotzko T, Jussaume JRA. 1998. Globalization of the Washington apple industry: its evolution and impacts. *Int. J. Sociol. Agric. Food.* 7:151–38

Tillotson JE. 2004. America's obesity: conflicting public policies, industrial economic development, and unintended human consequences. *Annu. Rev. Nutr.* 24:617–43

Tinker I. 1999. Street foods into the 21st century. *Agric. Hum. Val.* 16:327–33

Tomlinson J. 1999. *Globalization and Culture*. Chicago: Chicago Univ. Press

Trauger A. 2004. Because they can do the work: women farmers in sustainable agriculture in Pennsylvania, USA. *Gend. Place Cult.* 11(2):289–307

Tsing A. 2000. The global situation. *Cult. Anthropol.* 15(3):327–60

Van Esterik P. 1989. *The Breast-Bottle Controversy*. New Brunswick, NJ: Rutgers Univ. Press

Van Esterik P. 1999. Right to food; right to feed; right to be fed: the intersection of women's rights and the right to food. *Agric. Hum. Val.* 16:225–32

Wallace J. 2005. Terra madre: a global gathering of food producers. *Can. Org. Grow.* Winter:26–27

Walton J, Seddon D. 1994. *Free Markets and Food Riots: The Politics of Global Adjustment*. Oxford, UK: Blackwell

Waring M. 1988. *If Women Counted: A New Feminist Economics*. San Francisco: Harper Collins

Warman A. 2003. *Corn and Capitalism: How a Botanical Bastard Grew to Global Dominance*. Chapel Hill/London: Univ. N.C. Press

Watson JL, ed. 1997. *Golden Arches East: McDonald's in East Asia*. Stanford, CA: Stanford Univ. Press

Watson JI, Caldwell MI, eds. 2005. *The Cultural Politics of Food and Eating: A Reader*. Oxford, UK: Blackwell

Webb KL, Pelletier D, Maretzki AN, Wilkins J. 1998. Local food policy coalitions: evaluation issues as seen by academics, project organizers, and funders. *Agric. Hum. Val.* 15:65–75

Weismantel M. 1988. *Food, Gender and Poverty in the Ecuadoran Andes*. Philadelphia: Univ. Penn. Press

Weismantel M. 1999. Tasty meals and bitter gifts: consumption and production in the Ecuadoran Andes. In *Changing Food Habits*, ed. C Lentz, pp. 135–53. Amsterdam: Overseas Publ. Assoc.

Whatmore S, Thorne L. 1997. Nourishing networks: alternative geographies of food. In *Globalising Food: Agrarian Questions and Global Restructuring*, ed. D Goodman, M Watts, pp. 287–304. London: Routledge

WHO (World Health Organ.). 1998. *Obesity: Preventing and Managing the Global Epidemic*. Geneva: WHO

Yenal NZ. 1999. Food TNCs, intellectual property investments and post-Fordist food consumption: the case of Unilever and Nestlé in Turkey. *Int. J. Sociol. Agric. Food* 8:21–34

Archaeology of Overshoot and Collapse

Joseph A. Tainter

Global Institute of Sustainability and School of Human Evolution and Social Change, Arizona State University, PO Box 873211, Tempe, Arizona 85287-3211; email: Joseph.Tainter@asu.edu

Annu. Rev. Anthropol. 2006. 35:59–74

First published online as a Review in Advance on May 10, 2006

The *Annual Review of Anthropology* is online at anthro.annualreviews.org

This article's doi: 10.1146/annurev.anthro.35.081705.123136

Copyright © 2006 by Annual Reviews. All rights reserved

0084-6570/06/1021-0059$20.00

Key Words

intensification, Malthus, resources

Abstract

The literature on sustainability and the human future emphasizes the belief that population and/or mass consumption caused resource degradation and collapse in earlier societies. Archaeological literature proposing overshoot and collapse appears in current debates over resource conservation versus continued economic growth. The prominence of this debate, with its national and international dimensions, makes it important to assess whether there is evidence in the archaeological literature for overshoot and collapse brought on by Malthusian overpopulation and/or mass consumption.

Overshoot: the
outcome when a
trajectory is
unsustainable for
environmental,
technical, or social
reasons

Collapse: rapid loss
of an established
level of social,
political, and/or
economic complexity

INTRODUCTION

Overshoot is a term and concept in the wild. Like a computer virus in the wild, it proliferates in the public arena. It mutates like a biological virus, assuming altered forms and new meanings. Overshoot is part of contemporary politics, ideology, and public discourse. Many believe that humanity has overshot the carrying capacity of some resource or other (e.g., Rees 2004). Conversely, neoclassical economists and the politicians they influence argue that resources, and the concept of overshoot, can be left out of economic calculations. As a resource becomes scarce, they believe market prices will signal that there are rewards to innovation: A new resource or technology will emerge. This debate tinges public life and international relations. It also means that academic discourse, including archaeological and historical research, about overshoot has political connotations.

The concept of overshoot is often traced to Malthus' (1798) *Essay on the Principle of Population*. Malthus believed that whereas agricultural production increases linearly, population tends to grow geometrically. Population will overshoot food supply. Malthus was influenced by Wallace (1761), who argued that progress would undermine itself by filling the world with people. Stimulated by Malthus, Jevons (1866 [1865]) wrote *The Coal Question*, in which he proposed that Britain's industrial development would outrun the coal supply. Ehrlich (1968) brought Malthusian overshoot to public attention in *The Population Bomb*. The concept was systematized by Catton (1980) in *Overshoot: The Revolutionary Basis of Ecological Change*. Catton defines overshoot as follows:

> (v.) to increase in number so much that the habitat's carrying capacity is exceeded by the ecological load, which must in time decrease accordingly; (n.) the condition of having exceeded for the time being the permanent carrying capacity of the habitat (p. 278).

The concept of overshoot clearly depends on that of carrying capacity, which Catton (1980) defines as follows:

> the maximum population of a given species which a particular habitat can support indefinitely (under specified technology and organization, in the case of the human species) (p. 272).

Catton did not seem to realize that this qualifier may make the concept moot for humans. As an ecologist he emphasized population, whereas today's concerns are about both population and consumption.

Collapse, too, is in the wild, as shown by Diamond's (2005) popular book *Collapse: How Societies Choose to Fail or Succeed*. The term collapse has many meanings. Colloquially, collapse means everything from what happened to the Soviet Union to what a worker may do at the end of a hard day. Societies collapse, but then so do bridges, levees, and cardiovascular systems. Academically, the problem is not that definitions vary, but that scholars sometimes discuss the collapses of societies without defining the term. Authors assume that we know what it means, without individual, cultural, or temporal variation.

Where authors fail to define collapse, I use my own definition (Tainter 1988). Diamond (2005) does explicitly define collapse, giving priority to population: "By collapse, I mean a drastic decrease in human population size and/or political/economic/social complexity, over a considerable area, for an extended time" (p. 3).

The interest in Diamond's book suggests that, in the popular imagination, collapse results from overshoot. The belief that previous collapses did result from overshoot (Rees 2004) contributes to the debate over our own future. While recognizing a wider range of writings about resources and collapse, I concentrate on literature pertinent to the contemporary debate. Is there evidence in history or prehistory that population and/or mass consumption overshot carrying capacity and degraded resources, causing societies to collapse?

Although we commonly consider overshoot to be an excess of population and/or consumption relative to natural resources, overshoot may take several forms. A common theme in the study of early states is whether elite demands for taxes and/or labor exceeded the peasants' tolerance or capacity to produce (e.g., Lowe 1985). Agrarian empires may overshoot a sustainable size within the constraints of transportation and communication—a province too far, so to speak (e.g., Tainter 1988). Government costs may grow to the point that they undermine a state's ability to respond to crises (Phillips 1979). More broadly, social and political complexity carry costs, which may increase to the level of becoming unsustainable (Tainter 1988). These topics merit their own reviews.

STUDIES IN OVERSHOOT AND COLLAPSE

In 1931, Cooke proposed that the collapse in the southern Maya lowlands (Classic period ca. A.D. 250–830) was caused by soil erosion and land scarcity, encroachment of grasses, silting of lakes with attendant destruction of water transportation, decline in water supply in dry years, and an increase in mosquito populations along with the introduction of, or increase in, malaria. Thirty years later, Sanders (1962, 1963) conducted an extensive study of lowland ecology and reached similar conclusions. He argued that swidden agriculture in this region leads to soil depletion, weeds, and savanna formation. Between the times when Cooke and Sanders wrote, Betty Meggers (1954) proposed her environmental limitation theory: More productive environments can sustain more complex societies. Cultural complexity is limited by environmental potential, especially for agriculture. Meggers considered tropical rainforests to have insufficient agricultural potential to support much cultural complexity. This raised the problem of the Maya. Her solution was that Maya civilization

must have been introduced from elsewhere. By this circuitous reasoning, the Maya overshot the limits of the environment in which they found themselves, and so collapsed.

Culbert (1988) argues that the Maya could not achieve equilibrium because they "were a growth system" (p. 77). Population may have reached 200/km^2. Intensive agriculture could have supported such dense populations, but at a cost of grass invasion, fertility loss, and erosion. Sustaining such a system required high levels of continual labor. Yet labor was diverted into monument construction and warfare, depriving the agricultural sector of necessary maintenance. The resulting environmental degradation ultimately created the conditions for a collapse.

The most widely accepted archaeological cases of overshoot and collapse were proposed by Jacobsen & Adams (1958; Adams 1981). In ancient southern Mesopotamia, intensive irrigation could produce growing prosperity. The Third Dynasty of Ur (ca. 2100 to 2000 B.C.) expanded the irrigation system and encouraged growth of population and settlement. It established a bureaucracy to collect taxes and tribute. Unfortunately, after a few years of overirrigating, saline groundwaters rose and destroyed the basis of agricultural productivity. The political system lost its resource base and was destabilized. Large irrigation systems that required central management were useless once the state could not maintain them.

In the Early Dynastic period (ca. 2900 to 2300 B.C.), crop yields per hectare averaged 2030 liters. Under the Third Dynasty of Ur this declined to 1134 liters. Ur III farmers had to plant an average of 55.1 liters per hectare, double the previous rate. The Third Dynasty of Ur pursued intensification that yielded diminishing returns.

The Third Dynasty of Ur hung on through five kings and then collapsed. The consequences were catastrophic for the population. By 1700 B.C. yields were down to 718 liters per hectare. Of the fields still in production, more than one fourth averaged only about 370 liters per hectare. The labor to farm

Intensification: increase in the inputs to a productive system to obtain higher gross outputs

a hectare of land was constant, so for equal efforts cultivators took in harvests about one third the size of harvests in the previous millennium. Soon southern Babylonia was extensively abandoned. By a millennium or so after the Third Dynasty of Ur the number of settlements was down 40%, and the settled area contracted 77%. Population did not rebound to Ur III densities until the first centuries A.D. (Adams 1981).

The fullest development of Mesopotamian agriculture began in the sixth century A.D. Under the Abbasid Caliphate (750–1258) the needs of the state took precedence over peasants' ability to pay. Tax was fixed whatever the yield, so peasants had to cultivate intensively. Taxes were no longer remitted for crop failure. Fifty percent of a harvest was owed under the Caliph Mahdi (775–785), with many supplemental payments. Sometimes taxes were demanded before a harvest, even before the next year's harvest.

As the irrigation system grew in size and complexity, maintenance was no longer within local capacity. Communities depended on the government, which became unstable. Fields again developed problems of salinization. Peasants lacked reserves, and revolts were inevitable. Civil war meant that the hierarchy could not manage the irrigation system. Mesopotamia experienced an unprecedented collapse. In the period from 788 to 915 revenues fell 55%. At the center of the empire, the Sawad region had supplied 50% of the government's revenues. This dropped within a few decades to 10%. Most of this loss occurred between the years 845 and 915. In many areas there were revenue losses of 90% within a lifetime. State control contracted, which diminished any chance to resolve the agricultural problems. By the early tenth century irrigation weirs were limited to the vicinity of Baghdad.

In portions of Mesopotamia the occupied area had shrunk by 94% by the 11th century. Population dropped to the lowest level in five millennia. Urban life was eliminated

for centuries in 10,000 square kilometers of Mesopotamia.

Chew (2001) has employed the framework of World Systems Theory to explore ecological degradation between 3000 B.C. and the present. Chew believes that the relations between culture and nature are exploitative and that the outcomes include "civilizational collapse" (p. 1). More broadly, "[i]t is the interplay between the limits of Nature and the trends and dynamics of social, political, and economic relations that ultimately defines the historical tendencies of transformation and evolution of societal systems" (p. 2). Collapse is one kind of societal transformation and also an environmental interlude: "[D]ark ages should be appreciated as periods for the restoration of the ecological balance ..." (p. 10). Chew believes that during the Bronze Age of Mesopotamia and the Indus Valley, excess consumption produced environmental degradation that led to collapse.

In the Tigris and Euphrates valleys, argues Chew (2001, pp. 20–26), wood requirements for manufacturing, urban consumption, construction, implements, and shipbuilding caused deforestation in northern Mesopotamia. Combined with overgrazing, the result was siltation of irrigation systems. Canals had to be cleaned regularly. When there was unrest, agriculture declined. This decline was exacerbated by the problem of salinization. Overall, core-periphery relations coupled with high consumption to degrade the environment (p. 26). This problem was exacerbated when peripheral elites tried to emulate the lifestyles of core elites.

But human action was not the only factor. Between 3100 and 1200 B.C., Mesopotamia experienced declining precipitation (Chew 2001, pp. 36–39). This decline was combined with increases in evapotranspiration and salinization. Agriculture was intensified nonetheless. In Chew's assessment, the eventual decline in agricultural production brought collapse to southern Mesopotamia and a shift in power to the north.

The Harappan Civilization of the Indus Valley and beyond, asserts Chew (2001), had the same culture-nature relations as southern Mesopotamia (pp. 26–36). Demand for wood, including wood needed to manufacture fired brick, led to "extreme deforestation of the Harappan landscape and its hinterland" (p. 27). Increased aridity between 1800 and 1500 B.C. stressed the Harappans, as did a decline in Mesopotamian imports. Tectonic shifts diverted water courses. By ca. 1700 B.C., "overcultivation, overgrazing, salinity, deforestation, and flooding contributed to the decline of the Harappan urban complex" (p. 35). As southern Mesopotamia declined simultaneously, Harappan exports to the Gulf fell. People migrated to the north and south, until even small trading towns "merged into the countryside" (p. 36).

Chew sees the same processes in the Minoan and Mycenaean collapses (2001, pp. 41–61). Population on Crete increased until ca. 1600 B.C. Large volumes of wood were needed for construction and shipbuilding. Chew argues that deforestation led to erosion and flash flooding. Crete imported wood from Mycenaean Greece and metals from various places, in turn producing value-added exports. The environmental problems on the island weakened Cretan manufacturing, and also the island's political and economic strength, by the 15th century B.C.

Chew postulates that similar transformations occurred in Mycenaean Greece. Cretan wealth was transferred to the mainland in exchange for Mycenaean wood. But the Mycenaeans had to undertake extensive environmental engineering to combat erosion and siltation caused by deforestation. As with Mesopotamia and Harappa, "ceaseless accumulation of capital, core-hinterland relations, urbanization, population growth, deforestation, and intensive land use, ultimately led to severe constraints on the continued expansion of socioeconomic communities of the Aegean" (Chew 2001, p. 56). But other factors were involved: natural catastrophes, changes in climate, external invasion,

and perhaps internal rebellions. Mycenaean Greece ultimately had to import food and metals. The Hittite collapse disrupted the trade routes on which Mycenaean imports depended. Notwithstanding such exogenous factors, Chew concludes that "[e]cological scarcity required a downscaling of material and cultural lifestyles" (p. 60).

Chew (2001) continues his narrative into the Roman era. Forest loss was "predominant all over the Roman Empire" (p. 93). During 400 years of silver smelting in Iberia, some 500 million trees were cut. Morocco lost five million hectares of forest in the Roman period. Yet Chew refrains from linking this loss to the Roman collapse. Other scholars are less reticent. Hughes (1975) indicts the Romans for failing to establish harmonious relations among economy, society, and the environment. He believes that this was a major contributor to the Roman collapse. Deforestation led to erosion, the most accessible minerals were mined, lands were overgrazed, and agriculture declined. Food shortages and population decline sapped the Empire's strength. In later writing, Hughes & Thirgood (1982) focused particularly on deforestation as a cause of collapse.

Deforestation has also been implicated in the collapse of Cahokia in the American Midwest. A high volume of wood went into Cahokia's construction and occupation, and land was cleared for planting. Lopinot & Woods (1993) point out that in the Stirling phase (A.D. 1100–1200) wood use came to be increasingly localized and diversified. Intensified local cutting increased runoff and caused floods to become more frequent, severe, and unpredictable. Milner (1990) notes that after 1050 the area experienced rapid soil deposition, and he suggests that it was caused by increased runoff from cutting bluff-zone forests (p. 7). It appears that flood levels were increasing and that this increase reduced the area of bottomland suitable for farming and habitation (p. 7).

The most wide-ranging attempt to draw contemporary lessons from past ecological crises is Diamond's (2005) recent work. Diamond's working model is overshoot, followed by degradation and collapse:

> It has long been suspected that many of those mysterious abandonments were at least partly triggered by ecological problems: people inadvertently destroying the environmental resources on which their societies depended.... Unsustainable practices led to environmental damage.... Consequences for society included food shortages, starvation, wars among too many people fighting over too few resources, and overthrows of governing elites by disillusioned masses.... The risk of such collapses today is now a matter of increasing concern (pp. 6–7).

Diamond realized early on that collapses are more complex than simple overshoot. So he developed a more nuanced framework involving environment, climate, hostile neighbors, friendly trade partners, and societal responses. Yet slips of the pen betray his conviction that environmental deterioration is really to blame. A modern collapse would be "triggered ultimately by scarcity of environmental resources" (Diamond 2005, p. 7). Environmental problems "undermined preindustrial societies" (p. 35). "The Anasazi and Maya were ... undone by water problems" (p. 490). "Deforestation was a or *the* major factor in all the collapses of past societies described in this book" (p. 487, emphasis original). Today's Third World trouble spots all suffer from environmental deterioration: "[I]t's the problems of the ancient Maya, Anasazi, and Easter Islanders playing out in the modern world" (p. 516).

Diamond discusses six archaeological cases: Easter Island, Pitcairn Island, Henderson Island, the Anasazi (especially Chaco Canyon) of the U.S. Southwest, the Maya, and Norse Greenland. Some of these are places where subsistence producers could not have survived long-term and are thus unsuitable for deriving broader inferences, let alone lessons for the future. Pitcairn and Henderson islands, for example, are small, remote, and lacking critical resources. They could not be occupied for long without obtaining resources from elsewhere. The failure of attempts to occupy them (which I do not consider collapses) is attributed by Diamond as much to problems plaguing trade partners on Mangareva as to anything done by the occupants of Pitcairn and Henderson islands (pp. 120–35). For comparison, if the resupply of the International Space Station were to fail, future historians would not wonder at the fate of the astronauts, nor draw broader inferences. The cases of Pitcairn and Henderson islands are no more compelling.

Norse Greenland is not an enduring lesson for the same reason: Local resources could not indefinitely support a medieval European society. Add to this the problem of low-frequency events—rare but inevitable adverse climate fluctuations—and it is clear that the Norse settlements were temporary (although the Norse themselves did not recognize this). Although the Norse did put the local environment to use, and thereby degraded it, the great problem they faced was the Little Ice Age (e.g., McGovern 1994). As McGovern noted, the dilemma is not that the Greenland Norse went extinct or left, but that they need not have done either. The continued occupation of the area by the Inuit shows that alternative subsistence strategies and ways of life would have allowed the Norse to survive in Greenland. The Norse failure, argues McGovern, lay in not adopting Inuit ways. Diamond, like McGovern, wonders at the inflexibility of the Norse. Whatever the answer to that conundrum, Norse Greenland is not a simple example of overshoot and collapse. It may illustrate a limited kind of overshoot—overshoot in respect to extreme conditions.

Diamond's (2005, pp. 136–56) account of the Anasazi is a confused muddle, including Chaco Canyon as "the Anasazi capital," a Chaco "mini-empire," and perhaps "provincial capitals" elsewhere (pp. 148–49). Diamond alternates between discussions of

Chaco Canyon, "warfare-related cannibalism" (p. 151), and Long House Valley, with mention of other places that "also underwent collapses, reorganization, or abandonment at various times within the period A.D. 1100–1500" (p. 154). This includes the Mimbres, Mesa Verdeans, Hohokam, Mogollon, and others. One wonders what society, over a period of 400 years, would not experience some process that could be labeled "reorganization." Diamond concludes that Chaco Canyon was abandoned in the twelfth century because of human impact and drought. With centuries of population growth, demands on the environment grew, resources declined, and people lived precariously. The proximate reason was a drought beginning in A.D. 1130, which "pushed Chacoans over the edge" (p. 156). At a lower population density they might have survived it.

Diamond (2005) also considers collapses in the Maya region (pp. 157–77). The Maya damaged their environment, of course. They also fought among themselves over farmland, and, Diamond believes, emphasized "war and erecting monuments rather than . . . solving underlying problems" (p. 160). But climate also played a role. A drought beginning around A.D. 760, and peaking around 800, was "suspiciously associated with the Classic collapse" (p. 174). Diamond concludes that one strand in the Classic Maya collapse was population overshoot. This contributed to deforestation and erosion. More and more people fought over fewer and fewer resources. Elites fiddled while the lowlands burned. Drought then came to a system at the margins (pp. 176–77). Diamond's analysis of the Maya places them with the Anasazi and Norse Greenland: a society that overshot the level of population, consumption, and political complexity that could be sustained under rare, extremely adverse circumstances.

Thus Easter Island is Diamond's best case of overshoot, resource degradation, and collapse. It is not Diamond's case alone. "Easter Island," wrote Kirch (1984), "is an example of a society which—temporarily but brilliantly

surpassing its limits—crashed devastatingly" (p. 264). Many have come to regard Easter Island as a metaphor for "Spaceship Earth" (e.g., Flenley & Bahn 2002; Ponting 1991). Easter Island now figures in economic theory. Brandner & Taylor (1998) use the Lotka-Volterra predator-prey model to simulate overshoot and collapse on the island, whereas Dalton & Coats (2000) explore whether markets and a private-property regime could have saved Easter Island. Erickson & Gowdy (2000) use Easter Island to evaluate the consequences of substituting human for natural capital. Easter Island is in the wild.

Islands are useful laboratories for the study of some ecological processes. Cut off to varying degrees from the influence of larger land masses, islands permit ecologists to study such things as invasion, population growth, and extinctions in a more controlled environment than is otherwise possible. For this reason, and because scholars have recently discussed it at length, Easter Island merits review in some detail.

We do not know when Easter Island was first occupied. Flenley & Bahn (2002) cite a date of A.D. 690 ± 130 (p. 77). This is from a large platform, so it cannot record the earliest settlement. Kirch (2000) notes what may have been human forest clearance as early as 1630 ± 130 B.P. (p. 271). Initial settlement sometime in the first few centuries A.D. seems likely.

The settlers found an island that was poor in resources by the standards of Oceania. Its latitude is subtropical, so the climate is cool compared with the rest of Polynesia (Diamond 2005, pp. 83, 86). The ocean is too cold in winter to support a coral reef, so the population of marine fauna is depauperate (McCoy 1979, p. 140). Around the island there are 126 species of fish, compared with 450 species around Hawai'i and 1000 around Fiji. Sea mammals and turtles may never have been abundant (Flenley & Bahn 2002, p. 19). As happened elsewhere in Polynesia, the settlers (and the rats that they introduced) destroyed a diverse community of nesting birds (Steadman 1989, 1995).

An early faunal assemblage from the Ahu Naunau site was analyzed by Steadman et al. (1994). Radiocarbon dates ranged between 660 and 900 B.P. Dolphin was the most common marine species. Bones of the Polynesian rat (introduced for food where Polynesians settled) were second in abundance, and chicken bones were outnumbered by those of native birds. Overall, marine mammals, seabirds, and native land birds were more common than in later prehistoric sites, and bones of fish and chickens were much rarer.

The settlers found a forest dominated by a now-extinct palm that is related to the Chilean wine-palm (Flenley & King 1984). Historically this forest no longer exists. Its disappearance plays a large role in overshoot-and-collapse interpretations of Easter Island and in contemporary imaginings of humanity's future (e.g., Diamond 2005; Flenley & Bahn 2002).

Easter Island is known, of course, for its statues. The cessation of statue carving figures prominently in the idea that Easter Island underwent a collapse. Statues were placed on *ahu*, elongated platforms parallel to the shore. *Ahu* and statues may have been built over a period of 700 years (Kirch 1984, p. 271), starting probably no earlier than A.D. 900 (McCoy 1979, p. 152). Many statues were standing in 1722, when a Dutch ship commanded by Roggeveen made the first recorded European contact. A Spanish ship in 1770 saw much of the island but reported no fallen statues. Only four years later Cook found many statues toppled, and the *ahu* were no longer maintained. Subsequent visits continued to report toppled statues (Flenley & Bahn 2002, p. 150).

Society was hierarchical. The island was unified sufficiently to allow transport of statues from the Rano Raraku quarry to all coasts. The high-ranking Miru clan occupied the western and northern parts of the island. As is common in Polynesia, this group had a monopoly on fishing in deeper waters, where

marine mammals and larger fish could be found (Kirch 1984, pp. 270, 272).

Estimates of maximum population, reached most likely in the sixteenth century, range from 7000 to 10,000 (Van Tilburg 1994, p. 52), up to 15,000 (Diamond 2005, p. 91). Population declined to ~2000 by 1722 (Flenley & Bahn 2002, p. 169).

This decline in population qualifies under Diamond's definition as a collapse (2005, p. 3). Archaeologists point to concomitant changes in subsistence, and in the social, political, and economic spheres. In these realms, the essence of collapse is a marked reduction in complexity (Tainter 1988). The complexity of Easter Island society seems to have changed significantly after ~1500. Labor was no longer organized for corporate group projects. Rights to move statues across the island ceased to be exercised, along with the interclan political and/or ceremonial relations that this implies. Island-wide exchange and cooperation declined. The hereditary status system lost influence. Chiefs lost economic power, including the right to surplus production, and a rigid class structure gave way. Warfare became chronic. A warrior class emerged, largely supplanting the hereditary rank system. Late in prehistory the island had no high chief. Instead, the island's descent groups coalesced into opposing factions of the east and west (Flenley & Bahn 2002; Kirch 1984, 2000; McCoy 1979). The loss of organizational capacity makes it appropriate to label this a collapse.

Late in the island's occupation there was conflict over land, and defeated people risked dispossession or enslavement. Many lived in fortified caves. Late middens have a high frequency of fractured and charred human remains, many from juveniles. This is interpreted as cannibalism. In time the statues were overthrown and many were destroyed (McCoy 1979).

The Easter Islanders themselves ascribe the end of statue construction to the outbreak of war. Mulloy (1970) proposed that war resulted from overpopulation, which led to "competition for agricultural land and fishing rights.... With warfare came considerable cultural decline" (p. 5). In 1983, Flenley & King (1984) cored deposits in the three main craters and showed what had long been suspected: The island was once forested. Deforestation occurred since ca. 990 ± 70 B.P. The findings "do not conflict with the hypothesis that the decline of megalithic culture was associated with total deforestation" (p. 50). Mann et al. (2003), undertaking soil analyses, found that the island's primeval soils began to erode severely by A.D. 1200 and that there was forest clearance and erosion everywhere between 1200 and 1650. Deforestation presumably occurred as a result of cutting wood to build canoes, using wood for structural elements, fashioning wood into implements, cooking, cremating, perhaps moving and raising statues, and possibly early swiddening.

Several authors see the deforestation as the start of a cascading process that led to a decline in fishing and farming; changes in farming technology; increases in warfare and insecurity; changes in settlement patterns; population decline; and sociopolitical collapse. Forest depletion, in this view, led to a shortage of wood for canoe construction, and thus to a decline in the consumption of fish (especially deep, pelagic fish) and marine mammals. Soils eroded, and the fertility of forest soils was lost. Crops were exposed to the winds that blow at Easter Island most of the year. Soils lost moisture. Crop yields declined. Springs and streams dried up. People responded with agricultural intensification. Stone dams diverted water, while lithic mulch was employed to retain soil moisture. Stone-lined pits were created to shelter plants from the wind. Rocks were stacked to create windbreaks. Stone chicken houses up to 20 meters long were built to prevent theft. Fires were fueled by herbs and grasses (Ayres 1985; Diamond 2005; Flenley & Bahn 2002; Kirch 1984, 2000; McCoy 1976, 1979).

Easter Island, in this account, is the paradigmatic case of overshoot and collapse, the prototype Spaceship Earth. Diamond (2005) sketches the parallels between Easter Island and our own potential future:

> Polynesian Easter Island was as isolated in the Pacific Ocean as the Earth is today in space.... Earthlings have [no] recourse elsewhere if our troubles increase. Those are the reasons why people see the collapse of Easter Island as a metaphor, a worst-case scenario, for what may lie ahead of us in our own future (p. 119).

EVALUATING OVERSHOOT AND COLLAPSE IN ARCHAEOLOGY

The past is contested in many ways, including whether Malthusian overshoot caused earlier collapses. We can gather more data, refine chronologies, and develop new techniques to reconstruct paleoenvironments, but none of these will resolve the question of whether past collapses provide analogues for possible future ones. Fundamental beliefs and short-term well-being are at stake. Still, one can try to make the debate as rational as possible. To that end, this section evaluates whether those who see overshoot and collapse in past societies have made their case.

Betty Meggers' (1954) environmental limitation theory never found widespread favor and is today rarely discussed. In the Amazon Basin, where Meggers' own work stimulated her theory, we now know that some societies had levels of complexity that her theory predicted would be impossible (e.g., Heckenberger et al. 2003). Meggers did not consider the role of intensification in raising the productivity of land.

Intensification also undercuts the arguments of Cooke (1931) and Sanders (1962, 1963) regarding the consequences of swiddening in the southern Maya Lowlands. We have learned that the southern cities were not supported by low-production swiddening, but by a landscape that managed to give high agricultural yields (e.g., Turner 1974). It is sometimes suggested that this landscape was unsustainable (Culbert 1988), but that question cannot be divorced from the costs and consequences of sustaining urban centers, elites, monumental construction, and inter-polity warfare, coupled perhaps with drought. The Maya collapse cannot be explained by the simple overshoot of Cooke and Sanders.

Culbert (1988) believes the dramatic population loss of the Maya collapse suggests agricultural failure. Yet if, as he suggests, agricultural breakdown came from inept decision-making, what ultimately was the problem: population, competition, public construction, mismanagement, disaffection, or all these? If Maya elites had allocated labor better, would scholars today discuss overshoot? Culbert (p. 100) compares the Maya to Mesopotamia and reaches conclusions similar to those of Adams (1981). As with Mesopotamia, if the southern lowland cities collapsed from resource degradation, the main questions involve decision-making rather than procreation. This would mean that the Maya collapse is not an example of Malthusian overpopulation but of elite-driven intensification.

The Third Dynasty of Ur and the Abbasid Caliphate are two of history's best candidates for overshoot, degradation, and collapse. Powell (1985) questions the role of salinization in the Ur III collapse on textual grounds. Whether Powell's objections undermine the case, Ur III is poorly known. The political situation in Iraq has prevented archaeologists from acquiring data to address the questions that the case raises. This consideration applies also to the Abbasid Caliphate, but its collapse was more recent and is better documented. Still, both Mesopotamian cases have limited potential to give a broader understanding of overshoot and collapse. Neither is a Malthusian overshoot, nor an overshoot brought on by excess production for mass markets, today's primary concerns. The agricultural problems in both cases can be traced to elite mismanagement. The critical questions then involve not merely the resource, but the more fundamental question of why rulers would undermine the agricultural regime on which they and their societies depended. We cannot yet answer this question. For the Abbasid Caliphate, though, some pertinent factors can be discussed.

One factor in Abbasid tax policy may have been the need to fund the frequent wars with the Byzantine Empire. Another factor was that the Abbasid Caliphate was a costly regime. Under the Abbasids there was unprecedented urban growth. Baghdad grew to five times the size of tenth-century Constantinople. The capital was moved often, and each time built anew on a grand scale. The Caliph al-Mutasim (833–842) built a new capital at Samarra, 120 kilometers upstream from Baghdad. In 46 years, he and his successors built a city that stretched along the Tigris for 35 km. It would have dwarfed imperial Rome (Hodges & Whitehouse 1983, pp. 151–56).

Overshoot in these cases resulted from the failure of feedback loops. Negative feedback, which dampens excesses in a system's behavior, operates by feeding back information about the system's state or behavior to the control, which responds by altering its own state or behavior. The thermostat is a simple example. The Mesopotamian collapses resulted from a failure of this mechanism. Information about the deteriorating state of agriculture either failed to reach the government or was ignored. As agricultural yields faltered, these regimes demanded yet more production. What should have been a negative feedback system, dampening departures from sustainability, instead became a positive feedback system. The government responded to agricultural problems in a way that made the problems worse. Positive feedback forced the agricultural system, the regime, indeed the complexity of the society as a whole, into a downward spiral toward collapse.

The interpretation of overshoot and collapse in Bronze Age societies advanced by Chew (2001) is empirically weak. Chew provides no data, merely sweeping assertions, on the extent of deforestation or erosion in northern Mesopotamia, the Indus River watershed, Minoan Crete, and Mycenaean

Greece. In southern Greece, erosion does not correspond temporally to the Mycenaean collapse (van Andel et al. 1990). Paleoenvironmental studies may someday provide further data to test Chew's ideas. These cases have not yet been demonstrated to be examples of overshoot.

Deforestation did not cause the Roman collapse. To the end, Roman mints consumed tons of charcoal to produce millions of coins, even in places like North Africa. Builders fired millions of bricks to build the walls of Rome in the 270s. There is no evidence of wood shortages. Indeed, forests were regrowing in the late empire (Tainter 2000a).

It is unlikely that deforestation and flooding caused the collapse of Cahokia. The rulers of Cahokia had demonstrated extraordinary capacity to move people, relocate settlements, mobilize labor, and build massive earthworks (Dalan 1997). If flooding was a threat to Cahokia, the elites could have moved political centers, villages, agricultural production, and population to higher ground a short distance away. They had already accomplished similar feats of organization.

Diamond's inclusion of Pitcairn and Henderson islands, and Norse Greenland, illustrates problems in his conception of collapse. There was no loss of sociopolitical complexity in these places, with a less complex society succeeding. The occupants either died or left. Apparently any place that was abandoned is potentially, to Diamond, a collapse. When he includes Rwanda in his cases, he equates genocide with collapse. There is no logical consistency among these cases. Diamond's approach was seemingly to find cases where (*a*) bad things happened, and (*b*) he could construct a plausible environmental reason. The outcomes, however diverse their nature, are lumped into the category "collapse."

Diamond would have liked to have shown that Chaco Canyon, the Anasazi and other Southwesterners, and the Maya overshot the capacity of their environments, degraded them, and collapsed. In each case, though, he was confronted with the potential roles of climate and other factors. These were not Malthusian overshoots. In Diamond's formulation, these cases may illustrate overshoot in reference to extreme climatic conditions. If the extreme conditions had not occurred, the societies in question might not have collapsed. Sheets (1999) has argued that the ability to withstand extreme events (volcanism in his cases) varies with the complexity of the society. This idea suggests that the many archaeological studies that focus on extreme events such as drought merit their own review.

Easter Island again requires discussion: It is the last candidate for an overshoot resulting from excess population and/or consumption. Diamond (2005) considers Easter Island to be "as close as we can get to a 'pure' ecological collapse" (p. 20). Yet there are many questions about deforestation, deep-sea voyaging, social organization, agriculture, and statue production in the Easter Island collapse.

Diamond (2005) writes, "I have often asked myself, 'What did the Easter Islander who cut down the last palm tree say while he was doing it?'" (p. 114). In fact some scholars suggest that remnants of the island's forest may have survived in the volcano craters into the nineteenth century (Flenley and Bahn 2002, pp. 86–87; Ponting 1991, p. 5), after which the last trees may have been killed by sheep and goats (Flenley & Bahn 2002, p. 160). Seeds of the extinct indigenous palm have been found. These are important: Every seed discovered had been gnawed by the Polynesian rat and could not have germinated (Flenley & Bahn 2002, pp. 160–61). The rats ate these nuts systematically, and the Polynesians ate the rats. Once the Polynesian rat was introduced to Easter Island, the palm forest may have been doomed. Human use merely sped up the inevitable. This could explain why practices of sustainable forest use were not successful, if they were attempted.

The extinct palm was not uniformly useful. Palm wood is porous and would have been undesirable for fashioning canoes. The forest did contain other trees. Even so, "larger trees suitable for canoe construction may have been sparse or lacking" (Kirch 1984, p. 268). Diamond observes that canoes in the historic period were small, flimsy, and leaky. Yet when Roggeveen approached the island in 1722, a canoe came nearly 5 kilometers out to the Dutch ships. The marine zone where the Easter Islanders could obtain delphinids and pelagic fish was well within this radius. Moreover, Easter Islanders claimed that they regularly undertook voyages to the island of Salas-y-Gómez, to the east-northeast, a round-trip of 930 km (Flenley & Bahn 2002, p. 67). The Easter Islanders have a name for this island, and the claim is generally accepted. Salas-y-Gómez is considered Polynesia's easternmost tip. Boats could also have been made of reeds (Van Tilburg 1994, pp. 47–48). These facts challenge Diamond's (2005) claim that "Lack of timber . . . brought to an end . . . the construction of seagoing canoes" (p. 107). Still, unless the early faunal remains from Anakena are an unrepresentative sample, deep-sea catches seem to have declined in later prehistory (Steadman et al. 1994).

Even if lack of wood meant a decline in the availability of sea mammals and large fish, the entire population would not have been equally affected. As is common in Polynesia, the high-ranking Miru clan controlled fishing in deeper, offshore waters. High chiefs had the right to distribute prestigious fish. The Miru could place *tapu* (taboo) on marine resources from May through October, when only nobles could eat larger fish like tuna (Flenley and Bahn 2002, p. 100; Kirch 1984, p. 272). If deforestation did lead to a decline in the catch of larger fish and marine mammals, a large part of the population was only minimally affected.

A decline in agriculture would have been more serious than the loss of marine delicacies. Easter Island undoubtedly experienced erosion. It is a common mistake, though, to assume that erosion is always detrimental. Ancient Egypt and Mesopotamia were sustained by upstream erosion, as other places have been. No research has shown that erosion adversely affected Easter Island agriculture. Removing forest cover would have ex-

posed soils to drying and challenged young plantings. The islanders responded by digging pits, erecting small windbreaks, and employing lithic mulch. Problems of soil fertility could have been addressed by shifting cultivation and/or by use of night soil. In late prehistory, chickens were kept in stone structures with small runs. This was reportedly to deter theft, but it would also have the consequence of making chicken manure easier to collect. The chicken houses have small entrances and passageways (McCoy 1976, pp. 23–26), but not so small that a child could not crawl inside. Chicken manure could have been used to enhance soil fertility.

Nearly the entire surface of Easter Island is arable (Kirch 2000, p. 272), yet in recent centuries only the coast and the interior of Rano Kau crater were intensively cultivated (Flenley & Bahn 2002, pp. 96, 158; McCoy 1976, pp. 78–79, 84). The factor limiting agriculture may have been water (McCoy 1976, p. 142), rather than erosion, wind, or soil fertility. If agricultural productivity declined with deforestation, this could have been compensated for by increasing the area under intensive cultivation. Diamond (2005) cites Cook's 1774 description of the Easter Islanders as "small, lean, timid, and miserable" (p. 109) to support his view that deforestation led to starvation. Yet he ignores Roggeveen's statement in 1722 that the islanders were "well proportioned, generally large in stature, very sturdy with strong muscles, and extremely strong swimmers" (Flenley & Bahn 2002, p. 90). When people face agricultural problems, a common response is to intensify production. This is what the Easter Islanders did (McCoy 1976, pp. 145–146).

Finally there is the mystery of the end of statue production. Some scholars have suggested that production ceased because there was no longer wood to move and erect statues. Others have even suggested that moving the statues caused the deforestation. Perhaps 800 to 1000 statues had been produced, or partly produced, when work ceased (Flenley & Bahn 2002, p. viii). Of these, 324 statues were ultimately erected on 245 *ahu* around the coast (Kirch 2000, p. 272). Some 397 statues remain in the quarry zone of Rano Raraku crater (Van Tilburg 1994, p. 21). About 200 statues lie unfinished within the quarry (Kirch 2000, p. 272), some of which broke during production. Ninety-two statues were abandoned in transport (Van Tilburg 1994, p. 148). From these figures it is clear that statue-making continued at an undiminished rate until production ceased. It is even possible that the rate of production was increasing. When production ceased, it did so abruptly. Had production simply tapered off, we would expect to see fewer unfinished statues and fewer statues in the quarry zone. These figures contradict the interpretation that deforestation caused the end of statue production. It is inconceiveable that new statues would be commissioned at a constant or accelerating pace if the means to transport them was visibly dwindling. Clearly the end of statue production was linked to some factor other than the end of the forest. Even without trees, statues can be dragged over ground lubricated with sweet potatoes (Flenley & Bahn 2002, p. 122). This would take a lot of sweet potatoes, but that resource is more readily replenished than are trees.

In short, Easter Island may not qualify as a case of overshoot and collapse. The Polynesian rat had much to do with the decline of the palm forest, so human use affected the rate of deforestation but not the ultimate outcome. Diamond (2005) acknowledges that Easter Island's deforestation was due in part to its latitude, low rainfall, lack of volcanic ash, lack of dust from Asia, and small size (pp. 115–18). Even without tall trees, Easter Islanders made water craft capable of long voyages and deepsea fishing. Marine mammals and large fish did decline in the diet, but this decline primarily affected the elite segment of the population. Agriculture was probably compromised by deforestation, but Easter Islanders responded to this in time-honored fashion: They intensified production. Finally, the end of statue production seems to have occurred for reasons other than deforestation.

CONCLUSIONS

When the *ARA* Editorial Committee invited me to address the topic "Archaeology of Overshoot and Collapse," I assumed I could review only part of a voluminous literature. Although I have extensively read the collapse literature (Tainter 1988), I was surprised to realize that the literature has produced few cases that postulate overshoot of population and/or mass consumption, followed by degradation and collapse. Writers today prefer to explain collapse by the occurrence of extreme events (e.g., Binford et al. 1997). Within the small overshoot literature, many of the most ardent proponents are outside archaeology.

Some overshoot interpretations are not credible (environmental limitations), or have been proven wrong (savannah formation in the Maya Lowlands). Others are untested (Bronze Age core-periphery systems) or cannot explain collapse (deforestation in Rome and Cahokia). Other cases advanced as overshoot examples (Anasazi, Maya) prove to be overshoot in regard to extreme conditions. The collapses of the Third Dynasty of Ur and the Abbasid Caliphate seem to be cases of overshoot. Yet the proximate causes were not overpopulation nor mass consumption, but elite mismanagement and a failure of information feedback. The reasons why Mesopotamian elites acted detrimentally in regard to their long-term interests remain to be determined. This question pertains also to the Maya collapse. Easter Island, considered the paradigmatic case of overshoot and collapse, is equivocal. Easter Island may be such a case, but there is contradictory evidence. There does not presently appear to be a confirmed archaeological case of overshoot, resource degradation, and collapse brought on by overpopulation and/or mass consumption. As a personal aside, I consider myself to be conservation-minded, and I currently focus my research on sustainability (e.g., Allen et al. 2003). I realize the political and ideological implications of this conclusion and how it might be used.

With limited space, I briefly raise two questions: Why are there no cases of what Diamond (2005) calls "'pure' ecological collapse" (p. 20)? And does this mean that Spaceship Earth is reprieved? These are rich topics that cannot be explored here. A few words alone are possible, but the fundamental issues are quickly drawn.

The concept of overshoot is teleological, as if humans could set a target for population or consumption. Overshoot denies the human capacity for flexible adjustments, including intensifying production. Overshoot and depletion of megafauna, for example, occurred in many places (e.g., Barnosky et al. 2004) but seem not to have caused a single collapse. It is usually possible to coax more resource production by applying capital and technology, increasing labor, applying energy subsidies, and making production more knowledge-intensive. Irrigation, fertilization, and mechanization are all ways to increase production, as is putting in more hours or tilling more land. Wallace, Malthus, Jevons, and Ehrlich have, so far, been wrong.

As an alternative to intensifying, societies or institutions may simplify so that they are less costly, or people may otherwise reduce consumption. This was the strategy of the Byzantine Empire when it lost its wealthiest provinces in the seventh century A.D. and responded with what may be history's only example of a large, complex society systematically simplifying (Tainter 2000b).

The question for our time is whether intensification can continue indefinitely. Can we forever find some way to escape the Malthusian fate? Neoclassical economists assume that, with incentives and unfettered markets, there will always be new technologies and new resources. Humanity, in this view, need never face a crisis of overpopulation or overconsumption. The contrary view is well known: We must reduce our ecological footprint or eventually collapse. The neoclassical argument is based on faith that markets will always work and denial of diminishing returns to innovation (Rescher 1978). Should we base our future on faith and denial, or on rational planning? That is open for debate. It is a question in the wild.

ACKNOWLEDGMENTS

I am pleased to express my appreciation to the following colleagues for their suggestions: Jeanne Arnold, John Bintliff, Jeffrey Dean, Thomas Dillehay, Timothy Kohler, Barbara Mills, Ben Nelson, Charles Redman, Payson Sheets, and Sander van der Leeuw.

LITERATURE CITED

Adams RM. 1981. *Heartland of Cities*. Chicago: Aldine

Allen TFH, Tainter JA, Hoekstra TW. 2003. *Supply-Side Sustainability*. New York: Columbia Univ. Press

Ayres WS. 1985. Easter Island subsistence. *J. Soc. Ocean.* 80:103–24

Barnosky AD, Koch PL, Feranec RS, Wing SL, Shabel AB. 2004. Assessing the causes of late Pleistocene extinctions on the continents. *Science* 306:70–75

Binford MW, Kolata AL, Brenner M, Janusek JW, Seddon MT, et al. 1997. Climate variation and the rise and fall of an Andean civilization. *Quat. Res.* 47:235–48

Brandner JA, Taylor MS. 1998. The simple economics of Easter Island: a Ricardo-Malthus model of renewable resource use. *Am. Econ. Rev.* 88:119–38

Catton WR. 1980. *Overshoot: The Ecological Basis of Revolutionary Change*. Urbana: Univ. Ill. Press

Chew SR. 2001. *World Ecological Degradation: Accumulation, Urbanization, and Deforestation, 3000 B.C.–A.D. 2000*. Walnut Creek, CA: AltaMira

Cooke CW. 1931. Why the Mayan cities of the Peten district, Guatemala, were abandoned. *J. Wash. Acad. Sci.* 21(13):283–87

Culbert TP. 1988. The collapse of Classic Maya civilization. In *The Collapse of Ancient States and Civilizations*, ed. N Yoffee, GL Cowgill, pp. 69–101. Tucson: Univ. Ariz. Press

Dalan RA. 1997. The construction of Mississippian Cahokia. In *Cahokia: Domination and Ideology in the Mississippian World*, ed. TR Pauketat, TE Emerson, pp. 89–102. Lincoln: Univ. Neb. Press

Dalton TR, Coats RM. 2000. Could institutional reform have saved Easter Island? *J. Evol. Econ.* 10:489–505. **http://springerlink.metapress.com/link.asp?ID=2G7POXXAU7L8LA9G**

Diamond JD. 2005. *Collapse: How Societies Choose to Fail or Succeed*. New York: Viking

Ehrlich PR. 1968. *The Population Bomb*. New York: Ballantine

Erickson J, Gowdy JM. 2000. Resource use, institutions, and sustainability: a tale of two Pacific island cultures. *Land Econ.* 76:345–54

Flenley J, Bahn P. 2002. *The Enigmas of Easter Island*. Oxford: Oxford Univ. Press. 2nd ed.

Flenley JR, King SM. 1984. Late Quaternary pollen records from Easter Island. *Nature* 307:47–50

Heckenberger MJ, Kuikuro A, Kuikuro UT, Russell JC, Schmidt M, et al. 2003. Amazonia 1492: pristine forest or cultural parkland? *Science* 301:1710–14

Hodges R, Whitehouse D. 1983. *Mohammed, Charlemagne and the Origins of Europe*. Ithaca, NY: Cornell Univ. Press

Hughes JD. 1975. *Ecology in Ancient Civilizations*. Albuquerque: Univ. N.M. Press

Hughes JD, Thirgood JV. 1982. Deforestation in ancient Greece and Rome: a cause of collapse. *Ecologist* 12:196–208

Jacobsen T, Adams RM. 1958. Salt and silt in ancient Mesopotamian agriculture. *Science* 128:1251–58

Jevons WS. 1866. *The Coal Question*. London: Macmillan. 2nd ed.

Kirch PV. 1984. *The Evolution of the Polynesian Chiefdoms*. Cambridge, UK: Cambridge Univ. Press

Kirch PV. 2000. *On the Road of the Winds: An Archaeological History of the Pacific Islands*. Berkeley: Univ. Calif. Press

Lopinot N, Woods WI. 1993. Wood overexploitation and the collapse of Cahokia. In *Foraging and Farming in the Eastern Woodlands*, ed. CM Scarry, pp. 206–31. Gainesville: Univ. Press Fla.

Lowe JWG. 1985. *The Dynamics of Apocalypse: A Systems Simulation of the Classic Maya Collapse*. Albuquerque: Univ. N.M. Press

McCoy PC. 1976. Easter Island settlement patterns in the late prehistoric and protohistoric periods. *Int. Fund Monum., Easter Island Comm., Bull.* 5. New York: Int. Fund Monum

McCoy PC. 1979. Easter Island. In *The Prehistory of Polynesia*, ed. JD Jennings, pp. 135–66. Cambridge, MA: Harvard Univ. Press

McGovern TH. 1994. Management for extinction in Norse Greenland. In *Historical Ecology: Cultural Knowledge and Changing Landscapes*, ed. CL Crumley, pp. 127–54. Santa Fe, NM: Sch. Am. Res. Press

Malthus TR. 1798. *An Essay on the Principle of Population*. London: J. Johnson

Mann D, Chase J, Edwards J, Beck W, Reanier R, Mass M. 2003. Prehistoric destruction of the primeval soils and vegetation of Rapa Nui (Isla de Pascua, Easter Island). In *Easter Island: Scientific Exploration Into the World's Environmental Problems in Microcosm*, ed. J Loret, JT Tanacredi, pp. 133–53. New York: Kluwer Acad./Plenum

Meggers BJ. 1954. Environmental limitation on the development of culture. *Am. Anthropol.* 56:801–24

Milner G. 1990. The late prehistoric Cahokia cultural system of the Mississippi River Valley: foundations, florescence, and fragmentation. *J. World Prehist.* 4:1–43

Mulloy W. 1970. A speculative reconstruction of techniques of carving, transporting and erecting Easter Island statues. *Arch. Phys. Anthropol. Oceania* 5:1–23

Phillips DA. 1979. The growth and decline of states in Mesoamerica. *J. Steward Anthropol. Soc.* 10:137–59

Ponting C. 1991. *A Green History of the World*. New York: St. Martin's

Powell MA. 1985. Salt, seed, and yields in Sumerian agriculture. A critique of the theory of progressive salinization. *Zeitschrift für Assyriologie und Vorderasiatische Archaeologie* 75:7–38

Rees WE. 2004. Carrying capacity and sustainability: waking Malthus' ghost. In *Introduction to Sustainable Development*, ed. DVJ Bell. In *Encyclopedia of Life Support Systems*. Oxford, UK: EOLSS. **http://www.eolss.net**

Rescher N. 1978. *Scientific Progress: A Philosophical Essay on the Economics of Research in Natural Science*. Pittsburgh: Univ. Pitts. Press

Sanders WT. 1962. Cultural ecology of the Maya Lowlands, part I. *Estudios de Cultura Maya* 2:79–121

Sanders WT. 1963. Cultural ecology of the Maya Lowlands, part II. *Estudios de Cultura Maya* 3:203–41

Sheets PD. 1999. The effects of explosive volcanism on ancient egalitarian, ranked, and stratified societies in Middle America. In *The Angry Earth: Disaster in Anthropological Perspective*, ed. A. Oliver-Smith, SM Hoffman, pp. 36–58. New York: Routledge

Steadman DW. 1989. Extinction of birds in eastern Polynesia: a review of the record, and comparison with other Pacific island groups. *J. Archaeol. Sci.* 16:177–205

Steadman DW. 1995. Prehistoric extinction of Pacific island birds: biodiversity meets Zooarchaeology. *Science* 267:1123–31

Steadman DW, Casanova PV, Ferrando CC. 1994. Stratigraphy, chronology, and cultural context of an early faunal assemblage, Easter Island. *Asian Perspect.* 33:79–96

Tainter JA. 1988. *The Collapse of Complex Societies*. Cambridge, UK: Cambridge Univ. Press.

Tainter JA. 2000a. Global change, history, and sustainability. In *The Way the Wind Blows: Climate, History, and Human Action*, ed. RJ McIntosh, JA Tainter, SK McIntosh, pp. 331–56. New York: Columbia Univ. Press

Tainter JA. 2000b. Problem solving: complexity, history, sustainability. *Popul. Environ.* 22:3–41

Turner BL. 1974. Prehistoric intensive agriculture in the Mayan Lowlands. *Science* 185:118–24

van Andel TH, Zangger E, Demitrack A. 1990. Land use and soil erosion in prehistoric and historical Greece. *J. Field Archaeol.* 17:379–96

Van Tilburg J. 1994. *Easter Island: Archaeology, Ecology and Culture*. London: Br. Mus. Press

Wallace R. 1761. *Various Prospects of Mankind, Nature, and Providence*. London: A. Millar

The Research Program of Historical Ecology

William Balée

Department of Anthropology, Tulane University, New Orleans, Louisiana 70118;
email: wbalee@tulane.edu

Annu. Rev. Anthropol. 2006. 35:75–98

First published online as a Review in
Advance on April 26, 2006

The *Annual Review of Anthropology* is
online at anthro.annualreviews.org

This article's doi:
10.1146/annurev.anthro.35.081705.123231

Copyright © 2006 by Annual Reviews.
All rights reserved

0084-6570/06/1021-0075$20.00

Key Words

hard-core postulates, landscape transformation, historical
contingency, human-mediated disturbance, species diversity,
biological invasions

Abstract

Historical ecology is a new interdisciplinary research program concerned with comprehending temporal and spatial dimensions in the relationships of human societies to local environments and the cumulative global effects of these relationships. Historical ecology contains core postulates that concern qualitative types of human-mediated disturbance of natural environments and the effect of these on species diversity, among other parameters. A central term used in historical ecology to situate human behavior and agency in the environment is the landscape, as derived from historical geography, instead of the ecosystem, which is from systems ecology. Historical ecology is similar to nonequilibrium dynamic theory, but differs in its postulate of human-mediated disturbance as a principle of landscape transformation. Such disturbances counterintuitively may involve anthropogenic primary and secondary succession that result in net increases of alpha and even beta diversity. Applied historical ecology can supply the reference conditions of time depth and traditional knowledge to restore past landscapes.

INTRODUCTION

Historical ecology is a research program concerned with the interactions through time between societies and environments and the consequences of these interactions for understanding the formation of contemporary and past cultures and landscapes (Balée 1998b; Balée & Erickson 2006a,b; Crumley 1994, 1998, 2003; Redman 1999; Sutton & Anderson 2004). A research program is a set of interdependent postulates on which only a portion of the scientific community agrees (Lakatos 1980, Stengers 2000 [1993]). It is therefore unlike a paradigm, which in the Kuhnian sense of normal science assumes conflicting models purporting to explain that the same phenomena cannot coexist (Kuhn 1970, Stengers 2000 [1993]). In anthropology, research programs include cultural ecology and sociobiology; a generation ago, research programs in the social sciences would have included psychoanalysis and Marxism (Lakatos 1999 [1973]). In ecology, systems theory and nonequilibrium dynamics constitute separate research programs (Zimmerer 2000).

Research programs consist of three to five hard-core postulates (Lakatos 1999 [1973]). In historical ecology, the postulates are the following: (*a*) Practically all environments on Earth have been affected by humans, including in a broad sense behavioral activities of the genus *Homo* (Kidder & Balée 1998, Redman 1999, Sauer 1956), although others would limit the wide-ranging effect of humans on the environment to only the entire time dating from the beginning of the Holocene, that is, the time coinciding with the beginnings of agriculture (Dickinson 2000); (*b*) human nature is not programmed genetically or otherwise to lessen or augment species diversity and other environmental parameters (Crumley 2001, Hayashida 2005); (*c*) it follows that kinds of societies defined by various socioeconomic, political, and cultural criteria impact landscapes in dissimilar ways, as some landscapes are less disturbed (and richer in species) than others; and (*d*) human inter-

actions with landscapes in a broad variety of historical and ecological contexts may be studied as a total (integrative) phenomenon (Balée 1998b, Egan & Howell 2001b, Rival 2006, Sutton & Anderson 2004).

Historical ecologists take a long view of history and landscapes and thus tend to be at variance with earlier established research programs of environmental anthropology (Balée & Erickson 2006b; Braudel 1980; Crumley 1994, 1998, 2003; Kidder & Balée 1998; Russell 1997). Historical ecology exemplifies revisionism of earlier regnant concepts in cultural ecology, cultural evolutionism, cultural materialism, and ecological systems theory (Dove 2001; cf. Headland 1997, Rival 2006). It is an interdisciplinary means of grappling with applications from both the social sciences and life sciences (Balée 1998a,b; Crumley 1994, 1998, 2003), the most important of which for strategic environmental concerns is restoration ecology, a synonym of applied historical ecology (Anderson 2001, Egan & Howell 2001a,b, Higgs 2003).

Historical ecology arose out of empirical studies that showed problems in the application of ecological anthropology to complex societies. Peasantries and other complex societies exhibiting different socioeconomic strata could not be analyzed according to methodologies developed in cultural ecology because cultural ecology referred only to classless or simple societies, wherein it was thought a linear relationship existed between key features of indigenous technology and the environment on the one hand and low population size and simple political organization of society on the other (Boglioli 2000, Cole & Wolf 1974). Such societies were not seen to exert so much a long-term effect on the local environment as to be adapted to its putative constraints (Adams 1998; Balée 1989; Balée & Erickson 2006b; Cole & Wolf 1974; Stahl 1996; Wolf 1982, 1999). Systems theory in ecological anthropology was an attempt to bring more mathematical rigor to the subject matter, especially by conceiving of human societies as populations having exchanges of energy with other animal and plant populations in ecosystems (Rappaport 2000). Systems theory in anthropology, as in ecology, was ahistorical and excluded human agency and intentionality in the landscape (Dove 2001, Wolf 1999; cf. Biersaack 1999).

A SECOND WORLD

In historical ecology the landscape is a place of interaction with a temporal dimension that is as historical and cultural as it is evolutionary per se, if not more so, upon which past events have been inscribed, sometimes subtly, on the land (Crumley 2003, Ingold 1993, Marquardt & Crumley 1987, Neves & Petersen 2006, Russell 1997). Historical ecology registers simple foragers and swidden horticulturalists as agents of history manifesting cultural pasts that defy placement in a stage of political evolution (Cormier 2003, Crumley 2003, Politis 2001, Rival 2002, Rival 2006, Zent & Zent 2004). Wolf (1982) showed that cultural ecology lacked a unified theory and could not rise above explanations of single cases because of its emphasis on human adaptations to the environment, rather than deeming society engaged with that environment and acting, effectively, to change it over time. Wolf (1999) argued that environmental anthropology needed to abandon systems theory and become both political and historical ecology to assess changes in relations between human societies and their landscapes.

Historical ecology has challenged the notion of "pristine primitives" (Wolf 1982) and virgin rainforests (Balée 1989, Denevan 1992) through different but ultimately convergent strands of interdisciplinary thinking in anthropology, geography, history, and ecology (Hayashida 2005). The notion that landscapes have history, and that natural things in given environments are historiographic indices of those environments, has several precursors in diverse fields, especially in history and geography. Historian Cronon's (1983) classic study of the impact of precolonial Indians in New England in shaping the landscape thought by the Puritans to be pristine was a careful empirical challenge to the concept of pristine primitives harnessed to the restraints of virgin forests (Turner 2005). The principal mechanism that created the parkland landscapes noted by the Puritans was controlled (or broadcast) fire (Cronon 1983, Pyne 1998).

Indigenous societies molded not only mosaic-like environments with patches rich in utilitarian natural resources, but also in some cases enhanced local (alpha) species diversity. Specifically, controlled (broadcast) fires are now considered to have enhanced local landscape heterogeneity as well as species diversity (especially of rare species), partly by preventing fuel buildups and the ensuing possibility of destructive wildfires in numerous indigenous areas of North America, South America, and Australia (Anderson 1999; Bird et al. 2005; Boyd 1999a,b; Lunt & Spooner 2005; Mistry et al. 2005; Posey 1985; Pyne 1991, 1998; Robbins 1999; Storm 2002; Winthrop 2001; cf. Foster et al. 2004). That fire by human agents in controlled cases amplifies diversity, whereas wildfires and combustion by fossil fuels tend to have degrading effects, refers one back to the notion of landscape, where humans and the environment meet in an analytic whole, with a temporal dimension that defines the relationship (Balée 1998a; Crumley 1994, 2003; Ingold 1993; Marquardt & Crumley 1987; Pyne 1998).

This notion of landscape in its most recent version originates in cultural and historical geography (Denevan 2001, Doolittle 2000, Kates et al. 1990, Olwig 2003, Rival 2006, Sutton & Anderson 2004). Geographers early derived the idea of an inseparability of humans and the environment in the context of a landscape (*Landschaft*) partly from German landscape gardeners and architects of the nineteenth century (Crumley 1994, Hall 2005, Wolschke-Bulmahn 2004) and from schools of nineteenth-century landscape painters in Europe, North America, and Australia who sought to capture their ideas of wilderness and its embedded humanity, however savage, on canvas as well as in the Western psyche (Hirsch & O'Haulon 1995). The landscape in historical ecology is also influenced by the French *Annales* school of history in conceiving of the *paysage* as undergoing several forms of temporal change, both short- and long-term, as well as cyclical (Braudel 1980, Crumley 1998).

The thinking that humans are everywhere historical agents (apart from their consciousness of being so) of change in the landscape, by rendering it historical either by agriculture or some other recognizably human interference, dates from classical antiquity (Glacken 1967, Hall 2005, Hughes 1975). Herodotus proposed that historical events unfold in a physical place and that the characteristics of place, in turn, change through time—i.e., culture and the environment are in a sense intertwined and change together through time (Pitzl 2004). Cicero wrote of how through domestication, fertilization, and irrigation humans influenced the creation of a second world apart from the so-called natural one (Glacken 1967, Hughes 1975, Wolschke-Bulmahn 2004), a concept echoed 1700 years later in the Enlightenment (Roger 1997).

Cicero's second world was a built environment. He might not have recognized second worlds in sub-Saharan Africa, Australia, lowland South America, and much of North America, just as Renaissance and Enlightenment thinking did not, considering such regions to be wilderness (Raffles 2002, Roger 1997). The second world, from a nineteenth-century European perspective, incorporated natural and cultural things together, often in a garden-like setting, as seen especially in Italy and Germany (Hall 2005, Wolschke-Bulmahn 2004). The garden as a spatially defined landscape involving nature and culture antedates European civilization, having been borrowed by Hellenistic society from East Asia (Glacken 1967).

The garden is the underlying premise of a landscape, for there humans habitually interact with other living forms, both in a cyclical fashion, and in the long-term (involving at least decades) and very long-term (involving centuries), a concept known as *longue durée* (Braudel 1980). Historical ecologists have discerned gardens in the midst of seeming wilderness in both the Neotropics and Paleotropics and have referred to these as forest gardens, forest fields, trail gardens, war gardens, man-made tropical forests, cultural or anthropogenic forests, and domesticated landscapes (Balée 1989; Clement 1999a; Denevan 1992, 2001, 2006; Erickson 2006; Gómez-Pompa et al. 1987, 1990; Heckenberger et al. 2003; Janzen 1998; Posey 1985; Posey & Balée 1989; Rival 2006). These are distinguished from cultural landscapes, which are not so much disturbed by humans as indexical (by iconic biota and places discernible to the naked eye) of local societies and their long-term history in situ (Stoffle et al. 2003). Historical ecologists also examine indexical functions of biota in specific landscapes affected by human activity over time (Feely-Harnik 2001, Verheyen et al. 2004, Walker 2000).

There is a long-standing division among European geographers and foresters between domesticated (or culturalized) and natural landscapes (Alexander & Butler 2004). The concept of pristine forests is gradually being replaced with a more hedged notion of old growth forest. The notion of old growth forest in Europe as well as North America includes forests that may have been disturbed by humans although not for long periods of time, so-called first nature (Rudel 2002). Increasing evidence, however, suggests intermediate disturbance may have lasting legacies, of the *longue durée* sort, in terms of redefining vegetation patterns (Turner 2005). Europe's culturalized landscapes run the gamut from treeless zones to mature forests similar to former woodland, yet none is primary, although relic species, such as lichens, bryophytes, and mycorrhizal fungi, as well as a few ancient trees, may still be found (Myers & Bazely 2003). Historical geographer Sauer proposed that wherever humans had lived and impacted the environment by domestication, landscapes with determinate histories were the result (Olwig 2003, Rival 2006, Sauer 1956). In more recent times, a number of scholars have argued that agricultural impacts dating from the Holocene have essentially transformed the world so much that hardly any part of it is pristine per se and that, indeed, humans created the landscapes typically referred to as examples of Holocene environments (Denevan 1992, Dickinson 2000). The notion that certain species-rich forested landscapes of Greater Amazonia, Middle America, and West Africa were pristine wildernesses was challenged by new data and interpretations in the past two decades of the twentieth century from anthropologists, geographers, and biologists (Balée 1989; Balée & Campbell 1990; Denevan 1992, 2001; Fairhead & Leach 1996; Gómez-Pompa & Kraus 1992; Gómez-Pompa et al. 1987; Hayashida 2005; Leach & Fairhead 2000; Posey 1985; Posey & Balée 1989; Rival 2006; Stahl 1996; cf. Parker 1992), who supplied evidence of human activity in the origin of these landscapes.

In historical ecology, the concept of landscape transformation, resulting in so-called man-made forests (Campbell et al. 2006, Gómez-Pompa et al. 1987, Wiseman 1978), was derived initially from evidence of agriculture and agroforestry; more recent work suggests foraging and trekking societies have also influenced forest composition through activities such as sowing propagules of trees that attract honeybees without using fire for forest clearance (Zent & Zent 2004) and abandoning camp yet leaving changes in species composition that involve the coexistence of crops and noncrops (Politis 2001, Rival 2002, Rival 2006). The evidence of classless societies as disturbance agents that modified and managed environments earlier regarded as systemic concatenations of interactive, primeval biota and physical elements represents, in historical ecology, a divergence away from the core postulates of cultural ecology as well as equilibrium theory.

OTHER ECOLOGIES, OTHER HISTORIES

The distinction between historical ecology and other ecological viewpoints and disciplines has to do with anthropocentrism in one guise or another (Balée & Erickson 2006b). Historical ecology differs from cultural ecology principally on the criterion of human agency, as well as adaptation to the environment. Cultural ecology holds that the environment is not transformable. Rather, humans must adapt their cultures, technologies, and populations to it. Typically cultural ecology cannot explain higher-order social phenomena such as cities, states, and their dependent hinterlands because the core postulates are based on the environmental determinism of societies with simple technologies (cf. Cole & Wolf 1974). Historical materialism as a research program (Lakatos 1999 [1973]) allows for human agency in initial appropriations from and transformations of nature (Wolf 1982) but does not conceive of the environment, once changed by human hands, exerting a longer-term effect on subsequent human cultures in the region of the changes (Balée 1998a,b). Historical materialism lacked the *longue durée* notion of the *Annales* historical school, which would be developed a century later (Crumley 1998).

Historical ecology differs from anthropological systems ecology—itself a critique of cultural ecology—by moving away from a concern with the functionalist adaptations of human behavior to given environmental conditions and steady states of the ecosystem (Wolf 1999; cf. Biersaack 1999). Although historical ecology underscores the importance of time and contingency in environmental change (Botkin 1990, Scoones 1999, Zimmerer 2000), as does the new ecology, it is not a formulated record of geological changes that took place in the absence of humans, a study of human response to natural catastrophes (cf. Bilsky 1980), or merely recorded history or prehistory of any environment(s). It differs from the new ecology, moreover, which is not accepted as a term for a distinctive model in ecology (Zimmerer 2000), by emphasizing an anthropocentric history. Historical ecology involves a tripartite array of conceptions of human time, borrowed from the *Annales*, especially the following: (*a*) *événement* (event) as a short-term, episodic phenomenon; (*b*) *conjoncture* (cycle), involving repetitive statistical patterns over a decade, quarter-century, or half-century or so; and (*c*) *longue durée*, empirical patterns of history and prehistory occurring over centuries (Braudel 1980, Crumley 2003).

Historical ecology has been most often conflated with environmental history. Environmental history is a fairly well-established interdisciplinary subject (Beinart & McGregor 2003, Crosby 2004, Hughes 2001, Worster 1993), but it is not a perspective that articulates hard-core postulates, such as historical ecology does. In this sense, historical ecology is not a part of environmental history nor is it parallel to it as a separate way of thinking (cf. Moran 2000, Myllntaus 2001). Environmental history encompasses the following: the comparative history of human activity in widely separated but structurally similar environments having similar politico-economic and historical conditions seen as resulting in convergent behaviors, the history of green movements and the relation of these to government policy, the history of environmental sciences and forestry, and the historiography of environmental history writing (Beinart & Coates 1995, Crosby 2004, Hughes 2001, Worster 1994). Historical ecology of a landscape, such as the Llanos de Mojos of Bolivia or the Upper Xingu of Brazil (Erickson & Balée 2006, Heckenberger et al. 2003, Mann 2002), would not be coterminous with environmental history of the same because historical ecology subscribes to a single theory of history and offers a model of how and why the landscape underwent transformation, regardless of the unique chronology of events.

Historical ecology differs from landscape ecology (cf. Moran 2000). Landscape ecol-ogy focuses on spatial heterogeneity reflected in clusters of ecosystems and, with notable exceptions (Hayashida 2005, Turner 2005), tends to exclude, as a principle, intermediate human disturbance of environments and temporal changes in them as a qualitative factor in landscape transformation (e.g., Forman & Godron 1986, Turner 2005; see critiques by Crumley 1998, 2003; Denevan 2006). The concepts of design, ecology, and architecture of landscapes in the modern senses seem to envision re-education of human beings so they can live more harmoniously with self-contained natural systems and processes. Basically landscape ecology does not involve humans recapturing indigenous or local knowledge that could be of use to restoration ecology (Gunn 1994), which, in at least one of its crucial theoretical aspects, authenticity, is close to or the same as historical ecology (Anderson 2001, Egan & Howell 2001a,b, Higgs 2003, Jones 2004).

Historical ecology is sometimes compared with, or thought to be the same as, political ecology (e.g., Wolf 1999). Many have deemed the term political ecology a misnomer by stating that it concerns only politics and not ecology (Vayda & Walters 1999) and that it doesn't increase knowledge relevant to ecology and the life sciences (Scoones 1999). In some ways political ecology is more similar to environmental history with its emphasis on the critique of conservationist movements (Dove 2001). Political ecology does, however, comprise one feature relevant to historical ecology, to wit: the possibility of understanding and applying the critique of regnant folk models of nature and the environment for building a more enlightened approach to the reconstruction of past landscapes. Political ecology could be synonymous with applied historical ecology, but the term itself is perhaps still used too widely in disparate senses to refer to a single field or theory.

The anthropological ecology of practice (influenced by the sociology of Pierre Bourdieu) instantiates the third hard-core postulate of historical ecology by stressing the differential environmental results obtained from disjunct economic and political histories in given regions (Nyerges 1997, Porro 2005). The proposal of an evenemental (*sic*) or event ecology (Vayda & Walters 1999) is bound to the particularistic limitations of case-by-case studies, similar to cultural ecology (Wolf 1982), and the omission of human agency in landscape formation; therefore it does not represent a new concept. The notion of *événement* in the *Annales* is but the short-term episodic feature affecting the formation of new landscapes—the others are *conjonctures* and *longue durée* (Braudel 1980, Crumley 1998), concepts incorporated into the core postulates of historical ecology. These postulates are, moreover, at variance with equilibrium theory and systems theory—essentially synonyms—in ecology.

Historical ecology is unlike, and fundamentally at odds with, ecological systems theory by a similar logic—the logic of the behavior of sentient, sapient beings with cultural capacities not just to transform species-rich environments into barrens of low diversity and landscape homogeneity, which clearly humans can do and have done, but also in certain cases to heighten the species diversity of local environments through ongoing resource-management practices. Historical ecology answers the call for an anthropocentric as opposed to an ecocentric or geocentric ecology (Balée & Erickson 2006a,b, Erickson & Balée 2006). Some thinking in ecology interprets these practices as always destructive, but that view is derived from the misunderstanding of human agency as a principle of some disturbance of the environment, which at a given level of intensity may be essential to sustaining diversity itself, a finding comprehensible within a historical-ecological viewpoint, which has affinities, as such, with other models in contemporary ecology, including nonequilibrium dynamics (Botkin 1990, Huston 1994, Turner 2005, Zimmerer 2000).

HISTORICAL CONTINGENCY AND ECOLOGICAL SUCCESSION

Environments—ecosystems in systems theory—undergo histories of changes in their fundamental characteristics similar to suites or guilds of species of plants and animals over time. Disturbance is the nomothetic origin of change (called succession) in species composition in a locale, and without it, ecosystems do not evolve to display climax communities, defined as ecosystems in their most mature state, with the highest diversity of species. Equilibrium or systems theory in ecology holds that climatically stable, large-area (such as continental) environments support more readily climax communities that consist for the most part of organisms that are K-selected, that is, organisms with long life spans, low numbers of offspring, and slow growth rates. With regard to forest communities, these would be trees and other structural organisms (Huston 1994). In contrast, small (such as insular) ecosystems consist for the most part of r-selected organisms, that is, plants with short life spans, high numbers of offspring, and fast growth rates. These ecosystems are more easily invaded by species from continents. Because islands develop through genetic drift clines and endemism (as with Darwin's finches), they are also more prone to extinctions. The theory, called island biogeography theory (MacArthur & Wilson 1967), proposes that the further an island is from a continent, the higher its endemism and species diversity and the higher the number of K-selected organisms. In contrast, the closer an island is to a continent, all else being equal, the lower its diversity as a result of its susceptibility to invasions of organisms from the mainland that replace local biota in the same or similar niches and therefore cause their extirpation and possible extinction (i.e., an outcome of competitive exclusion). The theory is elegant as a qualitative model of the rise and fall of species diversity on islands (i.e., ecosystems) but has been deemed problematic in quantitative prediction (Peters 1991, Walker & del Moral 2003) because it does not specify a human or other historical parameter in the transport of many invasive species, some of which, as with the brown tree snake on Guam, have cascading effects in new environments (Fritts & Rodder 1998). The theory excludes history, and partly for that reason it has been hard to replicate in the real world of island diversity and invasion biology (Huston 1994, Lomolino 2000, Simberloff 1997).

Species invasion is one kind of disturbance. Disturbance traditionally, in fact, can be biotic or abiotic. It can also be cultural and historical. When they are demonstrably natural and unrelated to global warming, to ill-conceived levee and dike construction, and to other sorts of human error, hurricanes and floods are abiotic disturbance agents that can account for the reductions of forests with many K-selected species and the near grassland and savanna environments replete with r-selected species (Huston 1994). Hurricanes and floods can also cause terrestrial environments to become marine ones, for example, by splitting islands in two (Walker & del Moral 2003). Biotic factors include not only invasive species and their effects on local biodiversity (whether to lessen or replace it with new species), but also organisms that demonstrably alter the landscape inhabited by other life forms (Schmitz et al. 1997, Simberloff 1997).

Humans effect and are influenced by changes in the landscape. The ancient Greek dichotomy between *physis* (nature) and *nomos* (culture) (Glacken 1967, Hughes 2001) that foreshadows the Cartesian dualism of the body (material world) versus the mind (thinking) is inapplicable in understanding ecological succession as modified or interfered with by humans as the disturbance agency. Historical ecology deals not with the synthesis of humans and the environment, but focuses on the result of their cyclical interaction (*conjoncture*).

Historically the more centralized the political regime (i.e., the more it is similar to a state), the greater the potential for the reduction of species diversity. Advanced industrial technologies with fossil fuels have long been known to reduce the genetic diversity of crop plants (Kates et al. 1990). Ancient civilizations using intensive agriculture (with terracing, irrigation, and fertilizers) reduced the diversity of traditional cultivars in agricultural fields as a result of taxation exigencies on a narrow range of foodstuffs (Zimmerer 1993). Interestingly, human depopulation, as occurred in the Amazon (and in the Americas generally and Australia) after contact as a result of the introduction of new pathogens, can lower the agrodiversity of landraces in areas where local knowledge and behavior are key to the management of traditional crops, including tree crops (Clement 1999a,b). If genetic diversity below that of the species rank is considered part of a region's diversity, then gamma diversity has been diminished as a result of people being removed from the landscape. Depopulation and other consequences of contact have led to the loss of agriculture and other basic technology altogether, even the disappearance of a society's cultural ability to manufacture fire, a feature once thought a sociocultural universal (Balée 2000, Cormier 2003).

With regard to advanced industrial agriculture (Kates et al. 1990), fertilization alone tends to reduce biodiversity (Huston 1994) by increasing the competition for nutrients among species originally present on a plot. It is a paradox of enrichment: Areas of high primary productivity (rich in nutrients) are often impoverished (but not always) in species diversity (Huston 1994). Despite high rainfall, large tracts of tropical rainforests have been increasingly prone to wildfires as a result of deforestation and possibly global warming artifacts of the twentieth century to date. In the future, the spread of GMOs and their potential for uncontrolled gene flow with native crops (a result in part of efficient dispersal mechanisms, such as anemochory) may reduce agro-diversity (Altieri 2004, Burney 1995/1996, Pilson & Prendeville 2004). But the human impact on the environment is highly variable, and historical ecologists recognize that each landscape needs to be understood in terms of its specific cultural and historical influences on succession without prejudice toward human nature.

Ecologists recognize two basic kinds of succession: primary and secondary. Primary succession refers to the initial colonization of a substrate that had no life on it before, such as the succession of organisms on newly formed volcanic atolls or emergent deltaic islands on the point bars of meandering rivers. On a longer timescale, the succession of organisms in areas of former glaciation is an example of primary succession, as is the replacement of entire phyla by new ones over millions of years (Huston 1994). Secondary succession refers to the replacement of organisms by other types of organisms (such as K-selected by r-selected organisms) on a substrate that has been disturbed, as is the case with well-drained forest lands when subjected to hurricanes, tornadoes, droughts, blowdowns (wind shear), and, as has been especially well studied in the tropics, human disturbance by slash-and-burn cultivation or some other form of extensive agriculture. In all cases, both in systems theory and cultural ecology, the idea is that following the disturbance, the succession of guilds of organisms proceeds anew: In the case of tropical forests, for example, the succession proceeds from dominance by the r-selected species to the climax, the dominance and highest diversity of what are basically K-selected communities. This is the climax community, an ecological systems concept dating from the early twentieth century (Huston 1994). Although equilibrium theory has many defenders (Lomolino 2000), an increasing number of ecologists recognize disturbance not as an alien agent of change in an ecosystem, but as a basic part of the function and maintenance of diversity (Botkin 1990, Huston 1994, Perry & Amaranthus 1997, Petraitis et al. 1989, Smith & Wishnie 2000). The disturbance they prognosticate is not the removal of many species guilds (highly intense disturbance), but an ongoing disturbance of a much

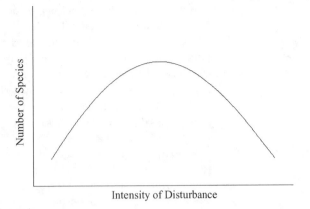

Figure 1

Simplified model of the intermediate disturbance hypothesis. Taken from Myers & Bazely 2003.

smaller scale, called intermediate disturbance, such as broadcast fire and chance treefalls in a forest without which local diversity (alpha diversity) may not be fully understood (**Figure 1**).

Intermediate disturbance (through broadcast burning, tree cultivation, settlement, and soil enrichment) has been seen to account for forest islands in West Africa (Fairhead & Leach 1996, Leach & Fairhead 2000). Evidence from Sierra Leone indicates resource exploitation and land use have varied over time, as have rangeland uses in southern Africa (Beinart & Coates 1995, Beinart & McGregor 2003), with the past use of forest sites for fortresses, the conversion of forests into charcoal for iron smelting, and the adoption of new cash crops (such as peanuts); such permutations of society explain forest composition and ecology today (Nyerges 1997, Scoones 1999; cf. Rudel 2002). Evidence from Namibia and Angola indicates that activities of historic kingdoms of the late nineteenth and early twentieth centuries expanded the frontier of orchards of fruit trees of palm, marula, birdplum, fig, and baobab at the expense of savanna (Kreike 2003). Historical variation in landscape features is probably conditioned by changes in political complexity. Savannas sometimes seem to result from human choice (Erickson 2006, Scoones 1999). Intermediate disturbance through controlled (broadcast) burning in African savannas, Brazilian *cerrados*, and the Bolivian Llanos de Mojos appears to promote the coexistence of trees and grasses by increasing landscape heterogeneity (Erickson 2006, Jeltsch et al. 1998, Mistry et al. 2005). Landscape heterogeneity induces edge effects that can reduce the diversity of species that require undisturbed forest for breeding, nesting, and reproduction (Renfrew et al. 2005), but sometimes habitat fragmentation leads to net increases of diversity (Fahrig 2003). Contrasting viewpoints hold that tropical forest islands on landscapes dominated by savanna species are relics of the Pleistocene and hence should be protected from human disturbance, the assumed cause of savannization, yet mechanisms of anthropogenic succession have been demonstrably associated with local structural and species diversity (Dove 2001, Fairhead & Leach 1996, Kreike 2003, Leach & Fairhead 2000).

Intermediate disturbance on a human scale involves the partial replacement of species of an episodic or cyclical nature on small plots of land, at times as small as treefall-sized light gaps and as large as 20 hectares (ha), as opposed to major perturbations such as clear-cutting, deforestation, selective logging, flooding, and eutrophication. Intermediate disturbance would not connote intensification, industrialization, or globalization, which can result in diminished species diversity per unit land area through overuse, fertilization, and erosion. The measurable effects of intermediate disturbance mediated by humans refer at least to one of the three types of species diversity recognized in ecology, alpha diversity. Alpha diversity is the number of species on a restricted locale with constant environmental parameters (such as drainage and soil type). Intermediate disturbance mediated by humans might also be seen in beta diversity, which is diversity over an environmental gradient such as slope or rainfall involving the distance between adjoining plots previously singled out by alpha diversity alone (Campbell et al. 2006, Erickson &

Balée 2006, Huston 1994). The third type of diversity, gamma, is the diversity of an entire region, such as the Amazon Basin. With regard to the Amazon Basin, because most of the species diversity predates the Pleistocene (Bush 1994, Vieira et al. 2001), prehistoric and early colonial societies probably had a negligible impact, except through the introduction of invasive species (biological invasions), these species occurring in inverse proportionality to pre-existing species diversity in the locales of introduction. Gamma diversity of Amazonia lacks a single, simple explanation (Bush 1994); it requires a complex model, grounded in historical ecology, capable of accounting not only for physical and temporal factors of diverse dimensions, but also for human-mediated ones impacting landscapes over time. The concept of ecological succession—the term originally used in systems and equilibrium theory—is still useful in a dynamic model of environmental change entailing increases and decreases of biological diversity (Huston 1994), the principal focus of inquiry in ecology, but for different reasons than in systems ecology. Ecological succession in historical ecology can be called landscape transformation (anthropogenic succession), of which there are several types.

Direct human impacts can be qualitatively assigned to a scale sensitive to time and place, indicative of least perturbation (e.g., by prehistoric foraging in the Arctic, the *puna* of the Andes, and the desert of the Great Basin), where a minimal human signature remains on the landscape from that time, to most perturbed (e.g., by advanced industrial agriculture and globalization), where prehistoric signatures are mostly erased as a result of complete replacements of guilds of species and the land-use intensity influenced by worldwide demand on agricultural labor and commodities (Kates et al. 1990, Rudel 2002). The intensity of human impacts on landscapes may lie in inverse proportionality to species diversity thereon (Burney 1995/1996), regardless of the rules that govern access to common resources of the landscape (Alvard & Kuznar 2001, Holt

2005, Smith & Wishnie 2000). The implicit corollary hypothesis is that where human-mediated disturbance was of the least intensity, species diversity would have been highest.

That viewpoint is a premise of wilderness areas. These are Western analogs to sacred groves (Russell 1997), and their implementation over time has passively affected species distribution and behavior on the landscape, for example, by converting hunted game to protected wildlife (Beinart & Coates 1995). Sacred groves have independent histories in sub-Saharan Africa, East and South Asia, and Mesoamerica (Byers et al. 2001, Gómez-Pompa et al. 1990, Russell 1997), and their function is to protect biotic diversity. Without sacred groves and wilderness areas, human-mediated disturbances may lessen diversity, especially if landscapes are not heterogeneous in situ (Turner 2005; cf. Renfrew et al. 2005). In other words, to maintain diversity, sacred groves in diverse cultural contexts suggest a folk belief that human-mediated disturbance ought to be excluded therein. Human disturbances of the environment, however, are ultimately scalar and temporal (Allenby 2000, Balée 1998b, Crumley 2001, Erickson 2000, Hayashida 2005, Peterson & Parker 1998, Sheuyange et al. 2005) and not in their genesis sociobiological.

Human-mediated disturbances of certain tropical forest landscapes in prehistory may have decreased alpha diversity, or had no measurable effect on it. Using the Shannon-Weaver index of biodiversity, Lentz et al. (2002) found that anthropogenic forests resulting from ancient Maya agriculture in Belize did not result in an increase in biodiversity, although forest composition is essentially anthropogenic on the study plots (see also Campbell et al. 2006, Gómez-Pompa et al. 1987, Wiseman 1978). Conversely, Lentz et al. (2002) do not show a reduction in alpha or beta diversity as a result of human impacts because prehistoric baseline inventories of all taxa are unavailable. Human-mediated disturbance of lowland Mesoamerica over time appears to have resulted in forests dominated by a few species [in terms of their relative biomass and other components (e.g., relative density and frequency) of ecological importance]. These guilds of dominant species are referred to as oligarchies (Campbell et al. 2006, Peters et al. 1989).

Oligarchic forests (usually replete with fruit trees and other economic plants) contrast with sacred groves or other relatively undisturbed forests existing in areas used by traditional societies to the extent that traditional patterns of human-mediated disturbance specifically involving broadcast and swidden burning result in a mosaic of landscapes. Recent work suggests such mosaics—landscape heterogeneity—tend to increase not only density of wildlife, but also beta diversity of flora and fauna. Intermediate disturbance by traditional societies employing broadcast fire in Australia, Africa, and the Neotropics has demonstrably resulted in increases of alpha diversity of vegetation (Bird et al. 2005, Lunt & Spooner 2005, Mistry et al. 2005, Pyne 1998, Sheuyange et al. 2005). In other words, in these instances, human-mediated intermediate disturbance and management of tropical forest biotas may be essential to the explanation of their diversity in situ. *Homo sapiens* in certain socioeconomic contexts with historically determined land-use strategies may act as a keystone species in which the diversity of entire landscapes over time is dependent (Balée & Erickson 2006b, Denevan 2001, Erickson & Balée 2006, Mann 2002, Storm 2002).

PRIMARY AND SECONDARY LANDSCAPE TRANSFORMATION IN AMAZONIA

Primary landscape transformation in the Central and Lower Amazon Basin involved mound building as well as changes in river courses to effectuate the ease of transportation, with seemingly negligible effects on species diversity (Neves & Petersen 2006, Raffles 2002). The effects, if any, on alpha and beta diversity are unknown from prehistoric manipulation of soils and drainage in the Upper Xingu (Lower Amazon) by approximately AD 1000 (Heckenberger et al. 2003), as well as in other areas of Amazon Dark Earth (anthropogenic soils) (Erickson 2003). Increases in alpha diversity of flora and fauna by indigenous resource management and use, however, have been reported in numerous environments in the Neotropics (Balée 1993, Fedick 1995, Politis 2001, Posey 1985, Rival 2002, Stahl 2000, Zent & Zent 2004). Landscapes of the Ka'apor, Guajá, and Tembé Indians of Pre-Amazonia (easternmost Amazonia, of approximately 10,000 km^2) include high forests (relatively undisturbed) and old fallow forests [of intermediate indigenous disturbance, dating from 40 to 150 years ago (cf. Myers & Bazely 2003)]. Old fallow forests instantiate anthropogenic secondary succession. Forest inventories (completed using standard biological inventory procedures as discussed in Campbell et al. 2006) of 4 ha of old fallow and 4 ha each of nearby high forest across Pre-Amazonia showed that (a) tree alpha diversity measures between fallow forest and high forest were insignificantly different; (b) adjacent plots of high forest and fallow forest shared only approximately one-half the number of shared species within inventory plots of either type regardless of distance between those more similar plots in the same category; and (c) the effect is a net gain in both alpha and beta diversity, the latter involving the gradient of time (Huston 1994), the high forest being older than the fallow forests (Balée 1993, Balée 1998b).

Secondary forests are not necessarily more impoverished in diversity than primary forests (Schulze et al. 2004). Even if soils in many secondary forests are significantly more fertile than those of primary forests (Denevan 2001, 2006; Erickson 2003; Erickson & Balée 2006; Neves & Petersen 2006), the secondary forest soils have not noticeably been reported to suffer from the paradox of enrichment. The habitat of the Sirionó Indians of the Bolivian Amazon encompasses a heterogeneous landscape of well-drained forests on relic mounds, slightly inundated forests at the base of such mounds (called pampa forest), and seasonally inundated and poorly drained savannas, which account for approximately two-thirds of the landscape (Erickson 2003, 2006; Erickson & Balée 2006; Townsend 1996). Mound forests are all anthropogenic and date from approximately 500 to 1000 years since the time of their construction and continuous habitation; pampa forests are also anthropogenic, artifacts of mound construction. Two 1-ha tree inventories, one of a mound forest 18 m in height and the other of a nearby pampa forest, showed (a) a similarity in the number of species, with 55 on the mound forest and 53 in the pampa forest; (b) a shared 24 species between the two forests (yielding a large percentage compared with Pre-Amazonia); (c) a total number of species in both forests of 84 $[(55 + 53) - (24) = 84]$; (d) and a dominance of oligarchies in both forest types (the 10 ecologically most important species on the mound inventory constitute 65.4% of all importance values of all trees on the plot, and the top 10 on the pampa inventory represent 70.9% of all importance values of all trees on that plot). The oligarchies are, however, somewhat different (with one species of palm having an importance value of 46.21 on the mound and 9.21 on the pampa and another palm species having an importance value of 41.2 on the mound and 83.27 on the pampa), which is probably a result of slope (Erickson & Balée 2006). Savannas are the original, oldest landscape, and these are maintained by periodic burning (Erickson 2006). Flooding occurs in the savanna every year, and it alternates with a marked dry season. The total number of vascular plant species in the savanna is less than 20 (Townsend 1996), with sedges and grasses by far most dominant.

The primary landscape transformation that accrued at the Ibibate Mound Complex (the mound and adjoining pampa forest) would be, in ecological terms, a primary succession, although that term most commonly excludes anthropogenesis of the landscape (e.g., Huston 1994). The transformation involved a sweeping replacement of savanna species with flood-intolerant trees, having an alpha diversity of several orders of magnitude higher than the savanna. Comparable mounds, specifically prehistoric shell middens (including gastropods and bivalves of many different species) in southwest Florida and southeastern Louisiana, which support higher diversity than any nearby marshes regardless of salinity levels, represent human-mediated increases in alpha diversity (Kidder 1998, Marquardt 1992). Therefore forest ecology in these cases of primary succession without natural causes is actually an artifact of culture and society. Perhaps to represent better and distinguish the impact of human-mediated disturbance of the environment, given that it is scalar and temporal (Peterson & Parker 1998, Sheuyange et al. 2005), one should therefore refer to primary and secondary landscape transformation when discussing biotic and environmental change on a human scale of time. In other words, alpha and beta diversity are amenable to analysis in all three modes of historical time (Braudel 1980) and are hence the definitive material of historical ecology.

INVASIVE SPECIES AND LANDSCAPE HISTORIES

Biological invasions sometimes refer only to invasive species that replace other (usually) structurally similar species in the new environment, but the term here refers both to invasive species in the conventional sense and invasive diseases (Turner 2005), including bacterial, protozoan, viral, and prion infections, that take on epidemic characteristics in regard to previously unexposed native flora and fauna, including humans (**Table 1**). The integration of landscape ecology and epidemiology (Turner 2005) is analogous to the recognition in historical ecology that human activity has been associated with a variety of new pathogens and their distribution and that human societies' political organization mirrors

their susceptibility to epidemic disease, as well as their potential to generate biological invasions in new environments (Newson 1998).

Biological invasions that involve the transfer and spread of invasive species from one point to another have been termed succession in action (Myers & Bazely 2003). Invasive species are introduced (exotic) species of plants and animals that have become weedy supplanters of existing (native) flora and fauna. Definitions vary, but usually weedy organisms are considered out of place; they multiply and spread rapidly at the expense of other organisms (Crosby 2004, Myers & Bazely 2003). Only a minority of introduced species became invasive. The success of invasive species, as weeds, depends on biotic and historical factors, alone or in combination, specific in each case. The invasive species may have no natural enemies in the place of introduction (as with the Brazilian rubber trees in Malaysia), a view originally proposed by Darwin (Hierro et al. 2005), or they may fill an empty niche in the place of introduction (Hierro et al. 2005). They may have higher numbers of duplicate chromosomes (such as tetraploids), which give them greater reproductive success, as is the case of all invasive grass species from Europe in North America (Myers & Bazely 2003). Structurally, invasive species are likely to be ruderal (Hierro et al. 2005, Huston 1994) rather than treelike, but there are many exceptions. They may exude secondary metabolites toxic to native biota but not to others in their place of origin (Hierro et al. 2005). Invasive species may have coexisted with humans longer than the affected (replaced) species in the place of their introduction and subsequent expansion (Burney 1995/1996, Hierro et al. 2005). Finally, propagules of many invasive species are located closer to shipping lanes in their points of origin and in their initial places of dispersion (Hierro et al. 2005) and hence are easily transported often as ballast (Burney 1995/1996, Crosby 2004, Russell 1997). Biological invasions since the emergence of modern humans usually have occurred with historical agency; these are called

Table 1 Some modern human-mediated invasive species and diseases

Taxon	Common name	Origin	New environment	Date established	Use (if any)
Agave sp.	Century plant	Mexico, Southwest United States	Southern Africa	Twentieth century	Fencing
Avian influenza (H5N1 virus type A influenza)	Bird flu	East Asia	?	Early twenty-first century	–
Boiga irregularis	Brown tree snake	South Pacific	Guam	1945–1950	–
Casuarina esquisetifolia	Australian pine	Australia	South Florida	Early twentieth century	Windbreak Scenic byway
Cerato stomellaulmii	Dutch elm disease	Europe	Northern United States	Late nineteenth century	–
Cryphonectria parasitica	Chestnut blight	Europe	Northeastern United States	Late nineteenth century	–
Melaleuca quinquenervia	Melaleuca	Australia	South Florida	1906	Ornamental
Myobacterium bovis	Bovine tuberculosis	North America	Southern Africa	Late twentieth century	–
Myocastor coypus	Nutria	South America	Louisiana, Florida	1941	Fur
Rattus rattus	Black rat	Asia via Europe	North America	Sixteenth century	–
Schinus terebinthifolius	Brazilian pepper	Southern Brazil	South Florida	Nineteenth century	Ornamental
Ulex europeaus	Gorse	Europe	New Zealand	Nineteenth century	–

Sources: Beinart & Coates 1995, Burney 1995/1996, Caron et al. 2003, Fritts & Rodder 1998, Hierro et al. 2005, Kidder 1998, Myers & Bazely 2003, Russell 1997, Schmitz et al. 1997, Simberloff 1997, Simberloff et al. 1997.

human-mediated invasions (Myers & Bazely 2003). [Note that not all of these biological invasions have been human mediated: For example, because of their superior swimming abilities, hippopotami, elephants, and deer hopped from one island to another across open seas during the Quaternary (Burney 1995/1996).] Regardless of the transport agent, biological invasions have been the principal proximate cause of extirpations and extinctions of native flora and fauna (Burney 1995/1996, Myers & Bazely 2003, Pimm 1991) when compared with others such as overexploitation (as with extinctions of the Carolina parakeet and the Giant Auk) and locally cascading effects of the removal of singularly important species (keystone species) on which other species depend.

Invasive species are often transported to new destinations accidentally (Crosby 2004, Myers & Bazely 2003) as in ship ballast (Crosby 2004, Myers & Bazely 2003, Pilson & Prendeville 2004, Russell 1997, Simberloff et al. 1997), the case, for example, with red tides (toxic dino-flagellates) (Burney 1995/1996), a phenomenon that increased significantly after approximately 1500 (Crosby 2004). Perhaps just as often, however, invasive species have been introduced intentionally (before their invasive features in the new environment were known) to fulfill desired functions, including as ornamentals, windbreaks, scenic byways, erosion control, fencing, and livestock feed (Beinart & Coates 1995, Myers & Bazely 2003, Simberloff et al. 1997). In some cases, these species are indicative of landscapes inhabited and modified by human societies in ancient times, as with the Kentucky coffee tree, American chestnut, and butternut, propagated at long distances from their original distribution in prehistoric North America, and the walnut and sweet chestnut in the British Isles, taken there by the Romans in the first millennium AD (Russell 1997).

The restorationist (and conservationist) notion that native species in situ are superior and preferable to introduced species is traceable to nineteenth-century European thinking that conjoined culture and wilderness into a single landscape (Hall 2005), such as the German *Naturgarten* (Wolschke-Bulmahn 2004). Specifically regarding diversity, goals of restoration ecology that include eradication of exotic species can be traced to antiquity, with Plato's doctrine on the desirability of high species diversity—"the world is the better, the more [living] things it contains" (Glacken 1967)—insofar as the richer the species diversity, the greater the resilience of the area to biological invasion (Pimm 1991; cf. Simberloff 1997). Plato further thought the state of nature was only bountiful when actively managed by humans (Hall 2005). More recent study of Mediterranean so-called ruined landscapes suggests many represent the anthropogenic expansion of forests rich in species diversity in the region, not the reverse (Grove & Rackham 2003).

Biological invasions have caused reductions and extirpations of numerous species through mechanisms including direct competitive exclusion (Burney 1995/1996, Simberloff et al. 1997). In the case of introduced pathogens, their success is only mitigated by the extent to which a host population survives and can be a reservoir for future endemic propagation (Newson 1998). The species barrier between humans and other animals is effectively broken down by diseases that are anthropozoonotic (the vector human, infecting other animals), such as tuberculosis, measles, and human herpes virus (Karesh & Cook 2005), and by habitat loss [an extreme example of habitat fragmentation, which in a general sense does not always cause reductions in species diversity (Fahrig 2003)], accounting for changes in relations between pathogens and hosts, as with chronic wasting disease of mule deer, white-tailed deer, and Rocky Mountain elk (Farnsworth et al. 2005). Malaria seems to be both zoonotic (the vector an animal, infecting humans) and anthropozoonotic in the relationship between the Guajá people and their pet monkeys in Amazonian Brazil. Specifically, the reservoir for malaria in this case seems to alternate between humans and monkeys (Cormier 2005). Some pathogens developed in livestock domesticates have jumped species barriers several times. Bovine tuberculosis (from domestic cattle) has infected wild bison in Canada, deer in Michigan, and Cape buffalo, lions, leopards, cheetahs, greater kudus, and chacma baboons in South Africa (Caron et al. 2003, Karesh & Cook 2005). Avian influenza (H5N1 type A influenza virus), which has potential to become pandemic, is notable for high morbidity as well as for having the potential for multiple vectors: wild birds, house cats, big cats, chickens, pigs, and humans, all of which have human-mediated distributions and interactions (Normile 2005). Scrapie (a prion disease) in sheep jumped the species barrier and became mad cow disease in cattle, a strain of which appears to have crossed the species barrier to humans as variant Creutzfeldt-Jakob disease (Karesh & Cook 2005). Disease ecology to the extent that it links humans and other biota, by affecting distributions on the landscape of both, becomes more fully comprehensible within the temporality of historical ecology (Newson 1998, Turner 2005).

The morphology and behavior of invasive biota may be predictable (they may be weedy, opportunistic, and genetically plastic with a capacity to mutate rapidly and, in some cases, to infect other organisms and jump species barriers), but biological invasions do not necessarily all result in net reductions of alpha, beta, or even gamma diversity. Indeed, many r-species invaded K-dominated environments before the advent of the *Homo* migrations out of Africa at the beginning of the Pleistocene, and initial modern humans did not have many invasive species other than head lice and a few others, none of which were domesticated, to transport with them (Burney 1995/1996). The question then is how long must a species exist in a given environment to no longer be considered invasive? An arbitrary classification for invasive plants is used in European forestry, whereby archaeotypes existed on the continent before 1500 and neophytes are those plants arriving after 1500; other species' origins are simply unknown, and the species are denoted as cryptogenic (Myers & Bazely 2003). Some invasive species in fact function as keystone species, and "even their removal may not cause a return to the 'uninvaded' state" (Myers & Bazely 2003). This is arguably the case with invasive species that have altered the fundamental structural characteristics of landscapes, such as melaleuca trees, which form woodlands in Florida where previously there were none, hence altering the distribution of numerous other species of flora and fauna (Schmitz et al. 1997, Simberloff 1997).

DISCUSSION AND CONCLUSIONS

On the basis of the notion that native species are more desirable than exotic ones, not only for aesthetics but for reasons related to protecting biotic diversity, efforts in restoration ecology have tended to focus on the removal and eradication of invasive species. These efforts have met with mixed results. Restoration ecology (applied historical ecology) essentially requires the knowledge of reference conditions of a past state of the landscape to attain authenticity (Egan & Howell 2001b, Hall 2005, Hayashida 2005, Higgs 2003, Jones 2004).

Historical ecology can supply the reference conditions needed for authenticity of landscape reconstruction (Egan & Howell 2001a,b, Hayashida 2005, Higgs 2003). The sources vary and are derived from research in paleoecology, ethnohistory, history, and archaeology (Crumley 1994, 2003; Erickson 2003; Hayashida 2005; Heckenberger et al. 2003; Kidder 1998; Turner 2005); from ethnography and ethnobiology (Balée 1993, Posey 1985, Posey & Balée 1989, Rival 2002, Zent & Zent 2004); from biological inventory work (Campbell et al. 2006, Erickson & Balée 2006, Turner 2005); and from research on symbols and language. Landscapes, as gardens, communicate meaning about their users and owners in the Peruvian Andes (Finerman

& Sackett 2003). Knowledge of archaic cultigens is retained in memory and reflected in ritual in Borneo and elsewhere in Southeast Asia (Dove 1999). Language catalogs past states of landscapes by current topographic terms (Russell 1997); it also embodies past methods of resource exploitation, such as agriculture in prehistoric equatorial Africa, reconstructed by historical-linguistic study of living Bantu languages (Vansina 1990). Language retains evidence of former economic valorization of species and landscapes, as with the cacao export cycle from the Amazon in the eighteenth century, reflected in the indigenous borrowing of a nonnative term for cacao even though the tree is native (Balée 2003). Marking reversals for biota represent a chronology of landscape transformation inscribed in vocabulary, such as the change, in many Mesoamerican languages, in the name for sheep, introduced from Spain, to the original name for white-

tailed deer, a native forest animal but increasingly rare as a result of the invasion of pasture for sheep grazing, and vice versa (Witkowski & Brown 1983). Historical ecology is interdisciplinary, and in one of its disciplines, anthropology, it is clearly intersubdisciplinary.

Applied historical ecology may become the holistic engagement of knowledge from diverse disciplines for the benefit of human societies and selected biota and landscapes. It is derived from several fields with the objective of determining reference conditions of past landscapes with the highest degree of authenticity for the period chosen for restoration. The remaining problem, in terms of the applications of historical ecology, concerns political questions as to who will be privileged in determining the desired time depth (Higgs 2003, Jones 2004) and the associated state of historical knowledge (Anderson 2001, Hall 2005) about the landscapes to be restored.

ACKNOWLEDGMENTS

For helpful discussion and suggestion of references, I am indebted to David Campbell, Clark L. Erickson, and Charbel Niño El-Hani. For initial bibliographic assistance, I thank Nathalie Dajko. I gratefully acknowledge the library staff and Ecology Division of Florida Gulf Coast University for making bibliographic resources available to me during the months when Tulane University libraries were closed as a result of Hurricane Katrina.

LITERATURE CITED

Adams WY. 1998. *The Philosophical Roots of Anthropology.* Stanford, CA: Center for the Study of Language and Information

Alexander KNA, Butler JE. 2004. Is the US concept of 'old growth' relevant to the cultural landscapes of Europe? A UK perspective. See Honnay et al. 2004, pp. 233–46

Allenby BR. 2000. The fallacy of "green technology." *Am. Behav. Sci.* 44:213–28

Altieri MA. 2004. *Genetic Engineering in Agriculture: The Myths, Environmental Risks, and Alternatives.* 2nd ed. Oakland, CA: Food First Books

Alvard MS, Kuznar L. 2001. Deferred harvests: the transition from hunting to animal husbandry. *Am. Anthropol.* 103:295–311

Anderson MK. 1999. The fire, pruning, and coppice management of temperate ecosystems for basketry material by California Indian tribes. *Hum. Ecol.* 27:79–113

Anderson MK. 2001. The contribution of ethnobiology to the reconstruction and restoration of historic ecosystems. See Egan & Howell 2001a, pp. 55–72

Balée W. 1989. The culture of Amazonian forests. See Posey & Balée 1989, pp. 1–21

Balée W. 1993. Indigenous transformation of Amazonian forests: an example from Maranhão, Brazil. *Homme* 33:231–54

Balée W, ed. 1998a. *Advances in Historical Ecology*. New York: Columbia Univ. Press

Balée W. 1998b. Historical ecology: premises and postulates. See Balée 1998a, pp. 13–29

Balée W. 2000. Antiquity of traditional ethnobiological knowledge in Amazonia: the Tupí-Guaraní family and time. *Ethnohistory* 47:399–422

Balée W. 2003. Historical-ecological influences on the word for cacao in Ka'apor. *Anthropol. Linguist.* 45:259–80

Balée W, Campbell DG. 1990. Evidence for the successional status of liana forest (Xingu River basin, Amazonian Brazil). *Biotropica* 22:36–47

Balée W, Erickson C, eds. 2006a. *Time and Complexity in Historical Ecology: Studies in the Neotropical Lowlands*. New York: Columbia Univ. Press

Balée W, Erickson C. 2006b. Time, complexity, and historical ecology. See Balée & Erickson 2006a, pp. 1–17

Beinart W, Coates P. 1995. *Environment and History: The Taming of Nature in the USA and Southern Africa*. London: Routledge

Beinart W, McGregor J, eds. 2003. *Social History and African Environments*. Athens: Ohio Univ. Press

Biersaack A. 1999. Introduction: from the "new ecology" to the new ecologies. *Am. Anthropol.* 101:5–18

Bilsky LJ, ed. 1980. *Historical Ecology: Essays on Environment and Social Change*. Port Washington, NY: Kennikat Press

Bird DW, Bird RB, Parker CH. 2005. Aboriginal burning regimes and hunting strategies in Australia's Western Desert. *Hum. Ecol.* 33:443–64

Boglioli MA. 2000. Civil conflict and savage unity: cross-cultural assumptions in ecological anthropology. *Anthropol. Work Rev.* 21:18–21

Botkin D. 1990. *Discordant Harmonies: A New Ecology for the Twenty-First Century*. New York: Oxford Univ. Press

Boyd R, ed. 1999a. *Indians, Fire and the Land in the Pacific Northwest*. Corvallis: Or. State Univ. Press

Boyd R. 1999b. Ecological lessons from Northwest Native Americans. See Boyd 1999a, pp. 292–97

Braudel F. 1980. *On History*. Transl. S Matthews. Chicago: Univ. Chicago Press

Burney DA. 1995/1996. Historical perspectives on human-assisted biological invasions. *Evol. Anthropol.* 4:216–21

Bush MB. 1994. Amazonian speciation: a necessarily complex model. *J. Biogeogr.* 21:5–17

Byers BA, Cunliffe RN, Hudak AT. 2001. Linking the conservation of culture and nature: a case study of sacred forests in Zimbabwe. *Hum. Ecol.* 29:187–218

Campbell DG, Ford A, Lowell KS, Walker J, Lake JK, et al. 2006. The feral forests of the Eastern Petén. See Balée & Erickson 2006a, pp. 21–55

Caron PC, Caron A, DuToit JT. 2003. Ecological implications of bovine tuberculosis in African buffalo herds. *Ecol. Appl.* 13:1338–45

Clement CR. 1999a. 1492 and the loss of Amazonian crop genetic resources. I. The relation between domestication and human population decline. *Econ. Bot.* 53:188–202

Clement CR. 1999b. 1492 and the loss of Amazonian crop genetic resources II. Crop biogeography at contact. *Econ. Bot.* 53:203–16

Cole JW, Wolf ER. 1974. *The Hidden Frontier: Ecology and Ethnicity in an Alpine Valley*. New York: Academic

Cormier LA. 2003. *Kinship with Monkeys: The Guajá Foragers of Eastern Amazonia*. New York: Columbia Univ. Press

Cormier LA. 2005. Um aroma no ar: a ecologia histórica das plantas anti-fantasma entre os Guajá da Amazônia. *Mana* 11:129–54

Cronon W. 1983. *Changes in the Land: Indians, Colonists, and the Ecology of New England.* New York: Hill & Wang

Crosby AW. 2004. *Ecological Imperialism: The Biological Expansion of Europe,* 900–1900. Cambridge, UK: Cambridge Univ. Press. 2nd ed.

Crumley CL, ed. 1994. *Historical Ecology: Cultural Knowledge and Changing Landscapes.* Santa Fe, NM: School of Am. Res. Press

Crumley CL. 1998. Foreword. See Balée 1998a, pp. ix–xiv

Crumley CL. 2001. Introduction. In *New Directions in Anthropology and Environment,* ed. CL Crumley, pp. vii–xi. Walnut Creek, CA: Altamira Press

Crumley CL. 2003. *Historical ecology: integrated thinking at multiple temporal and spatial scales.* Presented at World Syst. Hist. Glob. Environ. Change Conf., Lund University, Sweden. **http://www.humecol.lu.selwoshglec/** (accessed on November 14, 2005)

Denevan WM. 1992. The pristine myth: the landscape of the Americas in 1492. *Ann. Assoc. Am. Geogr.* 82:369–85

Denevan WM. 2001. *Cultivated Landscapes of Native Amazonia and the Andes.* New York: Oxford Univ. Press

Denevan WM. 2006. Pre-European forest cultivation in Amazonia. See Balée & Erickson 2006a, pp. 153–63

Dickinson WR. 2000. Changing times: the Holocene legacy. *Environ. Hist.* 5:483–502

Doolittle WF. 2000. *Cultivated Landscapes of Native North America.* Oxford: Oxford Univ. Press

Dove MR. 1999. The agronomy of memory and the memory of agronomy: ritual conservation of archaic cultigens in contemporary farming systems. In *Ethnoecology: Situated Knowledge/ Located Lives,* ed. V Nazarea, pp. 45–70. Tucson: Univ. Ariz. Press

Dove MR. 2001. Interdisciplinary borrowing in environmental anthropology and the critique of modern science. In *New Directions in Anthropology and Environment,* ed. CL Crumley, pp. 90–110. Walnut Creek, CA: Altamira Press

Egan D, Howell EA, eds. 2001a. *The Historical Ecology Handbook: A Restorationist's Guide to Reference Ecosystems.* Washington, DC: Island Press

Egan D, Howell EA. 2001b. Introduction. See Egan & Howell 2001a, pp. 1–23

Erickson CL. 2000. An artificial landscape-scale fishery in the Bolivian Amazon. *Nature* 408:190–93

Erickson CL. 2003. Historical ecology and future explorations. In *Amazonian Dark Earths: Origin, Properties, Management,* ed. J Lehmann, DC Kern, B Glaser, WI Woods, pp. 455–500. Dordrecht, The Netherlands: Kluwer

Erickson CL. 2006. The domesticated landscapes of the Bolivian Amazon. See Balée & Erickson 2006a, pp. 235–78

Erickson CL, Balée W. 2006. The historical ecology of a complex landscape in Bolivia. See Balée & Erickson 2006a, pp. 187–233

Fahrig L. 2003. Effects of habitat fragmentation in biodiversity. *Annu. Rev. Ecol. Evol. Syst.* 34:487–515

Fairhead J, Leach M. 1996. *Misreading the African Landscape: Society and Ecology in a Forest-Savanna Mosaic.* Cambridge, UK: Cambridge Univ. Press

Farnsworth ML, Wolfe LL, Hobbs NT, Burnham KP, Williams ES, et al. 2005. Human land use influences Chronic Wasting Disease in mule deer. *Ecol. Appl.* 5:119–26

Fedick SL. 1995. Indigenous agriculture in the Americas. *J. Archaeol. Res.* 3:257–303

Feely-Harnik G. 2001. *Ravenala madagascariensis:* the historical ecology of a "flagship species" in Madagascar. *Ethnohistory* 48:31–86

Finerman R, Sackett R. 2003. Using home gardens to decipher health and healing in the Andes. *Med. Anthropol. Q.* 17:459–82

Forman RTT, Godron M. 1986. *Landscape Ecology.* New York: Wiley & Sons

Foster D, Motzkin G, O'Keefe J, Boose E, Orwig D, et al. 2004. The environmental and human history of New England. In *Forests in Time: The Environmental Consequences of 1,000 Years of Change in New England,* ed. D Foster, JD Aber, pp. 43–100. New Haven, CT: Yale Univ. Press

Fritts TH, Rodder GH. 1998. The role of introduced species in the degradation of island ecosystems: a case history of Guam. *Annu. Rev. Ecol. Evol. Syst.* 35:149–74

Glacken CJ. 1967. *Traces on the Rhodian Shore: Nature and Culture in Western Thought from Ancient Times to the End of the Eighteenth Century.* Los Angeles: Univ. Calif. Press

Gómez-Pompa A, Kraus A. 1992. Taming the wilderness myth. *Bioscience* 42:271–79

Gómez-Pompa A, Flores JS, Sosa V. 1987. The 'pet-kot': a man-made tropical forest of the Maya. *Interciencia* 12:10–15

Gómez-Pompa A, Salvador Flores J, Alphat Fernández M. 1990. The sacred cacao groves of the Maya. *Lat. Am. Antiq.* 1:247–57

Grove AT, Rackham O. 2003. *The Nature of Mediterranean Europe: An Ecological History.* New Haven, CT: Yale Univ. Press

Gunn J. 1994. Introduction: a perspective from the humanities-science boundary. *Hum. Ecol.* 22:1–22

Hall M. 2005. *Earth Repair: A Translatlantic History of Environmental Restoration.* Charlottesville: Univ. of Va. Press

Hayashida FM. 2005. Archaeology, ecological history, and conservation. *Annu. Rev. Anthropol.* 34:43–65

Headland TN. 1997. Revisionism in ecological anthropology. *Curr. Anthropol.* 38:605–30

Heckenberger MJ, Kuikuro A, Kuikuro UT, Russell JC, Schmidt M, et al. 2003. Amazonia 1492: pristine forest or cultural parkland? *Science* 301:1710–14

Hierro JL, Maron JL, Callaway R. 2005. A biogeographical approach to invasions: the importance of studying exotics in the introduced and native range. *J. Ecol.* 93:5–15

Higgs E. 2003. *Nature by Design: People, Natural Process, and Ecological Restoration.* Cambridge, MA: MIT Press

Hirsch E, O'Haulon M, eds. 1995. *The Anthropology of Landscape: Perspectives on Place and Space.* Oxford: Clarendon Press

Holt FL. 2005. The catch-22 of conservation: indigenous peoples, biologists, and cultural change. *Hum. Ecol.* 33:199–215

Honnay O, Verheyen K, Bossuyt B, Hermy M, eds. 2004. *Forest Biodiversity: Lessons from History for Conservation.* IUFRO Research Series, 10. Cambridge, MA: CABI

Hughes JD. 1975. *Ecology in Ancient Civilizations.* Albuquerque: Univ. N. Mex. Press

Hughes JD. 2001. *An Environmental History of the World: Humankind's Changing Role in the Community of Life.* London: Routledge

Huston MA. 1994. *Biological Diversity: The Coexistence of Species on Changing Landscapes.* Cambridge, UK: Cambridge Univ. Press

Ingold T. 1993. The temporality of the landscape. *World Archaeol.* 25:152–74

Janzen D. 1998. Gardenification of wildland nature and the human footprint. *Science* 279:1312–13

Jeltsch F, Milton SJ, Dean WRJ, van Rooyen N, Moloney KA. 1998. Modelling the impact of small-scale heterogeneities on tree-grass coexistence in semiarid savannas. *J. Ecol.* 86:780–93

Jones ME. 2004. Historical ecology for conservation managers. *Conserv. Biol.* 18:281–82

Karesh WB, Cook R. 2005. The human-animal link. *Foreign Aff.* 84:38–50

Kates RW, Turner BL II, Clark WC. 1990. The great transformation. In *The Earth as Transformed by Human Action: Global and Regional Changes in the Biosphere Over the Past 300 Years*, ed. BL Turner II, pp. 1–17. New York: Cambridge Univ. Press

Kidder TR. 1998. The rat that ate Louisiana: aspects of historical ecology in the Mississippi River Delta. See Balée 1998a, pp. 141–68

Kidder TR, Balée W. 1998. Epilogue. See Balée 1998a, pp. 405–10

Kreike E. 2003. Hidden fruits: a social ecology of fruit trees in Namibia and Angola, 1880s–1990s. See Beinart & McGregor 2003, pp. 27–42

Kuhn TS. 1970. *The Structure of Scientific Revolutions*. Chicago: Univ. Chicago Press

Lakatos I. 1980. *The Methodology of Scientific Research Programmes*. Philosophical Papers, Vol.1. Cambridge, UK: Cambridge Univ. Press

Lakatos I. 1999 (1973). The methodology of scientific research programmes. (Linacre lecture #8). In *For and Against Method*, ed. M Motterlini, pp. 96–109. Chicago: Univ. Chicago Press

Leach M, Fairhead J. 2000. Challenging neo-Malthusian deforestation analyses in West Africa's dynamic forest landscapes. *Popul. Dev. Rev.* 26:17–43

Lentz DL, Haddad L, Cherpelis S, Joo HJM, Potter M. 2002. Long-term influences of Ancient Maya agroforestry practices on tropical forest biodiversity in Northwestern Belize. In *Ethnobiology and Biocultural Diversity*, ed. JR Stepp, FS Wyndham, RK Zarger, pp. 431–41. Athens: Univ. Ga. Press

Lomolino MV. 2000. A call for a new paradigm of island biogeography. *Global Ecol. Biogeogr.* 9:1–16

Lunt ID, Spooner PG. 2005. Using historical ecology to understand patterns of biodiversity in fragmented agricultural landscapes. *J. Biogeogr.* 32:1859–73

MacArthur RH, Wilson EO. 1967. *The Theory of Island Biogeography*. Princeton, NJ: Princeton Univ. Press

Mann C. 2002. 1491. *Atlantic Monthly* 289:41–53

Marquardt WH, ed. 1992. *Culture and Environment in the Domain of the Calusa Institute of Archaeology and Paleoenvironmental Studies*, Monograph 1. Gainesville: Univ. Fla.

Marquardt WH, Crumley CL. 1987. Theoretical issues in the analysis of spatial patterning. In *Regional Dynamics: Burgundian Landscapes in Historical Perspective*, ed. CL Crumley, WH Marquardt, pp. 1–18. San Diego: Academic

Mistry J, Berardi A, Andrade V, Krahô T, Krahô P, Leonardos O. 2005. Indigenous fire management in the *cerrado* of Brazil: the case of the Krahô of Tocantins. *Hum. Ecol.* 33:365–86

Moran EF. 2000. *Human Adaptability: An Introduction to Ecological Anthropology*. Boulder, CO: Westview Press. 2nd ed.

Myers JH, Bazely D. 2003. *Ecology and Control of Introduced Plants*. Cambridge, UK: Cambridge Univ. Press

Myllyntaus T. 2001. Environment in explaining history: restoring humans as part of nature. In *Encountering the Past in Nature: Essays in Environmental History*, pp. 141–60. Athens: Ohio Univ. Press. Rev. ed.

Neves EG, Petersen JB. 2006. Political economy and pre-Columbian landscape transformations in Central Amazonia. See Balée & Erickson 2006a, pp. 279–309

Newson LA. 1998. A historical-ecological perspective on epidemic disease. See Balée 1998a, pp. 42–63

Normile D. 2005. Pandemic influenza: global update. *Science* 309:370–73

Nyerges AE, ed. 1997. *The Ecology of Practice: Studies in Food Crop Production in Sub-Saharan West Africa.* New York: Gordon & Breach

Olwig K. 2003. Landscape: the Lowenthal legacy. *Ann. Assoc. Am. Geogr.* 93:871–77

Parker E. 1992. Forest islands and Kayapó resource management in Amazonia: a reappraisal of the apêtê. *Am. Anthropol.* 94:406–28

Perry DA, Amaranthus MP. 1997. Disturbance, recovery, and stability. In *Creating a Forest for the 21st Century: The Science of Ecosystem Management*, ed. KA Kohm, JF Franklin, pp. 31–56. Washington, DC: Island Press

Peters RH. 1991. *A Critique for Ecology.* Cambridge, UK: Cambridge Univ. Press

Peters CM, Balick MJ, Kahn F, Anderson A. 1989. Oligarchic forests of economic plants in Amazonia: utilization and conservation of an important tropical forest resource. *Conserv. Biol.* 3:341–49

Peterson DL, Parker VT. 1998. Dimensions of scale in ecology, resource management, and society. In *Ecological Scale: Theory and Application*, ed. DL Peterson, VT Parker, pp. 499–522. New York: Columbia Univ. Press

Petraitis PS, Latham RE, Niesenbaum RA. 1989. The maintenance of species diversity by disturbance. *Q. Rev. Biol.* 64:393–418

Pilson D, Prendeville HR. 2004. Ecological effects of transgenic crops and the escape of transgenes into wild populations. *Annu. Rev. Ecol. Evol. Syst.* 35:149–74

Pimm SL. 1991. *The Balance of Nature? Ecological Issues in the Conservation of Species and Communities.* Chicago: Univ. Chicago Press

Pitzl GR. 2004. *Encyclopedia of Human Geography.* Westport, CT: Greenwood

Politis G. 2001. Foragers of the Amazon: the last survivors or the first to succeed? In *Unknown Amazon: Culture in Nature in Ancient Brazil*, ed. C McEwan, C Barreto, EG Neves, pp. 26–49. London: British Museum Press

Porro R. 2005. Palms, pastures, and swidden fields: the grounded political ecology of "agro-extractive/shifting cultivator peasants" in Maranhão, Brazil. *Hum. Ecol.* 33:17–56

Posey DA. 1985. Indigenous management of tropical forest ecosystems. *Agroforestry Systems* 3:139–58

Posey DA, Balée W, eds. 1989. *Resource Management in Amazonia: Indigenous and Folk Strategies. Advances in Economic Botany*, Vol. 7. Bronx: New York Botanical Garden

Pyne SJ. 1991. *Burning Bush: A Fire History of Australia.* New York: Henry Holt

Pyne SJ. 1998. Forged in fire: history, land, and anthropogenic fire. See Balée 1998a, pp. 64–103

Raffles H. 2002. *In Amazonia: A Natural History.* Princeton NJ: Princeton Univ. Press

Rappaport RA. 2000. *Pigs for the Ancestors: Ritual in the Ecology of a New Guinea People.* Prospect Heights, Ill: Waveland Press. 2nd ed.

Redman CL. 1999. *Human Impact on Ancient Environments.* Tucson: Univ. Ariz. Press

Renfrew RB, Ribic CA, Nack JL. 2005. Edge avoidance by nesting grassland birds: a futile strategy in a fragmented landscape. *Auk* 122:618–36

Rival L. 2002. *Trekking Through History: The Huaorani of Amazonian Ecuador.* New York: Columbia Univ. Press

Rival L. 2006. Amazonian historical ecologies. *J. R. Anthropol. Inst.* 12:S79–94

Robbins WG. 1999. Landscape and environment: ecological change in the Intermontane Northwest. See Boyd 1999a, pp. 219–37

Roger J. 1997. *Buffon.* Trans. SL Bonnefoi. Ithaca, NY: Cornell Univ. Press

Rudel TK. 2002. Paths of destruction and regeneration: globalization and forests in the tropics. *Rural Sociol.* 67:622–36

Russell E. 1997. *People and the Land Through Time: Linking Ecology and History*. New Haven: Yale Univ. Press

Sauer CO. 1956. The agency of man on the Earth. In *Man's Role in Changing the Face of the Earth*, ed. WL Thomas Jr, CO Sauer, M. Bates, L Mumford, pp. 49–69. Chicago: Univ. Chicago Press

Schmitz DC, Simberloff D, Hofstetter RH, Haller W, Sutton D. 1997. The ecological impact of nonindigenous plants. See Simberloff et al. 1997, pp. 39–61

Schulze CH, Waltert M, Kessler PJA, Pitopang R, Shahabuddin Veddeler D, et al. 2004. Biodiversity indicator groups of tropical land-use systems: comparing plants, birds, and insects. *Ecol. Appl.* 14:1321–33

Scoones I. 1999. New ecology and the social sciences: what prospects for a fruitful engagement? *Annu. Rev. Anthropol.* 28:479–507

Sheuyange A, Oba G, Weladji RB. 2005. Effects of anthropogenic fire history on savanna vegetation in northeastern Namibia. *J. Environ. Manag.* 75:189–98

Simberloff D. 1997. The biology of invasions. See Simberloff et al. 1997, pp. 3–17

Simberloff D, Schmitz DC, Brown TC, eds. 1997. *Strangers in Paradise: Impact and Management of Nonindigenous Species in Florida*. Washington, DC: Island Press

Smith EA, Wishnie M. 2000. Conservation and subsistence in small-scale societies. *Annu. Rev. Anthropol.* 29:493–524

Stahl PW. 1996. Holocene biodiversity: an archaeological perspective from the Americas. *Annu. Rev. Anthropol.* 25:105–26

Stahl PW. 2000. Archaeofaunal accumulation, fragmented forests, and anthropogenic landscape mosaics in the tropical lowlands of prehispanic Ecuador. *Latin Am. Antiq.* 11:241–57

Stengers I. 2000 (1993). *The Invention of Modern Science*. Transl. DW Smith. Minneapolis: Univ. Minn. Press (From French)

Stepp JR, Wyndham FS, Zarger RK, eds. 2002. *Ethnobiology and Biocultural Diversity*. Athens: Univ. Georgia Press

Stoffle RW, Toupal R, Zedeño N. 2003. Landscape, nature, and culture: a diachronic model of human-nature adaptation. In *Nature Across Cultures: Views of Nature and the Environment in Non-Western Cultures*, ed. H Selin, pp. 97–114. Dordrecht: Kluwer Academic

Storm LE. 2002. Patterns and processes of indigenous burning: how to read landscape signatures of past human practices. See Stepp et al. 2002, pp. 496–508

Sutton MQ, Anderson EN. 2004. *Introduction to Cultural Ecology*. Walnut Creek, CA: Altamira Press

Townsend W. 1996. *Nyao Itõ: Caza y Pezca de los Sirionó*. La Paz, Bolivia: Instituto de Ecología, Universidad Mayor de San Andrés

Turner MG. 2005. Landscape ecology: What is the state of the science? *Annu. Rev. Ecol. Evol. Syst.* 36:319–44

Vansina J. 1990. *Paths in the Rainforests: Toward a History of Political Tradition in Equatorial Africa*. Madison: Univ. Wisc. Press

Vayda AP, Walters BB. 1999. Against political ecology. *Hum. Ecol.* 27:167–79

Verheyen K, Honnay O, Bossuyt B, Hermy M. 2004. What history can teach us about present and future forest biodiversity. See Honnay et al. 2004, pp. 1–9

Vieira ICG, Cardoso da Silva JM, Oren DC, D'Incao MA, eds. 2001. *Biological and Cultural Diversity of Amazonia*. Belém, Brazil: Museu Paraense Emílio Goeldi

Walker KJ. 2000. Historical ecology of the southeastern longleaf and slash pine flatwoods: a Southwest Florida perspective. *J. Ethnobiol.* 20:269–99

Walker LR, del Moral R. 2003. *Primary Succession and Ecosystem Rehabilitation*. Cambridge, UK: Cambridge Univ Press

Winthrop KR. 2001. Historical ecology: landscape of change in the Pacific Northwest. See Crumley 2001, pp. 203–22

Wiseman FJ. 1978. Agriculture and historical ecology of the Maya lowlands. In *Pre-Hispanic Maya Agriculture*, ed. PD Harrison, BL Turner II, pp. 63–115. Albuquerque: Univ. N. Mex. Press

Witkowski SR, Brown CH. 1983. Marking-reversals and cultural importance. *Language* 59:569–82

Wolf ER. 1982. *Europe and the People Without History*. Los Angeles: Univ. Calif. Press

Wolf ER. 1999. Cognizing "cognized models." *Am. Anthropol.* 101:19–22

Wolschke-Bulmahn J. 2004. All of Germany a garden? Changing ideas of wilderness in German garden design and landscape architecture. In *Nature in German History*, ed. C Mauch, pp. 74–92. New York: Berghahn Books

Worster D. 1993. *The Wealth of Nature: Environmental History and the Ecological Imagination.* New York: Oxford Univ. Press

Worster D. 1994. *Nature's Economy: A History of Ecological Ideas.* Cambridge, UK: Cambridge Univ. Press. 2nd ed.

Zent EL, Zent S. 2004. Amazonian Indians as ecological disturbance agents: the Hotï of the Sierra de Maigulaida Venezuelan Guayana. In *Ethnobotany and Conservation of Biocultural Diversity*, ed. L Maffi, TJS Carlson, pp. 79–111. Bronx: New York Botanical Garden

Zimmerer KS. 1993. Agricultural biodiversity and peasant rights to subsistence in the Central Andes during Inca rule. *J. Hist. Geogr.* 19:15–32

Zimmerer KS. 2000. The reworking of conservation geographies: nonequilibrium landscapes and nature-society hybrids. *Ann. Assoc. Am. Geogr.* 90:356–69

Anthropology and International Law

Sally Engle Merry

Department of Anthropology, New York University, New York, New York 10003;
email: sally.merry@nyu.edu

Annu. Rev. Anthropol. 2006. 35:99–116

First published online as a Review in
Advance on April 27, 2006

The *Annual Review of Anthropology* is
online at anthro.annualreviews.org

This article's doi:
10.1146/annurev.anthro.35.081705.123245

Copyright © 2006 by Annual Reviews.
All rights reserved

0084-6570/06/1021-0099$20.00

Key Words

human rights, globalization, indigenous rights, sovereignty, legal
pluralism

Abstract

International law, including human rights law, has expanded enormously in the past century. A growing body of anthropological research is investigating its principles and practices. Contemporary international law covers war and the treatment of combatants and noncombatants in wartime; international peace and security; the peaceful settlement of disputes; economic arrangements and trade agreements; the regulation of the global commons such as space, polar regions, and the oceans; environmental issues; the law of the sea; and human rights. This review demonstrates how anthropological theory helps social scientists, activists, and lawyers understand how international law is produced and how it works. It also shows the value of ethnographic studies of specific sites within the complex array of norms, principles, and institutions that constitute international law and legal regulation. These range from high-level commercial dispute settlement systems to grassroots human rights organizations around the world.

INTRODUCTION

International law has expanded enormously in the past century and has spawned a growing body of anthropological research on its principles and practices. Anthropological theory helps social scientists, activists, and lawyers to understand how international law is produced and how it works. International law originally focused on relations among states, but since World War II has expanded to include individuals, both as violators of international law and as bearers of rights defined by international law. The international law of human rights, in particular, defines a series of individual rights that states are obligated to uphold. Nevertheless, the existence and operation of international law depend primarily on nation-states and are embedded in the political relations of these states. This review focuses on the development of international law since the middle of the twentieth century and examines the contributions that anthropologists and other social scientists have made to understanding its operation and significance.

The principle domains of contemporary international law are war and the treatment of combatants and noncombatants in wartime; international peace and security; the peaceful settlement of disputes; economic arrangements and trade agreements; the regulation of the global commons such as space, polar regions, and the oceans; environmental issues; the law of the sea; and human rights. Human rights principles address rights such as free speech, rights to protection from torture and from extrajudicial killing, and rights to work, to development, to affordable housing, and to health. Since the 1940s, a series of international conventions have articulated and established this body of human rights.

International law creates a global legal order through conventions and treaties, monitoring and oversight, and social pressure. The sources of international law are primarily international conventions recognized by states, general principles of law recognized by states defined as "civilized," and customary international law (Bederman 2001, pp. 12–13). International law is increasingly based on a system of treaties, which nations enter into voluntarily. These are both bilateral treaties between two countries and multilateral ones between three or more countries (Bederman 2001, p. 26). Custom and treaties are coequal sources of international law; neither trumps the other. Because countries are joined by a large number of contracts, trade agreements, political alliances, academic networks, and other translational connections, they comply with international law because of reciprocity, the desire for membership in the international community, the wish to appear "civilized," pressure from other countries for trade agreements, and myriad other forms of indirect pressure (see Koh 1997).

International law aspires to universality but exists alongside and above domestic law—the law of nation-states. The domestic laws of nations have been incorporated into international law. Often the domestic law of nation-states serves as the basis for international legal arrangements. However, international law also shapes domestic law (Bederman 2001, pp. 6–7; Kingsbury 2003). Thus, despite the myth that international law is entirely separate from domestic law, in practice the systems are closely connected.

However, international law differs from domestic law in that it is grounded in a system of sovereign nations. Each nation is accountable to its own domestic order and not to a larger international community beyond what it consents to do (Bederman 2001, p. 50). According to the classic doctrine of sovereignty, no central authority has the power to force sovereign states to comply with its decisions. Short of war, no country can force another to change its practices toward its own citizens. However, sovereignty is not a matter of absolute autonomy, although the degree to which it is constrained by international law is a matter of ongoing debate among international lawyers (see Kingsbury 2003). In practice, within the present global order sovereignty is increasingly circumscribed (see Chayes &

Chayes 1998; Slaughter 2004). It is becoming contingent on compliance with a minimum of human rights principles toward a nation's own residents. The expansion of a rights discourse and enthusiasm for the rule of law facilitated by the 1990 collapse of the USSR and the establishment of liberal political orders in parts of Eastern Europe, against the backdrop of destructive ethnonationalism in the former Yugoslavia, facilitated this understanding of sovereignty (see Wilson 1997, p. 2; Cowan 2001). South Africa is a prime example of a country whose systematic violations of human rights principles under the apartheid system made it an international pariah state. However, less-powerful countries are more vulnerable to this pressure, whereas some of the most powerful, such as the United States, refuse to be bound by some aspects of international law at all. The United States, for example, typically complies with human rights conventions while refusing to ratify them (see Ignatieff 2001; Koh 2003).

In the absence of a central authority, how does international law work? Where do these laws come from? How are they enforced? Some legal scholars argue that this is not real law because it lacks centralized judicial institutions, police, and the means to enforce compliance. One of the basic questions about international law is why countries obey these laws. Realists claim that states comply only when it is in their self interest (see Dembour 2006). Conversely, research on social movements and nongovernmental organizations (NGOs) shows that civil society plays a role in holding governments accountable. Moreover, although violence by nonstate actors, such as paramilitaries or guerilla movements, poses dilemmas for a system of international law premised on controlling the actions of states, international legal institutions are beginning to define these actions as subject to their intervention (Alston 2005). Thus, international law is changing and developing at the same time as its enforcement mechanisms are am-biguous and dependent on a complex set of social processes. Anthropological analysis can illuminate some of these processes.

Some intriguing parallels can be found between the way international law works and the law of villages without centralized rule-making bodies and formal courts, the classic domain of legal anthropology. Both rely on custom, social pressure, collaboration, and negotiations among parties to develop rules and resolve conflicts (e.g., Nader 1969, Nader & Todd 1978, Redfield 1967). In both, law is plural and intersects with other legal orders, whether that of nation-states or other organizations or forms of private governance (Nader 1990). Each order constitutes a semiautonomous social field within a matrix of legal pluralism (Moore 1978). Both depend heavily on reciprocity and the threat of ostracism, as did the Trobrianders in Malinowski's (1926) account. Gossip and scandal are important in fostering compliance internationally as they are in small communities. Social pressure to appear civilized encourages countries to ratify international legal treaties (Hathaway 2002, Koh 1997) much as social pressure fosters conformity in small communities. Countries urge others to follow the multilateral treaties they ratify, but treaty monitoring depends largely on shame and social pressure (Bayefsky 2001, Merry 2003). Clearly there are many differences between social ordering in villages and in the world, but there are some similarities.

Some principles in international law are so widely accepted that they are known as customary law, *jus cogens* (compelling law), much as informal law and custom form the basis of social ordering in small communities (e.g., Nader 1969, 1990; Nader & Todd 1978). *Jus cogens* norms are so well established that they are no longer enforced and do not depend on consent. The 1969 Vienna Convention that defines international agreements calls *jus cogens* norms those "accepted and recognized by the international community of States as a whole as a norm from which no derogation is permitted."[1] The Universal Declaration of Human Rights (UDHR) is now considered *jus cogens*. According to a 2003 opinion of the Inter-American Court of Human Rights "the principle of equality before the law, equal protection before the law and nondiscrimination belongs to *jus cogens*, because the whole legal structure of national and international public order rests on it and it is a fundamental principle that permeates all laws."[2] *Jus cogens* norms trump other norms of customary or treaty law. Laws become established as customary when states announce them and other states do not complain or object (Bederman 2001, p. 20).

Similar to law in small communities, international law rules are produced through a process of deliberation and consensus formation rather than imposition (see Riles 2000, Merry 2006a). Global conferences, commission meetings, and trade negotiations all produce resolutions, declarations, and policy statements. The conventions that make up international law are produced by multiparty discussion and negotiation among many countries. Much of international law consists of multilateral treaties, developed collaboratively by individual countries. To some extent, the legitimacy of these international norms grows out of this process of international negotiation and compromise and the international consensus that emerges over time. This process parallels that occurring in local communities when they negotiate the rules they live by through disputing. For example, Comaroff & Roberts' (1981) study of disputing among the Tswana people in South Africa shows how the parties to the conflict draw on a repertoire of norms, general principles, and customs to resolve particular conflicts. The outcomes of the conflict and the rules that

they reinforce govern the repertoires available for future conflicts (Comaroff & Roberts 1981).

The norms of international law typically begin from nonbinding resolutions or statements of general principles, such as the Universal Declaration of Human Rights, which become solidified over time through subsequent resolutions and discussions. Only after a state ratifies a treaty is the state committed to complying with its terms. Non-binding declarations and treaties may well lead to binding treaties in the future (Bederman 2001, p. 27). Environmental law, for example, had no rules at all 60 years ago but gradually drew on general principles from domestic judicial systems and customary international law to begin treaty making. There are now a series of treaties and detailed regulatory regimes with conventions on acid rain, ozone depletion, fisheries management, wild-life preservation, and trade restrictions to promote these goals (Bederman 2001, p. 48; see Zerner 2003). In the terms used by international lawyers, environmental norms have moved from "soft law" to "hard law." In addition to global systems of treaties and regulatory regimes are a number of regional bodies and treaties.

THE DEVELOPMENT OF INTERNATIONAL LAW

Although international commercial law is quite ancient and there has long been concern about regulating war, the development of a set of international regulations governing political and social issues is relatively recent. Over the past century, the web of treaties, agreements, and contracts linking nations together has dramatically expanded. Members of different countries now participate in creating such global legal orders, whether concerning the regulation of sex trafficking or concerning the emission of greenhouse gases. However, now as in the past, powerful nations play a disproportionately large role in shaping these institutions.

---

[1] Art. 53, Vienna Convention on the Law of Treaties, 23 May 1969, U.N.T.S., vol. 1155, p. 331, quoted in Satterthwaite 2005, p. 43.

[2] Inter-American Court of Human Rights, *Juridical Condition and Rights of the Undocumented Migrants*, Advis. Opin. OC-18/03 (2003), para. 101, cited in Satterthwaite 2005, p. 43.

The formation of a system of international law generally dates to the international order of nation states created by the Treaty of Westphalia in 1648 in which the emerging nation states of Europe agreed to a system in which each state respected the autonomy and independence of other states (Bederman 2001, p. 2). Of course, at that time the majority of the world lay outside this system. Indeed, there was a close connection between the expansion of international law and the emergence of empire. Anghie (1999, 2004) argues that international law was shaped by the sixteenth-century encounter between the Spanish and the Indians. At that time, Francisco de Vitoria, one of the originators of international law, substituted a secular and universalizing basis for legal authority for religious papal authority. He argued that because the Indians had a capacity for reason, they could be incorporated under the same system of natural law as the Spanish. This natural law system allowed the Spanish to travel and sojourn in the Indians' territory and to respond to any Indian attempt at resistance as an act of war that justified retaliation. Thus, under Vitoria's theory, the Spanish gained the right to "defend" themselves against Indian resistance (Anghie 1999, p. 95). Rather than seeing international law as a preexisting system brought to the colonial encounter, Anghie shows how the encounter and the new problems it posed formed international law.

One of the central concerns of international law is the regulation of transnational economic activity. The expansion of transnational corporations and transnational economic activity has, over the past two decades, produced an enormous expansion of international mechanisms of managing disputes and negotiating rules (see Halliday & Osinsky 2006). With the expansion of the global production system and the global market for financial services has come global legal regulation, particularly commercial arbitration. New legal regimes to guarantee property rights and contracts for firms doing transna-

tional business are increasingly important (Sassen 1996, pp. 12–20). A series of institutions, such as the European Union, North American Free Trade Agreement (NAFTA), the World Trade Organization, the International Monetary Fund, and the World Bank (Halliday & Osinsky 2006), have developed in the postwar period to handle international economic and trade relations. Snyder's work on trade networks demonstrates the possibilities of an ethnography of the international trade system (Snyder 2005). A growing body of institutions works to resolve international commercial conflicts. Between 1970 and 1990, the system of international private justice shifted from relatively informal arbitration based on European scholars and the International Chamber of Commerce in Paris to "offshore litigation" with greater emphasis on Anglo-American law firms for resources and clients, on fact finding, and on adversarial lawyering (Dezalay & Garth 1995, pp. 34–36). Myriad systems exist for handling international conflicts such as the negotiation of disputes over rivers that cross national boundaries (Nader 2005).

Arup's (2000) study of the texts and impacts of the World Trade Organization, especially two of its new multilateral agreements—General Agreement on Trade and Services (GATS) and the Agreement on Trade-Related Aspects of Intellectual Property Rights (TRIPs)—examines how these new forms of global legal regulation operate. He analyzes them as examples of legal pluralism, or interlegality, to use Santos's term (1995). This term emphasizes how legalities clash, mingle, hybridize, and interact with one another. This takes place at several levels: between national legalities and among legalities not necessarily centered on any nation state (Arup 2000, p. 5). These legalities include the reemergence of a supranational *lex mercatoria* based on transnational contracts, model codes, and private arbitration.

The rapid development of offshore financial systems and tax havens provides ways to evade state control of financial transactions for purposes. Carried out under the aegis of the free market, such systems build on discourses of unique and distinctive places within a global market and the celebration of flexible persons who can readily move from one place to another (Maurer 1997). They provide places for escaping state regulation of financial transactions and tax payments, whereas the digitalizing of financial transactions makes them more difficult to trace and police. Although such changes are typically seen as an assault on state sovereignty, they may represent more fundamental shifts in the location of regulation. Investors in offshore locations still need to operate with high levels of trust and to have some guarantees of security of ownership and guarantees of contracts. The rapid proliferation of offshore financial systems raises new questions about the location and institutionalization of the regulatory systems that enable them to function (see Maurer 1997, 2005).

THE DEVELOPMENT OF INTERNATIONAL HUMAN RIGHTS LAW

Since World War II, an elaborate system of human rights documents and institutions for implementing these documents has developed internationally, focused largely on the United Nations (U.N.) and its subsidiary organizations (see generally Steiner & Alston 2000; Kingsbury 2003). The development of the human rights system means that not only states but also individuals are considered to have rights and responsibilities under international law. A series of conventions focused on specific spheres of rights, such as civil and political rights, economic and social rights, women's rights, children's rights, the rights of racial minorities, and the rights to protection from torture and genocide, constitutes the statutory basis of the human rights system (Bayefsky 2001, Peters & Wolper 1995). This system is built on the same formal structure of autonomous, sovereign states tied through treaties as the rest of international law. Only

states that ratify these conventions are bound by them, but the major conventions are widely ratified. Although no judicial body can enforce compliance with these norms, the conventions represent a transnational body of norms governing social justice and specifying the rights and obligations of states to their members.

The concept of human rights itself has been dramatically transformed over the past 50 years as activists have deployed it in a variety of innovative contexts. A major expansion has occurred from an individually based conception of legal and political rights adhering to individuals to protect them from the oppression of the state, such as rights to freedom from torture or the right to due process, to more collective rights to survival and well-being (see Messer 1993; Sarat & Kearns 1995). New human rights, many of which are more collective, are constantly being created by activists and leaders of the human rights system. These include the right to development, elaborated in the 1980s (Alston & Robinson 2005, Sen 1999), and women's rights in the 1990s (Peters & Wolper 1995).

During the 1980s and 1990s, indigenous peoples sought support from the U.N. Human Rights Commission for their claims to resources and self-determination, culminating in a draft declaration of rights of indigenous peoples (Coulter 1994, Tennant 1994, Trask 1993). The development of human rights documents dealing with indigenous peoples raised issues of group or community rights with particular force. Beginning from a movement by leaders of indigenous groups in the Americas, an initial declaration on principles for the defense of indigenous nations was formulated and presented at a U.N. conference in 1977. The U.N. Sub-Commission on the Prevention of Discrimination and Protection of Minorities, part of the U.N. Human Rights Commission, created the Working Group on Indigenous Populations in 1982. This soon became the leading international forum for hundreds of indigenous peoples' leaders and representatives as they met each year in July at the

Working Group meetings in Geneva (Coulter 1994, p. 37; see also Anaya 1994, 2000). Indigenous peoples incorporated into settler states such as the United States, Canada, Australia, and New Zealand drew on the language of self-determination developed in the late 1940s and 1950s to fight colonialism (see Nagengast & Turner 1997, Trask 1993, Turner 1997).

Although indigenous groups sought self-determination under international law, they were generally not seeking statehood or independence but survival of their cultural communities. They were searching for cultural identity and control over land and other resources rather than autonomy (Lam 1992). This has been a fundamentally legal struggle, using the language and institutions of the law rather than other forms of political contestation. One of the major objectives has been the establishment of some degree of legal autonomy and self-governance. The Draft Declaration on the Rights of Indigenous Peoples, finalized in 1994 after years of discussion among indigenous groups and U.N. representatives, includes the right to create and maintain indigenous peoples' own governments and their own laws and legal systems (Coulter 1994, p. 40). However, as of 2006, it was still not adopted.

By the 1990s, there were many national, regional, and international human rights commissions and organizations and a burgeoning civil society of human rights organizations. Strong regional human rights institutions existed in the Americas and Europe and were developing in Africa. However, the post-9/11 concern with terrorism may dampen human rights enthusiasm as security takes on greater significance (Wilson 2005a). In some ways, concerns with peace and security have long been antithetical. Peace may be achieved at the price of ignoring human rights violations, whereas respecting rights can lead to war, as some political leaders and scholars claim occurred when the United States invaded Iraq in 2003 (see Cushman 2005).

Human rights development was also buffeted by global political struggles such as the Cold War. Although the Universal Declaration included both civil and political rights and social and economic rights, it proved politically impossible to produce a convention with both sets of rights. The development of the human rights framework in the 1940s to 1960s followed two tracks, one supported by the capitalist and democratic West, which focused on civil and political rights, and the other advocated by socialist governments, which emphasized economic and social rights such as rights to food, housing, and health. Whereas the Soviets advocated the right to work and other social rights, the United States promoted civil and political rights such as free speech and freedom of religion. In the 1950s, worried that an international investigation into the economic, educational, and political disparities between whites and African Americans in the United States could prove deeply embarrassing and provide a platform for the Soviets to trumpet the importance of food and housing rights, U.S. State Department officials decided to emphasize free speech. This provided a platform to criticize the Soviet suppression of dissidents (Anderson 2003). The division between these categories of rights remains deep. Developing countries take the lead in asserting social and economic rights, and the United States focuses on civil and political rights. Sen's argument that development includes promoting human rights emphasizes the linkage among rights and the importance of social and economic rights (e.g., Sen 1999; see Alston & Robinson 2005).

Inequalities in wealth and power between the global North and the global South have a major impact on the shape and operation of the human rights system. As Rajagopal (2003) argues, international law changed in response to the demands made by Third World social movements. For example, the shift from economic growth to poverty reduction came in response to the politicization of poverty and demands for change. Although the development of international law is often described by legal scholars as the logical outgrowth of international legal deliberation, he argues that it responds to the pressure of poor and discontented people and their forms of resistance.

Despite worries that the human rights system is a new form of imperialism, it has produced very few interventions to protect human rights (Donnelly 2003). However, violations of human rights principles are increasingly being used as justifications for various forms of international military action, as in Kosovo. States and international NGOs sometimes pressure other states to protect the human rights of their populations. For example, during the 1990s the United States sought to use the U.N. High Commission on Human Rights to put pressure on China to reverse its poor human rights record (Foot 2000).

Thus, the human rights system represents a new international legal regime, although one constructed on the old international order of sovereignty. Although it is now the dominant language of global justice, the concern with terrorism and security post-9/11 may shrink its importance in the twenty-first century (Wilson 2005a). Because individuals are endowed with human rights on the basis of their human dignity rather than on the basis of their membership in a nation, it is more incorporative than nation-state law and valuable for the burgeoning populations of noncitizens such as illegal immigrants and refugees (see Coutin 2000). These are groups excluded from citizenship but still endowed with human rights, at least theoretically although not always in practice (see Dembour 2003; Sarat & Kearns 2001).

Nineteenth-century imperialism produced a transplantation of laws, courts, wigs, and many of the other mechanisms of European rule to the very different contexts of colonial society (see Comaroff & Comaroff 1991, 1997; Merry 2000). International law adds a new layer of legal pluralism to this legacy of colonialism. The British colonial government often encouraged the maintenance of separate personal laws governing family and marriage on the basis of religious

membership as a way of governing through existing institutions. This strategy minimized costs and reduced forms of resistance to colonial control. These legal distinctions fostered separatism and ethnic violence in the postcolonial period in places such as India, Malaysia, and Fiji (see Merry & Brenneis 2004). Bowen (2003) and Benda-Beckmann & Benda-Beckmann have studied the emergence of forms of postcolonial legal pluralism in Indonesia that include international law (e.g., Benda-Beckmann & Benda-Beckmann 2005, 2006; Benda-Beckmann 2001).

TOWARD AN ANTHROPOLOGY OF INTERNATIONAL LAW

Anthropology can make significant contributions to the understanding and analysis of international law. Its focus on the meanings and practices of small social spaces, whether in villages or the corridors of international tribunals, enables a far deeper understanding of how the various facets of international law actually work. The analogy to village law, despite vast differences in these forms of law, shows the analytic possibilities of focusing on particular situations, individual actions, wider structural inequalities, and systems of meaning. Although international lawyers recognize the historically produced and eclectic nature of international law, ethnography reveals the variations in the way it operates in many locations. For example, Coxshall's (2005) analysis of a group of Andean villagers' refusal to participate in the Peruvian Truth and Reconciliation Commission shows why they are indifferent to the commission, their difficulty in narrating the pain of state violence and conflict, and the gendered and racialized identities that shape these decisions. Her ethnography offers a valuable antidote to claims that narrating pain in such a forum promotes forgiveness and healing. Moreover, an anthropological perspective on international law leads to greater attention to the systems of meaning that shape international actions and their historical and structural origins. For example, Razack's (2004) recent study of the violence of Canadian peacekeepers in Somalia highlights the racial narratives that undergird the whole peacekeeping project, as the "civilized" North seeks to rescue the apparently chaotic and violent South from its inability to govern itself. She locates these narratives in the Canadian imperial conquest of native peoples and long-standing imperial narratives of white supremacy. The latter help to construct a Canadian self-identity as peacekeeper to the world.

A growing body of anthropological scholarship on human rights NGOs provides a rich and complex understanding of these organizations and the kinds of support they provide to the human rights system. Local, national, and transnational NGOs contribute to the drafting of documents and shoulder a significant portion of the burden of implementing human rights declarations (see Keck & Sikkink 1998; Risse et al. 1999). They do research, identify issues, generate media attention, define problems in human rights terms, and bring these issues to the attention of international political organizations (see Keck & Sikkink 1998; Otto 1999). McLagen (2005) shows how NGOs create media representations of human rights abuses, even providing technical expertise to other organizations for developing issues, preparing videos, and targeting publics by developing a range of specialized messages. Although NGOs and governments collaborate in these important ways, there are also significant tensions between them. Governments resist the criticism and exposure of violations that are the standard approach of human rights organizations (see Merry 2006a).

Human rights NGOs are caught between international and local normative commitments, pressures from international funders, the constraints of national and nationalist politics, and the limitations of human rights discourse itself (e.g., An-Na'im 2002, Berry 2003, Karim 2001, Leve 2001, Leve & Karim 2001, Pigg 1997, Rosga 2005, Samson 2001). As Rosga (2005) argues in her analysis of the challenges of producing a report on child trafficking in Bosnia/Herzogovina, creating human rights reports is deeply political. Her ethnography of writing a human rights report, a basic feature of human rights activism, delineates the political and social hurdles to producing this kind of knowledge. The obstacles include inequalities in resources, ambiguities about who is in control, and restrictions on what counts as expertise. She confronted the preferences of wealthy donors, their assumptions about the incompetence of local researchers, ambiguities and distrust in the construction of research budgets and methodologies, simmering tensions between Serbian and Muslim groups, and fundamental problems of translation (2005). There is, she notes, no word in the Bosnia language for trafficking.

Anthropologists play complex and sometimes contradictory roles as scholars and as activists in the chaotic, multilayered world of international and local human rights advocacy (Jean-Klein & Riles 2005, Coxshall 2005, Rosga 2005, Merry 2006a, Sharma 2006). Sometimes anthropologists work with human rights NGOs, merging their scholarship with activism in ways that challenge traditional notions of the anthropologist as outside observer but contributing to deeper insights and a more ethical engagement with their subjects. Anthropologists often play critical roles as advocates and supporters of indigenous claims. For example, an important victory in the Awas Tingni decision of the Inter-American Court of Human Rights in 2001, which established a principle of the right of indigenous peoples to the protection of their customary land and resources, depended on substantial background research by anthropologist Ted McDonald (Anaya & Grossman 2002, p. 1). The people of Awas Tingni in the Atlantic coast region of Nicaragua received substantial assistance from United States-based lawyers and anthropologists in their case, which produced the first legally binding decision by an international tribunal upholding the collective land and resource rights of indigenous people when the state failed to do so (Anaya & Grossman 2002, p. 2; see also Anaya 1994, 2000).

The transplantation and localization of concepts of rights and the rule of law are also central to disseminating human rights. Legal institutions, procedures, and laws are taken from one cultural context and recreated in quite another, usually by wealthy donor nations. Localization has been examined by anthropologists working in areas where human rights and other forms of international law have become increasingly important, such as Goodale's work in Bolivia (2002), An-Naim's on Africa (2002), and Merry's on women's rights in several Asia/Pacific countries (2006a), as well as by international relations scholars (Keck & Sikkink 1998, Risse Ropp & Sikkink 1999). Tate's (2004) study of human rights in Columbia reveals the opportunistic appropriation of this technology by groups on the political right as well as the left.

INTERNATIONAL LAW AND KNOWLEDGE PRACTICES

An anthropology of international law includes studying up; looking at transnational organizations concerned with trade, peacekeeping, human rights, and humanitarian aid to see how they create rules and impose pressure to support them; and looking at the larger political and economic contexts that shape international law, despite the claims of some practitioners that the system evolves according to its own principles and technologies. It can focus on the knowledge practices of law and their transnational circulation: particular points of intersection, technologies of legality, and sites of negotiation among multiple systems of law. The knowledge practices of law, including its technologies for producing truth and defining identity, often sit at the intersection of plural legalities. As Ong & Collier (2005) note, as global forms are articulated in specific situations, which they refer to as "global assemblages," they provide a site

where the conditions of individual and collective existence are problematized and open to technological, political, and ethical reflection and intervention (p. 4). Globally circulating legal concepts and practices become sedimented, fixed into documents, letters of intent, forms of agreement, contracts, and other legal forms (see Riles 2000, 2004; Pottage & Mundy 2004; Miyazaki & Riles 2005). As new situations emerge, such as the need to determine under which system of law conflicts over collateral will be judged, documents are developed which structure these decisions (A. Riles, unpublished manuscript). Similarly, negotiations around development projects in Africa take place through a technology of matrices and numbers, even when these are far removed from actual situations. The technology itself, as Rottenburg (2002) shows, produces the truth, which serves as the basis for further development planning. The knowledge practices produce particular forms of organizing information shaped by legal rules. These forms themselves then create representations of knowledge.

The transnationally mobile knowledge practices of international and domestic law reshape subjectivity in important ways, redefining persons as citizens, noncitizens, deportees, and adoptees, for example (Coutin 2000, Coutin Mauer & Yngvesson 2002). Because of law's capacity to define identity and establish the rights and duties of various statuses, its transnational dispersal has significant implications for persons who cross boundaries. As Kelly (2004) shows in Palestine, the lines that laws create serve to include and exclude, constituting identities and marginalities. The knowledge practices of law include multiple ways of defining selves and, as they become part of local consciousness, producing new subjectivities. The focus on knowledge practices as a domain of legality and the use of ethnographic methods to examine specific technologies and practices of law represent innovative anthropological contributions to understanding the impacts of international law.

INTERNATIONAL HUMAN RIGHTS LAW

A substantial body of research in the field of legal anthropology has developed theoretical frameworks useful for analyzing international human rights law. This work demonstrates the way law creates social order through defining relationships, punishing certain forms of behavior, and creating categories of meaning. Law empowers powerful groups to construct normative orders that enhance their control over resources and people, but also provides to less privileged people avenues for protest and resistance (Hirsch & Lazarus-Black 1994). Human rights law also has this two-sided impact, buttressing neoliberal political and economic regimes but providing some recourse for the powerless.

Legal anthropologists show how law makes persons and things (Pottage 2004, Pottage & Mundy 2004). Human rights law defines persons in terms of autonomy, choice, and bodily integrity, in contrast with other systems of law that focus on obligation and exchange. Strathern (2004) describes a situation in Papua New Guinea, for example, in which a young woman was slated to be given to another family to repay a tribal debt. The national human rights commission prevented the exchange on the grounds that it violated her human rights, even though she herself saw the exchange as an obligation she should fulfill and saw herself in terms of her relationships.

Anthropologists are now analyzing human rights as social practice. In contrast with earlier work that debated the ethical and theoretical advantages of universal moral principles or relativistic ones (An-Na'im 1992, Nagengast & Turner 1997, Zechenter 1997; but see Cowan et al. 2001, Dembour 2006, Messer 1993), this later work examines human rights as a social process of producing norms, knowledge, and compliance. It asks where human rights ideas and doctrines are made and by whom, how various groups seek to champion and implement them, and how actors who claim them think about these rights.

For example, Dembour (2006) reexamines the universalism/relativism debate through a study of human rights practice as revealed in cases at the European Court of Human Rights. She sees human rights as a matter of discourse and practice located in particular places and uses her analysis of practice to problematize the meanings of universalism and relativism.

Scholarship on the practice of human rights asks how human rights ideas and institutions make a difference in people's everyday lives and explores how they become locally meaningful (see Wilson 1996; Cowan et al. 2001; Goodale 2006; Goodale & Merry 2007; Merry 2006a,b). Ethnographic work on rights explores rights consciousness and asks when and why individuals choose to mobilize rights (see Merry & Stern 2005). One study of disabled Americans, for example, shows their reluctance to assert disability rights even when laws exist to define those rights (Engel & Munger 2003). In the field of indigenous rights, a growing body of scholarship examines the way customary forms of justice among indigenous groups interact with international human rights law (Sierra 1995, Speed & Collier 2000).

Some ethnographic research explores the phenomenon of state retreat and legal failure: of places where law is absent. In some of these places, international law may move in to replace failing domestic law. Ethnic conflict and violence are frequent markers of this situation, and some argue that weak states are more hazardous for human rights than are strong states (Ignatieff 2001). Work on violence, suffering, and lynching provides some insight into the effects of weak states (Das et al. 1998). In Bolivia, for example, Goldstein analyzes the expansion of collective community lynching as a response to the failure of state police and courts (Goldstein 2003, p. 2004). He attributes the withdrawal of the state from providing justice to neoliberal structural reform and its ideologies of privatization and devolution so that security becomes the responsibility of citizens (2005, p. 395).

INTERNATIONAL TRIBUNALS AND TRANSITIONAL JUSTICE

International tribunals of various kinds represent another form of global law. Here also anthropologists have done important work, such as challenging the concepts of justice and reconciliation that shape the tribunals. International criminal tribunals hold leaders accountable for offenses such as war crimes, genocide, or abuses connected with war, such as rape or sexual slavery. Tribunals to settle property and financial disputes between countries are at least two centuries old, but international criminal courts that hold war crimes violators to account date from the Nuremberg trials after World War II (Bederman 2001, p. 45). Special tribunals have been set up for Rwanda, the former Yugoslavia, Sierra Leone, and East Timor, with others under discussion. In 2002, the International Criminal Court came into existence to try war crimes, crimes against humanity, and genocide. Another form of international tribunal is the truth commission, which uses truthtelling and the search for forgiveness to heal societies shattered by armed conflict and ethnic division. Wilson's (2000, 2001) study of the South African Truth and Reconciliation Commission (TRC) shows how its message of redemption and reconciliation satisfied some but not others, who preferred streetlevel popular justice and punishment for wrongdoing.

Whether a criminal justice approach is more effective than a reconciliation model is currently a hotly debated issue. The former is better at holding individuals accountable but can handle only a few cases, whereas the latter may be better at healing social conflicts but fails to punish perpetrators. Hybrid models incorporate some aspects of both models. Another difficult issue for transitional justice is whether it should be managed by an international body or by the leaders of the nation experiencing ethnic conflict or state repression. If the same leaders are in power, a nationally based tribunal is problematic. Another issue is whether the goal is to hold individuals responsible or to produce a national narrative of the conflict. The proponents of the South African TRC saw it as the chance to tell the story of apartheid. Wilson (2005b) argues that the ongoing trial of Milosevic by the International Criminal Court for Yugoslavia is similarly producing a relatively objective history of the era, but that this is only possible because the tribunal is internationally created and managed.

Clearly, careful ethnographic work on such tribunals—including studies such as Coxshall's (2005), which explores the reasons victims choose not to testify, or Wilson's (2001), which shows some communities' preference for punishment rather than forgiveness—is essential in understanding how these tribunals operate and challenging assumptions about postconflict healing. Anthropological research can contribute knowledge that will address questions about the relative merits of criminal trials, with their delay and expense and small defendant rolls, and the more open, conciliatory, and amnesty-focused proceedings of truth commissions. In general, as Jean-Klein & Riles (2005) argue, anthropology has much to contribute to understanding human rights practices.

CONCLUSIONS

New global legal institutions for peacekeeping and collective security, commercial law, humanitarian law, human rights law, and more recently international criminal law are gradually emerging (Kingsbury 2003). Law's internationalization is a product of transnational movements such as colonialism, contemporary transnational activism, the creation of a new world order of negotiated contracts and agreements linking together diverse states, the expansion of human rights activism and institutions, and the transplanting of legal institutions themselves. The relationship between weak international systems and nation-state law remains deeply ambiguous, however. These new institutions incorporate in fluid and complicated ways laws, procedures, and practices from previously existing national and local systems of law. They contribute to the creation of a new legal order but are also deeply constrained in their authority by the system of sovereignty that underlies all transnational endeavors and inevitably reflects the global inequalities among rich and poor nations. Government aid programs, NGO activism, U.N. organizations, and social movements such as global feminism have all contributed to this internationalization of law and the transformations it evokes.

Given the ambiguity and novelty of these developments, anthropological research plays a critical role in examining how international law works in practice, mapping the circulation of ideas and procedures as well as examining the array of small sites in which international law operates, whether in Geneva, a local office of a human rights NGO, or the International Criminal Court. Despite the significant legal and social science scholarship on this system of law, its principles, and its practices, anthropology is particularly well equipped to provide insight into the individuals, the issues, the practices, and the meanings that constitute international law as a social process.

ACKNOWLEDGMENTS

My work in this area has benefited from a fellowship at the American Bar Foundation and a fellowship year at the Carr Center for Human Rights Policy at Harvard. My research on international human rights has been generously supported by the Law and Social Sciences and Cultural Anthropology programs of the National Science Foundation and by a Mellon Fellowship from Wellesley College.

LITERATURE CITED

Alston P, ed. 2005. *Non-State Actors and Human Rights*. Oxford, UK: Oxford Univ. Press

Alston P, Robinson M, eds. 2005. *Human Rights and Development: Towards Mutual Reinforcement*. Oxford, UK: Oxford Univ. Press

Anaya SJ. 1994. International law and indigenous peoples. *Cult. Surv. Q.* Spring:42–44

Anaya SJ. 2000. *Indigenous Peoples in International Law*. Oxford, UK: Oxford Univ. Press

Anaya SJ, Grossman C. 2002. The case of Awas Tingni v. Nicaragua: a new step in the international law of indigenous peoples. *Ariz. J. Int. Comp. Law* 19(1):1–15

Anderson C. 2003. *Eyes off the Prize: The United Nations and the African-American Struggle for Human Rights, 1944–1955*. Cambridge, UK: Cambridge Univ. Press

Anghie A. 1999. Francisco de Vitoria and the colonial origins of international law. In *Laws of the Postcolonial*, ed. E Darian-Smith, P Fitzpatrick, pp. 89–109. Ann Arbor: Univ. Mich. Press

Anghie A. 2004. *Imperialism, Sovereignty and the Making of International Law*. Cambridge, UK: Cambridge Univ. Press

An-Na'im AA. 1992. *Human Rights in Cross-Cultural Perspectives: A Quest for Consensus*. Philadelphia: Univ. Penn. Press

An-Na'im A, ed. 2002. *Cultural Transformation and Human Rights in Africa*. London: Zed Books

Arup C. 2000. *The New World Trade Organization Agreements: Globalizing Law through Services and Intellectual Property*. Cambridge, UK: Cambridge Univ. Press

Bayefsky AF. 2001. *The UN Human Rights Treaty System: Universality at the Crossroads*. Ardsley, NY: Transnational

Bederman DJ. 2001. *International Law Frameworks*. New York: Foundation

Benda-Beckmann FV, Benda-Beckmann KV. 2006. Transnationalization of law, globalization, and legal pluralism: a legal anthropological perspective. In *Globalization and Law in Asia*, ed. C Antons, V Gessner. Oxford, UK: Hart. In press

Benda-Beckmann FV, Benda-Beckmann KV. 2005. Democracy in flux: time, mobility and sedentarization of law in Minangkabau, Indonesia. In *Mobile People, Mobile Law: Expanding Legal Relations in a Contracting World*, ed. F von Benda-Beckmann, K von Benda-Beckmann, A Griffiths, pp. 111–31. Aldershot, UK: Ashgate

Benda-Beckmann KV. 1981. Forum shopping and shopping forums—dispute settlement in a Minangkabau village in West Sumatra. *J. Legal Plur.* 19:117–59

Benda-Beckmann KV. 2001. Transnational dimensions of legal pluralism. In *Begegnung und Konflikt—Eine Kulturanthropologische Bestandsaufname*, ed. W Fikentscher, pp. 33–48. Muenchen: Verlag der Bayerischen Akademie der Wissenschaften. C.H. Beck Verlag

Berry K. 2003. Developing women: the traffic in ideas about women and their needs in Kangra, India. In *Regional Modernities: The Cultural Politics of Development in India*, ed. K Sivaramakrishnan, A Agrawal, pp. 75–98. Stanford, CA: Stanford Univ. Press

Bowen JR. 2003. *Islam, Law, and Equality in Indonesia: An Anthropology of Public Reasoning*. Cambridge, UK: Cambridge Univ. Press

Chayes A, Chayes AH. 1998. *The New Sovereignty: Compliance with International Regulatory Agreements*. Cambridge, MA: Harvard Univ. Press

Comaroff J, Comaroff JL. 1991. *Of Revelation and Revolution: Christianity, Colonialism, and Consciousness in South Africa*. Vol. I. Chicago: Univ. Chicago Press

Comaroff JL, Comaroff J. 1997. *Of Revelation and Revolution: The Dialectics of Modernity on a South African Frontier*. Vol. II. Chicago: Univ. Chicago Press

Comaroff J, Roberts S. 1981. *Rules and Processes: The Cultural Logic of Dispute in an African Context*. Chicago: Univ. Chicago Press

Coulter RT. 1994. Commentary on the UN draft declaration on the rights of indigenous peoples. *Cult. Surv. Q.* 18(2):37–41

Coutin S. 2000. *Legalizing Moves: Salvadoran Immigrants' Struggle for U.S. Residency*. Ann Arbor: Univ. Mich. Press

Coutin SB, Maurer B, Yngvesson B. 2002. In the mirror: the legitimation work of globalization. *Law Soc. Inq.* 27:801–44

Cowan J, Dembour M, Wilson R, eds. 2001. *Culture and Rights*. Cambridge, UK: Cambridge Univ. Press

Cowan JK. 2001. Ambiguitie of an emancipatory discourse: the making of a Macedonian minority in Greece. See Cowan et al., pp. 152–77

Coxshall W. 2005. From the Peruvian reconciliation commission to ethnography: narratives, relatedness, and silence. *PoLAR: Polit. Legal Anthropol. Rev.* 28(2):203–23

Cushman T. 2005. The conflict of the rationalities: international law, human rights and the war in Iraq. *Deakin Law Rev.* 10(2):546–70

Das V, Kleinman A, Lock M, eds. 1998. *Social Suffering*. Berkeley: Univ. Calif. Press

Dembour MB. 2003. Human rights law and national sovereignty in collusion: the plight of quasi-nationals at Strasbourg. *Neth. Q. Hum. Rights* 21:63–98

Dembour MB. 2006. *Who Believes in Human Rights? Reflections on the European Convention*. Cambridge, UK: Cambridge Univ. Press

Dezalay Y, Garth B. 1995. Merchants of law as moral entrepreneurs: constructing international justice from the competition for transnational business disputes. *Law Soc. Rev.* 29:27–65

Donnelly J. 2003. *Universal Human Rights in Theory and Practice*. Ithaca, NY: Cornell Univ. Press. 2nd ed.

Engel D, Munger F. 2003. *Rights of Inclusion: Law and Identity in the Life Stories of Americans with Disabilities*. Chicago: Univ. Chicago Press

Foot R. 2000. *Rights Beyond Borders: The Global Community and the Struggle over Human Rights in China*. Oxford, UK: Oxford Univ. Press

Jean-Klein I, Riles A. 2005. Introducing discipline. *PoLAR: Polit. Legal Anthropol. Rev.* 28(2):173–202

Goldstein DM. 2003. "In our own hands": lynching, justice and the law in Bolivia. *Am. Ethnol.* 30(1):22–43

Goldstein DM. 2004. *The Spectacular City: Violence and Performance in Urban Bolivia*. Durham, NC: Duke Univ. Press

Goldstein DM. 2005. Flexible justice: neoliberal violence and 'self-help' security in Bolivia. *Crit. Anthropol.* 25(4):389–411

Goodale M. 2002. Legal ethnography in an era of globalization: the arrival of western human rights discourse to rural Bolivia. In *Practicing Ethnography in Law: New Dialogues, Enduring Methods*, ed. J Starr, M Goodale, pp. 50–72. New York: Palgrave Macmillan

Goodale M. 2006. Toward a critical anthropology of human rights. *Curr. Anthropol.* 47(3): In press

Goodale M, Merry SE, eds. 2007. *The Practice of Human Rights*. Cambridge, UK: Cambridge Univ. Press. In press

Halliday TC, Osinsky P. 2006. Globalization of law. *Annu. Rev. Sociol.* 32:447–70

Hathaway O. 2002. Do human rights treaties make a difference *Yale Law J.* 111:1935–2042

Hirsch SF, Lazarus-Black M. 1994. Introduction. In *Contested States: Law, Hegemony, and Resistance*, ed. M Lazarus-Black, SF Hirsch, pp. 1–31. New York: Routledge

Ignatieff M. 2001. *Human Rights as Politics and Idolatry*. Princeton, NJ: Princeton Univ. Press

Karim L. 2001. Politics of the poor? NGOs and grass-roots political mobilization in Bangladesh. *PoLAR: Polit. Legal Anthropol. Rev.* 24(1):92–107

Keck ME, Sikkink K. 1998. *Activists Beyond Borders: Advocacy Networks in International Politics*. Ithaca, NY: Cornell Univ. Press

Kelly T. 2004. Returning home? Law, violence, and displacement among West Bank Palestinians. *PoLAR: Polit. Legal Anthropol. Rev.* 27(2):95–112

Kingsbury B. 2003. The international legal order. In *Oxford Handbook of Legal Studies*, ed. P Cane, M Tushnet, pp. 271–91. Oxford, UK: Oxford Univ. Press

Koh HH. 1997. Why do nations obey international law? *Yale Law J.* 106:2599–59

Koh HH. 2003. On American exceptionalism. *Stanford Law Rev.* 55:1479–527

Lam MC. 1992. Making room for peoples at the United Nations: thoughts provoked by indigenous claims to self-determination. *Cornell Int. Law J.* 25:603–22

Leve L. 2001. Between Jesse Helms and Ram Bahadur: women, "participation," and "empowerment" in Nepal. *PoLAR: Polit. Legal Anthropol. Rev.* 24(1):108–28

Leve L, Karim L. 2001. Introduction: privatizing the state: ethnography of development, transnational capital, and NGOs. *PoLAR: Polit. Legal Anthropol. Rev.* 24(1):53–58

Malinowski B. 1926. *Crime and Custom in Savage Society*. London: Routledge & Kegan Paul

Maurer B. 1997. *Recharting the Caribbean: Land, Law, and Citizenship in the British Virgin Islands*. Ann Arbor: Univ. Mich. Press

Maurer B. 2005. *Mutual Life, Limited: Alternative Currencies, Islamic Banking, Lateral Reason*. Princeton, NJ: Princeton Univ. Press

McLagen M. 2005. Circuits of Suffering. *PoLAR: Polit. Legal Anthropol. Rev.* 28(2):223–40

Merry SE. 2000. *Colonizing Hawai'i*. Princeton, NJ: Princeton Univ. Press

Merry SE. 2003. Constructing a global law—violence against women and the human rights system. *Law Soc. Inq.* 284:941–79

Merry SE. 2006a. *Human Rights and Gender Violence: Translating International Law into Local Justice*. Chicago: Univ. Chicago Press

Merry SE. 2006b. Transnational human rights and local activism: mapping the middle. *Am. Anthropol.* 108(1):38–51

Merry SE, Brenneis D, eds. 2004. *Law and Empire in the Pacific: Hawai'i and Fiji*. Santa Fe, NM: Sch. Am. Res. Press

Merry SE, Stern R. 2005. The female inheritance movement in Hong Kong: theorizing the local/global interface. *Curr. Anthropol.* 46(3):387–409

Messer E. 1993. Anthropology and human rights. *Annu. Rev. Anthropol.* 22:221–49

Miyazaki H, Riles A. 2005. Failure as an endpoint. In *Global Assemblages: Technology, Politics, and Ethics as Anthropological Problems*, ed. A Ong, SJ Collier, pp. 320–31. Malden, MA: Blackwell

Moore SF. 1978. The semi-autonomous social field. In *Law as Process: An Anthropological Approach*. New York: Routledge

Nader L. 1969. Styles of court procedure: to make the balance. In *Law in Culture and Society*, ed. L Nader, pp. 69–92. Berkeley: Univ. Calif. Press

Nader L. 1990. *Harmony Ideology*. Stanford, CA: Stanford Univ. Press

Nader L. 2005. Civilization and its negotiations. In *Law and Anthropology: A Reader*, ed. SF Moore, pp. 330–43. Medford, MA: Blackwell

Nader L, Todd HF, eds. 1978. *The Disputing Process—Law in Ten Societies*. New York: Columbia Univ. Press

Nagengast C, Turner T. 1997. Introduction: universal human rights versus cultural relativity. *J. Anthropol. Res.* 53:269–72

Ong A, Collier SJ, eds. 2005. *Global Assemblages: Technology, Politics, and Ethics as Anthropological Problems*. Malden, MA: Blackwell

Otto D. 1999. Subalternity and international law: the problems of global community and the incommensurability of difference. In *Laws of the Postcolonial*, ed. E Darian-Smith, P Fitzpatrick, pp. 145–80. Ann Arbor: Univ. Mich. Press

Peters J, Wolper A, eds. 1995. *Women's Rights, Human Rights*. New York: Routledge

Pigg SL. 1997. Found in most traditional societies: traditional medical practitioners between culture and development. In *International Development and the Social Sciences: Essays on the History and Politics of* Knowledge, ed. F Cooper, R Packard, pp. 259–90. Berkeley: Univ. Calif. Press

Pottage A. 2004. Introduction: the fabrication of persons and things. In *Law, Anthropology, and the Constitution of the Social: Making Persons and Things*, ed. A Pottage, M Mundy, pp. 1–40. Cambridge, UK: Cambridge Univ. Press

Pottage A, Mundy M, eds. 2004. *Law, Anthropology, and the Constitution of the Social: Making Persons and Things*. Cambridge, UK: Cambridge Univ. Press

Rajagopal B. 2003. *International Law from Below: Development, Social Movements, and Third World Resistance*. Cambridge, UK: Cambridge Univ. Press

Redfield R. 1967. Primitive law. In *Law and Warfare: Studies in the Anthropology of Conflict*, ed. P Bohannan. pp. 3–25. Austin: Univ. Tex. Press

Riles A. 2000. *The Network Inside Out*. Ann Arbor: Univ. Mich. Press

Riles A. 2004. Law as object. See Merry & Brenneis 2004, pp. 187–213

Risse T, Ropp SC, Sikkink K, eds. 1999. *The Power of Human Rights: International Norms and Domestic Change*. Cambridge, UK: Cambridge Univ. Press

Rosga A. 2005. The traffic in children: the Funding of translation and the translation of funding. *PoLAR: Polit. Leg. Anthropol. Rev.* 28(2):258–82

Rottenburg R. 2002. *Weit hergeholte Fakten: Eine Parabel der Entwicklungshilfe*. (*Far-Fetched Facts*: *A Parable of Development*). Stuttgart, Germany: Lucius und Lucius

Samson C. 2001. Rights as the reward for simulated cultural sameness: the Innu in the Canadian colonial context. See Cowan et al., pp. 226–49

Santos BS. 1995. *Toward a New Common Sense*. New York: Routledge

Sarat A, Kearns T, eds. 2001. *Human Rights: Concepts, Contests, Contingencies*. Ann Arbor: Univ. Mich. Press

Sarat A, Kearns TR, eds. 1995. *Identities, Politics, and Rights*. Ann Arbor: Univ. Mich. Press

Sassen S. 1996. *Losing Control: Sovereignty in an Age of Globalization*. New York: Columbia Univ. Press

Sassen S. 1998. *Globalization and its Discontents*. New York: New Press

Satterthwaite ML. 2005. *Beyond Nannygate: Using the Inter-American Human Rights System to Advance the Rights of Migrant Domestic Workers*. Working Pap. Ser. (Data posted August 10, 2005). Available at SSRN: **http://ssrn.com/abstract=775006**. To be published in *Gender Migration*

Sen A. 1999. *Development as Freedom*. Westminster, MD: Knopf

Sharma A. 2006. Crossbreeding institutions, breeding struggle: women's empowerment, neoliberal governmentality, and state (re)formation in India. *Cult. Anthropol.* 21(1):60–95

Sherene HR. 2004. *Dark Threats and White Knights: The Somalia Affair, Peacekeeping, and the New Imperialism*. Toronto: Univ. Toronto Press

Sieder J, Witchell J. 2001. Advancing indigenous claims through the law: reflections on the Guatemalan peace process. See Cowan et al., pp. 201–26

Sierra MT. 1995. Indian rights and customary law in Mexico: a study of the Nahuas in the Sierra de Puebla. *Law Soc. Rev.* 29:227–55

Slaughter AM. 2004. *A New World Order*. Princeton, NJ: Princeton Univ. Press

Snyder F. 2005. Governing economic globalization: global legal pluralism and European Union law. In *Law and Anthropology: A Reader*, ed. SF Moore, pp. 313–30. Medford, MA: Blackwell

Speed S, Collier J. 2000. Limiting indigenous autonomy in Chiapas, Mexico: the state government's use of human rights. *Hum. Rights Q.* 22:877–905

Steiner HL, Alston P, eds. 2000. *International Human Rights in Context: Law, Politics, Morals*. Oxford, UK: Oxford Univ. Press

Strathern M. 2004. Losing (out on) intellectual resources. In *Law, Anthropology, and the Constitution of the Social: Making Persons and* Things, ed. A Pottage, M Mundy, pp. 201–34. Cambridge, UK: Cambridge Univ. Press

Tate W. 2004. *Counting the dead: human rights claims and counter-claims in Columbia*. PhD diss., Dep. Anthropol., New York Univ.

Teitel R. 2000. *Transitional Justice*. Oxford, UK: Oxford Univ. Press

Tennant C. 1994. Indigenous peoples, international institutions, and the international legal literature from 1945–1993. *Hum. Rights Q.* 16:1–57

Trask HK. 1993. *From a Native Daughter: Colonialism and Sovereignty in Hawai'i*. Monroe, ME: Common Courage

Turner T. 1997. Human rights, human difference: anthropology's contribution to an emancipatory cultural politics. *J. Anthropol. Res.* 53:273–91

Wilson RA. 1997. Introduction: human rights, culture and context. In *Human Rights, Culture and Context: Anthropological* Perspectives, ed. RA Wilson, pp. 1–28. London: Pluto

Wilson RA. 2000. Reconciliation and revenge in post-Apartheid South Africa: rethinking legal pluralism and human rights. *Curr. Anthropol.* 41:75–98

Wilson RA. 2001. *The Politics of Truth and Reconciliation in South Africa: Legitimizing the Post-Apartheid State.* Cambridge, UK: Cambridge Univ. Press

Wilson RA, ed. 2005a. *Human Rights in the 'War on Terror.'* Cambridge, UK: Cambridge Univ. Press

Wilson RA. 2005b. Judging history: the historical record of the international criminal tribunal for the former Yugoslavia. *Hum. Rights Q.* 27:908–42

Zechenter EM. 1997. In the name of culture: cultural relativism and the abuse of the individual. *J. Anthropol. Res.* 53:319–47

Zerner C, ed. 2003. *Culture and the Question of Rights.* Durham, NC: Duke Univ. Press

Institutional Failure in Resource Management

James M. Acheson

Departments of Anthropology and Marine Science, University of Maine, Orono, Maine 04469; email: acheson@maine.edu

Annu. Rev. Anthropol. 2006. 35:117–34

The *Annual Review of Anthropology* is online at anthro.annualreviews.org

This article's doi:
10.1146/annurev.anthro.35.081705.123238

Copyright © 2006 by Annual Reviews.
All rights reserved

0084-6570/06/1021-0117$20.00

Key Words

conservation rules, collective action, natural resources, devising institutions, rational choice

Abstract

Many of the world's natural resources are in a state of crisis. The solution to this crisis is to develop effective management institutions, but there is no consensus on what those institutions are. Some economists favor solving resource-management problems through the institution of private property; others advocate central government control; and many anthropologists see local-level management as the solution. In this review, I argue that all these governance structures fail under certain conditions. However, the factors contributing to failure in each of these institutional forms differ radically, and the causes of that failure are not always predicted on the basis of existing theory. This chapter contains a review of the literature on the factors identified as causing the failure of private-property regimes, government-controlled resources, and local-level management. We will have to learn to match the resource problems with governance institutions and specific management techniques if we are to manage resources effectively. We also will have to understand the complex biosocial factors influencing sustainability.

INTRODUCTION

Over the past 50 years it has become increasingly apparent the world is facing a resource management crisis. Large numbers of marine fisheries have been seriously depleted. Forests are being harvested at unsustainable levels; acid rain and smog are problems in widespread parts of the industrialized world; soil erosion threatens vast areas; parts of Africa and the Middle East are returning to desert; industrial waste dumps make life hazardous for large numbers of humans and other animals; many rivers and estuaries are polluted; and virtually every large lake in the world is in a precarious state.

There is increasing consensus that the cause of resource degradation is institutional. If we get the right rules and governance structures, natural resources will be used wisely and conservation goals will be met. Unfortunately, we clearly have not gotten those rules right. That so many resources are in such dire straits indicates we are witnessing widespread institutional failure.

Although there is agreement that institutions are needed to solve resource problems, there is no agreement as to what institutions would do the job best. At this point, it is generally agreed that three possible governance structures exist: private property, government management, and local community management. Each of these structures has strong advocates (Ostrom 1990).

A number of economists from the late 1950s to the 1970s, working on what became known as the common property problem, concluded that the primary cause of the destruction and inefficient use of natural resources was the absence of property rights. The solution was to put resources in private hands or to simulate private-property rights, for example, by establishing licenses or limiting entry schemes (Cheung 1970, Gordon 1954, Johnson 1972, Posner 1977, Scott 1955). Their insights have had no small effect on the management of natural resources.

Hardin (1968) advocated government management in his article "The Tragedy of the Commons." Many bureaucrats and environmentalists share Hardin's advocacy of strong and possibly repressive government action, and they have persuaded the U.S. Congress to enact a number of important conservation laws, including the Clean Air Act, the Clean Water Act, the Environmental Protection Act, and the Endangered Species Act.

Since the 1980s, many anthropologists and other social scientists have come to advocate management by local-level communities. They have buttressed their arguments by pointing to the large number of cases in which resources were managed well at the local level by communities around the world or by communities in partnership with governments (i.e., co-management) (Anderson & Hill 2004, Baland & Platteau 1996, Berkes 1989, McCay & Acheson 1987, Ostrom 1990, Pinkerton & Weinstein 1995).

Social scientists and others tend to lionize one of these solutions to resource dilemmas. I argue none of these is a general solution. All these different kinds of governance structures have succeeded in conserving natural resources in some instances, but they have all had their share of failures as well. In this review, I concentrate on the failures. Focusing on cases where these governance structures did not work gives some unusual insights into the resource-management problems we currently face. As discussed below, many institutions have failed to conserve resources, and the reasons for those failures are not always predicted on the basis of existing theory.

There is no well-developed literature on institutional failure because analysts far prefer to write about successful resource-management ventures rather than the failures. Nevertheless, there is a good deal of scattered information on cases where mismanagement occurred and the reasons for it.

One general cause of resource depletion is that people may not recognize that resources are being depleted or even that they are under stress, particularly in the first stages of overexploitation. The factors influencing changes in resources' stocks are so complex that genuine uncertainty may exist about the role of human activities on stock sizes (Berkes & Folke 1998, Wilson 2002). In aboriginal societies, where game is thought to be provided by spirits or other supernatural forces, the idea that shortages of fish and game could be a result of overexploitation may not even occur (Anderson 1996, p. 101; Brightman 1993). However, even in cases where people recognize the problem, they can fail to conserve. The primary reason for conservation failure is that they cannot devise effective institutions or rules.

Assessing institutions is difficult because several different criteria can be used to measure the success or failure of institutions designed to conserve renewable resources, ranging from economic efficiency and equity (Fehr & Gachter 2000) to adaptability and accountability. However, in this review I assess institutional failure in terms of resource sustainability. Although there are problems with this definition (see Singleton 1998, pp. 15–16), I do not believe we can judge rules to conserve renewable resources as being successful if the resource is not maintained in the long run. Before I discuss institutional failure, information is needed on some basic concepts and their application to resource management.

COMMON-POOL RESOURCES, COMMUNAL ACTION DILEMMAS, AND PROPERTY RIGHTS

The root of the resource-management problem, according to many social scientists, lies in the common-pool nature of many of our most important natural resources. Common-pool resources (such as water, air, grasslands, forests, and stocks of fish and wildlife) have two characteristics, which in combination cause serious problems. First, they are subtractable, which means the amount of the resource used by one person cannot be used by

another. Second, it can be difficult to exclude people from using these resources (Ostrom et al. 1994). As a result, oceans, rivers, lakes, air, parks, and wildlife can be exploited by large numbers of people, who, after a time, deplete the resource.

The solution to managing common-pool resources is to establish rules curtailing resource use in the interest of long-term sustainability. Such rules would presumably benefit everyone by preventing overexploitation of the resource and/or its complete destruction. However, even though such rules bring favorable results, there is no guarantee they will be provided. Olson (1965) first recognized this problem: He pointed out that even if rules or other public goods would benefit all, they would only be provided if special incentives exist. The basic problem, he argued, was that individuals have no incentive to voluntarily help to produce a public good because they will have the benefit of it regardless of whether they help to produce it. Because it is rational for everyone to free ride on the efforts of others, no one cooperates, and the rule or public good is not provided. Everyone is worse off than if they had cooperated, even though everyone has acted rationally.

More recently, the problem has been phrased in terms of a collective-action dilemma. This is a situation in which there is a divergence of what is in the interests of the individual and what is optimal for the community or larger group. In collective-action dilemmas, rational behavior by individuals leads them "to behave in ways that are collectively disastrous" (Elster 1989, p. 17; Taylor 1990). In the case of common-pool resources, it can be all too rational to refuse to cooperate in conserving natural resources, even though cooperation would have benefited everyone.

Collective-action dilemmas have received a good deal of attention from social scientists because they describe many of the most vexing problems facing humans. In fact, Taylor states, "politics is the study of ways of solving collective action problems" (Taylor 1990, p. 224.)

However collective-action dilemmas have not received much attention in anthropology. One exception is the work of Hawkes (1992), who uses concepts from rational-choice theory to study sharing among hunters and gatherers, and I use collective-action dilemmas to understand rule development in the Maine lobster industry (Acheson 2003).

Adding to the difficulty of managing common-pool resources is that two different kinds of rules must be put in place to solve two different kinds of collective-action dilemmas. First, property rights must be devised and enforced. If everyone is permitted to harvest a resource (i.e., open access), the resource is almost certain to be overexploited by all comers because there is little incentive to maintain it. Second, those permitted to exploit the resource have to agree to establish rules curbing their exploitation rate (i.e., management mechanisms). Doing one without the other will not suffice. From this perspective, effective management means that a group must solve a two-tier collective-action problem (Hechter 1990). Institutional failure is a situation in which a group cannot solve one, or both, of these collective-action problems.

Generally, two different kinds of rules can be used to control effort. The first kind are rules that limit how the resource is harvested, i.e., rules governing the time, place, and techniques that can be used (Acheson & Wilson 1996). The second kind are rules specifying how much of the resource may be taken (i.e., a quota). Currently, individual transferable quotas (ITQs), a solution that combines quotas with market-based solutions, are much in vogue (Rose 2002).

Property rights can be held by a wide variety of organizations (Acheson 1984, Hann 1998). Furthermore, rules giving access, management, inheritance, and exclusion rights can be combined in different configurations (Schlager & Ostrom 1993). In the resource-management literature, it is standard to see property as owned or affected by local communities, governments, or private individuals (Berkes 1989, p. 9). In this review, I follow this convention.

PRIVATE PROPERTY

The effect of private-property rights on natural resources was explored in some detail by economists working from the 1950s to the 1980s (Acheson 1989, Gordon 1954, Scott 1955), who made a distinction between private property (called sole owner in some of the literature) and common property. They concluded that owners of private property have an incentive to protect and make investments in it because they can be assured that they, and only they, receive the benefits. Common-property resources, by way of contrast, are overexploited because no one has any incentive to invest in those resources or conserve them for the future. Why conserve when the resource will likely be taken by someone else—perhaps in a matter of a few hours (Acheson 1989, Gordon 1954, Hardin 1968)? Ciriancy-Wantrup & Bishop (1975) challenged this analysis by pointing out that it was open-access resources that were subject to abuse and that communally owned resources could be managed quite well. No one has challenged the idea that complete private-property rights help to conserve resources, and it will be helpful to review what these economists claim are the benefits of sole ownership.

In addition to conservation, economists pointed out that private-property rights have a number of other virtues. Private ownership promotes efficient use because the owners of those resources are free to use them in ways that grant them the highest income and to reject less productive options. Owners of agricultural land, for example, can grow crops, lease the land, enter into an arrangement with a sharecropper, or sell the land outright—whichever choice is to their advantage. Users of open-access resources, conversely, cannot enter into any exchanges regarding resources they do not own. Their only recourse is to harvest the resource themselves as quickly as possible (Acheson 1989).

In addition, private property is said to promote efficient use of capital. Open-access resources are subject to overcapitalization, a situation where far more firms enter the industry with more equipment than is needed to harvest the resource, a situation that can facilitate overharvesting. Private property also lowers transaction costs by making it relatively easy for an owner to go to court and gain compensation if the property is damaged or destroyed by another person. Private-property rights make it possible to solve a number of resource problems by entering into market exchanges. Eggertsson (1993, p. 2) summarizes the deleterious effects of the absence of property rights: "It is obvious that the nature of control matters for economic actors: short-term control shortens the time horizon; uncertain control discourages potentially profitable projects; lack of control incites costly races for possession; restricted control allocates assets to inferior uses."

Because these economists see private property as having many advantages, they have long advocated solving resource-management problems by effecting private-property rights or by simulating such rights with mechanisms such as licensing or quotas (Acheson 1989). Contrary to what the theory suggests, the potential for managing natural resources by privatizing them is much more limited than assumed by the economists advocating this solution. If privatization is going to solve resource-management problems, property rights have to be complete and well defined, efficient markets for those resources have to exist, and enforcement of property rights must be possible at low cost. In the real world, some important resources, such as migratory species of fish, cannot be privatized. Moreover, market inefficiency and market failure are common (North 1990). There is no market for some resources such as air. The primary cause of market failure is incomplete property rights, which result in ex-

ternalities (Bates 1994). Negative externalities exist when firms are allowed to pass some of their production costs to others external to the firm (e.g., a polluter who damages the property of others downstream or downwind). Positive externalities exist when owners cannot capture all the benefits of their own productive activity (e.g., the owner of a beehive who cannot charge farmers for pollination services). (For a more complete discussion of these problems, see Baland & Platteau 1996, pp. 37–47). Privatization will not solve resource problems in many cases.

More important, even where complete property rights to a resource exist and markets are efficient, private-property rights do not always result in resource conservation. Under certain circumstances, people can and will overexploit resources they own privately, even when property rights are secure. The literature on pastoralists, farmers, and loggers shows that "resource conservation is not always ensured by the private property status of the resource" (McCay & Acheson 1987, p. 9). The dust-bowl conditions of the 1930s, soil erosion in more modern times, and depletion of industrial forests all underline the fact that at times private landowners are no more responsible than users of open-access resources. Such cases are not all that rare. What conditions make it rational for owners to overexploit their own resources? Four such circumstances are mentioned in scattered parts of the literature.

First, Clark (1973) has advanced the most widely known explanation of the failure of private property to conserve resources. He argues that "[a] corporate owner of property rights in a biological resource might actually prefer extermination to conservation, on the basis of maximization of profits" (p. 630). This occurs when the growth rate of the resource is less than the discount rate. It does not make sense to borrow money from the bank at 8% interest to invest in a resource that increases in value at only 4% per year. This would not be a rational investment. Under these circumstances, it would only be sensible to deplete the resource as fast as possible and invest the money where it will give higher returns.

Second, long time horizons—in and of themselves—make it rational to overexploit privately owned resources. Forests are an excellent example. Economic analyses of forests demonstrate that forests grow so slowly that money invested in them would get a far better return put into other industries. Regardless of what discount rate is used, the future value of forests is quite low (Mass & Vicary 1991).

Baskerville (1995) advances a closely connected time-horizon argument. He argues it is illogical to invest in slow-maturing resources if there are two, three, or more generations between resource investment and harvest. He points out that in the case of New Brunswick forests, there is a strong tendency to make decisions with the interests of the current generation in mind. This same point can be made of other resources. Most people—including most owners of firms—figure there is little sense investing in a resource that someone else is going to harvest far into the future.

Third, uncertainty about resource availability can lead to overexploitation. Forests and stocks of fish and wildlife are harvested in a complex and even chaotic environment, so rapid, unpredictable fluctuations occur owing to, for example, disease, predation, and weather (Wilson 2002). When biological systems are unpredictable, the incentive for people to invest in such stocks or curb their own exploitive behavior is reduced because of the uncertainty that these activities will result in any payoff.

Fourth, economic pressures also can force resource owners to overexploit them. With regard to the Third World, Baland & Platteau (1996, p. 46) state, "for people in 'extreme poverty'. . . all that matters is consumption today." Similar pressures can exist in industrialized countries. The economic situation of some private-property owners might be so precarious that they are forced to forego optimal strategies (e.g., selective cutting, crop rotation) in an effort to stay in business in the short run, even though this degrades their property in the long run.

Any one of these four circumstances can motivate owners of natural resources to overexploit or fail to maintain resources at optimal levels. When two or more of these circumstances occur together, strong incentives to degrade privately owned resources can be created.

In Maine, many of these circumstances exist in the pulp and paper industry, which owns a large percentage of the northern part of the state (Acheson 2000). In all the northern counties of the state, the rate of cutting is not sustainable. Recent studies found that the cut-to-growth ratio was 2 to 1 or higher, indicating at least twice as much wood was being cut as was growing back. In Piscataquis County, the ratio was 3.6 to 1. As a result, the quality of stands has decreased, while the amount of land in hardwoods and saplings has increased greatly (Gadzik et al. 1998, pp. 3–4; McWilliams 1997).

Why are companies in this industry in the process of destroying their own forests? First, the paper industry faces a variety of economic pressures that reduce profits to low levels. All forest landowners contend with economic returns on investment that are no more than 6%, given the low rates of forest growth. Second, the pulp and paper companies have cutthroat price competition from more modern mills built in the southern part of the United States and in foreign countries, lowered demand for paper products, and volatile prices (Legasse 1997, McDonald 1997).

To keep profits at an acceptable level, the paper companies have reacted to this situation by keeping costs low, keeping capital equipment as long as possible, and running their mills continually. They have successfully lobbied the state government for a variety of services, such as fire control, spruce budworm spraying, and low land taxes. Most important, the paper companies are cutting their own forests heavily, using low-cost techniques such as clear cutting and poor-quality partial cuts. These strategies avoid the full costs of investing in sustainable forests. In this case, it is private owners who are degrading their own forests.

GOVERNMENT

Governments do wonderful things. We have come to depend on them for a huge variety of services and goods. In the past few decades, we in the United States have come to see the government as our primary bulwark against environmental pollution and degradation.

Governments generally attempt to preserve resources in two ways: First they buy large amounts of land and resources to create parks, national forests, and biosphere reserves; second, they pass laws and regulations designed to protect resources. They generally have not been doing either for long. In the United States, the first national parks were established in the early twentieth century. Virtually all our important environmental legislation (including the Clean Air Act, the Clean Water Act, and the Fisheries Conservation and Management Act) was enacted in the 1970s. During most of our history, resource management has not been a primary goal of the government. I believe this is still the case in many, but not all, of the countries of the Third World, and in countries in the ex-Soviet block.

There is little question that these government efforts have borne fruit. Our environment is much cleaner now than it was a few decades ago. There are many people in the United States—especially professional managers and the conservation community—who assume resources can be managed only by the government.

But government can also fail in the resource area—sometimes massively. Some 70% of all marine fisheries are depleted or endangered. Countries such as Haiti, Bangladesh, Thailand, Pakistan, and the Philippines have lost over 40% of their forests in the past 20 years alone (Ascher 1995, pp. 3–4). Many of these resources have been under scientific management choreographed by central governments for decades (McGoodwin 1990). Wunsch (1999, p. 244) summarizes the situation by saying, "the centralized, hierarchical, bureaucratic administrative model has failed." Durrenberger & King (2000, p. 4) echo this conclusion by pointing out that "centralized management systems themselves can cause 'tragedies'." The government record in Third World countries is far worse. Baland & Platteau (1996, p. x) write of the "absolutely appalling record of most of the national governments of the poorest countries."

When discussing government failure, an important distinction exists between the destruction of resources in cases where governments do not perceive of natural resource conservation as a primary goal and cases where governments have accepted the responsibility for resource conservation. There are different kinds of government failure involved in each. Here I focus on cases where the government has tried to conserve natural resources and has failed.

There is a large body of literature on policy failure and government failure. On the whole, it does not provide an adequate explanation for the failure of government resource-management policy.

Why do so many government efforts to manage resources fail so miserably? In some cases, the problem lies in the open-access nature of the resources. Air, for example, is not owned, and this has made regulation difficult. But governments have property rights over many resources, including oceans in the exclusive economic zone and national forests and parks. In these cases, resource abuse is a result of the mismanagement of state-owned property, resulting from policy failure (Marchak 1987). For a variety of reasons, government agents cannot or will not generate effective management rules.

The literature on government failure mentions agency problems as the most important reason that the government works poorly. That is, the problems of governments stem, in the main, from the behavior of politicians and government officials who opt to serve their own interests rather than those of the public (Cook & Levi 1990, p. 411; Moberg 1994; Shleifer & Vishny 1998, p. 4). These activities can range from voting for the interests of constituents in ways that do not serve the public at large to outright bribery. Corruption is a particularly serious problem in Third World countries (Wade 1982, 1985). Baland & Platteau (1996, p. x) write of the people of rural communities as "oppressed and repressed by the autocratic leaders and kleptocratic civil and military officers of those countries."

Buchanan & Tullock (1962), Olson (1965), and Becker (1983) see the source of government failure in the interest groups or winning majorities that pressure the government into redistributing goods and services to them at enormous cost to the public. Others see the problem in terms of rent seeking, which occurs when an interest group "colonizes a government bureau so that the bureau promotes the specific interests of the organized group at the expense of the public as a whole" (Bickers & Williams 2001, p. 194; Yandle & Dewees 2003).

Others argue the organization of bureaucracies contains the seeds of failure. Bureaucratic incentives can make it difficult for agencies to cooperate (Sproule-Jones 2002) or even to work against each other (Gibson 1999). A number of authors, including Miller (1992, pp. 140–42), Williamson (1970, pp. 25–27), and Tullock (1965, pp. 142–93), have argued that all bureaucracies, including those of the government, have problems with asymmetrical information. That is, as information is transmitted from the bottom of a hierarchy to the top, it is simplified and distorted, resulting in top executives making decisions based on faulty information. Some eminent social scientists say government inefficiency can be the product of deliberate design. Moe (1990) argues politicians deliberately design government institutions to be inefficient to avoid having an efficient invention of their own making used against them when they

are out of power. North (1990, p. 59) points out that sometimes it serves the interests of rulers to allow inefficient institutions to exist, including monopolies, barriers to entry, and featherbedding rules.

However, I believe two additional factors play important roles in the failure of governments to effectively manage their resource: problems with science and top-down management. Neither has been given adequate attention.

Problems with Science and Engineering

In large numbers of cases, government efforts to manage resources fail because of the mistakes made by scientists and engineers. In the modern world, an aura of certainty and infallibility has come to surround science and scientists. Their advice is sought on all kinds of matters, and it is usually accepted because it is difficult for laypeople to challenge them. Unfortunately, the science involved in resource management is plagued with problems, making scientists all too fallible. When those advising government policy makers make mistakes, the results can be disastrous.

Scientific and engineering problems produce different kinds of problems in different resources. For example, reforestation attempts have failed, in part, because government foresters have imported foreign, fast-growing trees, which do not grow well or have been killed off owing to disease, insect infestations, and inadequate soil or water (Ascher 1995, p. 9).

Government-sponsored irrigation efforts have been plagued with errors. Irrigation officials and engineers have a penchant for large-scale projects, even when small projects are more cost efficient (Ostrom 1992, p. 6). In some cases, these poorly planned projects lost massive amounts of money or could not be sustained at all (Ostrom 1992, pp. 2–3); in others, they did not deliver adequate amounts of water to farmers who were forced to obtain water by illegal means (Chambers 1980).

In other projects, poor design problems were compounded by the unwillingness of governments to provide adequate money for maintenance. Interestingly, farmers are often blamed for the problems stemming from inadequate design (Freeman & Lowdermilk 1985).

Fisheries' scientists are not able to measure stock sizes accurately or understand the reasons that stocks change because of serious conceptual problems and problems in gathering data (Acheson 2003, Durrenberger 1996). Wilson (2002, p. 329) reports that when measuring stock size, "errors of measurement on the order of 30 to 50% are common." All too often, the advice of scientists falls far off the mark and leads to serious consequences. In the New England groundfishery, for example, scientists overestimated the stock size, which exacerbated the overfishing problem in the 1980s and 1990s. In the lobster fishery, scientific problems led fishery administrators to recommend the elimination of management measures that were effective (Acheson 2003). Fishermen are fully aware of these inadequacies, and as a result, they often give little support to fisheries management plans. This, in turn, increases enforcement problems.

Top-Down Management

In the past decade, there has been a litany of criticism of centralized government efforts to manage resources. Decentralized management efforts generally appear to work better in managing forests (Ascher 1995, p. 10; Gibson et al. 2000, p. 3), irrigation systems (Lam 1998, Ostrom 1992), and fisheries (Pinkerton & Weinstein 1995).

Centralized, hierarchical government units have a number of traits that in the long run work against effective resource management. Government agencies have a strong penchant for regulatory uniformity. As a result, central governments are apt to promulgate one set of rules for large areas that do not take into account variations in the local ecology. Agencies are invested with a good deal of power, which they often use to ride roughshod over the wishes of local government units. This can result in a lot of hostility and opposition from local government officials (Ascher 1995).

Government agencies concerned with resource management generally are staffed with well-educated engineers and scientists from urban areas who tend to have an interest only in scientific and technical aspects of their job and have little interest in the local culture. Many cannot communicate with peasants (Weeks 2000); others have contempt for local-level knowledge based on decades of experience (Ascher 1995, p. 125; Anderson 1996, p. 101; Coward 1985; Lam 1998, p. 37). Often, no attempt is made to organize the farmers, wood harvesters, or fishermen who are affected by these plans or to frame rules they will support (Freeman & Lowdermilk 1985). The plans produced by agency officials often have a negative effect on the resource and impose huge costs on the resource users as well (Takahashi 1970, p. 52). Peasants often react to this situation by working around officials in a variety of ways (Baland & Platteau 1996, pp. 238–241; Lam 1998, p. 43).

Far worse, government agents in innumerable cases have so little understanding of human social organization or behavior that they introduce changes in technology, rules, and subsidies in ways that motivate resource users to make decisions that result in disaster for the resources involved. There are many examples of such government-produced perverse incentives. Reforestation programs in many Third World countries have failed, in part, because the incentive system set up by the government did not induce people to plant trees and maintain forests (Ascher 1995, p. 8). In another example, the government of Kenya encouraged growing cattle (to provide beef for the urban markets) and having fewer goats, which are more drought resistant. When drought hit, large numbers of cattle died, putting the tribesmen into dire straights (Dyson-Hudson 1985, p. 178). Fisheries provide still more examples. In Maine and Hawaii, conservation laws motivated skippers to put more effort on the resource than they would have otherwise (Acheson 1984, Townsend & Pooley 1995). In California, a state law designed to increase the amount of sardines packed for human consumption resulted in a large amount of the catch being turned into fish meal (see also McEvoy 1986, p. 140).

In addition to failing to conserve the resource, governments actions have produced other deleterious effects. These range from loss of autonomy and control (Apostle & Barrett 1992) to conflicts over resources (Anderson 1987, Smith 2000). In addition, government policies all too often result in the concentration of the resource in the hands of local elites or corporations (Leslie 2000, Palsson & Helgason 1997, Polioudakis & Polioudakis 2000).

Finally, and most serious, central governments often "frustrate rather than facilitate" the local level or private efforts to provide public goods, including rules to manage resources (Ostrom 2000a, p. 138; Pinkerton & Weinstein 1995, pp. 177ff). By making it impossible for local governments to experiment in solving problems, top-down management policies stifle learning and curtail adaptive responses to problem solving (Wunsch 1999).

Government programs are sometimes plagued by both scientific problems and top-down management simultaneously. When this occurs, the result can be devastating. In perhaps the best example, Scott (1998) focuses his book *Seeing Like a State* on describing the failure of state enterprises designed to better the human condition in the twentieth century and the underlying causes of that failure. He analyzes such diverse disasters as China's great leap forward and Soviet collectivization, both of which resulted in massive starvation, along with less deadly enterprises, such as compulsory villagization in Tanzania and the planning of certain cities such as Brazilia.

Scott says four factors underlie these disastrous mistakes by governments. First, states must make complex, diverse social and ecological phenomena "legible." They invent, for example, tax lists, land maps, and census data to make the society they are in charge of understandable and hence controllable from the top. To do this they have to simplify complex phenomena. Second, Scott says, is "high modernism," an uncritical and unskeptical faith in science and technical progress. (Note that this is faith, not scientific practice.) The practitioners of high modernism are unwilling to admit to the high degree of uncertainty and complexity that surrounds human and ecological phenomena. Legibility and high modernism only become lethal, Scott says, when they are combined with the final two factors: a powerful, highly centralized state willing and eager to use its power to bring these high modernistic schemes into being and a "prostrate civil society lacking the capacity to resist these plans."

Of course Scott is referring to Lenin's Russia and Communist China, but his analysis also applies to cases in North America. One example is Canada's failed attempts to manage groundfish (i.e., cod, haddock, pollock) in Newfoundland, which has resulted in stocks of these fish being reduced to 500-year lows. According to Finlayson (1994), this disaster can be traced to decisions of the Canadian government. To develop the poor province of Newfoundland, the Canadian government financed the construction of 170 large offshore trawlers capable of taking far more fish than had been taken historically. Government scientists said the stock could support higher catches, although industry spokesmen warned against putting a lot more pressure on them. The result was overexploitation, leading to a devastating stock failure. The causes of the Newfoundland disaster are reminiscent of Scott's (1998) analysis. In the Newfoundland case, the roots of disaster are found in poor science in the form of an overly optimistic, politicized stock assessment used by a powerful, centralized bureaucracy determined to improve a poor and relatively weak province, with a poorly advised fleet expansion.

LOCAL-LEVEL MANAGEMENT

Although there are many instances in which local-level communities successfully organized to conserve the resources on which their livelihood depends (e.g., Berkes 1989, Berkes & Folke 1998, Dyer & McGoodwin 1994, McCay & Acheson 1987, Ostrom 1990, Pinkerton & Weinstein 1995), there are also many cases of failure. The problem is also not confined to industrial societies. Recent work has demonstrated that people in tribal societies have done a good deal of damage to land and wildlife in many parts of the world, in some cases long before contact with Western civilization (Jackson et al. 2001, Krech 1999).

Local-level efforts to conserve resources fail because the people of those communities either cannot devise rules to manage them or because the rules fail after they are established. Different sets of factors are involved in each.

There is a growing consensus that the failure to get rules is traceable in great part to the characteristics of communities. A number of characteristics are said to make the process of devising and enforcing rules easier: a sense of community, social capital, social homogeneity, dependence on the resource, leadership, and secure boundaries (North 1990, p. 12; Ostrom 1990, 2000a,b; Wade 1988). An absence of any one or a combination of these factors can result in the inability to develop effective conservation rules. (This is not to suggest there is complete agreement on the factors that predispose communities to be able to generate rules to manage natural resources. See Agrawal 2002 for good coverage of this debate.)

The reasons for the inability to get rules vary from case to case and resource to resource. In some instances, an inability to establish and enforce boundaries undermines efforts at local-level management (e.g., Ostrom 1992, 2000a; Pomeroy 1994). Where boundaries cannot be defended, outsiders can gain the benefits of any resource-management effort, making it senseless to invest time and energy in conservation. Social heterogeneity

can make it impossible to produce rules. In Nepal, for example, conflict owing to ethnic differences made it impossible to maintain and operate some of the local irrigation systems (Lam 1998, p. 68). Still other local efforts to manage resources failed owing to a decrease in the dependence on the resource. In Nepal, when rural people got other sources of income or part-time city jobs, the incentive to manage forests (Pradham & Parks 1995, p. 174) and irrigation systems (Lam 1998, p. 67) at the local level was reduced.

Singleton & Taylor (1992) note that many cases of failure are a result of an absence of a sense of community, which they stress is a key factor in solving communal action levels at the local level. A number of anthropologists suggest the inability to cooperate in peasant cultures is rooted in a complex of social and cultural factors that make it difficult for people to trust one another (Banfield 1958, Foster 1967). In some cultures, the incentive to free ride is so strong among so many groups in the community that there is no "demand for institutions to conserve resources" (Gibson & Becker 2000).

In many instances, efforts to manage resources locally fail because of a combination of such factors. A good example is the efforts of Maine lobster fishing communities to get informal trap limits at the local level. In the 1950s when the number of traps began to escalate rapidly, a high percentage of lobster fishermen came to favor trap limits (i.e., a cap on the number a single license holder could use) to reduce tangles and contain costs. When the legislature proved unable to pass a trap-limit law, large numbers of fishermen talked about getting informal trap-limit laws at the local level. The only communities able to devise such rules were five small islands, which were isolated, closely knit, with strong territorial boundaries. The other 92 harbors could not do so, and those that tried failed (Acheson 2003, chapter 3). The harbors that could not devise informal trap limits had such a large number of fishermen that they could not monitor each other. They were heterogeneous, with both full-time and part-time fishermen with different interests; the fishermen did not interact much and had little sense of community; and these towns were not primarily dependent on the lobster industry. Most important, none of these communities had much exclusive fishing area, nor could they limit entry to the waters they did control. With no boundaries or limits on those who could fish, it made little sense to erect local trap limits because traps taken out of the water by a group agreeing to the rules would only be replaced by traps put in by people from adjacent harbors.

In some cases, local-level management efforts fail because of factors outside the community. High on this list of factors is interference by government officials who are reluctant to give power to locals (Pinkerton & Weinstein 1995). Class antagonism can also make it impossible to establish and enforce local-level management rules. In Teelin, Ireland, for example, the local priest tried to get local fishermen to form a cooperative to buy out salmon-fishing rights and manage the salmon for their own benefit. His efforts failed because of an unwillingness to sanction other community members and a long tradition of poaching well-grounded in class hatred and antagonism to authority. In Teelin, enforcing rules would not only be difficult, it would undermine local solidarity (Taylor 1987).

There are many cases in the literature where rules were established by local communities and then went out of existence. In Third World countries, Western colonial governments may undermine the power of local political authorities and the resource-management rules they had enforced (Johannes 1978, Pradham & Parks 1995). Growing population, new technology, and new markets can result in growing competition for resources and can motivate people to disobey rules, invade areas of others, or increase their exploitive efforts to the detriment of the resource (Aswani 2002, Becker & Leon 2000, McGoodwin 1994, Pradham & Parks 1995). Becoming engaged in international markets, coupled with a weakening of traditional rules, can have an especially devastating effect (Rose 2002, p. 249).

Sometimes a number of cultural and social factors can conspire to undermine existing rules. For example, with the Orma of Kenya, social change made the elders unwilling to continue to enforce rules to control the number of cattle. This resulted in overgrazing, which Ensminger (1992, p. 151) describes as "a classic failure of collective action."

SUMMARY AND FUTURE RESEARCH NEEDS

Few generalizations can be made about the reasons humans are unable to manage natural resources, save for the fact that failure is traceable to a lack of willingness or ability to solve collective-action dilemmas to produce effective rules. As noted above, the authors of the literature on resource management and institutions have identified a large number of such factors that make it difficult to produce such rules. However, our knowledge is far from complete at this point. Our understanding of the conditions under which institutions fail is messy and poorly thought-out at best. This problem deserves far more attention than it has received to date.

In an effort to extend and modify this body of theory, I make three points about institutional failure. First, there is no universal solution to the problems of resource management. Private owners, governments, and local communities all can be effective in managing natural resources. They also can fail. Moreover, a large number of circumstances can cause that failure. For private-property institutions to work, a set of conditions are required that are not commonly found in reality. Property rights are often incomplete, so externalities abound. Even if private-property rights are secure and markets are efficient, poverty, economic competition, and problems associated with slow-growing resources can lead to overexploitation. State efforts to manage resources founder because of a wide variety of problems, ranging from rent seeking, winning majorities, and deliberately introduced design flaws to agency problems and outright corruption. Governments of industrialized countries often are stymied by problems stemming from poor science and top-down management. Local-level management is often a precarious enterprise, at best. Efforts to manage resources at the local level are likely to fail if communities do not have the right set of characteristics.

Management will be effective only if resources are matched with governance structures and management techniques. A governance structure using a technique on one resource might succeed, whereas the same governance organization using the same technique might fail miserably when applied to another resource. For example, tradable environmental allowances have worked well in controlling air pollution (Tietenberg 2002), but such programs (e.g., ITQs) have generally not done well in managing fisheries because they have motivated fishermen to high grade (discard all fish except the most desirable) (Leal 2002), have led to a concentration in control by a small elite (Palsson & Helgason 1997), and in many cases have not conserved the fish stocks (Organization for Cooperation and Development 1997, p. 82).

To manage resources effectively, we will have to be quite imaginative. We will need to combine various elements of privatization, government control, local control, and managerial techniques (e.g., selective cutting of forests, ITQs for fisheries) in ways we have not imagined could be done. The exact combination used will have to vary with the specific resource and place.

Second, one of the basic axioms running through the literature on resource management is that failure or success is a result of one factor or a few separate factors (see Agrawal 2002). There has been little attempt to discuss factor interdependence and the way that various complex factor combinations cause resource-management attempts to fail. This seems a strange oversight, given there is a growing consensus among environmental scientists that stocks of fish, wild animals, and other natural resources are part of complex and possibly chaotic systems (Ludwig et al. 2002). In either case these populations are subject to unpredictable changes in size in response to a complicated set of interactive factors (Acheson & Wilson 1996, Wilson 2002). If this is true, and I believe it is, the penchant of social scientists to see institutional failure in terms of single factors or a list of unconnected factors is simplistic. If we are going to modify and extend our understanding of institutional failure, we need to see such resource-management institutions as parts of complex socioenvironmental systems, and the success or failure of those institutions needs to be considered as the result of a complex of factors working in tandem. In many cases, the factors producing success or failure are quite subtle. Ostrom writes, "we have all seen in the field nearby villages facing similar circumstances sometimes succeeding in overcoming collective action problems and sometimes failing" (E. Ostrom, personal communication).

Moreover, the complex nature of these socioenvironmental systems also means it is going to be difficult to improve the science on which resource management is based. We may have to admit we cannot predict changes in the quantities of resources at all, and we may need to concentrate instead on developing ways to manage resources in the face of great uncertainty (Acheson & Wilson 1996, Ludwig et al. 2002, Wilson 2002).

Third, rules to manage resources and the enforcement of those rules are public goods. The provision of public goods is usually the purview of governments because such goods cannot be provided by markets and free rider problems abound (Ostrom et al. 1994). This means governments need to be involved in the management of many different kinds of natural resources in many parts of the world. Given the inevitability of government involvement, the failure of governments to manage many resources effectively is particularly disturbing. How can we improve the track record of governments? One way to begin is to ask the following questions: How much government do we need? What kind of government do we need? One set of scholars has answered these questions by calling for co-management that involves managerial authority being split between government units and industry groups (Baland & Platteau 1996, Pinkerton 1989, Pinkerton & Weinstein 1995). Another suggestion is polycentric governance, utilizing the federalist principle on which the U.S. government was formed. That is, resource management would be accomplished by a hierarchy of governmental units. Authority would be given to the smallest unit in the hierarchy possible (local government, state government), but it needs to be recognized that some functions can be performed only by central governments (Ostrom 1999).

ACKNOWLEDGMENTS

An earlier version of this article was presented as the keynote address at the meetings of the International Association for the Study of Common Property Resources, June 3, 2000, in Bloomington, Indiana. The author wishes to thank Elinor Ostrom for her comments on an earlier draft.

LITERATURE CITED

Acheson JM. 1984. Government regulation and exploitive capacity: the case of the New England groundfishery. *Hum. Org.* 43(4):319–29

Acheson JM. 1989. Management of common property resources. In *Economic Anthropology*, ed. S Plattner, pp. 351–78. Stanford, CA: Stanford Univ. Press

Acheson JM. 2000. Clearcutting Maine: implications for the theory of common property resources. *Hum. Ecol.* 28(2):145–69

Acheson JM. 2003. *Capturing the Commons: Devising Institutions to Manage the Maine Lobster Industry*. Hanover: Univ. Press N. Eng.

Acheson JM, Wilson JA. 1996. Order out of chaos. *Am. Anthropol.* 98(3):579–94

Agrawal A. 2002. Common resources and institutional sustainability. In *The Drama of the Commons*, ed. E Ostrom, T Dietz, N Dolsak, P Stern, S Stonich, EU Weber, pp. 41–85. Washington: Natl. Acad. Press

Anderson E. 1987. A Malaysian tragedy of the commons. See McCay & Acheson 1987, pp. 327–43

Anderson E. 1996. *Ecologies of the Heart*. New York: Oxford Univ. Press

Anderson T, Hill PJ. 2004. *The Not So Wild, Wild West: Property Rights on the Frontier*. Stanford, CA: Stanford Univ. Press

Apostle R, Barrett G. 1992. *Emptying Their Nets: Small Capital and Rural Industrialization in the Nova Scotia Fishing Industry*. Toronto: Univ. Toronto Press

Ascher W. 1995. *Communities and Sustainable Forestry in Developing Countries*. San Francisco: ISC Press

Aswani S. 2002. Assessing the effects of changing demographics and consumption patterns on sea tenure regimes in the Roviana Lagoon, Solomon Islands. *Ambio* 31(4):272–84

Baland JM, Platteau JP. 1996. *Halting Degradation of Natural Resources: Is There a Role for Rural Communities?* Oxford: Oxford Univ. Press

Banfield E. 1958. *The Moral Basis of a Backward Society*. New York: Free Press

Baskerville GL. 1995. The forestry problem: adaptive lurches of renewal. In *Barriers and Bridges to the Renewal of Ecosystems and Institutions*, ed. LH Gunderson, CS Hollings, SS Lights, pp. 37–102. New York: Columbia Univ. Press

Bates R. 1994. Social dilemmas and rational individuals. In *Anthropology and Institutional Economics, Monographs in Econ. Anthropol. No. 12*, ed. JM Acheson, pp. 43–66. Lanham: Univ. Press of America

Becker CD, Leon R. 2000. Indigenous forest management in the Bolivian Amazon: lessons from the Yuracare people. See Gibson et al. 2000, pp. 163–91

Becker G. 1983. A theory of competition among pressure groups for political influence. *Q. J. Econ.* 98(3):371–400

Berkes F. 1989. *Common Property Resources: Ecology and Community-Based Sustainable Development.* London: Belhaven Press

Berkes F, Folke C. 1998. *Linking Social and Ecological Systems: Management Practices and Social Mechanisms for Building Resilience.* New York: Cambridge Univ. Press

Bickers K, Williams JT. 2001. *Public Policy Analysis.* Boston: Houghton Mifflin

Brightman R. 1993. *Grateful Prey: Rock Cree Human-Animal Relationships.* Berkeley: Univ. Calif. Press

Buchanan J, Tullock G. 1962. *The Calculus of Consent.* Ann Arbor: Univ. Mich. Press

Chambers R. 1980. Basic concepts in the organization of irrigation. In *Irrigation and Agricultural Development in Asia: Perspectives from the Social Sciences*, ed. E Walter, pp. 28–50. Ithaca, NY: Cornell Univ. Press

Cheung SNS. 1970. The structure of a contract and the theory of a non-exclusive resource. *J. Law Econ.* 13(1):45–70

Ciriancy-Wantrup SV, Bishop RC. 1975. Common property as a concept. *Nat. Resour. J.* 15:713–27

Clark. 1973. The economics of over-exploitation. *Science* 181:630–34

Cook K, Levi M. 1990. *The Limits of Rationality.* Chicago: Univ. Chicago Press

Coward EW. 1985. Technical and social change in currently irrigated regions: rules, roles and rehabilitation. In *Putting People First: Sociological Variables in Rural Development*, ed. MM Cernea, pp. 27–51. Oxford: Oxford Univ. Press

Durrenberger EP. 1996. *Gulf Coast Soundings: People and Policy in the Mississippi Shrimp Industry.* Lawrence: Univ. Kans. Press

Durrenberger EP, King TD. 2000. *State and Community in Fisheries Management: Power, Policy and Practice.* Westport, CT: Bergin & Garvey

Dyer C, McGoodwin J, eds. 1994. *Folk Management in the World's Fisheries: Lessons for Modern Fisheries Management.* Niwot: Univ. Colo. Press

Dyson-Hudson N. 1985. Pastoral production systems and livestock development projects: an East African perspective. In *Putting People First: Sociological Variables in Rural Development.* ed. MM Cernea, pp. 157–88. New York: Oxford Univ. Press

Eggertsson T. 1993. *Economic perspectives on property rights and the economics of institutions.* Presented at the Beijer Int. Inst. Ecol. Econ. The Royal Swedish Acad. Sci.

Elster J. 1989. *The Cement of Society: A Study of Social Order.* Cambridge, UK: Cambridge Univ. Press

Ensminger J. 1992. *Making a Market: The Institutional Transformation of an African Society.* Cambridge, UK: Cambridge Univ. Press

Fehr E, Gachter S. 2000. Fairness and retaliation: the economics of reciprocity. *J. Econ. Perspect.* 14:159–81

Finlayson C. 1994. *Fishing for Truth.* Saint John's: Memorial Univ. Newfoundland/ Inst. Soc. Econ. Stud.

Foster G. 1967. *Tzintzuntzan: Mexican Peasants in a Changing World.* Boston: Little Brown

Freeman DM, Lowdermilk ML. 1985. Middle level organizational linkages in irrigation projects. In *Putting People First: Sociological Variables in Rural Development*. ed. MM Cernea, pp. 91–118. New York: Oxford Univ. Press

Gadzik CJ, Blanck J, Caldwell L. 1998. *Timber Supply Outlook for Maine: 1995–2045*. Augusta: Maine Forest Service

Gibson C. 1999. *Politicians and Poachers: The Political Economy of Wildlife Policy in Africa*. Cambridge, UK: Cambridge Univ. Press

Gibson C, Becker CD. 2000. A lack of institutional demand: why a strong local community in western Ecuador fails to protect its forest. See Gibson et al. 2000, pp. 135–61

Gibson C, McKean M, Ostrom E, eds. 2000. *People and Forests: Communities, Institutions and Governance*. Cambridge, MA: MIT Press

Gordon HS. 1954. The economic theory of a common property resource: the fishery. *J. Polit. Econ.* 62:124–42

Hardin G. 1968. The tragedy of the commons. *Science* 162:1243–48

Hann CM. 1998. *Property Relations: Reviewing the Anthropological Tradition*. Cambridge, UK: Cambridge Univ. Press

Hawkes K. 1992. Sharing and collective action. In *Evolutionary Ecology and Human Behavior*, ed. EA Smith, B Winterhalder, pp. 269–300. New York: Aldine De Gruyter

Hechter M. 1990. Comment: on the inadequacy of game theory for the solution of real-world collective action problems. See Cook & Levi 1990, pp. 240–49

Jackson JB, Kirby MX, Berger WH, Bjorndal KA, Botsford LW, et al. 2001. Historical over-fishing and the recent collapse of coastal ecosystems. *Science* 293:629–38

Johannes RE. 1978. Traditional marine conservation methods in Oceania and their demise. *Annu. Rev. Ecol. Syst.* 9:349–64

Johnson OEG. 1972. Economic analysis, the legal framework and land tenure systems. *Law Econ.* 15:259–76

Krech S. 1999. *The Ecological Indian: Myth and History*. New York: W.W. Norton

Lam WF. 1998. *Governing Irrigation Systems in Nepal: Institutions, Infrastructure and Collective Action*. San Francisco: ISC Press

Leal DR. 2002. *Fencing the Fishery: A Primer on Ending the Race for Fish*. Bozeman, MO: Polit. Econ. Res. Cent.

Legasse MA. 1997. Wall Street gem no community hero. *Bangor Daily News*, Dec. 30, A1

Leslie K. 2000. The privatization of common-property resources in a Mexican lobster cooperative: human ecological perspective. See Durrenberger & King 2000, pp. 41–56

Ludwig D, Walker B, Holling CS. 2002. Models and metaphors of sustainability, stability and resilience. In *Resilience and Behavior of Large Scale Systems*, ed. L Gunderson, L Pritchard Jr, pp. 21–47. Washington, DC: Island Press

Marchak P. 1987. Uncommon property. In *Uncommon Property: The Fishing and Fish Processing Industries of British Columbia*. ed. P Marchak, N Guppy, J McMullen, pp. 3–31. Toronto: Methuen

Mass D, Vicary B. 1991. The value of increased survival and stocking with herbicide treatments. *Proc. Northeast. Wood Sci. Soc. Meet.* 45:15–32

McCay B, Acheson J, eds. 1987. *The Question of the Commons*. Tucson: Univ. Ariz. Press

McDonald M. 1997. Paper industry struggles in ever-tougher market. *Bangor Daily News*, Dec. 27–28, A1

McEvoy AF. 1986. *The Fisherman's Problem: Ecology and Law in the California Fisheries*, 1850–80. Cambridge, UK: Cambridge Univ. Press

McGoodwin J. 1990. *Crisis in the World's Fisheries*. Stanford, CA: Stanford Univ. Press

McGoodwin J. 1994. "Nowadays, nobody has any respect": the demise of the folk management in a rural Mexican fishery. See Dyer & McGoodwin 1994, pp. 43–54

McWilliams WH. 1997. Results from the 1995 Maine forest inventory. *Spec. Rep. No. 97–07.* USDA For. Serv. Radnor, PA: Northeast. For. Experiment Station

Miller G. 1992. *Managerial Dilemmas: The Political Economy of Hierarchy.* New York: Cambridge Univ. Press

Moberg M. 1994. An agency model of the state. In *Anthropology and Institutional Economics, Monographs in Econ. Anthropol. No.12*, ed. JM Acheson, pp. 213–31. Lanham: Univ. Press of America

Moe T. 1990. The politics of structural choice: toward a theory of public bureaucracy. In *Organization Theory*, ed. O Williamson, pp. 116–53. New York: Oxford Univ. Press

North D. 1990. *Institutions, Institutional Change and Economic Performance.* Cambridge, UK: Cambridge Univ. Press

Olson M. 1965. *The Logic of Collective Action: Public Goods and the Theory of Groups.* Cambridge, MA: Harvard Univ. Press

Organization for Economic Co-operation and Development. 1997. *Towards Sustainable Fisheries: Economic Aspects of the Management of Living Marine Resources.* Paris: Org. Econ. Coop. Dev.

Ostrom E. 1990. *Governing the Commons: The Evolution of Institutions for Collective Action.* Cambridge, UK: Cambridge Univ. Press

Ostrom E. 1992. *Crafting Institutions for Self-Governing Irrigation Systems.* San Francisco: ICS Press

Ostrom E. 2000a. Collective action and the evolution of social norms. *J. Econ. Perspectives* 14(3):137–58

Ostrom E. 2000b. Reformulating the commons. *Swiss Polit. Sci. Rev.* 61(1):29–52

Ostrom E, Gardner R, Walker J. 1994. *Rules, Games and Common Pool Resources.* Ann Arbor: Univ. Mich. Press

Ostrom V. 1999. Polycentricity (part I). In *Polycentricity and Local Public Economies*, ed. MD McGinnis, pp. 52–74. Ann Arbor: Univ. Mich. Press

Palsson G, Helgason A. 1997. Figuring fish and measuring men: the ITQ system in the Icelandic cod fishery. In *Social Implication of Quota Systems in Fisheries*, ed. G Palsson, G Petursdottir, pp. 189–218. Copenhagen: TemaNord

Pinkerton E. 1989. *Co-operative Management of Local Fisheries: New Directions for Improved Management and Community Development.* Vancouver: Univ. Br. Columbia Press

Pinkerton E, Weinstein M. 1995. *Fisheries That Work: Sustainability Through Community-Based Management.* Vancouver: David Suzuki Found.

Polioudakis E, Polioudakis N. 2000. Resource management, social class, and the state at a Muslim fishing village in southern Thailand. See Durrenberger & King 2000, pp. 85–102

Pomeroy C. 1994. Obstacles to institutional development in the fishery of Lake Chapala, Mexico. See Dyer & McGoodwin 1994, pp. 17–41

Posner R. 1977. *Economic Analysis of Law.* Boston: Little Brown

Pradham AS, Parks PJ. 1995. Environment and socioeconomic linkages of deforestation and forest land use change in Nepal Himalaya. In *Property Rights in a Social and Ecological Context.* ed. S Hanna, M Munasinghe, pp. 167–80. Washington, DC: Beijer Inst. & World Bank

Rose CM. 2002. Common property, regulatory property, and environmental protection: comparing community-based management to tradable environmental allowances. In *The Drama of the Commons*, ed. E Ostrom, T Dietz, N Dolsak, P Stern, S Stonich, EU Weber, pp. 233–57. Washington, DC: Natl. Acad. Press

Schlager E, Ostrom E. 1993. Property rights regimes and coastal fisheries: an empirical analysis. In *Economy of Customs and Culture*, ed. TL Anderson, R Simmons, pp. 13–41. Lanham, MD: Rowan & Littlefield

Scott A. 1955. The fishery: objectives of sole ownership. *J. Polit. Econ.* 63:116–34

Scott JC. 1998. *Seeing Like a State*. New Haven, CT: Yale Univ. Press

Shleifer A, Vishny RW. 1998. *The Grabbing Hand: Government Pathologies and Their Cures*. Cambridge, MA: Harvard Univ. Press

Singleton S. 1998. *Constructing Cooperation: The Evolution of Institutions of Co-Management*. Ann Arbor: Univ. Mich. Press

Singleton S, Taylor M. 1992. Common property, collective action and the community. *J. Theor. Polit.* 4(3):309–24

Smith E. 2000. Managing resources: European union regional dilemmas. See Durrenberger & King 2000, pp. 117–30

Sproule-Jones M. 2002. *Restoration of the Great Lakes: Promises, Practices and Performances*. Vancouver: Univ. Br. Columbia Press

Takahashi A. 1970. *Land and Peasants in Central Luzon: Socio-Economic Structure of a Philippine Village*. Honolulu: East-West Cent. Press

Taylor L. 1987. "The river would run red with blood": community and common property in an Irish fishing settlement. See McCay & Acheson 1987, pp. 290–307

Taylor M. 1990. Cooperation and rationality: notes on the collective action problem and its solution. See Cook & Levi 1990, pp. 222–40

Tietenberg T. 2002. The tradable permits approach to protecting the commons: What have we learned? In *The Drama of the Commons*, ed. E Ostrom, T Dietz, N Dolsak, P Stern, S Stonich, EU Weber, pp. 197–232. Washington, DC: Natl. Acad. Press

Townsend R, Pooley S. 1995. Corporate management of the Northwestern Hawaiian Islands lobster fishery. *Ocean Coast. Zone Manage.* 28(1–3):63–83

Tullock G. 1965. *The Politics of Bureaucracy*. Washington, DC: Public Affairs Press

Wade R. 1982. The system of administration and political corruption: canal irrigation in south India. *J. Dev. Stud.* 18(2):287–27

Wade R. 1985. The market for public office: why the Indian government is not better at development. *World Dev.* 13(4):467–97

Wade R. 1988. *Village Republics: Economic Conditions for Collective Action in India*. Cambridge, UK: Cambridge Univ. Press

Weeks P. 2000. Language and limited entry: the formation of Texas shrimping policy. See Durrenberger & King 2000, pp. 103–16

Williamson O. 1970. *Corporate Control and Business Behavior*. Englewood Cliffs, NJ: Prentice-Hall

Wilson JA. 2002. Scientific uncertainty, complex systems and the design of common-pool institutions. In *The Drama of the Commons*, ed. E Ostrom, T Dietz, N Dolsak, P Stern, S Stonich, EU Weber, pp. 327–59. Washington, DC: Natl. Acad. Press

Wunsch JA. 1999. Institutional analysis and decentralization: developing an analytical framework for effective Third World administrative reform. In *Polycentric Governance and Development*, ed MD McGinnis, pp. 243–68. Ann Arbor: Univ. Mich. Press

Yandle T, Dewees C. 2003. Privatizing the commons...twelve years later: Fisher's experiences with New Zealand's market-based fisheries management. In *The Commons in the New Millennium*, ed. N Dolsak, E Ostrom, pp. 101–27. Cambridge, MA: MIT Press

Archaeology and Texts: Subservience or Enlightenment

John Moreland

Department of Archaeology, University of Sheffield, Sheffield, S1 4ET, United Kingdom; email: j.moreland@sheffield.ac.uk

Annu. Rev. Anthropol. 2006. 35:135–51

First published online as a Review in Advance on April 27, 2006

The *Annual Review of Anthropology* is online at anthro.annualreviews.org

This article's doi: 10.1146/annurev.anthro.35.081705.123132

Copyright © 2006 by Annual Reviews. All rights reserved

0084-6570/06/1021-0135$20.00

Key Words

contextual archaeology, material culture, literacy, Vindolanda

Abstract

An overview of the relationship between archaeology and history is presented as the context in which to situate the argument that a rapprochement between the disciplines can be achieved only if we begin to think of texts and objects as having had efficacy in the past rather than just as evidence about it. Discussions of the meaning of material culture and the power of texts conclude with the suggestion that historical archaeologists need to be more cognizant of the latter. A case-study from the Roman world is used to illustrate the fact that texts can be both instruments of oppression and vehicles for enlightenment and liberation.

INTRODUCTION

Scholars have for long subdivided study of the past into disciplines (archaeology, history, art history, etc.) (Burke 2000), but at the turn of the twenty-first century two countervailing tendencies are in operation. On the one hand, we have increased specialization as new methodologies and new technologies are applied to more and more narrowly focused research projects. On the other hand, we have an insistence on interdisciplinarity and the persistence of calls for a closer relationship between archaeology and history. In the sections that follow, I outline the history of the relationship between archaeology and texts to provide a context for the argument that the desired-for rapprochement can be sought most productively in a contextual (postprocessual) archaeology that sees both objects and texts as resources drawn upon in pursuit of human projects. Looking in particular at textual communities in the Roman empire, I highlight the limitations of arguments that see the written word primarily (or only) as an instrument of oppression.

HISTORY AND ARCHAEOLOGY—MASTER AND SERVANT

In 1880, on a lecture tour designed to highlight Darwin's monumental discoveries, Thomas Huxley noted that the disciplines of history, archaeology, geology, physical astronomy, and paleontology were linked by their need to reconstruct complex realities that cannot be experienced directly. All historical knowledge is therefore "indirect, presumptive, conjectural" (Ginzburg 1992, pp. 103, 106). Some historical knowledge, however, is deemed more indirect and more conjectural than others because, where both objects and texts are available, the written word is generally taken as providing us with more direct access to the past.

The subservience of archaeology to history began early (Andrén 1998; Moreland 2001, p. 11) and permeated all historical archaeologies. Assyriologists, classicists, and medievalists have all characterized the archaeological record as mute, as only able to illuminate certain aspects of the past (technology and subsistence) and never being able to challenge the truths told in the texts (Bottéro 1992, 2000; Grierson 1959, p. 129; Lloyd 1986). Nor are the historical archaeologies of the New World immune to such beliefs. Here too, texts communicate directly with the researcher while objects have to be coaxed to speak—about diet, technology, and the economy (Schrire 1991, p. 78; 1995, p. 3; Schuyler 1988, p. 38). On both sides of the Atlantic archaeologists have lamented the fact that historians set the agenda for the study of life in the historical past (Austin 1990, p. 13; Deagan 1991, p. 99).

Here, there is a master/servant relationship between history and archaeology—archaeology is the handmaiden of history (Moreland 2001, p. 10; Noël Hume 1964). Here the archaeologist provides the relics that illuminate historians' texts and add flavor to historical frameworks constructed on textual evidence (Arnold 1986, p. 35; Austin 1990, pp. 11–14). Although this understanding of the relationship between texts and artifacts persists (Geary 2002, pp. 1–14), it tends to be characteristic of the early phases of historical archaeologies (Gómez Romero 2005, p. 136; Pikirayi 1999, pp. 71–73; Trigger 1989), and advances in the discipline have emerged from archaeologists' rejection of the subservience it entails.

CORRUPT TEXTS AND OBJECTIVE ARTIFACTS

From the 1980s onward historical archaeologists, encouraged by the maturity that comes from experience and (in some cases) emboldened by the claims of the early New Archaeology to be able to reconstruct all aspects of past societies from the archaeological record (Binford 1983), sought to dispute the assertion that their practice was simply an expensive way of finding out what we already knew from texts, and to promote their claims to parity of esteem with historians. Many emphasized the possibility that, because they were produced by and for elites, texts give us a distorted picture of the past (Andrén 1998, p. 77; Hodges 1983; Moreland 2001, pp. 21–28; Trigger 1989, p. 315). Archaeologists warned that the texts contained only what the author wanted known and were designed to meet their economic and political needs (Austin 1990, p. 12; Kosso 2001, p. 30). The result was that some medieval archaeologists dismissed texts altogether and relied entirely on archaeological evidence (Arnold 1984, p. 6; Halsall 1997, p. 818). North American historical archaeologists too have highlighted the bias inherent in written texts because of elite control over their production and distribution (Deagan 1991, p. 103; Schrire 1995, p. 10). Some Mesoamerican archaeologists have used the idea of texts as propaganda as the central element in their discussion of these sources and this society (Marcus 1992, p. 143; but see Houston 2000, pp. 168–71).

A corollary of the idea that texts are partial and biased is the assertion that, because the objects recovered by archaeologists were not intended to communicate information, they cannot be distorted in the same way—"physical objects simply are what they are; they have no agenda" (Kosso 2001, p. 30; but see below). A version of this argument seems particularly prevalent in American historical archaeology where there are frequent references to the idea that archaeology deals with "the unintended, the subconscious," the "nonintentional material by-products" of past societies (Deagan 1988, p. 8; 1991, p. 103; Deetz 1991, p. 6; Deetz & Deetz 2000, pp. 209, 268–69). In some ways this idea resembles the psycho-analytical suggestion that it is in seemingly insignificant, half-forgotten details that real secrets can be uncovered (Ginzburg 1992).

From archaeologists' privileged access to these "nonintentional" objects [the material culture of the everyday life, the "small things forgotten" that are rarely noted in contemporary records (Deetz 1977; 1993, p. 13)] American historical archaeology claims its greatest strength: the capacity to give voice to the voiceless, to render articulate those who do not appear in the texts (Deagan 1991, pp. 101, 108; Deetz 1991, p. 6; 1993, p. 12; Hall 1993, pp. 186–91). Similar arguments have been expressed in European classical and postmedieval archaeology (Alcock 1993, pp. 3–8; Tarlow 1998, p. 263). This position is frequently extended to include the argument that historical archaeology is uniquely placed to uncover acts of resistance to elite domination—acts that, perhaps understandably, find little place in the written accounts (Deagan 1991, p. 109; Frazer 1999; Orser 1988, 2001b; Paynter & McGuire 1991). Some more recent analyses have drawn on critical cultural theory to locate the "third space," between those with power and those subjected to power, where resistance manifests itself in the appropriation, transformation, and negation of accepted codes (Hall 1999, 2000; Lydon 1999).

ARCHAEOLOGY AND HISTORY—PARALLEL SOURCES

In Graeco-Roman and medieval archaeology there has been a tendency to see material culture and texts as deriving from, and informing us about, different aspects of past societies (Arnold 1984, p. 163). Such arguments are emblematic of a long-standing and generally negative relationship between archaeology and history in the Old World in which each side devalues the significance of the other's evidence (Halsall 1997, pp. 817–20; and above). American historical archaeology also tends to treat written and artifactual materials as separate categories of data (Cleland 1988, p. 15; Deagan 1988, p. 8; Little 1992b p. 4; Potter 1992), but the written sources, rather than being ignored or opportunistically plundered (Halsall 1997, pp. 818, 821), tend in America to be seen as a parallel source of information about the past, contributing to what some have called text-aided archaeology (Deetz & Deetz 2000, pp. 268–69; Little 1992b; Paynter 2000a, pp. 13–17). Here the relationship between the sources includes the use of one as an empirical control for the veracity of the other, the use of archaeology to add "texture and dimensionality" to the laconic references in the texts, and the use of written sources to fill in absences from the archaeological record (Brown 1988, p. 82; Deetz & Deetz 2000, p. 264; Leone & Crosby 1987, p. 399).

What we also commonly find in North American historical archaeology (although it occurs elsewhere as well) is the assumption that texts provide an independent source against which theories derived from archaeology can be tested (Cleland 1988, pp. 15–16; Little 1994, pp. 14, 29; Paynter & McGuire 1991, p. 19). It also lies at the heart of Lewis Binford's naïve contention that historical documents constitute a New Archaeological "Rosetta stone" facilitating the inference of human behavior from material culture (Binford 1983). Critics of this position (Beaudry 1988b; Little 1994, pp. 11–12; Paynter 2000a; p. 14), however, tend not to remark on the fact that it implies some degree of archaeological inferiority—texts provide a standard against which it has to measure up (Moreland 2001, pp. 25–26).

There is a feeling among some archaeologists that this juxtaposition of text and artifact is insufficiently problematized, and they have sought methodological advances by developing an argument we have already encountered: that "even within one society, the artifacts and written records were used and produced by different people, for different purposes, and at different times and survived for different reasons" (Leone 1988b, p. 33; Leone & Crosby 1987, p. 399; Houston 2004c, p. 242). Following Binford, Leone argues that we construct different "organisational frameworks (contexts within which acts, customs, and behavior took place and must be understood) for texts and artifacts, that we bring these together, and that we seek out (and focus on) the discrepancies between them. These dis-

crepancies will, they argue, encourage the researcher to return to both the texts and the artifacts in search of new insights with which to resolve the ambiguity (Binford 1987; Leone 1988b, p. 33; see also Andrén 1998, pp. 102–3; Paynter 2000a, p. 15; Potter 1992; and Halsall 1997 for a very similar proposal emerging from a European context).

Leone's more recent work on Hoodoo (a variant of Voodoo) among communities of Americans of African descent in Virginia, North Carolina, and South Carolina uncovered a discrepancy, in terms of the materials used and the locations in which they were placed/found, between the archaeology and autobiographical descriptions of the practice (neither crystals nor placement in the northeast corners of houses are mentioned in the texts)—forcing a return to "reread the autobiographies in a different way, with a new slant" (Leone & Fry 2001, p. 154; see below). This is a very significant piece of work, and the methodology has much to recommend it, but we should note that the texts and objects cannot always be considered as having been produced and used by different people. As we shall see, even the illiterate interacted with and reacted to texts—and everyone used material culture!

MATERIAL CULTURE AND MEANING

These developments, particularly in New World historical archaeology, have moved the discipline some ways from the bad old handmaiden-of-history days. However, one could argue that we can go still further, and that to do so we need to evaluate critically how historical archaeologists have used objects and texts in their reconstructions of the past.

We have to begin by pointing out that the archaeological record cannot be considered an unmediated, unbiased source and that the "small things forgotten" recovered by historical archaeologists across the world cannot be considered as unintentional. It was never intended that a twelfth-century household's plates, spoons, rings, bottles, and jugs be recovered and analyzed by twenty-first-century archaeologists, but that it also true of much of the written material. The earliest writing systems in Sumeria and Egypt, like the archives of Louis XIV, were designed for the benefits of administrators, not future historians (Burke 2000, p. 140; Cooper 2004; Nissen Damerow & Englund 1993; Schmandt-Besserat 1992). Here lies the crux of the problem: It may never have been intended that the objects (and texts) survive as evidence about the past (the small things probably were forgotten), but we should not doubt that, in the context in which they were produced and used in the past, they were meaningful (Barrett 2001; Hines 2004, p. 11).

In 1990, Leone's team uncovered a seemingly mundane group of objects—rock crystals, perforated bone discs, a black river pebble, the base of a bowl, and two coins—in the corner of a room of an eighteenth-century house in Annapolis, Maryland (Leone & Fry 2001, p. 144). As we have seen, further documentary and archaeological research revealed the Annapolis find to be part of a wider phenomenon in which Americans of west African descent used objects to control the spirit world (Leone & Fry 2001, p. 151; also Johnson 1996, pp. 161–62). The significance for us here lies in the fact that, out of the context established by Leone & Fry, these objects could have been seen as "yard scatter or rubbish," as "unique and uninterpretable"—but in the eighteenth century they were deeply meaningful (Leone & Fry 2001, p. 151).

Clearly not all excavated objects were used to conjure spirits, but drawing on the raft of propositions emerging from postprocessual (contextual) archaeology, many historical archaeologists have moved from a position that sees objects merely as the residue of past cultures to one that attributes to them an active role in cultural practices (Paynter 2000a, p. 11). Objects are no longer simply evidence for the past, but are one of the media through which human beings constructed themselves and their communities in the past (the lit-

erature on postprocessualism is vast, but see Barrett 2001).

Postprocessualism emerged from a critique of a Binfordian New Archaeology by a group of British prehistorians (Trigger 1989, pp. 348–57), and the idea of objects as active in the construction and transformation of past societies has been widely applied in British late- and postmedieval archaeology (Austin 1998; Giles 1998; Johnson 1996, 2002; Tarlow 1999). However, it is in American historical archaeology (perhaps because of the anthropological context within which it is situated, archaeologists were already familiar with much of the anthropological and sociological literature that inspired postprocessualism) that it has been most successfully applied (Yentsch & Beaudry 2001, p. 226). Two generations of American (and latterly South African and South American) historical archaeologists have deepened our knowledge of the historical processes in operation not only within societies but also between them, serving to bind them to the emerging capitalist world system (Funari Hall & Jones 1999; Orser 1996).

Slavery (and resistance to it) has been at the heart of American historical archaeology's research agenda, and some of its best work is done here (McGuire & Paynter 1991; Leone LaRoche & Babiarz 2005; Orser 1988, 2001b; Paynter 2000b, pp. 182–86; Singleton 1988), although we should note that the enslaved and the poor can be just as inarticulate in the material as in the textual record (Bankoff & Winter 2005, p. 314; Hall 1999, p. 193). Closely related is the way in which material culture was used as a vital element in the construction of identities (Epperson 2001; Hall 2000; Rowlands 1999; Singleton 1999, 2001). Archaeologists have also shown how material culture was instrumental in the construction of community identities and in interactions between native and colonist across the New Worlds (Brenner 1988, Hall 1993, Schrire 1995), and they have laid bare the consequences of the industrialization that accompanied a community's entanglement in the world of global capitalism (Beaudry et al.

1996, Casella & Symonds 2005, Paynter 2000b). American historical archaeology is perhaps best known for highlighting the role of material culture in the operation of the Georgian order—a series of attitudes to living, knowledge, eating, and work that attended the transition to modernity in the eighteenth century (Leone 1988a, 1988b, 1995, 2005; Shackel 1992). The point here is that these archaeologists have analyzed the ways in which a whole range of objects had efficacy in the past—they have shown that even the humble thimble was redolent with "layered cultural knowledge" (Yentsch & Beaudry 2001, pp. 214–40; Hoskins 1998). What then of texts? What is their role in the historical process, and in our accounts of that process?

TEXT AS TECHNOLOGY

At the outset it is worth noting that archaeologists have not, in fact, been alone in their search for the poor and enslaved, the people rendered inarticulate by their omission from texts. These people have been the focus of generations of historians who have spent much time and exercised considerable ingenuity in locating "the people without history" among the words of the powerful—the voiceless are, in fact, enmeshed within texts. The villagers of Salem, Massachusetts, found the tiniest details of their lives recorded not just in the transcripts of the 1692 trials but also in the mundane records (wills, deeds, estate inventories, petitions, church accounts) from which historians reconstructed the network of relationships out of which the witchcraft accusations emerged (Boyer & Nissenbaum 1974). Like the inhabitants of Uruk (Sumeria) in the third millenium B.C., or the village of Tebtunis (Egypt) in the first century A.D. they were entangled in literacy, which was an active force in their world (see below).

That written texts were more than a passive medium for recording events is hardly in doubt—the primary function of writing was, according to Lévi-Strauss, to facilitate slavery (1973, p. 393). More positively, Goody & Ong have argued that writing was "the most momentous of all human technological inventions," a technology that "shaped and powered the intellectual activity of modern man" (Goody 1977, pp. 18, 36; Ong 2002, pp. 82, 84). Writing, especially alphabetic writing, affected human consciousness, they said, because it made it "possible to scrutinise discourse in a different kind of way by giving oral communication a semipermanent form; this scrutiny favoured the increase in the scope of critical activity, and hence of rationality, scepticism, and logic" (Goody 1977, pp. 36–51; 1987; Goody & Watt 1963; Ong 2002, pp. 77–114; Powell 2002). Other scholars have made the same connection between writing and changes in the way we think, but have placed it earlier, in the context of the development and use of Sumerian cuneiform (Bottéro 1992, pp. 32, 39; 2000, pp. 20, 66), or later, when the proliferation of printed texts in early modern Europe facilitated comparison of rival accounts (Burke 2000, pp. 11, 51).

Many commentators have, however, criticized both the notion that writing restructures thought and the implication that it was a monolithic force, having the same consequences regardless of historical context (Collins 1995, p. 78). We now know that some of the supposed features of textual analysis (scrutiny, detection of contradiction, etc.) are common in oral traditions and that others are the product of western schooling, not literacy (Halverson 1992, Harris 2000, Scribner & Cole 1981). The critics conclude that the "medium of communication has no intrinsic significance in the communication of ideas or the development of logical thought processes" (Halverson 1992, p. 314).

Goody and Ong have always denied seeing writing as a disembedded, monocausal force and have insisted that its potentialities depend on the social and historical context (Goody 1977 p. 147; 1986, p. xv; Ong 2002, p. 172). Furthermore, it is not difficult to locate examples in which the medium of communication does affect the message, or in which the use of writing was itself part of the message (Justice

1994, p. 25; Moreland 2001, pp. 86–87). However, even supporters have acknowledged the absence within Goody & Ong's literacy thesis of direct causal linkages between writing and thinking (Olson 1994, p. 16). In a series of recent publications Olson has sought to provide just such linkages and has demonstrated that significant cognitive consequences do flow (if indirectly) from reading and writing. He particularly emphasizes the consequences of the fact that writing turns speech into an object suitable for reflection and analysis and argues that its inability to capture the illocutionary force of a statement forces us into a "whole new world of interpretative discourse, of commentary and argument" (Olson 1986; 1994, pp. 257–71; 1996; 2001; Olson & Astington 1990; see also Hines 2004). The implications of these recent developments for how we evaluate the transformative power of writing in the past need to be explored through detailed case studies that account for the particular historical context, including the forms and distribution of writing resources within society. The excellent archaeological work already carried out there, the significance of the transformations traced, and the range of textual and artifactual materials available suggest that early modern New England or Annapolis may be rewarding contexts for such research.

Even if we leave aside these "cognitive" aspects of the literacy thesis, a very important residue remains (Halverson 1992, p. 315). Writing's preservative potentiality turns it into a technology with material effects on past societies. Writing transforms the "evanescent world of sound into the . . . quasi-permanent world of space"; it enables speech to be transmitted over space and preserved over time thereby significantly amplifying the possibilities for communicating and recording information (Goody 1986; Ong 2002, p. 90). Obligations and rights, thoughts, and actions could now be permanently documented and transmitted (if desired) to the ends of the earth and to those not yet born. The construction of this kind of permanent record also meant that a greater depth of knowledge/information

could be accumulated (Bottéro 2000, p. 20; Goody 1977, p. 37; Halverson 1992, p. 316; Hopkins 1991, p. 135; Olson 1994, pp. 17–18, 105). Another consequence of literacy is to effect a distance between author and subject (Ong 2002, p. 102), which could mean that knowledge of a person or community could be located other than with that person or community (in the state archives, for example), and for many this would have been "a frightening and alienating possibility" (Fentress & Wickham 1992, p. 10). However, as we shall see, individuals could accumulate their own archives, lengthening the depth of their knowledge and providing themselves with some certainty in their dealings with the state (for state and private archives, see papers in Brosius 2003; and below).

Goody argued that in enhancing memory capacity writing also allowed a state (or individual) to keep track of many more transactions (1986, p. 70; Ong 2002, p. 172). Here he was thinking primarily of economic transactions, of writing as an administrative tool; one of the most heated debates in earlier historical archaeologies is whether writing emerged to deal with economic and political complexity or whether it created the conditions for such complexity to emerge (Bagley 2004; Baines 1983, 2004; Cooper 2004; Houston 2004c, 2004d; Postgate et al. 1995; Schmandt-Besserat 1992). However, once a system of writing is invented or introduced, archaeologists tend to acknowledge it as a potent force in organizing and regulating human conduct (Bowman & Woolf 1994; Glassner 2003, pp. 183–93; Hines 2004, pp. 19–20; Hopkins 1991; Nissen Damerow & Englund 1993), although some scholars emphasize its use in ceremony and display (Baines 1989, 2004; Houston 2004d). Generally, it is accepted that writing provides elites with the capacity to generate (and store) more knowledge about their subjects and with the ability to exercise more control over them.

This tendency to see texts as an instrument of power is encouraged by the recognition that, up until fairly recent times, writing was socially restricted. Among the Maya this marked writing as special, and scribes were members of the elite, as were those who wrote the Linear B texts in Bronze Age Pylos, Greece (Bennet 2001; Houston 2000, p. 150). In Old Kingdom Egypt, writing was centrally controlled, and less than 1% of the population was literate (Baines 1983). Between 5% and 10% of the population in the western Roman Empire (and up to 15% of those in Italy) may have been able to read and write (to varying degrees) (Harris 1989, pp. 267, 272; Hopkins 1991, p. 134). At the beginning of the sixteenth century, ~90% of British males (and 99% of females) were unable to read and write and, despite a century of print and Protestantism, by 1680, 70% of males and 90% of females were illiterate (Moreland 2001, pp. 54–76; Wheale 1999, p. 2). In considering the implications of these figures, we must bear in mind that likely many more people could read than could write, and there were a huge range of competencies in each of these skills (Hall 1996, pp. 30–32). We must also remember that levels of both are likely to have been much higher in the upper ranks of society [literacy was nearly universal among London's seventeenth-century nobility (Wheale 1999, pp. 23, 31), but this fact just reinforces the point that literacy was a socially restricted practice].

Finally, throughout the historical periods a magical, supernatural significance has been attributed to writing, enhancing the esteem within which it was held and the efficacy attributed to it (Moreland 2001). Throughout the historical periods, elite control over the liturgical texts, calendars, inscriptions, and images through which access to the supernatural was effected reinforced the power of the elite in the world (Bahrani 2003, Beard 1991, Glassner 2003, Moreland 2001).

Some archaeologists and some historians have brought these features of writing together to make it a potent technology of power (Moreland 2001, pp. 88–92). And it seems it was so from the beginning of writing in Sumeria in the fourth millennium B.C.

where, Herrenschmidt (2000) argued, "people began to write because written accounts maintained social order" (p. 79) and where, from the end of the third millennium B.C., relations of authority and forms of power were imbibed at school (Glassner 2003, p. 225). In Mesoamerica, writing was a tool of the state (Marcus 1992, p. xvii; but see Houston 2004d), and in the Roman empire it was "an instrument of power" (Beard 1991, p. 58; Hopkins 1991, p. 142). Some medieval historians have referred to its "sinister role" and have seen it as a means to power for elites and "a corrosive" acting on communal bonds (Briggs 2000, p. 400). Finally, we are told that in the early modern period writing was a factor in "upper class hegemony and oppression" (Thomas 1986, p. 120), and, most graphically of all, the monopoly of information represented by seventeenth- and eighteenth-century state archives was likely a "means to achieve a monopoly of power" (Burke 2000, p. 141). The problem, as we see below, is that we find very little of this in even the best historical archaeologies.

ENSLAVEMENT OR ENLIGHTENMENT?

There seems to be a consensus, therefore, among archaeologists, philologists, anthropologists, historians, and sociologists that texts (like other objects) were an active force in the historical process. Most scholars would now agree that their impact is historically contingent and that, in each instance, they interacted with other modes of communication and other dimensions of authority—but all would confirm that texts (like other objects) are much more than neutral dispatches from the past (Collins 1995, Franklin 2002, Hines 2004, Messick 1993). A contextual approach, expansive enough to include the idea that people and communities constructed themselves through their engagement with objects and texts, would seem to transcend the disciplinary boundaries between archaeology and history.

We get a sense of this in some of the best work in the historical archaeology of the medieval and early modern worlds (contra Moreland 2001, pp. 102–11). Some scholars have articulated a theoretical position on texts and objects that closely parallels the position outlined above (Little 1992c; Hall 2000, p. 16) and have emphasized that texts are cultural products (Leone 1988a, p. 247; Schuyler 1988, p. 39). Scholars have provided practical demonstrations of how texts helped to constitute and reproduce kinship and community relations, of how they were an essential part of the process through which material wealth was distributed (Yentsch 1988a, p. 140; 1988b, p. 16), and of the power of words in constructing and organizing some of the cultural categories central to the eighteenth-century English world (Yentsch 1988b, p. 153; Beaudry 1988c). Others have highlighted the relationship between power and control over the flow of information via newspapers (Mrozowski 1988, p. 189). But despite the sophisticated approaches to material culture emerging in classical, medieval, and (especially) American historical archaeology there is still a tendency to see texts as providing evidence about the past rather than having efficacy within it. Despite the focus on the poor and marginalized, there is still comparatively little archaeological analysis of the ways in which texts contributed to the oppression and silence of the "voiceless." And despite the emphasis on agency within contextual archaeology, few scholars have addressed the possibility that texts may have been a vehicle for liberation and enlightenment.

To focus on texts only as instruments of oppression (and they certainly were that) is to ignore not just the fact that human beings are knowledgeable about the conditions within which they live and have the capacity to act on that knowledge, but also some good empirical data that demonstrates that texts could empower as well as enslave. Texts have been associated with resistance to oppression. In the 1381 Peasants' Revolt in England some of the insurgents communicated their demands in writing—in appropriating the discourse of their masters they were making the medium part of the message (Justice 1994; Moreland 2001, p. 87). However, even this focus on the moment of resistance does not do justice to the ways in which people (literate and illiterate) encountered, interacted with, and became entangled in texts on a day-to-day basis. As we see if we look at an example drawn from a moderately complex society, whereas on some occasions these encounters resulted in oppression, on other occasions they contributed to empowerment and/or enlightenment.

In A.D. 190, some time before July 20th, at the gateway leading from a small Egyptian village into the desert, a man leading two donkeys was stopped and asked to pay customs dues on the goods carried by the animals: six measures of lentils! The transaction was recorded on a piece of papyrus. Another text, from the middle of the first century A.D., records the fact that a peasant had worked for five days on the village irrigation system, and this fact is confirmed, in their own writing, by four villagers. The tax office in the nearby village of Karanis contained files listing tax payment by person; there were files for each tax, there were records of the payments made each day, and monthly summary accounts were submitted to the district capital, in multiple copies (Hopkins 1991). These texts are the product of, and a testimony to, an intrusive state that levied duty on lentils carried by a donkey on the margins of the desert—and recorded the fact! Imperial demands entangled these Egyptian peasants in the pages of the state archive (Moreland 2001).

At the other end of the Empire, excavations at the Roman fort of Vindolanda, northern England, recovered hundreds of very thin wooden tablets, about the size of a postcard, covered in ink writing (Birley 2002; Bowman 1991, 1994a,b; see Franklin 2002 for similar tablets from early medieval Russia). These are some of the texts produced by the military garrison (and families), and they are full of the "grinding detail" that characterizes the bureaucratic state. Some texts record troop location and rank, who was on duty and who was absent, and who was fit and who was sick. There are interim, daily, and monthly strength reports. Requests for leave were recorded in writing (Birley 2002; Bowman 1994a,b). Very much in line with the contention that writing was a technology that transformed the societies in which it was deployed, scholars have argued that the precise and detailed communication that writing facilitated explains how Rome was able to control such large areas with so few troops (Bowman 1994b, p. 119).

However, signs from both ends of the Empire show that writing was not just an instrument of oppression. One of the most evocative of the Vindolanda tablets contains a birthday invitation from Claudia Severa to her friend Lepidina (*Tab. Vindol.* II 291). The main body of this letter may have been written by a scribe, but Claudia herself supplied the signing-off, and, in any case, Claudia and her friends were using writing to construct social networks outside the military ones that dominated their lives.

Detailed analysis of the writing on the tablets reveals the presence of several hundred different hands (Bowman 1994b, p. 117). This does not demonstrate mass literacy, but it shows a community that encountered texts on a day-to-day basis—on the wooden tablets, in painted inscriptions on amphora, on coins, in dedications and inscriptions on altars and temples, and perhaps on inscribed curse tablets (Birley 2002, Tomlin 2002). It was a textual community for which it might be better to speak of literacies rather than literacy (Woolf 2002) and whose use of texts was much more instrumental than we might have expected—and the state (via the army) may have been crucial in this. Although we might expect the army to use writing extensively, scholars now argue that such institutional use was not necessarily restrictive but served to "open up channels of communication and methods of organisation...to create and encourage the communal use of texts"

(Bowman 1994b, pp. 119–21; Woolf 2002, p. 186).

As in Britain, in Roman Egypt, even if one could not read or write, one encountered and engaged with writing on a regular basis—from time to time one used writing. I've previously noted how four Egyptian peasants witnessed in writing the labor service of another. Like Claudia's letter, receipts for grain borrowed from the state granaries were generally written by two people: one part by an official, and the second by "some-one else," the person concerned, a friend, a literate brought along for the occasion. In the contracts signed in the village of Tebtunis during one month in A.D. 42 illiterate peasants called on the services of 25 different literates (Hopkins 1991, pp. 151–52). This fact is significant. On their own, isolated from community, illiterates ran the risk of deception when confronted by writing, so they used literate friends or acquaintances to mediate their encounters with the Word (and the state). In so doing they constructed alliances of self-protection, "private networks of trust"—a system of social relationships that emerged from the encounter with writing and which empowered both individual and community (Hanson 1991, p. 168).

For some scholars the archive is a physical manifestation of the intimate connection between writing and the power of the state (Burke 2000, pp. 138–41). However, it is now clear that private archives existed throughout the ancient world (Brosius 2003). Egyptian peasants collected texts as proof of obligations fulfilled and as supporting evidence to reinforce petitions to regional or imperial powers (Hanson 1991, p. 179). An early third-century A.D. edict of Soubatianos Akulas, prefect of Egypt, reveals that in three days of assizes at one regional center he received no fewer than 1804 petitions, and, astonishingly, he not only read and answered every one but he also "publicly posted the replies, as law required, within 2 months" (Harris 1989, p. 25; Hopkins 1991, p. 137). Again this situation shows people using texts, if not as a means of liberation then at least in an attempt to have grievances redressed. Roman subjects wrote an amazing number of petitions [there is one among the Vindolanda tablets (*Tab. Vindol.* II 344)], and they did so because, just like the Englishmen who made written demands during the Peasants' Revolt (see above), "they learned the language of the conquerors in order to borrow the conqueror's power, and to protect themselves from exploitation" (Hopkins 1991, p. 137; Justice 1994).

They may also have learned the conquerors' language in pursuit of enlightenment. One of the tablets from Vindolanda contains a line from Vergil's *Aeneid*; another may have a line from Catullus (*Tab. Vindol.* II 118, 119; Bowman 1994b, p. 117). These may be writing exercises, but they nonetheless point to the assimilation of the greatest Latin classics on the edge of Empire. The *Aeneid* is particularly significant; it recounts the origin-myth of Rome and lay at the heart of Rome's sense of its place in history. The Roman literary elite, who defined themselves through their exclusive knowledge of deliberately obtuse texts in Latin and Greek, would probably have sneered at the pretensions of those who read and copied it at Vindolanda, but the latter were nevertheless empowered by their endeavors (Hopkins 1991, Woolf 2003).

Lévi-Strauss (1973) continued his assertion that writing facilitated slavery by arguing that its use for pleasure and intellectual purposes was in fact a means of concealing and strengthening that oppression (p. 393). There can be no doubt that, in the hands of a bureaucratic state like the Roman Empire (and this is probably true of all historical societies), writing was a technology of power. But this was not its only manifestation. Here and elsewhere, people used this technology, this resource, for their own purposes. It empowered individuals, it created networks of trust, and in literature and religion, for example, it helped to construct them as Romans—in a context where that mattered (Beard 1991, Hopkins 1991, Tomlin 2002).

What is missing here, of course, is material culture. Studies of the impact of many different kinds of texts on early historic societies (Sumeria, Egypt, China, Rome, etc.) need to be integrated with analyses of the significance of material culture in the historical process (Bennet 2001, p. 27), like those that constitute best practice in New and Old World historical archaeology (Austin 1998; Deetz 1993, 2000; Leone 2005; Yentsch 1994). By recognizing that both material culture and texts are resources that can be drawn on in the pursuit of human projects we can construct more fully rounded pasts that recognize both the reality of oppression and the human desire for enlightenment.

ACKNOWLEDGMENTS

I am very happy to acknowledge the encouragement and support of John Barrett; John Bennet, for the loan of books and articles, and for the stimulus that flows from coteaching a module on archaeology and text; Barbara Little, for supplying me with references and for (gently) pointing out that some of my arguments were not quite as new as I thought; David Olson, for clarifying references, sending me articles, and inspiring the title; the organizers of the AHRC symposium on "Archaeology, Art and Text," held at Newcastle University in December 2004, for inviting me to speak and for helping me to consider some of these issues in a new light; and especially Prue and Tomàs for the sacrifices they made to allow me the time to finish this paper.

LITERATURE CITED

Alcock S. 1993. *Graecia Capta. The Landscapes of Roman Greece.* Cambridge, UK: Cambridge Univ. Press

Andrén A. 1998. *Between Artifacts and Texts. Historical Archaeology in Global Persepctive.* New York: Plenum

Arnold C. 1984. *Roman Britain to Saxon England*. London: Croom Helm

Arnold C. 1986. Archaeology and history: the shades of confrontation and cooperation. See Bintliff & Gaffney 1986, pp. 32–39

Austin D. 1990. The 'proper study' of medieval archaeology. See Austin & Alcock 1990, pp. 9–42

Austin D. 1998. Private and public: an archaeological consideration of things. See Hundsbichler et al. 1998, pp. 163–206

Austin D, Alcock L, eds. 1990. *From the Baltic to the Black Sea. Studies in Medieval Archaeology*. London: Unwin Hyman

Bagley RW. 2004. Anyang writing and the origin of the Chinese writing system. See Houston 2004a, pp. 190–249

Bahrani Z. 2003. *The Graven Image. Representation in Babylonia and Assyria*. Philadelphia: Univ. Penn. Press

Baines J. 1983. Literacy and ancient Egyptian society. *Man* 18:572–99

Baines J. 1989. Communication and display: the integration of early Egyptian art and writing. *Antiquity* 63:471–82

Baines J. 2004. The earliest Egyptian writing: development, context, purpose. See Houston 2004a, pp. 150–89

Bankoff HA, Winter FA. 2005. The archaeology of slavery at the van Cortlandt Plantation in the Bronx, New York. *Int. J. Hist. Archaeol.* 9:291–318

Barrett JC. 2001. Agency, the duality of structure and the problem of the archaeological record. See Hodder 2001, pp. 141–64

Beard M. 1991. Ancient Literacy and the function of the written word in Roman religion. See Humphrey 1991, pp. 35–58

Beaudry M, ed. 1988a. *Documentary Archaeology in the New World*. Cambridge, UK: Cambridge Univ. Press

Beaudry M. 1988b. Introduction. See Beaudry 1988a, pp. 1–3

Beaudry M. 1988c. Words for things: linguistic analysis of probate inventories. See Beaudry 1988a, pp. 43–50

Beaudry M, Mrozowski SA, Ziesing G. 1996. '*Living on the Boott': Historical Archaeology at the Boott Mills Boardinghouses in Lowell, Massachusetts*. Amherst: Univ. Mass. Press

Bennet J. 2001. Agency and bureaucracy: thoughts on the nature and extent of administration in Bronze Age Pylos. In *Economy and Politics in Mycenaean Palace States*, ed. S Voutsaki, J Killen, pp. 25–25. Cambridge, UK: Cambridge Philol. Soc., Suppl. Vol. 27

Binford L. 1983. *In Pursuit of the Past*. London: Thames and Hudson

Binford L. 1987. Researching ambiguity: frames of reference and site structure. In *Method and Theory for Activity Area Research*, ed. S Kent, pp. 449–512. New York: Columbia Univ. Press

Bintliff J, Gaffney C, eds. 1986. *Archaeology at the Interface*. Oxford: British Archaeol. Rep., Int. Ser. 300

Birley A. 2002. *Garrison Life at Vindolanda. A Band of Brothers*. Stroud, UK: Tempus

Bottéro J. 1992. *Mesopotamia. Writing, Reasoning and the Gods*. Chicago: Univ. Chicago Press

Bottéro J. 2000. Religion and reasoning in Mesopotamia. See Bottéro et al. 2000, pp. 3–66

Bottéro J, Herrenschmidt C, Vernant JP, eds. 2000. *Ancestor of the West. Writing, Reasoning and Religion in Mesopotamia, Elam and Greece*. Chicago: Univ. Chicago Press

Bowman AK. 1994a. *Life and Letters on the Roman Frontier*. London: Br. Mus.

Bowman AK. 1994b. The Roman imperial army: letters and literacy on the northern frontier. See Bowman & Woolf 1994, pp. 109–25

Bowman AK. 1991. Literacy in the Roman empire: mass and mode. See Humphery 1991, pp. 119–32

Bowman AK, Woolf G, eds. 1994. *Literacy and Power in the Ancient World*. Cambridge, UK: Cambridge Univ. Press

Boyer P, Nissenbaum S. 1974. *Salem Possessed. The Social Origins of Witchcraft*. Cambridge, MA: Harvard Univ. Press

Brenner EM. 1988. Socio-political implications of mortuary remains in seventeenth-century native southern New England. See Leone & Potter 1988, pp. 147–81

Briggs C. 2000. Literacy, reading and writing in the medieval West. *J. Medieval Hist.* 26:397–420

Brosius M, ed. 2003. *Ancient Archives and Archival Traditions*. Oxford, UK: Oxford Univ. Press

Brown MR. 1988. The behavioural context of probate inventories: an example from Plymouth colony. See Beaudry 1988a, pp. 79–82

Burke P. 2000. A *Social History of Knowledge*. Oxford, UK: Polity Press

Casella EC, Symonds J, ed. 2005. *Industrial Archaeology: Future Directions*. New York: Springer

Cleland C. 1988. Questions of substance, questions that count. *Hist. Archaeol.* 22:13–17

Collins J. 1995. Literacy and literacies. *Annu. Rev. Anthropol.* 24:75–93

Cooley A, ed. 2002. *Becoming Roman, Writing Latin? Literacy and Epigraphy in the Roman West*. Portsmouth, RI: JRA Suppl. Ser. 48

Cooper JS. 2004. Babylonian beginnings: the origin of the cuneiform writing system in comparative perspective. See Houston 2004a, pp. 71–99

Deagan K. 1988. Neither history nor prehistory: the questions that count in historical archaeology. *Hist. Archaeol.* 22:7–12

Deagan K. 1991. Historical archaeology's contributions to our understanding of early America. See Falk 1991, pp. 97–112

Deetz J. 1977. *In Small Things Forgotten*. New York: Anchor

Deetz J. 1991. Introduction: archaeological evidence of sixteenth and seventeenth century colonial encounters. See Falk 1991, pp. 1–9

Deetz J. 1993. *Flowerdew Hundred. The Archaeology of a Virginia Plantation 1619–1864*. Charlottesville: Univ. Va. Press

Deetz J, Deetz PS. 2000. *The Times of Their Lives. Life, Love and Death in Plymouth Colony*. New York: Anchor

Epperson TW. 2001. A separate house for the Christian slaves, one for the Negro slaves: the archaeology of race and identity in late seventeenth-century Virginia. See Orser 2001a, pp. 54–70

Falk L, ed. 1991. *Historical Archaeological in Global Perspective*. Washington, DC: Smithson. Inst. Press

Fentress J, Wickham C. 1992. *Social Memory*. Oxford, UK: Blackwell

Franklin S. 2002. *Writing, Society and Culture in Early Rus, c.950–1300*. Cambridge, UK: Cambridge Univ. Press

Frazer B. 1999. Reconceptualising resistance in the historical archaeology of the British Isles. *Int. J. Hist. Archaeol.* 3:1–10

Funari P, Hall M, Jones S, ed. 1999. *Historical Archaeology: Back from the Edge*. London: Routledge

Geary P. 2002. The *Myth of Nations: The Medieval Origins of Europe*. Princeton, NJ: Princeton Univ. Press

Giles K. 1998. The 'familiar' fraternity: the appropriation and consumption of medieval guildhalls in early modern York. See Tarlow & West 1998, pp. 87–102

Ginzburg C. 1992. Clues: roots of an evidential program. In *Clues, Myths and the Historical Method*, ed. C Ginzburg, pp. 96–125. Baltimore, MD: John Hopkins Univ. Press

Glassner JJ. 2003. *The Invention of Cuneiform. Writing in Sumer*. Baltimore, MD: Johns Hopkins Univ. Press

Gómez Romero F. 2005. A brief overview of the evolution of historical archaeology in Argentina. *Int. J. Hist. Archaeol.* 9:135–41

Goody J. 1968. *The Logic of Writing and the Organisation of Society*. Cambridge, UK: Cambridge Univ. Press

Goody J. 1977. *The Domestication of the Savage Mind*. Cambridge, UK: Cambridge Univ. Press

Goody J. 1986. *The Logic of Writing and the Organisation of Society*. Cambridge, UK: Cambridge Univ. Press

Goody J. 1987. *The Interface between the Written and the Oral*. Cambridge, UK: Cambridge Univ. Press

Goody J, Watt I. 1963. The consequences of literacy. *Comp. Stud. Soc. Hist.* 5, pp. 304–45

Grierson P. 1959. Commerce in the Dark Ages: a critique of the evidence. *Trans. R. Hist. Soc.* 9:123–40

Hall DD. 1996. *Cultures of Print. Essays in the History of the Book*. Amherst: Univ. Mass. Press

Hall M. 1993. The archaeology of colonial settlement in southern Africa. *Annu. Rev. Anthropol.* 22:177–200

Hall M. 1999. Subaltern voices? Finding spaces between things and words. See Funari et al. 1999, pp. 193–203

Hall M. 2000. *Archaeology and the Modern World. Colonial Transcripts in South Africa and the Chesapeake*. London: Routledge

Halsall G. 1997. Archaeology and historiography. In *Companion to Historiography*, ed. M Bentley, pp. 805–27. London: Routledge

Halverson J. 1992. Goody and the implosion of the literacy thesis. *Man* 27:301–17

Hanson AE. 1991. Ancient illiteracy. See Humphrey 1991, pp. 159–98

Harris R. 2000. *Rethinking Writing*. London: Continuum

Harris WV. 1989. *Ancient Literacy*. Cambridge, MA: Harvard Univ. Press

Herrenschmidt C. Writing between visible and invisible worlds in Iran, Israel, and Greece. See Bottéro et al. 2000, pp. 69–146

Hines J. 2004. *Voices in the Past. English Literature and Archaeology*. Cambridge, UK: DS Brewer

Hodder I, ed. 2001. *Archaeological Theory Today*. Oxford, UK: Polity

Hodges R. 1983. New approaches to medieval archaeology, part 2. In *25 Years of Medieval Archaeology*, ed. D Hinton, pp. 24–32. Sheffield, UK: Univ. Sheffield

Hopkins K. 1991. Conquest by book. See Humphrey 1991, pp. 133–58

Hoskins J. 1998. *Biographical Objects. How Things Tell the Stories of People's Lives*. London: Routledge

Houston S. 2000. Into the minds of the ancients: advances in Maya glyph studies. *J. World Prehist.* 14:121–201

Houston S, ed. 2004a. *The First Writing. Script Invention as History and Process*. Cambridge, UK: Cambridge Univ. Press

Houston S. 2004b. Final thoughts in first writing. See Houston 2004a, pp. 349–53

Houston S. 2004c. The archaeology of communication technologies. *Annu. Rev. Anthropol.* 33:223–50

Houston S. 2004d. Writing in early Mesoamerica. See Houston 2004a, pp. 274–309

Humphrey J, ed. 1991. *Literacy in the Roman World*. Ann Arbor, MI: J. Rom. Archaeol., Suppl. Ser. 3

Hundsbichler H, Jaritz G, Kühtreiber T, eds. 1998. *Die Vielfalt der Dinge: Neue Wege zur Analyse mittelalterlicher Sachkultur*. Vienna: Verlag der Österreich ischen Akademie der Wissenschaften

Johnson M. 1996. *An Archaeology of Capitalism*. Oxford, UK: Blackwell

Johnson M. 2002. *Behind the Castle Gate: From Medieval to Renaissance*. London: Routledge

Justice S. 1994. *Writing and Rebellion. England in 1381*. Berkeley: Univ. Calif. Press

Kosso P. 2001. *Knowing the Past. Philosophical Issues of History and Archaeology*. New York: Humanity Books

Leone M. 1988a. The Georgian order as the order of merchant capitalism in Annapolis, Maryland. See Leone & Potter 1988, pp. 235–61

Leone M. 1988b. The relationship between archaeological data and the documentary record: eighteenth-century gardens in Annapolis. *Hist. Archaeol.* 22:29–35

Leone M. 1995. A historical archaeology of capitalism. *Am. Anthropol.* 97:251–68

Leone M. 2005. *The Archaeology of Liberty in an American Capital: Excavations in Annapolis*. Berkeley: Univ. Calif. Press

Leone M, Crosby C. 1987. Middle range theory in historical archaeology. In *Consumer Choice in Historical Archaeology*, ed. S. Spencer-Wood, pp. 397–410. New York: Plenum

Leone M, Fry GM. 2001. Spirit management among Americans of African descent. See Orser 2001a, pp. 143–57

Leone M, LaRoche CJ, Babiarz JJ. 2005. The archaeology of black Americans in recent times. *Annu. Rev. Anthropol.* 34:575–98

Leone M, Potter PB, eds. 1988. *The Recovery of Meaning: Historical Archaeology in the Eastern United States*. Washington, DC: Smithson. Inst. Press

Lévi-Strauss C. 1973. *Tristes Tropiques*. London: Picador

Little B, ed. 1992a. *Text-Aided Archaeology*. Boca Raton: CRC Press

Little B. 1992b. Text-aided archaeology. See Little 1992a, pp. 1–6

Little B. 1992c. Texts, images, material culture. See Little 1992a, pp. 217–21

Little B. 1994. People with history: an update on historical archaeology in the United States. *J. Archaeol. Method Theory* 1:5–40

Lloyd J. 1986. Why should historians take archaeology seriously? See Bintliff & Gaffney 1986, pp. 40–51

Lydon J. 1999. Pidgin English: historical archaeology, cultural exchange and the Chinese in the Rocks, 1890–1930. See Funari et al. 1999, pp. 255–83

Marcus J. 1992. *Mesoamerican Writing Systems*. Princeton, NJ: Princeton Univ. Press

McGuire R, Paynter B, ed. 1991. *The Archaeology of Inequality*. Oxford, UK: Blackwell

Messick B. 1993. *The Calligraphic State. Textual Domination and History in a Muslim Society*. Berkeley: Univ. Calif. Press

Moreland J. 2001. *Archaeology and Text*. London: Duckworth

Mrozowski SA. 1988. For gentlemen of capacity and leisure: the archaeology of colonial news-papers. See Beaudry 1988a, pp. 184–91

Nissen HJ, Damerow P, Englund RK. 1993. *Archaic Bookkeeping. Writing and Techniques of Economic Administration in the Ancient Near East*. Chicago: Univ. Chicago Press

Noël Hume I. 1964. Archaeology: handmaiden to history. *N.C. Hist. Rev.* 41:215–25

Olson DR. 1986. The cognitive consequences of literacy. *Can. Psychol.* 27:109–21

Olson DR. 1994. *The World on Paper. The Conceptual and Cognitive Implications of Writing and Reading*. Cambridge, UK: Cambridge Univ. Press

Olson DR. 1996. Toward a psychology of literacy: on the relations between speech and writing. *Cognition* 60:83–104

Olson DR. 2001. What writing is. *Pragmat. Cogn.* 9:239–58

Olson DR, Astington JW. 1990. Talking about text: how literacy contributes to thought. *J. Pragmat.* 14:705–21

Ong WJ. 2002. *Orality and Literacy.* London: Routledge

Orser CE. 1988. Toward a theory of power for historical archaeology: plantations and space. See Leone & Potter 1988, pp. 313–43

Orser CE. 1996. *A Historical Archaeology of the Modern World.* New York: Plenum

Orser CE. 1998. The archaeology of the African diaspora. *Annu. Rev. Anthropol.* 27:63–83

Orser CE, ed. 2001a. *Race and the Archaeology of Identity.* Salt Lake City: The University of Utah Press

Orser CE. 2001b. Race and the archaeology of identity in the modern world. See Orser 2001a, pp. 1–13

Paynter R. 1988. Steps to an archaeology of capitalism: material change and class analysis. See Leone & Potter 1988, pp. 407–33

Paynter R. 2000a. Historical and anthropological archaeology: forging alliances. *J. Archaeol. Res.* 8:1–37

Paynter R. 2000b. Historical archaeology and the post-Columbian world of north America. *J. Archaeol. Res.* 8:169–217

Paynter R, McGuire R. 1991. The archaeology of inequality: material culture, domination and resistance. In *The Archaeology of Inequality*, ed. R McGuire, B Paynter, pp. 1–27. Oxford: Blackwell

Pikirayi I. 1999. Research trends in the historical archaeology of Zimbabwe. See Funari et al. 1999, pp. 67–84

Postgate JN, Wang T, Wilkinson T. 1995. The evidence for early writing: utilitarian or ceremonial? *Antiquity* 69:459–80

Potter PB. 1992. Middle-range theory, ceramics, and capitalism in nineteenth-century Rockbridge County, Virginia. See Little 1992a, pp. 9–23

Powell BP. 2002. *Writing and the Origins of Greek Literature.* Cambridge, UK: Cambridge Univ. Press.

Rowlands M. 1999. Black identity and sense of the past in Brazilian national culture. See Funari et al. 1999, pp. 328–44

Schmandt-Besserat D. 1992. *Before Writing, Volume 1: From Counting to Cuneiform.* Austin: Univ. Tex. Press

Schrire C. 1991. The historical archaeology of the impact of colonialism in seventeenth-century South Africa. See Falk 1991, pp. 69–96

Schrire C. 1995. *Digging through Darkness. Chronicles of an Archaeologist.* Charlottesville: Univ. Press Va.

Schuyler RL. 1988. Archaeological remains, documents, and anthropology: a call for a new culture history. *Hist. Archaeol.* 22:36–42

Scribner S, Cole M. 1981. *The Psychology of Literacy.* Cambridge, MA: Harvard Univ. Press

Shackel P. 1992. Probate inventories in historical archaeology: a review and alternatives. See Little 1992a, pp. 205–15

Singleton TA. 1988. An archaeological framework for slavery and emancipation, 1740–1880. See Leone & Potter 1988, pp. 345–70

Singleton TA. 1999. The formation of ethnic-American identities: Jewish communities in Boston. See Funari et al. 1999, pp. 284–307

Singleton TA. 2001. Class, race and identity among free blacks in the Antebellum South. See Orser 2001a, pp. 196–207

Tarlow S. 1998. Strangely familiar. See Tarlow & West 1998, pp. 263–72

Tarlow S. 1999. *Bereavement and Commemoration. An Archaeology of Mortality*. Oxford: Blackwell

Tarlow S, West S, eds. 1998. *The Familiar Past. Archaeologies of Later Historical Britain*. London: Routledge

Thomas K. 1986. The meaning of literacy in early modern England. In *The Written Word. Literacy in Transition*, ed. G. Baumann, pp. 97–131. Oxford, UK: Clarendon

Tomlin RSO. 2002. Writing to the gods in Britain. See Cooley 2002, pp. 165–80

Trigger B. 1989. *A History of Archaeological Thought*. Cambridge, UK: Cambridge Univ. Press

Wheale N. 1999. *Writing and Society. Literacy, Print and Politics in Britain 1590–1660*. London: Routledge

Woolf G. 2002. How the Latin West was won. See Colley 2002, pp. 181–88

Woolf G. 2003. The city of letters. In *Rome the Cosmopolis*, ed. C Edwards, G Woolf, pp. 203–21. Cambridge, UK: Cambridge Univ. Press

Yentsch A. 1988a. Farming, fishing, whaling, trading: land and sea as resource on eighteenth-century Cape Cod. See Beaudry 1988a, pp. 138–60

Yentsch A. 1988b. Legends, houses, families and myths: relationships between material culture and American ideology. See Beaudry 1988a, pp. 5–19

Yentsch A. 1994. *A Chesapeake Family and their Slaves: A Study in Historical Archaeology*. Cambridge, UK: Cambridge Univ. Press

Yentsch A, Beaudry M. 2001. American material culture in mind, thought and deed. See Hodder 2001, pp. 214–40

RELATED RESOURCES

The Advanced Papyrological Information System (APIS) at Columbia University provides access to some of the Egyptian records discussed. **http://www.columbia.edu/cu/lweb/projects/digital/apis/**

Vindolanda Tablets Online (Oxford) is a fantastic Web site making available the full range of texts (with photographs, translations, and commentary) so unexpectedly discovered at the Roman fort of Vindolanda. **http://vindolanda.csad.ox.ac.uk/**

The Ethnography of Finland

Jukka Siikala

Department of Anthropology, University of Helsinki, 00024 Helsinki, Finland;
email: jukka.siikala@helsinki.fi

Annu. Rev. Anthropol. 2006. 35:153–70

First published online as a Review in
Advance on May 25, 2006

The *Annual Review of Anthropology* is
online at anthro.annualreviews.org

This article's doi:
10.1146/annurev.anthro.35.081705.123206

Copyright © 2006 by Annual Reviews.
All rights reserved

0084-6570/06/1021-0153$20.00

Key Words

Finno-Ugric cultures, ethnology, folklore, nationalism

Abstract

Different national traditions define disciplines in different ways, and
ethnology, folklore, and anthropology are separated in the Finnish
university system. The great divide between the more universally oriented anthropological research and the local, especially Eastern and
Northern European ethnological traditions is sometimes conceptualized by defining the latter as nationalist. The emergence of Finnish
and Finno-Ugric studies in Finland complicates the difference in a
way that is relevant to urgent questions of globalization and its relationship to cultural diversity. At the same time this emergence raises
important questions about the significance of ethnographic knowledge. Historically oriented ethnological and folkloristic studies in
Finland have formulated a multidisciplinary approach analogical to
the four anthropological fields for research into the history of Finnish
and Finno-Ugric cultures and languages. Researchers have used the
accumulated data in new and novel ways, which has opened up perspectives instead of limiting them to the field of area studies. The
development of Finnish ethnographic studies clearly demonstrates
the necessity of comparison and the comparative perspective.

PRIVILEDGED AND UNPRIVILEDGED PLACES

Anthropology is a discipline constantly drawn apart by extremes. The present debate, as well as its historical development, is similar to a play of binary oppositions and the redefinition of their values. The place and the hierarchy of places compose a major role in this play. The anthropological discussions have been dominated at different times by problems that have emerged out of the research of different ethnographic regions. These regions have become priviledged places, which are connected to another hierarchical order of locations, the places where writing about those regions is done. The connection between the places of writing and the places of ethnographic data has been mostly political: The Americans studied the North American Indians, and the British studied their colonies in Africa, whereas the French, as Parkin (2005) notes, concentrated on general theory, and the Germans were left with nothing other than history. This organizing power of place for anthropological discourse has had ramifications at different research levels. According to the shifting power relations, the ethnographies of different cultural areas have had differential weight in theoretical argumentation, and it has been possible to ignore counterevidence from less-priviledged ethnographic areas. On the level of interpretation, questions derived from and determined by the priviledged places in the scholarly discussion have been dominant.

The relative importance of the sites of scholarly activities in the worldwide political scene and their relation to locations of ethnographic information has created enormous white areas on the world map as we imagine it ethnographically. The Eurasian north is one of the ethnographic areas that, for both political and theoretical reasons, has played an insignificant role in anthropological discussions in general. Politics limited fieldwork possibilities in the Soviet Union. For that reason, Siberia at the moment could be a new Klondike for ethnographers. One would expect that access to a huge cultural area, where few Western ethnographers have done research, would have resulted in a rush of anthropologists to the area. It did not happen, however. The reason is not only the crisis of ethnographic representation and the criticism of traditional field research (Clifford & Marcus 1986), but also the prevailing ideologies of the societies defining the relevant questions. Dumont (1986, p. 204) recognized this connection when he defined anthropological approaches that, "in the guise of a specific anthropology, are in reality intent on subjecting anthropology to nonanthropological concerns." Dumont was fully aware of the difficulties connected to the creation of a noncultural language to describe culture or a nonsocial language to analyze society. He was concerned about anthropologists imposing their own societies' construction and tensions on others.

At the moment, globalization and its consequences define the worldwide political discourse and its ideological underpinnings. The centers of world politics, which also dominantly define anthropological questions, are looking for the problem-generating areas in that process. Political and anthropological questions are thus collapsed together. If, for example, racism is an everyday experience and a commonsensical explanation for social tensions in the United States, racism is elevated to the level of analytic concept, and every tension or boundary construction is reduced to racism. Similarly, for imperial centers dominating the globalization process, nationalism poses a threat and has therefore been made into a major anthropological problem. The way in which the problems are defined creates a hierarchy of the interesting fields. An area such as the Balkans is much more important as a site of research and discussion than that of northern Eurasia (Cushman 2004, Hayden 2005).

One of the great dividing lines in ethnographic studies is the politically determined division between the German-dominated historically oriented ethnological tradition of northern and eastern Europe and the anthropological tradition in Britain, France, and the United States (Barth et al. 2005). Extreme anthropological positions characterize the differences of these traditions in several ways. One defining feature of the ethnological tradition is its persistent orientation toward historical interpretations and its focus on something that has been called national cultures. This has given rise to strong criticism by those on the other side of the dividing line. Ethnological research has been labeled as nationalist, with the aim of creating homogenous, permanent, primordial, essentialized, and expansionist national cultures (Gellner 1964, p. 168; Gellner 1983, pp. 48–49; Gellner 1987, p. 8). The political tendency to create universal citizens out of cultural people also forced the critics of ethnography to interpret the recognition of differences as creating hierarchies (Abu-Lughod 1991) and the attention to history as primordializing and essentializing (Besteman 1999). The political positions defining these extremes are obvious in the way that opposites are defined as nationalism. The creation of unity out of differences (such as when Benedict Anderson labels the Russification of the Russian Empire, as well as opposition to that process by cultural and linguistic minorities, as nationalism) collapses together the "universal-imperial" and the "national-particular" (Anderson 1991, pp. 84–85).

As Dirks & Ortner (1994, p. 38) note, the "construction of otherness and difference has for the last several hundred years been linked to projects of rule and domination." This construction has occurred not only in the field but also in the descriptions and characterizations of other ethnographic traditions. Ethnological/anthropological research in Finland is one field that illuminates some of the problems connected with the tendency to collapse together different levels of social discourse. This research has been labeled as nationalistic (Anttonen 2005, Wilson 1976), and therefore an overview of the national tradition's formative years is illuminative. This overview enables us to clarify some of the perennial binary oppositions in anthropology, as well as to highlight the importance of ethnographic data for the deep understanding of cultural phenomena and their place in our conceptualizations of the world.

INVENTING FINLAND

That anthropologists discover places and the people living in them is a logical contradiction because those living there have already found the place. In this example one can find many of anthropology's conceptual problems connected to the notions of place, culture, and people. Ethnographic discoveries have universally been preceded by political ones, and both discoveries have led to the encompassment of new areas into politico-administrative or conceptual schemes derived from the outside. Because discovery is foremost a conceptual process, it is also a continuous one, and the same places can and will be discovered again and again. Incorporation not only results in the addition of new elements to an existing system, but it also partly creates those elements. The ability of colonial power relations to create tribes, ethnic groups, and even nations has its limits, however. To make something out of nothing is difficult to accomplish, and the relationship between what already exists and what is created should be analyzed carefully.

This necessity for careful analysis applies clearly to the ethnology of Finland. In the present usage, the term Finland refers to a nation-state that became independent in 1917 and is at the moment a member of the European Union. Defining ethnology on the basis of existing political units, and thus limiting its scope within political borders, would mean a complete collapse of culture to modern forms of political organization and a definition of its place in terms of political geography. The shifting grounds of Finnish culture, and consequently its geographical location, can be understood from the fact that the area between the Scandinavian Peninsula and Russia was a battleground between the

Swedish kingdoms and Novgorod. Important trade routes to Russia passed through this area, and its population spoke a different language than the traders. These trade routes connected the Viking kingdoms to foreigners all the way back to Constantinople. During the twelfth and thirteenth centuries, Sweden was able to gain control of part of the geographic area of Finland. Politics and religion went hand in hand, and several military conquests resulted in the gradual conversion of the Finnish population to Christianity. Novgorod conquered the eastern part of Finland, and the 1323 Treaty of Pähkinäsaari established the important west-east divide that crossed through Europe and manifested itself on a religious level in the division of the Catholic Church into Western Roman Catholic and Eastern Orthodox.

Through discovery and conquest, the external powers not only defined the area of Finland but also divided it, and this division has had far-reaching consequences in the cultural history of the area. The cultural border crossing through Europe divided Finland into western and eastern cultural areas. Despite this divide, the political unification of the Finnish area continued as a result of the expansion of Swedish power toward the east. First only the southwestern part of the area was called Finland or Finland Proper in the treaty of Teusina in 1595; then in the 1616 Treaty of Stolbova between Sweden and Russia, even the eastern parts of Finland were incorporated into the Swedish Empire. The phrasing of these treaties reveals an important distinction between the political units and other levels of sociocultural integration. First, Sweden was defined as consisting of Sweden, Finland, and Estonia. Second, the power of the Swedish crown was said to extend over distinct nations, and the concept of folk was applied to the Finns. The unifying factor of the empire was the power of the crown, and different nations were subjects of it. The concepts of citizenship and nationality were clearly separate (Kemiläinen 1964, 2004).

Peace treaties in general belong to the field of diplomatic practice, and one can argue with good reason that the totalizing concept of nation or folk in the treaties has little to do with the way people conceptualized their own social belonging. From the point of view of external pressures, the church and its influences were directly connected to the lives of the people. In medieval kingdoms, religion was an essential legitimating factor for political power, and the church was an important instrument for the execution of local administration. Although the heavy emphasis on doctrinal orthodoxy had its basis in canonical and universally valid texts, the dissemination of the religious message required the use of language that the people could understand. This required, and still does, the translation of the religious message into local languages, as well as the standardization of the content in written form to guarantee its orthodoxy. Catholic priests and bishops already had translated some basic religious literature into Finnish, but there is no detailed information about the extent of that translation and publication activity. The Reformation, with its ideology of lay priesthood, diminished clerical control but increased the need for standardized texts for general consumption. The Reformation in the Swedish Empire was implemented with a political decision in 1527. After that, a major translation project began, and Bishop Michael Agricola, who is said to be the father of literary Finnish, became the leading figure in creating Finnish religious literature. He wrote the first Finnish ABC book (at approximately 1543), and translated the New Testament (1548) and parts of the Old Testament (1551) into Finnish. That Agricola addresses the 1551 translation of David's Psalm "To the Finns" refers to their unity and reflects the ecclesiastical unification of Finnish dialectical diversity. In the typical way of early modern empires, Sweden had thus discovered Finland and created it as a politico-legal, administrative, and ecclesiastical unit. A recognition of internal cultural differences and localized social formations was apparent in the way the area was administratively divided into provinces. The provinces also formed the basis for organizing the military troops drafted from Finland. Thus, despite the homogenizing effects, the empire also recognized internal diversity, which has been interpreted as reflective of the ancient tribal divisions of Finland (Lappalainen 2001; for general historical interpretations, see Kirkinen et al. 1994, Rasila 1993). The cultural, social, and linguistic differences between the populations of Sweden and Finland did not result in a homogenizing othering; rather, unity and diversity functioned on different levels of social integration.

DISCOVERING FINNISHNESS

The ethnographic imagining of Finnishness was a different project from the discovery of Finland as part of an empire. Away from the practicalities of politics and the concomitant unity of a governed population, the ethnographic project relativized its object from the beginning. The aim of the first grammar of the Finnish language was indicative of this difference. It was published in 1649, 50 years before the publication of the first Swedish grammar, and was intended to help the Swedish-speaking civil servants understand their subjects (Korhonen 1986, p. 17). Instead of the description of a single language, the main aim of the research on Finnish language was, according to the emerging historical philology, the relationship of Finnish to other languages spoken in the area. According to Korhonen's (1986, p. 29) exhaustive history of Finno-Ugrian language studies, the German philosopher G.W. Leibnitz, a significant figure in the shift from practical to humanistic and historical analysis, attempted to reveal the history of various people with the help of comparative language materials. This notion of the relationship between language and people and their mutual histories formed the basis for the emerging interest in philology and in fact separated the histories of empires from the histories of people, which ulti-

mately led to historical ethnography and the sharp distinction between universalism and particularism. The application of Latin normative grammar to different and separate languages was replaced by the study of the relationships between languages and their specific characters.

Despite the change of interest defined by the principal question to be answered, the institutional basis of discussions did not change immediately. As Korhonen notes, the discovery of the Finno-Ugrian language family during the eighteenth century led to an enormous interest in it in European intellectual centers, and research began to be organized at the University of Uppsala, the Imperial Academy of St. Petersburg, the University of Göttingen in Germany, as well as at several universities in the Austro-Hungarian Empire. The "ideas took a long time to filter through to Finland" (Korhonen 1986, pp. 30–31). All these centers were heavily influenced by German developments in historical philology, and the research in Finland was firmly tied to these discussions through the activities of Henrik Gabriel Porthan (1739–1804). His visit to Göttingen in 1779, and especially his familiarity with the work of August Ludwig (von) Schlözer, prompted a deepening interest in the comparative study of Finno-Ugric languages on the basis of field materials. Porthan's plan for an expedition to Russia to collect new unpublished materials was not realized during his lifetime. The plan itself, however, demonstrates the international character of the scientific community that planned its activities across imperial borders. Porthan's made his plan with scholars from St. Petersburg while Finland was still under Swedish rule.

Both Russian and Finnish initiatives led to extensive expeditions during the nineteenth century, and Anders Johan Sjögren was the first Finnish scholar to travel extensively in Russia to collect ethnographic and linguistic materials. Branch (1973) has thoroughly analyzed Sjögren's significance to the research. While working in St. Petersburg, Sjögren's state funding was authorized by Tsar

Alexander I, and he was able to undertake a five-year-long expedition from 1824 to 1829 through Karelia, Lapland, the Kola Peninsula, Archangel, and further east to the Perm area. The historical project proposed earlier by Porthan formed the basis of Sjögren's work, and in addition to documenting the Finno-Ugric languages, he formulated clearly the basis on which historical inferences should be made. In his analysis Branch (1973, p. 208) has stressed "the three tools" Sjögren saw necessary for any historical reconstruction: Beyond the written records and archaeological remains, one had to pay attention to onomastics, ethnography, and linguistics. Sjögren also made observations on physiognomy using the criteria of his time, thus gaining an early formulation of a multidisciplinary project analogous to the research practice that later became known as the four-field approach in anthropology.

Several Finnish expeditions to Russia during the nineteenth century continued the research practices established by Sjögren. Castrén's extensive travels during 1841–1844 and 1845–1849 resulted in a major contribution to Uralic linguistics and ethnography. His posthumously published collected works include grammars of the Yurak, Yenisei-Samoyed, Tavgi, Selkup, and Kamassian languages, along with ethnographic observations and folklore texts (Castrén 1853–1862). Castrén's work is of great theoretical importance when one analyzes the ethnographic invention of Finnishness. He worked comparatively and demonstrated the relationships between languages, thus connecting, rather than separating, cultural units into discrete and bounded species. Finnishness in this conceptualization was a point in a continuum of linguistic relations and, as such, an essentially historical formation.

Historical knowledge does not, however, serve the practical needs of governance. The research on Finno-Ugrian languages had been conducted in imperial intellectual centers, and the results had been published in Russian, German, French, and Latin. As a Grand

Dutchy of Russia since 1809, Finland was governed by a Swedish-speaking elite and the use of Finnish for official purposes was limited despite the fact that Swedish speakers were only 14% of the population (Suomen Tilastollinen Vuosikirja 1907, table 13). Russian was understood even less than Swedish. Literary Finnish had its basis in old religious texts and was neither linguistically satisfactory nor met the practical demands of the time. The Finnish language received an official, although still subordinated, status only in 1863. The official acknowledgment of Finnish was preceded by the establishment of the first professorship of Finnish Language in Finland in 1850. Several restrictions limited the activities of the professorship, and he was not allowed to participate in degree examinations and could be removed from office. Censorship was also applied, and only economic and religious publications were allowed in Finnish. The professorship in Finnish, the relationship of Finnish studies to Finno-Ugric studies, and the development of literary Finnish reveal analytically important distinctions in the process of inventing the national language. As Branch (1999) has pointed out, the previous center in St. Petersburg lost its monopoly in Finnish research, and the emphasis among the specialists partially shifted from theoretical and historical philology to a focus on the practical development of the Finnish language.

Anderson's (1991) well-known formulation about the importance of print capitalism in the formation of national, standardized literary languages does not apply well to the Finnish situation. Instead of merchants needing a unified language (Anderson 1991, p. 77), the administrative and educational sectors constituted the immediate demand for a standardized language. Thus the creation of Finnishness in the sense of a bounded language community resulted from an Enlightenment ideology developing a state bureaucracy (Goody 1986) instead of romantic ideas. The distinct trends of differentiation and unification characterized the study of Finnish in Finland. The Finno-Ugric tradition of relating speech communities continued in the Finnish dialectology while the Finnish specialists worked to create a language capable of meeting the needs of a growing national administration and economy. Instead of imagining the nation as a homogenous language community, the dialectical diversity was recognized to be not only a linguistic fact, but also a topic for internal discussions about which dialect would be the basis of a literary language.

FROM FINNO-UGRIC STUDIES TO THE ETHNOGRAPHY OF FINLAND

The systematic accumulation of Finnish ethnographic information has a long history. In 1630 Gustaf II Adolf gave an order for civil servants and the clergy to collect and preserve antiquities and descriptions of an ethnographic nature. In 1666 the College of Antiquities was founded in Sweden to manage this activity and preserve the collected information. Previously, the ecclesiastic recording of beliefs and ritual practices were regarded as superstitious and thus to be wiped out, but now historical interest determined this political interest and was supposed to form the basis for studying the ancestry of the populations subject to the crown. Instead of being wiped out, the antiquities were declared the property of the crown, and they were to be preserved "for the glory of the nation and for their intrinsic value" (Sihvo 1999, p. 186; Vuorela 1977, p. 11). The nationalistic "possessive individual" (Handler 1988) was thus preceded by the royal and imperial one. The research program formulated by the Academy of Sciences in St. Petersburg for Finno-Ugric philology included from the beginning the collection of ethnographic materials that were, besides the philological uses, intended for use by the state in its administrative functions (Branch 1999).

The application of systematic scientific methods of analysis to the randomly collected pieces of ethnographic information was tied to the emergence of historical philology in the eighteenth century. The basic premise was that of comparison, and only through the application of the comparative method was one supposed to reach any historical conclusions. Although the strict principles of the comparative method were formulated by the neogrammarians only in the late nineteenth century, the systematization of the treatment of research data and the aims of the analysis appear more than 100 years earlier (Bunzl 1996). This systematization had its basis in certain presuppositions, which followed from the underlying paradigm-constituting questions and notions of systematic regularities. The systematic changes in languages were supposed to reveal their historical relationships.

Sjögren (1861) illuminates the early ethnographic method with his conclusion that a historical relationship exists between the cultures of the Finns and the Komi. By comparing the languages, he concluded that lexical comparisons without structural similarities are insufficient. Structural similarities of languages were to be complemented by ethnographic affinity. In his ethnographic comparisons, Sjögren was much less systematic, and he was satisfied with finding corresponding singular cultural features and similarities in material culture and in the ornamentation of artifacts. As conclusive evidence for the supposed historical relationship, Sjögren looked for a correspondence between the different types of data. The main emphasis on language shaped not only the notion of the contingent nature of other kinds of ethnographic evidence, but also the practices of fieldwork. The field trips were long, lasting up to five years, but they did not consist of intensive studies of single communities. Rather, they involved working with single informants in several communities to collect data on the local vernaculars, which could then be described as synchronic and a virtual system. As Korhonen et al. (1983) demonstrate in the centennial publication for the Finno-Ugric Society, this field practice became the standard form of data collection. As a result, the linguistic data, besides lexical data, consisted of long narrative materials, songs, folk poetry, charms, and ritual texts, whereas observations of an ethnographic nature were more detached and decontextualized.

The notion of culture as a systematic and structured phenomenon that could be analyzed on the basis of structural properties and the realization of taxonomical differences between language families laid the foundation for the emergence of several key concepts that have played a significant role in anthropological theory development. The historical relationship between languages could be measured, different language families could be classified, and their history could thus be derived from a protolanguage. Taxonomically different protolanguages and their differentiation into several subspecies actually formed an evolutionary explanation that one could reach through the comparative method. The expected correspondence of different types of data had its basis in the presupposition of a close relationship between languages, populations, and their general cultures.

The early version of a linguistic analogy enabled researchers to extend expectations of its systematic nature to all linguistic materials. Therefore an important parallel development can be found in several scholarly discourses that also have their basis in lay practices. For nearly 2000 years, the Christian tradition systematized two discourses: It narrativized history beginning with the genealogical-tribal history of the Jews, which continues with the history of the church, and it created theology as the doctrinal systematization of beliefs. The Renaissance attempted to replace the grand sacred narrative with a secular one, but history in narrative form remained at the core, and history had only one significant origin, which was the classic culture of Greek and Roman antiquity. From Mcpherson's *The Highlander*, 1758, and *The Works of Ossian*, 1765, to their English counterparts *Reliquies of Ancient English Poetry*, 1765, and Herder's *Stimmen der Völker im Lieder*, 1778, various works aimed to replace the universal historical narrative with

particular ones. The history of the Jews and the church was thus replaced with histories of different nations, and correspondingly, the theology of the church was replaced by the mythologies of different nations. Just as researchers were to analyze language relationships and construct protolanguages using the comparative method, they were also to reconstruct mythologies comparatively from the fragments still circulating in oral discourse. The common organizing problem concerned the origin and historical development of different languages and mythologies. The comparative method and a quest for origins were thus tied together to solve clearly defined historical problems.

The vast geographic areas where the historically related languages and cultures could be found crossed several political borders. The Finno-Ugric languages were found in Sweden, Finland, and in numerous governments in Russia, Estonia, and the Austro-Hungarian Empire. The place of the Finno-Ugric cultures thus could not be bounded by political borders, nor was it possible to collapse political units and cultural ones. This notion was firmly established in the definition of the professorial chairs in the emerging disciplines of folklore and ethnology in Helsinki. Kaarle Krohn was appointed as Professor Extraordinarius for folklore research in 1889, and in 1908 the discipline was defined as Finnish and Comparative Folklore Research. The discipline also included the study of folk religion. Ethnology was institutionalized as an academic discipline in 1921 after Finland became independent, and this discipline covered "primarily the material culture and customs of Finno-Ugric people, provided that these do not impinge upon the Departments of Folklore or Folk Religion" (Vuorela 1977, p. 10). The way ethnology was tied to a linguistic group foreshadowed its later development in comparison with folklore studies, which was internationally oriented from its academic inception.

Fieldwork possibilities among Finno-Ugric people outside the Finnish borders became limited after the Russian revolution, and ethnology began to orient itself to the study of Finnish peasant culture on the basis of museological materials. Instead of a theoretical or methodological nationalism (Schiller 2005, p. 439), this limitation was of a practical kind, emerging out of the research practices and the nature of the data. The subsequent accumulation of research materials during the twentieth century was an important factor in formulating the paradigmatic research questions of the disciplines. Folklore studies remained, and parts still remain, internationally oriented, whereas ethnology became more localized and turned more toward the ethnology of Finland, with a strong orientation on the history of localities. Folklore studies retained their folkloristic nature in Finland, asking broad questions in a more comparative way.

RESCUE, RECONSTRUCTION, AND THE ETHNOGRAPHIC ARCHIVES

The criticism aimed at the "taxonomizing and museological traditions" in anthropology (Silverstein 2005) gives the impression that one can ignore all the results of this previous research despite the fact that this now-despised tradition created and accumulated the ethnographic knowledge that enables us to criticize its methods. The same reservation regarding the relevance of ethnographic information can be applied to the materials collected during different periods of Finnish ethnographic research. One of the main contributions of these previous ethnographic interests was the unearthing of materials intended to construct histories of cultural phenomena of varying order. Culture, people, language, and corresponding kinds of emerging entities, which organized the historical questions, required the expansion of the concept of conventional historical sources, and this expansion has had long-lasting effects on the way the past is constructed and the way in which the relationship between the past and present is understood.

The critical study of antiquity as formulated by Friedrich August Wolf at the end of the nineteenth century (Markner & Veltri 1999) and especially the Homeric question raised by his *Prologemena ad Homerum* in 1795 were seminal in the accumulation of ethnographic materials, especially folklore, in Finland. Wolf's works contained three main claims. First, in the spirit of the Renaissance, he claimed only the Greeks and Romans had contributed to the development of civilization, and the rest of the world's cultures were insignificant from the point of view of the present. Second, he claimed Homerian poetry was not the work of a single individual but instead a compilation of the poetic traditions of a cultural community. Third, he used the comparative method of philology to validate his interpretations.

The Homerian question, combined with the demands for cultural recognition, was the theoretical impetus for Elias Lönnrot's interest in Finnish folk poetry. After making an initial survey of available published folk poetry about the hero Väinämöinen, Lönnrot began a systematic collection of the poetry in the field. During 1831 to 1833, Lönnrot made five field trips to collect poetry in Kalevalaic metrics. On the basis of his field materials he decided to create the literary work *The Kalevala*, which then became known as the national epics of Finland. The first edition was published in 1835 and the second, and expanded version, in 1849. Thus Lönnrot's activities replicated all the elements of the Homerian question: He collected folk poetry, canonized it in a single literary work, and thus created a politically significant symbol of national culture. Lönnrot followed the methodological demand of comparative Homerian studies and was adamant in documenting all the variants of the poems. Thus he prepared the foundation for methodological and theoretical developments in Finnish folklore studies. The subsequent documentation of ethnographic data in the collections of the Folklore Archives of the Finnish Literature Society has been aimed at the same goal and, besides the canonical Kalevala, the Society has published all the collected variants of Kalevalaic poems in 34 volumes of *Suomen Kansan Vanhat Runot* (1908–1994) for research purposes.

The later collections of the Folklore Archives and the materials collected among other Finno-Ugric populations in Russia form a body of data that in its quantity and quality corresponds to the achievements of early Indianology (Adams 1998) and the subsequent text tradition in American anthropology (Darnell 1990). The nature of these archival materials as they were narrated or dictated in the field situation, and later even written down by the informants, made it suitable to apply the logic of historical philology to their analysis. The rendition thus priviledged a discourse that was "marking itself as detached from the local and is correspondingly more replicable and is therefore better culture, a distilled type that presents itself as decontectualized or polycontextual" (Urban 1996, p. 42). Metric poetry, fairy tales, songs, and corresponding genres thus constitute the majority of the materials. These materials formed the basis of the emergence of the Finnish method in folklore studies, which dominated the field for nearly a half-century since the publication of its paradigmatic work by Krohn (1918).

The main principles of the Finnish method and its development have been discussed in detail by Kuusi (1980), who derives the applicability of the method from the questions it was supposed to answer. The underlying problem, parallel to that of historical philology, concerns origin and development. The question of the origin's reconstruction derives from the early attempt to reconstruct the original forms of Homerian poetry by comparing all the available variants of the texts. The archivist of the Alexandria library, Aristarchon of Samo, defined the different stages of the method as the following: *recensio* (viewing the data), *examinatio* (examination of data), *divination* (solution), and finally *conjectura* (interpretation). With regard to folklore and ethnology, as well as language studies, the application of this method required collecting data and recording its geographic distribution, which was the method underlying the theory formulation of origin, even the one in the natural sciences that led to the theory of evolution. Conjectural history on the basis of the comparative method thus had an application both in the analysis of culture as well as the analysis of nature.

What is compared and identified as comparable depends on the identification of elements that are supposed to be variants of the same, be they natural species or cultural features. For the early formalizers of the Finnish method, Julius and Kaarle Krohn, the poem was the basic unit of folklore, which could be identified in different variations in several field documentations. The geographic distribution of the poems and a comparison of their features made it possible to construct a developmental series for a poem and reconstruct its original form (Kuusi 1980). The same logic was applied to nonmetric narrative materials in the seminal works of Aarne (1907, 1910), which then culminated in the worldwide catalog of folk narrative types (Thompson 1987). The comparative analysis of the identified items on the taxonomical level of a narrative or poem forced the research to establish lower levels. Aarne's comparisons of fairy tales led him to pay attention to the individual motifs from which they were composed. A motif, as Thompson (1951, pp. 415–16) later defined it, is "the smallest element in a tale having the power to persist in tradition." The worldwide comparison of folklore's elements at different taxonomical levels, from poems to motifs, revealed the ability of these elements to travel independently of population movements. The taxonomization and typologization thus broke down the correspondence of different types of data expected during the first half of the nineteenth century. Culture and people could thus not be conflated in any primordialist way into a permanent species (cf. Silverstein 2005) because both were changing combinations of complex historical processes.

The trend of deconstructing the relationship between people as nations and the ethnographic facts observable at any given time in any given place is obvious in the ethnological research of material culture. From the inception of the practice, researchers were concerned with observing distinct cultural features and their distribution. The institutional basis of the study of material culture was the museum, which was organized on an areal basis. The collection and preservation of antiquities had been organized as a state responsibility since the seventeenth century, and new forms of museum organization began to flourish in the middle of the eighteenth century. The antiquities collections of the University Museum in Helsinki were divided into two departments, one of which was an ethnographic museum, which later developed into The Museum of History and Ethnography. The provincially organized student organizations of the University in Helsinki were encouraged to collect ethnographic materials from their home provinces, and the museum collections and their organization by geographic area reflected this historical interest.

The museum organization and the notion that museum collections formed the proper object of ethnological studies seemed to determine the research interests of the Finnish ethnologists. The rich ethnographic data collected on Finno-Ugric houses (Heikel 1888, Valonen 1963), fishing methods (Schwindt 1905, Sirelius 1906a,b, Vilkuna 1974), and especially ornaments and the artistic features of handicrafts (Heikel 1910–1915; Sirelius 1903, 1904) have been extensively analyzed by ethnologists to the present day. *The Atlas of Finnish Folk Culture* (Vuorela 1976) comprehensively summarizes the geographic-historical treatment of the data, aimed at the reconstruction of possible historical contacts. The distributional studies and typological series of the individual items were analogical to the folkloristic deconstruction of folklore as a narrative whole depicting the past. Both provided only indirect materials for reconstructing the past.

The obvious emphasis on cultural features in the *Atlas* highlights the lack of interest in questions about social organization. This lack of interest becomes even more obvious if one looks at the ethnographic descriptions and analyses of customs connected to social structure, such as weddings or burials. Wedding and funeral rituals have been described in detail, and burial practices have been connected to the well-documented practices of ancestor worship (Hämäläinen 1913, Salminen 1916, Waronen 1898), but the orientation on the history of the practices has hampered any attempts to develop a systematic analysis of kinship. The remarkable exception to this trend is Harva (1940), who has documented kinship systems among the Finno-Ugric people and studied their religious pratices. Voionmaa (1915) also has analyzed the extended family system and its position in the social system in a way that provides a sound basis for the analysis of the dynamics of house society. Later Vilkuna (1964) tried to reconstruct the development of social structure on the basis of ethnographic and historical data with insightful notions about alliance formation.

Despite these exceptions, ethnology's main emphasis remained on cultural features, and the construction of a holistic notion of society and culture, which would have been necessary for the direct application of ethnological research to nationalistic purposes, is lacking. This emphasis is illustrated in all the general ethnographic descriptions of Finnish culture (Sirelius 1920/1921; Talve 1990; Vuorela 1964, 1975) that discuss separate cultural features with an emphasis on their histories and development, without any systematic attempt to create theories of either culture or society. In his review of Vuorela's 1964 book, Gjessing (1966, p. 280) stated that it "is arranged as an historical, atomistic inventory of culture traits among the peoples concerned, and the author has piled together an enormous mass of material...too often irrelevant to the understanding of the cultures dealt with." One can in fact claim that a description of cultures would have been against the presupposition of the ethnological research. As Vilkuna (1975) stressed, political, linguistic, and cultural borders are not congruent but are porous and shifting.

The ethnographic archives that have emerged out of the activities of philological, folkloristic, and ethnological studies in Finland are, as Gjessing rightly noted, enormous. As archives, they are reminiscent of the ethnographic data accumulated by the Boasian tradition in American anthropology. As Boas notes in the introduction to *Tsimshian Mythology*, "material of this kind does not represent a systematic description of the ethnology of a people, but it has the merit of bringing out those points which are of interest to the people themselves" (quoted in Darnell 1990, p. 135). This notion was familiar to Finnish folklorist Krohn (1885) more than 100 years ago when he stated that folk poetry does not consist of ready-made poems and their reproduction, but it consists of constant poetic creation. Thus in the relationship between a rune singer's performance and a rune as an example of a type in the archives, the singer and the rune are phenomena of different order (Hautala 1954, p. 195). The archival material consists of those cultural features that are of enough interest to be constantly replicated and thus form the basis of the cultural resources of creativity. The ethnographic collections in the archives of the National Board of Antiquities, folklore texts accumulated in the Folklore Archives of the Finnish Literary Society, or the materials published in the Journals and Memoirs of the Finno-Ugric Society thus form a bulk of primary sources. They provide the materials for constructing and reconstructing culture and social structure in Finland or among other Finno-Ugric people for anthropologists that are interested in the native's point of view instead of just imposing external categories on the cultures studied.

RECENT TRENDS OF RESEARCH

The formative years of Finnish ethnological studies clearly formulated questions of a historical nature and accumulated materials for finding these questions along the lines of the local version of a four-fields approach. The historical question of the emergence of Finnish culture has recently been discussed in two major symposia. The results of the first meeting were published in 1984 with the title "Suomen kansan esihistorialliset juuret" (Prehistoric Roots of Finnish Population) (Åström 1984). Despite the botanic concept in the title, the contributors looked at the problem from the point of view of different influences from linguistics, archaeology, ethnology, history, ethnography, and genetics. They formulated clearly the problems connected to simple migration theories and emphasized the necessity of taking into account both the continuities and discontinuities in the history of the population and culture. The second volume (Fogelberg 1999) complicates even further the puzzle of the origins, but at the same time it brings out clearly the nature of the historical reconstructions. As Janhunen (1999) stresses in his analysis of the relationship between languages, the notion of a language tree with its concomitant concepts of a protolanguage and an original homeland is a theoretical construct. A protolanguage was not a language used in a speech community, and a homeland was not a place; thus the relationship between present populations and these theoretical constructs is diffuse and indirect.

The utilization of accumulated ethnographic materials on the Finno-Ugric cultural area and different localities in Finland with an emphasis on peasant culture has been complemented to an increasing degree by questions of social history and cultural studies. Research on industrial communities (Spoof 1997), the formation of a working class lifestyle (Sappinen 2000), and the modernization of the Sami reindeer herding economy (Ruotsala 2002) have emphasized the differentiation of cultural practices and have thus changed the focus from historical reconstruction to present-day formations with an attention to social stratification.

Research in folklore, earlier dominated by the Kalevala questions, has transformed the use of accumulated archival materials. The change in orientation from texts to performance has forced researchers to re-evaluate the relationship between the texts in the archives and the practice of singing, telling, or interpreting the world by utilizing received categories and narrative schemes. Whereas the classic text-oriented analysis treated materials in a decontextualized way, new questions have demanded a contextualization at both the individual and social level. The study of traditional narratives such as fairy tales (Apo 1995b) was complemented by new questions. Narrating (Kaivola-Bregenhøj 1996, Siikala 1990) and epic singing (Harvilahti & Kazagaeva 2005, Honko 1998, Tarkka 2005) have been analyzed from the point of view of the dialectics of individuality, performativity, and textuality.

When research began to focus on the life of folklore in society, the different contextual factors determining the performances and their formation also received attention. Social differentiation according to age, social stratification, and gender has received increased attention. Virtanen (1978) has analyzed children's traditions on the basis of a wide range of contemporary materials, and the research has attracted attention among educators and child psychologists. Social differentiation and historical events in Finnish history have been analyzed from the point of view of the participant's experiences and the narrative devices forming the memory of those events. In addition to Armstrong's (2004) anthropological study of Karelian evacuees' memories, Peltonen (1996) has analyzed narrative materials from the Finnish civil war, Pöysä (1997) has researched the construction of the lumber jack's way of life, and Nenola (1982, 2002), Stark (1995), and Apo (1995a) have highlighted the gendered nature of folklore and its uses in definite social contexts.

The study of folk religion and mythology, which was supposed to form a coherent field, has not be superseded, but the interest in comparative studies of belief systems and ritual practices has continued. For this research the extensive ethnographic databases collected in the archives are valuable. Comparative studies of shamanism (Siikala 1978) and Finnish mythology (Siikala 2002) have demonstrated the ability of the old materials to answer contemporary questions.

THE PROBLEM OF NATIVE ANTHROPOLOGY

If we look at the problems of anthropology from the point of view of native anthropology as exemplified by the early Finnish ethnographic research, important qualifications have to be made. Instead of being nationalistic in any direct sense, Finnish research has led to a situation comparable with differences between American and British anthropology as highlighted by Adams. He cites Aidan Southall's claim that the American ethnographic database is so massive that it is impossible for Americans to "get under this pile and see straight into the Other, our anthropological Other" (Adams 1998, p. 363). Adams attributes this disbelief to a kind of chauvinism dating back to colonial times, but other understandings can be offered. The Boasian tradition, concentrating on Native Americans, crested with time into a brand of area studies, which turned inwards and thus lost interest in formulating general and comparative questions. The Finnish tradition provides two contrasting trends in this respect. Folklore remained comparative despite its main focus on Finnish materials. Ethnology, with its institutional basis in museums, narrowed its scope and became basically area studies. Thus one can claim the dividing line between anthropology and national ethnologies is constituted by the fact that the latter has turned into area studies.

If the ultimate aim of anthropology, and ethnology as well, is the immersion into another culture in such a way as to force one to question received ontological presuppositions (Kapferer 2001), one cannot derive the organizing questions of the research from one cultural area only. Crossing the border is a necessary prerequisite for this process. When native anthropology turns into local ethnology or when anthropology of the natives in any locality loses its outside, and thus questioning, perspective, they both turn into area studies with all the ramifications of a limited epistemological position. Area studies are always rich in data and well-informed about their details, but, despite this mastery, the ability to pose new questions is limited. In a bureaucratic welfare state such as Finland, two other factors can limit questions. The formulation of problems can begin to be dominated by local sociopolitical issues or the narcissism of the present as exemplified by most of cultural studies. Both lead to real restrictions and presentism. The limitation applies, however, to the anthropological tradition on the other side as well. Ignoring the local ethnographic data in all its richness leads to a glossing over of differences, however politically correct that may be. This ignoring creates a different kind of area-studies syndrome, where the whole world is the same area dominated by the same principles familiar from the researcher's own society. On both sides one has to have a comparative perspective and master the ethnography to know what it means and to expand anthropological analysis.

ACKNOWLEDGMENTS

I thank all the participants in the Departmental Seminar at the Department of Anthropology at the University of Helsinki for providing stimulus for clarifying my ideas about comparison and area studies.

LITERATURE CITED

Aarne A. 1907. *Vergleichende Märchenforschungen. Mémoirs de la Société Finno-Ougrienne XXV.* Helsinki: Finno-Ugric Soc.

Aarne A. 1910. Verzeichnis der Märchentypen. *Folklore Fellows Communications*, Vol. 1. Helsinki: Academia Scientiarum Fennica

Aarne A. 1961. *Antti Aarne, the Types of the Folktale: A Classification and Bibliography/Antti Aarne's Verzeichnis der Märchentypen. Folklore Fellows Communications No. 184.* Transl. S Thompson. Helsinki: Academia Scientiarum Fennica

Abu-Lughod L. 1991. Writing Against Culture. In *Recapturing Anthropology*, ed. R Fox, pp. 137–62. Santa Fe: SAR Press

Adams WY. 1998. *The Philosophical Roots of Anthropology.* Stanford, CA: CSLI Publications

Anderson B. 1991. *Imagined Communities. Reflections on the Origin and Spread of Nationalism.* London: Verso

Anttonen P. 2005. *Tradition Through Modernity: Postmodernism and the Nation-State in Folklore Scholarship.* Helsinki: Finnish Lit. Soc.

Apo S. 1995a. *Naisen Väki: Tutkimuksia Suomalaisten Kansanomaisesta Kulttuurista ja Ajattelusta.* Helsinki: Hanki ja Jää

Apo S. 1995b. *The Narrative World of Finnish Fairy Tales: Structure, Agency and Evaluation in Southwest Finnish Folktales. Folklore Fellows Communications No. 256.* Helsinki: Academia Scientiarum Fennica

Armstrong K. 2004. *Remembering Karelia. A Family's Story of Displacement During and After the Finnish Wars.* New York: Berghahn

Åström SE, ed. 1984. *Suomen Väestön Esihistorialliset Juuret.* Helsinki: Societas Scientiarum Fennica

Barth F, Gingrich A, Parkin R, Silverman S. 2005. *One Discipline, Four Ways: British, German, French, and American Anthropology*. Chicago: Univ. Chicago Press

Besteman C, ed. 1999. *Unraveling Somalia: Race, Class, and the Legacy of Slavery*. Philadelphia: Univ. Penn. Press

Branch M. 1973. *A.J. Sjögren Studies of the North*. Helsinki: Finno-Ugric Soc.

Branch M. 1999. The Academy of Sciences in St. Petersburg as a centre for the study of nationalities in the north-east Baltic. In *National History and Identity: Approaches to the Writing in the North-East Baltic Region Nineteenth and Twentieth Centuries*, ed. M Branch, pp. 122–37. Helsinki: Finnish Lit. Soc.

Bunzl M. 1996. Franz Boas and the Humbolftin tradition: from voklsgeist and national character to an anthropological concept of culture. In *Volksgeist as Method and Ethic: Essays on Boasian Ethnography and the German Anthropological Tradition*, ed. GW Stocking, pp. 17–78. Madison: Univ. Wisc. Press

Castrén M. 1853–1862. *Nordische Reisen un Forschungen von Dr. M.A. Castren Herausgegeben von Anton Schiefner 1–7*. St. Petersburg, Russia: Imperial Acad. Sci.

Clifford J, Marcus G, eds. 1986. *Writing Culture: The Poetics and Politics of Ethnography*. Berkeley: Univ. Calif. Press

Cushman T. 2004. Anthropology and genocide in the Balkans: an analysis of conceptual practices and power. *Anthropol. Theory* 4(1):5–28

Darnell R. 1990. Franz Boas, Edward Sapir, and the Americanist text tradition. *Historiogr. Linguist.* 17(1–2):129–44

Dirks NB, Ortner SB. 1994. Introduction. In *Culture/Power/History: A Reader in Contemporary Social Theory*, ed. NB Dirks, SB Ortner, pp. 3–45. Princeton, NJ: Princeton Univ. Press

Dumont L. 1986. *Essays on Individualism: Modern Ideology in Anthropological Perspective*. Chicago: Univ. Chicago Press

Fogelberg P, ed. 1999. *Pohjan Poluilla: Suomalaisten Juuret Nykytutkimuksen Mukaan*. Helsinki: Societas Scientiarum Fennica

Gellner E. 1964. *Thought and Change*. London: Weidenfeld & Nicolson

Gellner E. 1983. *Nationa and Nationalism*. London: Basil Blackwell

Gelner E. 1987. *Culture, Identity and Politics*. Cambridge, UK: Cambridge Univ. Press

Gjessing G. 1966. Review of Toivo Vuorela: the Fenno-Ugric peoples. *Man* 1(2):280–81

Goody J. 1986. *The Logic of Writing and the Organization of Society*. Cambridge, UK: Cambridge Univ. Press

Hämäläinen A. 1913. *Mordvalaisten, Tšeremissien ja Votjakkien Kosinta ja Häätavoista: Vertaileva Tutkimus*. Helsinki: Finnish Lit. Soc.

Handler R. 1988. *Nationalism and the Politics of Culture in Quebec*. Madison: Univ. Wisc. Press

Harva U. 1940. *Der Bau des Verwandschaftsnamensystems un die Werwanschaftshältnisse bei den Fenno-Ugrien. Finnisch-Ugrische Forschungen No. 26*. Helsinki: Finno-Ugric Soc.

Harvilahti L, Kazagsačeva ZS. 2003. *The Holy Mountain: Studies on Upper Altay Oral Poetry. Folklore Fellows Communications No. 282*. Helsinki: Academia Scientiarum Fennica

Hautala J. 1954. *Suomalainen Kansanrunoudentutkimus*. Helsinki: Finnish Lit. Soc.

Hayden RM. 2005. Inaccurate data, spurious issues and editorial failure in Cushman's "Anthropology and Genocide in the Balkans." *Anthropol. Theory* 5(4):545–54

Heikel AO. 1888. *Die Gebäude der Čeremissen, Mordwinen, Esten und Finnen*. Helsinki: Finno-Ugric Soc.

Heikel AO. 1910–1915. *Die Stickmuster der Tscheremissen*. Helsinki: Finno-Ugric Soc.

Honko L. 1998. *Textualising the Siri Epic. Folklore Fellows Communications No. 264.* Helsinki: Academia Scientiarum Fennica

Janhunen J. 1999. Euraasian alkukodit. In *Pohjan Poluilla: Suomalaisten Juuret Nykytutkimuksen Mukaan*, ed. P Fogelberg pp. 27–37. Helsinki: Societas Scientiarum Fennica

Kaivola-Bregenhøj A. 1996. *Narrative and Narrating: Variation in Juho Oksanen's Storytelling. Folklore Fellows Communications No. 261.* Helsinki: Academia Scientiarum Fennica

Kapferer B. 2001. Star Wars: About Anthropology, Culture and Globalisation. *Suom. Antr.* 26(3): 2–29

Kemiläinen A. 1964. *Nationalism: Problems Concerning the World. The Concept and Classification.* Jyväskylä: Jyväskylän Kasvatusopillinen Korkeakoulu

Kemiläinen A. 2004. Kansallinen identiteetti ruotsissa ja suomessa 1600 ja 1700 luvulla. *Tieteessä Tapahtuu* 8:22–31

Kirkinen H, Nevalainen P, Sihvo H. 1994. *Karjalan Kansan Historia.* Porvoo: WSOY

Korhonen M. 1986. *Finno-Ugrian Language Studies in Finland 1828–1918.* Helsinki: Societas Scientiarum Fennica

Korhonen M, Suhonen S, Virtaranta P. 1983. *Sata vuotta suomen sukua tutkimassa.* Espoo: Weilin & Göös

Krohn J. 1885. *Suomalaisen Kirjallisuuden Historia, Vol. 1.* Osa: Kalevala/Helsinki: Weilin & Göös

Krohn K. 1918. *Kalevalankysymyksiä: Opas Suomen Kansan Vanhojen Runojen Tilaajille ja Käyttäjille ynnä Suomalaisen Kansanrunouden Opiskelijoille ja Harrastajille.* Helsinki: Finno-Ugric Soc.

Kuusi M. 1980. Suomalainen tutkimusmenetelmä. In *Perinteentutkimuksen perusteita*, ed. O Lehtopuro, pp. 21–73. Porvoo: WSOY

Lappalainen JT. 2001. *Sadan Vuoden Sotatie: Suomen Sotilaat 1617–1721.* Helsinki: Finnish Lit. Soc.

Markner R, Veltri G. 1999. *Friedrich August Wolf: Studien, Dokumente, Bibliographie.* Stuttgart: Franz Steiner Verlag

Nenola A. 2002. *Inkerin Itkuvirret.* Helsinki: Finnish Lit. Soc.

Nenola-Kallio A. 1982. *Studies in Ingrian Laments. Folklore Fellows Communications No. 234.* Helsinki: Academia Scientiarum Fennica

Parkin R. 2005. The French-speaking countries. In *One Discipline, Four Ways: British, German, French, and American Anthropology*, ed. F Barth, A Gingrich, R Parkin, S Silverman, pp. 157–53. Chicago: Univ. Chicago Press

Peltonen UM. 1996. *Punakapinan Muistot: Tutkimus Työväen Muistelukerronnan Muotoutumisesta Vuoden 1918 Jälkeen.* Helsinki: Finnish Lit. Soc.

Pöysä J. 1997. *Jätkän Synty: Tutkimus Sosiaalisen Kategorian Muotoutumisesta Suomalaisessa Kulttuurissa ja Itäsuomalaisessa Metsätyöperinteessä.* Helsinki: Finnish Lit. Soc.

Rasila V. 1993. *Pirkanmaan Historia.* Tampere: Pirkaanmaanliitto

Ruotsala H. 2002. *Muuttuvat Palkiset: Elo, Työ ja Ympäristö Kittilän Kyrön Paliskunnassa ja Kuolan Luujärven Poronhoitokollektiiveissa Vuosina 1930–1995.* Helsinki: Suomen Muinaismuistoyhdistys

Salminen V. 1916. *Inkerin Kansan Häärunoelma Muinaisine Kosimis ja Häämenoineen.* Helsinki: Finnish Lit. Soc.

Sappinen E. 2000. *Arkielämän Murros 1960 ja 1970 Luvuilla: Tutkimus Suomalaisen Työväestön Elämäntavoista ja Niiden Paikallisista Raumalaisista Piirteistä.* Helsinki: Suomen Muinaismuistoyhdistys

Schiller NG. 2005. Transnational social fields and imperialism: bringing a theory of power to transnational studies. *Anthropol. Theory* 5(3):439–61

Schwindt Th. 1905. *Suomalainen Kansatieteellinen Kuvasto I. Metsänkäynti ja Kalastus*. Helsinki: Suomen Valtio

Sihvo H. 1999. Karelia: a source of Finnish national history. In *National History and Identity: Approaches to the Writing in the North-East Baltic Region Nineteenth and Twentieth Centuries*, ed. M Branch, pp. 181–201. Helsinki: Finnish Lit. Soc.

Siikala AL. 1978. *The Rite Technique of the Siberian Shaman. Folklore Fellows Communications No. 220*. Helsinki: Academia Scientiarum Fennica

Siikala AL. 1990. *Interpreting Oral Narrative. Folklore Fellows Communications No. 245*. Helsinki: Academia Scientiarum Fennica

Siikala AL. 2002. *Mythic Images and Shamanism: A Perspective on Kalevala Poetry. Folklore Fellows Communications No. 280*. Helsinki: Academia Scientiarum Fennica

Silverstein M. 2005. Languages/cultures are dead! Long live the linguistic-cultural! In *Unwrapping the Sacred Bundle: Reflection on the Disciplining of Anthropology*, ed. DA Segal, SJ Yanagisako, pp. 99–125. Durham, NC: Duke Univ. Press

Sirelius UT. 1903. *Die Handarbeiten der Ostjaken und Wogulen*. Helsinki: Finnish Lit. Soc.

Sirelius UT. 1904. *Ostjkkien ja Wogulien Tuohi ja Nahkakoristeita: Ornamente aud Birkenrinde und Fell bei den Ostjaken und Wogulen*. Helsinki: Finno-Ugric Soc.

Sirelius UT. 1906a. *Suomalaisten Kalastus*. Helsinki: Finnish Lit. Soc.

Sirelius UT. 1906b. *Über die Sperrfischerei bei den Fnnisch-Urischen Völkern: Eine Vergleichende Ethnographische Untersuchung mit 607 Figuren*. Helsinki: Finno-Ugric Soc.

Sirelius UT. 1920/1921. *Suomen Kansanomaista Kulttuuria: Esineellisen Kansatieteen Tuloksia*. Helsinki: Otava

Sjögren AJ. 1861. Die Syrjänen. In *Gesammelte Schriften, Vol. 1*, ed. FJ Wiedemann, pp. 234–459. St. Petersburg, Russia: Academy of Sciences

Spoof SK. 1997. *Savikkojen Valtias: Jokelan Tiilitehtaan Sosiaalinen ja Fyysinen Miljöö*. Helsinki: Suomen Muinaismuistoyhdistys

Stark L. 1995. *Gender, Magic and Social Order: Ideologies of Pairing, Household, and the Female Body in Finnish-Karelian Folklore*. Helsinki: Finnish Lit. Soc.

Suomen Tilastollinen Vuosikirja. 1907. Helsinki: Tilastokeskus

Talve I. 1990. *Suomen Kansankulttuuri*. Helsinki: Finnish Lit. Soc.

Tarkka L. 2005. *Rajarahvaan Laulu: Tutkimus Vuokkiniemen Kalevalamittaisesta Runokulttuurista 1821–1921*. Helsinki: Finnish Lit. Soc.

Thompson S. 1951. *The Folktale*. New York: Dryden Press

Thompson S. 1987. *Antti Aarne, the Types of the Folktale: A Classification and Bibliography/ Antti Aarne's Verzeichnis der Märchentypen (FFC No. 3) Translated and Enlarged*. Helsinki: Academia Scientiarum Fennica

Urban G. 1996. Entextualization, replication, and power. In *Natural Histories of Discourse*, ed. M Silverstein, G Urban, pp. 21–44. Chicago: Univ. of Chicago Press

Valonen N. 1963. *Zur Geschichte des Finnischen Wohnstubes*. Helsinki: Finno-Ugric Soc.

Vilkuna K. 1964. *Kihlakunta ja Häävuode: Tutkielma Suomalaisen Yhteiskunnan Järjestymisen Vaiheilta*. Helsinki: Otava

Vilkuna K. 1974. *Lohi: Kemijoen ja sen Lähialueen Lohenkalastuksen Historia*. Helsinki: Otava

Vilkuna K. 1975. Kieliraja, etninen raja, kulttuuriraja. Plenary lecture, IV International Fenno-Ugric Congress, Budapest. In *Pars I. Acta Sessionum*, ed. J Gulya, pp. 49–58. Budapest: Akademi Kiado

Virtanen L. 1978. *Children's Lore*. Helsinki: Helsinki: Finnish Lit. Soc.

Voionmaa V. 1915. *Suomen Karjalaisen Heimon Historia*. Helsinki: Kansanvalistusseura

Vuorela T. 1964. *The Finno-Ugric Peoples*. Bloomington: Indiana Univ. Press

Vuorela T. 1975. *Suomalainen Kansankulttuuri*. Porvoo: WSOY

Vuorela T. 1976. *Suomen Kansankulttuurin Kartasto. Atlas der Finnischen Volkskultur, Atlas of Finnish Folk Culture*, Vol. 1. Helsinki: Finnish Lit. Soc.

Vuorela T. 1977. *Ethnology in Finland Before 1920*. Helsinki: Societas Scientiarum Fennica

Waronen M. 1898. *Vainajainpalvelus Muinaisilla Suomalaisilla*. Helsinki: Finnish Lit. Soc.

Wilson WA. 1976. *Folklore and Nationalism in Finland*. Bloomington: Indiana Univ. Press

What Cultural Primatology Can Tell Anthropologists about the Evolution of Culture

Susan E. Perry

Cultural Phylogeny Group, Max Planck Institute for Evolutionary Anthropology, Deutscher Platz 6, 04103 Leipzig, Germany; Department of Anthropology/Behavior, Evolution, and Culture Group, University of California, Los Angeles, California 90095-1553; email: sperry@anthro.ucla.edu

Annu. Rev. Anthropol. 2006. 35:171–90

First published online as a Review in Advance on May 10, 2006

The *Annual Review of Anthropology* is online at anthro.annualreviews.org

This article's doi: 10.1146/annurev.anthro.35.081705.123312

Copyright © 2006 by Annual Reviews. All rights reserved

0084-6570/06/1021-0171$20.00

Key Words

primates, traditions, cultural transmission, social learning

Abstract

This review traces the development of the field of cultural primatology from its origins in Japan in the 1950s to the present. The field has experienced a number of theoretical and methodological influences from diverse fields, including comparative experimental psychology, Freudian psychoanalysis, behavioral ecology, cultural anthropology, and gene-culture coevolution theory. Our understanding of cultural dynamics and the evolution of culture cannot be complete without comparative studies of (*a*) how socioecological variables affect cultural transmission dynamics, (*b*) the proximate mechanisms by which social learning is achieved, (*c*) developmental studies of the role of social influence in acquiring behavioral traits, and (*d*) the fitness consequences of engaging in social learning.

INTRODUCTION

The study of culture has been central in the field of anthropology since the founding of the discipline. The question of how the human cultural capacity evolved is one of the few questions to which all four subfields of anthropology can make significant and complementary contributions. The purpose of this review is to describe the progress that cultural primatology has made in defining how cultural processes operate and how culture evolved, and to relate this progress to research efforts in other branches of anthropology.

One of the problems that has hampered anthropology's progress as a cohesive discipline in studying culture is the lack of a commonly shared definition of what culture is. There are hundreds of definitions, but most fall into two classes: those focusing on observable behavioral variation, and those focusing on the mental processes or constructs responsible for producing cultural variants. Because of the difficulty in directly accessing the contents of nonhuman primates' minds, cultural primatologists have adopted the former type of definition. Here I define culture as behavioral variation that owes its existence at least in part to social learning processes, social learning being defined as changes in behavior that result from attending to the behavior or behavioral products of another individual. This definition of culture will be viewed as overly simplified by some scholars, but it has the advantage of being easily operationalized and relevant to both humans and nonhumans. Also, it captures the core element of all previous definitions in cultural primatology and virtually all previous definitions within cultural anthropology: the idea that information, skills, practices, or beliefs are transmitted via social inheritance rather than through genetic inheritance [see Laland & Hoppitt (2003), Durham (1991), and Kroeber & Kluckhohn (1952) for further discussion of definitions of culture].

CULTURAL PRIMATOLOGY: HISTORY OF APPROACHES

Japanese Foundations

The field of cultural primatology was founded by the Japanese researcher Kinji Imanishi, who in his 1952 paper on "The Evolution of Human Nature" inspired Japanese primatologists to search for between-group differences in behavior in nonhuman primates. In the decades that followed, a group of dedicated researchers produced a steady stream of papers documenting interesting within- and between-site variability in the diet, food-processing techniques, courtship signals, bathing habits, grooming techniques, and solitary play habits of Japanese macaques, *Macaca fuscata* (reviewed in Itani & Nishimura 1973, McGrew 1998, Perry & Manson 2003). These papers are noteworthy for their richness of description of the transmission process; many report the precise order in which individuals acquired novel traits and discuss this finding in the context of the social organization of the group, reporting group members' kinship, rank, and spatial organization. In these early papers, researchers assumed that behavior was determined either by species-universal "instinct" or by "culture," i.e., that variability in behavior was necessarily a consequence of culture. They did not seriously consider the possibility that subtle variations in ecology or individual experience could induce individuals to behave differently from conspecifics at other places owing to asocial learning processes.

"Cultural Panthropology" and its Offshoots

With rare exceptions (e.g., Green 1975, Stephenson 1973, McGrew & Tutin 1978, Hannah & McGrew 1987), Western scientists ignored the developing field of cultural primatology until the 1990s, when the community of chimpanzee (*Pan troglodytes*) field researchers began reporting striking intersite behavioral variation, particularly with regard to tool use (e.g., Boesch 1996, Nishida 1987). This body of research received far more attention from the scientific community generally, in part because more of it was written in English and in part perhaps because anthropologists found it more plausible to accept the notion of culture in the closest living relative to humans than they did in a monkey species. The goal of many of these early chimp culture papers was apparently to convince cultural anthropologists that humans are not alone in exhibiting culture, that there is evolutionary continuity between humans and other primates regarding cultural diversity and reliance on social learning. These publications (particularly Boesch 1996, McGrew 1992, Whiten et al. 1999) focused on documenting the geographic distribution of behavioral variants across study sites, creating a sort of "chimpanzee relations area file." One strength of this body of work is the acknowledgment that not all between-site behavioral variation is necessarily cultural in origin; some variation may be due to intersite genetic variation or to ecological differences that lead individuals at different sites to arrive at different behavior patterns because of asocial learning processes (i.e., trial-and-error learning) (Nishida 1987, Whiten et al. 1999). However, in contrast with the earlier Japanese macaque research, the chimpanzee field researchers rarely described in their "culture" papers the relevant aspects of within-community social dynamics that may have produced the observed patterns of behavioral variation. Perhaps in part for this reason, nonprimatologists reading these lists of putative cultural differences (divorced from descriptions of the complex social dynamics of chimpanzees that are presumably involved in creating and maintaining these variations) perceived chimpanzee "culture" as rather sterile in comparison with their conceptions of human culture. It is not entirely clear why the chimpanzee researchers abandoned the Japanese researchers' tradition of supplementing discussions of social transmission sequences with richly detailed "simian so-ciology." Perhaps it is because transmission chains are harder to document accurately in a fission-fusion species like chimpanzees, in which all members of the same social group are rarely found in the same place at the same time, than in stable social groupings like those of macaques. Also, behavioral analyses that are relatively easy to accomplish for stable social groups can be methodologically more difficult in fission-fusion species, in which most group members are out of view of one another most of the time, and not all dyads have equal opportunities to interact with one another. Another factor may be that the two most prestigious scientific journals (*Science* and *Nature*) limit contributions to a few pages, making it impossible to report the contextual detail that was typical of early Japanese cultural primatology. Certainly the chimpanzee researchers writing about culture were well aware of the complexities of chimpanzee social structure and relationship negotiation; in fact, some of them had written extensively about these topics in other venues. They simply had not integrated this information into their articles on culture to the extent that Japanese researchers had.

The landmark publication of the "cultural panthropologists," to use Whiten's (2003) memorable phrase, appeared in *Nature* and included an impressive list of 39 behavior patterns (*a*) that were present in some chimpanzee communities but not others and (*b*) for which ecological explanations of the geographic variation seemed improbable (Whiten et al. 1999). This paper set chimpanzees apart from other nonhuman primates as the species having the most elaborate cultural diversity. However, similar collaborative studies had never been performed on other species; it is quite likely that the "behavioral diversity gap" between chimpanzees and other primates will shrink once equivalent studies are performed, just as the Whiten et al. (1999) study shrank the gap between chimpanzees and humans. One other study, on orangutans, of similar design has been published since Whiten's. Orangutans seem like unlikely candidates for cultural diversity because they lead a more solitary existence than practically any other anthropoid primate, yet van Schaik and his colleagues (2003) documented 24 behavioral variants suspected to be cultural in a study comparing 6 study sites in Sumatra and Borneo. The orangutan's virtually solitary life makes it, in some ways, an ideal candidate for documenting the acquisition of behavioral traits from particular social partners because each individual has extensive contact with only one or two other associates. Thus, Russon (2003) has the best data set documenting social influence on development of foraging techniques for any wild ape, and her data make more plausible the claim that the intersite variation seen in orangutans is truly cultural in nature. Recent work by Whiten et al. (2005) on captive chimpanzees also lends credence to the idea that observed patterns of variation in the field are possibly socially learned by demonstrating that (a) individuals can acquire new techniques for gaining food by watching a group member who has been trained by an experimenter, and (b) chimpanzees who know multiple techniques tend to conform to the technique predominantly used by their companions.

Many theoretical reasons show that traditions are as common in many monkey species as they are in apes and that they simply have not been discovered owing to lack of research effort by researchers interested in such questions (Perry & Manson 2003). In general, monkeys live in social settings in which they have a larger number of social contacts from whom they could acquire behavioral practices, relative to those apes (chimps and orangutans) in which cultural diversity has been documented best. Also, many monkeys are omnivorous (which should make social cues useful in making food choice decisions) and engage in extractive foraging (which would make tool use and other complex foraging techniques useful). Likewise, many monkeys exhibit cooperative social relationships and live in complex social environments of the type that might necessitate extensive communication about their relationships and promote the development of flexible bond-testing rituals (Perry et al. 2003a).

Mechanisms of Social Learning

While field researchers in the 1990s were busy documenting behavioral variations in chimpanzees, laboratory researchers were hard at work documenting the cognitive mechanisms underlying cultural transmission. Early work on the cognitive psychology of social learning was guided by two conflicting anthropomorphic assumptions, both of which turned out to be false to some degree. Because imitation (copying of a model's motor actions) comes so easily to human children, and because folklore about primates is riddled with "monkey see, monkey do" stories, some researchers (e.g., the early Japanese primatologists) started with the assumption that imitation must be easy, a cheap trick for learning many new skills quickly. Other researchers, noting that extreme cultural elaboration in humans greatly exceeded cultural capacities in nonhumans, assumed that some extremely complex cognitive machinery must be necessary to produce culture; therefore, they speculated that there would be sharp differences between humans and apes, and likewise between apes and monkeys, in their capacities to learn socially, innovate, and form traditions. Tomasello & Call (1997), in their review of the literature, found considerable evidence for simple forms of social learning such as local and stimulus enhancement (i.e., being attracted to a particular object or location with which a model is engaged) and emulation learning (observational learning of the cause-and-effect relationships created by a model's manipulations) in both monkeys and apes. The apes were better than monkeys at emulation, and human-raised apes were far better at imitation than either ape-reared apes or monkeys. The general conclusion by the early 1990s was that copying motor actions was easy for humans, difficult for apes (although present at least in human-reared, i.e., "enculturated," apes) and essentially absent in monkeys (Byrne 1995, Tomasello 1996).

Some of the most detailed and careful work on social learning was performed on captive brown capuchin monkeys (*Cebus apella*) by Fragaszy's and Visalberghi's labs (see Fragaszy et al. 2004 for a review of this body of work). The tasks that they gave their animals were all centered around food choice and food-processing techniques (some requiring merely dexterity, such as foraging on pumpkin seeds, and others requiring tool use such as nut cracking, obtaining peanuts from inside glass tubes with sticks, and operating a juice dispenser). The general conclusions from these experiments were that social influence is important in the development of particular skills and preferences but that relatively simple social-learning processes such as social facilitation (an increase in a behavioral element already present in the repertoire that is contingent on concurrent performance of the same behavior by others in the vicinity), stimulus enhancement, and local enhancement, rather than imitation, are typically employed by the monkeys. For example, in the food choice experiments, the subject monkeys were stimulated to increase their consumption of both novel and familiar foods when the demonstrator monkey was also eating, but they did not prefer the particular food eaten by the demonstrator (Visalberghi & Addessi 2003). They argued that capuchins' tendencies to coordinate their activities in space and time channel their behavior such that they are likely, in the wild, to end up trying the foods eaten by the more knowledgeable members of their social group, even if they do not attend very well to the specific properties of those foods. Capuchins who were given ample opportunity to observe experienced monkeys poking sticks through tubes to remove the peanuts inside them failed to show that they understood the relevant aspects of the tube, implying that they were not imitating the model. Again, it seems that capuchin monkeys do gain an enthusiasm for particular tasks and objects by watching others engage in them, even though they do not learn fine-grained details about the way in which objects are to be manipulated. Visalberghi (1993) and Fragaszy et al. (2004) concluded that the role of social influence is to channel the monkeys' attention toward particular objects and general activities, after which they gain knowledge of the task via trial-and-error learning.

Puzzlingly, however, results from wild *Cebus capucinus* in the field indicate that young capuchins do visually attend to the specific properties of foods being processed by groupmates: They show significant preferences for observing groupmates who are foraging on food items that are rarer in the diet, as well as those items that require more complex processing, which suggests that they are seeking out rather specific information about what to eat and how to process food (Perry & Ordoñez 2006). Data from wild *C. capucinus* also show that the more time pairs of monkeys spend in close association with one another, the more likely they are to share a particular foraging technique (Panger et al. 2002; S. Perry, unpublished observations); such results are difficult to reconcile with a social-learning model that excludes imitation entirely. Although imitation is difficult for most nonhuman primates, and it is not nearly so often employed in their daily lives as are the cognitively simpler social-learning mechanisms, imitation is nonetheless possible for many nonhuman primates under a narrow range of circumstances. This interpretation is consistent with one captive study that produced some suggestive evidence that capuchins can imitate under certain conditions, although they appear to do it quite rarely (Custance et al. 1999).

Numerous studies of imitation have been done in a variety of taxa in the past decade, and now the distinctions drawn previously are less well defined (see Whiten et al. 2004 for a review of social learning in apes). Researchers have documented imitative capacities not only in chimpanzees and orangutans, but even in callitrichids (Voelkl & Huber 2000) and in some nonprimates (e.g., birds: Zentall 2004).

To summarize the state of the literature on social-learning mechanisms, the picture is still murky as to which mechanisms are employed by which species and under which circumstances, and much work is still needed to sort out this mess (see for example Whiten et al. 2004). There are, however, some clear take-home messages. All primate species that have been thoroughly investigated rely on a number of social-learning mechanisms, some of them quite simple (e.g., attraction to locations occupied by groupmates or to objects being handled by groupmates) and others perhaps more cognitively challenging (such as association of an object with a particular behavioral goal; or imitation of fine motor details). The simpler mechanisms are more commonly employed than is true imitation in monkeys, apes, and even humans (Tomasello 1999). True imitation is not an exclusively human cognitive trick, but it is certainly more commonly used by humans than by other species (Boesch & Tomasello 1998, Tomasello 1999). One of the main challenges for psychologists working in this area will be to determine which factors trigger the use of certain types of social-learning mechanisms as opposed to others. Which features of the task, of the demonstrator, and of the social context stimulate the animal to pay attention to details such as the physical properties of the objects being manipulated (e.g., color, smell, size, shape), the motor movements of the demonstrator, the apparent behavioral goals of the demonstrator (as determined by the consequences of their actions), or the movements of manipulated objects relative to other objects?

Cultural Transmission Theory

The study of culture in nonhumans became far more interesting theoretically when behavioral ecologists began to focus on culture. Theoreticians such as Boyd & Richerson (1985), Cavalli-Sforza & Feldman (1981), and Laland (Laland & Kendal 2003) began to model gene-culture coevolution and to promote cultural transmission as a topic that had

relevance to biology (see Richerson & Boyd 2004 for an accessible account of the ideas expressed by these formal models, and Durham 1991 for empirical examples of gene-culture coevolution). For the first time, culture was viewed as a topic of serious scientific inquiry in biology, and behavioral biologists were captivated by the idea that certain behaviors could be inherited socially in a manner roughly analogous to the way in which genetic inheritance occurs. Laland and his colleagues (Laland & Kendal 2003, Odling-Smee et al. 2003) were particularly influential as ambassadors of gene-culture coevolution theory to primatologists, and they emphasized that socially learned behaviors could alter the environment in such a way that the modified environment exerted selective pressure on genetically inherited traits. This process by which animals can, by their own behavior, alter the selective pressures on future generations was dubbed niche construction (Odling-Smee et al. 2003). Although I know of only one empirical study in primatology that directly incorporates this idea (Flack et al. 2006), it was nonetheless an effective attention getter in that it branded social learning as a topic of evolutionary importance and thereby diverted research effort toward social learning in general.

The Socioecology of Animal Social Learning and Traditions: What, Why, When, and Who?

Once more behavioral ecologists joined the cultural primatology bandwagon, the research emphasis started to shift away from the question "Does Species X have culture?" to more theoretically interesting questions such as "Under which conditions should individuals engage in social learning?," "Who should an individual copy?," "How do various socioecological variables affect the dynamics of social transmission?," and "What adaptive benefits accrue to animals who engage in social learning?" (see Laland 2004 for a cogent discussion of the first two issues). Several research programs are actively engaged in answering the first three questions [see for example papers in Box & Gibson 1999, Fragaszy & Perry 2003a, Heyes & Galef 1996, as well as the special issue of *Learning and Behavior* (2004; vol. 32, number 1) devoted to social learning]. The latter question ("How is social learning adaptive?") remains difficult to answer in an empirically rigorous way, although it is the topic of frequent speculation. Clearly the social learning of new foraging strategies improves the efficiency of foraging, and perhaps opens up new resources that would otherwise be unavailable (e.g., Boesch & Boesch 1990). Some scholars have proposed that social learning may aid primates in identifying predators and medicinal plants, guide choices of where to look for food, determine appropriate travel routes, define group membership, determine appropriate mating or social partners, assess rivals, and communicate about the quality of social relationships (see review in Perry 2003). **Table 1** shows a few examples of putative traditions documented (with varying levels of certainty about the role of social influence) in the four best-studied primate genera. This is by no means an exhaustive review of wild primate traditions, but the review articles cited in the table will direct the reader to most well-documented primate traditions discovered prior to 2003.

Some researchers focused primarily on how the speed and extent of cultural transmission is affected by various sorts of demographic conditions or behavior types. For example, Huffman & Hirata (2003) found no consistent effect of group size on diffusion rates, although they did find that innovations regarding food type and experimental tasks spread more slowly than do play and food-processing innovations. Similarly, van Schaik & Pradhan (2003) created a model that suggests that group size has very little impact on the likelihood of social transmission. Other researchers emphasized how factors such as the rate of environmental change, the cost of acquiring a trait by trial-and-error learning, and the relative reliability of social versus asocial cues would affect the tendency of animals to engage in social learning (see reviews by Dewar 2003, Laland 2004, Laland & Kendal 2003, Richerson & Boyd 2004). These topics were also pursued by empirical researchers of birds, rodents, and other species (see for example Fragaszy & Perry 2003a). But the most quintessentially primatological topic to emerge during this time period was the study of how personality factors, emotions, and the quality of social relationships influence the probability that social learning will occur. Nonhuman primates, like humans, exhibit considerable interindividual variation in personality types and emotional expression, and they live in complex societies in which social relationships are often sharply differentiated (Aureli & Schaffner 2002, Capitanio 2004). For these reasons, it seems logical to assume that not all pairs of individuals are equally likely to learn from one another, and a good understanding of the social dynamics of a society will enhance our understanding of the dynamics of cultural transmission.

The Japanese primatologists recognized early on that there must be some link between factors such as personality, social dynamics, and the effectiveness of social transmission (Imanishi 1957). This early work was inspired by a Freudian theoretical framework rather than a socioecological one (the field of socioecology had yet to be created) and was supported more by case studies and anecdotes (as is typical in psychoanalytic research) rather than by more systematic quantitative tests of hypotheses. Imanishi's writings were somewhat vague on the mechanics of how identification (the "mechanism for introducing culture into personality") worked, and his assumptions regarding young animals' choices of role models (i.e., that cultural traits were learned almost exclusively from the mother and from the "leader male") were not rigorously tested. Kawamura (1959) also emphasized the importance of troop-specific attitudes as key factors determining the ease of social transmission and the importance of relationship quality in predicting the probability of transmission. He noted that the

Table 1 Examples of putative primate traditions in various behavioral domains

Genus	Food processing technique	Food choice	Interspecific interactions; hunting techniques	Courtship signal	Other communicative signal	Self-care	Other
Pan (Common chimpanzees, bonobos)[a,b,c]	Nut-cracking with hammer and anvil; termiting sticks			Leaf clipping	Leaf clipping; hand clasp grooming; different display styles	Rain hats; toothpicks; nest covers (bonobos)	
Pongo (orangutans)[d]	Stick tools for *Neesia* seed extraction or to probe treeholes; leaf gloves		Loris eating		Kiss squeaking	Scratching sticks	Raspberry sound during nest building
Cebus (capuchins)[e,f]	Nut cracking with hammer and anvil		Squirrel neck biting; army ant following		Handsniffing; "games"; eyeball poking; sucking body parts		
Macaca (macaques)[g,h]	Potato and wheat washing	Fish eating		(various)	Begging gesture	Louse handling techniques	Stone handling

[a]Whiten et al. 1999.
[b]Ingmanson 1996.
[c]Hohmann & Fruth 2003.
[d]van Schaik et al. 2003.
[e]Ottoni & Mannu 2001.
[f]Perry et al. 2003b and S. Perry, unpublished data.
[g]Itani & Nishimura 1973.
[h]see review of wild monkey traditions (Perry & Manson 2003).

monkeys of some troops were far more re-laxed around humans and also more curious about novel items being held by their group-mates, and those groups exhibiting more open attitudes were more likely to acquire and transmit new behaviors such as the adop-tion of novel dietary items. Kawamura, like Imanishi, thought that the social organization contributed to the acquisition of a basic atti-tude that was then adopted (somehow by so-cial transmission) by all group members (Itani & Nishimura 1973) and that this attitude facil-itated or inhibited social-learning processes. Subsequent work by researchers working with Japanese macaques were attentive to factors such as kinship, rank, class, and centrality in the group's spatial structure when describing patterns of social transmission [see Itani & Nishimura (1973) for an English review of this literature]. Itani emphasized the impor-tance of knowing the history of experiences for the members of each troop: For exam-ple, history of provisioning can have a pro-found effect on the openness of monkeys to trying new foods (Itani & Nishimura 1973). The patterns that emerged were fairly com-plicated, such that it was not possible to make strong generalizations about how particular social and demographic factors influenced so-cial transmission; rather, the type of cultural trait (e.g., food choice, food processing, play-related behavior) had a strong impact on the transmission speed, the type of innovator, and the pathway by which social transmission oc-curred (e.g., by mother to offspring, from peers to peers, etc.) (Huffman 1996, Huffman & Hirata 2003). This makes sense because no one individual is likely to be the most knowl-edgeable and skilled performer of all types of behaviors, nor do all group members have the same needs regarding the sorts of behaviors that are appropriate for them to learn at a particular time in their lives. A more sophis-ticated and flexible social-learning strategy is expected that takes into account the observer's current knowledge and skills, the availability of asocial cues for learning the necessary skills, the skill level and tolerance levels of avail-

able models, and the specifics of the task itself (Laland 2004).

After a long gap in which there was very little further discussion of the role of person-ality and social dynamics in social transmis-sion processes, an important theoretical pa-per was published emphasizing that "more extensive and more frequent behavioral co-ordination in time and space will be achieved among groups exhibiting an egalitarian or tol-erant style of social dynamics" (Coussi-Korbel & Fragaszy 1995, p. 1446) and that such be-havioral coordination is presumed to enhance the effectiveness of social learning. If two in-dividuals can relax in one another's presence without one fearing domination or food theft by the other, then there is more opportunity for the animals to associate frequently and to concentrate on learning a new task in one an-other's presence. The idea that the quality of social dynamics affects the probability of so-cial transmission began to receive more public recognition in anthropology when Boesch & Tomasello (1998) published their theories re-garding the relationship between social struc-ture and social transmission processes. For example, they emphasized that the extent to which social relationships are differentiated (i.e., extreme variation in the quality of rela-tionships between dyads) is expected to affect the homogeneity of cultural traits. Also, the extent to which the social structure is egalitar-ian is predicted to affect the degree to which some group members can impose social norms on others, which in turn will affect the homo-geneity and patterning of cultural transmis-sion. In 1999, van Schaik et al. published their model of the evolution of material culture. One of the central tenets of the van Schaik et al. model was that both gregariousness and interindividual tolerance during foraging ac-tivities are necessary for a tool use innovation to be propagated. Thus far, the van Schaik et al. model has been tested only in a broad-strokes sort of way, for example, by doing cross-site comparisons in which mean party size is used to predict the number of feed-ing traditions at a particular site (van Schaik

2003, van Schaik et al. 2003). No attempt has been made to do the far more time-consuming exercise of investigating within-group diversity of relationship quality, with direct measures of tolerance, and its effects on social transmission. However, this task is currently being undertaken at my field site for white-faced capuchins, as well as by experimental researchers working on social learning in captive brown capuchins (K. Bonnie and F.B.M. de Waal, personal communication).

CULTURAL PRIMATOLOGY AND CULTURAL ANTHROPOLOGY: PROSPECTS FOR MUTUAL INFLUENCE

One of the virtues of the theoretical orientation of cultural primatology that could profitably be imported into cultural anthropology is the tendency to examine multiple levels of explanation (following Tinbergen 1963) for the existence of culture (Fragaszy & Perry 2003b, McGrew 1998). An ethologist studying culture from Tinbergen's approach would ask such questions as the following:

1. Proximate level of analysis: By which mechanisms are cultural traits transmitted from one individual? Which factors enhance or inhibit the social transmission of information or skills?

2. Developmental level of analysis: Over the lifespan of an individual animal, how are new behavioral traits acquired? (e.g., To what extent is social learning involved in the acquisition of new behavioral traits, and from whom is the animal learning these traits?) Which factors speed the acquisition of socially learned traits?

3. Phylogenetic level of analysis: What is the evolutionary history of culture? To what extent was the human form of culture present in our ancestors and our closest living relatives (i.e., the great apes)? Looking across a broad taxonomic range, in what taxa do we see human-like social-learning abilities, and what can this taxonomic distribution tell us about the evolution of culture?

4. Ultimate or adaptive level of analysis (i.e., the typical genetic consequences of engaging in a particular behavior): What is culture good for? What is the adaptive value of having and employing social-learning mechanisms? Under which circumstances is it adaptive to rely on social cues as opposed to asocial cues for making behavioral decisions?

Cultural primatologists and other ethologists have addressed all these questions, whereas cultural anthropologists have tended, throughout the history of the discipline, to focus on a different set of questions. Cultural anthropologists have focused more on the patterning of cultural elements across culture groups (a topic rarely addressed by cultural primatologists, although see Whiten et al. 1999 and van Schaik et al. 2003 for some quite preliminary explorations in this direction). The early diffusionists were interested in how cultural elements were patterned geographically (e.g., Ratzel 1896–1898) and in the way core cultural elements cohered into "worldviews" (Frobenius 1933) or trait complexes (Herskovits 1926). Other scholars, including many archaeologists (e.g., Flannery 1972, 1973) and linguists (e.g., Croft 2000; Labov 1994, 2001; Thomason & Kaufman 1988) examined cultural macroevolution—e.g., the phylogeny of languages and horizontal diffusion of linguistic traits. Ratzel, for example, discusses how migrations and conquests by one ethnic group or another influence cultural diffusion. In this early work, the emphasis was on cultures or cultural traits as the unit of analysis, and the issue of how individual actors come to adopt the customs of their culture was ignored. Later anthropologists such as Kroeber (1963) and Gluckman (1955) emphasized culture change as a product of internal sociopolitical changes rather being primarily a product of contact between culture groups. The emphasis on cultural traits as the unit of analysis is shared by biologically inspired research on memetics (see papers in Aunger 2000 for a critical evaluation of the "meme" concept). Although there is much to be gained from such an approach, it is important to realize that cultural traits do not have a life of their own; they are expressed and transmitted by individual actors, who vary in interesting ways according to their psychological characteristics, developmental histories, and positions in a social network. Both the properties of the "memes" (or cultural traits) and the properties of the individual actors are important when considering the probability of cultural transmission.

Only relatively recently in the history of anthropology have anthropologists begun to localize cultural concepts in the minds of individuals and to consider which factors might make some concepts and practices more stable and transmissible than others. Cognitive anthropologists [e.g., Atran (1990), Boyer (1999), Sperber & Hirschfeld (2004)] discuss this issue at length, as do many linguistic anthropologists [see, for example, Blevins (2004) for proximate and developmental factors affecting the transmission quality of phonological traits, and also references cited in Richerson & Boyd (2004)]. In addressing this issue of the interface between the psychology of learning and the characteristics of cultural traits, cultural primatology is of most use to anthropology generally. Researchers such as Whiten (2002), Tomasello (1999), and Greenfield (Greenfield et al. 2000) have done comparative work with both humans and nonhuman primates examining the cognitive processes involved in social learning. Although our understanding of the specific mechanisms involved in learning is still far from perfect (see above), much headway has been made in determining the similarities and differences between species in their social-learning capacities and also in determining the factors affecting within-species variation in the contexts in which individuals depend on particular types of social cues. New research on the neurobiology of social learning (e.g., work on mirror neurons, which fire both when an action is observed and when it is performed) will no doubt enhance our understanding of the proximate mechanisms underlying social transmission (Williams et al. 2001).

The second important contribution of cultural primatology is the focus on how social and ecological variables (such as those to be described in the final section of this review) affect individuals' tendencies to adopt particular sorts of cultural traits and the focus on how social dynamics affect diffusion of cultural traits. Scholars presume that relationships between these variables will hold in humans as well as in nonhuman primates. Very little work has been done on the precise way in which different relationship qualities and interaction styles (such as tolerance of the teacher or model, history of cooperation and hence trust between the model and learner, dominance style, and mutual emotional engagement/joint attention during the activity) affect the ease of social transmission in humans. However, evidence from studies of Italian schoolchildren demonstrates that early prosocial behavior in humans (whether rated by self, peers, or teachers) is a better predictor of academic performance than is prior academic performance or aggressive tendencies (Caprara et al. 2000). It is not clear which components of prosocial behavior cause this enhancement of sociocognitive abilities. It is extraordinarily difficult to obtain longitudinal data on the details of social dynamics, personality factors, and learning opportunities (not just of academic skills but also of the skills important for daily life) over the course of an individual's development. The fission-fusion nature of human society and the strong objection that privacy-valuing humans exhibit to being followed constantly by a researcher make these sorts of data hard to collect. Although such data are time consuming to collect in any species, it is easier to collect them in nonhuman primates than in humans. Because they share many of those human characteristics that are critical for the emergence of culture, nonhuman primates can provide a useful model for explaining which factors promote social transmission.

Cultural primatologists and cultural anthropologists alike would do well to think more about the role of emotions in facilitating cultural transmission. The subfield of cultural anthropology known as psychological anthropology has addressed this issue in ways that are roughly analogous to the way Japanese primatologists looked at personality and culture. However, psychological anthropologists have used a variety of approaches to study the relationship between personality and culture, some focusing more on individual decision making and others focusing more on broader cultural patterns and culture-specific personalities (see Bock 1988 for a review of the early history of this field). Clearly the types of emotions displayed by models influence the amount and quality of attention they receive from observers, which affects what they learn. Emotions are likely to be particularly important in establishing social norms, in which case the type of emotional display affects the way the two participants in an interaction respond to one another. For example, conformist transmission in humans is likely to be emotionally mediated via shame (Fessler 1999): People are ashamed to be different or to be ridiculed by others, and this simple mechanism is important in giving rise to all sorts of traditions that are seemingly arbitrary, such as which hand to hold your fork in. Shame, pride, and the self-righteousness associated with punishing people for not conforming to social norms may be essential for creating the cultural complexity we see in humans. These emotions are thought to be lacking in nonhuman primates (Fessler 1999), and this lack may explain (proximately and phylogenetically) some of the differences between human cultures and simpler nonhuman cultures. Another factor that may be important in differentiating nonhuman cultures from human cultures is the prevalence of prestige-biased transmission in humans (Henrich & Gil-White 2001); prestige (freely conferred deference based on respect, as opposed to dominance, which is deference due to fear of aggression) is likely a phenomenon that is rare or nonexistent in nonhuman primates, although this is a relatively unexplored area of research in primatology (but see Ottoni et al. 2005). The range of emotions possible in a species may be correlated with the types of cultural transmission, social complexity, and cultural complexity that are possible.

And what can cultural primatologists learn from cultural anthropologists? Cultural anthropologists have always emphasized the importance of historical perspective. Cultural primatology is such a new field that very few currently ongoing studies can claim to have a historical perspective on culture change [although Huffman's (1996) study of stone handling in macaques and the study by Perry et al. (2003a) of the appearance and dissolution of social conventions in capuchins are a step in the right direction]. Primatologists who have studied culture should, research resources permitting, maintain long-term data collection on these topics in the same populations to add a temporal component to their studies. Another important contribution by cultural anthropologists is the emphasis on the patterning of cultural elements [i.e., the study of how certain cultural elements seem to co-occur consistently owing to an underlying symbolically based ideology (Frobenius 1933) or for functional reasons (Harris 1979)]. For example, a particular subsistence style (e.g., horticulture or pastoralism) and its associated technologies tend to co-occur with a particular descent system (e.g., matrilineality or patrilineality) and a particular religion that contains symbolic elements that help organize and reinforce that descent system. Among the most striking differences between human culture and nonhuman primate traditions, given our current understanding of these issues, are (*a*) the difference in the degree to which symbolic communication is inherent in the cultural traits and degree to which cultural traits are clustered around a conceptual core, (*b*) the degree to which active teaching is part of the social transmission process in humans (although it is important to consider the possibility that active teaching plays a more important role in Western cultures than in other human populations), and (c) the extent to which human culture is cumulative—i.e., that new cultural variants are modifications of past cultural variants rather than brand new innovations (Richerson & Boyd 2004, Tomasello 1996, Whiten et al. 2003). Although these differences are important, it nonetheless seems that humans and nonhuman primates have much in common regarding their social transmission processes and that further comparative work will be crucial to understand the evolution of human cultural capacities.

A WORKING MODEL OF HOW CULTURAL TRAITS ARISE

Here I present a model (**Figure 1**) of how most (or at least many) cultural primatologists conceptualize the process of how cultural traits are formed and maintained in nonhuman primates and humans. Although this model has not been presented in its entirety in any other place, work by other authors has developed particular links in this model, as articulated earlier in this paper. Of course, many other aspects of the cultural process have been omitted from this model—for example, I have not explicitly discussed gene-culture coevolution here. The reason is because this topic has not yet been addressed empirically in nonhuman primate studies; nor do I know of any researcher who has imminent plans to do so. A complete model of cultural processes would, of course, have to integrate genetic feedback (Richerson & Boyd 2004).

Basically, cultural primatologists are interested in how external variables (i.e., aspects of the physical and social world) affect particular psychological attributes of animals (i.e., attitudes toward particular tasks and individuals, and also mental representations of particular actions), which in turn affect the tendency for them to exhibit behavior patterns that are either similar to, or different from, the behav-

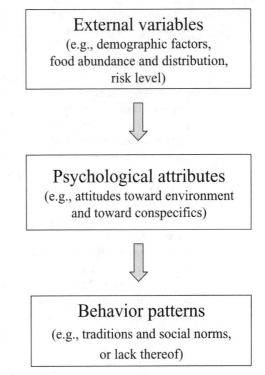

Figure 1

Model of factors affecting the propensity to develop traditions and social norms.

iors of their groupmates in similar contexts. The external variables can exert an effect on psychological attributes and behavior on an evolutionary time scale (via natural selection) and/or on an ontogenetic time scale. Let me first describe in more detail what I mean by each of these three categories and then give some specific examples of how particular sorts of traditions and social norms could arise.

The sorts of external variables I have in mind consist primarily of those variables that have long interested primate socioecologists: aspects of the demography and ecology of the animals. For example, variables such as sex ratio, group size, birth cohort size, and the ratio of adults to immatures in a group will affect the number and type of models from which any particular individual can learn. Availability of models is likely to affect the probability and speed of social transmission of traits, as well as the patterning of the spread of the trait through the group. Ecological variables of interest include food abundance, distribution, and diversity. Variables such as food abundance and distribution influence aspects of primates' social relationships, such as tolerance, dominance style, and propensity to cooperate (van Schaik 1989, 1996). The degree of risk in the environment (e.g., prevalence of exposure to toxins, predators, and dangerous conspecifics) is likely to affect individuals' levels of caution in testing new foods or interacting with unknown animals, which in turn could affect their abilities and propensities to learn about novel foods or animals via asocial means (trial-and-error learning). Another potentially important influence on group dynamics that has not so often been considered is the role of individual personalities, and particularly the personalities of long-term alpha males and females, who set the tone for how tolerant group dynamics can be, in general. To give an example, the successive alpha males of one of my capuchin groups consistently engage in separating interventions, punishing attempts by other males to associate with one another. In contrast, the males of some of my other groups are tolerant of other males' affiliations, such that these males are free to associate and cooperate frequently, and the group has a more relaxed social atmosphere overall. Such influences could persist even after the death or emigration of the animal(s) whose personality created the norm, as in Sapolsky & Share's (2004) documentation of a founder's effect on a culture of peacefulness in baboons.

Psychological attributes include at least two types of phenomena: (*a*) attitudes (e.g., emotional responses to particular types of situations) and (*b*) mental representations of tasks. The first, attitudes, is of primary interest to socioecologists interested in determining how external variables such as those discussed above translate into patterns of behavioral responses because some attitudes are more conducive to social learning than others. Examples of attitudes are tolerance, neophobia, and emotional engagement (high interest level in

an object, task, or individual animal). Tolerance has been hypothesized to enhance the probability of social learning (Coussi-Korbel & Fragaszy 1995, van Schaik et al. 1999). Neophobia decreases the odds that an animal will learn about a new food by trial-and-error learning. Strong expression of emotion by models toward the objects with which they are engaged increases the salience of objects to the observer such that observers are more likely to explore the objects (Fragaszy et al. 2004). And high emotional engagement between participants seems to be a critical feature of traditional bond-testing rituals in capuchins (Perry et al. 2003a) and interaction rituals in humans (Collins 1993). It seems clear that emotions add salience to learning situations, focusing the observer's attention on particular aspects of its environment. Being sensitive to the emotional states and gaze directions of others enables joint attention of the model and the observer on the same aspects of an activity pattern, thereby enhancing the probability that some aspect of the model's knowledge and/or behavior will be acquired by the observer.

The second type of psychological attribute, mental representations, refers to the animal's conceptualization of (*a*) a particular object's properties, (*b*) a particular course of action, (*c*) a cause-and-effect relationship between two objects or individuals, or (*d*) a particular type of social interaction. For one individual to learn socially from observing a demonstrator's actions, the observer will have to produce a mental representation that is at least partially overlapping with the demonstrator's mental representation of the task, although the degree of overlap may be very slight (Richerson & Boyd 2004). It is this particular black box that most concerns those cultural primatologists who do experimental work to discern the precise social learning mechanisms employed by primate species in specific contexts. Of course, it is quite difficult to know what mental representations are present in animals' minds because the only clues we have are their behavioral outputs.

Typically when one primate observes another performing some task and learns socially from these observations, it does not exhibit a perfect replication of what it has observed, which implies that the primate is not conceptualizing the task in exactly the same way as the model. The aspects of a behavioral sequence that seem salient to one observer may not be the same aspects that are salient to another. To give a hypothetical example, if three animals were watching a fourth conspecific crack open nuts with a stone and eat them, one might learn from this observation that nuts are good to eat, the second might learn that combining uncracked nuts and stones produces cracked nuts (without appreciating the importance of the specific motor actions involved), and the third might learn that the specific act of pounding yields food (but may fail to understand why a stone is a particularly good item to pound with). All three of these observers might take the different bits of information they acquired from watching the model and then modify those mental representations with further information acquired from subsequent trial-and-error learning, until they devised their own subtly different techniques for opening nuts. It is devilishly difficult to know exactly how an animal conceptualizes its understanding of a particular task and the exact extent to which one animal's mental representation overlaps with another animal's. But it is important to understand that even if two animals have only partial overlap in their mental representations, they can converge on similar or identical behavior patterns such that a tradition is formed.

Finally let us consider the behavioral patterns that cultural primatologists are trying to explain: traditions and social norms. I define a tradition as a relatively long-lasting behavior pattern shared by multiple practitioners owing to some form of social learning. Most of the traditions that have been studied by cultural primatologists consist of readily identifiable, discrete behaviors (e.g., quirky foraging techniques such as nut cracking or potato washing) that can be reliably coded as present

or absent in a particular individual. Foraging techniques, and material culture in particular, have been a focus of study both in humans and nonhumans because of the ease with which such traits can be identified. But there is another whole type of behavioral patterns, which consists of group-typical responses to particular social situations, that can perhaps be defined best as social norms. Such behavior patterns would technically fit my definition of tradition because of the role of social learning in their establishment, but I distinguish them from traditions merely because they are harder to identify and operationalize. Social norms are patterns of social behavior that typify particular groups and are variable between groups, but which each individual within a group can follow to varying degrees, such that it is difficult to classify any particular individual as possessing or lacking the trait. The acquisition of social norms is directly influenced by social interaction with others but not necessarily by copying what has been observed: The process of internalizing a norm could come about by taking a complementary role in an interaction rather than by adopting the same role as the model. Although the term social norm would imply punishment for violation of a social rule to many scholars, that condition is not a necessary part of my definition for the purposes of this discussion.

A well-documented human example of a social norm is the culture of honor in the southern United States, in which southerners are far more polite than northerners in general but also are far more likely to respond to insults with extreme physiological stress responses and impulsive violence (Nisbett & Cohen 1996). Some nonhuman primate examples of social norms would be peacefulness in the forest baboon troop of Masai Mara (Sapolsky & Share 2004) and matrilineal inheritance of dominance rank in macaques, in which a monkey socially inherits the rank just below her mother and just above the older sister that is closest to her in dominance rank (Chapais 1988). Some primatologists have produced experimental evidence for social norms. For example, rhesus macaques (*Macaca mulatta*) rarely reconcile, yet when de Waal & Johanowicz (1993) housed rhesus juveniles with juvenile stumptail macaques (*M. arctoides*), which reconcile far more frequently, the young rhesus developed a stumptail-like reconciliation rate that persisted after the rhesus were placed back in all-rhesus groups. Yet the rhesus juveniles did not acquire species-typical stumptail reconciliation gestures, suggesting that social attitudes rather than motor patterns were transmitted between individuals of the two species. Also, Kummer (1996) found that female hamadryas baboons (which are accustomed to exclusive relationships with a single male) can quickly adapt to the different consort style of savanna baboons (in which male-female sexual relationships are more fluid and transient and males are less controlling) and vice versa when females from one species are transplanted into groups of the other species.

Further possibilities for cognitive rules in primates in which the role of social learning may prove to be influential are the acquisition of decision rules determining which animal to side with in a coalition (Perry et al. 2004) or the tendency to punish certain behaviors. Social norms are slowly established over time, as maturing animals or immigrants adjust their behaviors in accordance with the behavior patterns exhibited by the majority of animals (or, perhaps, with the behavior patterns exhibited by particular influential animals). Because an individual is unlikely to conform to the norm in 100% of its opportunities to do so, it is difficult to say with certainty when any particular animal has internalized a social norm. Likewise, it is hard to say at a group-wide level when a social norm has been clearly established. For these methodological reasons, and for the reason that vast amounts of behavioral data are necessary to document changes in social norms over the history of a group or in the course of an individual's ontogeny, very few primatologists have devoted research effort to studying social norms. Nonetheless, they are a fascinating topic of inquiry and one that is likely to shed light on the origins of human culture (de Waal 2004). Although most of the empirical anthropological work on the dynamics of human culture change has also focused on material culture and subsistence technology (Richerson & Boyd 2004), perhaps for the same methodological reasons that have created this research bias in cultural primatology, the most profound and subtle aspects of cultural variation clearly center around differences in status relations and appropriate means of negotiating social relationships in a complex society. Although much human relationship negotiation employs symbolic communication in the form of language, many aspects of human social norms consist primarily of gestures, postures, and appropriate behavioral coordination in space and time (for example, culture-specific ways of greeting a socially dominant individual or of resolving a conflict). Social norms of these types may prove not to be so different from social norms in nonhuman primates.

ACKNOWLEDGMENTS

Thanks are given to the Max Planck Institute for Evolutionary Anthropology for funding me while I wrote this review. I also thank Filippo Aureli, Josep Call, Richard Lesure, and Mike Tomasello for helpful discussions, and Joseph Manson for comments on the manuscript.

LITERATURE CITED

Atran S. 1990. *Cognitive Foundations of Natural History: Towards an Anthropology of Science.* Cambridge, UK: Cambridge Univ. Press. 360 pp.

Aunger R. 2000. *Darwinizing Culture: The Status of Memetics as a Science.* Oxford, UK: Oxford Univ. Press. 242 pp.

Aureli F, Schaffner C. 2002. Relationship assessment through emotional mediation. *Behaviour* 139:393–420

Blevins J. 2004. *Evolutionary Phonology: The Emergence of Sound Patterns*. Cambridge, UK: Cambridge Univ. Press. 386 pp.

Bock PK. 1988. *Rethinking Psychological Anthropology: Continuity and Change in the Study of Human Action*. New York: Freeman/Times Books/Holt. 254 pp.

Boesch C. 1996. Three approaches for assessing chimpanzee culture. In *Reaching into Thought: The Minds of the Great Apes*, ed. AE Russon, K Bard, ST Parker, pp. 404–29. Cambridge, UK: Cambridge Univ. Press. 464 pp.

Boesch C, Boesch H. 1990. Tool use and tool making in wild chimpanzees. *Folia Primatol.* 54:86–99

Boesch C, Tomasello M. 1998. Chimpanzee and human cultures. *Curr. Anthropol.* 39:591–614

Box H, Gibson K. 1999. *Mammalian Social Learning: Comparative and Ecological Perspectives*. Cambridge, UK: Cambridge Univ. Press. 438 pp.

Boyd R, Richerson PJ. 1985. *Culture and the Evolutionary Process*. Chicago: Univ. Chicago Press. 340 pp.

Boyer P. 1999. Human cognition and cultural evolution. In *Anthropological Theory Today*, ed. HL Moore, pp. 206–33. Cambridge, UK: Polity/Blackwell. 292 pp.

Byrne R. 1995. *The Thinking Ape*. Oxford, UK: Oxford Univ. Press. 266 pp.

Capitanio J. 2004. Personality factors. In *Macaque Societies: A Model for the Study of Social Organization*. ed. B Thierry, M Singh, W Kaumanns, pp. 13–33. Cambridge, UK: Cambridge Univ. Press. 434 pp.

Caprara GV, Barbaranelli C, Pastorelli C, Bandura A, Zimbardo PG. 2000. Prosocial foundations of children's academic achievement. *Psychol. Sci.* 11:302–6

Cavalli-Sforza LL, Feldman MW. 1981. *Cultural Transmission and Evolution: A Quantitative Approach*. Princeton, NJ: Princeton Univ. Press. 388 pp.

Chapais B. 1988. Rank maintenance in female Japanese macaques: experimental evidence for social dependency. *Behaviour* 104:41–59

Collins R. 1993. Emotional energy as the common denominator of rational action. *Ration. Soc.* 5:203–30

Coussi-Korbel S, Fragaszy D. 1995. On the relation between social dynamics and social learning. *Anim. Behav.* 50:1441–53

Croft W. 2000. *Explaining Language Change: An Evolutionary Approach*. London: Pearson Educ., 287 pp.

Custance DM, Whiten A, Fredman T. 1999. Social learning of an artificial fruit task in capuchin monkeys (Cebus apella). *J. Comp. Psychol.* 113:1–11

De Waal FBM. 2004. Peace lessons from an unlikely source. *PLoS Biol.* 2:434–36

De Waal FBM, Johanowicz DL. 1993. Modification of reconciliation behavior through social experience: an experiment with two macaque species. *Child Dev.* 64:897–908

Dewar G. 2003. The cue reliability approach to social transmission: designing tests for adaptive traditions. See Fragaszy & Perry 2003a, pp. 127–58

Durham WH. 1991. *Coevolution: Genes, Culture and Human Diversity*. Stanford, CA: Stanford Univ. Press. 629 pp.

Fessler D. 1999. Toward an understanding of the universality of second order emotions. In *Biocultural Approaches to the Emotions*, ed. A Hinton. pp. 75–116. New York: Cambridge Univ. Press. 383 pp.

Flack JC, Girvan M, de Waal FBM, Krakauer DC. 2006. Policing stabilizes construction of social niches in primates. *Nature* 439:426–29

Russon AE. 2003. Developmental perspectives on great ape traditions. See Fragaszy & Perry 2003a, pp. 329–64

Sapolsky RM, Share LJ. 2004. A pacific culture among wild baboons: its emergence and transmission. *PLoS Biol.* 2:534–41

Sperber D, Hirschfeld LA. 2004. The cognitive foundations of cultural stability and diversity. *Trends Cogn. Sci.* 8:40–46

Stephenson GR. 1973. Testing for group specific communication patterns in Japanese macaques. *Proc. Fourth Int. Congr. Primatol.* 1:51–75. Basel: Karger

Thomason S, Kaufman T. 1988. *Language Contact, Creolization and Genetic Linguistics.* Berkeley: Univ. Calif. Press. 411 pp.

Tinbergen N. 1963. On aims and methods of ethology. *Z. Tierpsychol.* 20:410–33

Tomasello M. 1996. Do apes ape? See Heyes & Galef 1996, pp. 319–46

Tomasello M. 1999. *The Cultural Origins of Human Cognition.* Cambridge, MA: Harvard Univ. Press. 248 pp.

Tomasello M, Call J. 1997. *Primate Cognition.* Oxford, UK: Oxford Univ. Press. 517 pp.

van Schaik CP. 1989. The ecology of social relationships among female primates. In *Comparative Socioecology: The Behavioural Ecology of Humans and Other Animals*, ed. V Standen, RA Foley, pp. 241–69. Oxford, UK: Blackwell Sci. 424 pp.

van Schaik CP. 1996. Social evolution in primates: the role of ecological factors and male behavior. *Proc. Br. Acad.* 88:9–31

van Schaik CP. 2003. Local traditions in orangutans and chimpanzees: social learning and social tolerance. See Fragaszy & Perry 2003a, pp. 297–328

van Schaik CP, Ancrenaz M, Borgen G, Galdikas B, Knott C, et al. 2003. Orangutan cultures and the evolution of material culture. *Science* 299:102–5

van Schaik CP, Deaner RO, Merrill MY. 1999. The conditions for tool use in primates: implications for the evolution of material culture. *J. Hum. Evol.* 36:719–41

van Schaik CP, Pradhan GR. 2003. A model for tool-use traditions in primates: implications for the coevolution of culture and cognition. *J. Hum. Evol.* 44:645–64

Visalberghi E. 1993. Tool use in a South American monkey species: an overview of the characteristics and limits of tool use in *Cebus apella*. In *The Use of Tools by Human and Non-Human Primates*, ed. A Berthelet, J Chavaillon, pp. 118–31. Oxford, UK: Clarendon. 424 pp.

Visalberghi E, Addessi E. 2003. Food for thought: social learning about food in capuchin monkeys. See Fragaszy & Perry 2003a, pp. 187–212

Voelkl B, Huber L. 2000. True imitation in marmosets. *Anim. Behav.* 60:195–202

Whiten A. 2002. Imitation of sequential and hierarchical structure in action: experimental studies with children and chimpanzees. In *Imitation in Animals and Artifacts*, ed. K Dautenhahn, CL Nehaniv, pp. 191–209. Boston: MIT Press. 625 pp.

Whiten A, Goodall J, McGrew WC, Nishida T, Reynolds V, et al. 1999. Cultures in chimpanzees. *Nature* 399:682–85

Whiten A, Horner V, de Waal FBM. 2005. Conformity to cultural norms of tool use in chimpanzees. *Nature* 437:737–40

Whiten A, Horner V, Litchfield CA, Marshall-Pescini S. 2004. How do apes ape? *Learn. Behav.* 32(1):36–52

Whiten A, Horner V, Marshall-Pescini S. 2003. Cultural panthropology. *Evol. Anthropol.* 12(2):92–105

Williams JHG, Whiten A, Suddendorf T, Perrett DI. 2001. Imitation, mirror neurons and autism. *Neurosci. Biobehav. Rev.* 25:287–95

Zentall TR. 2004. Action imitation in birds. *Learn. Behav.* 32(1):15–23

Indigenous People and Environmental Politics

Michael R. Dove

School of Forestry Studies and Environmental Studies and Department of Anthropology, Yale University, New Haven, Connecticut 06511-2189; email: michael.dove@yale.edu

Annu. Rev. Anthropol. 2006. 35:191–208

First published online as a Review in Advance on July 12, 2006

The *Annual Review of Anthropology* is online at anthro.annualreviews.org

This article's doi: 10.1146/annurev.anthro.35.081705.123235

Copyright © 2006 by Annual Reviews. All rights reserved

0084-6570/06/1021-0191$20.00

Key Words

environmental knowledge, environmental conservation, social movements, ethnographic representation, NGOs

Abstract

Modernity has helped to popularize, and at the same time threaten, indigeneity. Anthropologists question both the validity of the concept of indigeneity and the wisdom of employing it as a political tool, but they are reluctant to deny it to local communities, whose use of the concept has become subject to study. The concept of indigenous knowledge is similarly faulted in favor of the hybrid products of modernity, and the idea of indigenous environmental knowledge and conservation is heatedly contested. Possibilities for alternate environmentalisms, and the combining of conservation and development goals, are being debated and tested in integrated conservation and development projects and extractive reserves. Anthropological understanding of both state and community agency is being rethought, and new approaches to the study of collaboration, indigenous rights movements, and violence are being developed. These and other current topics of interest involving indigenous peoples challenge anthropological theory as well as ethics and suggest the importance of analyzing the contradictions inherent in the coevolution of science, society, and environment.

DEFINITIONS OF INDIGENOUS

Whereas the connotations of popular use of the term indigenous focus on nativeness, formal international definitions focus more on historic continuity, distinctiveness, marginalization, self-identity, and self-governance.

Oxford English Dictionary (1999): 1. Born or produced naturally in a land or region; native or belonging naturally to (the soil, region, etc.). (Used primarily of aboriginal inhabitants or natural products.) 2. Of, pertaining to, or intended for the natives; "native," vernacular.

International Labor Organization (1989): (a) Tribal peoples in independent countries whose social, cultural, and economic conditions distinguish them from other sections of the national community, and whose status is regulated wholly or partially by their own customs or traditions or by special laws or regulations; (b) peoples in independent countries who are regarded as indigenous on account of their descent from populations which inhabited the country, or a geographical region to which the country belongs, at the time of conquest or colonization or the establishment of present state boundaries and who, irrespective of their legal status, retain some or all of their own social, economic, cultural and political institutions. [ILO 1989: Article 1.1]

United Nations (1986): Indigenous communities, peoples, and nations are those which have a historical continuity with preinvasion and precolonial societies that developed on their territories, consider themselves distinct from other sectors of societies now prevailing in those territories, or parts of them. They form at present nondominant sectors of society and are determined to preserve, develop, and transmit to future generations their ancestral territories, and their ethnic identity, as the basis of their continued existence as peoples, in accordance with their own cultural patterns, social institutions, and legal systems. [Cobo 1986, 5: para.379]

INTRODUCTION: THE RISE OF INTERNATIONAL INDIGENISM

Over the past quarter-century, much of anthropology's interest in local, native, autochthonous peoples has been framed in terms of indigeneity, with its focus on history and place. Many local movements that once would have been represented as revolving around race, ethnicity, or religion, have come to be seen—by the participants as well as by analysts—as indigenous rights movements. Subjects of study and debate that would formerly have been represented as peasants or tribesmen have come to be represented as indigenous peoples. Jung (2003) writes that indigenous subjects in Latin America have replaced peasants as the privileged interlocutors of the capitalist state; Tsing (2003) writes of a reimagining in South and Southeast Asia of economically and educationally disadvantaged peasants as culturally marked and naturally wise tribals. The rubber tappers of the Amazon exemplify this shift with their rise to global attention accompanied by their rearticulation as indigenous people of the forest (Keck 1995). Another equally successful rearticulation was that of the Zapatistas of Chiapas: Their little-known peasant land reform movement rose to global prominence after it became reframed as a movement about Indian indigeneity (Nugent 1995).[1] The increasing global importance of indigeneity was reflected in the development of its definition by the United Nations in 1986 and by the International Labor Organization in 1989 (the latter binding on signatories)—both of which defined indigeneity in terms of historic continuity, distinctiveness, marginalization, self-identity, and self-governance—and by the United Nations' declaration of 1995 to 2004 as the "indigenous peoples' decade."

The confluence of forces leading to the conception of indigeneity with such global force has been surprisingly little studied (in contrast to the concept itself). Niezen (2003) attributes the origins of international indigenism to the intersecting development of identity politics and universal human rights laws and principles. Other analyses focus on the delocalizing impact of modernity (Appadurai 1996,

---

[1] See the collected papers on the Zapatistas' movement in *Identities* 3(1–2).

Giddens 1984). Hornborg (1996), for example, suggests that dissatisfaction with the fate of localized systems of resource use under totalizing systems of modernity stimulated interest in indigeneity and indigenous systems of resource knowledge and management. Hirtz (2003) suggests modernity makes indigeneity possible in the first place. He writes, "it takes modern means to become traditional, to be indigenous"; as a result, "through the very process of being recognized as 'indigenous', these groups enter the realms of modernity" (p. 889).

THE CRITIQUE OF INDIGENEITY

The Concept of Indigeneity

The rise of popular international interest in indigeneity is noteworthy, in part, because it was so opposed to theoretical trends within anthropology. During the 1970s and 1980s, anthropological thinking about indigenous peoples was radically altered by world system studies (Wolf 1982) even argued even isolated communities were caught up in global historical processes, which were even responsible for this isolation. Many scholars began to argue that indigenous identity itself was a product of historic political processes. Writing of contemporary Indonesia (and in particular Sulawesi), Li (2000) asserts that unlike the National Geographic vision of tribal peoples, there is a political nature to group formation. Where clear tribal identities are found today, she says, they can be traced to histories of confrontation and engagement, warfare and conflict. Also writing of Southeast Asia, Benjamin (2002, p. 9) similarly argues that, "[o]n this view, all historically and ethnographically reported tribal societies are *secondary* formations." The academic conception of indigeneity also was impacted by influential scholarship on the invention of tradition (Hobsbawm & Ranger 1983) and by the related argument that culture itself is but a construction (Linnekin 1992), so the search

for cultural authenticity is pointless.[2] Drawing on the work of the sociologist and cultural theoretician Stuart Hall, Clifford (2001) and Li (2000) have suggested that one way to elide this debate over authenticity is to focus on the articulation of indigeneity.

The debate over indigeneity came to a head with the publication of Kuper's (2003) critique "The Return of the Native" in which he questioned the empirical validity of claims to this status.[3] The debate that followed indicated that referring to indigeneity as invented was much more controversial than referring to tradition (or perhaps even culture) as invented, suggesting there may be more political capital invested in the former concept than the latter. The impact of Kuper's article came, in part, from making the tensions between science and politics within anthropology explicit and public. He challenged the discipline: "Should we ignore history for fear of undermining myths of autochthony? Even if we could weigh up the costs and benefits of saying this or that, our business should be to deliver accurate accounts of social processes" (Kuper 2003, p. 400). Many who disagreed with Kuper did so on the basis of the politics of science as opposed to the concept of indigeneity itself, which most agree is problematic.

Many anthropologists have commented on the negative political implications of the concept of indigeneity. Some have said it is too exclusive. Gupta (1998, p. 289) writes,

> I fear that there is a heavy price to be paid for the emphasis placed by proponents of indigenous knowledge on cultural purity, continuity, and alterity. Such efforts at cultural conservation make no room for the vast majority of the world's poor, who live on the margins of subsistence and the most degraded ecological conditions but who cannot

---

[2]Compare with Clifford's (1988, p. 1) critique of "pure products."

[3]There was an extended debate regarding Kuper's argument and, more generally, the whole question of indigeneity in 2002–2004 in *Anthropology Today.*

claim to be 'indigenous people' in the limited definition accorded that term.

Similarly, Li (2000, p. 151) writes, "one of the risks that stems from the attention given to indigenous people is that some sites and situations in the countryside are privileged while others are overlooked, thus unnecessarily limiting the field within which coalitions could be formed and local agendas identified and supported." These risks are especially great for people who move about, which reflects the importance of place in conceptions of indigeneity (Li 2000). Whereas nomadism and transhumance fit into a recognized indigenous niche, there are far greater numbers of people involved in resettlement, migration, and flight. Thus the resource knowledge and management skills of urban squatters (Rademacher 2005) and frontier colonists (Brondizio 2004, Campos & Nepstad 2006) have tended to be less visible, less privileged, and less studied.

Plasticity and Insecurity

Even for those people who are eligible for indigenous status, the concept can be a double-edged sword. Rangan (1992) has written of the negative local impact of the global embrace of the Chipko indigenous rights movement in northern India, and Conklin (1997) has written about the downside of Amazonian peoples' strategic adoption of global images of indigeneity. Aspirations for and articulations of indigenous identity that appear inauthentic and opportunistic may elicit official disdain and sanction, which Li (2000) sees as a real threat in Indonesia. Indigenous identity is in any case a narrow target, which is easily over- or undershot. Thus, Li (2000) writes that if people present themselves as too primitive, they risk resettlement, whereas if they present themselves as not primitive enough, they risk resettlement on other grounds. Once indigenous status has been attained, official expectations of appropriate behavior can be exacting. Li (2000, p. 170) writes, "[c]andidates for the

tribal slot who are found deficient according to the environmental standards expected of them must also beware."

In sharp contrast to the increasingly cautious academic approach to indigeneity, however, the concept has traveled, been transformed, and enthusiastically deployed the world over (Béteille 1998). The same potential that makes anthropologists anxious about the concept makes it attractive to many local peoples.[4] Niezen's (2003) term international indigenism is an ironic comment on this mobility. Most alarming to anthropologists is that local communities are not just adapting the concept to their own uses but are doing the reverse. Jackson (1995, 1999) has written about how local notions of history and culture in Vaupés, Columbia, are being changed to fit the received global wisdom of what constitutes Indianness; Pulido (1998) writes of the deployment of romanticized ecological discourses and culturalism in the southwestern United States as a means of resistance using the master's tools; and Li (2002) worries about the feedback loop through which an external sedentarist metaphysics is shaping the belief and practices of those called indigenous in Indonesia.

Obviously calculated instances of the deployment of indigenous status have, predictably, generated some political backlash. But, more interestingly, they have also generated adjustments by those doing the deploying. Conklin (2002) writes of a shifting emphasis in Brazil from indigenous rights to indigenous knowledge and shamanism to counter this backlash [compare with Hornborg's (2005) related observation that it is increasingly legitimate for Native Americans in Nova Scotia to invoke images of sacredness in defense of their resource rights]. Anthropologists have also adjusted to this

---

[4]Compare Hodgson's (2002) recommendation that instead of engaging in debates over the definition, construction, and authenticity of indigenous claims, anthropologists should instead ask how and why indigenous groups are deploying the concept (pp. 1040, 1044).

evolving situation by beginning to study the emic meaning of the articulation of indigenous status. Thus Oakdale (2004) has studied the meaning that externally oriented displays of culture and ethnicity by the Kayabi of Brazil hold for the Kayabi themselves. And Graham (2005), intriguingly, suggests the globally oriented articulation of indigenous status by the Xavante of Brazil is driven not by identity politics but by a quest for existential recognition. These feedback dynamics are not unexpected. Giddens (1984) has examined what he calls the interpretive interplay between social science and its subjects, and he concludes that theory cannot be kept separate from the activities composing its subject matter, a relationship that he aptly terms the double hermeneutic.

INDIGENOUS KNOWLEDGE AND THE ENVIRONMENT

Indigenous Knowledge

The twentieth century's high-modern, global discourse of development was dismissive of local knowledge (Scott 1998), including knowledge of the environment. Just as the development of the concept of indigeneity (Brokensha et al. 1980) was a reaction to modernity's delocalizing impacts, so was the rise in interest in indigenous knowledge in part a response to modernity's deskilling vision of and consequences for local communities. In an explicit effort to counter the dominant development discourse, indigenous knowledge scholars argued that indigenous peoples possess unique systems of knowledge that can serve as the basis for more successful development interventions (Nazarea 1999, Sillitoe et al. 2002). Interest in this concept became so powerful so quickly (it was invoked in principle 22 of the 1992 Rio Declaration) that in 1996 the World Bank declared its own commitment to indigenous knowledge by committing itself to becoming the knowledge bank. Proponents of the concept of indigenous knowledge initially had high hopes for it, as illustrated by Sillitoe's (1998) claim that it could serve as

the foundation for a new applied anthropology by promoting collaborative development with anthropology's subjects as well as improved north-south collaboration. Scholars in other disciplines pursued parallel lines of inquiry, with Scott (1998) developing a distinction between scientific knowledge on the one hand, and partisan, situated, practical knowledge, which he glossed as "mētis" on the other.

Similar to the concept of indigeneity, indigenous knowledge soon became the subject of a wide-ranging critique. In a pioneering and influential analysis, Agrawal (1995, p. 422) writes

> Certainly, what is today known and classified as indigenous knowledge has been in intimate interaction with western knowledge since at least the fifteenth century. In the face of evidence that suggests contact, variation, transformation, exchange, communication, and learning over the last several centuries, it is difficult to adhere to a view of indigenous and western forms of knowledge being untouched by each other.

Ellen & Harris (2000) point out that the epistemic origins of much knowledge, whether folk or scientific, are hidden, and they argue this anonymity has contributed to the emergence of a perceived divide between scientific practice and indigenous knowledge. When the origins of knowledge can be revealed, the label of indigenous knowledge often becomes more questionable. In the case of smallholder rubber cultivation in Southeast Asia, closer study reveals that although this is indeed an impressive system of agro-ecological knowledge, it could hardly be less indigenous in nature (Dove 2000). Hornborg (2005) points out that so-called indigenous knowledge systems are reified by the structures of modernity that marginalize them. The concept of a chasm instead of a confluence between local and extralocal systems of knowledge is not sociologically neutral.[5] By problematizing a purported division between local and extralocal, the concept of indigenous knowledge obscures existing linkages or even identities between the two and may privilege political, bureaucratic authorities with a vested interest in the distinction (whether its maintenance or collapse).

Many scholars argue for replacing this concept of a neat divide with something more complicated. On the basis of his work with migrants in southeastern Nicaragua, Nygren (1999) argues for replacing the perceived dichotomy between local and universal knowledge with an understanding of knowledge as heterogeneous, negotiated, and hybrid. Similarly, Gupta (1998, pp. 264–65), on the basis of his work in Uttar Pradesh in northern India, maintains that "postcolonial modernities" are characterized by a "mix of hybridity, mistranslation, and incommensurability." Historical studies of how such incommensurabilities or contradictions arise are perhaps most promising of all, as in Ellen's (1999) analysis of the internal contradictions in contemporary Nuaulu views of the environment, which reflect recent and ongoing changes in their environmental relations.

An important locus of debate over indigenous knowledge involves the issue of intellectual property rights. The traditional anthropological focus on plant knowledge, coupled with the development of interest in the conservation of biodiversity in general and plants with pharmaceutical value in particular, led to interest in assigning market-oriented intellectual property rights to indigenous peoples for biogenetic resources (Brush & Stabinsky 1996, Moran et al. 2001). This also

represented a reaction against a history of free appropriation of such resources, coupled with patenting in Western countries and then sale back to indigenous peoples in some of the most egregious cases. The concept of assigning intellectual property rights to indigenous peoples proved to not be as simple as it appeared, however. I previously suggested the concept's premises were disingenuous with respect to the national politics and structural marginality of many indigenous communities (Dove 1996). Brown (1998) similarly concluded intellectual property rights were an inappropriate, romantic, and politically naive way of defending indigenous communities. Actual attempts to deploy intellectual property rights, and engage indigenous communities in global bio-prospecting partnerships, have been less than successful. Greene (2004) analyzes the problems of a controversial ethnopharmaceutical project of the International Cooperative Biodiversity Group in Peru's high forest, and Berlin & Berlin (2004) regretfully describe the much-publicized collapse of a bioprospecting project in Chiapas, Mexico, which they subtitle "How a Bioprospecting Project That Should Have Succeeded Failed."

Environmental Conservation by Indigenous Peoples

Much of the interest in indigenous knowledge has focused on natural resources and the environment, which was reflected in the emergence of the concept of indigenous environmental knowledge. The emergence of this concept represented a reaction to the historical proliferation of discourses that largely and uncritically blamed local populations for environmental degradation. Most of these discourses were driven by a neo-Malthusian view of population growth outstripping available resources, a view now widely critiqued for being overly simplistic and, in particular, ignoring overarching political-economic drivers. The field of political ecology

---

[5]The constructed division between indigenous and nonindigenous knowledge is an example of what Foucault (1982) calls "dividing practices," referring to the many ways by which societies objectify the other and privilege the self (e.g., by distinguishing between mad and sane, sick and healthy, criminals and law-abiding citizens) (p. 208).

established itself, in part, through the critique of these degradation discourses, notable examples of which include Blaikie's (1985) work on soils, Fairhead & Leach's (1996) work on forests, and Thompson et al.'s work (1986) on the Himalayan ecosystem.

Although there was both some historical justice and empirical validity to this correction, the concept of indigenous environmental knowledge was also flawed. As a proponent, Berkes (1999) wrote, it embodied three essentialized myths about indigenous peoples: that of the exotic other, the intruding wastrel, and the noble savage or fallen angel. As a result, this concept too became the subject of fierce debates. Iconic cases of indigenous environmentalism such as that of the Kayapó of Brazil have been subjected to exacting critiques. Posey's analysis (1985) of the anthropogenic forest islands (*apete*) of the Kayapó was one of the most powerful visions of environmental knowledge and management by indigenous peoples ever presented. The geographer Parker (1992), however, countered that these islands were really the natural products of the advance and retreat of the forest at the edges of the Brazilian savanna. An equally robust debate broke out in the wake of Krech's (1999) publication in which he claimed that, although there is evidence Native Americans had possessed both indigenous knowledge of and an ecological perspective on the environment, there is no evidence they had ever actually, intentionally conserved natural resources. Indeed, a debate was launched as to whether any indigenous people anywhere in the world had ever practiced anything that could properly be called conservation (Stearman 1994). One glaring lacuna in these debates is the lack of critical attention to the cross-cultural translation and interpretation of the concept of conservation itself, especially in non-Western societies and outside of the major world religions. Studies similar to that of Tuck-Po (2004), who explores the indigenous concept of environmental degradation among the Batek of peninsular Malaysia,

or West (2005), who compares emic and etic views of Gimi relations with their forests in Papua New Guinea, are relatively rare.[6]

For many scholars, intention is the key criterion for the presence versus the absence of conservation. Thus Stearman (1994) questions the accuracy of claims for resource management in the absence of conscious awareness, and Smith & Wishnie (2000) similarly argue conservation must be an intended outcome not an unintended by-product. However, much behavior that has the effect of conserving natural resources is not intentional (just as much religious behavior does not constitute religiosity). Fairhead & Leach (1996, pp. 285), in their pioneering reinterpretation of perceived deforestation in West Africa, attribute the actual afforestation taking place to "the sum of a much more diffuse set of relations, a constellation more than a structure." They write that, "While villagers do intentionally precipitate these vegetational changes, their agency in this is not always so overt. Short-term agricultural and everyday activities can sometimes in themselves lead unintentionally to these long-term and beneficial vegetational results; villagers know the results and appreciate them, but do not necessarily work for them" (p. 207). Although Posey, in his work with the Kayapó, was perhaps inclined for political reasons to exaggerate the consciousness of their resource-management practices, he too recognized that some practices with important consequences were of the everyday, unconscious variety. It is illuminating to look at how unconscious practices have been transformed in the modern era to conscious ones, as Ellen (1999) does for the Nuaulu of eastern Indonesia. He distinguishes an older, local, embedded system of Nuaulu environmental knowledge from a newer system of knowledge of higher-order environmental processes, and he does so partly on the

---

[6]West (2005, p. 632) calls for placing the "politics of translation" at the center of environmental anthropology.

ICDP: integrated
conservation and
development project

basis of self-consciousness.[7] Taken together, these studies suggest any perceived divide between intention and nonintention in resource management is more likely a reflection of difference between modernity and premodernity than between conservationist and nonconservationist practices.

Integrated Conservation and Development Projects and Extractive Reserves

The debate over indigenous conservation reached its most critical juncture with regard to integrated conservation and development projects (ICDPs). Widespread failure of the traditional fences and fines approach to protected area management led the International Union for the Conservation of Nature, the World Wildlife Fund, and the United Nations Environmental Program to call for a shift away from the strict separation of conservation and human development to a combination of the two in their 1980 World Conservation Strategy.[8] This led to the global proliferation of ICDPs, defined by Wells (1992), which typically were committed to raising the standards of living of communities located next to or within protected areas, with the premise that this was the primary determinant of the amount of pressure on natural resources. ICDPs proved to be complex to implement, however, and often failed to achieve their dual social and environmental objectives (see Naughton-Treves et al. 2005 for a recent assessment). In-depth studies of specific project histories have been rare (for exceptions, see Neumann 1997, Gezon 1997, West 2006). Whatever the case,

this new paradigm elicited a sharp counterattack from conservationists who, disputing the basic principle of tying conservation success to human development, demanded a return to the fortress nature approach (Oates 1999, Redford & Sanderson 2000, Terborgh 1999), which helped propel a shift in the late 1990s from the community level to ecoregions. Defenders of the basic principle of ICDPs have responded equally vigorously (Wilshusen et al. 2002). Holt (2005) points out that there is a catch-22 in the resurgent protectionist paradigm, in that only groups lacking technology, population growth, and market ties are seen as conservation friendly, but only groups that have all of these characteristics are likely to have the incentive to practice conservation.[9] Shepard (2006), drawing on long-term research in Manu National Park in Peru, questions the claim that local communities do not conserve resources, and Schwartzman et al. (2000) present a convincing political argument that local people are actually the best defenders of tropical forests against the threats to them from both public and private sectors.[10]

One of the best-known examples of ICDPs is the so-called extractive reserves of the Amazon, which were designed to address both conservation and development goals through the noninvasive, sustainable extraction of forest products (Allegretti 1990, Schwartzman 1989). Heavily promoted but little studied

---

[7] Related studies have looked at how indigenous peoples, as part of this process of conscious environmentalism development, have strategically deployed claims to indigenous environmental wisdom (Conklin & Graham 1995, Li 2000, Zerner 1993).

[8] The history of the separation of society and environment in U.S. protected area management, which set the model for much of the rest of the world, is detailed in Spence (1999).

[9] In a related argument, Fisher (1994) observes that the Kayapó's articulation of an ecomystical attachment to the land was suited only to a specific political-economic juncture in time.

[10] The debate over ICDPs notwithstanding, there is considerable convergence today between environmental anthropologists and conservation scientists, beginning with their mutual commitment to a nonequilibrium paradigm and a related rethinking of simplistic concepts of community, nature, and culture (cf. Scoones 1999). Both fields share an interest in the prospects for community-based resource management and skepticism regarding the benefits of market involvement; both are re-examining the overlooked agency of local social as well as natural actors; and both are asserting the merits of an engaged versus disengaged science.

(Ehringhaus 2005),[11] it soon transpired that some of the indigenous communities involved found extractive reserves too constraining and began logging instead of conserving their forests [as happened with the Kayapó (Turner 1995)]. Zimmerman et al. (2001) report somewhat more optimistic results from a second-generation extractive reserve project, supported by Conservation International, which is attempting to present the Kayapó with improved economic alternatives to logging.

INDIGENEITY, AGENCY, SOVEREIGNTY

Community and State

A number of observers have commented on a fundamental shift in thinking within environmental anthropology over the past quarter of a century with respect to the study of power, politics, and sovereignty.[12] Thus, Brosius (1999a) argues that a major discontinuity between the ecological anthropology of the 1960s and 1970s and the environmental anthropology of today is that the latter draws on poststructural theory. This discontinuity is perhaps reflected in the distinction between Posey's (1985) analysis of forest islands in the Amazon, which began in the late 1970s, and Fairhead & Leach's (1996) analysis of forest islands in West Africa, carried out in the early 1990s (Dove & Carpenter 2006). Both studies correct the idea that forest islands are remnants of natural forest, but whereas Posey emphasizes the correction, Fairhead and Leach emphasize the mistake. Posey emphasizes the political importance to policy makers of valuable indigenous environmental

knowledge, whereas Fairhead and Leach emphasize the importance to scholars of studying the politics of the deflected knowledge of policy makers.

The new paradigm is reflected in the poststructurally driven rethinking of state hegemony, exemplified in the recent set of essays published in the *American Anthropologist* on the work of James C. Scott (Sivaramakrishnan 2005). A complementary development is heightened interest in the agency of local people and communities (Brosius 1999a,c), defined as "the socioculturally mediated capacity to act" (Ahearn 2001, p. 112). Scholars such as Li (2000) have looked at the way agency is exercised in the articulation of indigeneity, which she says opens up room to maneuver that might otherwise be unavailable, even if some of the elements employed in this articulation are essentialized. Li (2000, p. 163) writes, "the telling of this story [of indigeneity] in relation to Lindu or any other place in Indonesia has to be regarded as an accomplishment, a contingent outcome of the cultural and political work of articulation through which indigenous knowledge and identity were made explicit, alliances formed, and media attention appropriately focused."

One site of traditionally perceived agency, the local community, is increasingly problematized. Many anthropologists have contributed to a revisionist view of the community as much less homogeneous, harmonious, and integrated and much more historically contingent than formerly thought. Writing on south Indian irrigation systems, for example, Mosse (1997, p. 471) argues, counterintuitively, that older, supralocal social systems have actually been replaced by more localized ones in recent times because of the demands of the modern state:

> The newly theorized 'community management' ideas stressing locally autonomous, internally sustained and self-reliant community institutions have emerged within a global discourse (policy and practice)

---

[11] A recent assessment by Godoy et al. (2005) concluded that the available evidence still does not allow any definitive conclusions to be drawn regarding the impact of extractive reserves on the well-being of indigenous communities or the success of their resource-conservation practices.

[12] Agrawal (2005b) maintains that the literature on indigeneity is still marked by the absence of any theory of power.

oriented towards finding community solutions to the perceived problems of state and market-based irrigation management; solutions that are capable of addressing the policy imperatives of cost-sharing, recovery, and reducing the financial liability of the state.

The hegemonic global discourse of community-based natural resource management (CBNRM), which helped to promote the development of this concept of community, is undermined by its shaky empirical basis. The problems and prospects of CBNRM are reviewed by Agrawal & Gibson (2001) and Brosius et al. (2005). Leach et al. (1999), on the basis of a comparative global study, critique the premise of a consensual community in CBNRM, and Berry (2004), reviewing cases in Africa, argues the CBNRM process of deciding who and what are local creates more problems than it solves.

One of the most debated cases of community identity and autonomy involves the San of the Kalahari, who were long taken to be an iconic case of isolated, timeless, indigenous people, a view now under revision and debate. The most influential revisionist Wilmsen (1989) argues the San were integrated into modern capitalist economies materially, as the British colonial administration strengthened the Tswana tribute system, which extracted surplus from the San, and they were also integrated discursively in a way that obfuscated their real history (cf. Sylvain 2002). In rejoinder, Solway & Lee (1990) argue that, although some San were dependent on non-San, others were, if not isolated and timeless, at least substantially autonomous and actively resisting incorporation into world capitalism.[13]

---

[13] An analogous debate, known as the wild yam debate, focused on whether these and other tubers constituted a sufficiently robust source of wild carbohydrates for tropical forests to support people without extraforest ties and dependencies (Headland & Bailey 1991, McKey 1996).

Collaboration

Much scholarship has tried to move beyond the concept of local resistance, as seen in the work of Scott (1985, 1989) (which was itself an early and central contribution to the study of agency). Some felt Scott was overly optimistic in his assessment of local resistance possibilities, whereas others believed he was not optimistic enough and local communities did not simply resist powerful extracommunity actors but also collaborated with them in more complex ways than had been imagined. For example, in a departure from a long history of studies of opposition between forest departments and indigenous peoples, Mathews (2005) and Vasan (2002) analyze the everyday ways in which foresters and farmers actually get along to mutual advantage. Others, taking a Foucaultian view of decentered relations of power and the making of subjects, are more negative. For example, Agrawal (2005a) suggests the widely lauded granting of forest rights to villagers in India is really a way of making them into environmental subjects.

Collaboration and complicity are distinguished from participation in this literature. As interest in revealing informal patterns of collaboration has waxed, so too has a critique of formal developmental structures of participation. Over the past quarter-century, there has been a major discursive shift in global development circles toward ensuring the participation of indigenous communities in their own development, which was reflected in the emergence of purportedly more participatory techniques of research (e.g., participatory rural appraisal and local mapping), as well as CBNRM (discussed above).[14] But critics have questioned just how participatory these measures really are (Mosse 1994). Trantafillou & Nielsen (2001), for example, argue that participatory empowerment simply leads to greater enmeshment in relations of power.

---

[14] Compare Rademacher & Patel's (2002) analysis of the political genesis of the rise of the participatory paradigm.

Much of the scholarship on collaboration has focused on relations between indigenous communities and nongovernmental organizations (NGOs). Tsing (1999, p. 162) is hopeful about the prospect of such collaborations, writing that they "offer possibilities for building environmental and social justice in the countryside as exciting as any I have heard of." Others, such as Conklin & Graham (1995), who have also studied the shifting middle ground between NGOs and indigenous peoples, place somewhat greater emphasis on its insecurity. The capacity of the oldest and most powerful international NGOs to benefit indigenous peoples has especially been questioned. Chapin (2004) and Bray & Anderson (2005) set off a firestorm of debate by claiming several of the world's leading environmental NGOs were no longer (if indeed they ever had been) defenders of indigenous rights. In her case study of fishing in the Central Amazon of Brazil, Chernela (2005) builds on this critique by arguing the problem is a more subtle but equally problematic shift in the NGOs' role from mediation to domination and from local partnering to local production.

Indigenous Rights Movements

The expression of agency in indigenous rights movements has become of great interest to anthropologists. Jackson & Warren (2005) have reviewed the literature on such movements in Latin America, and Hodgson (2002) has reviewed the literature for Africa and the Americas. Well-studied cases include the Chipko movement (Rangan 1992), the Narmada dam (Baviskar 1995), the Zapatistas (Jung 2003, Nugent 1995), and the rubber tappers of Brazil (Allegretti 1990, Ehringhaus 2005, Keck 1995). There has also been great interest in the relationships of such movements to extralocal NGOs, led by Brosius's (1999a,c) study of the Penan logging blockades in Sarawak. Brosius became interested in the implications for governmentality raised by such relations. He writes that as environmental NGOs displace grassroots environmental movements, they "might be viewed as engaged in projects of domestication, attempting to seduce or to compel" grassroots groups "to participate in statist projects of environmental governmentality," projects that envelop movements "within institutions for local, national, and global environmental surveillance and governance" (Brosius 1999b, pp. 37, 50).[15]

Complementing the interest in social movements has been new interest in the study of violence involving indigenous peoples. A prominent focus of scholarship on this topic has been what Richards (1996, pp. xiii) terms the new barbarism or Malthus-with-guns interpretation of tribal violence in terms of unchecked population/resource pressures (Homer-Dixon 1999, Kaplan 1994). This interpretation has drawn a sharp rebuttal from anthropologists who argue, first, that violence is more likely to result in degradation of local resources and impoverishment of local peoples than the reverse and, second, that extralocal political-economic forces—often involving industrialized Western countries—are frequently implicated in the causes of such violence (Fairhead 2001, Richards 1996). A number of contributors to this debate have argued for the need to articulate emic understandings of violence (Fairhead 2001, Harwell & Peluso 2001). I have analyzed the discontinuity in Kalimantan, Indonesia, between academic explanations of ethnic violence in terms of political economy and indigenous explanations in terms of culture (Dove 2006).

INDIGENOUS PEOPLES AND ANTHROPOLOGY

Problems

The study of indigenous movements and violence, indigenous resource rights and knowledge, and the deployment of indigenous status

NGOs: nongovernmental organizations

---

[15] Compare Escobar & Paulson's (2005) analysis of the discontinuity between dominant biodiversity discourses and the political ecology of social movements.

and identity all raise questions about the politics and ethics of research. That the topics of anthropological interest have become the tools by which indigenous peoples articulate their identities, stake claims to local resources, and fight for their rights in regional, national, and international arenas poses moral and ethical challenges to anthropologists—challenges that require new responses. As Brosius (1999c, p. 368) writes, "[w]ith but a few exceptions, anthropologists have yet to address seriously the political implications of the difference between mapping the life of a village . . . and mapping the contours of a social movement." The debate regarding these implications reveals that a sea change has already taken place within the discipline with respect to the admixture of morality and science. The debate over Kuper's (2003) article on indigeneity, for example, revealed that simple disavowal of politics and insistence on distance have become a minority stance, whereas an explicit, subjective, moral positioning is increasingly common. Kottak (1999) argues that anthropologists' personal witnessing of threats to their subjects imposes a moral responsibility, and Hodgson (2002) points out that the uneven topography of power in the world makes neutral representation by anthropologists impossible.

One consequence of this moral positioning is ethnographic refusal, which is as little discussed as it is common. Ortner (1995) coined this term to refer to the refusal by ethnographers to write thickly about their subjects' own views in cases of resistance. This refusal is especially marked with respect to behavior that violates the political norms of most anthropologists, including violence and biases on the basis of ethnicity, gender, caste, class, religion, and race. It is further complicated when what is at issue is not simply behavior seen as politically incorrect, but representations of behavior (as in some of the self-deployments of indigenous status) deemed politically nonastute. As Li (2002, p. 364) writes, "[w]hat does it mean for scholars, to generate knowledge intended to counter understandings framed in ethnic or religious terms, when these understandings are generated not by misguided outsiders (the media, scholars or politicians highlighting primordial identities and exotic tribal rituals) but by everyday 'indigenous' experience?" Ortner (1995, p. 190) attributes ethnographic refusal, in part, to a "failure of nerve surrounding questions of the internal politics of dominated groups." It not only results in "ethnographic thin-ness" (p. 190), but it also reflects a lack of respect for people's own understanding of their motives (Baviskar 1996).

Prospects

The implications of academic critique grow ever more complex. Thus, Latour (2004) supports a shift from critical scholarship discrediting matters of fact to an acceptance of the reality of matters of concern, using global warming as an example. He writes, "[i]n which case the danger would no longer be coming from an excessive confidence in ideological arguments posturing as matters of fact—as we have learned to combat so efficiently in the past—but from an excessive *distrust* of good matters of fact disguised as bad ideological biases!" (p. 227). Latour is troubled by the fact that environment-despoiling political actors are borrowing the tools of academic deconstruction to attack the thesis of global warming. Potentially troubling for the same reason is the coincidence of popular interest in indigeneity and its academic critique, raising questions as to how anthropology's erasure of locality relates to the rise of indigenous rights (and, more generally, what role the decontextualizing trend in academia plays in modernity's larger project of decontextualization).

Gidden's (1984) double hermeneutic describes a similar sort of feedback process. For environmental anthropology, however, these theories are complicated by the addition of the environment as an active agent. Science, society, and environment clearly coevolve. This is illustrated by what we know of the Kayapó over the past generation, for example. Their environment and their regimes for managing it, their identity and their modes of representing it, as well as scholarly understandings of all of this, all have changed in a mutually influencing and constantly evolving process, which presents a host of contradictions at any given time. We see these same sorts of contradictions among the Nuaulu, who became a people of nature precisely as they became more distanced from it (Ellen 1999). There are many other examples of modernity making possible articulation of indigeneity and indigenous conservation at the very time as it renders actual achievement of these things impossible. Such contradictions should be the future focus of environmental anthropology, or, to put it another way, an understanding of the coevolution of science, society, and environment that shows why these are not really contradictions at all should be the future goal of the anthropology of the environment.

ACKNOWLEDGMENTS

I am grateful to Carol Carpenter for a number of ideas that contributed to this essay, as well as the students of the advanced seminar that we co-teach at Yale, "The Social Science of Development and Conservation," in which an earlier version of this review was presented. I am also grateful to my indomitable student research intern for the past two years, Caroline Simmonds, and my stalwart secretary, Ann Prokop. None of the aforementioned people or institutions is responsible for the content of this essay, however, whose shortcomings are mine alone.

LITERATURE CITED

Agrawal A. 1995. Dismantling the divide between indigenous and scientific knowledge. *Dev. Change* 26:413–39

Agrawal A. 2005a. Environmentality: community, intimate government, and the making of environmental subjects in Kumaon, India. *Curr. Anthropol.* 46(2):161–90

Agrawal A. 2005b. *Indigenous knowledge/power*. Presented at Agrarian Stud. colloq., Dec. 2, Yale University

Agrawal A, Gibson CC, eds. 2001. Communities and the Environment: Ethnicity, Gender, and the State in Community-Based Conservation. New Brunswick, NJ: Rutgers Univ. Press

Ahearn LM. 2001. Language and agency. *Annu. Rev. Anthropol.* 30:109–38

Allegretti MH. 1990. Extractive reserves: an alternative for reconciling development and environmental conservation in Amazonia. In *Alternatives to Deforestation: Steps Toward Sustainable Use of the Amazonia Rain Forest*, ed. AB Anderson, pp. 252–64. New York: Columbia Univ. Press

Appadurai A. 1996. *Modernity at Large: Cultural Dimensions of Globalization*. Minneapolis: Univ. Minn. Press

Baviskar A. 1995. *In the Belly of the River: Tribal Conflicts Over Development in the Narmada Valley*. Delhi: Oxford Univ. Press

Baviskar A. 1996. Reverence is not enough: ecological Marxism and Indian adivasis. In *Creating the Countryside: The Politics of Rural and Environmental Discourse*, ed. EM DuPuis, P Vandergeest, pp. 204–24. Philadelphia: Temple Univ. Press

Benjamin G. 2002. On being tribal in the Malay world. In *Tribal Communities in the Malay World: Historical, Cultural, and Social Perspectives*, ed. G Benjamin, C Chou, pp. 7–76. Leiden(Singapore: IIAS/ISAS

Berkes F. 1999. *Sacred Ecology: Traditional Ecological Knowledge and Resource Management*. Philadelphia, PA: Taylor & Francis

Berlin B, Berlin EA. 2004. Community autonomy and the Maya ICBG project in Chiapas, Mexico: how a bioprospecting project that should have succeeded failed. *Hum. Org.* 63(4):472–86

Berry S. 2004. Reinventing the local? Privatization, decentralization and the politics of resource management: examples from Africa. *Afr. Study Monogr.* 25(2):79–101

Béteille A. 1998. The idea of indigenous people. *Curr. Anthropol.* 39(2):187–91

Blaikie P. 1985. *The Political Economy of Soil Erosion in Developing Countries.* New York: Longman

Bray D, Anderson AB. 2005. *Global conservation, non-governmental organizations, and local communities.* Work. Pap. No.1, Conserv. Dev. Ser. Inst. Sustainable Sci. Lat. America Caribbean, Fla. Int. Univ.

Brokensha D, Warren DM, Werner O, eds. 1980. *Indigenous Knowledge Systems and Development.* Washington, DC: Univ. Press of America

Brondizio ES. 2004. Agriculture intensification, economic identity, and shared invisibility in Amazonian peasantry: caboclos and colonists in comparative perspective. *Cult. Agric.* 26(1–2):1–24

Brosius JP. 1999a. Analyses and interventions: anthropological engagements with environmentalism. *Curr. Anthropol.* 40(3):277–309

Brosius JP. 1999b. Green dots, pink hearts: displacing politics from the Malaysian rain forest. *Am. Anthropol.* 101(1):36–57

Brosius JP. 1999c. Locations and representations: writing in the political present in Sarawak, east Malaysia. *Identities* 6(2–3):345–86

Brosius JP, Tsing AL, Zerner C, eds. 2005. *Communities and Conservation: History and Politics of Community-Based Natural Resource Management.* Walnut Creek, CA: AltaMira Press

Brown MF. 1998. Can culture be copyrighted? *Curr. Anthropol.* 39(2):193–222

Brush SB, Stabinsky D, eds. 1996. *Valuing Local Knowledge: Indigenous People and Intellectual Property Rights.* Washington, DC: Island Press

Campos MT, Nepstad DC. 2006. Smallholders: The Amazon's new conservationists. *Conserv. Biol.* 20:In press

Chapin M. 2004. A challenge to conservationists. *World Watch* (Nov./Dec.): 17–31

Chernela J. 2005. The politics of mediation: local-global interactions in the Central Amazon of Brazil. *Am. Anthropol.* 107(4):620–31

Clifford J. 1988. *The Predicament of Culture.* Cambridge, MA: Harvard Univ. Press

Clifford J. 2001. Indigenous articulations. *Contemp. Pac.* 13(2):468–90

Conklin BA. 1997. Body paint, feathers, and VCRs: aesthetics and authenticity in Amazonian activism. *Am. Ethnol.* 24(4):711–37

Conklin BA. 2002. Shamans versus pirates in the Amazonian treasure chest. *Am. Anthropol.* 104(4):1050–61

Conklin BA, Graham LR. 1995. The shifting middle ground: Amazonian Indians and eco-politics. *Am. Anthropol.* 97(4):215–29

Dove MR. 1996. Center, periphery and bio-diversity: a paradox of governance and a developmental challenge. In *Valuing Local Knowledge: Indigenous People and Intellectual Property Rights*, ed. S Brush, D Stabinsky, pp. 41–67. Washington, DC: Island Press

Dove MR. 2000. The life-cycle of indigenous knowledge, and the case of natural rubber production. In *Indigenous Environmental Knowledge and its Transformations*, ed. RF Ellen, A Bicker, P Parkes, pp. 213–51. Amsterdam: Harwood

Dove MR. 2006. 'New barbarism' or 'old agency' among the Dayak? Reflections on post-Soeharto ethnic violence in Kalimantan. *Soc. Anal.* 50(1): In press

Dove MR, Carpenter C, eds. 2006. *Environmental Anthropology: An Historical Reader.* Boston: Blackwell. In press

Ehringhaus C. 2005. *Post-victory dilemmas: land use, development policies, and social movement in Amazonian extractive reserves.* PhD thesis. Yale Univ. 425 pp.

Ellen RF. 1999. Forest knowledge, forest transformation: political contingency, historical ecology and the renegotiation of nature in Central Seram. In *Transforming the Indonesian Uplands*, ed. TM Li, pp. 131–57. Amsterdam: Harwood

Ellen RF, Harris P. 2000. ed. Introduction. In *Indigenous Environmental Knowledge and its Transformations*, ed. RF Ellen, A Bicker, P Parkes, pp. 213–51. Amsterdam: Harwood

Escobar A, Paulson S. 2005. The emergence of collective ethnic identities and alternative political ecologies in the Columbian rainforest. In *Political Ecology Across Spaces, Scales and Social Groups*, ed. S Paulson, L Gezon, pp. 257–77. New Brunswick, NJ: Rutgers Univ. Press

Fairhead J. 2001. International dimensions of conflict over natural and environmental resources. In *Violent Environments*, ed. NL Peluso, M Watts, pp. 213–36. Ithaca: Cornell Univ. Press

Fairhead J, Leach M. 1996. *Misreading the African Landscape: Society and Ecology in Forest-Savanna Mosaic*. Cambridge: Cambridge Univ. Press

Fisher WH. 1994. Megadevelopment, environmentalism, and resistance: the institutional context of Kayapó indigenous politics in Brazil. *Hum. Org.* 53(3):220–32

Foucault M. 1982. Afterword: the subject and power. In *Michel Foucault: Beyond Structuralism and Hermeneutics*, ed. H Dreyfus, P Rabinow, pp. 208–26. Chicago: Univ. Chicago Press

Gezon L. 1997. Institutional structure and the effectiveness of integrated conservation and development projects: case study from Madagascar. *Hum. Org.* 56(4):462–70

Giddens A. 1984. *The Constitution of Society: Outline of the Theory of Structuration*. Berkeley: Univ. Calif. Press

Godoy R, Reyes-García V, Byron E, Leonard WR, Vadez V. 2005. The effects of market economies on the well-being of indigenous peoples and their use of renewable natural resources. *Annu. Rev. Anthropol.* 34:121–38

Graham LR. 2005. Image and instrumentality in a Xavante politics of existential recognition. *Am. Ethnol.* 32(4):622–41

Greene S. 2004. Indigenous people incorporated? Culture as politics, culture as property in pharmaceutical bioprospecting. *Curr. Anthropol.* 45(2):211–37

Gupta A. 1998. *Postcolonial Developments: Agriculture in the Making of Modern India*. Durham, NC: Duke Univ. Press

Harwell E, Peluso N. 2001. The ethnic violence in west Kalimantan. In *Violent Environments*, ed. N Peluso, M Watts, pp. 83–116. Ithaca: Cornell Univ. Press

Headland TN, Bailey RC. 1991. Introduction: Have hunter-gatherers ever lived in tropical rain forest independently of agriculture? *Hum. Ecol.* 19(2):115–22

Hirtz F. 2003. It takes modern means to be traditional: on recognizing indigenous cultural communities in the Philippines. *Dev. Change* 34(5):887–914

Hobsbawm E, Ranger T, eds. 1983. *The Invention of Tradition*. Cambridge: Cambridge Univ. Press

Hodgson DL. 2002. Introduction: comparative perspectives on the indigenous rights movement in Africa and the Americas. *Am. Anthropol.* 104(4):1037–49

Holt FL. 2005. The catch-22 of conservation: indigenous peoples, biologists, and cultural change. *Hum. Ecol.* 33(2):199–215

Homer-Dixon TF. 1999. *Environment, Scarcity, and Violence*. Princeton: Princeton Univ. Press

Hornborg A. 1996. Ecology as semiotics: outlines of a contextualist paradigm for human ecology. In *Nature and Society: Anthropological Perspectives*, ed. P Descola, G Pálsson, pp. 45–62. London: Routledge

Hornborg A. 2005. Undermining modernity: protecting landscapes and meanings among the Mi'kmaq of Nova Scotia. In *Political Ecology Across Spaces, Scales and Social Groups*, ed. S Paulson, L Gezon, pp. 196–214. New Brunswick, NJ: Rutgers Univ. Press

Jackson JE. 1995. Culture, genuine and spurious: the politics of Indianness in the Vaupés, Columbia. *Am. Ethnol.* 22(1):3–27

Jackson JE. 1999. The politics of ethnographic practice in the Columbian Vaupés. *Identities* 6(2–3):281–317

Jackson JE, Warren KB. 2005. Indigenous movements in Latin America, 1992–2004: controversies, ironies, new directions. *Annu. Rev. Anthropol.* 34:549–73

Jung C. 2003. The politics of indigenous identity: neoliberalism, cultural rights, and the Mexican Zapatistas. *Soc. Res.* 70(2):433–62

Kaplan RD. 1994. The coming anarchy: how scarcity, crime, overpopulation, and disease are rapidly destroying the social fabric of our planet. *Atlan. Mon.* (Feb.):44–76

Keck ME. 1995. Social equity and environmental politics in Brazil: lessons from the rubber tappers of Acre. *Comp. Pol.* 27:409–24

Kottak C. 1999. The new ecological anthropology. *Am. Anthropol.* 101(1):23–35

Krech S III. 1999. *The Ecological Indian: Myth and History*. New York: Norton

Kuper A. 2003. The return of the native. *Curr. Anthropol.* 44:389–402

Latour B. 2004. Why has critique run out of steam? From matters of fact to matters of concern. *Crit. Inq.* 30:225–48

Leach M, Mearns R, Scoones I. 1999. Environmental entitlements: dynamics and institutions in community-based natural resource management. *World Dev.* 27(2):225–47

Li TM. 2000. Articulating indigenous identity in Indonesia: resource politics and the tribal slot. *Comp. Stud. Soc. Hist.* 42(1):149–79

Li TM. 2002. Ethnic cleansing, recursive knowledge, and the dilemma of sedentarism. *Int. Soc. Sci. J.* 173:361–71

Linnekin J. 1992. On the theory and politics of cultural construction in the Pacific. *Oceania* 62:249–63

Mathews AS. 2005 Power/knowledge, power/ignorance: forest fires and the state in Mexico. Hum. Ecol. 33(6):795–820

McKey DB. 1996. Wild yam question. In *Encyclopedia of Cultural Anthropology*, Vol. 4, ed. D Levinson, M Embers, pp. 1363–66. New York: Henry Holt

Moran K, King SR, Carlson TJ. 2001. Biodiversity prospecting. *Annu. Rev. Anthropol.* 30:505–26

Mosse D. 1994. Authority, gender and knowledge: theoretical reflections on the practice of participatory rural appraisal. *Dev. Change* 25:497–526

Mosse D. 1997. The symbolic making of a common property resource: history, ecology, and locality in a tank-irrigated landscape in south India. *Dev. Change* 28:467–504

Naughton-Treves L, Holland MB, Brandon K. 2005. The role of protected areas in conserving biodiversity and sustaining local livelihoods. *Annu. Rev. Environ. Res.* 30:219–52

Nazarea V, ed. 1999. *Ethnoecology: Situated Knowledge/Local Lives*. Tucson: Univ. Ariz. Press

Neumann RP. 1997. Primitive ideas: protected area buffer zones and the politics of land in Africa. *Dev. Change* 28:559–82

Niezen R. 2003. *The Origins of Indigenism: Human Rights and the Politics of Identity*. Berkeley: Univ. Calif. Press

Nugent D. 1995. Northern intellectuals and the EZLN. *Mon. Rev.* 47(3):124–38

Nygren A. 1999. Local knowledge in the environment-development discourse: from dichotomies to situated knowledges. *Crit. Anthropol.* 19(3):267–88

Oakdale S. 2004. The culture-conscious Brazilian Indian: representing and reworking Indianness in Kayabi political discourse. *Am. Ethnol.* 31(1):60–75

Oates JF. 1999. *Myth and Reality in the Rain Forest: How Conservation Strategies Are Failing in
West Africa.* Berkeley: Univ. Calif. Press

Ortner S. 1995. Resistance and the problem of ethnographic refusal. *Comp. Stud. Soc. Hist.*
37(1):173–93

Parker E. 1992. Forest islands and Kayapo resource management in Amazonia: a reappraisal
of the Apete. *Am. Anthropol.* 94(2):406–28

Posey DA. 1985. Indigenous management of tropical forest ecosystems: the case of the Kayapó
Indians of the Brazilian Amazon. *Agrofor. Syst.* 3:139–58

Pulido L. 1998. Ecological legitimacy and cultural essentialism. In *The Struggle for Ecological
Democracy: Environmental Justice in the United States*, ed. D Faber, pp. 293–311. New York:
Guilford

Rademacher A. 2005. *Culturing urban ecology: development, statemaking, and river restoration in
Kathmandu.* PhD thesis, Yale Univ. 341 pp.

Rademacher A, Patel R. 2002. Retelling worlds of poverty: reflections on transforming participatory research for a global narrative. In *Knowing Poverty: Critical Reflections on Participatory
Research and Policy*, ed. K Brock, R McGee, pp. 166–88. London: Earthscan

Rangan H. 1992. Romancing the environment: popular environmental action in the Garhwal
Himalayas. In *Defense of Livelihoods: Comparative Studies in Environmental Action*, ed. J
Friedmann, H Rangan, pp. 155–81. West Hartford: Kumarian

Redford K, Sanderson SE. 2000. Extracting humans from nature. *Conserv. Biol.* 14:1362–64

Richards P. 1996. *Fighting for the Rain Forest: War, Youth and Resources in Sierra Leone.* Oxford:
Int. Afr. Inst.

Schwartzman S. 1989. Extractive reserves: the rubber tappers' strategy for sustainable use of the
Amazon rain forest. In *Fragile Lands in Latin America: Strategies for Sustainable Development*,
ed. JO Browder, pp. 150–65. Boulder, CO: Westview Press

Schwartzman S, Moreira A, Nepstad D. 2000. Rethinking tropical forest conservation: perils
in parks. *Conserv. Biol.* 14(5):1351–57

Scoones I. 1999. New ecology and the social sciences: what prospects for a fruitful engagement?
Annu. Rev. Anthropol. 28:479–507

Scott JC. 1985. *Weapons of the Weak: Everyday Forms of Peasant Resistance.* New Haven: Yale
Univ. Press

Scott JC. 1989. *Domination and the Arts of Resistance: Hidden Transcripts.* New Haven: Yale Univ.
Press

Scott JC. 1998. *Seeing Like a State: How Certain Schemes to Improve the Human Condition Have
Failed.* New Haven: Yale Univ. Press

Shepard GHJ. 2006. Trouble in paradise: indigenous populations and biodiversity conservation
in Manu National Park, Peru. *J. Sustain. For.* In press

Sillitoe P. 1998. The development of indigenous knowledge: a new applied anthropology. *Curr.
Anthropol.* 39(3):223–52

Sillitoe P, Bicker A, Pottier J. 2002. *Participating in Development: Approaches to Indigenous Knowledge.* London: Routledge

Sivaramakrishnan K. 2005. Introduction to "moral economies, state spaces, and categorical
violence." *Am. Anthropol.* 107(3):321–30

Smith EA, Wishnie M. 2000. Conservation and subsistence in small-scale societies. *Annu. Rev.
Anthropol.* 29:493–524

Solway JS, Lee RB. 1990. Foragers, genuine or spurious? Situating the Kalahari San in history.
Curr. Anthropol. 33(1):187–224

Spence MD. 1999. *Dispossessing the Wilderness: Indian Removal and the Making of the National Parks*. New York: Oxford Univ. Press

Stearman AM. 1994. "Only slaves climb trees": revisiting the myth of the ecologically noble savage in Amazonia. *Hum. Nat.* 5(4):339–57

Sylvain R. 2002. Land, water, and truth: San identity and global indigenism. *Am. Anthropol.* 104(4):1074–85

Terborgh J. 1999. *Requiem for Nature*. Washington, DC: Island Press

Thompson M, Warburton M, Hatley T. 1986. *Uncertainty on a Himalayan Scale: An Institutional Theory of Environmental Perception and a Strategic Framework for the Sustainable Development of the Himalaya*. London: Ethnographica

Trantafillou P, Nielsen MR. 2001. Policing empowerment: the making of capable subjects. *Hist. Hum. Sci.* 14(2):63–86

Tsing AL. 1999. Becoming a tribal elder and other green development fantasies. In *Transforming the Indonesian Uplands: Marginality, Power and Production*, ed. TM Li, pp. 159–202. London: Berg

Tsing AL. 2003. Agrarian allegory and global futures. In *Nature in the Global South: Environmental Projects in South and Southeast Asia*, ed. P Greenough, AL Tsing, pp. 124–69. Durham, NC: Duke Univ.

Tuck-Po L. 2004. *Changing Pathways: Forest Degradation and the Batek of Pahang, Malaysia*. Lanham, MD: Lexington Books

Turner TS. 1995. An indigenous people's struggle for socially equitable and ecologically sustainable production: the Kayapó revolt against extractivism. *J. Latin Am. Anthropol.* 1:98–121

Vasan S. 2002. Ethnography of the forest guard: contrasting discourses, conflicting roles and policy implementation. *Econ. Polit. Wkly* 37(40):4125–33

Wells BK 1992. People and Parks: Linking Protected Area Management with Local Communities. Washington, DC: World Bank

West P. 2005. Translation, value, and space: theorizing an ethnographic and engaged environmental anthropology. *Am. Anthropol.* 107(4):632–42

West P. 2006. *Conservation Is Our Government Now: The Politics of Ecology in Papua New Guinea*. Durham, NC: Duke Univ. Press

Wilmsen EN. 1989. *Land Filled with Flies: A Political Economy of the Kalahari*. Chicago: Univ. Chicago Press

Wilshusen PR, Brechin SR, Fortwangler CL, West PC. 2002. Reinventing a square wheel: critique of a resurgent "protecting paradigm" in international biodiversity conservation. *Soc. Nat. Res.* 15:17–40

Wolf ER. 1982. *Europe and the People Without History*. Berkeley: Univ. Calif. Press

Zerner C. 1993. Through a green lens: the construction of customary environmental law and community in Indonesia's Maluku Islands. *Law Soc. Rev.* 28(5):1079–1122

Zimmerman B, Peres CA, Malcolm JR, Turner T. 2001. Conservation and development alliances with the Kayapó of south-eastern Amazonia, a tropical forest indigenous people. *Environ. Conserv.* 28(1):10–22

Diet in Early *Homo*:
A Review of the Evidence and a New Model of Adaptive Versatility

Peter S. Ungar,[1] Frederick E. Grine,[2] and Mark F. Teaford[3]

[1] Department of Anthropology, University of Arkansas, Fayetteville, Arkansas 72701; email: pungar@uark.edu

[2] Departments of Anthropology and Anatomical Sciences, Stony Brook University, Stony Brook, New York 11794; email: fgrine@notes.cc.sunysb.edu

[3] Center for Functional Anatomy and Evolution, Johns Hopkins University School of Medicine, Baltimore, Maryland 21205; email: mteaford@jhmi.edu

Annu. Rev. Anthropol. 2006. 35:209–28

First published online as a Review in Advance on May 17, 2006

The *Annual Review of Anthropology* is online at anthro.annualreviews.org

This article's doi: 10.1146/annurev.anthro.35.081705.123153

Copyright © 2006 by Annual Reviews. All rights reserved

0084-6570/06/1021-0209$20.00

Key Words

Hominin, feeding adaptations, *Homo habilis*, *Homo rudolfensis*, *erectus*

Abstract

Several recent studies have stressed the role of dietary change in the origin and early evolution of our genus in Africa. Resulting models have been based on nutrition research and analogy to living peoples and nonhuman primates or on archeological and paleoenvironmental evidence. Here we evaluate these models in the context of the hominin fossil record. Inference of diet from fossils is hampered by small samples, unclear form-function relationships, taphonomic factors, and interactions between cultural and natural selection. Nevertheless, craniodental remains of *Homo habilis*, *H. rudolfensis*, and *H. erectus* offer some clues. For example, there appears to be no simple transition from an australopith to a *Homo* grade of dietary adaptation, or from closed forest plant diets to reliance on more open-country plants or animals. Early *Homo* species more likely had adaptations for flexible, versatile subsistence strategies that would have served them well in the variable paleoenvironments of the African Plio-Pleistocene.

INTRODUCTION

Over the past few years, scholars have paid increased attention to the evolution of diet in the Plio-Pleistocene hominins of Africa, especially the earliest members of our genus, *Homo rudolfensis*, *H. habilis*, and *H. erectus*. Resulting models have been based largely on nutritional studies combined with direct analogy (to living peoples or nonhuman primates) or on contextual evidence, such as archeological and paleoenvironmental indicators. Although many of these models are elegantly constructed and well reasoned, they do not tell us what the hominins actually ate. They form hypotheses that may or may not be testable given the nature of the fossil record.

Here, we review and evaluate some recent models for dietary adaptations of early *Homo* in the context of the hominin fossil record, the archeological record, and evidence for environmental dynamics during the Plio-Pleistocene. The most notable point from this exercise is the limited scope of what can actually be said about the diets of these early hominins. Nevertheless, the jaws and teeth of early *Homo* do offer some clues to the diets of these species. A synthetic view of this evidence, in the context of archeological and paleoenvironmental indicators, suggests that the origin and early evolution of *Homo* are most likely associated with biological and cultural adaptations for a more flexible, versatile subsistence strategy. This strategy would have put the earliest members of our genus at an advantage given climatic fluctuation and a mosaic of different microhabitats in Africa during the late Pliocene.

THE FOSSIL EVIDENCE FOR PLIO-PLEISTOCENE *HOMO*

The temporal ranges, taxonomy, and hypodigms of early *Homo* species have all been the subject of intense debate over the past couple of decades, and any meaningful discussion of the role of diet in the origin and early evolution of our genus must be grounded in a firm understanding of these issues.

Homo habilis and *Homo rudolfensis*

Many researchers recognize two early species within our genus, *Homo habilis* and *H. rudolfensis* (Stringer 1986, Lieberman et al. 1988, Wood 1991, Rightmire 1993, Strait et al. 1997, Leakey et al. 2001, Dunsworth & Walker 2002, contra Tobias 1991). For the purposes of this review, we accept the hypodigms set forth by Wood (1991) for *H. habilis* and *H. rudolfensis*.

Temporal ranges for these taxa are presented in **Figure 1**. *Homo habilis* and *H. rudolfensis* were largely synchronous. Most *H. habilis* specimens come from Olduvai and Koobi Fora and date to between 1.87 and c. 1.65 Myr, although A.L. 666-1 from the Hadar extends its range back to 2.33 Myr (Kimbel et al. 1997). Specimens attributed to *H. habilis* at Sterkfontein (Tobias 1991) come mostly from Member 5, which probably also dates to between 2.3 and 1.8 Myr. Most *H. rudolfensis* specimens come from Koobi Fora and date to between 1.90 and 1.85 Myr, although specimens from the Omo Shungura Formation extend this range to 2.02 Myr and perhaps back even to 2.40 (Suwa et al. 1996). If the UR 501 mandible from Malawi and KNM-BC 1 temporal from Chemeron are attributable to *H. rudolfensis* (Bromage et al. 1995, Sherwood et al. 2002), this lends further support to a first appearance date for this taxon of c. 2.4 Myr. Furthermore, if KNM-ER 819 from Koobi Fora is *H. rudolfensis* (Wood 1991), that would extend the range for this taxon forward to between 1.65 and 1.55 Myr (**Figure 1**). Even so, there is little doubt that, as with other paleontological species, the fossil record does not accurately sample the entire geochronological ranges of either *H. habilis* or *H. rudolfensis*.

Homo erectus

Whereas Wood (1991) has argued for taxonomic distinction of *Homo ergaster* from *H. erectus* and other early *Homo* species, other workers have noted continuous morphological variation between specimens attributed

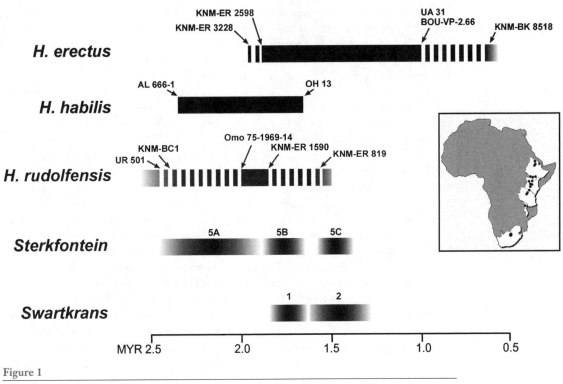

Figure 1

Early *Homo* timeline.

to *H. ergaster* and *H. erectus* (Wolpoff 1984, Kramer 1993, Rightmire 1998, Anton 2002, Asfaw et al. 2002, Dunsworth & Walker 2002). We here concur with these workers, who regard the earlier and later African specimens as sampling a single evolving species, *H. erectus*.

Homo erectus was a long-lived species, with a temporal range in Africa extending well over a million years (**Figure 1**). It was synchronous in the earlier part of its range with both *H. habilis* and *H. rudolfensis*. The oldest undisputed *H. erectus* specimen (the KNM-ER 2598 cranial fragment) dates to 1.89 Myr, well within the ranges of both *H. habilis* and *H. rudolfensis* (Feibel et al. 1989). The enigmatic KNM-ER 3228 hipbone might extend the range of this taxon as far back as 1.95 Myr (Susman et al. 1983, Rose 1984). The youngest African *H. erectus* fossils came from Baringo, and probably date to less than 660 Kyr (Wood & Van Noten 1986), and from Tighenif, Alge-

ria, between 800 Kyr and 600 Kyr (Geraads et al. 1986). *Homo erectus* has also been identified in Member 2 at Swartkrans (Robinson 1961, Rightmire 1990, Wood 1991, Tobias 1991), dating to between 1.9 and 1.65 Myr and perhaps younger (Vrba 1985, McKee et al. 1995).

ENVIRONMENTAL DYNAMICS AND DIETS OF EARLY *HOMO*

Given that diet is a direct link between an animal and its environment, environmental dynamics likely played an important role in dietary changes related to the origin and evolution of early *Homo*. Recent investigators have attempted to explain the origins of individual hominin species by relating first appearances of taxa during the late Pliocene to major episodes of global cooling and drying (see Vrba et al. 1995). Although researchers debate the tempo of faunal turnover at the time (see Potts 1998), most agree that cooler and more variable climatic conditions had a broad effect on mammalian diversity. Conventional wisdom associates adaptive radiations of *Paranthropus* and *Homo* to these environmental changes.

Cerling (1992) has noted that after 2.5 Myr, C$_4$ grasslands spread across East Africa, concomitant with periodic fluctuations in climate. If any of the early hominins had critical keystone foods (i.e., foods essential for survival and reproduction) found only in more closed habitats, then extinction would likely have followed. By contrast, if early hominins developed craniodental specializations for consuming savanna resources, such as roots, seeds, and tubers, they would have flourished. An alternative would be to face environmental change with versatility rather than specialization (e.g., Teaford et al. 2002, Wood & Strait 2004). This act would have been advantageous given variable, unpredictable environments, or a mosaic environment comprised of many different microhabitats (Behrensmeyer et al. 1997, Potts 1998, Wood & Strait 2004).

THE ARCHEOLOGICAL RECORD

The archeological record can provide important evidence for the diets of Plio-Pleistocene hominins. The earliest archeological remains, both lithic and faunal, probably relate directly to feeding activities. Modern orangutans and chimpanzees use hammerstones and wooden probes to open hard-husked fruits, sticks for digging and probing for insects in hard-to-reach places, and other implements fashioned to allow procurement or preparation of foods that would otherwise be inaccessible to them (Fox et al. 1999, Whiten et al. 1999). The earliest hominins likely also used such tools (Panger et al. 2002).

The earliest evidences we have for tool manufacture and use by hominins are stone artifacts from Gona, Ethiopia, dated to at least 2.5 Myr (Semaw et al. 1997) and faunal remains with cut marks from Bouri, Ethiopia, dated to about the same age (De Heinzelin et al. 1999). The actual origin of material culture is almost certainly much older, however, because the earliest tools were likely perishable (Mann 1972, Panger et al. 2002). The archeological record also likely underestimates the functional versatility of the early hominin tool kit. The use of stone tools in butchery is evinced by cut marked bones, but tools were probably also used to process many other types of foods, as is evident from microwear of slightly younger Oldowan artifacts used to prepare vegetation, presumably for consumption, and perhaps to make other tools from plant tissues (Keeley & Toth 1981). Furthermore, we cannot assume that early stone tools served the same functions for all early hominin groups, especially given differences in both material toolkits and diet among living chimpanzee groups (Whiten et al. 1999) and human foragers (Milton 2002). Indeed, we might reasonably view early stone tools as indicative of an expanded toolkit that included perishable and durable implements, thus reflecting increased dietary versatility and flexibility (e.g., Mann 1972, Schick & Toth 1993). Increasing distances by which stones were transported and the recovery of artifacts from a broader range of environments through the late Pliocene (Rogers et al. 1994, Potts 1998) also suggest increasing adaptive versatility for hominins.

Nevertheless, we are limited to the available evidence, and this evidence indicates that by 2.5 Myr, Pliocene hominins were making and using stone tools to process animal remains, almost certainly for consumption. Many researchers have thus argued that the earliest stone tools indicate the beginnings of a substantive increase in meat consumption by hominins (e.g., Dart 1953, Isaac 1971, Harris 1983). Although the early evidence is limited, additional possible cut marked bones have been found in deposits dated to 2.33–2.34 Myr in both West Turkana and the Hadar (Kibunjia 1994, Kimbel et al. 1997).

At first glance, it would seem that the near synchrony of appearances of *Homo* and the first stone tools and cut marked bones are connected, particularly in light of long-standing assumed associations between *H. habilis* and Oldowan artifacts (Leakey et al. 1964). However, there were at least three genera and four species of hominins in East Africa around 2.4–2.5 Myr, and there is no way to know which one(s) was responsible for these artifacts. The earliest known cut marks, for example, are found in the same stratigraphic horizon as hominin fossils referred to "*Australopithecus*" *garhi* (Asfaw et al. 1999). Also, the earliest evidence for *Paranthropus* (Walker et al. 1986) dates to 2.5 Myr, and some scholars have suggested that at least *P. robustus* used durable, identifiable tools (Susman 1988, Backwell & d'Errico 2001). At this point, then, we cannot argue that durable tool manufacture reflects a new, unique adaptive zone that can help define and distinguish the genus *Homo*. Regardless of whether *Australopithecus* or *Paranthropus* left an archeological record, however, most would agree that one or more species of early *Homo* probably did make and use Oldowan tools.

What about associations between major archeological advances and the appearance of *Homo erectus*? The first major technological innovation, the Acheulean, appears at ~1.4 Myr (Asfaw et al. 1992), and so it postdates the appearance of *H. erectus*. Furthermore, we cannot associate *Homo erectus* with the control of fire for cooking (another important advance in food-processing technology). Although early evidence for fire at Plio-Pleistocene sites includes reddened patches at Chesowanja and Koobi Fora, and burnt bones at Swartkrans (Gowlett et al. 1981, Brain 1993, Bellomo 1994), most researchers question whether this indicates controlled use of those fires (see Bunn 1999). The oldest unequivocal hearths date only to the middle Pleistocene of Eurasia and are attributed to *Homo heidelbergensis* (James 1989), and even the most recent finds do not push control of fire back beyond 790 Kyr (Goren-Inbar et al. 2004).

On the other hand, the earliest large concentrations of stone tools and modified bones at sites such as DK and FLK 22 at Olduvai and FxJj 1 at Koobi Fora are approximately coincident with the appearance of *Homo erectus* (Blumenschine & Masao 1991). Such sites show that animal tissues had become an important part of early hominin diets by the beginning of the Pleistocene (Potts 1983, Shipman 1983, Blumenschine 1995, Bunn 2001). Still, because *H. habilis*, *H. rudolfensis*, and *Paranthropus boisei* are also found at these sites, it is not possible to associate these concentrations definitively with any specific hominin. Nevertheless, it is reasonable to assume that *H. erectus* did make and use stone tools for animal processing, given similar sites outside of Africa, where no other hominins have been found (e.g., Dennell et al. 1988, Gabunia & Vekua 1995).

DIET MODELS AND EARLY *HOMO*

The apparent contemporaneity of the earliest *Homo*, Oldowan technology and the spread of C_4 grasslands across East Africa have made for compelling models of the origin and evolution of diet in early *Homo*. The argument suggests that environmental change during the late Pliocene (whether directional or an increase in fluctuation) would have led to changes in resources available to hominins. If early *Homo* used a greater range of habitats, or more variable habitats, an expanded toolkit would have allowed these hominins to process and consume foods that would have been otherwise unavailable. Environmental change provides the motive, and technological innovation offers the opportunity for new dietary adaptations. There remains, however, no consensus on which foods were key and how these foods contributed to the evolution of more human-like subsistence practices. Most models stress increased reliance on either animal products or on savanna-based plant resources.

USO: underground
storage organ

Meat Eating and Human Evolution

For more than a half century, researchers have stressed the predatory nature of humankind and the key role that hunting must have played in human evolution (e.g., Dart 1953). The basic idea has been that, as savannas began to spread, forest resources became increasingly scarce, and grassland-adapted ungulates became more abundant. Hominins began to incorporate more meat into their diets, with improved hunting abilities following from an expanding toolkit and increasing intelligence. A feedback loop followed, as the new high-protein diet allowed for larger brains, and hunting strategies led to a division of labor, more complex social systems, and selection for yet greater intelligence (Washburn 1963, Isaac 1971; see Lee & DeVore 1968).

Models emphasizing the role of meat eating in human evolution continue to dominate the literature today, but they approach the issue from a variety of perspectives (see Stanford & Bunn 2001). Models relating diet to brain size, for example, have suggested that meat became an increasingly important nutritional resource for early *Homo*, especially *H. erectus* (Milton 1987; Leonard & Robertson 1992, 1994). According to Aiello & Wheeler (1995), we maintain our basal metabolic rates by balancing brain size with gut size. Splanchnic organs and brains are roughly equally expensive tissues to maintain, so decreasing our guts would have allowed brain expansion without the need for a marked increase in energy intake. Animal products would provide readily digestible nutrients for hominins with small guts, so an increase in meat consumption may be tied, indirectly, to the evolution of a large brain. At the same time, animal fat would also provide important nutrients, such as long-chain polyunsaturated fatty acids used to form brain tissue (Hayden 1981, Speth 1989, Eaton et al. 2002).

Eaton and coauthors (2002) argue that as hunting and/or scavenging assumed greater significance, increased complexity of interpersonal and social interactions, together with animal fat, provided the necessary "psychonutritional nexus" for brain expansion. Indeed, many scholars have emphasized the role of changing subsistence strategies in division of labor and food sharing (Washburn & Lancaster 1968, Isaac 1978, Milton 1987). In this regard, increased meat consumption is seen as having been important to the origins and early evolution of a more human-like adaptive strategy. Recent work on nonnutritional aspects of hunting and meat consumption by chimpanzees and human foragers provides elaborate models for exploring possible roles of food in the evolution of human sociality (Kaplan et al. 2000, Stanford 2001).

Plant Eating and Human Evolution

Whereas most researchers have stressed increasing animal consumption as the savannas spread across eastern and southern Africa, others have proposed that early *Homo* included more xeric plants in their diets and that gathering was a motive force in human evolution (Linton 1971, Coursey 1973, Wolpoff 1973). As Zihlman & Tanner (1978) noted, plants often account for 60%–70% of the human forager diet. Thus, tools may well have been used first to gather and process plants.

More recent models emphasizing the role of xeric plant foods [especially underground storage organs (USOs) such as tubers, roots, corms, and bulbs] in early hominin evolution have followed, taking their leads from studies of human and nonhuman primate behavioral ecology. O'Connell and coauthors (1999) suggested that after 2 Myr, environmental changes led to reduced access to foods that children could gather themselves. The authors argued that these hominins showed a shift from ape-like to human-like life-history patterns in early *Homo* and that this shift implies an extended postmenopausal life span, allowing grandmothers to help gather food for their grandchildren. They proposed that USOs are the most likely keystone resource

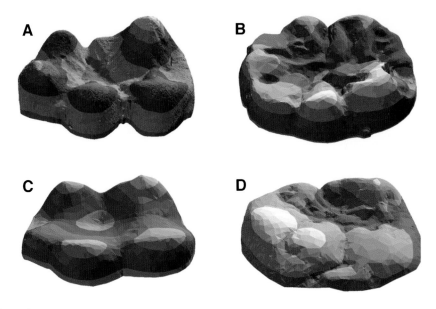

Figure 2

Triangulated irregular network models of surface data for similarly worn M₂s of (*A*) *Gorilla gorilla*, (*B*) *Pan troglodytes*, (*C*) *Homo erectus* (KNM-WT 15,000), and *D*) *Praeanthropus afarensis* (AL 266-1).

Figure 4

KNM-ER 3220. Note the taphonomic damage to the teeth. Image copyright by the National Museums of Kenya.

for early *Homo* and that increased reliance on material culture, such as digging sticks and ultimately cooking fires, would have improved access to these foods and the nutrients they contain. Although subsequent work casts doubt on life-history changes in early *Homo* (Dean et al. 2001), other work has also suggested USOs were important parts of early hominin diets.

Wrangham et al. (1999) proposed, as an alternative, that cooking appeared with early *Homo* and that associated delays in food consumption might have selected for a more human-like social system to protect food from theft. Like O'Connell and coauthors, Wrangham and coauthors emphasized the role of plant foods, especially USOs, in early *Homo* diets. Cooking, they argued, can increase digestibility of USOs and break down their mechanical and chemical defenses. It should be noted, however, that Schoeninger and coauthors (2001) have shown that USOs are of limited nutritional value in any case.

O'Connell's and Wrangham's models both suggest a transition from ape-like *Homo habilis* and *H. rudolfensis* subsistence strategies to a more human-like strategy for *H. erectus*. Furthermore, both models suggest larger female body mass and reduction of tooth size in *H. erectus*, compared with earlier *Homo*, as evidence for this transition (although we know of no data for relative female body mass in any of these taxa). Finally, both suggest that because evidence for the consumption of vertebrate tissues (cut marks on faunal remains found at hominin sites) predates *H. erectus*, meat eating is not likely central to the origins of a more human-like substance strategy.

PALEONTOLOGICAL EVIDENCE FOR DIET IN EARLY *HOMO*

The above-mentioned foraging models may generate testable hypotheses, but they do not provide any direct evidence of what *Homo rudolfensis*, *H. habilis*, or *H. erectus* actually ate. The archeological evidence is also important but is of limited utility given its bias toward durable resources and a lack of associations between artifact accumulations and specific hominin taxa. Furthermore, ecological models tell us about available resources but not about which ones were actually exploited. Nutritional models and those derived from human and nonhuman behavioral ecology suggest possible scenarios but do not allow us to choose among them.

The only direct source of data on the diets of early *Homo* is the fossil record of the hominins themselves. Researchers have developed a number of tools for teasing aspects of diet from these fossils. This work has focused on both biological adaptations (tooth size, shape and structure, and jaw biomechanics) and nonadaptive lines of evidence relating to the effects of foods on individuals during their lifetimes (dental microwear and mineralized tissue chemistry) (Ungar 1998, 2002). Although applications of these approaches to early *Homo* have been limited, some investigators have looked to the fossils for evidence of diet.

Tooth Size

Researchers have argued for more than a half century that tooth size differences among hominins reflect dietary differences (Robinson 1954, Jolly 1970, Kay 1985). Recent work has taken an allometric approach, evaluating data for fossil hominins relative to regressions of tooth size over body weight for extant primates with known diets. Relative incisor breadths suggest that *Homo habilis* and *H. rudolfensis* had large front teeth, with values above the 95% confidence limits of the extant regression line, whereas *H. erectus* fell on the line, along with the australopith species (Teaford et al. 2002). Because extant taxa with larger front teeth tend to eat foods requiring more extensive or intensive incisal preparation, we posited that *H. habilis* and *H. rudolfensis* probably also consumed foods requiring more anterior tooth use than did their australopith predecessors or *H. erectus*. We speculated that larger incisor sizes of *H. habilis* and *H. rudolfensis* compared with the australopiths relate to changes in diet and that incisor breadth reduction from *H. habilis* and *H. rudolfensis* to *H. erectus* reflects changing selective pressures with increasing tool use to prepare foods prior to ingestion. However, we also cautioned that the small samples for early *Homo* were "embarrassingly small" (see below) and that these inferences should be viewed with caution.

Other work has focused attention on molar allometry, suggesting that bigger cheek teeth provided larger working surfaces to process more low-quality foods. Researchers have noted a trend toward reduction in molar surface area through time in the *Homo* lineage (see Brace et al. 1991, McHenry 1994). Wood & Collard (1999) suggested, for example, that *Homo habilis* and *H. rudolfensis* have relatively large, australopith-sized molar teeth and, like their predecessors, had a "mechanically more demanding" diet than did *H. erectus*. They argued partly on this basis that *H. habilis* and *H. rudolfensis* occupied the same adaptive zone as did australopiths and should be reassigned to the genus *Australopithecus*. McHenry & Coffing (2000) challenged this assertion, however, suggesting that *H. habilis* and *H. rudolfensis* evince reduced cheek tooth area relative to reconstructed body size compared with australopiths and that this relative decrease is actually a key unique feature that *H. habilis* and *H. rudolfensis* share with later species of *Homo*.

Tooth Shape

The shapes of primate molar teeth reflect the fracture properties of foods that these animals eat. Taxa that often eat tough leaves, for example, have more occlusal relief than do species adapted to consume hard objects (e.g., Kay 1984, Meldrum & Kay 1997). Recent work confirms that dental topography differences between ape species track diet even for worn teeth (M'Kirera & Ungar 2003; Ungar & M'Kirera 2003, Ungar 2006a).

Dental topographic analysis on a mixed sample of early *Homo* specimens suggests occlusal relief and surface slope values intermediate between those of like-worn *Pan troglodytes* and *Gorilla gorilla* (**Figure 2**, see color insert) (Ungar 2004). Further, the early *Homo* sample had higher occlusal relief and surface slope values than did *Praeanthropus afarensis*,[1] with differences on the same order as those between chimpanzees and gorillas. These apes differ mostly in fallback foods in places where they are sympatric; gorillas rely more on tougher foods such as leaves and stems when preferred resources are less available. Perhaps then, early *Homo* species "fell back" on tougher foods, such as pliant plant parts or meat, than would have their predecessors (see Lucas & Peters 2000). Still, no hominin has reciprocally concave shearing blades like gorillas and siamangs, whose molars are specialized for fracturing tough foods (Kay 1985). Unfortunately, sample sizes of available undamaged molars of each individual *Homo* species are too small to compare *H. habilis*, *H. rudolfensis*, and *H. erectus*.

Enamel Thickness

Tooth enamel thickness has been argued to be an adaptation to protect teeth against breakage given a diet including hard, brittle foods requiring high occlusal forces to initiate fracture (Kay 1981, Dumont 1995). Notwithstanding methodological differences between studies, scholars generally agree that the australopiths and early *Homo* had relatively thick enamel on their molar crowns compared with modern humans and most other living primates. Although it is difficult to separate early *Homo* from australopiths given isolated measures of enamel thickness from various sources (Tobias 1991, Ramirez-Rozzi 1998), *H. erectus*

---

[1]The genus *Australopithecus* as advocated by many to include *A. africanus*, *A. afarensis*, and other species is most probably paraphyletic. Strait et al (1997) adopted the name *Praeanthropus africanus* for this taxon, which was later changed to *Praeanthropus afarensis* (ICZN 1999).

specimens had the absolutely thinnest enamel of those Plio-Pleistocene hominins analyzed by Beynon & Wood (1986). Thinner enamel facilitates quicker dentin exposure, which can increase surface jaggedness. This might therefore suggest another adaptation for efficient fracturing of tough foods (Kay 1981, Ungar & M'Kirera 2003).

Jaw Biomechanics

Mandibular corpus shape likely reflects forces acting on the jaw during chewing, potentially providing important clues concerning mechanical properties of foods eaten by early hominins (Hylander 1988, Daegling & Grine 1991). Although *Homo erectus* corpora are somewhat thinner than those of *H. habilis* and *H. rudolfensis*, all early *Homo* mandibular corpora are thicker than those of any extant ape and comparable in robusticity to those of "gracile" australopiths. If thicker corpora resist extreme torsion associated with high bite forces and/or muscle activity during chewing, early *Homo*, and especially *H. habilis* and *H. rudolfensis*, retained the ability to dissipate unusually high masticatory stresses.

Dental Microwear

The patterns of microscopic use-wear on primate molar teeth also relate to food preferences. Diets dominated by hard, brittle foods, for example, tend to leave large pits in teeth, whereas those dominated by tougher foods tend to leave more microwear striations and perhaps smaller pits (Teaford 1988, Teaford & Runestad 1992). Our own study of dental microwear in early *Homo* showed that these specimens tend to group with extant primates that do not regularly eat very fracture-resistant foods (Ungar et al. 2006). Nevertheless, we noted variation within the sample, such that *H. erectus* had, on average, more small pits than did *H. habilis* specimens (**Figure 3**). This finding suggests that *H. erectus* may have, at least on occasion, consumed more brittle or tough items than did *H. habilis*.

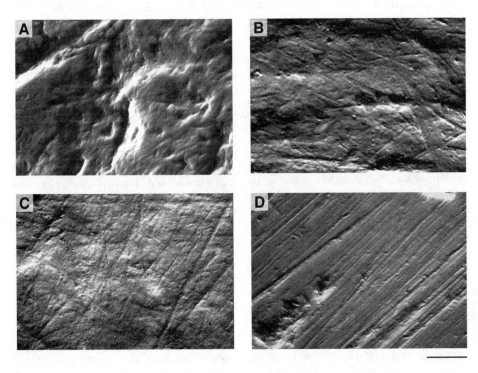

Figure 3

Dental microwear of (*A*) *Lophocebus albigena* (NMNH 220086), (*B*) *Homo erectus* (KNM-ER 820), (*C*) *Homo habilis* (OH 15), (*D*) *Gorilla gorilla* (NMNH 545027). Scale bar = 30 μm.

Mineralized Tissue Chemistry

Because stable isotope ratios and trace elements in animal tissues relate to foods eaten, studies of tooth and bone chemistry in early hominins may also give us insight into diet and habitat (Sillen & Kavanagh 1991, Schoeninger et al. 1997). Elevated Sr/Ca in *Homo erectus* suggested to Sillen and coauthors (1995), for example, that these hominins ate underground storage organs, which are high in strontium. However, the ability of stable isotope studies to distinguish hominin taxa has been limited. Indeed, specimens of *Australopithecus africanus*, *Paranthropus robustus*, and early *Homo* all show δ^{13}C and δ^{18}O values similar to one another and to other primates, with values between those of extant grazers and browsers, perhaps suggesting a comparable mix of C_3- and C_4-based foods (Lee-Thorp et al. 2000, van der Merwe et al. 2003).

LIMITS TO INTERPRETATION

Although studies such as these help us glean insights about the diets of early *Homo*, we must acknowledge the limitations of what we can infer from the fossil evidence (Ungar 2006b). Small samples reduce the power of statistical analyses. Relationships between form and function are often unclear when applied to the fossil record. Taphonomic processes alter remains, making interpretations difficult. And, in the case of hominins, there are few appropriate living analogs, particularly for comparative studies on how technological innovation affects selective pressures on biology.

Sample Size

The single greatest obstacle to reconstructing diet in early *Homo* is sample size. For example, only five I^{1}s have been reported for early *Homo* (one for *H. rudolfensis*, two for *H. habilis*, and two for *H. erectus*). This limitation, along with typical variation of about ±20% for hominoids (see Plavcan 1990), makes it difficult to consider how incisor size relates to diet in these hominins. Small sample sizes further hamper dental allometry studies because of their dependence on postcranial elements to reconstruct body weights. *H. rudolfensis* has no definitively associated craniodental and postcranial remains. Even if samples were sufficient, Smith (1996) has argued convincingly that confidence intervals for reconstructed weight estimates are so great that most allometric studies of fossil hominins would have to be viewed very cautiously. McHenry (1994), for example, lists a species average body weight for *H. habilis* of 51.6 kg ± 22.6 kg for males and 31.5 kg ± 22.5 kg for females.

Unclear Relationships between Function and Morphology

Diet cannot be inferred from fossils where form-function relationships are unclear in living primates (Kay 1984). Molar size presents one case in point. Recent studies have used this attribute to help define adaptive zones for early hominins (Wood & Collard 1999, Leakey et al. 2001), with the basic idea that larger cheek teeth indicate lower-quality diets. Although this may explain why folivorous platyrrhines have relatively larger molars than do frugivorous New World monkeys, it is not clear why frugivorous catarrhines have larger molars than do closely related folivores (Kay 1977, Lucas 1980). Mandibular corpus robusticity provides another example. If thick mandibular corpora are expected to resist stresses and strains associated with a diet involving heavy chewing, why do colobines and gorillas have such thin corpora compared with early hominins? It is no surprise, then, that Brown (1997) found "not a single useful formula whereby a given mandible can be associated with a specific diet" (p. 269).

Taphonomic Effects

Bones and teeth are exposed to taphonomic agents that can alter them, making the inference of diet difficult or impossible. Dental microwear, for example, is often obliterated by surface etching or erosion (**Figure 4**, see color insert)—molars of only 18 of 83 early *Homo* specimens examined from East and South Africa retain antemortem dental microwear (Ungar et al. 2006). This is a problem because large samples are important to infer dietary breadth, given that individual wear features can be worn away and replaced by others in only days (Teaford & Oyen 1989).

The problem is even worse with studies of mineralized tissue chemistry, where it is often difficult to identify and control for the diagenetic effects of fossilization (Schoeninger et al. 2003). Furthermore, there are limitations to the antiquity of fossil specimens suitable for such analyses given current technology, particularly for those elements (e.g., nitrogen) found in the organic phases of bones and teeth. Also, because a specific food type can yield varying results depending on the environment from which it comes, accumulation from different times and places can be especially problematic—particularly for hominins who likely moved among microhabitats during life. One related problem with tissue chemistry studies is that different foods can yield similar results. For example, a folivore can have Sr/Ca levels indistinguishable from those of a carnivore (Sealy & Sillen 1988). Different foods can likewise confer the same $\delta^{13}C$ values (see Burton & Wright 1995).

Technological Innovation and Natural Selection

Conventional wisdom suggests that one key adaptive shift in early *Homo* was an increased reliance on tools for food acquisition and processing (Oakley 1962). As tools began to take on an increasingly important role in obtaining and preparing foods, selective pressures on hominin jaws and teeth probably changed (Brace et al. 1991). Cutting implements, for example, change the mechanical properties of foods before they enter the mouth and, hence, change the demands placed on the craniodental toolkit for food processing. Tools, therefore, become a confounding variable in assessing form-function relationships between teeth and jaws, on the one hand, and food properties, on the other.

We are further limited by our lack of understanding of the roles that tools played in food acquisition and processing by early *Homo*. Even if we could reasonably reconstruct stone (and bone) tool function, we have no perishable elements of the early Oldowan toolkit, and we have no way of knowing how common and important these tools were to early *Homo*. We cannot, therefore, adequately assess the probable effects of tools on the jaws and teeth of early *Homo*. This problem is further exacerbated by a lack of extant analogs with which to compare effects of habitual tool use on craniodental morphology; there is a substantive gap between chimpanzees and modern humans in degree of tool use in food acquisition and processing.

DISCUSSION

Although a number of problems limit our ability to reconstruct the diets of early *Homo*, the evidence we have is still valuable for evaluating competing models and generating new hypotheses. It is difficult to assess changes between the australopiths and their early *Homo* successors. Claims of larger incisors and smaller molars in *H. habilis* and *H. rudolfensis* are difficult to evaluate without larger samples and more precise body-weight estimates. Preliminary observations of cheek tooth crown shape hint that early *Homo* had more occlusal relief than did some australopiths (e.g., *Praeanthropous afarensis*). If so, early *Homo* would have been able to process tougher foods better than could *Pr. afarensis*. Technological innovations may have further allowed the consumption of a broader spectrum of foods.

Small samples prohibit assessment of morphological differences between *H. erectus* and *H. habilis* or *H. rudolfensis*. Still, *H. erectus* may have had thinner dental enamel, narrower mandibular corpora, and more small microwear pits in their cheek teeth. These observations suggest that *H. erectus* may have been less capable of crushing hard objects but better able to shear through tougher foods with their molar teeth than *H. rudolfensis*, *H. habilis*, and earlier hominins. This possible reduction in ability to process a broad spectrum of foods would, at first glance, seem to be a reversal of the trend toward selection for an increasingly flexible diet suggested for "gracile" australopiths (Teaford & Ungar 2000). Alternatively, this evidence may simply reflect changing selective pressures resulting from food preparation using tools prior to ingestion and mastication, thus indicating the increasing role of technology as an adaptive strategy (Teaford et al. 2002).

Dietary Versatility as an Adaptive Strategy

The fossil, archeological, and paleoenvironmental evidence taken together suggest a model of increasing dietary versatility with the appearance and early evolution of *Homo*. The concurrence of stone tools, cut marked bones, and early *Homo* by ~2.4 Myr suggests that regardless of what other hominins were doing, *H. rudolfensis* and *H. habilis* probably used durable and perishable tools to increase the range of foods to which they would have had access. Technological innovation likely played a relatively minor role in the dietary adaptations of these taxa, though, because *H. rudolfensis* and *H. habilis* show little evidence of the changing selective pressures expected if tools replaced jaws and teeth in initial food processing. These hominins retain fairly thick molar enamel and broad mandibular corpora perhaps for processing hard foods or those foods requiring repetitive loading, yet they show more molar cusp relief than at least *Praeanthropus afarensis*, suggesting an improved ability to fracture tough foods such as pliable plant parts and meat. Tools would have allowed for more dietary flexibility, but in-

creased dietary versatility still may have been driven more by biological (i.e., dental) than by cultural evolution.

On the other hand, the earliest major concentrations of tools and tool-modified bones coincide roughly with the appearance of *H. erectus*. Although other hominins may have been involved, *H. erectus* almost certainly contributed to these sites, especially given similar accumulations outside Africa. *H. erectus* may also show adaptive changes, such as thinning enamel, to further improve efficiency in shearing and slicing tough foods such as pliable plant parts or meat. Although increasing efficiency for fracturing tougher foods may have resulted in decreased ability to crush hard and brittle foods, tools such as the hammerstones observed for Taï Forest chimpanzees (Boesch & Boesch 1990) could have easily compensated. Thus, a combination of tools and morphological change would have allowed increased dietary versatility for *H. erectus*.

Dietary versatility would have been especially useful given environmental changes, such as the spread of C_4 grasslands across East Africa following 2.5 Myr, when *H. habilis* and *H. rudolfensis* first appear. It would also have served *H. erectus* well because this taxon emerged at the midpoint of a significant faunal turnover spanning 2.1–1.7 Myr. Potts (1998) argued that locomotor versatility was a crucial adaptation to Pliocene climatic fluctuation and mosaic habitats. We suggest that dietary flexibility may have been equally important as an adaptive strategy under these environmental conditions. Craniodental adaptations and material culture would have allowed early *Homo*, and especially *H. erectus*, to eat a broader spectrum of foods than could earlier hominins.

This does not mean that early *Homo* individuals had particularly varied diets, but rather that they may have been capable of eating a broader range of foods. Chimpanzees and gorillas show significant differences in their diets, depending on the individual population and the seasonal availability of resources within home ranges (e.g., Goodall & Groves 1977, Vedder 1984, Wrangham et al. 1991, Yamagiwa et al. 1992, Tutin et al. 1997, Yamakoshi 1998). Ethnographic studies over the past century have shown human foragers to have an even greater range of diets, from nearly all animal products (e.g., Ho et al. 1972) to mostly wild plant parts (e.g., Gould 1980). This finding led Milton (2002) to argue vehemently against a single hypothetical "Paleolithic diet."

Perhaps then, early *Homo*, and especially *H. erectus*, had an adaptive strategy of dietary versatility. This versatility would have been advantageous in an unpredictable, changing environment or an environment dominated by many different microhabitats. Perhaps *H. erectus* was the first hominin to leave Africa because it was the first with sufficient dietary versatility to allow it to do so. It may be no coincidence that this species spread into habitats as far north as the Republic of Georgia, and perhaps as far east as Indonesia, so quickly following its origin and first appearance in Africa (Swisher et al. 1994, Gabunia et al. 2000).

Evaluation of Common Models

A versatility model for early *Homo* diets differs from most published models, which focus on specific keystone resources. Most reconstructions involve a shift from closed-forest C_3 vegetation to meat or more xeric plant underground storage organs. But how important was meat to early *Homo*? Because investigators have found few cut marked bones at archeological sites predating 1.9 Myr, meat-eating by hominins may not have been widespread when early *Homo* first evolved. *Homo rudolfensis* and *H. habilis* retain thick tooth enamel and wide mandibular corpora, indicative of an ability to process hard, brittle foods, but appear to show greater occlusal relief, suggesting increased efficiency for ingesting and shearing tough foods, including meat. Thus, although meat-eating could have remained opportunistic under some condi-

tions, animal tissues may have started to become a more important resource under other conditions.

Evidence of an important role for meat eating is more compelling for *H. erectus*. Large concentrations of stone tools and modified bones after 1.9 Myr combined with thinner enamel may suggest improved abilities to slice and shear tough foods, including meat. A higher incidence of small pits in the enamel may indicate the consumption of soft, tough foods such as meat (Teaford & Runestad 1992). However, did meat dominate their diets? Not necessarily. The little lithic microwear evidence we have suggests that early Pleistocene tools were used to process animal and plant tissues (Keeley & Toth 1981).

What about underground storage organs? Thick tooth enamel, flat occlusal surfaces, and broad mandibular corpora of *Homo rudolfensis* and *H. habilis* are consistent with crushing hard and brittle foods, such as USOs (assuming that these are, in fact, hard and brittle). However, the fact that early *Homo* had more occlusal relief than did their hominin predecessors suggests they were not adapted to hard and brittle roots and tubers. Furthermore, cheek tooth microwear data suggest lower pit percentages than expected of a hard object specialist (Ungar et al. 2006). Although tools might certainly have been used to dig out edible bulbs and roots and to crush them prior to ingestion, the archeological record does not offer evidence for this (see Backwell & d'Errico 2001). In sum, there is little evidence that *H. rudolfensis* and *H. habilis* would have specialized on these foods. Nutritional considerations also make a USO specialization unlikely (Schoeninger et al. 2001).

One could make a similar argument for *H. erectus*. Although tools could have allowed these hominins to procure and process USOs, some morphological evidence may suggest that these hominins would have been less able to process hard, abrasive roots and tubers within the mouth. These hominins simply do not show clear morphological adaptations suggesting specialization on such resources.

SUMMARY AND CONCLUSIONS

Many models exist for the origins and early evolution of the genus *Homo*. Most models note an environmental shift to drier, more open conditions in the late Pliocene. Authors argue that the roughly concurrent appearances of early *Homo* and an archeological record suggest that these hominins evolved subsistence strategies to process xeric resources, be they animal or plant tissues, with the help of tools. Resulting hunting or gathering strategies are said to have set in motion psychosocial changes that led from a more ape-like to a more human-like adaptive strategy.

The fossil and archeological evidence offer little support for adaptive strategies that focus on such specific foods. We propose that the fossil evidence, combined with archeological remains and paleoenvironmental indicators, suggests a more flexible, versatile subsistence strategy. This is not to say that *H. rudolfensis*, *H. habilis*, or *H. erectus* individuals necessarily had very broad diets at any given time. These species were more likely adapted to subsist in a range of different environments with different resources in each. This strategy would have put them at an advantage given climatic fluctuation and a mosaic of different microhabitats in Africa during the late Pliocene.

ACKNOWLEDGMENTS

We are grateful to the governments and National Museums of Ethiopia, Kenya, and Tanzania for permission to study early hominin specimens in their care and to the curators at the University of the Witwatersrand and the Transvaal Museum for permission to study early hominin materials from South Africa. We also thank Luci Betti for her work on **Figure 1**. This work was supported by the L.S.B. Leakey Foundation and the U.S. National Science Foundation.

LITERATURE CITED

Aiello LC, Wheeler P. 1995. The expensive tissue hypothesis. *Curr. Anthropol.* 36:199–221

Antón SC. 2002. Evolutionary significance of cranial variation in Asian *Homo erectus*. *Am. J. Phys. Anthropol.* 118:301–23

Asfaw B, Beyenne Y, Suwa G, Walter RC, White TD, et al. 1992. The earliest Acheulian from Konso-Gardula. *Nature* 360:730–35

Asfaw B, Gilber WH, Beyene Y, Hart WK, Renne PR, et al. 2002. Remains of *Homo erectus* from Bouri, Middle Awash, Ethiopia. *Nature* 416:317–20

Asfaw B, White TD, Lovejoy O, Latimer B, Simpson S, Suwa G. 1999. *Australopithecus garhi*: a new species of early hominid from Ethiopia. *Science* 284:629–35

Backwell LR, d'Errico F. 2001. Evidence of termite foraging by Swartkrans early hominids. *Proc. Natl. Acad. Sci. USA* 98:1358–63

Behrensmeyer AK, Todd NE, Potts R, McBrinn GE. 1997. Late Pliocene faunal turnover in the Turkana Basin, Kenya and Ethiopia. *Science* 278:1589–94

Bellomo RV. 1994. Methods of determining early hominid behavioral activities associated with the controlled use of fire at FxJj 20 Main, Koobi Fora, Kenya. *J. Hum. Evol.* 27:173–95

Beynon AD, Wood BA. 1986. Variations in enamel thickness and structure in East African hominids. *Am. J. Phys. Anthropol.* 70:177–93

Blumenschine RJ. 1995. Percussion marks, tooth marks, and experimental determinants of the timing of hominid and carnivore access to long bones at FLk *Zinjanthropus*, Olduvai Gorge, Tanzania. *J. Hum. Evol.* 29:21–51

Blumenschine RJ, Masao FT. 1991. Living sites at Olduvai Gorge, Tanzania?: Preliminary landscape archaeology results in the basal Bed II lake margin zone. *J. Hum. Evol.* 21:451–62

Boesch C, Boesch H. 1990. Tool use and tool making in wild chimpanzees. *Fol. Primatol.* 54:86–99

Brace CL, Smith BH, Hunt KD. 1991. What big teeth you had grandma! Human tooth size, past and present. In *Advances in Dental Anthropology*, ed. MA Kelley, CS Larsen, pp. 33–57. New York: Wiley-Liss

Brain CK. 1993. The occurrence of burnt bones at Swartkrans and their implications for the control of fire by early hominids. In *Swartkrans: A Cave's Chronicle of Early Man*, ed. CK Brain, pp. 229–42. Pretoria: Transvaal Mus.

Bromage TG, Schrenk F, Zonneveld FW. 1995. Paleoanthropology of the Malawi Rift: an early hominid mandible from the Chiwondo Beds, northern Malawi. *J. Hum. Evol.* 28:71–108

Brown B. 1997. Miocene hominoid mandibles: functional and phylogenetic perspectives. In *Function, Phylogeny, and Fossils: Miocene Hominoid Evolution and Adaptations*, ed. DR Begun, CV Ward, MD Rose, pp. 153–71. New York: Plenum

Bunn HT. 1999. Reply to Wrangham et al. *Curr. Anthropol.* 40:579–80

Bunn HT. 2001. Hunting, power scavenging, and butchering by Hadza foragers and by Plio-Pleistocene *Homo*. In *Meat-Eating and Human Evolution*, ed. CB Stanford, HT Bunn, pp. 199–218. Oxford, UK: Oxford Univ. Press

Burton JH, Wright LE. 1995. Nonlinearity in the relationship between bone Sr/Ca and diet: Paleodietary implications. *Am. J. Phys. Anthropol.* 96:273–82

Cerling TE. 1992. Development of grasslands and savannas in East Africa during the Neogene. *Paleogeogr. Palaeoclimatol. Palaeoecol.* 97:241–47

Coursey DG. 1973. Hominid evolution and hypogeous plant foods. *Man* 8:634–35

Daegling DJ, Grine FE. 1991. Compact bone distribution and biomechanics of early hominid mandibles. *Am. J. Phys. Anthropol.* 86:321–39

Dart RA. 1953. The predatory transition from ape to man. *Int. Anthropol. Ling. Rev.* 1:201–17

Dean C, Leakey MG, Reid D, Schrenk F, Schwartz GT, et al. 2001. Growth processes in teeth distinguish modern humans from *Homo erectus* and earlier hominins. *Nature* 414:628–31

De Heinzelin J, Clark JD, White T, Hart W, Renne P, et al. 1999. Environment and behavior of 2.5-million-year-old Bouri hominids. *Science* 284:625–29

Dennell RW, Rendell H, Hailwood E. 1988. Early tool making in Asia: two million year old artefacts in Pakistan. *Antiquity* 62:98–106

Dumont ER. 1995. Enamel thickness and dietary adaptation among extant primates and chiropterans. *J. Mammal.* 76:1127–36

Dunsworth H, Walker AC. 2002. Early genus *Homo*. In *The Primate Fossil Record*, ed. W Hartwig, pp. 419–35. New York: Cambridge Univ. Press

Eaton SB, Eaton SB III, Cordain L. 2002. Evolution, diet, and health. In *Human Diet: Its Origin and Evolution*, ed. PS Ungar, MF Teaford, pp. 7–18. Westport, CT: Bergen and Garvey

Feibel C, Brown FH, McDougall I. 1989. Stratigraphic context of fossil hominids from the Omo Group deposits: northern Turkana Basin, Kenya and Ethiopia. *Am. J. Phys. Anthropol.* 78:595–622

Fox EA, Sitompul AF, van Schaik CP. 1999. Intelligent tool use in wild Sumatran orangutans. In *The Mentality of Gorillas and Orangutans*, ed. S. Parker, L Miles, A Mitchell, pp. 99–117. Cambridge, UK: Cambridge Univ. Press

Gabunia L, Vekua A. 1995. A Plio-Pleistocene hominid from Dmanisi, East Georgia, Caucasus. *Nature* 373:509–12

Gabunia L, Vekua A, Lordkipanidze D, Swisher CC, Ferring R, et al. 2000. Earliest Pleistocene hominid cranial remains from Dmanisi, Republic of Georgia: taxonomy, geological setting, and age. *Science* 288:1019–25

Geraads D, Hublin JJ, Jaeger JJ, Tong H, Sen S, Tourbeau P. 1986. The Pleistocene hominid site of Ternifine, Algeria: new results on the environment, age, and human industries. *Quaternary Res.* 25:380–86

Goodall AG, Groves CP. 1977. The conservation of eastern gorillas. In *Primate Conservation*, ed. Prince Rainier III of Monaco, GH Bourne, pp. 599–637. New York: Academic

Gould RA. 1980. *Living Archeology.* Cambridge, UK: Cambridge Univ. Press

Gowlett JA, Harris JWK, Walton D, Wood BA. 1981. Earliest archeological sites, hominid remains and traces of fire from Chesowanja, Kenya. *Nature* 292:125–29

Harris JWK. 1983. Cultural beginnings: Plio-Pleistocene archaeological occurrences form the Afar, Ethiopia. In *African Archaeological Review*, ed. N David, pp. 3–31. Cambridge, UK: Cambridge Univ. Press

Hayden B. 1981. Subsistence and ecological adaptations of modern hunter/gatherers. In *Omnivorous Primates: Gathering and Hunting in Human Evolution* ed. RSO Harding, G Teleki, pp. 344–421. New York: Columbia Univ. Press

Ho KJ, Mikkelson B, Lewis LA, Feldman SA, Taylor CB. 1972. Alaskan arctic Eskimos: response to a customary high fat diet. *Am. J. Clin. Nutr.* 25:737–45

Hylander WL. 1988. Implications of in vivo experiments for interpreting the functional significance of "robust" australopithecines' jaws. In *Evolutionary History of the "Robust" Australopithecines*, ed. FE Grine, pp. 55–83. New York: Aldine de Gruyter

Goren-Inbar N, Alperson N, Kislev ME, Simchoni O, Melamed Y, et al. 2004. Evidence of hominin control of fire at Gesher Benot Ya'aqov, Israel. *Science* 304:725–27

ICZN. 1999. *Australopithecus afarensis* Johanson, 1978. (Mammalia, Primates): specific name conserved. Opinion 1941. *Bull. Zool. Nomen.* 56:223–24

Isaac GL. 1971. The diet of early man: aspects of archaeological evidence from lower and middle Pleistocene sites in Africa. *World Archaeol.* 1:1–28

Isaac GL. 1978. Food-sharing and human evolution: archaeological evidence from the Plio-Pleistocene of East Africa. *J. Anthropol. Res.* 34:311–25

James S. 1989. Hominid use of fire in the Lower and Middle Pleistocene: a review of the evidence. *Curr. Anthropol.* 30:1–26

Jolly CJ. 1970. The seed-eaters: a new model of hominid differentiation based on a baboon analogy. *Man* 5:1–26

Kaplan H, Hill K, Lancaster J, Hurtado AM. 2000. A theory of human life history evolution: diet, intelligence and longevity. *Evol. Anthropol.* 9:156–85

Kay RF. 1977. The evolution of molar occlusion in the Cercopithecidae and early catarrhines. *Am. J. Phys. Anthropol.* 46:327–52

Kay RF. 1981. The nut-crackers: a new theory of the adaptations of the Ramapithecinae. *Am. J. Phys. Anthropol.* 55:141–51

Kay RF. 1984. On the use of anatomical features to infer foraging behavior in extinct primates. In *Adaptations for Foraging in Nonhuman Primates: Contributions to an Organismal Biology of Prosimians, Monkeys and Apes*, ed. PS Rodman, JGH Cant, pp. 21–53. New York: Columbia Univ. Press

Kay RF. 1985. Dental evidence for the diet of *Australopithecus. Annu. Rev. Anthropol.* 14:315–41

Keeley LH, Toth N. 1981. Microwear polishes on early stone tools from Koobi Fora, Kenya. *Nature* 293:464–65

Kibunjia M. 1994. Pliocene archeological occurrences in the Lake Turkana Basin. *J. Hum. Evol.* 27:159–71

Kimbel WH, Johanson DC, Rak Y. 1997. Systematic assessment of a maxilla of *Homo* from Hadar Ethiopia. *Am. J. Phys. Anthropol.* 103:235–62

Kramer A. 1993. Human taxonomic diversity in the Pleistocene: Does *Homo erectus* represent multiple hominid species? *Am. J. Phys. Anthropol.* 91:161–71

Leakey LSB, Tobias PV, Napier JR. 1964. A new species of the genus *Homo* from Olduvai Gorge. *Nature* 202:7–9

Leakey MG, Spoor F, Brown FH, Gathogo PN, Kiarie C, et al. 2001. New hominin genus from eastern Africa shows diverse middle Pliocene lineages. *Nature* 410:433–40

Lee RB, DeVore I. 1968. *Man the Hunter*. Chicago: Aldine

Lee-Thorp JA, Thackeray JF, van der Merwe NJ. 2000. The hunters or the hunted revisited. *J. Hum. Evol.* 39:565–76

Lieberman DE, Pilbeam DR, Wood BA. 1988. A probabilistic approach to the problem of sexual dimorphism in *Homo habilis*: a comparison of KNM-ER 1470 and KNM-ER 1813. *J. Hum. Evol.* 17:503–12

Leonard WR, Robertson ML. 1992. Nutritional requirements and human evolution: a bioenergetics model. *Am. J. Hum. Biol.* 4:179–95

Leonard WR, Robertson ML. 1994. Evolutionary perspectives on human nutrition: the influence of brain and body size on diet and metabolism. *Am. J. Hum. Biol.* 6:77–88

Linton S. 1971. Woman the gatherer: male bias in anthropology. In *Woman in Cross-Cultural Perspective: A Preliminary Sourcebook*, ed. SE Jacobs, pp. 9–21. Urbana: Univ. Ill. Press

Lucas PW. 1980. *Adaptation and form of the mammalian dentition with special reference to the evolution of man*. PhD thesis, Univ. College, London

Lucas PW, Peters CR. 2000. Function of postcanine tooth shape in mammals. In *Development, Function and Evolution of Teeth*, ed. MF Teaford, MM Smith, MWJ Ferguson, pp. 282–89. Cambridge, UK: Cambridge Univ. Press

Mann AE. 1972. Hominid and cultural origins. *Man* 7:379–86

McHenry HM. 1994. Behavioral ecological implications of early hominid body size. *J. Hum. Evol.* 27:407–31

McHenry HM, Coffing K. 2000. *Australopithecus* to *Homo*: transformations in body and mind. *Annu. Rev. Anthropol.* 29:125–46

McKee JK, Thackeray JF, Berger LR. 1995. Faunal assemblage serration of southern African Pliocene and Pleistocene fossil deposits. *Am. J. Phys. Anthropol.* 106:235–50

Meldrum DJ, Kay RF. 1997. *Nuciruptor rubricae*, a new pitheciin seed predator from the Miocene of Colombia. *Am. J. Phys. Anthropol.* 102:407–28

Milton K. 1987. Primate diets and gut morphology: implications for hominid evolution. In *Food and Evolution: Toward a Theory of Human Food Habits*, ed. M Harris, EB Ross, pp. 93–115. Philadelphia: Temple Univ. Press

Milton K. 2002. Hunter-gatherer diets: wild foods signal relief from diseases of affluence. In *Human Diet: Its Origin and Evolution*, ed. PS Ungar, MF Teaford, pp. 111–22. Westport, CT: Bergen & Garvey

Oakley KP. 1962. The earliest tool-makers. In *Evolution und Hominisation*, ed. G Kurth, pp. 157–69. Stuttgart: Geburtstage von Gerhard Heberer

O'Connell JF, Hawkes K, Blurton-Jones NJ. 1999. Grandmothering and the evolution of *Homo erectus*. *J. Hum. Evol.* 36:461–85

Panger MA, Brooks AS, Richmond BG, Wood B. 2002. Older than the Oldowan? Rethinking the emergence of hominin tool use. *Evol. Anthropol.* 11:235–45

Plavcan JM. 1990. *Sexual dimorphism in the dentition of extant anthropoid primates*. PhD thesis, Duke Univ., Durham, NC

Potts R. 1983. Foraging for faunal resources by early hominids. In *Animals and Archaeology*, Volume 1, ed. J Clutton-Brock, C Grigson, pp. 51–62. London: Br. Archaeol. Rep.

Potts R. 1998. Environmental hypotheses of hominin evolution. *Yrbk. Phys. Anthropol.* 41:93–136

Ramirez-Rozzi F. 1998. Can enamel microstructure be used to establish the presence of different species of Plio-Pleistocene hominids from Omo, Ethiopia? *J. Hum. Evol.* 35:543–76

Rightmire GP. 1990. The evolution of *Homo erectus*. Cambridge, UK: Cambridge Univ. Press

Rightmire GP. 1993. Variation among early *Homo* crania from Olduvai Gorge and the Koobi Fora region. *Am. J. Phys. Anthropol.* 90:1–33

Rightmire GP. 1998. Evidence from facial morphology for similarity of Asian and African representatives of *Homo erectus*. *Am. J. Phys. Anthropol.* 106:61–85

Robinson JT. 1954. Prehominid dentition and hominid evolution. *Evolution* 8:324–34

Robinson JT. 1961. The australopithecines and their bearing on the origin of Man and of stone tool making. *S. Afr. J. Sci.* 57:3–16

Rogers M, Feibel CS, Harris JWK. 1994. Changing patterns of land use by Plio-Pleistocene hominids in the Lake Turkana Basin. *J. Hum. Evol.* 27:139–58

Rose MD. 1984. A hominine hip bone, KNM-ER 3228., from East Lake Turkana, Kenya. *Am. J. Phys. Anthropol.* 63:371–78

Schick KD, Toth N. 1993. *Making Silent Stones Speak*. Phoenix: Orion Books

Schoeninger MJ, Bunn HT, Murray SS, Marlett JA. 2001. Composition of tubers used by Hadza foragers of Tanzania. *J. Food Compos. Anal.* 14:15–25

Schoeninger MJ, Iwaniec UT, Glander KE. 1997. Stable isotope ratios indicate diet and habitat use in New World monkeys. *Am. J. Phys. Anthropol.* 103:69–84

Schoeninger MJ, Reeser H, Hallin K. 2003. Paleoenvironment of *Australopithecus anamensis* at Allia Bay, East Turkana, Kenya: evidence from mammalian herbivore enamel isotopes. *J. Anthropol. Archaeol.* 22:200–07

Sealy J, Sillen A. 1988. Sr and Sr/Ca in marine and terrestrial foodwebs in the southwestern Cape, South Africa. *J. Archaeol. Sci.* 15:425–38

Semaw S, Renne P, Harris JWK, Feibel CS, Bernor RL, et al. 1997. 2.5 million-year-old stone tools from Gona, Ethiopia. *Nature* 385:333–36

Sherwood RJ, Ward SC, Hill A. 2002. The taxonomic status of the Chemeron temporal (KNM-BC 1). *J. Hum. Evol.* 42:153–84

Shipman P. 1983. Early hominid lifestyle: hunting and gathering or foraging and scavenging? In *Animals and Archaeology*, Vol. 1, ed. J Clutton-Brock, C Grigson, pp. 31–50. London: Br. Archaeol. Rep.

Sillen A, Hall G, Armstrong R. 1995. Strontium calcium ratios (Sr/Ca) and strontium isotope ratios (^{87}Sr/^{86}Sr) of *Australopithecus robustus* and *Homo* sp. from Swartkrans. *J. Hum. Evol.* 28:277–85

Sillen A, Kavanagh M. 1991. Stronium and paleodietary research: a review. *Yrbk. Phys. Anthropol.* 25:67–90

Smith RJ. 1996. Biology and body size in human evolution. *Curr. Anthropol.* 37:451–81

Speth JD. 1989. Early hominid hunting and scavenging: the role of meat as an energy source. *J. Hum. Evol.* 18:329–43

Stanford CB. 2001. A comparison of social meat-foraging by chimpanzees and human foragers. In *Meat-Eating and Human Evolution*, ed. CB Stanford, HT Bunn, pp. 122–40. Oxford, UK: Oxford Univ. Press

Stanford CB, Bunn HT. 2001. *Meat-Eating and Human Evolution*. Oxford, UK: Oxford Univ. Press

Strait DS, Grine FE, Moniz MA. 1997. A reappraisal of early hominid phylogeny. *J. Hum. Evol.* 32:17–82

Stringer CB. 1986. The credibility of *Homo habilis*. In *Major Topics in Primate and Human Evolution*, ed. BA Wood, LV Martin, P Andrews, pp. 266–94. New York: Liss

Susman RL. 1988. Hand of *Paranthropus robustus* from member 1, Swartkrans: fossil evidence for tool behavior. *Science* 240:781–84

Susman RL, Stern JT, Rose MD. 1983. Morphology of KNM-ER 3228 and OH 28 innominates from East Africa. *Am. J. Phys. Anthropol.* 60:259

Suwa G, White TD, Howell FC. 1996. Mandibular postcanine dentition from the Shungura Formation, Ethiopia: crown morphology, taxonomic allocations, and Plio-Pleistocene hominid evolution. *Am. J. Phys. Anthropol.* 101:247–82

Swisher C, Curtis G, Jacob T, Getty A, Suprijo A, Widiasmoro. 1994. Age of the earliest known hominids in Java. *Science* 263:1118–21

Teaford MF. 1988. A review of dental microwear and diet in modern mammals. *Scan. Microsc.* 2:1149–66

Teaford MF, Oyen OJ. 1989. In vivo and in vitro turnover in dental microwear. *Am. J. Phys. Anthropol.* 80:447–60

Teaford MF, Runestad JA. 1992. Dental microwear and diet in Venezuelan primates. *Am. J. Phys. Anthropol.* 88:347–64

Teaford MF, Ungar PS. 2000. Diet and the evolution of the earliest human ancestors. *Proc. Natl. Acad. Sci. USA* 97:13506–11

Teaford MF, Ungar PS, Grine FE. 2002. Paleontological evidence for the diets of African Plio-Pleistocene hominins with special reference to early *Homo*. In *Human Diet: Its Origins and Evolution*, ed. PS Ungar, MF Teaford, pp. 143–66. Westport, CT: Bergin and Garvey

Tobias PV. 1991. *The Skulls, Endocasts and Teeth of* Homo habilis. *Olduvai Gorge*, Vol. 4. Cambridge, UK: Cambridge Univ. Press

Tutin CEG, Ham R, White LJT, Harrison MJS. 1997. The primate community of the Lopé Reserve in Gabon: diets, responses to fruit scarcity and effects on biomass. *Am. J. Primatol.* 42:1–24

Ungar PS. 1998. Dental allometry, morphology and wear as evidence for diet in fossil primates. *Evol. Anthropol.* 6:205–17

Ungar PS. 2002. Reconstructing diets of fossil primates. In *Reconstructing Behavior in the Primate Fossil Record*, ed. JM Plavcan, RF Kay, WL Jungers, CP van Schaik, pp. 261–96. New York: Kluwer Academic

Ungar PS. 2004. Dental topography and diets of *Australopithecus afarensis* and early *Homo*. *J. Hum. Evol.* 46:605–22

Ungar PS. 2006a. Dental topography and human evolution: with comments on the diets of *Australopithecus africanus* and *Paranthropus robustus*. In *Dental Perspectives on Human Evolution: State of the Art Research in Dental Anthropology*, ed. S Bailey, JJ Hublin. New York: Springer-Verlag. In press

Ungar PS. 2006b. Limits to knowledge on the evolution of hominin diet. In *Evolution of the Human Diet: The Known, the Unknown, and the Unknowable*, ed. PS Ungar. New York: Oxford Univ. Press. In press

Ungar PS, Grine FE, Teaford MF, El-Zaatari S. 2006. Dental microwear and diets of African early *Homo*. *J. Hum. Evol.* 50:78–95

Ungar PS, M'Kirera F. 2003. A solution to the worn tooth cunundrum in primate functional anatomy. *Proc. Natl. Acad. Sci. USA* 100:3874–77

Ungar PS, Teaford MF, Grine FE. 2001. A preliminary study of molar microwear of early *Homo* from East and South Africa. *Am. J. Phys. Anthropol.* 32(Suppl.):153

Van der Merwe NJ, Thackeray JF, Lee-Thorp JA, Luyt J. 2003. The carbon isotope ecology and diet of *Australopithecus africanus* at Sterkfontein, South Africa. *J. Hum. Evol.* 44:581–97

Vedder A. 1984. Movement patterns of a group of free-ranging mountain gorillas (*Gorilla gorilla beringei*) and their relation to food availability. *Am. J. Primatol.* 7:73–88

Vrba ES. 1985. Early hominids in southern Africa: updated observations on chronological and ecological background. In *Hominid Evolution: Past, Present and Future*, ed. PV Tobias, pp. 165–70. New York: Liss

Vrba ES, Denton GH, Partridge TC, Gurkle LH (eds.). 1995. *Paleoclimate and Evolution with Emphasis on Human Origins*. New Haven, CT: Yale Univ. Press

Walker A, Leakey RE, Harris JM, Brown FH. 1986. 2.5 Myr *Australopithecus boisei* from West of Lake Turkana, Kenya. *Nature* 322:517–22

Washburn SL. 1963. Behavior and human evolution. In *Classification and Human Evolution*, ed. SL Washburn, pp. 190–203. Chicago: Aldine

Washburn SL, Lancaster CS. 1968. The evolution of hunting. In *Man the Hunter*, ed. RB Lee, I DeVore, pp. 293–303. Chicago: Aldine

Whiten A, Goodall J, McGrew WC, Nishida T, Reynolds V, et al. 1999. Cultures in chimpanzees. *Nature* 399:682–85

Wolpoff MH. 1973. Posterior tooth size, body size, and diet in South African gracile australopithecines. *Am. J. Phys. Anthropol.* 39:375–94

Wolpoff MH. 1984. Evolution of *Homo erectus*: the question of stasis. *Paleobiol.* 10:389–406

Wood BA. 1991. *Hominid Cranial Remains. Koobi Fora Research Project*, Vol. 4. Oxford, UK: Clarendon

Wood BA, Collard M. 1999. The human genus. *Science* 284:65–71

Wood BA, Strait D. 2004. Patterns of resource use in early *Homo* and *Paranthropus*. *J. Hum. Evol.* 46:119–62

Wood BA, Van Noten FL. 1986. Preliminary observations on the BK 8518 mandible from Baringo, Kenya. *Am. J. Phys. Anthropol.* 69:117–27

Wrangham RW, Conklin NL, Chapman CA, Hunt KD. 1991. The significance of fibrous foods for Kibale Forest chimpanzees. *Phil. Trans. R. Soc. London Ser. B* 334:171–78

Wrangham RW, Holland Jones J, Laden G, Pilbeam D, Conklin-Brittain NL. 1999. The raw and the stolen: cooking and the ecology of human origins. *Curr. Anthropol.* 40:567–94

Yamagiwa J, Mwanza N, Yumoto T, Maruhashi T. 1992. Travel distances and food habits of eastern lowland gorillas: a comparative analysis. In *Topics in Primatology, Volume 2: Behavior, Ecology and Conservation*, ed. N Itoigawa, Y Sugiyama, GP Sackett, RKR Thompson, pp. 267–81. Tokyo: Univ. Tokyo Press

Yamakoshi G. 1998. Dietary responses to fruit scarcity of wild chimpanzees at Boussou, Guinea: possible implications for ecological importance of tool use. *Am. J. Phys. Anthropol.* 106:283–95

Zihlman AL, Tanner NM. 1978. Gathering and hominid adaptation. In *Female Hierarchies*, ed. L Tiger, HT Fowler, pp. 163–94. Chicago: Beresford Food Serv.

Alcohol: Anthropological/ Archaeological Perspectives

Michael Dietler

Department of Anthropology, University of Chicago, Chicago, Illinois 60637;
email: m-dietler@uchicago.edu

Annu. Rev. Anthropol. 2006. 35:229–49

First published online as a Review in
Advance on May 11, 2006

The *Annual Review of Anthropology* is
online at anthro.annualreviews.org

This article's doi:
10.1146/annurev.anthro.35.081705.123120

Copyright © 2006 by Annual Reviews.
All rights reserved

0084-6570/06/1021-0229$20.00

Key Words

material culture, colonialism, feasts, gender, identity

Abstract

Alcohol is a special form of embodied material culture and the most
widely used psychoactive agent in the world. It has been a fundamentally important social, economic, political, and religious artifact
for millennia. This review assesses trends in the anthropological engagement with alcohol during the past two decades since the *Annual
Review* last covered this subject. It highlights the growing archaeological contributions to the field, as well as recent developments by
sociocultural anthropologists and social historians. Increasing historicization has been a useful corrective to the earlier functionalist
emphasis on the socially integrative role of drinking. Recent studies tend to employ a more strategic/agentive analytical framework
and treat drinking through the lens of practice, politics, and gender.
Moreover, alcohol has come to be seen as an important component
of the political economy and a commodity centrally implicated in
strategies of colonialism and postcolonial struggles over state power
and household relations of authority.

INTRODUCTION

It has been nearly two decades since the *ARA* published an overview of the anthropology of alcohol (Heath 1987a). The current review seeks to complement this excellent earlier study by selectively assessing some major trends in the field during the intervening period. This includes highlighting archaeological contributions to the study of the history of alcohol, something that has been largely absent from works on alcohol by sociocultural anthropologists. Space limitations preclude any attempt at comprehensive coverage, and several important themes, such as medical anthropology's engagement with alcohol studies, are left to other venues and more capable hands (e.g., Bennett & Cook 1996, Marshall et al. 2001).

As Heath (1987a) pointed out in his review, the study of alcohol was experiencing a transformation in perspective at the time he was writing (see also Heath 1976, 1987b, 1995, 2000). The dominant approach, grounded almost exclusively in the disciplines of biology/medicine, public health, and social psychology, had focused on alcohol consumption primarily as an individual pathology or a social problem. This view began essentially with the emergence of the temperance movement in the early nineteenth century, the corresponding creation of alcohol as a collective category and dangerous substance, and the discursive construction of drinking as a problem and then alcoholism as a disease (Blocker 1989, Harrison 1971, Heather & Robertson 1989, McDonald 1994c). However, by the 1980s the orthodoxy of this alcoholism-and-addiction literature was being challenged by a growing anthropological engagement with the subject, which had begun in the 1960s, that focused instead on normal drinking and on alcohol as an integrated social artifact and culturally valued good. Moreover, for the first time, anthropologists were undertaking ethnographic research specifically designed to focus on alcohol rather than simply reporting on it as a secondary by-product of studies designed to meet other goals.

Since that time, anthropological studies of alcohol have proliferated, and several new developments in theoretical orientation have both guided and grown out of this work. To be sure, alcohol has remained a minority research field within anthropology, and anthropologists have never achieved more than a minority voice in the broader field of alcohol studies, nor have they shared much in the abundant research funding supporting this field (see Hunt & Barker 2001). However, they have made important contributions in highlighting the cultural understanding of drinking practices and patterns and in exposing the ethnocentric assumptions underlying much other work. In this sense, both anthropologists and social historians have played similarly subversive roles in alcohol studies by challenging entrenched orthodoxies of more powerful disciplines from the margins (Barrows & Room 1991b, Bennett & Cook 1996).

Much of the earlier alcohol research in sociocultural anthropology evinced a somewhat defensive tone in response to two trends. The first was a foundational subtext of ethnocentric moralizing and individualism in the dominant alcohol-as-pathology literature, and the second was an earlier widespread colonial discourse about the predilection for inebriation and disorder among colonized peoples. Hence, early anthropological analyses often were drawn by the logic of (at least implicit) polemic into a functionalist orientation that focused predominantly on the socially integrative role of drinking. This is evident even in works as late as Douglas (1987a). More recent studies, however, have tended to give equal emphasis to conflict and contradiction and to treat drinking in a more agentive/strategic framework through the lens of practice, politics, and gender. Moreover, the criticism that anthropologists had ignored the dysfunctional aspects of drinking (e.g., Room 1984) has been countered by studies that seek to define and understand culturally and historically specific forms of abnormal problem drinking within particular normal drinking patterns (Bennett & Cook 1996, Colson &

Scudder 1988, Eber 2000, Heath 2000, Huby 1994, Marshall 1991, Spicer 1997). Furthermore, since Singer's (1986) critique of the field for neglecting the broader political economy in which drinking is embedded, alcohol increasingly has come to be recognized as an important component of the political economy and as a commodity centrally implicated in strategies of colonialism and postcolonial economic and political struggles over state power and in household relations of authority (e.g., Bryceson 2002a, Crush & Ambler 1992, Dietler 1990, Jankowiak & Bradburd 2003). Social historians and some anthropologists have also contributed to a crucial historicization of drinking that has been important in overcoming some of the problems inherent in functionalist interpretations (e.g., Akyeampong 1996, Barrows & Room 1991a, Colson & Scudder 1988, Willis 2002). Finally, another significant new development is the extension of research on alcohol into the deep past through the emergence of a sustained archaeological engagement with drinking (e.g., Dietler 1990, Milano 1994, Vencl 1994) and a recent flourishing of work by archaeologists on feasting (e.g., Bray 2003a, Dietler & Hayden 2001, Wright 2004).

This review examines several of these trends, with a special effort made to highlight the archaeological exploration of alcohol. The intention is to suggest that alcohol research represents a fruitful conjuncture of interests and actually has the potential to serve as a mutually heuristic bridge across the subdisciplines of anthropology.

ALCOHOL AS EMBODIED MATERIAL CULTURE

One issue that demands immediate attention is the nature of the category that defines the subject of this review. What, precisely, is meant by alcohol, and what are the implications of using this term? In the first place, it should be clear that the term does not describe a single, self-evident object. Rather, alcohol is a culturally specific, and quite re-

cent, analytical category that lumps together an astonishing variety of disparate substances on the sole basis of the common presence of a chemical named ethanol (C_2H_5OH) that produces psychoactive effects. However, the chemical composition and properties of ethanol were identified only in the twentieth century, and, as noted above, the concept of alcohol as a collective term linking such things as beer, wine, and whiskey is a discursive product of the nineteenth-century temperance movement (Blocker 1989, Harrison 1971, Roberts 1984). This is not necessarily a universally shared folk category, especially among peoples who had/have not been exposed to the recent Euro-American demonization and medicalization of drinking that arose in the context of an emerging urban-industrial social order and the demands of capitalist work discipline. Even in societies that use the category, culturally specific patterns of inclusion and exclusion can, for example, create fatal problems for epidemiological survey studies when researchers are unaware of such variations. Strunin (2001), for instance, found that young Haitians did not consider two favorite rum-based beverages (*kremas* and *likay*) to be alcoholic drinks.

Ethanol can be produced from an impressively wide range of sugary or starchy foods by a variety of techniques (Bruman 2000, Huetz de Lemps 2001, Jennings et al. 2005). Moreover, some varieties of alcoholic drinks have substantial nutritional value, and they may form a significant component of the diet of many peoples (Platt 1955, 1964; Steinkraus 1995). In fact, it is perhaps more appropriate to think of alcohol as a special class of food with psychoactive properties resulting from the application of alternative culinary techniques: The same grain can become porridge, bread, beer, or whiskey, depending simply on the techniques applied to it. It is clear that many peoples think of their traditional forms of alcohol in this way. Despite the British conception of alcohol as a kind of antifood that marks a discrete sphere of consumption (Douglas 1975), one shared by ancient Greeks

(Murray 1990), many peoples consider it an especially valued form of food.

Furthermore, similar to other foods, alcohol is a form of what may be called embodied material culture (Dietler 2001). That is, it is a special kind of material culture created specifically to be destroyed, but destroyed through the transformative process of ingestion into the human body. Hence, it has an unusually close relationship to the person and to both the inculcation and the symbolization of concepts of identity and difference in the construction of the self. Moreover, because of their psychotropic properties, alcoholic beverages often have a heightened valuation in ritual contexts, and they frequently even serve as a crucial indexical sign of ritual. As one Tanzanian informant succinctly summed it up, "If there's no beer, it's not a ritual" (Willis 2002, p. 61). Consequently, the consumption of alcohol is usually enveloped by a set of cultural rules and beliefs that is even more emotionally charged than with other foods and drinks (Douglas 1987b; Heath 1987a, 1987b, 2000; Wilson 2005b). Furthermore, because sustaining the process of alcohol consumption requires continual replenishing production through both agricultural and culinary labor, this domain of material culture reveals especially intimate dialectical linkages between the domestic and political economy. These features also assure that the consumption of embodied material culture constitutes a prime arena for the negotiation, projection, and contestation of power, or what may be called commensal politics (Dietler 1996).

In brief, alcoholic drinks are not simply reducible to a uniform chemical substance with physiological effects. They constitute a form of material culture subject to almost unlimited possibilities for variation in terms of ingredients, techniques of preparation, patterns of association and exclusion, modes of serving and consumption, aesthetic and moral evaluations, expected behavior when drinking, styles of inebriation, and so forth. They form a versatile and highly charged symbolic medium and social tool that are operative in the playing out of ritual and politics, and in the construction of social and economic relations, in crucial ways. Hence, alcohol, as a special class of embodied material culture, is a particularly salient example of what Mauss referred to as a "total social fact," and it constitutes an especially revealing focus of analysis for anthropologists and historians.

THE (PRE)HISTORY OF ALCOHOL

Alcohol is currently the most widely used human psychoactive agent around the world, and this is a social fact with a deep history. At the time of European colonial expansion, only parts of the Pacific and North America seem to have been without indigenous versions of alcoholic drinks, and European forms were quickly adopted in those regions as well. Furthermore, although religious prohibitions against alcohol consumption currently are widespread in the Islamic Middle East, this was certainly not the case in antiquity. Some of the oldest archaeological evidence for beer and wine comes from precisely this region (McGovern et al. 1995, Michel et al. 1993), and the word alcohol is even of Arabic origin (al'kohol, originally meaning a powdered essence).

The investigation of the early history of alcohol by archaeologists and ancient historians has developed greatly in recent years. That is not to say that earlier scholars ignored alcohol in antiquity (e.g., see Braidwood et al. 1953). But what distinguishes recent work is a more systematic, concerted effort both to develop the theoretical understanding of drinking as a social practice (e.g., Dietler 1990, 2001; Murray 1995; Poux 2004) and to improve techniques for detecting alcohol production and consumption in the archaeological record (e.g., Biers & McGovern 1990, Michel et al. 1993). Part of this effort has also involved the ethnoarchaeological investigation of alcohol, in which researchers undertake ethnographic studies that pay systematic attention to the material dimension of alcohol in its social context as a way of aiding archaeological interpretation (Arthur 2003; Bowser 2003; Dietler & Herbich 2001, 2006).

Archaeologists have several potential lines of evidence to explore the production and consumption of alcohol in the past, and the best results come from triangulating multiple strands of data. These strands include the excavated material-culture traces of consumption, production, and trading practices (e.g., brewing, drinking, serving, and transport vessels; feasting ritual sites and domestic kitchens; breweries and wineries; and shipwrecks laden with wine amphorae), iconographic and textual representations of drinking, models and test implications derived from experimental and ethnographic research, and the chemical traces of alcoholic beverages preserved in ancient vessels.

Archaeometric techniques for analyzing chemical residues from ancient vessels have seen remarkable progress over the past couple of decades, and these techniques have been instrumental in the recent detection of alcohol in Neolithic China, demonstrating the production of a fermented beverage of rice, honey, and fruit as early as the seventh millennium B.C.E. This beverage was the precursor of the cereal-based alcohol of the second millennium B.C.E. that has been preserved inside sealed bronze vessels of the Shang and Western Zhou dynasties (McGovern et al. 2004). The earliest chemical traces of alcohol found elsewhere date to the early sixth millennium B.C.E. and come from the Middle East and Transcaucasia. The oldest residues of grape wine come from Georgia, and residues of both wine and barley beer have been found in Iranian ceramics dating a few centuries later (McGovern 2003, Michel et al. 1993), although the origin of these beverages is probably even older. It has even been suggested that the desire for beer may have been responsible for the original domestication of cereals in the eighth millennium B.C.E. (Braidwood et al. 1953, Katz & Voigt 1986). In any case, archaeological evidence of wine and beer drinking is widespread in Mesopotamia, Assyria, and Anatolia by the third millennium B.C.E., and this demonstrates both that wine was an object of trade from an early date and that it was generally a costly good consumed only by elite strata of these societies, whereas the lower classes drank beer (Joffe 1998, McGovern et al. 1995, Milano 1994, Pollock 2003).

Wine had also spread to beer-drinking Egypt by the third millennium B.C.E., despite the absence of native wild grapes in Egypt. The evidence for alcohol in ancient Egypt is particularly rich: It includes tomb paintings and models illustrating the complete wine-making and beer-making processes. The evidence also shows that wine was, again, present as an important elite drink and that it had important religious roles (James 1995, Lesko 1995, Poo 1995). Wine jars demonstrate that a complex labeling system was already in operation in ancient Egypt by the New Kingdom. Writing on the shoulders of jars and stamps on clay seals indicated the year of the vintage, the region, the vineyard, the vintner, and even the quality of the wine (Lesko 1995). Barley and wheat beer, however, remained the popular drink of the masses, and there is evidence for its production on a large scale, such as the brewery excavated at Hierakonpolis (Geller 1993).

In Europe, credible evidence for alcoholic beverages, especially drinking vessels in funerary contexts, dates back to at least the Neolithic, although it is probable that forms of alcohol such as fermented honey (mead) may have existed even earlier (Dietler 1990, 1996; Sherratt 1991; Vencl 1994). Both grain beers and mead are attested during the Iron Age (first millennium B.C.E.) through historical texts, chemical residues, and the traces of a possible brewery in Germany (Arnold 1999, Dietler 1990, 1999, Stika 1996). Wine was also introduced to Early Bronze Age Greece in the third millennium B.C.E. and served as an elite beverage in Minoan and Mycenaean contexts (Hamilakis 1999; Wright 1995, 2004). It subsequently spread to Italy with Greek colonization during the eighth and seventh centuries B.C.E. Unlike its role in other societies, wine eventually replaced beer and other drinks altogether among Greeks (except Spartans), Etruscans, and Romans of all social classes (Murray 1990, Murray & Tecusan 1995, Tchernia 1986, Tchernia & Brun 1999). Meanwhile, Phoenician colonists carried the practice of making wine from the Levant to Carthage and their colonies in southern Spain during the eighth century B.C.E. (Greene 1995). By 700 B.C.E., native Iberian societies in Spain (where beer was the indigenous drink) began to make their own wine and to trade it in amphorae modeled after the Phoenician type (Guérin & Gómez Bellard 1999). France was the last region in the Mediterranean to begin consuming wine. The introduction of wine to this region was the result of an Etruscan wine trade that began in the late seventh century B.C.E. and the founding of the Greek colony of Massalia (modern Marseille) in approximately 600 B.C.E., which produced the first wine in France (Bertucchi 1992, Dietler 1990). By the second to first centuries B.C.E., the Mediterranean wine trade had expanded dramatically, such that an estimated 55–65 million amphorae of Roman wine were imported into France over a period of a century (Poux 2004, Tchernia 1986). By the second century C.E., France, now a Roman province, had become a major wine-producing region that was even exporting wine back to Rome (Amouretti & Brun 1993, Brun 2003).

The origins of alcohol distillation are still somewhat obscure. Greeks in Alexandria had already developed the distillation of plant essences for medicinal purposes by the fourth century C.E. The technique was further developed by Arab chemists for the extraction of essential oils for perfumes, and it probably was passed back to Europe during the medieval period, perhaps through Spain. The distillation of alcohol from wine seems to have emerged in the medical schools of Salerno and/or Montpellier during the twelfth century (although see Allchin 1979). Distilled alcohol remained primarily for medicinal uses until the sixteenth and seventeenth centuries, although some recreational consumption seems to have begun as early as the fifteenth century, especially in Germany. During the sixteenth century, production began to shift from apothecaries and monasteries to merchants and commercial distillers. By the seventeenth century, consumption was widespread and production increased dramatically, especially once cheaper sugar- and grain-based alcohols began to be produced in northern Europe (Braudel 1979, pp. 241–49; Forbes 1970; Matthee 1995).

Little archaeological research has been conducted on ancient alcohol in Africa outside of Dynastic Egypt, although Edwards (1996) has identified credible evidence for the ritual importance of sorghum beer in Kushite society from the late first millennium B.C.E. However, sub-Saharan Africa does have an immense range of indigenous alcoholic beverages made from various cereals, bananas, palm sap, honey, and other ingredients that were an important part of African cultures everywhere at the time of European and Arabic contact (Huetz de Lemps 2001). These are probably of considerable antiquity in most areas, a fact attested by an eleventh-century reference by the geographer Al-Bakri to alcoholic drinks as part of a royal funerary ritual in Ghana (Pan 1975, pp. 20–21). As in most other places, the technique of distilling alcohol is a by-product of European colonialism and dates only to the late nineteenth century in most parts of Africa. However, indigenous materials were quickly adapted to make distillation devices and produce local varieties of distilled spirits in many areas (Dietler & Herbich 2006, Huetz de Lemps 2001, Tanzarn 2002, Willis 2002).

In India, textual evidence demonstrates that barley and rice beers extend back to at least the Vedic period (second millennium B.C.E.), and alcoholic beverages made from a variety of grasses, fruits, and other substances are also attested in ancient texts (Prakash 1961). On the basis of Sanskrit texts and possible small pottery stills, Allchin (1979) has even claimed that the process of alcohol distillation may have been invented in India and Pakistan at approximately 500 B.C.E., although the evidence for this is ambiguous.

The New World also has a range of traditional alcoholic drinks made from very different ingredients: principally maize and agave, but many other kinds of roots, fruits, and stalks as well (Bruman 2000). In the Americas, less research has been conducted on identifying the earliest traces of these drinks. However, it is clear that maize-based *chicha* was an important element of feasting and state politics in the Inca empire and in several earlier expansionary polities of South America from at least the third century B.C.E. (Bray 2003b, Cook & Glowacki 2003, Goldstein 2003, Lau 2002, Moore 1989, Morris 1979). Moreover, *chica* may have been a significant implement of feasting and status differentiation as early as the ninth century B.C.E. (Clark & Blake 1994). It has even been argued that the desire for alcohol made from sweet stalks (rather than grain) may have been responsible for the original domestication and spread of maize as early as the sixth millennium B.C.E. (Smalley & Blake 2003). In Central America, the Maya also drank maize beer, as well as a fermented drink called *balché* made from honey and bark that was additionally spiked with hallucinogens (Coe 1994, pp. 134, 166; LeCount 2001). Fermented agave formed the base for the alcohol of choice (*pulque*) of the Aztec state (Smith et al. 2003). This drink presumably had a greater antiquity as well, although clear evidence is lacking. Distilled alcohol and the production of wine from grapes in the New World are products of the Spanish conquest (Bruman 2000, Rice 1996).

Recent archaeological and historical research of this kind has succeeded in enriching our understanding of the deep antiquity and near ubiquity of alcohol on a worldwide scale, as well as illuminating the social, political, and economic roles of alcohol in ancient societies. These latter insights are discussed below with related contributions from sociocultural anthropologists and social historians.

ALCOHOL, IDENTITY, AND GENDER

The integrative role of alcohol in maintaining social cohesion and drinking as a constructive social act are themes stressed by most anthropologists who have studied alcohol since the 1960s, and these need little further comment here (see Douglas 1987b; Heath 1987a, 1987b, 2000). Another longstanding theme has been the way in which drinking serves to mark social categories, boundaries, and identity. However, what distinguishes more recent work is that drinking patterns are not viewed simply as reflections of social organization, manifestations of deep cognitive structure (in the structuralist mode), nor as simple expressions of cultural identity, but rather as practices through which personal and group identity are actively constructed, embodied, performed, and transformed. In other words, drinking is seen as a significant force in the construction of the social world, both in the sense of creating an ideal imagined world of social relationships and in the pragmatic sense of strategically crafting one's place within that imagined world, or challenging it. This theme has, in fact, tended to dominate a number of recent edited volumes on drinking by both anthropologists and historians (e.g., de Garine & de Garine 2001, Douglas 1987a, Gefou-Madianou 1992, McDonald 1994b, Scholliers 2001, Wilson 2005a).

This kind of identity construction and marking through drinking occurs along a variety of social category and boundary distinctions, including age, gender, class, family or lineage, occupation, ethnicity, and religion (e.g., Martin 2001, Mars 1987, McDonald 1994a). Regional, national, and cosmopolitan identities also frequently involve drinking practices (e.g., Guy 2001, Hall 2005, Wilson 2005b). The relationship between alcohol and identity can also shift over time, as, for example, in contexts of increasing commoditization in which traditional associations with age/seniority and community may be overridden by new associations with class distinctions

(Suggs 1996). In all these cases, drinking serves simultaneously to construct both a sense of communal identity for those drinking together or sharing tastes and a sense of difference and boundaries from others.

It is not only types of alcohol that serve as indexical signs of identity. Drinking is a learned *technique du corps*, in the sense of Mauss (1936), and all aspects are relevant in embodying and discerning identity and difference. Hence, in addition to such qualitative distinctions (i.e., aesthetic dispositions people develop about preferred kinds of alcohol, drinking paraphernalia, and styles of drinking and the cultural capital derived from embodied knowledge about proper consumption practices), various other symbolic diacritica converge in complex permutations in the construction of identity through drinking practices. These include the following: (*a*) spatial distinctions (i.e., segregation into separate drinking places or other structured differential positioning of groups or individuals while drinking together), (*b*) temporal distinctions (such as the order of serving or consumption, or the timing of drinking events), (*c*) quantitative distinctions (in the relative amounts of drink consumed or served), and (*d*) behavioral distinctions (i.e., differences in expected bodily comportment during and after drinking, including such things as permissible signs of intoxication or expected modes of drunken comportment and serving or being served). Such distinctions are not only part of an embodied Bourdieuean habitus, but they can be consciously manipulated on a microscale to make statements about relative status or sentiments of inclusion and exclusion at various levels. Feasts and other kinds of drinking rituals can be an especially powerful theater for such politically charged symbolic assertions and contestations (Dietler & Hayden 2001).

Gender is perhaps the most widespread dimension of identity in which alcohol plays an obvious role (Gefou-Madianou 1992, McDonald 1994b). Masculinity is frequently defined around the capacity to drink within associations of male drinkers, from the ancient Greek *symposion* to the Irish pub (Driessen 1992, Murray 1990, Peace 1992, Suggs 1996). In many societies, women may be expected to drink less than men (or to abstain completely), to behave differently from men when drinking or intoxicated, to prefer different kinds of alcohol than men, or to drink in different places than men (Dietler & Herbich 2006, Eber 2000, Hendry 1994, Huby 1994, Macdonald 1994, Suggs 1996). Male and female practices may also vary by class within the same society (González Turmo 2001). These features are not static but change in response to a variety of factors, including the use of drinking as a form of resistance to male authority (Papagaroufali 1992) and the commoditization of alcohol (Suggs 1996).

Another gendered dimension of drinking is that, at least in contexts of nonindustrial production, women have often been the primary suppliers of alcohol predominantly consumed by men. Some researchers have viewed this as exploitation, although female brewing labor (and male dependence on it) may also be overtly recognized and valued, and women may derive considerable categorical and individual status from their central role in the furnishing of hospitality or in maintaining commensal relations with the gods (March 1998). Furthermore, with the commoditization of alcohol, women have frequently benefited from their role as brewers by developing a new source of economic power and independence (see below).

Alcohol has also played a frequent role in the distinction of class boundaries and the embodiment of class identities through both the development of tastes for different types of alcohol and styles of drinking, and sometimes the imposition of sumptuary laws restricting access to symbolically charged drinks or drinking paraphernalia. In contemporary Africa, for example, factory-brewed bottled beer and traditional ferments commonly distinguish the consumption patterns of urban workers and provincial salaried professionals on the one hand, and rural agriculturalists on the other, whereas imported distilled liquor is consumed exclusively by urban elites (e.g., Colson & Scudder 1988, Diduk 1993, Partanen 1991). These specific distinctions represent a postcolonial shift in African patterns, but this is not a new phenomenon. As noted above, the distinction between wine and beer was a common class marker in ancient Mesopotamia and Egypt, and diacritical styles of drinking also characterized, for example, some European Iron Age societies (Arnold 1999; Dietler 1990, 1999). In other contexts, distinctions between wine and beer, for instance, may be associated more with regional identity than class (e.g., Hall 2005), although class may be marked by other aspects of drinking practices.

ALCOHOL AND POLITICS

Alcohol has long been a prime political tool. Its importance in this domain is related to its widespread association with hospitality and ritual, and to its status as a socially valued good and form of embodied material culture that acts as a social marker. There are numerous paths by which alcohol is deployed in the micropolitics and macrostrategies of the manipulation of power and the construction of authority (see Dietler 1990, 2001; Willis 2002). However, especially in the context of rituals of public consumption (feasts), alcohol has been equally crucial to the operation of politics at all scales: from societies without formal political roles or institutions, to societies with centralized chiefly authority, to imperial states (Bray 2003a, Dietler & Hayden 2001).

In contexts where the exercise of power is not vested in formal political institutions or roles, the manipulation of drinking frequently serves as a significant avenue to the creation of prestige and social capital that are fundamental to the conditions of possibility for leadership in influencing group decisions and actions. The production of this kind of power may occur in the context of the subtle small-scale engineering of social indebtedness through the manipulation of hospitality (e.g., in small beer drinks in the home), the lavish hosting of community ceremonies, or the overtly agonistic mounting of competitive feasts (e.g., Dietler & Herbich 2006, Rehfisch 1987). Hosting drinking feasts may also be essential for climbing the social hierarchy by acquiring formal titles or ritual positions, where these exist (e.g., Arthur 2003, de Garine 1996).

In societies with formal centralized leadership roles, the generous public provision of alcohol on a regular basis frequently is seen as a duty of the person who performs that role, as it symbolically institutionalizes a patron-client relationship. Failure to lavishly dispense alcohol will result in loss of authority, and political challenges may be orchestrated through the mounting of rival drinking feasts. This public largesse can impose considerable demands on such leaders for agricultural surplus and brewing labor (Jennings 2005), and it is one of the main reasons often cited for a connection between political power and polygyny in Africa (see Dietler 2001). Such leaders also frequently have a right to tribute in alcohol and to corvée labor from subjects that serves to ease the burden of such obligatory hospitality. However, corvée labor also requires the provision of beer in compensation for participation (see below). Researchers have observed this kind of political role for alcohol in cases ranging from petty chiefs and royalty in Africa (e.g., Akyeampong 1996, Crush 1992, Willis 2002) to the Inca imperial state. So important was alcohol to the operation of the Inca state that it maintained vast storehouses and compounds of female brewers specifically to produce *chicha* for large consumption events (Moore 1989, Morris 1979).

ALCOHOL, POLITICAL ECONOMY, AND COLONIALISM

Alcohol has also been an object of major economic importance and a significant component of the political economy in a wide variety of contexts. It has been a particularly prominent factor in colonial situations, both ancient and modern (Dietler 1990, Jankowiak & Bradburd 2003, Pan 1975). To understand the roles of alcohol in this domain, it is necessary to first briefly consider the properties of alcohol as an economic good.

Most traditional forms of alcohol are made for immediate consumption: They will spoil within a few days of fermentation. This is true for most forms of grain beer before the addition of hops as a preservative (a European invention of the ninth century) and for most other fruit-, sap-, or starch-based alcohols before the invention of distillation (Bruman 2000, Huetz de Lemps 2001, Jennings et al. 2005). The major ancient exception is wine, which could be preserved in amphorae for years. Modern exceptions include distilled spirits and hopped beers. Consequently, most traditional indigenous forms of alcohol could not be traded over great distances or stockpiled: Production and consumption were usually spatially and temporally proximate. These drinks necessitated control of a large labor force for hosting a significant consumption event, and they were of limited value as trade goods. Moreover, these drinks were usually made from products that were a common part of the household agrarian base, and production was often a domestic activity. Wine (as with distilled liquor), on the other hand, could be accumulated for years and traded over vast distances. It had a stronger potential to become a circulating commodity—that is, a good produced for exchange rather than immediate consumption in a social event (see Dietler 1990). The brief window of consumption for most traditional alcoholic beverages is one reason that ancient breweries have been relatively rare archaeological finds, and those that have been identified, for example, in Egypt and South America (Geller 1993, Moore 1989), are facilities for state-sponsored feasting at an adjacent location rather than for trade. Wineries, on the other hand, as specialized commodity-production facilities separated from consumption sites, have been far more commonly detected (Amouretti &

Brun 1993, Brun 2003, Rice 1996). As Willis (2002, p. 237) further observed in regard to distilled alcohol, "when compared with informal-sector ferments, spirits have encouraged more complex economic linkages and a tendency to more overtly commercialized labor relations within production." But, as he also observed, distillation in contexts such as the African countryside has remained a small-scale affair, often as a complement to brewing. It solves the problem of localized oversupply for sellers, as, rather than spoiling, excess alcohol can be kept for sale at another time (Willis 2002, p. 237). The elevated psychoactive effects owing to a much higher alcohol content have also been an obvious source of attraction.

Traditional forms of alcohol have tended to constitute a major component of the domestic economy, with a significant proportion of agricultural resources devoted to brewing. Where quantitative measures have been attempted in smallholder and peasant households, it is clear that 15%–30% (and often considerably more) of the household grain supply is commonly dedicated to the production of alcohol (de Garine 1996, Dietler 2001, Jennings 2005, Platt 1964, Saul 1981). Moreover, this production also frequently requires large quantities of fuel. For example, Saul (1981) noted that, during one week in Manga (a Mossi town of 7000 inhabitants), five beer feasts held in one ward required 1400 kg of wood for brewing and cooking for one of these feasts alone, in addition to 1900 kg of red sorghum required for beer. Other figures from different parts of Africa indicate that 10%–50% of fuelwood consumption is a common figure for brewing (McCall 2002).

Alcohol production of this type is usually a labor-intensive process and one performed predominantly by women. However, alcohol also performs a crucial role in maintaining interhousehold flows of labor through its use in work feasts (see Dietler & Herbich 2001). The work feast is the most-common practice by which large collective-labor projects have been mobilized before the advent of capitalist wage labor: It is an event in which a group of people is called together to work on a project for a day (or more) and, in return, is treated to drink and/or food, after which the host owns the proceeds of the day's labor. This mechanism has both a voluntary form, in which the workers/guests are drawn by the host's reputation for lavish hospitality, and a more obligatory form, called corvée, in which labor tribute is seen as a duty. However, both forms operate through the idiom of generous hospitality providing the context for collective labor. Such practices have been instrumental in mobilizing everything from agricultural labor, house and wall construction, cash cropping, and trade expeditions in acephalous societies to large-scale building and mining projects in imperial states (e.g., Colson & Scudder 1988; Crush 1992; Dietler & Herbich 2001, 2006; Garine 2001; Jennings 2005; McAllister 2001; Milano 1994; Morris 1979; Moore 1989).

Given the common political and economic importance of alcohol, it is not surprising that it should have come to play a major role in the operation of the political economy and in the articulation of colonial encounters in various parts of the ancient and modern worlds (Crush & Ambler 1992, Dietler 1990, Jankowiak & Bradburd 2003). In fact, the roles of alcohol in colonial situations have been extremely complex and even contradictory, ranging (sometimes simultaneously) from an intended implement of seduction and control to an imagined vector of disorder, a source of colonial and postcolonial state revenue, and a major component of a subversive alternative economy (i.e., bootleg production, smuggling, etc.). What is crucial in each context is to understand the nature of cross-cultural demand (or indifference) for specific types of alcohol and the shifting unintended consequences of consumption of an alien beverage. The meaning, use, and value of particular forms of alcohol usually change as the drinks traverse cultural and social frontiers (Bryceson 2002b, Dietler 1990).

In the ancient world, wine was a form of alcohol implicated in various colonial encounters around the Mediterranean. For example,

it was a trade commodity that served as the primary element articulating relations between the indigenous peoples of Gaul and alien Etruscans, Greeks, and Romans over several centuries (Dietler 1990, Poux 2004). This relationship eventually reached such proportions that ships carrying up to 10,000 amphorae of wine maintained a trade that pumped up to 16 million liters of Roman wine per year into Gaul over nearly a century (Tchernia 1986). Careful analysis of the regionally distinctive nature of consumption of imported wine and the often-unintended social and cultural consequences has been extremely helpful in understanding the historical transformation of the colonial encounter as a whole (Dietler 1990, 1996; Poux 2004).

The analysis of *chicha* production and consumption in the Andes has been equally helpful in revealing the operation of the Inca imperial state, which depended on the massive production of *chicha* to organize state labor projects and consolidate power through state-sponsored commensal rituals. It was largely the brewing and weaving labor of a select group of women (*aclla*) appropriated from around the empire that underwrote this system of state control (Bray 2003b, Jennings 2005, Moore 1989, Morris 1979). *Chicha* was equally important in several earlier Andean polities, although often in somewhat different ways (e.g., Lau 2002). For example, a comparative analysis of the Tiwanaku core area and peripheral regions suggests a prominent role for feasting in what Goldstein (2003) suggests may have been a soft form of Tiwanaku state expansion in which agency resided with multiple competing corporate groups operating independently of any state design.

Alcohol has been an equally important element in the expansion of modern European colonialism in both the Old and New Worlds and in the operation of postcolonial states in the age of globalization (e.g., see Angrosino 2003, Eber 2000, Mancall 2003, Scaramelli & De Scaramelli 2005). However, Africa offers perhaps the richest set of analyses of this phenomenon by anthropologists and social historians (e.g., Akyeampong 1996; Ambler 1991, 2003; Bryceson 2002a; Colson & Scudder 1988; Crush & Ambler 1992; Diduk 1993; Holtzman 2001; Pan 1975; Partanen 1991; Willis 2002). In West Africa, distilled spirits (brandy, rum, and gin) played a major role in the Atlantic slave trade from its beginning, serving as a commodity, a currency, and a lubricant for establishing exchange relationships (Ambler 2003, Diduk 1993, Pan 1975). Cities such as Liverpool even built special distilleries specifically to service the African market. Liquor became a key trade item in the triangle that linked Europe, Africa, and the Americas: It was traded for African slaves who worked the American sugar plantations that provided the raw material for rum that was used to obtain more slaves. By the 1770s, North American rum exports to Africa alone are estimated at an annual average of over 1.1 million liters (Smith 2001). Moreover, the growing slave-sugar economy of the seventeenth century also made cheap rum readily available to the working classes of England and Holland for the first time (Matthee 1995).

With the imposition of European colonial control over Africa in the nineteenth century (and earlier in South Africa), alcohol became a subject of ambivalence, conflicting discourses, and shifting policies and alliances—but was always of major concern. On the one hand, the colonial state in most regions began to rely on taxes on alcohol for both a substantial part of its operating revenues (Akyeampong 1996, Crush & Ambler 1992, Diduk 1993, Heap 2002, Pan 1975) and for the mobilization and pacification of a native labor force (Crush & Ambler 1992, Diduk 1993, Holtzman 2001, Suggs & Lewis 2003). For example, French West Africa derived approximately 70% of its revenues from alcohol duties in the early twentieth century (Pan 1975, p. 16). On the other hand, anxiety about the effects of alcohol in producing an unruly subject population and disrupting work discipline also became pervasive. Moreover, the prevalence of a strong temperance ideology among Protes-

tant missionaries led to both political agitation for state limitations on alcohol and direct attempts to influence African drinking practices and beliefs through religious conversion. These conflicting forces resulted in alcohol becoming a constant subject of colonial legislation and (usually unsuccessful) attempts to control native consumption and production of alcohol while promoting the sale of revenue-producing imported varieties or state monopolies. Not surprisingly, alcohol also became a central object of contestation between the colonial state and both African leaders and local brewers. This struggle has continued in postcolonial African states (Akyeampong 1996, Ambler 1991, Colson & Scudder 1988, Crush & Ambler 1992, Diduk 1993, Gewald 2002, Partanen 1991, Willis 2002).

A major consequence of the colonial engagement with Africa, and other regions, has been shifts toward the commercialization of alcohol and toward new contexts of consumption, which have often altered the cultural meaning of drinking. In Europe, domestic production of alcohol was gradually replaced between the fourteenth and nineteenth centuries by specialist alewives selling out of homes and eventually by commercial establishments that became a primary locus for public consumption—alehouses, taverns, or public houses (Clark 1983, Kümin & Tlusty 2002). Similar processes are seen in nineteenth and twentieth century Africa, particularly in urban contexts where new forms of public culture emerged in which public drinking was a major element. These transformations toward commercialization have often provided women, as the primary traditional brewers (at least for grain beers), with a new source of economic power and independence, although one with limitations (Akyeampong 1996, Colson & Scudder 1988, Dietler & Herbich 2006, Green 1999, Haggblade 1992, Holtzman 2001, Roberts 2000, Saul 1981, Suggs 1996). In many cases, income from commoditized brewing and distilling has become decisive for the survival of poorer households, especially female-headed ones (Green

1999). The dependence on alcohol production has also frequently propelled women into resistance against the state (Bradford 1992, Gewald 2002, Haggblade 1992).

Commoditization also produced new contexts of consumption (beer halls, shebeens, etc.) that the state has often seen as potential centers of subversive politics and has tried, usually without success, to control. Shifting alcohol from ritual to market contexts also sometimes has set off conflict between generations and genders (as senior men have felt their power challenged by liberalized access to a potent political symbol and tool) and, for example, between traditionalists and Christian converts (e.g., Quintero 2002). This shift sometimes has produced curious alliances of interest as well, as in the case of senior women and young male drinkers uniting in opposition to official alcohol restrictions in Windhoek (Gewald 2002), or in the case of colonial officials enacting restrictive liquor laws in Ghana, despite the loss of considerable revenues, to support the desire of local chiefs for selective access to alcohol and to shore up the social control of these senior men on whom the state depended (Akyeampong 1996). Commoditization has also frequently altered the cultural meaning of drinking toward the celebration of individual prowess and away from community cooperation, although the continuities and transformative play on traditional symbols are complex (Bryceson 2002b, Suggs 1996). Despite the intricacies of local histories of the intersection of alcohol, colonialism, and globalization, as Colson & Scudder (1988, p. 96) noted in Zambia, a frequent long-term result of commercialization has been the recruitment of new categories of drinkers (e.g., young men and women), an increase in the overall quantities of alcohol available, and an increase in the proportion of the population involved in heavy drinking.

ALCOHOL AND RELIGION

Because inebriation induces altered states of consciousness, alcohol has frequently played a prominent role in rituals of both a religious and secular nature. Indeed, it is often treated as an indexical sign of a ritual event. But the relationship of alcohol to religion is complex. On the one hand, it is, and has been, an integral part of many religious practices around the world and throughout history, from the ritual consumption of wine in the Catholic mass to ancestor and spirit propitiation with beer in Africa (Carlson 1990, Colson & Scudder 1988, Green 1999, Luning 2002). On the other hand, its consumption is proscribed by some religions (e.g., Islam and several Protestant Christian sects) to such an extent that abstention can become one of the most important defining symbols of piety and group membership.

The association between alcohol and religion is one with a deep antiquity. Information on this relationship is especially abundant in the case of ancient Greece, which has left us a rich and diverse textual and iconographic archive on the subject of wine. Wine was not only the crucial element of the Greek social ritual of the *symposion*, but it was directly associated with the divine power of Dionysus, and ritual libations were an essential part of religious practice (Brun et al. 2005, Lissarrague 1990, Murray 1990, Murray & Tecusan 1995). Wine was also a fundamental aspect of ancient Egyptian religion: It had many theological associations, and wine offerings were made in divine cults and funerary rituals (Poo 1995). Archaeologists have also been able to reconstruct the pervasive use of alcohol in funerals and other religious rituals of ancient societies that did not leave texts, such as Iron Age European societies (Arnold 1999; Dietler 1990, 1999; Forenbaher & Kaiser 2001; Poux 2004), ancient Kushite society (Edwards 1996), and various Andean polities (Lau 2002). Religion is not only intimately entwined with alcohol consumption, but often with its production as well. Perhaps the most salient case is the preservation of wine production on monastic estates in Europe after the decline of the Roman Empire and the longstanding tradition of monasteries as centers of beer production and experimentation with techniques of herbal additives to alcoholic drinks (Vess 2004).

As noted above, some Protestant Christian sects depict alcohol as an evil and dangerous substance that defiles the drinker and forbid its consumption. Aside from its prominent role in the temperance movements of Europe and the United States (Blocker 1989, Harrison 1971, Roberts 1984), this belief has been transported by missionaries to many colonial encounters and postcolonial situations. In those contexts, alcohol has often acquired the additional stigma of being associated with traditional ritual practices and the power of what missionaries view as pagan superstition and prior networks of communal identity. Hence, for example, Christian fundamentalists in Malawi have mandated that alcohol must be avoided to attain salvation both because of its evil nature and because of its association with the traditional extended family relations and obligations that thwart the attainment of worldly success in the Western individualist model (van Dijk 2002). Spier (1995) offers the telling example of Andean women opposing the conversion of their husbands to Protestantism precisely because abstinence from drinking would sever household connections to mutual aid networks. Such examples are widespread in Africa, Latin America, and other places where missionaries have been active (e.g., Eber 2000, Heath 2000, Willis 2002). This has frequently resulted in alcohol serving as a highly charged focus of symbolic contestation in identity struggles between not only traditionalists and Christian converts, but also between Protestant and Catholic converts (Luning 2002).

CONCLUSION

Alcohol, as an especially prized form of embodied material culture and the most widely used type of psychoactive agent in the world, has been a fundamentally important social, economic, and political artifact for millennia. Hence, alcohol should be a subject of crucial interest to the social sciences, both for what it can tell us about social life and culture and for our ability to understand its potential dangers and benefits. Although still marginal to the dominant perspectives in alcohol studies, sociocultural anthropologists, archaeologists, and social historians have made a variety of important contributions and are expanding research in several directions. A few major themes among those contributions over the past couple of decades have been reviewed here in a highly selective fashion. Although far from comprehensive in its coverage, it is hoped that this discussion serves both to highlight the potential of an anthropological engagement with alcohol and to suggest the interconnections and the mutually heuristic benefits of this subject as a bridge between the subdisciplines.

ACKNOWLEDGMENTS

This piece is dedicated jointly to Dwight Heath and André Tchernia. Dwight Heath has been the most important analyst of the anthropology of alcohol for nearly three decades, and his generosity and encouragement in reviewing an article early in my career have remained a model for emulation. André Tchernia has been, also for decades, the foremost expert on ancient Roman wine in all its dimensions, as well as a constant source of stimulation and discovery in matters oenological, both ancient and modern. I also want to thank my early guides to the modern wine trade when I briefly participated in that enjoyable milieu in Berkeley nearly two decades ago, Oliver McCrum and Paul Marcus.

LITERATURE CITED

Akyeampong E. 1996. *Drink, Power, and Cultural Change: A Social History of Alcohol in Ghana, c. 1800 to Recent Times.* Oxford: James Currey

Allchin FR. 1979. India: the ancient home of distillation? *Man* 14:55–63

Ambler C. 1991. Drunks, brewers, and chiefs: alcohol regulation in colonial Kenya 1900–1939. See Barrows & Room 1991a, pp. 165–83

Ambler C. 2003. Alcohol and the slave trade in West Africa, 1400–1850. See Jankowiak & Bradburd 2003, pp. 73–87

Amouretti MC, Brun JP, eds. 1993. *La production du vin et de l'huile en Méditerranée.* Paris: Boccard

Angrosino MV. 2003. Rum and ganja: indenture, drug foods, labor motivation, and the evolution of the modern sugar industry in Trinidad. See Jankowiak & Bradburd 2003, pp. 101–15

Arnold B. 1999. "Drinking the feast": alcohol and the legitimation of power in Celtic Europe. *Camb. Archaeol. J.* 9:71–93

Arthur JW. 2003. Brewing beer: status, wealth and ceramic use alteration among the Gamo of south-western Ethiopia. *World Archaeol.* 34(3):516–28

Barrows S, Room R, eds. 1991a. *Drinking Behavior and Belief in Modern History.* Berkeley: Univ. Calif. Press

Barrows S, Room R. 1991b. Introduction. See Barrows & Room 1991a, pp. 1–25

Bennett LA, Cook PW. 1996. Alcohol and drug studies. In *Medical Anthropology: Contemporary Theory and Method*, ed. CF Sargent, TM Johnson, pp. 235–51. Westport, CT: Praeger. Rev. ed.

Bertucchi G. 1992. *Les amphores et le vin de Marseille, VIe s. avant J.-C. - IIe s. après J.-C.* Paris: CNRS

Biers WR, McGovern PE, eds. 1990. *Organic Contents of Ancient Vessels: Materials Analysis and Archaeological Investigation.* Philadelphia: MASCA Res. Pap. Sci. Archaeometry

Blocker J. 1989. *American Temperance Movements: Cycles of Reform.* Boston: Twayne

Bowser B. 2003. *The perceptive potter: beer bowls and political action in the Ecuadorian Amazon.* Presented at Annu. Meet. Soc. Am. Archaeol., 68th, Milwaukee

Bradford H. 1992. "We women will show them": beer protests in the Natal countryside, 1929. See Crush & Ambler 1992, pp. 208–34

Braidwood R, Sauer JD, Helbaek H, Mangelsdorf PC, Cutler C, et al. 1953. Symposium: Did man once live by beer alone? *Am. Anthropol.* 55:515–26

Braudel F. 1979. *Civilization and Capitalism, 15th–18th Century. Volume 1: The Structures of Everyday Life.* Trans. S Reynolds. New York: Harper & Row

Bray T, ed. 2003a. *The Archaeology and Politics of Food and Feasting in Early States and Empires.* New York: Kluwer

Bray T. 2003b. To dine splendidly: imperial pottery, commensal politics, and the Inca state. See Bray 2003a, pp. 93–142

Bruman JH. 2000. *Alcohol in Ancient Mexico.* Salt Lake City: Univ. Utah Press

Brun JP. 2003. *Le vin et l'huile dans la Méditerrannée antique.* Paris: Errance

Brun JP, Poux M, Tchernia A, eds. 2005. *Le vin: nectar des dieux, génie des hommes.* Gollion, Switzerland: InFolio

Bryceson DF, ed. 2002a. *Alcohol in Africa: Mixing Business, Pleasure, and Politics.* Portsmouth, NH: Heinemann

Bryceson DF. 2002b. Changing modalities of alcohol usage. See Bryceson 2002a, pp. 23–52

Carlson RG. 1990. Banana beer, reciprocity, and ancestor propitiation among the Haya of Bukova, Tanzania. *Ethnology* 29:297–311

Clark J, Blake M. 1994. The power of prestige: competitive generosity and the emergence of rank societies in lowland Mesoamerica. In *Factional Competition and Political Development in the New World*, ed. EM Brumfiel, JW Fox, pp. 17–30. Cambridge, UK: Cambridge Univ. Press

Clark P. 1983. *The English Alehouse: A Social History, 1200–1830*. New York: Longman

Coe SD. 1994. *America's First Cuisines*. Austin: Univ. Texas Press

Colson E, Scudder T. 1988. *For Prayer and Profit: The Ritual, Economic, and Social Importance of Beer in Gwembe District, Zambia, 1950–1982*. Stanford, CA: Stanford Univ. Press

Cook AG, Glowacki M. 2003. Pots, politics, and power: Huari ceramic assemblages and imperial administration. See Bray 2003a, pp. 173–202

Crush J. 1992. The construction of compound authority: drinking at Havelock, 1938–1944. See Crush & Ambler 1992, pp. 367–94

Crush J, Ambler C, eds. 1992. *Liquor and Labor in Southern Africa*. Athens: Ohio Univ. Press

de Garine I. 1996. Food and the status quest in five African cultures. In *Food and the Status Quest: An Interdisciplinary Perspective*, ed. P Wiessner, W Schiefenhövel, pp. 193–218. Oxford: Berghahn

de Garine I, de Garine V, eds. 2001. *Drinking: Anthropological Approaches*. New York: Berghahn

Diduk S. 1993. European alcohol, history, and the state in Cameroon. *Afr. Stud. Rev.* 36(10):1–42

Dietler M. 1990. Driven by drink: the role of drinking in the political economy and the case of Early Iron Age France. *J. Anthropol. Archaeol.* 9:352–406

Dietler M. 1996. Feasts and commensal politics in the political economy: food, power, and status in prehistoric Europe. In *Food and the Status Quest: An Interdisciplinary Perspective*, ed. P Wiessner, W Schiefenhövel, pp. 87–125. Oxford: Berghahn

Dietler M. 1999. Rituals of commensality and the politics of state formation in the "princely" societies of Early Iron Age Europe. In *Les princes de la protohistoire et l'émergence de l'état*, ed. P Ruby, pp. 135–52. Naples: Cahiers du Centre Jean Bérard, Inst. Français de Naples

Dietler M. 2001. Theorizing the feast: rituals of consumption, commensal politics, and power in African contexts. See Dietler & Hayden 2001, pp. 65–114

Dietler M, Hayden B, eds. 2001. *Feasts: Archaeological and Ethnographic Perspectives on Food, Politics, and Power*. Washington, DC: Smithsonian

Dietler M, Herbich I. 2001. Feasts and labor mobilization: dissecting a fundamental economic practice. See Dietler & Hayden 2001, pp. 240–64

Dietler M, Herbich I. 2006. Liquid material culture: following the flow of beer among the Luo of Kenya. In *Grundlegungen. Beiträge zur Europäischen und Afrikanischen Archäologie für Manfred K.H. Eggert*, ed. HP Wotzka, pp. 395–408. Tübingen, Germ.: Francke Verlag

Douglas M. 1975. Deciphering a meal. *Daedalus* 101:61–82

Douglas M, ed. 1987a. *Constructive Drinking: Perspectives on Drink from Anthropology*. Cambridge, UK: Cambridge Univ. Press

Douglas M. 1987b. A distinctive anthropological perspective. See Douglas 1987a, pp. 3–15

Driessen H. 1992. Drinking on masculinity: alcohol and gender in Andalusia. See Gefou-Madianou 1992, pp. 71–79

Eber CE. 2000. *Women and Alcohol in a Highland Maya Town: Water of Hope, Water of Sorrow*. Austin: Univ. Texas Press. Rev. ed.

Edwards DN. 1996. Sorghum, beer, and Kushite society. *Norwegian Archaeol. Rev.* 29:65–77

Forbes RJ. 1970. *Short History of the Art of Distillation*. Leiden, The Netherlands: E.J. Brill

Forenbaher S, Kaiser T. 2001. Nakovano Cave: an Illyrian ritual site. *Antiquity* 75:677–78

Garine E. 2001. An ethnographic account of the many roles of millet beer in the culture of the Duupa agriculturalists, (Poli Mountains) northern Cameroon. See de Garine & de Garine 2001, pp. 191–204

Gefou-Madianou D, ed. 1992. *Alcohol, Gender and Culture*. London: Routledge

Geller J. 1993. Bread and beer in fourth-millennium Egypt. *Food Foodways* 5(3):255–67

Gewald JB. 2002. Diluting drinks and deepening discontent: colonial liquor controls and public resistance in Windhoek, Namibia. See Bryceson 2002a, pp. 117–38

Goldstein P. 2003. From stew-eaters to maize-drinkers: the chicha economy and the Tiwanaku expansion. See Bray 2003a, pp. 143–72

González Turmo I. 2001. Drinking: an almost silent language. See de Garine & de Garine 2001, pp. 130–43

Green M. 1999. Trading on inequality: gender and the drinks trade in southern Tanzania. *Africa* 69:404–25

Greene JA. 1995. The beginnings of grape cultivation and wine production in Phoenician/Punic North Africa. See McGovern et al. 1995, pp. 311–21

Guérin P, Gómez Bellard C. 1999. La production du vin dans l'Espagne préromaine. In *Els productes alimentaris d'origen vegetal al'etat del Ferro de l'Europa Occidental: de la producció al consum*, ed. R Buxó, E Pons, pp. 379–88. Girona, Spain: Museu d'Arqueologia de Catalunya

Guy KM. 2001. Wine, champagne and the making of French identity in the Belle Epoque. See Scholliers 2001, pp. 163–77

Haggblade S. 1992. The shebeen queen and the evolution of Botswana's sorghum beer industry. See Crush & Ambler 1992, pp. 395–412

Hall TM. 2005. Pivo at the heart of Europe: beer-drinking and Czech identity. See Wilson 2005a, pp. 65–86

Hamilakis Y. 1999. Food technologies, technologies of the body: the social context of wine and oil production and consumption in Bronze Age Crete. *World Archaeol.* 31(1):38–54

Harrison B. 1971. *Drink and the Victorians: The Temperance Question in England*, 1815–72. London: Faber & Faber

Heap S. 2002. Living on the proceeds of a grog shop: liquor revenue in Nigeria. See Bryceson 2002a, pp. 139–59

Heath DB. 1976. Anthropological perspectives on alcohol: an historical review. In *Cross-Cultural Approaches to the Study of Alcohol: An Interdisciplinary Perspective*, ed. M Everett, J Waddell, D Heath, pp. 41–101. The Haugue: Mouton

Heath DB. 1987a. Anthropology and alcohol studies: current issues. *Annu. Rev. Anthropol.* 16:99–120

Heath DB. 1987b. A decade of development in the anthropological study of alcohol use: 1970–1980. See Douglas 1987a, pp. 16–69

Heath DB, ed. 1995. *International Handbook on Alcohol and Culture*. Westport, CT: Greenwood Press

Heath DB. 2000. *Drinking Occasions: Comparative Perspectives on Alcohol and Culture*. Philadelphia: Brunner/Mazel

Heather N, Robertson I. 1989. *Problem Drinking*. Oxford: Oxford Univ. Press. 2nd ed.

Hendry J. 1994. Drinking and gender in Japan. See McDonald 1994a, pp. 175–90

Holtzman J. 2001. The food of the elders, the "ration" of women: brewing, gender, and domestic processes among the Samburu of northern Kenya. *Am. Anthropol.* 103:1041–58

Huby G. 1994. Drinking and the management of problem drinking among the Bari, southern Sudan. See McDonald 1994b, pp. 235–47

Huetz de Lemps A. 2001. *Boissons et civilsations en Afrique*. Bordeaux, France: Presses Univ. de Bordeaux

Hunt GP, Barker JC. 2001. Socio-cultural anthropology and alcohol and drug research: towards a unified theory. *Soc. Sci. Med.* 53:165–88

James TGH. 1995. The earliest history of wine and its importance in ancient Egypt. See McGovern et al. 1995, pp. 197–213

Jankowiak W, Bradburd D, eds. 2003. *Drugs, Labor, and Colonial Expansion.* Tucson: Univ. Ariz. Press

Jennings J. 2005. La chichera y el patrón: chicha and the energetics of feasting in the prehistoric Andes. In *Archaeological Papers of the American Anthropological Association*, vol. 14, pp. 241–59. Washington, DC: Am. Anthropol. Assoc.

Jennings J, Antrobus KL, Atencio SJ, Glavich E, Johnson R, et al. 2005. "Drinking beer in a blissful mood": alcohol production, operational chains, and feasting in the ancient world. *Curr. Anthropol.* 46(2):275–304

Joffe AH. 1998. Alcohol and social complexity in ancient western Asia. *Curr. Anthropol.* 39(3):297–322

Katz SH, Voigt MM. 1986. Bread and beer: the early use of cereals in the human diet. *Expedition* 28(2):23–34

Kümin B, Tlusty BA, eds. 2002. *The World of the Tavern: Public Houses in Early Modern Europe.* Burlington, VT: Ashgate

Lau G. 2002. Feasting and ancestor veneration at Chinchawas, North Highlands of Ancash, Peru. *Lat. Am. Antiq.* 13:387–402

LeCount LJ. 2001. Like water for chocolate: feasting and political ritual among the Late Classic Maya at Xunantunich, Belize. *Am. Anthropol.* 103:935–53

Lesko LH. 1995. Egyptian wine production during the New Kingdom. See McGovern et al. 1995, pp. 215–30

Lissarrague F. 1990. *The Aesthetics of the Greek Banquet: Images of Wine and Ritual.* Princeton, NJ: Princeton Univ. Press

Luning S. 2002. To drink or not to drink: beer brewing, rituals, and religious conversion in Maane, Burkina Faso. See Bryceson 2002a, pp. 231–48

Macdonald S. 1994. Whisky, women and the Scottish drink problem. A view from the Highlands. See McDonald 1994b, pp. 125–44

Mancall PC. 2003. Alcohol and the fur trade in New France and English America, 1600–1800. See Jankowiak & Bradburd 2003, pp. 89–99

March KS. 1998. Hospitality, women, and the efficacy of beer. In *Food and Gender: Identity and Power*, ed. CM Counihan, SL Kaplan, pp. 45–80. Amsterdam: Harwood Acad.

Marshall M. 1991. "Problem deflation" and the ethnographic record: interpretation and introspection in anthropological studies of alcohol. *J. Subst. Abuse* 2:353–67

Marshall M, Ames GM, Bennett LA. 2001. Anthropological perspectives on alcohol and drugs at the turn of the new millennium. *Soc. Sci. Med.* 53:153–64

Martin AL. 2001. Old people, alcohol and identity in Europe, 1300–1700. See Scholliers 2001, pp. 119–37

Mars G. 1987. Longshore drinking, economic security and union politics in Newfoundland. See Douglas 1987a, pp. 91–101

Matthee R. 1995. Exotic substances: the introduction and global spread of tobacco, coffee, cocoa, tea, and distilled liquor, sixteenth to eighteenth centuries. In *Drugs and Narcotics in History*, ed. R Porter, M Teich, pp. 24–51. Cambridge, UK: Cambridge Univ. Press

Mauss M. 1936. Les techniques du corps. *J. Physiol. (Paris)* 32:271–93

McAllister P. 2001. *Building the Homestead: Agriculture, Labour and Beer in South Africa's Transkei.* Leiden, The Netherlands: Ashgate

McCall MK. 2002. Brewers, woodfuel, and donors: an awkward silence as the fires blaze. See Bryceson 2002a, pp. 93–114

McDonald M. 1994a. Drinking and social identity in the west of France. See McDonald 1994b, pp. 99–124

McDonald M, ed. 1994b. *Gender, Drink and Drugs.* Oxford: Berg

McDonald M. 1994c. Introduction: a social-anthropological view of gender, drink and drugs. See McDonald 1994b, pp. 1–30

McGovern PE. 2003. *Ancient Wine: The Search for the Origins of Viticulture.* Princeton, NJ: Princeton Univ. Press

McGovern PE, Fleming SJ, Katz SH, eds. 1995. *The Origins and Ancient History of Wine.* Amsterdam: Gordon & Breach

McGovern PE, Zhang JH, Tang JG, Zhang ZQ, Hall GR, et al. 2004. Fermented beverages of pre- and proto-historic China. *Proc. Natl. Acad. Sci. USA* 101(51):17593–98

Michel RH, McGovern PE, Badler VR. 1993. The first wine and beer: chemical detection of ancient fermented beverages. *Anal. Chem.* 65:408–13

Milano L, ed. 1994. *Drinking in Ancient Societies: History and Culture of Drinks in the Ancient Near East. Papers of a Symposium Held in Rome, May 17–19, 1990.* Padova, Italy: Sargon

Moore JD. 1989. Pre-Hispanic beer in coastal Peru: technology and social context of prehistoric production. *Am. Anthropol.* 91:682–95

Morris C. 1979. Maize beer in the economics, politics and religion of the Inca empire. In *Fermented Foods in Nutrition*, ed. C Gastineau, W Darby, T Turner, pp. 21–34. New York: Academic

Murray O, ed. 1990. *Sympotica: A Symposium on the Symposion.* Oxford: Clarendon

Murray O. 1995. Histories of pleasure. See Murray & Tecusan 1995, pp. 3–17

Murray O, Tecusan M, eds. 1995. *In Vino Veritas.* London: British School at Rome

Pan L. 1975. *Alcohol in Colonial Africa.* Helsinki: Finn. Found. Alcohol Stud.

Papagaroufali E. 1992. Uses of alcohol among women: games of resistance, power, and pleasure. See Gefou-Madianou 1992, pp. 48–70

Partanen J. 1991. *Sociability and Intoxication: Alcohol and Drinking in Kenya, Africa, and the Modern World.* Helsinki: Finnish Foundation for Alcohol Studies

Peace A. 1992. No fishing without drinking: the construction of social identity in rural Ireland. See Gefou-Madianou 1992, pp. 167–80

Platt B. 1955. Some traditional alcoholic beverages and their importance in indigenous African communities. *Proc. Nutr. Soc.* 14:115–24

Platt B. 1964. Biological ennoblement: improvement of the nutritive value of foods and dietary regimens by biological agencies. *Food Technol.* 18:662–70

Pollock S. 2003. Feasts, funerals, and fast food in early Mesopotamian states. See Bray 2003a, pp. 17–38

Poo MC. 1995. *Wine and Wine Offering in the Religion of Ancient Egypt.* London: Kegan Paul

Poux M. 2004. *L'Age du vin: rites de boisson, festins et libations en Gaule indépendente.* Montagnac, France: Editions Monique Mergoil

Prakash OM. 1961. *Food and Drinks in Ancient India (From Earliest Times to 1200 A.D.).* Delhi: Munshi Ram Manohar Lal

Quintero G. 2002. Nostalgia and degeneration: the moral economy of drinking in Navajo society. *Med. Anthropol. Q.* 16:3–21

Rehfisch F. 1987. Competitive beer drinking among the Mambila. In *Constructive Drinking: Perspectives on Drink from Anthropology*, ed. M Douglas, pp. 135–45. Cambridge: Cambridge Univ. Press

Rice PM. 1996. The archaeology of wine: the wine and brandy haciendas of Moquegua, Peru. *J. Field Archaeol.* 23:187–204

Roberts BD. 2000. Always cheaply pleasant: beer as a commodity in rural Kenyan society. In *Commodities and Globalization: Anthropological Perspectives*, ed. A Haugerud, PM Stone, PD Little, pp. 179–96. Boulder, CO: Rowman & Littlefield

Roberts J. 1984. *Drinking, Temperance and the Working Class in Nineteenth-Century Germany*. Boston: Allen & Unwin

Room R. 1984. Alcohol and ethnography: a case of problem deflation? *Curr. Anthropol.* 25:169–91

Saul M. 1981. Beer, sorghum, and women: production for the market in rural Upper Volta. *Africa* 51:746–64

Scaramelli F, De Scaramelli KT. 2005. The roles of material culture in the colonization of the Orinoco, Venezuela. *J. Soc. Archaeol.* 5:135–68

Scholliers P, ed. 2001. *Food, Drink and Identity: Cooking, Eating, and Drinking in Europe Since the Middle Ages*. Oxford: Berg

Sherratt A. 1991. Sacred and profane substances: the ritual use of narcotics in later prehistoric Europe. In *Sacred and Profane: Proceedings of a Conference on Archaeology, Ritual and Religion*, ed. P Garwood, D Jennings, R Skeates, J Toms, pp. 50–64. Oxford: Oxford Univ. Comm. Archaeol.

Singer M. 1986. Toward a political-economy of alcoholism: the missing link in the anthropology of drinking. *Soc. Sci. Med.* 23(2):113–30

Smalley J, Blake M. 2003. Sweet beginnings—stalk sugar and the domestication of maize. *Curr. Anthropol.* 44(5):675–703

Smith FH. 2001. Alcohol, slavery, and African cultural continuity in the British Caribbean. See de Garine & de Garine 2001, pp. 212–24

Smith ME, Wharton JB, Olson JM. 2003. Aztec feasts, rituals, and markets: political uses of ceramic vessels in a commercial economy. See Bray 2003a, pp. 235–68

Spicer P. 1997. Toward a (dys)functional anthropology of drinking: ambivalence and the American Indian experience with alcohol. *Med. Anthropol. Q.* 11:306–23

Spier F. 1995. *San Nicolas de Zurite: Religion and Daily Life of a Peruvian Andean Village in a Changing World*. Amsterdam: VU Univ. Press

Steinkraus KH, ed. 1995. *Handbook of Indigenous Fermented Foods*. New York: Marcel Dekker

Stika HP. 1996. Traces of a possible Celtic brewery in Eberdingen-Hochdorf, Kreis Ludwigsburg, southwest Germany. *Veg. Hist. Archaeobotany* 5:81–88

Strunin L. 2001. Assessing alcohol consumption: development from qualitative research methods. *Soc. Sci. Med.* 53(2):215–26

Suggs DN. 1996. Mosadi Tshwene: the construction of gender and the consumption of alcohol in Botswana. *Am. Ethnol.* 23:597–610

Suggs DN, Lewis SA. 2003. Alcohol as a direct and indirect labor enhancer in the mixed economy of the Batswana, 1800–1900. See Jankowiak & Bradburd 2003, pp. 135–49

Tanzarn NB. 2002. Liquid gold of a lost kingdom: the rise of waragi production in Kibaale District, Uganda. See Bryceson 2002a, pp. 75–91

Tchernia A. 1986. *Le vin de l'Italie romaine: essai d'histoire économique d'après les amphores*. Paris: Boccard

Tchernia A, Brun JP. 1999. *Le vin romain antique*. Grenoble, France: Glénat

van Dijk R. 2002. Modernity's limits: pentacostalism and the moral rejection of alcohol in Malawi. See Bryceson 2002a, pp. 249–64

Vencl S. 1994. The archaeology of thirst. *J. Eur. Archaeol.* 2(2):299–326

Vess D. 2004. Monastic moonshine: alcohol in the Middle Ages. In *Religion and Alcohol: Sobering Thoughts*, ed. CK Robertson, pp. 147–75. New York: Peter Lang

Willis J. 2002. *Potent Brews: A Social History of Alcohol in East Africa, 1850–1999*. Nairobi: Brit. Inst. East. Afr.

Wilson TM, ed. 2005a. *Drinking Cultures: Alcohol and Identity*. New York: Berg

Wilson TM. 2005b. Drinking cultures: sites and practices in the production and expression of identity. See Wilson 2005a, pp. 1–24

Wright JC. 1995. Empty cups and empty jugs: the social role of wine in Minoan and Mycenaean societies. See McGovern et al. 1995, pp. 287–309

Wright JC, ed. 2004. *The Mycenaean Feast*. Athens: Am. School Class. Stud.

Parks and Peoples: The Social Impact of Protected Areas

Paige West,[1] James Igoe,[2] and Dan Brockington[3]

[1] Department of Anthropology, Barnard College, Columbia University, New York, New York 10027; email: cw2031@columbia.edu,

[2] Department of Anthropology, University of Colorado, Denver, Colorado 80217-3364; email: jigoe@cudenver.edu

[3] Institute for Development Policy and Management, University of Manchester, Manchester M13 9QH, United Kingdom; email: daniel.brockington@manchester.ac.uk

Annu. Rev. Anthropol. 2006. 35:251–77

First published online as a Review in Advance on June 5, 2006

The *Annual Review of Anthropology* is online at anthro.annualreviews.org

This article's doi: 10.1146/annurev.anthro.35.081705.123308

Copyright © 2006 by Annual Reviews. All rights reserved

0084-6570/06/1021-0251$20.00

Key Words

conservation, environment, virtualism, displacement, governmentality

Abstract

This review examines the social, economic, and political effects of environmental conservation projects as they are manifested in protected areas. We pay special attention to people living in and displaced from protected areas, analyze the worldwide growth of protected areas over the past 20 years, and offer suggestions for future research trajectories in anthropology. We examine protected areas as a way of seeing, understanding, and producing nature (environment) and culture (society) and as a way of attempting to manage and control the relationship between the two. We focus on social, economic, scientific, and political changes in places where there are protected areas and in the urban centers that control these areas. We also examine violence, conflict, power relations, and governmentality as they are connected to the processes of protection. Finally, we examine discourse and its effects and argue that anthropology needs to move beyond the current examinations of language and power to attend to the ways in which protected areas produce space, place, and peoples.

INTRODUCTION

NGO:
nongovernmental
organization

Over the past 25 years, anthropologists' focus has expanded from local social lives to included experiences of larger-scale processes. New areas of ethnography and analysis have proliferated as a result, with titles such as transnationalism, colonialism, postcolonialism, and globalization. One area that has also received increasing attention in recent years is environmentalism. Within this topic converge our discipline's recent interest in interactions between the local and the global and its long-standing concern with the relationships between peoples and their surroundings. This convergence, as well as the increasing involvement of anthropologists in applied issues, is at the heart of anthropologists' interests in conservation dating back to the 1970s (Orlove & Brush 1996).

By "surroundings" we mean the world around us that we, as human beings, have material, intellectual, and symbolic access to and that we work to alter and make sense of through our daily actions (Carrier 2004, p. 1). The term surroundings takes for granted that the world is made materially and symbolically through human action, a proposition anthropologists and other social scientists have accepted since Escobar's (1995) merging of political ecology and poststructuralism. By using the term we forgo conversations about the social construction of nature versus the material nature of the environment because the term allows for both: The world is out there, and we interact with it in ways that reproduce it, often altering it in the process (Smith 1990), yet the world only has meaning for us as language-using and symbol-making animals owing to how we intellectually apprehend it.

Within this disciplinary interest in environmentalism lies a subset of studies on the social effects of protected areas. The recent interest in protected areas as an anthropological subject also reflects a profound increase in the extent and complexity of protected areas. Official records list over 105,000 protected areas in the world, covering 20.3–21.5 million km², depending on how it is measured. Terrestrial protected areas cover 16.8 million km², or 11% of the world's land area (**Table 1**), whereas marine protected areas cover 4.7 million km². Of the former, approximately 6.4 million km² (4.3% of the land surface) are found in categories that can impose considerable restrictions on human use and occupancy. Globally, the spatial distribution and size-class distribution of protected areas are highly uneven (**Table 1**). Furthermore, many protected areas are recent creations (**Figure 1**). The establishment rate jumped to a new level in 1970 and peaked between 1985 and 1995. In the past ten years we have seen global activity on a par with levels in the 1970s.

Clearly, owing to this recent growth of protected areas, a review is timely, albeit demanding. Here we structure our work around two key questions and a central contention. Our questions are the following: What are the social, material, and symbolic effects of protected areas, and how do protected areas impact people's lives and their surroundings? Our contention is that protected areas matter because they are a way of seeing, understanding, and (re)producing the world. As such, they are rich sites of social production and social interaction. Contemporary protected areas not only affect the people living in them, adjacent to them, and displaced by them, but also the people working for the nongovernmental organizations (NGOs) and government agencies that create and manage the protected areas. They also change the face of the Earth by renaming places, drawing boundaries around areas, and erasing boundaries between states. In this review we begin by examining how protected areas are a form of "virtualism" (Carrier & Miller 1998). Then we review the anthropological literature on their social effects. Finally we offer suggestions for future research trajectories for anthropologists who wish to examine the social effects of protected areas.

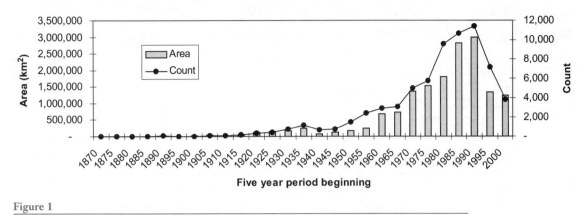

The global growth of protected areas

Figure 1

The global growth of protected areas.

THE STATE OF ANTHROPOLOGICAL ANALYSIS OF PROTECTED AREAS

In their review, Orlove & Brush (1996) found that the published literature on protected areas was limited primarily to journals of applied anthropology. A decade later, however, we also find relevant publications in the more-mainstream anthropology journals such as *Current Anthropology*, *American Anthropologist*, *American Ethnologist*, and *Cultural Anthropology*. There are also numerous edited volumes concerned with protected areas (Anderson & Berglund 2003, Anderson & Ikeya 2001, Brechin et al. 2003, Brosius et al. 2005, Chatty & Colchester 2002, Ghimire & Pimbert 1997, Greenough & Tsing 2003, Hulme & Murphree 2001), several single-author monographs (Adams 2004, Brockington 2002, Haenn 2005, Igoe 2004, Neumann 1998, Orlove 2002, Ranger 1999, Walley 2004, West 2006), an important overview work (Borgerhoff Mulder & Coppolillo 2005), and numerous recent dissertations (Austin 2003, Castagna 2005, Doane 2001, Ediger 2005, Erazo 2003, Garner 2002, Gustavo 2005, Kohler 2005, Nyhus 1999, Palmer 2001, Paudel 2005, Peterson 2005, Sodikoff 2005, Stern 2006, Stronza 2000, Van Helden 2001, Wagner 2002, Weiant 2005). Finally,

anthropologists have become increasingly involved in the creation of institutions concerned with relationships between people and protected areas, including the International Union for the Conservation of Nature and Natural Resources (IUCN) Commission on Environmental, Economic, and Social Policy and the Society for Conservation Biology's Social Science Working Group.

PROTECTED AREAS AS A FORM OF VIRTUALISM

The growth and extent of protected areas are recorded in the World Database on Protected Areas (**http://sea.unep-wcmc.org/wdbpa/**), hereafter referred to as the Database, and have been reported periodically in the anthropological literature (Borgerhoff Mulder & Coppolillo 2005, Geisler & de Sousa 2001, Orlove & Brush 1996, Zimmerer et al. 2004). These reports, however, use relatively old data, the most recent of which coming from the 1996 version of the Database. The current version of the Database contains over three times as many records as it did in 1996. The extent of protected areas reported has increased by at least 50%. This increase is not just a consequence of new growth, but also reflects improved surveillance of already existing protected areas.

IUCN:
International Union for the Conservation of Nature and Natural Resources, The World Conservation Union

Table 1 Distribution of marine and terrestrial protected areas in different IUCN regions

	Terrestrial		Marine		Total		Proportion of land protected (%)[2]			
IUCN region[1]	Count	Area (km^2)	Count	Area (km^2)	Count	Area (km^2)	Category 1–4[3]	Category 5–6[3]	No category	Total
Antarctica	67	2265	59	68,054	126	70,318	0.00	0.00	0.01	0.02
Australia & New Zealand	9085	798,684	467	702,165	9552	1,500,849	6.88	3.11	0.04	10.04
Pacific	199	55,311	288	33,451	487	88,762	0.80	1.23	7.98	10.01
South Asia	1076	327,247	184	28,832	1260	356,079	5.41	0.30	1.59	7.30
Southeast Asia	2238	656,193	420	213,546	2658	869,740	5.11	4.50	4.99	14.60
East Asia	2986	1,921,762	295	64,675	3281	1,986,437	1.92	14.12	0.26	16.30
North Eurasia	17,642	1,610,320	82	430,708	17,724	2,041,027	5.24	0.48	1.56	7.29
Europe	43,159	662,995	745	162,969	43,904	825,964	3.13	6.30	3.28	12.70
North Africa & Middle East	1230	1,204,928	141	161,356	1371	1,366,284	2.11	6.85	0.41	9.37
Eastern & southern Africa	3924	1,789,578	152	116,942	4076	1,906,520	5.92	4.63	4.90	15.46
Western & central Africa	2554	1,290,420	43	60,908	2597	1,351,328	5.46	0.77	3.86	10.09
North America	12,863	3,147,172	760	2,189,346	13,623	5,336,519	6.07	5.09	3.08	14.23
Central America	548	117,954	129	38,317	677	156,271	6.90	8.01	7.64	22.55
Caribbean	494	18,836	473	69,309	967	88,145	5.22	1.55	1.25	8.02
South America & Brazil	2500	3,206,623	202	369,987	2702	3,576,609	4.65	4.48	8.87	18.01
Total	100,565	16,810,289	4440	4,710,564	105,005	21,520,853	4.35	4.09	2.91	11.34
										Area (km^2)

[1] The countries that make up each region are available at **http://sea.unep-wcmc.org/wdbpa/** (accessed September 23, 2005). We have modified these categories slightly in the following ways. The IUCN classifies Comoros, Djibouti, Madagascar, and Mauritius as part of as western and central Africa. We have assigned them to eastern and southern Africa. Brazil forms an entire IUCN region on its own, but we have grouped it with South America. Sao Tome and Principe, Anguilla, and the British Indian Ocean Territories have not been allotted regions by the IUCN, and we placed them in western and central Africa, the Caribbean, and South Asia, respectively.

[2] Only terrestrial protected areas are included as we only have data for the size of land areas within each country and therefore cannot express marine protected areas as a proportion of country size.

[3] The categories refer to IUCN protected area categories, defined as follows: category 1a, strict nature reserve. Protected area managed mainly for science; category 1b, wilderness area. Protected area managed mainly for wilderness protection; category 2, national park. Protected area managed mainly for ecosystem protection and recreation; category 3, national monument. Protected area managed mainly for conservation of specific natural features; category 4, habitat/species management area. Protected area managed mainly for conservation through management intervention; category 5, protected landscape/seascape. Protected area managed mainly for landscape/seascape conservation and recreation; category 6, managed resource protected area: protected area managed mainly for the sustainable use of natural resources.

Nevertheless, by its own standards, the Database could still be much improved. Size data for protected areas are not known for 12% of the records. Furthermore 35% of the entries lack an establishment date. Indeed, although in 2003 the fifth World Parks Congress celebrated the achievement of protecting 10% of the planet's land surface with some ceremony, the target may have actually already been reached when the fourth World Parks Congress set that goal in 1992. There are also clearly anomalies in the categorization systems the IUCN uses in the database. Chape et al. (2005) eschewed the marine/terrestrial classification and mapped existing protected areas onto a GIS (geographic information system) model of the Earth's lands and seas. They found that 18.4 million km^2 of protected areas

covered the land, substantially more than the categorization system states.

The Database, therefore, is clearly a clumsy machine, but even if it was finely tuned, we would need to use it with caution. The Database is not just a record of practice, it is also a way of seeing the world with blindspots and blurred vision not easily perceived by its operators, but these blindspots become darker and fuzzier as the machine becomes better. For the Database to work best, it could erase or exclude precisely the sort of local practices that fuel our interests in the first place (Brosius 1999b).

The Database only records state activity. It is blind to individual, and informal collective, activity. For example, private protected areas are not included in the data. In South

Table 1 (*Continued*)

			Count of all protected areas in each size class			
<1 km²	≥1 km² <10 km²	≥10 km² <100 km²	≥100 km² <1000 km²	≥1000 km² <10,000 km²	≥10,000 km² <100,000 km²	≥100,000 km² <1000,000 km²
40	40	14	8	2	1	0
5242	2559	1165	425	123	20	2
83	101	93	43	23	1	0
161	236	370	384	63	5	0
230	509	831	786	166	12	0
259	413	1542	812	181	20	2
7166	3083	1507	1158	289	33	1
26,885	7678	2908	1137	141	2	0
223	217	303	239	57	13	2
527	926	1290	831	300	31	0
90	629	875	643	179	28	0
3118	3568	3069	1553	525	69	2
66	157	225	162	32	1	0
373	236	140	55	14	1	0
285	418	716	623	410	82	1
44,748	20,770	15,048	8859	2505	319	10
10,612	75,767	539,300	2,895,756	7,591,812	6,960,583	3,447,024

Africa. over 13% of the country is set aside as privately run game farms compared with only 6% set aside as state and provincial protected areas. Diverse forms of informal community conservation and natural resource management, from sacred groves to calf pastures and community conservation areas, are also omitted (Pathak et al. 2004). The Database can only recognize what its constituent countries providing information recognize as official conservation.

None of these observations mean we should disregard these data; all facts are shaped by the circumstances of their creation. Rather, as discussed below, records such as the Database become more interesting because they often transform the world into their own image. Although the goal to set aside 10% of the world's land surface was, probably, launched after that milestone had already been reached, it galvanized a large number of NGOs to actively extend protected-area networks in the early 1990s. Their activity and fund-raising gained authority and success be-

cause of the need to meet this target. The category system adopted by the IUCN (**Table 1**, footnote 3) is being used to rewrite and modify protected-area legislation in an increasing number of countries (Bishop et al. 2004). Management categories intended to describe a park's status are now used to prescribe and proscribe activities within it. Protected areas provide a means of seeing and governing the world that have myriad social effects.

Protected areas have increasingly become the means by which many people see, understand, experience, and use the parts of the world that are often called nature and the environment. This virtualizing vision (Carrier & Miller 1998), although rarely uncontested, has imposed the European nature/culture dichotomy on places and people where the distinction between nature and culture did not previously exist (Strathern 1980). As such, protected areas have become a new cosmology of the natural—a way of seeing and being in the world that is now seen as just, moral, and right. In effect, protected areas are the material and discursive means by which conservation and development discourses, practices, and institutions remake the world (Brosius 1999a, Watts 1993). The implications of this cannot be analyzed merely by giving greater attention to the social construction of nature (see Nygren 1998), but also by examining the material effects of the production of our surroundings.

SEPARATION OF NATURE AND CULTURE

Throughout the literature one finds instances of the discursive and material separation of people and their surroundings into the categories nature, culture, environment, and society (Wilshusen et al. 2002). Chape et al. (2003, p. 10) show that through the IUCN process of listing and cataloging protected-area types, and IUCN's attempt to create a worldwide category system, national governments have to fit their protected lands into these international categories that separate people from their surroundings. This is a form of the generification (Errington & Gewertz 2001, West & Carrier 2004) of the external world—the IUCN takes an externally imagined set of categories and restructures the world to fit these categories with limited regard for national or local descriptive categories. Anthropologically speaking, these separations mirror Western imaginaries of nature and culture and impose them on much of the world (Gillison 1980, Johnson 2000, Seeland 1997, Strathern 1980).

Nygren (1998, p. 213) shows that NGOs rely heavily on the "western division between nature and culture." NGO publications frequently present nature as a static object, separate from human beings. By extension, they present the ecological effects of human activities—as part of culture—as unnatural. In other cases, they may present indigenous peoples as ecologically noble savages, whose cultures are somehow closer to nature. Whether indigenous peoples are imagined, or project themselves (see Adams 2003), as inside or outside nature, however, the imposition of this putative nature/culture dichotomy has had significant material and social impacts, either by forcefully excluding people from their land or holding them to discursive standards that are nearly impossible to live up to in practice (Igoe 2005, West 2001).

Some authors show how the discursive creation and subsequent separation of nature and culture are tied to the different worldviews of actors involved in conservation and the different kinds of liberation and sustainability narratives available on the global discursive scale (Dove 2003, Igoe 2005, MacDonald 2004, West 2001). Baviskar (2003) examines the ideas of Indian environmental activists and rural tribal peoples concerning relationships between people and their surroundings and shows that the negioations over discursive productions have material effects of land rights and land use. Stegeborn (1996) demonstrates how the idea of poachers, a discursive production of people as separate from and damaging to their surroundings, led to the removal of Wanniya-Laeto peoples from protected forests in Sri Lanka.

Goldman (2001), using materials from the Mekong region of Laos, shows how new definitions of land and land use imposed by the World Bank separate people and their surroundings in ways that do not clearly lead to sustainable development. Roth (2004) demonstrates that the Thai concept of nature includes humans but that international NGOs impose Western ideas about the separation of nature and culture in their work with Thai protected areas. This has led, on the one hand, to local people resisting the creation of protected areas. On the other hand, it has led to alliances between NGOs and local people built upon discourses of human rights and sustainable development (Roth 2004).

The idea of wilderness as a place that should not be commercially developed has presented other opportunities for alliances between local people and conservationists. The creation of Gates of the Arctic National Park in Alaska, for instance, was brought about by an alliance between Inuit activists and conservationists seeking to block an oil pipeline (Catton 1997). Kakadu National Park in Australia's Northern Territory was brought about by a similar alliance to block uranium mining (Lawrence 2000). West (2005) further demonstrates the connections between these separations of people and surroundings and a neoliberal conservation agenda that needs biodiveristy or nature to become commodities and natives to become labor. In such settings, natives may also become commodities, as their culture becomes part of the selling point for people-centered conservation initiatives or ecotourism marketing (Igoe 2004).

CHANGING USE RIGHTS, DISPLACEMENT, AND CONFLICT

The Durban Action Plan, the central outcome of the fifth World Parks Congress, emphasizes the connection between dispossession and poverty, culture change, and social and subsistence losses on the part of people living in and around protected areas (MacKay & Caruso 2004). The creation of protected areas alters land-use rights in general (Agrawal & Ostrom 2001, Albers & Grinspoon 1997, Jim & Xu 2003, Panusittikorn & Prato 2001, Roth 2004, Wilshusen et al. 2002). Specifically we see the following examples: instances of increased elite control of resources historically (Cleary 2005, Sivaramakrishnan 2003) and contemporarily (Brothers 1997, Colchester 2003, Daily & Ellison 2002, Hitchcock 1995, Jeffery et al. 2003, Peluso 1993, Silori 2001), the alienation from land and sea and the influx of alien land and sea uses in places surrounding protected areas (Foale & Manele 2004, Haenn 2005, Peters 1998), and the criminalization of native peoples because of their land-use practices (Freedman 2002, Geisler et al. 1997). The overwhelming impression protected-area creation leaves is of restricted access and use for rural peoples through legislation, enforcement, and privatization (Greenough 2003, Horowitz 1998,

Igoe 2003, Mahanty 2003, Negi & Nautiyal 2003, Santana 1991). Displacement from protected areas is one of the most controversial and contested aspects of protected areas. It has received a great deal of attention in recent years, particularly from anthropologists, but the literature is far from straightforward. Borgerhoff Mulder & Coppolillo (2005, p. 36) claim the literature on displacement represents a "massive cataloguing of past, recent and on-going abuses." This statement is simply wrong and surprising in a work devoted to tackling the problems conservation can cause. First, there are few studies compared with the number of protected areas; we have found just under 250 reports covering just under 200 protected areas. Second, the literature is not a catalog, for there is no system or order in the literature. Third, and most seriously, much of what is written is simply not informative. Nearly 50% of the works we examined merely mention the fact of removal, either to announce the establishment of protection or to warn activists that marginal rural groups, especially indigenous peoples, are facing further threats to their livelihood. Barely 25% undertake detailed examinations of the anatomy of the livelihood change experienced by rural groups following displacement (see Brockington 2001). This is unfortunate because these issues are often denied by states, NGOs, and others with an interest in the displacment of people from these areas. Defenders of protected areas complain, legitimately, of anecdotal critiques (Sanderson & Redford 2004).

Only a handful of individual studies detail the economic costs and/or the social impacts of people displaced by protected areas (Emerton 2001, Geisler 2003, Ghimire 1997, Olwig & Olwig 1979, Overton 1979, Shyamsundar & Kramer 1997, Tacconi & Bennett 1995). Only recently has there been any attempt to apply established means of assessing the impacts of displacement to cases of conservation-induced displacement and representatively assess its consequences (Cernea 2005, Schmidt-Soltau 2003, 2005).

The most productive bodies of literature give particular attention to select regions or individual protected areas. For example, there has been a flourish of studies in India (Ganguly 2004, Guha 1997, Rangarajan 1996, Saberwal et al. 2000). There has also been considerable attention given to Nepal, especially the Royal Chitwan National Park. McLean & Straede's (2003) work there is the source for probably the best study we have found of the ongoing consequences of eviction as it takes place.

There also have been many environmental histories reinterpreting the history of national parks and protected areas in the United States, focusing on the simultaneous containment of Native Americans onto reservations and the creation of national parks in the American West at the end of the nineteenth century (Burnham 2000, Catton 1997, Jacoby 2001, Keller & Turek 1998, Nabakov & Lawrence 2004, Spence 1999). Most notoriously, the creation of Yellowstone, the world's premiere national park, was instigated by eastern elites, but keeping it free of hostile indigenes required the services of the U.S. Army, and convincing tourists it was safe required the services of marketing experts (Burnham 2000, Spence 1999). Maintaining Yellowstone as the quintessential American wilderness experience has entailed the systematic erasure of this history. The Yellowstone model was quickly replicated throughout the American West (Stevens 1997), and American parks in turn "served as models for preservationist efforts and native dispossession all over the world" (Spence 1999, p. 5). More insidiously, Yellowstone became a model for the creation of virtual landscapes, in the form of theme parks, malls, international hotels, and other spaces designed to present consumers with generic experiences of sanitized histories and landscapes (Wilson 1992).

South Africa's unusual history of thorough eviction under apartheid means it has both remarkably good records of who was moved where, and at what cost, and a restitution program of lands lost to biodiversity conservation. These records have been explored with detailed individual histories of specific protected areas (Carruthers 1995, Palmer et al. 2002), as well as overview studies (Fabricius & de Wet 2002, Magome & Fabricius 2004). Elsewhere in Southern Africa, the San bushmen's plight as a result of eviction from protected areas has received considerable attention (Hitchcock 2001, Ikeya 2001, Kuper 2003, Suzman 2002/2003). In East Africa, a great deal has been written about Maa-speaking pastoralists and conservation (Gavlin et al. 2002; Homewood & Rodgers 1991; Igoe 2003, 2004; Igoe & Brockington 1999; McCabe 2002).

The absence of some regions from the protected-area literature may reflect differences between countries. The lack of European regions in the literature demonstrates the relative lack of hardship created by protected areas on this continent. The plethora of African material, however, is testimony to the large individual size of African protected areas (**Table 1**), the continent's predominantly rural population, and the combination of weak states and colonial imposition, which makes planning for displacement so difficult. In Australia and Latin America, the lack of studies reflects the fact that protected-area dynamics and policies work differently in these areas. Australia has witnessed less displacement owing to conservation than places such as Africa and North America. However, there are significant conflicts over park-management authority and tourism's impact on aboriginal cultures and sacred places (Cordell 1993, Lawrence 2000, Toyne & Johnston 1991). In Latin America, indigenous communities have treated protected areas as an opportunity to protect their traditional homelands (Chapin 2000, Winer 2003), but they have also learned protected areas can be a front for outside commercial interests (Nugent 1994, Zamarenda 1998).

One surprising conclusion from our survey is that work on indigenous peoples is particularly uninformative as to the precise impacts of eviction. Although the achievements of indigenous peoples' activists in challenging displacement are considerable (Brosius 2004), relatively few accounts provide detailed observations. Moreover, as Igoe (2005, pp. 7–8) has argued elsewhere, this conceptual enclosure of indigenous peoples as the primary victims of protected-area displacement conceals two fundamental inequalities. First, between indigenous groups, some indigenous people are more indigenous than others. San groups in Namibia, for instance, have become a permanent underclass of agricultural workers. Members of this group are unable to articulate the same claims to indigeneity as San groups in neighboring Botswana (Sylvain 2002). Second, indigenous people are not always the most-marginal people displaced and impoverished by protected areas. Studies from Indonesia (Li 2000, 2005) and South Africa (Kuper 2003) demonstrate that people descended from displaced groups frequently are a significant minority of the rural populations in developing countries. They are also frequently the most marginal and least ethnically distinct. Nevertheless, their relationships to the environment have profound implications for conservation.

There is a final lacuna with respect to our knowledge of displacement from protected areas: We have little knowledge of the protected areas' rates of use and occupation. Instead of a global overview of these rates, we have a smattering of individual surveys showing occupation rates of 56%–72% for national parks and wildlife sanctuaries in India (Kothari et al. 1989); 85% for national parks in South America (Amend & Amend 1995); 70% for protected areas in well-populated tropical areas (Bruner et al. 2001), and 70%–100% for protected areas in Myanmar, Mongolia, and East Kalimantan (Bedunah & Schmidt 2004, Jepson et al. 2002, Rao et al. 2002). Remote sensing of agricultural activities inside protected areas (using protected-area data from 2000, which had approximately 44,000 records) illustrates that agriculture is practiced in 29% of known protected areas (McNeely & Scherr 2003). Clearly it is difficult to understand the con-

sequences of displacement from protected areas if a good overview of protected-area occupancy rates does not exist in the first place. If these surveys are representative, however, then current protest is but the thin end of the wedge. If existing conservation legislation is applied strictly in many countries, the level and rate of evictions should increase remarkably. Recent reports from India, for example, suggest that nearly 4 million people face eviction following amendments to protected-area policy (Kothari 2004). Geisler & de Sousa (2001) estimate that between 1 and 16 million people in Africa could become environmental refugees from protected areas. If this becomes true, the real challenge facing anthropology and conservation is how to deal with this portending displacement (Brockington et al. 2006).

Displacement then is more elusive and complex than it might otherwise seem. Indeed the ambiguities protected areas can create are remarkable. Protected areas can produce new sorts of lands that are owned by the state but used by local people for subsistence and social needs (Sato 2000). National parks are often ambiguous in this way because they turn historic hunting and grazing zones into areas that local people cannot use (Knudsen 1999). In Nepal buffer zones restrict traditional access rights and land use, lead to conflict and economic loss, and destroy traditional land-tenure systems, yet there is no evidence that buffer zones lead to conservation (Heinen & Mehta 2000). Chatty (2002) demonstrates that an oryx-reintroduction project on the Arabian Peninsula, although lauded a conservation success story, actually changed land-use rights, so the Harasiis people who have shared space with the oryx for centuries are now denied grazing rights and are put into a position where poaching is a financial and subsistence option. Rae et al. (2002) show how protected areas in Syria replace customary land-tenure systems with new regulatory systems that dispossess pastoral groups, alter intra- and intertribal relations, and affect local community dynamics. In Nepal and

Bhutan, land-management techniques used by national parks to protect wildlife disrupt local agriculture and create hostility among local people toward conservation in general (Seeland 2000).

Conflict is often at the heart of protected-area establishment and maintenance. In part this is because of clumsy top-down approaches by states that fail to appreciate, or work with, local practices and interests. Orlove (2002) has shown how villagers effectively resisted attempts to establish a national reserve in the reedbeds of Lake Titicaca in Peru either from the outset or because the new controls proved difficult to reconcile with the villagers' management of the reedbeds. The reedbeds were thoroughly anthropogenic environments with villagers planting, cutting, and tending the beds in accordance with fluctuating lake levels. On other occasions, protected-area creation hinges on the physical and symbolic erasure of former residents (Neumann 1998, Ranger 1999, Spence 1999). One central feature of the Yellowstone Model was the erasure of the social history of Native American land use and even Native Americans themselves (Meyer 1996, Rasker 1993). Native Americans, as with people displaced by protected areas around the world, were then made to reappear in these landscapes as purveyors of arts and craft, entertainment, and other services required by visitors. The policing and funding of protected areas require continued state violence (Neumann 2004, Peluso 1993).

Protected areas, as with any development intervention, are also instrumental in fueling social conflict between groups. African transboundary conservation areas, which can require displacement and fuel ethnic tensions, ironically have sought popular support as peace parks (Duffy 2005, Wolmer 2003). Contests develop over the fortunes and misfortunes that protected areas can distribute. This can be between rich and poor (e.g., McLean & Straede 2003), castes (e.g., Paudel 2005), or ethnic groups (e.g., Nelson & Hossack 2003). Protected areas are frequently cited as one of the means by which violence is

done to indigenous peoples (Colchester 2003, Colchester & Erni 1999, Gray et al. 1998, Nelson & Hossack 2003).

The creation of wilderness spaces, however, has often also resulted in the creation of liminal spaces, beyond the control of the state. Parks in Africa and Latin America have served as staging grounds for guerilla movements (Dunn 2003), as well as for drug trafficking (Stepp 2005). U.S. parks shelter marijuana plantations and methamphetamine labs, as well as being a preferred route for people seeking to enter the country illegally (Igoe 2005). Parks sometimes offer indigenous communities opportunities to elude state control and other incursions onto their land. The Ute Mountain Tribal Park in Colorado was created to preempt the expropriation of Ute land by the U.S. National Park Service (Igoe 2004). The Kuna Park in Panama was created to preempt the invasion of Kuna land by peasant agriculturalists entering the Atlantic coast from the center of the country (Chapin 2000). Some conservation areas are created in partnership with local people and still change land- and sea-use patterns. The Seaflower Biosphere Reserve in Columbia was created as a result of the local identification of overfished areas and the local agreement to turn these areas into no-take reserves (Friedlander et al. 2003). In some cases protected areas meant to change land-use rights create a joint land management with rights and responsibilities falling to both residents of reserves and wildlife managers, but local people still lose important rights to agricultural lands (Maikhuri et al. 2000). This loss affects local lifeways and subsistence practices and often has negative consequences.

CHANGES IN SOCIAL PRACTICES

Protected areas and conservation efforts have profound effects on gender relationships worldwide (Agarwal 1997, Ghimire & Pimbert 1997, Schroeder 1993). In the Maya Biosphere Reserve in Guatemala, project planners targeted the men as the "primary agents of social change," whereas the planners initially virtually ignored the women (Sundberg 2003, p. 733). The project worked, however, to "disrupt local power structures and gender relations, thereby creating spaces for new forms of environmental activism and political alliances" (p. 734). Because they were ignored, women began to build alliances and work outside of their immediate family. This allowed women new ways of constituting themselves as persons. Instead of making self only through family interactions, women broadened their social networks and their networks of self (Sundberg 2004). Similarly, in Costa Rica, women's participation in handicraft production projects aimed at tourist markets has given them economic power that they did not have in the past (Vivanco 2001). The kinds of handicraft projects that have emerged because of conservation and ecotourism in Costa Rica have changed the way women produce crafts and the imagery used in the crafts. Women now incorporate images of the quetzal into their designs, even if they have never seen the birds before (Vivanco 2001). In Tanzania, bride-price conventions and women's income earning have changed over time because of the fall in cattle numbers following displacement (Brockington 2001). Sullivan's (2000) work in Namibia has shown that attempts to deal with the economic exclusions of conservation policies discriminated against and devalued women's resource use.

Conservation efforts also change the ways people see themselves in relation to their surroundings. In the past, the Huaorani Indians saw the natural environment as inextricable from their social world (Holt 2005). Today, nature and culture are separate for them because of their involvement in conservation. In some instances local people have begun to monitor their own wildlife consumption (Noss et al. 2004). Peters (1998) demonstrates that deeply embedded socioecological practices such as tavy in Madagascar have been approached by conservation actors as environmental practices that have little or no so-

cial significance. These practices, seen as simply environmental usage by ecologists and conservationists, are stopped or changed to the detriment of local social life and custom. In some cases, of course, resource depletion causes social changes such as intensification of land use and dependence on market economies (Putsche 2000). Some authors show that the language of environmentalism and protection has come to permeate local language and speech. This appropriation of environmentalist discourse is used in Cerro Azul Meambar National Park in Honduras when people wish to gain access to the benefits of the park, yet it also works to change local views of peoples' relationships with their surroundings (Pfeffer et al. 2001).

In many projects people are made less complicated so as to make them understandable to outsiders and managers and so their socioecological practices will fit within the IUCN categories of protected landscapes (Harmon 2003). We take this process to be one of both generification, making people fit into already existing categories, and decomplexification, simplifying people's social practices and beliefs so they fit within certain policy structures. Conservation efforts often do not effectively respond to the changing social, political, and economic needs of communities (Egenter & Labo 2003). These efforts tend to fix communities and peoples in time and space and not allow for change. People are often judged as difficult and projects as failures when they do not conform to their created image at the project's inception (West 2001, 2006). In other instances indigenous peoples and their ecological knowledge and practice are fixed temporally in the past, and little attention is paid to their current understandings and uses of their surroundings (English 2000). A kind of virtualism is at play here—people are produced one way, and when they are not that way or change, they are seen as failing.

We also see shifting identity claims on the part of nonindigenous actors. In Australia there has been conflict over forest-protection planning because of the ways in which white

Australians react to arguments about Aboriginal spiritual and social ties to the land (Trigger & Mulcock 2005). With regard to the Aboriginal peoples' assertion of historic ties to the land, whites have begun to assert their social and spiritual connections to the land. Others show how people in wealthy nations come to configure their identity as environmentalists through NGO media representations of indigenous peoples and their use and understandings of their surroundings (Weeks 1999).

Some of the most pervasive and far-reaching changes wrought by protected areas are visible in the spread of ecotourism and commodification. Ecotourism enterprises are symbiotic with protected areas. If there is a protected area, some form of ecotourism likely uses it, and if ecotourism enterprises are present, some protected areas likely exist in the vicinity. Because of this connection, people living in and around protected areas interact with ecotourism as a revenue source, as a set of social relationships that bring nature and culture to areas where they did not exist before, and as a conduit for visitors from other places. It brings new ways of seeing and using people's surroundings to already existing socioecological landscapes and creates new boundaries (Forbes 1995, Vivanco 2001, West & Carrier 2004).

Ecotourism works to create simplistic images of local people and their uses and understanding of their surroundings. Through the lens of these simplified images, officials direct policies and projects toward the local people, and the local people are blamed with the projects fail (Belsky 1999). Ecotourism also works to change the ways people understand their surroundings (Vivanco 2001), and it can lead to pressure on local resources because of the numbers of tourists and increasing tourist activities (Panusittikorn & Prato 2001, Puntenney 1990). Ecotourism can also lead to increased economic expectations on the part of local people (Chapin 1990, Foucat 2002). In the Yucatan, it has contributed to changes in Mayan diets that include increased

dependency on purchased items and a decline in overall nutrition (Leatherman & Goodman 2005).

The money that tourism can generate often ties parks and park management to ecotourism (Walpole et al. 2001). But there is a tension in this relationship because ecotourism often causes conflict and changes in land-use rights (Bookbinder et al. 1998), fails to deliver promises of community-level benefits (Alexander 2000, Kiss 2004, Kruger 2005, Stone & Wall 2004), actually damages environments (Carrier & Macleod 2005, Karan & Mather 1985, Quiros 2005, Savage 1993, Zurick 1992), and has myriad other social impacts (Wallace & Diamante 2005). Indeed, many argue repeatedly that ecotourism is neither ecologically nor socially beneficial (Carrier & MacLeod 2005, West & Carrier 2004), yet it persists as a strategy for conservation and development.

In Cuc Phuong National Park, where some Muong villagers have been relocated outside the park to buffer zones, ecotourism has caused conflict between Muong villages by creating class differences between people who have money because of tourism and those who do not; it created images of people living in the park as indigenous and those moved outside of it as villagers; and it created a dependency on conservation for jobs and income (Rugendyke & Son 2005). This park is not the only place where people have been displaced by ecotourism (Weinberg et al. 2002) or where an economic dependency on tourism exists (Macleod 2001, Putsche 2000). In Costa Rica, 70% of regional income near Monte Verde comes from ecotourism (Vivanco 2001). We also see the creation of socioeconomic differences between communities involved in park-related ecotourism enterprises and those not given the same opportunities in Jordan (Schneider & Burnett 2000) and Neapl (Mehta & Kellert 1998), and unequal benefit distribution in Nepal (Bookbinder et al. 1998) and Indonesia (Walpole et al. 2001). Conflict also arises over ecotourism in Australia (Slattery 2002),

Tasmania (Kirkpatrick 2001), and Papua New Guinea (West 2006, West & Carrier 2004). Abel (2003) demonstrates that, in Bonaire, ecotourism presents an enormous disruption to socioecological systems by changing social relations between peoples and relations of production across the island. Abel also shows how ecotourism internationalizes economies in ways that are not necessarily beneficial to people living in and around protected areas, whereas Dixon et al. (1993) demonstrate how dive tourism in Bonaire has negatively affected reef health and thus subsistence for some people.

Even without ecotourism, protected areas at times provide employment for rural peoples (Whitesell 1996), although in some instances protected areas turn people into labor in ways that create new sorts of subjectivities (Sodikof 2005), employment for expatriates (Peters 1998), and employment for in-country elites (Baviskar 2003). Protected areas also provide some in-country scientific-capacity building (Aguilar-Stoen & Dhillion 2003, Danielsen et al. 2005, Sivaramakrishnan 2003). However, NGOs do not always meet these promises of capacity building (Haley & Clayton 2003). Protected areas also, at times, create a dependency on conservation projects for employment opportunities for both rural peoples and landholders (Brandon et al. 2005, Charles 1999, Lane 2002, Lawson 2003, Westman 1990).

More significant than the creation or distribution of employment, however, are the consequences of commodification that incorporation into market systems can bring. (Peters 1998, Sundberg 2003, Toly 2004, West 2006, Wilshusen et al. 2002). Ecotourism can make protected areas, and experience and interaction with them, into things that have an economic value on the basis of visitors' consumption of them (Alexander 2000, King & Stewart 1996, Panusittikorn & Prato 2001, Vaughan 2000). Whereas rural peoples' previous interactions with plants and animals were unique social ways of relating to their surroundings, these plants and animals' instillation into economic valuation erases local ways of seeing and being (Brown 1998, Jeffery et al. 2003, King & Stewart 1996, Tsing 2003).

MacDonald (2004) has shown that the international sport hunting of ibex in Pakistan, driven by shaky narratives of scarcity, displaces local hunting practices and beliefs. The commodity of trophy species becomes a means of control and domination. Indeed, integrated conservation and development projects (referred to as ICDPs or ICADs) are premised on the idea that people living in and around protected areas can come to value their surroundings as "in situ biological diversity" if they intellectually connect it to markets and cash income (Filer 2004; Van Helden 1998, 2001; Wagner 2003; West 2005, 2006).

These projects always focus on some sort of commercialization of plants, animals, places, or peoples (Brandon & O'Herron 2004, Cameron 1996), but they rarely take local systems of evaluation into account (Sillitoe 2001, West 2005). In addition, ICAD projects often exacerbate already existing social differences (Cameron 1996, Horowitz 1998) and create expectations that are not met (Foale 2001). The conservation literature can be skeptical of these projects' effectiveness for conservation (Wells et al. 1999).

In some instances, when animals are turned into commodities in local peoples' minds, they retaliate against national parks because of the financial burdens imposed on them through the killing of wildlife (Seeland 2000). Certain species have gone from being little known or valued by local people to being highly valued commodities (Vivanco 2001). The commodification of plants may erase their social value and lead to overproduction within protected areas (Merlin & Raynor 2005). Local people and their image can also be turned into commodities (Krech 2005), as can their intellectual property that is concerned with their surroundings (Brush 1993, Filer 2000).

CONCLUSIONS

How might anthropologists think more carefully about the material effects of protected areas in future research? Lefebvre (1991), Smith (1990, 1996), and Harvey (1989) all argue that space is produced through social practices, science, planning, and technology, and space is lived and understood through symbols, language, and images (see Lefebvre 1991, pp. 38–39). By space these authors mean the world around us as it is experienced materially and symbolically. Here we take space to mean the same as surroundings, the term we use to think about how one should describe the world people live in and with when discussing protected areas, so as to not replicate culturally biased terms such as environment, nature, natural resources, or wilderness.

Anthropologists have used ideas about spatial production productively to move beyond debates about social construction and material effects in other nonenvironmental realms of analysis (Low 1996), and geographers have used these ideas to think about the production of natural spaces in preservation projects (Katz 1998). We would like to see more analysis of the ways in which protected areas produce space both discursively, as Brosius (1999a) suggests, and materially. How do protected areas bring particular types of space into being? What does the creation of new places through conservation intervention do to the places being symbolically and materially remapped by conservation topologies? How do these productions of space alter local social relations with people's surroundings? How do they alter how people use and make meaningful their surroundings?

Some of this type of analysis exists in the literature on protected areas in an embedded form, but it is not, for the most part, explicitly discussed as the formation of new kinds of space and place (Arias & Nations 1992, Austin et al. 1997, Baviskar 2003, Bryant 2000, Duffy 2005, Silori 2001, Slattery 2002, Westman 1990). Some authors have specifically addressed spatial productions with regard to the following: the creation of na-

ture in general (Braun 2002, West 2006), ecotourism (Carrier & Macleod 2005), mapping and conservation (Hughes 2005, Sletto 2002), the fixation of local people in particular kinds of spaces (Whitesell 1996), implications of and for NGOs (Sundberg 1998), displacement (McLean & Straede 2003), and finally the work of discursive practices online and in offices in New York and Washington, D.C., to remake the world (Weeks 1999).

Moore's (1998) study of the environmental politics and history surrounding the Kaerezi River Protected Area in Zimbabwe's Eastern Highlands serves as a good example of where we would like to see future work headed. He argues for "viewing the landscape as the historical sedimentation of symbolic and material processes," emphasizing "competing cultural constructions that assert resource rights and environmental entitlements" (p. 379). He demonstrates the ways in which landscapes come into being, how they are profoundly social, and how the push for conservation changes the social nature of people's surroundings. He also problematizes the state, the community, peasants, and conservationists in ways that show the complexity of social productions of space.

Additionally, Brockington (2002, p. 18, 25, 28) shows how these sorts of spatial productions then work to mold and shape who claims to have membership in or is claimed by others to be of a particular ethnic group. The social is made to seem less complex so it can fit into the new spatial productions of conservation. This is done for ease of policy making and management (Brockington 2002, p. 25) and to make people's socioecological practices fit within the IUCN categories of protected landscapes (Harmon 2003). Therefore, conservation, similar to colonialism, solidifies certain identities and ethnicities (Hodgson 2001, Li 2000) and incarcerates them in space and place (Appadurai 1988).

These spatial productions also affect what kinds of evaluation systems of the surroundings' value are in place and/or taken seriously. Kaus (1993) demonstrates that the Mapimi

Biosphere Reserve in Mexico, with its division into eight different zones, is a new production of space that is profoundly different from local peoples' divisions of lands. She also shows that local people and researchers have vastly different ideas about what the land in the reserve contains and its importance and that they have vastly different systems for evaluation of the value of plants, animals, and natural processes.

Additionally, we also want to encourage more work on the production of value by and for people living outside of protected areas. Harmon (2003) discusses 11 intangible values derived from protected areas: recreational, therapeutic, spiritual, cultural, identity, existence, artistic, aesthetic, educational, peace, and scientific research and monitoring. These values can be seen as social effects of protected areas as they change the social lives and well-being of the people who visit parks and the people living in them. The recreationists, tourists, artists, scientists and others who use protected areas need to be studied.

Finally, we would like to see more work specifically focused on what we see as a simplification process that takes place when biologists and other natural scientists write about, think about, and attempt to legislate the social relations between people and their surroundings. In this simplification process, rich and nuanced social interactions connected to what natural scientists see as the environment are condensed to a few easily conveyable and representable issues or topics. We see this process

taking place on two levels. First, people's uses of and understandings of their surroundings are simplified so they are seen as resource use (Tsing 2003, West 2005), and, second, people's uses of their surroundings are simplified so that they are seen as falling on a scale of authenticity that ranges from ecologically pristine native to fallen-from-grace native to peasant, and so on (see Igoe 2005, West 2001). In some ways this is a retelling of the unilinial evolution paradigm from eighteenth-century anthropology.

To conclude, we reiterate our assertion that protected areas are a form of what has been called globalization. The contemporary focus on the technological aspects of globalization (such as the rapid communication and information systems and networks, rapid transportation, and the movements of people, money, and ideas) has perhaps made globalization seem less relevant in a field where the aim appears to be the preservation of a natural state. At the same time, political economic critiques such as those of Marxist geographers are cast at such a scale as to not take into account the individual (idiosyncratic) practices and beliefs of local populations. We argue for an anthropology of protected areas that bridges this gap, one that attends to the political economies of globalization and the subtle but profound local social effects of the creation of nature and environment in places where those categorizations of people's surroundings did not exist until recently.

ACKNOWLEDGMENTS

The authors jointly wish to thank the editors of the *Annual Review of Anthropology* and the members of Paige West's Parks and Protected Areas seminar in the fall of 2006. Paige West wishes to acknowledge the American Association of University Women and the American Council of Learned Socieites whose fellowships she held while working on this chapter. Dan Brockington wishes to acknowledge the support of an ESRC Fellowship (RES 000 27 0174) held while working on this chapter.

LITERATURE CITED

Abel T. 2003. Understanding complex human ecosystems: the case of ecotourism on Bonaire. *Conserv. Ecol.* 7(3):10–26

Adams C. 2003. Pitfalls of synchronicity: a case study of the *Caicaras* in the Atlantic rainforest of south-eastern Brazil. See Anderson & Berglund 2003, pp. 19–31

Adams WM. 2004. *Against Extinction: The Story of Conservation*. London: Earthscan

Agrawal A, Ostrom E. 2001. Collective action, property rights, and decentralization in resource use in India and Nepal. *Polit. Soc.* 29(4):495–514

Agarwal B. 1997. Environmental action, gender equity and women's participation. *Dev. Change* 28(1): 1–28

Aguilar-Stoen M, Dhillion SS. 2003. Implementation of the convention on biological diversity in Mesoamerica: environmental and developmental perspectives. *Environ. Conserv.* 30(2):131–38

Albers HJ, Grinspoon E. 1997. A comparison of the enforcement of access restrictions between Xishuangbanna Nature Reserve (China) and Khao Yai National Park (Thailand). *Environ. Conserv.* 24:351–62

Alexander SE. 2000. Resident attitudes towards conservation and black howler monkeys in Belize: the Community Baboon Sanctuary. *Environ. Conserv.* 27(4):341–50

Amend S, Amend T. 1995. *National Parks Without People? The South American Experience*. Gland, Switzerland: IUCN

Anderson DG, Berglund E, eds. 2003. *Ethnographies of Conservation: Environmentalism and the Distribution of Privilege*. New York: Bergahn Books

Anderson DG, Ikeya K. 2001. *Parks, Property and Power: Managing Hunting Practice and Identity Within State Policy Regimes. Senri Ethnological Studies No. 59*. Osaka, Japan: Nat. Museum Ethnol.

Appadurai A. 1988. Putting hierarchy in its place. *Cult. Anthropol.* 3(1): 36–49

Arias O, Nations JD. 1992. A call for Central American peace parks. In *Poverty, Natural Resources, and Public Policy in Central America*, ed. S Annis, pp. 43–58. Washington, DC: Overseas Dev. Counc.

Austin D, Stoffle R, Nieves Zedeno M. 1997. Landmark and landscape: a contextual approach to the management of American Indian resources. *Cult. Agric.* 19(3):123–29

Austin R. 2003. *Environmental movements and fisherfolk participation on a coastal frontier, Palawan Island, Philippines*. PhD thesis. Univ. Ga., Athens

Baviskar A. 2003. States, communities and conservation: the practice of ecodevelopment in the Great Himalayan National Park. In *Battles Over Nature: Science and the Politics of Conservation*, ed. V Saberwal, M Rangarajan, pp. 256–83. Delhi: Permanent Black

Bedunah DJ, Schmidt SM. 2004. Pastoralism and protected area management in Mongolia's Gobi Gurvansaikhan National Park. *Dev. Change* 35(1):167–91

Belsky JM. 1999. Misrepresenting communities: the politics of community-based rural ecotourism in Gales Point Manatee, Belize. *Rural Sociol.* 64(4):641–67

Bishop K, Dudley N, Phillips A, Stolton S. 2004. *Speaking a Common Language: The Uses and Performance of the IUCN System of Management Categories for Protected Areas*. Cardiff, UK: Cardiff Univ., IUCN, UNEP-WCMC

Bookbinder MP, Dinerstein E, Rijal A, Caule H, Rajouria A. 1998. Ecotourism's support of biodiversity conservation. *Conserv. Biol.* 12(6):1399–404

Borgerhoff Mulder M, Coppolillo P. 2005. *Conservation: Linking Ecology, Economics and Culture*. Princeton, NJ: Princeton Univ. Press

Brandon K. 2004. The policy context for conservation in Costa Rica: model or muddle? In *Biodiversity Conservation in Costa Rica: Learning the Lessons in a Seasonal Dry Forest*, ed. G Frankie, A Mata, SB Vinson, pp. 299–311. Berkley: Univ. Calif. Press

Brandon K, Gorenflo LJ, Rodrigues ASL, Waller RW. 2005. Reconciling biodiversity conservation, people, protected areas, and agricultural suitability in Mexico. *World Dev.* 33(9):1403–18

Brandon K, O'Herron M. 2004. Parks, projects, and policies: a review of three Costa Rican ICDPs. In *Getting Biodiversity Projects to Work*, ed. TO McShane, MP Wells, pp. 154–80. New York: Columbia Univ. Press

Braun B. 2002. *The Intemperate Rainforest: Nature, Culture, and Power on Canada's West Coast.* Minneapolis: Univ. Minn. Press

Brechin SR, Wilshusen PR, Fortwangler CL, West PC, eds. 2003. *Contested Nature: Promoting International Biodiversity with Social Justice in the Twenty-First Century.* Albany: State Univ. N.Y. Press

Brockington D. 2001. Women's income and livelihood strategies of dispossessed pastoralists. The case of Mkomazi Game Reserve. *Hum. Ecol.* 29:307–38

Brockington D. 2002. *Fortress Conservation: The Preservation of the Mkomazi Game Reserve, Tanzania.* Oxford, UK: James Currey

Brockington D, Igoe J, Schmidt-Soltau K. 2006. Conservation, human rights, and poverty reduction. *Conserv. Biol.* 20(1):250–52

Brosius JP. 1999a. Analyses and interventions: anthropological engagements with environmentalism. *Curr. Anthropol.* 40(3):277–309

Brosius JP. 1999b. Green dots, pink hearts: displacing politics from the Malaysian rain forest. *Am. Anthropol.* 101(1):36–57

Brosius JP. 2004. Indigenous peoples and protected areas at the World Parks Congress. *Conserv. Biol.* 18(3):609–12

Brosius JP, Tsing A, Zerner C, eds. 2005. *Communities and Conservation: Histories and Politics of Community-Based Natural Resource Management.* Walnut Creek, CA: Altamira Press

Brothers TS. 1997. Deforestation in the Dominican Republic: a village level view. *Environ. Conserv.* 24:213–23

Brown K. 1998. The political ecology of biodiversity, conservation and development in Nepal's Terai: confused meanings, means and ends. *Ecol. Econ.* 24(1):73–87

Bruner AG, Gullison RE, Rice RE, da Fonseca GAB. 2001. Effectiveness of parks in protecting tropical biodiversity. *Science* 291(5501):125–28

Brush SB. 1993. Indigenous knowledge of biological resources and intellectual property rights: the role of anthropology. *Am. Anthropol.* 95(3):653–71

Bryant RL. 2000. Politicized moral geographies: debating biodiversity conservation and ancestral domain in the Philippines. *Polit. Geogr.* 19:673–705

Burnham P. 2000. *Indian Country God's Country: Native Americans and National Parks.* Washington, DC: Island Press

Cameron MM. 1996. Biodiversity and medicinal plants in Nepal: involving untouchables in conservation and development. *Hum. Org.* 55(1):84–86

Carrier JG. 2004. Introduction. In *Confronting Environments: Local Environmental Understanding in a Globalising World*, ed. JG Carrier, pp. 1–29. Walnut Creek, CA: Altamira Press

Carrier JG, Macleod DVL. 2005. Bursting the bubble: the socio-cultural context of ecotourism. *J. R. Anthropol. Inst.* 11(2):315–33

Carrier JG, Miller D. 1998. *Virtualism: A New Political Economy.* Oxford, UK: Berg

Carruthers J. 1995. *The Kruger National Park: A Social and Political History.* Pietermaritzburg, South Africa: Univ. Natal Press

Castagna CN. 2005. *The 'wylding' of Te Urewera National Park: analysis of (re)creation discourses in Godzone (Aotearoa/New Zealand).* PhD thesis. Univ. Hawaii

Catton T. 1997. *Inhabited Wilderness: Indians, Eskimos, and National Parks in Alaska.* Albuquerque: Univ. N. Mex. Press

Cernea MM. 2005. Concept and method. Applying the IRR model in Africa to resettlement and poverty. In *Displacement Risks in Africa: Refugees, Resettlers and Their Host Population,* ed. I Ohta, YD Gebre, pp. 195–258. Kyoto, Japan: Kyoto Univ. Press

Chape S, Blyth S, Fish L, Fox P, Spalding M, eds. 2003. *United Nations List of Protected Areas.* Cambridge, UK: UNEP-WCMC

Chape S, Harrison J, Spalding M, Lysenko I. 2005. Measuring the extent and effectiveness of protected areas as an indicator for meeting global biodiversity targets. *Philos. Trans. R. Soc. Lond. B* 360:443–55

Chapin M. 1990. The silent jungle: ecotourism among the Kuna indians of Panama. *Cult. Surv. Q.* 14(1):42–45

Chapin M. 2000. *Defending Kuna Yala.* Washington, DC: USAID Biodivers. Support Program

Chapin M. 2004. A challenge to conservationists. *Worldwatch* 17(6):17–31

Charles JN. 1999. Involvement of Native Americans in cultural resources programs. *Plains Anthropol.* 44(170):25–35

Chatty D. 2002. Animal reintroduction projects in the Middle East: conservation without a human face. See Chatty & Colchester 2002, pp. 227–43

Chatty D, Colchester M, eds. 2002. *Conservation and Mobile Indigenous Peoples: Displacement, Forced Settlement and Sustainable Development.* New York: Berghahn Books

Cleary M. 2005. Managing the forest in colonial Indochina c. 1900–1940. *Mod. Asian Stud.* 39(2):257–83

Colchester M. 2003. *Salvaging Nature: Indigenous Peoples, Protected Areas and Biodivesity Conservation.* Moreton-in-Marsh, UK: World Rainforest Movement, Forest Peoples Programme

Colchester M, Erni C. 1999. *Indigenous Peoples and Protected Areas in South and Southeast Asia: From Principles to Practice.* Copenhagen: IWGIA

Cordell J. 1993. Who owns the land? Indigenous involvement in protected areas. In *The Law of the Mother: Indigenous Peoples and Protected Areas,* ed. E Kempf, pp. 104–13. London: Earthscan

Daily GC, Ellison K. 2002. Costa Rica: paying mother nature to multitask. In *The New Economy of Nature: The Quest to Make Conservation Profitable,* ed. GC Daily, K Ellison, pp. 165–88. Washington, DC: Island Press/Shearwater

Danielsen F, Burgess N, Balmford A. 2005. Monitoring matters: examining the potential of locally-based approaches. *Biodivers. Conserv.* 14:2507–42

Dixon JA, Scura LF, Vanthof T. 1993. Meeting ecological and economic goals—marine parks in the Caribbean. *Ambio* 22(2–3):117–25

Doane M. 2001. *Broken grounds: the politics of the environment in Oaxaca, Mexico.* PhD thesis. City Univ. N.Y., New York

Dove MR. 2003. Forest discourses in South and Southeast Asia: a comparison with global discourses. See Greenough & Tsing 2003, pp. 103–23

Duffy R. 2005. The politics of global environmental governance: the powers and limitations of transfrontier conservation areas in Central America. *Rev. Int. Stud.* 31(2):307–23

Dunn K. 2003. National parks and human security in East Africa. *Proceedings of Beyond the Arch: Community Conservation in Greater Yellowstone and East Africa,* ed. A Biel, pp. 61–74. Mammoth Springs, WY: Natl. Parks Service

Ediger VL. 2005. *Natural experiments in conservation ranching: the social and ecological consequences of diverging land tenure in Marin County, California.* PhD thesis. Stanford Univ., Stanford

Egenter C. Labo M. 2003. In search of equitable governance models for indigenous peoples in protected areas—the experience of Kayan Mentarang National Park. *Policy Matters* 12:248–53

Emerton L. 2001. The nature of benefits and the benefits of nature. Why wildlife conservation has not economically benefitted communities in Africa. See Hulme & Murphree 2001, pp. 208–26

English A. 2000. An emu in the hole: exploring the link between biodiversity and aboriginal cultural heritage in New South Wales, Australia. *Parks* 10:13–25

Erazo JS. 2003. *Constructing autonomy: indigenous organizations, governance, and land use in the Ecuadorian Amazon, 1964–2001.* PhD thesis. Univ. Mich., Ann Arbor

Errington F, Gewertz D. 2001. On the generification of culture: from blow fish to Melanesian. *J. R. Anthropol. Inst.* 7:509–25

Escobar A. 1995. *Encountering Development: The Making and Unmaking of the Third World.* Princeton: Princeton Univ. Press

Fabricius C, de Wet C. 2002. The influence of forced removals and land restitution on conservation in South Africa. See Chatty & Colchester 2002, pp. 142–57

Filer C. 2000. *How can Western conservationists talk to Melanesian landowners about indigenous knowledge?* RMAP Work. Pap. No. 27., Res. School for Pac. Asian Stud., Australian Natl. Univ.

Filer C. 2004. *Hotspots and handouts: illusions of conservation and development in Papua New Guinea.* Presented at Bridging Scales and Epistimologies: Linking Local Knowledge with Global Science Conf., Alexandria, Egypt

Foale S. 2001. 'Where's our development?' Landowner aspirations and environmentalist agendas in Western Solomon Islands. *Asia Pac. J. Anthropol.* 2(2):44–67

Foale S, Manele B. 2004. Social and political barriers to the use of Marine Protected Areas for conservation and fishery management in Melanesia. *Asia Pac. Viewp.* 45:373–86

Forbes AA. 1995. Heirs to the land: mapping the future of the Makalu-Barun. *Cult. Surv. Q.* 18(4):69

Foucat VSA. 2002. Community-based ecotourism management moving towards sustainability, in Ventanilla, Oaxaca, Mexico. *Ocean Coast. Manage.* 45(8):511–29

Freedman E. 2002. When indigenous rights and wilderness collide: prosecution of Native Americans for using motors in Minnesota's Boundary Waters Canoe Wilderness Area. *Am. Indian Q.* 26(4):378–92

Friedlander A, Nowlis JS, Sanchez JA, Appeldoorn R, Usseglio P, et al. 2003. Designing effective marine protected areas in Seaflower Biosphere Reserve, Colombia, based on biological and sociological information. *Conserv. Biol.* 17(6):1769–84

Ganguly V. 2004. *Conservation, Displacement and Deprivation: Maldhari of Gir Forest of Gujarat.* New Delhi: Indian Soc. Inst.

Garner A. 2002. *Contemporary forest landscapes in Britain: ownership, environmentalism and leisure.* PhD thesis. Univ. College London

Gavlin KA, Ellis J, Boone RB, Magennis AL, Smith NM, et al. 2002. Compatibility of pastoralism and conservation? A test case using integrated assessment in the Ngorongoro Conservation Area, Tanzania. See Chatty & Colchester 2002, pp. 36–60

Geisler C. 2003. Your park, my poverty. Using impact assessment to counter displacement effects of environmental greenlining. See Brechin et al. 2003, pp. 217–29

Geisler C, de Sousa R. 2001. From refuge to refugee: the African case. *Public Adm. Dev.* 21:159–70

Geisler C, Warne R, Barton A. 1997. The wandering commons: a conservation conundrum in the Dominican Republic. *Agric. Hum. Values* 14:325–35

Ghimire K, Pimbert M, eds. 1997. *Social Change and Conservation*. London: James & James/Earthscan

Ghimire KB. 1997. Conservation and social development: an assessment of Wolong and other panda reserves in China. See Ghimire & Pimbert 1997, pp. 187–213

Gillison G. 1980. Images of nature in Gimi thought. In *Nature, Culture and Gender*, ed. C MacCormack, M Strathern, pp. 143–73. Cambridge, UK: Cambridge Univ. Press

Goldman M. 2001. Constructing an environmental state: eco-governmentality and other transnational practices of a 'green' world bank. *Soc. Prob.* 48(4):499–523

Gray A, Parellada A, Newing H. 1998. *From Principles to Practice. Indigenous Peoples and Biodiversity Conservation in Latin America. Proceedings of the Puscallpa Conference*. Copenhagen: IWGIA

Greenough P. 2003. Pathogens, pugmarks, and political emergency: The 1970s South Asian debate on nature. See Greenough & Tsing 2003, pp. 201–30

Greenough P, Tsing A. eds. 2003. *Nature in the Global South: Environmental Projects in South and South East Asia*. Durham, NC: Duke Univ. Press

Guha R. 1997. Radical American environmentalism and wilderness preservation: a Third World critique. In *Varieties of Environmentalism: Essays North and South*, ed. R Guha, J Martinez-Alier, pp. 71–83. London: Earthscan

Gustavo A. 2005. *Conservation, sustainable development, and 'traditional' people: Pataxo ethnoecology and conservation paradigms in southern Bahia, Brazil*. PhD thesis. Cornell Univ., Ithaca

Haenn N. 2005. *Fields of Power, Forests of Discontent: Culture, Conservation, and the State in Mexico*. Tucson: Univ. Ariz. Press

Haley M, Clayton A. 2003. The role of NGOs in environmental policy failures in a developing country: the mismanagement of Jamaica's coral reefs. *Environ. Values* 12(1):29–54

Harmon D. 2003. Intangible values of protected areas. *Policy Matters* 12:9–22

Harvey D. 1989. *The Condition of Postmodernity: An Enquiry Into the Origins of Cultural Change*. Cambridge, UK: Blackwell

Heinen JT, Mehta JN. 2000. Emerging issues in legal and procedural aspects of buffer zone management with case studies from Nepal. *J. Environ. Dev.* 9(1):45–67

Hitchcock RK. 1995. Centralisation, resource depletion and coercive conservation among the Tyua of the northeastern Kalahari. *Hum. Ecol.* 23:168–98

Hitchcock RK. 2001. 'Hunting is our heritage': the struggle for hunting and gathering rights among the San of southern Africa. See Anderson & Ikeya 2001, pp 139–56

Hodgson DL. 2001. *Once Intrepid Warriors: Gender, Ethnicity, and the Cultural Politics of Maasai Development*. Bloomington: Indiana Univ. Press

Holt FL. 2005. The Catch-22 of conservation: indigenous peoples, biologists, and cultural change. Hum. Ecol. 33(2):199–215

Homewood KM, Rodgers WA. 1991. *Maasailand Ecology: Pastoralist Development and Wildlife Conservation in Ngorongoro, Tanzania*. Cambridge, UK: Cambridge Univ. Press

Horowitz LS. 1998. Integrating indigenous resource management with wildlife conservation: a case study of Batang Ai National Park, Sarawak, Malaysia. *Hum. Ecol.* 26(3):371–403

Hughes DM. 2005. Third nature: making space and time in the Great Limpopo Conservation Area. *Cult. Anthropol.* 20(2):157–84

Hulme D, Murphree M, eds. 2001. *African Wildlife and Livelihoods: The Promise and Performance of Community Conservation*. Portsmouth, NH: Heinemann

Igoe J. 2003. Scaling up civil society: donor money, NGOs and the pastoralist land rights movement in Tanzania. *Dev. Change* 34:863–85

Igoe J. 2004. *Conservation and Globalisation: A Study of National Parks and Indigenous Communties from East Africa to South Dakota*. Belmont, CA: Wadsworth/Thomson Learning

Igoe J. 2005. Global indigenism and spaceship earth: convergence, space, and re-entry friction. *Globalizations* 2:1–13

Igoe J, Brockington D. 1999. *Pastoral Land Tenure and Community Conservation: A Case Study from North-East Tanzania. Pastoral Land Tenure Series 11*. London: IIED

Ikeya K. 2001. Some changes among the San under the influence of relocation plan in Botswana. See Anderson & Ikeya 2001, pp. 183–98

Jacoby K. 2001. *Crimes Against Nature: Squatters, Poachers, Thieves and the Hidden History of American Conservation*. Berkeley: Univ. Calif. Press

Jeffery R, Sundar N, Mishra A, Peter N, Tharakan PJ. 2003. A move from minor to major: competing discourses of nontimber forest products in India. See Greenough & Tsing 2003, pp. 79–102

Jepson P, Momberg F, van Noord H. 2002. A review of the efficacy of the protected area system of East Kalimantan Province, Indonesia. *Nat. Areas J.* 22(1):28–42

Jim CY, Xu SS. 2003. Getting out of the woods: quandries of protected area management in China. *Mt. Res. Dev.* 23:222–26

Johnson LM. 2000. A place that's good: Gitksan landscape perception and ethnoecology. *Hum. Ecol.* 282:301–25

Karan PP, Mather C. 1985. Tourism and environment in the Mount Everest region. *Geogr. Rev.* 75(1):93–95

Katz C. 1998. Whose nature, whose culture? Private productions of space and the preservation of nature. In *Remaking Reality: Nature at the End of the Millenium*, ed. B Braun, N Castree, pp. 46–63. London: Routledge

Kaus A. 1993. Environmental perceptions and social relations in the Mapimi Biosphere Reserve. *Conserv. Biol.* 7:398–406

Keller R, Turek M. 1998. *American Indians and National Parks*. Tuscon: Univ. Ariz. Press

King DA, Stewart WP. 1996. Ecotourism and commodification: protecting people and places. *Biodivers. Conserv.* 5(3):293–305

Kirkpatrick JB. 2001. Ecotourism, local and indigenous people, and the conservation of the Tasmanian Wilderness Heritage Area. *J. R. Soc. N. Z.* 31:819–29

Kiss AG. 2004. Is community-based ecotourism a good use of biodiversity conservation funds? *Trends Ecol. Evol.* 19(5):232–37

Knudsen A. 1999. Conservation and controversy in the Karakoram: Khunjerab National Park, Pakistan. *J. Polit. Ecol.* 56:1–30

Kohler NP. 2005. *Protected areas and landscape change in mainland Southeast Asia (Cambodia, Laos, Thailand, Vietnam)*. PhD thesis. Univ. Oregon, Eugene

Kothari A. 2004. Displacement fears. *Frontline*. **http://www.frontlineonnet.com/fl2126/stories/20041231000108500.htm**

Kothari A, Pande P, Singh S, Variava D. 1989. *Management of National Parks and Sancturies in India: A Status Report*. New Delhi: Indian Inst. Public Admin.

Krech IIIS. 2005. Reflections on conservation, sustainability, and environmentalism in indigenous North America. *Am. Anthropol.* 107:78–86

Kruger O. 2005. The role of ecotourism in conservation: panacea or Pandora's box? *Biodivers. Conserv.* 14(3):579–600

Kuper A. 2003. The return of the native. *Curr. Anthropol.* 44(3):389–402

Lane MB. 2002. Buying back and caring for country: institutional arrangements and possibilities for indigenous lands management in Australia. *Soc. Nat. Res.* 15:827–46

Lawrence D. 2000. *Kakadu: The Making of a National Park*. Melbourne, Australia: Melbourne Univ. Press

Lawson HM. 2003. Controlling the wilderness: the work of wilderness officers. *Soc. Animals* 114:329–51

Leatherman TL, Goodman A. 2005. Coca-colonization of diets in the Yucatan. *Soc. Sci. Med.* 61(4):833–46

Lefebvre H. 1991. *The Production of Space*. Trans. D Nicholson-Smith. Oxford, UK: Blackwell

Li T. 2000. Articulating indigenous identity in Indonesia: resource politics and the tribal slot. *Comp. Stud. Soc. Hist.* 421:149–79

Li T. 2005. Engaging simplifications: community-based natural resource management, market processes, and state agendas in upland Southeast Asia. See Brosius et al., pp. 427–57

Low SM. 1996. Spatializing culture: the social production and social construction of public space in Costa Rica. *Am. Ethnol.* 23(4):861–79

MacDonald K. 2004. Developing 'nature': global ecology and the politics of conservation in Northern Pakistan. *In Confronting Environments: Local Environmental Understanding in a Globalising World*, ed. J Carrier, pp. 71–96. Lantham, MD: Altamira Press

MacKay F, Caruso E. 2004. Indigenous lands or national parks? *Cult. Surv. Q.* 28(1):14

Macleod DVL. 2001. Parks or people? National parks and the case of Del Este, Dominican Republic. *Prog. Dev. Stud.* 1(3):221–35

Magome H, Fabricius C. 2004. Reconciling biodiversity conservation with rural development: the Holy Grail of CBNRM. In *Rights, Resources and Rural Development: Communty-Based Natural Resource Management in Southern Africa*, ed. C Fabricius, E Koch, H Magome, S Turner, pp. 93–111. London: Earthscan

Mahanty S. 2003. Insights from a cultural landscape: lessons from landscape history for the management of Rajiv Gandhi (Nagarahole) National Park. *Conserv. Soc.* 1(1):23–45

Maikhuri RK, Nautiyal S, Rao KS, Chandrasekhar K, Gavali R, Saxena KG. 2000. Analysis and resolution of protected area—people conflicts in Nanda Devi Biosphere Reserve, India. *Environ. Conserv.* 27(1):43–53

McCabe JT. 2002. Giving conservation a human face? Lessons from forty years of combining conservation and development in the Ngorongoro Conservation Area, Tanzania. See Chatty & Colchester 2002, pp. 61–76

McLean J, Straede S. 2003. Conservation, relocation and the paradigms of park and people management—a case study of Padampur Villages and the Royal Chitwan National Park, Nepal. *Soc. Nat. Res.* 16:509–26

McNeely JA, Scherr SJ. 2003. *Ecoagriculture: Strategies to Feed the World and Save Wild Biodiversity*. Washington, DC: Island Press

Mehta JN, Kellert SR. 1998. Local attitudes toward community-based conservation policy and programmes in Nepal: a case study in the Makalu-Barun Conservation Area. *Environ. Conserv.* 25(4):320–33

Merlin MD, Raynor W. 2005. Kava cultivation, native species conservation, and integrated watershed resource management on Pohnpei Island. *Pac. Science* 59(2):241–60

Meyer J. 1996. *The Spirit of Yellowstone: The Cultural Evolution of a National Park*. London: Rowman & Littlefield

Moore DS. 1998. Clear waters and muddied histories: environmental history and the politics of community in Zimbabwe's eastern highlands. *J. South. Afr. Stud.* 24(2):377–404

Nabakov P, Lawrence L. 2004. *Restoring a Presence: A Documentary Overview of Native Americans and Yellowstone National Park*. Norman, OK: Univ. Okla. Press

Negi CS, Nautiyal S. 2003. Indigenous peoples, biological diversity and protected area management-policy framework towards resolving conflicts. *Int. J. Sustain. Dev. World Ecol.* 10:169–79

Nelson J, Hossack L, eds. 2003. *Indigenous Peoples and Protected Areas in Africa*. Moreton-in-Marsh, UK: Forest Peoples Programme

Neumann R. 1998. *Imposing Wilderness: Struggles Over Livelihood and Nature Preservation in Africa*. Berkeley: Univ. Calif. Press

Neumann R. 2004. Moral and discursive geographies in the war for biodiversity in Africa. *Polit. Geogr.* 23:813–37

Noss AJ, Cuellar E, Cuellar RL. 2004. An evaluation of hunter self-monitoring in the Bolivian Chaco. *Hum. Ecol.* 32(6):685–702

Nugent S. 1994. *Big Mouth: The Amazon Speaks*. San Francisco: Brown Trout Press

Nygren A. 1998. Environment as discourse: searching for sustainable development in Costa Rica. *Environ. Values* 7(2):201–22

Nyhus P. 1999. *Elephants, tigers and transmigrants: conflict and conservation at Way Kambas National Park, Sumatra, Indonesia*. PhD thesis. Univ. Wisc., Madison

Olwig KF, Olwig K. 1979. Underdevelopment and the development of 'natural' park ideology. *Antipode* 11(21):16–25

Orlove B. 2002. *Lines in the Water: Nature and Culture in Lake Titicaca*. Berkley: Univ. Calif. Press

Orlove BS, Brush SB. 1996. Anthropology and the conservation of biodiversity. *Annu. Rev. Anthropol.* 25:329–52

Overton J. 1979. A critical examination of the establishment of national parks and tourism in underdeveloped areas: Gros Morne National Park in Newfoundland. *Antipode* 11(2):34–47

Palmer L. 2001. *Kakadu as an aboriginal place: tourism and the construction of Kakadu National Park*. PhD thesis. Northern Territory Univ., Australia

Palmer R, Timmermans H, Fay D. 2002. *From Conflict to Negotiation. Nature-Based Development of the South African Wild Coast*. Pretoria, South Africa: Hum. Sci. Res. Counc.

Panusittikorn P, Prato T. 2001. Conservation of protected areas in Thailand: the case of Khao Yai National Park. *Protected Areas East Asia* 18(2):67–76

Pathak N, Bhatt S, Tasneem B, Kothari A, Borrini-Feyerabend G. 2004. *Community conservation areas. A bold frontier for conservation*. CCA Briefing Note 5, Nov. IUCN WCPA-CEESP Theme on Indig. Local Comm., Equity, and Protected Areas (TILCEPA) and with financial support of GEF, Iran: CENESTA

Paudel NS. 2005. *Conservation and livelihoods: an exploration of the local responses to conservation interventions in Royal Chitwan National Park in Nepal*. PhD thesis. Univ. Reading, United Kingdom

Peluso NL. 1993. Coercing conservation: the politics of state resource control. *Glob. Environ. Change* 3(2):199–218

Peters J. 1998. Transforming the integrated conservation and development project (ICDP) approach: observations from the Ranomafana National park project, Madagascar. *J. Agr. Environ. Ethics* 11(1):17–47

Peterson ND. 2005. *Casting a wide net: decision-making in a Mexican marine park*. PhD thesis. Univ. Calif., San Diego

Pfeffer MJ, Schelahs JW, Day LA. 2001. Forest conservation, value conflict, and interest formation in a Honduran National Park. *Rural Sociol.* 66(3):382–402

Puntenney PJ. 1990. Defining solutions: the Annapurna experience. *Cult. Surv. Q.* 14(2):9

Putsche L. 2000. A reassessment of resource depletion, market dependency, and culture change on a Shipibo Reserve in the Peruvian Amazon. *Hum. Ecol.* 28(1):131–40

Quiros A. 2005. Whale shark ecotourism in the Philippines and Belize: evaluating conservation and community benefits. *Trop. Res. Bull.* 24:42–48

Rae J, Arab G, Nordblom T. 2002. Customs excised: arid land conservation in Syria. See Chatty & Colchester 2002, pp. 212–26

Rangarajan M. 1996. *Fencing the Forest: Conservation and Ecological Change in India's Central Provinces 1860–1914*. New Delhi: OUP

Ranger T. 1999. *Voices from the Rocks: Nature, Culture and History in the Matapos Hills of Zimbabwe*. Oxford: James Currey

Rao M, Rabinowitz A, Khaing ST. 2002. Status review of the protected-area system in Myanmar, with recommendations for conservation planning. *Conserv. Biol.* 16(2):360–68

Rasker R. 1993. Rural development, conservation and public policy in the Greater Yellowstone Ecosystem. *Soc. Nat. Res.* 6:109–26

Roth R. 2004. On the colonial margins and in the global hotspot: park-people conflicts in highland Thailand. *Asia Pac. Viewp.* 45(1):13–32

Rugendyke B, Son NT. 2005. Conservation costs: nature-based tourism as development at Cuc Phuong National Park, Vietnam. *Asia Pac. Viewp.* 46(2):185–200

Saberwal V, Rangarajan M, Kothari A, eds. 2000. *People, Parks and Wildlife: Towards Co-Existence*. Hyderabad, India: Orient Longman Limited

Sanderson S, Redford KH. 2004. The defense of conservation is not an attack on the poor. *Oryx* 38(2):146–47

Santana EC. 1991. Nature conservation and sustainable development in Cuba. *Conserv. Biol.* 5(1):13–17

Sato J. 2000. People in between: conversion and conservation of forest lands in Thailand. *Dev. Change* 31:155–77

Savage M. 1993. Ecological disturbance and nature tourism. *Geogr. Rev.* 83(3):290–300

Schmidt-Soltau K. 2003. Conservation-related resettlement in central Africa: environmental and social risks. *Dev. Change* 34:525–51

Schmidt-Soltau K 2005. The environmental risks of conservation-related displacements in Central Africa. In *Displacement Risks in Africa: Refugees, Resettlers and Their Host Population*, ed. I Ohta, YD Gebre, pp. 282–311. Kyoto, Japan: Kyoto Univ. Press

Schneider IE, Burnett GW. 2000. Protected area management in Jordan. *Environ. Manage.* 25(3):241–46

Schroeder R. 1993. Shady practice: gender and the political ecology of resource stabilization in Gambian garden/orchards. *Econ. Geogr.* 69(4):349–65

Seeland K, ed. 1997. *Nature Is Culture: Indigenous Knowledge and Socio-Cultural Aspects of Trees and Forests in Non-European Cultures*. London: Intermediate Technol.

Seeland K. 2000. National park policy and wildlife problems in Nepal and Bhutan. *Popul. Environ.* 22(1):43–62

Shyamsundar P, Kramer R. 1997. Biodiversity conservation—at what cost? A study of households in the vicinity of Madagascar's Mantandia National Park. *Ambio* 26(3):180–84

Sillitoe P. 2001. Hunting for conservation in the Papua New Guinea highlands. *Ethnos* 66(3):365–93

Silori CS. 2001. Status and distribution of anthropogenic pressure in the buffer zone of Nanda Devi Biosphere Reserve in Western Himalaya, India. *Biodivers. Conserv.* 10(7):1113–30

Sivaramakrishnan K. 2003. Scientific forestry and genealogies of development in Bengal. See Greenough & Tsing 2003, pp. 253–88

Slattery D. 2002. Resistance to development at Wilsons Promontory National Park (Victoria, Australia). *Soc. Nat. Res.* 15:563–80

Sletto B. 2002. Producing space(s), representing landscapes: maps and resource conflicts in Trinidad. *Cult. Geogr.* 9(4):389–420

Smith N. 1990. *Uneven Development: Nature, Capital and the Production of Space*. Oxford, UK: Basil Blackwell

Smith N. 1996. The production of nature. In *Future/Natural: Nature, Science, Culture*, ed. G Robertson, M Marsh, L Tickneret, J Bird, B Curtis, T Putnam, pp. 35–54. London: Routledge

Sodikoff G. 2005. *Reserve labor: a moral ecology of conservation in Madagascar*. PhD thesis. Univ. Mich., Ann Arbor

Spence M. 1999. *Dispossessing the Wilderness: Indian Removal and the Making of the National Parks*. New York: Oxford Univ. Press

Stegeborn W. 1996. Sri Lanka's forests: conservation of nature versus people. *Cult. Surv. Q.* 20(1):16–24

Stepp R. 2005. *Documenting Garifuna traditional ecological knowledge for park co-management in Southern Belize*. Presented at Annu. Meet. Soc. App. Anthropol., 65th, Santa Fe

Stern MJ. 2006. *Understanding local reactions to national parks: the nature and consequences of local interpretations of park policies, management, and outreach*. PhD thesis. Yale Univ., New Haven

Stevens S, ed. 1997. *The Legacy of Yellowstone: Conservation Through Cultural Survival. Indigenous Peoples and Protected Areas*. Washington, DC: Island Press

Stone M, Wall G. 2004. Ecotourism and community development: case studies from Hainan, China. *Environ. Manage.* 33:12–24

Strathern M. 1980. No nature, no culture: the Hagen case. In *Nature, Culture and Gender*, ed. C MacCormack, M Strathern, pp. 174–222. Cambridge, UK: Cambridge Univ. Press

Stronza A. 2000. *"Because it is ours": community-based ecotourism in the Peruvian Amazon*. PhD thesis. Univ. Florida, Gainesville

Sullivan S. 2000. Gender, ethnographic myths and community-based conservation in a former Namibian 'homeland'. In *Rethinking Pastoralism in Africa: Gender, Culture and the Myth of the Patriarchal Pastoralist*, ed. ED Hodgson, pp. 142–64. Oxford, UK: James Currey

Sundberg J. 1998. NGO landscapes in the Maya Biosphere Reserve, Guatemala. *Geogr. Rev.* 88(3):388–412

Sundberg J. 2003. Conservation and democratization: constituting citizenship in the Maya Biosphere Reserve, Guatemala. *Polit. Geogr.* 22(7):715–40

Sundberg J. 2004. Identities in the making: conservation, gender and race in the Maya Biosphere Reserve, Guatemala. *Gender, Place and Culture* 11(1):43–66

Suzman J. 2002/2003. Kalahari conundrums: relocation, resistance, and international support in the Central Kalahari Botswana. *Before Farming* 4(12):1–10

Sylvain R. 2002. Land, water, and truth: San identity and global indigenism. *Am. Anthropol.* 104(4):1074–85

Tacconi L, Bennett J. 1995. Biodiversity conservation: the process of economic assessment of a protected area in Vanuatu. *Dev. Change* 26:89–110

Toly NJ. 2004. Globalization and the capitalization of nature: a political ecology of biodiversity in Mesoamerica. *Bull. Sci. Technol. Soc.* 24(1):47–54

Toyne P, Johnston R. 1991. Reconciliation or new dispossession? Aboriginal land rights and nature conservation. *Habitat Aust.* 193:8–10

Trigger D, Mulcock J. 2005. Forests as spiritually significant places: nature, culture, and 'belonging' in Australia. *Aust. J. Anthropol.* 16(3):306–20

Tsing A. 2003. Cultivating the wild: honey-hunting and forest management in Southeast Kalimantan. In *Culture and the Question of Rights: Forests, Coasts and Seas in Southeast Asia*, ed. C Zerner, pp. 24–55. Durham, NC: Duke Univ. Press

Van Helden F. 1998. *Between Cash and Conviction: The Social Context of the Bismarck-Ramu Integrated Conservation and Development Project. NRI Monograph 33.* Port Moresby, Papua New Guinea: Natl. Res. Inst. & United Nations Dev. Programme

Van Helden F. 2001. *Through the thicket: disentangling the social dynamics of an integrated conservation and development project on mainland Papua New Guinea.* PhD thesis. Wageningen Universiteit, The Netherlands

Vaughan D. 2000. Tourism and biodiversity: a convergence of interests? *Int. Aff.* 76:283–97

Vivanco LA. 2001. Spectacular quetzals, ecotourism, and environmental futures in Monte Verde, Costa Rica. *Ethnology* 402:79–92

Wagner J. 2002. *Commons in transition: an analysis of social and ecological change in a coastal rainforest environment in rural Papua New Guinea.* PhD thesis. McGill University, Montreal

Wagner J. 2003. The politics of accountability: an institutional analysis of the conservation movement in Papua New Guinea. *Soc. Anal.* 45(2):78–93

Wallace T, Diamante DN. 2005. Keeping the people in the parks: a case study from Guatemala. *Natl. Assoc. Pract. Anthropol. Bull.* 23(1):191–218

Walley C. 2004. *Rough Waters: Nature and Development in an African Marine Park.* Princeton: Princeton Univ. Press

Walpole MJ, Goodwin HJ, Ward KGR. 2001. Pricing policy for tourism in protected areas: lessons from Komodo National Park, Indonesia. *Conserv. Biol.* 15(1):218–27

Watts M. 1993. Development I: power, knowledge and discursive practice. *Prog. Hum. Geogr.* 17(2):257–72

Weeks P. 1999. Cyber-activism: World Wildlife Fund's campaign to save the tiger. *Cult. Agric.* 21(3):19–30

Weiant PA. 2005. *A political ecology of marine protected areas (MPAs): case of Cabo Pulmo National Park, Sea of Cortez, Mexico.* PhD thesis. Univ. Calif., Santa Barbara

Weinberg A, Bellows S, Ekster D. 2002. Sustaining ecotourism: insights and implications from two successful case studies. *Soc. Nat. Res.* 15(4):371–80

Wells M, Guggenheim S, Kahn A, Wardojo W, Jepson P. 1999. *Investing in Biodiversity: A Review of Indonesia's Integrated Conservation and Development Projects.* Washington, DC: World Bank

West P. 2001. Environmental non-governmental organizations and the nature of ethnographic inquiry. *Soc. Anal.* 45(2):55–77

West P. 2005. Translation, value, and space: theorizing an ethnographic and engaged environmental anthropology. *Am. Anthropol.* 107(4):632–42

West P. 2006. *Conservation Is Our Government Now: The Politics of Ecology in Papua New Guinea.* Durham, NC: Duke Univ. Press

West P, Carrier JG. 2004. Getting away from it all? Ecotourism and authenticity. *Curr. Anthropol.* 45(4):483–98

Westman WE. 1990. Managing for biodiversity. *Bioscience* 40(1):26–33

Whitesell EA. 1996. Local struggles over rain-forest conservation in Alaska and Amazonia. *Geogr. Rev.* 86(3):414–36

Wilshusen P, Brechin SR, Fortwangler C, West PC. 2002. Reinventing a square wheel: a critique of a resurgent protection paradigm in international biodiversity conservation. *Soc. Nat. Res.* 15:17–40

Wilson A. 1992. *The Culture of Nature: North American Landscapes from Disney to the Exxon Valdez.* Cambridge, MA: Blackwell

Winer N. 2003. Co-management of protected areas, the oil and gas industry and indigenous empowerment—the experience of Bolivia's Kaa Iya del Gran Chaco. *Policy Matters* 12:181–91

Wolmer W. 2003. Transboundary conservation: the politics of ecological integrity in the Great Limpopo Transfrontier Park. *J. South. Afr. Stud.* 29:261–78

Zamarenda A. 1998. *Cuyabeno Wildlife Production Reserve: Indigenous People and Bio-Diversity Conservation in Latin America*. Copnehagen: IWGIA

Zimmerer KS, Ryan EG, Buck MV. 2004. Globalisation and multi-spatial trends in the coverage of protected-area conservation (1980–2000). *Ambio* 33(8):520–29

Zurick DN. 1992. Adventure travel and sustainable tourism in the peripheral economy of Nepal. *Ann. Assoc. Am. Geogr.* 82(4):608–28

RELATED REVIEWS

Agrawal A. 2003. Sustainable governance of common-pool resources: context, methods, and politics. *Annu. Rev. Anthropol.* 32:243–62

Little PE. 1999. Environments and environmentalisms in anthropological research: facing a new millennium. *Annu. Rev. Anthropol.* 28:253–84

Orlove BS. 1980. Ecological anthropology. *Annu. Rev. Anthropol.* 9:235–73

Smith EA, Wishnie M. 2000. Conservation and subsistence in small-scale societies. *Annu. Rev. Anthropol.* 29:493–524

Mayan Historical Linguistics and Epigraphy: A New Synthesis

Søren Wichmann

Department of Linguistics, Max Planck Institute for Evolutionary Anthropology,
D-04103 Leipzig, Germany; Languages and Cultures of Indian America (TCIA),
Leiden University, 2300 RA Leiden, The Netherlands; email: wichmann@eva.mpg.de

Annu. Rev. Anthropol. 2006. 35:279–94

First published online as a Review in
Advance on June 5, 2006

The *Annual Review of Anthropology* is
online at anthro.annualreviews.org

This article's doi:
10.1146/annurev.anthro.35.081705.123257

Copyright © 2006 by Annual Reviews.
All rights reserved

0084-6570/06/1021-0279$20.00

Key Words

Maya writing, evolution of writing, sociolinguistics

Abstract

Recent years have seen rapid advancement in our understanding of
the phonology and grammar of Classic Ch'olan and the distribution
of Lowland Mayan languages in the Classic period. The control over
the data has advanced to such an extent that Classic Ch'olan should
no longer be considered chiefly a product of reconstruction, but
rather a language in its own right, providing fresh input to historical reconstruction. The interpretation of writing system principles
has moved into the forefront of research, and recent discussions of
these and other major issues are summarized here. This review suggests that the exceptional phonological transparency of the Maya
script, which is a precondition for the current advances in linguistic
epigraphy, is rooted in the need of scribes to spell out regional linguistic variants, and a sociolinguistically oriented theory of the evolution of writing in general is formulated and tested on the Mayan
hieroglyphic materials.

Proto-language:
reconstructed by
comparing elements
of attested languages
that are cognate and
making inferences
regarding the
original forms
and/or functions of
these elements

Classic Maya:
originally defined as
the period when
hieroglyphic
monuments were
erected; for the
present purposes c.
300–900 A.D.

Lowland Mayan
languages:
languages of the
Ch'olan and
Yucatecan subgroups
of the Mayan family

Ch'olan: subgroup
of Mayan; is closely
related to Tzeltalan
(Tzeltal and Tzotzil)
and consists of
Western Ch'olan
(Ch'ol and Chontal)
and Eastern Ch'olan
(Ch'orti' and
Ch'olti')

Classic Ch'olan:
the early form of
Ch'olan represented
in the monumental
inscriptions of the
Classic period

Yucatecan: appears
to have descended
directly from
proto-Mayan and
consists of Yucatec,
Lacandon, Mopan,
and Itza

INTRODUCTION

Two decades ago, two Mayan historical linguists asked themselves, "where are we now?" (Campbell & Kaufman 1985). Their paper represented the culmination of a productive period of research during which many Mayan languages had become documented, new members of the language family had been discovered, major phonological developments had been worked out, grammar and lexicon of the proto-language had, to some extent, been reconstructed, and a classification had been reached, most aspects of which still enjoy a large degree of consensus. The authors, however, could not foreshadow that an entirely new approach to Mayan historical linguistics was beginning to take shape, namely the synthesis of historical linguistics and the epigraphy of Maya writing. Advances in epigraphy have allowed us to move beyond pure diachronic reconstruction into the realms of observation and explanation. Because many monuments are dated and securely placed in space, their texts expose language change before our very eyes, and one can now see how such changes are sensitive to geographical and social factors. The purpose of this review is to discuss the major, current issues in studying the development of the languages of the hieroglyphic inscriptions and to illustrate how the study of the script is affecting the practice of Mayan historical linguistics.

LANGUAGE IDENTIFICATION

Whereas early epigraphic studies mostly relied on geographical arguments in regard to the identification of languages involved in the Classic Maya inscriptions, it became clear from the 1980s onward that such identifications should preferably be made by matching morphological elements in the inscriptions to data from extant Mayan languages. Given the high degree of lexical diffusion among Mayan languages in general and Lowland Mayan languages in particular (Kaufman 1980, Justeson et al. 1985, Wichmann & Brown 2003),

the recurrence in a particular language of some lexeme found in an inscription does not provide sufficient evidence to argue that the inscription is written in the language in question. The foundation for the linguistic identification of the script as chiefly Ch'olan was provided mainly by Schele (1982), MacLeod (1984, 1987), and Bricker (1986), who identified certain Ch'olan verbal grammatical morphemes in the inscriptions, as well as by Campbell (1984), who pointed out phonological parallels. Subsequent studies, in particular Wald (1994), Lacadena (1997a, 1997b, 2000a, 2003, 2004), MacLeod (1987, 2004), and Houston et al. (2000, 2001), have identified an ever-increasing range of Ch'olan grammatical affixes in the inscriptions.

Along with a steadily more detailed picture of Classic Ch'olan grammar acknowledged as being present throughout the lowlands linguists have also recognized that features of other languages, including early forms of Yucatecan and Tzeltalan, have left traces in or among texts that are otherwise written in Classic Ch'olan (Lacadena & Wichmann 2000, 2002; Lacadena 2000b), and variation within Classic Ch'olan itself has also been observed (Lacadena & Wichmann 2002, Wichmann 2002a). **Table 1** gives an overview of these features, and **Figure 1** (see color insert) shows their distribution. Examples of how this linguistic model has led to other types of distributional studies are provided by the onomastic studies of Colas (2004a, b), where the author notes that differences in naming patterns also have an eastern-versus-western distribution. In the west, rulers are usually named after animals, objects, and social roles, and the names function syntactically as noun phrases, whereas in the east, rulers carry names mostly based on those of gods, and the names function as sentences.

Linguists have debated where to place the otherwise essentially unitary language of the Classic-period inscriptions within the part of the family tree of Mayan languages that comprises the Greater Tzeltalan (Ch'olan and Tzeltalan) group. As an alternative to what

Table 1 Variable and vernacular linguistic features

Ch'olan variable features	
Strong Eastern versus Western Ch'olan features	**WINAL-la** versus **WINAK-ki** for "month"
	AJAW-li versus **AJAW-le(-le)** for "rulership"
Strong unilateral Eastern Ch'olan features	Loss of vowel length
	Passive in -*w-aj*
Weak unilateral Eastern Ch'olan features	-**b'i**-complement to **HAB'** or **WINAKHAB'**
	-**he-na** rather than -**he-wa** in distance numbers
	-**na**, not -**ta** complement to "Wo" and "Sip"
Strong unilateral Western Ch'olan features	-**wa-ni** rather than -**la-ja** on positional verbs
Weak unilateral Western Ch'olan features	CV1-CV1-**ja** spellings of passive verbs
	-**b'u**, not -**wa** on **K'AN-HAL** spelling "Pop"
	Positionals in –*(V₁)l-iiy*

Yucatecan vernacular features	
Strong features	Passive in -*(a)b'*
	Titles preceding, not following, personal names
	Inchoative in -*(a)j-al*
	Causative in -*kun*
	Various lexical traits
Weak features	-*ik* and -*(i)k-i* suffixes
	Suffixation of –**ya**, not -**yi** to verb **T'AB'**
	Final -C**e** spellings

Possible Tzeltalan vernacular features	
Stronger features	Positional in -*h-...-(a)j*
	WINIK-li, winikil for "month"
Weaker features	-**na** complement to month name "Wo"
	Synharmonic spelling **i-la-ja** "was seen"

I have denominated by the neutral term Classic Ch'olan (Hieroglyphic Ch'olan or Epigraphic Ch'olan would serve equally well), Houston et al. (2000) introduced the term Classic Ch'olti'an because they believe that they have found grammatical evidence for a specifically Eastern Ch'olan affiliation of Classic Ch'olan and furthermore, following Robertson (1992, 1998), see Ch'olti' as an ancestral form of Ch'orti'. Mora-Marín (2005), however, argues against Houston et al. that their 'Ch'olti'an' grammatical markers are in fact proto-Ch'olan retentions and therefore cannot count as evidence for a specifically Eastern Ch'olan affiliation of the inscriptions, and Wichmann (2002a) argued against the view that Ch'orti' is a descendant of Ch'olti' (a view that Robertson 2004 subsequently formulated somewhat differently). Various important issues are raised but not necessarily resolved in these recent contributions.

How is the internal Ch'olan linguistic variation in the inscriptions of the Lowlands to be interpreted? Did scribes more or less write the kind of Ch'olan that they spoke at that time, or did they suppress their linguistic identities in favor of some prestige norm and only occasionally, and perhaps unconsciously, let features of their local dialect or vernacular percolate into written texts? How great is the differentiation among the different variants of Ch'olan? Should we be speaking of different languages or just of different dialects? If there was some kind of prestige norm, to which historical stratum of Ch'olan did it belong?

The evidence for the existence of a specifically Eastern Ch'olan norm, as correctly seen by Mora-Marín (2005), crucially hinges on whether certain features used throughout the inscriptions of the Maya lowlands can be proven to be Eastern Ch'olan innovations. The existence of a norm representing a conservative form of Ch'olan, on the other hand, would hinge on the identification of features known to have changed in vernacular languages or dialects but retained in written inscriptions. Lacadena & Wichmann (2002) were positive toward the Eastern Ch'olan prestige language hypothesis although cautioning that "it is still too early to make final judgments about the totality of the picture" (p. 282).

Today I would be less positive, given that the following six problems with the hypothesis still remain and no new evidence in its favor have emerged. (*a*) It is not clear at all that the three "Ch'olti'an" features of Houston et al. (2000), which are composed of a passive, a mediopassive, and a transitivizing verbal derivation, were indeed innovated by Eastern Ch'olan. The authors themselves show for the first two features that the suffixes involved have pre-Ch'olan ancestry, so claims regarding innovations rest entirely on interpretations on changes in functions making such claims difficult to verify; for the last feature there is Tzeltalan evidence for also reconstructing the derivational process in question for proto-Ch'olan, so this feature cannot be brought to bear on Eastern Ch'olan innovations. (*b*) Several of the features observed by Lacadena & Wichmann (2002) to originate in the Western Lowlands spill over into the east (see **Figure 1**), whereas eastern linguistic features are not adopted by westerners. This contrasts a picture according to which Eastern Ch'olan is somehow more prestigious than is the western variant. (*c*) Both eastern and western features spread in a more-or-less systematic fashion in time and space from different centers of innovation and do not pop up in a haphazard manner, as would be expected if they represented unconscious "slips of the chisel"; thus, they seem to attest to linguistic changes indicative of an emerging Eastern versus Western Ch'olan differentiation rather than old isoglosses. (*d*) The domi-

nation of one part of the Maya Lowlands over all of the rest is not expected from the political picture, which rather suggests constant competition among different regions, great and small (Martin & Grube 2000). (*e*) Positional and passive morphology documented in Early Classic inscriptions such as Tikal Stela 31 show the language of this period to be so archaic (Hruby & Robertson 2001, Lacadena 2002) that it hardly makes sense to imagine a full-blown Eastern versus Western Ch'olan differentiation to be in place simultaneously by then. (*f*) When we do find linguistic features, such as the passive suffix –*w* occurring at Copan (Lacadena 1997b) or the deverbalizing instrumental derivation in –*ib'* also from Copan (Wichmann 2002a), that are identifiably Eastern Ch'olan and cannot be traced to proto-Ch'olan or beyond, then these features exclusively occur in inscriptions of the eastern region. Particularly interesting is the mediopassive –k'–$a(j)$, found at Tikal (Beliaev & Davletshin 2003). A salient characteristic of Eastern Ch'olan is the occurrence of a suffix –*a* on derived intransitives, including passives and mediopassives. The origin of this characteristic clearly must be the –*aj*, which, together with infixed –*h*–, forms the passive and which has a proto-Mayan origin. Thus, the ancestry of the suffix can be traced, but its spread to derived intransitives in general in Eastern Ch'olan is an innovation. The –k'–aj mediopassive, then, could be yet another possible Eastern Ch'olan marker, but again we find it just where we would expect it, namely in the eastern part of the lowlands. Thus, even though some possible Eastern Ch'olan innovations exist, they cannot be brought to bear on an Eastern Ch'olan prestige language hypothesis.

Even if there are many reasons to doubt a specifically Eastern Ch'olan affiliation of a prestige language, the written language may still have preserved features of some early kind of Ch'olan that no longer existed in the spoken language at that time or may have been preserved only in a part of the Ch'olan speech community. Such features would also support a prestige language hypothesis, although the affiliation of this prestige language would be somewhat different, representing an earlier form of Ch'olan before any significant differentiation. We do find scattered evidence of returns to previous norms. For instance, Hruby & Child (2004) observe a return to the use of –laj suffixation to positional verbs in the inscriptions of Palenque after the reign of K'ihnich Janaab' Pakal, which saw the introduction of the innovative Western Ch'olan –waan suffix (scholars have assumed that –waan is a specifically Chontal affix, but Vázquez Alvarez 2002 attests a cognate Ch'ol affix –wañ, now used only in negative imperatives of positionals). Clearly, tendencies exist to preserve an archaic norm in the written language. Moreover, it is obviously correct to talk about prestige norms when scribes write in Ch'olan even if they are identifiable as mother-tongue speakers of Tzeltalan or Yucatecan by the sporadic vernacular influences they leave in their texts. Clearly there were norms for writing that were often distinct from local vernaculars, but we also see that scribes were flexible enough to accommodate linguistic changes.

One final issue is the degree of differentiation within Ch'olan in the Classic period. Given that we cannot use tests such as mutual intelligibility or counts of differences in standard word lists, it is really a moot question whether we are dealing with different languages or different dialects at a given stage of the Classic period. Because Eastern versus Western Ch'olan differentiation had set in by 400 A.D. we could perhaps speak of different dialects at this point. Around 600 A.D., in the Late Classic, there is evidence for a further differentiation within Eastern Ch'olan foreboding the Ch'orti' versus Ch'olti' split (Wichmann 2002a). At this point, then, we might talk about Eastern versus Western Ch'olan languages, and about dialects within these languages. Eventually, at least four Ch'olan languages would emerge. This emergence may have happened around the transition to the Post-Classic. Although I

suggest using the terms dialect and language in the manner specified in the context of the Ch'olan group, I do not insist on such terminology and would rather suggest speaking of variants and leave out altogether use of the terms dialect and language whenever such a use would stimulate purposeless controversy.

Terminology becomes even more contentious when stages of written, hieroglyphic Ch'olan are assigned labels such as "preproto-Ch'olan," "proto-Ch'olan," or other such labels that refer to reconstructed stages. Identifying an attested language with a reconstructed one is fallacious because the two are qualitatively different objects. Reconstructions can be made bottom up, if descendant forms are well attested within the subgroup, and top down, if they are attested in at least one language of the subgroup plus languages of other subgroups of the family. If none of these conditions holds, it is not possible to make a reconstruction. Thus, there will inevitably be features that would have been present in the given, early-language stratum but simply cannot be reconstructed because the formal criteria for establishing the reconstruction are not met; thus, any proto-language will necessarily be an impoverished version of the language, which it is supposed to approximate (Wichmann 2003b). The hieroglyphic inscriptions sometimes present features that are not reconstructible to proto-Ch'olan on the basis of the alphabetically recorded Ch'olan languages, even if they can be reconstructed to proto-Mayan. Thus, we find at any one stage of Classic Ch'olan a mixture of features, some of which would have to be called preproto-Ch'olan, others proto-Ch'olan, and yet others Eastern or Western Ch'olan if the guideline for their classification were the framework of reconstructions. This kind of classification can lead to confusion and discussions that are meaningless because the premise is incorrect. While debates revolve around whether Classic-period Hieroglyphic Ch'olan is preproto-Ch'olan, proto-Ch'olan, or something else, the correct answer is that it is none of these but rather a language in

Syllabic sign:
represents a
consonant-vowel
sequence and is
conventionally
transcribed using
bold, small letters

its own right. It would be a terminological fallacy to call the language proto-Ch'olan or preproto-Ch'olan. Instead, one should label it Classic Ch'olan—or Pre-Classic, Early Classic, Late Classic, Ch'olan if one needs to be more specific.

PHONOLOGY

Once scholars had agreed that a component of the Maya writing system consisted of syllabic signs, a syllabary (or inventory of syllabic signs) could be drawn up as a way of summarizing existing hypotheses about readings and indicating, by means of empty cells, the scope and aims of future decipherment. A comparison of an early syllabary, such as that of Mathews (1984), with the most recent one, by Stuart (2005), reveals tremendous progress in decipherment and in the understanding of the phonology of the script. As late as a few years ago, Grube (2004) added a column to the syllabary, having assembled evidence for a systematic distinction among velar and glottal fricatives. Reversely, the column left open in the grid as of 1984 for signs representing ejective *p'* plus vowel has never been filled. Partly with the aim of explaining why that might be, Wichmann (2003a) considers the comparative linguistic evidence for the innovation of the phoneme *p'* and concludes that it dates to a period hardly earlier than the transition to the Post-Classic. Another feature of the syllabic grid, which scholars have discussed, is the traditional column for vowel-only signs. In Wichmann (2002b) I propose that the column could be split in two, given that at least within each of the cells for **a** and **u** some signs are in complementary or near-complementary distribution; I suggest as a very tentative explanation that there could be a vowel length distinction in play. Whether such an explanation is tenable—this is still a very open question—the distributional facts remain and pose a challenge to interpretation.

Much recent attention has been given to orthographical conventions. Words in Mayan languages usually end in closed syllables; the syllabic signs of the writing system, however, invariably represent open (CV) syllables. Thus, whenever a syllabic sign is involved in the spelling of a word-final consonant (as in **TUN-ni** "stone"), the final written vowel is "silent." Although Knorozov (1965) stipulated that this final vowel would normally be identical to the preceding one—a principle he called "synharmony"—this is by no means always true. Searches for any governing principle for the different patterns observed were unsuccessful until Stuart in 1997 suggested to close colleagues that disharmony might be a way to indicate vowel length (compare Stuart 2005). This suggestion developed into the hypothesis of Houston et al. (1998) that disharmony could be a way to indicate that the syllable preceding the complement was complex, i.e., consisted of a long vowel, a vowel plus *h*, or a vowel plus glottal stop. The only vowels that occur in disharmonic complements are **i**, **a**, and **u**. Synharmony, the authors contended, is a sort of default or unmarked spelling mode also occurring both with short and complex vowels. Lacadena & Wichmann (2004b) suggested a refinement of this proposal. They noted first that no consistent pattern, neither synharmonic nor disharmonic, is associated with a preconsonantal *h* (e.g., **k'a-k'a** "fire," known to have been pronounced *k'ahk'*). In comparison, specific and distinct patterns of disharmony are associated with glottal stops as opposed to vowel length. Synharmony indicates the presence of a short vowel (rule 1). Disharmony involving a complement vowel **i** indicates vowel length (rule 2), and disharmony involving a complement vowel **a** indicates the presence of a glottal stop (Rule 3). Because these rules sometimes conflict, some supplementary rules are needed. Thus, when the spoken vowel is *i* and the scribe needs to indicate a long vowel, Rules 1 and 2 stand in conflict: Normally the complement vowel **i** would indicate a long vowel, but in this case synharmony would arise; for this reason, a supplementary rule specifies that the complement vowel **a** indicates a long vowel when the spoken vowel is *i*. When Rules 1 and 3 are in conflict the complement vowel used is **u**. Thus, to express a glottal stop when the spoken vowel is *a*, the complement vowel is **u** rather than synharmonic **a**. Finally, a complement vowel **u** will also be used when the spoken vowel is *i* because the pattern **i-a** already is occupied by the supplementary rule for expressing vowel length. Lacadena & Wichmann (2004b) found good overall agreement with their orthographic interpretations and phonological reconstructions but do note that almost a third of the synharmonic spellings are potentially problematic because they apply to forms that have been reconstructed with vowel length or glottal stops. They also note exceptions to rules 2 and 3, but only in the order of 12%–16%. Several types of explanations for the possible exceptions are offered. Some orthographical forms may record late Ch'olan phonological developments. Others may really be underspelled (abbreviated), as is possibly the case with **yu-ha** "his necklace." Harmony rule 3 requires the interpretation *y-u'h*, which conflicts with the reconstruction of Brown & Wichmann (2004) (although not with that of Kaufman & Norman 1984). Nevertheless, the form ceases to be problematic if we consider that it could be an underspelling of **yu-ha-la** for *y-uh-al*. Mayan scribes commonly left out a final sign spelling the last consonant of a suffix (Zender 1999). Finally, some scholars argue that some synharmonic spellings may have been retained by mere force of cultural habit from earlier periods of the script. Lacadena & Wichmann (2004b) hypothesize that the harmony rules were not established until the Early Classic, when they replaced earlier conventions of always either using synharmonic complementation or complementation involving **Ca** signs. Some of the earlier spellings, however, would have become so ingrained that they were maintained even after the spelling reform. Additionally, one could argue that Classic inscriptions sometimes contribute phonological information about proto-Mayan lexemes not to be retrieved from any other source. It is a com-

monplace experience in reconstruction using the comparative method that new data will require existing reconstructions to change.

A different approach would be simply to broaden the spelling rules such as to accommodate exceptions. For instance, if we stipulate that synharmonic spellings do not necessarily imply a short vowel, most exceptions would disappear. But it would be hard to see the motivation for a system where one and the same word form could be spelled using different patterns of complementation. Moreover, apart from changes in spellings that were motivated by phonological changes known to have occurred (loss of vowel length and glottal stops), we actually do not see fluctuations in spelling patterns that would suggest vague rules. Finally, a theory encompassing all spellings observed throughout the history of the writing system in a single framework of orthographic rules would come at the cost of losing hypotheses about orthographic and phonological changes. The hypothesis of an Early Classic spelling reform would no longer have any basis, and Late Classic changes in spellings from earlier disharmonic patterns to synharmonic ones (e.g., **b'a-ki** > **b'a-ka** "captive") would not necessitate a hypothesis about the loss of vowel length because both types of spellings would be licensed by the rules. More generally, spelling rules that seek to accommodate all historical developments in a single system fall victim to what Houston (2000, p. 144) calls the "synoptic fallacy," defined as "the belief that a script in use over centuries or millennia can be understood as a synchronic phenomenon" (Houston 2004, p. 239). Nevertheless, in a recent manuscript reacting to Lacadena & Wichmann (2004b), Robertson, Houston, Zender, and Stuart advocate such an approach. In their new proposal the orthographic rules of Houston et al. (1998) are revised to accommodate some of Lacadena & Wichmann's insights; however, they are kept vague to avoid conflicts with phonological reconstructions. The new proposals represent a small step toward a consensus. But

Spelling rule: convention governing the relationship between how signs are combined and the way the sequences are pronounced

Logogram:
represents a lexeme;
conventionally
transcribed using
bold, capital letters

the two camps are far from reconciled. There are crucial differences in the degree to which different scholars are willing to see Maya spellings directly reflecting phonological distinctions. Lacadena & Wichmann's approach may be said to operate with radical phonological transparency and that of Robertson et al. with moderate phonological transparency.

MORPHOLOGY

In regard to the interpretation of the way that Mayan scribes rendered suffixes, the differences widen between proponents of moderate versus radical phonological transparency. In spite of Stuart's (1987, p. 45) warnings against "dangerously" assuming that certain signs could represent grammatical affixes, Houston et al. (2001, pp. 14–23) introduced a category of signs labeled "morphosyllables." They are graphically identical to various syllabic signs, but when they are involved in spelling affixes they are to be interpreted as having morphemic values. Thus, a sign such as **li** can occur at the end of a word with the value **–IL**, as in **AK'AB'-IL** "darkness," which is derived from **AK'AB'** "night."

Several problems arise with the concept of morphosyllables, the major ones being the following, which have been identified in collaboration with Lacadena. First, such a category of signs is typologically rare. Sporadically one does find signs representing grammatical morphemes, as in the Egyptian script where two or three vertical strokes represent the plural, but there is no script in which several such signs form a whole category. Second, if signs were to be read backward (as when **li** is read *–il*) it would require the Maya reader to be able to operate with phonemes, which is hardly possible for someone trained to use a logosyllabic system (Read et al. 1986, Morais et al. 1986). Third, one and the same sign, e.g., **ja/-AJ**, would correspond to several distinct morphemes (e.g., *-aj* "inchoative," *-aj* "thematic of derived intransitives," *-aj* "nominalizer"). Thus, one would have to allow for polyvalency as a general feature of the script

despite that extremely few logograms are known to have more than one logogrammatic value. Fourth, there is not always a one-to-one correspondence between a "morphosyllable" used and the morpheme it represents. Thus, **ja** is used only to spell the thematic suffix on derived intransitives in the absence of a following suffix having a vowel different from *a*. When the future participial *–o'm* follows, **jo** is used (e.g., **TZUTZ-jo-ma** "it would be ended") and when the temporal deictic enclitic *–iiy* follows, **ji** is used (e.g., **TZUTZ-ji-ya** "it had been ended"). If **ja** represented the suffix in the same way that a logogram represents a lexeme it would be inexplicable that other signs could replace it.

Houston et al. (2001) claim that morphosyllables "underspecify the phonological content of the morphemes they reference. They underspecify since their spoken counterparts are suffixes, taking the form VC (not CV), the vowel being unwritten and variable," and they "underspecify by suspending disharmony" (p. 15). If the putative morphosyllables indeed both underspecify the vowel of the suffix and block harmony rules from operating, no phonological information but the consonant of the suffix would be given orthographically. Thus, very little input would be found in the inscriptions for the study of diachronic phonological developments of Mayan suffixes. Lacadena & Wichmann (2004a), however, are more optimistic about the amount of phonological information to be gleaned from the hieroglyphic inscriptions. They see the spelling rules as working in the normal ways, supplying information about vowel length and glottal stops. In the following three examples each of the three harmony rules are operative in the domain of suffixes:

> **K'UH-lu / k'u-hu-lu**, *k'uh-ul* "holy"
> **u-K'UH-li**, *u-k'uh-uul* "his god"
> **ma-su-la**, *Ma[h]s-u'l* "place where the cricket abounds" (toponym)

The inscriptions are rich in such contrastive forms where affixes that share the same vowel and consonant are spelled

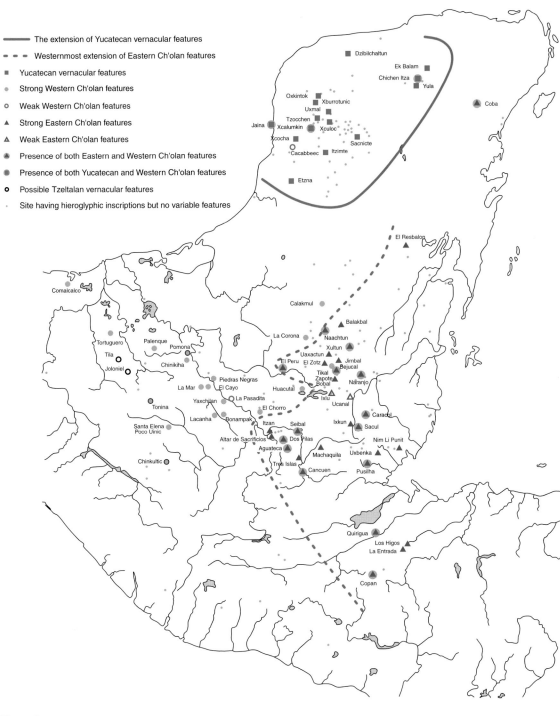

Legend:
- ——— The extension of Yucatecan vernacular features
- – – – Westernmost extension of Eastern Ch'olan features
- ■ Yucatecan vernacular features
- ● Strong Western Ch'olan features
- ○ Weak Western Ch'olan features
- ▲ Strong Eastern Ch'olan features
- △ Weak Eastern Ch'olan features
- ◆ Presence of both Eastern and Western Ch'olan features
- ◆ Presence of both Yucatecan and Western Ch'olan features
- ◉ Possible Tzeltalan vernacular features
- · Site having hieroglyphic inscriptions but no variable features

Figure 1

The distribution of Lowland Mayan languages as revealed through inscriptions of the Classic period.

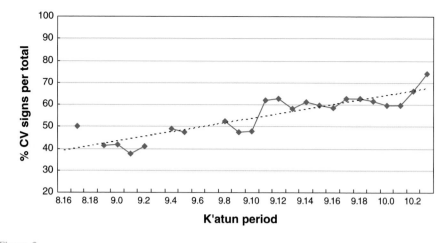

Average regional development of phoneticism during the Classic period.

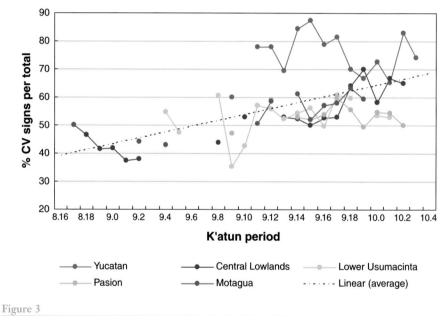

The regional development of phoneticism during the Classic period.

according to different patterns of syn- or disharmony, something that can indicate only that the scribes were carefully distinguishing different types of syllable nuclei, exactly as they did when writing lexemes. In many cases the quality of the vowel of the suffix may be inferred from alternative spellings elsewhere in the corpus. Thus, "holy" may be spelled **K'UH-lu**. Because the vowel of the complement **lu** is silent, and we do not consider it possible to read **lu** backwards as **ul**, there is no way of knowing which of the five Ch'olan vowels are present. This information, however, is provided by the alternative spelling **k'u-hu-lu**. Here the vowel *u* of the suffix is spelled syllabically as part of the **hu** syllabic sign. For **u-K'UH-li** we have evidence from the Ch'olti' expression <vchuul ahitzaob> "the idols of the Itzas," recorded by Morán (1695, p. 37), that the high back rounded vowel is intended (Zender 2004a, p. 259, n. 94). The $-VV_1l$ possessive suffix is found in other hieroglyphically recorded forms, e.g., in the expression **yo-lo-li** (on a Tikal bone tube published by Laporte 1999), which likely refers to "its center" and contains the same vowel-harmonic suffix seen in a fossilized form in modern Tzotzil *'o'lol* "middle, center" (Laughlin 1975, p. 64). Thus, the writing system may, indeed, underspecify the quality of the vowel but only in the special case in which a syllabic sign spelling part of a suffix is directly preceded by a logogram. Once the quality of the vowel is provided by the reader, the harmony rules operate as usual. For instance, if the underspecified suffix vowel of **K'UH-li** is the high back one, the "silent" **i**-vowel of **li** tells us that the high back vowel is long and we can transliterate the spelling as *k'uhuul*. For **K'UH-lu**, however, once we know that the vowel intended is the high back one, we also know that that vowel is short because of the synharmony pattern.

The following case study may illustrate the importance of a correct understanding of spelling rules for the decipherment of grammatical elements. The inscriptions of the Naj Tunich cave contain a recurrent verb alternately spelled **pa-ka-xi** and **pa-ka-xa**. MacLeod related this to the Ch'olti' forms <pacxi> and <pacxiel> "to return" in MacLeod & Stone (1995), and epigraphers have been on the lookout for morphemes of the shape *–xi* or *–xa* that might explain the Naj Tunich forms. Knowing how spelling rules operate, however, the obvious strategy is to look for a verb of the shape *pakaax*, corresponding to **pa-ka-xi**, later developed into *pakax* owing to loss of vowel length. Standard lexicographical sources for Tojolab'al and Ch'orti' offer the verb *pakax* "to return." Therefore, it is likely that a suffix *–aax* ~*–ax* is directly reflected in the Naj Tunich drawings and that the cognate Ch'olti' form <pacxi(el)> contains a syncopated version of the suffix with further suffixation of an *–i*, which in this language is found on other intransitive motion verbs as well. The suffix *–aax* ~ *–ax* can now be directly related to the ones seen on three different verbs on Copan Stela J, the most semantically transparent being **ma-ka-xa** "got (or will get) covered," from the transitive *mak* "to cover." These verbs represent intransitives derived from transitive roots and have a mediopassive function. Going back to *paka(a)x*, we also discern a mediopassive origin for this form, given the existence of a verb root *pak* "to fold," attested in Ch'orti', Tzeltal, and Q'anjob'al. The suffix must surely be related to one that has been reconstructed to proto-Mayan by T.S. Kaufman (unpublished comparative work) and whose reflexes include Huastec *–x* "reciprocal," Tojolab'al *–x* "mediopassive," Chuj *–ax* "nonagentive passive," and Mocho *–Vx* "reflexive," as well as several Eastern Mayan cognates. Notice that none of the attestations include Ch'olan or even Tzeltalan languages. Thus, similar to the nominal absolutive *–is* identified by Zender (2004b), the suffix *–aax* (or *–VV_1x*) represents an instance of a Classic Ch'olan suffix with clear cognates beyond Ch'olan but none (or, at most, a fossilized instance) in alphabetically recorded Ch'olan languages. As such, it is an excellent example of the new synthesis of epigraphy and historical linguistics, showing how a good understanding of the mechanisms of the writing system combined with the use of comparative evidence may aid decipherment, which in turn produces new data that contribute to further historical reconstruction.

To date, an excess of 70 different Classic Ch'olan and Classic Yucatecan affixes have been deciphered, a great many within the past few years. The near future will likely see the publication of grammatical overviews, just as the first Classic Ch'olan vocabularies have recently seen the light of day (Boot 2002, Montgomery 2002, Stuart 2005). Currently the most direct way of acquiring an overview of grammatical morphemes is probably by reference to Stuart (2005), with supplementary use of Wichmann's (2004a) index.

MORPHOSYNTAX

An issue often pondered by epigraphers is whether Classic Ch'olan had a split ergative system. Kaufman & Norman (1984) asserted that proto-Ch'olan had "a verbal agreement system of the so-called split ergative type in which subject agreement with intransitive verbs is marked by ergative morphemes in the incompletive aspect but by absolutive morphemes in the completive aspect" (p. 90) and furthermore ascribed the split to Yucatecan influence. Others, such as Hofling (2000) and Mora-Marín (2005), concur with Kaufman & Norman. This view, however, is challenged by Law et al. (2006), who argue that split ergativity is restricted to Western Ch'olan, whereas Ch'olti' is only incipiently split ergative. They propose to distinguish between the progressive in Ch'olti', which does show the use of ergative pronominals with intransitive verbs, and the incompletive, which does not. Although these arguments are reasonable, several details of the Eastern Ch'olan developments still need to be worked out, and the argument begs the question of what the Classic Ch'olan incompletive construction would have looked like. We cannot exclude that intransitives in the incompletive did, in fact, carry ergative inflection. Because the texts nearly always describe completed actions, no clear instances of incompletive intransitive predicates have been discerned. However, texts such as the direct speech utterances embedded in the cartoon-like illustrations on painted vessels will someday likely yield just the right kind of data to settle the issue conclusively.

SYNTAX AND DISCOURSE

Research on syntactic structures of the hieroglyphic inscriptions and the larger discourse structures they comprise has, somewhat surprisingly, been largely neglected in recent years. Thus, I limit myself very briefly to signaling some areas in which new insights are likely to be harvested. Mora-Marín's (2004) work on preferred argument structure, which focuses on texts from Palenque, could be followed up by studies of a larger corpus. Another area that still deserves more scrutiny is the syntactic structure of personal names. Finally, the calendrical sequences, which form a large part of the inscriptions, should be studied more closely with a view to their syntactic organization. As revealed by the presence of the deictic enclitics –ij and –iiy studied by Wald (2004), long count dates and time intervals (so-called distance numbers) should be regarded as linguistic expressions just like sentences describing historical events, and their internal syntactic structure as well as their syntactic relationship to other text segments need more study.

WRITING WITH AN ACCENT: PHONOLOGY AS A MARKER OF ETHNIC IDENTITY

The phonological transparency of the Maya writing system is what makes possible a close integration of Mayan historical linguistics and epigraphy. But why is the system so transparent in the first place?

The Maya script is a unitary one. Its orthographic rules are the same throughout the area where writing was practiced, and its basic sign inventory, although it developed over time (Grube 1990), was shared among all sites. Nevertheless, there is some variation in the degree of phoneticism. Because it operates with both syllabic signs and logograms, the Maya writing system in many cases offers different possibilities of writing the same word, i.e., using a logogram, using a combination of a logogram and one or more syllabic signs, or using syllabic signs only. Although all these possible ways of spelling the word would be equally adequate, they represent different degrees of phonological specification. How can we account for different preferences among scribes for one over the other type of spelling?

A very general hypothesis about the evolution of writing systems would be that developments toward greater phonological transparency are often triggered by the wish of scribes to set off clearly their pronunciations of words from other possible pronunciations by speakers of other dialects or languages. Such a need to indicate clearly phonological differences arises only in situations of language contact, most pressingly in diglossic situations in which different languages are used by speakers for different purposes. Writing with an accent is not, however, equally opportune under all sociolinguistic circumstances. In the city-states of Ancient Greece or the petty kingdoms of the Classic Maya it was natural to express differences in the pronunciations of cognate morphemes, and the writing systems that developed under these circumstances were therefore relatively phonologically transparent. However, in a large, centralized state subsuming many ethnic groups such as China, Ancient Egypt, or the Aztec Triple Alliance, it would be a disadvantage to have a writing system designed to indicate subtle differences of pronunciation. Under these circumstances, contact among different languages produces the opposite effect, namely writing systems that are relatively opaque phonologically. Because the Maya writing system allows for variation concerning the degree of phonological transparency of individual spellings, it offers an opportunity to investigate whether degrees of language contact correlate with phonological transparency.

As a simple way of quantifying the degree of phonological transparency in different inscriptions, Wichmann & Davletshin (2004) counted the number of syllabic signs versus the total number of signs, logograms included, in a sample of 245 provenanced and dated texts. Regional differences in phoneticism were studied with reference to Sharer's (1994) overall division of the Classic Maya realm into three major zones: the Northern Lowlands (here labeled "Yucatan"), including such sites as Dzibilchaltun, Chichen Itza, and Tulum, the Central Lowlands (Calakmul, Tikal, Naranjo, etc.), and the Southern Lowlands. The last was divided into the Lower Usumacinta (Palenque, Tonina, Yaxchilan, etc.), Pasión (Dos Pilas, Cancuen, Machaquila, etc.), and Motagua (Copan, Quirigua) regions. The cells in the datasheet represent the number of syllabic signs out of all signs in all texts during a given k'atun period (20×360 days) at a given site.

The overall, average development of phoneticism is shown in **Figure 2** (see color insert), the stippled line representing the average increase throughout the history of the inscriptions studied (8.17 = 376 A.D. to 10.3 = 889 A.D.). Disregarding the earliest point at 8.17, which is based on materials too limited to be statistically reliable, the increase may be described as neatly step-like with an average of ~40% during the Early Classic period of 8.19–9.2 (416–476 A.D.), ~50% by the transition to the Late Classic (9.4–9.10 or 514–633 A.D.), ~60% during most of the Late Classic (9.11–10.1 or 652–849 A.D.), and ~70% during the Terminal Classic period of 10.2–10.3 (869–889 A.D.).

Not included in the graph are the earliest and latest attestations of Maya writing. A count of the glyphs on a small sample of proto-Classic objects shows a 30.8% proportion of CV signs, which is roughly what we would expect. Some representative sections of Codex Dresden showed a 59.9% proportion of CV signs. If the stippled line in **Figure 2** is extended, the prediction is a 90% proportion for the time the Dresden Codex was produced (assigning the date to ~1500 A.D.). Instead, we find an amount corresponding to the average of the greater part of the Late Classic. This finding suggests that the glyphic texts of the codices relate to the actual language spoken by the scribes in ways that are different from the Late Classic texts and/or that the writing system has somehow stagnated.

Figure 3 (see color insert) gives an overview of differences among the different regions. The clearest result is that Yucatan has a much higher overall degree of phoneticism than do other areas. The Central and Southern Lowland regions do not show any marked mutual differences. All undergo a gradual increase in phoneticism with only slight differences in how steep the average rise is. The fact that the Northern Lowlands stand out as markedly more phonologically transparent is explained by our theory that language contact will lead to a higher degree of phoneticism, provided that the sociopolitical circumstances allow it. The studies referenced above show that there was a diglossic situation in northeastern and north-central Yucatan. This situation would have spurred the greater degree of phoneticism. For example, scribes here would prefer syllabic spellings if the Ch'olan pronunciation of a logogram did not correspond to the Yucatecan pronunciation of the corresponding word. Thus, the equivalent of the Ch'olan hieroglyphic expression **yo-OTOT-ti** "his house" is **yo-to-che** in Yucatan. We would similarly attribute the overall increase of phoneticism in the Central and Southern Lowlands to an increasing need to spell out regional variants in the wake of the gradual differentiation of Ch'olan.

CONCLUSION

Whereas the mid-1980s saw the great boom in the phonetic decipherment of the Maya script, the late 1990s and the turn of the century have witnessed the culmination of its linguistic interpretation (Wichmann 2004b). By now, a very detailed picture of the development of language distribution in the Classic Maya Lowlands has been worked out, the morphology of Classic Ch'olan is reasonably well understood, and highly refined interpretations of orthographical rules of the script as well as improved phonological reconstructions based on the extant spoken Mayan languages have become available. Classic Ch'olan has crystallized to such a degree that it forms a dataset in its own right, providing a unique new input to the diachronic study of Mayan languages.

Although the dedication of many scholars has brought us this far, it is interesting to realize that the ultimate condition for the success is due to the Mayas themselves. The decipherment of monumental inscriptions could not have happened without the existence of alternative spellings of identical words, producing so-called substitution patterns. These patterns have allowed epigraphers to identify the phonetic values of particular signs by their equivalence to other, already deciphered signs. It is almost as if ancient Mayan scribes had tried to give us hints at how to read their texts when the texts suddenly deviate from common practice and begin to complement a logogram with syllabic signs or substitute it entirely for such signs. These hints, however, are of course not directed at us, but rather at contemporary readers. They represent an awareness of language that is ultimately rooted in an awareness of regional identity. By exposing features of who they considered themselves to be, the Classic Maya have indirectly helped modern scholars improve their understanding of Maya history and society through the linguistically controlled scrutiny of the ancient hieroglyphic texts.

ACKNOWLEDGMENTS

I would like to thank Alfonso Lacadena, Mark Zender, Stanley Guenter, Albert Davletshin, Peter Biro, and John Robertson for constructive comments on an earlier draft of this paper.

LITERATURE CITED

Beliaev D, Davletshin A. 2003. Possible mediopassive suffix –k'-a(j) in the Maya script? *PARI J.* 3(3):12

Boot E. 2002. *A preliminary Classic Maya-English/English-Classic Maya vocabulary of hieroglyphic readings.* http://www.mesoweb.com/resources/vocabulary/Vocabulary.pdf

Bricker V. 1986. *A Grammar of Mayan Hieroglyphs*. Middle Am. Res. Inst., Publ. 56. New Orleans: Tulane Univ.

An early, large-scale attempt to integrate relevant information on the languages of the Classic inscriptions from both hieroglyphic sources and modern Mayan languages.

Brown CH, Wichmann S. 2004. Proto-Mayan syllable nuclei. *Int. J. Am. Linguist.* 70:128–86

Campbell L. 1984. The implications of Mayan historical linguistics for glyphic research. See Justeson & Campbell 1984, pp. 1–17

Campbell L, Kaufman T. 1985. Mayan linguistics: Where are we now? *Annu. Rev. Anthropol.* 14:187–98

Colas PR. 2004a. *Personal names: one aspect of an ethnic boundary among the Classic Maya.* Presented at Eur. Maya Conf., 9th, Univ. Bonn

Colas PR. 2004b. *Sinn und Bedeutung Klassischer Maya-Personennamen: Typologische Analyse von Anthroponymphrasen in den Hieroglyphenin-schriften der Klassischen Maya-Kultur als Beitrag zur allgemeinen Onomastik.* Acta Mesoam. 15. Markt Schwarben: Anton Saurwein

Grube N. 1990. *Die Entwicklung der Mayaschrift. Grundlagen zur Erforschung des Wandels der Mayaschrift von der Protoklassik bis zur spanischen Eroberung.* PhD Diss. Univ. Hamburg. Acta Mesoam. 3. Berlin: Verlag Von Flemming

Grube N. 2004. The orthographic distinction between velar and glottal spirants in Maya hieroglyphic writing. See Wichmann 2004c, pp. 61–81

Hofling CA. 2000. Response to Houston et al. 'The language of the Classic Maya inscriptions'. *Curr. Anthropol.* 41(3):339–21

Houston SD. 2000. Into the minds of ancients: advances in glyph studies. *J. World Prehist.* 14:121–201

Houston SD. 2004. The archaeology of communication technologies. *Annu. Rev. Anthropol.* 33:223–50

Houston SD, Robertson J, Stuart D. 2000. The language of Classic Maya inscriptions. *Curr. Anthropol.* 41(3):321–56

Houston SD, Robertson J, Stuart D. 2001. Quality and quantity in glyphic nouns and adjectives. Res. Rep. Anc. Maya Writ. 47, Cent. Maya Res. Washington, DC

Houston SD, Stuart D, Robertson J. 1998. Disharmony in Maya hieroglyphic writing: linguistic change and continuity in Classic society. In *Anatomía de una Civilización. Aproximaciones Interdisciplinarias a la Cultura Maya*. Publ. S.E.E.M., 4, ed. A Ciudad Ruiz, Y Fernández, JM García Campillo, MJ Iglesias Ponce de León, A Lacadena García-Gallo, LT Saenz Castro, pp. 275–96. Madrid: Sociedad Española de Estudios Mayas

An important breakthrough toward a new understanding of the orthographical conventions of the Maya script.

Hruby ZX, Child MB. 2004. Chontal linguistic influence in Ancient Maya writing: intransitive verbal affixation. See Wichmann 2004c, pp. 13–26

Hruby ZX, Robertson JS. 2001. *Evidence for language change in ancient Maya writing: a case study of the verb tzutz.* Res. Rep. Anc. Maya Writ. 50, Cent. Maya Res. Washington, DC

Proceedings of a 1979 conference at which consensus was reached on the phonetic nature of the Maya script and the importance of Ch'olan languages.

Justeson J, Campbell L, ed. 1984. *Phoneticism in Mayan Hieroglyphic Writing.* **Inst. Mesoam. Stud., Publ. No. 9. Albany: State Univ. NY**

Justeson JS, Norman WM, Campbell L, Kaufman TS. 1985. *The Foreign Impact on Lowland Mayan Language and Script.* Middle Am. Res. Inst., Publ. 53. New Orleans: Tulane Univ.

Kaufman TS. 1980. Pre-Columbian borrowings involving Huastec. In *American Indian and Indo-European Studies: Papers in Honor of Madison S. Beeler*, ed. K Klar, M Langdon, S. Silver, pp. 101–12. The Hague: Mouton

Kaufman TS, Norman WM. 1984. An outline of Proto-Cholan phonology, morphology and vocabulary. See Justeson & Campbell 1984, pp. 77–166

Knorozov YV. 1965. Principios para descifrar los escritos mayas. *Estud. Cult. Maya* 5:153–88

Lacadena A. 1997a. Bilinguismo en el Códice de Madrid. In *Los Investigadores de la Cultura Maya*, No. 5, pp. 184–204. Campeche: Universidad Autónoma de Campeche y Secretaría de Educación Pública

Lacadena A. 1997b. On Classic -*w* suffix morphology. *Yumtzilob* 9(1):45–51

Lacadena A. 2000a. Antipassive constructions in the Maya glyphic texts. *Written Lang. Liter.* 3(1):155–80

Lacadena A. 2000b. Nominal syntax and the linguistic affiliation of Classic Maya texts. In *The Sacred and the Profane: Architecture and Identity in the Maya Lowlands*, Acta Mesoam. 10, ed. PR Colas, K Delvendahl, M Kuhnert, A Schubart, pp. 119–28. Markt Schwaben: Anton Sauerwein

Lacadena A. 2002. *Vestiges of the Preclassic stage of the language of Classic Maya inscriptions.* Presented at Maya Meet., Austin

Lacadena A. 2003. El sufijo verbalizador –*Vj* (-*aj* ∼ -*iij*) en la escritura jeroglífica maya. In *De la Tablilla a la Inteligencia Artificial*, ed. A González Blanco, JP Vita, JA Zamora, pp. 847–65. Zaragoza: Instituto de Estudio Islámicos y del Oriente Próximo

Lacadena A. 2004. Passive voice in Classic Mayan text: CV-*h*-C-*aj* and -*n*-*aj* constructions. See Wichmann 2004c, pp. 165–94

Lacadena A, Wichmann S. 2000. *The dynamics of language in the Western Lowland Maya region.* Presented at Chacmool Conf., Calgary

Draws precise geographical boundaries between Classic Yucatecan and Classic Ch'olan and demonstrates an east-west differentiation of Ch'olan vernacular variants.

Lacadena A, Wichmann S. 2002. The distribution of Lowland Maya languages in the Classic period. In *La Organización Social Entre los Mayas. Memoria de la Tercera Mesa Redonda de Palenque*, **Vol. II, ed. V Tiesler, R Cobos, M Greene Robertson, pp. 275–314. México D.F.: Instituto Nacional de Antropología e Historia and Universidad Autónoma de Yucatán**

Lacadena A, Wichmann S. 2004a. *Harmony rules in the suffix domain: a study of Maya scribal conventions.* http://email.eva.mpg.de/%7EWichmann/harm-rul-suf-dom7.pdf

Lacadena A, Wichmann S. 2004b. On the representation of the glottal stop in Maya writing. See Wichmann 2004c, pp. 103–62

Laporte JP. 1999. Contexto y función de los artefactos de hueso en Tikal, Guatemala. *Rev. Esp. Antropol. Am.* 29:31–64

Laughlin RM. 1975. *The Great Tzotzil Dictionary of San Lorenzo Zinacantán.* Washington, DC: Smithson. Inst. Press

Law D, Robertson J, Houston SD. 2006. Split ergativity in the history of the Ch'olan branch of the Mayan language family. *Int. J. Amer. Linguist.* 72: In press

MacLeod B. 1984. Cholan and Yucatecan verb morphology and glyphic verbal affixes in the inscriptions. See Justeson & Campbell 1984, pp. 233–62

MacLeod B. 1987. *An Epigrapher's Annotated Index to Cholan and Yucatecan Verb Morphology.* Univ. Mo. Monogr. Anthropol., No. 9. Columbia: Univ. Mo.

MacLeod B. 2004. A world in a grain of sand: transitive perfect verbs in the Classic Maya script. See Wichmann 2004c, pp. 291–325

MacLeod B, Stone A. 1995. The hieroglyphic inscriptions of Naj Tunich. In *Images from the Underworld: Naj Tunich and the Tradition of Maya Cave Painting*, ed. A Stone, pp. 155–84. Austin: Univ. Tex. Press

Martin S, Grube N. 2000. *The Chronicle of Maya Kings and Queens*. London: Thames and Hudson

Mathews P. 1984. Appendix A: a Maya hieroglyphic syllabary. See Justeson & Campbell 1984, pp. 311–14

Montgomery J. 2002. *Dictionary of Maya Hieroglyphs*. New York: Hippocrene

Mora-Marín DF. 2004. The preferred argument structure of Classic Lowland Mayan texts. See Wichmann 2004c, pp. 339–61

Mora-Marín DF. 2005. *Proto-Ch'olan as the standard language of Classic Lowland Mayan texts.* http://www.unc.edu/~davidmm/ProtoCholanHypothesis.pdf

Morais J, Alegria J, Content A. 1986. Literacy training and speech segmentation. *Cognition* 24:45–64

Morán F. 1695. *Arte y Vocabulario de la Lengua Cholti que Quiere Desir la Lengua de Milperos.* Manuscr. Coll. 497.4/M79. Philadelphia: Am. Philos. Soc.

Read C, Yun-Fei Z, Hong-Yin N, Bao-Qin D. 1986. The ability to manipulate speech sounds depends on knowing alphabetic readings. *Cognition* 24:31–44

Robertson JS. 1992. *The History of Tense/Aspect/Mood/ Voice in the Mayan Verbal Complex*. Austin: Univ. Tex. Press

Robertson JS. 1998. A Ch'olti'an explanation for Ch'orti'an grammar: a postlude to the language of the Classic Maya. *Mayab* 11:5–11

Robertson JS. 2004. *A brief response to Wichmann's "Hieroglyphic evidence for the historical configuration of Eastern Ch'olan" (RRAMW 51)*. Res. Rep. Anc. Maya Writ., 51a, pp. 1–13. Cent. Maya Res., Barnardsville, NC

Schele L. 1982. *Maya Glyphs: The Verbs*. Austin: Univ. Tex. Press

Sharer RJ. 1994. *The Ancient Maya*. Stanford, CA: Stanford Univ. Press. 5th ed.

Stuart D. 1987. *Ten Phonetic Syllables*. Res. Rep. Anc. Maya Writ. 14. Washington, DC: Cent. Maya Res.

Stuart D. 2005. *Sourcebook for the 29th Maya Hieroglyph Forum, March 11–16, 2005*. Austin: Dep. Art and Art Hist., Univ. Tex. Austin

Vázquez Alvarez JJ. 2002. *Morfología del verbo de la lengua chol de Tila, Chiapas*. MA thesis, Cent. Investig. Estud. Super. Antropol. Soc., Mexico City

Wald RF. 1994. *Transitive verb inflection in Classic Maya hieroglyphic texts: its implication for decipherment and historical linguistics*. MA thesis, Univ. Tex. Austin

Wald RF. 2004. Telling time in Classic-Ch'olan and Acalan-Chontal narrative: the linguistic basis of some temporal discourse patterns in Maya hieroglyphic and Acalan-Chontal texts. See Wichmann 2004c, pp. 211–58

Wichmann S. 2002a. *Hieroglyphic Evidence for the Historical Configuration of Eastern Ch'olan*. Res. Rep. Anc. Maya Writ. 51. Washington, DC: Cent. Maya Res.

Wichmann S. 2002b. Questioning the grid: a new distinction among the syllabic signs of the Maya hieroglyphic script? *Mexicon* 24(5):98–106

Wichmann S. 2003a. A new look at linguistic interaction in the lowlands as a background for the study of Maya codices. Presented at 8th Eur. Maya Conf., Madrid

Wichmann S. 2003b. Contextualizing proto-languages, homelands and distant genetic relationship: some reflections on the comparative method from a Mesoamerican perspective. In *Examining the Farming/Language Dispersal Hypothesis*, ed. P Bellwood, C Renfrew,

A classic paper containing some of the most beautiful demonstrations of decipherment methodology ever published.

pp. 321–29. McDonald Inst. Monogr. Cambridge, MA: McDonald Inst. Archaeol. Res.

Wichmann S. 2004a. Index of grammatical morphemes in the inscriptions. See Wichmann 2004c, pp. 451–52

Wichmann S. 2004b. The linguistic epigraphy of Mayan writing: recent advances and questions for future research. See Wichmann 2004c, pp. 1–11

Wichmann S, ed. 2004c. *The Linguistics of Maya Writing*. Salt Lake City: Univ. Utah Press

Wichmann S, Brown CH. 2003. Contact among some Mayan languages: inferences from loanwords. *Anthropol. Linguist.* 45:57–93

Wichmann S, Davletshin A. 2004. *Writing with an accent: phonology as a marker of ethnic identity.* Presented at Eur. Maya Conf., 9th, Univ. Bonn

Zender MU. 1999. *Diacritical marks and underspelling in the Classic Maya script: implications for decipherment.* MA thesis. Univ. of Calgary

Zender MU. 2004a. *A study of Classic Maya priesthood.* Ph.D. diss. Univ. of Calgary

Zender MU. 2004b. On the morphology of intimate possession in Mayan languages and Classic Mayan glyphic nouns. See Wichmann 2004c, pp. 195–209

Contains many important contributions to the linguistically oriented study of Maya writing from the mid-1980s to the turn of this century.

Sovereignty Revisited

Thomas Blom Hansen[1] and Finn Stepputat[2]

[1] Department of Anthropology, Yale University, New Haven, Connecticut 06520-8277; email: blomhansent@hotmail.com

[2] Danish Institute for International Studies, Copenhagen DK-1401, Denmark; email: fst@diis.dk

Annu. Rev. Anthropol. 2006. 35:295–315

First published online as a Review in Advance on June 7, 2006

The *Annual Review of Anthropology* is online at anthro.annualreviews.org

This article's doi: 10.1146/annurev.anthro.35.081705.123317

Copyright © 2006 by Annual Reviews. All rights reserved

0084-6570/06/1021-0295$20.00

Key Words

political anthropology, violence, kingship, authority, body, government

Abstract

Sovereignty has returned as a central concern in anthropology. This reinvention seeks to explore de facto sovereignty, i.e., the ability to kill, punish, and discipline with impunity. The central proposition is a call to abandon sovereignty as an ontological ground of power and order in favor of a view of sovereignty as a tentative and always emergent form of authority grounded in violence. After a brief account of why the classical work on kingship failed to provide an adequate matrix for understanding the political imaginations of a world after colonialism, three theses on sovereignty—modern and premodern—are developed. We argue that although effective legal sovereignty is always an unattainable ideal, it is particularly tenuous in many postcolonial societies where sovereign power historically was distributed among many forms of local authority. The last section discusses the rich new field of studies of informal sovereignties: vigilante groups, strongmen, insurgents, and illegal networks. Finally, the relationship between market forces, outsourcing, and new configurations of sovereign power are explored.

INTRODUCTION

NGO:
nongovernmental
organizations

The current reevaluation of the meanings of sovereignty—critically informed by the work of Giorgio Agamben—resonates in profound ways with an intensified global crisis of the nation-state as the main vehicle of sovereign power.

Transnational corporations, the "soft" global network power of nongovernmental organizations (NGOs) and Internet communities, as well as the proliferation of ethnic conflicts in the post–Cold War age seemed to undermine the naturalness of the idea of national sovereignty in the 1990s. The aftermath of 9/11 made it clear that national sovereignty, war, and security regimes still remained the hard kernel of modern states. It was also clear, however, that the new threat to the established world order would come from forces that were difficult to conceptualize—highly mobile, evanescent, and resolutely global networks, akin to what Deleuze & Guattari (1987 [1980]) call "nomadic war machines," rhizomes of force (*puissance*) that leave institutionalized power (*pouvoir*) highly vulnerable. There is no clearer example of the paradoxes of sovereignty in the twenty-first century than Iraq since the United States–led invasion in 2003. Here, multiple, fragile, and contested centers of military might, welfare, and ethnoreligious and local loyalties claim sovereignty over people and land—both legal sovereignty as in the legitimate right to govern and de facto sovereignty as the right over life (to protect or to kill with impunity).

Recent work on sovereignty addresses, and maybe transcends, two long-standing theoretical impasses in anthropology: the decline of political anthropology with its emphasis on kingship, sacrifice, and ritual in "primitive" societies. This once influential strand in anthropological debates was so steeped in an ahistorical mode of analysis that it all but disappeared with the emergence of historical anthropology and the many critiques of colonialism since the 1980s. The subsequent reinvention of the anthropology of the political

and the state in the 1990s has been heavily indebted to Foucault's attempt to cut off the King's head in the social sciences (Foucault 1980) and to develop a nonessentialist ontology of power beyond notions of origins and centers or the continuity of cultural forms.

The triumph of a Foucauldian view of power has in many ways created an impasse of its own. If power is dispersed throughout society, in institutions, disciplines, and rituals of self-making, how do we, for instance, account for the proliferation of legal discourse premised on the widespread popular idea of the state as a center of society, a central legislator, and an adjudicator? How do we understand popular mythologies of power, corruption, secrecy, and evil as emanating from certain centers, people, or hidden domains? How do we interpret how violence destroys social ties but also produces informal authority? How can we understand war as a totalizing logic of life and society, as Foucault himself pointed out in the late 1970s (2003)?

The return to sovereignty, often via Agamben's writings on banished life (*homo sacer*), desymbolized and "bare," as the included outside upon which a community or a society constitutes itself and its moral order (Agamben 1998), promises a new and fruitful focalization—maybe another strategic reductionism—of ongoing debates on the nature of power and violence.

In the following, we offer an interpretation of what has prompted this revisiting of sovereignty as a central concern in anthropology; what possibilities this move has offered; and which new fields of inquiry it promises to open. This revisiting differs from the past endeavors in anthropology, and from the debates on sovereignty in political science and history, in two important respects: It is, in the main, oriented toward exploring de facto sovereignty, i.e., the ability to kill, punish, and discipline with impunity wherever it is found and practiced, rather than sovereignty grounded in formal ideologies of rule and legality. This does not preclude studies of legal practices or state practices but may help to reorient such studies away from the law as text, or the courtroom spectacle, toward exploring more quotidian notions of justice, of "legal consciousness," and of punishment as they occur in everyday life. The key move we propose is to abandon sovereignty as an ontological ground of power and order, expressed in law or in enduring ideas of legitimate rule, in favor of a view of sovereignty as a tentative and always emergent form of authority grounded in violence that is performed and designed to generate loyalty, fear, and legitimacy from the neighborhood to the summit of the state.

The second difference is the focus on the body as the site of, and object of, sovereign power. Agamben's work has made it possible to understand that it is not only the King who has two bodies, a natural body and a political body as in medieval political theology (Kantorowicz 1957). This duality is a generalized condition in modern societies where the citizen has an included body, a body that has itself (*habeas corpus*) and an array of rights by virtue of its inclusion into the political community, and simultaneously a biological body, a life that can be stripped of symbolization and humanity and reduced to "bare life" by decree or bio-political fiat. This is, Agamben shows, the nature of modern sovereign power of which the camp, designed for extermination, waiting, or infinite detention, is the most poignant expression (see Fiskesjö 2003). The larger point is of course that the body is always the site of performance of sovereign power, which becomes most visible in states of war, extreme conditions, fragmentation, and marginality. Sovereign power can be fruitfully regarded as the central, if often unacknowledged, underside of modern and liberal forms of highly codified and regulated (self) government (Agamben 2005, Hindess 2005).

We are, in other words, charting and advocating an ethnographic approach to sovereignty in practice. This may turn out to be every bit as destabilizing to formal and legal notions of sovereignty as ethnography has been with respect to the idea of religion, the state, and the market.

We start with a brief and critical account of why the political anthropology inspired by Frazer, Hocart, and Evans-Pritchard produced many striking insights but failed to provide an adequate matrix for understanding the political imaginations of a world after colonialism. We also offer a brief assessment of how various assumptions about sovereignty persisted, if rarely in an enunciated form, in much of the influential work on colonialism and its legacies. The anthropology of colonialism has demonstrated that the anxieties of colonial rule were centered on its body politics, the imprinting of rule on the bodies of natives, and the protection of white bodies: the fears of miscegenation, the performance of European dignity, the presentation of the European family and domesticity, the taming and disciplining of immoral practices, etc. We also suggest that through the lens of sovereignty in practice, colonial rule appears less hegemonic and effective than in its self-presentations in official texts and plans. A key feature of the colonial world was that different kinds and registers of sovereignty coexisted and overlapped. Most modern states claim effective legal sovereignty over a territory and its population in the name of the nation and the popular will. Although this is always an unattainable ideal, it is particularly tenuous in many postcolonial societies in which sovereign power was historically fragmented and distributed among many, mostly informal but effective, forms of local authority.

The last section provides a discussion of the rich new field of studies of informal sovereignties such as vigilante groups, strongmen, insurgents, and illegal networks. We also address, albeit in a more tentative form, more recent work exploring the relationship between market forces, privatization, outsourcing, and the new configuration of sovereign power it produces in the present.

CORPUS MYSTICUM: ON KINGSHIP AND ENDURING CULTURAL FORMS

By and large, anthropologists have understood political authority, often studied under the rubric of kingship, in two different ways: either as embedded in the wider structures of production, kinship, and clan or as a distinct and centralizing institution, reproduced through public ritual, constituting a symbolic center of society. The former is commonly associated with work on segmentary and acephalous polities with relatively low levels of functional and institutional differentiation. In such societies, "the law" does not have an existence separate from procedures or injunctions outside the ethos of everyday life: "[T]he basis of law is force," writes Evans-Pritchard and continues, "the club and the spear are sanctions of rights" (Evans-Pritchard 1969 [1940], p. 169). The functionalist thrust of this tradition posited a fundamental consonance between political symbols and rituals and the meanings and sentiments they evoked among subjects. "An African ruler," Evans-Pritchard & Fortes write in their introduction to the classical collection *African Political Systems*, "is not to his people merely a person who can enforce his will on them. He is . . . the embodiment of their essential values. . . . His credentials are mystical and are derived from antiquity" (Evans-Pritchard & Fortes 1940). There is no history in this perspective, only incessant feuds and conflicts that nonetheless follow intricate rules and patterns that in the end ensure the permanence and indivisibility of the realm or the community (Evans-Pritchard 1969 [1940], pp. 142–47; see also Barth 1959, Fortes 1945, Gulliver 1963).

This is ultimately a Durkheimian view of the integrative mechanisms in "primitive" societies, a view of political authority as expressing a deep and collective political will and sovereignty. Gluckman writes on the hierarchically organized Zulu Kingdom with its powerful chiefs and aristocracy: "There-fore, despite the apparent autocracy of kings and chiefs, ultimately, sovereignty in the State resided in the people" (Gluckman 1940). In this tradition, the body of the king is identical to the body of the people, the body-politic, and "political behavior" hardly exists as a distinct practice. Schapera (1969) suggests that the influence of colonial administration and missionaries accorded more law-making authority to the chiefs and thus opened a rift between the force of the law, backed by the modern state, and the legitimacy of a more consensual custom/tradition. In a Melanesian context, Sahlins' distinction between the chief and the big man (Sahlins 1963) referred to the difference between societies hierarchically organized around a powerful chiefly or royal institution (see Valeri 1985, Thomas 1994) and the more unstable character of political authority in acephalous societies (see Sillitoe 1978, Godelier & Strathern 1991).

The second view of political authority sets it apart from the moral frameworks of ordinary life, either as chiefly or royal power. Although indebted to the countless examples of the mythical origin of kings in Frazer's *The Golden Bough* (Frazer 1959), Hocart's writings on kingship have exerted considerable, if not always acknowledged, influence on many anthropologists. Hocart was resolutely comparative, and often quite evolutionist, in his focus on the process of centralization of societies around the royal institution. He drew an analogy between human society and the evolution of the body. In lower forms of life, each unit of the body is relatively self-contained and independent, whereas mammals are incredibly centralized organisms where the head (and the brain) is the indispensable center of everything. In the place of segmentary organization of societies grows centralized and functionally specialized systems of rule and control. Thus, centralized and functionally specialized systems of rule and control supersede the segmentary organization of societies (Hocart 1936, pp. 38–39).

Drawing on examples from Fiji, South Asia, Africa, and Europe, Hocart's central propositions are that kingship originates in ritual; that kings are people endowed with, and entrusted with, special powers of symbolic representation and of moral transgression; and that kings carry the burden of impurities of a community in his body. The king is thus both divine and impure, and the realm of kingly behavior is constitutively different from that of his subjects. Kings are indispensable, both benevolent and dangerous (Hocart 1936). These insights have spawned debates on the differences between royal sovereignty and ritual purity in South Asia (e.g., Inden 1978, Raheja 1988, Dirks 1987, Quigley 1993); on notions of the generalized duality of royal power (Sahlins 1985, Scubla 2002); on the place of sacrifice and scapegoats in producing the sacred (Girard 1977); and on divine kingship, ritual murder, and the king as scapegoat (de Heusch 1982, Simonse 1991).

These two streams of work on political authority reflect two models of sovereignty—sovereignty as intrinsic to the community/people or as extrinsic—an alien and potentially threatening force that ensures renewal but also needs to be ritually domesticated. In philosophical terms, it corresponds to the distinction between Durkheim, Herder, and Rousseau on one side, and Hobbes, Hocart, and Schmitt on the other. Yet, matters are not so simple. Hobbes' famous idea of "the State of Warre" as the origin of sovereign power [Hobbes (1651) 1996] seems to be widely accepted in the anthropology of "primitive" or nonmodern kingship. This state of war is seen as an ongoing practice or tension that reproduces society, say among the Nuer or Zulus; an ever-present threat that has to be warded off through the labor of balance and ritual perfection in Bali (Geertz 1980); a potential that can be preempted through constant exchange and gift giving, as Sahlins (1974) pointed out in his perceptive essay on Mauss' *Essai sur le don*; or a memory of conquest and foundational violence that is ritually enacted as in Bloch's study of kingship in eighteenth-century Madagascar, a study that creatively attempts to combine the two mod-

els of sovereignty mentioned above (Bloch 1987).

Yet, for most anthropologists, it is imperative to show that a Hobbesian and Hegelian teleology of state formation does not apply to "primitive societies." A permanent state of war, or threat of war, may be a powerful impulse in consolidating and reproducing societies and the authority of kings, but these conditions necessarily produce neither a modern state nor a semblance of a covenant. The work of Clastres is particularly interesting in this respect. In his work on the Guayani in Paraguay, he rejects the evolutionist view that the many dispersed and highly mobile societies in the region have been unable to develop more complex forms of organization. These societies—organized as relatively egalitarian and acephalous bands of mobile warriors—were organized, argues Clastres (1989), in exactly such a way as to prevent them from ossifying and becoming settled and hierarchical structures. Permanent warfare and the constant elections and dismissals of war chiefs aimed to prevent any submission to the various forms of sovereign power that have existed in the region from pre-Columbian times to the contemporary state forms. In his efforts to reject a Euro-centric teleology of state formation and to account for such societies in their own terms, Clastres tended nonetheless to embrace Rousseau, another European thinker, and his idealization of the purity and equality of savage society (Clastres 1989 [1974]).

FROM KINGSHIP TO MODERN FORMS OF POWER

How useful has this substantial body of work on kingship been in subsequent work on what in the 1960s became known as "new states" in the postcolonial world? The answer is that it has been surprisingly absent, as if the conceptual gulf posited between the traditional and the modern became quite accurately applied to the distinction between colonizer and colonized, Western and Eastern/African, modern modalities of power versus traditional registers. In a recent meditation on how anthropology was forced to adjust itself and be more sensitive to history and to the new tumultuous world of postcolonial states and their polities, Geertz (2004) suggests that anthropologists have been so beholden to an idea of the homogenous nation-state as the essential form of modern power that they have failed to understand actual states "against the background of the sort of society in which it is embedded—the confusion that surrounds it, the confusion it confronts, the confusion it causes, the confusion it responds to" (p. 580). Geertz calls for an understanding of states and sovereignties as cultural constructs but not necessarily as entities whose nature and practices can be derived from, or reduced to, any cultural logic. To push the point further, it was historians and a few distinguished anthropologists of Latin America and the Caribbean (Wolf 1982, Mintz 1985) who, in their interrogation of colonial history, began to blur these distinctions and pointed toward a more complex and necessarily globally entangled history of the formation of states and sovereignties, as we discuss below.

There were some, if relatively rare, attempts to project "traditional" cultural logics of authority and sovereignty onto modern, postcolonial forms of state and political authority. Some of these studies have demonstrated that cultural holism and the concomitant assumptions about ideological cohesion and shared cultural meanings throughout a society—whether of a Boasian/Herderian or Durkheimian/Rousseauian provenance—are ineffective as analytical templates for analyzing modern societies and polities. For all its perceptive analysis of royal ritual and symbols, Combs-Schilling's (1989) work on Moroccan kingship has little to tell us about how royal sovereignty and ritual actually connects and combines with modern forms of governance in Morocco. Kapferer's (1988) attempt to explain ethnic conflict in Sri Lanka by projecting ideas of corporate religious identity onto entire groups, i.e., to equate the religious body of

Buddhism with the political body of the state, appear unduly totalizing and curiously insensitive to the intricacies of actual politics and modern government in the country (Kapferer 1988). Other attempts have been more felicitous, such as Apter on Nigeria (Apter 1992), Burghart on Nepal (Burghart 1990) and Anderson on Indonesia (Anderson 1990), but the work on premodern kingship has generally been sitting uncomfortably with much of the recent anthropology of nationalism, power, and the state.

The inability of anthropologists to understand "primitive societies" as historical formations is a main reason for this impasse, and the singular focus on symbolic forms and cohesion is another. However, a third reason has been a poor and undifferentiated understanding of the specificity of modern forms of power, and more particularly the forms of sovereignty that developed around the colonial encounter. Hutchinson's ethnography of the Nuer (Hutchinson 1996) is exemplary in its attention to the salient forces of war, weapons, and the presence of the state in contemporary Nuer life, and thus is an unusually well-crafted corrective to the rarefied timelessness in which much older anthropological work was set.

Much of anthropology has juxtaposed a thick description of the practices and symbolic forms of the exotic other and a thin, ahistorical, if not bland, symbolic representation of the West—as if, say, the nature of modern sovereignty could be understood through a reading of Hobbes. The result has been a formulaic reproduction of a distinction between a homogenized realm of modern/Western/capitalist concepts of power and government and another deep, rich, and heterogeneous realm of the traditional/primitive/uncolonized/authentic notions of power and agency. This work has been useful for rhetorical clarity but detrimental to a nuanced understanding of our contemporary world. Abeles' otherwise excellent analysis of Mitterand's presidential practices and performances through a prism of royal ritual aiming at symbolic integration of society is a relatively rare attempt to dissolve this analytical boundary. Abeles focuses exclusively on ritual form and myth created by and around Mitterrand to show that modern political forms, like traditional ones, are deeply infused with religious imagery and sentiment. Yet, Abeles has little to say about the forms of sovereign power and modern government—invested in the nation and the state—that made Mitterand's performance both possible and credible (Abeles 1988). In the absence of a conceptualization of the deep importance of spectacle and performance in modern politics (see for example Wedeen 1999), Abeles's analysis gets no further than pointing out an analogy.

The challenge seems to engage in a double movement: on the one hand to develop a deeper, more historically attuned and theoretically sophisticated understanding of the nature of modern sovereignty, including how it developed and morphed in the colonial encounter, and on the other hand, to chart and understand the de facto configurations of sovereignty both within and beyond the modern state and its constitutive idea of the rule of territory and people through a formal language of law, which by the mid-twentieth century had become the dominant horizon for political authority and imagination across the world.

Before engaging the question of colonial sovereignty, let us briefly sketch an outline of a stronger and more universal understanding of sovereignty, which we developed in more detail elsewhere (Hansen & Stepputat 2005). Let us summarize it in three theses:

1. The duality inherent in royal power and its promise to conjoin opposites—*celeritas* versus *gravitas* (Sahlins 1985), wild and fecund versus dry and contemplative (Bloch), or the natural and fallible body of the king versus the *corpus mysticum*, the transcendent body-politic (Kantorowicz 1957)—is also at the heart of modern sovereignty. Here it takes

the form of the tension between the sovereign in its ideal and transcendent form (nation, state, the people), which amounts to "empty places" that never can be fully represented (Lefort 1988), and their always transient and imperfect embodiment in a specific leader, party, movement, or institution. The essays in Bornemann's recent (2004) collection on the "the death of the father" all address the failure of embodiment of the national community in a supreme leader. Modern sovereign power has both sublime and profane dimensions, and both modern and premodern political communities have two bodies: a fully human included into political-cultural life, and another biological body, potentially stripped of dignity and desymbolized as "bare life" (Agamben).

2. The origin of sovereign power is the "state of exception"—the suspension of rules and conventions creating a conceptual and ethical zero-point from where the law, the norms, and the political order can be constituted. This exception can be legal (see Schmitt 1985 [1922]), ethical (Agamben 2005), a Hobbesian "State of Warre," or mythical origin of royalty. Yet, sovereign power is fundamentally premised on the capacity and the will to decide on life and death, the capacity to visit excessive violence on those declared enemies or on undesirables. Sovereignty is intrinsically linked to life as a biological force and to the body, either to the will to take life or to the willingness to disregard one's body and one's own life (Bataille 1991). The emaciated body of the hunger striker (Aretxaga 2001) or the blood of the jihadist martyr (Devji 2005) remains a powerful weapon in what Mbembe calls modern "necropolitics" (Mbembe 2003).

3. In spite of these fundamental continuities between archaic/premodern sovereignty and modern sovereignty,

the latter is marked by an unprecedented desire to become not merely a legal or symbolic reign but a comprehensive, effective, and totalizing form of detailed government of territories and their populations. Many of the disciplines of modern institutions, the technologies of government, and the technologies of the self characteristic of modern societies did indeed aim at creating an ostensibly depoliticized government in the name of scientific rationality and improvement of the life of citizens and populations (Burchell et al. 1991). These new bio-political regimes reconfigured rather than superseded sovereignty as a mode of power. Modern disciplines are driven by a powerful idea of defending, purifying, and protecting the new locus of sovereignty—society, the nation, the people, and/or the community—often defined in ethnic and racial terms (Foucault 2003). Modern techniques of government thus made possible much more exhaustive, ambitious, and effective forms of sovereignty, culminating in ethnic cleansing, in such systematic exterminations as the Holocaust, the invention of a new doctrine of mass extermination of populations in colonial wars (Hull 2005), in mass internments, mass incarcerations of "antisocial elements," etc. Whereas Jean Bodin in the sixteenth century advised monarchs to reserve the "marks of sovereignty" exclusively for themselves (Bodin 1992 [1588]), the regime of modern sovereignty and its mirror image, the sovereign community, have made bodily marks, pigmentation, language, and dress the markers that decide whether a person is included in the polis/community as a political body (Balibar 2002) or whether a body merely counts as biological life subjected to the whims of the executive.

COLONIAL POWER, GOVERNMENTALITY, AND MODERN SOVEREIGNTY

The colonial world was not a stage whereupon a fully formed cultural idea of "realist" Western sovereignty clashed with, and superseded, other forms of ritual or sacred sovereignty. The colonies became the site where European powers tested and developed their techniques of government. It was here that the notion of the natural sovereignty, and the right to rule, of the "civilized," Christian, white nations emerged over several centuries (Pagden 1995). The colonial world was therefore a twilight zone of multiple, indeterminate configurations of power and authority. It was in part a zone of exception and lawlessness (Thomson 1989), allowing for unrestrained violence and exploitation, in part a realm believed to be ruled by excessive despotism that at times was emulated in order to indigenize colonial rule (Cohn 1983, Apter 1999) and at other times that served as an imaginary canvas on which liberal arguments of the necessity of rights and the rule of law in the West could be made (Grosrichard 1998). This peculiar articulation of different registers of sovereign power in the colonial world is fundamentally important to any understanding of the character of postcolonial states and political formations in postcolonial societies.

Colonial domination developed slowly, tentatively, and unevenly. Most of the early colonial enterprises in Asia and Africa were from the outset in the hands of private trading companies, privateers, and semiofficial armies and naval forces. Although acting in accordance with a royal charter, or in the name of their sovereign, they were in reality forces in their own right. Accountability, risk taking, and also the prudence of military actions and civil administration by these companies were often hotly debated in Britain and the Netherlands in the eighteenth century (see Sen 2002). At the center of these debates was the question of which standards of government and punishment should apply to the colonial world: those of "civilized men" or those of the native rulers? The colony constituted a zone of exception in a double sense: both as not being directly under the sovereign power of the Crown or the republic and as being "beyond the pale," an alien world whose populations were not accorded full humanity or membership of a community of civilized men entitled to *habeas corpus* and other rights of the subjects of European powers. As a result, colonial sovereignty was generally marked by an excess of violence and much harsher forms of punishment than were administered in the European world at the time (for a general argument along these lines, see Arendt 1968; for South Asia, see Chandavarkar 1998, Hussain 2003).

In India, for example, the local jurisprudence and forms of punishment administered by local princes and courts were generally seen as both ineffective and inconsistent (Cohn 1983). The East India Company decided to erect public gallows and open new prisons across the colony. The frequent use of capital punishment intended to create an all-important aura of fortitude and rigor that remained a cornerstone of British rule in India in the nineteenth and twentieth centuries. The protracted campaigns against the infamous Thuggees in central India in the 1840s were indeed part of a general effort at disarmament of Indian society. But they also had performative functions designed to demonstrate the British ability and will to both rule and reform with a firm hand (van Woerkens 2002). Similar considerations applied to colonial Malaya where the native Islamic courts were seen as too inconsistent to provide a coherent structure of justice and civil order. Only after a thorough reconstruction and codification that introduced more rigorous punishments were these local courts allowed to play an integral, if minor, role in the overall administration of justice in Malaya (Peletz 2002). Similar rationalizations took place with the formation of personal law codes across India. Codification and systematization of local jurisprudence subsequently became the cornerstone of the institutionalization of legal pluralism in most of colonial Africa in the twentieth century (Moore 1978, Gluckman 1965, Chanock 1998).

In the Dutch Indies and in French Indochina, colonial governments were faced with an ever-growing population of "mixed race." Causing not merely a problem of classification and appropriateness, these populations were regarded as a potential threat to the moral cohesion of the Dutch and French settlers. Those in power also feared that the mixing of races undermined the stature and prestige of the colonial masters in the eyes of the natives. The systematic encouragement of emigration of white women to the colonial world at the end of the nineteenth century aimed at strengthening the racial community of colonists which, in tune with the dominance of scientific racism at the time, was seen as the very basis of colonial sovereignty (Stoler 2002).

Until the end of the nineteenth century, colonial enterprises in Africa were mainly of a simple and extractive nature, first based on the slave trade and later on extraction of minerals and timber. As in Asia, but employing much more random and excessive violence, these enterprises were mainly private and only loosely associated with European states through royal charters (Coquery-Vidrovitch 1977, Sen 1998). This "private indirect government" (Mbembe 2001) operated in what, in every sense of the word, was a state of exception—in areas outside the control of any state and using methods and levels of violence that would have been unacceptable in most others parts of the world. If Leopold's Congo is the most widely known example (Ewans 2002), the massacres at Maji-Maji and the crushing of the Herero revolt in South West Africa and the massacres in Rhodesia in 1899 are other cases in point. The slave trade was sanctioned and encouraged by European states, but the actual operations were run almost entirely by private companies. These companies operated with near-complete impunity, attacking some existing states and kingdoms on the Atlantic coast, collaborating with others, and in the process transforming these states into predatory slave economies wreaking terror and disorder upon populations deep into the interior (Meillassoux 1991). As has been characteristic of state formation in much of the world, these entrepots, privateers, and maverick entrepreneurs became included into the colonial states or became their enemies as bandits or pirates, when these began to firm up in the latter half of the nineteenth century (Gallant 1999). Similar oscillation between inclusion and assertion of autonomy applied to many of the mission stations across Africa. While spearheading a civilizing mission and thus supporting the overall goals of colonial rule, missions in outlying areas were very often in conflict with the colonial administration over issues of punishment and harsh rule of their flocks (Comaroff & Comaroff 1991).

Even as modern forms of government were imported and implemented in the colonial territories, their effects were always uneven and extraordinarily dispersed. Many different forms of sovereignty coexisted within the colonial territories. The colonies were never governed as intensely and with the same devotion to registering and monitoring its subjects as was the case in Europe—not even in settler colonies such as Kenya and South Africa. Substantial parts of the colonized populations lived under native rule—chiefs, rajas, local regents—which enforced brutal labor and penal regimes under the supervision of the colonial state. In much of Africa, a major part of the rural population lived under such regimes (Mamdani 1996); in India, about one-third of the territory and population in the subcontinent lived under indirect rule until 1947, and in Malaya, most of the rural Malay population was governed by the Malay aristocracy throughout the colonial period.

Agamben's interventions have forced many social scientists to rethink generally the relationship between sovereignty and the disciplinary modalities of power explored by Foucault (for a good discussion of this, see Cohen 2004, Das & Poole 2004). Sovereign power exists in modern states alongside, and intertwined with, bio-political rationalities aiming at reproducing lives and societies as an ever-present possibility of losing one's citizenship and rights and becoming reduced to a purely biological form. This insight is even more pertinent and important in the colonial and postcolonial world where bio-political rationalities were always predominantly configured around maintaining public order and governing communities and collectivities rather than individual subjects. Although the deployment of a Foucauldian optic in the analysis of colonial rule has produced major insights (Chatterjee 1993, Mitchell 2002), it is obvious that however interesting and compelling it is to explore the mentalities and blueprints of colonial officials, such analysis tells us relatively little about how government and sovereign power was configured in practice and in everyday life. Colonial states were indeed "ethnographic states" that employed scientific data collection and categorization to generate a governable reality amenable to interventions, as Dirks noted in the context of India (Dirks 2001) and Chaikov noted in his analysis of both the imperial and Soviet paradigms of knowledge and rule in Siberia (Ssorin-Chaikov 2003).

These designs and intentions should not blind us, however, to the fact that the reach and efficacy of colonial states was uneven and often severely limited. This limitation was especially true of border areas in which local elites and freebooters often enjoyed effective autonomy (Nugent 1999, Sivaramakrishnan 1999). The incompleteness, tentativeness, and fragmented nature of colonial states and the excessive forms of violence they frequently visited on their subject populations have structured postcolonial states in profound ways. A fast-growing literature on the culture of different postcolonial states seeks to historicize specific states, to set them in their wider context, and to get beyond universalist notions of state functions. Many of these studies have sought to conceptualize and document the consequences of sovereignty moving away from being rhetorically invested in the state and the law to being invested in new entities in the postcolonial situation—the nation, the people, "society" as such, the national economy (see for instance, Coronil 1997, Fuller & Benei 2000, Tarlo 2003, Goswami 2004). Other works have attempted in creative ways to shed light on how both elite and popular ontologies of power—as something hidden, magical, fetishised, realist, or ultimately violent—intersected and clashed in everyday encounters between the postcolonial state, its subjects, and other sovereign powers (Siegel 1997, Taussig 1997, Navaro-Yashin 2002).

The fetishization of sovereign power is by no means limited to societies beyond the West, however. This was forcefully noted by the exiled German philosopher Ernst Cassirer in his critique of Nazism (Cassirer 1946) and explored anthropologically in a range of recent publications (Verdery 1999, Meyer & Pels 2003). The historically complex and often unsettled configurations of sovereignty in many postcolonial societies—and we include Latin America in this category—have given rise to a complex range of informal sovereignties. The tentative rule and local despotisms of these forces often structure the lives of ordinary people more profoundly and effectively than does the distant and far-from-panoptic gaze of the state. We turn now to this body of work.

BENEATH THE PANOPTIC GAZE: INFORMAL SOVEREIGNS AND OTHER OPAQUE POWERS

As Durkheim (1933) noted, the production of state authority, and the law as an expression of its sovereignty, is dependent on the production of an unlawful underside of the state. Thus, a murky, secretive underworld of pirates, bandits, criminals, smugglers, youth gangs, drug lords, warlords, Mafiosi, traitors, terrorists, *en fin* of outlaws and liminal figures seems to persist and mutate despite state laws and powerful institutions entrusted with the

responsibility of eliminating them. The persistence of this underworld is true of highly developed and powerful states and even more pronounced in much of the postcolonial world in which multiple and segmented sovereignties was always the reality for large sections of the population.

Anthropologists have increasingly insisted that this underworld and its shadow networks cannot be understood without reference to their specific relations to states and hegemonic discourses of social order (e.g., Nordstrom 2000, Parnell & Kane 2003). They have described how illegal organizations often work with the "studied ignorance or tacit consent" of the authorities (Schneider & Schneider 1999), how state officials receive bribes in their "dirty togetherness" with criminals, or how they have vested interest in upholding zones of exception where illegal groups operate with impunity. State institutions may even forge "unruly coalitions" (Verdery 1996) with illegal groups that control territories or populations where the state does not have the capacity or will to exercise its sovereignty. In an attempt to characterize the wide range of illegal/state relations, Smart (1999) talked of a "continuum of persistence" of illegality, ranging from tranquil conviviality to open challenges of state sovereignty.

Historically we find examples of informal sovereignties at agricultural, highland, and sea frontiers where "military entrepreneurs" operated in a highly ambiguous relationship with states in the making, such as the Lords of the Marches in Lebanon (Gilsenan 1996), mestizo settlers at the Northern Mexican frontier (Alonso 1994), or *gamonales* at the highland frontiers in Peru (Poole 2004). From a world-system perspective, Gallant (1999) argues that the phenomenon is associated with primitive accumulation and the extension and intensification of markets, with armed groups and individuals sometimes assisting and sometimes resisting central state authorities. Poole (2004) insists that the gamonales cannot be interpreted as autonomous sovereigns operating in and of themselves beyond the reach of the state. They helped, represented, and abused people in their area of influence while also representing the state and the law, as well as the transgression of law. Thus, they personified the two sides of state making: the law and the violence on which it rests, employing both the "law making" and the "law preserving" violence, to use Benjamin's (1978) famous distinction.

Turning to the issue of informal sovereignty in the present, we find that the use of illegal and often violent practices by local strongmen, staunch bureaucrats, vivid politicians, businessmen or vigilantes is widespread. As they operate with impunity within their "jurisdictions" they become a law unto themselves, in a sense representing a legacy of colonial indirect government. The question is what the sources and attributes of informal sovereignty are, and whether such practices may be meaningfully characterized as sovereign practices being exercised within, beside, or against formally sovereign states?

Hobsbawm's (1969) social bandits constitute a celebrated ideal type of outlaws who base their quasi-legitimate rule on the perceptions of state law as being unenforced or immoral, unjust, arbitrary or in other ways out of tune with reality. In some aspects, Mafiosi, gangs and, other "violent entrepreneurs" (Blok 1974) have fulfilled vital state functions such as the provision of security, credits, and conflict mediation. In postcolonial and postsocialist states, arbitrary laws and bureaucratic procedures that increase unnecessarily the transaction costs of exchange and production have served to explain the extension of protection rackets and criminal organizations that control, but also enable the working of transport systems, trade, and other sectors using patronage and predatory practices. However, as Schneider & Schneider (1999) warned us, this functionalist view comes very close to the self-perceptions of these predatory organizations.

While effectively challenging the state's monopoly of violence, these organizations are engaging in sovereign practices themselves, as argued for example by Humphrey (2004) in her analysis of transport entrepreneurs in postsocialist Ulan-Ude. Drawing heavily on Agamben's insights, she identifies "localized forms of sovereignty" that are "nested" within "higher sovereignties" but nevertheless "retain a domain within which control over life and death is operational" (p. 420). In the early 1990s mafia-like organizations took over control of transportation after a period of violent accumulation and boundary marking, but the structure stabilized and gave room for "ways of life" of taxi entrepreneurs. As long as they paid their tributes to the organization they could even experience a certain "*joie de vivre*" (p. 434). However, they do not have rights within the system and risk being excluded or just abandoned without access to urban survival. As the system works, its dynamics are generated more by the rationales of the way of life and the fear of abandonment than by the fear of violent repression and exclusion.

Similar fragmented systems of authority are found all over the postcolonial world where local strongmen occupy strategic positions between state institutions and the population. One such example is found in metropolitan squatter areas and slum cities, where proper land titling never has been undertaken and where access to entitlements is contingent on having a well-connected patron who can channel claims and applications (e.g., Parnell 2003). In many cases, such local slumlords, strongmen, and quasi-legal networks have been de facto sovereigns from colonial times. They have at times been tamed and incorporated into governmental structures and have at other times been nodes of opposition to the state (Adelkhah 2000, Hansen 2001, Plissart & de Boeck 2006).

Such persons command discretionary powers deciding when to punish illegalities and when to make the customary exception from the law. The figure of the criminal is often faceless or assumes a spectral and yet enormously powerful form as reported by

Siegel (1998) from Jakarta. In other cases, the criminal figure can be well known and highly visible, operating between the zones of illegality and legality, deploying rumors of his violent past or connections to powerful and hidden underworld forces to style himself as a heroic protector of communities and common people. Not only are such figures central to the regulation and adjudication of everyday life, but police departments, civic administrations, and political parties must also rely on them to govern and regulate life in slums and popular neighborhoods (Hansen 2005).

The interpretation of de facto sovereignty as being related to the exercise of violence with impunity resonates with numerous ethnographic descriptions of ruthless men (seldom women) of force, particular individuals or groups with the reputation of being unpredictably, arbitrarily, and excessively violent. As Gilsenan (1996) notes, "at the extreme such men were said to show a sovereign pleasure in violating others by deed or word arbitrarily, gratuitously, 'just like that' without any reason but their own personal will and pleasure" (pp. xi–xii). The apparently immanent attributes of such individuals, Gilsenan argues, were crucial and personalized elements of people's experience of power at the Lebanese frontier. The narratives of these men's force and violence depicted the foundational violence of the current social order and contributed to the constitution of social relations of contest and domination.

Such narratives of ruthless and violent individuals and organizations develop around key performances of sacrifice or heroism at the expense of "savages" or outcasts at the frontiers, the violent suppression of rivals, or the depuration of traitors from within the political or moral community in question (McCoy 1999, Jensen 2005). Similar to nationalist narratives, they may be analyzed as constitutive of solidarity and identity in the Durkheimian vein or as being nurtured by the anxieties of contamination, impurity, and blurred identities (Appadurai 1998).

Another strand of analysis focuses on the role of secrecy and magic in narratives of invincibility and unrestrained "wild" power. Leaders have often been associated with ambiguous, occult forces that may harm as well as benefit others (e.g., West 2005), but the mastery of occult forces is seen as not only reinforcing but also subverting existing power structures (Geschiere 1997). Thus, guerrilla forces in Zimbabwe, Sierra Leone, and Liberia were seen as having access to the power of spirits (Lan 1985, Richards 1996, Ellis 1999); today, vigilantes in Nigeria are described in popular discourse as magically empowered superheroes who can mobilize symbolic registers of the unknown and supernatural (Smith 2004); in Caracas the spirits of renown dead criminals are seen to posses the bodies of the living in a spirit cult (Ferrandiz 2004); and as Taussig (1991) famously showed in the case of the rubber economy at the Putomayo River, narratives of the supernatural powers of the Indians inspired acts of excessive violence in the "space of terror" mirroring and appropriating these powers for the men at the frontier.

As commonly noted, imaginations of occult forces seem to be particularly salient in contexts of rapid change in which power relations are unclear or incomprehensible, such as the current phase of globalization and modernization (Comaroff & Comaroff 1999). Whereas these forces lie beyond the jurisdiction and powers of state institutions, communal or popular bodies engaging in everyday policing—by default or through outsourcing arrangements—will often have to deal with rumors of witchcraft and sorcery.

Particularly in postcolonial or postsocialist states, we find the phenomenon of "nested" or "outsourced" (Buur 2005) sovereignty. Whether the effect of an inherently limited capacity for law enforcement or the conscious definition of zones and times of exception where state law is suspended for practical purposes, we find state officials or their substitutes engaging in de facto exercise of sovereign practices in the interstices of laws and formal procedures, between the real and the legal. "Free-fire zones" or "zones of transgression," for example, are found at international borders and metropolitan areas where paramilitary groups or semiprivate death squads engage in cleansing operations beyond formal accountability (Scheper-Hughes 1992). As several authors suggest, the excessively violent practices commonly used in authoritarian states such as Brazil and Nigeria are being reproduced by vigilantes and clandestine security organizations in formally democratic states (Linger 2003).

The past decade of simultaneous state decay and democratic reforms of security and justice sectors in the wake of armed conflicts in some areas has turned the attention of anthropologists toward issues of everyday security, community policing, communal and popular justice, and private security companies (e.g., Ruteere & Pommerolle 2003, Gore & Pratten 2003, Buur & Jensen 2004). Studies suggest a wide range of relationships from tight control and regulation to complete autonomy that goes much beyond a simple state-society divide. Furthermore we may see the outsourcing of everyday policing less as a sign of weakness of the state than as a way of incorporating segments and zones where state sovereignty never was effective, and where low-cost forms of policing poor neighborhoods are developed. But the new (or rather re-emerging) policies of outsourcing sovereignty are also a sign of the increasing importance of market forces in regard to practices of informal as well as formal sovereignty.

CONCESSIONS, FIRMS, AND THE SOVEREIGNTY OF THE MARKET

The trading company, the concession, and the royal charter were the main vehicles for early colonial expansion. Later, privately owned enterprises were of equal importance in the consolidation and administration of the colonies. In the Caribbean, the planter soon emerged as the preeminent symbol and daily adminis-

trator of colonial economy and terror. On the plantations and estates from the Caribbean to Sri Lanka, Fiji, and Malaya, the planter was the crucial node in the colonial administration: the sovereign of his land who either literally owned the bodies of his labor force or held workers in such tight control and wielded such influence in the colony that colonial officials rarely found it opportune, neither politically nor economically, to intervene or to protect slaves or indentured laborers (Mintz 1989).

This de facto outsourcing of colonial sovereignty had deep and enduring effects in areas dominated by European settlers or plantation economies. Populations were kept separated along ethnic and racial lines, and economic power continued to be held by very small elites controlling vast tracts of land and vast pools of labor. This historical predicament laid the ground for a range of different conflicts—from violent oppression in Haiti (Trouillot 1995) to the isolation and vulnerability of the "estate Tamils" in Sri Lanka (see Daniel 1996) and the deep racial and cultural divides of present day Fiji (Kelly & Kaplan 2001), to mention a few examples.

The emergence of "special economic zones" devoted to labor-intensive production or tourism across Asia in the 1970s and 1980s represented in some ways a return of the concession in a new form, and an outsourcing, or maybe "grading," of sovereignty (Ong 1999). The difference was, however, that these zones and their interaction with the rest of society were often controlled rather effectively by the states in which they were located. Some states, particularly in Africa, were unable to control mining, oil, and timber companies, and the proliferating development and NGO sector, mainly because many states were already parceled out and their resources effectively privatized by military elites and leading members of the political elite (Bayart et al. 1999). In Zimbabwe, the theme of sovereignty has dominated campaigns against white settlers seen as alien and exploitative and as remnants of the colonial regime. The plundering of the state by the political elite and the takeover of private white-owned farms by war veterans and youth brigades still loyal to Mugabe have explicitly been organized as assertions of popular sovereignty—the protection and communal retaking of the ancestral land from the private control of the settlers (Worby 2003, Moore 2005).

Because the nation-state is no longer the privileged locus of sovereignty—always doubtful in much of the postcolonial world—sovereignties are found in multiple and layered forms around the world. Outsourcing of vital infrastructural services and security operations to major corporations, and an almost-religious belief in the self-regulating forces of the market, is at the heart of America's new imperial adventures in Afghanistan, Iraq, and elsewhere (Harvey 2005). In the age of the great concessions Western rulers believed that military and trading entrepreneurs would ultimately serve the interests and consolidate the sovereignty of the king or state that had certified and encouraged their pursuit of private accumulation. Similarly, today substantial tasks—from protecting the Green Zone in Baghdad to overseeing the rebuilding of the Iraqi infrastructure—are outsourced to companies based in the United States or in "friendly" nations (Klein 2004). Across the world, major development projects funded by developed nations in the West and in East Asia are operated and implemented by private contractors and NGOs, often with multinational personnel, on behalf of sovereign nation states. International agencies are tied into coordinating mechanisms and contracts with military agencies and private contractors in a rapidly developing "security-development network" (Duffield 2001).

Whereas sovereign power has always depended on the capacity for deployment of decisive force, it seems that the control over territory and bodies that marked the nation-state model of sovereignty is now supplemented by a powerful drive to control the "legal contract"—the modern-day concession that empowers private companies to carry out state functions. It echoes Sassen's (1996) suggestion that the most decisive form of citizenship within states, and internationally, now belongs to firms and market forces, rather than to individuals or groups of citizens. This emerging and complex configuration of sovereignties calls not only for historical analogies but also for new anthropological studies and critical reflection on how the circulation of capital, that ubiquitous fiction we call "the market," is an evermore powerful sovereign force: magical and redemptive (Comaroff & Comaroff 2000) but also unpredictable and pitiless in its punishment of those who fail to perform or those who fall behind.

LITERATURE CITED

Abeles M. 1988. Modern political ritual. *Curr. Anthropol.* 29:391–404

Adelkhah F. 2000. *Being Modern in Iran*. New York: Columbia Univ. Press

Agamben G. 1998. *Homo Sacer: Sovereign Power and Bare Life*. Stanford, CA: Stanford Univ. Press

Agamben G. 2005. *State of Exception*. Chicago: Univ. Chicago Press

Alonso A. 1994. *Thread of Blood: Colonialism, Revolution, and Gender on Mexico's Northern Frontier*. Tucson: Univ. Ariz. Press

Anderson B. 1990. *Language and Power. Exploring Political Cultures in Indonesia*. Ithaca, NY: Cornell Univ. Press

Appadurai A. 1998. Dead certainty: ethnic violence in the era of globalization. *Dev. Change* 29:905–25

Apter A. 1992. *Black Critics and Kings: The Hermeneutics of Power in Yoruba Society*. Chicago: Univ. Chicago Press

Apter A. 1999. The subvention of tradition. A genealogy of the Nigerian durbar. In *State/Culture: State Formation after the Cultural Turn*, ed. G Steinmetz, pp. 213–52. Ann Arbor: Univ. Mich. Press

Arendt H. 1968. *The Origins of Totalitarianism*. New York: Harvest

Aretxaga B. 2001. *Shattering Silence*. Princeton, NJ: Princeton Univ. Press

Ashforth A. 2005. *Witchcraft, Violence and Democracy in South Africa*. Chicago: Univ. Chicago Press

Balibar E. 2002. *We, the People of Europe? Reflections on Transnational Citizenship*. Princeton, NJ: Princeton Univ. Press

Barth F. 1959. *Political Leadership among Swat Pathans*. London: Althone

Bataille G. 1991. (1970–1988). *The Accursed Share*. Vols. II and III. New York: Zone

Bayart J, Ellis S, Hibou B. 1999. *The Criminalization of the State in Africa*. Oxford, UK: Currey

Benjamin W. 1978. *Reflections: Essays, Aphorisms, Autobiographical Writings*. New York: Schocken

Bloch M. 1987. The ritual of the royal bath in Madagascar: the dissolution of death, birth and fertility into authority. In *Rituals of Royalty: Power and Ceremonial in Traditional Societies*, ed. D Cannadine, S Price, pp. 271–97. Cambridge, UK: Cambridge Univ. Press

Blok A. 1974. *The Mafia of a Sicilian Village, 1860–1960: A Study of Violent Peasant Entrepreneurs*. New York: Harper and Row

Bodin J. 1992. *On Sovereignty: Four Chapters from the Six Books on Commonwealth*. Cambridge, UK: Cambridge Univ. Press

Borneman J, ed. 2004. *The Death of the Father: An Anthropology of the End of Political Authority*. Oxford, UK: Berghahn

Burchell G, Gordon C, Miller P, eds. 1991. *The Foucault Effect: Studies in Governmentality*. Chicago: Univ. Chicago Press

Burghart R. 1990. *The Condition of Listening: Essays on Religion, History and Politics in South Asia*. New York: Oxford Univ. Press

Buur L. 2005. The sovereign outsourced: local justice and violence in Port Elizabeth. See Hansen & Stepputat 2005, pp. 192–217

Buur L, Jensen S. 2004. Introduction: vigilantism and the policing of everyday life in South Africa. *Afr. Stud.* 63:139–52

Cassirer E. 1946. *The Myth of the State*. Garden City, NY: Doubleday

Chandavarkar R. 1998. *Imperial Power and Popular Politics*. Cambridge, UK: Cambridge Univ. Press

Chanock M. 1998. *Law, Custom and Social Order: The Colonial Experience in Malawi and Zambia*. London: Heinemann

Chatterjee P. 1993. *The Nation and its Fragments: Colonial and Postcolonial Histories*. Princeton, NJ: Princeton Univ. Press

Clastres P. 1989 [1974]. *Society Against the State*. New York: Zone

Cohen L. 2004. Operability: surgery at the margin of the state. See Das & Poole 2004, pp. 165–90

Cohn B. 1983. Representing authority in Victorian India. In *The Invention of Tradition*, ed. E Hobsbawm, T Ranger, pp. 165–209. Cambridge, UK: Cambridge Univ. Press

Cohn B. 1987. *An Anthropologist among the Historians and Other Essays*. New Delhi: Oxford Univ. Press

Comaroff J. 1997. Contests of conscience: models of colonial domination in South Africa. In *Tensions of Empire*, ed. F Cooper, A Stoler, pp. 163–97. Berkeley: Univ. Calif. Press

Comaroff J, Comaroff J. 1991. *Of Revelation and Revolution*. Vol. I. Chicago: Chicago Univ. Press

Comaroff J, Comaroff J. 1999. Occult economies and the violence of abstraction. Notes from the South African postcolony. *Am. Ethnol.* 26:279–303

Comaroff J, Comaroff J. 2000. Millennial capitalism: first thoughts on a second coming. *Publ. Cult.* 12:291–343

Combs-Schilling M. 1989. *Sacred Performances: Islam, Sexuality and Sacrifice.* New York: Columbia Univ. Press

Coquery-Vidrovitch C. 1977. *Le Congo au Temps des Grandes Compagnies Concessionaires, 1898–1930.* Paris: Mouton

Coronil F. 1997. *The Magical State. Nature, Money, and Modernity in Venezuela.* Chicago: Chicago Univ. Press

Daniel EV. 1996. *Charred Lullabies: Chapters in an Anthropology of Violence.* Princeton, NJ: Princeton Univ. Press

Das V, Poole D, eds. 2004. *Anthropology in the Margins of the State.* Santa Fe: Sch. Am. Res. Press

de Heusch L. 1982. *The Drunken King or The Origin of the State.* Bloomington: Indiana Univ. Press

Deleuze G, Guattari F. 1987 [1980]. *A Thousand Plateaus: Capitalism and Schizophrenia.* Minneapolis: Univ. Minn. Press

Devji F. 2005. *Landscapes of the Jihad: Militancy, Morality, Modernity.* London: Hurst

Dirks N. 1987. *The Hollow Crown. Ethno-History of an Indian Kingdom.* Ann Arbor: Univ. Mich. Press

Dirks N. 2001. *Castes of Mind: Colonialism and the Making of Modern India.* New Delhi: Permanent Black

Duffield M. 2001. *Global Governance and the New Wars.* London: Zed

Durkheim E. 1933 [1893]. *The Division of Labor in Society.* New York: Free

Ellis S. 1999. *The Mask of Anarchy. The Destruction of Liberia and the Religious Dimension of an African Civil War.* London: Hurst

Evans-Pritchard EE. 1969 [1940]. *The Nuer: A Description of the Modes of Livelihood and Political Institutions of a Nilotic People.* New York: Oxford Univ. Press

Evans-Pritchard EE, Fortes M, eds. 1940. *African Political Systems.* Oxford, UK: Oxford Univ. Press

Ewans M. 2002. *European Atrocity, African Catastrophe: Leopold II, the Congo Free State and Its Aftermath.* London: Routledge

Ferrandiz F. 2004. The body as wound: possession, malandros and everyday violence in Venezuela. *Crit. Anthropol.* 24:107–33

Fiskesjö M. 2003. *The Thanksgiving Turkey Pardon, the Death of Teddy's Bear, and the Sovereign Exception of Guantánamo.* Chicago: Prickly Paradigm

Fortes M. 1945. *The Dynamics of Clanship among the Tallensi.* London: Oxford Univ. Press

Foucault M. 1980. *Power/Knowledge.* New York: Pantheon

Foucault M. 2003 [1997]. *"Society Must Be Defended": Lectures at the College de France, 1975–1976.* New York: Picador

Frazer JG. 1959. *The New Golden Bough: A New Abridgement of the Classic Work.* New York: SG Phillips

Fuller C, Benei V, eds. 2000. *The Everyday State and Society in Modern India.* London: Hurst

Gallant TW. 1999. Brigandage, piracy, capitalism, and state-formation: transnational crime from a historical world-systems perspective. See Heyman 1999b, pp. 25–62

Geertz C. 1980. *Negara: The Theatre State in Nineteenth Century Bali.* Princeton, NJ: Princeton Univ. Press

Geertz C. 2004. What is a state if it is not a sovereign? Reflections on politics in complicated places. *Curr. Anthropol.* 45:577–86

Geschiere P. 1997. *Modernity and Witchcraft: Politics and the Occult in Postcolonial Africa*. Charlottesville: Univ. Va. Press

Gilsenan M. 1996. *Lords of the Lebanese Marches: Violence and Narrative in an Arab Society*. London: I.B.Tauris

Girard R. 1977. *Violence and the Sacred*. Baltimore, MD: Johns Hopkins Univ. Press

Gluckman M. 1940. The kingdom of the Zulu of South Africa. In *African Political Systems*, ed. M Fortes, EE Evans-Pritchard, pp. 25–55. Oxford, UK: Oxford Univ. Press

Gluckman M. 1965. *The Ideas in Barotse Jurisprudence*. New Haven, CT: Yale Univ. Press

Godelier M, Strathern M, eds. 1991. *Big Men and Great Men: Personifications of Power in Melanesia*. Cambridge, UK: Cambridge Univ. Press

Gore C, Pratten D. 2003. The politics of plunder: the rhetorics of order and disorder in Southern Nigeria. *Afr. Aff.* 102:211–40

Goswami M. 2004. *Producing India. From Colonial Economy to National Space*. Chicago: Chicago Univ. Press

Grosrichard A. 1998. *The Sultan's Court. European Fantasies of the East*. London: Verso

Gulliver P. 1963. *Social Control in an African Society*. Boston: Boston Univ. Press

Hansen T. 2005. Sovereigns beyond the state: on legality and authority in Urban India. See Hansen & Stepputat 2005, pp. 169–91

Hansen T, Stepputat F, eds. 2005. *Sovereign Bodies. Citizens, Migrants and States in the Postcolonial World*. Princeton, NJ: Princeton Univ. Press

Hansen TB. 2001. *Wages of Violence: Naming and Identity in Postcolonial Bombay*. Princeton, NJ: Princeton Univ. Press

Hansen TB, Stepputat F, eds. 2001. *States of Imagination: Ethnographic Explorations of the Postcolonial State*. Durham, NC: Duke Univ. Press

Harvey D. 2005. *The New Imperialism*. New York: Oxford Univ. Press

Heyman J. 1999a. State escalation of force: a Vietnam/US-Mexico border analogy. See Heyman 1999b, pp. 285–314

Heyman J, ed. 1999b. *States and Illegal Practices*. Oxford: Berg

Hindess B. 2005. Citizenship and empire. See Hansen & Stepputat 2005, pp. 241–56

Hobbes T. 1996[1651]. *Leviathan*. Cambridge, UK: Cambridge Univ. Press

Hobsbawm E. 1969. *Bandits*. London: Weidenfeld & Nicholson

Hocart A. 1936. *Kings and Councillors*. Chicago: Univ. Chicago Press

Hull I. 2005. *Absolute Destruction: Military Culture and the Practices of War in Imperial Germany*. Ithaca, NY: Cornell Univ. Press

Humphrey C. 2004. Sovereignty. In *A Companion to the Anthropology of Politics*, ed. D Nugent, J Vincent, pp. 418–36. Oxford: Blackwell

Hussain N. 2003. *The Jurisprudence of Emergency. Colonialism and the Rule of Law*. Ann Arbor: Univ. Mich. Press

Hutchinson S. 1996. *Nuer Dilemmas. Coping with Money, War and the State*. Berkeley: Univ. Calif. Press

Inden R. 1978. Ritual, authority, and cyclic time in Hindu kingship. In *Kingship and Authority in South Asia*, ed. J Richards, pp. 41–91. Madison: Univ. Wisc. Press

Jensen S. 2005. Above the law: practices of sovereignty in Surrey Estate, Cape Town. See Hansen & Stepputat 2005, pp. 218–38

Kantorowicz E. 1957. *King's Two Bodies; a Study in Medieval Political Theology*. Princeton, NJ: Princeton Univ. Press

Kapferer B. 1988. *Legends of People, Myths of State: Violence, Intolerance and Political Culture in Sri Lanka and Australia.* Washington, DC: Smithson. Inst. Press

Kelly J, Kaplan M. 2001. *Represented Communities: Fiji and World Decolonization.* Chicago: Univ. Chicago Press

Klein N. 2004. Baghdad year zero. *Harper's.* **http://www.harpers.org/BaghdadYearZero.html**

Lan D. 1985. *Guns and Rain. Guerillas and Spirit Mediums in Zimbabwe.* London: Currey

Lefort C. 1988. *Democracy and Political Theory.* Cambridge, UK: Polity Press

Linger D. 2003. Wild power in postmilitary Brazil. In *Crime's Power. Anthropologists and the Ethnography of Crime*, ed. P Parnell, S Kane, pp. 99–124. New York: Palgrave Macmillan

Mamdani M. 1996. *Citizen and Subject: Contemporary Africa and the Legacy of Late Colonialism.* Princeton, NJ: Princeton Univ. Press

Mbembe A. 2001. *On the Postcolony.* Berkeley: Univ. Calif. Press

Mbembe A. 2003. Necropolitics. *Publ. Cult.* 15:11–40

McCoy A. 1999. Requiem for a drug lord: state and commodity in the life of Khun Sa. See Heyman 1999b, pp. 129–68

Meillassoux C. 1991. *The Anthropology of Slavery: The Womb of Iron and Gold.* London: Athlone

Meyer B, Pels P, eds. 2003. *Magic and Modernity. Interfaces of Revelation and Concealment.* Stanford, CA: Stanford Univ. Press

Mintz S. 1986 [1985]. *Sweetness and Power: The Place of Sugar in Modern History.* New York: Penguin

Mintz S. 1989. *Caribbean Transformations.* New York: Columbia Univ. Press

Mitchell T. 2002. *Rule of Experts: Egypt, Techno-Politics, Modernity.* Berkeley: Univ. Calif. Press

Moore D. 2005. *Suffering for Territory: Race, Place and Power in Zimbabwe.* Durham, NC: Duke Univ. Press

Moore SF. 1978. *Law as Process. An Anthropological Approach.* London: Routledge and Kegan Paul

Navaro-Yashin Y. 2002. *Faces of the State: Secularism and Public Life in Turkey.* Princeton, NJ: Princeton Univ. Press

Nordstrom C. 2000. Shadows and Sovereigns. *Theory Cult. Soc.* 17:35–54

Nugent D. 1999. State and shadow state in Northern Peru circa 1900: illegal political networks and the problem of state boundaries. See Heyman 1999b, pp. 63–98

Ong A. 1999. *Flexible Citizenship: The Cultural Logic of Transnationality.* Durham, NC: Duke Univ. Press

Pagden A. 1995. *Lords of All the World. Ideologies of Empire in Spain, Britain and France c. 1500–1800.* New Haven, CT: Yale Univ. Press

Parnell P. 2003. Criminalizing colonialism: democracy meets law in Manila. In *Crime's Power. Anthropologists and the Ethnography of Crime*, ed. P Parnell, S Kane, pp. 197–220. London: Palgrave Macmillan

Parnell P, Kane S, eds. 2003. *Crime's Power. Anthropologists and the Ethnography of Crime.* New York: Palgrave Macmillan

Peletz M. 2002. *Islamic Modern. Religious Courts and Cultural Politics in Malaysia.* Princeton, NJ: Princeton Univ. Press

Plissart M, De Boeck F. 2006. *Kinshasa: Tales of the Invisible City.* London: Ludion

Poole D. 2004. Between threat and guarantee: justice and community in the margins of the Peruvian state. See Das & Poole 2004, pp. 35–66

Quigley D. 1993. *The Interpretation of Caste.* Oxford: Clarendon

Raheja G. 1988. *The Poison in the Gift. Ritual, Prestation and the Dominant Caste in a North Indian Village.* Chicago: Chicago Univ. Press

Richards P. 1996. *Fighting for the Rainforest: War, Youth and Resources in Sierra Leone*. Oxford, UK: James Currey

Ruteere M, Pommerolle ME. 2003. Democratizing security or decentralizing repression? The ambiguities of community policing in Kenya. *Afr. Aff.* 102:587–604

Sahlins M. 1963. Poor man, rich man, big man, chief: political types in Melanesia and Polynesia. *Compar. Stud. Soc. Hist.* 5:285–303

Sahlins M. 1974. *Stone Age Economics*. Chicago: Aldine-Atherton

Sahlins M.1985. *Islands of History*. Chicago: Univ. of Chicago Press

Sassen S. 1996. *Losing Control? Sovereignty in an Age of Globalization*. New York: Columbia Univ. Press

Schapera I. 1969. Uniformity and variation in chief-made law. In *Law, Culture and Society*, ed. L Nader, pp. 230–44. Berkeley: Univ. Calif. Press

Scheper-Hughes N. 1992. *Death Without Weeping. The Violence of Everyday Life in Brazil*. Berkeley: Univ. Calif. Press

Schmitt C. 1985. *Political Theology: Four Chapters on the Concept of Sovereignty*. Cambridge, MA: MIT Press

Schneider J, Schneider P. 1999. Is transparency possible? The political-economic and epistemological implications of Cold-War conspiracies and subterfuge in Italy. See Heyman 1999b, pp. 169–98

Scubla L. 2002. Hocart and the royal road to anthropological understanding. *Soc. Anthropol.* 10:359–76

Sen S. 1998. *Empire of Free Trade. The East India Company and the Making of the Colonial Marketplace*. Philadelphia: Univ. Penn. Press

Sen S. 2002. *Distant Sovereignty*. New York: Routledge

Siegel J. 1997. *Fetish, Recognition, Revolution*. Princeton, NJ: Princeton Univ. Press

Siegel J. 1998. *The New Criminal Type in Jakarta: Counter-revolution Today*. Durham, NJ: Duke Univ. Press

Simonse S. 1991. *Kings of Disasters. Dualism, Centralism and the Scapegoat King in Southeastern Sudan*. Leiden: J. Brill

Sivaramakrishnan K. 1999. *Modern Forests: Statemaking and Environmental Change in Colonial Eastern India*. Stanford, CA: Stanford Univ. Press

Smart A. 1999. Predatory rule and illegal economic practices. See Heyman 1999b, pp. 99–128

Smith D. 2004. The Bakassi boys: vigilantism, violence and political imagination in Nigeria. *Cult. Anthropol.* 19:429–55

Ssorin-Chaikov N. 2003. *The Social Life of the State in Subarctic Siberia*. Stanford, CA: Stanford Univ. Press

Sillitoe P. 1978. Big men and war in New Guinea. *Man* 13:252–71

Stoler AL. 2002. *Carnal Knowledge and Imperial Power: Race and the Intimate in Colonial Rule*. Berkeley: Univ. Calif. Press

Tarlo E. 2003. *Unsettling Memories: Narratives of the Emergency in Delhi*. London: Hurst

Taussig M. 1991 [1986]. *Shamanism, Colonialism, and the Wild Man: A Study in Terror and Healing*. Chicago: Univ. Chicago Press

Taussig M. 1997. *The Magic of the State*. New York: Routledge

Thomas N. 1994. Kingship and hierarchy. Transformation of polities and ritual in eastern Oceania. *Hist. Anthropol.* 7:109–31

Thomson J. 1989. Sovereignty in historical perspective: the evolution of state control over extraterritorial violence. In *The Elusive State: International and Comparative Perspectives*, ed. JA Caporaso, pp. 227–55. London: Sage

Trouillot MR. 1995. *Silencing the Past: Power and the Production of History*. Boston: Beacon

Valeri V. 1985. *Kingship and Sacrifice. Ritual and Society in Ancient Hawaii*. Chicago: Univ. Chicago Press

Van Woerkens M. 2002. *The Strangled Traveler: Colonial Imaginings and the Thugs of India*. Chicago: Univ. Chicago Press

Verdery K. 1996. *What Was Socialism, and What Comes Next?* Princeton, NJ: Princeton Univ. Press

Verdery K. 1999. *The Political Lives of Dead Bodies. Reburial and Postsocialist Change*. New York: Columbia Univ. Press

Volkov V. 2002. *Violent Entrepreneurs. The Use of Force in the Making of Russian Capitalism*. Ithaca: Cornell Univ. Press

Wedeen L. 1999. *Ambiguities of Domination. Politics, Rhetoric and Symbols in Contemporary Syria*. Chicago: Univ. Chicago Press

West H. 2005. *Kupilikula: Governance and the Invisible Realm in Mozambique*. Chicago: Univ. Chicago Press

Wolf E. 1982. *Europe and the People without History*. Berkeley: Univ. Calif. Press

Worby E. 2003. The end of modernity in Zimbabwe: passages from development to sovereignty. In *Zimbabwe's Unfinished Business: Rethinking Land, State and Nation in the Context of Crisis*, ed. A Hammer, B Raftopoulos, S Jensen, pp. 49–82. Harare: Weaver

Local Knowledge and Memory in Biodiversity Conservation

Virginia D. Nazarea

Department of Anthropology, University of Georgia, Athens, Georgia 30602;
email: vnazarea@uga.edu

Annu. Rev. Anthropol. 2006. 35:317–35

The *Annual Review of Anthropology* is
online at anthro.annualreviews.org

This article's doi:
10.1146/annurev.anthro.35.081705.123252

Copyright © 2006 by Annual Reviews.
All rights reserved

0084-6570/06/1021-0317$20.00

Key Words

cultural memory, indigenous knowledge, sensory embodiment,
landscape, place

Abstract

For the past two decades, biodiversity conservation has been an area
of concerted action and spirited debate. Given the centrality of biodiversity to the earth's life support system, its increasing vulnerability
is being addressed in international conservation as well as in research by anthropologists and other social scientists on the cultural,
economic, political, and legal aspects of human engagement with biological resources. The concepts of biodiversity as a social construct
and historical discourse, of local knowledge as loaded representation
and invented tradition, and of cultural memory as selective reconstruction and collective political consciousness have also been the
foci of recent critical reflection.

If we can live in memory, we would not have to
consecrate sites of memory in its name.
Pierre Nora (1997 [1984–1992])

INTRODUCTION

Local knowledge and cultural memory are crucial for the conservation of biodiversity because both serve as repositories of alternative choices that keep cultural and biological diversity flourishing. As scholarly foci, both have undergone similar transitions from obscurity, to prominence, to some form of crisis. This review stresses the continuity and authenticity of local knowledge and memory despite, or because of, their fluidity, contingency, situatedness, and resilience. It points to some directions for restoration of diversity that is rooted in place.

Although the evolution of our species has been driven primarily by human curiosity, appreciation, and exploitation of the variability of plants and animals, the term biodiversity is of recent coinage. First used in 1986 when the National Forum on BioDiversity was organized under the auspices of the National Academy of Sciences and the Smithsonian Institution in Washington, D.C., it had captured public imagination and attracted enough attention worldwide by 1992 to be a rallying point at the Rio Earth Summit (Wilson 1988, 1997). Biodiversity is "the variety of life forms, the ecological roles they perform, and the genetic diversity they contain" (Wilcox 1984, p. 71). It has a wide range of direct uses for food, medicine, ritual, construction, and commerce (Patrick 1997) and performs critical environmental services such as maintenance of nutrient and hydrologic cycles, regulation of air quality and water purity, preservation of habitat, and reservoir of evolutionary change (Hawkes 1991, Chapin et al. 2000). Because "the natural wealth of our planet is being lost at an estimated rate of 5% per decade" (Raven & McNeely 1998, p. 13), there is growing concern among scientists and policymakers over an impending crisis of genetic erosion and extinction. This crisis is driven by growth in population and rates of consumption, which in turn drives habitat destruction, introduction of exotic species, and overharvesting of the earth's resources (Myers 1996, Lovejoy 1997). The dominance of economic considerations over ethical-ecological ones only exacerbates these environmental and cultural vulnerabilities (Norgaard 1988, Ehrlich 2002).

By the mid-1990s, the twin ideas of biodiversity and biodiversity conservation became the subject of impassioned, albeit at times tangential, critiques aimed mainly at biodiversity's correspondence to some real entity or phenomenon, or—more to the point—the lack thereof. Is biodiversity a thing that exists in nature or just a conceptual and opportunistic sleight-of-hand to serve some hidden agenda? For anthropologists, a closely related question was, Is this thing that scientists and policy makers are preoccupied with recognized by local people (as in, Aha! Group So-and-So does not have a term for "biodiversity"!). Energetically questioned, too, was the purported urgency of stemming biodiversity loss. Because evolution is an ongoing process with species lost and species gained all the time, is biodiversity conservation simply an alarmist call to create mass hysteria or a charismatic lure to generate funding or sell books? Perhaps because of its bumper sticker aplomb, "erosion is real, extinction is permanent" did not particularly sit well with poststructuralist thinking, which pointed out that deeper understanding of the problem requires theorizing beyond the obvious and the absolute to penetrate created realities and demand for solutions. Some scholars argued further that biodiversity is a social/political construct (Takacs 1996, Ribiero 1997) and a "historically produced discourse" (Escobar 1998, p. 54). Indeed, in the hands of these critical scholars, biodiversity and its conservation became something good to think rather than something good to do.

A review of anthropology and the conservation of biodiversity emphasized the increasing contribution of anthropologists to the understanding of human impact on biodiversity

Figure 1

V. Nazarea with members of culinary revival group in Cusco, Peru.

Figure 2

Mother, daughter, tubers, and seeds in Cotacachi, Ecuador.

(Orlove & Brush 1996). Underlining human cognition, decision making, and behavior, the authors surveyed anthropological perspectives on biodiversity under four themes: ethnobiology of agricultural diversity, cultural ecology of plant genetic resources, participatory conservation, and politics of genetic resources. Aside from this review, several books and edited volumes have been published on the cultural, economic, political, and legal dimensions of biodiversity conservation in the past decade (Zimmerer 1996, 2003; Collins & Qualset 1999; Nazarea 1998, 2005; Brush 2000, 2004; Dutfield 2000, 2004; Cleveland & Soleri 2002). Interest in exploring the complex web of interactions among culture, society, and biodiversity can be expected to grow with increasing recognition of the need for complementing formal or institutional approaches like ex situ conservation in gene banks with more informal or local initiatives like in situ conservation in homegardens. It will also intensify with the demand for intersectoral negotiations on access and benefits in relation to plant genetic resources and associated local knowledge.

In light of these developments, this review's objective is to examine anthropological investment on the subject of biodiversity conservation and loss while recognizing the questioning that has been going on since the concept gained some degree of prominence in environmental conservation. I also take into account local knowledge and memory and examine how they reinforce cultural and biological diversity. Local knowledge and memory have followed a similar course of ascendancy, crisis, and renaissance as has the notion of biodiversity. The deconstruction of these concepts has provoked serious reexamination, which continues to lead us to deeper insights. But it has also provoked doubt and sown confusion, leading to a palpable malaise in both theory and practice. Recent developments in anthropological thought, particularly in the areas of sensory memory or sensuous scholarship (Seremetakis 1994, Stoller 1997, Sutton 2001), marginality and mime-

sis (Taussig 1993, Tsing 1993, Nazarea 2005), and landscape or place (Basso 1996, Stewart 1996, Gold & Gujar 2002) offer a way out of misplaced essentialism, which demands strict adherence to what does or does not count as biodiversity, knowledge, and memory. This emerging body of research and scholarship enjoins us to explore different avenues of engagement with ecology and conservation or to return to comforting old haunts of deeply sited ethnography and thick description.

CBD: Convention on Biological Diversity

CONSERVING BIODIVERSITY OR IMAGINING BIODIVERSITY?

Whether the problem of biodiversity loss was cast in a straight and narrow economic mode or in a more encompassing biocentric mode, the result was to galvanize the scientific and policy community into action. International organizing and advocacy made a strong case for the urgency of the problem. One watershed document, the Convention on Biological Diversity (CBD), was signed in the 1992 Rio Earth Summit. The CBD defined biodiversity as "the variability among living organisms from all sources and the ecological complexes of which they are part; this includes diversity within species, between species, and of ecosystems" (UNEP 1994, p. 4). It recognized national sovereignty over plant genetic resources and bound signatory countries to "regulate and manage biological resources important for the conservation of biological diversity" and "respect, preserve, and maintain knowledge, innovations, and practices of indigenous and local communities embodying traditional lifestyles relevant to the sustainable use and conservation of biological diversity" (UNEP 1994, pp. 8–9). There are still unresolved issues associated with rights and responsibilities, but the CBD has made it difficult to ignore the enormous challenge of biodiversity conservation and the crucial role of local knowledge and local custodians in maintaining it.

Since the first call to arms in the 1980s, biological and social scientists have been analyzing causes and trends and fashioning solutions (Altieri & Merrick 1987, Brush 1991, Soule 1993, Beattie & Ehrlich 2001). Some of the measures that have been put in place are ex situ and in situ gene banks, buffer zones and protected areas, and biological corridors (Plucknett et al. 1987, Cohen et al. 1991, Maxted et al. 1997). Repatriation of germplasm collected from centers of diversity and conserved in gene banks to communities from which they originated but from which they have since been lost is another promising mechanism being explored. In Cusco, Peru, efforts are underway to return to Quechua farmers hundreds of potato landraces from the International Potato Center. Reintegrating these native potatoes into Quechua farming systems is complemented by initiatives to document customary laws and revive culinary traditions in the Andes (**Figure 1**; see color insert). Repatriation and in situ conservation are parts of an ongoing paradigm shift in biodiversity conservation toward less-centralized and more on-the-ground efforts that acknowledge the contribution of indigenous populations, women, and elderly farmers (Wilkes 1991, Soleri & Smith 1999, Jarvis & Hodgkin 2000). Complementation of scientific and cultural approaches to conservation, inclusion of neglected or underutilized crops in conservation mandates, and integration of conventional functions of gene banks with new ones as dictated by discoveries and political situations have likewise been stressed (Pimbert 1994, Hammer 2003).

In a more critical vein, the problem has been recast in the constructivist sense as the specter of biodiversity being an environmental workhorse under threat and in its conservation as a nascent social movement with broader political ends. From this perspective, the "idea" of biodiversity and the call for its conservation are seen as means to renegotiate the dominant discourse on nature and culture—one that reinforces the interconnectivity between identity and ethnicity, territoriality, autonomy, and natural resource claims (Takacs 1996, Escobar 1998, Hayden 2003).

These claims and counterclaims travel across various locations and conversations and in no time assume a life of their own (certainly a language of their own) not unlike the constructs they critique. Still, it is heartening to note that while the concept of biodiversity is being problematized and its attendant issues debated on the big stage of science, technology, and society, while biologists and anthropologists ponder deeply and nongovernmental organizations organize zealously, local farmers and gardeners go about their daily round—exchanging, renewing, and connecting through seeds and memories—surrounding themselves with familiarity and comfort and defying the somber politics of loss.

In biodiversity conservation, resilience can be found in diverse genetic compositions internal and external to disturbed ecosystems. Of prime importance here are biological legacies and reservoirs that are redundant and self-renewing, a point to which I return later. But it is fostered as well in small, reverberating acts of human defiance to the homogenizing forces that erode identity, agency, and diversity (Richards 1986, 1996; Nabhan 1989; Zimmerer 1996; Nazarea 1998, 2005). While intellectual and policy debates may stress loss, surrender, and abandonment associated with sweeping habitat fragmentation and agricultural development—an emptying not only of forests and fields but also of reserves of local knowledge and memory—it is important to acknowledge a powerful counter in marginal fields and uncaptured spirits. For the most part, this counter is lodged not in rhetoric and text but in the senses and the flesh—in the dance, pungency, and grittiness of everyday life. Sensuous recollection in marginal niches and sovereign spaces that people carve out of uniformity and predictability constantly replenishes what modernity drains. One example is women's intimate relationship to their seeds in Cotacachi, Ecuador, where, according to Rosa Ramos (**Figure 2**; see color insert), seeds are gathered in the aprons of their skirts and transported in the folds of their clothes, to be hidden, displayed, and/or shared as they see fit. In Paucartamba, Peru, where women control seed storage, they closely observe and sort maize landraces on the basis of use, planting, and ripening and keep men from drawing any consumption-seed ears out of storage areas (Zimmerer 1996).

INDIGENOUS KNOWLEDGE AND ITS TRANSFORMATIONS

Anthropology's engagement with environmental conservation has been rooted in local or indigenous knowledge. In many respects, local knowledge has always been at the core of anthropology, but it ascended to prominence in development anthropology in the early 1980s. Three intellectual waves precipitated this ascent. The first we can call the "ethnoscientific wave." The concentration on understanding of local understanding had its beginnings in the mid-1950s and early 1960s (Conklin 1954, 1961; Goodenough 1957; Frake 1962), but it crested in the 1970s and 1980s (Berlin et al. 1974; Hunn 1977, 1982; Ford 1978; Posey 1984; Atran 1985; Berlin 1992; Ellen 1993). Based primarily on cognitive/linguistic principles, ethnoscience systematized data collection and analysis, effectively eticizing the emic. Because of its promise of methodological rigor and theoretical significance, supporters dubbed it as the "new ethnography." However, its detractors found dubious the idea of cognitively based behavior and referred to it more as "science of trivia" or rules for the "anemic" and "emetic" (Harris 1974). The debate also raged among ethnoscientists themselves, between the structural/intellectualist camp (represented by Brent Berlin and Scott Atran) and the utilitarian/adaptationist camp (represented by Eugene Hunn and Roy Ellen). Questions of correspondence between ethnobiological categories and Linnean taxonomies continue to animate these exchanges, but some form of synthesis has been achieved in other areas. Among other things, ethnobiology and ethnoecology provided a framework for linking categories with action plans and, in effect, environmental perception with resource management practices (see Hunn 1989 and Nazarea 1999 for further discussion). Research in this direction shed light on "classifications as situationally adapted and dynamic devices of particular importance to their users, reflecting an interaction... between culture, psychology, and discontinuities in the natural world" (Ellen 1993, p. 3).

By stressing the adaptive nature of classificatory systems, ethnoscience caused a radical reorientation in viewing the relationship between humans and their habitats. Following on its wings, the appropriate technology wave utilized methods and findings originating from more esoteric pursuits focused on figuring out "how the natives think" and applied these to agricultural development and environmental conservation. That local people who have lived in a particular environment and dealt with its constraints over time have acquired sophisticated knowledge that needs to be considered to make development and conservation projects more contextually sensitive and appropriate was practically intuitive, but it took awhile for it to become influential. Also known in the literature as indigenous knowledge (IK)—or traditional environmental knowledge (TEK) when more specifically applied to beliefs and practices in relation to nature—local knowledge was celebrated in a revalorization of the small, the beautiful, and the brown. Efforts by anthropologists in the academic and development arenas successfully demonstrated how anthropology can provide a major contribution in directing development toward a more sustainable course by allowing local perspectives to shape its priorities (Rhoades 1982, Ashby 1985, Warren 1989, Bentley & Andrew 1991, Rhoades & Bebbington 1995). Indigenous or local knowledge and technologies were vigorously documented and promoted and became information currency in the international agricultural research centers and the World Bank. While this was going on, an underlying theme, local knowledge as subject matter, developed

IK: indigenous knowledge

TEK: traditional environmental knowledge

from anthropology of development (Dove 1986, DeWalt 1994, Nazarea-Sandoval 1995, Sillitoe 1996). Generated in the academe and frequently in the context of interdisciplinary research, these works compared local knowledge with Western science, examined the equivalences and particularities, and made recommendations for mutually beneficial integration or mainstreaming.

In the 1990s, a postmodern critical wave questioned what it deemed to be a static, overly romanticized image of local knowledge (Brosius 1999, Li 1999, Ellen & Harris 2000, Parkes 2000). Local knowledge came to be regarded as practical and partial, even contingent, and attempts to document and bank it were viewed as misguided at best and suspect at worst (Escobar 1998, Agrawal 2002). Arguably, most of the caveats raised in these critiques were valid; to abstract local knowledge from its context and to "refunctionalize" it to Western ideas of conservation could be a disservice not only to local knowledge but also to conservation and science. However, the postmodern wave glossed over the original intention of documenting local knowledge, which was to foreground the cultural dimension that development and conservation programs often overlooked and to make sure that there is a library of previously unwritten beliefs and practices in case there was ever any need to revive, disperse, or retool this valuable pool of information (Knight 1980, Brokensha et al. 1982, Oldfield & Alcorn 1987, Nazarea 1998). The critics also forgot to mention that most of these efforts were intended to be ethnographically grounded and participatory, with local perspectives checking the excesses of decontextualization and "scientisation." At its extreme, critical scholarship interrogated the very existence of local knowledge, arguing that local discourse could be simply a reflection of global rhetoric and agenda: generalized, embellished, framed. It was not that the love affair with local knowledge in anthropology and development ended, it simply "grew up" and culminated in a doubt-ridden marriage.

One way to look at the transformations in IK and its discontents is in terms of generation one and generation two IK (or TEK) studies. First-generation IK studies focused on content, comparing and contrasting local knowledge with scientific knowledge and legitimizing it in terms of Western standards (see, for example, Warren et al. 1995). Rigorous testing and verification of the scientific basis of soil classification and enhancement, water conservation and distribution, crop preferences and cultivation, pest identification and management, and other domains of indigenous knowledge subjected local beliefs and practices to the burden of legitimacy. From this standpoint, IK was regarded as a bundle of instrumentalities for "complementation" and "integration." This was true not only in the development arena where IK promised to redeem top-down strategies that violated and further diminished would-be beneficiaries, but also in academic research. Numerous publications on the significance and relevance of IK appeared in the *Journal of Economic Botany*, *Journal of Ethnobiology*, *Human Ecology*, *Human Organization*, and *Agriculture and Human Values* during this period. Ethnoscientific approaches became the cornerstone for understanding and explaining local knowledge, particularly of the natural world. Views of local knowledge as distributed and situated challenged the heretofore dominant belief in invariant, acultural systems of encoding such knowledge.

Second-generation IK studies focused on process and transformation, noting that local knowledge is not just intrinsically dynamic and situated but is often contingent on external opportunities and constraints (see, for example, Ellen et al. 2000). The emphasis on understanding local knowledge in the context in which it evolved freed it from the demands of comparison and verification and highlighted the agency of local people. However, although it freed IK from the burden of legitimacy, it imposed a burden of a different sort: authenticity. With utmost vigilance, we now dissect local knowledge to check if it is reified or commodified and imagined or invented. Thus, this reservoir of strength and resilience called local knowledge that anthropologists endeavored, with considerable success, to bring to the attention of planners, policy makers, and scholars in other disciplines is often lost in a conceptual quagmire that submerges scientific measures and ethnographic insights under cross-cutting ripples of political discourse. Although agency still echoes somewhere in the background, a disquieting aspect of the more immediate intellectual cosmovision has local people swimming in swift and overwhelming currents of power—hapless, witless victims with neither knowledge nor memory. As I see it, the danger in conceptually stripping local knowledge of its adaptiveness and reducing it to little more than political currency and intellectual fodder to be complicated ad infinitum is that we can lose sight of both the human actors and the environment and ultimately negate the agency we have taken pains to foreground.

LOCAL ETHNOECOLOGIES AND GLOBAL CONSERVATION

With regards to biodiversity conservation, we as anthropologists find ourselves contending not only with our ambivalence about local knowledge but also with inherent tensions between local fit and global standards, between diversity and design. The basic problem in trying to reconcile local knowledge with global science is one of incommensurability (Fairhead & Leach 1996, Espeland and Stevens 1998). Local knowledge is experiential and embodied in everyday practice. It is not logically formulated apart from what makes sense from living day to day in one's environment; nor is it inscribed as a set of processes or rules. To treat it solely as information to be tested, or text to be deconstructed, is to ignore the sensory embodiment of local knowledge as well as the attendant emotion and memory that is its power. In short, local knowledge is cosmos more than corpus, praxis and pulse more than precision and plan. Global science and other essentialisms—including, paradoxically, the critical kind—disempower place and agency in its treatment of local knowledge.

The literature makes promising attempts to reinsert an appreciation of knowing that is acquired in place. This kind of deep, affective knowledge cannot be subject to the same standard or design as global science. Geertz (1983) put it succinctly, "No one lives in the world in general" and leaves no doubt about the significance of dwelling not in a generalized space but rather in a specific place, "local knowledge . . . presents locally to locals a local frame of mind" (p. 12). In arguing why place conceptually precedes space, Casey (1996) noted that, "Local knowledge is at one with lived experience . . . . To live is to live locally, and to know first of all, the places one is in" (p. 18). According to Casey, this sense of place "imbues a coherence at the primary level, one supplied by the horizons and depth of experience." People have to trust this coherence and integrity or they cannot function. They construct and defend memory and identity because without this internal coherence, all faith, hope, agency, and action are impossible. The fact that these are always in the process of construction and repair does not make them any less authentic; one can argue that the emotional investment involved makes them even more so.

The pivotal significance of context and coherence is central to phenomenology, sociology of knowledge, and ethnoecology. Beyond the purely cognitive, or the purely rational, a "feeling" for one's surroundings comes from an intensive apprenticeship in its idiosyncracies and demands and endows one with a habit of mind and a bodily orientation that is honed in place. Merleu-Ponty's "presences" (1962), Bourdieu's "dispositions in positions" and "habitus" (1980, 1987), Ellen's "prehensions" and "affordances" (1993), and Ingold's "dwelling" and "enskillment"(1996, 2000) underline subconscious or preattentive frameworks that emanate from one's locality or sense of place. These predispositions inform practice; they also suggest perceived latitudes and boundaries of decision making and behavior.

Orientation and navigation in space suggest not only movement but also maneuvering and play. In *Mimesis and Alterity*, Taussig (1993) argues that "this medley of the senses bleeding into each other's zone of expectations . . . recalls mimesis, the magical power of replication . . . wherein the representation shares in or takes power from the represented" (p. 57). We must keep in mind the magic of this maneuverability to appreciate the situated and dynamic nature of local knowledge. For instance, the Wamira of Papua New Guinea believed in the multiple powers of Tauribariba, "a small stone, no bigger than a person's outstretched hand" that formed part of a large circle of stones on the seaside hamlet of Irene (Kahn 1996, p. 180). To the local people, Tauribariba recalled their past, established their rights to the land, anchored their taro, and assured them that their gardens would yield abundant food. As he took care of things, they would say, "he walked the night." To the missionaries, however, Tauribariba was nothing more than a striped rock resembling a chocolate cake. In 1936, when the cathedral was completed, they decided to cement Tauribariba to the pulpit wall to signify the transference of Wamirans' "worship of stone" to worship of God. As Tauribariba was being consecrated to the church, Wamirans remembered that "he walked the night" and stole him back. Using the stone that "walked the night" as a metaphor for local knowledge, we can ask, to what extent are its attributed powers "real," or is this question even relevant? Can it be reduced in a colonial encounter to a mere instrumentality; and, if it can, for how long? What purpose does it serve to consecrate it to a higher knowing and fix its character once and for all, especially if it can at any moment be pried free and stolen back?

To argue that knowledge has to be just so for it to qualify as local or indigenous and that anything deviating from this standard of authenticity is not to be taken seriously is like cementing Tauribariba, the stone that walks, to a church wall. Likewise, to insist on systematic and rational design as a requisite for conservation is to declare all institutional initiatives as legitimate conservation and to denigrate all informal efforts as haphazard sustainability or conservation by default. Although Smith & Wishney's (2000) theory of conservation specifies that "to qualify as conservation, any action or practice must not only prevent or mitigate resource overharvesting or environmental damage, it must be designed to do so" (p. 493), in Cotacachi, Ecuador, men and women "know" their crops by remembering. They also "walk their seeds," displaying and exchanging them along the way to enrich and revitalize their germplasm. For Andean farmers, biodiversity conservation is what they do (or, with great sadness, fail to do) as they cultivate their fields and cook their meals. Thus, according to Pedro Lima, a 45-year-old farmer (Nazarea 2005),

> [w]hen I was a child, we used to grow everything we ate. My favorite food was quinoa and corn soup. We ate chuchuca, barley, wheat, morocho (a kind of corn), corn gruel with brown sugar, and salty corn gruel . . . To make a favorite salty dish, we used yellow and white carrots, potatoes, and wild potatoes that we gathered in the mountain. It was small and not bitter and harvested the same time as corn . . . I would like to have mashua (an Andean tuber) again, I like it because it is sweet. When one is tired, it is nice to have something sweet. The oca (another Andean tuber) is like that, although when the harvest is coming to an end, it must be cooked with salt . . . . Yesterday's foods also had less spices. We used lard, salt, onions, cabbage, aliyuyo, and rabano (wild herbs) from the stream. (p. 131)

MEMORY AND COUNTERMEMORY

Like local knowledge, memory has risen from obscurity to a legitimate scholarly focus and then assailed by some form of crisis. With respect to the former, the burden of legitimacy debunked as folk anything that failed to meet scientific verification, and subsequently, the burden of authenticity dismissed as false anything that was contaminated with outside influences or motivations. With respect to the latter, doubts about continuity, reliability, and authenticity—at times lumped together as the "afterwardness" of memory (Laplanche 1992; Radstone 2000)—brought into question the genuineness and accuracy of memory. Lately, both have undergone some form of renaissance. Rigney (2005) noted that we need to look at cultural memory as "working memory," one that is "constructed and reconstructed in public acts of remembrance and evolves according to distinctly cultural mechanisms" (p. 11). What is important to remember, particularly in relation to biodiversity conservation, is that memory in use (no less than knowledge in use) metamorphoses constantly and is thus never rigid, uncontaminated, or strictly "authentic." Cultural memory embedded in food and place enables small-scale farmers and gardeners to resist the vortex of agricultural commercialization and monoculture by continuing to nurture a wide variety of species and varieties in their home gardens and their fields, sustained by sensory recollections regarding the plants' aesthetic appeal, culinary qualities, ritual significance, and connection to the past (Nazarea 1998, Villadolid & Apffel-Marglin 2001, Oakley & Momsen 2005).

The resurgence of interest in memory is fueled by the desire to recover personal narratives that have been fragmented or erased and to understand better how the past is recalled or reconstructed. This is especially so with regard to periods of colonization and genocide as well as specific events such as the Holocaust and the two world wars, which do not completely yield to historical analysis (Zerubavel 1995, Assman 1997, Uehling 2004). Memory is not history; to expect it to possess the same virtues is to underrate seriously its potential to deliver more insights but of a different kind.

Some scholars have even argued that the concept of memory stands in opposition to, and tension with, the concept of history: "History seemed to claim Truth and to vouch for an 'objective' reality that would correct memory's seemingly subjective, unreliable stance in a world of objects" (Weissberg 1999, p. 11). But a new scholarly interest predicated on longing to recall if not to relive the past took root, ironically, in history itself with the publication of Nora's *Les Lieux de Memoire* (1984–1992). Nora mourned the loss of what he called "*milleux de memoire*" or the milieu of memory represented by rural life before the advent of modernity. He noted that "the real environments of memory are gone" but that present-day memory "crystallizes and secretes itself in the *lieux de memoire*, or sites of memory" and lamented that "modern day memory is archival memory" (p. 7).

From interest in philosophy on the phenomenology of remembering and forgetting, to the preoccupation in psychoanalysis with seduction, trauma, and fantasy, to anthropology's fascination with identity politics in relation to transnationalism and postcolonial memories, and finally to history's own inspired quest for "history from below" and "history of everyday life," the study of memory became a consuming "past-time" (Tonkin 1992, Sutton 1998, Harkin 2003, Gordillo 2004, Moran 2004). But as memory's stock rose, its nature and function became even more enigmatic. As Boutin et al. (2005) observed,

> [i]t has become increasingly clear that the construction of memory is imbricated in a complex network of social, psychological, political and cultural practices spanning a wide range of scholarly disciplines. We cannot understand how collective memories gain currency or, a contrario, slip into oblivion, without understanding the dynamics of power within the societies in which they circulate. Equally important is an understanding of the cultural forms in which memories are inscribed. (p. 5)

Pre-dating Nora, Maurice Halbwachs was interested in how memory is generated and sustained within groups such as those based on kinship, religion, and class. In *La Memoire Collective* (1950) he emphasized that memory is social, collective, and "lived." For Halbwachs, "people acquire or construct memory not as isolated individuals but as members of society" so much so that the analytical distinction between individual memory and social memory is meaningless. For social or collective memory to cohere, communication between individuals belonging to the same social group and transmission across generations are crucial. Connerton, writing *How Societies Remember* (1989), sought an explanation for how this communication of social memories works and suggested that, "if we are to say that a social group, whose duration exceeds that of the lifespan of any single individual, is able to 'remember' in common, it is not sufficient that the various members who compose that group at any given time should be able to retain the mental representation relating to the past of that group. It is necessary also that the older members of that group should not neglect to transmit these representations to the younger members of the group" (p. 38). The key, according to Connerton, is in commemorative ceremonies that are performative, enacted in ritual and incorporated in the body as a form of "habit memory."

Although memory was conceptualized by Halbwachs as "collective," and by Connerton as "performative," the concern eventually shifted to the construction of cultural memory. Following a shift in emphasis from the social group to its mode of production, "a social constructivist model of memory evolved taking, as its starting point, the idea that memories of a shared past are collectively constructed and reconstructed in the present rather than resurrected from the past" (Rigney 2005, p. 14). Cultural memory is vital for people underserved by history, referred to by Wolf (1982) in relation to Western Europe as "people without history." Borne of unofficial accounts of people who are persecuted, converted, displaced, and in other ways marginalized, it is essentially counter-hegemonic and subversive, thus constituting a countermemory (Boddy 1989, Lipsitz 1991). Selective and embellished to secure the present and engineer the future, cultural memory forms an alternative consciousness and identity. Thus, according to Zerubavel (1995), "The master commemorative narrative represents the political elites' construction of the past which serves its special interests and promotes its political agenda. Countermemory challenges this hegemony by offering a different commemorative narrative representing the views of marginalized individuals or groups within society" (pp. 10–11).

If repressive hegemony imparts wounds, countermemory assuages the pain and can lead to recovery by foregrounding healing narratives, performances, and practices. Seduction and trauma in relation to memory is more frequently addressed in terms of experiences of sexual abuse and repression of sexual fantasies that lead to later neuroses (Freud & Breuer 1974 [1893–1895], Freud 1976 [1900]) and hardly in terms of larger seductive and cataclysmic events such as those that concern us here. Nevertheless, it is a viable framework from which to view political upheavals and global climate changes that threaten whole landscapes rich in biodiversity as well as the initially hypnotic but ultimately disorienting effects of development and commercialization (Steinberg & Taylor 2003, McDowell 2004, Cruikshank 2005). With respect to plant genetic erosion, trauma can come from vigorous extension of modern varieties and technological packages to the extent that all choices in crops, their cultivation, and their preparation are "disappeared" (Fowler & Mooney 1990, Shiva 1993, Dove 1999). These trends, along with the ubiquity and glamour of Western-style, store-bought consumables, banish attachment to origin and anticipation of seasons, thereby precipitating an "epoch of tastelessness" (Seremetakis 1994). The centrality of rape as metaphor for ill-conceived development projects, for politically uninformed (or politically motivated) plant breeding and introduction, and for unethical bioprospecting and biopiracy can hardly be called inappropriate. As Connerton (1989) pointed out,

> [a]ll totalitarianisms behave in this way: the mental enslavement of the subjects of a totalitarian regime begins when their memories are taken away. When a large power wants to deprive a small country of its national consciousness, it uses the method of organized forgetting....What is horrifying about a totalitarian regime is not only the violation of human dignity but the fear that there may remain nobody who could ever again bear witness to the past." (pp. 12–14)

Research into cultural memory is usually approached through the analysis of texts, events, and rituals where memories of the dominated sediment. In reflections on postcolonial memories and identity politics, there is a gradient from countermemories inscribed in subversive discourse to those incorporated in performative ceremonies. To give just a few examples, in *Fragmented Memories*, Saika (2004) examined "buranjis" or chronicles of glorious exploits written on the bark of aloe wood to unearth a distinctive Assamese identity in the context of contemporary India; in *The Politics of Memory*, Rappaport (1998) highlighted native historian's oral accounts of changes in the Colombian Andes as opposed to official historical accounts; in *Embodying Colonial Memories*, Stoller (1995) considered Songhay spirit possession and broader social relations as a sensual reconciliation of history, and in *The Weight of the Past*, Lambek (2002) focused on Sakalava spirit mediums who "bear" the past through ritual performances that give body and voice to the ancestors. Stoller (1994) argues that there is a significant difference between the merely discursive and the performative because "... embodiment is not primarily textual; rather, the sentient body is culturally consumed by a world filled with forces, smells, textures, sights, sounds and tastes, all of which trigger cultural memory" (p. 636).

Texts, events, and rituals encode memory and powerfully evoke marginality and resistance, but they require a stage and a group of experts, minimally setting up a distinction between messenger and audience. More important in relation to biodiversity are memories of places and food, of trails followed, gardens tended, and meals savored in solitude or in the company of one's folks. These sensory memories constitute "a vast social unconscious of sensory-emotive experience that potentially offers up hidden and now inadmissible counter-narratives of once-valued lifeworlds" (Seremetakis 1994, p. 10). Like fairy tales, they help visualize and congeal a "wish landscape" (Bloch 1988) over a constraining one thereby enlivening alternatives—including an odd array of plants and other living things— that may have been buried or purged. Subsistence farmers, indigenous peoples, heirloom seedsavers, and women homegardeners nurture memory in private, more sovereign places such as sacred groves, tangled plots, and steaming kitchens. In these interior landscapes, cultural memory is not simply articulated or performed; it is materialized in "old timey" or archaic plants that persist, in seeds and stories that travel, in recipes that recall intimacies and comforts of the past and reinvigorate the present.

In secret recesses close to the heart, strength and hope emanate from invisible depths of connection to the past. Thus, the Kalymnians in Greece insist that their guests partake of grilled octopus and roasted goat "to remember Kalymnos by" (Sutton 2001), and Sardinians in Orgosolo consume and serve only bread baked, and meat roasted, in wood-fired rustic ovens and refuse to pay attention to any political talk that is not "cooked," meaning simmered in the intimacy of local social relations (Heatherington 2001). As for immigrants, Malaysians of Peranakan descent in Australia gather the ingredients for *satay babi* (skewered pork) in the ethnic market and prepare the dish the traditional way as a "means of 'regaining touch' through sensory relocation" (Choo 2004), and Vietnamese in

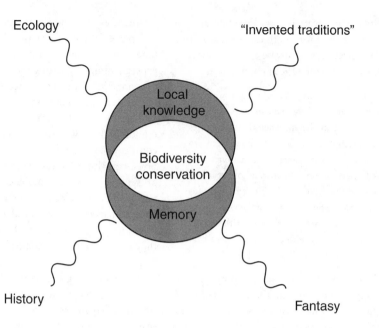

Ecology

"Invented traditions"

Local knowledge

Biodiversity conservation

Memory

History

Fantasy

Figure 3

Recreating the milieu of biodiversity.

Exterior landscape

Interior landscape

the United States layer sweet potatoes, lemon grass, bitter melon, and banana plants in furrows and trellises in their yards and stir herb-flavored *pho* (noodle soup) in their kitchens to summon an "out of place sense of place" (Nazarea 2005). In a book eventually published by her daughter under the title, *In Memory's Kitchen*, a starving Jewish artist gathered recipes of rich cakes and savory dumplings from other women in the German concentration camp of Thereseinstadt to send to her daughter beyond the prison walls and across life and death with the injunction, "Let fantasy run free" (de Silva 1996). What is special and promising about sensory memories in connection with biodiversity conservation is that it is difficult to tell if we are dealing with sites of memory or with the milieu of memory itself, one that allows for both recollection and experience. Definitely, it is not "archival memory," and it challenges rather than surrenders to the purposeful straightening and organized forgetting imposed by modernity and other totalitarianisms (**Figure 3**). It seems possible that comfort food and familiar places

enwrap people with warmth, flavors, and aromas that make the milieu itself transcendent and tangible.

CONSERVATION AS MEMORY WORK

In the field of environmental conservation and landscape restoration, ecologists have come to the conclusion that the ability of ecosystems to rebuild after large-scale natural and human-induced disturbances is dependent on "ecological memory." According to Bengtsson and her coworkers (2003), ecological memory is the network of species, their dynamic interactions, and the combination of structures that make reorganization possible. They further pointed out that there are two principal components of ecological memory: one internal or within-patch and the other external or outside reserves. The former consists of "biological legacies" that serve as foci for regeneration and growth, whereas the latter consists of resources outside the disturbed area such as ecological fallows and dynamic reserves in the surrounding landscape. Hence, "for a nature reserve to function in the longer term, there has to be a buffer to disturbance in the landscape that conserves the capacity to reorganize and recover from perturbations. There has to be ecological resilience" (2003, p. 390).

In cultural terms, "living" or "working" memory is the equivalent of within-patch legacies on which reconstruction can be based. But just as important are external reserves of memory from dynamic repositories outside the traumatized sphere. Therefore, reconstruction for biodiversity conservation should not only recover internal "pockets of memory" (Nazarea 1998) but also draw on archived memory, to the extent of copying and recycling from other communities. Memory work or active "re-membrance" is called for because of the gravity of historical events that bring about repression or loss of memory (Haug 2000, Radstone 2000). Colonialism, for instance, can pose such a disorienting dialectic between European and indigenous consciousness that the only recourse for dealing with postcolonial trauma is to artfully hybridize or purposely forget (Comaroff & Comaroff 1997, Abercrombie 1998, Cole 2001). Restorative memory work should facilitate not only transmission from one generation to another but also jump across memory gaps where transmission has failed or was thwarted. Boutin et al. (2005) referred to these gaps as "cognitive and ethical void(s) arising

from irreparable loss" and pointed to the need to "mobilize an imaginary relation to the past for fundamentally different conceptions of the present" (p. 8). Repair and circulation of cultural memory to underwrite conservation of biological and cultural diversity can start with local historians and bards who are "relentless recorders" of an alternative past (Connerton 1989) or with ordinary men and women who hold on to their cherished seeds and commensal rituals and pass these along to their children. The goal of memory work in this case is to summon aesthetics, emotion, and imagination to inspire a swell of pride and a sense of possibility that can effectively counter "monocultures of the mind" or hegemonic knowledge structures that destroy diversity by dismissing local alternatives from consideration (Shiva 1993). In this manner, communities can fan memory's own diaspora to engage the silence and counter the trauma of the displaced, the disinherited, and "the disappeared" (**Figure 4**).

In *Defacement*, Taussig (1999, p. 78) referred to Pitt-Rivers' (1971) characterization of the north (typified by the British) as honest, industrious, and repressed and the south (typified by the Andalusians, or the people of the Sierra) as "anything but," as "the mischief of distinction." This form of mischief can put up insidious dichotomies and arbitrary standards of purity and authenticity that diminish local knowledge and memory and their potential

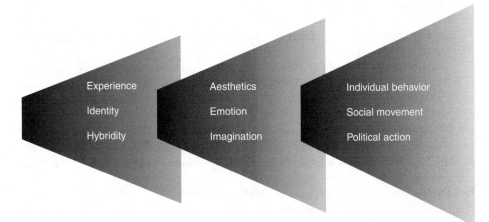

Figure 4

Interlinked concepts in memory work

contribution to biodiversity conservation, and environmental conservation in general. Mischievous polarization is "anything but" helpful in revitalizing the agency and resistance as well as the memory and resilience needed for countering the erosion of biodiversity. It is incongruous that while today essentialism is deemed highly objectionable in most areas of concern for anthropologists, it is demanded in others, and although dynamism and situatedness are lauded in most cases, continuity of transformed or transferred forms is rarely accepted. Trauma, repression, and silence are very real consequences of encounters characterized by significant power differentials, be these sexual, economic, or technological in nature. Reinscription and reembodiment countering loss of cultural memory and biological diversity can come in the form of "concrete utopias" (Bloch 1988) where interior landscapes are mapped onto exterior landscapes through objects and stories that stimulate sensory recall and affective engagement. This cross-mapping will have to tolerate a certain degree of ambiguity and fantasy, of borrowing and bricolage. Where communities have suffered from the loss of variability, a contagion of emotion can conceivably bring about restorative social movements of a subdued but no less powerful kind.

LITERATURE CITED

Abercrombie TA. 1998. *Pathways of Memory and Power: Ethnography and History among an Andean People*. Madison: Univ. Wisc. Press

Agrawal A. 2002. Indigenous knowledge and the politics of classification. *Int. Soc. Sci. J.* 173:287–97

Altieri MA, Merrick LC. 1987. Agroecology and in situ conservation of native crop diversity in the third world. In *Biodiversity*, ed. EO Wilson, pp. 361–69. Washington, DC: National Academy Press

Ashby JA. 1985. The social ecology of soil erosion. *Rural Sociol.* 50(3):337–96

Assman J. 1997. *Das Kulturelle Gedachtnis: Schrift, Erinnerung und Politische Identitat in Fruhen Hochkulturen*. Munich: Beck

Atran S. 1985. The nature of folk-biological life forms. *Am. Anthropol.* 87(2):289–315

Basso K. 1996. Wisdom sits in place: notes on a western Apache landscape. See Feld & Basso 1996, pp. 53–90

Beattie A, Ehrlich PR. 2001. *Wild Solutions: How Biodiversity Is Money in the Bank*. New Haven, CT: Yale Univ. Press

Bengtsson J, Angelstam P, Elmqvist T, Emanualson U, Folke C, et al. 2003. Reserves, resilience, and dynamic landscapes. *Ambio* 32(6):389–96

Bentley J, Andrew KL. 1991. Pests, peasants, and publications: anthropological and entomological views of an integrated pest management program for small-scale Honduran farmers. *Hum. Org.* 50(2):113–24

Berlin B. 1992. *Ethnobiological Classification: Principles of Categorization of Plants and Animals in Traditional Societies*. Princeton, NJ: Princeton Univ. Press

Berlin B, Breedlove DE, Raven PH. 1974. *Principles of Tzeltal Plant Classification*. New York/London: Academic

Bloch E. 1988 [1930]. The fairy tale moves on its own in time. In *The Utopian Function of Art and Literature: Selected Essays*, ed. J. Zipes, pp. 163–66. Cambridge, MA: MIT Press

Boddy J. 1989. *Wombs and Alien Spirits: Women, Men, and the Zar Cult in Northen Sudan*. Madison: Univ. Wis. Press

Bourdieu P. 1980. *The Logic of Practice*. Stanford, CA: Stanford Univ. Press

Bourdieu P. 1987. What makes a social class?: On the theoretical and practical existence of groups. *Berk. J. Sociol. Crit. Rev.* 31:1–18

Boutin A, Hargreaves AG, Leushuis R, Walters LJ. 2005. Introduction. *J. Eur. Stud.* 31(1):5–9

Brokensha D, Warren DM, Werner O, eds. 1982. *Indigenous Knowledge Systems and Development.* Washington, DC: Univ. Press Am.

Brosius P. 1999. Analyses and interventions: anthropological engagements with environmentalism. *Curr. Anthropol.* 40:277–309

Brush SB. 1991. A farmer-based approach to conserving crop germplasm. *Econ. Bot.* 45:153–65

Brush SB, ed. 2000. *Genes in the Field: On-Farm Conservation of Crop Diversity.* Rome: Int. Dev. Res. Cent. Int. Plant Gen. Resour. Inst.

Brush SB. 2004. *Farmers' Bounty: Locating Crop Diversity in the Contemporary World.* New Haven/London: Yale Univ. Press

Casey ES. 1996. How to get from space to place in a fairly short stretch of time: phenomenological prolegomena. See Feld & Basso 1996, 1:13–52

Chapin FS, Osvaldo ES, Ingrid CB, Grime JP, Hooper DU, et al. 2000. Consequences of changing biodiversity. *Nature* 405:234–42

Choo S. 2004. Eating *satay babi*: sensory perception of transnational movement. *J. Intercul. Stud.* 25(3):203–13

Cleveland DA, Soleri D, eds. 2002. *Farmers, Scientists and Plant Breeding: Integrating Knowledge and Practice.* New York/London: CABI

Cohen JI, Williams JT, Plucknett DL, Shands H. 1991. Ex situ conservation of plant genetic resources: global development and environmental concerns. *Science* 253:866–72

Cole J. 2001. *Forget Colonialism? Sacrifice and the Art of Memory in Madagascar.* Berkeley/Los Angeles: Univ. Calif. Press

Collins WW, Qualset CO, ed. 1999. *Biodiversity in Agroecosystems.* Washington, DC: CRC Press

Comaroff J, Comaroff J. 1997. *Of Revelations and Revolutions: The Dialectics of Modernity in a South African Frontier.* Chicago: Univ. of Chicago Press

Conklin H. 1954. *The relation of Hanunuo culture to the plant world.* PhD diss. Yale Univ.

Conklin H. 1961. The study of shifting cultivation. *Curr. Anthropol.* 2:27–61

Connerton P. 1989. *How Societies Remember.* New York/London: Cambridge Univ. Press

Cruikshank J. 2005. *Do Glaciers Listen? Local Knowledge, Colonial Encounters, and Social Imagination.* Vancouver/Toronto: Univ. Br. Columbia Press

DeSilva C, ed. 1996. In *Memory's Kitchen*, trans. BS Brown. Northvale, NJ: Aronson

DeWalt B. 1994. Using indigenous knowledge to improve agriculture and natural resource management. *Hum. Org.* 53(2):540–52

Dove M. 1986. The practical reason of weeds in Indonesia: peasant vs state views of Imperata and Chromolaena. *Hum. Ecol.* 14(2):163–89

Dove M. 1999. The agronomy of memory and the memory of agronomy: ritual conservation of archaic cultigens in contemporary farming. In *Ethnoecology: Situated Knowledge/Located Lives*, ed. VD Nazarea, 4:45–69. Tucson: Univ. Ariz. Press

Dutfield G. 2000. *Intellectual Property Rights, Trade and Biodiversity.* London: Earthscan

Dutfield G. 2004. *Intellectual Property, Biogenetic Resources and Traditional Knowledge.* Sterling, VA/London: Earthscan

Ehrlich PR. 2002. Human natures, nature conservation, and environmental ethics. *BioScience* 52:31–43

Ellen R. 1993. *The Cultural Relations of Classification: An Analysis of Nuaulu Animal Categories from Central Seram.* Cambridge, UK: Cambridge Univ. Press

Ellen R, Harris H. 2000. Introduction. In *Indigenous Environmental Knowledge and its Transformations: Critical Anthropological Perspectives*, ed. R Ellen, P Parkes, A Bicker, pp. 1–33. Amsterdam: Harwood Acad.

Ellen R, Parkes P, Bicker A, eds. 2000. *Indigenous Environmental Knowledge and Its Transformations: Critical Anthropological Perspectives*. Amsterdam: Harwood

Escobar A. 1998. Whose knowledge? Whose nature? Biodiversity, conservation, and the political ecology of social movements. *J. Polit. Ecol.* 5:54–82

Espeland WN, Stevens ML. 1998. Commensuration as a social process. *Annu. Rev. Sociol.* 24:313–43

Fairhead J, Leach M. 1996. *Misreading the African Landscape: Society and Ecology of a Forest–Savanna Mosaic*. New York: Cambridge Univ. Press

Feld S, Basso KH, eds. 1996. *Senses of Place*. Santa Fe: Sch. Am. Res. Press

Ford RI. 1978. Ethnobotany: historical diversity and synthesis. In *The Nature and Status of Ethnobotany*, ed. RI Ford, Anthropol. Pap., 67:33–49. Ann Arbor: Univ. Mich. Press, Mus. Anthropol.

Fowler C, Mooney P. 1990. *Shattering: Food, Politics, and Loss of Genetic Diversity*. Tucson: Univ. Ariz. Press

Frake CO. 1962. Cultural ecology and ethnography. *Am. Anthropol.* 64:53–59

Freud S. 1976 [1900]. *The Interpretation of Dreams. Penguin Freud Library*, vol. 4. Harmondsworth: Penguin

Freud S, Breuer J. 1974 [1893–1895]. *Studies on Hysteria. Penguin Freud Library*, vol. 3. Harmondsworth: Penguin

Geertz C. 1983. *Local Knowledge: Further Essays in Interpretive Anthropology*. New York: Basic Books

Gold A, Gujar B. 2002. *In Time of Trees and Sorrows*. Ithaca/London: Cornell Univ. Press

Goodenough WH. 1957. Cultural anthropology and linguistics. In *Report of the Seventh Annual Table Meeting on Linguistics and Language Study*, ed. PL Garvin. Washington, DC: Georgetown Univ. Monogr. Ser. Lang. Ling.

Gordillo GR. 2004. *Landscape of Devils: Tensions of Place and Memory in the Argentinean Chaco*. Durham/London: Duke Univ. Press

Halbwachs M. 1992. *On Collective Memory*, ed./trans. LA Coser. Chicago: Univ. Chicago Press

Hammer K. 2003. A paradigm shift in the discipline of plant genetic resources. *Genet. Res. Crop. Evol.* 50:3–10

Harkin ME. 2003. Feeling and thinking in memory and forgetting: toward an ethnohistory of the emotions. *Ethnohistory* 50(2):261–84

Harris M. 1974. Why a perfect knowledge of all the rules one must know to act like a native cannot lead to a knowledge of how natives act. *J. Anthropol. Res.* 30:242–51

Haug F. 2000. Memory work: the key to women's anxiety. In *Memory and Methodology*, ed. S Radstone, 7:155–78. New York: Berg

Hawkes J. 1991. The importance of genetic resources in plant breeding. *Biol. J. Linn. Soc.* 43:3–10

Hayden C. 2003. *When Nature Goes Public: The Making and Unmaking of Bioprospecting in Mexico*. Princeton/Oxford: Princeton Univ. Press

Heatherington T. 2001. In the rustic kitchen: real talk and reciprocity. *Ethnology* 40(4):329–45

Hunn E. 1977. *Tzeltal Folk Zoology: The Classification of Distcontinuities in Nature*. New York: Academic

Hunn E. 1982. The utilitarian in folk biological classification. *Am. Anthropol.* 84:830–47

Hunn E. 1989. Ethnoecology: the relevance of cognitive anthropology for human ecology. In *The Relevance of Culture*, ed. N Freilich, pp. 143–60. New York: Bergin and Garvey

Ingold T. 1996. Hunting and gathering as ways of perceiving the environment. In *Redefining Nature: Ecology, Culture, and Domestication*, ed R Ellen, K Fukui, 5:117–56. Oxford/Washington, DC: Berg

Ingold T. 2000. *The Perception of the Environment: Essays on Livelihood, Dwelling and Skill*. London: Routledge

Jarvis D, Hodgkin T. 2000. Farmer decision making and genetic diversity: linking multidisciplinary research to implementation on-farm. In *Genes in the Field: On-Farm Conservation of Crop Diversity*, ed. SB Brush, pp. 261–78. Rome: Int. Dev. Res. Cent. Int. Plant Gen. Resour. Inst.

Kahn M. 1996. Your place and mine: sharing emotional landscape in Wamira, Papua New Guinea. See Feld & Basso 1996, 5:167–98

Knight CG. 1980. Ethnoscience and African farmers: rationale and strategy. In *Indigenous Knowledge Systems and Development*, ed. DW Brokensha, DM Warren, pp. 203–30. Boston, MA: Univ. Press Am.

Lambek MJ. 2002. *The Weight of the Past: Living with History in Mahajanga, Madagascar*. New York: Palgrave Macmillan

Laplanche J. 1992. Notes on Afterwardness. In *Jean Laplanche: Seduction, Translation, Drives*, ed. J Fletcher, M Stanton, pp. 217–23. London: Inst. Contemp. Arts

Levitt P. 2001. *Transnational Villagers*. Berkeley: Univ. Calif. Press

Li TM. 1999. Marginality, power and production: analysing upland transformations. In *Transforming the Indonesian Uplands: Marginality, Power and Production*, ed. TM Li, 1:1–44. Amsterdam: Harwood Acad.

Lipsitz G. 1991. *Time Passages*. Minneapolis: Univ. Minn. Press

Lovejoy TE. 1997. Biodiversity: What is it? See Reaka-Kudla et al. 1997, pp. 7–14

Maxted N, Ford-Lloyd B, Hawkes JG. 1997. Complementary conservation strategies. In *Plant Genetic Conservation: The In Situ Approach*, ed. N Maxted, B Ford-Lloyd, JG Hawkes, pp. 15–40. London: Chapman and Hall

McDowell L. 2004. Cultural memory, gender and age: young Latvian women's narrative memories of war-time Europe, 1944–1947. *J. Hist. Geogr.* 30:701–28

Merleau-Ponty M. 1962. *Phenomenology of Perception*. Trans. C Smith. London: Routledge/Kegan Paul

Moran J. 2004. History, memory and the everyday. *Rethink. Hist.* 8(1):51–68

Myers N. 1996. The biodiversity crisis and the future of evolution. *Environmentalist* 16:37–47

Nabhan G. 1989. *Enduring Seeds: Native American Agriculture and Wild Plant Conservation*. San Francisco: North Point

Nazarea V. 1998. *Cultural Memory and Biodiversity*. Tucson: Univ. Ariz. Press

Nazarea V. 1999. A view from a point: ethnoecology as situated knowledge. In *Ethnoecology: Situated Knowledge/Located Lives*, ed. VD Nazarea, 1:3–19. Tucson: Univ. Ariz. Press

Nazarea V. 2005. *Heirloom Seeds and Their Keepers: Marginality and Memory in the Conservation of Biological Diversity*. Tucson: Univ. Ariz. Press

Nazarea-Sandoval V. 1995. *Local Knowledge and Agricultural Decision Making in the Philippines: Class, Gender, and Resistance*. Ithaca/London: Cornell Univ. Press

Nora P, ed. 1997 [1984–1992]. *Les Lieux de Memoire*. Paris: Gallimard

Norgaard RB. 1988. The rise of the global exchange economy and the loss of biological diversity. In *Biodiveristy*, ed. EO Wilson, pp. 206–11. Washington, DC: Natl. Acad. Press

Oakley E, Momsen JH. 2005. Gender and agrobiodiversity. *Geogr. J.* 171(3):195–208

Oldfield M, Alcorn JB. 1987. Conservation of traditional agroecosystems. *Bioscience* 37:199–208

Orlove BS, Brush SB. 1996. Anthropology and the conservation of biodiversity. *Annu. Rev. Anthropol.* 25:329–52

Parkes P. 2000. Enclaved knowledge: indigent and indignant representations of environmental management and development among the Kalasha of Pakistan. In *Indigenous Environmental*

Knowledge and its Transformations, ed. R Ellen, P Parkes, A Bicker, 9:253–91. Amsterdam: Harwood Acad.

Patrick R. 1997. Biodiversity: Why is it important? See Reaka-Kudla et al. 1997, 3:15–24

Pimbert M. 1994. The need for another research paradigm. *Seedling* 11:20–32

Pitt-Rivers J. 1971. *The People of the Sierra*. Chicago: Univ. Chicago Press. 2nd ed.

Plucknett DL, Smith NJH, Williams JT, Anishetty NM. 1987. *Gene Banks and the World's Food*. Princeton, NJ: Princeton Univ. Press

Posey DA. 1984. Ethnoecology as applied anthropology in Amazonian development. *Hum. Org.* 43:95–107

Radstone S. 2000. Screening trauma: Forrest Gump, film, and memory. In *Memory and Methodology*, ed. S Radstone, 4:79–110. New York: Berg

Rappaport J. 1998. *The Politics of Memory: Native Historical Interpretation in the Colombian Andes*. Durham, NC: Duke Univ. Press

Raven PH, McNeely JA. 1998. Biological extinction: its scope and meaning for us. In *Protection of Global Biodiversity*, ed. LD Guruswamy, JA McNeely, pp. 13–32. Durham, NC/London: Duke Univ. Press

Reaka-Kudla ML, Wilson DE, Wilson EO, eds. 1997. *Biodiversity II*. Washington, DC: Joseph Henry

Rhoades RE, Booth R. 1982. Farmer-back-to-farmer. *Agric. Admin.* 11:127–37

Rhoades RE, Bebbington A. 1995. Farmers who experiment: an untapped resource for agricultural research and development. In *Indigenous Knowledge Systems: The Cultural Dimension of Development*, ed. PM Warren, D Brokensha, LJ Slikkerveer, pp. 296–307. London: Intermed. Technol.

Ribíero GL. 1997. Transnational virtual community? Exploring implications for culture, power, and language. *Organization* 4(4):496–505

Richards P. 1986. *Coping with Hunger: Hazard and Experiment in a West African Farming System*. London: Allen and Unwin

Richards P. 1996. Culture and community values in the selection and maintenance of African rice. In *Valuing Local Knowledge: Indigenous People and Intellectual Property Rights*, ed. SB Brush, D Stabinsky, pp. 209–29. Washington, DC: Island

Rigney A. 2005. Plentitude, scarcity and circulation of cultural memory. *J. Eur. Stud.* 35(1):11–28

Saikia Y. 2004. *Fragmented Memories: Struggling to be Tai-Ahom in India*. Durham, NC/London: Duke Univ. Press

Seremetakis NC. 1994. *The Senses Still: Perception and Memory as Material Culture in Modernity*. Chicago: Univ. Chicago Press

Shiva V. 1993. *Monocultures of the Mind: Perspectives on Biodiversity and Biotechnology*. London/Penang: Zed Books

Sillitoe P. 1996. *A Place Against Time: Land and Environment in the Papua New Guinea Highlands*. Amsterdam: Harwood Acad.

Smith EA, Wishnie M. 2000. Conservation and subsistence in small-scale societies. *Annu. Rev. Anthropol.* 29:493–524

Soleri D, Smith SE. 1999. Conserving folk crop varieties: different agricultures, different goals. In *Ethnoecology: Situated Knowledge/Located Lives*, ed. VD Nazarea, 8:133–54. Tucson, AZ: Univ. of Ariz. Press

Soulé M. 1993. Conservation: tactics for a constant crisis. In *Perspectives on Biodiversity: Case Studies of Genetic Resource Conservation and Development*, ed. CS Potter, JI Cohen, D Janczewski, pp. 3–17. Washington, DC: Am. Assoc. Adv. Sci.

Steinberg M, Taylor MJ. 2003. Public memory and political power in Guatemala's postconflict landscape. *Geogr. Rev.* 93(4):449–68

Stewart K. 1996. *A Space on the Side of the Road*. Princeton, NJ: Princeton Univ. Press

Stoller P. 1994. Embodying colonial memories. *Am. Anthropol.* 96(3):634–48

Stoller P. 1995. *Embodying Colonial Memories: Spirit Possession, Power and the Hauka in West Africa*. New York/London: Routledge

Stoller P. 1997. *Sensuous Scholarship*. Philadelphia, PA: Univ. Penn. Press

Sutton DE. 1998. *Memories Cast in Stone: The Relevance of the Past in Everyday Life*. New York: Berg

Sutton DE. 2001. *Remembrance of Repasts: An Anthropology of Food and Memory*. New York: Berg

Takacs D. 1996. *The Idea of Biodiversity: Philosophies of Paradise*. Baltimore, MD: Johns Hopkins Univ.

Taussig M. 1993. *Mimesis and Alterity*. New York: Routledge

Taussig M. 1999. *Defacement*. Stanford, CA: Stanford Univ. Press

Tonkin E. 1992. *Narrating Our Pasts: The Social Construction of Oral History*. New York/London: Cambridge Univ. Press

Tsing AL. 1993. *In the Realm of the Diamond Queen: Marginality in an Out-of-the-Way Place*. Princeton, NJ: Princeton Univ. Press

Uehling GL. 2004. *Beyond Memory: The Crimean Tartars' Deportation and Return*. New York: Palgrave Macmillan

UNEP (United Nations Env. Program.). 1994. *Convention on Biological Diversity: Text and Annexes*. UNEP/CBD/94/1. Geneva: Interim Secret. Am. Biol. Divers.

Valladolid J, Apffel-Marglin F. 2001. Andean cosmovision and the nurturing of biodiversity. In *Interbeing of Cosmology and Community*, ed. J Grim, pp. 639–70. Cambridge, MA: Harvard Univ. Press

Warren DM. 1989. Linking scientific and indigenous systems. In *The Transformation of International Agricultural Research and Development*, ed. JL Compton, pp.153–70. Boulder, CO: Lynne ReRienner

Warren DM, Slikkerveer LJ, Brokensha D, eds. 1995. *The Cultural Dimension of Development: Indigenous Knowledge Systems*. London: Intermed. Technol.

Weissberg L. 1999. Introduction. In *Cultural Memory and the Construction of Identity*, ed. D. Ben-Amos, L Weissberg, pp. 7–26. Detroit: Wayne State Univ. Press

Wilcox BA. 1984. *Conservation Biology: An Evolutionary-Ecological Perspective*. Sunderland, MA: Sinauer

Wilkes G. 1991. In situ conservation of agricultural systems. In *Biodiversity, Culture, Conservation and Ecodevelopment*, ed. M Oldfield, J Alcorn, pp. 86–101. Boulder, CO: Westview

Wilson EO. 1988. The current state of biological diversity. In *Biodiveristy*, ed. EO Wilson, pp. 3–18. Washington, DC: Natl. Acad. Press

Wilson EO. 1997. Introduction. See Reaka-Kudla et al. 1997, 1:1–3

Wolf E. 1982. *Europe and the People without History*. Berkeley: Univ. Calif. Press

Zerubavel Y. 1995. *Recovered Roots: Collective Memory and the Making of Israel National Tradition*. Chicago/London: Univ. Chicago Press

Zimmerer K. 1996. *Changing Fortunes: Biodiversity and Peasant Livelihood in the Peruvian Andes*. Berkeley/Los Angeles: Univ. Calif. Press

Zimmerer K. 2003. Just small potatoes (an ulluco)? The use of seed-size variation in "native commercialized" agriculture and agrobiodiversity conservation among Peruvian farmers. *Agric. Hum. Val.* 20:107–23

Obesity in Biocultural Perspective

Stanley J. Ulijaszek and Hayley Lofink

Institute of Social and Cultural Anthropology, University of Oxford,
Oxford OX2 6PF, United Kingdom; email: stanley.ulijaszek@anthro.ox.ac.uk,
hayley.lofink@anthro.ox.ac.uk

Annu. Rev. Anthropol. 2006. 35:337–60

First published online as a Review in
Advance on July 6, 2006

The *Annual Review of Anthropology* is
online at anthro.annualreviews.org

This article's doi:
10.1146/annurev.anthro.35.081705.123301

Copyright © 2006 by Annual Reviews.
All rights reserved

0084-6570/06/1021-0337$20.00

Key Words

population trends, socioeconomic status, nutrition transition,
genetics, evolution, neurophysiology, food security

Abstract

Obesity is new in human evolutionary history, having become possible at the population level with increased food security. Across the past 60 years, social, economic, and technological changes have altered patterns of life almost everywhere on Earth. In tandem, changes in diet and physical activity patterns have been central to the emergence of obesity among many of the world's populations, including the developing world. Increasing global rates of obesity are broadly attributed to environments that are obesogenic, against an evolutionary heritage that is maladaptive in these new contexts. Obesity has been studied using genetic, physiological, psychological, behavioral, cultural, environmental, and economic frameworks. Although most obesity research is firmly embedded within disciplinary boundaries, some convergence between genetics, physiology, and eating behavior has taken place recently. This chapter reviews changing patterns and understandings of obesity from these diverse perspectives.

Human genetics likely have undergone selection for traits that promote energy intake and storage and minimize energy expenditure. Thus it is no surprise that there are a great many obesity-related genotypes. Models linking genetic susceptibilities with physiology and feeding behavior are emerging, and although they only explain a small proportion of global obesity rates, might underlie the more-common and genetically complex forms of human obesity. Human physiology can only exert weak control on the reduction of food intake and the increase of energy expenditure when energy stores are replete and food security is high, and obesity is almost an inevitable human biological outcome in the environments that have been constructed in industrialized nations over the past 60 years and that have emerged with modernization elsewhere.

INTRODUCTION

Obesity is the condition in which excess body fat has accumulated to a degree that health and function are negatively affected. It is new in human evolutionary history, having been essentially nonexistent until approximately 10,000 years ago (Brown 1991, Brown & Krick 2001). Across history, individuals and groups of privilege have been able to display embodied wealth by above-average body size, including weight and fatness (Brown & Konner 1987, Brown 1991, de Garine & Pollock 1995). Obesity was known in ancient Greece (Bevegni & Adami 2003) and was a common condition among the English upper classes in the late eighteenth century (Trowell 1975). It emerged more generally among North American men in the nineteenth century (Kahn & Williamson 1994), increasing in successive surveys in both the United States and Britain across the twentieth century (Garrow 1978). Across the past 60 years, social, economic, and technological changes have altered patterns of life worldwide. During post–World War II reconstruction, economic development grew on a more-global scale, as colonial models of economic management fell from favor. In tandem, changes in diet and activity patterns have been central to the emergence of obesity among many of the world's populations, including poorer ones (Popkin & Doak 1998). In the vast majority of nations for which comparative data are available, rates of obesity are increasing (de Onis 2005, Nishida & Mucavele 2005). It is estimated that over 300 million adults are currently obese, as defined by having a body mass index (BMI) above 30 kg/m^2. A further 700 million people are considered overweight, with BMIs between 25 kg/m^2 and 30 kg/m^2. The prevalence of obesity among children is also rising.

Increasing rates of obesity across the world are broadly attributed to environments that are obesogenic (French et al. 2001, Brownell 2002, Hill et al. 2003), against an evolutionary heritage that is maladaptive in these new contexts (Neel 1962, Eaton et al. 1998, Neel et al. 1998, Lev-Ran 2001). The term obesogenic environment was coined by Swinburn et al. (1999), who argued that the physical, economic, social, and cultural environments of the majority of industrialized nations encourage positive energy balance in their populations. A dominant explanatory framework for the emergence of obesogenic environments is that of nutrition transition (Popkin 2004), which relates globalization, urbanization, and westernization to changing food environments across the populations of the world (Drewnowski & Popkin 1997, Griffiths & Bentley 2001, Contaldo & Pasanisi 2004). Central to this transition are shifts in diet toward increased consumption of energy-dense foods (Drewnowski & Popkin 1997) and declines in physical activity (Erlichman et al. 2002). In this formulation, global food supply becomes increasingly abundant, less expensive, and more-aggressively marketed; coupled with declines in physical activity, this has led to higher prevalences of obesity (Nielsen et al. 2002, Drewnowski & Darmon 2005). In addition, economic inequalities within and between nations have ensured food security for significant sectors of society and for some nations as a whole, while denying food security for many others (Dyson 1996). Underpinning such global phenomena are interrelated physiological, genetic, and behavioral factors (Shuldiner & Munir 2003, Clegg & Woods 2004, Flier 2004), as well as cultural norms that make humans susceptible to obesity (Brown 1991, de Garine & Pollock 1995). How food use is structured socially and culturally has been slow to adjust to changing patterns of food security, as have perceptions of appropriate body size for health and beauty, which has contributed to the emergence of obesity in various societies (de Garine & Pollock 1995).

Obesity has been studied using genetic, physiological, psychological, behavioral, cultural, environmental, and economic frameworks. Although most obesity research is firmly embedded within disciplinary boundaries, some convergence between the study of genetics, physiology, and eating behavior has taken place recently (Barsh & Schwartz 2002, Flier 2004, de Castro 2006). Anthropologists use biocultural perspectives to understand the interacting factors that may have made fatness-related traits advantageous across evolutionary time and in relation to cultural change (Brown 1991). Much has happened in obesity research since 1991, making a review from biocultural perspectives timely. In this chapter, we place new observations in the genetics and physiology of obesity (and the social, cultural, and behavioral forces that interact with them) in an updated biocultural description of this phenomenon. We rely heavily on research carried out in the United States, largely because this is where most of the best work has been carried out. Our focus is predominantly on obesity among adults.

We begin by defining measures of obesity and continue by considering its health implications and population trends. We use a definition of obesity as a BMI greater than 30 kg/m^2, and its age equivalent for children, which is recommended for international use (Shetty & James 1994, Cole et al. 2000), although this measure is not independent of stature, lean body mass, or body proportion (Norgan 1994a,b). This index is widely used largely because of the need for a simple comparative measure of obesity in the world's populations.

MEASUREMENT OF OBESITY AND FATNESS

Measures used to assess body fatness and obesity include (*a*) visual appearance; (*b*) anthropometry; (*c*) body density by underwater weighing, isotopic dilution, dual X-ray absorptiometry, or bioelectrical impedance; and (*d*) body imaging by ultrasound, computed tomography, or magnetic resonance imaging (Poskitt 1995). The most-frequently used measures for population-based work are anthropometric; the most common of these is the BMI, which is derived by dividing body weight in kilograms by the square of height in meters. It has been adopted for epidemiological and public health usage because it reflects body energy stores and shows strong associations with morbidity and mortality from a number of chronic diseases and disorders.

Relationships between BMI and both morbidity and mortality are usually either J- or U-shaped, with risk increasing outside of a normative range. At the lower end of the BMI distribution, increased morbidity risk owing to infectious disease has been demonstrated for populations in India (Campbell & Ulijaszek 1994), Pakistan and Kenya (Garcia & Kennedy 1994), but not in the Philippines or Ghana (Garcia & Kennedy 1994). At the upper end of the distribution, the BMI has been shown to be associated with chronic disease risk and mortality (Shetty & James 1994). These include coronary heart disease; high blood pressure; stroke; noninsulin-dependent diabetes (NIDDM) (World Health Organization 2000, Li et al. 2002); endometrial, ovarian, cervical, and postmenopausal breast cancer in women; and prostate cancer in men (Bianchini et al. 2002). The normative

BMI range of 18.5–25 kg/m^2 is likely to be maintained in many populations by way of balancing selection. The BMI cut-offs are used to define overweight and obesity in adults are 25 kg/m^2 and 30 kg/m^2, respectively (Shetty & James 1994). However, the relationship between BMI and fatness varies across populations, as do relationships between morbidity and BMI. In some Chinese (Li et al. 2002) and South Asian populations (Gill 2001, Sullivan 2001, Wahlqvist 2001), increased chronic disease risk occurs at lower BMIs than among European populations (Li et al. 2002). The BMI does not give a measure of intra-abdominal (visceral) or lower-body fatness, however. High levels of intra-abdominal fatness are independently associated with risk markers of cardiovascular disease, NIDDM, and various cancers (World Health Organization 2000). High lower-body fatness relative to waist size is associated with lower risk of the same disorders, and among females it is important for buffering the energetic stresses of pregnancy and lactation (Garaulet et al. 2000).

Classification of childhood obesity using BMI is more problematic than for adults because of the variability in the growth rates of children both within and between populations. The BMI changes with age, and Cole et al. (2000) have proposed for international use age-specific cut-offs for childhood overweight and obesity that pass through BMIs of 25 kg/m^2 and 30 kg/m^2, respectively, at the age of 18, using a normative distribution that varies by age and sex. However, unlike in adults where it is possible to establish increased health risks associated with an increased BMI, most health effects of childhood obesity are manifested in adult life and not childhood, with the possible exception of risk markers for NIDDM.

POPULATION TRENDS IN OBESITY

Obesity at the population level was largely unknown in the 1950s. However, by the 1990s,

33 nations had obesity rates exceeding 10% of their adult populations (**Figure 1**, see color insert) (Nishida & Mucavele 2005). Currently, obesity is most prevalent in some Pacific Island nations; the United States; most European, many Middle Eastern, and some Latin American nations; and South Africa. Four Pacific Island nations (Nauru, Tonga, the Cook Islands, and French Polynesia) have the highest rates of obesity in the world, in all cases exceeding 40% of their adult populations. Obesity rates for Bahrain and Kuwait lie close to that of the United States, at a little below 30% of the adult population. The rate for Canada is approximately half that of the United States. For the adult South African population, the rate is 22%, similar to Egypt, Turkey, Hungary, and Germany, the latter two having the highest rates in Europe. The lowest rate in Europe, 5%, is among adults in Norway and Switzerland. Of Latin American populations, Mexico, Uruguay, and Peru have rates that exceed 15%. Rates among wealthier Asian nations vary from 6% in Singapore to 3% of adult populations in Japan and South Korea. In the vast majority of nations, obesity rates among females are higher than for males by an average of 5%. Obesity rates of females exceed those of males by more than 2% in 32 of the 66 nations for which data exist for both sexes, whereas obesity rates of males exceed those of females in only 4 nations.

Rising obesity rates have varied in different nations. In Pacific Island nations, rates of obesity were already high by the 1960s and continued to increase dramatically into the 1990s (Ulijaszek 2005). The United States and Canada had similar rates of obesity 40 years ago, at approximately 10% of the adult population; subsequently, rates became higher in the United States than in Canada (Nishida & Mucavele 2005). In the past 20 years, obesity rates have risen in the majority of nations with available data. Of 28 nations for which data are available, increased obesity rates have been observed for adult males in 20 and for adult females in 19 (Nishida & Mucavele 2005). The fastest increases have taken place in Hungary, Russia, Ireland, Turkey, and Nauru. Of the nations with no increase or a decrease in obesity, three of them (France, Italy, and Japan) continued to have the low levels of obesity they experienced approximately 20 years ago and are economically advanced nations with excellent food security. The extensive emergence and rise of obesity among most of the world's populations indicate that the ability to become obese is universal (Lev-Ran 2001). Furthermore, the great variation in obesity rates between nations in the same regions with different economic standing supports the view that increasing food security is but one component of the recent emergence of obesity.

Although previously a condition predominantly of the wealthy, the relationship between social class and obesity has become inverted in wealthier and economically emerging nations (Sobal & Stunkard 1989, Kirchengast et al. 2004, Rennie & Jebb 2005, Stamatakis et al. 2005). Similar inversions are also found in urban areas of less-developed countries (Monteiro et al. 2000, Peña & Bacallao 2002), as increased food security and sedentization of life have increasingly permeated poorer sectors of society, as well as wealthier ones. Within more-affluent nations, minority populations and rural communities show the highest rates of obesity (Swinburn et al. 2004). For example, obesity rates among adult Pacific Islanders living in New Zealand in the early 1990s were above 65% (Swinburn et al. 2004), compared with nationwide values of 15%. In the United States, Native Americans, African Americans, Puerto Ricans, and Mexican Americans have higher body mass than European Americans (Denney et al. 2004). Nearly 40% of black non-Hispanic adults have a BMI above 30 kg/m^2, much higher than obesity rates for Mexican American and white non-Hispanic adults, who have rates of 35% and 29%, respectively (Flegal et al. 2002).

FATNESS AND HUMAN EVOLUTION

Larger body mass and increased ability to accumulate fat relative to other nonhuman primates in seasonal environments are two key adaptive features of human life history (Aiello & Wells 2002). The rapid brain evolution observed with the emergence of *Homo erectus* at approximately 1.6–1.8 million years ago is likely associated with increased body fatness as well as diet quality (Leonard et al. 2003), i.e., the greater availability of animal fat and cholesterol that would have come with increased diet quality, possibly facilitating encephalization (Horrobin 1999). Whereas Cunnane & Crawford (2003) proposed that the modern human brain was an outcome of earlier natural selection for greater fatness in neonates and infants, Kuzawa (1998) has argued that the two phenomena coevolved in feedback with each other. Regardless of whether fatness preceded encephalization, greater levels of body fatness and reduced levels of muscle mass relative to other primate species allow human infants to accommodate brain growth by having adequate stored energy for brain metabolism when intake is limited and by reducing the total energy costs of the rest of the body (Aiello & Wells 2002). Compared with apes, humans have a similar proportion of maternal daily nonmaintenance energy budget invested in fetal tissue, but humans have a much higher diet quality. This allows both larger brain size and higher body fatness at birth (Ulijaszek 2002a). Energy stored in adipose tissue buffers against mortality risk soon after birth and at weaning, when nutrition is often disrupted (Kuzawa 1998).

Fatness in human females is linked to fertility (Brown & Konner 1987, Norgan 1997), female ovarian function being particularly sensitive to energy balance and energy flux (Ellison 2003). At any BMI, females have a greater proportion of body weight as fat than males. Furthermore, they have a greater proportion of lower-body fat than males. This has importance in reproductive function: Lower-body fat is less-readily available for everyday energetic needs than upper-body or abdominal fat, but lower-body fat is mobilized during pregnancy and lactation (Garaulet et al. 2000). Reproductive effort during pregnancy and lactation is thus buffered from environmental energetic constraints (Ellison 2003).

Human genetics are likely to have undergone selection for traits that promote energy intake and storage and minimize energy expenditure (Rosenbaum & Leibel 1998). There is great diversity in obesity-related genotypes (Perusse et al. 2005). However, the vast majority of obesity is related to more than one locus, each accounting for only part of the phenotypic variance (Comuzzie 2002). Because all aspects of metabolism are under genetic control, and the expression of obesity phenotypes is much more limited than the expression of peptides that regulate metabolism, natural selection for the capacity to save and store energy is likely to have taken place for different genes with the same phenotypic result (Lev-Ran 2001), perhaps ultimately to defend the energy needs of large brain size. Neel et al. (1998) argued that many different genes underwent such selection in different populations and geographic areas and under different kinds of environmental pressure. Against this microevolutionary scenario, that most mammals are able to overeat to high levels of body fatness suggests the genetic basis for the majority of human obesity lies in deeper evolutionary time, although the greater normative level of body fatness of humans relative to other primates and most mammals is likely to have evolved with the encephalization that took place with *H. erectus*.

Seasonality of food availability likely was a major environmental pressure, given that it occurred during hominid evolution (Foley 1993) and is common in primate (Hladik 1988) and human subsistence ecologies of all kinds (de Garine & Harrison 1988). Human genotypes for obesity, however, are not incompatible with present environments of good food security and sedentary lifestyle, given that the almost-worldwide increases in survivorship and longevity have taken place often in tandem with the emergence of obesity (Eaton et al. 1998).

Because energy stores are vital to survivorship and reproduction, the ability to conserve energy as adipose tissue would have conferred selective advantage to *Homo sapiens*. Neel (1962) suggested the existence of thrifty genotypes that code for efficient and potentially excessive energy accumulation. This formulation has undergone modification, with alternative terms proposed for conditions associated with genes for diabetes, obesity, and hypertension considered to have been adaptive in the remote past but now compromised by changed environments. These terms include syndromes of impaired genetic homeostasis, civilization syndromes, and altered lifestyle syndromes (Neel et al. 1998). Genes corresponding to such syndromes may be called stockpiling (Garrow 1993), greedy, or acquisitive instead because little obesity is caused by thrifty metabolism (Lev-Ran 2001).

The biological drives of feeding, hunger, and the dietary regulation of macronutrient intake may have shared physiological and behavioral bases with other animals (Ulijaszek 2002b, Berthoud 2004). Various mammals are susceptible to overeating and increased body-fat deposition when presented with diets that are plentiful, palatable, and/or high in fat, indicating that the tendency to overeat in response to food-portion size, palatability, energy density and to overeat fat passively are general mammalian evolutionary traits. Furthermore, social aspects of feeding are far from unique to humans; the social facilitation of food intake (in which social interaction during eating increases food intake) has long been known to take place among animals from chickens to primates.

Body size in the genus *Homo* was greater than that of most australopithecines, and although meat and nutritionally dense plant foods were the major dietary components most likely to have fueled body-size increase

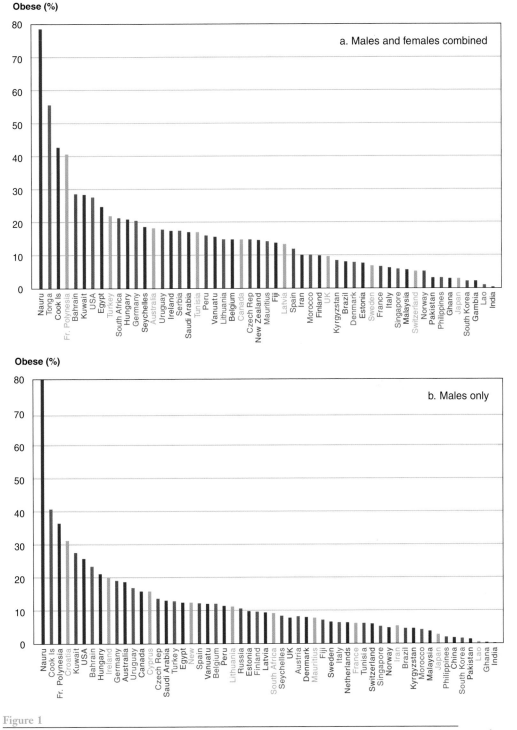

Obese (%)

a. Males and females combined

Nauru, Tonga, Cook Is, Fr. Polynesia, Bahrain, Kuwait, USA, Egypt, Turkey, South Africa, Hungary, Germany, Seychelles, Australia, Uruguay, Ireland, Serbia, Saudi Arabia, Tunisia, Peru, Vanuatu, Lithuania, Belgium, Canada, Czech Rep, New Zealand, Mauritius, Fiji, Latvia, Spain, Iran, Morocco, Finland, UK, Kyrgyzstan, Brazil, Denmark, Estonia, Sweden, France, Italy, Singapore, Malaysia, Switzerland, Norway, Pakistan, Philippines, Ghana, Japan, South Korea, Gambia, Lao, India

Obese (%)

b. Males only

Nauru, Cook Is, Fr. Polynesia, Croatia, Kuwait, USA, Bahrain, Hungary, Ireland, Germany, Australia, Uruguay, Canada, Cyprus, Czech Rep, Saudi Arabia, Turkey, Egypt, New, Spain, Vanuatu, Belgium, Peru, Lithuania, Russia, Estonia, Finland, Latvia, South Africa, Seychelles, UK, Austria, Denmark, Mauritius, Fiji, Sweden, Italy, Netherlands, France, Tunisia, Switzerland, Singapore, Norway, Iran, Brazil, Kyrgyzstan, Morocco, Malaysia, Japan, Philippines, China, South Korea, Pakistan, Lao, Ghana, India

Figure 1

Obesity rates by nation (body mass index greater than 30 kg/m²). Figure created using data from Nishida & Mucavele 2005.

Obese (%)

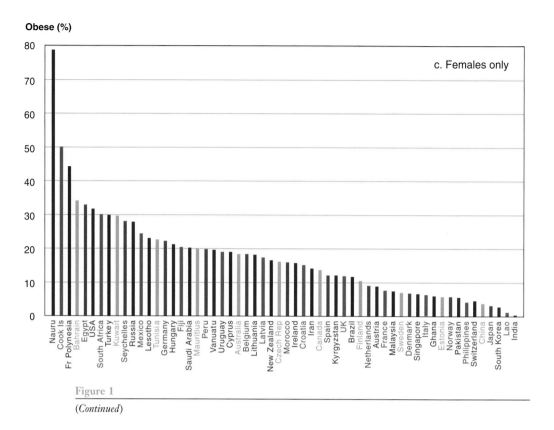

c. Females only

Figure 1

(*Continued*)

and encephalization in *Homo* (Plummer 2004), decreased taste sensitivities associated with greater body size would have also favored increased diet breadth. Low sweetness and bitterness sensitivities allow larger primate species to find food sources of lower-energy density palatable and to eat them more frequently than among primate species of small body size (Simmen & Hladik 1998). Furthermore, basal metabolic rate per unit of body mass scales negatively with body weight among primates (Martin 1993), making the energy requirement per unit of body size lower in large primates than in small ones.

Human eating behavior differs from other mammalian species in the extent to which (*a*) food availability is controlled, (*b*) social and cultural norms of diet and eating exist, and (*c*) personal feeding constraints operate (Ulijaszek 2002b). Social and cultural norms of diet and eating are likely to have increased in complexity only with the emergence of complex symbolic behavior among *H. sapiens* by 75,000 years ago (Henshilwood et al. 2004). With cooking, the emergence of cuisine, and increased complexity of food use, great diversity in the social patterning of feeding has taken place. Social feeding may have been a behavioral adaptation of early *Homo* that has continued to have implications for the energy balance of contemporary human populations.

GENETICS OF OBESITY

Various types of evidence have been used to identify genetic contributions to human obesity. These include (*a*) familial clustering of body fatness (Allison et al. 1996), (*b*) estimates of heritability for obesity and fatness phenotypes in twin studies (Stunkard et al. 1986, Keller et al. 2003), (*c*) identification of monogenic severe early-onset obesity (Flier 2004), and (*d*) genotyping of polygenic obesity (Clement et al. 2002).

The heritability of human adiposity (estimated in most studies from BMI, but also from skinfolds) varies from 0.49 to 0.93 (Keller et al. 2003). Heritability of food in-

take is lower, generally varying between 0.11 to 0.65 (Keller et al. 2003). With respect to eating behaviors and styles, heritabilities of 0.44 and 0.65 have been reported for meal frequency and size, respectively (de Castro 1999), 0.40 and 0.45 for disinhibition (Neale et al. 2003, de Castro & Lilenfeld 2005), 0.44 for cognitive restraint, and 0.24 for perceived hunger (de Castro & Lilenfeld 2005).

Over 600 genes, markers, and chromosomal regions have been associated with human obesity phenotypes (Perusse et al. 2005), and the numbers continue to grow. By October 2004, 173 human obesity cases owing to single-gene mutations in 10 different genes had been reported, whereas 49 loci related to Mendelian syndromes relevant to human obesity had been mapped to a genomic region, with causal genes or strong candidate genes identified for most of them. Furthermore, 204 quantitative trait loci (single genes with large effects on a given quantitative trait) for obesity-related phenotypes had been identified from 50 genome-wide scans (Perusse et al. 2005). Several single-point mutations have also been associated with various obesity phenotypes (Bouatia-Naji et al. 2006, Wilson et al. 2006). At the population level, obesity is mainly polygenic, with genetic variations influencing metabolism. There are interactions of different obesity genes, and gene-dosage effects in heterozygotes of obesity genotypes, such that intermediate phenotypes are less extreme than homozygotes (Chung & Leibel 2005). Success in the identification of polygenic determinants of obesity across human populations has been limited (Comuzzie 2002), although genome-wide scans in different populations have localized major obesity loci on chromosomes 2, 5, 10, 11, and 20 (Clement et al. 2002). The study of polygenic obesity requires the analysis of genotype-phenotype associations while taking into account the influence of environmental factors such as diet and sedentary lifestyle (Clement 2005). However, such an integrated approach requires large samples and the expansion of biocomputing tools for the analysis of

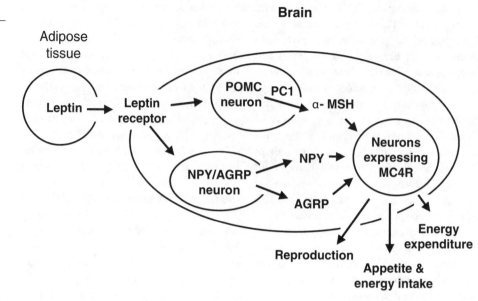

Figure 2

Genetic regulation of energy balance by way of leptin signaling and agouti related protein (AGRP). Modified from Mizuno et al. 2003 and Flier 2004. α-MSH, α-melanocyte stimulating hormone; MC4R, melanocortin 4 receptor; NPY, neuropeptide Y; PC1, prohormone convertase 1; POMC, pro-opiomelanocortin.

multiple interactions with no a priori hypotheses (Clement 2005).

For over 50 years, monogenic rodent models of obesity have been used widely in attempts to understand body-weight regulation in humans. Linkages between the genetic and physiological study of obesity became possible with the identification of (*a*) the *ob* gene product leptin (Zhang et al. 1994) and the leptin receptor (Tartaglia et al. 1995), and (*b*) the *agouti* gene and agouti related protein (AGRP) (Zemel et al. 1995, Mizuno et al. 2003). Leptin is a cytokine secreted from adipose tissue at a rate proportional to the size of body-fat stores and is the principal physiological indicator of nutritional state and fatness. AGRP, along with neuropeptide Y (NPY) and α-melanocyte stimulating hormone (α-MSH), is a central mediator of leptin action. The melanocortin 4 receptor (MC4-R) plays a central regulatory role in the action of leptin and is influenced by levels of α-MSH, NPY, and AGRP. The signaling pathways involving leptin and MC4-R influence the regulation of all aspects of energy balance (Barsh & Schwartz 2002, Fan et al. 2005). Several types of monogenic human obesity owing to genetic disruption of the leptin-signaling

pathway identified more recently include deficiency syndromes of leptin, leptin receptor, pro-opiomelanocortin (POMC), MC4-R, and prohormone convertase 1 (Farooqi & O'Rahilly 2005). These peptides function in a central nervous system pathway for energy-balance regulation (**Figure 2**) (Mizuno et al. 2003, Flier 2004). Although the mechanism whereby MC4R influences food intake is reasonably elaborated, its influence on energy expenditure is not. However, in the Quebec Family Study, Loos et al. (2005) have identified a DNA-sequence variation at the MC4R gene locus that may contribute to physical inactivity. Although the major leptin-regulatory arm of this model accounts for less than 4% of severe early-onset obesity, quantitative differences in the expression or function of these same genes, either alone or in combination with one another, may underlie the more-common and genetically complex forms of human obesity (Flier 2004).

PHYSIOLOGY AND BEHAVIOR

Physiologically, obesity can only develop if food consumption is high and/or energy expenditure is low, resulting in positive energy balance across months or years. A positive energy balance of 10% can lead to approximately a 13.5-kg increase in body weight within a year (Bray 1987). The increasing rates of obesity among adults in many industrialized populations across the second half of the twentieth century are a result of a disregulation of energy balance of less than 1% per year. The physiology of energy accumulation is that of neuroendocrine, gut- and adipose-tissue regulation of energy balance, the maintenance of which involves coordinated and physiologically linked changes in energy intake and expenditure (Moore 2000). Both leptin- and melanocortin-signaling pathways are upstream of nervous system–effector mechanisms that regulate both appetite and energy expenditure (Flier 2004).

Much less is known about the neurophysiological mechanisms by which reduced energy expenditure influences energy balance than about altered appetite and energy balance (Flier 2004). There is no dominant physiological pathway of the desire to eat in relation to nutritional requirement or environmental constraint of intake through availability. Rather, a range of physiological signals regulates intake. Over 60 obesity-related peptides are known, many identified as either promoting increased or decreased energy intake. Various models have been put forward that link energy-balance endocrinology of the gut, pancreas, adipose tissue to the central nervous system and the brain (Tschop et al. 2000, Schwartz & Morton 2002, Flier 2004), and **Figure 3** gives a simplified consensus view.

In the absence of food (**Figure 3a**), there are falling levels of leptin from adipose tissue, insulin from the pancreas, and peptide YY-36 from the gut, as well as increasing levels of ghrelin from the gut and upregulated NPY/AGRP neurons in the hypothalamus, the physiological system that links the nervous and endocrine systems. Upregulated NPY/AGRP neurons cause the release of NPY and AGRP that inhibit downstream neurons in the paraventricular nucleus of the hypothalamus and the ventromedial hypotha-

lamus (often thought of as the satiety center of the brain), stimulating appetite. Stimulation of NPY/AGRP neurons also causes cellular and tissue growth and appetite-stimulating effects in the lateral hypothalamus, which in turn upregulate energy intake and downregulate energy expenditure. Decreasing leptin and insulin concentrations also lead to reduced stimulation of POMC neurons, resulting in lowered secretion of α-MSH in the pituitary. α-MSH is a secondary peptide product of the POMC gene, one of eight yielded by differential processing of the primary peptide product of this gene. This in turn lowers its stimulation of the downstream neurons in the hypothalamus. Inhibition of these downstream neurons reduces metabolic breakdown of larger molecules to smaller ones. The NPY/AGRP neurons are stimulated by starvation but are not significantly affected by overfeeding (**Figure 3b**), whereas POMC neurons are affected by both starvation and overfeeding. Thus there would have been stronger natural selection against starvation than overfeeding.

Other gut peptides involved in appetite regulation include cholecystokinin (CCK), glucagon-like peptide 1, and bombesin-like peptides (similar in structure to a family of short peptides widely distributed among mammals with potent physiological effects on feeding and satiety). Bombesin-like peptides include gastrin-releasing peptide, originally named so for its ability to release gastrin in the gut but also expressed in the pituitary gland, and neuromedin B, whose physiological effects include the regulation of feeding, blood pressure, blood glucose, body temperature, and cellular growth. CCK is involved in the control of the amount of food eaten at any time and is released from the small intestine into the circulation in response to nutrients in the lumen of the gut, such as fatty acids (Moran 2000). Glucagon-like peptide 1 is released after feeding and produces loss of appetite (Yamamoto et al. 2002). As well as its involvement in the regulation of energy balance, MC4R has been implicated in the regulation

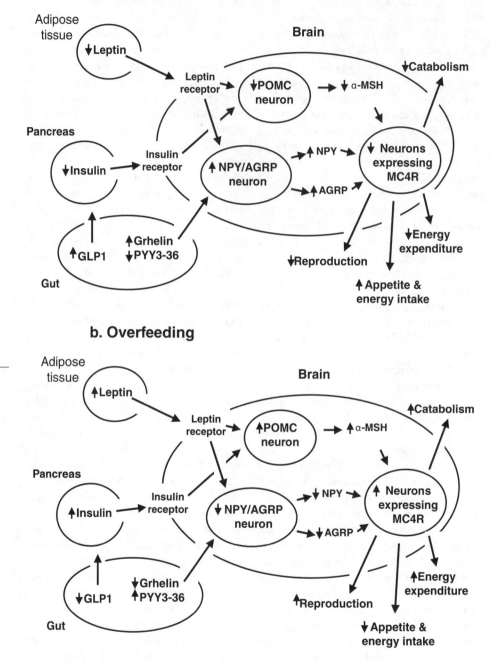

a. Starvation

Adipose tissue
↓Leptin

Brain

Leptin receptor → ↓POMC neuron → ↓α-MSH

↑Catabolism

Pancreas
↓Insulin → Insulin receptor

↑NPY/AGRP neuron → ↑NPY → ↓Neurons expressing MC4R

↑AGRP

Gut
↑GLP1
↑Grhelin
↓PYY3-36

↓Reproduction

↑Appetite & energy intake

↓Energy expenditure

b. Overfeeding

Figure 3

Neuroendocrine regulation of energy balance. Modified from Schwartz & Morton 2002, Tschop et al. 2000, and Flier 2004. AGRP, agouti related protein; α-MSH, α-melanocyte stimulating hormone; GLP1, glucagon-like peptide 1; MC4-R, melanocortin 4 receptor; NPY, neuropeptide Y; POMC, pro-opiomelanocortin.

Adipose tissue
↑Leptin

Brain

Leptin receptor → ↑POMC neuron → ↑α-MSH

↑Catabolism

Pancreas
↑Insulin → Insulin receptor

↓NPY/AGRP neuron → ↓NPY → ↑Neurons expressing MC4R

↓AGRP

Gut
↓GLP1
↓Grhelin
↑PYY3-36

↑Reproduction

↑Energy expenditure

↓Appetite & energy intake

of reproduction by way of the hypothalamo-pituitary-gonadal axis (Schioth et al. 2003).

The neurophysiological system described in **Figure 3** strongly controls feeding and reduced energy expenditure when energy reserves are depleted and fuel security is low. However, it can only exert weak control on reducing food intake and increasing energy expenditure when energy stores are replete and food security is high (Ahima et al. 1996).

Environmental factors associated with modern life and good food security create constant pressures on food intake that are not compensated by equivalent increases in energy expenditure, with surplus energy stored overwhelmingly in adipose tissue (Berthoud 2004). This model is a partial one, however, because food intake is driven by additional cognitive and environmental factors (Berthoud 2004). At the low end of the BMI distribution, considerable research has been conducted on low food intake and adaptation to low energy intakes (Waterlow 1990, Shetty 1993), showing energy balance at low intakes to be strongly defended. The major components are feedforward mechanisms between the brain and gut that anticipate the nutritional needs of the body (Myers & Sclafani 2003) by responding to the abundance of food cues in food-secure and socially enhanced environments (de Castro & Stroebele 2002, Ulijaszek 2002b, Rolls 2003). Such cues include perceived qualities of potential foods, including (a) smell; (b) associations with pleasure, displeasure, or disgust; (c) expectations from foods; and (d) sensory properties while eating. Thus the neuroendocrine pathways regulating energy balance must intersect with systems regulating pleasure and reward (Saper et al. 2002). Leptin is known to inhibit sweet-sensitive taste cells in the tongue (Kawai et al. 2000). Thus, when leptin levels increase (as in overfeeding), perception of the sweetness of food declines and with it the range of food intake because of the reduced palatability of foods with sweetness as a component of their flavor. Furthermore, the gut peptide CCK is a physiological satiety factor in humans. However, little else is known of the links between the pathways for pleasure and reward and those regulating hunger and satiety (Flier 2004).

Food cues involve learning because there are few unlearned sensory preferences for foods and taste among humans (Mela & Catt 1996). Although infants have innate preferences for sweetness in food and aversions to sour and bitter tastes, food preferences are molded from birth, both culturally and behaviorally. At any given time they are highly stable but are heavily determined by social contexts of eating, in addition to expectations from foods prior to eating (Mela 1999). In the absence of food limitation in either volume, weight, or energy, the most-powerful behavioral influences on the amounts of food eaten by humans include (a) other individuals at a meal (de Castro 1999, Bell & Pliner 2003, Wansink 2004), (b) television viewing (Stroebele & de Castro 2004), (c) the size of food packages and portion sizes (Rolls et al. 2004, Wansink 2004), (d) palatability (Spitzer & Rodin 1981), (e) the energy density of food (Stubbs 1998), and (f) the consumption of caloric beverages with a meal (Della Valle et al. 2005). In all cases, the greater the size or dose of the influence, the more is eaten. Influences on the energy intake and density of food eaten in societies where there is food insecurity include (a) economic constraints (Darmon et al. 2002, 2003; Drewnowski & Darmon 2005), (b) consumption of energy-containing beverages (Bray et al. 2004), (c) passive overconsumption of fat in high-fat diets (Blundell & Stubbs 1997), and (d) social and cultural mores (de Garine & Pollock 1995). There remains, however, great within-population variation in food-consumption behavior not explained by these factors. Both food novelty and palatability play to powerful behavioral influences on the size of food intake. Many industrial food products appeal to the palate as well as being energy dense, whereas the range of novel food items marketed in the industrialized world has increased dramatically in the past 20 years. Furthermore, technology in such societies has now divorced the sensory and nutritional attributes of foods in a way that prevents learning by associative conditioning of palatability, appetite, and satiety (Stubbs & Whybrow 2004). The extent to which this uncoupling between sensory and nutritional properties of food is responsible for overconsumption is not known, however (Stubbs & Whybrow 2004).

Two theories have been proposed to explain between-individual differences in food consumption behaviors and the tendency to overeat. The first, that of externality, postulates that obese people are more reactive to external cues (such as the time of day, presence of food, and situational effects) and less sensitive to internal physiological hunger and satiety signals than are lean subjects (Schachter & Rodin 1974). According to this view, high reactivity to external cues encourages overeating and the development of obesity in environments in which highly palatable food is readily available. However, evidence confirming such an eating style among obese subjects is not conclusive (Brownell & Wadden 1991). If it exists, externality may be an antecedent of obesity and not a consequence or correlate of overeating (Mela 1996). The second theory, that of psychosomatic feeding, focuses on emotional eating (Allison & Heshka 1993). The usual response to arousal (such as fear, anxiety, or anger) is loss of appetite. However, some individuals respond by overeating. This may be a result of an inability to differentiate between the need for food and other uncomfortable sensations and feelings, probably as a result of early learning experiences. The balance of conflicting evidence suggests relative overeating in obese individuals during negative emotional states (Geliebter & Aversa 2003). However, people can counteract their externally or emotionally induced tendency to overeat by cognitive restraint of their food intake. Obese people are less likely to practice restraint in eating, however (Herman & Mack 1975), regardless of any psychological reason as to why they might overeat.

CULTURAL, BEHAVIORAL, AND ECONOMIC PERSPECTIVES

Although good food security and sedentization of life are central to the generation of obesogenic environments, various other factors also contribute to them. The maintenance of parsimonious food behaviors, involving avoidance of waste or getting the best value for money, becomes maladaptive in the context of good food security. Indirect evidence for waste avoidance comes from studies in the

United States and Mexico that show humans are largely blind to portion size (Rolls et al. 2004, Mrdjenovic & Levitsky 2005, Levitsky et al. 2005, Wansink & Cheney 2005), with increased portion size predicting increased energy consumption (Fisher et al. 2003, Dilberti et al. 2004, Levitsky & Youn 2004, McConahy et al. 2004, Rolls et al. 2004, Wansink & Cheney 2005). In the United States, portion sizes of prepackaged and restaurant-prepared foods have increased greatly across the past two decades (Harnack et al. 2000, McConahy et al. 2002, Young & Nestle 2002, Smiciklas-Wright et al. 2003, Kral & Rolls 2004). Increased snacking and decreased structure of meals have also taken place in many industrialized (Decarli et al. 2000, Samuelson 2000, Jahns et al. 2001, Zizza et al. 2001, Crooks 2003, St-Onge et al. 2003) and industrializing nations. Children in the United States eat more food away from home, drink more soft drinks, and snack more frequently than 20 years ago (Jahns et al. 2001, Nielsen et al. 2002, St-Onge et al. 2003). Snack foods are often densely caloric, prepared, processed, and packaged foods (Nielsen et al. 2002). Both adults (Tucker & Friedman 1989, Tucker & Bagwell 1991, Jeffrey & French 1998) and children (Dietz & Gortmaker 1985, Del Toro & Greenberg 1989, Renders et al. 2004, van den Bulck & van Mierlo 2004,) often snack without feeling physically hungry, especially when distracted by an external stimulus, such as watching television (Stroebele & de Castro 2004). It is more difficult for humans to accurately monitor how much they have eaten when distracted (Wansink 2004). Television also increases exposure to the commercial marketing of energy-dense foods. In the 1990s, children in the United States watched on average approximately 10,000 television advertisements for food each year, 95% of which were for foods in one of four categories: sugared cereals, sweets/chocolate, fast food, and soft drinks (Brownell 2002). However, although both time spent watching television and rates of obesity increased concurrently in the United States since the 1960s, a causal link between the two has yet to be demonstrated (Gorely et al. 2004).

Fast food has characteristics that favor the development of obesity, including its high-energy density, fat, and fructose content (Isganaitis & Lustig 2005), and Jebb (2003) has proposed a possible mechanistic link between fast foods, energy density, and obesity. However, Bandini et al. (1999) found that obese adolescents in the United States eat no more fast food than nonobese adolescents, emphasizing that excess energy intake may come from a variety of food sources and not solely from energy-dense snack foods. Although the globalization of fast food is beginning to affect children's eating patterns in many countries undergoing nutrition transition, the contribution of fast food and soft drinks to children's diet remains relatively small compared with the United States (Adair & Popkin 2005).

Increasing time constraints on home cooking in food-secure nations also likely contribute to obesity rates because of high female engagement in the workforce (St-Onge et al. 2003). A consequence of this has been the emergence and rise in demand for prepackaged convenience foods with short preparation times (Schluter & Lee 1999) and of food consumption away from the home (Lin et al. 1996, McCrory et al. 1999, French et al. 2001, Nielsen et al. 2002, Critser 2003, St-Onge et al. 2003). Both phenomena have increased dependence on industrialized food in many countries. Other time-saving devices (including drive-through, 24-hour, take-away, and home-delivery food services) have helped make food ubiquitous in everyday life in the United States (Brownell 2002) and increasingly elsewhere.

In the United States, Sweden, United Kingdom, Poland, and other industrialized nations, the inverse relationship between socioeconomic status and obesity has been explained by class differences in obesity-relevant health behaviors that have persisted, with people of higher social class eating diets with lower fat content, exercising more, and being

more likely to diet to control weight (Jeffrey et al. 1991, Molarius 2003, Bielicki et al. 2005, Stamatakis et al. 2005). It has also been linked to dietary energy density and energy cost (Darmon et al. 2002, French 2003). In the United States, the price of fresh fruit and vegetables has increased as a proportion of disposable income across time, whereas the price of refined grains, sugars, and fats has declined (Sturm 2005). Diets that are more energy-dense are associated with lower daily food consumption costs (Drewnowski & Darmon 2005). However, they also have lower effects on satiety and can result in passive overeating and weight gain (Prentice & Poppitt 1996). Obesity may thus be linked with disparities in food choice because affordability and accessibility to foods recommended or seen as healthy may be limited by financial constraints in low-income groups. In an ecological study of obesity in 21 developed nations, Pickett et al. (2005) found income inequality to be positively associated with energy intake and obesity.

Low levels of physical activity are associated with an increased risk of obesity (Erlichman et al. 2002), and obesogenic environments not only discourage physical activity but also encourage inactivity both occupationally and during leisure time (Hill & Peters 1998, Brownell 2002, Hill & Wyatt 2005). There has been a great decline in occupationally related activity since the turn of the twentieth century (Popkin et al. 2005). In industrialized nations and urban areas of developing countries, jobs requiring heavy manual labor have been largely replaced by jobs in service and high-technology sectors, which require minimal physical exertion (French et al. 2001). The increased use of automobiles and public-transportation systems encourages inactivity, whereas increased time spent watching television, playing electronic games, and/or using computers has increased sedentary behavior of both adults and children (Hill & Peters 1998, Jeffrey & French 1998, Brownell 2002). Obesity is uncommon among occupational groups that undertake high levels of physical activity during working hours. In one population with high levels of obesity, Keighley et al. (2006) found that adults in American Samoa engaged in farm work had lower BMIs than those not engaged in such work. In the United States and elsewhere, children participate less in physical activity at school (Hill & Peters 1998), whereas unsafe neighborhoods and limited access to recreation areas in some urban environments discourage leisure-time physical activity (Pucher & Dijkstra 2003).

Cultural variations of appropriate and preferable body image (de Garine & Pollock 1995) also may have contributed to obesity rates. In some societies, larger body size has traditionally been seen as attractive and indicative of attributes such as health, fertility, beauty, wealth, and power. In a cross-cultural comparison of appropriate body size in different traditional societies, Brown (1991) found that the vast majority favored plumpness as being attractive. Such societies include ones in Nauru, Samoa, and Malaysia (de Garine & Pollock 1995). Various societies across the world practice or have practiced ritual fattening to promote fertility, marriageability, and embodied social status. These include groups in Africa, Central and North America (Mexican Americans and African Americans in particular), Japan, and the Pacific (de Garine & Pollock 1995). Among these, only populations in the Pacific now experience widespread obesity.

Relationships between obesity and perceived attractiveness vary among communities and societies. African American women prefer body size that is larger, on average, than similar groups of European American women (Stevens et al. 1994, Flynn & Fitzgibbon 1998, Becker et al. 1999, Fitzgibbon et al. 2000). Furthermore, overweight and obese African American women perceive themselves as healthier, more attractive, and more attractive to the opposite sex than white women of similar weight and age (Stevens et al. 1994, Flynn & Fitzgibbon 1998, Becker et al. 1999), whereas European Americans experi-ence dissatisfaction with their own body size at lower BMIs than either Hispanic Americans or African Americans (Fitzgibbon et al. 2000).

Studies showing an increased value of thinness and increased awareness of the risk factors associated with overweight and obesity suggest that sociocultural factors, such as participation in the global economy and exposure to western ideas, may influence body-image perceptions worldwide. A number of communities and societies in which obesity has risen in recent decades and that previously were shown to desire and/or accept larger bodies and obesity now prefer thinner bodies (Madrigal et al. 2000, Anderson et al. 2002, Tur et al. 2005). This has been observed among African American girls (Katz et al. 2004) and women with diabetes (Anderson et al. 1997, Lieberman et al. 2003), British Bangladeshis with diabetes (Greenhalgh et al. 2005), Turkish adolescents (Canpolat et al. 2005), Pacific Islanders (Wilkinson et al. 1994, Craig et al. 1996, Brewis et al. 1998, Becker et al. 2005), the Ojibway-Cree in Canada (Gittelsohn et al. 1996), urban Native American youth (Rinderknecht & Smith 2002), and Korean children (Lee et al. 2004). Among Europeans, the desire for thinner body size is increasingly observed in children and adolescents and is not confined to females of upper-socioeconomic status (Story et al. 1995, Katz et al. 2004, Lee et al. 2004, Canpolat et al. 2005). Although high cultural valuation of body fatness may contribute to the emergence of obesity, it may possibly cease to be an important contributor in subsequent generations.

CONCLUSIONS

Increasing rates of obesity across the world are broadly attributed to environments that are obesogenic, against an evolutionary heritage that is maladaptive in these new contexts. The extensive emergence and rise of obesity among most of the world's populations indicate that the ability to become obese is universal, whereas great variation in obesity rates across geographical regions indicates possible population differences in genetic susceptibility to obesity. Human genetics are likely to have undergone selection for traits that promote energy intake and storage and that minimize energy expenditure, and there are a great many obesity-related genotypes. Current models linking genotypes with physiology and feeding behavior are only able to explain a small proportion of all obesity, but they may underlie the more-common and genetically complex forms of human obesity. Studies of the regulation of energy balance show that human physiology exerts strong control of feeding under conditions of fasting or food shortage, but only weak control on reducing food intake and increasing energy expenditure under conditions of replete energy stores and good food security. Thus it is almost inevitable that obesity should have emerged as a major human biological phenomenon in the environments that have been constructed in industrialized nations over the past 60 years and that have been transferred across the world with modernization since.

Because of the diverse contexts in which obesity has emerged and the complex environments in which it persists, a ubiquitous reversal in the prevalence of obesity at any stage is unlikely in the near future. Any ceiling on the potential for obesity in the majority of the world's populations is clearly far from being reached. However, we should avoid the danger of extrapolating from the recent past into the future because present obesity patterns are outcomes of conjoining forces: (*a*) a continuing economic development with compara-tively few serious setbacks; (*b*) an increased food security for much of the world's populations, yet unchanged or significantly declined food security for the rest; (*c*) the penetration of the world food system into the remotest parts of the world; (*d*) declining prices for energy-dense foods; (*e*) the progressive mechanization of the vast majority of labor-intensive tasks; (*f*) the urbanization and sedentization of work in the form of service-oriented jobs as replacements for labor-intensive production jobs; (*g*) the mechanization of transport; and (*h*) the sedentization of leisure time. That humans have biological tendencies to maximize food intake and use it efficiently is clear and increasingly elaborated by physiologists, but the picture is still far from complete. The human tendency to minimize energy expenditure where possible is well-known but even less well understood biologically than food intake. However, many of the economic trajectories of the second half of the twentieth century may be environmentally unsustainable (Parker 1993, Kasun 1999, von Geibler et al. 2004) because they rely on ever-increasing consumption of global resources. Economic systems create and respond to markets, and these will change as sustainability issues become more important and new technologies emerge. These undoubtedly will be reflected in changes in human body size and nutritional status into the future. If food security continues to improve across the twenty-first century, obesity rates possibly may at least stabilize in the richer nations, while emerging and increasing at greater rates in nations that emerge economically.

LITERATURE CITED

Adair LS, Popkin BM. 2005. Are child eating patterns being transformed globally? *Obes. Res.* 13:1281–99

Ahima RS, Prabakaran D, Mantzoros C, Qu D, Lowell B, et al. 1996. Role of leptin in the neuroendocrine response to fasting. *Nature* 382:250–52

Aiello LC, Wells JCK. 2002. Energetics and the evolution of the genus *Homo*. *Annu. Rev. Anthropol.* 31:323–38

Allison DB, Faith MS, Nathan JS. 1996. Risch's lambda values for human obesity. *Int. J. Obes. Relat. Metab. Disord.* 20:990–99

Allison DB, Heshka S. 1993. Emotion and eating in obesity? A critical analysis. *Int. J. Eat. Disord.* 13:289–95

Anderson LA, Eyler AA, Galuska DA, Brown DR, Brownson RC. 2002. Relationship of satisfaction with body size and trying to lose weight in a national survey of overweight and obese women aged 40 and older, United States. *Prev. Med.* 35:390–96

Anderson LA, Janes GR, Ziemer DC, Phillips LS. 1997. Diabetes in urban African Americans. Body image, satisfaction with size, and weight change attempts. *Diabetes Educ.* 23:301–8

Bandini LG, Vu D, Must A, Cyr H, Goldberg A, Dietz WH. 1999. Comparison of high-calorie, low-nutrient-dense food consumption among obese and nonobese adolescents. *Obes. Res.* 7:438–43

Barsh GS, Schwartz MW. 2002. Genetic approaches to studying energy balance: perception and integration. *Nat. Rev. Genet.* 3:589–90

Becker AE, Gilman SE, Burwell RA. 2005. Changes in prevalence of overweight and in body image among Fijian women between 1989 and 1998. *Obes. Res.* 13:110–17

Becker DM, Yanek LR, Koffman DM, Bronner YC. 1999. Body image preferences among urban African Americans and whites from low income communities. *Ethn. Dis.* 9:377–86

Bell R, Pliner PL. 2003. Time to eat: the relationship between the number of people eating and meal duration in three lunch settings. *Appetite* 41:215–18

Berthoud HR. 2004. Mind versus metabolism in the control of food intake and energy balance. *Physiol. Behav.* 81:781–93

Bevegni C, Adami GF. 2003. Obesity and obesity surgery in ancient Greece. *Obes. Surg.* 13:808–9

Bianchini F, Kraaks R, Vainio H. 2002. Overweight, obesity and cancer risk. *Lancet Oncol.* 3:565–74

Bielicki T, Szklarska A, Koziel S, Ulijaszek SJ. 2005. Changing patterns of social variation in stature in Poland: effects of transition from a command economy to the free-market system? *J. Biosoc. Sci.* 37:427–34

Blundell JE, Stubbs J. 1997. Diet composition and the control of food intake in humans. In *Handbook of Obesity*, ed. GA Bray, C Bouchard, WPT James, pp. 243–72 New York: Marcel Dekker

Bray G. 1987. Obesity—a disease of nutrient or energy balance? *Nutr. Rev.* 45:33–43

Bray GA, Nielsen SJ, Popkin BM. 2004. Consumption of high-fructose corn syrup in beverages may play a role in the epidemic of obesity. *Am. J. Clin. Nutr.* 79:537–43

Brewis AA, McGarvey ST, Jones J, Swinburn BA. 1998. Perceptions of body size in Pacific Islanders. *Int. J. Obes. Relat. Metab. Disord.* 22:185–89

Brown PJ. 1991. Culture and the evolution of obesity. *Hum. Nat.* 2:31–57

Brown PJ, Konner M. 1987. An anthropological perspective of obesity. *Ann. N. Y. Acad. Sci.* 499:29–46

Brown PJ, Krick SV. 2001. Culture and ethnicity in the etiology of obesity: diet, television and the illusion of personal choice. In *Obesity, Physical Growth and Development*, ed. FE Johnston, G Foster, pp. 111–57. London: Smith-Gordon

Brownell KD. 2002. The environment and obesity. In *Eating Disorders and Obesity: A Comprehensive Handbook*, ed. CG Fairburn, KD Brownell, pp. 433–38. New York: Guilford Press. 2nd ed.

Brownell KD, Wadden TA. 1991. The heterogeneity of obesity: fitting treatments to individuals. *Behav. Ther.* 22:153–77

Bouatia-Naji N, Meyre D, Lobbens S, Seron K, Fumeron F, et al. 2006. ACDC/adiponectin polymorphisms are associated with severe childhood and adult obesity. *Diabetes* 55:545–50

Campbell P, Ulijaszek SJ. 1994. Relationships between anthropometry and retrospective morbidity in poor men in Calcutta, India. *Eur. J. Clin. Nutr.* 48:507–12

Canpolat BI, Orsel S, Akdemir A, Ozbay MH. 2005. The relationship between dieting and body image, body ideal, self-perception, and body mass index in Turkish adolescents. *Int. J. Eat. Disord.* 37:150–55

Chung WK, Leibel RL. 2005. Molecular physiology of syndromic obesities in humans. *Trends Endocrinol. Metab.* 16:267–72

Clegg DJ, Woods SC. 2004. The physiology of obesity. *Clin. Obs. Gynecol.* 47:967–79

Clement K. 2005. Genetics of human obesity. *Proc. Nutr. Soc.* 64:133–42

Clement K, Boutin P, Froguel P. 2002. Genetics of obesity. *Am. J. Pharmacogenomics* 2:177–87

Cole TJ, Bellizzi MC, Flegal KM, Dietz WH. 2000. Establishing a standard definition for child overweight and obesity world wide: international survey. *Br. Med. J.* 320:1240–43

Comuzzie AG. 2002. The emerging pattern of the genetic contribution to human obesity. *Best Pract. Res. Clin. Endocrinol. Metab.* 16:611–21

Contaldo F, Pasanisi F. 2004. Obesity epidemics: secular trend or globalization consequence? Beyond the interaction of genetic and environmental factors. *Clin. Nutr.* 23:289–91

Craig P, Swinburn B, Matenga-Smith T, Matangi H, Vaughan F. 1996. Do Polynesians still believe that big is beautiful? Comparison of body size perceptions and preferences of Cook Islands, Maori and Australians. *N. Z. Med. J.* 14:200–3

Critser G. 2003. *Fat Land*. New York: Houghton Mifflin

Crooks DL. 2003. Trading nutrition for education: nutritional status and the sale of snack foods in an eastern Kentucky school. *Med. Anthropol. Q.* 17:182–99

Cunnane SC, Crawford MA. 2003. Survival of the fattest: fat babies were the key to evolution of the large human brain. *Comp. Biochem. Physiol. A Physiol.* 136:17–26

Darmon N, Ferguson EL, Briend A. 2002. A cost constraint alone has adverse effects on food selection and nutrient density: an analysis of human diets by linear programming. *J. Nutr.* 132:3764–71

Darmon N, Ferguson EL, Briend A. 2003. Do economic constraints encourage the selection of energy dense diets? *Appetite* 41:315–22

Decarli B, Cavadini C, Grin J, Blondel-Lubrano A, Narring F, Michaud PA. 2000. Food and nutrient intakes in a group of 11 to 16-year-old Swiss teenagers. *Int. J. Vitam. Nutr. Res.* 70:139–47

de Castro JM. 1999. Measuring real world eating behavior. *Prog. Obes. Res.* 8:215–21

de Castro JM. 2006. Heredity influences the dietary energy density of free-living humans. *Physiol. Behav.* 87:192–98

de Castro JM, Lilenfeld LR. 2005. Influence of heredity on dietary restraint, disinhibition, and perceived hunger in humans. *Nutrition* 21:446–55

de Castro JM, Stroebele N. 2002. Food intake in the real world: implications for nutrition and aging. *Clin. Geriatr. Med.* 18:685–97

de Garine I, Harrison GA, eds. 1988. *Coping with Uncertainty in Food Supply*. Oxford, UK: Oxford Univ. Press

de Garine I, Pollock NJ. 1995. *Social Aspects of Obesity*. Amsterdam: Gordon & Breach

Della Valle DM, Roe LS, Rolls BJ. 2005. Does the consumption of caloric and noncaloric beverages with a meal affect energy intake? *Appetite* 44:187–93

Del Toro W, Greenberg BS. 1989. Television commercials and food orientations among teenagers in Puerto Rico. *Hisp. J. Behav. Sci.* 11:168–77

Denney JT, Krueger PM, Rogers RG, Boardman JD. 2004. Race/ethnic and sex differentials in body mass among US adults. *Ethn. Dis.* 14:389–98 de Onis M. 2005. The use of anthropometry in the prevention of childhood overweight and obesity. *United Nations Syst. Standing Comm. Nutr.* 29:5–12

Dietz WH, Gortmaker SL. 1985. Do we fatten our children at the television set? Obesity and television viewing in children and adolescents. *Pediatrics* 75:807–12

Dilberti N, Bordi PL, Concklin MT, Roe LS, Rolls BJ. 2004. Increased portion size leads to increased consumption in a restaurant meal. *Obes. Res.* 12:562–68

Drewnowski A, Darmon N. 2005. The economics of obesity: dietary energy density and energy cost. *Am. J. Clin. Nutr.* 82:S265–73

Drewnowski A, Popkin BM. 1997. The nutrition transition: new trends in the global diet. *Nutr. Rev.* 55:31–43

Dyson T. 1996. *Population and Food*. London: Routledge

Eaton SB, Konner M, Shostak M. 1998. Stone agers in the fast lane: chronic degenerative diseases in evolutionary perspective. *Am. J. Med.* 84:739–49

Ellison PT. 2003. Energetics and reproductive effort. *Am. J. Hum. Biol.* 15:342–51

Erlichman J, Kerbey AL, James WPT. 2002. Physical activity and its impact on health outcomes. Paper 2: Prevention of unhealthy weight gain and obesity by physical activity: an analysis of the evidence. *Obes. Rev.* 3:273–87

Fan W, Voss A, Cao WH, Morrison SF. 2005. Regulation of thermogenesis by the central melanocortin system. *Peptides* 26:1800–13

Farooqi IS, O'Rahilly S. 2005. Monogenic obesity in humans. *Annu. Rev. Med.* 56:443–58

Fisher JO, Rolls BJ, Birch LL. 2003. Children's bite size and intake of an entrée are greater with large portions than with age-appropriate or self-selected portions. *Am. J. Clin. Nutr.* 77:1164–70

Fitzgibbon ML, Blackman LR, Avellone ME. 2000. The relationship between body image discrepancy and body mass index across ethnic groups. *Obes. Res.* 8:582–89

Flegal KM, Carroll MD, Ogden CL, Johnson CL. 2002. Prevalence and trends in obesity among US adults, 1999–2000. *J. Am. Med. Assoc.* 288:1723–27

Flier JS. 2004. Obesity wars: molecular progress confronts an expanding epidemic. *Cell* 116:337–50

Flynn KJ, Fitzgibbon M. 1998. Body images and obesity risk among black females: a review of the literature. *Annu. Behav. Med.* 20:13–24

Foley RA. 1993. The influence of seasonality on hominid evolution. In *Seasonality and Human Ecology*, ed. SJ Ulijaszek, SS Strickland, pp. 17–37. Cambridge, UK: Cambridge Univ. Press

French SA. 2003. Pricing effects on food choice. *J. Nutr.* 133:S841–43

French SA, Story M, Jeffrey RW. 2001. Environmental influences on eating and physical activity. *Annu. Rev. Public Health* 22:309–35

Garaulet MP, Pérez-Llamas F, Fuente T, Zamora S, Tebar FJ. 2000. Anthropometric, computer tomography and fat cell data in an obese population: relationship with insulin, leptin, tumor necrosis factor-α, sex hormone-binding globulin and sex hormones. *Eur. J. Endocrinol.* 143:657–66

Garcia M, Kennedy E. 1994. Assessing the linkages between low body mass index and morbidity in adults: evidence from four developing countries. *Eur. J. Clin. Nutr.* 48(Suppl.): S90–97

Garrow JS. 1978. *Energy Balance and Obesity in Man*. Amsterdam: Elsevier. 2nd ed.

Garrow JS. 1993. The thrifty genotype and noninsulin dependent diabetes. *Br. Med. J.* 306:933–34

Geliebter A, Aversa A. 2003. Emotional eating in overweight, normal weight, and underweight individuals. *Eat. Disord. Resour.* 3:341–47

Gill TP. 2001. Cardiovascular risk in the Asia-Pacific region from a nutrition and metabolic point of view: abdominal obesity. *Asia Pac. J. Clin. Nutr.* 10:85–89

Gittelsohn J, Harris SB, Thorne-Lyman AL, Hanley AJ, Barnie A, Zinman B. 1996. Body image concepts differ by age and sex in an Ojibway-Cree community in Canada. *J. Nutr.* 126:2990–3000

Gorely T, Marshall SJ, Biddle SJ. 2004. Couch kids: correlates of television viewing among youth. *Int. J. Behav. Med.* 11:152–63

Greenhalgh T, Chowdhury M, Wood G. 2005. Big is beautiful? A survey of body image perception and its relation to health in British Bangladeshis with diabetes. *Psychol. Health Med.* 10:126–38

Griffiths PL, Bentley ME. 2001. The nutrition transition is underway in India. *J. Nutr.* 131:2692–700

Harnack LJ, Jeffery RW, Boutelle KN. 2000. Temporal trends in energy intake in the United States: an ecologic perspective. *Am. J. Clin. Nutr.* 71:1478–84

Henshilwood C, d'Errico F, Vanhaeren M, van Niekerk K, Jacobs Z. 2004. Middle stone age shell beads from South Africa. *Science* 304:404

Herman CP, Mack D. 1975. Restrained and unrestrained eating. *J. Personality* 43:647–60

Hill JO, Peters JC. 1998. Environmental contributions to the obesity epidemic. *Science* 280:1371–74

Hill JO, Wyatt HR. 2005. Role of physical activity in preventing and treating obesity. *J. Appl. Physiol.* 99:765–70

Hill JO, Wyatt HR, Reed GW, Peters JC. 2003. Obesity and the environment: Where do we go from here? *Science* 299:853–55

Hladik CM. 1988. Seasonal variations in food supply for wild primates. In *Coping with Uncertainty in Food Supply*, ed. I de Garine, GA Harrison, pp. 1–25. Oxford, UK: Oxford Univ. Press

Horrobin DF. 1999. Lipid metabolism, human evolution and schizophrenia. *Prostaglandins Leukot. Essent. Fatty Acids* 60:431–37

Isganaitis E, Lustig RH. 2005. Fast food, central nervous system insulin resistance, and obesity. *Arterioscler. Thromb. Vasc. Biol.* 25:2451–62

Jahns L, Siega-Riz AM, Popkin BM. 2001. The increasing prevalence of snacking among US children from 1977 to 1996. *J. Pediatr.* 138:493–98

Jebb SA. 2003. Fast foods, energy density and obesity: a possible mechanistic link. *Obes. Rev.* 4:187–94

Jeffrey RE, French SA. 1998. Epidemic obesity in the United States: Are fast foods and television viewing contributing? *Am. J. Public Health* 88:277–80

Jeffrey RW, French SA, Firster JL, Spry VM. 1991. Socioeconomic status differences in health behaviors related to obesity—the healthy worker project. *Int. J. Obes.* 15:689–96

Kahn HS, Williamson DF. 1994. Abdominal obesity and mortality risk among men in nineteenth century North America. *Int. J. Obes.* 18:686–91

Kasun JR. 1999. Doomsday every day: sustainable economics, sustainable tyranny. *Independent Rev.* 4:91–106

Katz ML, Gorden-Larsen P, Bentley ME, Kelsey K, Shields K, Ammerman A. 2004. "Does skinny mean healthy?" Perceived ideal, current, and healthy body sizes among African-American girls and their female caregiver. *Ethn. Dis.* 14:533–41

Kawai K, Sugimoto K, Nakashima K, Miura H, Ninomiya Y. 2000. Leptin as a modulator of sweet taste sensitivities in mice. *Proc. Natl. Acad. Sci. USA* 97:11044–49

Keighley ED, McGarvey ST, Turituri P, Vial S. 2006. Farming and adiposity in Samoan adults. *Am. J. Hum. Biol.* 18:112–22

Keller KI, Pietrobelli, Faith MS. 2003. Genetics of food intake and body composition: lessons from twin studies. *Acta Diabetol.* 40:S95–100

Kirchengast S, Schober E, Waldhor T, Sefranek R. 2004. Regional and social differences in body mass index, and the prevalence of overweight and obesity among 18-year-old men in Austria between the years 1985 and 2000. *Coll. Antropol.* 28:541–52

Kral TV, Rolls BJ. 2004. Energy density and portion size: their independent and combined effects on energy intake. *Physiol. Behav.* 82:131–38

Kuzawa CW. 1998. Adipose tissue in human infancy and childhood: an evolutionary perspective. *Am. J. Phys. Anthropol.* 27(Suppl.):177–209

Lee K, Sohn H, Lee S, Lee J. 2004. Weight and BMI over 6 years in Korean children: relationships to body image and weight loss efforts. *Obes. Res.* 13:1959–66

Leonard WR, Robertson ML, Snodgrass JJ, Kuzawa CW. 2003. Metabolic correlates of hominid brain evolution. *Comp. Biochem. Physiol. A Physiol.* 136:5–15

Levitsky DA, Obarzanek E, Mrdjenovic G, Strupp BJ. 2005. Imprecise control of energy intake: absence of a reduction in food intake following overfeeding in young adults. *Physiol. Behav.* 84:669–75

Levitsky DA, Youn T. 2004. The more young adults are served, the more they overeat. *J. Nutr.* 134:2546–49

Lev-Ran A. 2001. Human obesity: an evolutionary approach to understanding our bulging waistline. *Diabetes Metab. Res. Rev.* 17:347–62

Li G, Chen X, Jang Y, Wang J, Xing X, et al. 2002. Obesity, coronary heart disease risk factors and diabetes in Chinese: an approach to the criteria of obesity in the Chinese population. *Obes. Rev.* 3:167–72

Lieberman LS, Probart CK, Schoenberg NE. 2003. Body image among older, rural, African-American women with type 2 diabetes. *Coll. Antropol.* 27:79–86

Lin B, Guthrie J, Blaylock JR. 1996. The diets of America's children: influences on dining out, household characteristics, and nutritional knowledge. *Agric. Econ. Rep.* 746:1–37

Loos RJF, Rankinen T, Tremblay A, Perusse L, Chagnon Y, Bouchard C. 2005. Melanocortin-4 receptor gene and physical activity in the Quebec Family Study. *Int. J. Obes.* 29:420–28

Madrigal H, Sanchez-Villegas A, Martinez-Gonzalez MA, Kearney J, Gibney MJ, Irala J. 2000. Underestimation of body mass index through perceived body image as compared to self-reported body mass index in the European Union. *Public Health* 114:468–73

Martin RD. 1993. Scaling. In *The Cambridge Encyclopedia of Human Evolution*, ed. S Jones, R Martin, D Pilbeam, p. 42. Cambridge, UK: Cambridge Univ. Press

McConahy KL, Smiciklas-Wright H, Birch LL, Mitchell DC, Picciano MF. 2002. Food portions are positively related to energy intake and body weight in early childhood. *J. Pediatr.* 140:340–47

McConahy KL, Smiciklas-Wright H, Mitchell DC, Picciano MF. 2004. Portion size of common foods predicts energy intake among preschool-aged children. *J. Am. Diet. Assoc.* 104:975–79

McCrory MA, Fuss PJ, Hays NP, Vinken AG, Greenberg AS, Roberts SB. 1999. Overeating in America. Association between restaurant food consumption and body fatness in healthy adult men and women ages 19 to 80. *Obes. Res.* 7:564–71

Mela DJ. 1996. Eating behavior, food preferences and dietary intake in relation to obesity and body-weight status. *Proc. Nutr. Soc.* 55:803–16

Mela DJ. 1999. Food choice and intake: the human factor. *Proc. Nutr. Soc.* 58:513–21

Mela DJ, Catt S. 1996. Ontogeny of human taste and smell preferences and their implications for food selection. In *Long-Term Consequences of Early Environment: Growth,*

Development and the Lifespan Developmental Perspective, ed. CJK Henry, SJ Ulijaszek, pp. 139–54. Cambridge, UK: Cambridge Univ. Press

Mizuno TM, Makimura H, Mobbs CV. 2003. The physiological function of the agouti-related peptide gene: the control of weight and metabolic rate. *Ann. Med.* 35:425–33

Molarius A. 2003. The contribution of lifestyle factors to socioeconomic differences in obesity in men and women: a population-based study in Sweden. *Eur. J. Epidemiol.* 18:227–34

Monteiro CA, D'A-Benicio MH, Conde WL, Popkin BM. 2000. Shifting obesity trends in Brazil. *Eur. J. Clin. Nutr.* 54:342–46

Moore MS. 2000. Interactions between physical activity and diet in the regulation of body weight. *Proc. Nutr. Soc.* 59:193–98

Moran TH. 2000. Cholecystokinin and satiety: current perspectives. *Nutrition* 16:858–65

Mrdjenovic G, Levitsky DA. 2005. Children eat what they are served: the imprecise regulation of energy intake. *Appetite* 44:273–82

Myers KP, Sclafani A. 2003. Conditioned acceptance and preference but not altered taste reactivity responses to bitter and sour flavors paired with intragastric glucose infusion. *Physiol. Behav.* 78:173–83

Neale BM, Mazzeo SE, Bulik CM. 2003. A twin study of dietary restraint, disinhibition and hunger: an examination of the eating inventory (three factor eating questionnaire). *Twin Res.* 6:471–78

Neel J. 1962. Diabetes mellitus: a "thrifty" genotype rendered detrimental by "progress"? *Am. J. Hum. Genet.* 14:353–62

Neel JV, Weder AB, Julius S. 1998. Type II diabetes, essential hypertension, and obesity as "syndromes of impaired genetic homeostasis": The "thrifty genotype" hypothesis enters the 21st century. *Perspect. Biol. Med.* 42:44–74

Nielsen SJ, Siega-riz AM, Popkin BM. 2002. Trends in energy intake in U.S. between 1977 and 1996: Similar shifts seen across age groups. *Obes. Res.* 10:370–78

Nishida C, Mucavele P. 2005. Monitoring the rapidly emerging public health problem of overweight and obesity: the WHO global database on body mass index. *United Nations Syst. Standing Comm. Nutr.* 29:5–12

Norgan NG. 1994a. Population differences in body composition in relation to the BMI. *Eur. J. Clin. Nutr.* 48(Suppl.):S10–27

Norgan NG. 1994b. Relative sitting height and the interpretation of the body mass index. *Ann. Hum. Biol.* 21:79–82

Norgan NG. 1997. The beneficial effects of body fat and adipose tissue in humans. *Int. J. Obes. Relat. Metab. Disord.* 21:738–46

Parker K. 1993. Economics, sustainable growth, and community. *Environ. Values* 2:233–45

Peña M, Bacallao J. 2002. Malnutrition and poverty. *Annu. Rev. Nutr.* 22:241–53

Perusse L, Rankinen T, Zuberi A, Chagnon YC, Weisnagel SJ, et al. 2005. Human obesity gene map: the 2004 update. *Obes. Res.* 13:381–490

Pickett KE, Kelly S, Brunner E, Lobstein T, Wilkinson RG. 2005. Wider income gaps, wider waistbands? An ecological study of obesity and income inequality. *J. Epidemiol. Comm. Health* 59:670–74

Plummer T. 2004. Flaked stones and old bones: biological and cultural evolution at the dawn of technology. *Am. J. Phys. Anthropol.* 125(Suppl.):118–64

Popkin BM. 2004. The nutrition transition: an overview of world patterns of change. *Nutr. Rev.* 62:S140–43

Popkin BM, Doak CM. 1998. Obesity is a worldwide phenomenon. *Nutr. Rev.* 56:106–14

Popkin BM, Duffey K, Gorden-Larsen P. 2005. Environmental influences on food choice, physical activity and energy balance. *Physiol. Behav.* 86:603–13

Poskitt EME. 1995. Assessment of body composition in the obese. In *Body Composition Techniques in Health and Disease*, ed. PSW Davies, TJ Cole, pp. 146–55. Cambridge, UK: Cambridge Univ. Press

Prentice AM, Poppitt SD. 1996. Importance of ED and macronutrients in the regulation of energy intake. *Int. J. Obes. Metab. Disord.* 20:S18–23

Pucher J, Dijkstra L. 2003. Promoting safe walking and cycling improve public health: lessons from The Netherlands and Germany. *Am. J. Public Health* 93:1509–16

Renders CM, Henneman L, Timmermans DR, Hirasing RA. 2004. Television watching and some eating habits of 6–14 year-old children in Amsterdam, the Netherlands; a cross sectional study. *Ned. Tijdschr. Geneeskd.* 148:2072–76

Rennie KL, Jebb SA. 2005. Prevalence of obesity in Great Britain. *Obes. Rev.* 6:11–12

Rinderknecht K, Smith C. 2002. Body image perceptions among urban Native American youth. *Obes. Res.* 10:315–27

Rolls BJ. 2003. The supersizing of America: portion size and the obesity epidemic. *Nutr. Today* 38:42–53

Rolls BJ, Roe LS, Kral TV, Meengs JS, Wall DE. 2004. Increasing the portion size of a packaged snack increases energy intake in men and women. *Appetite* 42:63–69

Rosenbaum M, Leibel RL. 1998. The physiology of body weight regulation: relevance to the etiology of obesity in children. *Pediatrics* 101:525–39

Samuelson G. 2000. Dietary habits and nutritional status in adolescents over Europe. An overview of current studies in the Nordic countries. *Eur. J. Clin. Nutr.* 54(Suppl. 1):S21–28

Saper CB, Chou TC, Elmquist JK. 2002. The need to feed: homeostatic and hedonic control of eating. *Neuron* 36:199–211

Schachter S, Rodin J. 1974. *Obese Humans and Rats*. Washington, DC: Erlbaum/Halsted

Schioth HB, Lagerstrom MC, Watanobe H, Jonsson L, Vergoni AV, et al. 2003. Functional role, structure, and evolution of the melanocortin-4 receptor. *Ann. N.Y. Acad. Sci.* 994:74–83

Schluter G, Lee C. 1999. Changing good consumption patterns: their effects of the US food system, 1972–92. *Food Rev.* 22:35–37

Schwartz MW, Morton GJ. 2002. Obesity: keeping hunger at bay. *Nature* 418:595–97

Shetty PS. 1993. Chronic undernutrition and metabolic adaptation. *Proc. Nutr. Soc.* 52:267–84

Shetty PS, James WPT. 1994. *Body Mass Index: A Measure of Chronic Energy Deficiency in Adults*. Rome: Food Agric. Org.

Shuldiner AR, Munir KM. 2003. Genetics of obesity: more complicated than initially thought. *Lipids* 38:97–101

Simmen B, Hladik CM. 1998. Sweet and bitter taste discrimination in primates: scaling effects across species. *Folia Primatol.* 69:129–38

Smiciklas-Wright H, Mitchell DC, Mickle SJ, Goldman JD, Cook A. 2003. Foods commonly eaten in the United States, 1989–1991 and 1994–1996: Are portion sizes changing? *J. Am. Diet. Assoc.* 103:41–47

Sobal J, Stunkard AJ. 1989. Socioeconomic status and obesity: a review of the literature. *Psychol. Bull.* 105:260–75

Spitzer L, Rodin J. 1981. Human eating behavior: a critical review of studies in normal weight and overweight individuals. *Appetite* 2:293–329

Stamatakis E, Primatesta P, Chinn S, Rona R, Falascheti E. 2005. Overweight and obesity trends from 1974 to 2003 in English children: What is the role of socioeconomic factors? *Arch. Dis. Child.* 90:999–1004

Stevens J, Kumanyika SK, Keil JE. 1994. Attitudes toward body size and dieting: differences between elderly black and white women. *Am. J. Public Health.* 84(8):1322–25

St-Onge M, Keller KL, Heymsfield SB. 2003. Changes in childhood food consumption patterns: a cause for concern in light of increasing body weights. *Am. J. Clin. Nutr.* 78:1068–73

Story M, French SA, Resnick MD, Blum RW. 1995. Ethnic/racial and socioeconomic differences in dieting behaviors and body image perceptions in adolescents. *Int. J. Eat. Disord.* 18:173–79

Stroebele N, de Castro JM. 2004. Television viewing is associated with an increase in meal frequency in humans. *Appetite* 42:111–13

Stubbs RJ. 1998. Appetite feeding behavior and energy balance in human subjects. *Nutr. Rev.* 57:1–16

Stubbs RJ, Whybrow S. 2004. Energy density, diet composition and palatability: influences on overall food energy intake in humans. *Physiol. Behav.* 81:755–64

Stunkard AJ, Fock TT, Hrubec Z. 1986. A twin study of human obesity. *J. Am. Med. Assoc.* 256:51–54

Sturm R. 2005. Childhood obesity—what we can learn from existing data on societal trends, part 2. *Prev. Chronic Dis.* 2:A20

Sullivan DR. 2001. Cardiovascular risk in the Asia-Pacific region from a nutrition and metabolic point of view: visceral obesity. *Asia Pac. J. Clin. Nutr.* 10:82–84

Swinburn BA, Caterson I, Seidell JC, James WPT. 2004. Diet, nutrition and prevention of excess weight gain and obesity. *Public Health Nutr.* 7:123–46

Swinburn BA, Egger G, Raza F. 1999. Dissecting obesogenic environments: the development and application of a framework for identifying and prioritizing environmental interventions for obesity. *Prev. Med.* 29:563–70

Tartaglia LA, Dembski M, Weng X, Deng N, Culpepper J, et al. 1995. Identification and expression cloning of a leptin receptor, OB-R. *Cell* 83:1263–71

Trowell H. 1975. Obesity in the Western world. *Plant Foods Man* 1:157–65

Tschop M, Smiley DL, Heiman ML. 2000. Ghrelin induces adiposity in rodents. *Nature* 407:908–13

Tucker LA, Bagwell MRN. 1991. Television viewing and obesity in adult females. *Am. J. Public Health* 81:908–11

Tucker LA, Friedman GM. 1989. Television viewing and obesity in adult males. *Am. J. Public Health* 79:516–18

Tur JA, Serra-Majem L, Romaguera D, Pons A. 2005. Profile of overweight and obese people in a Mediterranean region. *Obes. Res.* 13:527–36

Ulijaszek SJ. 2002a. The comparative energetics of primate fetal growth. *Am. J. Hum. Biol.* 14:603–8

Ulijaszek SJ. 2002b. Human feeding from an evolutionary ecological perspective. *Proc. Nutr. Soc.* 61:517–26

Ulijaszek SJ. 2005. Modernisation, migration, and nutritional health of Pacific Island populations. *Environ. Sci.* 12:167–76

van den Bulck J, van Mierlo J. 2004. Energy intake associated with television viewing in adolescents, a cross sectional study. *Appetite* 43:181–84

von Geibler J, Kuhndt M, Seifert E, Lucas R, Lorek S, Bleischwitz R. 2004. Sustainable business and consumption strategies. In *Eco-Efficiency, Regulation and Sustainable Business: Towards a Governance Structure for Sustainable Development*, ed. R Bleischwitz, P Hennicke, pp. 116–64. ESRI Stud. Ser. Environ. Cheltenham, UK: Elgar

Wahlqvist ML. 2001. Nutrition and diabetes in the Asia-Pacific region with reference to cardiovascular disease. *Asia Pac. J. Clin. Nutr.* 10:90–96

Wansink B. 2004. Environmental factors that increase the food intake and consumption volume of unknowing consumers. *Annu. Rev. Nutr.* 24:455–79

Wansink B, Cheney MM. 2005. Super bowls: serving bowl size and food consumption. *Obes. Res.* 293:1727–28

Waterlow JC. 1990. Mechanisms of adaptation to low energy intakes. In *Diet and Disease*, ed. GA Harrison, JC Waterlow, pp. 5–23. Cambridge, UK: Cambridge Univ. Press

Wilkinson J, Ben-Tovim D, Walker M. 1994. An insight into the personal significance of weight and shape in large Samoan women. *Int. J. Obes. Relat. Metab. Disord.* 18:602–6

Wilson SG, Adam G, Langdown M, Reneland R, Braun A, et al. 2006. Linkage and potential association of obesity-related phenotypes with two genes on chromosome 12q24 in a female dizygous twin cohort. *Eur. J. Hum. Genet.* 14:340–43

World Health Organization. 2000. Obesity: preventing and managing the global epidemic. *WHO Tech. Rep. Ser., No. 894.* Geneva

Yamamoto H, Lee CE, Marcus JN, Williams TD, Overton JM, et al. 2002. Glucagon-like peptide-1 receptor stimulation increases blood pressure and heart rate and activates autonomic regulatory neurons. *J. Clin. Invest.* 110:43–52

Young LR, Nestle M. 2002. The contribution of expanding portion sizes to the US obesity epidemic. *Am. J. Public Health* 92:246–49

Zemel MB, Kim JH, Woychik RP, Michaud EJ, Kadwell SH, et al. 1995. Agouti regulation of intracellular calcium: role in the insulin resistance of viable yellow mice. *Proc. Natl. Acad. Sci. USA* 92:4733–37

Zhang Y, Proenca R, Maffei M, Barone M, Leopold L, Friedman JM. 1994. Positional cloning of the mouse obese gene and its human homologue. *Nature* 372:425–32

Zizza C, Siega-Riz AM, Popkin BM. 2001. Significant increase in young adults' snacking between 1977–1978 and 1994–1996 represents a cause for concern! *Prev. Med.* 32:303–10

Food and Memory

Jon D. Holtzman

Department of Anthropology, Western Michigan University, Kalamazoo,
Michigan 49008; email: jon.holtzman@wmich.edu

Annu. Rev. Anthropol. 2006. 35:361–78

First published online as a Review in
Advance on June 14, 2006

The *Annual Review of Anthropology* is
online at anthro.annualreviews.org

This article's doi:
10.1146/annurev.anthro.35.081705.123220

Copyright © 2006 by Annual Reviews.
All rights reserved

0084-6570/06/1021-0361$20.00

Key Words

sensuality, nostalgia, identity, invented traditions, history

Abstract

Much of the burgeoning literature on food in anthropology and
related fields implicitly engages with issues of memory. Although
only a relatively small but growing number of food-centered studies
frame themselves as directly concerned with memory—for instance,
in regard to embodied forms of memory—many more engage with
its varying forms and manifestations, such as in a diverse range of
studies in which food becomes a significant site implicated in social
change, the now-voluminous body relating food to ethnic or other
forms of identity, and invented food traditions in nationalism and
consumer capitalism. Such studies are of interest not only because
of what they may tell us about food, but moreover because particular
facets of food and food-centered memory offer more general insights
into the phenomenon of memory and approaches to its study in
anthropology and related fields.

INTRODUCTION

In considering how notions of memory are infused within the food literature, one may feel somewhat in a role imagined by Jorge Luis Borges (1970) in his short story *Tlön, Uqbar, Orbis Tertius*. Critics, writes Borges, "often invent authors: [T]hey select two dissimilar works—the *Tao Te Ching* and the *1001 Nights*, say—attribute them to the same writer and then determine most scrupulously the psychology of this interesting *homme de lettres*...[.]"

I will, of course, be inventing neither authors nor a subject. Yet the topic of food and memory is in several ways far less conventionally defined and bounded than would be, for example, "Kinship Studies Since the 90s" or "Change in African Pastoralist Societies." First, few anthropological studies explicitly frame their focus as food and memory—books by Sutton (2001) and Counihan (2004) are the principal full-length works. Consequently there is, by and large, not a self-defined and readily contained literature that need merely be surveyed to assess the current state of the field. Rather, the strands of significantly varying processes commonly construed as "memory" implicitly inform much of the literature on food, such that the task becomes largely to tease out and to disentangle these strands within differing approaches focusing on differing processes. Specifically, my goal is to understand how varied notions of memory emerge within much of the burgeoning literature on food in anthropology and related fields, with a secondary goal of understanding how the processes described in these works could provide some broader insights into more general approaches to memory.

I do not question that a powerful connection exists between food and memory. Their inexorable relationship is frequently offered to us initially in short-hand, via Proust, in which the canonized taste of the squat little madeleines is the catalyst for remembrances to fill dense, thick volumes. Yet precisely what the relationships are between food and memory (as phenomena and as objects of study) is complexified by a second critical issue. Each half of this relationship—food and memory—is something of a floating signifier, although in rather different ways. As for food, we may readily define it in a strictly realist sense—that stuff that we as organisms consume by virtue of requiring energy. Yet it is an intrinsically multilayered and multidimensional subject—with social, psychological, physiological, symbolic dimensions, to name merely a few—and with culturally constructed meanings that differ not merely, as we naturally assume, in the perspectives of our subjects, but indeed in the perspectives of the authors who construct and construe the object of food in often very different ways, ranging from the strictly materialist to the ethereal gourmand. And memory is much thornier. What we homonymically label as "memory" often refers to an array of very different processes which not only has a totally different dynamic, but which we aim to understand for very different reasons—everything from monumental public architecture to the nostalgia evoked by a tea-soaked biscuit. In a sense, then, exploring approaches to food and memory is akin to examining the neck of the Great Roe—Woody Allen's mythological beast with the head of the lion and the body of the lion, although not the same lion—the intersection of two objects that are potently linked but each is, to varying degrees, shifting and indeterminate.

This chapter focuses principally on the anthropological literature, although both food and memory are subjects that intrinsically demand a cross-disciplinary approach. Memory ties anthropology to history, and in a different sense psychology, whereas food studies cross-cut sociology, literature, and even culinary science. I thus seek to address the ways that key questions concerning memory have been treated (explicitly or implicitly) in the study of food in anthropology and related fields. For instance, which facets of food—or what configuration of its varying facets—render it a potent site for the construction of memory?

Which kinds of memories does food have the particular capacity to inscribe, and are there other ways that food may be implicated in a conscious or unconscious forgetting? How are food-centered forms of memory—conscious or unconscious, publicly validated or privately concealed—linked to other mediums for memory? How does dietary change become linked in complex, and perhaps contradictory, ways to broader understandings of change? Or how, alternatively, does real or perceived resilience in foodways speak to understandings of the present and imaginings of the future through reference to a mythic or historicized conception of past eating?

Before turning to these questions, however, I first survey the parameters of my two floating signifiers.

DEFINING MEMORY

Despite the recent surge in memory studies, the concept is often treated in quite disparate ways. This review cannot fully engage with—much less resolve—all the issues incumbent in these disparities. However, I briefly address some key tensions in approaches to memory, both to clarify how I treat it and to foreground reasons why food provides a particularly rich arena to explore memory's complexities.

As some have suggested, the current scholarly excitement over the study of "memory" is to a great extent framed in juxtaposition to its older, frumpier sibling "history"—although history is frequently tied to empiricism, objectivity, and as Hodgkin & Radstone (2003) note, "a certain notion of truth" (p. 3), memory intrinsically destablilizes truth through a concern with the subjective ways that the past is recalled, memorialized, and used to construct the present. This, of course, occurs through a diverse range of processes, both individual and social, some of which constitute quite different faculties within remembering subjects, whereas others concern social processes that mark, inscribe, or interpret the past. That such diverse processes are often considered under the single rubric of memory—some literal forms of remembering, some more metaphorical uses of the term—infuses a fuzziness into many studies of memory that can be intrinsically problematic. Beyond this, however, the fact that the disparate nature of these different processes is not often acknowledged can lead to a failure to underscore the multiple readings and affective ambivalence that often characterizes even a single individual's reading of the past, much less social renderings of it. Thus, even the most nuanced treatments of memory can, perhaps inadvertently, imply that the complex intersecting messages elucidated in their studies might be ultimately interpreted as being principally about some main thing in particular, such as colonialism (Cole 2001) or the state (Mueggler 2001). Although ambivalences and dissonances are sometimes noted in anthropological treatments of memory (e.g., Jackson 1995, Ong 2003, Ganguly 2001), only rarely are they treated as deeply fundamental to the fabric and texture of memory, as in Smith's (2004) treatment of heteroglossic memory.

For reasons I return to near the conclusion of this review, I see food as a particularly rich arena in which to explore such complexities of memory, but for now I simply highlight the fairly broad parameters I employ while exploring it. In my own uses of the term memory I take as fundamental to its definition the notion of experience or meaning in reference to the past. This working definition nonetheless includes quite a broad array of disparate processes, including (although not exhaustively) events that subjects recall or emotionally re-experience, the unconscious (perhaps embodied) memories of subjects, how a sense of historicity shapes social processes and meanings, nostalgia for a real or imagined past, and invented traditions. From this I exclude historically sedimented practices that neither reflect the (conscious or unconscious) captured experience of remembering subjects, nor the experience of temporality or historicity in subjects' present engagement with the world. Examples of such "unremembered forms of memory" would include such notions as Shaw's (2002) "practical memory" or James' (1988) notion of a cultural archive, and within food studies a broad range of scholarship which is principally interested in history in the strict sense of how processes unfolded over time rather than how subjects in the present remember or construe these processes [e.g., Cwiertka 2000, 2002; Mintz 1985 (and to a great extent 1996); Lentz 1999; Brandes 1997; Plotnicov & Scaglion 1999; Trubek 2000].

I now turn from memory to a brief discussion of food, before returning to their confluence.

WHAT IS FOOD?

This is not a stupid question. If the answer seems obvious (we can point to food; we have all eaten food) we should consider the extent to which the anthropological enterprise has aimed to destabilize categories drawn from the commonsense architecture of Western thought. Thus, food—like the family, gender, or religion—must be understood as a cultural construct in which categories rooted in Euro-American experience may prove inadequate. Although space does not allow a full elaboration of this assertion, I would contend that as a collective body the scholarly treatment of food often relies fairly explicitly on Western constructions of it; however, certainly many individual scholars rely on more culturally specific (e.g., Meigs 1984) or highly theorized notions (Sutton 2001).

An important aspect of this is that the scholarly literature on food has the blessing and the curse of having potential carryover to an educated lay market. That is, where a book on structural adjustment programs, for instance, has little potential for popular appeal, a book on camembert (Boisard 2003) has potential marketability among high-brow, deep-pocketed cheese lovers. Venues, such as the intriguing new journal *Gastronomica*, similarly have a vision that combines "luscious imagery" and "a keen appreciation for the pleasures and aesthetics of food" with "smart, edgy analysis" and "the latest in food studies," a vision that can, therefore, encompass not only articles by anthropologists and historians, but also special issues devoted to the life of Julia Child. Ethnographic cookbooks (e.g., Roden 1974, Goldstein 1993) might be viewed in a similar light.

This natural potential link to a popular audience has implications for food studies in anthropology and elsewhere. Thus, I argue, that although the rise in anthropological interest in food is quite consonant with Stoller's (1989) call for a more sensuous, experience-near ethnography elaborated in the *Taste of Ethnographic Things* (see also Classen 1997), often what emerges is the ethnography of tasty things—food-centered analysis that feeds on Western epicurean sensibilities, popular culture notions concerning how foods serve as markers for immigrant communities, the nostalgia that wafts from home-cooked broths, and the connections forged between mothers and daughters through food. Indeed, it is notable that Stoller's (1989) discussion of an intentionally awful meal cooked for him in Mali is atypical by virtue of its focus on unappealing food. In sum, then, I argue that a limitation of food studies (anthropology not wholly excluded) is a tendency to construct the multidimensional object of food within a particular Euro-American framework.

I now consider some of the dominant relationships between food and memory, which have been explored within anthropology and related fields. These relationships include embodied memories constructed through food; food as a locus for historically constructed identity, ethnic or nationalist; the role of food in various forms of "nostalgia"; dietary change as a socially charged marker of epochal shifts; gender and the agents of memory; and contexts of remembering and forgetting through food. In conclusion, I consider some themes and directions for further study, which may enhance our understanding of both food and memory and the relationship between them.

FOOD AND SENSUOUS MEMORY

Sutton's (2001) *Remembrance of Repasts* is an important starting point for considering the relationship between food and memory by virtue of his efforts to deal with issues of memory from a variety of perspectives. Framed as a prospective and theoretical look at a little-explored topic, his starting point is what he terms a "Proustian anthropology," derived from his observation that his informants on the Greek Island of Kalymnos frequently remember far-off events through food—for instance, the apricots they were eating while exploring an abandoned synagogue during the Nazi occupation. One important dimension to this book is that he deals with many of the varied phenomena that we label memory. For instance, how the seasonal food cycle shapes "prospective memory" by causing one to looking forward (e.g., pears in August) in reference to past events: how the repetition of everyday habits [such as Seremetakis's (1996) account of drinking a cup of coffee] in some sense still time, by recreating past occurrences; how the longstanding anthropological interest of exchange can be understood through reference to memory, since social relations are constructed through narratives of past generosity (or lack thereof); and how (per Douglas 1975) one meal is understood in reference to previous meals. This broad-ranging treatment of memory offers a range of creative insights into the phenomena we term memory, although also to some extent elides the above-discussed ambiguities concerning the disparities among the varying phenomena we term "memory."

Sutton's (2000, 2001) most central concern is how the sensuality of food causes it to be a particularly intense and compelling medium for memory. The experience of food evokes recollection, which is not simply cognitive but also emotional and physical, paralleling notions such as Bourdieu's (1977) habitus, Connerton's (1989) notion of bodily memory, and Stoller's (1995) emphasis on embodied memories. Indeed, varied examples show food to be an important engine for the construction of intense bodily memories. Powles (2002) argues that the collective memory of displacement for refugees she studied in Zambia is constructed most poignantly through the corporeal experience of the absence of fish. Harbottle (1997) considers how the taste responses of Iranians in Britain are embodied experiences of pollution, purity, and ethnicity, seeing the mouth "as a gateway through which a person guards and protects the self from the outside." Giard (1998 with De Certeau) construes the everyday practice of eating as making "concrete one of the specific modes of relation between a person and the world, thus forming one of the fundamental landmarks in space-time" (p. 183). Batsell et al. (2002) have found that in the United States childhood experiences of being forced to clean one's plate form compelling "flashbulb memories," recalling in vivid detail aspects of early childhood when little else may be remembered, while Lupton (1994, 1996) similarly examines how the emotional embodied memories surrounding particular foods are implicated in structuring eating habits. And Seremetakis's (1993) reflexive montage aims at developing a memory of the senses—for instance, the exchange of saliva in the mushed bread that passes from grandmother to child's mouth—to understand the lost experiences that are not part of the public culture of Greek modernization.

Thus, the sensuousness of food is central to understanding at least much of its power as a vehicle for memory. Yet, as with food studies generally, we need to be wary of taking for granted Euro-American constructions both of this sensuousness and the body experiencing it. If recalling through the sweet, moist delights of a fig (Sutton 2001) is of a piece with Western Epicurean sensuality, the sensuality associated with the sorcery-induced diarrhea central to the political contestation of memory at Lelet mortuary feasts in New Ireland (Eves 1996) is rather not. Thus, while concurring that the power of food in constructing memory is intrinsically tied to its sensuality, we need be remain wary of too readily relying on familiar constructions of it.

FOOD AND ETHNIC IDENTITY

Ethnic identity forms a central arena in which food is tied to notions of memory, although not necessarily framed in those terms. Notably, even if an identity is constructed through a historical consciousness, it is quite possible to make a synchronic analysis of how it is marked or performed. Thus, for example, although Bahloul's (1989) analysis of the Seder shows Algerian Jewish ethnicity to be constructed by multistranded historical elements, the study does so through a somewhat ahistorical structuralist framework. Similarly, Searls's (2002) ethnography richly shows the historical elements in aspects of Inuit collective identity constructed through contrasts between Inuit and "white" food but does not emphasize how Inuit people experience this through a lens of historicity.

A vast literature—some in anthropology, although much in folklore and other fields—has been concerned with how American ethnic identities in particular are maintained and performed through food. Thus, a plethora of studies demonstrate how various ethnic American groups use food—in festivals or in the family—to maintain a historically validated ethnic identity (e.g., Brown & Mussel 1984, Comito 2001, Douglas 1984, Gabbacia 1998, Gillespie 1984, Humphrey & Humphrey 1988, Kalcik 1984, Lockwood & Lockwood 2000, Powers & Powers 1984, Shortridge & Shortridge 1998) Although a rich and engaging literature exists, many studies tend toward the atheoretical, relying on popular culture notions of the resilience of ethnic difference within the melting pot, rather than theorizing this phenomenon. There are, of course, exceptions, such as Spiro's (1955) Freudian-inspired argument that "the oral zone is, of course, the first to be socialized" (p. 1249) (and hence less easily acculturated) or Goode's (Goode et al. 1984) use of Mary Douglas' (1975) notion of meal

format, to explain what they saw as greater resilience in prosaic, everyday eating than in the festive contexts typically emphasized. Diner's (2003) historical study of nineteenth- and early-twentieth-century immigration to the United States also provides an interesting counterpoint to the widespread focus on food as a valorized site of ethnic resilience, emphasizing memories of hunger—rather than tasty ethnic dishes—in structuring immigrant experience. Thus, Diner suggests, "as hungry people found food within their reach, they partook of it in ways which resonated with their earlier deprivations. How they remembered those hungers allows us to see how they had once lived them, and how they then understood themselves in their new home without them" (pp. 220–21). Tuchman & Levine (1993) also present an interesting twist on stereotyped versions of American ethnic identity, by pointing out through the New York Jewish love of Chinese food that even self-defined traditions need not be of great historical depth, tied to a mythical past, nor some essentialized notion of core identity.

One important question that the American ethnic literature tends to elide is what the significance is of this identity—everyone has origins and ancestors, but not everyone performs them through food—particularly when such an identity may not have much life outside festivals or public displays. This is a question that Brown & Mussel (1984) allude to, although mainly in an empiricist sense of striving to identify their unit of analysis of "ethnic" or "regional" foodways. Buckser's (1999) analysis of Kosher practices in Denmark also problematizes the significance of identity by exploring how Jews do (or do not) maintain a historically validated identity through food in a context where a Jewish "community" arguably does not exist. Abarca (2004) is also useful in problematizing notions of identity through a contrast of notions of "the authentic," an overly essentialized historical identity, versus "the original," which acknowledges the agency of cooks within that identity.

THE GASTRONOMIC MEMORY OF DIASPORA

Food-centered nostalgia is a recurring theme in studies of diasporic or expatriate populations. Unlike the just-discussed examples, here the emphasis is on experience of displacement rather than construction of identity. Sutton (2000, 2001) emphasizes the longing evoked in diasporic individuals by the smells and tastes of a lost homeland, providing a temporary return to a time when their lives were not fragmented. Such sentiments can be found in direct texts, such as Roden's (1974) *Book of Middle Eastern Food*, inspired by memories of her Cairo childhood evoked by brown beans. Composed of recipes and stories/ethnographies collected from other displaced Middle Easterners, it is both cookbook and work of nostalgia. Apropos to this is Appadurai's (1988) characterization of Indian cookbooks as the literature of exiles.

The theme of gustatory nostalgia is particularly evident in analyses of Indian immigrants, such as Roy's (2002) (mainly literary) analysis of the "Gastropoetics of South Indian Diaspora." Mankekar (2002) argues that Indian customers do not go to ethnic markets in the Bay Area simply to shop for groceries, but also to engage with representations of their (sometimes imagined) homeland. Like Sutton and others, she sees the gustatory as central to the creation of memory, ranging from the sensory clues the shops evoke, the cultural mnemonics of the commodities purchased, and how the goods acquired allow for practices that foster historically validated forms of identity. Ray's (2004) full-length work takes food as a potent and broad-ranging realm to understand changes in everyday life brought about by migration and globalization among Bengali-American households, with particular emphasis on the ways that food becomes a nexus of nostalgia and diasporic identity. In a different ethnographic context, Lee (2000) provides an interesting contrast to notions of diasporic gustatory nostalgia in showing how the inability of older Korean migrants to Japan to stomach spicy Korean food as they age problematizes self-identity because they interpret their changing tastes as the moral failure of not remaining sufficiently Korean.

GUSTATORY NOSTALGIA, EXPERIENCED AND INVENTED

As a form of memory, "nostalgia" has several different senses, generally and in respect to food. Some food literature (particularly outside anthropology) relies on a lay notion of sentimentality for a lost past, viewing food as a vehicle for recollections of childhood and family. Winegardner et al. (1998) contains varied accounts by mostly American writers reflecting on their family histories through the lens of food. Similar themes are developed in several interesting and creative pieces by contributors in Weiss (1997), blending a range of artistic and humanistic genres in exploring aspects of childhood nostalgia. Food-centered reminiscence is articulated within genres of food-centered memoirs (e.g., Clarke 1999, Keith 1992), the most well-known within this genre being Fisher's (1943) classic *The Gastronomical Me*.

Yet, in contrast with viewing nostalgia as a re-experiencing of emotional pasts it may also be seen as a longing for times and places that one has never experienced. Appadurai (1996) characterizes this as "armchair" nostalgia, suggesting that in late capitalist consumerism "the merchandiser supplies the lubricant of nostalgia" and the consumer "need only bring the faculty of nostalgia to an image that will supply the memory of a loss he or she has never suffered" (p. 78). The literature on food is rich with such nostalgia. Kugelmass' (1990) playful analysis of the carnivalesque in a New York Jewish restaurant offers a particularly rich description of the evocation of a schmaltz-based version of nostalgia for experiences that patrons at the restaurant never had. This type of nostalgia is also not discrete from the experience of actual loss. Mankekar (2002) emphasizes the extent to which the gustatory nostalgia Indian shoppers experience is for representations of a homeland that is largely imagined. Lupton (1994, 1996) argues that the nostalgic remembering of comfort foods need not be linked to a happy childhood but can serve to create the fiction of one, a theme also developed in Duruz's (1999) analysis of "Eating the 50s and 60s" in Australia.

Several studies emphasize a kind of false colonial nostalgia entailed in eating "ethnic food" sometimes construed as "eating the Other." Narayan's (1995) multilayered analysis of the invention and meanings of curry speaks directly to such issues. Cook & Crang (1996) employ a cultural studies approach to the ways in which geographical knowledge is constructed in encounters with exotic "ethnic" foods, cooked by Others who were once in the distant reaches of Empire, but who now constitute London as the quintessential globalized city (see also Goldman 1992, Heldke 2001). Bal (2005) takes a novel approach to similar issues concerning how *glub*—a kind of seed eating prevalent among immigrants in Berlin—is part of the aesthetic that shapes the Berlin art world, suggesting that it stands for cultural habits through which artists "participate in other people's memories" (p. 66). Notably, to Bal the exposure to culturally deep culinary habits, rather than the literal consumption of "ethnic food," is central here.

The link of Appadurai's "armchair nostalgia" to consumerism is seen in studies that illustrate how "tradition"—often invented—serves in the selling of consumer goods, using notions of history to convey a particular unique panache to a product. Most analyses focus on elite foods, although certainly the idiom is not limited to them; that Budweiser has been brewed since 1876 is significant to its slogan "The King of Beers," but it makes no parallel claim to being the "Beer of Kings." Typically, however, historical notions construct claims of distinction. Thus Ulin (1995, 1996) has analyzed the political maneuvering of French wine producers in arguing that "Bordeaux's paramount reputation follows from a social history and a

hegemonic, invented winegrowing tradition that enabled winegrowing elites to replicate and profit from the cultural capital associated with the aristocracy" (1995, p. 519). Terrio's (2000) examination of the history of French chocolate also notes the ways that chocolatiers romanticize their history through an "ideology of craft" expressed in memoirs, public histories, lectures, and window plays that are integral to selling their chocolate.

FOOD, NATIONALISM, AND INVENTED TRADITIONS

Many studies consider the creation of nation through the invention, standardization, or valorization of a national cuisine, often drawing on Anderson's (1983) conception of the imagined community and Hobsbawm's (1983) conception of invented tradition. Cookbooks are one important avenue for this process, for instance in Appadurai's (1988) classic study of the creation of Indian national cuisine through cookbooks from the 1960s–1980s, where forging the nation out of distinct regions is a prominent trope. Zubaida & Tapper (1994) note the shared tendency among nationalist ideologues and many writers on food "to be drawn to explanations in terms of origin and to assumptions of cultural continuity in the history of a people or a region" (p. 7). Roden (1974), for instance, unabashedly ties contemporary everyday Middle Eastern cooking methods, from Iran to Morocco, to the medieval al-Baghdadi cookbook, whereas Perry (1994) similarly enters into nationalist debates concerning origins of baklava. In a more critical vein, Fragner (1994) looks historically at Persian cookbooks as a form of literature and the agendas to which historical ethnography is employed within them.

Food is often used explicitly in the invention of national identities, a prominent theme in many of the contributions to Bellasco & Scranton's (2002) collection on the role of food in consumer societies. Murcott (1996) also emphasizes food as a symbol for creating imagined communities of nation in Europe.

Wilk's (1999) analysis of the recent rise of Belizean cuisine is particularly interesting because both nation and cuisine are more intrinsically imagined than in most contexts. Developed in response to the perceived need for a culture of nationhood after independence in 1981, Wilk contrasts 1970s meals of bland, imported food with the 1990s, when Belizean "local food" had become an important imagined tradition of Belizean authenticity. The need for "authenticity" in the tourist industry is a second driving force, a theme also emphasized in Howell's analysis of the lamb dish *mansaf*—traditionally the quintessential Bedouin food of hospitality—as a symbol of Jordanian national identity, constructing nostalgic identities based in notions of Bedouin hospitality, which serve both nationalist discourse and the tourist industry. Closer to home, Siskind (1992) elucidates the invention of Thanksgiving (a.k.a. Turkey Day) as a ritual of American nationality.

Boisard's (2003) study of camembert explores how this smelly cheese has become a concrete mythic symbol of the Republic and French national identity. Through a range of historical transformations camembert is a malleable symbol upon which other struggles are layered: For instance, pasteurized versus unpasteurized camembert comes to represent a struggle of tradition versus modernity within such anxieties as the impact of the European Union. Similar themes form an important dimension in Ohnuki-Tierney's (1993) nuanced study of rice in Japan, explicating how rice constructs Japanese conceptions of self in ways that are intensely historical and mythic, both overdetermined and invented. Rice has diffuse symbolic and material significance ranging from cosmogony, the aesthetics of consumption, the centrality of the rural rice paddy in nationalist natural aesthetic, and of course dietary staple. Yet it is also a metaphor viewed through a highly selective lens, particularly because it was not always the staple food, especially for nonelites in central Japan.

Integration into the European Union (EU) has been a particularly important arena tying food to notions of memory and historical consciousness, particularly the threat of homogenization of national and regional difference—both in scholarship and within the popular culture slow food movement. Seremetakis (1996), for instance, considers what she sees as the erasure of unconscious memory, as special varieties of food are lost through standardization. Leitch (2000, 2003) provides a particularly rich analysis of the politics of memory in regard to a specific food item, *lardo di Colonatta*, a pork lard native to a town in Italy. Both the food and its artisanal production techniques were valorized in the town's collective memory through annual lardo festivals until health standards imposed by the EU placed restrictions on production techniques. Its identification by the slow food movement as an endangered food subsequently enhanced its marketability, in what Leitch argues was (as in some studies cited above) a commodification of tradition, where the nostalgia surrounding lardo became the commodity sold.

Other studies, although of a more literary or historical bent, offer to constructions of nationalism other insights into the relationship of food-centered memory. Lyngo (2001) examines the public construction of memory in nutritional exhibitions in Norway in the 1930s using a lens of modernity to contrast the science incumbent in a "new Norwegian diet" with supposed nutritional problems found in past methods of Norwegian eating. In a different vein, Morton's (2004) collection ties food to notions of English romanticism, and although many of the pieces are restricted to literary analysis, others elucidate vivid forms of nostalgia historically or in contemporary life. Fulford (2004), for instance, focuses on the importance of breadfruit in the imagination of Empire by evoking mythic images of lost Eden in which Tahitian islanders could supposedly get bread without work. In the contemporary context, Roe (2004) examines how the recent foot and mouth epidemic was read through the lens of nostalgic notions of Romantic England, being not just an animal epidemic but a threat to the romantic notion of the countryside as "a haven, a blessed sanctuary" (p. 110).

FOOD, GENDER, AND THE AGENTS OF MEMORY

Gender forms a central theme within many analyses of food and memory, emphasizing its role as a vehicle for particularly feminine forms of memory. Thus, for instance, Counihan (2002a, 2004) explicitly uses her food-centered life-history approach as a means to "give voice to traditionally muted people... *especially women*" (2004, pp. 1–2; emphasis added). Christensen (2001) views the kitchen as a repository for memory; describing his mother's experience he asserts that "to open the skin of a garlic and dice its contents into grains allowed her to become a daughter again, to reenter the female world of her childhood" (p. 26). Thus, a wide body of literature emphasizes memory structured through what is construed as women's special relationship to food, providing access to histories and memories not found in other types of accounts. Meyers (2001) sees "food heritage" as a gift that mothers give to their daughters in an account that seeks to correct for the widespread emphasis on dysfunction in mother-daughter relationships. Berzok (2001) similarly provides a very reflexive recounting of memories encompassed in recipes her mother has given her. Innes's (2001a) varied edited collection examines how gender politics and memory are constructed through food. Thus, for instance, Blend (2001) construes tortilla making as a prosaic, but ritualized activity, which ties Latina women to a historically constituted subjectivity grounded in a gendered cultural identity, "tortilla/tamale making as a woman-centered, role-affirming communal ritual that empowers women as the carriers of tradition." Kelly (2001) takes as her starting point a grave marker memorializing "Helga, the Little Lefse Maker," deftly offering a more ambivalent view on the forms of memory laden with the contradictions entailed in women's valorization through

activities that simultaneously index their subordination.

These studies, many reflexive, and most not by anthropologists, illustrate both the strengths and weaknesses of food scholarship discussed earlier in this review. Although the insights they reveal about food are accessible and appealing to a student and educated lay audience, their familiarity may not push food studies to uncharted terrain. Most deal with American contexts and can imply stereotypical notions of Western womanhood by suggesting the natural feminine gendering of memories surrounding food. In contrast with the significant body of woman-centered food literature, relatively few studies examine masculinized memories through food, such as Taggart's (2002) use (per Counihan) of food-centered life histories among Latino men in the American southwest or Weiner's (1996) historical study of the role of Coca Cola in the nostalgic yearnings (and subsequent wartime memories) of American soldiers in World War II (see also Mintz 1996). Moving beyond Western contexts, however, one may encounter forms of food-centered memory that are far more masculine, such as memory creation enacted through the feasts of Melanesian big men (e.g., Eves 1996, Foster 1990) or in memories of male food-centered communitas among Samburu pastoralists in Kenya (Holtzman 1999).

A handful of studies examine more novel figures who serve as the mediators of memory and tradition through food. Chatwin (1997), for instance, engages in an extended discussion of the *tamada*, the head of the table at Georgian drinking occasions, seen as a "world maker," a mediator of tradition and nostalgia who has the authority to construct a particular vision of the past. In a different context, Prosterman (1984) presents an interesting view on public memory by focusing on the kosher caterer as a professional who stores, refracts, and mediates collective ideas about a historically validated identity, through the selection of arrays of foods appropriate to particular groups and particular events, tailoring "tradition" to the individualized tastes of particular clients.

FOOD AS THE MARKER OF EPOCHAL TRANSFORMATIONS

Dietary change marks epochal social transformations in a wide range of contexts, serving as a lens both to characterize the past and to read the present through the past (e.g., Holtzman 2003). Often this entails "memories of Gemeinschaft" (Sutton 2001), where previous foods tasted better or where food was shared more freely in precapitalist relations. Sometimes this feeling is expressed by the subjects themselves, but other times it is inferred by anthropologists and other writers on food. Thus, for instance, the desperation to acquire food is the central trope in Turnbull's (1972) narrative concerning the total dissolution of sociality, love, and kindness among the Ik, although absent is an account of how the Ik viewed themselves in relation to food and their past. In a different sense, Watson's (1997) collection implicitly engages with arguably nostalgic discourses concerning the loss of the unique non-Western Other, by looking at the localization of the quintessential symbol of cultural imperialism and homogenization—McDonalds—in a range of East Asian contexts. Field (1997) employs a genre blending cookbook with "salvage ethnography," although the nostalgia that laces her account is mainly that of the older Italian women who serve as her informants.

Past ways of eating can alternatively contrast the present to a better past, or an inferior past to an enlightened modernity. These alternating themes are developed in contributions to Kahn & Sexton' (1988) collection on change and continuity in Pacific foodways, where traditional foods serve as cultural markers in the context of dietary change. Flinn (1988), for instance, examines how Pulpalese assert moral superiority in relation to others on Truk through their comparatively greater reliance on traditional foods, whereas Lewis (1988) looks at "gustatory subversion" on

Kiribati, where the local cuisine is undermined by associating new foods with a superior modernity. I, however, argue that among Samburu pastoralists, the same individuals ambivalently mix these themes, viewing new ways of eating on the basis of purchased agricultural products simultaneously as markers of diffuse cultural decay and as the triumph of practical reason over the irrational cultural practices of an unenlightened past (J.D. Holtzman, unpublished manuscript). In a different sense Noguchi (1994) argues that the same food—ekiben, or train station lunch boxes—can simultaneously represent "high speed Japan" and a venerated past.

Counihan's *Around the Tuscan Table* (2004)—one of the few full-length works specifically concerned with food and memory—employs "food-centered life history" to use food as a window into the key changes in the lives of late twentieth century Florentines. Focusing on experiences and memories concerning all manners of eating, and changes in food over time, Counihan shows that food serves as a vivid medium for understanding perspectives on modernity often invisible within public debates. Many of the essays in Wu & Tan's (2001) edited collection on changing Chinese foodways develop similar themes, including the ways foods are used to define both tradition and the hybridity/syncretism of modernity.

Several studies look through the lens of food at epochal transformations in post-Socialist societies. Farquhar's (2002) full-length work addresses the question of "appetites" (encompassing food and sex) in postsocialist China. Emphasizing an embodied approach to history and memory, Farquhar examines the changing meanings and contexts of desire, in which 1990s consumerism is read in reference to the embodied asceticism and altruism that characterized Maoist ideology. Chatwin (1997) describes the "urgency and nostalgia" that accompanied food insecurity in post-Soviet Georgia. In the context of growing chaos, nostalgia emerged both for the distant culinary past—partially a

Hobsbawmian tradition for the new Georgian nation—and for the more recent orderliness of the Soviet system.

Specific foods can also be vehicles for reconnecting with a lost past. Pollock (1992) notes how traditional Polynesian foods, once viewed in negative terms, are now revalorized as the "roots of tradition." Erikson (1999) focuses on the controversy surrounding renewed whaling by Makah native Americans who, in the face of often racially charged opposition, viewed it as a means for reinvigorating a historically validated identity centered both on food procurement and consumption, contending both that the hunt is a "cultural necessity" and that adding whale back to their diet would ameliorate health problems.

RITUALS OF REMEMBERING AND FORGETTING THROUGH FOOD

Ritual has been viewed as a potent site for constructing food-centered memory—and food-centered forgetting. Dove (1999), for instance, looks at the ritual encoding of "archaic" plant foods as a mythic means for perpetuating cultural memory. In contrast, Singer (1984) shows how within a Hindu sect food is used as a medium for forgetting, creating new identities through the intentional erasure of the sediments of other ones.

Mortuary feasting is a particularly important arena for memorializing and forgetting through food, viewed in some instances as a context that creates a space of temporary memorialization, after which the person can be (at least publicly) forgotten (Munn 1986, Battaglia 1990). In contrast with public forgetting, Sutton (2001) suggests that the offering of mortuary food (and later devotions to dead relatives) begins the creation of a new person, by reediting memories of the deceased in reference to their generosity while alive. Hamilakis (1998) comparatively draws from Melanesian ethnography in his archaeological examination of funerary feasting from the Bronze Age Aegean, concerning how food

may offer a range of devices to generate memory and forgetting. Foster (1990) argues that forms of ceremonial exchange—ambiguously read as nurturing and/or forced feeding—is the medium for creating matrilineal continuity through time among Tangans of New Ireland. Eves (1996) also focuses on the memories created by and concerning the givers and receivers of mortuary feasts, specifically how the embodied experience of the feast (particularly sorcery-induced diarrhea) serves to create a remembrance of the feast that is transformed into fame for the feast giver.

An additional context is the literal or figurative eating of the dead themselves. Bloch (1985) focuses not on eating the dead, per se, but on metaphorical quasi-cannibalism when Merina "almost eat the ancestors" in the form of rice and beef, in an intriguing analysis of how particular foods become tied to mythic forms of identity. A range of studies focuses on funerary cannibalism, (e.g., Conklin 2001, McCallum 1999) and the culturally variant ways that eating the dead serves to deal with issues of grief, remembering, and forgetting in culturally specific ways. Stephen (1998) presents a more general psychological argument that funerary cannibalism (and other forms of corpse abuse) is tied to deeply embedded memories of other types of bereavement and loss, particularly the severing of the mother-child bond.

CONCLUSION

Here I have sought to discuss a confluence that is powerful, yet also in many ways is indeterminate. On one hand, we have food, which may be construed as principally fuel, a symbol, a medium of exchange, or a sensuous object experienced by an embodied self. On the other hand, memory may be private remembrance, public displays of historically validated identity, an intense experience of an epochal historical shift, or reading the present through the imagining of a past that never was—all processes in which food is implicated. In conclusion, I aim to consider some questions and themes that may provide further insight into what dynamic could link these various processes in ways that are generalizable or particular to specific contexts and historical/cultural milieus.

The most central question, sometimes addressed quite deliberately, but sometimes elided, is, "why food?" What makes food such a powerful and diffuse locus of memory? The most compelling answer, as many studies discussed here illustrate, is that the sensuality of eating transmits powerful mnemonic cues, principally through smells and tastes. However, this answer also has limitations. I suggest that scholars tend to emphasize forms of bodily memory consonant with Western views of food and the body—the pleasant smells and tastes of good food with far less attention to other types of sensualities, less epicurean, and sometimes less pleasant—whether fullness, energy, lethargy, hunger, sickness, or discomfort. This is less a critique of an approach based on sensuality than a call to problematize it deliberately. However, the sensuousness of food does not fully explain the widespread "armchair nostalgia" surrounding many foods nor how rarely eaten "heritage foods" are sometimes those most closely tied to collective memory. Indeed many studies successfully emphasize the symbolic importance of food without reference to its bodily experiences.

One potential, though so far underdeveloped, theme that might illuminate some of these linkages is the extent to which food intrinsically traverses the public and the intimate. Although eating always has a deeply private component, unlike our other most private activities food is integrally constituted through its open sharing, whether in rituals, feasts, reciprocal exchange, or contexts in which it is bought and sold. One might consider then the significance of this rather unique movement between the most intimate and the most public in fostering food's symbolic power, in general, and in relation to memory, in particular. At the same time, we must maintain an awareness of the fact that this attribute has a particular cultural-historical dynamic in the Euro-American contexts that are disproportionately represented in food studies. In America (unlike in some cultural/historical contexts), for instance, what one eats at home is relatively unmarked—even valorized, as an enduring symbol of the melting pot—whereas in the public sphere ethnic food is a particularly palatable form of multiculturalism, in contrast with the conformity expected, demanded, or even legislated in areas such as language and clothing. One might, then, consider what the ubiquity of food in maintaining historically constituted identities owes not only to the properties of food itself, but also to the social and cultural conditions that allow or encourage this to be a space for resilient identities where other arenas are far more stigmatized.

Viewed from the other side, one may ask, conversely, what food could illuminate about memory as a more general phenomenon or set of phenomena. As Wiley (2006) has recently noted, food studies is one area that remains relatively at ease among the often fractious debates concerning the continuing value, or inevitable unbundling, of anthropology's four fields. Few dispute that the salience of food emanates not only from its material centrality as the nutritional source of life, but also from the ways that this key facet articulates with densely intersecting—yet to some degree discrete—lines of causality and meaning in ways that are deeply symbolic, sensuous, psychological, and social. It has the uncanny ability to tie the minutiae of everyday experience to broader cultural patterns, hegemonic structures, and political-economic processes, structuring experience in ways that can be logical, and outside of logic, in ways that are conscious, canonized, or beyond the realm of conscious awareness. And so too are many of the disparate phenomena we term memory—social, psychological, embodied, invented, private and political, discrete yet also interconnected and reinforcing. Food, thus, offers a potential window into forms of memory that are more heteroglossic, ambivalent, layered, and textured. I, thus, suggest that understandings of food and memory would benefit from studies that more deliberately aim to understand the interconnections among the varying aspects of food, the varying phenomena of memory, and their confluences—how these in some senses constitute a whole, albeit a messy and ambiguous one.

LITERATURE CITED

Abarca M. 2004. Authentic or not, its orginal. *Food Foodways* 12(1):1–25

Anderson B. 1983. *Imagined Communities*. London: Verso

Appadurai A. 1988. How to make a national cuisine: cookbooks in contemporary India. *Comp. Stud. Soc. Hist.* 30(1):3–24

Appadurai A. 1996. *Modernity at Large: Cultural Dimensions of Globalization*. Minneapolis: Univ. Minn. Press

Bahloul J. 1989. From a Muslim banquet to a Jewish seder: foodways and ethnicity among North African Jews. In *Jews Among Arabs: Contacts and Boundaries*, ed. M Cohen, A Udovitch, pp. 85–96. Princeton, NJ: Darwin

Bal M. 2005. Food, form and visibility: glub and the aesthetics of everyday life. *Postcolon. Stud.* 8(1):51–73

Batsell WR, Brown A, Ansfield M, Paschall G. 2002. "You will eat all of that!": a retrospective analysis of forced consumption episodes. *Appetite* 38:211–19

Battaglia D. 1990. *On the Bones of the Serpent: Persons, Memory and Mortality in Sabarl Island Society*. Chicago, IL: Univ. Chicago Press

Bellasco W, Scranton P, eds. 2002. *Food Nations: Selling Taste in Consumer Societies*. London: Routledge

Berzok L. 2001. My mother's recipes. See Innes 2001b, pp. 84–101

Blend B. 2001. "I am an act of kneading": food and the making of Chicana identity. See Innes 2001a, pp. 41–62

Bloch M. 1985. Almost eating the ancestors. *Man* (n.s.) 20:631–46

Boisard P. 2003. *Camembert: A National Myth*. Berkeley: Univ. Calif. Press

Borges JL. 1941. Tlön, Uqbar, Orbis Tertius. In *Labyrinths: Selected Stories and Other Writings*. New York: Penguin

Bourdieu P. 1977. *Outline of a Theory of Practice*. Cambridge, UK: Cambridge Univ. Press

Brandes S. 1997. Sugar, colonialism and death: on the origins of Mexico's Day of the Dead. *Comp. Stud. Soc. Hist.* 39(2):266–95

Brown L, Mussell K, eds. 1984. *Ethnic and Regional Foodways in the United States*. Knoxville: Univ. Tenn. Press

Buckser A. 1999. Keeping kosher: eating and social identity among the Jews of Denmark. *Ethnology* 38:191–209

Chatwin ME. 1997. *Socio-Cultural Transformation and Foodways in the Republic of Georgia*. Commack, NY: Nova Sci.

Christensen P. 2001. Mac and gravy. See Innes 2001b, pp. 17–39

Clarke A. 1999. *Pig Tails 'n Breadfruit*. New York: New Press

Classen C. 1997. Foundations for an anthropology of the senses. *Int. Soc. Sci. J.* 153:401–12

Cole J. 2001. *Forget Colonialism? Sacrifice and the Art of Memory in Madagascar*. Berkeley: Univ. Calif. Press

Comito J. 2001. *Remembering Nana and Papu: the poetics of pasta, pane and peppers among one Iowan Calabrian family*. PhD Diss., Univ. Iowa

Conklin B. 2001. *Consuming Grief: Compassionate Cannibalism in an Amazonian Society*. Austin: Univ. Tex. Press

Connerton P. 1989. *How Societies Remember*. Cambridge, UK: Cambridge Univ. Press

Cook I, Crang P. 1996. The world on a plate: culinary culture, displacement and geographical knowledges. *J. Mater. Cult.* 1(2):131–53

Counihan C. 2002a. Food as woman's voice in the San Luis Valley of Colorado. See Counihan 2002b, pp. 295–304

Counihan C, ed. 2002b. *Food in the USA*. New York: Routledge

Counihan C. 2004. *Around the Tuscan Table: Food, Family and Gender in Twentieth Century Florence*. London: Routledge

Cwiertka K. 2000. From Yokohama to Amsterdam: meidi-ya and dietary change in modern Japan. *Japanstudien* 12:45–63

Cwiertka K. 2002. Popularising a military diet in wartime and postwar Japan. *Asian Anthropol.* 1(1):1–30

Diner H. 2003. *Hungering for America: Italian, Irish and Jewish Foodways in the Age of Migration*. Cambridge, MA: Harvard Univ. Press

Douglas M. 1975. *Implicit Meanings*. London: Routledge

Douglas M, ed. 1984. *Food in the Social Order: Studies of Food and Festivities in Three American Communities*. New York: Russell Sage

Dove M. 1999. The memory of agronomy and the agronomy of memory. In *Ethnoecology: Situated Knowledges/Located Lives*, ed. V Nazarea pp. 45–66. Tuscon: Univ. Ariz. Press

Duruz J. 1999. Food as nostalgia: eating the fifties and sixties. *Aust. Hist. Stud.* 113:231–50

Erikson P. 1999. A-whaling we will go: encounters of knowledge and memory at the Makah Cultural and Research Center. *Cult. Anthropol.* 14(4):556–83

Eves R. 1996. Memories of things passed: memory, body and the politics of feasting in New Ireland. *Oceania* 66(4):266–77

Farquhar J. 2002. *Appetites: Food and Sex in Postsocialist China*. Durham, NC: Duke Univ. Press

Field C. 1997. *In Nonna's Kitchen: Recipes and Traditions from Italy's Grandmothers*. New York: Harper Collins

Fisher MFK. 1943. *The Gastronomical Me*. New York: Duell, Sloan and Pierce

Flinn J. 1988. Tradition in the face of change: food choices among Pulapese in Truk state. *Food Foodways* 3(1,2): 19–37

Foster R. 1990. Nurture and force feeding: mortuary feasting and the construction of collective individuals in a New Ireland society. *Am. Ethnol.* 17(3):431–48

Fragner B. 1994. Social reality and culinary fiction. See Zubaida & Tapper 1994, pp. 63–72

Fulford T. 2004. The taste of paradise: the fruits of romanticism in the empire. In *Cultures of Taste/Theories of Appetite: Eating Romanticism*, ed. T Morton, pp. 41–57. London: Palgrave

Gabbacia D. 1998. *We Are What We Eat: Ethnic Food and the Making of Americans*. Cambridge, MA: Harvard Univ. Press

Ganguly K. 2001. *States of Exception*. Minneapolis: Univ. Minn. Press

Giard L. 1998. Part II: doing-cooking. In *The Practice of Everyday Life*, Vol. 2, *Living and Cooking*, ed. L Giard with M de Certeau P Mayol, pp. 149–48. Minneapolis: Univ. Minn. Press

Gillespie A. 1984. A wilderness in the megalopolis: foodways in the Pine Barrens of New Jersey. See Brown & Mussell 1984, pp. 145–68

Goldman A. 1992. I yam what I yam: cooking, culture and colonialism. In *De/Colonizing the Subject*, ed. S Smith, J Watson, pp. 169–95. Minneapolis: Univ. Minn. Press

Goldstein D. 1993. *The Georgian Feast: The Vibrant Culture and Savory Food of the Republic of Georgia*. New York: Harper Collins

Goode J, Curtis K, Theopano J. 1984. Meal formats, meal cycles and menu negotiation in the maintenance of an Italian-American community. See Douglas 1984, pp. 143–218

Hamilakis Y. 1998. Eating the dead: mortuary feasting and the political economy of memory in the Bronze Age Aegean. In *Cemetary and Society in the Aegean Bronze Age*. ed. K Branigan, pp. 115–32. Sheffield, UK: Sheffield Acad. Press

Harbottle L. 1997. Taste and embodiment: the food preferences of Iranians in Britain. In *Food Preference and Taste: Continuity and Change* ed. H MacBeth, pp. 175–85. Providence, RI: Berghahn

Heldke L. 2001. Let's cook Thai: recipes for colonialism See Innes 2001b, pp. 164–85

Hensel C. 1996. *Telling Ourselves: Ethnicity of Discourse in Southwestern Alaska*. Oxford, UK: Oxford Univ. Press

Hobsbawm E. 1983. Introduction: inventing traditions. In *The Invention of Tradition*, ed. E Hobsbawm, T Ranger, pp. 1–14. Cambridge, UK: Cambridge Univ. Press

Hodgkin K, Radstone S, eds. 2003. *Contested Pasts: The Politics of Memory*. London: Routledge

Holtzman JD. 1999. Cultivar as civilizer: Samburu and European perspectives on cultivar diffusion. *Ethnology* (Monogr.) 17:11–19

Holtzman JD. 2003. In a cup of tea: commodities and history among Samburu pastoralists in northern Kenya. *Am. Ethnol.* 30(1):136–55

Howell S. 2003. Modernizing Mansaf: the consuming contexts of Jordan's national dish. *Food Foodways* 11(4):215–43

Humphrey T, Humphrey L, eds. 1988. *"We Gather Together": Food and Festival in American Life*. Ann Arbor: UMI Res.

Innes S, ed. 2001a. *Cooking Lessons*. Lanham, MD: Rowman and Littlefield

Innes S, ed. 2001b. *Pilaf, Pozole and Pad Thai*. Amherst: Univ. Mass. Press

Jackson M. 1995. *At Home in the World*. Durham, NC: Duke Univ. Press

James W. 1988. *The Listening Ebony*. Oxford, UK: Clarendon Press

Kahn M, Sexton L, eds. 1988. Continuity and change in Pacific foodways. *Food Foodways* (Spec. Issue) 3(1–2)

Kalcik S. 1984. Ethnic foodways in America: symbol and performance of identity. See Brown & Mussell 1984, pp. 37–65

Keith N. 1992. Nonnibutibus: the sociolcultural messages of the Jamaican tea meeting. *Anthropol. Hum. Q.* 17(1):2–9

Kelly TM. 2001. Honoring Helga, "The Little Lefsa Maker": regional food as social marker, tradition and art. See Innes 2001a, pp. 19–40

Kugelmass J. 1990. Green bagels: an essay on food, nostalgia, and the carnivalesque. *YIVO Annu.* 19:57–80

Lee SSJ. 2000. Dys-appearing tongues and bodily memories: the aging of first-generation resident Koreans in Japan. *Ethos* 28(2):198–223

Leitch A. 2000. The social life of Lardo: slow food in fast times. *Asian Pac. J. Anthropol.* 1(1):103–18

Leitch A. 2003. Slow food and the politics of pork fat: Italian food politics and European identity. *Ethnos* 68:4

Lentz C, ed. 1999. *Changing Food Habits: Case Studies from Africa, South America, and Europe*. Amsterdam: Harwood Acad.

Lewis DEJ. 1988. Gustatory subversion and the evolution of nutritional dependency in Kiribati. *Food Foodways* 3(1,2):79–98

Lockwood W, Lockwood YR. 2000. Finnish American milk products in the northwoods. In *Milk: Beyond the Dairy. Oxford Symposium on Food and Cookery 1999 Proceedings*, ed. H Walker, pp. 232–39. Oxford: Prospect

Lupton D. 1994. Food, memory, and meaning: the symbolic and social nature of food. *Sociol. Rev.* 42(4):664–87

Lupton D. 1996. *Food, the Body and the Self*. New York: Sage

Lyngo IJ. 2001. The national nutrition exhibition: a new nutritional narrative in Norway in the 1930s. In *Food, Drink and Identity: Cooking, Eating and Drinking in Europe Since the Middle Ages*, ed. P Scholliers, pp. 141–61. London: Berg

Macbeth H, ed. 1997. *Food Preferences and Taste: Continuity and Change*. Providence, RI: Berghahn

Mankekar P. 2002. "India shopping": Indian grocery stores and transnational configuration of belonging. *Ethnos* 67(1):75–98

McCallum C. 1999. Consuming pity: the production of death among the Cashinua. *Cult. Anthropol.* 14(4):443–71

Meigs A. 1984. *Food, Sex and Pollution: A New Guinea Religion*. New Brunswick, NJ: Rutgers Univ. Press

Meyers M. 2001. *A Bite off Mama's Plate: Mothers' and Daughters' Connections Through Food*. New York: Bergin and Garvey

Mueggler E. 2001. *The Age of Wild Ghosts: Memory, Violence and Place in Southwest China*. Berkeley: Univ. Calif. Press

Mintz S. 1985. *Sweetness and Power*. New York: Penguin

Mintz S. 1996. *Tasting Food, Tasting Freedom*. Boston, MA: Beacon Press

Morton T, ed. 2004. *Cultures of Taste/Theories of Appetite: Eating Romanticism*. London: Palgrave

Munn N. 1986. *The Fame of Gawa*. Cambridge, UK: Cambridge Univ. Press

Murcott A. 1996. Food as an expression of identity. In *The Future of the National State: Essays on Cultural Pluralism and Political Integration*, ed. S Gustafsson, L Lewin, pp. 49–77. Stockholm: Nerenius and Santerus

Narayan U. 1995. Eating cultures: incorporation, identity and Indian food. *Soc. Ident.* 1(1):63–86

Noguchi P. 1994. Savor slowly: *EKIBEN*—the fast food of high-speed Japan. *Ethnology* 33(4):317–30

Ohnuki-Tierney E. 1993. *Rice as Self: Japanese Identities Through Time*. Princeton, NJ: Princeton Univ. Press

Ong A. 2003. *Buddha is Hiding*. Berkeley: Univ. Calif. Press

Perry C. 1994. The taste for layered bread among the nomadic Turks and the Central Asian origins of baklava. See Zubaida & Tapper 1994, pp. 87–92

Pollock N. 1992. *These Roots Remain: Food Habits in Islands of the Central and Eastern Pacific*. Laie, Hawaii: Inst. Polynes. Stud.

Powers W, Powers P. 1984. Metaphysical aspects of Oglala food systems. See Douglas 1984, pp. 40–94

Plotnicov L, Scaglion R, eds. 1999. *Consequences of Cultivar Diffusion. Ethnol. Monogr. No. 17*

Powles J. 2002. *"Like baby minnows we came with the current": social memory among Angolan refugees in Meheba settlement, Zambia*. Presented at Annu. Meet. Assoc. Soc. Anthropol. Great Britain and the Commonwealth. Arusha, Tanzania

Prosterman L. 1984. Food and celebration: a kosher caterer as the mediator of communal traditions. See Brown & Mussel 1984, pp. 127–42

Ray K. 2004. *The Migrant's Table: Meals and Memories in Bengali-American Households*. Philadelphia: Temple Univ. Press

Roden C. 1974. *Book of Middle Eastern Food*. New York: Vintage Books

Roe N. 2004. Eating romantic England: the foot and mouth scare and its consequences. In *Cultures of Taste/Theories of Appetite: Eating Romanticism*, ed. T Morton, pp. 97–112. London: Palgrave

Roy P. 2002. Reading communities and culinary communities: the gastropoetics of south Indian diaspora. *Positions* 10(2):471–502

Searls E. 2002. Food and the making of modern Inuit identities. *Food Foodways* 10(1):55–78

Seremetakis CN. 1993. The memory of the senses: historical perception, commensal exchange and modernity. *Vis. Anthropol. Rev.* 9(2):2–18

Seremetakis CN. 1996. *The Senses Still.* Chicago, IL: Univ. Chicago Press

Shaw R. 2002. *Memories of the Slave Trade.* Chicago, IL: Univ. Chicago Press

Shortridge B, Shortridge J, eds. 1998. *The Taste of American Place.* Lanham, MD: Rowan and Littlefield

Singer E. 1984. Conversion through foodways enculturation: the meaning of eating in an American Hindu sect. See Brown and Mussell 1984, pp. 195–214

Siskind J. 1992. The invention of Thanksgiving: a ritual of American nationality. *Crit. Anthropol.* 12(2):167–91

Smith A. 2004. Heteroglossia, "common sense" and social memory. *Am. Ethnolog.* 31(2):251–69

Spiro M. 1955. The acculturation of American ethnic groups. *Am. Anthropol.* 57(6):1240–52

Stephen M. 1998. Devouring the mother: a Kleinian perspective on necrophagia and corpse abuse in mortuary ritual. *Ethos* 26(4):387–409

Stoller P. 1989. *The Taste of Ethnographic Things.* Philadelphia: Univ. Penn. Press

Stoller P. 1995. *Embodying Colonial Memories.* New York: Routledge

Sutton D. 2000. Whole foods: revitalization through everyday synesthetic experience. *Anthropol. Hum.* 25(2):120–30

Sutton D. 2001. *Remembrance of Repasts: An Anthropology of Food and Memory.* London: Berg

Taggart J. 2002. Food, masculinity and place in the American Southwest. See Counihan 2002b, pp. 305–14

Terrio S. 2000. *Crafting the Culture and History of French Chocolate.* Berkeley: Univ. Calif. Press

Trubek A. 2000. *Haute Cuisine: How the French Invented the Culinary Profession.* Philadelphia: Univ. Penn. Press

Tuchman G, Levine H. 1993. New York Jews and Chinese food: the social construction of an ethnic pattern. *J. Contemp. Ethnog.* 22(3):362–407

Turnbull C. 1972. *The Mountain People.* New York: Simon and Schuster

Ulin R. 1995. Invention and representation as cultural capital: Southwest French winegrowing history. *Am. Anthropol.* 97(3):519–27

Ulin R. 1996. *Vintages and Traditions. An Ethnohistory of Southwest French Wine Cooperatives.* Washington: Smithson. Inst. Press

Watson J, ed. 1997. *Golden Arches East: McDonald's in East Asia.* Stanford, CA: Stanford Univ. Press

Weiner M. 1996. Consumer culture and participatory democracy: the story of Coca Cola during World War II. *Food Foodways* 6(2):109–29

Weiss A, ed. 1997. *Taste Nostalgia.* New York: Lusitania Press

Wiley A. 2006. The breakdown of holism and the curious fate of food studies in anthropology. *Anthropol. News* 47(1):9, 12

Wilk R. 1999. 'Real Belizean food': building local identity in the transnational Caribbean. *Am. Anthropol.* 101(2):244–55

Winegardner M. 1998. *We Are What We Ate.* Fort Washington, PA: Harvest Books

Wu DYH, Tan CB, eds. 2001. *Changing Chinese Foodways in Asia.* Hong Kong: Chinese Univ. Press

Zubaida S, Tapper R, eds. 1994. *Culinary Cultures of the Middle East.* London: Taurus

Evolution of the Size and Functional Areas of the Human Brain

P. Thomas Schoenemann

Department of Behavioral Sciences, University of Michigan–Dearborn, Dearborn, Michigan 48128; email: ptoms@umich.edu

Annu. Rev. Anthropol. 2006. 35:379–406

First published online as a Review in Advance on June 16, 2006

The *Annual Review of Anthropology* is online at anthro.annualreviews.org

This article's doi: 10.1146/annurev.anthro.35.081705.123210

Copyright © 2006 by Annual Reviews. All rights reserved

0084-6570/06/1021-0379$20.00

Key Words

neuroanatomy, encephalization, behavior, adaptation, selection

Abstract

The human brain is one of the most intricate, complicated, and impressive organs ever to have evolved. Understanding its evolution requires integrating knowledge from a variety of disciplines in the natural and social sciences. Four areas of research are particularly important to this endeavor. First, we need to understand basic principles of brain evolution that appear to operate across broad classes of organisms. Second, we need to understand the ways in which human brains differ from the brains of our closest living relatives. Third, clues from the fossil record may allow us to outline the manner in which these differences evolved. Finally, studies of brain structure/function relationships are critical for us to make behavioral sense of the evolutionary changes that occurred. This review highlights important questions and work in each of these areas.

INTRODUCTION

The evolution of the human brain has been one of the most significant events in the evolution of life. Although the outline of how and why this happened is being filled in, many fundamental questions remain to be answered. The fossil record, in concert with a comparative neuroanatomical analysis of closely related species, shows that the hominid brain increased in size more than threefold over a period of approximately 2.5 million years. However, it has become increasingly clear that the human brain is not simply a large ape brain: Important qualitative and quantitative changes occurred as well. Some of these changes are a result of broad patterns of brain evolution that appear across species, either for developmental reasons or because of patterns of adaptation that are inherent in the nature of life. Some are presumably a result of direct selection for specific behavioral abilities of various kinds. Unraveling which adaptational explanations are possible or likely requires understanding as much as we can about how brain structure relates to behavioral variation. Unraveling the story of human evolution requires research in each of these areas: (*a*) general patterns of brain evolution, (*b*) comparative assessment of brain anatomy across species, (*c*) the fossil history of human-brain evolution, and (*d*) brain structure/function relationships.

This review focuses on trying to understand evolutionary changes in brain size as well as the proportions of different brain areas. It highlights conceptual areas and questions that are prone to misunderstanding, need particularly careful assessment, are of current controversy, or present important avenues for future research. It necessarily leaves out some research areas that are both important and interesting, such as deep cortical and brainstem nuclei, the evolution of specific neuron types and their

specializations, and possible gene-expression changes.[1]

PATTERNS OF BRAIN EVOLUTION

Brain/Body Scaling

How should species be compared with respect to brain size? It has long been known that brain size scales with body size across broad groups of animals (Dubois 1913). For this reason, some measure of relative brain size has usually been favored in comparative studies. Empirically the relationship between brain and body size can be estimated using a function of the form [brain] $= c$[body]^a, where c and a are empirically derived constants. Because the brain/body relationship is nonlinear, a simple ratio of brain to body is problematic (e.g., small animals have larger ratios than larger animals on average). Encephalization quotients (EQs) are widely used measures of relative brain size that take this empirical relationship between brain and body size into account. They are simply the ratio of a species' actual brain size to the brain size expected for an animal of its body size (Jerison 1973). The expected brain size for a given species is usually derived using a regression (or other method, e.g., reduced major axis) of log brain to log body size for the comparison group of species, resulting in a formula of the type [log brain] $= \log c + a$[log body]. Jerison (1973) used mammals as the comparison group, but one can estimate EQs, for example, on the basis of primates only. One can also extend the concept to subcomponents of the brain and scale them either against

---

Encephalization quotient (EQ): calculated as the ratio of a species' actual brain size to the size expected given its body weight

[1] I encourage those interested in extended reviews of human brain evolution to consult Allman 1999, Deacon 1997, Falk 1992, Geary 2005, Holloway et al. 2004a, and Striedter 2005.

body size or brain size (see, e.g., Schoenemann 1997).

Because EQs are calculated on the basis of empirical estimates of brain/body-scaling relationships, they are sensitive to the particular sample used to derive a and c parameters. Jerison (1973) originally estimated the scaling parameter a (i.e., slope) for mammals as ~0.67, but Martin (1981) estimated it to be 0.76 using a larger sample. Using Jerison's (1973) equation, human EQs are ~7, whereas Martin's (1981) equation gives the values at ~5. Regardless of the slope estimate used, however, humans consistently have the highest values among mammals.

Figure 1 (see color insert) shows brain/body-size relationships for a sample of 52 primate species and illustrates different scaling estimates for separate primate subtaxa. Primates as a group tend to have larger brains than the average mammal, with EQs for anthropoids (all primates excluding prosimians) averaging ~2 (i.e., anthropoids have brains approximately twice the size of the average mammal of their body size). Even though absolute brain size is significantly larger in pongids (chimpanzee, bonobo, gorilla, orangutan) than in all other anthropoids except humans, they do not have substantially larger EQs, indicating their brains are scaling approximately similar to other anthropoids. Human brain sizes, by contrast, are not explained by brain/body scaling in either mammals or primates.

Although EQs are superficially appealing as a measure of comparative brain size, it is unclear exactly how to interpret EQ differences between species. The behavioral relevance of EQ has long been questioned (Holloway 1966), yet it is often incorrectly assumed that it must be the most behaviorally relevant variable of brain size—as if it were some coarse estimate of intelligence or other behavioral ability (e.g., Kappelman 1996). Others have uncritically assumed that increases in absolute brain size may not be meaningful if EQs remain the same (e.g., Wood & Collard 1999, Wynn 2002). Unfor-

tunately, EQs are not so easily interpreted. If EQ really tells us something about intelligence or general behavioral complexity, what are we to make of the large whales, who have the lowest EQs of all mammals [e.g., humpback whales (*Megaptera nodosa*) have EQs of 0.18 (Schoenemann 1997)]? Humpback whales display a variety of complex behaviors, including structured vocal sequences (songs?) that last 5–25 min before repeating, and complex feeding techniques, including the use of bubble clouds to encircle prey (Rendell et al. 2001).

Other species comparisons further highlight the problem: Guinea pigs (*Cavia cutleri*) have significantly higher EQs (0.95) than do elephants (*Loxodonta africana*, 0.63). This is true even though guinea pig brains weigh only ~3.3 g, whereas elephant brains can weigh over 5700 g (Schoenemann 1997). If EQ really tells us something important about behavior, this should be evident in a comparison of guinea pig versus elephant behavior, yet this does not appear to be the case. If anything, given the variety of complex social behaviors known in elephants (e.g., McComb et al. 2001), absolute brain size appears more behaviorally relevant in this comparison.

In fact, a number of studies suggest that—for some behavioral domains—absolute brain size is more relevant than EQ. This is true for measures of the ease of learning abstract rules as opposed to simple associations (Rumbaugh et al. 1996), as well as the speed of learning object-discrimination tasks (Riddell & Corl 1977). In addition, although relative brain size is often emphasized in brain/behavior studies, associations are invariably also significant if absolute brain volumes are used (e.g., Dunbar 1995, Reader & Laland 2002). Jerison (1973) recognized this when he suggested an alternative to EQ: an estimate of extra neurons, which is the absolute amount of neural tissue beyond that predicted empirically by body mass (e.g., two species with identical EQs but different body masses also differ in number of extra neurons). This measure is, however,

Pongids: larger-bodied apes, part of the taxonomic superfamily Hominoidea, which include common and bonobo chimpanzees, gorillas, and orangutans

not commonly used in discussions of hominid brain evolution.

The incorrect assumption that absolute brain size is not particularly behaviorally relevant may stem from the fact that, because brain size scales with body size, it is assumed growth of the two must be tightly constrained together developmentally (e.g., Finlay et al. 2001). Such developmental constraints would require that a larger-bodied species have a larger brain, so simply comparing species in absolute brain size would improperly conflate brain size with body-size differences. The problem with this view is that brain/body scaling does not, in fact, necessarily imply developmental constraint. Although the correlation between brain and body size is high (typically $r > 0.95$), at least a tenfold range of variation in absolute brain size exists at a given body size in mammals (Finlay et al. 2001, Schoenemann 1997). Thus, any developmental constraint would not appear to be strong. In addition, it is not often recognized that brain/body scaling could be the result of body size constraining brain size, rather than the brain and body being tightly developmentally linked. Jerison's (1973) explanation for the brain/body relationship is that larger bodies need larger brains both to control greater muscle mass and to process greater amounts of sensory information. Other explanations emphasize the limiting role of metabolic resources in brain growth across species (Armstrong 1983, Martin 1981). In either case, absolutely larger brains might always be adaptive if they can be paid for metabolically (and hence ecologically). Because brains are metabolically expensive [i.e., having high metabolic rates per gram of tissue (Aiello & Wheeler 1995, Hofman 1983b)], brain sizes tend to vary at a given body size as a function of the usefulness of brains for a particular species niche. Larger animals generally have larger brains because they have more metabolic resources available to put toward brain development and maintenance, not because of developmental constraints (Schoenemann 2004).

Under this model, body size varies according to a variety of ecological constraints and tends to put upper limits on possible brain size, which in turn tend toward the high end, particularly in social species (see below). The human condition is explained by behavioral adaptations that lead to a relaxation of ecological constraints. This behavioral-selection/body-size-limiting model of brain-size evolution is more consistent with the wide range of brain sizes at a given body size in mammals, and it also explicitly does not assume that EQ is the only behaviorally relevant comparative measure. In addition, this model is consistent with the finding that two genetic loci known to be important to brain size development, ASPM and microcephalin, both show signatures of strong selection specifically at the evolutionary divergence of the line leading to pongids and hominids (away from all other primates) even though pongids do not show an increase in relative brain size over other primates (as noted above) (see Evans et al. 2004, Wang & Su 2004).

In summary, brain size does scale with body size, and EQ differences do suggest something about the relative importance brains have had during a species' evolutionary history, but they should not be used uncritically as proxies of species' behavioral capacities. That brain size scales with body size across mammals does not constitute strong evidence of developmental constraints tying the two together. Absolute brain size itself appears to be behaviorally relevant.

Patterns of Internal Brain Allometry

Larger brains have more neurons (Haug 1987), but for these neurons to remain equally well connected to each other (in the sense of a signal having the same average number of synapses to traverse to travel between any two neurons), the number of connections (axons) must increase much faster than the number of neurons (Ringo 1991). Hofman's (1985) data show that white matter increases faster than gray matter with increasing brain size. (White matter contains longer-distance axonal connections between cortical areas, whereas gray matter contains most neuronal cell bodies and dendritic connections.) However, the increase is not fast enough to maintain equal degrees of connectivity between neurons (Ringo 1991). As brain size increases, therefore, there is a concomitant increase in the separation between existing areas, leading to a strong correlation between brain volume and the number of distinguishable cortical areas across mammals (Changizi & Shimojo 2005). These scaling relationships predict ~150 distinct cortical areas in humans. Although the human cortex is not yet completely mapped, this predicted number is broadly consistent with what is thought to be the actual number (Van Essen et al. 1998).

HUMAN BRAINS IN COMPARATIVE PERSPECTIVE

Understanding human brain evolution requires the assessment of exactly how human brains differ with respect to the size of various components from those of other living animals, particularly our closest evolutionary relatives: the pongids. Empirically mapping all the possible differences across many species is an extraordinarily time-consuming task, and at present we are nowhere near a complete understanding of all the differences that may exist. Below I review the brain components that have been studied in enough detail to give at least preliminary assessments about the relative status of human brains. The neuroanatomical variables studied to date are either relatively easy to measure or have been thought to be particularly interesting behaviorally. Because conscious awareness is localized to areas of the cortex (the outermost layer of gray matter of the cerebral hemispheres), much comparative research has focused on cortical subdivisions. In some areas, only the size of an entire cortical lobe has been estimated in enough species to allow any comparison; in other areas, studies exist of more-localized (and presumably functionally specific) areas.

Because humans differ from other species on a number of interesting behavioral dimensions (e.g., communication, ability to harness technology, problem solving, complexity of social relationships; see below), and because the neural processing underlying these is often located in different brain regions, there is no general agreement about what components are most important to study a priori. For this reason, this review covers most of the components for which information is available. These include overall brain size, olfactory bulb, cerebellum, visual cortex, temporal lobe, and the overall frontal cortex and its components (primary motor, premotor, and prefrontal cortices). Because of space limitations, noncortical areas other than the cerebellum (e.g., deep cortical and brainstem nuclei) are not discussed here. Behavioral implications of anatomical differences are reviewed in the subsequent sections. Our knowledge of anatomical differences is further advanced than our knowledge of what these differences might mean behaviorally. In general, however, it is generally assumed, implicitly or explicitly, that more tissue translates into greater sophistication in neural processing in some way, which in turn suggests increased complexity of the behaviors mediated by that particular area (or areas). Actual direct tests of this assumption are relatively rare, however.

Brain Size

The most obvious evolutionary change during human evolution, as noted above, has been an increase in both absolute and relative brain size (Holloway 1995). Estimated brain sizes of our closest living relatives, the pongids (large-bodied apes), are as follows: common chimpanzee (*Pan troglodytes*), 337 ($\pm$16) cc; pygmy chimpanzee (*P. paniscus*), 311 ($\pm$11) cc; gorilla (*Gorilla gorilla*), 397 ($\pm$67) cc; and orangutan (*Pongo pygmaeus*), 407 ($\pm$29) cc (Rilling & Insel 1999). Modern human brain sizes vary widely, but average ~1330 cc (Dekaban 1978, Garby et al. 1993, Ho et al. 1980a, Pakkenberg

& Voigt 1964).[2] Modern human brains are 3.1 times larger than predicted on the basis of primate brain/body-size allometric scaling (Schoenemann 1997).

Olfactory bulb. The olfactory bulb is the first major processing area for the sense of smell. Stephan et al.'s (1981) data show that the olfactory bulb is only ~30% as large as predicted for primate brains of our size (Schoenemann 1997). Because overall brain size is approximately three times larger in modern humans, this suggests the olfactory bulb has lagged behind overall brain-size evolution. This finding is consistent with the belief that olfaction is relatively poor in humans, comparatively. However, the human olfactory bulb is ~1.6 times larger than expected for a primate of our body size (Schoenemann 1997). Exactly how one should interpret differences relative to body size versus differences relative to brain size is a major unresolved issue. It would appear that olfaction is not unimportant.

Cerebellum. The cerebellum plays a key role in modulating patterns of muscle movements and appears to play a role in timing generally. It may be involved in aspects of language processing as well (Gazzaniga et al. 1998). The human cerebellum is ~2.9 times as large as expected for a primate of our body size (calculated from data in Stephan et al. 1981) and as such has increased only slightly more slowly than the brain as a whole. MacLeod et al. (2003) have shown that there is a grade shift in hominoids with respect to the size of the cerebellar hemispheres, with hominoids as a group (humans included) showing greatly enlarged cerebella compared with monkeys. The cerebellum's participation in language presumably explains why it has not lagged behind as has the olfactory bulb, for example.

---

[2] Original data in grams was converted to estimated cc using the formula (brain volume in cc) = (brain mass in grams)/ 1.036. European-derived samples only.

Visual cortex. The visual cortex is so named because it is the site of the initial conscious processing of visual information. It is located in the occipital lobe, which is the most posterior portion of the cortex. The human primary visual cortex (the initial cortical area devoted to processing visual information) is only ~60% the size it should be for a primate brain that size (Holloway 1992), but it is ~1.5 times larger in absolute terms than it is in chimpanzees (Stephan et al. 1981). The human primary visual cortex is 5% larger than expected given a primate of our body size (Deacon 1997, Schoenemann 1997). It is not clear whether this says anything about relative visual processing abilities in humans. However, given that the human primary visual cortex is smaller in relative terms, but larger in absolute terms, it could be used to test which is more behaviorally relevant: If humans have behavioral advantages over apes in the visual domain (specifically in those known to be mediated by the primary visual cortex), it would suggest that absolute amounts of neural tissue would be more important than relative amounts, at least for visual processing. Such a study has not been done.

Preuss & Coleman (2002) have documented a variety of changes of the neurons in the primary visual cortex in humans, particularly a population of interneuronal connections in layer 4a that appears to have expanded significantly in human evolution. The exact behavioral significance is not known, but these changes emphasize that human-brain evolution involved more than simple changes in size (relative or absolute) of brain regions.

Temporal lobe. The temporal lobe plays a critical role in auditory information, as well as memory (through the hippocampal formation and associated areas), emotion (amygdala), and conceptual understanding (Carpenter & Sutin 1983). As a result, it also plays an important role in language processing. Rilling & Seligman (2002) report that humans have significantly larger overall volumes, white matter volumes, and surface areas of their temporal lobes than predicted on the basis of ape scaling relationships. This suggests an elaboration in humans of the behaviors mediated in this lobe.

Frontal lobe. The frontal lobe consists of all cortical areas anterior to the central sulcus (which angles inferoanteriorly to superoposteriorly along the midlateral convexity of the cortex on both hemispheres).[3] It contains a number of different functional areas, including the primary motor area (also known as Brodmann's area 4 to neuroanatomists, located immediately anterior and adjacent to the central sulcus), which directly controls conscious muscle movements; the premotor area (known as Brodmann's area 6, located immediately anterior to the primary motor area), which plans complex muscle-movement sequences; and the prefrontal cortex (everything anterior to the premotor area), which mediates a number of higher cortical functions important for planning, language, and social interactions, as well as having a general executive oversight of other brain regions (see below). A number of studies have quantified the entire frontal cortex (which is relatively easy to delineate across species), without subdividing it into its functional subdivisions. Overall, the frontal lobe in humans appears to be as large as expected, given a primate brain of our size (Bush & Allman 2004, Semendeferi et al. 2002, von Bonin 1963). Semendeferi et al. (2002) report that human frontal cortex averaged 37.7 (±0.9)% of the entire brain, compared with 35.4 (±1.9)% for common chimpanzees, 34.7 (±0.6)% for bonobo, 36.0% for gorilla, and 37.6 (±1.1)% for orangutan.

However, recent data suggest a difference with respect to gray matter/white matter proportions of the frontal lobe, which suggest potentially important behavioral implications. Schenker et al. (2005) report that humans have significantly more white matter volume in areas close to the cortical surface than hominoid (pongids plus the smaller-bodied apes such as gibbons and siamangs) data predict. Calculating from their data (Schenker et al. 2005), human frontal cortical gray matter is 3.6 times larger than the average for their pongid sample, but human frontal gyral white matter is 4.7 times larger. This suggests a bias toward white matter expansion in humans, although the extent to which this is explained statistically by allometric-frontal/nonfrontal (or some other) scaling cannot be determined (e.g., total brain sizes are not reported). Because allometric explanations have neither straightforward behavioral implications nor developmental-constraint implications, as discussed above, it is not clear what an allometric explanation would mean in any case. However, it may reflect increased functional distinctions of areas within the frontal lobe. In any case, the frontal lobe is, at a minimum, more than three times larger than it is in pongids, and this likely has important behavioral implications of some kind. To understand what these might be, it is useful to look at specific subdivisions of the frontal lobe.

Primary motor and premotor areas. Although the sample sizes are small ($N = 7$), the primary motor area in humans appears to be only ~33% as large as predicted for a primate brain our size (Blinkov & Glezer 1968). This suggests our primary motor cortex has scaled approximately with absolute body size during human evolution (Deacon 1997). Given that this area mediates the direct conscious control of muscle movements, and given that humans do not seem particularly gifted or particularly poor comparatively with respect to muscle control, this approximate scaling with body size (but not brain size) argues against the importance of relative amounts of neural tissue for behavioral ability, at least for this area.

The human premotor area, just anterior to the primary motor area, also appears smaller than predicted given absolute brain size, although not to the same extent. The premotor

---

[3] The surface of the cortex is not smooth but is folded back and forth upon itself, resulting in patterns of indentations referred to as sulci (singular, sulcus) separated by ridges referred to as gyri (singular, gyrus).

area is ~60% as large as predicted for a primate brain our size (Blinkov & Glezer 1968).[4] This suggests the premotor area has not lagged as far behind as the primary motor area as brain size increased. Taken together, these two findings suggest an elaboration of motor planning but not an increase in motor control per se. No direct tests of these suggestions have been reported, however.

Prefrontal. If the entire frontal lobe is approximately as large as expected given overall human brain size, yet the two portions of the frontal lobe reviewed above (the primary motor and premotor areas) are significantly smaller, then the rest of the frontal lobe (i.e., the prefrontal) must necessarily be larger than expected (Preuss 2000). There is nevertheless currently some controversy over this point. Brodmann's original cytoarchitectural studies, which form the basis for much of our knowledge of cortical areas, strongly point to significantly larger prefrontal cortices in humans compared with other primates (Brodmann 1909). Allometrically, Brodmann's data suggest the human prefrontal is ~2 times larger than predicted on the basis of the size of the rest of the brain (Deacon 1997). The suggestion of biased expansion is also supported by research quantifying the degree of folding in different parts of the cortex: Humans appear to have substantially more convoluted (and hence, a greater volume of) cortex in prefrontal regions (Armstrong et al. 1991, Rilling & Insel 1999).

Studies using magnetic resonance imaging (MRI) to quantify prefrontal cortex also support this contention. Because the posterior boundary of the prefrontal cortex does not follow obvious sulcal/gyral gross morphological features, it is not possible to exactly delineate it using structural MRI. However, a proxy for prefrontal cortex volume can be used: cortical volume anterior to the corpus callosum (the major tract of white matter connecting the two hemispheres). This proxy is commonly applied to both human (e.g., Raz et al. 2005, Sax et al. 1999) and nonhuman primate (Lyons et al. 2002; variant in McBride et al. 1999) studies. Estimated in this way, human prefrontal cortex was shown to be significantly larger than in pongids (Schoenemann et al. 2005b). Specifically, human values averaged 12.7% of total brain volume, compared with an average of 10.3% for the four pongid species. Nonprefrontal cerebral volume in humans averaged 3.7 times larger than the average of *P. paniscus* and *P. troglodytes*, but the prefrontal portion averaged 4.9 times larger.

Assessing both Semendeferi et al.'s (2002) data on the total frontal lobe and our own data, it appears that if the analysis is restricted to increasingly anterior regions of the frontal (keeping in mind that the prefrontal occupies the most-anterior portions of the frontal lobe), humans appear increasingly disproportionate. With respect to allometric scaling, total human frontal cortex is slightly smaller than predicted (Semendeferi et al. 2002), but the prefrontal (using our proxy) is slightly larger than predicted (Schoenemann et al. 2005b). Given that the prefrontal proxy used appears to underestimate human values much more so than other primates (Schoenemann et al. 2005a), this strongly suggests that human prefrontal is in fact larger, both as a percentage of total brain volume, as well as allometrically. Our data do not allow a clear confirmation of whether human prefrontal cortex is actually twice the predicted size, however.

In addition, the human difference appeared biased toward white matter rather than gray matter (Schoenemann et al. 2005b). Comparing humans with chimpanzees, prefrontal gray volumes averaged 4.8 times larger in humans, whereas nonprefrontal gray

---

[4]Semendeferi et al. (2002) report that human precentral gyrus volumes (expressed as percent of total cortex; i.e., not allometrically) fall within the range of their hominoid sample. However, because the precentral gyrus does not contain all of the motor cortex, and only contains a small portion of the premotor cortex, it is not clear exactly what this suggests about either motor or premotor cortex size in humans.

volumes averaged 4.2 times larger. By contrast, prefrontal white volumes averaged 5.0 times larger in humans, whereas nonprefrontal white volumes averaged only 3.3 times larger. Furthermore, the human average value was significantly allometrically larger as well, although not to the extent found in Brodmann's original data. Sherwood et al. (2005) point out that prefrontal white volume is predicted by prefrontal gray volume in our dataset, suggesting that the difference appears to be in proportions of prefrontal versus nonprefrontal. Given that a critically important role of the prefrontal is to moderate activity in posterior cortical areas, this apparent shift in proportions likely has important behavioral implications, as discussed below.

Additional support for the biased expansion of the prefrontal comes from work morphing primate brains into human brains. Deformation maps describing the necessary transformations allow for detailed, global assessments of morphological differences. Comparisons between humans and bonobo (*P. paniscus*) (Zilles 2005), common chimpanzees (*P. troglodytes*) (Avants et al. 2005), and macaque monkeys (Van Essen 2005) have been reported. In all three cases, substantial increases in the prefrontal region were reported. Our own group found that the average common chimp–human difference was approximately twofold for some prefrontal areas (Avants et al. 2005). To date, these studies involve comparisons between only two species, so scaling trends across primates cannot be estimated. However, it should be possible to extend these analyses to multiple species comparisons, resulting in separate allometric-scaling estimates—and extent of human divergence, if any—for individual areas at high resolution. Furthermore, the morphing algorithms can be applied to collections of cell-stained brain sections, thereby combining the resolution of detailed cytoarchitectural analyses (studies of patterns of neurons in the cortex) with the ability of morphing algorithms to quantify changes in shape.

Within the prefrontal itself, studies suggest a mosaic of evolutionary changes. A cytoarchitectural study of Brodmann's area 13, a subdivision of the prefrontal that mediates aspects of social behavior (particularly emotional dimensions), suggests that this area lagged behind the expansion of the brain as a whole: It is only 1.5 times larger than the average pongid value (Semendeferi et al. 1998). By contrast, another subdivision of the prefrontal, Brodmann's area 10, which is known to mediate tasks involving planning and organization of thought and future behavior (Carpenter & Sutin 1983), is 6.6 times larger in humans than in pongids (Semendeferi et al. 2001). Holloway (2002) notes this is actually only slightly more than one would predict given how area 10 scales with brain size. This is because the relationship is strongly positively allometric (i.e., as brain size increases, area 10 seems to increase much faster).

How should we interpret these findings in subareas of the prefrontal? First, as discussed above, even if allometry statistically predicts some increase in humans, this does not license us to conclude that the increase is behaviorally irrelevant (Schoenemann et al. 2005a). Nor does the existence of allometric scaling constitute a demonstration of the existence of inherent developmental constraints. Larger brains may have larger prefrontal cortices (or subregions therein) because selection places greater demands on the oversight role of prefrontal areas as posterior regions become more complex. As discussed above, absolute amounts of cortical tissue have been shown to be correlated with a variety of behavioral dimensions. Thus, even though area 13 is relatively smaller than one would predict, it might nevertheless indicate an important behavioral change, particularly given the enhanced interactive sociality that has increasingly characterized the human condition (see below). Increases in area 10 almost surely suggest increased importance in the various dimensions of behavioral planning.

FOSSIL EVIDENCE OF HUMAN BRAIN EVOLUTION

What is known about the evolutionary history of these apparent differences in brain anatomy? The goal of research in this area is to determine exactly what can be inferred about the behavior of fossil hominids from imprints on the inside surface of their braincases. This is of central importance to understanding human brain evolution. Because of this intrinsic interest in the behavior of fossil hominids, a great deal of effort has been spent trying to extract maximal inference out of minimal data. Because brains do not fossilize, the richness of comparative data is always greater than the fossil data. The following subsections highlight these limitations and serve to illustrate the inherent difficulty of the task. At present, the fossil record is clearest for overall brain size as indexed by cranial capacity, although other suggestive clues have been found regarding possible early changes in different brain regions related to visual processing and language.

Cranial Capacity

Cranial capacity is by far the most well-attested change in human brain evolution in the fossil record. **Figure 2** (see color insert) plots cranial capacity estimates against estimated specimen age for published hominid fossils dating from 15 KYA to 4 MYA, a total of 145 individual specimens. It is apparent from **Figure 2** that changes in hominid brain size began sometime between 3 and 2 Mya.

Although it has been argued that brain size has undergone punctuational (i.e., not continuous and gradual) change at various points during hominid evolution (e.g., Hofman 1983a), **Figure 2** suggests the range of variation at any particular point in time (best exemplified in modern species) combined with the sparse sampling evident for particular time periods of our evolutionary history (e.g., between 1.0 and 0.5 Mya) indicate that it may be premature to assess the likelihood of punctuational events. Recent empirical analyses of cranial capacity changes over time support this notion (De Miguel & Henneberg 2001, Lee & Wolpoff 2003). Furthermore, it is not clear how important species designations (which are inherently problematic for fossils) are for understanding brain-size evolution. De Miguel & Henneberg (2001) showed that 90% of the variation in fossil hominid brain size can be explained simply by the age of fossils, leaving only 10% to be explained by species differences and/or measurement error. This suggests that most of the brain size increase during hominid evolution was not closely tied to speciation events.

Lunate Sulcus

The portion of the cortex that has received perhaps the greatest amount of attention in fossil specimens is the visual cortex. A sulcus known as the lunate marks the anterior boundary of the primary visual cortex in nonhuman primates, although it is often missing in humans (Allen et al. 2005a, Connolly 1950). In relative terms, an anterior position of the lunate (and therefore anterior extent of the primary visual cortex) is characteristic of the general pongid condition, whereas a posterior placement is characteristic of modern humans. As discussed above, the primary visual cortex is a relatively smaller portion of the human brain in comparison with chimpanzee brains, even though in absolute terms it is ~1.5 times larger than that of either chimpanzees or gorillas (Stephan et al. 1981).

The evolutionary history of this change has been the source of considerable controversy over the years: Did it occur early in hominid evolution (e.g., in early Australopithecines), thereby signaling some form of early reapportionment (Holloway prefers the term reorganization) of neural resources? Or was it simply the result of the primary visual cortex lagging behind as brain size increased during human evolution? Holloway and Falk have, over the years, disagreed on the possible positioning of the lunate sulcus on brain endocasts attributed to both *Australopithecus africanus* (Taung) and *A. afarensis* (AL 162–28, 3.2 Mya) (e.g., Falk 1987, Holloway 1995). Holloway believes the lunate either cannot be seen (Taung) or is likely in a modern human posterior position (AL 162–28) in early Australopithecines, long before substantial changes in absolute brain size occurred. Falk and others have argued that it likely occurred later, as a result of brain size increases in other cortical regions. Debates over the position of the lunate have not been resolved, in part because it is difficult to assess its location unequivocally on endocast specimens and because of disagreements about the proper orientation of the AL 162–28 specimen. Holloway and colleagues (Holloway et al. 2004b) have recently reported on another *A. africanus* specimen, STW 505, which they show appears to have a relatively posterior lunate.

In addition, Holloway et al. (2003) discuss the brains of two apparently normal chimpanzees that nevertheless have lunates in human-like posterior locations. They note this finding demonstrates the possibility of a posterior lunate in the absence of increased brain size, which means Holloway's long-held contention of a posterior shift in early small-brained hominids is certainly possible. However, these specimens also complicate behavioral interpretations of the apparent change. Holloway et al. (2003) argue that the reduction of the primary visual cortex has no behavioral implications. However, if a chimpanzee can have a human lunate pattern (presumably indicating a reduced primary visual cortex), this pattern is not a clear indicator of human-like behavior, and therefore the location of the lunate in fossil endocasts may not be behaviorally interpretable, rendering the lunate sulcus debate moot.

However, Holloway and colleagues (Holloway et al. 2004b, p. 6) argue that a posterior lunate in Australopithecines "indicates an expanded posterior parietal cerebral cortex [anterior to the primary visual cortex], and was most likely associated with enhanced social behavior including communication." Thus cortical expansion anterior to the lunate is argued to have behavioral implications, but reduction posterior to the lunate is argued to be behaviorally meaningless. If the size of the primary visual cortex really is irrelevant, why do humans have 1.5 times as much primary visual cortex, given the evolutionary costs of brain tissue (see below)? If Holloway and colleagues are right about the location of the lunate in AL 162–28 and STW 505 (which they seem to be), it is either behaviorally meaningless, or Australopithecines had reduced visual processing capabilities of some kind. Both these alternatives are problematic. Thus, at this point it is not clear how to interpret the position of the lunate in fossil specimens.

Broca's Area

Evidence relevant to the origin of language is intrinsically of great interest. There is some suggestion of the elaboration of Broca's area (a key cortical region that plays a central role in language processing, located in the left prefrontal portion of the inferior frontal lobe) in fossil hominids. Holloway (1983) noted that a Broca's cap (an endocranial bump over what would be Broca's area) is present—although inconsistently—in pongids. Thus, the presence of a Broca's cap does not definitively indicate the existence of language, unfortunately. Tobias (1975) and Holloway (1983) argue that Broca's cap becomes increasingly present in early *Homo*, however (see also Broadfield et al. 2001). Tobias (1983) argues this indicates early *Homo* had language. Both Falk (1983) and Holloway (1995) agree that the endocast of the early *Homo* specimen KNM-ER 1470 (1.8 Mya) looks more modern-human-like in the inferior frontal region. Although this does not prove that KNM-ER 1470 had a Broca's area or that it had language, it nevertheless suggests something important is occurring in this region. Broadfield et al. (2001) report that the specimen Sambungmacan 3 has asymmetrical Broca's caps, which they speculate may indicate a level of language ability beyond

Petalias: areas
where the brain
extends farther in
some direction for
one hemisphere over
another

that found in earlier hominids. This specimen is assumed to be Middle Pleistocene *Homo erectus*, although it is unfortunately not well provenienced (Marquez et al. 2001). Thus, suggestive (but equivocal) evidence exists of possible language-related changes in the brains of early *Homo*, dating back to almost 2 Mya.

Asymmetry

Because important aspects of behavior are asymmetrically organized (e.g., key components of language are usually processed in the left hemisphere, which is usually also the dominant hemisphere for hand movements), it is of interest to determine whether cortical asymmetries can be found that predict these behavioral asymmetries, thereby possibly allowing us to infer behavior from fossil specimens. Research to date has centered on particular anatomical asymmetries known as petalias. Holloway & de la Coste-Lareymondie (1982) report that only modern and fossil hominids (including australopithecines, *H. erectus*, and Neanderthals) show a consistent, distinct right-frontal and left-occipital petalial pattern. Pongids also show petalias, but they did not display the same degree of consistency, particularly in the combination of right-frontal and left-occipital petalias. Only 25% of pongids assessed displayed this pattern, compared with 82% of hominids. Falk et al. (1990) demonstrated that Rhesus monkeys (*Macaca mulatta*) show a significant tendency toward right-frontal petalias (although not to the same consistency as found in modern and fossil hominids) but not for left-occipital petalias. Thus it appears that petalias in general are common in anthropoids, but the particular pattern of petalias and the degree of consistency appear unique to hominids.

Holloway & de la Coste-Lareymondie (1982) speculate this right-frontal/left-occipital petalial pattern may be related to right-handedness, language-related symbol manipulation, and spatio-visual integration.

However, because the hominid pattern occurs in a fair number of pongid specimens, the functional significance of this finding is obviously not clear. It cannot be considered definitive evidence of any particular behavior in individual specimens.

Summary of the Fossil Evidence

It is clear that brain evolution started in earnest sometime between 2 and 3 Mya. Although punctuated models of brain size increase can be fit to the data, there is no compelling reason to assume anything other than a reasonably constant trend toward increasing brain size over time. Apart from cranial capacity, only suggestive, equivocal clues of possible behavioral patterns are evident in the fossil record of hominid brain evolution, mostly relating to the question of language evolution. Although definitive statements are not currently warranted, we do not presently know the limits of possible inferences about the behavior of fossil hominids from their endocranial remains. The intrinsic interest in reconstructing hominid behavior ensures that every possible avenue of inference will be explored in the future. It is certainly possible that additional associations between cranial form and brain anatomy (and ultimately behavior) will eventually be uncovered using modern morphometric methods.

EVOLUTION OF BRAIN AND BEHAVIOR

Explaining the anatomical changes in the human brain reviewed in the sections above remains a central question in human evolutionary studies. Exactly why these changes happened, and what they might mean behaviorally, is a question of fundamental importance. As with any evolutionary change, there are two basic kinds of explanation: adaptive change (the result of selection) and nonadaptive change (the result of genetic drift). Adaptive explanations are probably the strongest for questions of brain evolution as compared

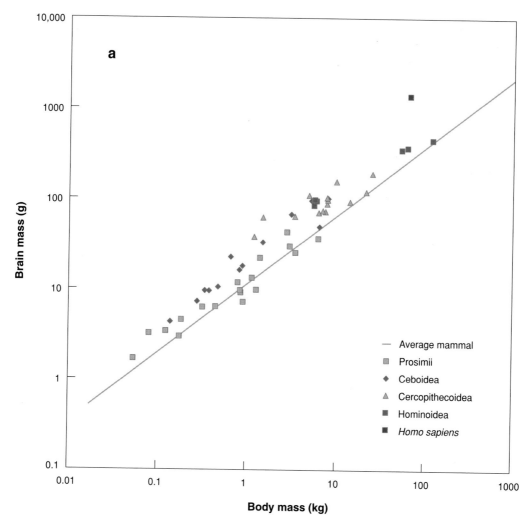

Figure 1

Brain/body relationships among primates. (*a*) Individual species plotted with Martin's (1981) estimate for the average mammal. (*b*) Least squares–regression estimates for various primate subtaxa. All primates (excluding humans): [log brain g] = 1.24 + 0.761 [log body kg], r^2 = 0.92, N = 51; Hominoidea (excluding humans): [log brain g] = 1.548 + 0.553 [log body kg], r^2 = 0.99, N = 6; Cercopithecoidea: [log brain g] = 1.54 + 0.477 [log body kg], r^2 = 0.87, N = 14; Ceboidea: [log brain g] = 1.35 + 0.765 [log body kg], r^2 = 0.94, N = 13; Prosimii: [log brain g] = 1.111 + 0.659 [log body kg], r^2 = 0.92, N = 18. Data extracted from literature sources (see Schoenemann 1997 for details); pongid data estimated from cranial capacities using [brain weight g] = [cranial capacity cc]/ 1.14 (following Kappelman 1996).

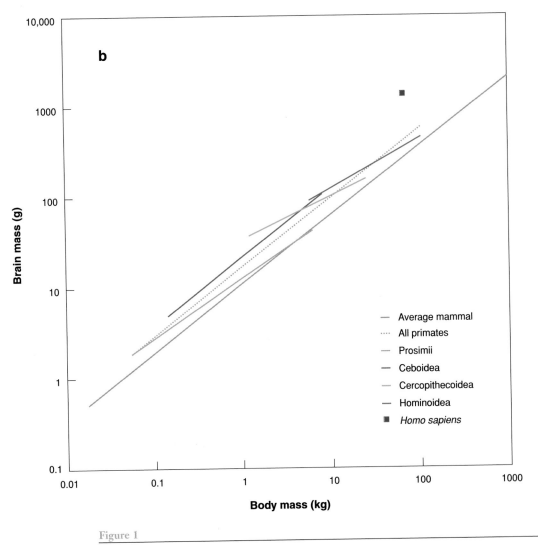

Figure 1

(*Continued*)

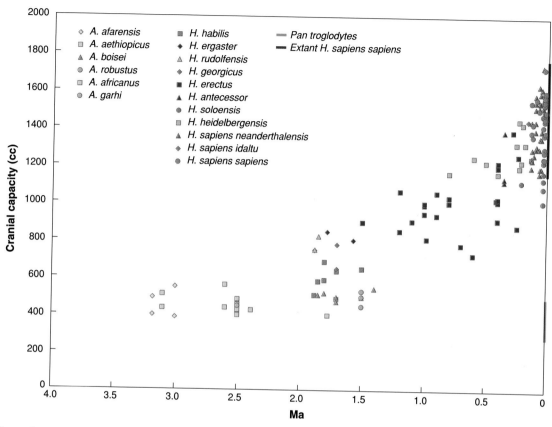

Figure 2

Cranial capacity in fossil hominids over time. Extant chimpanzees (*Pan troglodytes*) and humans (*Homo sapiens sapiens*) are included for comparison. Fossil data and species designations from Holloway et al. 2004a. *Pan* and *Homo* species data compiled from literature sources listed in Schoenemann (1997).

with almost any other biological characteristic. This is partly because of the pattern of changes and partly because of the apparent evolutionary costs involved in the changes, both of which strongly argue for adaptive explanations.

Although genetic drift can lead to the fixation of particular alleles at a single locus by chance, the odds that an evolutionary succession of alleles at a variety of loci (e.g., see Gilbert et al. 2005) leads progressively in a particular direction (e.g., larger brain size) is extraordinarily unlikely. In addition, these changes have occurred in the face of apparently strong evolutionary costs (Smith 1990). Costs in this context refer to correlated effects that—everything else being equal—ultimately translate into decreased numbers of offspring produced per unit time. These costs have to be paid every generation. First, as noted above, the brain is among the most metabolically expensive organs in the body [i.e., neural tissue has among the highest metabolic rates per gram (Aiello & Wheeler 1995, Hofman 1983b)]. Second, increasing brain size in primates is strongly correlated with longer gestation periods, an increased period of infant dependency, and delayed reproduction (Harvey & Clutton-Brock 1985), which all decrease the number of offspring an individual can produce per unit time. Third, there is an apparent trade-off in bipedal hominids between locomotor efficiency and ease of childbirth (Lovejoy 1975). Fourth, there is potentially a problem of cooling a larger brain (Falk 1990). If there were no counterbalancing advantages to larger amounts of brain tissue, individuals with smaller brains would necessarily have a selective advantage.

For adaptive evolutionary change to occur, reproductive benefits must have consistently (or at least on average) accrued to individuals—within successive populations connecting ancestral and descendent populations—who varied anatomically from the average of their populations. Of course, brain size may not have uniformly and gradually increased in every successive population. If so, there would have been some ancestral populations in which individuals with larger-than-average brain sizes did not have reproductive advantages. [This might explain the possible decrease in brain size from Neanderthal to modern humans (Schoenemann 2004).] However, on average over our evolutionary history, reproductive benefits needed to have been at least marginally greater for larger-brained individuals.

Brain Evolution Through Behavioral Selection

As the various mental faculties gradually developed themselves the brain would almost certainly become larger. No one, I presume, doubts that the large proportion which the size of man's brain bears to his body, compared to the same proportion in the gorilla or orang, is closely connected with his higher mental powers.

Darwin 1871, p. 145

Given that larger brain sizes must have provided individuals with reproductive advantages during significant portions of our evolutionary history, it is reasonable to ask both (*a*) what exactly the advantages were, and (*b*) whether these advantages still exist within modern humans (and/or other living primates). Although Gould (1981) suggested that variation in brain size is behaviorally meaningless in modern populations, it is not at all clear why we should expect brain size above some threshold to have absolutely no advantage. The simplest a priori model would posit a behavioral benefit (or usefulness), on average, to larger brains that would be present regardless of whether the particular benefit translated into reproductive advantages in any given environment. The behavioral benefit might be, for example, greater memory ability, planning ability, or linguistic ability. Whether such benefits were evolutionarily meaningful depends on the degree to which they helped pay (reproductively) for the evolutionary costs associated with larger brains. This, in turn, depends on the specific ecological and social conditions characteristic of a given

Genetic
correlation: occurs
when changes in the
genetic effects on
one trait have the
effect of changing
the other trait

Heritability: the
proportion of
phenotypic
(observable) variance
of a characteristic in
a population that is
explained by genetic
variance in that
population

population. An increasingly powerful linguistic processor is likely not worth the costs for a species that is not highly socially interactive, for example. More complex models regarding costs and benefits of increasing brain size are of course possible (e.g., wildly nonlinear relationships between behavioral abilities and brain size). However, parsimony requires investigating simpler explanations first.

For selection on some behavioral ability to cause evolutionary changes in brain anatomy, there must necessarily have been a genetic correlation between them. Failing this, selection on behavior would have no evolutionary effect on brain anatomy, and we would lack an explanation for evolutionary changes in the brain. Attempts to assess such brain/behavior correlations are therefore central for any model that posits the evolutionary importance of behavior in human brain evolution.

It is also not generally appreciated, however, that the genetic correlation between behavior and brain size does not actually have to be large to explain human brain-size evolution (Schoenemann et al. 2000). This is partly because the rate of change in brain size per generation is only ~8 mm^3 (assuming a 1000-cc increase in brain size over 2.5 million years and a 20-year average generation length) (see **Figure 2**), or approximately 0.0002 standard deviations of chimpanzee-brain size (see also Holloway et al. 2004a). The size of the genetic correlation needed to account for this amount of change per generation is partly a function of the strength of selection operating on the hypothesized correlated (directly selected) variable (e.g., some behavioral ability), as well as of the extent to which both brain size and the selected variable are genetically influenced, or heritable (Falconer 1981).[5] If

we posit a small genetic correlation of only $r = 0.05$ and heritabilities (i.e., the proportion of phenotypic variation in a population explained by genetic variation) of 0.3, the selected individuals (i.e., those who contribute to the subsequent generation) only have to differ from their overall population average by less than 0.006 standard deviations on the hypothesized directly selected characteristic (Schoenemann et al. 2000). This is so small that it would be extremely difficult to demonstrate empirically. Although the strength of selection could have varied over time during our evolutionary history, these estimates clearly demonstrate that we do not need to hypothesize more than a weak genetic correlation to explain the dramatic change in brain size via selection on correlated behavioral characteristics.

This does not mean, however, that the genetic correlation must therefore be small and that there is no justification for assessing genetic correlations within humans without massive sample sizes. It simply shows that it need not be large. Because of the evolutionary costs described above, it is highly unlikely that the correlation was in fact zero (or negative), as that would require some unknown nonbehavioral explanation for increasing brain size.

Evidence of Genetic Correlations Between Brain and Behavior

There is substantial evidence that many features of brain anatomy are influenced by genetic factors. In a number of studies, researchers have reported heritability of brain size to be significant, with estimates ranging from 0.66 to 0.94 (reviewed in Winterer & Goldman 2003). Heritability estimates of the patterns of sulci and gyri on the cortical surface are generally significantly lower, although this may be an artifact of the difficulty of quantifying them (Winterer & Goldman 2003). Thompson et al. (2001) estimated independent heritabilities for each voxel (the smallest unit of volume in an MRI image) of

---

[5] The strength of selection and the size of the genetic correlation interact to determine the likely amount of change per generation. Assuming reasonable heritabilities, the same amount of change can occur if either selection is strong and the genetic correlation is weak, or if selection is weak but the genetic correlation is strong.

cortical gray matter in a sample of monozygotic and dizygotic twins and found evidence for widespread genetic influence. Volumes of the left and right frontal lobes have estimated heritabilities of between 0.52 and 0.66 (Geschwind et al. 2002), and a number of Brodmann areas (including some prefrontal regions) appear to have at least moderate heritabilities (Wright et al. 2002). Thus, brain anatomy appears to be under genetic influence.

Similarly, cognitive abilities have been shown to have genetic influence. Although intelligence is a controversial concept in some areas of the social sciences, the consensus among those who research individual differences in cognitive ability is that genetic influences on general cognitive ability (g)[6] are substantial, although environmental influences are also clearly evident (Neisser et al. 1996). Genetic influences have also been demonstrated for other cognitive domains, such as verbal and spatial factors, although the degree to which these genetic factors are independent of g is not always clear (Plomin et al. 1997).

Although there is evidence of genetic influences on both brain and behavior, to what extent are these influences genetically correlated? A large number of studies reported finding phenotypic (not genetic) correlations between brain size and behavioral ability (usually g, or other IQ-related abilities). Obviously, our ancestors were not selected to do well on modern IQ tests, but some of the abilities tapped by these tests possibly were selected for. Studies using MRI to estimate actual brain size report correlations averaging $r = \sim0.45$ (Rushton & Ankney 1996).

However, these are phenotypic correlations, not genetic correlations, and are therefore not necessarily evolutionarily relevant. Phenotypic correlations could be caused by a third variable affecting both the brain and behavior (or other hypothesized evolutionarily relevant correlate) in similar directions. Socioeconomic status, for example, is correlated with both IQ scores (Herrnstein & Murray 1994) and growth of the body (Bogin 1999), and one might therefore predict a spurious correlation between brain size and IQ on this basis. In addition, cross-assortative mating can result in phenotypic correlations between characteristics that actually have completely independent genetic influences (Jensen & Sinha 1990). If the correlation between brain size and some behavior is spurious, selection on that behavior cannot explain evolutionary changes in brain size. It is therefore critically important to assess the strength of the genetic correlation, not just the phenotypic correlation, between the brain and behavior.

One way to control for possible confounds is by assessing the strength of the association between brain size and behavior among siblings within families. Family members share essentially the same socioeconomic status (this can be directly assessed), and meiosis ensures siblings contain random associations of alleles at different loci, thereby eliminating cross-assortative mating effects. To date, only a few studies have used this methodology. Two within-family studies using head circumference as a proxy for brain size have reported equivocal results (Jensen 1994, Jensen & Johnson 1994; see discussion in Schoenemann et al. 2000). Only a few MRI studies have been reported to date. Our own group found essentially no correlation $(r = -0.05, \text{NS})$ within families between brain size and an estimate of g in 36 pairs of adult sisters (Schoenemann et al. 2000). Another study of male-sibling pairs reported a nonsignificant but positive within-family correlation of $r = 0.23$ between brain size and g (Gignac et al. 2003). In addition, a recent study using a genetically informative cohort of 24 monozygotic pairs, 31 dizygotic pairs, and 25 additional nontwin siblings estimated a genetic correlation between g and both gray and white matter volumes of $r = 0.29$ and

[6]Performance on a wide variety of cognitive tests is correlated. g is a measure that statistically explains these correlations and as such is typically interpreted as a measure of general cognitive ability. IQ tests are good measures of g.

$r = 0.24$, respectively (both $p < 0.05$) (Posthuma et al. 2002). The genetic correlation for overall brain size was not reported, unfortunately, but was presumably similar (given that gray + white = total brain).

One unresolved issue is the direction of causality. It has long been known that environmental influences can affect brain volume, specifically cortical gray matter volume in rats (Diamond 1988). This means that genes with higher g could be causing individuals to experience more-stimulating and complex environmental situations, which may in turn cause developmental (not genetic) increases in their brain sizes and cortical gray volumes (Posthuma et al. 2003). If this were the sole reason for the brain size/g correlation, then selection for g is not likely the explanation for our increased brain sizes during our evolutionary history because it implies brain-size variation is solely a developmental response. However, some of the brain size/g correlation is likely explained through g influencing brain size, which means that the evolutionarily critical association—in which brain size causes (or allows for) changes in g—is likely smaller than the $r = 0.24$ to $r = 0.29$ genetic correlations suggested by Posthuma et al.'s (2002) study.

Taken together, these studies suggest the genetic correlation between brain size and g is not zero but is not as large as the phenotypic correlations typically reported for MRI studies of brain volume and g mentioned above. The proportion of genetic variance in g explained by genetic variance in brain volume appears substantially less than 8.5%. This is still large enough to explain the evolution of brain size in hominids, however.

Other behavioral measures. Although most research has focused on correlations with behaviors associated with general cognitive ability, natural selection may have acted on other unrelated behavioral dimensions as well as (or instead of) general cognitive ability. Associations between neuroanatomical variation and other behavioral dimensions

that are conceivably evolutionarily relevant have also been found, including spatial ability, working memory, and the ability to extract relevant information from a distracting environment.

Spatial ability has been the focus of research partly because it was proposed to help explain sex differences in brain size, which average ~1 standard deviation (Ho et al. 1980b). Some but not all of this difference is explained by body weight (Ankney 1992, Falk et al. 1999) and/or fat-free weight (Schoenemann 2004). Because males and females differ on average in spatial ability, in Western populations at least (Halpern 1987), if spatial ability correlates strongly with brain size, the residual sex difference in brain size might therefore be explained. However, many studies, including the more recent genetically informative MRI-based ones, have failed to find a significant association between brain size and spatial abilities (Posthuma et al. 2003, Schoenemann et al. 2000, Wickett et al. 2000).

Spatial-ability differences still may explain differences in the shape of the corpus callosum, which in women appears to be larger in the posterior region (e.g., Davatzikos & Resnick 1998, de Lacoste-Utamsing & Holloway 1982). This portion of the corpus callosum, known as the splenium, connects areas of the parietal lobes known to mediate spatial tasks. Thus, Holloway and colleagues (Holloway et al. 1993) have suggested the anatomical difference in corpus callosum morphology may therefore be explained by sex differences in spatial abilities. Consistent with this suggestion, our own group has recently found that women with smaller (more male-like) splenia score better on a test of mental rotation–spatial ability (P.T. Schoenemann, A. Dubb, J. Hu, J. Lewis & J. Gee, unpublished manuscript).

Working-memory abilities (i.e., the ability to manipulate information in short-term memory to solve particular problems or goals) appear to be associated with dimensions of brain size ($r = 0.40$, $p < 0.05$ for gray matter; $r = 0.33$, $p < 0.05$ for white matter)

(Posthuma et al. 2003). Because the prefrontal cortex is known to be particularly important to the mediation of working memory (Goldman-Rakic 1996), Posthuma et al.'s finding is of particular interest in light of the possible biased increase in the prefrontal cortex during human evolution discussed above. Working memory abilities have been shown to correlate with the length of the main prefrontal sulcus (principal sulcus) across a variety of Old and New World monkeys, and this correlation completely explains the association between working-memory ability and cranial capacity across these species (Redmond 1999). This raises the question of whether the association found by Posthuma et al. (2003) in humans is actually more properly localized to the prefrontal cortex (which unfortunately was not separately delineated in their study).

The size of the prefrontal cortex in humans has been shown to correlate with the Stroop task within families (Schoenemann et al. 2000). This test measures the extent of linguistic interference in naming colors, when ink color and word name are mismatched (e.g., the word red written in blue ink). It is generally considered a test of the ability to extract (and focus on) the relevant information from an environment and is known to be mediated by prefrontal areas.

The prefrontal cortex also mediates a variety of additional particularly interesting behaviors, including planning (Damasio 1985), memory for serial order and temporal information (Fuster 1985), aspects of language (Deacon 1997), and social information processing (de Bruin 1990). The importance of serial-order memory is generally not appreciated in discussions of human behavioral evolution. One of the clearest behavioral advantages humans have over other organisms is the ability to reconstruct, understand, and utilize causal information. All human technological sophistication is dependent on this ability. In turn, causality is dependent on the ability to remember the serial order of past events. Without this, it is impossible to reconstruct (remember) what actions or behaviors lead to exactly which outcomes. Thus serial-order memory likely played a key role in human behavioral evolution. Although no studies have addressed whether serial-order memory is associated with prefrontal size (or size of some other region), this would seem to be a fruitful direction to pursue.

Brain Size and Conceptual Complexity

A general argument can be made that increasing brain size brought with it an increase in conceptual or semantic complexity (Gibson 2002). Jerison (1985, p. 30) suggested that "[g]rades of encephalization presumably correspond to grades of complexity of information processing. These, in turn, correspond in some way to the complexity of the reality created by the brain, which may be another way to describe intelligence."

A number of observations support this view. First, concepts are instantiated in the brain as webs or networks of activation between different areas (see Pulvermuller 2001). Most of our subjectively experienced concepts are actually complex combinations of sensory information processed in various ways by the different cortical centers. Taste, for example, is actually a complex interaction of olfactory (smell) and gustatory (taste) inputs (e.g., the flavor of a banana is largely olfactory). Similarly, the auditory perception of a phoneme can be altered if it is paired with a mismatched visual input (McGurk & MacDonald 1976). This means there must be networks connecting differing regions as well as areas that mediate the integration of this information.

To what extent is brain size relevant to conceptual complexity? Larger-brained species have more complicated networks of interconnection, thereby leading to greater potential conceptual complexity (Lieberman 2002). It has long been known that certain areas of the body (e.g., the lips and hands) are disproportionately represented in the somatosensory and primary motor areas of the brain and that these match differences in the degree of sensitivity and/or motor control for different parts of our body (Penfield & Rasmussen 1950). Thus, even within species, we have a clear association between the amount of cortical tissue and behavioral dimensions (Gibson 2002). Animals with specific behavioral specializations (e.g., bat echolocation) have correlated increases in areas of the brain known to mediate those behaviors (Krubitzer 1995).

We can then add to this the tendency for larger-brained animals to display greater degrees of cortical specialization: Individual areas tend to be more specific in function and less directly connected to other areas. This is critical to conceptual complexity because it increases the brain's potential to differentiate complex sensory information into diverse constituent parts, thereby helping to magnify subtle differences between different streams of sensory input. The argument can be summarized as follows: Increasing brain size leads to increasingly complex processing within areas, greater degrees of autonomy between areas, and greater complexity of the possible interactions between areas. This leads to a greater complexity of possible network-activation states, which is equivalent to a greater degree of conceptual subtlety and sophistication possible in the organism's representations of reality. Whatever else increasing brain size led to in hominid evolution, it is difficult to escape the conclusion that conceptual complexity increased substantially during this time. Furthermore, given the fundamentally socially interactive nature of humans, as well as the general association between degree of sociality and brain size (discussed below), this increase in conceptual complexity is likely directly relevant to the evolution of language.

Brain Evolution and Language

Although the exact evolutionary changes in the brain necessary to allow for language are not known, language clearly relies on a large number of neural resources. The importance for language of Broca's and Wernicke's areas has been known for more than a century, but it has become increasingly clear that language requires the cooperation of a wide range of cortical areas, including the cerebellum (Gazzaniga et al. 1998), right-hemisphere areas [important for processing logical inferences encoded in language (Beeman et al. 2000)], prefrontal cortex [important for higher-level language functioning (Novoa & Ardila 1987)], and areas of the frontal lobe outside Broca's area (Alexander et al. 1989). Functional brain imaging studies suggest the prefrontal cortex also plays a critical role in conceptual/semantic processing (Gabrieli et al. 1998). All of this indicates that language draws on a wide array of neural resources, which suggests that important features of brain evolution may be explained by the coevolution of language (Deacon 1997).

That language evolution is specifically relevant to brain-size evolution has been suggested many times (e.g., Dunbar 1996, Gibson 2002, Wang 1991, Washburn 1960). Darwin (1871, p. 57) himself argued that, although language use during human evolution likely had effects on the elaboration of the vocal organs, "the relation between the continued use of language and the development of the brain has no doubt been far more important." Brain size, in this view, is itself an index of language evolution. This suggests language has origins that are substantially older than the appearance of anatomically modern H. sapiens, which date to perhaps ~160,000 years ago (White et al. 2003). As reviewed above, the trend toward increasing brain size began sometime before 2 Mya (**Figure 2**). Although there is widespread disagreement about how far back language extends in human evolution (for a review, see Schoenemann 2005), it is difficult to escape the conclusion that language likely played a major role in the evolution of the human brain. The evidence of the relationship between brain size and conceptual complexity at a minimum suggests that fundamental changes in human cognition critical to language evolution began prior to ~2 Mya.

Sociality and Brain Evolution

Primates in general, and humans in particular, are socially interactive animals. Our ability to survive and reproduce is at least as dependent on successfully navigating social arrangements as it is navigating the physical environment (Holloway 1975, Humphrey 1984). Social interactions are intrinsically complicated, and the complexity increases with increasing social group size. Humphrey (1984) pointed out that the increasing complexity of the social world selects for increasing cognitive sophistication (social intelligence) in individuals, which in turn creates even more complex social interactions. This creates a cycle of ever-increasing social complexity, leading to ever-increasing intellect among individuals—what Humphrey refers to as an evolutionary ratchet. Because of the apparent benefits of being skilled at social manipulation in such an increasingly complex social existence, this has become known as the Machiavellian intelligence hypothesis.

It appears likely that selection for social abilities was an important influence on brain evolution. A number of comparative studies of primates have confirmed an association between measures of brain and/or neocortex size (both absolute and relative) and a variety of measures of social complexity, including mean social group size, social clique size, frequency of reported acts of deceptive behavior, amount of social play (but not nonsocial types of play), and the degree to which male-dominance rank fails to accurately predict mating success (see review in Dunbar 2003, and references therein). All of this is consistent with the idea that brain size is a factor in social ability, broadly defined, although there are glaring exceptions: Orangutans are relatively large-brained but relatively asocial. Clearly, brain size is not a perfect function of social complexity. However, there is no other known behavioral variable that correlates as highly with brain size across species.

Dunbar (1996) has further argued that human language represents a form of social grooming that allowed the increase in group size beyond that otherwise possible. Although there are a number of extrapolations needed to arrive at this conclusion, language clearly serves a highly social function in humans.

Although the comparative evidence that social complexity correlates with brain size is strong, the specific abilities crucial to social ability within humans (or any other species) are not clearly defined or understood. Some people are more social than others, and some social people are better at understanding and/or manipulating social interactions than others. However, there does not appear to have been much research into this question from a neurocognitive and/or neuroanatomical standpoint. Presumably social competence depends on a wide variety of abilities, including language, nonverbal-cue processing, memory (particularly of past interactions and the order of past events), and probably many other basic cognitive abilities. Interestingly, intact prefrontal cortex (unlike other cortical areas) appears to be crucial for the maintenance of high position in dominance hierarchies in monkeys (de Bruin 1990, Myers et al. 1973). Given that this area seems to have undergone disproportionate increase, as discussed above, this appears to be a promising avenue of investigation with respect to brain evolution. Other parts of the brain that appear to be important for social behavior include the amygdaloid nuclei and overlying temporal pole (tip of the temporal lobe) and the posterior medial orbital cortex (including Brodmann's area 13, located in the inferior prefrontal cortex) (Kling 1986). As reviewed above, Brodmann's area 13 shows a moderate increase in absolute terms, although it does lag behind the increase of the brain as a whole. Piecing together the effects the social environment had on modifying the brain during human evolution will likely continue to be the focus of significant research in the future.

Ecological Hypotheses

An alternative (but not mutually exclusive) hypothesis is that adaptation for ecological challenges influences brain evolution. Milton (1981) pointed out that different types of diet vary with respect to the cognitive demands they place on individuals. Fruit is patchily distributed in both time and space, whereas leaves are much less cognitively demanding to obtain. This suggests that species that specialize in fruit (or, more generally, any food source that is cognitively demanding to obtain) are expected to have larger brains than species that do not. Dunbar (1995) did not find a significant association between a measure of relative brain size (ratio of the neocortex to the rest of the brain) and percent of fruit in diet in anthropoid primates. However, Barton (1996) did find a significant association within diurnal haplorhines (specifically, diurnal monkeys and apes) between absolute and relative brain size and percent of fruit in the diet. This discrepancy is possibly a result of a difference in neuroanatomical variables used.

It is also possible that the causality runs the other way: Because larger brains are more metabolically expensive, some sort of dietary accommodation may be necessary to pay for it nutritionally. The expensive-tissue hypothesis (Aiello & Wheeler 1995) argues for a trade-off between brain and gut size. If larger brains mean smaller guts, then one would predict a higher quality diet. This hypothesis is supported in primates (Fish & Lockwood 2003). It also fits the human case, in which brain size started increasing at about the same time as meat became increasingly important in hominid diets (as indexed by the initial appearance of stone tools).

Tools and Brain Evolution

Is it possible that the cognitive demands of tool making itself spurred brain evolution? Reader & Laland (2002) showed that frequency of tool use in primates is positively correlated with both absolute and relative brain volume. Although early hominid stone-tool industries are not highly complex technologically, they may have required cognitive abilities beyond that shown by apes, for example, in the sequencing of required actions (Toth & Schick 1993). A preliminary functional brain-imaging study of stone-tool manufacturing suggests the activation of cortical areas mediating spatial cognition, as well as motor, somatosensory, and cerebellar areas (as might be expected given the nature of the task), although prefrontal areas known to be relevant to planning were not significantly activated (Stout et al. 2000). If this finding can be replicated, given that spatial ability does not appear significantly correlated with brain size in modern humans (as discussed above), it may argue against early stone-tool manufacturing specifically spurring brain-size evolution (although the spatial abilities tested involved paper-and-pencil tests, rather than hands-on, three-dimensional manipulation as in the stone-tool study). Research on the possible importance of stone-tool manufacturing is clearly in its infancy, and future functional-imaging studies are needed to clarify the issue.

It has also been suggested that the development of accurate throwing might have spurred brain evolution. Calvin (1983) pointed out that human throwing accuracy requires timing abilities (for the release of the thrown object) that far exceed the probable timing accuracies of neurons (judging from measurements of the intrinsic variability in neuronal signals). He pointed out that increasingly accurate timers could be built by putting greater and greater numbers of even inaccurate neurons in parallel in a timing circuit. He also suggested that, given the cortical areas in the primary motor cortex controlling the mouth and tongue (involved in language) and the hand (involved in throwing) were reasonably close to each other, selection for throwing ability may have led to changes that preadapted the brain for language. This hypothesis has proven difficult to test, but it may be consistent with the tentative finding that the premotor cortex in humans may not have lagged as far behind as the primary motor cortex during human brain evolution. It is also consistent with the finding that sequential finger tapping is disrupted by concurrent speech (which depends on the left hemisphere in most individuals) only if the tapping is done with the right hand (which is also controlled by the left hemisphere) and not the left hand (which is controlled by the right hemisphere) (Ikeda 1987).

The Cognitive Reserve Hypothesis

An additional explanation for the increase in brain size in human evolution is that it may have allowed for an increase in longevity (Allen et al. 2005b, Humphrey 1999). The argument is that larger brains would buffer individuals against a variety of inevitable brain insults as individuals age, thereby increasing the useful cognitive lifespan. The results of a variety of clinical studies are consistent with the idea that larger brain size has a protective effect for a number of brain diseases and types of injury (reviewed in Allen et al. 2005b). Why (and whether) longevity would be evolutionarily adaptive in humans is unclear, although the survival of older, postreproductive individuals has been argued to be important (e.g., the grandmother hypothesis). The cognitive reserve hypothesis and the idea that more neural resources translate into better cognitive functioning of some kind are not mutually exclusive, of course.

Summary of the Evolution of Brain and Behavior

Explaining why the human brain changed as it did requires determining the behavioral implications of changing brain size and/or the proportions of various brain components. To be evolutionarily relevant, associations between the brain and behavior must be genetic correlations. These correlations can be quite small, however. Although both brain morphology and behavioral dimensions have been

shown to be genetically influenced, genetic correlations between brain anatomy and behavior appear to be quite modest. The genetic correlation between overall brain size and general cognitive ability appears to be substantially smaller than overall phenotypic correlation. Associations between specific functional areas and specific behavioral abilities appear to be somewhat more robust.

A number of general behavioral models of brain evolution have been proposed that have theoretical and/or cross-species empirical support. These include the idea that brain size is associated with increased conceptual complexity, language ability, social ability, ecological challenges, the development of tools, and the need for a cognitive reserve. Direct tests of these hypotheses await future research.

CONCLUSION

Over the past 2 to 3 million years, our brain has changed in dramatic and behaviorally interesting ways. Although brain size and body size are correlated, absolute increases in neural tissue are likely behaviorally relevant, and the overemphasis on EQ needs to be tempered. There is substantial evidence that the human brain is also not simply a larger version of a generic primate brain, with some areas showing evidence of lagging behind (such as the olfactory bulb, primary visual cortex, primary motor and premotor areas) and some accounting for disproportionate increases (such as the prefrontal). We should expect to find clues about the details of the behavioral evolution of our species from these patterns. Given the evolutionary costs of neural tissue, disproportional increases (even in absolute terms) would not likely have occurred unless they conferred some sort of adaptive (reproductive) advantages, on average, to individuals in the successive populations. The advantages could be slight, however, making our task as scientists potentially difficult. General cognitive ability appears to show weak associations with brain size, and a number of behavioral dimensions appear to be associated with specific brain areas. Hypotheses involving conceptual complexity, social abilities, language, ecological challenges, tool use, and the cognitive reserve hypothesis all appear to have merit for explaining human brain evolution

Filling out the history of human brain evolution will continue to utilize an intensively interdisciplinary approach in which information, methods, and resources from a wide variety of fields will increasingly be marshaled to the task of squeezing every last possible bit of valid inference out of the data. Fundamentally, our arguments will always necessarily be statistical judgments. At present, we do not even know the limits of what we can and cannot know about this history. Discovering these limits is a central task for the future.

ACKNOWLEDGMENTS

I wish to thank Vincent Sarich, John Allen, Ralph Holloway, Dean Falk, Tim White, Thomas Budinger, Arthur Jensen, Bruce Lahn, Karen Schmidt, Janet Monge, Dan Glotzer, Michael Sheehan, and Reina Wong for stimulating discussions on the topics discussed in this review. Any errors that remain are my own, of course.

LITERATURE CITED

Aiello LC, Wheeler P. 1995. The expensive tissue hypothesis: the brain and the digestive system in human and primate evolution. *Curr. Anthropol.* 36:199–221

Alexander MP, Benson DF, Stuss DT. 1989. Frontal lobes and language. *Brain Lang.* 37:656–91

Allen JS, Bruss J, Damasio H. 2005a. MRI analysis of the calcarine and lunate sulci in modern humans. *Am. J. Phys. Anthropol.* 126(S40):67

Allen JS, Bruss J, Damasio H. 2005b. The aging brain: the cognitive reserve hypothesis and hominid evolution. *Am. J. Hum. Biol.* 17:673–89

Allman JM. 1999. *Evolving Brains*. New York: W.H. Freeman

Ankney CD. 1992. Sex differences in relative brain size: the mismeasure of woman, too? *Intelligence* 16:329–36

Armstrong E. 1983. Relative brain size and metabolism in mammals. *Science* 220:1302–4

Armstrong E, Zilles K, Curtis M, Schleicher A. 1991. Cortical folding, the lunate sulcus and the evolution of the human brain. *J. Hum. Evol.* 20:341–48

Avants BB, Schoenemann PT, Gee JC. 2005. Lagrangian frame diffeomorphic image registration: morphometric comparison of human and chimpanzee cortex. *Med. Image Anal.* 10:397–412

Barton RA. 1996. Neocortex size and behavioral ecology in primates. *Proc. R. Soc. London Ser. B* 263:173–77

Beeman MJ, Bowden EM, Gernsbacher MA. 2000. Right and left hemisphere cooperation for drawing predictive and coherence inferences during normal story comprehension. *Brain Lang.* 71:310–36

Blinkov SM, Glezer II. 1968. *The Human Brain in Figures and Tables*. New York: Plenum. 482 pp.

Bogin B. 1999. *Patterns of Human Growth*. Cambridge, UK: Cambridge Univ. Press. 2nd ed.

Broadfield DC, Holloway RL, Mowbray K, Silvers A, Yuan MS, Márquez S. 2001. Endocast of Sambungmacan 3 (Sm 3): A new *Homo erectus* from Indonesia. *Anat. Rec.* 262:369–79

Brodmann K. 1909. *Vergleichende Lokalisatiesiehre der Grosshirnrinde in ihren Prinzipien Dargestellt auf Grund des Zellenbaues*. Leipzig: Johann Ambrosius Barth Verlag

Bush EC, Allman JM. 2004. The scaling of frontal cortex in primates and carnivores. *Proc. Natl. Acad. Sci. USA* 101:3962–66

Calvin WH. 1983. A stone's throw and its launch window: timing precision and its implications for language and hominid brains. *J. Theor. Biol.* 104:121–35

Carpenter MB, Sutin J. 1983. *Human Neuroanatomy*. Baltimore, MD: Williams & Wilkins

Changizi MA, Shimojo S. 2005. Parcellation and area-area connectivity as a function of neocortex size. *Brain Behav. Evol.* 66:88–98

Connolly CJ. 1950. *External Morphology of the Primate Brain*. Springfield, IL: C.C. Thomas

Damasio AR. 1985. The frontal lobes. In *Clinical Neuropsychology*, ed. K Heilman, E Valenstein, p. 339–75. Oxford, UK: Oxford Univ. Press

Darwin C. 1871. *The Descent of Man and Selection in Relation to Sex*. Vol. 1. London: John Murray

Davatzikos C, Resnick SM. 1998. Sex differences in anatomic measures of interhemispheric connectivity: correlations with cognition in women but not men. *Cereb. Cortex* 8:635–40

Deacon TW. 1997. *The Symbolic Species: The Coevolution of Language and the Brain*. New York: W.W. Norton

de Bruin JPC. 1990. Social behavior and the prefrontal cortex. In *Progress in Brain Research*, ed. HBM Uylings, CG Van Eden, JPC de Bruin, MA Corner, MGP Feenstra, pp. 485–97. New York: Elsevier Science

Dekaban AS. 1978. Changes in brain weights during the span of human life: relation of brain weights to body heights and body weights. *Ann. Neurol.* 4:345–56

de Lacoste-Utamsing C, Holloway RL. 1982. Sexual dimorphism in the human corpus callosum. *Science* 216:1431–32

De Miguel C, Henneberg M. 2001. Variation in hominid brain size: How much is due to method? *Homo* 52:3–58

Diamond MC. 1988. *Enriching Heredity: The Impact of the Environment on the Anatomy of the Brain*. New York: Free Press

Dubois E. 1913. On the relation between quantity of brain and the size of the body in vertebrates. *Verh. Kon. Akad. Wetenschappen Amsterdam* 16:647

Dunbar R. 1996. *Grooming, Gossip and the Evolution of Language*. London: Faber & Faber

Dunbar RIM. 1995. Neocortex size and group size in primates: a test of the hypothesis. *J. Hum. Evol.* 28:287–96

Dunbar RIM. 2003. The social brain: mind, language, and society in evolutionary perspective. *Annu. Rev. Anthropol.* 32:163–81

Evans PD, Anderson JR, Vallender EJ, Gilbert SL, Malcom CM, et al. 2004. Adaptive evolution of ASPM, a major determinant of cerebral cortical size in humans. *Hum. Mol. Genet.* 13:489–94

Falconer DS. 1981. *Introduction to Quantitative Genetics*. New York: Longman. 2nd ed.

Falk D. 1983. Cerebral cortices of East African early hominids. *Science* 221:1072–74

Falk D. 1987. Hominid paleoneurology. *Annu. Rev. Anthropol.* 16:13–30

Falk D. 1990. Brain evolution in *Homo:* the "radiator" theory. *Behav. Brain Sci.* 13:333–81

Falk D. 1992. *Braindance: New Discoveries About Human Origins and Brain Evolution*. New York: Henry Holt

Falk D, Froese N, Sade DS, Dudek BC. 1999. Sex differences in brain/body relationships of Rhesus monkeys and humans. *J. Hum. Evol.* 36:233–38

Falk D, Hildebolt C, Cheverud J, Vannier M, Helmkamp RC, Konigsberg L. 1990. Cortical asymmetries in frontal lobes of Rhesus monkeys (*Macaca mulatta*). *Brain Res.* 512:40–45

Finlay BL, Darlington RB, Nicastro N. 2001. Developmental structure in brain evolution. *Behav. Brain Sci.* 24:263–308

Fish JL, Lockwood CA. 2003. Dietary constraints on encephalization in primates. *Am. J. Phys. Anthropol.* 120:171–81

Fuster JM. 1985. The prefrontal cortex, mediator of cross-temporal contingencies. *Hum. Neurobiol.* 4:169–79

Gabrieli JD, Poldrack RA, Desmond JE. 1998. The role of left prefrontal cortex in language and memory. *Proc. Natl. Acad. Sci. USA* 95:906–13

Garby L, Lammert O, Kock KF, Thobo-Carlsen B. 1993. Weights of brain, liver, kidneys, and spleen in healthy and apparently healthy adult Danish subjects. *Am. J. Hum. Biol.* 5:291–96

Gazzaniga MS, Ivry RB, Mangun GR. 1998. *Cognitive Neuroscience: The Biology of the Mind.* New York: W.W. Norton

Geary DC. 2005. *The Origin of Mind: Evolution of Brain, Cognition, and General Intelligence.* Washington, DC: Am. Psychol. Assoc.

Geschwind DH, Miller BL, DeCarli C, Carmelli D. 2002. Heritability of lobar brain volumes in twins supports genetic models of cerebral laterality and handedness. *Proc. Natl. Acad. Sci. USA* 99:3176–81

Gibson KR. 2002. Evolution of human intelligence: the roles of brain size and mental construction. *Brain Behav. Evol.* 59:10–20

Gignac G, Vernon PA, Wickett JC. 2003. Factors influencing the relationship between brain size and intelligence. In *The Scientific Study of General Intelligence: Tribute to Arthur R. Jensen,* ed. H Nyborg, pp. 93–106. London: Elsevier

Gilbert SL, Dobyns WB, Lahn BT. 2005. Genetic links between brain development and brain evolution. *Nat. Rev. Genet.* 6:581–90

Goldman-Rakic PS. 1996. The prefrontal landscape: implications of functional architecture for understanding human mentation and the central executive. *Philos. Trans. R. Soc. London Ser. B* 351:1445–53

Gould SJ. 1981. *The Mismeasure of Man.* New York: Norton. 352 pp.

Halpern DF. 1987. *Sex Differences in Cognitive Abilities.* Hillsdale, NJ: Erlbaum

Harvey PH, Clutton-Brock TH. 1985. Life history variation in primates. *Evolution* 39:559–81

Haug H. 1987. Brain sizes, surfaces, and neuronal sizes of the cortex cerebri: a stereological investigation of man and his variability and a comparison with some mammals (primates, whales, marsupials, insectivores, and one elephant). *Am. J. Anat.* 180:126–42

Herrnstein RJ, Murray C. 1994. *The Bell Curve.* New York: Free Press

Ho K, Roessmann U, Straumfjord JV, Monroe G. 1980a. Analysis of brain weight. I. Adult brain weight in relation to sex, race, and age. *Arch. Pathol. Lab. Med.* 104:635–39

Ho K, Roessmann U, Straumfjord JV, Monroe G. 1980b. Analysis of brain weight. II. Adult brain weight in relation to body height, weight, and surface area. *Arch. Pathol. Lab. Med.* 104:640–45

Hofman MA. 1983a. Encephalization in hominids: evidence for the model of punctuationalism. *Brain Behav. Evol.* 22:102–17

Hofman MA. 1983b. Energy metabolism, brain size, and longevity in mammals. *Q. Rev. Biol.* 58:495–512

Hofman MA. 1985. Size and shape of the cerebral cortex in mammals. I. The cortical surface. *Brain Behav. Evol.* 27:28–40

Holloway. 1966. Cranial capacity and neuron number: a critique and proposal. *Am. J. Phys. Anthropol.* 25:305–14

Holloway RL. 1975. *The Role of Human Social Behavior in the Evolution of the Brain.* New York: Am. Mus. Nat. Hist.

Holloway RL. 1983. Human paleontological evidence relevant to language behavior. *Hum. Neurobiol.* 2:105–14

Holloway RL. 1992. The failure of the gyrification index (GI) to account for volumetric reorganization in the evolution of the human brain. *J. Hum. Evol.* 22:163–70

Holloway RL. 1995. Toward a synthetic theory of human brain evolution. In *Origins of the Human Brain*, ed. J-P Changeux, J Chavaillon, pp. 42–54. Oxford: Clarendon Press

Holloway RL. 2002. Brief communication: How much larger is the relative volume of area 10 of the prefrontal cortex in humans? *Am. J. Phys. Anthropol.* 118:399–401

Holloway RL, Anderson PJ, Defendini R, Harper C. 1993. Sexual dimorphism of the human corpus callosum from three independent samples: relative size of the corpus callosum. *Am. J. Phys. Anthropol.* 92:481–98

Holloway RL, Broadfield DC, Yuan MS. 2003. Morphology and histology of chimpanzee primary visual striate cortex indicate that brain reorganization predated brain expansion in early hominid evolution. *Anat. Rec. A Discov. Mol. Cell Evol. Biol.* 273:594–602

Holloway RL, Broadfield DC, Yuan MS. 2004a. *The Human Fossil Record, Volume 3. Brain Endocasts: The Paleoneurological Evidence.* Hoboken, NJ: Wiley & Sons

Holloway RL, Clark RJ, Tobias PV. 2004b. Posterior lunate sulcus in *Australopithecus africanus*: Was Dart right? *C. R. Palevol.* 3:287–93

Holloway RL, de la Coste-Lareymondie MC. 1982. Brain endocast asymmetry in pongids and hominids: some preliminary findings on the paleontology of cerebral dominance. *Am. J. Phys. Anthropol.* 58:101–10

Humphrey N. 1984. The social function of intellect. In *Consciousness Regained*, ed. N. Humphrey, pp. 14–28. Oxford, UK: Oxford Univ. Press

Humphrey N. 1999. Why human grandmothers may need large brains. *Psycholoquy* 10:24. **http://psycprints.ecs.soton.ac.uk/archive/00000659/**

Ikeda K. 1987. Lateralized interference effects of concurrent verbal tasks on sequential finger tapping. *Neuropsychologia* 25:453–56

Jensen AR. 1994. Psychometric *g* related to differences in head size. *Pers. Individ. Dif.* 17:597–606

Jensen AR, Johnson FW. 1994. Race and sex differences in head size and IQ. *Intelligence* 18:309–33

Jensen AR, Sinha SN. 1990. Physical correlates of human intelligence. In *Biological Approaches to the Study of Human Intelligence*, ed. PA Vernon. Norwood, NJ: Ablex

Jerison HJ. 1973. *Evolution of the Brain and Intelligence.* New York: Academic

Jerison HJ. 1985. Animal intelligence as encephalization. *Philos. Trans. R. Soc. London Ser. B* 308:21–35

Kappelman J. 1996. The evolution of body mass and relative brain size in fossil hominids. *J. Hum. Evol.* 30:243–76

Kling AS. 1986. Neurological correlates of social behavior. *Ethol. Sociobiol.* 7:175–86

Krubitzer L. 1995. The organization of neocortex in mammals: Are species differences really so different? *Trends Neurosci.* 18:408–17

Lee SH, Wolpoff MH. 2003. The pattern of evolution in Pleistocene human brain size. *Paleobiology* 29:186–96

Lieberman P. 2002. On the nature and evolution of the neural bases of human language. *Yearb. Phys. Anthropol.* 45:36–62

Lovejoy CO. 1975. Biomechanical perspectives on the lower limb of early hominids. In *Primate Functional Morphology and Evolution*, ed. RH Tuttle, pp. 291–326. The Hague: Mouton

Lyons DM, Afarian H, Schatzberg AF, Sawyer-Glover A, Moseley ME. 2002. Experience-dependent asymmetric variation in primate prefrontal morphology. *Behav. Brain Res.* 136:51–59

MacLeod CE, Zilles K, Schleicher A, Rilling JK, Gibson KR. 2003. Expansion of the neocerebellum in Hominoidea. *J. Hum. Evol.* 44:401–29

Marquez S, Mowbray K, Sawyer GJ, Jacob T, Silvers A. 2001. New fossil hominid calvaria from Indonesia—Sambungmacan 3. *Anat. Rec.* 262:344–68

Martin RD. 1981. Relative brain size and basal metabolic rate in terrestrial vertebrates. *Nature* 293:57–60

McBride T, Arnold SE, Gur RC. 1999. A comparative volumetric analysis of the prefrontal cortex in human and baboon MRI. *Brain Behav. Evol.* 54:159–66

McComb K, Moss C, Durant SM, Baker L, Sayialel S. 2001. Matriarchs as repositories of social knowledge in African elephants. *Science* 292:491–94

McGurk H, MacDonald J. 1976. Hearing lips and seeing voices. *Nature* 264:746–48

Milton K. 1981. Distribution patterns of tropical plant foods as an evolutionary stimulus to primate mental development. *Am. Anthropol.* 83:534–48

Myers RE, Swett C, Miller M. 1973. Loss of social group affinity following prefrontal lesions in free-ranging macaques. *Brain Res.* 64:257–69

Neisser U, Boodoo G, Bouchard TJJ, Boykin AW, Brody N, et al. 1996. Intelligence: knowns and unknowns. *Am. Psychol.* 51:77–101

Novoa OP, Ardila A. 1987. Linguistic abilities in patients with prefrontal damage. *Brain Lang.* 30:206–25

Pakkenberg H, Voigt J. 1964. Brain weight of the Danes. *Acta Anatom.* 56:297–307

Penfield W, Rasmussen T. 1950. *Cerebral Cortex of Man: A Clinical Study of Localization of Function*. New York: Macmillan

Plomin R, DeFries JC, McClearn GE, Rutter M. 1997. *Behavioral Genetics*. New York: W.H. Freeman. 3rd ed.

Posthuma D, Baare WF, Pol HEH, Kahn RS, Boomsma DI, De Geus EJ. 2003. Genetic correlations between brain volumes and the WAIS-III dimensions of verbal comprehension, working memory, perceptual organization, and processing speed. *Twin Res.* 6:131–39

Posthuma D, De Geus EJ, Baare WF, Pol HEH, Kahn RS, Boomsma DI. 2002. The association between brain volume and intelligence is of genetic origin. *Nat. Neurosci.* 5:83–84

Preuss TM. 2000. What's human about the human brain? In *The New Cognitive Neurosciences*, ed. MS Gazzaniga, pp. 1219–34. 2nd ed. Cambridge, MA: Bradford Books/MIT Press

Preuss TM, Coleman GQ. 2002. Human-specific organization of primary visual cortex: alternating compartments of dense Cat-301 and calbindin immunoreactivity in layer 4A. *Cereb. Cortex* 12:671–91

Pulvermuller F. 2001. Brain reflections of words and their meaning. *Trends Cogn. Sci.* 5:517–24

Raz N, Lindenberger U, Rodrigue KM, Kennedy KM, Head D, et al. 2005. Regional brain changes in aging healthy adults: general trends, individual differences and modifiers. *Cereb. Cortex* 15:1676–89

Reader SM, Laland KN. 2002. Social intelligence, innovation, and enhanced brain size in primates. *Proc. Natl. Acad. Sci. USA* 99:4436–41

Redmond JCJ. 1999. Cranial capacity and performance on delay-response task correlated with principal sulcus length in monkeys. *Am. J. Phys. Anthropol.* 109:33–40

Rendell L, Whitehead H, Rendell L, Whitehead H. 2001. Culture in whales and dolphins. *Behav. Brain Sci.* 24:309–24; discussion 324–82

Riddell WI, Corl KG. 1977. Comparative investigation of the relationship between cerebral indices and learning abilities. *Brain Behav. Evol.* 14:385–98

Rilling JK, Insel TR. 1999. The primate neocortex in comparative perspective using magnetic resonance imaging. *J. Hum. Evol.* 37:191–223

Rilling JK, Seligman RA. 2002. A quantitative morphometric comparative analysis of the primate temporal lobe. *J. Hum. Evol.* 42:505–33

Ringo JL. 1991. Neuronal interconnection as a function of brain size. *Brain Behav. Evol.* 38:1–6

Rumbaugh DM, Savage-Rumbaugh ES, Wasburn DA. 1996. Toward a new outlook on primate learning and behavior: complex learning and emergent processes in comparative perspective. *Jpn. Psychol. Res.* 38:113–25

Rushton JP, Ankney CD. 1996. Brain size and cognitive ability: correlations with age, sex, social class, and race. *Psychon. Bull. Rev.* 3:21–36

Sax KW, Strakowski SM, Zimmerman ME, DelBello MP, Keck PEJ, Hawkins JM. 1999. Frontosubcortical neuroanatomy and the continuous performance test in mania. *Am. J. Psychiatry* 156:139–41

Schenker NM, Desgouttes AM, Semendeferi K. 2005. Neural connectivity and cortical substrates of cognition in hominoids. *J. Hum. Evol.* 49:547–69

Schoenemann PT. 1997. *An MRI study of the relationship between human neuroanatomy and behavioral ability*. PhD diss. Univ. of Calif., Berkeley

Schoenemann PT. 2004. Brain size scaling and body composition in mammals. *Brain Behav. Evol.* 63:47–60

Schoenemann PT. 2005. Conceptual complexity and the brain: understanding language origins. In *Language Acquisition, Change and Emergence: Essays in Evolutionary Linguistics*, ed. WS-Y Wang, JW Minett, pp. 47–94. Hong Kong: City Univ. of Hong Kong Press

Schoenemann PT, Budinger TF, Sarich VM, Wang WS. 2000. Brain size does not predict general cognitive ability within families. *Proc. Natl. Acad. Sci. USA* 97:4932–37

Schoenemann PT, Glotzer LD, Sheehan MJ. 2005a. Reply to "Is prefrontal white matter enlargement a human evolutionary specialization?" *Nat. Neurosci.* 8:538

Schoenemann PT, Sheehan MJ, Glotzer LD. 2005b. Prefrontal white matter volume is disproportionately larger in humans than in other primates. *Nat. Neurosci.* 8:242–52

Semendeferi K, Armstrong E, Schleicher A, Zilles K, Van Hoesen GW. 1998. Limbic frontal cortex in hominoids: a comparative study of area 13. *Am. J. Phys. Anthropol.* 106:129–55

Semendeferi K, Armstrong E, Schleicher A, Zilles K, Van Hoesen GW. 2001. Prefrontal cortex in humans and apes: a comparative study of area 10. *Am. J. Phys. Anthropol.* 114:224–41

Semendeferi K, Lu A, Schenker N, Damasio H. 2002. Humans and great apes share a large frontal cortex. *Nat. Neurosci.* 5:272–76

Sherwood CC, Holloway RL, Semendeferi K, Hof PR. 2005. Is prefrontal white matter enlargement a human evolutionary specialization? *Nat. Neurosci.* 8:537–38; author reply 538

Smith BH. 1990. The cost of a large brain. *Behav. Brain Sci.* 13:365–66

Stephan H, Frahm H, Baron G. 1981. New and revised data on volumes of brain structures in insectivores and primates. *Folia Primatologica* 35:1–29

Stout D, Toth N, Schick K. 2000. Stone tool-making and brain activation: position emission tomography (PET) studies. *J. Archaeol. Sci.* 27:1215–23

Striedter GF. 2005. *Principles of Brain Evolution*. Sunderland, MA: Sinauer Associates

Thompson PM, Cannon TD, Narr KL, van Erp T, Poutanen VP, et al. 2001. Genetic influences on brain structure. *Nat. Neurosci.* 4:1253–58

Tobias PV. 1975. Brain evolution in the Hominoidea. In *Primate Functional Morphology and Evolution*, ed. RH Tuttle, p. 353–92. The Hague: Mouton

Tobias PV. 1983. Recent advances in the evolution of the hominids with especial reference to brain and speech. In *Recent Advances in the Evolution of Primates*, ed. C Chagas, p. 85–140. Vatican City: Pontificia Acad. Sci.

Toth N, Schick K. 1993. Early stone industries and inferences regarding language and cognition. In *Tools, Language and Cognition in Human Evolution*, ed. KR Gibson, T Ingold, pp. 346–62. Cambridge, UK: Cambridge Univ. Press

Van Essen DC. 2005. Surface-based comparisons of macaque and human cortical organization. In *From Monkey Brain to Human Brain*, ed. S Dehaene, J-R Duhamel, MD Hauser, G Rizzolatti, pp. 3–19. Cambridge, MA: MIT Press

Van Essen DC, Drury HA, Joshi S, Miller MI. 1998. Functional and structural mapping of human cerebral cortex: Solutions are in the surfaces. *Proc. Natl. Acad. Sci. USA* 95:788–95

von Bonin G. 1963. *The Evolution of the Human Brain*. Chicago: Univ. Chicago Press

Wang WSY. 1991. Explorations in language evolution. In *Explorations in Language*, pp. 105–31. Taipei, Taiwan: Pyramid Press

Wang YQ, Su B. 2004. Molecular evolution of microcephalin, a gene determining human brain size. *Hum. Mol. Genet.* 13:1131–37

Washburn SL. 1960. Tools and evolution. *Sci. Am.* 203:63–75

White TD, Asfaw B, DeGusta D, Gilbert H, Richards GD, et al. 2003. Pleistocene *Homo sapiens* from Middle Awash, Ethiopia. *Nature* 423:742–47

Wickett JC, Vernon PA, Lee DH. 2000. Relationships between factors of intelligence and brain volume. *Pers. Individ. Dif.* 29:1095–22

Winterer G, Goldman D. 2003. Genetics of human prefrontal function. *Brain Res. Brain Res. Rev.* 43:134–63

Wood B, Collard M. 1999. The human genus. *Science* 284:65–71

Wright IC, Sham P, Murray RM, Weinberger DR, Bullmore ET. 2002. Genetic contributions to regional variability in human brain structure: methods and preliminary results. *Neuroimage* 17:256–71

Wynn T. 2002. Archaeology and cognitive function. *Behav. Brain Sci.* 25:389–438

Zilles K. 2005. Evolution of the human brain and comparative cyto- and receptor architecture. In *From Monkey Brain to Human Brain*, ed. S Dehaene, J-R Duhamel, MD Hauser, G Rizzolatti, pp. 41–56. Cambridge, MA: MIT Press

Early Mainland Southeast Asian Landscapes in the First Millennium A.D.

Miriam T. Stark

Department of Anthropology, University of Hawai'i, Manoa, Honolulu,
Hawaii 96822; email: miriams@hawaii.edu

Annu. Rev. Anthropol. 2006. 35:407–32

First published online as a Review in
Advance on June 27, 2006

The *Annual Review of Anthropology* is
online at anthro.annualreviews.org

This article's doi:
10.1146/annurev.anthro.35.081705.123157

Copyright © 2006 by Annual Reviews.
All rights reserved

0084-6570/06/1021-0407$20.00

Key Words

Southeast Asia, early states, archaeology, complexity

Abstract

Southeast Asia's earliest states emerged during the first millennium
A.D. from the Irawaddy River of Myanmar to the Red River delta of
northern Vietnam. Developments during this time laid the ground-
work for the florescence of the region's later and better-known civilizations such as Angkor and Pagan. Yet disciplinary and language
barriers have thus far precluded an anthropological synthesis of
cultural developments during this time. This review uses a landscape focus to synthesize current knowledge of mainland Southeast Asia's earliest states, which emerged in the first millennium A.D.
Research from archaeology and history illuminates articulations between physical and social factors in several kinds of Early Southeast
Asian landscapes: economic, urban, and political. Social and ideological forces that shaped these first-millennium-A.D. landscapes are
discussed as integral aspects of early state formation.

On ne saurait écrire de bonne histoire sans savoir comment une civilization organize son espace naturel pas plus, bien sûr, que la géographe ne comprendre un paysage humain s'il ne suit, étape par étape, sa genèse. (Groslier 1973, p. 338)

INTRODUCTION

For several reasons, research on the origins of complex societies in the Old World gives little attention to Southeast Asia relative to other geographic regions (e.g., Cowgill 2004, Stein 2001). The paucity of published material and a prevailing emphasis on insular, rather than mainland, Southeast Asia, particularly after the fifth century A.D. (Christie 1995; Manguin 2000, 2004; Miksic 2000), has dwarfed our knowledge of the Southeast Asian mainland. Significant organizational changes occurred, however, in mainland Southeast Asia between 500 B.C. and A.D. 500 that established the foundation for the region's earliest states along its South China Sea coasts and major inland river valleys, from Myanmar to Vietnam (**Figure 1**). Few archaeologists have ventured into this territory, which has traditionally been controlled by historians and philologists. Yet the Southeast Asian mainland, similar to its island neighbors to the south (Lape 2003), was an important cultural crossroads, and archaeological research is essential for deciphering local, regional, and macroregional developments that involved the Near East, South Asia, and East Asia.

This review article examines physical and cultural parameters of early state formation because these landscapes shaped, and were shaped by, their human inhabitants. This chapter has three central goals: (*a*) to provide a historical background on the study of early Southeast Asian landscapes; (*b*) to discuss the scale and nature of Southeast Asian landscapes that scholars have studied, examining both social and economic forces that structured their production; and (*c*) to discuss key themes for future research.

Conceptual Issues

Several conceptual terms that frame this discussion require limited consideration. The first involves scalar issues, which include both the size and the configuration of effective regions (following Crumley & Marquardt 1990, pp. 76–77) at different points in the sequence and the nature of these early "states." The configuration, durability, and typologies of early states are the subject of perennial research (e.g., Feinman 1998; Feinman & Marcus 1998; Nichols & Charlton 1997; Trigger 2003; Yoffee 1997, 2005). Whether these early polities across mainland and peninsular Southeast Asia were predominantly city-states (Manguin 2004), chiefdoms (Wheatley 1983), or kingdoms (Coedès 1968, Gutman & Hudson 2004) remains unclear and is examined below.

The term landscape also requires elaboration, given its polysemous definitions by previous scholars (Anschuetz et al. 2001, pp. 160–64). People constructed, inhabited, and imagined their landscapes in the past through a series of social and spatial practices, but the archaeological record is more amenable to historical ecological studies than to research on idealized landscapes. Viewing landscapes instead as materialized histories of decision-making helps sidestep the dichotomy that opposes landscapes as records of land-use strategies versus records of social history (Ashmore 2004, p. 260). This review uses landscape approaches to study the formation of both anthropogenic landscapes and archaeologies of "place," with a decided emphasis on the former.

Mainland Southeast Asia's archaeological record, not documentary records, offers the most accurate information for reconstructing the first millennium A.D., but it has been underutilized. Reliance on external documentary sources and on the region's art and epigraphy led earlier scholars to externalize influences on the region's earliest state formation (Bentley 1986, Kulke 1990, Mabbett 1997); more recent discussions

Figure 1

Mainland Southeast
Asia in the first
millennium A.D.
Adapted from Hall
(1985, map 1, p. 22)
with permission from
Univ. Hawaii Press.

incorporate internal factors as well (Reynolds
1995, Wolters 1999). The lack of systematic
archaeological research on post–A.D. 500 settlement patterns (Miksic 1995, p. 56) has hin-
dered progress. Until recently, political unrest and its accompanying hazards (such as
land mines) have favored the use of remote
sensing rather than pedestrian field survey and
test excavations (but see Welch 1989, 1997).
This chapter reconstructs mainland Southeast
Asia's first millennium A.D. history by triangulating between archaeological, art historical, epigraphic, and paleoenvironmental data
sources.

Methodological Considerations

Several types of source materials provide the
basis for this review of early Southeast Asia's
landscapes. Within archaeology, sources include archaeological survey and excavation,
sediment coring, and the analysis of remote-
sensing data. Source materials beyond archaeology include art historical, documentary records (both indigenous and external)
and paleoenvironmental data. Each source informs on different kinds of landscapes, in
sometimes contradictory ways. Yet one without the others is incomplete, particularly
because most interpretations of this period

have been dominated by documentary sources [as one example see Schweder (2000) versus Southworth (2000)].

Northeast Thailand and, through remote sensing, northwestern Cambodia are two of the best-documented archaeological regions in mainland Southeast Asia (e.g., Moore 1992, Welch 1989). Huge gaps exist in geographic coverage of the rest of the mainland. The emphasis on excavating large sites, rather than on survey projects, has informed on such topics as the nature of South-Southeast Asia interaction over time (Bellina & Glover 2004, Glover 1998, Theunissen et al. 2000) but has overlooked most landscape issues. Such work has focused on later periods in Thailand and Cambodia (Mudar 1999, Pottier 1999) and rarely includes a focus on the first millennium A.D. Substantial art historical research, from the colonial era to the present day, has concentrated on this period, which coincides with the appearance of the earliest Indic-inspired art (Brown 1996, Dalsheimer & Manguin 1998, Jacq-Hergoualc'h 1992). The focus on objects, rather than also on their locational contexts, has limited art history's contributions to our understanding of ancient landscapes.

Indigenous and nonindigenous documentary records also inform on early Southeast Asia. Chinese dynastic annals, which had a dominant role in shaping interpretations of the period (Ishizawa 1995, Wheatley 1983), describe diplomatic and trading missions to the land of the "southern barbarians." Some accounts also describe terrestrial and maritime routes from China to these locales (e.g., Southworth 2000). Problems inherent in these external sources have been described previously (Jacques 1979, 1995; Stark 1998), including intergenerational copying errors, a focus on trade centers that had relationships with China, and problems with linking Chinese toponyms to geographic points on the landscape (Jacq-Hergoual'ch 2002, pp. 163–64; Leong 1990, pp. 19–20).

Indigenous texts are also available for several of the region's early states: the Pyu (Myanmar), the pre-Angkorian Khmer (Cambodia), and the Cham (Vietnam). They tend to inform more on dynastic sequences than on political and economic organization (but see Vickery 1994, 1998). In a few cases, the names assigned to these early states have been found in contemporary indigenous sources (inscriptions or coins): the "Cham" of coastal Vietnam (Southworth 2004, p. 209), and "Dvaravati" (Indrawooth 2004, pp. 128–29) and the purported state of "Sri Canasa" in Thailand (Saraya 1992, p. 133; compare Brown 1996, pp. 25–27). However, most polities are known instead from outside sources, and increasingly, from the archaeological record. The next section offers time-space systematics to contextualize the study of landscapes in the first millennium A.D. across mainland Southeast Asia.

BACKGROUND

Timing

The period under study concentrates on the first seven centuries of the first millennium A.D. This period has elsewhere included the Iron Age (Higham 2002), the protohistoric period (Bronson & White 1992), or the early historic and Pre-Angkorian periods (M. Smith 1999; Stark 1998). Settlement hierarchies (or heterarchies?) formed during the first millennium B.C. in almost all regions where complex polities subsequently emerged (Higham 2002, pp. 168–227; O'Reilly 2003; White 1995).

China had intensive political and commercial relations with mainland Southeast Asia during much of the first millennium A.D. (Hall 1985), before political events in Tang China cut the southern Chinese ports off from their northern markets in the Tang dynasty (Southworth 2004, p. 226). A terrestrial "Southwest Silk Road" also linked Southwest China to much of mainland Southeast Asia from the Han period onward and linked China to India through upper Myanmar (Moore 2004b, p. 6; Yang 2004, pp. 287–89). A maritime Silk Road linked south and southeast China to the South China Sea coasts. This maritime route gained importance when the independent state of Wu arose and controlled territories south of the Yangzi River (including parts of northern Vietnam) in A.D. 221–280. As keen observers of early Southeast Asia, the Chinese have provided some of the most informative documentary evidence for the region's polities.

At least three phases of South-Southeast Asia contact characterize this period. In the first phase, sporadic interaction between the fourth century B.C. and second century A.D. (Bellina 2003, Bellina & Glover 2004) may be linked to the rise of Buddhism and Jainism in South Asia and resultant investment in international trade (Ray 1994, 1997, 2005). Tin, found throughout much of Southeast Asia (Bronson 1992, p. 80), was a major attraction to South Asians, whose metallurgical tradition incorporated high-tin bronzes. The Bay of Bengal formed the nexus of such interaction; by the second century B.C., a string of coastal entrepôts emerged along India's eastern coast (Ray 1997). The second phase of interaction (i.e., the second through the fourth centuries A.D.) was characterized by higher-volume, more regularized commodity circulation (Bellina 2003, Bellina & Glover 2004). Intensified ideological contact after the fourth century A.D. constitutes the third phase, in temporal parallel to the rise of the Guptas in South Asia. Whether South Asian events were causal in Southeast Asia, through unidirectional influence or competitive emulation, is a matter of some debate (e.g., Michell 2000, pp. 44–47; Morrison 1997, p. 95; Smith 1999, pp. 12–16). Differing interpretations largely reflect varying levels of reliance on documentary, rather than archaeological, evidence (e.g., Sinopoli 2005).

The period's end point of A.D. 750–800 approximately coincides with political transformations throughout the region that are associated with the onset of Thailand's Dvaravati phase (Brown 1996; Suchitta 1992; Vickery 1994, 1998; Welch 1997). Economic and ideological changes within Southeast Asia characterize this period because its trading focus shifted to island Southeast Asia, and particularly toward Buddhist kingdoms in southern Sumatra (Manguin 2004, pp. 301–4). Beyond Southeast Asia, the beginning of the Tang dynasty in China, the Gupta Empire's decline in South Asia, and the rise of regionalism in the Tamil country of southern India also affected (but did not unilaterally determine) developments that were internal to Southeast Asia. Despite some ethnolinguistic discontinuities, most first-millennium-A.D. states in mainland Southeast Asia established the template for subsequent "classical civilizations" (Bagan/Pagan, Sukothai, Angkor, Nam Viet) that emerged in the ninth through fourteenth centuries. Thus the first-millennium polities share close historical links with the region's contemporary nation-states.

Late Holocene Geography and Environment

Variation in climate, geography, and environment during the Late Holocene (here defined as 3000 BP to the present) affected both settlement and economic patterns across mainland Southeast Asia. This period's climatic variability remains poorly documented, although research in Vietnam's Red River delta suggests a shift from a cool wet climate around 2100–1540 BP to a drier and cooler climate around 540–640 BP (Li et al. 2006; see also Godley 2002). Debate continues about the nature and relative impact of a mid-sixth-century-A.D. catastrophic event that produced exceptionally low solar activity (Gunn 2000) and about its potential role in structural transformations that several mainland Southeast Asian polities underwent shortly after that time.

Marine transgressions and delta progradation constrained human settlement across the Southeast Asian mainland during this time. Sea levels in northern Vietnam lowered and stabilized to current levels about 2000 years ago (Boyd & Lam 2004); this stabilization occurred in peninsular Thailand/Malaysia about 1500 years ago (Tjia 1996, p. 99). Dvaravati settlements were established along the fringes of the swampy Chao Phraya plain (**Figure 2**;

see color insert) because its center was swampy and uninhabitable until 1000–1500 years ago (Sinsakul 2000); so were the southern reaches of the ever-expanding Mekong delta before the appearance of intensive cultivators with knowledge of water control techniques. At any rate, the delta's edge was 20–60 km inland of its current coastline at the beginning of the first millennium A.D. (Nguyen et al. 2000, p. 437; figure 5).

Researchers assume that much of mainland Southeast Asia was forested at 2000 BP, except for areas along its major drainages, their tributaries, and the region's coastlines. Paleoenvironmental research indicates that several key areas underwent cyclical vegetational changes between forest and open grassland, which have been correlated with increased intensity of land use. These include Thailand from its peninsular to its northern and northeastern reaches (e.g., Boyd & McGrath 2001, Kealhofer 2002, Maloney 1999, Penny & Kealhofer 2005), northern Vietnam (Li et al. 2006), and southern Cambodia (Bishop et al. 2003). Reliable studies of first millennium A.D. anthropogenic change, however, remain rare for at least two reasons: (a) Many of the region's best pollen cores lack late Holocene dates; and (b) few areas with high-quality paleoenvironmental data also contain well-documented archaeological evidence of settlement. Collaborative paleoenvironmental-archaeological research is currently underway in southern Cambodia [the Lower Mekong Archaeological Project (Bishop et al. 2003, Stark & Bong 2001)] and in Northeast Thailand [The Origins of Angkor Project (Boyd and McGrath 2001; Higham 2002)], but work is still needed across the rest of the region.

GEOGRAPHY OF EARLY SOUTHEAST ASIA

Geopolitical Landscapes

Archaeological landscape studies generally rely on regions as the scalar unit of research

(Ashmore 2004, p. 262), although archaeologists differ in their definitional criteria. Reliance on Chinese and Sanskrit ethnonyms identifies at least seven major geographic regions across mainland Southeast Asia in the first millennium A.D. (**Figure 1**). Stark (2001) summarizes their archaeological configuration and attributes; the following comments offer additional insights based on work published since that time.

The Pyu of Myanmar/Burma. Major sites include Beikthano, Halin, Mongmao, Sri Ksetra, and Otein Taung/Pagan (Gutman & Hudson 2004, pp. 158–69; Hudson et al. 2001, pp. 59–61; Moore 2004b). The archaeology of Myanmar/Burma for the first millennium A.D. remains poorly known for political as well as historical reasons. A small number of site reports from the Archaeological Survey of Burma (summarized in Stargardt 1990) and a few research projects in the past decade have generated more questions than answers. Yet the region's interstitial location between South and Southeast Asia, its emerging record of continuity from the prehistoric to historic periods, and its early and Buddhist material manifestations make research along Myanmar's major river valleys essential for understanding developments across mainland Southeast Asia.

Peninsular Myanmar/Burma around the Gulf of Martaban and Arakan. Although this region's role in the Bay of Bengal interactional network could have been very important during the first millennium A.D., no major site has been the subject of systematic archaeological investigation (Gutman & Hudson 2004, pp. 161–63; Moore 2004b).

The Pre-Dvaravati and early Dvaravati Central Thailand. Major sites from the Chao Phraya basin include Ban Don Ta Phet, Chansen, and U-Thong. Far more sites, however, have been documented for the succeeding Dvaravati period (Higham 2002, pp. 254–60; Indrawooth 2004, p. 120; Mudar 1999;

Vallibhotama 1992, p. 126). A marine transgression that coincides with the beginning of this period submerged substantial portions of central Thailand into marshy lowlands (Tanage et al. 2003), precluding extensive settlement in that area until later in the first millennium A.D.

Peninsular Thailand and Malaysia. Major sites include Kedah, Kuala Selinsing, Khao Sam Kaeo, and Khuan Lukpad. Perhaps ten or more coastal centers may have developed along the Malay Peninsula's coasts during this time, if Chinese reports are taken at face value (Christie 1995; Leong 1990, 1993; but see Allen 1997). The process of "Indianization" may have begun as early as the second century A.D. in peninsular Thailand. Qualitative changes occurred, however, in the fifth century A.D. as Indic statuary, writing, and architecture appeared across the Malay peninsula (Jacq-Hergoualc'h 2002, p. 105).

The late Iron Age of Northeast Thailand. No specific sites associated with this period have been thoroughly reported, although some "Iron Age" sites like Noen-U-Loke have associated water features that date to the first millennium A.D. (Higham 2004, p. 63). In addition, sixth- through eleventh-century Dvaravati sites in this region are commonly constructed on Iron Age predecessors (Higham 2002, pp. 193–212).

The "Funan" and pre-Angkorian periods of Cambodia and southern Vietnam. A few key sites such as Angkor Borei and Oc Eo have been documented in great detail (e.g., Stark 2003, Stark et al. 1999, Trinh 1996, Vo 1998); in addition, the "Oc Eo" culture sites of southern Vietnam fit into this period. In the Mekong basin, state-like polities also emerged that have been (problematically) glossed as Funan and Chenla (Coedès 1968; Vickery 1994, 1998). In Chinese accounts, the first millennium A.D. "Funan" arose largely through the intraregional and international maritime trade networks, and various Funan rulers controlled parts of the Malay Peninsula, central and southern Thailand, and the lower Irrawaddy valleys (e.g., Wheatley 1973, pp. 15–21). These documentary-based scenarios, however, have been questioned recently (Jacques 1995, Stark 1998, Stark et al. 1999, Vickery 1998).

The Cham civilization of central Vietnam. Major sites include Tra Kieu, My Son, Thanh Ho, and Go Cam. The earliest Cham occupations date to the mid–first millennium A.D., exhibit continuity from the prehistoric Sa Huynh culture, and bear a substantial Han Chinese imprint after 111 B.C. during the Han occupation of northern Vietnam (Glover & Yamagata 1998, Glover et al. 1996, Southworth 2004, Yamagata & Glover 1994). Third-century Chinese annals describe the state of "Linyi" in mid–third century A.D. (Yamagata 1998) that was a major political force (or collection of polities). Scholars believe Linyi's southern limit during this time lay at the Hai Van pass (between Thua Thien-Hue and Quang Nam province), that it incorporated areas as far southward as the Tra Kieu area by the fifth or sixth century A.D., and that Linyi was surrounded by multiple, competing trading states that acted independently of Linyi.

Northern Vietnam lies largely beyond this review because few western-language publications are available for the region and period (but see Nguyen et al. 2004). Its close political engagement with China during this time involved prolonged periods of Chinese control; the imposition of a preordained Chinese template generated northern Vietnamese landscapes quite distinct from those that developed elsewhere in mainland Southeast Asia.

Settlement Patterns and Interaction

Early Southeast Asian settlements concentrated primarily in one of three geographical settings: coastal areas, floodplains along tributaries, and areas in proximity to large freshwater lakes (Stark 2001). Areas of coastal settlement were situated near freshwater sources and potential harbors; inland riverine communities were found at interfaces between floodplain and upland areas (Vallibhotama 1992, p. 125). Settlements on floodplains were located on island-like elevated areas in central Thailand and the Mekong delta, which could support relatively large populations through either intensive or flood recession agriculture (Ng 1979, van Liere 1980). Phytolith evidence from central Thailand suggests reliance on rice agriculture well before 2000 BP (Kealhofer 2002, p. 187). The only major lake in the region, the Tonle Sap of northwestern Cambodia, has an increasingly robust record of first-millennium-A.D. settlement.

Interactional networks of this period integrated coastal and inland settlements through roads, rivers, and seaways. These transportation linkages have been most intensively documented for the Mekong delta from the French colonial period to the present in both Cambodia (Bishop et al. 2004) and Vietnam (Bourdonneau 2003, p. 270). Ostensible ancient canal traces, which Stargardt (1998) recorded around the Satingpra area (peninsular Thailand), may have served transportation as well as agricultural functions; these "canal" traces, however, lack sufficient chronometric dates at present. Given their morphology and locations, early- to mid-first-millennium-A.D. canals in the Mekong delta and peninsular Thailand were more likely designed for transportation than irrigation (Allen 1997, p. 81).

Intraregional trade networks likely preceded Southeast Asia's participation in an international trade network. Excavations of several first-millennium-A.D. sewn-plank boats (Manguin 1993, 1996) suggest active trade within South China Sea and Java sea networks. In the mid to late first millennium B.C., accelerating trading activity in the Malacca Straits and in the Java Sea (Christie 1995, pp. 246–51) involved mainland Southeast Asia, and particularly the Dongson region of northern Vietnam. That such networks con-

tinued their operation is evident from third-century-A.D. reports by Chinese envoys about the South China Sea metals trade in iron and tin (Harrison & O'Connor 1969, p. 307). The widespread use of Sanskrit-derived scripts, Indic-influenced statuary, and brick architectural styles suggests that ideas moved rather freely within this interactional sphere. So do similarities in archaeological assemblages that are found among sites located from peninsular Malaysia and the Melaka Straits to the Indochinese peninsula (Christie 1995, pp. 248–49; Manguin 2004; Stargardt 2003).

Southeast Asia's involvement in international maritime trade affected settlement distributional patterning, particularly for coastal settlements that participated in what Jacq-Hergoualc'h (2002) calls the "maritime silk route." We do not have enough evidence yet to document the nature of early Indian shipbuilding technologies in the Bay of Bengal. Investigations of several waterlogged vessels in island Southeast Asia, however, indicate that Southeast Asians possessed the technology to construct and sail watercraft to and from South Asia. Chinese Buddhist pilgrims described *bo* sea-going ships (>50 m in length) in Southeast Asia that could carry 600–700 people and 10,000 bushels of cargo (Manguin 1993, p. 262, 1996; for review see also Ray 1994, pp. 182–85).

Southeast Asians sought cotton cloth, sugar, and agricultural products from South Asians who plied their shores (Ray 1994, p. 117); from the Chinese came silk and porcelains, among other products. The Chinese, in turn, sought sumptuary goods (such as glass and precious stones), forest products, and spices from Southeast Asians. By the end of the period, the Chinese also sought religious icons and texts from Southeast Asia (Brown 1996). Small coastal settlements were established along the Malay peninsula, which exported local products and acted as "feeder points" (Leong 1990). These feeder points, in turn, supplied "collecting centers" that have prehistoric roots. The nature, directionality, and scale of this trade network changed

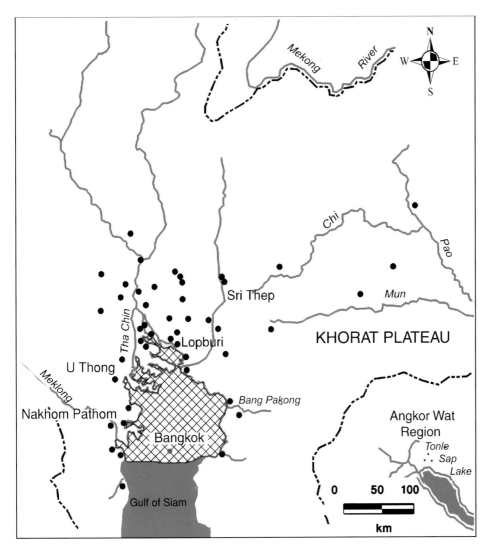

Figure 2

Relationship between marine transgression and Dvaravati site settlement patterns in the Chao Phraya basin, first millennium A.D. Reprinted from *J. Anthropol. Archaeol.* 18(1):1–28, Mudar, K. M., "How many author(s), how many Dvaravati kingdoms? Locational analysis of first millennium A.D. moated settlements in central Thailand." Copyright (1999), with permission from Elsevier.

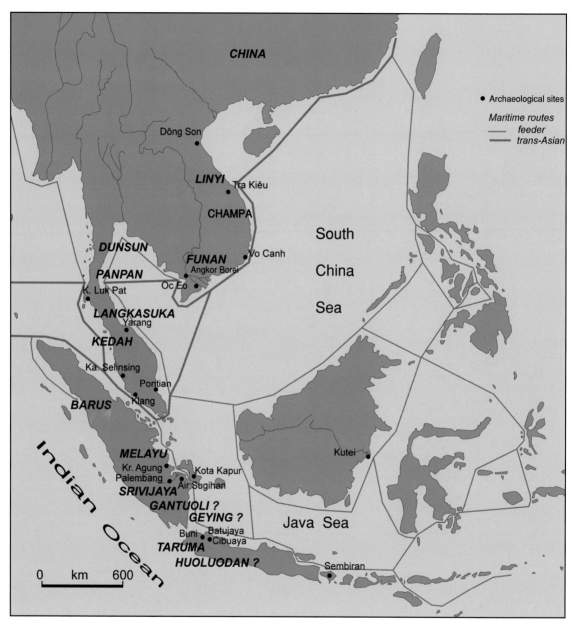

CHINA

Dông Son

LINYI
Tra Kiêu

CHAMPA

South

China

Sea

DUNSUN

PANPAN
K. Luk Pat

FUNAN
Angkor Borei
Oc Eo

Vo Canh

LANGKASUKA
Yarang

KEDAH

Ka. Selinsing

Pontian
Klang

BARUS

MELAYU
Kr. Agung
Palembang
Air Sugihan
SRIVIJAYA
GANTUOLI ?
GEYING ?

Kota Kapur

Kutei

Java Sea

Indian Ocean

Buni
Batujaya
Cibuaya
TARUMA
HUOLUODAN ?

Sembiran

0   km   600

• Archaeological sites

Maritime routes
——— feeder
——— trans-Asian

Figure 3

Manguin's "city-states" and hypothesized trade networks in first-millennium-A.D. Southeast Asia.
Reprinted from Figure 12.1 on p. 284 of "The archaeology of early maritime polities of Southeast Asia"
by P.-Y. Manguin in *Southeast Asia: From Prehistory to History* (Glover & Bellwood 2004) with permission from RoutledgeCurzon.

substantially after the eighth century A.D. in the Malay Peninsula, when true entrepôts emerged in areas with good natural harbors (also see Jacq-Hergoualc'h 2002, Leong 1993).

Coastal settlements also developed among the Cham of central Vietnam. The economic base of the earliest Cham state relied on coastal trade with China (Southworth 2004, p. 209), and this trading network may have prehistoric roots in the first-millennium-B.C. Sa Huynh culture of Vietnam (Yamagata et al. 2001). Cham settlements offered safe harbors and fresh water for trading ships between Southeast Asia and China. Overland trade with South Asia and China also played a role in settlement location in what is today Myanmar (formerly Burma). The Dry Zone of the Upper Irawaddy river basin was the only area of direct contact between South and Southeast Asia; this region boasts the highest site densities in the country in the first millennium A.D. Chinese overland routes also reached Myanmar via Sichuan and Yunnan by the second century B.C. (Gutman & Hudson, p. 157).

First millennium A.D. Southeast Asian landscape changes reflect, but are not determined by, the region's involvement in intraregional and international trade networks. The current skew toward historical (rather than archaeological) approaches has led to the persistence of explanations of "Indianization" (Kulke 1990, Mabbett 1997). Paleoenvironmental research (Bishop et al. 2003) suggests that some cultural developments also responded to regional environmental shifts from the mid–fifth millennium A.D. onward. Additional archaeological and paleoenvironmental research can provide a more balanced and nuanced explanation of changes during this period.

LANDSCAPES OF LIVELIHOOD

Agrarian and Craft Economies

Archaeological research can inform on the geography of economic systems, and early states throughout mainland Southeast Asia may have developed similar agrarian and craft production landscapes (see also White & Pigott 1996). First-millennium populations could have utilized complementary strategies in their "agro-ecosystems" (following Kealhofer 2002): (a) flood recession farming in lowland floodplains and the backswamps; (b) garden horticulture and arboriculture along the river levees; (c) livestock grazing in fallow fields within and beyond field areas; and (d) back swamps, which may have provided fish, fowl, and other raw materials (see also van Liere 1980, p. 265). No published research has systematically documented field systems, although several scholars contend that premodern agricultural features (which tend to be smaller and aligned differently than contemporary fields) are visible in remote-sensing data for both the Mekong delta and the Tonle Sap basin.

Locations of these agro-ecosystems shared several characteristics that were key to their success during the early- to mid–first millennium A.D.: (a) access to potable water in noninundated areas for settlement; (b) availability of good rice-growing soils in proximity to deep basins used during dry-season farming; and (c) a climate with a pronounced dry season (see also Ng 1979). Some of these zones were ideal for rice cultivation with significant hydraulic intervention using tanks, reservoirs, and canals. Trade and exchange, rather than agriculture, provided the basis of early state polities along the Malay peninsula (Manguin 2000, p. 415). Areas lacking sufficiently large and arable floodplains, such as the peninsular Malaysian settlement of Kedah (Allen 1997, pp. 81, 83), had trade-based, rather than agrarian-based economies.

Whether this intervention involved true intensification (replete with irrigation canals) remains unclear. Scholars working in the Pyu area of Myanmar (Stargardt 1990), Peninsular Thailand (Stargardt 1998), and the Mekong delta (Fox & Ledgerwood 1999) contend that irrigation-based agriculture was viable without substantial labor input (also see van Liere 1980). Were these claims verified, irrigation agriculture could have tripled the potential rice yield (Stargardt 1998, pp. 170–217). Promising environmental indicators have been identified in Thailand for rice cultivation (Kealhofer 2002, Mudar 1995, Penny & Kealhofer 2005), and perhaps also for forest clearance associated with upland agriculture (Kealhofer 1998, Maloney 1999). Convincing paleoenvironmental evidence documents the intensification of rice agricultural systems in other areas. Research in Northeast Thailand that associates forest recovery with a shift to controlled burns of ground cover during the early first millennium B.C. (White et al. 2004, p. 129), for example, provides a model methodology.

Little is known about the organization of craft production that structured community and regional economic systems, although White & Pigott (1996) contend that communities were engaged in "independent" (sensu Costin 2001), village-based specialization from the first millennium B.C. By the seventh century A.D., potters used the wheel in central and Northeast Thailand (Indrawooth 2004, p. 135) and in central Cambodia (Groslier 1981, pp. 14–15). Still higher-fired ceramic technologies are documented in Northeast Thailand (Welch & McNeill 1990, pp. 113–14). Evidence for glass bead production has also been recovered (or inferred) from sites in the Mekong delta (Dussubieux & Gratuze 2003, Malleret 1959). Work in central and Northeast Thailand also suggests that iron production may have been specialized at the village level by the sixth century A.D. (Moore 1992, Suchitta 1992).

A variety of specialists was likely required for the brick monumental construction underway by mid–fifth century A.D. The sheer volume of bricks manufactured for such projects suggests specialization in brick manufacture. Additionally, Hindu temple construction in contemporaneous South Asia required architects, artisans, and laborers, who were apparently organized into guild-like groups (Michell 1988, p. 55). Even religious special-

ists (Brahmans) were needed at various points in the construction process.

The foregoing discussion indicates how little is currently known about mainland Southeast Asian craft economies during the early first millennium A.D. Studies have not yet investigated evidence for elite control of production, such as through the recovery of evidence for specialized workshops in or near elite power centers (Schortman & Urban 2004, p. 191). Nor has much work concentrated on the contexts of production beyond White & Pigott's (1996; see Costin 2001) discussion concerning the circulation and consumption of both utilitarian and nonutilitarian goods. Work is also needed on the production and distribution contexts of smaller settlements in "hinterland" areas that surrounded large centers as an integral part of political economic reconstructions of early Southeast Asia.

Intraregional and Interregional Networks

Intraregional economic landscapes are also poorly documented for the first millennium A.D., although the circulation of both utilitarian commodities [such as earthenware ceramics, salt, and iron (Nitta 1997, Welch 1989, White & Pigott 1996)] and nonutilitarian commodities [copper and tin (traded both in raw and finished form), silver, horses, and cowry shells (Yang 2004)] probably continued from preceding centuries. That intraregional circulation of these goods ultimately moved them into the regional South China sea network seems clear (Higham 2002), but no research has systematically focused on production, distribution, or consumption contexts for these goods.

The emergence of Southeast Asia's earliest states with its incorporation into an international maritime trade network that linked China to South Asia and Rome has already been discussed. This network witnessed the development (or expansion) of a trade-based landscape that moved goods to Southeast

Asia's coasts from its interior areas, and that stimulated the establishment of inland and upland resource extraction settlements. Upland populations harvested the aromatic woods, camphor, and tin resources sought by the Chinese and Indians, whereas inland settlement of arable regions generated agricultural surpluses that could be transported to the coasts to feed traveling merchants and their entourages (Hall 1985, Ray 1994, pp. 115–17; Smith 1999, p. 20). Local labor, including artisans, was also needed to construct coastal settlements, to supply visiting traders, and to transport Southeast Asian goods into trading ships.

South and East Asian contact had an impact on first-millennium-A.D. Southeast Asia differentially. Although the Chinese never abandoned their attempts to control the "southern barbarians" of mainland Southeast Asia, they rarely established footholds south of northern Vietnam. Accordingly, Southeast Asia remained more a resource zone (for which Chinese envoys bartered gold and silk) than it did a vassal state or commandery. Perhaps this mercantile relationship explains Southeast Asian elites' reluctance to adopt (and resistance against adopting?) Chinese models of social, political, and religious structures that they associated with direct political control (Smith 1999, p. 18). In any event, Southeast Asian contact with South Asia may have been perceived as more benign, and the South Asian signature on the Southeast Asian landscape became increasingly pronounced through time. One of the areas with the clearest imprint lies in the form of mainland Southeast Asia's earliest urban landscapes.

URBAN ENVIRONMENTS IN EARLY SOUTHEAST ASIA

Urbanism, similar to "state" and "landscape," has been defined multifariously by previous scholars; most definitions, however, include site permanence, a clear urban-rural distinction, and a shared urban identity (Cowgill 2004; see also Smith 2003b). Early Southeast

Asian urbanism poses additional difficulties because its hallmarks diverge from the Chinese examples that Paul Wheatley (Wheatley 1971) used to construct a general model of urbanism. And although recent comparative research on ancient Old World urbanism emphasizes its social construction (A. Smith 2003, M. Smith 2003b), rather than its origins as unintended consequences of gradual aggregation processes (Cowgill 2004, pp. 535–36), the origins of Southeast Asian cities remain largely unstudied.

Mainland Southeast Asia's earliest large nucleated communities appeared rather abruptly. A pervasive focus on Iron Age burial sites (rather than on their habitation areas) and on aerial data (rather than ground-truthing) limits the sample of Iron Age settlements from which settlement size can be derived. However, three of the larger and well-dated Iron Age sites in Northeast Thailand—Ban Chiang Hian, Non Chai, Noen U-Loke—range in size from 18 to 50 hectares in size, with a mean of ~35 hectares (data from Higham 2002, pp. 187–208). In contrast, mid-first-millennium-A.D. centers in the "Funan" region of the Mekong delta (Stark 2003, Stark et al. 1999) and the "Pyu" region of Myanmar's Dry Zone (Moore 2003, table 2) ranged in area from 222–300 ha (Moore 2003) (**Table 1**). The scale of these urban cores parallels that documented in several of the world's earliest cities, including some found in Egypt, Mesopotamia, and the Late Preclassic (Yoffee 2005, p. 43, table 3.1). The end of this period ushered in even larger settlements in Thailand's Chao Phraya basin and Cambodia's Lower Mekong region. In the former region, the seventh- through eleventh-century Dvaravati site of U-Thong measured ~1420 hectares (Indrawooth 2004, p. 128). In the latter region, Angkorian cities like Angkor Thom enclosed ~900 hectares by the thirteenth and fourteenth centuries A.D. (Gaucher 2003, p. 234).

That first millennium A.D. centers bore an Indic imprint in their configuration and construction techniques seems clear. Earlier

Table 1 Locational and scalar information on selected early centers in mainland Southeast Asia occupied A.D. 1–700 (sites in table whose occupation span continues after A.D. 700 are noted)

Region	Geographic location	Approximate date range	Site name	Site area	Source
Myanmar/Burma	Dry zone	A.D. 1–500?	Maingmaw	222 ha	Moore 2003, table 2; 2004b
Myanmar/Burma	Dry zone	A.D. 1–500 (Pyu)	Beikthano	291.7 ha	Moore 2003, table 2; 2004b
Myanmar/Burma	Dry zone	A.D. 1000–780 (Pyu)	Halin	208 ha[1]	Aung Thaw 1972; Moore 2003, table 2, 2004b
Myanmar/Burma	Dry zone	A.D. 400–800 (Pyu)	Sriksetra	1477 ha[2]	Moore 2003, table 2
Myanmar/Burma	West coast	A.D. 450–800 (Pyu)	Dhanyawadi	572 ha[2]	Calculated from Gutman & Hudson 2004, figure 7.9
Vietnam	Central coast	A.D. 400–700 (Linyi/Cham)	Thanh Ho	490 ha	Parmentier 1909, pp. 137–138, pl. XXVII; Southworth (personal communication, 2006)
Vietnam	Central coast	A.D. 600–800? (Linyi/Cham)	Chau Sa[2]	160 ha	Parmentier 1909, pp. 235–36, pl. LV; Southworth (personal communication, 2006)
Vietnam	Central coast	A.D. 500–600? (Linyi/Cham)	Thanh Loi	250 ha	Parmentier 1909, pp. 512–14, pl. CVI
Vietnam	Central coast	A.D. 100–800 (Linyi/Cham)	Tra Kieu	850 ha[2]	Claeys 1928, pp. 469–70, pl. XXXVIII)
Vietnam	Mekong delta	A.D. 1–1000 (Funan)	Oc Eo[2]	450 ha[4]	Malleret 1959; Manguin & Vo 2000, p. 113
Cambodia	Mekong delta	A.D. 1–1000 (Funan)	Angkor Borei	300 ha[1,4]	Stark et al. 1999
Cambodia	Central Mekong	A.D. 500–800 (Chenla)	Sambor Prei Kuk (Isanapura)	400 ha[1]	I. Shimoda, personal communication, 2005
Thailand	Chao Phraya basin	(early Dvaravati)	Nakhon Pathom	300 ha[3]	Mudar 1999, p. 7
Thailand	Chao Phraya basin	(early Dvaravati)	Sri Thep	176	Indrawooth 2004, p. 131
Thailand	Chao Phraya basin	(early Dvaravati)	U-Thong	142	Indrawooth 2004, p. 127

[1] Size only includes walled area; substantial settlement also found beyond the walls.
[2] Site occupation span extends beyond A.D. 700, which in some cases may explain the large area reported.
[3] Area listed is Phase I site size (Mudar 1999, appendix I), which is the earliest Dvaravati phase.
[4] Site occupation extends beyond A.D. 700; area listed refers specifically to A.D. 1–600 occupational span.

scholars instead emphasized the imposition of South Asians and their ideas on Southeast Asia (e.g., Coedès 1968, Wheatley 1983). More recently, some scholars have argued that these early cities were deliberately created to legitimize and constitute political authority (e.g., Jacq-Hergoualc'h 2002, p. 96, for the Thai-Malay peninsula). Yet little systematic research on the configuration and developmental history of individual centers, which could provide insight on this issue, has yet been undertaken.

Settlement Morphology

Settlement morphology is remarkably redundant throughout mainland Southeast Asia. Settlements were moated, with earthen embankments that were topped by wooden palisades, brick walls, and/or laterite walls.

Settlement form varied, in part owing to the location of the river that often formed one bank of the settlement. These enclosed areas contained multiple and diverse precincts, often including an interior walled area or citadel that sometimes contained an inner moat and wall (Saraya 1992, p. 135; Vallibhotama 1992, p. 125). Multiple reservoirs have been documented within enclosed settlements or immediately beyond settlements' walls. Mudar (1999, p. 6) contends that sixth- through eleventh-century-A.D. moated settlements throughout central Thailand indicate the ability to mobilize labor for such public works.

Research has identified the development of networks of satellite communities (residential, ritual, and mortuary) within a 3-km radius of the center. This configuration of an urban core and rural hinterland has been documented in central Thailand (Mudar 1999, p. 5; Vallibhotama 1992) and southern Cambodia (Stark 2003) but may characterize much of mainland Southeast Asia when other regions become the subject of systematic investigation.

Myanmar's Pyu settlements offer one of the better-documented examples of first millennium A.D. (Gutman & Hudson 2004, Moore 2003, Stargardt 1990). These settlements varied in shape (quadrangular, circular, rhomboid) and were enclosed by brick walls that were segmented into as many as 12 curved gates, with openings that might once have been used for wooden gates and iron fittings (Moore 2003, p. 32). Pyu sites generally had elite enclosures along their outer walls (Gutman & Hudson 2004, Moore 2003), and some had earthenware urn burial areas outside the city's walls (Moore 2003, p. 34).

Settlement Functions

The nature of early Southeast Asian urbanism has been the subject of some discussion, particularly regarding the centers' primary functions and their organization (Wheatley 1983). Emphasis has been given to the cere-monial qualities of the region's ninth- through fourteenth-century centers such as Angkor and Pagan (Higham 2000, Mannika 1996) and their arguable adherence to city specifications outlined in the Arthasastra, a South Asian text generally attributed to the third century B.C. or first century A.D. (see Coningham 2000). Whether the region's earliest urban centers conformed to such ground plans is unclear. That developments associated with secondary urbanization in South Asia (Morrison 1997, pp. 89–91) took place only a few centuries before they appeared in Southeast Asia is intriguing and may suggest a less pronounced South Asian influence on Southeast Asia than scholars previously imagined.

Miksic (2000, 2001) offers the terms orthogenetic and heterogenetic to characterize differing types of urban centers in early mainland Southeast Asia. In his framework, orthogenetic settlements in the Mekong basin were stable centers associated with ritual activity, surplus agrarian production, low population sizes, and a concentration of elites and their monuments (Miksic 2001, pp. 94–96). In contrast, the delta's coastal settlements were heterogenetic and characterized by entrepreneurial and manufacturing activities and dense populations (pp. 97–98). Although such models are useful on an heuristic level, empirical data are needed to examine their efficacy. As one example, the inland orthogenetic center of Angkor Borei may have been more densely populated than the Miksic model presupposes: Using the lowest estimates from five similarly sized early urban centers provided by Yoffee (2005, table 3.1, p. 43), Angkor Borei could have easily housed 20,000 inhabitants.

The coastal location of many of Southeast Asia's urban settlements has prompted Manguin (2000, 2004) to argue that these polities were city-states (**Figure 3**; see color insert). Most of the world's earliest states may have been city-states rather than territorial states (Charlton & Nichols 1997; Yoffee 1997, p. 263; but see Yoffee 2005, pp. 45–62), and mainland Southeast Asia's first-millennium polities share many characteristics with other ancient city-states. Documentary records throughout mainland Southeast Asia describe multiple small competing principalities or kingdoms whose power rarely transferred to the rulers' offspring (Jacques 1986, p. 90).

GEOPOLITICAL LANDSCAPES OF EARLY SOUTHEAST ASIA

Understanding political forces that structured the production of early mainland Southeast Asian polities is essential; as in early states elsewhere, the political merged with the sacred. First millennium cities contained large brick temples, and smaller brick shrines located throughout the hinterlands marked localities with specific meanings. These monuments held sacred statuary, were sponsored by the region's elite, and reflected a syncretism of indigenous and Indic ideologies. Buddhism seems to have predominated in settlements and regions to the west (in central Myanmar and in central/western Thailand), and Hinduism predominated in areas further to the east in central Thailand, Cambodia, Laos, and coastal Vietnam.

Yet the co-occurrence of Buddhist and Hindu deities and architectural styles throughout mainland Southeast Asia suggests a selective adoption of Indic ideas that did not precisely duplicate their origin areas in South Asia. In peninsular Thailand/Malaysia, Brahmanical beliefs may have preceded Buddhist ideas (Jacq-Hergoualc'h 2002, p. 97), but both ideologies are evident after the fourth century A.D. (Bhattacharya 1997; Christie 1995, p. 256; Dalsheimer & Manguin 1998, p. 109; Ray 1994). In the Mekong delta, the Chinese considered Funan a great center of Buddhism (Pelliot 1903, pp. 284–85), yet its pre-Angkorian statuary tradition is largely Hindu in content. Similar developments occurred in the Late Phimai phase in Northeast Thailand between A.D. 300–600 (Welch & McNeill 1990, pp. 113–14). Perhaps groups in certain regions favored one Hindu sect over the other until the seventh century A.D.: Vishnu statues throughout the Mekong delta to the tip of peninsular Thailand/Malaysia bear close similarities to each other (Dalsheimer & Manguin 1998), while Siva images were worshipped throughout central and northern Cambodia.

Monumentality and Political Economy

Emergent ideologies and their material manifestations are key to establishing order and legitimacy in early civilizations (Baines & Yoffee 2000, pp. 14–15; DeMarrais et al. 1996). Monumental constructions are one medium for this process, and mainland Southeast Asia's first monumental arrangements (where the term monumental includes settlement embankments, settlement and enclave enclosure walls and moats, as well as a variety of brick constructions) were constructed in the mid–first millennium A.D. That earthen-walled and moated settlement precedents were constructed in the late prehistoric period is clear for both Thailand and Cambodia (Higham 2002; Moore 1992, p. 43). Among contemporary South Asian populations, settlement walls served multiple purposes: They protected against flooding and invaders, they restricted access by outsiders to the centers' markets, and they served as emblems of civic identity (Smith 2003a, pp. 278–79). Whether the emergent Southeast Asian monumental tradition reflected an "architecture of consensus," as Smith (p. 282) argues it did in South Asia, requires additional research.

India's Hindu temples also emerged as centers of social and economic activity under the Guptas by the fourth and fifth centuries A.D., when they were awarded royal land grants (Ray 1994, p. 161; 1997, p. 45). Brick monuments also appeared among the Pyu of Myanmar by the mid–first millennium A.D. In the Mekong delta and the Cham regions, brick and stone foundations that once supported wooden superstructures date between the fourth and seventh centuries A.D. (Gutman

& Hudson 2004, Southworth 2004, Vo 1998). In the Mekong delta, some brick shrines housed Hindu statuary (Dalsheimer & Manguin 1998, p. 100), whereas others served as mortuary monuments for cremations (Dao 1998). Southeast Asian shrines bear some resemblance to apsidal shrines that were established in the Indian subcontinent by the early first millennium A.D. (for latter see Ray 2004, p. 348). Mekong basin monuments also marked political and economic centers (Vickery 1998).

What forms of political leadership structured this cycle of monumental construction and use? Two general models have been proposed to explain leadership structure during this time: the "man of prowess" or mandala structure, and the galactic polity model (Tambiah 1985, Wolters 1999). In both models, power was fluid and contingent. As with early city-states elsewhere in the ancient world (Charlton & Nichols 1997, p. 11), power was diffuse in early Southeast Asia and few rulers were successful in passing their rule to their offspring (Vickery 1998).

Comparative research on early states in Africa, for example, suggests that leadership was closely linked to the supernatural (McIntosh et al. 2000, p. 29). This pattern holds true for first-millennium-A.D. mainland Southeast Asia in the linkage of Hindu images with royal authority. Fifth- and sixth-century mitered Vishnu statues have been recovered from the Mekong basin, areas to the south along the Malay Peninsula, and west Java (Dalsheimer & Manguin 1998, p. 90). Pre-sixth-century art forms bear clear similarities to art from southeastern India (specifically Tamil Nadu and Andhra Pradesh) but were manufactured within Southeast Asia (Dalsheimer & Manguin 1998; Stargardt 2003, pp. 107–9). Whether the popularity of Vishnu reflects the importance of Vaishnavism in first-millennium trading networks (Dalsheimer & Manguin 1998), such Hindu images were emblematic of the Indic ideology among these Southeast Asian populations. Elites commissioned and dedicated Indic im-

ages and the monuments that housed them (Brown 1996, p. 195); as elite-sponsored images of power, statuary and structures conferred order and legitimacy to the ruling elite and materialized their wealth (Baines & Yoffee 2000; Schortman & Urban 2004, pp. 192–94).

Lavy (2003) contends that the distribution of Vishnu and Siva iconography reflects the differential participation of ethnically and politically discrete groups before the seventh century A.D.: some in Vaishnavite cults and the others in Saivite cults. In this scenario, the appearance of the composite figure Harihara in the seventh century A.D. signaled efforts toward political unification between north and south and the emergence of new forms of leadership. Organizational changes during the seventh century A.D. include the expansion of Khmer culture into central, east, and Northeast Thailand and also Vietnam. Systematic documentation of the timing and nature of changes in regional settlement systems, accomplished primarily through regional survey, is required to evaluate this model.

Southeast Asian Ritual Terrains

Monumental architecture constitutes a politico-religious feature of the Early Southeast Asian landscape whose ritual meanings have persisted through time (Groslier 1973, p. 366; see also Knapp & Ashmore 1999, p. 19). Other features likely included rivers, springs, mountains, and caves, which ancient Hindu texts like the *Brihatsamita* describe as playgrounds of the gods (Michell 1988, p. 69) and which served as pilgrimage locations. Brick and stone temples were built atop natural promontories as far east as the Mekong delta (Vo 1998, p. 213) and west into lower Myanmar (Moore 2004a); so, too, were the region's first rock-cut caves. Buddhist residential monastic complexes appeared in South Asia in the second and first centuries B.C. (Ray 2005, pp. 313–14), and Cambodian hermitages may have been present as early as the fifth century (Coedès 1968, p. 60). Despite concerted survey efforts, archaeologists working in Cambodia have been unable to find archaeological evidence of these ashrams (Pou 2002, p. 318).

Aggregations of individual dedicatory events stimulated the growth of some of southern Cambodia's and Northeast Thailand's first-millennium-A.D. settlements. Each time a temple was constructed, water control structures like tanks, dikes, and moats were also built. The temples embodied sacred mountains, and the moats, sacred waters. Such sites in Northeast Thailand contained multiple mounds and reservoirs (Welch 1997). Settlements such as Muang Phet contained moats and earthen and brick walls (constructed partially or wholly with bricks) that served as landscape and ritual architecture (McNeill 1997). Unlike residential structures, which were constructed of perishable materials, these sacred sites were made from durable materials. Both the nature of the archaeological record and difficulties in archaeologists' access to many monuments (which are still considered sacred and therefore inviolable) make disarticulating the sacred from the secular difficult, if not impossible.

RECONCEPTUALIZING MAINLAND SOUTHEAST ASIA IN THE FIRST MILLENNIUM A.D.

Thousands of first-millennium-A.D. mounds are scattered across mainland Southeast Asia today, and most remain to be discovered. Material from multiple data sources provides an intriguing yet frustratingly incomplete picture of urbanism, political transformation, and ideological structure for this period. Might a fundamental resilience have existed at the level of local sociopolitical units that counterbalanced macrolevel political instabilities that involved shifting polities and their centers (see Stark 2006)? Multidisciplinary approaches are needed to examine political, social, economic, and environmental contexts of state development.

The idea that first-millennium-A.D. Southeast Asia witnessed the emergence of a series of city-states in both the mainland and insular regions (Manguin 2000, 2004) is intriguing. We still know too little, however, about the nature of the region's earliest cities to place particular examples into one or another of the current, competing models of early urbanism and early state formation (see also Cowgill 2004, pp. 534–37, Smith 2003b). Such knowledge is best gained by investigating the spatial organization of economic activities (i.e., production, distribution, and consumption) within and between its early centers. Understanding early urbanism is particularly urgent to tracing continuities and discontinuities in the regional pattern, given what appears to be the relatively dispersed nature of some ninth- to fourteenth-century-A.D. urban centers such as Angkor (Greater Angkor Project 2003).

Archaeological work is also needed to evaluate models, drawn from historical sources (e.g., Bentley 1986, Wolters 1999), that suggest a cyclical quality of early Southeast Asian states. These models resemble patterns that archaeologists have documented elsewhere in the Old and New Worlds (Feinman 1998), but archaeological work is necessary to understand the existence, nature, and implications of this cycling. Such work is also key to understanding political cycling within its broader context of subsistence economy, ethnic identities, lower-level administrative structures, and ideology.

Mainland Southeast Asia is an excellent and underutilized region for comparative studies of early state formation, with great potential for examining changing spatial configurations of human-environment relations through time. Theoretical frameworks of archaeological landscape studies elsewhere vary widely (e.g., Anschuetz et al. 2001; Smith 2003), yet mainland Southeast Asia remains largely untouched by these debates, to its detriment. Understanding changing landscapes of mainland Southeast Asia in the first millennium A.D. requires attention to at least three research themes: (*a*) late Holocene human-environmental and land-use histories, (*b*) changing patterns of settlement, and (*c*) economic networks at the regional and macroregional levels.

Late Holocene Human-Environmental and Land-Use Histories

Collaborative archaeological and paleoenvironmental research is also sorely needed to evaluate the nature of human impact on the environment with the rise of complex societies. Extant research on deltaic formations and changing sea levels, summarized in this review, has limited utility until they are examined against an archaeological backdrop. Work on climatic variability (both low-frequency and high-frequency processes) remains to be done in much of the mainland before we can examine the relative impact of climate on human decision-making.

Historical ecological approaches could articulate paleoenvironmental studies with anthropological questions and place settlement pattern studies more explicitly within their broader natural and ecological settings. Do we see long periods of landscape stability, or does evidence exist for changing patterns of land use (and agricultural intensification) through time? If so, what was its impact on local and regional watersheds? How did populations intentionally or unintentionally shape their landscapes at the local and regional scales? In turn, how did landscape elements constrain or direct human decision-making at different points during the first millennium A.D.? Such work should also distinguish anthropogenic from natural patterns to facilitate analysis of the relative importance of human action versus environmental factors in a variety of socioecological transitions.

Changing Patterns of Settlement

Systematic archaeological survey, combined with judicious test excavations to refine regional ceramic chronologies, is sorely needed

to understand the first millennium A.D. Such work should encompass both major urban centers and their rural catchments, combine archaeological with epigraphic and art historical information, and incorporate paleoenvironmental data. The sociopolitical contexts of rice agroecosystems require further investigation. What was the potential for agricultural surplus generation within particular regions? To what extent was this surplus dedicated for export (to support maritime traders along the South China Sea coast), and to what extent did this surplus underwrite intraregional activities? That urban centers arose and grew suggests that populations generated sufficient surplus to support food collectors (fisherfolk and hunters) and craft specialists. Across pre-Angkorian Cambodia, at least, this surplus production was a form of social production: It supported ritual, ceremonial, and construction activities by religious officials (Stark 2004, Vickery 1998). Archaeological evidence, however, is needed to understand better the relative importance of each form of production.

Studying changing patterns of land use will also inform on the nature of urban-hinterland configurations. Not only are center-periphery configurations structured differently under discrete kinds of political economies, but also these may change through time. What was the effective scale of these early Southeast Asian polities? How did centers articulate with their peripheries? To what extent did they control their rural hinterlands and the potential agricultural yields (following Manguin 2000, p. 414)? Only settlement surveys offer the potential to understand the timing, nature, and extent of urbanization in various river valleys and deltas across the region.

At least two landscape-based studies that focus instead on the second millennium A.D. provide models for this work. One project, undertaken in northern Thailand (Grave 1995), uses the political region (or mandala) as its analytical scale and focuses on links between lowland Buddhist populations (seen in their monuments) and upland non-Buddhist groups (seen in their mortuary sites). A second project, based in the Tonle Sap region of northwestern Cambodia (Greater Angkor Project 2003), uses the effective urban Angkor complex as its scale and is in the process of mapping the palimpsest of shrines, water features, and associated house-mound clusters, channels, and embankments (whether roads or banks of canals and water tanks) that comprise this ninth- to fourteenth-century landscape. Whether these second-millennium-A.D. systems had precursors in the previous millennium should also be a topic of archaeological investigation.

Political Economies and a "World System" of the First Millennium A.D.

That mainland Southeast Asia was embedded in broader economic, political, and social networks during the early to mid–first millennium A.D. is clear from Chinese documentary records that describe envoy journeys between southern China and various Southeast Asian polities (Coedès 1968, Ishizawa 1995, Southworth 2004, Wheatley 1983). More work, however, is needed to elucidate the nature and changing contexts of these systems at the intraregional, interregional, and macroregional levels. What kinds of communication and transportation networks linked subregions into broader interactional networks? Were regions structured into systems of village-based specialization and exchange of utilitarian goods, as White & Pigott (1996) suggested? Bellina & Glover (2004) have summarized our knowledge of goods imported from South Asia, but comparable scholarship remains to be conducted on a range of "prestige" goods (from precious metals, porcelains, and beads to horses and cowries) that originated in China and also circulated through the region.

Comparative studies of material culture could inform on the configuration of several interactional networks: within South China Sea communities, between mainland and island Southeast Asian regions, and between mainland Southeast Asia and its neighbors (southern India, southern China). Because art historical traditions have dominated such analyses, interpretations emphasize South Asian influence and the religious/ideological realm; more work is needed on the vernacular world. Documenting material culture homogeneity versus heterogeneity within and across regions and through time also informs on the nature, tempo, and directionality of organizational change versus cultural stasis.

A practice-theory approach to comparing technological traditions, as Bellina (2003) has initiated with bead studies, offers a holistic methodology that could benefit even more by incorporating compositional analysis. Work could compare and contrast technological styles in multiple material culture media, from ceramics (particularly the fine-paste wares found throughout island and mainland Southeast Asia after A.D. 300) and beads (glass and semiprecious gemstones) to brick manufacturing technology and architectural construction techniques. This work requires technological reconstructions of manufacturing sequences, stylistic comparisons of decoration, and provenience research.

First-millennium mainland Southeast Asia remains one of the world's richest and most underexploited areas of research for archaeologists studying early state formation. That this work must be undertaken at the regional and macroregional levels is clear, and close collaboration is needed between specialists in archaeology and those in ancillary disciplines. Also required are the energy and resources of a new generation of archaeologists who are committed to international collaboration with, and training of, archaeologists from the countries under study. Such interdisciplinary research blends archaeology, art history, and philology with the natural sciences and will greatly enhance our knowledge of mainland Southeast Asia's changing landscapes during the first millennium A.D.

ACKNOWLEDGMENTS

My thanks are extended to Ian Glover, William Southworth, Elizabeth Moore, Michael Aung-Thwin, and Karen Mudar for their generosity in providing unpublished information. I am also grateful to James Bayman, Lisa Kealhofer, Peter Lape, and Carla Sinopoli for their comments on a previous version of this manuscript. Jo Lynn Gunness drafted **Figure 1**, and Alexander Morrison provided graphics assistance with **Figures 2** and **3**. All errors in this manuscript remain my own.

LITERATURE CITED

Allen J. 1997. Inland Angkor, coastal Kedah: landscapes, subsistence systems, and state development in early Southeast Asia. *Bull. Indo-Pacific Prehist. Assoc.* 16(3):79–87

Allen J. 1999. Managing a tropical environment: state development in early historical-era Kedah, Malaysia. In *Complex Polities in the Ancient Tropical World*, ed. EA Bacus, LJ Lucero, pp. 131–50. Washington, DC: Archeol. Papers Am. Anthropol. Assoc. No. 9

Anschuetz KF, Wilshusen RH, Scheick CL. 2001. An archaeology of landscapes: perspectives and directions. *J. Archaeol. Res.* 9(2):157–211

Ashmore W. 2004. Social archaeologies of landscape. In *A Companion to Social Archaeology*, ed. L Meskell, RW Preucel, pp. 255–71. Malden, MA: Blackwell

Aung Thaw U. 1972. *Historical Sites of Burma*. Rangoon: Ministr. Union Cult.

Baines J, Yoffee N. 2000. Order, legitimacy and wealth: setting the terms. In *Order, Legitimacy and Wealth in Ancient States*, ed. J Richards, M Van Buren, pp. 13–17. Cambridge: Cambridge Univ. Press

Bellina B. 2003. Beads, social change and interaction between India and South-east Asia. *Antiquity* 77:285–97

Bellina B, Glover IC. 2004. The archaeology of early contact with India and the Mediterranean world, from the fourth century B.C. to the fourth century A.D. See Glover & Bellwood 2004, pp. 21–40

Bentley GC. 1986. Indigenous states of Southeast Asia. *Annu. Rev. Anthropol.* 15:275–305

Bhattacharya K. 1997. The religions of ancient Cambodia. In *Sculpture of Angkor and Ancient Cambodia: Millennium of Glory*, ed. HI Jessup, T Zéphir, pp. 34–52. Washington, DC: Natl. Gallery Art

Bishop P, Penny D, Stark MT, Scott M. 2003. A 3.5 Ka record of paleoenvironments and human occupation at Angkor Borei, Mekong Delta, Southern Cambodia. *Geoarchaeology* 18(3):359–93

Bishop P, Sanderson DCW, Stark MT. 2004. OSL and radiocarbon dating of a pre-Angkorian canal in the Mekong delta, southern Cambodia. *J. Archaeol. Sci.* 31(3):319–36

Bourdonneau E. 2003. The ancient canal system of the Mekong delta: preliminary report. See Karlström & Källén 2003, pp. 257–70

Boyd WE, Doan Dinh L. 2004. Holocene elevated sea levels on the North coast of Vietnam. *Austr. Geogr. Stud.* 42(1):77–88

Boyd WE, McGrath RJ. 2001. Iron Age vegetation dynamics and human impacts on the vegetation of Upper Mun River floodplain, N.E. Thailand. *N. Z. Geogr.* 57(2):21–32

Bronson B. 1992. Patterns in the early Southeast Asian metals trade. See Glover et al. 1992, pp. 63–114

Bronson B, White J. 1992. Southeast Asia. In *Chronologies in Old World Archaeology*, ed. RW Ehrich, pp. 475–15. Chicago: Univ. Chicago Press

Brown RL. 1996. *The Dvaravati Wheels of the Law and the Indianization of South East Asia.* Leiden/New York/Köln: Brill

Charlton TH, Nichols DL. 1997. The city-state concept: development and applications. See Charlton & Nichols 1997, pp. 1–14

Christie JW. 1995. State formation in early maritime Southeast Asia: a consideration of the theories and the data. *Bijdragen Tot De Taal-, Land- en Volkenkunde* 151:235–88

Claeys JY. 1928. 'Fouilles à Tra-Kieu'. *Bull. Ecole Française Extrême Orient* 27:468–82

Coedès G. 1968. *The Indianized States of Southeast Asia*, transl. SB Cowing, ed. WF Vella. Honolulu: Univ. Hawaii Press

Coningham R. 2000. Contestatory urban texts or were cities in South Asia built as images? *Camb. Archaeol. J.* 10:348–54

Costin CL. 2001. Craft production systems. In *Archaeology at the Millennium: A Sourcebook*, ed. GM Feinman, TD Price, pp. 273–328. New York: Kluwer Academic/Plenum

Cowgill G. 2004. Origins and development of urbanism: archaeological perspectives. *Annu. Rev. Anthropol.* 33:525–49

Crumley CL. 1994. Historical ecology: a multidimensional ecological orientation. In *Historical Ecology: Culture, Knowledge, and Changing Landscapes*, ed. CL Crumley, pp. 1–16. Santa Fe: Sch. Am. Res.

Crumley CL, Marquardt WH. 1990. Landscape: a unifying concept in regional analysis. In *Interpreting Space: GIS and Archaeology*, ed. K Allen, S Green, E Zubrow, pp. 73–79. London: Taylor & Francis

Dalsheimer N, Manguin PY. 1998. Visnu mitrés et réseaux marchands en Asie du Sud-est: nouvelles données archéologiques sur le I millénaire Apr. J.-C. *Bull. École Française Extrême Orient* 85:87–124

Dao LC. 1998. The Oc Eo Burial group recently excavated at Go Thap (Dong Thap Province, Viêt Nam). See Manguin 1998, pp. 111–17

DeMarrais E, Castillo LJ, Earle T. 1996. Ideology, materialization, and power strategies. *Curr. Anthropol.* 37:15–31

Dussubieux L, Gratuze B. 2003. Non-destructive characterization of glass beads: an application to the study of glass trade between India and Southeast Asia. See Karlström & Källén 2003, pp. 135–48

Feinman GM. 1998. Scale and social organization: Perspectives on the archaic state. See Feinman & Marcus 1998, pp. 95–134

Feinman GM, Marcus J, eds. 1998. *Archaic States.* Santa Fe: Sch. Am. Res.

Fox J, Ledgerwood J. 1999. Dry-season flood-recession rice in the Mekong delta: two thousand years of sustainable agriculture? *Asian Perspect.* 38:37–50

Gaucher J. 2003. New archaeological data on the urban space of the capital city of Angkor Thom. See Karlström & Källén 2003, pp. 233–42

Glover IC. 1998. The role of India in the later prehistory of Southeast Asia. *J. SE Asian Archaeol.* 18:21–49

Glover IC, Bellwood P, eds. 2004. *Southeast Asia: From Prehistory to History.* London/New York: RoutledgeCurzon

Glover IC, Suchitta P, Villiers J, eds. 1992. *Early Metallurgy, Trade and Urban Centres in Thailand and Southeast Asia.* Bangkok: White Lotus

Glover IC, Yamagata M. 1998. Excavations at Tra Kiêu, Viêt Nam 1993: Sa Huynh, Cham and Chinese influences. See Manguin 1998, pp. 75–93

Glover IC, Yamagata M, Southworth W. 1996. Excavations at Buu Chau Hill, Tra Kieu, Quangnam-Danang province, Vietnam, 1993. *Bull. Indo-Pacific Prehistory Assoc.* 14:166–76

Godley D. 2002. The reconstruction of flood regimes in SE Asia from El Niño-Southern Oscillation (ENSO) related records. In *Bridging Wallace's Line: The Environmental and Cultural History and Dynamics of the SE Asian-Australian Region*, ed. P Kershaw, B David, N Tapper, D Penny, J Brown, pp. 229–54. Reiskrichen, Germ.: CATENA VERLAG GMBH

Grave P. 1995. Beyond the *mandala*: Buddhist landscapes and upland-lowland interaction in north-west Thailand A.D. 1200–1650. *World Archaeol.* 27:243–65

Greater Angkor Project. 2003. Redefining Angkor: structure and environment in the largest low density urban complex of the preindustrial world. *Udaya* 4:107–25

Groslier BP. 1973. Pour une géographie historique du Cambodge. *Cahiers Outre-Mer* 104:337–79

Groslier BP. 1981. Introduction to the ceramic wares of Angkor. In *Khmer Ceramics, Ninth-Fourteenth Century*, ed. D. Stock, pp. 9–40. Singapore: SE Asian Ceramic Soc.

Gunn JD, ed. 2000. *The Years Without Summer: Tracing A.D. 536 and its Aftermath*. BAR Int. Ser. 872. Oxford: BAR

Gutman P, Hudson B. 2004. The archaeology of Burma (Myanmar) from the Neolithic to Pagan. See Glover & Bellwood 2004, pp. 149–76

Hall KR. 1985. *Maritime Trade and State Formation in Early Southeast Asia*. Honolulu: Univ. Hawaii Press

Harrison T, O'Connor SJ. 1969. *Excavations of the prehistoric iron industry in West Borneo, vol. II: associated artifacts and ideas*. Data Pap. No. 72. Ithaca, NY: Southeast Asia Program, Cornell Univ.

Higham CFW. 2000. The symbolism of the Angkorian city. *Camb. Archaeol. J.* 10:355–57

Higham CFW. 2002. *Early Cultures of Mainland Southeast Asia*. Bangkok, Thailand: River Books

Higham CFW. 2004. Mainland Southeast Asia from the Neolithic to the Iron Age. See Glover & Bellwood 2004, pp. 41–67

Hudson B, Nyein L, Win M. 2001. The origins of Bagan: new dates and old inhabitants. *Asian Perspect.* 40:48–74

Indrawooth P. 2004. The archaeology of the early Buddhist kingdoms of Thailand. See Glover & Bellwood 2004, pp. 120–48

Ishizawa Y. 1995. Chinese chronicles of the first-fifth century A.D. Funan, Southern Cambodia. In *South East Asia & China: Art, Interaction & Commerce*, ed. R Scott, J Guy, pp. 11–31. Colloquies on Art & Archaeology in Asia No. 17. London: Percival David Found. Chinese Art, Univ. London

Jacq-Hergoualc'h M. 1992. *La Civilisation de Ports-Entrepôts du Sud Kedah (Malaysia): Ve-XIVe siècle*. Paris: Harmattan

Jacq-Hergoualc'h M. 2002. *The Malay Peninsula: Crossroads of the Maritime Silk Road (100 B.C.–1300 A.D.)*, transl. V Hobson. Leiden/Boston: Brill

Jacques C. 1979. 'Funan,' 'Zhenla': the reality concealed by these Chinese views of Indochina. In *Early South East Asia: Essays in Archaeology, History, and Historical Geography*, ed. RB Smith, W Watson, pp. 371–79. New York: Oxford Univ. Press

Jacques C. 1986. Le pays Khmer avant Angkor. *J. Savants* Jan./Sept.:59–95

Jacques C. 1995. China and ancient Khmer history. In *South East Asia and China: Art, Interaction and Commerce*, ed. R Scott, J Guy, pp. 32–40. Colloquies on Art & Archaeology in Asia No. 17. London: Percival David Found. Chinese Art, Univ. London

Karlström A, Källén A, eds. 2003. *Fishbones and Glittering Emblems: Southeast Asian Archaeology 2002*. Stockholm: Mus. Far East. Antiq.

Kealhofer L. 1998. Evidence for cultural impact on the environment during the Holocene: two phytolith sequences from the Lopburi region, Thailand. In *South-East Asian Archaeol., 1992*, ed. R. Ciarla, F Rispoli, pp. 1–20. Rome: Istituto Italiano per l'Africa e l'Oriente

Kealhofer L. 2002. Changing perceptions of risk: the development of agro-ecosystems in Southeast Asia. *Am. Anthropol.* 104(1):178–94

Knapp AB, Ashmore W. 1999. Archaeological landscapes: constructed, conceptualized, ideational. In *Archaeologies of Landscape: Contemporary Perspectives*, ed. W Ashmore, AB Knapp, pp. 1–32. Malden, MA: Blackwell

Kulke H. 1990. Indian colonies, Indianization or cultural convergence? Reflections on the changing image of India's role in South-East Asia. In *Onderzoek in Zuidoost-Azie: Agenda's voor de Jaren Negentig*, ed. HS Nordholt, pp. 8–32. Leiden: Rijksuniversiteit te Leiden, Vakgroep Talen en Culturen van Zuidoost-Azie en Oceanie

Lape P. 2003. A highway and a crossroads: Island Southeast Asia and culture contact archaeology. *Archaeol. Oceania* 38(2):102–10

Lavy PA. 2003. As in heaven, so on earth: the politics of Visnu, Śiva and Harihara images in preangkorian Khmer civilization. *J. SE Asian Stud.* 34(1):21–39

Leong SH. 1990. Collecting centres, feeder points and entrepôts in the Malay Peninsula, 1000 B.C.–A.D. 1400. In *The Southeast Asian Port and Polity: Rise and Demise*, ed. J Kathirithamby-Wells, J Villiers, pp. 17–38. Singapore: Singapore Univ. Press, National Univ.

Leong SH. 1993. Ancient trading centres in the Malay Peninsula. *J. Arkeol. Malays.* 6:1–9

Lertrit S. 2003. On chronology-building for central Thailand through an attribute-based ceramic seriation. *Asian Perspect.* 42:41–71

Li Z, Saito Y, Matsumoto E, Wang Y, Tanabe S, Quang LV. 2006. Climate change and human impact on the Song Hong (Red River) Delta, Vietnam, during the Holocene. *Quat. Int.* 144:4–28

Lobo W, Reimann S, eds. 2000. *Southeast Asian Archaeology 1998*. Berlin: Cent. South-East Asian Stud., Univ. Hull Ethnol. Mus., Staatliche Museen zu Berlin, Stiftung Preußischer Kulturbesitz

Mabbett I. 1997. The "Indianization" of mainland Southeast Asia: a reappraisal. In *Living a Life in Accord with Dhamma: Papers in Honor of Professor Jean Boisselier on his Eightieth Birthday*, ed. N Eilenberg, MC Subhadradis Diskul, RL Brown, pp. 342–55. Bangkok: Silpakorn Univ.

Malleret L. 1959. *L'Archéologie du Delta du Mékong, Part 1. L'Exploration Archéologique et Les Fouilles d'Oc-Èo*. Paris: École Française Extrême-Orient

Maloney B. 1999. A 10,600 year pollen record from Nong Thale Song Hong, Trang Province, south Thailand. *J. Siam Soc.* 86:201–17

Manguin PY. 1993. Trading ships of the South China Sea. *J. Econ. Social Hist. Orient* 36:253–80

Manguin PY. 1996. Southeast Asian shipping in the Indian Ocean during the first millennium A.D. In *Tradition and Archaeology: Early Maritime Contacts in the Indian Ocean*, ed. HP Ray, J-F Salles, pp. 181–96. New Delhi: Manohar

Manguin PY, ed. 1998. *Southeast Asian Archaeology 1994*, Vol. 1. England: Cent. SE Asian Stud., Univ. Hull

Manguin PY. 2000. City-states and city-state cultures in prefifteenth century Southeast Asia. In *A Comparative Study of Thirty City-State Cultures*, ed. MH Hansen, pp. 409–16. Copenhagen: Historisk-filosofiske Skrifter, R. Danish Acad. Sci. Lett.

Manguin PY. 2004. The archaeology of early maritime polities of Southeast Asia. See Glover & Bellwood 2004, pp. 282–313

Manguin PY, Vo SK. 2000. Excavations at the Ba The/Oc Eo complex (Viet Nam): a preliminary report on the 1998 campaign. See Lobo & Reimann 2000, pp. 107–21

Mannika E. 1996. *Angkor Wat. Time, Space and Kingship*. Honolulu: Univ. Hawai'i Press

McIntosh RJ, Tainter JA, McIntosh SK. 2000. Climate, history, and human action. In *The Way the Wind Blows: Climate, History, and Human Action*, ed. RJ McIntosh, JA Tainter, SK McIntosh, pp. 1–42. New York: Columbia Univ. Press

McNeill JR. 1997. Muang Phet: Quaritch Wales' moated site excavations reappraised. *Bull. Indo-Pacific Prehistory Assoc.* 16:167–75

Michell G. 1988. *The Hindu Temple*. Chicago/London: Univ. Chicago Press

Michell G. 2000. *Hindu Art and Architecture*. London: Thames and Hudson

Miksic JN. 1995. Evolving archaeological perspectives on Southeast Asia 1970–95. *J. SE Asian Stud.* 26(1):46–62

Miksic JN. 2000. Heterogenetic cities in premodern Southeast Asia. *World Archaeol.* 32(1):107–22

Miksic JN. 2001. Early Burmese urbanization: research and conservation. *Asian Perspect.* 40:88–107

Moore E. 1992. Water enclosed sites: links between Ban Takhong, Northeast Thailand and Cambodia. In *The Gift of Water: Water Management, Cosmology and the State in South East Asia*, ed. J Rigg, pp. 26–46. London: SOAS

Moore E. 2003. Bronze and Iron Age sites in Upper Myanmar: Chindwin, Samon and Pyu. *SOAS Bull. Burma Res.* 1(1):24–39

Moore E. 2004a. Ancient knowledge and the use of landscape: walled settlements in lower Myanmar. In *Traditions of Knowledge in Southeast Asia, Part I*, pp. 1–28. Yangon: Myanmar Hist. Comm., Ministr. Educ.

Moore E. 2004b. Interpreting Pyu material culture: royal chronologies and finger-marked bricks. *Myanmar Hist. Res. J.* 13:1–57

Morrison KM. 1997. Commerce and culture in South Asia: perspectives from archaeology and history. *Annu. Rev. Anthropol.* 27:87–108

Mudar KM. 1995. Evidence for prehistoric dryland farming in mainland Southeast Asia: results of regional survey in Lopburi province, Thailand. *Asian Perspect.* 34:157–94

Mudar KM. 1999. How many Dvaravati kingdoms? Locational analysis of first millennium A.D. moated settlements in central Thailand. *J. Anthropol. Archaeol.* 18:1–28

Ng RCY. 1979. The geographical habitat of historical settlements in mainland Southeast Asia. In *Early South East Asia: Essays in Archaeology, History, and Historical Geography*, ed. RB Smith, W Watson, pp. 262–72. New York: Oxford Univ. Press

Nguyen KS, Pham MH, Tong TT. 2004. Northern Vietnam from the Neolithic to the Han period. See Glover & Bellwood 2004, pp. 177–208

Nichols D, Charlton T, eds. 1997. *The Archaeology of City-States*. Washington, DC: Smithson. Inst. Press

Nitta E. 1997. Iron-smelting and salt-making industries in northeast Thailand. *Bull. Indo-Pacific Prehistory Assoc.* 16:153–60

O'Reilly D. 2003. Further evidence of heterarchy in prehistoric Thailand. *Curr. Anthropol.* 44:300–7

Parmentier H. 1909. *Inventaire descriptif des Monuments Cams de l'Annam*. Paris: Imprimerie Nationale, École Française Extrême-Orient

Penny D, Kealhofer L. 2005. Microfossil evidence of land-use intensification in north Thailand. *J. Archaol. Sci.* 32:69–82

Pottier C. 1999. *Carte archéologique de la région d'Angkor. Zone Sud*. Ph.D. thesis, 3 vols. Univ. Paris III—Sorbonne Nouvelle (UFR Orient et Monde Arabe)

Pou S. 2002. Āśrama dans l'Ancien Cambodge. *J. Asiatique* 290:315–39

Pelliot P. 1903. Le Fou-nan. *Bul. École Française Extrême Orient* 3:248–303

Ray HP. 1994. *The Winds of Change: Buddhism and the Maritime Links of Early South Asia*. Delhi: Oxford Univ. Press

Ray HP. 1997. The emergence of urban centres in Bengal: implications for the late prehistory of Southeast Asia. *Bull. Indo-Pacific Prehistory Assoc.* 16:43–48

Ray HP. 2004. The apsidal shrine in early Hinduism: origins, cultic affiliation, patronage. *World Archaeol.* 36(3):343–59

Ray HP. 2005. The Axial Age in Asia: the archaeology of Buddhism (500 B.C. to A.D. 500). See Stark 2005, pp. 303–23

Reynolds CJ. 1995. A new look at Old Southeast Asia. *J. Asian Stud.* 54:419–46

Saraya D. 1992. The hinterland state of Sri Thep Sri Deva—a reconsideration. See Glover et al. 1992, pp. 131–47

Schortman EM, Urban P. 2004. Modeling the roles of craft production in ancient political economies. *J. Archaeol. Res.* 12:185–226

Schweyer AV. 2000. La dynastie d'Indrapura (Quang Nam, Viet Nam). See Lobo & Reimann 2000, pp. 205–17

Sinopoli CM. 2005. Imperial landscapes of South Asia. See Stark 2005, pp. 324–49

Sinsakul S. 2000. Late Quaternary geology of the Lower Central Plain, Thailand. *J. Asian Earth Sci.* 18:415–26

Smith AT. 2003. *The Political Landscape: Constellations of Authority in Early Complex Polities*. Berkeley: Univ. Calif. Press

Smith ML. 1999. "Indianization" from the Indian point of view: trade and cultural contacts with Southeast Asia in the early first millennium C.E. *J. Econ. Soc. Hist. Orient* 42:1–26

Smith ML. 2003a. Early walled cities of the Indian subcontinent as "small worlds." See M. Smith 2003b, pp. 269–89

Smith ML. 2003b. *The Social Construction of Cities*. Washington, DC: Smithson. Inst. Press

Southworth WA. 2000. Notes on the political geography of Campa in central Vietnam during the late eighth and early ninth centuries A.D. See Lobo & Reimann 2000, pp. 237–44

Southworth WA. 2004. The coastal states of Champa. See Glover & Bellwood 2004, pp. 209–33

Stargardt J. 1990. *The Ancient Pyu of Burma, Volume One: Early Pyu Cities in a Man-Made Landscape*. Cambridge, UK: Publ. Anc. Civ. SE Asia

Stargardt J. 1998. Earth, rice, water: 'reading the landscape' as a record of the history of Satingpra, South Thailand. In *Nature and the Orient: the Environmental History of South and Southeast Asia*, ed. RH Grove, V Damodaran, S Sangwan, pp. 127–83. New Delhi: Oxford Univ. Press

Stargardt J. 2003. Mapping the mind—some cultural cargoes of the sea-trade in Southeast Asia, fifth-thirteenth century. See Karlström & Källén 2003, pp. 103–18

Stark MT. 1998. The transition to history in the Mekong delta: a view from Cambodia. *Int. J. Hist. Archaeol.* 2(3):175–204

Stark MT. 2001. Southeast Asia Late Prehistoric: 2500–1500BP. In *Encyclopedia of Prehistory*, Vol. 3: *East Asia and Oceania*, ed. P Peregrine, pp. 160–205. New York: Plenum

Stark MT. 2003. Angkor Borei and the archaeology of Cambodia's Mekong Delta. In *Art and Archaeology of Fu Nan: Pre-Khmer Kingdom of the Lower Mekong Valley*, ed. J Khoo, pp. 87–106. Bangkok: Orchid

Stark MT, ed. 2005. *Archaeology of Asia*. Malden, MA: Blackwell

Stark MT. 2006. From Funan to Angkor: collapse and regeneration in ancient Cambodia. In *After Collapse: The Regeneration of Complex Societies*, ed. GM Schwartz, JJ Nichols, pp. 144–67. Tucson: Univ. Ariz. Press

Stark MT, Bong S. 2001. Recent research on the emergence of early historic states in Cambodia's lower Mekong. *Bull. Indo-Pac. Prehistory Assoc.* 19:85–98

Stark MT, Griffin PB, Chuch P, Ledgerwood J, Dega M, et al. 1999. Results of the 1995–1996 field investigations at Angkor Borei, Cambodia. *Asian Perspect.* 38: 1:7–36

Stein G. 2001. Understanding ancient state societies in the Old World. In *Archaeology at the Millennium: A Sourcebook*, ed. GM Feinman, TD Price, pp. 353–80. New York: Kluwer Academic/Plenum

Suchitta P. 1992. Early iron smelting in Thailand and its implications. See Glover et al. 1992, pp. 115–22

Tambiah S. 1985. The galactic polity in Southeast Asia. In *Culture, Thought, and Social Action: An Anthropological Perspective*, pp. 252–86. Cambridge, MA: Harvard Univ. Press

Tanage S, Saito S, Sato Y, Suzuki Y, Sinsakul S, et al. 2003. Stratigraphy and Holocene evolution of the mud-dominated Chao Phraya delta, Thailand. *Q. Sci. Rev.* 22:789–807

Theunissen R, Grave P, Bailey G. 2000. Doubts on diffusion: challenging the assumed Indian origin of Iron Age agate and carnelian beads in Southeast Asia. *World Archaeol.* 32:84–105

Tjia HD. 1996. Sea-level changes in the tectonically stable Malay-Thai Peninsula. *Quat. Int.* 31:95–10

Trigger B. 2003. *Understanding Early Civilizations: A Comparative Study*. New York: Cambridge Univ. Press

Trinh TH. 1996. Réflexions sur les vestiges de la culture d'Óc Eo. *Etudes Vietnamiennes* N. S. 50:111–23

Vallibhotama S. 1992. Early urban centres in the Chao Phraya Valley of central Thailand. In *Early Metallurgy, Trade and Urban Centres in Thailand and Southeast Asia*, ed. IC Glover, P Suchitta, J Villiers, pp. 123–29. Bangkok: White Lotus

Nguyen VL, Thi KOT, Tateishi M 2000. Late Holocene depositional environments and coastal evolution of the Mekong River Delta, Southern Vietnam. *J. Asian Earth Sci.* 18:427–39

van Liere WJ. 1980. Traditional water management in the lower Mekong basin. *World Archaeol.* 11:265–80

Vickery M. 1994. What and where was Chenla? In *Recherches Nouvelles sur le Cambodia*, ed. F Bizot, pp. 197–212. Paris: École Française Extrême-Orient

Vickery M. 1998. *Society, Economics, and Politics in Pre-Angkor Cambodia*. Tokyo: Cent. East Asian Cult. Stud. Unesco, The Toyo Bunko

Vo SK. 1998. Plans architecturaux des ancients monuments du Delta du Mékong du 1er au 10e siècles AD. See Manguin 1998, pp. 207–14

Welch D. 1989. Late prehistoric and early historic exchange patterns in the Phimai Region, Thailand. *J. SE Asian Stud.* 10(1):11–26

Welch D. 1997. Archaeology of Northeast Thailand in relation to the pre-Khmer and Khmer historical records. *Int. J. Hist. Archaeol.* 2:205–34

Welch D, McNeill J. 1990. Excavations at Ban Tamyae and Non Ban Kham, Phimai Region, Northeast Thailand. *Asian Perspect.* 28:99–123

Wheatley P. 1971. *Pivot of the Four Quarters: a Preliminary Enquiry into the Origins and Character of the Ancient Chinese City*. Edinburgh: Edinburgh Univ. Press

Wheatley P. 1973. *The Golden Khersonese: Studies in the Historical Geography of the Malay Peninsula before* A.D. *1500*. Kuala Lumpur: Univ. Malaya Press

Wheatley P. 1983. *Nagara and Commandery: Origins of the Southeast Asian Urban Traditions*. Res. Pap. 207–208. Chicago: Dep. Geogr., Univ. Chicago

White JC. 1995. Incorporating heterarchy into theory on socio-political development: the case from Southeast Asia. In *Heterarchy and the Analysis of Complex Societies*, ed. RM Ehrenreich, CL Crumley, JE Levy, pp. 101–24. Washington, DC: Archeol. Pap. Am. Anthropol. Assoc. 6

White JC, Penny D, Kealhofer L, Maloney B. 2004. Vegetation changes from the late Pleistocene through the Holocene from three areas of archaeological significance in Thailand. *Quaternary Int.* 113:111–32

White JC, Pigott V. 1996. From community craft to regional specialization: intensification of copper production in prestate Thailand. In *Craft Specialization and Social Evolution: In Memory of V. Gordon Childe*, ed. B Wailes, pp. 151–75. Philadelphia: Univ. Mus. Archaeol. Anthropol., Univ. Penn.

Wolters OW. 1999. *History, Culture and Region in Southeast Asian Perspectives.* Ithaca, NY: SE Asia Program, Cornell Univ. Rev. ed.

Yamagata M. 1998. Formation of Lin Yi: internal and external factors. *J. SE Asian Archaeol.* 18:51–89

Yamagata M, Glover IC. 1994. Excavation at Buu Chau Hill, Tra Kieu, Quangnam-Danang Province, Vietnam, 1993. *J. SE Asian Archaeol.* 14:48–57

Yamagata M, Pham DM, Hoang BC. 2001. Western Han bronze mirrors recently discovered in central Vietnam. *Bull. Indo-Pac. Prehistory Assoc.* 21:99–106

Yang B. 2004. Horses, silver and cowries: Yunnan in global perspective. *J. World Hist.* 15:281–322

Yoffee N. 1997. The obvious and the chimerical: city-states in archaeological perspective. See Nichols & Charlton 1997, pp. 255–63

Yoffee N. 2005. *Myths of the Archaic State.* Cambridge: Cambridge Univ. Press

Creolization and Its Discontents

Stephan Palmié

Department of Anthropology, University of Chicago, Chicago, Illinois 60637;
email: palmie@uchicago.edu

Annu. Rev. Anthropol. 2006. 35:433–56

The *Annual Review of Anthropology* is
online at anthro.annualreviews.org

This article's doi:
10.1146/annurev.anthro.35.081705.123149

Copyright © 2006 by Annual Reviews.
All rights reserved

0084-6570/06/1021-0433$20.00

Key Words

culture, language, Caribbean region, globalization, theory

Abstract

In the past two decades, analogies drawn from supposedly Caribbean
processes of creolization have begun to command increasing interest
in anthropology. Examining historical as well as contemporary social
uses of this terminology in its region of origin, as well as linguistic,
sociocultural, and archaeological extrapolations from such usages,
this review argues that although, as an analytical metaphor, "creolization" may appear to remedy certain deficits in long-standing
anthropological agendas, the current unreflexive use of it is neither
defensible on empirical grounds nor theoretically well advised. Yet
while this review argues against further uncritical extensions of such
metaphorics, it analyzes their current proliferation as a social phenomenon worthy of anthropological analysis in its own right.

INTRODUCTION

Once exclusively part of the vocabulary of Caribbean and Latin American regionalists or linguists specializing in language contact, terms such as "creole" and "creolization" have recently experienced a remarkable diffusion into all kinds of discourses on "culture," local or global. Although this trend has been observable in other disciplines as well (most notably literary criticism, but also history[1]), as far as anthropology is concerned, the attractiveness of deploying generalized conceptions built on such terminology seems fairly obvious. Dovetailing with a variety of late-twentieth-century projects aiming to dismantle prior localizing strategies and ethnographic objectifications, the proliferation of concepts of "creolization" (along with related notions of "hybridity," "syncretism," and "mestizaje")[2] appeared to offer a theoretical opening toward a critique of certain foundational fictions of our discipline, while allowing for a characterization of presumably global "postmodern" conditions and sensibilities: As processes of globalization unravel what we previously imagined as a world of pelagic cultures and identities, and dissolve hitherto seemingly non-negotiable differences into intersystemic continua of hybrid forms and states of being, some of us are discovering that the postmodern "conditio humana" resembles what has been the "conditio Caribbeana"

since at least the sixteenth century (Mintz 1996, Trouillot 1998).[3] Thus, supposedly "creole" phenomena have been sighted in as different ethnographic and historical contexts as, for example, modern South India (Caplan 1995), the Solomon Islands (Jourdan 1996), and Stockholm's Botkyrka quarter (Hannerz 1996, pp. 150–59), among female immigrant entrepreneurs in Milan (Lunghi 2003), in the development of sport in Singapore (Horton 2001) as well as in that country's food industry (Davis 2003), during Catholic masses in Ibadan (Salamone 1991), among nineteenth-century U.S. Mormons (Rodseth & Olsen 2000), in Roman Gaul (Webster 2001), in aboriginal southern Australia (Birmingham 2000), and in late-eighteenth-century Haida society (Mullins & Paynter 2000), lending ostensible credence to Hannerz's (1987) assertion that the world is (or perhaps has always been) "in creolization."[4]

Of course, the portent of such discoveries would seem to depend on what semantic work predicates such as "creole," "creolized," or "in creolization" are expected to perform. Are they meant to index a distinct class or group of objectively occurring phenomena that can be unambiguously distinguished from other "noncreole," "uncreolized," or "-creolizing" ones on the basis of specifiable criteria (Gundaker 2000, Khan 2001)? Or are we dealing with the products of a perspectival shift generative of a "now you

---

[1]See for example the collections edited by Condé & Cottenet-Hage (1995), Balutansky & Sourieu (1998), Collier & Fleischmann (2003), Buisseret & Reinhardt (2000), or Shepherd & Richards (2002). This overlap is not insignificant because several of the authors frequently referenced in the anthropological literature are themselves writers and critics from the Caribbean (e.g., Brathwaite 1971, 1974, 1984; Glissant 1989; 1995, 1997; Bernabé et al. 1989; Benítez Rojo 1992, 1995; Nettleford 1978; Condé & Cottenet-Hage 1995).

[2]On which see, e.g., García Canclini (1990), Young (1995), Werbner & Modood (1997), Kapchan & Turner (1999), Brah & Coombes (2000), Stewart & Shaw (1994), Stewart (1999), Johnson (2002), Hale (1996, 1997, 1999), Smith (1995, 1996), Wade (1997), Poole (1997), Martínez Echazábal (1998), de la Cadena (2000) and Yelvington (2001).

[3]This became strikingly clear when, in 2002, the international art event Documenta 11 featured as one of its Platform a workshop on "Créolité and Creolization" held in St. Lucia (Enwezor et al. 2003). The Web is saturated with entries for "creolization": A Google search will generate some 26,000 instant hits (as of December 2004). There one can find such gems as a serious debate about whether liberal political philosophy is a "moral pidgin" or on its way to full-blown "creolization." (**http://www.ed.uiuc.edu/EPS/PES-yearbook/92_docs/Bull.HTM**)

[4]Perhaps one of the most curious applications of the term known to me can be found in a recent festschrift for Hannerz, in which the editors come close to vaunting that Hannerz himself is a creole phenomenon (Stade & Dahl 2003).

see it, now you don't" effect that reflects the specificity of changing form of awareness on our part, rather than the specificity of facts that have simply come under novel descriptions (Strathern 1992; Parkin 1993; Friedman 1994; Maurer 1997, 2002; compare Sahlins 1993, 1999)? Given the generally undertheorized use of creolization terminology, it is perhaps unsurprising that both views have been articulated. Although most authors favoring such language tend to fall toward one or the other end of a spectrum of analytical intentionalities, it may be fair to say that the deployment of this terminology is supposed to both generate novel analytical insights about a world we have long been accustomed to consider in other terms (think of Roman Gaul or the Mormons) and render more adequate descriptions of substantially "new" cultural configurations and developments than previous anthropological discursive conventions might have produced (think of Nigerians or Swedes watching American TV soaps).

In either case, however, current creolization discourse in anthropology recurs to a language rooted in highly specific geohistorical as well as intellectual contexts. It extrapolates localized and historically situated social usages (including more restricted scholarly abstractions thereof) and elevates them to the status of generalized descriptive or analytical instruments.[5] Different from terms such as "hybrid" or "syncretic" (but not "mestizo/a"!), there are people for whom the term creole has served as an immediately significant predicate (whether imposed or self-selected) of selfhood and social practice for close to half a millennium. People and practices so named were, and often still are, found in the core areas of European colonial overseas expansion, and so, at least arguably, in those regions which historically functioned as the cradle of global capitalist modernity (James 1963 [1939]; Williams 1944; Mintz 1971a, 1974, 1985, 1996; Gilroy 1993; Blackburn 1997)—a point to which I return below. A list of localities where people, at one time or another, have been called "creole" (or called themselves thus) would have to include not just the Antilles and much of Latin America, but also parts of the southeastern United States (and Alaska), several island groups off the Atlantic and Pacific coast of Africa, a number of mainland regions on that continent (including Sierra Leone, Equatorial Guinea, Angola, and Mozambique), and a few pockets in the former Portuguese and Dutch colonial spheres in southeast Asia. Yet the common point of reference in the contemporary literature tends to be the post-Columbian Caribbean. When Clifford (1988, p. 173) thus proposed—in what appears now to be one of the founding texts for contemporary "creolization" discourse—that "we are all Caribbeans now in our urban archipelagoes," he implied that "our" current world (and we should ask, who is this "we"?) has come to share important qualities or characteristics with the one(s) people in the Caribbean inhabit. Although Clifford did not explicitly say so, given the subsequent outpouring of literature coming to essentially similar conclusions, one might argue that what "we" now share with the "Caribbeans" is a common "creoleness"—whatever that may be taken to mean.

A META-ARCHIPELAGO?

As a result, the Caribbean region has seen a surprising transformation in relation to changing anthropological structures of interest: From a long-neglected (Mintz 1970, 1971a, 1977), seemingly anomalous (Trouillot 1992) net-importer of metropolitan theory (Appadurai 1986, 1988; Fardon 1991) and a distinctly low-prestige zone of anthropological inquiry (Abu-Lughod 1989) that, as late

---

[5]This is not to disparage such strategies of concept formation as a matter of principle: Unlike natural scientists whose objects of study cannot name themselves, anthropologists have no choice but to fight an uphill battle against interferences from vernacular nominalism. Nevertheless it may be well to recall here the history of concepts such as "mana," "tapu," "totem," "shaman," or "caste" (or, alternatively, "witchcraft," "politics," "the state," or "the economy") in our discipline.

as the early 1990s, had seemed to have been all but abandoned to developmental sociology and political science (Carnegie 1992), the Caribbean has mutated into a prime object of anthropological cathexis, a region that, for various and often unstated reasons, is now understood as an "open frontier" (Trouillot 1992) for an anthropology promising to deliver timely and relevant forms of "cultural criticism" as well as impulses for intradisciplinary theoretical renewal (Slocum & Thomas 2003). If the societies and cultures of the Caribbean never quite fit the "savage slot" (Trouillot 1991) so crucial for the development of anthropology's disciplinary identity—if they were never quite "other" enough, but rather perceived as odd and largely uninteresting "hybrid" formations, then it should not come as much of a surprise that once we began to abandon the strategies of epistemic purification that had once underwritten our intellectual practice (Latour 1993; compare Maurer 1997, Palmié 2002) their former "hybrid" irrelevance to the discipline's central concerns instantly transformed as well. Once regarded as insufficiently differentiated from the "West" to warrant ethnographic attention, just such attention to the "creolized" cultures of the Caribbean now seem to be warranted, not because these cultures have become any more different from ours in the meantime, but because we feel ours are becoming increasingly similar to theirs: "creolized, creolizing" as Hannerz (1988) put it in reference to the United States, a densely rhizomatic mangrove of potentialities (Bernabé et al. 1989, Glissant 1989) that irreversibly dissolves all rooted certainties into contingent routes toward indeterminate cultural futures (Clifford 1997).

At least in the view of most advocates of Caribbean analogies (but see Maurer 1997), we are now witnessing the birth of a world more adequately rendered by an ethnographic "poetics of relation," an analytics of "transversality" (Glissant 1997) and "traveling theory" more generally (Clifford 1997), than by those ideas of discretely distributed human cultural difference, which our discipline iron-ically managed to contribute to the identity politics characterizing self-consciously multicultural Western societies or those "postcolonies" in which identity politics and violent strategies of "disambiguation" increasingly appear to be capturing the public sphere. At the same time, the imagery of intermeshing networks of spatially dispersed economic and political relations and transcontinental flows of goods and people—so dear to theorists of globalization—appears to sit well with a region that literally emerged (as an entity culturally legible not just to the West but to its own post-Columbian inhabitants) only from the operation of what the historian Philip Curtin (1969) called the "South Atlantic system," and pithily defined as "a complex economic organism centered on the production in the Americas of tropical staples for the consumption in Europe and grown by the labor of Africans" (p. 3). Initial focus and early fulcrum of the capitalist world system, the Caribbean was literally remade by market forces. Within a century after the plantation complex had finally taken hold in the region (∼1650), most of its aboriginal population had succumbed to violence and disease and had been replaced by heterogeneous, demographically nonself-reproducing cohorts of migrants from three continents—few of whom arrived willingly, fewer of whom still stayed out of their own volition, and none of whom were able to transfer their previous world views and social practices unaltered (Mintz 1971a, Mintz & Price 1992). Yet precisely the tragic nature of this rootless, restless place where everything was always already new, necessarily made up on the spot, and "primordially syncretic" (Amselle 1998) now only imbues it with added value as a source of language resonant with our contemporary concerns. In fact, the peculiarly "modern" historicity and inevitable artificiality[6] of all that can count as "Caribbean culture" even appears to indicate a way out of

---

[6]As opposed to notions of "organic" cultural "growth" as a "natural" process rather than human "artifice" (compare Strathern 1992, Latour 1993, Maurer 1997).

the moral and political dilemma we created for ourselves when we began to arbitrate the authenticity or "inventedness" of others' cultures and pasts. Holding out the promise of "postauthentic pluralism" (Thomas 1996)— or, alternatively—that of "postplural" authenticity (Strathern 1992), at the current post-millennarian juncture things "Caribbean" and "creole" are, or so it seems, "good to think" for an anthropology questioning some of its own disciplinary foundations.

The result is not just that Caribbean creoleness is fast approaching the status of a "native category" among European and North American academics [indeed, Howes (1996) already speaks of a "creolization paradigm"]. Rather, as Sheller (2003) charges, what may be at work here could well consist in "theoretical piracy on the high seas of global culture" (p. 188). In her view, a whole range of "contemporary claims to mobility, hybridity, and creative cultural adaptation draw on Caribbean antecedents of 'creolization' [that are] borrowed via the work of Caribbean diaspora theorists, but gutted of many of the original connotations of the term" through metaphorical overextension to inappropriate conceptual domains and analytical contexts. Of course, the claim that some of the characteristics of peripheral societies and cultures, which once anticipated important features of modernity in the core (Mintz 1985, 1996), may also prefigure the symptomatology of modernity's global denouement is intriguing, although obviously not empirically debatable. Yet what clearly is emerging in contemporary anthropological creolization discourse is a system of interactive metaphors [in Black's (1962) sense, with all its implications of unforeseeable performativity and semantic hybridization][7]—one that allows for near unlimited, and in fact quite promis-

cuous, semantic transfer not just between "Caribbeanness" and "creoleness" (which increasingly are being treated as coextensive in the nonregionalist literature), but also between those predicates and others presumed to apply to the global "postmodern condition," such that an objectified hyperfluid and -flexible "Caribbean" indeed comes to function as the "meta-archipelago" (Benítez Rojo 1992) for "our urban archipelagos" where, in the eyes of some of our colleagues, the identification of all that seems to melt in the air is now the hallmark of epistemological solidity.

More concretely, the reasoning behind such metropolitan tropological uptake from this particular peripheral world would seem to go somewhat like this: Once (say, 30 years ago) phenomena (people and/or cultures) exhibiting essential quality x ("creoleness") were thought to exist only in region y (the Caribbean). Now we have either (a) changed our minds and regard their occurrence in y as merely an instance of a hitherto-overlooked class of phenomena that all exhibit quality x (and can so be identified irrespective of space and time, e.g., in the archaeological record, or contemporary Milan) or (b) come to realize that the distribution of individual cases of phenomena characterized by x is so steadily approaching ubiquity that x has increasingly become essential (or at least typologically salient) to a historically specific group of phenomena—e.g., those forming part of what Hannerz (1996) calls the "global cultural ecumene" of the late twentieth and early twenty-first centuries (compare Appadurai 1996, but see also Friedman 1995, Mintz 1996 and Cooper 2001). Irrespective, however, of the tint of logical irreconcilability exposed by formulating matters this way,[8] the immediately salient question is not only

---

[7]We should be clear in regard to what is being exported from the Caribbean: We are not dealing with full-fledged sets of explicit models—as in the well-known case where attempts to apply African kinship models to Melanesia not only did not deliver any cargo empirically, but irreversibly damaged lineage theory itself (compare Barnes 1962, Karp 1978). Rather, we are facing a far more amorphous con-

geries of evocative associations that are (largely) beyond empirical falsification.

[8]It might now be considered pedantic to note that membership in classes composed of instances implies something logically very different than belonging to groups composed of historical particulars. Boas (e.g., 1966 [1887], pp. 639–47) was still well aware that one cannot quite have it both ways and remain argumentatively consistent.

whether the recent anthropological creolization literature identifies a panhuman potentiality, or the (somehow comparable) local outcomes of a set of historically specific processes. The question is, instead, what has all or any of this to do with the Caribbean? Have we simply (re)invented the region under the sign of "creolization" (Khan 2001)?[9] And if not, how (if at all) might the regionalist literature support either claim [for both claims have, in effect, been made (compare, for example, Drummond 1980, Bernabé et al. 1989 or Glissant 1989, 1997 on universality with Williams 1991, Mintz 1996, or Price & Price 1997, Price 2001, and Hall 2003a,b on historical specificity)]. What then does the "creoleness" of the Caribbean consist in, and how has it been named and conceptualized?

REGIONALIST PERSPECTIVES: INDIGENIZATION, NOSTRIFICATION, ALTERITY, EXCLUSION

Two distinct, although historically interrelated, sources spring to mind here: first, the rich, but contradictory body of documented historical and contemporary usages on which anthropologists and historians working on the region initially performed largely untheorized extrapolations to categorize their data (e.g., Gillin 1947, 1949; Tschopik 1948; Simmons 1955; Pearse 1956; Adams 1959; Crowley 1960; Smith 1965; Goveia 1965 or even Brathwaite 1971); and second, an important body of theory linguists have, since at least the 1950s, erected on the "protolinguistic" observations of speech patterns preva-

lent in the region and elaborated on in a variety of equally diverse and often contradictory ways (see below). What seems to link them most closely is a sense of novelty and exceptionality, but one that, in both cases, was relational and contrastive rather than absolute. Right from the beginning, "the creole" was a figure on someone else's— oftentimes quite alien—conceptual ground. In the first instance, we thus see terms such as "criollo" emerging in the context of a metropolitan folk sociology within decades of the onset of Iberian colonization of the Americas: Although their etymology continues to be the subject of lively debates,[10] their first appearance in the documentary record tends to be traced to the early Spanish and Portuguese Atlantic. By the second half of the sixteenth century such terms began to designate fairly consistently the modifications that Old World life forms (i.e., people, plants, and animals, probably in that order) were perceived to undergo upon becoming "native" to the Americas, thus highlighting a certain sense of surprise at the plasticity of biotic and social forms (Boyd-Bowman 1971, Bacigalupo 1981, Brading 1991, Alberro 1992, Allen 1998, Cañizares Esguerra 1999, Schwartz & Salomon 1999, Oscar Acevedo 1999, Chaplin 2007, Stewart 2007, Palmié 2007). Although polemically charged from its inception, and burdened with speculations about climatic, astrological, or other environmental influences, for example, on the processes of differentiation between Old World populations and their New World progeny, such terminology tended more often to evoke its own antitheses (i.e., the uncreole Indian or metropolitan European) than to indicate specific properties on the part of people so qualified. What it certainly did not imply were notions of explicitly racial or ethnic difference and least of all any form of hybridity or mixedness—at least not before such

---

[9]Mintz's (1971a) magisterial and still eminently pertinent analysis of the Caribbean as a "sociocultural area" notwithstanding, Sheller (2003) may well have a point when she argues for a view of the Caribbean as a category integrated more by long histories of Western thought and social practice (including the legalities of colonial slavery, the consumption of Caribbean products, and forms of exoticistic desire that became attached to ideas about the region) than by any realities on Antillean grounds (compare Palmié 2002).

[10]See for example Arrom (1951), Corominas & Pascual (1980), Perl (1982), Stein (1982, 1998), Woll (1997), Warner-Lewis (1997), or Eckkrammer (2003).

terminology was snatched up by the rhetoric of Latin American liberators in search of post-colonial nations (Palmie 2007) or brought into conjunction with rigidly corporative (e.g., North American) ideologies of racial hypodescent (e.g., Domínguez 1986).[11] What early usages of "criollo" tend to connote is a sense of alterity from the metropolitan view and of indigenization or nostrification from that of self-identified peripherals; and on a vernacular level the term continues to hold such meaning to this day.[12] This is also the sense that such terminology continued to carry when diffusing, by the second half of the seventeenth century, into British (but not British North American) English and French as a referent to American-born Europeans and Africans and, at times, those real or imputed peculiarities that set both apart from first-generation migrants from the metropolis or newly imported slaves (Stein 1998, Chaudenson 2001, Chaplin 2007, Stewart 2007).

Here we note an important shift in local historical semantics, which current anthropological creolization discourse consistently tends to disregard or blur. By the end of the eighteenth century, and especially upon the founding of the first Latin American nation-states in the early nineteenth century, the

semantic cargo transported by the term criollo in continental American Spanish began to diverge dramatically from the older meanings it continued to hold in Spain's remaining Caribbean colonies, as well as those of other European nations. In the former case, it now begins to take on the ideological weight of designating the citizenship requirements of—theoretically as of yet unimaginable—nations composed of racially heterogeneous populations (a conundrum prevented in the United States by categorical exclusion of nonwhites from the national project). Especially in situations involving large and still corporately organized Native American communities, it begins to perform the exclusionary work once discharged by Spanish colonial estate-based legal disqualifications, although now in the service of the ostensibly egalitarian liberal ideologies of indigenized postcolonial elites of allogenic origin. Often but not always yoked to conceptions of a "mestizo nation" developed in reaction to the rise of biologistic racism in nineteenth-century Europe and North America, by the twentieth century, Latin American "criollismo" mutated into an "all inclusive ideology of exclusion" (Stutzman 1981), serving to demarcate supposedly "uncreole" collective identities defined by performative failure apposite locally varying ideals of prescriptive hybrid homogeneity and entailing severe restrictions of resource access, civic status, and political empowerment for those who whether by choice or default remain "pure," and so "outside the nation" (Stutzman 1981; Knight 1990; Casimir 1992; Klor de Alva 1995; Smith 1995; Hale 1996, 1999; Martínez-Echazábal 1998; de la Cadena 2000; Sabato 2001; Palmie 2007a).

Casimir (1992) sees such postcolonial ideological elaboration of concepts of "creoledom" as characteristic of those regions of mainland Ibero-America and the Hispanic Caribbean that became incorporated into the capitalist world system not just in the form of socially essentially unviable peripheral production sites based on the creative destruction

---

[11] Much confusion has been generated by hasty assimilations of the term criollo to the Spanish-American "casta"—terminology that essentially designated debased legal statuses within the "república de los Españoles" (as opposed to corporate Native American groups) and did draw on an older, although originally not racially but culturally conceived, notion of "limpieza de sangre" (compare Schwartz & Salomon 1999, Stallaert 2000, Silverblatt 2002).

[12] So that "comida criolla," for example, designates regional notions of "homestyle" cooking, i.e., a cuisine distinctly uncontaminated by foreign influence, or a "gallina criolla" is a chicken raised in one's backyard rather one bought in a store (compare Dawdy 2002, Schwegler 2003). In fact, as Schwegler notes, contemporary adjectival use of the term can express ideas of purity [as in "this animal is a genuine creole (i.e., local) breed, unmixed with others from abroad"] that do not sit well with our preconceptions about the term as a designator of heterogeneity and hybridity—unless we wanted to presume that the speakers have simply forgotten that their world is necessarily impure and mixed and mistake historical hybridity for present purity.

of coerced plantation labor (as was the case of much of the Caribbean), but that also functioned *both* as settler and exploitation colonies until the end of the colonial period and so generated early and lasting senses of local identity among indigenized migrant populations (compare Mintz 1971a,b; Klor de Alva 1995). Contrariwise, in the case of the non-Iberian Caribbean, Casimir (1992) suggests that the qualifier "creole" mainly designated a structural position: namely that of the island-born slave sufficiently socialized into the violent extractive process "of a societal project lacking any local base" and productive only of forms of social cohesion in "those social spaces which did not adversely affect the colonial exploitation system" (p. 44) (compare Smith 1965, Mintz & Price 1992, Palmié 1993).[13] To be sure, it was in precisely such marginal social spaces that enslaved Africans transformed themselves from mere collectivities of deracinated individuals into viable communities integrated by cultural forms that, although selectively drawing on Old World resources, were nevertheless wholly the products of locally eventuating and locally inflected histories of struggle (Mintz & Price 1992, Trouillot 1998, Price 2001). Also true is that in what to this day remains the most powerful attempt to model these processes of African American "culture building," Mintz & Price (1992) recurred to an analogy to the emergence of forms of verbal communication among slaves and maroons, which linguists have classified as "creole" languages (see below). Nonetheless, to call these cultures "creole" or "creolized" may be to retroject anachronistically a modern terminology.

Contemporaries rarely portrayed such emergent patterns of Afro-Caribbean social practice as "creole," i.e., "locally nostrified" developments, but tended to see them as African holdovers or the racially determined—and so principally alien—patterns of behavior on the part of members of structurally defined groups (such as island-born "creole" slaves or freedpeople). Even after the end of slavery, the term creole, in certain regions, remained long unclaimed as an intentional predicate of Afro-Caribbean collective identities associated with such cultural forms and instead merely continued to mark categories of subalterns in official discourse.

For these reasons, Mintz (1971b, p. 487) urged that the emergence of "creole" identities in the insular Caribbean be studied "comparatively and differentially." Yet his call for specificity has gone unheeded to this day. Instead, we see a massive blurring not just of modern and historical usages and meanings; even on a level of historical semantics, regional differences tend to get ironed out to, at times, genuinely obscurantist degrees. As Casimir (1992) charges, for example, transferring the postcolonial Latin American sense of "lo criollo" to the social institution and cultural form that emerged among the enslaved in the colonial Antilles would seem to imply "confusing the creations of the dominated ethnic groups with the adaptations of European institutions by the dominant ethnic group." It was only when, and to the extent that, the ending of the slave trade, emancipation, and the absolute decline of Caribbean plantation economies after the middle of the nineteenth century cut off the constant African input that had demographically stabilized Caribbean plantation societies and submitted their elites to a similarly irreversible localization process by undercutting their political power vis à vis the metropolis that we begin to see the emergence of rhetorical uses of creole terminology that superficially—but not historically—resemble those of the Iberoamerican world. And it is at this point that two distinct

---

[13] It may, thus, be no accident that the French term *créol* lost all its meaning as a referent to social identities in postrevolutionary Haiti, where the ending of the slave trade and the destruction of the plantation industry obliterated the structural foundations of distinctions between the foreign and the indigenized, and instead gave rise to more localized postcolonial regimes of domination and value extraction in which, as Mintz (1974, p. 271; compare Trouillot 1990) once put it, the physical appearance of the elite became a historical expression of its power.

but interrelated processes begin to impart specificity to local conceptions of Caribbean "creoleness." The first of these relates to—once more structurally grounded—differentiating (rather than homogenizing) semantic functions, which the terminology often acquired in the context of postemancipation attempts to inhibit the growth of landed but wage labor–dependent peasantries by large-scale importation of coerced Asian labor power. The second has to do with, as Bolland (1998; compare Thomas 2004) puts it, the absorption, in the twentieth century, of creolization discourse with its populist "emphasis upon the origins of a distinctive common culture as a basis for national unity" into the "ideology of a particular social segment, namely a middle class intelligentsia that seeks a leading role in an integrated, newly independent society" (p. 4).

In regard to the operation of the first of these semantic moments, we thus face a situation in which, in Drummond's (1980) words, the term creole begins to locally articulate with "generalized belief system[s] based on the principle of ethnic difference: the notion that the social setting is populated by distinct kinds of people, who are what they are as a consequence of inborn qualities or deeply held beliefs manifest in their everyday behavior and difficult or impossible to renounce" (p. 354). As Lowenthal (1972) once observed, in the contemporary Caribbean, attributions of "creoleness" evoke an entire spectrum of locally varying patterns of "ethnic" boundary maintenance:

> In Jamaica "Creole" designates anyone of Jamaican parentage except East Indians, Chinese, and Maroons (back-country descendants of runaway slaves, who are considered "African"). In Trinidad and Guyana it excludes Amerindians and East Indians; in Suriname it denotes the "civilized" coloured population, as apart from tribes of rebel-slave descent called Bush Negroes. In the French Antilles "Creole" refers more to local-born whites than to colored or black

persons; in French Guyana, by contrast, it is used exclusively for nonwhites. (p. 32)

Notionally highlighting endemic divisions rather than suggesting their transcendence even in its "native habitat," as a designator of Caribbean "identities," the term creole would thus appear to create but illusory contrasts to the seemingly more rigidly exclusionary folk typologies of human kinds and communities observed elsewhere.[14] Indeed, as Stewart (2007) wryly puts it, if "the world is in creolization the Caribbean, paradoxically, might have some catching up to do."

From a regionalist perspective, it is therefore not surprising that the first systemic bodies of social theory produced by scholars from the Caribbean who aimed to capture analytically the peculiarities, prospects, and predicaments of the region—the "plantation society" and "plural society" theories most closely associated with George Beckford (1972) and Lloyd Best (1968) in the first case and M.G. Smith (1965) and his persistent critic R.T. Smith (1967) in the second—emphasized not just lasting structural inequalities held in place by the region's global economic functions. They also foregrounded deep-seated cultural cleavages between population segments separated by complex hierarchies of race and class and united only in as far as systems of domination insured their participation in the one single institution they shared: the market. To be sure, the rigidity of both models has been roundly criticized.[15] Yet even the more optimistic "creole society" thesis initially

---

[14]Perhaps expectably, the creolization terminology has come under the most sustained criticism from students of Trinidad, where the descendants of Indian indentured laborers now not only form a demographic majority, but where such language, for historical as well as contemporary reasons, denotes either exclusion of Indo-Trinidadians from the national project or otherwise denigrates their identity in highly gender-specific ways (compare Mohammed 1988; Segal 1994; Reddock 1998; Gregg 2002; Munasinghe 2001; Khan 2001, 2004). See also Burton 1993 for the case of Martinique and Guadeloupe).

[15]For particularly astute treatments of this debate see Berleant-Schiller (1981) and Austin (1983).

associated with the Barbadian historian and poet Edward Kamau Brathwaite (1971, 1974, 1984) has come under severe criticism not just because, as Bolland (1998) argues, it lacks a consistent theoretical basis and so tends to pass over the very structural contradictions and social conflicts that engendered the formation of uniquely Caribbean cultural constellations in the first place, but also because it "has functioned in the interest of the powerful, whether represented by the colonial or nationalist elite" by ideologically organizing locally "[c]ompeting interests and relations of exploitation and privilege [. . .] in a fluid clinal system of racial and cultural hierarchy" that erases the historicity of, and synchronically normalizes, locally prevailing patterns "of allocation of economic, cultural, symbolic, and social values" in the ostensible service of national viability (Hintzen 2002, p. 477; compare Thomas 2004).

More damaging even is Williams's (1991) charge that Caribbean creolization rhetoric masks the strategic incorporation on the part of local elites of cultural forms associated with subordinate groups into self-consciously "creole" cultural projects, while not only continuing to marginalize the originators of such cultural forms but also excluding them from the national project if they resist such appropriation. Although focused on Guyana, her remarks hold equally true in the case of the Jamaican elite's protracted incorporation of symbols deriving from the Rastafari movement (Waters 1985, van Dijk 1988), for example, or the Cuban state's policy of belatedly laying claims on the nation's "African heritage" while suppressing the public circulation of signs of "blackness" when taken as emblematic of collective forms of identity (compare Moore 1997, Hansing 2001, Hagedorn 2001, Brown 2003, Fernandes 2003):

Under these conditions, those groupings associated with objects, acts, and ideas treated in this manner are placed at both a pragmatic and ideological disadvantage. If they continue to insist on the root identity [sic]

of their selves and the objects, acts, and ideas associated with those selves, they are not "true" members of the ideologically defined nation. (Williams 1991, p. 30)

Similarly troubling for those of us who expect creolization terminology to deliver the analytical "open specificity" (Bernabé et al. 1989) of a "Third Space" (Bhabha 1990) beyond both ideological capture and empiricist reductionism is the critique leveled by Burton (1993), Arnold (1994), Condé & Cottenet-Hage (1995), and Price & Price (1997) against the proponents of the Martiniquan literary "créolité" movement and the glottopolitical programmatics advanced through its academic incarnation GEREC (Groupe d'Études et de Recherches en Espace de la Créolophonie). In the views of these critics, the claim that Caribbean "créolité" (as launched in the manifesto *Éloge de la Créolité* by Bernabé et al.) designates a "new dimension of man, whose prefigured shadow we are," a "nontotalitarian consciousness of a preserved diversity" for which "complexity is the very principle of [. . .] identity" (Bernabé et al. 1989, p. 88) reflects the historically specific, ultimately provincial (and masculinist) concerns of a local intellectual elite operating within the context of a culturally highly homogeneous society that constitutes a *département* of France—and so effectively is a part of the European community with all the economic and cultural implications this political status entails. "Prospective and progressive in theory," writes Burton (1993), "Créolité is in practice often retrospective, even regressive, in character, falling back, *in a last desperate recourse against decreolization*, into the real or imagined creole plenitude of *an tan lontan* (olden times)" (p. 23, emphasis added) of a Martiniquan culture whose agricultural base "has been eroded beyond all possibility of restoration, leaving that culture—where it survives at all—increasingly bereft of any anchorage in the actual lived experience of contemporary French West Indians and, as such, subject to a fatal combination of folklorization, exoticization, and commodification" (pp. 7–8).[16] Hence Price & Price's (1997) vitriolic charge that the intensely politicized debates about linguistic practice (and particularly orthography) in Martinique represent a shadow-boxing match between an-organic intellectuals struggling to counteract the assimilatory effects contingent on the privileges of Martinique's departmental status and inclusion in the European Union. Constituting a "rhetorical wish list" rather than "an examination of creolization on the ground" (Khan 2001, p. 282), or offering a theoretically consistent analytics, the *Éloge* is perhaps better understood as an expression of a particular constellation of political and cultural contradictions specific to the French Départements d'Outre Mèr than as an empirically grounded analysis thereof—let alone anything that could easily be generalized beyond its contextual conditions of articulation.

As should be evident from even such a cursory examination of the history of terms such as "creole," "creolization," and "créolité," and their functionalization in indigenously Caribbean analytical and political projects, it is difficult to understand how—other than by retrospectively constructing a "Caribbean" of the (nonregionalist) anthropological imagination—we could ever have regarded the region as a "prototype" (in both temporal and evolutionary senses) of an allegedly global postmodern condition. Unless, that is, we understand—as Khan (2001) argues—"creolization's reputed specificity to the Caribbean" as "a particular fiction that invents the region" (p. 272) in the service of no less particular ideological and theoretical projects originating outside of it. But, of course, indigenously Caribbean conceptual

language is not the only source of the proliferating mangrove of metaphors in which anthropologists eager to transcend older descriptive and analytical vocabularies are casting about. Another powerful strain of "creolization" tropes has been emanating from a specific branch of linguistics for at least four decades now. Hence it is probably not accidental that, in his first influential formulation of what some of us now regard as a veritable "creolization paradigm," Hannerz (1987) recurred not to a single intellectual (or social scientist) from the Caribbean. Instead, his main sources of inspiration would seem to have been a brief formulation by Johannes Fabian (1978) who merely suggested exploring pidgin and creole linguistics as a source of theoretical inspiration in the study of African popular culture and a more ambitious text by Drummond (1980) that explicitly analogized a, then as now, hotly contested universalist theory of linguistic processes to similarly universalistically conceived cultural dynamics in the context of a Guyanese case study. And this, indeed—rather than the matrix of historical usage and limited ethnographic generalization—is where we, too, should look for some of the features that have made the metaphorics of "creolization" (for we really are dealing with intermeshing figures of speech rather than disciplined forms of comparison) so attractive to some of us.

UN-NATURAL LANGUAGES, CULTURAL GRAMMARS, FEEDBACK LOOPS

Restrictions of space do not permit an adequate exploration of the vast and highly contentious literature on linguistic theories of "creolization" and their transfer to social theory. However, linguists were, in fact, the first scholars who plucked the term creole from New World vernaculars and aimed to operationalize it as the designation of an analytically identifiable class of phenomena (rather than a mere congeries of historically contingent local "individualities," which, given

---

[16]Compare Segal (1994) for a similar argument concerning the disjunctions between Trinidadian perceptions of pluralism as the effect of a "particular memorialization of the past" and the island's historical and contemporary social and cultural realities. Hagedorn (2001) and Brown (2003) provide examples for the operation of a similar moment in contemporary Cuban cultural politics.

the above, tended to be the case in the ethnographic literature on Latin America and the Caribbean, at least until quite recently). Descriptive use of the term for linguistic phenomena arguably originates with Moravian lexicographical efforts in the eighteenth-century Danish West Indies (Stein 1998, Palmié 2007b). But it took at least another century before their missiologically motivated and entirely pragmatic adjectival usage of "creole" for the language of the heterogeneous population locally designated as "the Creoles"[17] became the basis for systematic efforts, on the part of scholars such as van Name, Coelho, or Schuchart, at classifying the languages developed by subaltern colonial populations and isolating them (from the rest of supposedly "natural" languages) as a theoretically salient anomaly.[18] In light of the conceptual linkages between language, culture, and peoplehood that had been gaining ground in Europe since the days of Condillac and Herder, these languages now not only appeared to disrupt those modern linguistic ideologies[19] that eventually came to undergird what Barth (1969, p. 11) once summed up as the traditional proposition that "a race = a culture = a language," but also significantly disturbed the reigning arboreal, proto-Darwinian metaphorics of an emergent historical linguistics, and did so precisely because their origin could not be retrojected into (even only a fictive Rousseauian) state of nature in which the "volksgeist" of a people became irrevocably attached to a homogeneous linguistic medium, subject only to gradual

and continuous evolutionary branching and change (Alter 1999; compare Olender 1992, Mufwene 2002).[20] Hence, far from stimulating a revaluation of postenlightenment conceptions of languages as "natural kinds" (or, at least, "objective" entities) discretely distributed in social space, creole linguistics was firmly anchored in precisely such conceptions right from the start: Whatever else studies of Caribbean (and other colonial) sociolects contributed to the linguistic enterprise before the 1950s largely consisted in isolating specific "linguistic defects" (from the viewpoint of the reigning evolutionary school of thought, that is) common to these seemingly anomalous and artificial subaltern vernaculars to characterize negatively what a "proper" language should look like, how it ought to be acquired, and who should be speaking it.

This initially descriptive and, at best, vaguely typologizing concept of languages associated with some (but by no means all!) populations designated as "creole" subsequently underwent rather thoroughgoing mutations. By the time the second international conference on creole linguistics was held in Mona (Jamaica) in 1968, the designator "creole" had become transformed in at least three distinct ways: It began to function as a classificatory device for isolating certain types of hybrid languages originating in colonial contexts; it became complemented by a novel nominalized verb form to represent the linguistic processes from which such languages emerged ("creolization"); and it attained analytical significance as a concept claimed by various theoretical "schools" purporting to explain the structural and phonological features of creole languages in relation to widely divergent

---

[17]Calling "criolisch" the language of the Creoles ("die Sprache der Criolen"), Oldendorp (1777, p. 232) thus obviously modeled the heterogeneous origins of the sociolect he was trying to codify in analogy to the heterogeneous origins of the population: Irrespective of their origins (in Africa or Europe), or their social positions (as slaves or free person), the creoles were of diverse origin. So were the linguistic forms in which they communicated.

[18]See Holm (1989, Ch. 2) for an introduction to the European "discovery" of creole languages.

[19]On which see LePage & Tabouret-Keller (1985), Crowley (1990), Olender (1992), Gal & Irvine (1995), Woolard (1998), Alter (1999), and DeGraff (2003).

---

[20]As Jourdan (1991, p. 189) sums up the matter in an important review of the state of creole linguistics in the late twentieth century, the way linguists "came to reify pidgins and creoles sufficiently to create homogenizing analytical tools and categories is without doubt linked to our intellectual tradition." But, she continues, this has nevertheless "led to a surprising conception of pidgins and creoles as a special group of languages, almost extraneous to the rest of human languages, those that are 'natural.'"

hypotheses about their origins.[21] This move from description to analysis undoubtedly was a fruitful one as far as linguistics is concerned. But it proved eminently problematic once anthropologists and historians began to import linguistic theory into their studies of what came to be called "creole cultures" and processes of "cultural creolization" as a sort of "magic bullet" (Briggs 2002). It is clear today that, no less than in the case of earlier theoretical borrowings from structural and transformative linguistics, the transposition of sequences initially postulated on a typological plane to the level of historical process created a massive confusion of analytical tongues.

Why this would have been the case is fairly obvious. Linguists, at least, seem well prepared to acknowledge that their attempts at generalizing about the genesis and development of creole languages as media of communicative praxis (rather than as abstract systems of phonological or morphosyntactical features) stand and fall with sociolinguistic inferences impossible to draw in the absence of detailed historical data. Referring to the so-called pidginization/creolization cycle, which, to this day, underlies most anthropological attempts to harness linguistic models to historicistically conceived questions of cultural dynamics, Holm (1989), for example, gingerly admits that the "process of *creolization* or *nativization* (by which a pidgin acquires native speakers) is still not completely understood, but it is thought to be the opposite of pidginization: a process of expansion rather than reduction" (p. 7, emphasis in the original). The problem here becomes immediately evident when one considers that reduction and expansion or complexification refer to logical sequences on a classificatory or taxonomic plane that cannot possibly be directly diachronized let alone mapped onto (empirically insufficiently known) his-

torical processes. How ironic, then, that the very typological transitions sociocultural anthropologists are aiming to "calque" (Silverstein 2005) were themselves initially formulated on the basis of speculative extrapolation from inadequately understood local histories.

Jourdan (1991) thus notes that in positing a seemingly predicable transition from highly restricted pidgins developed by speakers of mutually unintelligible languages to full-blow creoles among their descendants, linguists "relied heavily, and of necessity, on 'Just So' stories from the Caribbean and other plantation settings" (p. 192)—contexts in which concrete evidence of precisely such transformations is notoriously lacking. McWhorter (2000) consequently speaks of an "inevitable post hoc-ness in tracing the emergence of a creole" (p. 38) and suggests that the vague and ambiguous nature of the historical record for the Caribbean has given linguists near-unlimited interpretative leeway in concocting explanations for the presence or absence of creole languages in certain regions. Harris & Rampton (2002) likewise argue that the substratist-universalist debate is based in speculative theorizing and ideological contention driven by a "search for *total* explanation, licensed by the paucity of the historical record" (p. 35) and marked by widespread reification of language as mere "system output" rather than as the product of historically contextualized human communicative agency. Their conclusion about the usefulness of creolization as a conceptual tool in social and historical analysis comes as no surprise: "[T]here do seem to be good grounds for doubting the value of traditional creole language study as a ground-breaking model or template for the analysis of cultural contact" (Harris & Rampton 2002, p. 38).[22]

---

[21] See DeCamp (1971) for a fairly balanced overview of the issues involved at the time when anthropologists first began to borrow explicitly from creole linguistics.

[22] This is to say nothing about the opinions of those creolists who are now arguing that the creole language/creolization concepts have overreached or exhausted their usefulness for linguists (e.g., Sankoff 1983 and Muysken 1988, both cited in Jourdan 1991, p. 191; Mufwene 1997; Parkvall 2002).

Painful as this may be to those of us who rely on linguistically derived modeling devices for ordering their data, the fact is that linguistic theories of creolization now do not stand and fall on the kind of abstract predictive potential we expect from them when we import them into our work, but rather thrive on the sketchy and oftentimes rather problematic primary data linguists in turn cull from the anthropological and historical literature. Bakker (2002) thus laments that creole genesis scenarios, in many instances, are "purely speculative, but they are quoted as fact by other creolists" (p. 75) and exasperatedly charges that creolists "should be forbidden from making any claims on history or life on plantations without reference to the work of historians" (p. 75). The trouble is, however, that those historians may already have been reading creolist texts. For what we are facing is a strange cross-disciplinary feedback loop in which anthropologists and historians recycle as theory the speculations linguists generate from anthropological and historical data increasingly produced and organized on the basis of linguistic hypotheses.[23]

Perhaps predictably, this is most glaringly evident in the study of Caribbean and, more generally, African American cultures. Here the moment of theoretical "calquing" goes all the way back to the Herskovits' (Herskovits & Herskovits 1936, pp. 114–35; Herskovits 1941, pp. 280–81) initial supposition that "substrate" theories about how African linguistic structures (of wider or narrower definition) provided the morphoyntactical and phonological molds into which European lexical items were poured ("superlexification") could help account for the features ('traits') shared among geographically dispersed African American cultures (compare Palmié 2007b). Given the metatheoretical linkages Boas himself had established between language and culture (Briggs 2002, Silverstein 2005), it was only a small step down a well-prepared metaphorical slope for Herskovits to assert the comparability of the "similarities in the grammar of language over the entire West African region with what may be termed the *grammar of culture*, one finds in a similar situation [i.e., in the same 'culture area']" (p. 281, emphasis added). Variously picked up by linguists (e.g., Turner 1949, Hall 1950) who, by the 1950s, had begun a vigorous debate about the viability of "substrate" hypotheses,[24] elements of this conception ironically gained a new lease on life in cultural anthropology when, in the early 1970s, Mintz & Price (1992 [1976]) launched a thoroughgoing methodological critique of prior scholarship on the historical anthropology of African American cultures. Arguing from sociological and historicist perspectives Mintz & Price strongly emphasized processually induced discontinuities in Atlantic cultural transmission and the importance of New World syntheses in the creation of those cultural forms that came to integrate African American communities (Yelvington 2001, Palmié 2007b). Yet while they dealt a vigorous blow to Neo-Herskovitsian searches for New World "Africanisms" based merely on the comparison of decontextualized data from both sides

---

[23] This irony is compounded in the following statement by a linguist whose work does not always evidence particular fastidiousness in his use of historical and ethnographic materials himself: " . . . [I]n terms of our knowledge of creole cultures, we are precisely where we were with creole languages a century ago. The absence of reliable descriptions of these cultures, and our ignorance of the sociohistorical conditions of creolization and the terminus a quo, are such that anyone at all can say whatever he or she pleases about creole cultures. As a result, purely ideological positions, which are harder and harder to defend in the linguistic domain, have been freely advanced in the domain of culture, where everybody believes they can dream or wander as they please" (Chaudenson 2001, p. 196).

[24] Substrate-influence arguments had been launched in linguistics at least since the late 1920s. The most spectacular case certainly was that of the Haitian linguist Suzanne Sylvain who, in 1936, famously described Haitian creole as "an Ewe language with a French vocabulary" (Holm 1989, p. 37). For the debate ensuing after ~1950, see, e.g., DeCamp (1971, p. 20), Alleyne (1980), Muysken & Smith (1986), Holm (1989, pp. 37–44), Arends et al. (1995), Arends (2002).

of the Atlantic, they nevertheless revived the notion that widely shared "deep structural" or "grammatical" principles of generalized West African provenance had been operative in the formation of African American cultures.[25] Perhaps wisely, Mintz & Price never mentioned the word "creolization" in the original text of their contribution (but see the preface of the 1992 edition and Price 2001). Yet such was the tenor of the stream of metaphors busily interacting at the interface of linguistics and cultural anthropology since Herskovits' time that their call for a rigorous historicization of African Americanist scholarship was almost immediately assimilated to (oftentimes highly bowdlerized) versions of linguistic substrate theory.

Although historians of North American slavery were first to succumb to the power of the linguistic metaphors Mintz & Price appeared to have put at their disposal (see the literature cited in Palmié 2007b), archaeologists soon followed suit. In a surprisingly influential formulation, Ferguson (1992) thus suggested that in "cultural creolization" processes, "material things are part of the lexicon of culture while the ways they were made, used, perceived are part of the grammar" (p. xlii). It is, of course, not inconceivable to represent object distributions metaphorically as a kind of vocabulary sample of material culture. Yet it is hard to see how the large number of unknowns involved in archaeological inference about use (let alone meaning) could possibly lead to an understanding of a body of formal rules governing the syntactical articulation of objects independent of the particular "utterances" represented by a specific site—unless, that is, an independently preconceived "grammar" (culled, in this case, from African ethnography) governs the organization of data in the first place. Singleton (1995), who is by no means unsympathetic to Ferguson's approach, thus readily admits that it deliberately

overplays certain types of evidence and may not, after all, represent "the best approach to understanding the archaeological record of many African-American sites" (p. 133). Nevertheless, even a cursory glance at the "creolization" literature produced in this field makes clear that the genie is out of the bottle. Not only is "creolization" the subject of a recent special issue of *Historical Anthropology* (Dawdy 2000a), but it is also rapidly diffusing out of its geohistorical context of origin, having reached, as of now, Roman Gaul (Webster 2001) and aboriginal Australia (Birmingham 2000). No doubt, some of these newer archaeological deployments of the creolization metaphor are far more subtle than Ferguson's crude analogy to dubious linguistics, and often express criticism of the decontextualizing, reductionist, and ultimately depoliticizing tendencies inherent in "creole" metaphorics (e.g., Ewen 2000, Dawdy 2000b, Gundaker 2000, Armstrong 2003). But they nevertheless raise troubling questions about the velocity of feedback within the interdisciplinary metaphoric loops in which "creolization" research has become entangled. Once processed by one discipline or subfield, what is now occasionally still recognized as linguistically inspired output in history, archaeology and cultural anthropology may well attain the status of data input in those branches of creole linguistics dependent on precisely the kinds of "primary data" historians, cultural anthropologists, and archaeologists are cobbling together on the basis of outmoded, and sometimes ill-understood, linguistic hypotheses.

CONCLUSION: BACK TO (HUMAN) NATURE?

There remains, of course, a final position to consider, and it allows me to return to the question about universalism and historical particularism raised at the beginning of this review. It is probably not accidental that most cultural anthropologists keen on theorizing about "creolization" (with the notable exception of Drummond 1980) have steered clear

---

[25] For a fuller treatment of their pathbreaking contribution and its—all but unproblematic—reception in African Americanist scholarship, see Palmié (2007b).

of literal transpositions of Bickerton's (e.g., 1981, 1984) so-called "language bioprogram hypothesis" to the cultural level. This may be the case because we have increasingly become wary of "human universals." Given our discipline's long history of ideological complicity in the normalization of peculiarly Western folk anthropologies as "human nature," and given also our current skepticism toward totalizing analytical narratives more generally, it may, perhaps, be perceived as not altogether surprising that even the staunchest advocates of extending a "creolization" terminology to the ends of the earth appear reluctant to follow up fully the implications of Bickerton's original formulation—or even to take Drummond at his word when he suggested that once rigorously conceptualized along Bickertonian lines we may, in fact, no longer be able to speak of separate cultures. Once we let go of the conceit of, even only analytically, separable cultures (or languages, for that matter) and treat cultures and languages as artificially reified instances of variations produced by humanity's universal faculty to symbolize in infinitely diverse ways, we *eo ipso* lose purchase on all senses in which we could use the term "creolization" to express anything (we feel is) novel about the particular world we inhabit. Once viewed from the perspective of the inevitable continua of meaningful communicative forms produced by humanity's innate signifying capacity, precisely those criteria that some hold as indicative of our world's being "in creolization" would ultimately reduce to those that differentiate *Homo sapiens sapiens* from other higher primates. If so, there would be no surprise in anyone's discovery of "creolization" processes in, say, Ulan Bator and Kinshasa—or in Minoan Crete and Pre-Incan Highland South America, for that matter.

Chances are that such discoveries are merely a matter of time. If so, however, it may behoove us to rethink the very epistemological grounds on which such "discoveries" could become distinguishable from—or enabled by—"normal science" in the first place. The matter arguably boils down to a metatheoretical question of conceptual politics, which *mutatis mutandis* bespeaks the inevitable politicization of concepts at the interface not just between intra- and interdisciplinary discourses but also between extradisciplinary ones as well. If we accept that entities called languages or cultures are themselves sociocultural constructs that are "only stable—hence, when perduring, classifiable—outcomes of dialectical valorization processes among populations of people," including anthropological communities of discourse (Silverstein 1998, p. 402), then the question of what "creolization" metaphors (whether of "Caribbean" or "linguistic" tenor) can or cannot do for us needs to be rephrased. This is so not only because the figure of the universal, hence boundless, "postplural" creole continuum exposes to "unmarked" indeterminacy the nature-culture distinction on which cultural anthropology has long built its fiction of cultures as discretely speciating artifacts natural to the human condition (Strathern 1992, Maurer 1997) but also because it throws into sharp relief the nature of those discriminating technologies by which those differences that make a difference within institutionally anchored structures of awareness are established and authorized. Viewed thus, "creolization theory" (whatever that may be) is neither a remedy for the alleged or real reifications of an older anthropology construed as a postmodern whipping boy nor an effective antidote against the kind of contemporary "culture talk" among metropolitan intellectuals at both ends of the political spectrum; least of all is it anything that we ought to project carelessly into peripheral scenarios—whether such language has played an explicitly politicized role there or not. This is so, because "creolization theory" is ultimately a mere reflex of the very conditions it seeks to denounce and supercede—and so, once properly conceptualized, might itself be more profitably regarded as an object of, rather than a tool for, anthropological inquiry.

ACKNOWLEDGMENTS

Comments on earlier versions of this review were generously offered by Greg Beckett, Jean Comaroff, Kesha Fikes, Robert Hill, Aisha Khan, Sidney Mintz, Salikoko Mufwene, Michael Silverstein, Charles Stewart, and Bonno Thoden van Velzen. Responsibility for all errors and misrepresentations rests with me.

LITERATURE CITED

Abu-Lughod L. 1989. Zones of theory in the anthropology of the Arab World. *Annu. Rev. Anthropol.* 18:267–306

Adams RN. 1959. On the relation between plantation and "Creole" cultures. In *Plantation Systems of the New World*, ed. V Rubin, pp. 73–79. Washington, DC: Pan Am. Union

Alberro S. 1992. *Del Gachupín al Criollo. O de Cómo los Españoles de México Dejaron de Serlo.* México, DF: El Col. Méx.

Allen C. 1998. Creole then and now: the problem of definition. *Caribb. Q.* 44:33–49

Alleyne MC. 1980. *Comparative Afro-American.* Ann Arbor, MI: Karoma

Alter SG. 1999. *Darwinism and the Linguistic Image.* Baltimore, MD: The Johns Hopkins Univ. Press

Amselle JL. 1998. *Mestizo Logics.* Stanford, CA: Stanford Univ. Press

Anderson B. 1983. *Imagined Communities.* London: Verso

Appadurai A. 1986. Theory in anthropology: center and periphery. *Comp. Stud. Soc. Hist.* 28:356–61

Appadurai A. 1988. Putting hierarchy in its place. *Cult. Anthropol.* 3:36–49

Appadurai A. 1996. *Modernity at Large.* Minneapolis: Univ. Minn. Press

Arends J. 2002. The historical study of Creoles and the future of Creole studies. See Gilbert 2002, pp. 48–68

Arends J, Kouwenberg S, Smith N. 1995. Theories focussing on the non-European input. In *Pidgins and Creoles*, ed. J Arends, P Muysken, N Smith, pp. 99–109. Amsterdam: Benjamins

Armstrong DV. 2003. *Creole Transformations from Slavery to Freedom.* Gainesville: Univ. Fla. Press

Arnold JA. 1994. The gendering of *créolité*: the erotics of Colonialism. *New West Indian Guide* 68:5–22

Arrom JJ. 1951. Criollo: definición y matices de un concepto. *Hispania* 34:172–76

Austin D. 1983. Culture and ideology in the English-speaking Caribbean: a view from Jamaica. *Am. Ethnol.* 19:223–40

Bacigalupo MH. 1981. *A Changing Perspective.* London: Thamesis

Bakker P. 2002. Some future challenges to Pidgin and Creole studies. See Gilbert 2002, pp. 69–92

Balutansky K, Sourieu MA, eds. 1998. *Caribbean Creolization.* Gainesville: Univ. Fla.

Barnes JA. 1962. African models in the New Guinea Highland. *Man* 62:5–9

Baron R, Cara AC, eds. 2003. Introduction: creolization and folklore—cultural creativity in process. *J. Am. Folk.* 116(459):4–8

Barth F. 1969. Introduction. In *Ethnic Groups and Boundaries: The Social Organization of Culture Difference*, ed. F Barth, pp. 1–38. Boston: Little, Brown

Beckford G. 1972. *Persistent Poverty: Underdevelopment in Plantation Economies of the Third World.* New York/London: Oxford Univ. Press

Benítez Rojo A. 1992. *The Repeating Island.* Durham, NC: Duke Univ. Press

Benítez Rojo A. 1995. The polyrhythmic paradigm: the Caribbean and the postmodern era. In *Race, Discourse, and the Origin of the Americas*, ed. VL Hyatt, R Nettleford, pp. 255–67. Washington, DC: Smithson. Inst. Press

Berleant-Schiller R. 1981. Plantation society and the Caribbean present. Part I: History, anthropology. *Plant. Soc. Am.* 1:387–409

Bernabé J, Chamoiseau P, Confiant R. 1989. *Éloge de la créolité/In Praise of Creoleness*. Paris: Gallimard

Best L. 1968. Outlines of a model of pure plantation economy. *Soc. Econ. Stud.* 17:283–326

Bhabha HK. 1990. The third space. In *Identity: Community, Culture, Difference*, ed. J Rutherford, pp. 207–21. London: Lawrence & Wishart

Bickerton D. 1981. *Roots of Language*. Ann Arbor, MI: Karoma

Bickerton D. 1984. The language bioprogram hypothesis. *Behav. Brain Sci.* 7:173–221

Birmingham J. 2000. Resistance, creolization or optimal foraging at Killalpaninna Mission, South Australia. In *The Archaeology of Difference*, ed. R Torrence, A Clarke, pp. 360–405. New York: Routledge

Black M. 1962. *Models and Metaphor*. Ithaca, NY: Cornell Univ. Press

Blackburn R. 1997. *The Making of New World Slavery*. London: Verso

Boas F. 1966 (1887). The study of geography. In *Race, Language and Culture*. New York: Free Press

Bolland NO. 1998. Creolization and Creole societies: a cultural nationalist view of Caribbean social history. *Caribbean Q.* 44:1–32

Boyd-Bowman P. 1971. *Léxico Hispanoamericano del Siglo XVI*. London: Tamesis

Brading DA. 1991. *The First America*. Cambridge, UK: Cambridge Univ. Press

Brah A, Coombes AE, eds. 2000. *Hybridity and Its Discontents*. London: Routledge

Brathwaite EK. 1971. *The Development of Creole Society in Jamaica, 1770–1820*. Oxford: Clarendon

Brathwaite EK. 1974. *Contradictory Omens: Cultural Diversity and Integration in the Caribbean*. Mona, Jamaica: Savacou

Brathwaite EK. 1984. *History of the Voice: The Development of Nation Language in Anglophone Caribbean Literature*. London/Port of Spain: New Beacon

Briggs C. 2002. Linguistic magic bullets in the making of a modernist anthropology. *Am. Anthropol.* 104:481–98

Brightman R. 1995. Forget culture: replacement, transcendence, relexification. *Cult. Anthropol.* 10:509–46

Brown DH. 2003. *The Light Inside: Abakuá Society Arts and Cuban Cultural History*. Washington, DC: Smithson. Inst. Press

Buisseret D, Reinhardt SG, eds. 2000. *Creolization in the Americas*. College Station: Tex. A&M Univ. Press

Burton RDE. 1993. *Ki moun nou yé?* The idea of difference in contemporary French West Indian thought. *New West Indian Guide* 67:5–32

Cañizares Esguerra J. 1999. New world, new stars: patriotic astrology and the invention of Indian and Creole bodies in Colonial Spanish America, 1600–1650. *Am. Hist. Rev.* 104:33–68

Caplan L. 1995. Creole world, purist rhetoric: Anglo-Indian cultural debates in colonial and contemporary Madras. *J. R. Anthropol. Inst.* 1:743–62

Carnegie C. 1992. The fate of ethnography: native social science in the English-speaking Caribbean. *New West Indian Guide* 66:5–26

Casimir J. 1992. *The Caribbean: One and Divisible*. Santiago, Chile: UN Comm. Latin Am. Caribbean

Chaplin J. 2007. Creoles in British America: from denial to acceptance. See Stewart 2007. In press

Chaudenson R. 2001. *Creolization of Language and Culture*. London: Routledge

Clifford J. 1988. *The Predicament of Culture*. Cambridge, MA: Harvard Univ. Press

Clifford J. 1997. *Routes: Travel and Translation in the Late Twentieth Century*. Cambridge, MA: Harvard Univ. Press

Collier G, Fleischmann U, eds. 2003. *A Pepper Pot of Cultures: Aspects of Creolization in the Caribbean. Matatu* 27/28 (Spec. Issue)

Condé M, Cottenet-Hage M, eds. 1995. *Penser La Créolité*. Paris: Karthala

Cooper F. 2001. What is the concept of globalization good for. An Africanist historian's perspective. *Afr. Aff.* 100:189–213

Corominas J, Pascual JA. 1980. *Diccionario Crítico Etimológico Castellano Hispánico*. Madrid: Gredos

Crowley DJ. 1960. Cultural assimilation in a multiracial society. *Ann. NY Acad. Sci.* 83:850–54

Crowley T. 1990. That obscure object of desire: a science of language. In *Ideologies of Language*, ed. JE Joseph, TJ Taylor, pp. 27–50. London: Routledge

Curtin PD. 1969. *The Atlantic Slave Trade*. Madison: Univ. Wis. Press

Davis T. 2003. Creolization or prodigalization? The many avatars of an Indo-Singaporean food consumptionscape. *Adv. Consum. Res.* 30:284–88

Dawdy SL, ed. 2000a. Creolization. *Hist. Archaeol.* 34, No. 3, Fall (Spec. Issue)

Dawdy SL. 2000b. Understanding cultural change through the vernacular: Creolization in Louisiana. *Hist. Archaeol.* 34:107–23

Dawdy SL. 2002. La comida mambisa: food, farming, and Cuban identity, 1839–1999. *New West Indian Guide* 76:47–80

DeCamp D. 1971. Introduction: the study of Pidgin and Creole languages. See Hymes 1971, pp. 13–39

DeGraff M. 2003. Against Creole exceptionalism. *Language* 79:391–410

de la Cadena M. 2000. *Indigenous Mestizos*. Durham, NC: Duke Univ. Press

Domínguez VA. 1986. *White By Definition*. New Brunswick, NJ: Rutgers Univ. Press

Drummond L. 1980. The cultural continuum: a theory of intersystems. *Man* 15:352–74

Eckkrammer EM. 2003. On the perception of 'Creole' language and identity in the Netherlands Antilles. See Collier & Fleischmann 2003, pp. 85–108

Enwezor O, Basualdo C, Bauer UM, Ghez S, Maharaj S, et al., eds. 2003. *Creolité and Creolization: Documenta 11 Platform 3*. Kassel: Documenta

Ewen CR. 2000. From colonist to Creole: archaeological patterns of Spanish colonialism in the New World. *Hist. Archaeol.* 34:36–45

Fabian J. 1978. Popular culture in Africa: findings and conjectures. *Africa* 48:315–34

Fardon R. 1991. Localizing strategies: the regionalization of ethnographic accounts. In *Localizing Strategies*, pp. 1–35. Washington, DC: Smithson. Inst. Press

Ferguson L. 1992. *Uncommon Ground*. Washington, DC: Smithson. Inst. Press

Fernandes S. 2003. Fear of a Black Nation: local rappers, transnational crossings, and state power in contemporary Cuba. *Anthropol. Q.* 76:575–608

Friedman J. 1994. *Cultural Identity and Global Process*. London: Sage

Friedman J. 1995. Global system, globalization, and the parameters of modernity. In *Global Modernities*, ed. M Featherstone, S Lash, R Robertson, pp. 69–90. London: Sage

Gal S, Irvine JT. 1995. The boundaries of languages and disciplines: how ideologies construct difference. *Soc. Res.* 62:967–1001

García Canclini N. 1990. *Culturas Híbridas: Estrategías Para Entrar y Salir De La Modernidad*. Mexico: Grijalbo

Gilbert G, ed. 2002. *Pidgin and Creole Studies in the Twenty-First Century*. New York: Lang

Gillin J. 1947. *Moche: A Peruvian Coastal Community*. Washington, DC: Smithson. Inst., Inst. Soc. Anthropol., Publ. No. 3

Gillin J. 1949. Mestizo America. In *Most of the World*, ed. R Linton, pp. 156–211. New York: Columbia Univ. Press

Gilroy P. 1993. *The Black Atlantic*. Cambridge, MA: Harvard Univ. Press

Glissant E. 1989. *Caribbean Discourse*. Charlottesville: Univ. Va. Press

Glissant E. 1995. Creolization in the making of the Americas. In *Race, Discourse, and the Origins of the Americas*, ed. V Lawrence Hyatt, R Nettleford, pp. 268–75. Washington, DC: Smithson. Inst. Press

Glissant E. 1997. *Poetics of Relation*. Ann Arbor: Univ. Mich. Press

Goveia E. 1965. *Slave Society in the British Leeward Islands at the End of the Eighteenth Century*. New Haven: Yale Univ. Press

Gregg V. 2002. Yuh know bout coo-coo? Where yuh know bout coo-coo? Language and representation, creolization and confusion in 'Indian Cuisine'. See Shepherd & Richards 2002, pp. 148–64

Gundaker G. 2000. Discussion: Creolization, complexity, and time. *Hist. Archaeol.* 34:124–33

Hagedorn K. 2001. *Divine Utterances: The Performance of Afro-Cuban Santería*. Washington, DC: Smithson. Inst. Press

Hale CR. 1996. Mestizaje, hybridity, and the cultural politics of difference in post-revolutionary Central America. *J. Latin Am. Anthropol.* 2:34–61

Hale CR. 1997. Cultural politics of identity in Latin America. *Annu. Rev. Anthropol.* 26:567–90

Hale CR. 1999. Travel warning: elite appropriations of hybridity, mestizaje, antiracism, equality, and other progressive-sounding discourses in Highland Guatemala. *J. Am. Folk.* 112:297–315

Hall RA. 1950. The African substratum in Negro English: a review of Turner 1949. *Am. Speech* 25:51–54

Hall S. 2003a. Creolité and the process of Creolization. See Enwezor et al. 2003, pp. 27–41

Hall S. 2003b. Creolization, diaspora, and hybridity in the context of globalization. See Enwezor et al. 2002, pp. 185–98

Hannerz U. 1987. The world in Creolization. *Africa* 57:546–59

Hannerz U. 1988. American culture: Creolized, creolizing. In *North American Studies*, ed. E Asard, Rep. 4, pp. 7–30. Uppsala, Sweden: Uppsala Univ.

Hannerz U. 1992a. *Cultural Complexity*. New York: Columbia Univ. Press

Hannerz U. 1992b. The global ecumene as a network of networks. In *Conceptualizing Society*, ed. A Kuper, pp. 34–56. London: Routledge

Hannerz U. 1996. *Transnational Connections*. New York: Routledge

Hansing K. 2001. Rasta, race and revolution: transnational connections in socialist Cuba. *J. Ethnic Migr. Stud.* 27:733–47

Harris R, Rampton B. 2002. Creole metaphors in cultural analysis: on the limits and possibilities of (socio-) linguistics. *Crit. Anthropol.* 22:31–51

Herskovits MJ. 1941. *The Myth of the Negro Past*. New York: Harper

Herskovits MJ, Herskovits FS. 1936. *Suriname Folk-Lore*. New York: Columbia Univ. Press

Hintzen PC. 2002. The Caribbean: race and creole ethnicity. In *A Companion to Racial and Ethnic Studies*, ed. DT Goldberg, J Solomos, pp. 475–94. Oxford: Blackwell

Holm JA. 1989. *Pidgins and Creoles*. Cambridge, UK: Cambridge Univ. Press

Horton PA. 2001. Complex creolization: the evolution of modern sport in Singapore. *Eur. Sports Hist. Rev.* 3:77–104

Howes D. 1996. Introduction: commodities and cultural borders. In *Cross-Cultural Consumption: Global Markets, Local Realities*, ed. D Howes, pp. 1–16. London: Routledge

Hymes D, ed. 1971. *Pidginization and Creolization of Languages*. Cambridge, UK: Cambridge Univ. Press

James CLR. 1963 (1939). *The Black Jacobins*. New York: Random House

Johnson PC. 2002. Migrating bodies, circulating signs: Brazilian Camdomblé, the Garifuna of the Caribbean, and the category of Indigenous religion. *Hist. Relig.* 41:301–27

Jourdan C. 1991. Pidgins and Creoles: the blurring of categories. *Annu. Rev. Anthropol.* 20:187–209

Jourdan C. 1996. Where have all the cultures gone? In *Melanesian Modernities*, ed. J Friedman, JG Carrier, pp. 34–52. Lund: Lund Univ. Press

Kapchan DA, Turner Strong P, eds. 1999. Theorizing the hybrid. *J. Am. Folk.* 112(445):239–53

Karp I. 1978. New Guinea models in the African Savannah. *Africa* 48:1–16

Khan A. 2001. Journey to the center of the Earth: the Caribbean as master symbol. *Cult. Anthropol.* 16:271–302

Khan A. 2004. *Callaloo Nation: Metaphor of Race and Religious Identity among South Asians in Trinidad*. Durham, NC: Duke Univ. Press

Klor de Alva JJ. 1995. The postcolonization of the (Latin) American experience: a reconsideration of 'colonialism', 'postcolonialism', and 'mestizaje'. In *After Colonialism*, ed. G Prakash, pp. 241–78. Princeton, NJ: Princeton Univ. Press

Knight A. 1990. Racism, revolution, and Indigenismo: Mexico, 1910–1940. In *The Idea of Race in Latin America*, ed. R Graham, pp. 71–113. Austin: Univ. Tex. Press

Latour B. 1993. *We Have Never Been Modern*. Cambridge, MA: Harvard Univ. Press

LePage R, Tabouret-Keller A. 1985. *Acts of Identity: Creole-Based Approaches to Language and Ethnicity*. Cambridge, UK: Cambridge Univ. Press

Lowenthal D. 1972. *West Indian Societies*. Oxford: Oxford Univ. Press

Lunghi C. 2003. *Culture Creole: Imprenditrici Straniere a Milano*. Milano: Franco Angeli

Martínez-Echazábal L. 1998. Mestizaje and the discourse of national/cultural identity in Latin America, 1845–1959. *Latin Am. Res. Rev.* 25:21–42

Maurer B. 1997. *Recharting the Caribbean*. Ann Arbor: Univ. Mich. Press

Maurer B. 2002. Fact and fetish in Creolization studies: Herskovits and the problem of induction, or, Guinea Coast, 1593. *New West Indian Guide* 76:5–22

McWhorter JH. 2000. *The Missing Spanish Creoles*. Berkeley: Univ. Calif. Press

Mintz SW. 1970. Foreword. In *Afro-American Anthropology*, ed. NE Whitten Jr, JF Szwed, pp. 1–16. New York: The Free Press

Mintz SW. 1971a. The Caribbean as a sociocultural area. In *Peoples and Cultures of the Caribbean*, ed. MM Horowitz, pp. 17–46. Garden City: The Natl. Hist. Press

Mintz SW. 1971b. The socio-historical background to pidginization and Creolization. See Hymes 1971, pp. 481–96

Mintz SW. 1974. *Caribbean Transformations*. New York: Columbia Univ. Press

Mintz SW. 1977. North American anthropological contributions to Caribbean studies. *Bol. Estud. Latinam. Caribe* 22:68–82

Mintz SW. 1985. *Sweetness and Power*. New York: Penguin

Mintz SW. 1996. Enduring substances, trying theories: the Caribbean region as *Oikumene*. *J. R. Anthropol. Inst.* 2:289–311

Mintz SW, Price R. 1992 (1976). *The Birth of African American Culture*. Boston: Beacon Press

Mohammed P. 1988. The 'Creolization' of Indian women in Trinidad. In *Trinidad and Tobago: The Independence Experience, 1962–1987*, ed. S Ryan, pp. 381–97. St. Augustine: ISER/UWI

Moore R. 1997. *Nationalizing Blackness: Afrocubanismo and Artistic Revolution in Havana, 1920–1940*. Pittsburgh, PA: Univ. Pittsburgh Press

Mufwene SS. 1997. Jargons, pidgins, creoles, and koines: What are they? In *The Structure and Status of Pidgins and Creoles*, ed. AK Spears, D Winford, pp. 35–70. Amsterdam: Benjamins

Mufwene SS. 2002. Competition and selection in language evolution. *Selection* 3:45–56

Mullins PR, Paynter R. 2000. Representing colonizers: an archaeology of creolization, ethnogenesis, and indigenous material culture among the Haida. *Hist. Archaeol.* 34:73–84

Munasinghe V. 2001. *Callaloo or Tossed Salad? East Indians and the Cultural Politics of Identity in Trinidad*. Ithaca, NY: Cornell Univ. Press

Muysken P, Smith N, eds. 1986. *Substrata Versus Universals in Creole Genesis*. Amsterdam: Benjamins

Nettleford R. 1978. *Caribbean Cultural Identity: The Case of Jamaica*. Kingston: Inst. Jamaica

Oldendorp CGA. 1777. *Geschichte der Mission der Evangelischen Brüder auf den Caraibischen Inseln S. Thomas, S. Croix und S. Jan*. Barby, Switz.: Christian Friedrich Laur

Olender M. 1992. *The Languages of Paradise*. Cambridge, MA: Harvard Univ. Press

Oscar Acevedo E. 1999. *Baroco y terminología en Hispanoamerica*. Buenos Aires: Ciudad Argentina

Palmié S. 1993. Ethnogenetic processes and cultural transfer in Caribbean slave population. In *Slavery in the Americas*, ed. W Binder, pp. 337–63. Würzburg: Königshausen Neumann

Palmié S. 2002. *Wizards and Scientists: Explorations in Afro-Cuban Modernity and Tradition*. Durham, NC: Duke Univ. Press

Palmié S. 2007a. On the 'C-Word', again: from colonial to postcolonial semantics. See Stewart 2007. In press

Palmié S. 2007. Is there a model in the muddle? "Creolization" in African American history and anthropology. See Stewart 2007. In press

Parkin D. 1993. Nemi in the modern world: return of the exotic? *Man* 28:79–99

Parkvall M. 2002. Cutting off the branch. See Gilbert 2002, pp. 355–67

Pearse A. 1956. Carnival in nineteenth century Trinidad. *Caribbean Q.* 4:176–93

Perl M. 1982. Los dos significados de la voz 'crioulo/criollo'. *Islas* 73:169–78

Poole D. 1997. *Vision, Race, and Modernity*. Princeton, NJ: Princeton Univ. Press

Price R. 2001. The miracle of Creolization: a retrospective. *New West Indian Guide* 75:35–64

Price R, Price S. 1997. Shadowboxing in the mangrove. *Cult. Anthropol.* 12:3–36

Reddock R. 1998. Contestation over culture, class, gender and identity in Trinidad and Tobago: 'the little tradition.' *Caribbean Q.* 44:62–80

Rodseth L, Olsen J. 2000. Mystics against the market: American religions and the autocritique of capitalism. *Crit. Anthropol.* 20:265–88

Sabato H. 2001. On political citizenship in nineteeth-century Latin America. *Am. Hist. Rev.* 106:1290–315

Sahlins M. 1993. Goodbye to *Tristes Tropes*: ethnography in the context of modern world history. *J. Mod. Hist.* 65:1–25

Sahlins M. 1999. Two or three things that I know about culture. *J. R. Anthropol. Inst.* 5:399–421

Salamone FA. 1991. Creole performance and the mass—the Creolization process. In *Art and Culture in Nigeria and the Diaspora* (Stud. Third World Soc. 46), pp. 21–35. Williamsburg: Dep. Anthropol., Coll. William and Mary

Schwartz SB, Salomon F. 1999. New peoples and new kinds of people: adaptation, readjustment, and ethnogenesis in South American indigenous societies (Colonial Era). In *The Cambridge History of the Native Peoples of the Americas*. Vol. III: *South America*, Part 2, ed. F Salomon, SB Schwartz, pp. 443–501. Cambridge, UK: Cambridge Univ. Press

Schwegler A. 2003. The linguistic geography of 'criollo' in Spanish America: a case of enigmatic extension and restriction. See Collier & Fleischmann 2003, pp. 45–65

Segal DA. 1994. Living ancestors: nationalism and the past in postcolonial Trinidad and Tobago. In *Remapping Memory*, ed. J Boyarin, pp. 221–39. Minneapolis: Univ. Minn. Press

Shaw R, Stewart C. 1994. Introduction: Problematizing syncretism. See Stewart & Shaw 1994, pp. 1–26

Sheller M. 2003. *Consuming the Caribbean*. London: Routledge

Shepherd VA, Richards GL, eds. 2002. *Questioning Creole*. Kingston: Randle

Silverblatt I. 2002. New Christians and New World fears in Seventeenth century Peru. In *From the Margins*, ed. BK Axel, pp. 95–121. Durham, NC: Duke Univ. Press

Silverstein M. 1998. Contemporary transformations of local linguistic communities. *Annu. Rev. Anthropol.* 27:401–26

Silverstein M. 2005. Languages/cultures are dead! Long live the linguistic-cultural. In *Unwrapping the Sacred Bundle: Reflections on the Disciplining of Anthropology*, ed. D Segal, S Yanagisako, pp. 99–125. Durham, NC: Duke Univ. Press

Simmons OG. 1955. The Criollo outlook in the Mestizo culture of Coastal Peru. *Am. Anthropol.* 57:107–17

Singleton TA. 1995. The archaeology of slavery in North America. *Annu. Rev. Anthropol.* 24:119–40

Slocum K, Thomas DA. 2003. Rethinking global and area studies: insights from Caribbeanist anthropology. *Am. Anthropol.* 105:553–65

Smith CA. 1995. Race-class-gender ideology in Guatemala: modern and anti-modern forms. *Comp. Stud. Soc. Hist.* 37:723–49

Smith CA. 1996. Myths, intellectuals, and race/class/gender distinctions in the formation of Latin American nations. *J. Latin Am. Anthropol.* 2:148–69

Smith MG. 1965. *The Plural Society in the British West Indies*. Berkeley: Univ. Calif. Press

Smith RT. 1967. Social stratification, cultural pluralism, and integration in West Indian societies. In *Caribbean Integration*, ed. S Lewis, TG Mathews, pp. 226–58. Rio Piedras: Inst. Caribbean Stud.

Stade R, Dahl G. 2003. Introduction: globalization, creolization, and cultural complexity. *Global Netw.* 3:201–6

Stallaert C. 2000. 'Biological' christianity and ethnicity: Spain's construct from past centuries. In *The Dynamics of Emerging Ethnicities*, ed. J Leman, pp. 113–45. Frankfurt: Lang

Stein P. 1982. Quelques dates nouvelles de l'histoire du môt *créole*. *Étud. Créoles* 5:162–65

Stein P. 1998. Romanische Kreolsprachen I.b.) Begriffsbestimmung und Bezeichnungen. In *Lexikon der Romanistischen Linguistik*, ed. G Holtus, M Metzelin, C Schmitt, 7: 610–18. Tübingen: Max Niemeyer

Stewart C. 1999. Syncretism and its synonyms: reflections on cultural mixture. *Diacritics* 29:40–62

Stewart C. 2007. *Creolization: History, Ethnography, Theory*. London: UCL Press. In press

Stewart C, Shaw R, eds. 1994. *Syncretism/Anti-Syncretism: The Politics of Religious Synthesis*. London: Routledge

Stolke V. 1995. Talking culture: new boundaries, new rhetorics of exclusion in Europe. *Curr. Anthropol.* 36:1–24

Strathern M. 1992. *Reproducing the Future*. New York: Routledge

Stutzman R. 1981. El Mestizaje: an all-inclusive ideology of exclusion. In *Cultural Transformations and Ethnicity in Modern Ecuador*, ed. NE Whitten, Jr, pp. 445–94. Urbana: Univ. Ill. Press

Thomas DA. 2004. *Modern Blackness: Nationalism, Globalization, and the Politics of Culture in Jamaica*. Durham, NC: Duke Univ. Press

Thomas N. 1996. Cold fusion. *Am. Anthropol.* 98:9–16

Thomas N. 2000. Technologies of conversion: cloth and Christianity in Polynesia. In *Hybridity and Its Discontents*, ed. A Brah, AE Coombes, pp. 198–215. London: Routledge

Trouillot MR. 1990. *Haiti: State Against Nation*. New York: Mon. Rev. Press

Trouillot MR. 1991. Anthropology and the savage slot: the poetics and politics of otherness. In *Recapturing Anthropology*, ed. RG Fox, pp. 17–44. Santa Fe: Sch. Am. Res. Press

Trouillot MR. 1992. The Caribbean region: an open frontier in anthropological theory. *Annu. Rev. Anthropol.* 21:19–42

Trouillot MR. 1998. Culture on the edges: Creolization in the plantation context. *Plant. Soc. Am.* 5:8–28

Tschopik H. 1948. On the concept of Creole culture in Peru. *Trans. NY Acad. Sci.* 1:252–61

Turner LD. 1949. *Africanisms in the Gullah Dialect*. Chicago: Univ. Chicago Press

van Dijk FJ. 1988. The twelve tribes of Israel: Rasta and the Middle Class. *New West Indian Guide* 62:1–26

Wade P. 1997. *Race and Ethnicity in Latin America*. London: Pluto

Warner-Lewis M. 1997. Posited Kikoongo origins of some Portuguese and Spanish words from the slave era. *Am. Negra* 13:83–97

Waters AM. 1985. *Race, Class and Political Symbols: Rastafari and Reggae in Jamaica*. New Brunswick, NJ: Transaction Books

Webster J. 2001. Creolizing the Roman provinces. *Am. J. Archaeol.* 105:209–25

Werbner P, Modood T, eds. 1997. *Debating Cultural Hybridity*. London: Zed

Williams B. 1991. *Stains on My Name, War in My Veins*. Durham, NC: Duke Univ. Press

Williams E. 1944. *Capitalism and Slavery*. Chapel Hill: Univ. NC Press

Woll D. 1997. Esp. *criollo* y port. *crioulo*: volviendo la cuestión del origen y la história de las dos palabras. In *Latinitas et Romanitas*, ed. A Bolleé, J Kramer, pp. 517–35. Bonn: Romanistischer Verlag

Woolard KA. 1998. Introduction: language ideology as a field of inquiry. In *Language Ideologies*, ed. B Schieffelin, KA Woolard, PV Kroskrity, pp. 3–47. New York: Oxford Univ. Press

Yelvington K. 2001. The anthropology of Afro-Latin America and the Caribbean: diasporic dimensions. *Annu. Rev. Anthropol.* 30:227–60

Young RJ. 1995. *Colonial Desire*. London: Routledge

Environmental Discourses

Peter Mühlhäusler[1] and Adrian Peace[2]

[1] Linguistics Discipline, University of Adelaide, SA 5005 Australia;
email: peter.muhlhausler@adelaide.edu.au

[2] Discipline of Anthropology, University of Adelaide, SA 5005 Australia;
email: adrian.peace@adelaide.edu.au

Annu. Rev. Anthropol. 2006. 35:457–79

First published online as a Review in
Advance on July 6, 2006

The *Annual Review of Anthropology* is
online at anthro.annualreviews.org

This article's doi:
10.1146/annurev.anthro.35.081705.123203

Copyright © 2006 by Annual Reviews.
All rights reserved

0084-6570/06/1021-0457$20.00

Key Words

ecolinguistics, ethnography of communication, environmental
metaphor, biocultural diversity, greenspeak

Abstract

Discourses concerned with the perceived global environmental crisis have increased dramatically over the past couple of decades. This
review consists of an ethnographic analysis of the principal components of environmental discourses as well as a discussion of the
approaches employed to analyze them. These include linguistic discourses (ecolinguistics, ecocritical linguistics, discourse analysis) as
well as approaches developed within other disciplines (anthropology,
literary studies, philosophy, and psychology).

Over the years, the structural properties of environmental discourses have developed into a distinct discourse category. It remains
unclear to what extent the numerous environmental discourses and
metadiscourses significantly contribute to improving the health of
the natural environment.

INTRODUCTION

Environmental discourse: the linguistic devices articulating arguments about the relationship between humans and their environment.

Discourses about the contemporary environment, and the economic and political processes that impact upon it, are by no means of concern solely to environmental anthropologists. Such is the reach and depth of disquiet and anxiety about the environmental future in both Northern and Southern hemispheres; it seems unlikely that the concerns of local and regional populations will not surface, at some point or other, during most anthropologists' periods in the field. At the same time, such is the linguistic complexity of environmental discourses that the need to marry anthropological perspectives with those prominent in other disciplines appears distinctly pressing. In recent years, we have spent considerable time as a linguist-anthropologist tag team unpacking the natural discourses with which people make sense of a unique island environment off the east coast of Australia. Convinced of the merits of pooling the strengths of our disciplines and taking the ethnography of speaking in new directions, we have more recently turned our attention to the competing and contentious discourses focused on environmental crisis at the global level.

Our main problem is the sheer quantity of environmental discourses, which has vastly increased in recent decades in response to worldwide awareness of the global environmental crisis, and which is produced from numerous disciplinary and linguistic backgrounds. Anthropology, linguistics, philosophy, sociology, and other disciplines now address the question of how environmental discourses work. A blurring of disciplinary boundaries is paralleled by a blurring between discourse and metadiscourse. In our terms, discourse refers to specific ways of talking about particular environments and their futures. Metadiscourse refers to practices of theorizing, which categorize issues to establish their significance.

DEFINITIONS

We define environmental discourse as comprising the linguistic devices articulating arguments about the relationship between humans and the natural environment, but we restrict the definition further. Language has always been used to explore this relationship. But until recently most discourse took place in the belief that a largely self-regulating nature could be taken for granted. The new discourse differs in that its principal focus is the endangerment of nature and the human species in a global context.

The ambiguity of the terms environment and nature is central to understanding this global discourse. Environment in essence is an anthropocentric notion: "The term has increasingly come to mean a nature tangibly important only to human health and livelihood" (Hochman 1997, p. 82). Rowe (1989, p. 123) and Fill (1993) criticize the vagueness of the term, and Howard includes it among his "weasel words" (1978, pp. 81–84). As examples, he cites U.S. game parks, where "visitors can see bears not, as we used to say in our old-fashioned way, in natural surroundings, but in the environmental habitat," and aerosol cans, which "kill most household germs on 'environmental' surfaces."

Williams (1983) calls nature "perhaps the most complex word in the language"; its meaning is far removed from the technical notion of "entities and processes uninterfered with by human agency" (p. 219). In a study of "naturalness" as it is applied to Australian ecosystems, Taylor (1990) concludes that "failure to recognize that naturalness is a culturally constructed concept, rather than a universal one, has produced . . . inconsistency and ambiguity in the terminology used for these assessments" (p. 411).

Jagtenberg (1994) says "we are confronting both ecological decline and an explosion of discourses about nature" (p. 14). However, this explosion is evidence not for some direct influence of environmental factors on language, but rather for the emergence of risk society (Beck 1992) and technologies such as nuclear power, which no insurance companies dare touch. We interpret environmental discourse as an attempt by risk society members to make sense of the global changes that affect them (Spaargen et al. 2000). Another task is to explore how the study of environmental discourse can make contributions to environmental understanding.

Our key questions are as follows:

- Are there any salient properties of environmental discourse?
- Which linguistic approaches are most suited to analyzing them?
- What contribution can the previous points make to environmental sustainability?

CLASSIFICATION

To reduce the polyphony of environmental voices to the common denominator of "political discourse" (Leuthold 1999, p. 5) seems too simplistic. Harré et al. (1999) distinguish between scientific, moral, economic, and aesthetic macro discourse. Clear distinctions exist between such micro discourses as green economic policies (Gerbig 2000), green consumerism (Elkington et al. 1988), and green advertising (Mühlhäusler 1996, Luke 1997). Herndl & Brown (1996) separate pretheoretical classifications into ethnocentric, ecocentric, and anthropocentric discourse. Dryzek (1997) adds a political discourse with four subcategories: problem solving, survivalism, sustainability, and green radicalism.

Such pretheoretical taxonomies are indicative of a nascent field of inquiry. We approach the salient features of environmental discourse in terms of an ethnography of speaking (Hymes 1972) such that

- the ethnography of communication lends itself to organizing large bodies of observation;

- the result is etic rather than emic, and therefore facilitates comparative study;
- the main level of analysis has been the event, a unit well provided for by the ethnography of communication; and
- an ethnographic approach highlights areas that have received insufficient attention.

SPEECH COMPONENTS IN DISCOURSE ABOUT ENVIRONMENTAL EVENTS

Participants

Hymes observes (1972), "[T]he common dyadic model of speaker-hearer specifies sometimes too many, sometimes too few, sometimes the wrong participants" (p. 59) and advocates a distinction between addresser, sender, hearer, and addressee. These distinctions are relevant to understanding global environmental discourses.

The addresser. Addressers are the source of a message, and a number of analysts have shown that speaking on behalf of the Earth ("vicarious advocacy" in Harré et al. 1999, p. 182) is a salient feature of environmental discourses. It entails assigning intelligence "to nonhuman entities such as ecosystems" (Dryzek 1997, p. 17) or a personified goddess such as Gaia (Lovelock 1979). Earlier black and white categorization between two addresser groups, environmentalists and developers, persists in more recent discourses, but others (Killingsworth & Palmer 1992) offer more complex classifications.

Addressers have been classified in terms of their key metaphors (Dryzek 1997) or dominant behaviors: ecofreaks, tree-huggers, ferals, greenies, NIMBY (not in my backyard), and NIABY (not in anybody's backyard) (see Mühlhäusler 2003). Dryzek (1997) emphasizes the discourses of principal "agents" such as survivalists, prometheans, democratic pragmatists, and green rationals, whereas Jamison

(2001) distinguishes activists, academics, and practitioners.

Increasing the number of addressers would seem timely; environmental discourses are no longer dominated by a small coterie of Western professionals. But addressers have also changed over time from concerned individuals (Carson 1962, Ehrlich 1969) to national and international organizations. Collective addressers fall into two main categories: those concerned with management and government, and those focused on moral and aesthetic aspects of the environment.

Big business has succeeded in repackaging its ideology by promoting green consumerism (Alexander 2002, Doyle 1991, Beder 1997, Gerbig 2000, Stauber & Rampton 1995). This is often green tokenism, but the actions of ethical enterprises differ markedly from traditional big business. Governments have become the most powerful producers of environmental messages. Transnational bodies such as the European Union, World Bank, and UNESCO increasingly broadcast environmental messages. Alongside powerful organizations such as Greenpeace, World Wildlife Fund, and the Sierra Club, we find concerned groups of scientists, the Club of Rome (Meadows et al. 1972), and green political parties.

The idea that there is a genuine global discourse remains problematic. Jamison (2001) comments that in the 1970s such a discourse appeared to "transcend the ideological disputes and other sources of division, like class, race, gender, and national identity" (p. 1) but comes to the conclusion that national identity defines discourse communities. The notion of global discourse also sits uneasily with incompatible value systems in intercultural settings. Jones (1994) details the incommensurability of Maori and Pakeha languages in environmental debates. Marnham (1981) observes, "African opinion would be hostile to every assumption" upon which an expatriate notion of "game parks" is based (p. 8). "Wilderness" is particularly problematic, as Burnett &

Kamuyu wa Kang'ethe (1994) have illustrated for east African languages. Richards (1992) highlights the problems with "wildlife conservation" (p. 1) in Sierra Leone. Genske & Hess-Lüttich (2002) underscore intercultural eco-semiotic problems between developing and developed nations; similar conclusions can be found in Mühlhäusler (2003). Rhetorical claims about globalization have resulted in a hyperbolic emphasis on integration and interdependence, which undervalues the persistence of national and local forces.

Speaker. The mainstreaming of environmentalism has resulted in a disjunction between the roles of addresser and speaker. The media are important speakers, and their role has attracted considerable attention (Dyer & Dyer 1990, Gerbig 2000, Hansen 1996, Rissel & Douglas 1993). A survey of the media's role in sustaining environmental discourse is given in Mühlhäusler (2003).

Speakers who represent large organizations can be found on all sides of the environmental debate. CEOs and professional environmental communicators, speakers for large corporations, spokespersons representing organizations such as Greenpeace, and green politicians increasingly speak with the voice of their party rather than as individuals.

Hearer. Hymes (1972) subscribes to a mechanistic metaphor of messages being sent and received that equates hearers and addressees with passive recipients. In reality, environmental meanings emerge in active or interactive discourses between all players. We do not develop this criticism but note that a mechanistic view of communication is shared by numerous producers of environmental messages.

One design feature of human language is that it is broadcast and that an uttered message can be heard by all and sundry. In the West, environmental discourses are heard all the time as the media untiringly churn out stories about environmental disasters.

The concept of risk society implies a lack of certainty on all sides (Caplan 2000). Hearers are exposed to messages they do not completely understand even when "ecoliterate" and numerous conflicting messages are encountered. This concept suggests a classification of hearers into those who are ecoliterate or earthliterate (Verhagen 2000) and those who ignore or filter out messages, or suffer from ecofatigue.

Corporate discourses about the environment are capable of manipulating even the ecoliterate. Ehrlich & Ehrlich (1996) have drawn attention to the practice of brownlash, which minimizes the severity of environmental problems; Brosius (1999) explains how greenwashing by public relations firms manufactures "uncertainty about environmental threats" (p. 28).

The ability of hearers to filter out information depends on whether they are directly affected by environmental issues. Farrell & Goodnight (1998) observe that during disasters a rhetorical crisis occurs where "audiences struggle to understand information, set criteria for policy evaluation, and locate viable options for action.... [T]he crisis does not so much invite discourse as defy it" (p. 76). In the wake of Three Mile Island, people simply fled. In other disaster situations such as Bhopal (Fortun 2001) or Exxon Valdez (Browning & Shetler 1992), hearers' reactions were influenced by patchy understanding and an inability to act rationally in the face of conflicting messages.

Addressee. Addressees are members of target audiences. Given the economic and ideological importance of green discourse, identifying target audiences is a central task of environmental rhetoric. Environmentalists tend to assume their message alone will appeal to the commonsense of those waiting to be enlightened. But their lack of attention to the question of how to target particular audiences has rendered them less effective than expected. Penman (1994) has drawn attention

to their failure to acknowledge limited environmental awareness.

Businesses and politicians have adopted more sophisticated strategies. Public opinion surveys (Luke 1993, pp. 165–66) increasingly shape the agenda of corporations and political parties, and the appeal of environmental messages has become important in electioneering and market research on green consumer behavior (Elkington et al. 1988, Lenz 2003, Mühlhäusler 2000). Limited consumer interest slows down the production of environmentally friendly vehicles and green television programs.

Ends

The gap between goals and outcomes is particularly noticeable in the area of environmental policy-making, in which policies are a substitute for, rather than a means of, achieving desired outcomes (Schiewer 2002, Strang 2004).

Goals/Purpose. Much environmental discourse elaborates the theme that human actions are detrimental to the survival of humanity. Each speech act warns that it is in the interest of the individual to desist from such activities. Waddell (1998) argues that the ultimate purpose is "the preservation of future choice" (p. xiii). Changes in individual behavior or government policy range from single topic (do not chop down more trees in the parkland) to generalist ones (save the planet/world).

"Proper conduct of the relation between society and nature" (Rutherford 1994, p. 40) has grown in importance, and it is to be achieved by government control and manipulation of environmental awareness. Neuwirth (2002) details the rhetorical strategies used by the Austrian government and the British Broadcasting Corporation (BBC) in support of nuclear power and in downplaying the risk of launching plutonium-laden spacecraft. Schultz (2001) analyzes the linguistic devices (euphemism, vagueness, hyperbole) employed by big government and large corporations to control public opinion.

One important discourse goal is to locate the speaker on the high moral ground, for example, in promoting vegetarianism (Marko 2000): To what extent vegetarianism is any better for animals than animal husbandry remains unclear, and it goes hand in hand with habitat destruction, use of pesticides, and high storage costs. Harré et al. (1999) have used narratology to explore the general principles of taking the moral high ground: The narratives of opposing groups (e.g., supporters and opponents of nuclear energy) are structurally identical; the only difference lies in the roles assigned (hero, helper, innocent bystander).

In spite of widely held views on the centrality of discourse in constructing reality, discourse often seems to postpone action. Talk about the plight of the River Murray in Australia, for instance, is not matched by comparable action; as we are running out of water, we are also running out of time. Adam (1997) comments on the difficulties humans experience when calibrating time. Environmental consequences of human actions can occur with a time lag varying between milliseconds and millennia. Humans typically perceive consequences that occur a few hours, at most a few years, after the event.

Outcomes. Bruner & Oelschlaeger (1994) emphasize the relative lack of consequential change in environmental discourses compared with those of antienvironmentalists who "have been effective in accomplishing their objectives at least in part, because of their ability to articulate persuasive rationales through slogans, myths and narratives" (p. xviii). This contrast in degree of linguistic adaptation was anticipated by earlier writers who commented on the way environmental rhetoric leaves a reality gap "because it uses old language to derive the terms of a new condition" (Segal 1991, p. 3). Continued exposure to more alarming facts about topics such as global warming does not lead to enhanced alertness but

rather to "an atmosphere of fading interest" (Killingsworth & Palmer 1992, p. 270).

The new discourse about the environment comprises the greening of the language of industrial societies, the proliferation of new lexical resources, the emergence of green word formation, and green metaphors becoming root cultural ones. Green language heightens peoples' awareness of environmental issues. As Hajer (1995) notes, "the discursive power of ecological modernization manifests itself in the degree to which its implicit future scenarios permeate through society and actors reconceptualize their interests and recognize new opportunities and new trouble spots" (p. 261).

Act Sequences

In Hymes's (1972) model, act sequences are concerned with the form messages conventionally take as well as their semantic content. The model separates formal from semantic properties, a separation difficult to uphold in discourse analysis. We nevertheless try to separate form and content, noting first that the intensity of environmental discourses is characterized by peaks (Rio, Kyoto) and troughs.

Ecolinguists argue that the contours of Western languages are increasingly at odds with the contours of their speakers' environments. According to Halliday (2001), modern Western languages are the outcome of past developments and their grammars are memories of past experience: Their layers reflect our past as hunter gatherers through to modern bureaucratic modes of existence. This memory of the past influences how we perceive the world today, although what seemed functional in the past is now no longer so. The notion that bigger is better (in English we typically find conjuncts where bigger comes first, as in "all creatures great and small") is deeply entrenched in most languages, but in the current crisis such "growthism" is dysfunctional.

Forms of speech. The greening of modern languages manifests in the changing norms for using lexical items. Lexical innovations in English combine deliberate creation of terminology with spontaneously evolving terms. There has been a proliferation of specialist dictionaries for environmental words (surveyed in Mühlhäusler 2003), which reveal substantial changes in everyday language.

Formally, most new lexical items are (*a*) morphologically complex, (*b*) built predominantly from Latin and Greek roots, (*c*) of limited transparency, or (*d*) misleading. The fact that major Western languages have in excess of 100,000 words for environmental matters does not mean that many of them enter into everyday discourse. Where specialist communities have redefined popular words such as "trash," "garbage," or "rubbish," miscommunication is frequently the result.

Like other unpleasant phenomena, environmental degradation has promoted the use of euphemisms which either replace existing terms—"to harvest" rather than "to hunt," "landfill" rather than "rubbish dump," "to cull" rather than "to kill"—or take the form of formalized collocation, as in "sustainable development" or "green business." The trends outlined in English are paralleled elsewhere. Stork (1998) has documented the environmental lexicon of French, whereas Trampe (2001) takes on the German lexicon of agribusiness.

Message content. Lanthier & Olivier (1999) observed that "the environmentalist discourse originates in the environmental and human disasters provoked by technology" (p. 67). These origins can be traced back to debates about deforestation, drought, and water shortages following the economic and cultural conquest of the earth by European colonizers (Grove 1992). The impact of mining, overgrazing, and overuse of forests has been discussed by Weigl (2004). The following areas have been identified by Trampe (2001, p. 233): pollution and waste problems, habitat destruction, species extinction, and nuclear energy. New topics are constantly

added, bearing out Sapir's (1912) observation as to the social dimension of all discourses about nature. In the discourses about animal extinction, a small number of charismatic species (whales, seals, wolves, tigers, koalas, pandas, and dingoes) prevail (Knight 2000), biologically equal or more important species (scavengers, dung beetles, weevils, or wasps) rarely feature, nor do equally endangered domestic subspecies (Penman 1994).

Brosius (1999) discussed the criticism that Euro-American discourses often ignore the plight of inhabitants of developing nations and pointed out that "environmental discourses are changing in response to critiques of elitism, to charges that they ignore social justice issues, to accusations that they are a form of neo-colonialism" (p. 282). The emergence of discourses of biocultural diversity (Maffi 2001) illustrates this change.

Tone or Key

The key of a message on one hand is a product of choices made in the domains of language form, content, and channel; on the other hand it impacts on the norms of interpretation and interaction. Although the terms key and tone are used interchangeably, our preference is for the latter.

Tone. Different macro discourses about the environment vary with respect to tone, although most are distinctly serious. In Kahn's (2001) summary, "Scientific discourses about the environment have been criticized for their 'cold, dry-as-dust objectivity, their antiseptic gaze on death and indignity, their consistent use of the passive voice to avoid the appearance of responsibility'" (p. 242). Killingsworth & Palmer (1992) observe that the attempt by scientists to write in a neutral detached tone is undermined by "anthropomorphizing the effect of scientific language" and their use of a "teleological kind of language for nonteleological concepts" (p. 114). Halliday & Martin (1993) criticize scientific discourse similarly: It constructs a reality that

> **Biocultural diversity:** implies that the well-being of languages is a prerequisite for the well-being of natural species

is "fixed and determinate, in which objects predominate and processes seem merely to define and classify them" (p. 20). However, this register gives scientific discourse its authoritative tone.

Whereas Myerson & Rydin (1996) have drawn attention to the frequent use of irony in environmental discourse, others have characterized it as irrational and emotional (Schiewer 2002) and as hysterical (Killingsworth & Palmer 1992). Harré et al. (1999) note that often "there is a coupling of terms such as 'global warming' and the 'rise of sea level' in disaster stories, such as the scenarios in which 'densely populated low-lying areas are flooded,' which in their view justifies characterizing such discourses as 'apocalyptic'" (p. 68).

INSTRUMENTALITIES

Environmental discourse involves both numerous channels and numerous speech forms. With increasing global involvement by more participants, further greening of communication can be anticipated. A range of studies addresses the production of environmental messages, but these studies are not matched by a similar concern with perception.

Channels/Media

The emergence of environmental discourses coincides with the proliferation of new media and their globalization. A brief survey by Mühlhäusler (2003, Ch. 11) reveals that environmental discourse is fully embedded in this global multimedia structure.

One exception is Phillips, who illustrates (2000) how six couples try to cope discursively with the proliferation of ecological risks. He maintains, "People's sense of responsibility is limited by being constituted within discourse, which constructs political action beyond a limited amount of political consumption as belonging to a separate realm to which they have access only via mass media" (pp. 171–207).

Environmental discourse in the mainstream and alternative press has received some attention. Dyer & Young (1990) and Doyle & Kellow (1995) provide accounts of the media treatment of environmental issues in Australia, including coverage of a northern Australian World Heritage Site, the Daintree Forest. They explain (Doyle & Kellow 1995) that once the researcher leaves the realm of major newspapers and enters the arena of small rural ones, antienvironmental bias appears well-entrenched. All papers created and perpetuated stereotypes; sympathetic portrayal of green issues by the media became widespread only recently.

In a critical review of *Time's* special edition (2 February 1989) on "The Planet of the Year, Our Endangered Earth," Grossman (1989) comments on the language therein, which perpetuates the myth that the environmental crisis is caused by the recklessness, carelessness, sloppy handling, and profligacy of individuals. It did not include the deliberate decisions of governments and corporations, nor that of criminal organizations, which continue to exacerbate the crisis.

In the realm of television and video, the imperative of newsworthiness is even more pronounced. As Delli et al. (1994, p. 79) have pointed out, most environmental degradation, unlike much less frequent eco-catastrophe, is an ongoing and slowly changing process and is therefore low on the scale of newsworthiness. Specially nominated days provide the media with an opportunity to compress slow-moving events into a fast-moving story. The green calendar is full of days focusing on particular issues or inviting particular actions, such as "Buy Nothing Day" or "Clean Up Australia Day." Public perceptions of major "crises" in American domestic life do little more than occasionally heighten public interest to alleviate boredom (Downs 1972, p. 89).

The main problem with such media coverage is that it articulates the view that sufficient information is known about

environmental problems for successful ame-
liorative measures to be undertaken. Nothing could be further from the truth, but
the ideological impact is understandably
substantial.

One principled linguistic limitation of environmental media is that the subject matter
is immensely complex and that most language
is ill suited to expressing the connectivity between relevant factors. This kind of discrete
linguistic restriction accounts for the radical
simplification of environmental information
by stereotyping, accumulating ill-digested
information on the Internet, and portraying
complex information in new ways. Jagtenberg
& McKie (1997) and McKie (2000) have
developed the notion of media scape or media
ecology to examine the complex feedback
relations between messages and audiences.
They note considerable differences between
public and private media. Eco-advocacy texts
emerge primarily from public television,
whereas commercial networks generate few
texts of that type. These divergences and
discrepancies reflect the limited appeal of
environmental reporting compared with light
entertainment and bear out that television is
not an effective medium of mass education
(Vivanco 2002). McKie (2000) adds that
the anthropocentric properties of human
languages are reinforced by unconscious and
deliberate selection.

Forms of Speech

The forms of speech component refers to
the dialect, accent, and variety used in speech
events, all of which have received little
attention.

Environmental discourses are predominantly in English and other major Western languages. As environmental concerns
are most prominent among the middle
classes, standard varieties of the language
are the norm. Such circumstances are compounded by the fact that standard written forms are used in print and electronic
media. Protest movements attempt to employ nonstandard forms of speaking as a
kind of antilanguage against the establishment. The protest against the proposed nuclear power station at Whyl was voiced in
Alamannic, the shared vernacular of Swiss,
German, and French citizens affected by the
development.

Genre

Environmental discourses employ traditional
genres such as narrative, myth, and sermon
and add new ones such as Environment Impact Assessments. Rose (2004) states, "it may
be that narrative is the method through which
the reason of connectivity will find its most
powerful voice" (p. 6). Killingsworth et al.
(1992) share this "hope for a generally accessible narrative, the story of how human action
reconciles conflicting demands and the search
for a good life" (p. 21).

Narratives are employed because of their
important role in creating sense, reducing
complex phenomena to accessible texts, and
maximizing on their rhetorical force. Harré
et al. (1999) focus on the first aspect, narratives as frameworks, "for our attempt to
come to terms with the nature and conditions
of our existence" (p. 20). This idea of narrative includes folk tales, fairy stories, nov-
els, and insider autobiographies (Kelly 1984).
Harré et al. (1999) note the importance of
the *Bildungsroman*, a novel reflecting the three
German meanings of *Bildung*: "formation,
education and creation" (p. 72): It is concerned with the development of the protag-
onist's mind in the passage to maturity, for
example, Lovelock's (1979) earnest biologist
who realizes too late the consequences of his
meddling with nature. Similar narratives are
discussed by Bowerbank (1999).

Cronon (1992) argues that narratives impose a single vision of reality when the
complexity of issues facilitates the production of several possibilities. Harré et al.
(1999) show how the same formal narrato-
logical structures are used in constructing
a range of stories about the environment.

Factors that militate against normative consensus in environmental discourse include its novelty, its global nature, and the constant changes in issues, ideologies, and participants. Agreed norms take time to develop. One can observe the gradual emergence of norms within regional and wider communities, but the presence of environmentalist and antienvironmentalist discourses limits emergence of shared norms. At the global level, there is little chance of norms developing from below: Contact between participants is insufficient. National and regional norms (Hajer 1995) for different European countries remain because they take place in widely different languages that favor different perspectives on the environment.

Bruner & Oelschlager (1994) argue, "Antienvironmentalists play to the established cultural narrative that 'Man' is over nature, that nature is nothing more than an ecomachine which we technologically manipulate, and that a good society is one which totally fulfils itself through market preferences" (p. 383).

Nature writing is another established genre that continues to inspire environmental discourse. This genre precedes all others, although, as Raglan (1991) observes, environmental thought is underrepresented in the Western canon, despite writers such as Thoreau, Rousseau, or the German Romantics having been influential. Early nature writers are nevertheless attacked as dangerous sentimentalists by others (Weissman 1996). We note that their modern equivalents have become semantically bleached and trivialized when Suzuki's or Attenborough's television series become items of popular culture.

Environmental history has emerged as an important genre over recent years, ranging from large-scale surveys such as Crosby's (1986) account of the biological consequences of European colonization, through to more focused accounts of the histories of commodities such as sugar, coffee, cod, or the history of landscapes (Worster 1990, Cronon 1996).

Although normative expectations can be imposed by those who define the global agenda, such as the Western educated and elite organizers of the 1992 Earth Summit (Harré et al. 1999, pp. 12–17), when a global message was whisked around the world from Rio (Conca & Dabelko 1998) and comprised "a fusion of local discourses into one media event" (Harré et al. 1999), no genuine norms resulted: "[A]s yet, it is far from the expression of a unified voice" (p. 20).

Norms of Interaction

The validity of environmental discourses depends on their accreditation as defined by assumptions about commonsense and shared metaphors. As Carbaugh (1992) has illustrated, outsiders have difficulty in making their voice heard. Western experts pronouncing on environmental matters in the developing world are at times accused of being neo-imperialists and eco-missionaries (Agarwal & Narain 1991). For their part, Western experts frequently ignore the proposition that scientific knowledge can be culture bound and provincial.

Interaction on environmental matters is characteristically defined by two opposing models of communication. The model used in scientific, economic, and political discourse is the conduit metaphor (Reddy 1979) of messages generated by experts being passed on to the unenlightened. But the assumption of passive hearers is an inadequate view of communication and yields undesirable consequences.

Environmentalists also subscribe to this model, but there are some within their ranks who instead aim to generate genuine collaboration and recognize that input never equals intake in human communication. In such models, knowledge-flow from the developing to the developed world is called for (Peet & Watts 1996).

Norms of Interpretation

The title of Taylor & Buttel's (1992) paper "How Do We Know that We Have Global Environmental Problems?" suggests that the central problem is one of making sense of complex, conflicting information. One key problem again is accreditation, that is "on relations obtaining between what is said or written and the circumstances in which it is being produced and/or interpreted" (Harris 2001, p. 154). Alexander (2000) writes, "Part of the problem of changing people's behavior regarding environmental and ecological issues is appreciating that differing social, economic and political forces employ language and discourse in persuasive terms in different ways" (p. 186).

One reason for the lack of common interpretive norms is the different time perspectives of different communities (Harré et al. 1999). The proportion of the world's population who do not think ahead for more than a few days at a time is large and growing, whereas those who understand the consequences of events in the distant future remain a small minority. As Posner (1990) summarizes, "Given that this generation has created technologies and technological problems that will be around for very long periods of time (e.g., nuclear waste, genetically engineered species), what will be the code, message and medium necessary to alert future generations to potential dangers?" (pp. 7–8).

The norms governing environmental discourse again draw heavily on those emanating from powerful institutions in society. Thus, the view in the West that one can trust scientists more than politicians also holds for green discourses and is one of the principal reasons why "greenspeaking" draws extensively on scientific language. The greening of business and the emergence of green consumers pose additional problems of interpretation. Almost all products offered for sale now have environmental claims attached to them, which makes informed decision making increasingly difficult. Interpretation is hugely problematic when it comes to complex disasters such as Three Mile Island, Chernobyl, or Bhopal. Farrell & Goodnight (1998) detail the insufficiency of official and private discourses to make sense of them and conclude

that "no one understood all that was going on" (p. 76).

SURVEY: ANALYTICAL APPROACHES TO ENVIRONMENTAL DISCOURSES

Environmental discourse concerns the relationship between language and the world. Mühlhäusler (2003, p. 2) highlights four different linguistic approaches to this relationship:

- Language is for cognition: It exists in a social and environmental vacuum (Chomsky).
- Language is constructed by the world (Marr).
- The world is constructed by language (structuralism, poststructuralism).
- Language is interconnected with the world: It both constructs and is constructed by it (ecolinguistics).

These approaches recognize that what one can know about the global environment is inextricably linked with language inasmuch as knowledge is dependent on effability. We begin with language because one can use language about all effable aspects of the world; but the converse is not the case. There is discourse about the environment, but no environment about discourse. The first perspective (Chomsky's independence hypothesis) takes the position that language is a neutral tool or that all human languages (potentially or actually) have the same capacity for talking about the environment. But both Saussurian structuralists and Chomskyan generativists disconnect language from external influences. This disconnection has been labeled "limiting the arbitrary" by Joseph (2000), who offers an incisive critique of modern linguistics, as does the ecolinguist Finke (2002).

The inability of modern linguists to address environmental discourses is compounded by their largest unit of analysis being a single sentence. Moreover, the meaning of sentences has been established with reference

Greenspeaking: replacing or postponing environmental action by just speaking about it in "green" language

Ecolinguistics: a branch of linguistics that integrates the study of language with its cultural and natural environment

Ecology of
language: the study
of interactions
between any given
language and its
cultural and political
environment

to internal sense relations, not external referents. The view that languages are constructed by the external physical or social world has not been popular in mainstream linguistics, but it continues to be argued in connection with language origins.

Saussurian structuralism was in part a reaction against a historical approach to language, which sought to explore how linguistic differences could be explained in terms of different environmental factors. The marginalization of onomatopoeia (Nuckolls 1999) and iconicity of signs further widened the gap between language and the world. When language change was considered, its explanation remained restricted to internal factors such as system organization, reanalysis, or faulty transmission.

External actors in language change were considered by the "ecology of language" approach pioneered by Haugen (1972), who focused on the deliberative man-made political ecologies in which languages compete with one another. Haugen defined language ecology as "the study of interactions between any given language and its environment" (p. 336), but he restricted this to the cultural and political environment while also emphasizing the survival of the fittest. This somewhat skewed perspective was followed by several European scholars (surveyed by Fill 2003 and Mühlhäusler 2003). Contemporary ecolinguists have modified Haugen by emphasizing the cooperative principle in ecology and the value of linguistic diversity.

More effective approaches emerged in other disciplines or in the still-marginalized critical linguistics (Fairclough 1992), integrational linguistics (Harris 1981, Toolan 1996), and ecolinguistics (Fill 2003, Mühlhäusler 2003). Critical linguistics and critical discourse linguistics are based on the poststructuralist notion that perceptions of the environment are discursively constructed.

Ecolinguistics can be traced back to the 1980s when a group of linguists asked whether the looming environment crisis was due in part to language. Early writers such as Fill

(1993) drew on the experience of language and gender studies because the linguistic denigration of women is, in many languages, accompanied by a denigration of nonhuman life forms (Leach 1968, Tansley 1991, Dunayer 2001).

One issue that drew much attention was the development of a new lexicon for talking about environmental matters. Mühlhäusler (1983) in a review of Landy (1979) proposed that this new language is characterized by three problems:

- semantic vagueness: e.g., terms like pollution, progress, and pest.
- semantic underdifferentiation: e.g., growing, which can refer to natural growth, man-made growth, arithmetic growth, exponential growth, etc.
- misleading encoding: e.g., zero-growth (which fails to recognize what is being added), labor saving (which does not say whose labor is being saved), and fertilizers (which can render soil unproductive).

Mühlhäusler (1983) detected a widespread unease among environmentalists who became aware of their linguistic limitations. Alternative discourse approaches such as Johnson (1991) and Jung (1996) became available in due course, whereas an address by Halliday in 1990 (published 2001) brought the nonecological nature of many languages to the attention of applied linguists. His proposal combined a detailed critique of lexical and grammatical categories of contemporary English in an attempt to correlate different types of grammar with different stages in cultural and technological development. Emphasis was given to the role of nominalization, transitivity, and countability of nominal expressions in distorting the fit between the contours of language and the contours of the environment (Martin 1986, Goatly 2001, Fill 2003).

The Whorfian notion that lexicon and grammar of individual languages are the root causes of our environmental crisis is a recurrent theme (surveyed by Mühlhäusler 1998). It has promoted the search for ecologically more adequate ways of speaking in non-Western cultures and has suggested ways in which an ecologically correct biocentric language can be developed. The first kind of suggestion, surveyed by Little (1999), ranges from romanticizing tribal languages considered to have privileged environmental insight to selectively mining them for traditional ecological knowledge.

That environmental language was a new area for language planning was suggested by Halliday in 1990; others have taken up the challenge. Stibbe (2004) surveys studies on environmental verbal hygiene and concludes that tinkering with language is unlikely to produce "a consistent and effective overall discourse for expressing ecological issues" (p. 4). However, in view of widespread ecofatigue, a robust discourse about speciesism, growthism, and other linguistic shortcomings could drive the wider adoption of environmental discourse. An examination of how different meanings of "sustainable development" prevent intelligent discourse about the subject (Alexander 2000, Redclift 1987) certainly seems worthwhile, likewise with the terminology applied to charismatic species (Lee 1988, Peace 2005).

Two principal resources for ecocritical analysis are rhetorical studies and critical analysis. Several publications deal with rhetoric (Killingsworth & Palmer 1992; Herndl & Brown 1996; Muir & Veenendall 1996; Myerson & Rydin 1996; Waddell 1998; Harré et al. 1999). Waddell (1998) has argued that environmental discourse must be cognitively plausible, evoke sentiment, and relate to most people. He implies the rhetorical study of current discourse rarely meets these criteria. Segal (1991) argues that "all arguments represent themselves as arguments for environmental protection. The absence of a clearly identifiable opposition means we encounter gestures in support for the environment, even from those who would despoil it" (p. 2). The result is a blurring of boundaries and the appropriation of "ecospeak" (Killingsworth & Palmer 1992) and "greenspeak" (Harré et al. 1999) by antienvironmentalists. The new rhetoric is one of appropriation and manipulation by big business and government. "We perceive, in the increasing greening of English and other Western languages, a kind of linguistic *Ersatzhandlung*, with the very real danger of talk replacing or postponing action" (Harré et al. 1999, p. ix).

A common focus in rhetorical studies is that environmental discourse involves a multitude of voices, a "new hybrid discourse" (Rojas 2001, p. 8) involving a "Babel of discourse communities" (Killingsworth & Palmer 1992, p. 21).

METAPHOR STUDIES

Given the limitations on environmental understanding, it comes as no surprise that scholars pay a great deal of attention to metaphor. Myerson & Rydin (1996) and Harré et al. (1999) devote a chapter to it. It is most commonly analyzed from the perspective of Lakoff & Johnson (1980). Root metaphors are used either as convenient parameters for distinguishing different types of environmental discourses (Drysek 1997) or as targets for criticism. Bullis (1992) for example attacks mechanistic metaphors as "having outlived their usefulness" (p. 347) and criticizes metaphors such as eco-defense and eco-warrior for constructing confrontation "as a means of achieving peace and harmony" (p. 352).

The centrality of medical metaphors in the construction of environmental awareness has been emphasized by Stratford (1994) and Lanthier & Olivier (1999). A concern for health is shared across a wide range of ideological positions. Metaphors of healing or preventive medicine are widely employed, but the main interest lies in showing how metaphors can fudge discursive differences.

Mills (1982) identifies three core metaphors by which Western societies have lived for the past 1000 years: nature

Ecocritical analysis: studies how the dynamics of social processes such as racism, sexism, or speciesism shape discourses and perceptions of ecological matters

as a book written by God (Middle Ages); nature as a reflection of the human body (Renaissance); and nature as a machine, first a clock, then a steam engine, and most recently a (bio)computer (the present). Ecofeminists have drawn attention to the root metaphor of rape (Schaffer 1988) in expressions such as "opening up virgin territory" or "penetrating the land."

Two principal reasons for the proliferation of metaphor are the novelty of the subject matter, which brings into being new heuristic possibilities, and the conflicting agendas of those who use environmental discourse. As Harris (2001) observes, "There is a fundamental division about the role of language, which can surface in all kinds of ways. At its sharpest, it emerges in where you draw the line between sense and nonsense . . . . For some people, undoubtedly, the claim *trees have rights* is nonsense, or at least utterly confused" (pp. 155–56).

Döring (2002, 2004) illustrates that the metaphors by which certain groups live are important factors in influencing people's environmental actions. The use of metaphor in greenwashing has been described by several analysts and surveyed by Mühlhäusler (2003, Ch. 10). Farrell & Goodnight (1998) have looked at the use of metaphors in relation to Three Mile Island, and Liebert (2001) similarly compares the emergence of the money-equals-water metaphor in the construction of nineteenth-century public water systems.

A recent trend looks at the total commodification of nature. Mühlhäusler & Peace's (2001) analysis of the language of ecotourism has highlighted the metaphorical tendency to anthropomorphize animals and to portray nature as a battlefield where the nonhuman combatants are in a permanent struggle for survival. Marko (2002) observes that although the sexuality of whales and their rearing practices are talked about in zoological terms, discourse about their communicative and social abilities is couched in anthropomorphic metaphor (see also Peace 2005). That disassociation is employed when animals are exploited or hunted

is a common theme, as in the case of baby seals versus seal pups (Martin 1986, Lee 1988).

Waddell (1998) comments on synecdoche (the part stands for the whole), and this deserves more scrutiny, as charismatic creatures typically stand for "nature" while endangered species are talked about as "miners' canaries" (p. xvi). That metonymy (being next to makes something similar to) plays an important role in naturalizing nonnatural practices and products has been shown for environmental advertising (Mühlhäusler 1999). Characteristically, such advertisements visually locate products or trademarks in unspoiled nature.

CRITICAL DISCOURSE ANALYSIS (ECOCRITICISM) AND CULTURAL STUDIES

What unites the varied contributions to ecocriticism is the objective of creating awareness of the cultural roots of the environmental crisis and the hope that such discourses will result in action. There is also an emphasis among ecocritics on connectivity, as Estok (2001) explains: "Ecocriticism at its best seeks understanding about the ways that dynamics of subjugation, persecution, and tyranny are mutually reinforcing, the ways that racism, sexism, homophobia, speciesism and so on are, to use Ania Loomba's term, interlocking" (p. 9).

Ecological discourse has featured prominently in green cultural studies with its emphasis on popular culture and the mechanisms that define common sense, as illustrated by a special issue of the *Australian Journal of Communication* (1994). Contributions range from analysis of media stories (Lucas 1994) and films (McKie 1994) to governmental appropriation of environmental discourse. Other objects of analysis are listed on a resource site at Warbaugh State University (**http://www.wsu.edu/~amerstu/ce/ce.html** accessed 10 October 2004).

One recurrent theme of green cultural studies is the limited efficacy of environmental discourse and the call for more active involvement in the environment.

Penman (1994) shows how the discursive practices of environmentalists and farmers have enabled her to become a better farmer, an experience shared by Trampe (2001).

THE BIOCULTURAL DIVERSITY APPROACH

Concern for the loss of biodiversity can be traced back to Carson (1962), but it has only recently become a topic of ecolinguistics. The equally dramatic disappearance of cultural and linguistic diversity is also a more recent focus for attention. That the two phenomena are causally connected was argued independently by Harmon (1996), Mühlhäusler (1995), and Thompson (1994). Mühlhäusler (1995) argued that life in a particular human environment is dependent on people's ability to talk about it. Maffi's (2001) edited volume contains several programmatic, empirical studies suggestive of interdependencies between language knowledge and environmental management. Given that 96% of languages are spoken by 4% of the world's population, almost three quarters of which are endangered or highly endangered, further acceleration of environmental degradation is probable.

The biocultural diversity approach considers a wider range of parameters than is common to discourse analysis, but its findings are tentative. One attempt to limit the range is Mühlhäusler's (1996) study of young languages among small populations on small islands such as Norfolk Island and Pitcairn Island. Preliminary findings suggest unnamed life forms have a considerably greater chance of becoming extinct than do named ones. The converging environmental and linguistic crises and their causes have been examined by Harmon (2002).

In the domain of language planning (e.g., Liddicoat & Bryant 2000), arguments in favor of biocultural diversity have become mainstream in a short period. The assimilationist and rationalist approach has recently begun to give way to ecological language planning, which favors maximum linguistic diversity.

The relations between linguistic diversity and biological diversity are now being discussed by major bodies such as UNESCO. May (2003) detailed the scepticism among those linguists and language planners who question the link and argued that speakers must be free to choose to abandon their language in favor of global culture. The concept of free choice is not problematized by these advocates.

CONCLUSIONS

When considering the relationship between discourse and the environment, one can start either at the linguistic end and explore how linguistic devices are employed in talking about the environment or at the environmental end and ask to what extent languages are shaped by environmental correlates. Our choice was motivated by the fact that the bulk of the literature surveyed here starts at the language end.

The first question of our survey concerned the salient properties of environmental discourses. We noted

- there is a tendency to equate the notion of environment with what sustains human life and what pleases humans. Most discourses are anthropocentric.
- most discourses are focused on local concerns and issues covering no more than a human life span.
- there are discursive attempts to globalize environmental discourse, but this is a small part of the totality of possible ones.

One further salient property is widespread uncertainty under conditions of risk society, which leads to a greater use of narratives and rhetoric than in many other discourse genres.

As environmental discourses are concerned with the everyday, so they are becoming institutionalized and bureaucratized, the more so as discourse analysis becomes part of environmental management programs being promulgated by big business or big government.

The most noticeable feature of green discourse is lexical choice. In addition to new descriptive expressions, many loaded terms are currently available for rhetorical purposes. Euphemisms, buzz words, weasel words, and emotive terms are prolific; their translation equivalents are beginning to spread, although European and American ones remain prominent. One of the outcomes of the greening of linguistics is the emergence of a new applied linguistics, which, according to Halliday (2001), may not hold the key to solving environmental problems. But it is assuredly imperative for us to write instructions for the use of the key.

The emergence of environmental discourse in the 1980s coincided with the disintegration of a single paradigm of modern linguistics. Practitioners of new approaches to linguistics began to ask new questions and employ new analytic methods. The emergence of ecolinguistics was likely inevitable, as has been exploration of the interconnectedness of language endangerment and biocultural diversity more recently.

Our final question concerned the contribution environmental discourses can make to environmental sustainability. We concur with Waddell (1998), who comments on the role of language in revitalizing the public at large and underlines the need to discover language "for both experts and generalists alike" (p. xv). Language may not be the key, and focusing on the nature of the linguistic code to produce an ecofriendly dialect is unlikely to prove successful. Renaming the vulgar names for life forms in the English language of the eighteenth century and replacing them with scientific ones did little to improve Britain's natural environment (Thomas 1983). What is important rather is to recognize the importance of multiple perspectives, dynamic dialects (Døør & Bang 1996), and the inevitability of change. This requires adopting Halliday's instructions to be critically aware of the instrument of language and its uses. Green approaches to discourse can promote awareness that the language one uses privileges certain perceptions and actions and that expressing matters differently will privilege others. The view that perfection is not in any single entity, but requires a diversity of expressions (Harmon 2002), is one of the central insights of ecological thinking and ecological approaches to language.

SUMMARY POINTS

1. The study of environmental discourse requires a number of approaches. It is necessarily an interdisciplinary exercise.

2. The study of environmental discourses is typically carried out by scholars who have agendas other than merely describing such discourses. As a consequence, there is a blurring between discourse and metadiscourse.

3. The vastness of the topic requires a descriptive framework that can accommodate a maximum number of properties of environmental discourses. An ethnography of communication approach was chosen for this reason.

4. The study of environmental discourses is a relatively recent phenomenon dating from the late 1980s. Most studies challenge the mainstream view of language as found in structuralist and generative linguistics.

FUTURE ISSUES TO BE RESOLVED

1. It remains to be established how precisely and to what extent discursive practices impact on the natural environment. One particular problem is that human discourses selectively focus on only a small subset of environmental phenomena.

2. It is not clear to what extent the anthropocentrism of human languages can be overcome by deliberate acts of language planning.

3. The efficacy of environmental discourse for resolving the global environmental crisis remains ill understood.

LITERATURE CITED

Adam B. 1997. Running out of time: global crisis and human engagement. In *Social Theory and Global Environment*, ed. M Redclift, T Benton, pp. 92–112. London: Routledge

Agarwal A, Narain S. 1991. Global warming in an unequal world: a case of environmental Colonialism. *Earth Island J.* 6:39–40

Alexander RJ. 2000. The framing of ecology: some remarks on the relation between language and economics. See Ketteman & Penz 2000, pp. 173–90

Alexander RJ. 2002. Everyone is talking about 'sustainable development.' Can they all mean the same thing? Computer discourse analysis of ecological texts. See Fill et al. 2002, pp. 239–54

Benton LM. 1995. Selling the natural or selling out? Explaining environmental merchandising. *Environ. Ethics* 17(1):3–22

Beck U. 1992. *Risk Society: Towards a New Modernity*. London: Sage

Beder S. 1997. *Global Spin: The Corporate Assault on Environmentalism*. Melbourne: Scribe

Bowerbank S. 1999. Nature writing as self-technology. In *Discourses of the Environment*, ed. E Darier, pp. 163–78. Oxford: Blackwell

Brosius JP. 1999. Analyses and interventions: anthropological engagements with environmentalism. *Curr. Anthropol.* 40(3):277–309

Browning LD, Shetler JC. 1992. Communication in crisis, communication in recovery: a postmodern commentary on the Exxon Valdez disaster. *Int. J. Mass Emerg. Disasters* 10(2):477–98

Bruner M, Oelschlaeger M. 1994. Rhetoric, environmentalism, and environmental ethics. *Environ. Ethics* 16:377–95

Bullis C. 1992. Retalking environmental discourses from feminist perspectives: the radical potential of ecofeminism. See Oravec & Cantrill 1992, pp. 346–59

Burnett GW, Kamuyu wa Kang'ethe. 1994. Wilderness and the Bantu mind. *Environ. Ethics* 16(2):145–60

Caplan P, ed. 2000. *Risk Revisited*. London: Pluto Press

Carbaugh D. 1992. 'The mountain' and 'the project': dueling depictions of a natural environment. See Oravec & Cantrill 1992, pp. 360–76

Carson R. 1962. *Silent Spring*. Boston: Houghton Mifflin

Conca K, Dabelko GD, eds. 1998. *Green Planet Blues: Environmental Politics from Stockholm to Kyoto*. Boulder, CO: Westview

Cronon W. 1992. A place for stories: nature, history, and narrative. *J. Am. Hist.* 78:1347–76

Cronon W, ed. 1996. *Uncommon Ground: Rethinking the Human Place in Nature*. New York: Norton

Crosby AW. 1986. *Ecological Imperialism: The Biological Expansion of Europe 900–1900*. Cambridge, UK: Cambridge Univ. Press

Delli C, Michael X, Williams BA. 1994. "Fictional" and "nonfictional" television celebrates Earth Day: or politics in comedy plus pretence. *Cult. Stud.* 8(1):74–98

Døør J, Bang JC. 1996. Ecology and truth: dialogue and dialectics. See Fill 1996, pp. 17–25

Döring M. 2002. "Vereint hinterm Deich"—die metaphorische konstruktion der wiedervereinigung in der deutschen presseberichterstatttung zur oderflut 1997. See Fill et al. 2002, pp. 255–73

Döring M. 2004. Rinderwahnsinn: das Unbehagen in der kultur und die metaphorischdiskursive ordnung ihres risikomaterials. **http://www.metaphorik.de/aufsaetze/doeringbse.htm**

Downs A. 1972. Up and down with ecology-the 'issue-attention' cycle. *Public Interest* 28:38–51

Doyle J. 1991. *Hold the Applause*. Washington, DC: Friends Earth Monogr.

Doyle T, Kellow AJ. 1995. *Environmental Politics and Policy Making in Australia*. Melbourne: Macmillan

Dryzek JS. 1997. *The Politics of the Earth: Environmental Discourses*. Oxford/New York: Oxford Univ. Press

Dunayer J. 2001. *Animal Equity: Language and Liberation*. Derwood, MD: Ryce

Dyer K, Dyer J. 1990. The print media and the environment. See Dyer & Young 1990, pp. 530–47

Dyer K, Young J, eds. 1990. *Changing Directions: The Proceedings of Ecopolitics IV*. Adelaide: Cent. Environ. Stud.

Ehrlich PR. 1969. *The Population Bomb*. San Francisco: Sierra Club

Ehrlich PR, Ehrlich AH. 1996. *Betrayal of Science and Reason: How Anti-Environmental Rhetoric Threatens Our Future*. Washington, DC: Island Press

Elkington J, Knight P, Hailes J. 1988. *The Green Consumer Guide: From Hairspray to Hamburgers—Shopping for a Better Environment*. Melbourne: Penguin Books

Estok SC. 2001. A report card on ecocriticism. *AUMLA: J. Aust. Univ. Lang. Lit. Assoc.* 96:220–38. **http://www.asle.umn.edu/archive/intro/estok**

Fairclough N, ed. 1992. *Critical Language Awareness*. London: Longman

Farrell TB, Goodnight GT. 1998. Accidental rhetoric: the root metaphors of Three Mile Island. See Waddell 1998, pp. 75–105

Fill A. 1993. *Ökolinguistik–Eine Einführung*. Tübingen: Narr

Fill A, ed. 1996. *Sprachökologie und Ökolinguistik*. Tübingen: Stauffenburg

Fill A. 2003. Language and ecology: ecolinguistic perspectives for 2000 and beyond. *AILA Rev.: Appl. Linguist. 21st Century* 14:60–75

Fill A, Mühlhäusler P, eds. 2001. *The Ecolinguistics Reader*. London/New York: Continuum

Fill A, Penz H, Trampe W, eds. 2002. *Colourful Green Ideas*. New York: Peter Lang

Finke P. 2002. Die nachhaltigkeit der sprache-fünf ineinander verschachtelte puppen der linguistischen Ökonomie. See Fill et al. 2002, pp. 29–58

Fortun K. 2001. *Advocacy After Bophal*. Chicago: Univ. Chicago Press

Genske DD, Hess-Lüttich EWB. 2002. Gespräche übers wasser ein ökosemiotisches projekt zur umweltkommunikation im Nord-Süd-Dialog. See Fill et al. 2002, pp. 299–326

Gerbig A. 2000. Patterns of language use in discourse on the environment: a corpus-based approach. See Ketteman & Penz 2000, pp. 191–216

Goatly A. 2001. Green grammar and grammatical metaphor, or language and myth of power, or metaphors we die by. See Fill & Mühlhäusler 2001, pp. 203–25

The first book-length introduction to ecolinguistics contains both a history of the field and numerous suggestions for future research.

Compiles important documents addressing the ecology of language and ecolinguistics. Many were published in inaccessible places and had not attracted the attention deserved.

Was compiled on the occasion of 30 years of ecolinguistic studies. Contains a number of important articles illustrating ecolinguistic analysis as well as suggestions for future research.

Grossman R. 1989. Of time and tide: media and the environment. *Chain React.*, Winter, pp. 18–19

Grove RH. 1992. Origins of western environmentalism. *Sci. Am.* 267:22–27

Hajer MA. 1995. *The Politics of Environmental Discourse: Ecological Modernization and the Policy Process.* Oxford: Clarendon

Halliday MAK. 2001. New ways of meaning: the challenge to applied linguistics. See Fill & Mühlhäusler 2001, pp. 175–202

Halliday MAK, Martin J. 1993. *Writing Science, Literacy and Discursive Power.* London: Falmer

Hansen A, ed. 1996. *The Mass Media and Environmental Issues.* Leicester: Leicester Univ. Press

Harmon D. 1996. Losing species, losing languages: connections between biological and linguistic diversity. *Southwest J. Linguist.* 15:89–108

Harmon D. 2002. *In Light of Our Differences: How Diversity in Nature and Culture Makes Us Human.* Washington, DC/London: Smithson. Inst. Press

Harré R, Brockmeier J, Mühlhäusler P. 1999. *Greenspeak: A Study of Environmental Discourse.* **California/London/New Delhi: Sage**

> Brings together philosophical, psychological, and linguistic insights into environmental discourse. Addresses the structure of environmental narratives and environmental metaphor.

Harris R. 1981. *The Language Myth.* London: Duckworth

Harris R. 2001. A note on the linguistics of environmentalism. See Fill & Mühlhäusler 2001, pp. 154–58

Haugen E. 1972. The ecology of language. In *The Ecology of Language: Essays by Einar Haugen,* ed. AS Dill, pp. 325–39. Stanford, CA: Stanford Univ. Press

Herndl CG, Brown SC, eds. 1996. *Green Culture: Environmental Rhetoric in Contemporary America.* Madison: Univ. Wis. Press

Hochman J. 1997. Green cultural studies: an introductory critique of an emerging discipline. *Mosaic* 30(1):81–97

Howard P. 1978. *Weasel Words.* London: Hamilton

Hymes D. 1972. The ethnography of speaking. In *Anthropology and Human Behavior,* ed. T Gladwin, WC Sturtevant, pp. 15–53. Washington, DC: Anthropol. Soc. Wash.

Jagtenberg T. 1994. The end of nature? *Aust. J. Commun.* 21(3):14–25

Jagtenberg T, McKie D. 1997. *Eco-Impacts and the Greening of Postmodernity: New Maps for Communication Studies, Cultural Studies, and Sociology.* Thousand Oaks, CA: Sage

Jamison A. 2001. *The Making of Green Knowledge: Environmental Politics and Cultural Transformation.* Cambridge: Cambridge Univ. Press

Johnson C. 1991. *Green Dictionary.* London: Macdonald

Jones D. 1994. Nga Kaitaki and the managers: bicultural communication and resource management in Aotearoa/New Zealand. *Aust. J. Commun.* 21(3):105–16

Joseph JE. 2000. *Limiting the Arbitrary: Linguistic Naturalism and Its Opposites in Plato's Cratylus and Modern Theories of Language.* Amesterdam/Philadelphia: Benjamins

Jung M. 1996. Ökologische Sprachkritik. See Fill 1996, pp. 149–73

Kahn M. 2001. The passive voice of science: language abuse in the wildlife profession. See Fill & Mühlhäusler 2001, pp. 241–44

Kelly P. 1984. *Fighting for Hope.* London: Chatto & Windus

Ketteman B, Penz H, eds. 2000. *ECOnstructing Language, Nature and Society: The Ecolinguistic Project Revisited.* Tübingen: Stauffenburg

Killingsworth JM, Palmer SP. 1992. *Ecospeak: Rhetoric and Environmental Politics in America.* Carbondale: South. Ill. Univ. Press

Knight J, ed. 2000. *Natural Enemies: People-Wildlife Conflicts in Anthropological Perspective.* London: Routledge

Lakoff J, Johnson M. 1980. *Metaphors We Live By.* Chicago: Univ. Chicago Press

Landy M, ed. 1979. *Environmental Impact Statement Glossary: A Reference Source for EIS Writers, Reviewers and Citizens*. New York: IFI/Plenum

Lanthier I, Olivier L. 1999. The construction of environmental 'awareness.' In *Discourses of the Environment*, ed. E Darier, pp. 63–78. Malden, PA: Blackwell

Leach E. 1968. Anthropological aspects of language: animal categories and verbal abuse. In *New Directions in the Study of Language*, ed. EH Lenneberg, pp. 23–63. Cambridge, MA: MIT Press

Lee JA. 1988. Seals, wolves, and words: loaded language in environmental controversy. *Alternatives* 15(4):21–29

Lenz T. 2003. 'How to get consumer trust in food? Approaches of governmental authorities and food producers.' *Hamburg Conf. "Does Discourse Matter? Discourse, Power and Institutions in the Sustainability Transition."* Hamburg: Res. Cent. Biotechnol. Soc. Environ./Inst. Polit. Sci. Univ. Hamburg

Leuthold M. 1999. Eco-knowledge for the future or "interference is the only way to stay realistic." In *Paradigms and Contentions, IWM Junior Visiting Fellows Conferences*, ed. M Gomez, A Guthmiller, S Kalt, Vol. 7. **http://www.iwm.at/publ-jvc/jc-07–08.pdf**

Liddicoat AF, Bryant P. 2000. Language planning and language ecology: a current issue in language planning. *Curr. Issues Lang. Plan.* 1(3):303–5

Liebert WA. 2001. The sociohistorical dynamics of language and cognition: the emergence of the metaphor model 'money is water' in the Nineteenth Century. See Fill & Mühlhäusler 2001, pp. 101–6

Little PE. 1999. Environments and environmentalisms in anthropological research: facing a new millennium. *Annu. Rev. Anthropol.* 28:253–84

Lovelock J. 1979. *Gaia: A New Look at Life on Earth*. Oxford: Oxford Univ. Press

Lucas A. 1994. Lucas Heights revisited: the framing of a major scientific controversy by the *Sydney Morning Herald. Aust. J. Commun.* 21(3):72–91

Luke TW. 1993. Green consumerism: ecology and the ruse of recycling. In *In the Nature of Things: Language, Politics and the Environment*, ed. J Bennett, W Chaloupka, pp. 154–71. Minneapolis: Univ. Minn. Press

Luke TW. 1997. *Ecocritique: Contesting the Politics of Nature, Economy and Culture*. Minneapolis: Univ. Minn. Press

Maffi L, ed. 2001a. *On Biocultural Diversity*. Washington, DC: Smithson. Inst. Press

Maffi L. 2001b. Introduction: on the interdependence of biological and cultural diversity. See Maffi 2001a, pp. 1–50

Marko G. 2000. Go veggie! A critical discourse analysis of a text for vegetarian beginners. See Ketteman & Penz 2000, pp. 217–39

Marko G. 2002. Whales and language—critically analysing whale-friendly discourse. See Fill et al. 2002, pp. 341–60

Marnham. 1981. *Dispatches from Africa*. London: Abacus

Martin JR. 1986. Grammaticalizing ecology. The politics of baby seals and kangaroos. In *Semiotics, Ideology, Language*, ed. T Threadgold, EE Grosz, G Kress, MAK Halliday, pp. 235–67. Sydney: Sydney Assoc. Stud. Soc. Cult.

May S. 2003. Rearticulating the case for minority language rights. *Curr. Issues Lang. Plan.* 4(2):95–125

McKie D. 1994. Telling stories: unnatural histories, natural histories, and biopolitics. *Aust. J. Commun.* 21(3):92–104

McKie D. 2000. Informing environmental citizens: media technologies public relations and public understandings. *Eur. J. Commun.* 15(2):171–207

Compiles more than 30 papers addressing the interrelationship between the loss of the world's linguistic heritage and the loss of biological diversity.

Meadows DH, Meadows DL, Randers J, Behrens WW III. 1972. *The Limits to Growth*. London: Earth Island

Mills WT. 1982. Metaphorical vision: changes in western attitudes to the environment. *Ann. Assoc. Am. Geogr.* 72:237–53

Mühlhäusler P. 1983. Talking about environmental issues. *Lang. Commun.* 3(1):71–81

Mühlhäusler P. 1995. The interdependence of linguistic and biological diversity. See Myers 1995, pp. 154–61

Mühlhäusler P. 1996. Linguistic adaptation to changed environmental conditions: some lessons from the past. See Fill 1996, pp. 105–30

Mühlhäusler P. 1998. Some recent developments in Whorfian linguistics with special reference to environmental language. In *Sprache in Raum und Zeit. In Memoria Johannes Bechert*, K Wagner, W Wilden, W Boeder, C Schrieder, 2:35–43. Bremen: Universitäetsverlag

Mühlhäusler P. 1999. Metaphor and metonymy in environmental advertising. *AAA-Arb. Angl. Am.* 24(2):167–80

Mühlhäusler P. 2000. Language planning and language ecology. *Curr. Issues Lang. Plan.* 1(3):306–67

Mühlhäusler P. 2003. *Language of Environment, Environment of Language: A Course in Ecolinguistics*. London: Battlebridge

Mühlhäusler P, Peace A. 2001. Discourses of ecotourism: the case of Fraser Island. *Lang. Commun.* 21:359–80

Muir S, Veenendall T, eds. 1996. *Earthtalk: Community Empowerment for Environmental Action*. Westport, CT: Praeger

Müller M. 1855. *The Languages of the Seat of War in the East with a Survey of the Three Families of Language, Semitic, Arian, and Turanian*. London: Williams & Norgate

Myers D, ed. 1995. *The Politics of Multiculturalism in Oceania and Polynesia*. Darwin: Univ. North. Territory Press

Myerson G, Rydin Y. 1996. *The Language of Environment: A New Rhetoric*. London: UCL Press

Neuwirth G. 2002. Eco-linguistics–going beyond the text. See Fill et al. 2002, pp. 361–71

Nuckolls JB. 1999. The case for sound symbolism. *Annu. Rev. Anthropol.* 28:225–52

Oravec CL, Cantrill JG, eds. 1992. *The Conference on the Discourse of Environmental Advocacy*. Utah: Univ. Utah Humanit. Cent.

Peace A. 2005. Loving leviathan: the discourse of whale watching in an Australian eco-tourist location. In *Animals in Person: Cultural Perspectives on Human-Animal Intimacies*, ed. J Knight, pp. 191–210. London: Routledge

Peet R, Watts M, eds. 1996. *Liberation Ecologies: Environments, Development, Social Movements*. London: Routledge

Penman R. 1994. Environmental matters and communication challenges. *Aust. J. Commun.* 21(3):26–39

Phillips L. 2000. Mediated communication and the privatization of public problems: discourse on ecological risks and political action. *Eur. J. Commun.* 15(2):171–207

Posner R. 1990. *Warnungen an die Ferne Zukunft: Atommüll als Kommunikiationsproblem*. München: Raben Verlag

Raglan R. 1991. Re-establishing connections. *Alternatives* 17(4):28–35

Redclift M. 1987. *Sustainable Development: Exploring the Contradictions*. London/ New York: Methuen

Reddy MJ. 1979. The conduit metaphor: a case of frame conflict in our language about language. In *Metaphor and Thought*, ed. A Ortony, pp. 284–324. Cambridge, MA: Cambridge Univ. Press

Book-length introduction to ecolinguistics containing chapters about environmental discourse and environmental metaphor.

An interdisciplinary study of environmental debates concentrating on the rhetorical devices employed in them. Contains numerous examples of environmental texts.

An early document containing more than 30 contributions on the language of environmental advocacy. Many of the themes first addressed here have been taken up by subsequent analysts.

Richards P. 1992. *Conversation about conservation.* Ms. thesis. Dep. Anthropol., Kings College, London

Rissel C, Douglas W. 1993. Environmental issues as prime time television. *Media Inf. Aust.* 68:86–92

Rojas CE. 2001. *Discourses of the environment in the Northern Expansion of Santafé de Bogotá.* MA thesis. Univ. Cincinnati, Cincinnati

Rose D. 2004. The ecological humanities in action: an invitation. *Aust. Humanit. Rev.*, Issue 31–32. **http://www.lib.latrobe.edu.au/AHR/archive/Issue-April-2004./rose.html**

Rowe SJ. 1989. What on earth is environment? *Trumpeter* 6(4):123–26

Rutherford P. 1994. The administration of life: ecological discourse as 'intellectual machinery of government.' *Aust. J. Commun.* 21(3):40–55

Sapir E . 1912. Language and Environment. *Am. Anthropol.* 14:226–42

Schaffer K. 1988. *Women and the Bush. Faces of Desire in the Australian Cultural Tradition.* Cambridge, UK: Cambridge Univ. Press

Schiewer GL. 2002. Sind gesellschaftliche diskurse über technikfolgen rational? Kooperative verständigung in kommunikationstheoretischer perspektive. See Fill et al. 2002, pp. 395–412

Schultz B. 2001. Language and the natural environment. See Fill & Mühlhäusler 2001, pp. 109–14

Segal JZ. 1991. The structure of advocacy: a study of environmental rhetoric. *Can. J. Commun.* 16(3/4). **http://www.wlu/ca/~wwwpress/jrls/cj/BackIssues?16.3/segal.html**

Spaargaren G, Mol APJ, Buttel FH, eds. 2000. *Environment and Global Modernity.* London: Sage

Stauber J, Rampton S. 1995. *Toxic Sludge is Good for You! Lies, Damned Lies and the Public Relations Industry.* Monroe, ME: Common Courage Press

Stibbe A. 2004. Moving away from ecological 'political correctness'. *Lang. Ecol. Online J.* pp. 1–6. **http://www.ecoling.net/magazine.html**

Stork Y. 1998. *Ecologie: Die Geschichte zentraler Lexien des französischen Umweltvokabulars seit 1968.* Germany: Tübigen

Strang V. 2004. *The Meaning of Water.* Oxford: Berg

Stratford E. 1994. Disciplining the feminine, the home, and nature in three Australian public health histories. *Aust. J. Commun.* 21(3):56–71

Tansley AG. 1991. The use of abuse of vegetational concepts and terms. In *Foundations of Ecology*, ed. LA Real, JH Brown, pp. 318–41. Chicago: Univ. Chicago Press

Taylor PJ, Buttel FH. 1992. How do we know we have global environmental problems? Science and globalization of environmental discourse. *Geoforum* 23(3):405–16

Taylor SG. 1990. Naturalness: the concept and its application to Australian ecosystems. *Proc. Ecol. Soc. Aust.* 16:411–18

Thomas K. 1983. *Man and the Natural World: Changing Attitudes in England 1500–1800.* Harmondsworth: Penguin Books

Thompson JN. 1994. *The Coevolutionary Process.* Chicago: Univ. Chicago Press

Toolan M. 1996. *Total Speech: An Integrational Linguistic Approach to Language.* Durham: Duke Univ. Press

Trampe W. 2001. Language and ecological crisis: extracts from a dictionary of industrial agriculture. See Fill & Mühlhäusler 2001, pp. 232–40

Verhagen FC. 2000. Ecolinguistics: a retrospect and a prospect. See Ketteman & Penz 2000, pp. 33–48

Vivanco LA. 2002. Seeing green: knowing and saving the environment on film. *Am. Anthropol.* 104(4):1195–1204

Waddell C, ed. 1998. *Landmark Essays on Rhetoric and the Environment.* Mahwah, NJ: Hermagoras

Weigl E. 2004. Wald und Klima: Ein Mythos aus dem 19. Jahrhundert. *(Humboldt im Netz) Int. Rev. Humboldt. Stud.* 9:1–20

Weissmann G. 1996. Ecosentimentalism: the summer dream beneath the tamarind tree. *Ann. NY Acad. Sci.* 27:483–89

Williams R. 1983. *Keywords: A Vocabulary of Culture and Society.* New York: Oxford Univ. Press

Worster D. 1990. Seeing beyond culture. *J. Am. Hist.* 36:1142–47

Old Wine, New Ethnographic Lexicography

Michael Silverstein

Department of Anthropology, University of Chicago, Chicago, Illinois 60637-1580;
email: m-silverstein@uchicago.edu

Annu. Rev. Anthropol. 2006. 35:481–96

First published online as a Review in
Advance on June 21, 2006

The *Annual Review of Anthropology* is
online at anthro.annualreviews.org

This article's doi:
10.1146/annurev.anthro.35.081705.123327

Copyright © 2006 by Annual Reviews.
All rights reserved

0084-6570/06/1021-0481$20.00

Key Words

lexical registers, word-meaning, cultural knowledge,
sociolinguistics, wine connoisseurship, oenology and viticulture

Abstract

The interests of anthropologists, focused on using the "meaning" of
words and expressions as an entrée into understanding cultures, and
of linguists, focused on the grammatically relevant sense components of abstract lexical forms, can be differentiated. A multicompo-
nential lexicography is outlined for investigating various *oinoglossic*
("wine-talk") registers of language, adequate to exploring this sociologically complex field of discourse spanning wine production, marketing, consumption, and connoisseurship. This approach builds on
developments of the past 30 years in linguistic anthropology and related areas that have clarified the relations of structural sense, stereo-
typy (cultural concepts), and indexicality in language, and how and
where to investigate these very different semiotic partials of language
use.

INTRODUCTION

Culture is, in some sense, encyclopedic knowledge unevenly distributed over socio-historically specific groups of people who actualize their groupness through interaction, principally, discursive interaction. Here, I bring together some considerations for how linguistic anthropology can investigate that group-specific knowledge by combining linguistic and cognitive science's concern with lexicographic semantics (the meanings of words and expressions) with the study of language use in interactional contexts (how a central medium of social action is precipitating texts-in-contexts, "doing things with words").

RECUPERATING AN ETHNOGRAPHIC LEXICOGRAPHY: CULTURAL CONCEPTS

What I term the psychophysical theory of language—shared by Franz Boas and his descendents down to the older tradition of cognitive anthropology—saw words and fixed expressions as implicit responses, in the realm of denotation, that rest on classifications or categorizations of the universe of experience-able stimuli, from the sensorial to the imagined. Boas himself developed this into the fruitful tradition of semantic analysis of the structural grammatical categories immanent in the presenting words and expressions of language. Out of these insights, among others, grew the American descriptivist tradition of Edward Sapir, Leonard Bloomfield himself (though not all Bloomfield's followers), Benjamin Lee Whorf, and their descendents (among them, this author). Saussure had, equivalently, adumbrated all this in his epistemological doctrine that our ability to describe the signifier–signified relation depends on the logically prior establishment of systems of relative "value" among signifiers themselves (syntagmatic and paradigmatic distributional relations), which project as structures of difference onto differences among signifieds, that is, onto normative conceptual distinctions. Within anthropological circles, by contrast, notwithstanding the prestige of structural linguistics at several historical moments, these fundamental structural lessons were eclipsed.

Instead, some anthropologists attempted to study the cognitive realm of cultural concepts in a linguistically prestructural, Stimulus-Response inspired field lexicology (see Tyler 1969; repudiated in Tyler 1978; see the introductory essay in Laughlin 1975, and compare D'Andrade 1995). It attempted to square the semantic circle by taking the very nomenclaturist view of words and lexemic expressions that Saussure had shown to be incoherent as a scientific approach to denotational meaning, whatever people feel intuitively about the applicability of words directly to "reality." According to methods proposed, all one needed to do was to hold up sets of objects and see which term people—What people? When? Under what conditions?—would use to label these objects "literally," whether the objects were flora and fauna, manufactured items, or kinspeople "held up" by proper name in the genealogical method. One could sort the denotata by response pattern (word used to refer to them) and attempt then, presumably with one's necessarily independent and autonomous "scientific" knowledge of the denotata themselves, somehow to extract the categorical semantics implicit in this approach, that is, the fixed and literal senses differentially cued by each of the lexical forms. (Somewhat more sophisticated versions in the psychological mode used hierarchical cluster analysis and/or multivariate statistical models to group denotata, but the nature of these factorial groupings still rests on supposed autonomous knowledge of them offered by the scientist.)

Needless to say, any approach to lexically coded categories that ignores grammar is anathema to the linguist, just as any such approach that ignores the local semiotic processes by which people seem to attain, maintain, and transform their ongoing alignments one to another in respect of reference groups and categories would be anathema to the sociocultural anthropologist. Attacked thus both within anthropology and beyond by all manner of critique, some of it interesting, some merely at the outer fringe of what I term nihilistic relativism, e.g., Schneider 1976, 1984—the last always leading to the epistemological hypochondria of the would-be student of another culture ever afraid of formulating an analytical truth-claim about it!—these well-intentioned cognitive categorial tentatives were mostly abandoned or at least marginalized within anthropology more widely (but generally for the wrong reasons).

Yet such eclipsed approaches deal with perhaps the most important methodological issue of anthropology: how to investigate how cultural knowledge manifests in the most important "official" semiotic mode of culture, discursive language. This report attempts, within a particular domain of our own contemporary sociocultural life in mass, stratified societies, to demonstrate how to study cultural concepts manifest in language-in-use for a realm of conceptual distinctions only marginally approachable in the chemistry or biology laboratory—even if we still have a positivist's faith in the clarity with which these can explain psychophysical reality. It is the domain of wine, "culturally" experienced by involving the human body in an aesthetic as well as gustatory encounter.

TALKING ABOUT WINE AS A CULTURAL OBJECT AND DENOTATIONAL DOMAIN

Traditionally counting as a prestige, almost sacralized comestible—certainly a continuing factor anchoring its cultural and economic position in the American and other contexts (Fuller 1993, 1996)—wine lives a cultural life at once as commodity produced, marketed, and consumed, and as aesthetic form one experiences with a sensorium and judgment, however "naturally" sensitive, as well

potentially "refined" through training, cumulative experience, and the subtlety of aesthetic memory.

As a drinkable commodity, it is, of course, the emergent product of refined, sometimes "boutique" agricultural techniques—depending on market-segment destination (Ulin 2002, p. 698)—of growing, harvesting, pressing, vat or barrel fermenting, and bottling, followed by distribution at wholesale and retail levels, reaching consumers as a measured, packaged, labeled substance with a history and even a future bound up with numbers: bottle volume in standard sizes, year of vintage (harvesting and final release), quantity of production, number of exemplars still in commodity circulation at any given moment, etc. Market forces of supply and demand, manipulated by advertising and other discursive techniques of salesmanship, as well as risk forces in the market mode of futures, as for any traded agricultural commodity, frame the value of this commodity at every stage, even, only in memory, as an ultimate metric of distinction (or its lack) applied against other, comparable exemplars (as, for example, a past vintage one has experienced of otherwise the "same" wine).

As an art form, wine is indeed subject to a social organization of value-determining connoisseurship, in which, at various stages of its existence, the licensed exercise of "the judg[e]ment of taste" (Bourdieu 1984) is the central performative act, a "representative declarative" one (Hancher 1979, p. 3), like that of an umpire in a game, with repercussions that vary in their subtended domain of effectiveness. Like connoisseurship in other realms—think of European painting, or African carving, or period furniture—there is a structure of authority to judgments that radiate from the representative-declarative acts of some to inform those of others by a kind of interdiscursivity. One quotes or cites or alludes to authority in orienting oneself to the object of aesthetic judgment. (Think Clement Greenberg in relation to having to judge a Jackson Pollock painting.)

Professional connoisseurs, those in the business itself, begin to interact with wine early in its commodity career, potentially setting price at wholesale as well as retail planes of circulation for many years to come. There is a whole critical apparatus that has emerged around (retail) wine consumption as an aesthetic experience, manifest even to the occasional consumer in the "food" or "living," a.k.a. "lifestyle" sections of newspapers and magazines. Quotation of authorities in retail shops brings the texts of connoisseurship to the very site of in-person marketing, an on-site, subtle form of advertising. For the more seriously devoted, there is a whole apparatus of newsletters, magazines, and Web sites devoted to wine. For a certain stratum of clientele, these publications reflect a lifestyle orientation emphasizing wine, including variously staged tastings with or without an accompanying meal that are frequently built around a thematic grape type, wine variety, grower, shipper, region, or country of origin, and are frequently followed—compare the author's tour with readings, book sales, and signings—by purchases or auctions. (There are comparable, generally elite, male-oriented endeavors for almost any prestige comestible, from microbrewery beer to scotch whisky to cigars, just as there have been for collectibles in realms such as automobiles and old technology). These, in turn, influence the market at the more rarefied orders of distinction.

Again, as in other realms of art, connoisseurship judgments change over time, values increasing and decreasing as particular labeled wines, particular vintages of wines, particular geographical regions, or particular styles of vinification come to be reevaluated, all with effects on then-current value in futurities of the commodity within its subsequent market phases. Like unique objects of plastic and graphic art, or heirloom and pedigreed items, which derive at least part of their marketable uniqueness from association ("wine once in the cellar of . . . !"), wine is continuously sold and resold at auction, for example, estate sales. Hence, just as for other auctioned aesthetic

commodities and collectible rarities, one can follow curves of appreciation and depreciation in value for a particular wine relative to its fields of comparison.

WINE TALKS: OUR BOUQUETS-AND-BODIES, OUR SELVES

At each of the phases of the sociocultural life of wine, interested people come together in various kinds of events that centrally involve discourse, using language in genre-specific interactional events. As in many similar cases, then, language in use thus becomes a mediating *tertium a quo* between humans and their fashioned agricultural and aesthetic commodity, wine. And in this process, organized around representations of their relationships to it, they become aligned one to another mediated not directly by wine in its physicochemical or even directly sensorial presence, so much as by the discursive processes of representation of it—at the last stage, critically peaking in the authoritatively structured tasting note communicated in dense, *oinoglossic* ("wine talk") register—on particular occasions of social relationality.

This sociolinguistic situation can be recognized by how its semiotic processes operate in both directions. On the one hand, to the extent that intersubjective alignments are achieved in interaction by negotiating relevant aspects of how wine is described in language, wine's dimensions of evaluation over its existential course are, in effect, thus projectively constructed as much as reflectively construed (compare Bourdieu 1991, pp. 127–36; Latour 1987, pp. 179–213; Silverstein 2004, pp. 640–44; Viechnicki 2002). Studying how such descriptive construals/constructions arise reveals the cultural bases for the aesthetic experience of what seems, merely, to be "there," comprising the object of denotation. On the other hand, studying how people use the discursive machinery for representing wine, chiefly lexemes and certain constructions with them—Who uses it, and with what kind and degree of control? With what authority and authoritativeness of judgment so rendered?—reveals the sociolinguistically nonhomogeneous distribution of facility with "wine-talk" even within a single language community, in effect providing an index of various relationally achieved identities made relevant in the act of using language to communicate about the object at hand.

The important fact, then, is that "I" *am* to a certain extent what "I" say about "what" "I" drink as much as what "I" say about "it" reflects what "I" can discern "what" "it" *is*. In the representative-declarative communication of judgment or evaluation, this semiotic consubstantiality facilitates the transduction of value across the realms of commodity/experience and commodity-experiencer, in a moment of reversible fetishization. Interested institutional forces are, however, hard at work to give directionality to this process, seeking to establish a solid foundation of "true" worth of the object by naturalizing (essentializing) hierarchies of distinction across these realms. Is one's palate or sensorium subtle enough for the exquisite subtleties of a viniferous experience? Has one a sufficient comparative tasting experience to judge a particular vintage at hand? These are the kinds of increments that place humans in hierarchical series parallel to the objects of connoisseurship and description. The proof of it all is, of course, one's fluent, fluid, textually conforming verbal usage.

The sociocultural study of language use as event and as process in a macrosocial formation is, thus, interested, in principle, in tracking the ways in which all this takes place, exemplifying the transduction of values across the realms of commodities and humans in this particularly interesting domain of practice. Interestingly, the traditional semantically centered study of words and fixed lexical expressions (lexemes) also rapidly discovers the complexities of what seems, at first, like the aggregated vocabulary of the language that just happens to be specialized for the deno-

tational domains of viticulture and enology. This is true both of lexicology, the word-root-and-stem-focused complement of the linguist's morphosyntactic study of language structure, and of practical lexicography, organized information about words with a view to dictionary making. Some writers on wine terminology—e.g., Brochet & Dubourdieu 2001; Lehrer 1975, 1983; Magalhães 2000; Teil 2001—seem to be disturbed at the indexical semiosis involved.

SENSES OF LEXICAL PRIMES OF GRAMMAR VERSUS MEANINGS OF WORDS AND LEXICAL EXPRESSIONS

This chapter does not elaborate all the considerations of lexical semantics as a part of linguistics (see, e.g., Cruse 1986, 2004; Hüllen & Schulze 1988; Lieber 2004; Lyons 1995, pp. 46–130), but certainly one distinction must be stressed. A linguist's analysis of the structure of a language as a formal system proceeds under the assumption of sense-compositionality corresponding to constructional complexity. That is, the sense of every complex construction made up of simpler forms in determinate grammatical arrangement is assumed to be computable, a regular function of the senses of the simpler forms entering into the construction according to the way they are combined under their grammatical arrangement. This grammatical analysis ultimately leads to the identification of major and minor classes of lexical primes, the apparently simplest elements of sense compositionality, in what is termed the lexicon of a language (actually, the lexicon under a particular grammatical analysis of form). The classes of major lexical primes, serving as the constructional centers of phrases and words and generally termed parts of speech, range from two (basic distinction of open-class lexical primes, frequently with some restrictions on use in both referring and predicating parts of a sentence, and particles, as opposed to the closed-class, paradigmatic material with which the open-class items occur) to eight or nine (think of Indo-European noun, verb, adjective, adverb, preposition, conjunction, particle, interjection).

During the late 1960s and years following, a movement within then-current generative grammar, so-called generative semantics, proposed—correctly, under the Boasian and Saussurean assumptions about structure—that the systematic distributional properties of many or most of what at first appear to be lexical primes under grammatical analysis are, in fact, complex structural configurations of nonpatent (deeply underlying) semantic components: Thus, the seeming lexical prime [kill-]$_V$, as in A killed B, a transitive verb in English under the usual analysis, seems to have many distributional parallels—and sense-projections—in common with the complex construction [cause-$_V$ [[X]$_{NP}$ [die-]$_V$]$_S$]$_{VP}$, as in A caused B to die, suggesting that the sense-complexity visible for the latter is, in fact, implicitly the sense of the former and that therefore the sense-components of "causative" and "die," ordered into a constructional complex like that shown, really do comprise the lexical primes—now the lexicosemantic primes—of grammatical analysis communicated in the seemingly simplex prime kill-. (Note how this parallels, and generalizes, the much more agreed-upon notion that the sense-components of "female" and "human" are communicated by the simple lexical prime woman-, only here in simple Boolean additive combination.) Indeed, much fruitful work in the semantic decompositional mode was done along these lines, whatever are the shortcomings of generative semantics as a whole (see Goldsmith & Huck 1995; Harris 1993; Newmeyer 1986; Silverstein 1972 and references therein), leading to some of the positive aspects of its descendents, among them "cognitive linguistics" (Croft & Cruse 2004, Janssen & Redeker 1999, Talmy 2000, Taylor 2002).

By contrast, consider the totality of what one might term the "meaning" of a word or expression, the quarry of the layperson, of

the philosopher, of the philologist, and especially, for our purposes, of the anthropologist. Words and expressions occur in texts-in-contexts. Texts and their segments, even their "sentence-length" segments, are objects of a very different ontic sort from the grammarian's maximal, sense-compositional construction type, i.e., grammatical sentence, even though the lexicosemantic contribution of lexical primes in constructional (grammatical) arrangement can be discerned as one among the factors determining a word's or expression's actual meaning (what a user knows about how to use it). [The philosophy of language and mind was given a great reformational boost when Hilary Putnam (e.g., 1975, 1978) realized this.] The lexicographer, in particular, is concerned with such full meanings of words and fixed expressions, and modern dictionaries strive to provide information about the various components of meaning of these kinds of lexical objects—let us call them lexemes—ranging over several kinds (see Hartmann 2001, Jackson 2002, Landau 2001, Svensén 1993; also note Bergenholtz & Tarp 1995). To be sure, dictionaries do describe the properties of forms as grammaticosemantic units (as above). But additionally, through usage notes (synonymy, phrasal collocations including a particular form, etc.) and register alerts ("slang," "obscene"), they give normative indexical properties of a lexeme's appropriateness-to and effectiveness-in co(n)texts (abbreviating "contexts and/or cotexts") of occurrence: where to use it, and what, socially speaking, will happen if you do.

Through sometimes lengthy attempts at paraphrase and the use of "–onomic" differentiators (see below), dictionary entries try to delimit what conceptual distinctions are associated with, or cued by, the use of a word or expression as it can be applied to differentially denoting an object (or objects) in universes of reference and predication. Note that illustrations—photographs of "type specimens," charts organizing areas of denotable knowledge, labeled diagrams of constructional innards, the usual stuff of manuals and handbooks—are increasingly in use as well in dictionaries as accompaniments to the verbal material to serve as iconic aids in communicating the specific normative denotation of lexemes. A lexicographic treatment of "the meaning" of lexemes is thus a study of norms of use of words and expressions in various discursive co(n)texts, such norms including a great deal in addition to grammaticosemantic properties abstracted through the methods of lexical primes of structural distribution.

And yet, with all of these varied and useful pieces of information, the construction of the usual layperson's dictionary is not based on a systematic theorization of how words and expressions get their denotational norms and figurative extensions in the pragmatics—the practicalities—of situated verbal communication as sociocultural action. Part of the problem has rested on the laboriousness of lexicographic work, giving rise to the parody of the lexicographer as a "harmless drudge." We all know the story of the *New* (now *Oxford*) *English Dictionary* (*on Historical Principles*) and its painstaking, decades-long collection from diligent participants far and wide of slips with examples of English word usage (Mugglestone 2005, Willinsky 1994, Winchester 2003). (The current administration still encourages submission of new data by lay correspondents, as in the beginning, by the way, even in the digital age of the Internet!) Newer technologies for the creation of data-banks of digital text, and their automated concordancing, have alleviated at least some of this phase of drudgery (see for example Atkins et al. 2003 and Fillmore et al. 2003, among many). Large corpora of keyboarded running text can be searched to retrieve all tokens of some lexical form, together with their immediate collocational cotexts. People are even using sophisticated Boolean keyword searches through the Internet search engines, e.g., Google™, to collect instances of usage of particular lexemes and collocations with them. (Warning! Such a search with the phrase "wine terminology" in late December 2005 yielded more than 128,000 sites in 0.8 s.)

But since the very concept of a dictionary has long been projected from that of the grammarian's lexicon—which, in much structuralist dogma was associated with the "content" of language, grammar being merely its "form" of arrangement—without further input little more than collocational frequencies emerge from this mining of cotextuality, and perhaps nuances of constructional co-occurrence ["Is it 'practice in' or 'practice of' law?" (see now Hoey 2005)]. As vitally important and useful as is such information, it should be clear that its universe is that of textual form, cotextuality, narrowed to sequences of text sentences and their parts (Normand 1998), and that it never can get to contextuality in the wider sense except, perhaps, in the way of some genre data about the texts in which forms occur and some demographic information about the creators and targeted receivers of the texts where this is available, a kind of hit-or-miss archival philology.

HOW TO STUDY THE "MEANING" OF WINE TALK: LEXEMES AND "COHERENCE"

Only in the past 30 years or so have the parameters emerged of a more adequate and systematic treatment of "the meaning of 'meaning'" of words and expressions, one that grounds a truly anthropological lexicography, that is, a lexicography actually useful to—in fact, a central enterprise of—the ethnographic task of understanding cultures (see Putnam 1975; Silverstein 1976, pp. 51–54). Its roots lie (*a*) in seeing that what we would term cultural concepts as part of cultural knowledge—frequently implicit, sociohistorically group-specific understandings of the world that make up anything one would want to term a group's "culture"—are cued in coherent patterns involving words and expressions of language organized in textual form; (*b*) in seeing what are the contexts in which such textual forms occur and how they sometimes come to function as the mediators of group-forming and -sustaining social relations; and (c) in seeing that there are large-scale macroformations of politicoeconomic and similar institutional forces that structure the relations of interdiscursivity across contexts of use of textual genres and thus of the words and expressions of which they consist.

The first area concerns empirically discoverable patterns of textual coherence of at least two fundamental sorts involving arrangements of lexemes. One was long ago observed in a paper by Charles O. Frake (1969 [1964]), which he wittily titled, "Notes on Queries in Ethnography," aiming, apparently, to make clear some of the assumptions of the "white room ethnography" of the old cognitive anthropology. What Frake actually succeeds in demonstrating is that discourse in (or influenced by) various terminologized realms of cultural knowledge—his focus is Subanun *gasi* ("beer") making and beer connoisseurship—manifests implicit coherence relations among the terms that index or cue specialized cultural knowledge. Such coherence relations obtain both within text sentences, where mutual selectional restrictions limit which lexemes can occur with which others in certain construction types (English: * ... pregnant man ... in the "attribute + object" construction under "literal" denotational reading) and across text-sentences, according to the "poetics" of textually cohesive lexical ligatures (see below; compare Halliday & Hasan 1976). This "ethnoscience," as we might well apply the term, lying behind people's ability to understand the difference between coherent and incoherent use of terminology, can be subjected to explicit question (query) and answer routines using the privileged metasemantic operators that occur in the language itself, the schematic frames of which relate two or more denotational lexemes in such semantic relations as taxonomy [... is a kind of ...], partonomy (meronomy) [... is part of ...], n-dimensional paradigm [... differs from ... along ... dimension(s)],

series [... occurs before/after ... (in respect of ... dimension)], etc. In short, the varied kinds of conceptual structures of ordered knowledge are indexed—revealed to native users of the language—by how someone communicates using conceptual labels, lexicalized terms, in the flow of discourse that is produced and interpreted with implicit measures of coherence licensed by the locally relevant conceptual knowledge. The conceptual knowledge underlies one's ability to produce and to interpret discourse constructed with the domain-specific terms.

Cultural concepts in this view are points of relational conceptual distinction in knowledge structures; as senses conveyed in the process of using language, such concepts are indexed or cued by certain terms (words of consistent and recurrent denotational applicability). Thus, having a serial conceptual structure of the life stages of a species, say bovines, that includes, in order, "calf" and "cow/bull," we can use the words "calf-" and "bull-" consistently with this knowledge, such that we can even answer test questions about relative age of critters called (denoted) by the words: "True or false? A calf is older than a bull." These coherence relations are of the form of what I term the -onomic knowledge; using the terms according to such coherence relations at the same time indexes the status of individuals as warranted participants in discursive interactions that depend on the authority of such knowledge. The terms, in short, cue specific areas of cultural knowledge the manifesting of possession or control over which is frequently critical to identifiability of someone's group membership or one's status within a group or position in a network.

Moreover, as Putnam (1975) gestured toward with his phrase "the division of linguistic labor"—better corrected to "the sociolinguistic division of (denotational) labor" for our purposes—or as Bakhtin (1981, pp. 263, 291) suggested with his concept of heteroglossia at the level of lexicon, -onomic knowledge and its manifestation in essentially terminologized denotational usage is unevenly distributed in society. Not only do we use lexemic words and expressions with different "meanings," but we do so as a constantly shifting function of our biographical histories of participation in one or another social group, at one or another institutional site at which we live out our discursive lives as speakers (writers, signers) and hearers (readers, viewers). Some of this history is in fact indexed by the very patterns we inscribe in or ascribe to the denotational text that mediates our interactions with others. Whether we use certain kinds of vocabulary with the same degree of terminologized precision as our interlocutor(s), if at all (this article perhaps an example of the problem?); whether we control comparable structures of -onomic knowledge indexically referenced or cued by the use of particular words and expressions; whether the coherence structures built up in our discourse are manifest to our interlocutors, and ones to which they can contribute in the coconstruction of an intersubjective understanding of what is being represented in an event of communication, these kinds of variability are all documented in the use of lexemes both in our intuitive everyday experience and in the systematic work of gathering examples from actual discourse in lexicographic work. The sociological dividing lines tend to be marked particularly for areas of experience and conceptualization with sharp register characteristics, where -onomy-indexing denotational consistency of lexical usage transparently differentiates expertise from nonexpertise. Scientific discourse, whether in words or in mathematicized formulaics, is one such area, of course; discourses of connoisseurship, such as winetalk, or *oinoglossia* as I have dubbed it, are certainly others.

Observe the two-sided character of the indexical relationship between coherence structures of denotational discourse and -onomic knowledge. On the one hand, to the degree that discourse can be processed as coherent with respect to the -onomic knowledge it indexes, it relies on the social existence of that knowledge, a necessary conceptual underpinning of communication presumed to be shared among participants in a discursive interaction. On the other hand, note that certain important features of the coming-to-textual-formedness of discourse itself allow what we might term asymmetric -onomic communication, in which, in effect, new -onomic knowledge can be both created and taught by one person to another.

This partly depends on there being available in the language used a whole set of semantically structuring syntactic schemata [Tyler (1978, pp. 255–300) terms them structures with "[semantic] ordering functions"] that in effect "place" lexemes, and the concepts differentially associable with each, one with respect to another. Without a way of communicating, "The calf is a younger version (or earlier life-stage) of the cow/bull," invoking the seriality inherent in adjectival comparison [English, ... ADJ-er than ...] to relate the denotatum of the term calf- to that of the terms cow- or bull-, we could not teach someone who did not already have this -onomic knowledge the facts of bovine life. So being able to put lexemes pairwise (or multiply) into explicitly -onomically structuring syntactic constructions and equivalent cross-sentence textual structures is essential to creating new -onomic knowledge as sharable culture. Learning a new area of -onomic knowledge is focally a question of learning new coherence relations among its lexemes that become, to this extent, terminologized ways of using language (in text) to think about a particular area of concern. One can learn a new area of -onomic knowledge by learning to represent it, that is, to talk coherently about it: coherence measured by the way those with prior, recognizedly authoritative knowledge do. One can learn to be an expert.

Here, crucially, is also where the second aspect comes in of how lexemes are arranged in emergent structures of denotational text. This aspect depends on generalizing to the entire range of denotational discourse Jakobson's (1960) insights about "poetic function," that is, the coming of discourse ("message") to coherence as cotextual form as such. What Jakobson discerned is that special structures of semantic relationship—generally understood as tropic figures, like those of classical rhetoric and poetry—are communicated for elements of text that stand one to another in special metrical positions. Such positions can be a function of highly explicit canons of division of discourse into units, as in poetry and the poetries of ritual, or they can be implicit, as in so-called ordinary discourse. In the latter case, the systems of what are termed deictic elements—forms in languages that correspond to English word-forms now/here/this versus then/there/that and to various other word and phrase categories—provide structures of relational "placing" of lexemes one with respect to another, and therefore these suggest semantic structurings that coordinate the -onomic concepts associable with these lexemes one with respect to another. The order of occurrence of otherwise comparable lexemes in discourse suggests seriality in some domain, e.g., temporal or causal or order of importance; phrasings differentiating this...versus that...suggest asymmetric opposition within a taxonomy or meronomy of, for example, something more versus less immediate or even important. In this way, denotational textual structure, organized by principles of arrangement distinct from, but interacting with, those of grammar contributes to creating and transforming intersubjectively projectible -onomic structure (Silverstein 2004, pp. 627–31). Observe how a whole layer of metaphors of body and bodily cultivation used to describe wine itself has recently crept into French oinoglossic register (Coutier 1997), paralleling, and probably influenced by, the "poetically" organized Anglo-American register documented in Silverstein (2003 [1996], pp. 222–27; 2004, pp. 640–45). Compare as well the discursve and visual poetry of bodily "seduction" in Portuguese wine advertisements (Agua-Mel 2000).

OINOGLOSSIA AS GENRED DISCOURSE IN INTERACTIONAL CONTEXT

The second area of concern to an ethnographic lexicography is, perhaps, more familiarly sociolinguistic to those familiar with the earlier literatures (Gumperz & Hymes 1972, Hymes 1974, Labov 1972). It seeks to establish the genre characteristics of communicational events in which people engage in the interactional work associated with certain ways of using language. Key here is the work of defining, maintaining, and transforming people's group-relative interactional identities in the course of making text, as one is also accomplishing other institutionalized ends of which communication is part. (See now Agha 2006, Bucholtz & Hall 2004, Hastings & Manning 2004, Kiesling 2006, Manning 2003, and Silverstein 2004 for modern statements on this.) In realms of technical knowledge and the subtleties of connoisseurship, being able to communicate like someone with expertise, being able to place some communicating other in respect of regimes of expertise, are all part of one's communicative competence in respect of this factor in identity formation and maintenance.

Several factors must be singled out among all the complexities of these essentially indexical processes. Asymmetric distribution of such ways of communicating over a population organizes the population relative to a division by indexically signaled knowledge in any area of life. Wine-growers have special terminologized lexemes in their dialects and sociolects (Alanne 1957a, 1957b, 1961; Ezquerro 2000; Fierobe 1993; Henry 1996; Kadel 1928; Kies 1999; Kleiber 1980, 1990-; Martin 1977; Nuţă 1981, 1992). This is an expected part of the above-cited "sociolinguistic division of denotational labor," to be sure. Yet, both the competence in indexical practices—facility in sending signals of one's position—and the metapragmatic knowledge of what, precisely, such indexicals signal about a person—thus, being able to interpret with whom one is interacting—are involved here so that one can have grosser or finer abilities at both these planes of social knowledge. ("She sounds like a professor, but I can't fathom what might be her field of expertise!"; "Listen to his acute analysis of Kant's *Critique*, all in one-syllable words! He is clearly intellectual, but he doesn't sound like an intellectual or realize he is one!") So we see that in addition to the projection of denotational context that includes an information structure of communicable -onomic knowledge about some area of experience, there is a second, sociologically anchored layer of context created by indexical shibboleths among all the verbiage, points of salience as social indexes that mark in-group versus out-group membership, perhaps by degrees, of the individuals discoursing about the topic in which expertise and therefore authority come to reside as a possible social differentiator.

Among all the verbiage of communication, which kinds of key, potent, or active semiotic shibboleths accomplish these ends? In exploring this question, we observe that language used in particular contexts comes to form a register of expected, recurring collocations of words and expressions in particular kinds of constructional (grammatical) arrangements and semantic (-onomic) coherence structures, in short a lexicosyntactic register with generative properties (Whorf [1956] termed this a "fashion of speaking"), the mastery of which is part of demonstrating identity as such, and hence in-group/out-group distinctions across social boundaries (compare the classic paper of Ferguson 1983 on "sports announcer talk," for example). Mastery of a register, a characteristic way of talking about some area of experience, indexes one's membership in the social group that characteristically does so; professional or avocational registers (medicine, plumbing, computers, linguistic anthropology, oenology and viticulture, sports enthusiasts, bird watchers, etc.) are highly salient divisions of the total vocabulary and phraseology of a language such as English.

The fact of enregisterment, the generation of new registers and maintenance of a leading edge of innovation in registers that already exist, emerges from the sociolinguistic dialectic pointed out long ago by Gumperz (1968, pp. 383–84) and emphasized by Labov (1972, pp. 192–206). Within a linguistic community, the fact is that indexical variation is perceived through the lens of "different ways of 'saying the same thing,'" alternants coming to sociolinguistic salience for the community by being understood to be parts of distinct registers. As explained in Silverstein (2003 [1996], p. 212) or Agha (1998; 2004, pp. 36–38), in the interdiscursivity across contexts of usage speakers develop a stereotypic -onomic knowledge of genres of discourse and associate these with particular institutionalized sites, roles, and kinds of people recruited to these roles. The fact of ideological stereotypification transforms what Gumperz called "dialectal" indexicality, indicating that a certain demographically identifiable kind of person was sending a message, into "superposed" indexicality, indicating which identity-conferring role-relationship is currently inhabited by the sender of a message among a whole repertoire of roles that such an individual could instantiate. The oscillation from the first to the second essentially involves stereotypification (Agha 1998), generally as a function of larger-scale ideological formations sweeping linguistic variation up into processes producing widespread knowledge of how people of certain social types interacting in certain roles use or ought to use language. Needless to say, this also becomes the stuff of parody and imitation.

So the identity work associated with wine-talk or any other expert discourse needs analysis as part of the fractionation of any so-called language into a union of registers, in terms of which the language users understand indexical variability. Who, that is, what type of person, is recruited to such occasions of usage, and how? How do degrees of competence from full through partial terminologization of wine-talk (and beyond) indicate something about the enregisterment of connoisseurship? Why is it attractive to people—what sociocultural value accrues to them—to control such discourses of expertise and connoisseurship? Through which network effects of participation do such registers spread across groups and categories of people, and across objects of denotation? How did oinoglossia become, in fact, generative as a model of what a prestige comestible ought to be, that is, a model of how one should describe a prestige comestible, with discourse organized as or inspired by the register usage of the "tasting note?"

OINOGLOSSIA AS MACROSOCIOLOGICALLY SANCTIONED ENREGISTERMENT OF LANGUAGE

This leads us to the third major area of research in an ethnographic lexicography. Here, we seek to place such enregistered language within networks of institutional authorization: Which institutional structures depend on, and in turn are renewed and substantiated, by people following the norms of usage of specialized registers and the textual genres they inhabit? Are there complex intersections of forces at privileged sites of social life that emerge as nodal licensers of usage, of identity, of value? Something like wine, a prestige comestible that starts life in agriculture, exists through the workings of a whole organized trajectory of cultivation, production, storage, circulation through tiers of marketing, and, finally, consumption in the first instance. It also intersects with institutions of collecting and preservation, much as in antiques and other like collectibles. An organized structure of connoisseurship, both professional and avocational, informs wine in both these respects, with a market that is structured by futurities and their risks from the moment grapes are grown.

Hence there is a kind of dialectic of the life cycle of commodity process and evaluative market-making from the very beginning of any cycle in which wine comes into being. Various kinds of experts are involved at every phase. During growing and pressing of grapes, soil scientists and industrial chemists pronouncing on growing conditions and the chemical characteristics of the pressed juice; local folk traditions have their own terminologies of techniques and paraphernalia without the numerical testing. As wine is aged in oak barrels or stainless steel vats—a function of aspiration in the market—tastings yield descriptive evaluations in the form of early tasting notes by experts, both in-house and beyond, that begin to set the price that a particular vintage will fetch, both wholesale and retail; note the fact that this may happen a few years before any wine will actually be released to purchasers, having thus an effect on an agricultural future much as in the commodity exchanges around the world. As wines come into the retail orbit, wine critics come into their own, writing for magazines, newspapers, and Web sites and giving both descriptive evaluations in the form of professional tasting notes on the particular wine and, increasingly, a numerical rating on some not entirely arbitrarily assumed scale (e.g., out of 100 "points" in interdiscursive relation with American school grades and the like). There is even a growing discursive re"medicalization" of wine as well, supposed health-conferring benefits of its consumption rediscovered by science (see Fournier 2003).

Afficionados at the retail level will subscribe to magazines or Web sites that evaluate, and hence make a market in, not only specific wines, elaborately reviewed and commented on in theme articles, but also in the whole connection to the sites of production, boutique agriculture at the more rarefied end of things, and to a lifestyle that thus is made palpably connected to it. (Compare here the trend in menus of a certain class pretension to give a prestige "denomination of origin" for all major ingredients of boutique cooking, whether by geographical locale or agricultural producer's name or equivalent.) Reports of recent trends in wine auction prices and comparable events emphasize the investment aspect of wine at the higher levels of the market. Discussions of, and advertisements for purchasing of, various gadgets, appurtenances, and paraphernalia for the full display of one's relationship to the prestige comestible also fill the publication spaces of such material. Here, wine becomes the center of a lifestyle self-definition, perhaps along with other "finer things" such as cognac—distilled from wine!—and can have all the intensity of hobbies, avocational sports, and other foci of what are institutionally cast into modes of investing in "leisure." As Sapir (1949 [1933], p. 11) long ago pointed out about hyperterminologized register usage among the avocationally committed, the -onomic knowledge of such leisure foci and their verbal counterpart in minute nomenclatural distinctions and evaluative statistics and other facts (including evaluative comparisons) becomes an end in itself, indexically potent as a means of psychologically satisfying validation of identity.

LEXICOLOGY AND LEXICOGRAPHY FINALLY GO ETHNOGRAPHIC

As a consequence of understanding the richer, multiple, and interacting partial systematicities involved in how it is that words and expressions occur in discourse—in particular texts in their sociocultural contexts of use—lexicography as such becomes, in part, an ethnographic undertaking. It blurs the boundary, if ever one wanted to invoke one, between what was intended by the "dictionary" of a language and by the "encyclopedia" of knowledge of a culture (see Peeters 2000).

This is, of course, to be expected once we understand how large a role cultural concepts, as we have termed them, play in the totality of communicatively relevant meanings of words and expressions. However, it also implies that we investigate such cultural concepts where they live, with methods that can reveal them to us. For something like the lexical registers for denoting a product and an experience as

complex as wine, we have to be prepared to encounter terms in discourse in all the contexts in which the denotatum is conjured as the focus of interaction, whether physically present or not. Observe that for most people, the experience of wine is purely retail, that is, centers on actual consumption and preparing, in one or another way, for it. But there is a whole set of interlocking organizational structures that bring the average retail consumer to wine (and vice versa) at a site of consumption. At every culturally recognizable node in the trajectory from production to consumption, then, there will be special lexical registers that conceptually define the object of discourse, frequently with a view back or forward to other nodes in the chain of sites. Physical and political geography, as well as fermentation history and methods, are frequently invoked on bottle labels destined to be read and understood by connoisseurs. These earlier stages in the emergence of something now being drunk are understood to be causally related to the experience and to the actualized tasting note, the structured text describing the object of aesthetic experience in consumption. And yet the descriptors come, etymologically, from completely different cultural schemata—the body, breeding, and character of persons and of gentlemanly cultigens, critters, and commodities—that are, like so much of a cultural sort, tropically brought into alignment with the psychophysical and psychochemical experiences in the encounter, from visual to olfactory to gustatory-tactual. Among the noncognoscienti, in fact, those who are sociologically far removed from the rarefied worlds of oenology, viticulture, and oenophilia, these tropes—with all their peformative potency of value-transduction from commodity-experience to humans—are, perforce, confused with the stuff itself (see Silverstein 2004, pp. 644–45). Wine-talk, like wine, thus is a cause of anxiety and ultimately nervous humor, as classic cartoons from James Thurber on demonstrate.

Wine, however, is not only good to think; it is good to drink. *A votre santé*!

LITERATURE CITED

Agha A. 1998. Stereotypes and registers of honorific language. *J. Ling. Anthropol.* 27:151–93

Agha A. 2004. Registers of language. In *A Companion to Linguistic Anthropology*, ed. A Duranti, pp. 23–45. Malden, MA: Blackwell

Agha A. 2006. *Language and Social Relations*. Cambridge, UK: Cambridge Univ. Press

Agua-Mel C. 2000. The dull, the conventional, and the sexist: Portuguese wine advertising. In *Advertising and Identity in Europe: The I of the Beholder*, ed. J. Cannon, PAO de Baubeta, IR Warner, pp. 76–84. Bristol/Portland, OR: Intellect

Alanne E. 1957a. Das fortleben der mhd. Ausdrücke für den Weinberg, Weinbergsarbeiten und Weinsorten am Oberrhein. *Mém. Soc. Néophilol. Hels.* 20(2). Helsinki: Soc. Néophilol.

Alanne E. 1957b. Observations on the development and structure of English wine-growing terminology. *Mém. Soc. Néophilol. Hels.* 20(3). Helsinki: Soc. Néophilol.

Alanne E. 1961. Der ursprung und die Entwicklung der niederländischen Weinbauterminologie: mit besonderer Berücksichtigung der mittelniederländischen Zeit. *Mém. Soc. Néophilol. Hels.* 25(1). Helsinki: Soc. Néophilol.

Atkins S, Rundell M, Hiroaki S. 2003. The contribution of FrameNet to practical lexicography. *Int. J. Lexicogr.* 16:333–57

Bakhtin MM. 1981. Discourse in the novel. In *The Dialogic Imagination*, ed. M Holquist, transl. C Emerson, M Holquist, pp. 259–422. Austin: Univ. Tex. Press

Basso KH, Selby HF, eds. 1976. *Meaning in Anthropology*. Albuquerque: Univ. N.M. Press

Bergenholtz H, Tarp S. 1995. *Manual of Specialized Lexicography: The Preparation of Specialised Dictionaries*. Amsterdam/Philadelphia: Benjamins

Bourdieu P. 1984. *Distinction: A Critique of the Judgement of Taste*. Transl. R Nice. Cambridge, MA: Harvard Univ. Press

Bourdieu P. 1991. *Language and Symbolic Power*, ed. JB Thompson, transl. G Raymond, M. Adamson. Cambridge, MA: Harvard Univ. Press

Brochet F, Dubourdieu D. 2001. Wine descriptive language supports cognitive specificity of chemical senses. *Brain Lang.* 77:187–96

Bucholtz M, Hall K. 2004. Theorizing identity in language and sexuality research. *Lang. Soc.* 33:469–515

Coutier M. 1997. Le champs du corps dans le vocabulaire de la dégustation du vin. *Cah. Lexicol.* 71:67–99

Croft W, Cruse DA. 2004. *Cognitive Linguistics*. Cambridge, UK: Cambridge Univ. Press

Cruse DA. 1986. *Lexical Semantics*. Cambridge, UK: Cambridge Univ. Press

Cruse DA. 2004. *Meaning in Language: An Introduction to Semantics and Pragmatics*. Oxford, UK: Oxford Univ. Press

D'Andrade R. 1995. *The Development of Cognitive Anthropology*. Cambridge, UK: Cambridge Univ. Press

Ezquerro AM. 2000. Usos lingüisticos de las actividades vinícolas riojanas. *Rev. Dialectol. Trad. Popul.* 55:241–57

Ferguson CA. 1983. Sports announcer talk: syntactic aspects of register variation. *Lang. Soc.* 12:153–72

Fierobe N. 1993. Les mots du Champagne. *La Banque des mots*, 46:57–93. Paris: Presses Univ. France

Fillmore CJ, Johnson CR, Petruck MRL. 2003. Background to FrameNet. *Int. J. Lexicogr.* 16:235–50

Fournier V. 2003. Médicalisation et médiatisation du vin: note de recherche. *Anthropol. Soc.* 27:155–65

Frake CO. 1969 [1964]. Notes on queries in ethnography. In *Cognitive Anthropology: Readings*, ed. SA Tyler, pp. 123–37. New York: Holt, Rhinehart and Winston

Fuller RC. 1993. Religion and ritual in American wine culture. *J. Am. Cult.* 16:39–45

Fuller RC. 1996. *Religion and Wine: A Cultural History of Wine Drinking in the United States*. Knoxville: Univ. Tenn. Press

Goldsmith JA, Huck G. 1995. *Ideology and Linguistic Theory: Noam Chomsky and the Deep Structure Debates*. London/New York: Routledge

Gumperz JJ. 1968. Linguistics, III. The speech community. In *International Encyclopedia of the Social Sciences*, ed. DL Sills, 9:381–86. New York: Macmillan

Gumperz JJ, Hymes DH. 1972. *Directions in Sociolinguistics: The Ethnography of Communication*. New York: Holt, Rinehart and Winston

Halliday MAK, Hasan R. 1976. *Cohesion in English*. London: Longman

Hancher M. 1979. The classification of cooperative illocutionary acts. *Lang. Soc.* 8:1–14

Harris RA. 1993. *The Linguistics Wars*. New York: Oxford

Hartmann RRK. 2001. *Teaching and Researching Lexicography*. London: Longman

Hastings AM, Manning P. 2004. Introduction: acts of alterity. *Lang. Comm.* 24:291–311

Henry A. 1996. Contributions à l'étude du langage oenologique en langue d'oïl (XIIe-Xve s.). *Mém. Classe Lettre, Acad. R. Belg.* 2 vols. Brussels: Belg. R. Acad.

Hoey M. 2005. *Lexical Priming: A New Theory of Words and Language*. London/New York: Routledge

Hüllen W, Schulze R. 1988. *Understanding the Lexicon: Meaning, Sense, and World Knowledge in Lexical Semantics*. Tübingen: Niemeyer

Hymes DH. 1974. *Foundations in Sociolinguistics: An Ethnographic Approach*. Philadelphia: Univ. Penn. Press

Jackson H. 2002. *Lexicography: An Introduction*. London/New York: Routledge

Jakobson R. 1960. Closing statement: linguistics and poetics. In *Style in Language*, ed. TA Sebeok, pp. 350–77. Cambridge, MA: MIT Press

Janssen T, Redeker G. 1999. *Cognitive Linguistics: Foundations, Scope, and Methodology*. Berlin/New York: Mouton de Gruyter

Kadel P. 1928. *Beiträge zur rheinhessischen Winzersprache. Beiträge zur deutschen Philologie*, nr. 25. Giessen: O. Kindt

Kies O. 1999. Weingärtnersprache in Lauffen am Neckar. *Muttersprache* 1:75–80

Kiesling S. 2006. Identity in sociocultural anthropology and language. In *Encyclopedia of Language and Linguistics*, ed. K Brown, 5:495–502. Amsterdam/Oxford: Elsevier. 2nd ed.

Kleiber W. 1980. *Zur sprachgeographischen Struktur der deutschen Winzerterminologie. Abhandlungen der Geistes- und Sozialwissenschaftlichen Klasse, Jahrg. 1980.*, Akademie der Wissenschaften und der Literatur von Mainz, nr. 6. Wiesbaden: F. Steiner

Kleiber W. 1990-. *Wortatlas der Kontinentalgermanischen Winzerterminologie*. Tübingen: Niemeyer

Labov W. 1972. *Sociolinguistic Patterns*. Philadelphia: Univ. Penn. Press

Landau SI. 2001. *Dictionaries: The Art and Craft of Lexicography*. Cambridge, UK: Cambridge Univ. Press. 2nd ed.

Latour B. 1987. *Science in Action: How to Follow Scientists and Engineers Through Society*. Cambridge, MA: Harvard Univ. Press

Laughlin RM. 1975. *The Great Tzotzil Dictionary of San Lorenzo Zinacantán. Smithson. Contrib. Anthropol., No. 19*. Washington, DC: Smithson. Inst. Press

Lehrer A. 1975. Talking about wine. *Language* 51:901–23

Lehrer A. 1983. *Wine and Conversation*. Bloomington: Indiana Univ. Press

Lieber R. 2004. *Morphology and Lexical Semantics*. Cambridge, UK: Cambridge Univ. Press

Lyons J. 1995. *Linguistic Semantics: An Introduction*. Cambridge, UK: Cambridge Univ. Press

Magalhães DMG. 2000. Vinho: práticas, elogios, cultos e representações em questão na sociedade portuguesa. *Sociol. Probl. Práticas* 32:9–21

Manning P, ed. 2003. Words and beyond: linguistic and semiotic studies of sociocultural order. *Lang. Comm.* 23(3–4)

Martin JB. 1977. Etude du vocabulaire de la viticulture et de la vinification employé à Roisey (Loire). *Trav. Ling. Litt.* 15:151–59

Mugglestone L. 2005. *Lost for Words: The Hidden History of the Oxford English Dictionary*. New Haven, CT/London: Yale Univ. Press

Newmeyer FJ. 1986. *Linguistic Theory in America*. Orlando, FL: Academic

Normand S. 1998/99. Etude de la terminologie de la dégustation du champagne par analyze de corpus. *Terminology* 5:251–69

Nuță I. 1981. De la nume proprii la nume commune în terminologia viticolă. *Ling. Rom.* 30:201–10

Nuță I. 1992. Denumiri pentru varietăți de vin în limba română. *Anuar Lingvistica Istorie Literara* 33:143–87

Peeters B. 2000. *The Lexicon-Encyclopedia Interface*. Amsterdam/Oxford: Elsevier

Putnam H. 1975. The meaning of "meaning." In *Philosophical Papers*, Vol. 2: *Mind, Language, and Reality*, 2:215–71. New York: Cambridge Univ. Press

Putnam H. 1978. *Meaning and the Moral Sciences*. London/Boston: Routledge and Kegan Paul

Sapir E. 1949 [1933]. Language. In *Selected Writings of Edward Sapir in Language, Culture, and Personality*, ed. DG Mandelbaum, pp. 7–32. Berkeley/Los Angeles: Univ. Calif. Press

Schneider DM. 1976. Notes toward a theory of culture. See Basso & Selby 1976, pp. 197–220

Schneider DM. 1984. *A Critique of the Study of Kinship*. Ann Arbor: Univ. Mich. Press

Silverstein M. 1972. Linguistic theory: syntax, semantics, pragmatics. *Annu. Rev. Anthropol.* 1:349–82

Silverstein M. 1976. Shifters, linguistic categories, and cultural description. See Basso & Selby 1976, pp. 11–55

Silverstein M. 2003 [1996]. Indexical order and the dialectics of sociolinguistic life. *Lang. Comm.* 23:193–229

Silverstein M. 2004. "Cultural" concepts and the language-culture nexus. *Curr. Anthropol.* 45:621–52

Svensén B. 1993. *Practical Lexicography: Principles and Methods of Dictionary-Making*. Oxford/New York: Oxford Univ. Press

Talmy L. 2000. *Toward a Cognitive Semantics*. 2 vols. Cambridge, MA: MIT Press

Taylor JR. 2002. *Cognitive Grammar*. New York: Oxford Univ. Press

Teil G. 2001. La production du jugement esthétique sur les vins par la critique vinicole. *Sociol. Travail* 43:67–89

Tyler SA. 1969. *Cognitive Anthropology: Readings*. New York: Holt, Rinehart and Winston

Tyler SA. 1978. *The Said and the Unsaid: Mind, Meaning, and Culture*. New York: Academic

Ulin RC. 2002. Work as cultural production: labour and self-identity among southwest French wine-growers. *J. R. Anthropol. Inst.* (n.s.) 8:691–712

Viechnicki GB. 2002. *Evidentiality in scientific discourse*. PhD thesis. Univ. Chicago, Dept. Ling.

Whorf BL. 1956. *Language, Thought, and Reality: Selected Writings of Benjamin Lee Whorf*, ed. JB Carroll. Cambridge, MA: MIT Press

Willinsky J. 1994. *Empire of Words: The Reign of the OED*. Princeton, NJ: Princeton Univ. Press

Winchester S. 2003. *The Meaning of Everything: The Story of the Oxford English Dictionary*. Oxford/New York: Oxford Univ. Press

The Maya Codices

Gabrielle Vail

Division of Social Sciences, New College of Florida, Sarasota, Florida 34243;
and Florida Institute for Hieroglyphic Research, Palmetto, Florida 34221;
email: gvail@ncf.edu

Annu. Rev. Anthropol. 2006. 35:497–519

The *Annual Review of Anthropology* is
online at anthro.annualreviews.org

This article's doi:
10.1146/annurev.anthro.35.081705.123324

Copyright © 2006 by Annual Reviews.
All rights reserved

0084-6570/06/1021-0497$20.00

Key Words

archaeoastronomy, Borgia codices, Postclassic rituals, scribes,
textual analysis

Abstract

Research over the past decade has significantly advanced our understanding of the prehispanic Maya codices, both in terms of their content (i.e., hieroglyphic texts, calendrical structure, and iconography)
as well as the physical documents themselves (where and when they
were painted, and by whom). Recent avenues of exploration include
a new emphasis on linguistic and textual analyses; novel methodologies for interpreting calendrical structure; and comparisons with
other manuscript traditions, in particular those from highland central Mexico. As a result of these studies, researchers have found that
some codical almanacs functioned as real-time instruments to document important astronomical events; others were used to schedule
rituals as part of the 52-year calendar that guided civic and religious life in Mesoamerica during the Late Postclassic period (circa
A.D. 1250 to 1520). Evidence of connections with central Mexico,
documented in terms of interchange among codical scribes, suggests the need for a more thorough exploration of Maya–highland
Mexican interaction during this time period.

INTRODUCTION

almanac: records
rituals, astronomical
events, and
prophecies. Contains
one or more frames
that include
hieroglyphic
captions, dates in the
tzolk'in, and pictures

D.: Dresden Codex

P.: Paris Codex

M.: Madrid Codex

B.: Borgia Codex

The extant Maya codices are screenfold manuscripts of varying lengths, which contain ritual and divinatory almanacs, as well as astronomical tables, that incorporate hieroglyphic captions, dates within one or several calendar systems, and pictures featuring deities in anthropomorphic and animal form. Three codices attributed to the prehispanic Maya area came to light in European collections in the eighteenth and nineteenth centuries: the Dresden, Paris, and Madrid manuscripts, named for the cities where they are currently housed.[1] Although tantalizing clues have been offered, their histories before reaching Europe remain unknown. All three are generally attributed to the Late Postclassic period (circa 1250–1520), although this assumption has been questioned recently (see discussion below). A fourth codex, known as the Grolier following its exhibition by the Grolier Club in New York in 1971, was recovered from a cave believed to be in Chiapas, Mexico, in the 1960s, along with several pre-Columbian artifacts, including sheets of blank fig bark paper. Until recently, research by Carlson (1983) was accepted by many scholars as indicating the authenticity of the codex, although new studies have questioned this assumption.

The basic structure of codical almanacs and tables has been understood since the 1880s as a result of the acumen of scholars such as Ernst Förstemann, Eduard Seler, and Cyrus Thomas.[2] Additionally, several early studies were highly successful in their efforts to disambiguate the iconography of codical instruments and to identify the deities pictured. However, attempts to decipher the hi-eroglyphic texts met with limited success until the introduction of the phonetic method of decipherment in the 1950s. These developments are considered briefly in the section that follows to provide a context for the discussion of current research.

A BRIEF HISTORY OF CODICAL RESEARCH

Pioneering studies in codical research include Förstemann (1880, 1906), Schellhas (1904), Seler (1902–1923), and Thomas (1882, 1884). [For a complete list of their publications relating to the Maya codices, see Vail & Hernández (2005).] Förstemann's (1880) facsimile of the Dresden Codex (D.) remains the finest ever produced, and de Rosny's photographs of the Paris Codex (P.) and of the Cortesianus section of the Madrid Codex (M.) (also published in the 1880s) likewise include details that are sometimes difficult to see on later facsimiles.[3] Drawings of the Troano portion of the Madrid Codex published by Brasseur de Bourbourg in 1869–1870 formed the basis for early studies of the manuscript.

To Förstemann goes the credit for elucidating the calendrical structure of codical almanacs and tables. Seler and Thomas likewise made significant advances in interpreting codical almanacs, as demonstrated in their discussions of M. 75–76, which has a cognate in one of the codices of the Borgia (B.) group believed to derive from highland Mexico, and of the yearbearer almanacs (those celebrating the end of one year and the start of the next) in the Dresden and Madrid codices (Seler 1901, Thomas 1884). Seler made important contributions to the study of the Borgia as well as the Maya codices, including a number of perceptive observations about structural parallels among the Borgia almanacs and similar

---

[1] For more detailed information about their current locations, see Cabello Carro (1986) and entries in Carrasco (2001).

[2] Unlike tables, which are placed in absolute time by reference to dates in the Maya Long Count calendar, almanacs typically are structured on the basis of the 260-day ritual calendar (the *tzolk'in*), which combines 13 numbers with a series of 20 named days. The term instrument is used to encompass both almanacs and tables.

[3] The Madrid Codex was discovered in two parts, known originally as the Cortesianus and Troano manuscripts. They were recognized as belonging to the same codex by de Rosny in the 1880s. For this reason, many European scholars refer to the codex as the Tro-Cortesianus or Spanish Tro-Cortesiano.

instruments in the Maya manuscripts (see, e.g., Seler 1902–1923, I:618–67; 1904).

Seler also undertook some of the earliest studies of the codical deities, as did the German scholar Paul Schellhas (1904). Both researchers drew interesting parallels between Maya deities and their central Mexican counterparts, and Schellhas is still remembered for the lettering system he developed to group representations of the same deity under a single rubric before it was possible to identify them according to their hieroglyphic names. Thomas (1892) made some astute decipherments under the assumption that Maya hieroglyphs were phonetic in nature, but he later recanted his proposals in the face of sustained criticism from Seler (1902–1923, I:558–61, 562–67 [orig. 1892]). Although they did not always agree with each other, all subsequent research has built on the discoveries and methodologies of these four founding fathers.

The key figure in the early part of the twentieth century was Eric Thompson, who undertook studies of the codical deities (see, e.g., Thompson 1950, 1970), developed a comprehensive catalog of inscriptional and codical glyphs (Thompson 1962), and published a commentary of the Dresden Codex (Thompson 1972). Other important contributions were made by Tozzer & Allen (1910), who catalogued the animals represented in the Maya codices along with their glyphs; Günter Zimmermann (1956), who developed a catalog of codical glyphs and categorized the attributive glyphs of the Maya deities; and Herbert Spinden (1924), John Teeple (1931), and Robert Willson (1924), who worked with the astronomical tables in the codices.

Little progress was made in deciphering the hieroglyphic texts—with the exception of the day and month glyphs, colors and directions, and some of the deity names—until the 1950s, with the advent of the phonetic methodology of Yurii Knorozov (1952, 1955, 1958). Early proponents of Knorozov's work, including David Kelley (1962, 1976), James Fox, and John Justeson (Fox & Justeson 1984), made initial forays, many of them highly suc-

cessful, into interpreting the codical texts. Kelley (1976, Ch. 4) is known especially for his insightful analysis of the codical deities.

The 1970s and early 1980s marked the turning point in codical studies, highlighted by the introduction of new research methodologies that helped shape our current understanding of the Maya codices. The publication of color photographic facsimiles of the Dresden, Madrid, and Paris codices in the 1960s and 1970s by the Akademische Druck-und Verlagsanstalt in Graz, Austria, proved invaluable to furthering codical research (Anders 1967, 1968; Deckert & Anders 1975), as did a compilation of the three Graz facsimiles published in the 1980s (Lee 1985).

The following discussion summarizes the state of research leading up to the current decade in codical studies. It serves as a prelude to the discussion of significant advances from 1996 to 2006.

Decipherment of Hieroglyphic Texts

The initial forays into phonetic decipherment cited above were followed by two seminal publications in the late 1980s (see V. Bricker 1986, Stuart 1987). Decipherment of additional codical glyphs rapidly followed, with contributions made by many researchers, including V. Bricker, Closs, Grube, Love, Nahm, Schele, and numerous others (Macri & Looper 2003, pp. 9–11). Participants in the Maya Meetings at the University of Texas, Austin, chaired by Schele until her death in 1998, were also actively involved in deciphering and transcribing texts from the Maya codices (their studies are published in the *U Mut Maya* series).

The culmination of earlier research has been the transcription and translation of the complete codical corpus (Davoust 1997, Schele & Grube 1997, Vail 2002b, Vail & Hernández 2005, Vail & Macri 2004).[4]

---

[4]Despite the promise of his early work, Knorozov's (1982) decipherments of the codical texts are not considered reliable.

Although most of the hieroglyphic texts can be read, their underlying metaphorical meaning is more difficult to determine. Researchers hope to make progress on this front by applying techniques used by ethnohistorians and linguists working with Colonial texts such as the Popol Vuh or the Books of Chilam Balam. Significant progress has been achieved in terms of analyzing the textual and linguistic structure of codical clauses, based on the pioneering research of V. Bricker (1985, 1986) and Hofling (1989). Additionally, online databases of the codices (Vail & Hernández 2005, Vail & Macri 2004) offer researchers the capability to search the entire codical corpus by T number [the cataloging system developed by Thompson (1962)], phonetic transcription, English gloss, or Maya (Yucatec or Ch'olan) gloss.

Studies of Deities

The most significant findings since the 1970s concerning the anthropomorphic figures depicted in the codices have been (*a*) the discovery that they are, indeed, deities, as demonstrated by Ringle's (1988) decipherment of the T1016c glyph that is frequently paired with name glyphs in codical texts as *k'uh*, a Yucatec word meaning "god" as well as "holy" and "sacred",[5] and (*b*) the realization that these figures are best understood not as individual entities, but rather in terms of their relationships with each other and as groupings of related deities (see, e.g., Closs 1979; Vail 1996, 2000b). The delineation of deity complexes forms the subject of publications by various authors, including Bill, Closs, Ciaramella, Kocyba, Love, Milbrath, Paxton, Stone, Taube, and Vail. A complete list of sources is included in Vail & Hernández's (2005) annotated bibliography.

Coe's (1989a) survey of representations of the Hero Twins from the Popol Vuh creation story in Classic and Postclassic Maya art is one of the earliest forays into identifying creation imagery in the codices (see discussion in Current Trends below). Taube (1992) provides additional examples of codical counterparts to the Hero Twins and notes connections between Maya and central Mexican deities in the tradition of Seler. His study also establishes links between Classic and codical variants of the same deity.

Sotelo Santos (2002) and Vail (1996) focus specifically on deities from the Madrid Codex, whereas Riese (1982), Taube & Bade (1991), and Whittaker (1986) document the presence of several central Mexican divinities in the Dresden Codex Venus table.

Astronomical and Calendrical Studies

Investigations of the astronomical tables in the Dresden Codex have been some of the most fruitful avenues of codical exploration since Thompson's (1972) commentary. Research has focused on the Venus table (Aveni 1992a, 2001, pp. 184–93; H. Bricker & V. Bricker, submitted manuscript; Closs 1977; Lounsbury 1983; Milbrath 1999, Ch. 5; Schele & Grube 1997; Tedlock & Tedlock 2002/2003), the eclipse table (Aveni 2001, pp. 173–84, H. Bricker & V. Bricker 1983, Milbrath 1999, pp. 111–15, Schele & Grube 1997), the Mars table (Aveni 2001, pp. 196–200, H. Bricker & V. Bricker 1997, V. Bricker & H. Bricker 1986b, Love 1995), the seasonal table (V. Bricker & H. Bricker 1988), and more recently the water tables on pages 69–74 (V. Bricker & H. Bricker 2005).[6] The Dresden astronomical tables are also the focus of studies by Justeson (1989) and Everson (1995), and they are discussed in Galindo Trejo's (2000) summary of the current state of archaeoastronomical research in Mesoamerica. Additionally, two full-length monographs are concerned with Maya astronomy: Aveni's

---

[5]Maya deities are primarily personifications of natural elements or forces, including rain, maize, wind or breath, death and destruction, etc.

[6]Space considerations preclude a comprehensive list of sources. For additional references, see Vail & Hernández (2005).

Skywatchers of Ancient Mexico (1980, 2001) and Milbrath's (1999) *Star Gods of the Maya*. Although neither focuses exclusively on the codices, they both include extensive discussions of Maya astronomical tables. A third monograph, *Astronomy in the Maya Codices* by Harvey and Victoria Bricker, is currently in preparation.

As a result of these studies, we know that the Maya tracked the synodic cycles of Venus and Mars (i.e., the period required for a planet to return to the same position—such as its predawn rise—with respect to the sun), as well as the retrograde period of Mars; used tables to chart the seasons (solstices and equinoxes) in relation to their civic year (*haab'*); predicted solar and lunar eclipses; and tracked the motion of the planets against the background of the stars. The latter discovery is especially significant because it shows that observations were made in relation to other celestial bodies and not just to the earth. Despite the century since Förstemann's initial research, however, scholars still cannot agree about how to interpret and date the Dresden astronomical tables (compare, for example, H. Bricker & V. Bricker 1997, V. Bricker & H. Bricker 1986b, and Love 1995 regarding the Mars table).

New models to emerge during the past two decades include the belief that Maya tables were designed to have an observational function, rather than serving only for computations or as a record of past events (H. Bricker & V. Bricker 1983, 1992; V. Bricker & H. Bricker 1986b), and the recognition that Maya astronomers tracked the sidereal, as well as the synodic, intervals of celestial bodies (Aveni et al. 2003, H. Bricker et al. 2001, Tedlock & Tedlock 2002/2003).[7] The latter discovery allows us to develop models for understanding positional (as opposed to horizon-based) astronomy in ancient cultures.

Another object of intensive inquiry in recent years is the "zodiac" on P. 23–24 (Aveni 2001, pp. 200–5; H. Bricker & V. Bricker 1992; Johnson & Quenon 1994; Justeson 1989; Kelley 1976, pp. 45–50; Love 1994, Ch. 10; Milbrath 1999, Ch. 7; Paxton 1992; Schele 1992; Severin 1981; Tedlock 1999; Tedlock & Tedlock 2002/2003).[8] As with the Dresden astronomical tables, scholars disagree about how it should be interpreted and dated. Tedlock (1999), for example, uses the same framework as that of her contemporary K'iche' informants from Momostenango, Guatemala, to interpret the sequence of Paris constellations, resulting in a model that differs from that proposed by other researchers (see, e.g., H. Bricker & V. Bricker 1992).

Another instrument that has engendered controversy is the Venus almanac found in the Grolier Codex. As Carlson (1983) and others have shown (Aveni 1980, pp. 193–95; 2001, pp. 193–95), it mirrors the structure of the Dresden Venus table (although it has pages devoted to all four stations of the planet, rather than just to heliacal rise). Nevertheless, a number of scholars believe that the codex is a recent forgery and not an authentic prehispanic document (Baudez 2002, Milbrath 2002, Thompson 1975). This question is examined in the discussion of Provenience and Dating below.

Only recently have other instruments lacking Long Count dates been considered as having possible astronomical content. Examples include the almanac on pages 12b–18b of the Madrid Codex (H. Bricker et al. 1997; Milbrath 1981, 1999, pp. 259–62; Wulfing 1994); almanacs from the Dresden Codex that may refer to eclipse cycles (Hofling & O'Neil 1992), Venus (Hofling 1988), or the moon's sidereal location (Tedlock & Tedlock 2002/2003); and possible references to Venus on the Madrid yearbearer pages (Closs 1992).

haab': Maya 365-day solar calendar consisting of 18 months of 20 days, followed by a five-day period called Wayeb'

Long Count: calendar used by the Maya to place dates in absolute time, on the basis of a starting date in 3114 B.C.

---

[7]The sidereal interval is the amount of time it takes for a planet or other celestial body to return to the same point in the sky relative to the background of stars, as observed from the earth.

[8]Love (1994, Ch. 10) objects to labeling this almanac a "zodiac" because some of the constellations depicted fall outside the path approximately 18 degrees wide that represents the zodiac, i.e., the course traveled by the sun, moon, and planets as seen by observers on earth.

Another almanac from the Madrid Codex, on pages 75–76, has long been interpreted as a cosmogram mapping the four-quadrant-plus-center structure of the Maya universe onto time and space. New models for interpreting its calendrical structure suggest that it incorporates a *haab'* as well as a *tzolk'in* cycle (Paxton 2001) and that it may visually represent the 52 years of the Maya Calendar Round (Vail 2004, Vail & Hernández 2006).

Other studies have focused on the calendrical structure of Maya almanacs and new methodologies for interpreting relationships among almanacs both within a particular codex and across codices. Some of the more innovative include Aveni's (Aveni et al. 1996) examination of interval structures shared among almanacs in the Dresden and Madrid codices; V. Bricker's (1998) analysis of agricultural almanacs and their placement within a 52-year cycle; and studies by the Brickers and their colleagues using a methodology of "cross-dating" almanacs with astronomical tables (see discussion in Current Trends below). Additionally, Graña-Behrens (2002) recently documented *haab'* dates (references to 7 and 12 Pop) on the Madrid yearbearer pages, and Jüngel (1999) commented on what have been interpreted as scribal errors in a Madrid almanac and how they should be interpreted.

Commentaries and Iconographic Studies

Substantial research has been devoted to understanding the content of the Maya codices over the past 20 years. Publications of note include two new facsimiles: one of the Dresden Codex (Códice de Dresde 1998), published by Cholsamaj in Guatemala using Förstemann's 1887 photographs, and an edition of the Madrid Codex (Códice Tro-Cortesiano 1991) that reproduces the composition and layering of the original in the Museo de América. Additionally, commentaries of the Dresden (Davoust 1997, Schele & Grube 1997), Madrid (V. Bricker & Vail 1997, Vail 2002b), and Paris (Love 1994, Treiber 1987) codices greatly extend our understanding of these manuscripts, with considerable emphasis focused on the context behind the activities and events depicted in the almanacs. Other book-length monographs treat the following subjects: the Madrid Codex from a descriptive perspective (Escalante 1992, Rivera Dorado 1991) and trees in the Dresden Codex (Salgado Ruelas 2001). Entries in the *Oxford Encyclopedia of Mesoamerican Cultures* (Carrasco 2001) provide a summary of research pertaining to the four codices as of 2001.

A number of thematic studies, especially of the Madrid almanacs, have been undertaken, focusing on topics including yearbearer rituals (Bill et al. 2000, Love 1991, Taube 1988, Vail 1997b), weaving (Ciaramella 1999), hunting and trapping (Colas 1999, Vail 1997a, von Nagy 1997), and apiculture (Ciaramella 2002, Vail 1994).[9] What distinguishes these studies from those of earlier scholars is the emphasis on placing them within a contextual framework through a careful sifting of the ethnohistoric and ethnographic literature pertaining to similar activities or rituals, or through a calendrical analysis of interrelationships among almanacs, as described below.

New areas of investigation include an examination of material culture depicted in the Maya codices; studies of the scribal tradition; and references to creation cosmology. Analyses of the types of artifacts depicted in the codices have been extremely helpful in dating these manuscripts (see, e.g., Graff 1997, 2000; Paxton 1986, 1991; and discussion in Provenience and Dating below). Research by Lacadena (1995, 2000) and his colleagues (Ciudad Ruiz 2000, Ciudad Ruiz & Lacadena 1999, Sanz Castro 2000), although focused on the Madrid Codex, has filled in some

[9]See Vail & Hernández (2005) for a list of additional studies.

tzolk'in: Maya 260-day ritual calendar, consisting of 20 named days, each paired with a number ranging from 1 to 13 (i.e., 1 Imix, 2 Ik', 3 Ak'b'al, etc.)

Calendar Round: cycle of 52 years formed by pairing the *tzolk'in* and *haab'*

cross-dating: used to anchor undated astronomical and seasonal events in absolute time by linking them to dated occurrences of the same events in astronomical tables

important but long neglected gaps in our knowledge of the people responsible for drafting the Maya codices. Paleographic studies suggest that nine scribes were involved in painting the Madrid (Ciudad Ruiz 2000, Lacadena 2000).[10] Earlier studies of the Dresden Codex suggest that it was painted by eight separate hands (Zimmermann 1956, Tafel 5; but see Lacadena 1995, pp. 182–85). Ciudad Ruiz & Lacadena's (1999, pp. 1000) studies indicate that the codices were composed and used by scribes who were also priests.

Groundbreaking research by Freidel, Grube, Looper, MacLeod, Schele, Villela, and others (see, e.g., Freidel et al. 1993, Schele 1992), focusing on how the events of creation are played out in the night sky and in prehispanic foundation rituals, offers researchers fertile ground for continuing investigation for years to come. Only recently have scholars begun to focus on representations of these events in the Maya codices and their calendrical significance. Of special interest is an emphasis on 4 Ahaw dates in the Madrid Codex. Vail (G. Vail, submitted manuscript) considers how the activities depicted may be a replication of the events of the original creation that took place on the Calendar Round date 4 Ahaw 8 Kumk'u.

CURRENT TRENDS IN CODICAL RESEARCH

The most significant developments during the past decade include new evidence concerning the provenience and dating of the Maya codices; new methodologies for dating Maya almanacs; linguistic analyses of codical texts; and connections among codices in the Maya and Borgia groups that provide evidence for Maya–highland Mexican interaction during the Late Postclassic period. Following a discussion of these topics individually, the review concludes by considering what these trends promise for future research.

---

[10]Sotelo Santos (2002, p. 46) believes that at least eight scribes were involved.

Provenience and Dating

One of the primary areas of investigation in recent years involves using evidence internal to the manuscripts to determine when and where they were painted. The Dresden Codex contains a number of Long Count dates that can be correlated with the Gregorian calendar. The earliest, ranging from the eighth to the tenth centuries, appear to be records of historical events (V. Bricker & H. Bricker 1992, pp. 82–83; Lounsbury 1983). Dates believed to be contemporaneous with the use of the codex fall in the fourteenth and early fifteenth centuries (V. Bricker & H. Bricker 1992, p. 83). These dates contrast with those proposed by earlier studies. Thompson (1972, pp. 15–16), for example, suggested that the codex was painted between A.D. 1200 and 1250 largely on the basis of stylistic evidence, which Paxton (1986, Ch. 6) found consistent with dates recorded in the astronomical tables. Nevertheless, her study of ceramic forms depicted in the codex indicates similarities to those manufactured throughout the Late Postclassic period in the northern lowlands, suggesting that the Dresden Codex may have been painted after the thirteenth century (Paxton 1991, p. 307). Lacadena (1995, p. 362; Ciudad Ruiz & Lacadena 1999, p. 1000) proposes a late date for the codex, whereas Grube (2001, p. 337) notes that, although it was painted during the Postclassic period, it probably represents a copy of a Classic period manuscript. Where it was painted remains unknown, although analyses by Paxton (1986, 1991, 2004) support a provenience in the Yucatán peninsula. She suggests the following possible locations: Mayapán, Chichén Itzá, Tulum, Santa Rita Corozal, or possibly Kabah (Paxton 1991, p. 307). Earlier, Thompson (1972, p. 16) suggested that it was composed at Chichén Itzá, and Coe (1989b) proposed that it may have been one of the codices acquired by Cortés and his men on Cozumel Island in 1519, which later reached Spain as part of the "royal fifth."

Scholars generally agree that the Paris Codex originated at Mayapán (**Figure 1**) or

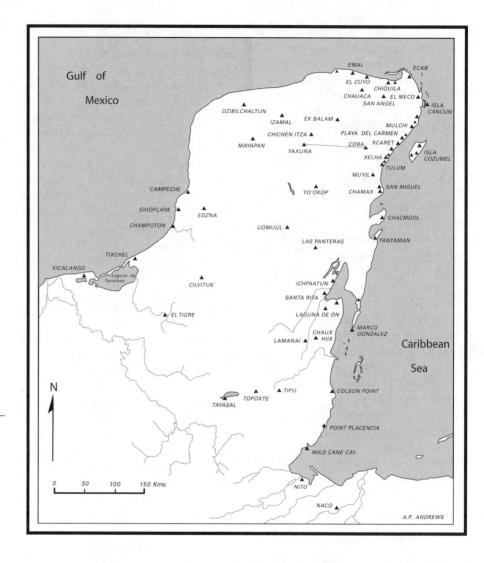

Figure 1

Sites occupied during the Postclassic period in the Maya lowlands. Illustration courtesy of Anthony P. Andrews.

k'atun: period consisting of 20 *tuns* of 360 days. One of the units of the Long Count calendar

in a nearby area [Love 1994, Ch. 2; but see Thompson (1972, p. 16), who alternately proposed an eastern Caribbean provenience]. Suggestions that it originated at Mayapán stem from similarities between *k'atun* ceremonies depicted in the codex (a *k'atun* is a period of approximately 20 years) and those recorded on stone monuments from Mayapán. Love (1994, p. 13) dates the codex to around 1450 on the basis of studies that place Mayapán Stela 1 in 1441. A recent re-analysis, however, suggests that the stela may date to 1185 instead (Schele & Mathews 1998, p. 367). Milbrath & Peraza Lope (2003, p. 39)

accept this earlier dating because it supports their interpretations of Mayapán's architectural sequence. The Paris *k'atun* pages, therefore, may refer to an earlier cycle than that proposed by Love. V. Bricker (1995) notes that calendrical and astronomical data provide support for a Classic period date, A.D. 731–987, as originally proposed by Treiber (1987). In this case, similar to the Dresden examples previously cited, it is necessary to separate historical texts copied from earlier manuscripts from the painting of the physical codex itself. As Love (1994, p. 8) and Lacadena (Ciudad Ruiz & Lacadena 1999, p. 1000) point out, the physical documents referred to today as the Maya codices were probably painted within 100 years or so of the conquest.

Two different theories have been proposed in recent years concerning the dating and provenience of the Madrid Codex. Iconographic evidence, including what he interpreted as a Spanish sword and a statue of a horse deity (Tz'iminchak), persuaded Porter (1997, pp. 41, 43) that the Madrid Codex was painted after Spanish contact in Tayasal, an Itzá Maya settlement in the Petén region (see **Figure 1**) that was visited by several expeditions in the sixteenth and seventeenth centuries but not "conquered" until 1697. Other recent studies (see Graff 2000, Graff & Vail 2001) interpret the same imagery as consistent with a Yucatecan provenience for the Madrid Codex. Paxton (2004) notes a close similarity between the material culture depicted in the codex and that found in the northern lowlands during the Late Postclassic period. Nevertheless, as Graff (2000, p. 28) notes, the portrayal of Late Postclassic artifacts, although suggesting that the codex was painted then, does not preclude a later date because it was not uncommon for artifacts from earlier periods to be depicted.

Coe & Kerr (1997, p. 181) also posited a postconquest date for the Madrid Codex and a Tayasal origin on the basis of a piece of European paper with a Latin text associated with M. 56. Coe & Kerr's dating of the codex to the Colonial period rests on their assumption that the European paper is embedded within the codex itself, something that later studies have shown not to be the case: The paper is clearly attached to the outer layer of the codex [H. Bricker 2004; Vail & Aveni 2004, Ch. 1, note 12; see also Anders (1967, pp. 37–38), who reached a similar conclusion when he examined the page in question in the 1960s].

Coe & Kerr suggested a Tayasal provenience on the basis of their belief that the name "...riquez" in the Latin text referred to Fray Juan Enríquez, a Spanish friar who was killed following a visit to Tayasal in 1624. Chuchiak (2004), after making a de-

THE M. 56 PATCH

Chuchiak's (2004) analysis of the handwritten Latin text on M. 56 leaves little doubt that it is a Bula de la Santa Cruzada, a type of papal bull sold by the hundreds in colonial New Spain. The style of handwriting indicates that it was written between 1570 and 1610, when the Yucatán peninsula experienced a shortage of printed bills. Handwritten copies were prepared by a select group of notaries; of these, Chuchiak (2004, pp. 70–72) believes he can identify the person who drafted the Bula attached to the Madrid Codex: Gregorio de Aguilar, cousin to the ecclesiastical judge Pedro Sánchez de Aguilar. Sánchez de Aguilar is best known for his passionate denunciation of Maya idolatry, which was undoubtedly strengthened by his confiscation of several Maya codices from the eastern Yucatán peninsula between 1603 and 1608. Chuchiak (2004, pp. 79–80) proposes that one of these may have been the Madrid Codex, given to King Philip III in 1619 when Sánchez de Aguilar returned to Spain. Although its subsequent history remains undocumented, Cabello Carro (1986) discusses the years leading to its acquisition by the Museo Arqueológico in Madrid (it was later transferred to the Museo de América, where it is currently housed).

tailed study of the same text, concludes that it represents part of a Bula de la Santa Cruzada, a type of papal bull produced by the colonial clergy and sold to the Maya of Yucatán (see Marhenke 1997 for her interpretation of the text's content). The 25 legible words of the text support Chuchiak's interpretation.

Chuchiak points out that the papal bull could not have derived from Tayasal because the Itzá settlement was located outside the area controlled by New Spain during the sixteenth century. Instead, his study supports a provenience in the northern Maya lowlands. Beginning in the 1590s, bulls of the Santa Cruzada were sold to inhabitants of the Yucatán peninsula in large numbers. Although initially viewed with suspicion, they soon were revered as sacred objects. It is therefore possible "that a Maya scribe or noble placed his copy of a bull into the codex to 'bless' it" (Chuchiak 2004, p. 77). When this may have occurred is not known, but the bull itself can be dated, using the two different styles of handwriting it contains, to a relatively short period between 1570 and 1610 (Chuchiak 2004, p. 68) (see The M. 56 Patch).

The codex itself contains no Long Count dates that would place it in absolute time. Several of its almanacs have been dated, however, using a methodology developed by the Brickers in the 1980s. These almanacs record astronomical and seasonal events in the tenth and fifteenth centuries (H. Bricker et al. 1997; V. Bricker 1997a,b; V. Bricker & H. Bricker 1988). It has been suggested that the earliest dated events were included because they were considered historically significant (i.e., they represent later copies of almanacs originally composed in the tenth century), whereas the later events are likely contemporaneous with the painting of the physical manuscript itself.

Because of its distinctive style and the circumstances surrounding its discovery, many scholars are reluctant to accept the Grolier Codex as an authentic prehispanic Maya codex. To settle the debate, in the 1970s Coe submitted a fragment of bark paper found in association with the codex for radiocarbon dating. It yielded a date of 1230 ± 130 years (Carlson 1983; Coe & Kerr 1997, p. 175). Nevertheless, Thompson (1975) considered the codex a forgery, largely on stylistic grounds, a conclusion that has been echoed in recent years by Milbrath (2002) and Baudez (2002). Milbrath (2002) notes that "the numerous irregularities in iconography seem suspicious, as does the fresh appearance of the paint in a manuscript presumably hidden in a cave for over seven hundred years" (p. 61).

On the other hand, Carlson (1983) argues that, at the time it was discovered, knowledge about Venus iconography and its relation to the calendrical cycle was not sophisticated enough for someone to have produced a forgery as detailed as the Grolier Codex. Other scholars, including Boone (2001) and Coe (Coe & Kerr 1997, p. 175), likewise believe the codex dates to the prehispanic period. Following Carlson, Boone (2001, p. 443) sees

its oddities as evidence of a hybrid manuscript produced in a borderland region where both Mayan and highland Mexican conventions were known and used. This is certainly a viable hypothesis, but one that will ultimately be resolved only when the findings of a study being performed by the Universidad Nacional Autónoma de México are published. Although third-hand accounts suggest that scissors were used to cut some of the pages (see Milbrath 2002, p. 60), it is premature to speculate about the results of the analysis until they are made public.

Also relevant to a discussion of the provenience and dating of the Maya codices are studies of the linguistic structure and languages represented in the codical texts.

Linguistic and Textual Analysis

Some of the most innovative research on the Maya codices in recent years has resulted from an examination of the morphology and syntactic structure of their hieroglyphic texts. Although much of this research is ongoing (Vail & Macri 2004), published studies focus on comparing the structure of codical texts with Mayan languages believed to be descendants of the languages recorded hieroglyphically (members of the Ch'olan and Yucatecan language families) (Figure 2).

Early research on the codical texts was based on the assumption that they were written by Yucatec scribes in their native language. This belief derived from the then-untested proposition that the hieroglyphic codices were painted in the northern Maya area, where the heaviest concentrations of lowland Maya populations resided at the time of Spanish contact in the early sixteenth century. Only recently have these assumptions been questioned.

In a proposal initially circulated informally in the late 1990s, Houston et al. (2000) asserted that the majority of Maya hieroglyphic texts, whether they were composed in Yucatec- or Ch'olan-speaking regions (see Figure 2), were written in a language they

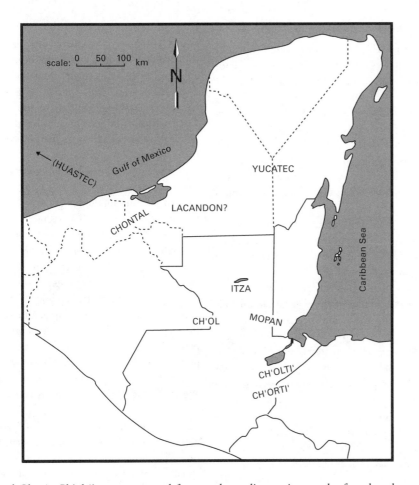

Figure 2

Linguistic groupings in the lowland Maya area at the time of the Spanish conquest. Yucatec, Lacandón, Itzá, and Mopán belong to the Yucatecan language family, whereas Chontal, Ch'ol, Ch'olti', and Ch'orti' are members of the Ch'olan family. Illustration courtesy of Victoria R. Bricker.

termed Classic Ch'olti'an, an ancestral form of the eastern Ch'olan languages Ch'olti' and Ch'orti' (Ch'orti' is still spoken in the vicinity of the archaeological site of Copán in Honduras). They propose that Classic Ch'olti'an represented a *lingua franca* that was known to and used by the elite as a means of communicating across a wide area inhabited by speakers of several different Mayan languages.

Also during the 1990s, researchers first questioned the idea that hieroglyphic texts in the Maya codices were written exclusively in Yucatec (Lacadena 1997, Wald 2004 [1994]) on the basis of the discovery of texts in the Dresden and Madrid codices that reflected Ch'olan rather than Yucatecan morphological patterning, as well as both Yucatecan and Ch'olan vocabulary. Evidence internal to the codices points to the fact that they contain almanacs that were composed at various points in time (see, e.g., V. Bricker & H. Bricker 1992, V. Bricker & Vail 1997). Almanacs would have been copied—and frequently reworked and updated—from older documents, much as occurred with texts from the colonial Yucatec Books of Chilam Balam (V. Bricker 2000). Therefore, an almanac or text may have been composed originally by a Ch'olan speaker, but the same text appearing in the Madrid or Dresden Codex may have been recopied by a Yucatec speaker, or vice versa. In other words, the language recorded in codical texts does not necessarily reflect that of the scribes who copied and drafted the almanacs and tables composing what we know of today as the Maya codices (V. Bricker 2000, Vail 2000a).

Astronomical and Calendrical Studies

In the late 1980s, there was a significant shift in our understanding of the astronomical content of the Maya codices as a result of V. Bricker & H. Bricker's (1986a, 1988, 1992) discovery that, as some Maya almanacs depict astronomical and seasonal events, they, like tables, can be dated in real (absolute) time. This absolute dating can be accomplished by cross-dating depictions of astronomical and/or seasonal events with those from astronomical tables that can be securely dated. However, because such events recur at various intervals, one must also have information relevant to the Maya *haab'* (365-day year) to provide a unique date for an almanac.

By way of example, the almanac on D. 38b–41b includes seasonal information (depictions of rainfall and planting) as well as references to eclipses. With these data as a guide, the Brickers suggest that the initial date of the almanac is May 20, 775. They then interpret the iconography and hieroglyphic captions associated with the almanac's eleven frames, showing that "the almanac describes what happened during the planting season in A.D. 775, chronicling in graphic detail the drought that must have resulted in a poor harvest that year" (V. Bricker & H. Bricker 1992, p. 76).

The Brickers' cross-dating approach has been the source of considerable debate (much of it unpublished) by codical researchers over the years. Nevertheless, scholars have made significant advances in the past decade in furthering our understanding of the astronomical content and calendrical structure of codical almanacs (see, e.g., Aveni 2004; H. Bricker et al. 1997; V. Bricker 1997a,b, 1998; Closs 1992; Drapkin 2002; Graff 1997; Knowlton 2003; Milbrath 1999; Paxton 2001; Vail 1994, 1997a; Wulfing 1994), as well as their ritual component (see below). Many of these studies were directly influenced by the Brickers' work. Additionally, analysis of the iconography and calendrical structure of Maya almanacs (Aveni 2004; Aveni et al. 1996;

Drapkin 2002; Love 1994, Ch. 5) has revealed a number of cognate instruments in the Dresden, Madrid, and Paris codices (i.e., almanacs that have many structural and calendrical similarities but may differ in significant ways).[11] These studies point to the importance of scribal interchange and/or the existence of archetypal almanacs that were copied by later generations of scribes.

Studies of the ritual component of the Maya codices have also benefited from the cross-dating methodology introduced by the Brickers. Their approach relies on identifying "like" elements in the iconography and hieroglyphic texts of almanacs and tables and interpreting these within the context of the calendrical data. Studies using this methodology rely on an integrative approach—i.e., an almanac's meaning may be understood only by reference to all of its components. This method of analysis represents a sharp departure from the approach, taken by many researchers, of divorcing the iconography and/or hieroglyphic text from its calendrical context.

The Brickers' work has fostered a new emphasis in codical studies on the identification of iconographic elements with apparent ritual meaning that crosscut different codical instruments (see, e.g., V. Bricker 1997b; V. Bricker & H. Bricker 1988, 1992). Researchers have found that many of the rituals depicted in Maya almanacs can be related to *haab'* ceremonies described in ethnohistoric sources such as Landa's *Relación de las cosas de Yucatán* (Tozzer 1941). A number of these almanacs depict rituals related to the yearbearer ceremonies, those that concern the final five days of the year (Wayeb') and the first day of the new year in the month Pop (Bill 1997; Bill et al. 2000; Graff 1997; Hernández & Bricker 2004; Taube 1988; Vail 2002a, 2004; Vail & Bricker 2004). These activities are depicted on D. 25–28 and M. 34–37, almanacs first

---

[11] Seler (1902–1923, 3:695–709) was the first to identify and comment on many of these cognates.

recognized as having yearbearer associations in the late nineteenth century (see previous discussion). The almanac on M. 51b (**Figure 3**, see color insert) has been identified as one such example (Bill 1997, pp. 114–16; Vail 1997b, p. 96, 2004, pp. 243–45). Its iconography can be compared with that from the middle register of the Dresden yearbearer pages, which has been interpreted as showing offerings to the deity patron associated with the outgoing year before he is retired (Taube 1988, pp. 235–36). Rituals performed during other months of the *haab'*, including ceremonies associated with planting, hunting and trapping, the preparation of wooden deity images, and care of the stingless bees (Bill 1997; Ciaramella 2002, 2004; Graff 1997; Vail 1997a, 2002a, 2004; Vail & Bricker 2004; von Nagy 1997), are also depicted in the Maya codices.

Another recent development, sparked by the research discussed above, is the *haab'* model developed by Vail (2002a, 2004). She proposes that many almanacs previously believed to be 260-day instruments were instead used within the 52-year Calendar Round, which represents a pairing of the 260- and 365-day calendars. According to this model, almanacs with iconography that repeats from frame to frame (in which the deity shifts but the activity remains constant) are likely to be 52-year instruments. As an example, she points to M. 16a (**Figure 4**, see color insert), which can be linked to a ritual discussed in Landa's *Relación* that took place every *haab'* (365 days) at roughly the same point in time (similar to our yearly holidays). Termed *ok nah*, it involved renovating the temples in honor of the Chaaks (rain gods) and gods of the field (Tozzer 1941, p. 161). M. 16a includes iconographic links to the ceremony described by Landa—a series of temples painted blue, the color associated with rain and fertility—as well as textual correspondences, as suggested by the phrase *ok nah* beginning each clause.

A traditional interpretation of the almanac's calendrical structure calls for the rep-

etition of the renovation ceremony every 10 to 16 days, as indicated by the black bar-and-dot numbers associated with each frame (see **Table 1a**, see color insert). This makes little sense given the ethnohistoric data, which suggest that the temple was renovated annually. However, a different reading of the same calendrical information allows the events to be interpreted as occurring at intervals of *haab's* rather than days. The four frames are separated by 15, 10, 11, and 16 *haab's*, respectively (see **Table 1b**). Why these particular intervals were chosen remains unclear; however, this is true whether they are interpreted as *haab's* or days. In almanacs of this type, a *haab'* interpretation provides a better explanation of the activities pictured than do models based on reading the intervals as days.

Vail's model calls for the reinterpretation of dozens of almanacs in the Maya codices. This reinterpretation, coupled with an emphasis on the relationship among almanacs, serves as the focus of a new commentary of the Madrid Codex by G. Vail & C. Hernández (unpublished manuscript). Their research encompasses not only the Maya codices, but also the Borgia group of codices (discussed below) because of cognates occurring in the two manuscript traditions. The best known of these are on page 1 of the Codex Fejérváry-Mayer (FM) from the Borgia group and M. 75–76. Vail & Hernández (2006) interpret both almanacs as Calendar Round instruments depicting Wayeb' and New Year's ceremonies.

In concert with the research described above, Vail & Bricker (2004) recently documented the presence of more than 40 possible *haab'* dates in almanacs from the Madrid Codex (several of them had been previously noted; see Graña-Behrens 2002 and Vail & Bricker 2004, table 7.1). This finding adds weight to recent proposals that Maya almanacs were not necessarily intended as repeating 260-day instruments but that many of them were anchored in time either seasonally or according to the civic year (see

FM: Codex Fejérváry-Mayer

V. Bricker & H. Bricker 1992, Vail & Aveni 2004).

Maya–Highland Mexican Connections

Another significant development in Maya codical studies involves a new perspective on scribal and elite interchange in Late Postclassic Mesoamerica, as suggested by the shared intellectual content of almanacs in the Maya and Borgia group of codices from highland Mexico. The seven members of the latter group share components of a similar style as well as a number of cognate almanacs, despite the fact that they were very likely produced over a broad region including the Valley of Mexico, Tlaxcala, Puebla, Oaxaca, and possibly the Gulf coast (Boone 2003, p. 214).

Thomas (1884) and Seler (1902–1923, I:618–67; 1904) were the first to comment on parallels between almanacs in the Borgia group and those in the Maya codices, including the correspondences between FM 1 and M. 75–76 discussed above and others between the Venus table in the Dresden Codex and a series of almanacs in the Borgia and Vaticanus B. codices. Studies by twentieth-century commentators also drew attention to ties between the two codex traditions. Rather than focusing on specific almanacs, however, they are of a more general nature, emphasizing parallels between Maya and Mexican deities, religion, and cosmology (see, e.g., Nowotny 1961; Taube 1992; Thompson 1934, 1970). Specific comparisons include the identification of central Mexican deities in the Dresden Venus table (Riese 1982, Taube & Bade 1991, Whittaker 1986), the use of the A-O year sign (a Mixtec convention) in several almanacs in the Madrid Codex (H. Bricker et al. 1997, Vail 1997b), spacers similar to those used in the Borgia group in the Grolier Codex (Carlson 1983), and closely similar intervallic patterning in the two manuscript traditions (Aveni 2004).

More recently, scholars have begun to apply the methodology used for dating Maya almanacs to the Borgia group (Aveni 1999, V. Bricker 2001, Hernández 2004) and have returned to the earlier focus on documenting specific connections between almanacs in the Maya codices (particularly the Madrid) and the Borgia group (Boone 2003; Drapkin 2002; Hernández & Bricker 2004; Just 2000, 2004; Vail & Hernández 2006). Just (2000, 2004) comments on four almanacs in the Madrid Codex that share a format typical of members of the Borgia group: an *in extenso* layout that allows the explicit recording of each day of the 260-day ritual calendar. His interest centers on why the Late Postclassic Maya adopted particular central Mexican forms such as this one. One possibility he proposes is that an *in extenso* format permits the recording of a variety of events or activities for a given interval of time, allowing multiple cycles to be represented simultaneously.

Just (2000, p. 14) believes that the use of central Mexican calendrical structures provides evidence for interaction between the Maya area and highland Mexico that was based not solely on political or military concerns, but also on the exchange of ideas about time and methods for recording it. M. Macri (submitted manuscript) examines other evidence for Maya–central Mexican connections in her study of possible borrowings from a Nahua language in the Maya codical texts. Research by Drapkin (2002) and Hernández & Bricker (2004) demonstrates that a number of the Madrid almanacs can be understood in terms of a highland Mexican model. Hernández & Bricker (2004, pp. 306–9) note, for example, that the Madrid yearbearer pages incorporate dates that occur throughout the year (*haab'*) in question, not simply those related to the inauguration of a new yearbearer. This is similar to almanacs in the Borgia Codex, such as B. 49–52, which reference both planting and New Year's events.

The iconographic, calendrical, and structural parallels detailed in these studies have led

Figure 3

A yearbearer ceremony depicted on M. 51b. Illustration after Anders (1967); courtesy of the Museo de América, Madrid.

Figure 4

An *ok nah* ceremony, similar to that described by Landa (in Tozzer 1941, p. 161) on M. 16a. Illustration after Anders (1967); courtesy of the Museo de América, Madrid.

Table 1   Calendrical structure of the almanac on M. 16a[1]

A. 260-day structure of almanac			
4 + 15 days	6 + 10 days	3 + 11 days	1 + 16 days
Ahaw	Men	Chikchan	Kib'
Eb'	Manik'	Kab'an	Lamat
K'an	Kawak	Muluk	Ahaw
Kib'	Chuwen	Imix	Eb'
Lamat	Ak'b'al	B'en	K'an
[frame 1]	[frame 2]	[frame 3]	[frame 4]
B. 52-year structure of almanac			
4 + 15 *haab's*	6 + 10 *haab's*	3 + 11 *haab's*	1 + 16 *haab's*
Ahaw	**Men**	**Chikchan**	Kib'
Eb'	Manik'	Kab'an	Lamat
K'an	Kawak	Muluk	**Ahaw**
Kib'	Chuwen	Imix	Eb'
Lamat	Ak'b'al	B'en	K'an
4 Ahaw (3 Yax) + 15 *haab's*	6 Men (3 Yax) + 10 *haab's*	3 Chikchan (3 Yax) + 11 *haab's*	1 Ahaw (3 Yax) + 16 *haab's*
[frame 1]	[frame 2]	[frame 3]	[frame 4]

[1]Note: The *haab'* date 3 Yax in Part B was chosen on the basis of Landa's attribution of the renovation ceremony to the months of Yax or Ch'en (Tozzer 1941, p. 161). Boldface is used to indicate where the dates in Part B are recorded in the almanac.

researchers to conclude that they are not the result of a pan-Mesoamerican tradition, but rather that "some form of scribal translation took place, in which the author or authors of the Madrid Codex reconfigured the information on several pages of the Borgia Codex (or a closely related manuscript) into a Maya format" (Hernández & Bricker 2004, p. 314). How this happened remains to be determined. We know that there were extensive commercial ties between parts of highland Mexico and the northern Maya lowlands during the Postclassic period (see, e.g., Milbrath & Peraza Lope 2003, Smith & Berdan 2003). Perhaps as a result, other exchange networks developed, including one that focused on intellectual interchange among scribes, artists, and other members of the elite. To address this question more fully, Dumbarton Oaks is sponsoring a symposium in the fall of 2006 concerning Late Postclassic interaction between the Mexican highlands and the Yucatán peninsula. Researchers will examine the relevant archaeological, iconographic, linguistic, and textual data to develop testable hypotheses about the types and levels of interaction that may have played a role in the composition of the Late Postclassic codices.

Online Resources and Future Directions for Research

Another recent innovation in codical studies is the online Maya Codices Database (Vail & Hernández 2005), developed with funding from the National Endowment for the Humanities. The first version, consisting of a searchable database of the Madrid Codex, was made available online in the fall of 2002 (Vail 2002b) on Dumbarton Oak's Web site. It was recently updated to expedite research inquiries pertaining to the manuscript's hieroglyphic texts.

Among the resources available to codical specialists, the database is unique in providing a comprehensive "catalog" of the content of the Maya codices (organized accord-

ing to dates, iconography, hieroglyphic texts, and themes) and a mechanism to search for particular data sets (e.g., all examples of the rain deity Chaak) or the intersection of such sets (e.g., all examples of Chaak holding an axe, or all examples of Chaak that occur on a particular date in the *tzolk'in* or *haab'*). Data from the Madrid Codex are currently available for searching; data entry for the other three Maya codices is scheduled for completion by December 2006.

The database offers exciting opportunities for future research, allowing the possibility of making further breakthroughs in each of the areas currently under investigation (calendrical interrelationships among codical almanacs, linguistic studies of the hieroglyphic texts, etc.), as well as in areas of study that may emerge in the coming years. Vail and Hernández envision a series of similar databases—pertaining to the Borgia group codices, Maya mural art, and Late Postclassic material culture—to facilitate research concerning religion, ideology, trade, and related topics in the Late Postclassic Mesoamerican world.

SUMMARY AND CONCLUSIONS

The past decade of research has been characterized by innovative methodologies for contextualizing iconographic studies of the Maya codices through new techniques for analyzing the hieroglyphic texts and calendrical structures of codical almanacs. Discussions of the scribal tradition and provenience and dating issues have served to reintegrate codical research into the broader tradition of Mesoamerican studies. The emphasis on Maya–highland Mexican interaction opens the door to a reexamination of issues of exchange and interchange among Late Postclassic cultures in Mesoamerica in ways not previously possible. Future research along these lines will broaden our perspective not only of the Mesoamerican world, but also of cultural interaction more generally.

ACKNOWLEDGMENTS

I am grateful to the National Endowment for the Humanities for their support of my research on the Maya codices in the form of grants RZ-20724-01 (2001–2002), FB-50332-04 (2004–2005), and RZ-50311-04 (2004–2006); to Ty Giltinan and Christine Hernández for collaborating with me on the Maya Codices Database Project; to Cynthia Vail and William Werner for their editorial assistance; and to the following colleagues for their comments on an earlier draft of my review: Anthony Aveni, Harvey M. Bricker, Victoria R. Bricker, Christine Hernández, and Martha J. Macri. My interest in the Maya codices first arose through a seminar taught by Victoria Bricker, and I thank her especially, as well as the colleagues named above, for many enjoyable years of collaboration. Any views, findings, conclusions, or recommendations expressed in this publication do not necessarily represent those of the National Endowment for the Humanities.

LITERATURE CITED

Anders F. 1967. *Codex Tro-Cortesianus (Codex Madrid). Museo de América Madrid.* Graz: Akad. Druck Verlag

Anders F. 1968. *Codex Peresianus (Codex Paris).* Graz: Akad. Druck Verlag

Aveni AF. 1980. *Skywatchers of Ancient Mexico.* Austin: Univ. Tex. Press

Aveni AF. 1992a. The moon and the Venus table: an example of commensuration in the Maya calendar. See Aveni 1992b, pp. 87–101

Aveni AF, ed. 1992b. *The Sky in Mayan Literature.* New York/Oxford: Oxford Univ. Press

Aveni AF. 1999. Astronomy in the Mexican Codex Borgia. *Archaeoastronomy* 24:S1–20

Aveni AF. 2001. *Skywatchers: A Revised and Updated Version of* Skywatchers of Ancient Mexico. Austin: Univ. Tex. Press

Aveni AF. 2004. Intervallic structure and cognate almanacs in the Madrid and Dresden codices. See Vail & Aveni 2004, pp. 147–70

Aveni AF, Bricker HM, Bricker VR. 2003. Seeking the sidereal: observable planetary stations and the ancient Maya record. *J. Hist. Astron.* 34:145–61

Aveni AF, Morandi SJ, Peterson PA. 1996. The Maya number of time: intervalic time reckoning in the Maya codices, part II. *Archaeoastronomy* 21:S1–32

Baudez C-F. 2002. Venus y el Códice Grolier. *Arqueol. Mex.* X(55):70–79

Bill CR. 1997. The roles and relationships of God M and other black gods in the codices, with specific reference to pages 50–56 of the Madrid Codex. See Bricker & Vail 1997, pp. 111–45

Bill CR, Hernández CL, Bricker VR. 2000. The relationship between early colonial Maya New Year's ceremonies and some almanacs in the *Madrid Codex. Anc. Mesoam.* 11:149–68

Boone EH. 2001. Grolier, Codex. See Carrasco 2001, 1:442–44

Boone EH. 2003. A web of understanding: pictorial codices and the shared intellectual culture of Late Postclassic Mesoamerica. See Smith & Berdan 2003, pp. 207–21

Bricker HM. 2004. The paper patch on page 56 of the Madrid Codex. See Vail & Aveni 2004, pp. 33–56

Bricker HM, Aveni AF, Bricker VR. 2001. Ancient Maya documents concerning the movements of Mars. *Proc. Natl. Acad. Sci. USA* 98(4):2107–10

Bricker HM, Bricker VR. 1983. Classic Maya prediction of solar eclipses. *Curr. Anthropol.* 24:1–23

Bricker HM, Bricker VR. 1992. Zodiacal references in the Maya codices. See Aveni 1992b, pp. 148–83

Bricker HM, Bricker VR. 1997. More on the Mars table in the Dresden Codex. *Lat. Am. Antiq.* 8(4):384–97

Bricker HM, Bricker VR, Wulfing B. 1997. Determining the historicity of three astronomical almanacs in the Madrid Codex. *Archaeoastronomy* 22:S17–36

Bricker VR. 1985. Noun incorporation in the Dresden Codex. *Anthropol. Linguist.* 27(4):413–23

Bricker VR. 1986. *A Grammar of Mayan Hieroglyphs*. Middle Am. Res. Inst., Publ. 56. New Orleans: Tulane Univ.

Bricker VR. 1995. Review of *The Paris Codex: Handbook for a Maya Priest*, by Bruce Love. *Lat. Am. Antiq.* 6(3):283–84

Bricker VR. 1997a. The "calendar-round" almanac in the Madrid Codex. See Bricker & Vail 1997, pp. 169–80

Bricker VR. 1997b. The structure of almanacs in the Madrid Codex. See Bricker & Vail 1997, pp. 1–25

Bricker VR. 1998. La función de los almanaques en el Códice de Madrid. In *Memorias del Tercer Congreso Internacional de Mayistas*, pp. 433–46. Mexico, D.F.: Cent. Estud. Mayas, Univ. Nac. Autón. Mex.

Bricker VR. 2000. Bilingualism in the Maya codices and the books of Chilam Balam. *Writ. Lang. Lit.* 3(1):77–115

Bricker VR. 2001. A method for dating Venus almanacs in the Borgia Codex. *Archaeoastronomy* 26:S21–44

Bricker VR, Bricker HM. 1986a. Archaeoastronomical implications of an agricultural almanac in the Dresden Codex. *Mexicon* 8:29–35

Bricker VR, Bricker HM. 1986b. The Mars table in the Dresden Codex. In *Research and Reflections in Archaeology and History: Essays in Honor of Doris Stone*, ed. EW Andrews V, pp. 51–80. Middle Am. Res. Inst., Publ. 57. New Orleans: Tulane Univ.

Bricker VR, Bricker HM. 1988. The seasonal table in the Dresden Codex and related almanacs. *Archaeoastronomy* 12:S1–62

Bricker VR, Bricker HM. 1992. A method for cross-dating almanacs with tables in the Dresden Codex. See Aveni 1992b, pp. 43–86

Bricker VR, Bricker HM. 2005. Astronomical references in the water tables on pages 69 to 74 of the Dresden Codex. In *Painted Books and Indigenous Knowledge in Mesoamerica: Manuscript Studies in Honor of Mary Elizabeth Smith*, ed. EH Boone, pp. 213–29. Middle Am. Res. Inst., Publ. 69. New Orleans: Tulane Univ.

Bricker VR, Vail G, eds. 1997. *Papers on the Madrid Codex*. Middle Am. Res. Inst., Publ. 64. New Orleans: Tulane Univ.

Cabello Carro P. 1986. Un siglo de coleccionismo Maya en España: de 1785–1787 a 1888. In *Los Mayas de los Tiempos Tardíos*, ed. M Rivera, A Ciudad, pp. 99–120. Madrid: Publ. Soc. Esp. Estud. Mayas, No. 1

Carlson JB. 1983. The Grolier Codex: a preliminary report on the content and authenticity of a thirteenth-century Maya Venus almanac. In *Calendars in Mesoamerica and Peru: Native American Computations of Time*, ed. AF Aveni, G Brotherston, pp. 27–57. BAR Int. Ser. 174. Oxford: Br. Archaeol. Rep.

Carrasco D, ed. 2001. *The Oxford Encyclopedia of Mesoamerican Cultures: The Civilizations of Mexico and Central America*, 3 Vols. New York: Oxford Univ. Press

Chuchiak JF. 2004. Papal bulls, extirpators, and the Madrid Codex: the content and probable provenience of the M. 56 patch. See Vail & Aveni 2004, pp. 57–88

Ciaramella MA. 1999. The weavers in the codices. *Res. Rep. Anc. Maya Writ.* 44. Washington, DC: Cent. Maya Res.

Ciaramella MA. 2002. The bee-keepers in the Madrid Codex. *Res. Rep. Anc. Maya Writ.* 52. Washington, DC: Cent. Maya Res.

Ciaramella MA. 2004. The idol-makers in the Madrid Codex. *Res. Rep. Anc. Maya Writ.* 54. Barnardsville, NC: Cent. Maya Res.

Ciudad Ruiz A. 2000. El códice tro-cortesiano del Museo de América de Madrid. *Rev. Esp. Antropol. Am.* 30:9–25

Ciudad Ruiz A, Lacadena García-Gallo A. 1999. El códice tro-cortesiano de Madrid en el contexto de la tradición escrita Maya. In *XII Simposio de Investigaciones Arqueológicas en Guatemala, 1998*, ed. JP Laporte, HL Escobedo, AC Monzón de Suasnávar, 2:997–1010. Guatemala: Minist. Cult. Deport., Inst. Antropol. Hist., Asoc. Tikal

Closs MP. 1977. The date-reaching mechanism in the Venus table of the Dresden Codex. In *Native American Astronomy*, ed. AF Aveni, pp. 89–99. Austin: Univ. Tex. Press

Closs MP. 1979. Venus in the Maya world: glyphs, gods and associated astronomical phenomena. In *Tercera Mesa Redonda de Palenque*, ed. MG Robertson, DC Jeffers, IV:147–65. Monterey, CA: Pre-Columbian Art Res. Cent.

Closs MP. 1992. Some parallels in the astronomical events recorded in the Maya codices and inscriptions. See Aveni 1992b, pp. 133–47

Códice D. 1998. *Kumatzim Wuj Jun: Códice de Dresde*. Guatemala: Cholsamaj

Códice TC. 1991. *Códice Tro-Cortesiano*. Introducción de Manuel Ballesteros Gaibrois; estudio crítico de Miguel Rivera Dorado. Colección Tabula Americae 12. Madrid: Testimonio Compañía Ed.

Coe MD. 1989a. The Hero Twins: myth and image. In *The Maya Vase Book*, ed. J Kerr, 1:161–84. New York: Kerr Assoc.

Coe MD. 1989b. The royal fifth: earliest notices of Maya writing. *Res. Rep. Anc. Maya Writ.* 28. Washington, DC: Cent. Maya Res.

Coe MD, Kerr J. 1997. *The Art of the Maya Scribe*. London: Thames & Hudson

Colas PR. 1999. *Auf der Jagd im Codex Madrid: Ikonographische und epigraphische Analyse der Seiten 38a und 39–49 des Codex Tro-Cortesianus*. MA thesis. Univ. Hamburg

Davoust M. 1997. *Un Nouveau Commentaire du Codex de Dresde: Codex Hiéroglyphique Maya du XIVe Siècle*. Paris: CNRS Ed.

Deckert H, Anders F. 1975. *Codex Dresdensis*. Graz: Akad. Druck Verlag

Drapkin J. 2002. *Interpreting the dialect of time: a structural analysis and discussion of almanacs in the Madrid Codex*. Honors thesis. Dept. Anthropol., Tulane Univ., New Orleans

Escalante R. 1992. *Códice Madrid Tro-Cortesiano*. Puebla: Museo Amparo

Everson GD. 1995. *The celestial Dresden: archaeoastronomy in Late Post-Classic Yucatán*. PhD thesis. Dept. Anthropol., Univ. Calif., Riverside

Förstemann E. 1880. *Die Mayahandschrift der Königlichen öffentlichen Bibliothek zu Dresden*. Mit 74 Tafeln in Chromo-Lichtdruck. Leipzig: Verlag Naumann

Förstemann E. 1906. *Commentary on the Maya Manuscript in the Royal Public Library of Dresden*. Pap. Peabody Mus. Am. Archaeol. Ethnol., Vol. 4, No. 2. Cambridge, MA: Harvard Univ.

Fox JA, Justeson JS. 1984. Polyvalence in Mayan hieroglyphic writing. In *Phoneticism in Mayan Hieroglyphic Writing*, ed. JS Justeson, L Campbell, pp. 17–76. Inst. Mesoam. Stud., Publ. 9. Albany: State Univ. NY

Freidel D, Schele L, Parker J. 1993. *Maya Cosmos: Three Thousand Years on the Shaman's Path*. New York: Morrow

Galindo Trejo J. 2000. Recent advances in Mesoamerican archaeoastronomy. *Archaeoastron.: J. Astron. Cult.* 15:32–42

Graff D. 1997. Dating a section of the Madrid Codex: astronomical and iconographic evidence. See Bricker & Vail 1997, pp. 147–67

Graff D. 2000. Material culture in the Madrid Codex. *Hum. Mosaic* 33(1):17–32

Graff D, Vail G. 2001. Censers and stars: issues in the dating of the Madrid Codex. *Lat. Am. Indian Lit. J.* 17(1):58–95

Graña-Behrens D. 2002. *Die Maya-Inschriften aus Nordwestyukatan, Mexiko.* PhD thesis. Univ. Bonn. **http://hss.ulb.uni-bonn.de/diss_online/phil_fak/2002/grana_behrens_daniel/**

Grube N. 2001. Dresden, Codex. See Carrasco 2001, 1:337–39

Hernández C. 2004. "Yearbearer pages" and their connection to planting almanacs in the Borgia Codex. See Vail & Aveni 2004, pp. 321–64

Hernández C, Bricker VR. 2004. The inauguration of planting in the Borgia and Madrid codices. See Vail & Aveni 2004, pp. 277–320

Hofling CA. 1988. Venus and the miscellaneous almanacs in the Dresden Codex. *J. Mayan Linguist.* 6:79–102

Hofling CA. 1989. The morphosyntactic basis of discourse structure in glyphic text in the Dresden Codex. In *Word and Image in Maya Culture: Explorations in Language, Writing, and Representation,* ed. WF Hanks, DS Rice, pp. 51–71. Salt Lake City: Univ. Utah Press

Hofling CA, O'Neil T. 1992. Eclipse cycles in the moon goddess almanacs in the Dresden Codex. See Aveni 1992b, pp. 102–32

Houston S, Robertson J, Stuart D. 2000. The language of Classic Maya inscriptions. *Curr. Anthropol.* 41(3):321–56

Johnson RE, Quenon M. 1994. A Maya zodiac: comments on the *Paris Codex* pages 23 and 24. In *U Mut Maya V,* ed. C Jones, T Jones, pp. 207–28. Arcata, CA: U Mut Maya

Jüngel P. 1999. An unique almanac in the *Codex Madrid:* a mistakological study. *Estud. Cult. Maya* 20:117–30

Just BR. 2000. Concordances of time: *in extenso* almanacs in the Madrid and Borgia group codices. *Hum. Mosaic* 33(1):7–16

Just BR. 2004. *In extenso* almanacs in the Madrid Codex. See Vail & Aveni 2004, pp. 255–76

Justeson JS. 1989. Ancient Maya ethnoastronomy: an overview of hieroglyphic sources. In *World Archaeoastronomy,* ed. AF Aveni, pp. 76–129. Cambridge/New York: Cambridge Univ. Press

Kelley DH. 1962. A history of the decipherment of Maya script. *Anthropol. Linguist.* 4(8):1–48

Kelley DH. 1976. *Deciphering the Maya Script.* Austin: Univ. Tex. Press

Knorozov Y. 1952. Drevniaia pis'mennost' Central'noi Ameriki [The ancient script of Central America]. *Sovietskaia etnografiia* 3:100–18. Moscow: Acad. Sci.

Knorozov Y. 1955. A brief summary of the studies of the ancient Maya hieroglyphic writing in the Soviet Union [Engl. transl.]. *Rep. Sov. Deleg. X Int. Congr. Hist. Sci., Rome.* Moscow: Acad. Sci.

Knorozov Y. 1958. The problem of the study of the Maya hieroglyphic writing. *Am. Antiq.* 23:284–91

Knorozov Y. 1982. *Maya Hieroglyphic Codices.* Transl. SD Coe. Inst. Mesoam. Stud., Publ. 8. Albany: State Univ. NY

Knowlton T. 2003. Seasonal implications of Maya eclipse and rain iconography in the Dresden Codex. *J. Hist. Astron.* 34:291–303

Lacadena A. 1995. *Evolución formal de las grafías escriturarias Mayas: implicaciones históricas y culturales.* PhD thesis. Univ. Complutense Madrid

Lacadena A. 1997. Bilingüismo en el Códice de Madrid. In *Los Investigadores de la Cultura Maya.* Publ. No. 5, pp. 184–204. Mexico: Univ. Autón. Campeche

Lacadena A. 2000. Los escribas del Códice de Madrid: metodología paleográfica. *Rev. Esp. Antropol. Am.* 30:27–85

Lee TA, ed. 1985. *Los Códices Mayas*. Tuxtla Gutiérrez, Mex: Univ. Autón. Chiapas

Lounsbury FG. 1983. The base of the Venus table of the Dresden Codex, and its significance for the calendar-correlation problem. In *Calendars in Mesoamerica and Peru: Native American Computations of Time*, ed. AF Aveni, G Brotherston, pp. 1–26. BAR Int. Ser. 174. Oxford: Br. Archaeol. Rep.

Love B. 1991. A text from the Dresden new year pages. See Robertson & Fields 1991, pp. 293–302

Love B. 1994. *The Paris Codex: Handbook for a Maya Priest*. Austin: Univ. Tex. Press

Love B. 1995. A Dresden Codex Mars table? *Lat. Am. Antiq.* 6(4):350–61

Macri MJ, Looper MG. 2003. *The New Catalog of Maya Hieroglyphs*. Vol. 1: *The Classic Period Inscriptions*. Norman: Univ. Okla. Press

Marhenke R. 1997. Latin in the Madrid Codex. In *U Mut Maya VI*, ed. C Jones, T Jones, pp. 199–201. Bayside, CA: U Mut Maya

Milbrath S. 1981. Astronomical imagery in the serpent sequence of the Madrid Codex. In *Archaeoastronomy in the Americas*, ed. RA Williamson, pp. 263–84. Ballena Press Anthropol. Pap., No. 22. Los Altos, CA: Ballena Press

Milbrath S. 1999. *Star Gods of the Maya: Astronomy in Art, Folklore, and Calendars*. Austin: Univ. Tex. Press

Milbrath S. 2002. New questions concerning the authenticity of the Grolier Codex. *Lat. Am. Indian Lit. J.* 18(1):50–83

Milbrath S, Peraza Lope C. 2003. Revisiting Mayapan: Mexico's last Maya capital. *Anc. Mesoam.* 14:1–46

Nowotny KA. 1961. *Tlacuilolli. Die Mexikanischen Bilderhandschriften. Stil und Inhalt, Mit Einem Katalog der Codex Borgia-Gruppe*. Berlin: Verlag Gebr. Mann

Paxton M. 1986. *Codex Dresden: stylistic and iconographic analysis of a Maya manuscript*. PhD thesis. Dept. Art Hist., Univ. N.M., Albuquerque

Paxton M. 1991. Codex Dresden: Late Postclassic ceramic depictions and the problems of provenience and date of painting. See Robertson & Fields 1991, pp. 303–8

Paxton M. 1992. The Books of Chilam Balam: astronomical content and the Paris Codex. See Aveni 1992b, pp. 216–46

Paxton M. 2001. *The Cosmos of the Yucatec Maya: Cycles and Steps from the Madrid Codex*. Albuquerque: Univ. N.M. Press

Paxton M. 2004. Tayasal origin of the Madrid Codex: further consideration of the theory. See Vail & Aveni 2004, pp. 89–127

Porter JB. 1997. Drawing the Maya screenfold books: preliminary observations. In *Latin American Indian Literatures: Messages and Meanings*, ed. MH Preuss, pp. 33–46. Lancaster, CA: Labyrinthos

Riese B. 1982. Eine mexikanische Gottheit im Venuskapitel der Mayahandschrift Codex Dresdensis. *Bull. Soc. Suisse Am.* 46:37–39

Ringle WM. 1988. Of mice and monkeys: the value and meaning of T1016c, the God C hieroglyph. *Res. Rep. Anc. Maya Writ.* 18. Washington, DC: Cent. Maya Res.

Rivera Dorado M. 1991. Estudio Crítico. In *Códice Tro-Cortesiano*, Tabula Americae 12, pp. 51–129. Madrid: Testimonio Compañia Ed.

Robertson MG, Fields VM, eds. 1991. *Sixth Palenque Round Table, 1986*. Norman: Univ. Okla. Press

Salgado Ruelas SM. 2001. *Análisis semiótico de la forma arbórea en el Códice de Dresde*. Mexico, D.F.: Univ. Nac. Autón. Mex.

Sanz Castro LT. 2000. Los escribas del Códice de Madrid: metodología y análisis pre-iconográfico. *Rev. Esp. Antropol. Am.* 30:87–103

Schele L. 1992. *Workbook for the XVIth Maya Hieroglyphic Workshop at Texas*. Austin: Dept. Art & Art Hist., Inst. Lat. Am. Stud., Univ. Tex.

Schele L, Grube N. 1997. The Dresden Codex. In *Notebook for the XXIst Maya Hieroglyphic Workshop*, pp. 79–247. Austin: Dept. Art & Art Hist., Coll. Fine Arts/Inst. Lat. Am. Stud., Univ. Tex.

Schele L, Mathews P. 1998. *The Code of Kings: The Language of Seven Sacred Maya Temples and Tombs*. New York: Scribner

Schellhas P. 1904. *Representation of Deities of the Maya Manuscripts*. Pap. Peabody Mus. Am. Archaeol. Ethnol., Vol. 4, No. 1. Cambridge, MA: Harvard Univ.

Seler E. 1901. *Codex Fejérváry-Mayer: eine altmexikanische Bilderhandschrift der Free Public Museums in Liverpool (12014/M)*. Berlin

Seler E. 1902–1923. *Gesammelte Abhandlungen zur Amerikanischen Sprach- und Alterthumskunde*, 5 Vols. Berlin: Asher

Seler E. 1904. Venus period in the picture writings of the Borgian Codex group. In *Mexican and Central American Antiquities, Calendar Systems, and History*, ed. CP Bowditch, pp. 355–91. Bur. Am. Ethnol. Bull. 28. Washington, DC: GPO

Severin GM. 1981. *The Paris Codex: Decoding an Astronomical Ephemeris*. Trans. Am. Philos. Soc., Vol. 71, Part 5. Philadelphia: Am. Philos. Soc.

Smith ME, Berdan FF, eds. 2003. *The Postclassic Mesoamerican World*. Salt Lake City: Univ. Utah Press

Sotelo Santos LE. 2002. *Los Dioses del Códice Madrid: Aproximación a las Representaciones Antropomorfas de un Libro Sagrado Maya*. Mexico, D.F.: Univ. Nac. Autón. Mex.

Spinden H. 1924. *The Reduction of Mayan Dates*. Pap. Peabody Mus. Am. Archaeol. Ethnol., Vol. 6, No. 4. Cambridge, MA: Harvard Univ.

Stuart D. 1987. Ten phonetic syllables. *Res. Rep. Anc. Maya Writ.* 14. Washington, DC: Cent. Maya Res.

Taube KA. 1988. *The ancient Yucatec new year festival: the liminal period in Maya ritual and cosmology*. PhD thesis. Yale Univ., New Haven, CT

Taube KA. 1992. *The Major Gods of Ancient Yucatan. Stud. Pre-Columbian Art Archaeol.*, No. 32. Washington, DC: Dumbarton Oaks

Taube KA, Bade BL. 1991. An appearance of Xiuhtecuhtli in the Dresden Venus pages. *Res. Rep. Anc. Maya Writ.* 35. Washington, DC: Cent. Maya Res.

Tedlock B. 1999. Maya astronomy: what we know and how we know it. *Archaeoastron.: J. Astron. Cult.* 14(1):39–58

Tedlock D, Tedlock B. 2002/2003. The sun, moon, and Venus among the stars: methods for mapping Mayan sidereal space. *Archaeoastron.: J. Astron. Cult.* 17:5–22

Teeple JE. 1931. *Maya Astronomy*. Contr. Am. Archaeol., Vol. 1, No. 2. *Carnegie Inst. Wash. Publ.* 403. Washington, DC: Carnegie Inst. Wash.

Thomas C. 1882. *A Study of the Manuscript Troano. U.S. Dept. Inter., Contrib. N. Am. Ethnol.*, Vol. 5, pp. 1–237. Washington, DC: GPO

Thomas C. 1884. Notes on certain Maya and Mexican manuscripts. In *3rd Annu. Rep. Bur. Am. Ethnol., 1881–82*, pp. 3–65. Washington, DC: GPO

Thomas C. 1892. Key to the Maya hieroglyphs. *Science* 20(494):44–46

Thompson JES. 1934. *Sky Bearers, Colors and Directions in Maya and Mexican Religion. Contrib. Am. Archaeol.*, Vol. 2, No. 10. *Carnegie Inst. Wash. Publ.* 436. Washington, DC: Carnegie Inst. Wash.

Thompson JES. 1950. *Maya Hieroglyphic Writing: Introduction. Carnegie Inst. Wash. Publ.* 589. Washington, DC: Carnegie Inst. Wash.

Thompson JES. 1962. *A Catalog of Maya Hieroglyphs*. Norman: Univ. Okla. Press

Thompson JES. 1970. *Maya History and Religion*. Norman: Univ. Okla. Press

Thompson JES. 1972. *A Commentary on the Dresden Codex: A Maya Hieroglyphic Book*. Mem. Am. Philos. Soc., Vol. 93. Philadelphia: Am. Philos. Soc.

Thompson JES. 1975. The Grolier Codex. In *Studies in Ancient Mesoamerica II*, ed. JA Graham, pp. 1–9. Contrib. Univ. Calif. Archaeol. Res. Facil., No. 27. Berkeley: Univ. Calif.

Tozzer AM. 1941. *Landa's Relación de las Cosas de Yucatan*. Pap. Peabody Mus. Am. Archaeol. Ethnol., Vol. 18. Cambridge, MA: Harvard Univ. (Landa's orig. ms. dates to c. 1566)

Tozzer AM, Allen GM. 1910. *Animal Figures in the Maya Codices*. Pap. Peabody Mus. Am. Archaeol. Ethnol., Vol. 4, No. 3. Cambridge, MA: Harvard Univ.

Treiber H. 1987. *Studien zur Katunserie der Pariser Mayahandschrift*. Acta Mesoam., Band 2. Berlin: Verlag Von Flemming

Vail G. 1994. A commentary on the bee almanacs in Codex Madrid. See Vega Sosa 1994, pp. 37–68

Vail G. 1996. *The gods in the Madrid Codex: an iconographic and glyphic analysis*. PhD thesis. Dept. Anthropol., Tulane Univ., New Orleans

Vail G. 1997a. The deer-trapping almanacs in the Madrid Codex. See Bricker & Vail 1997, pp. 73–110

Vail G. 1997b. The yearbearer gods in the *Madrid Codex*. In *Códices y Documentos sobre México. Segundo Simposio*, Vol. I, ed. S Rueda Smithers, C Vega Sosa, R Martínez Baracs, pp. 81–106. Mexico, D.F.: Inst. Nac. Antropol. Hist./Dir. Gen. Publ. Cons. Nac. Cult. Artes

Vail G. 2000a. Issues of language and ethnicity in the Postclassic Maya codices. *Writ. Lang. Lit.* 3(1):37–75

Vail G. 2000b. Pre-hispanic Maya religion: conceptions of divinity in the Postclassic Maya codices. *Anc. Mesoam.* 11:123–47

Vail G. 2002a. *Haab'* rituals in the Maya codices and the structure of Maya almanacs. *Res. Rep. Anc. Maya Writ.* 53. Washington, DC: Cent. Maya Res

Vail G. 2002b. *The Madrid Codex: A Maya Hieroglyphic Book, Version 1.0*. **http://www. doaks.org/Pre-Columbian.html**

Vail G. 2004. A reinterpretation of *tzolk'in* almanacs in the Madrid Codex. See Vail & Aveni 2004, pp. 215–52

Vail G, Aveni A, eds. 2004. *The Madrid Codex: New Approaches to Understanding an Ancient Maya Manuscript*. Boulder: Univ. Press CO

Vail G, Bricker VR. 2004. *Haab* dates in the Madrid Codex. See Vail & Aveni 2004, pp. 171–214

Vail G, Hernández C. 2005. *The Maya Hieroglyphic Codices, Version 2.0*. Available online at **http://www.doaks.org/pc_research_projects.html** or **http://www.mayacodices.org**

Vail G, Hernández C. 2006. Fire drilling, bloodletting, and sacrifice: yearbearer rituals in the Maya and Borgia group codices. In *Sacred Books, Sacred Languages: Two Thousand Years of Ritual and Religious Maya Literature. 8th European Maya Conference, Museo de América, Madrid, November 2003*, ed. R Valencia, G Le Fort, pp. 35–49. Markt Schwaben, Germany: Verlag Anton Saurwein. In press

Vail G, Macri MJ. 2004. *Maya Hieroglyphic Database: The Codices*. Davis: Dept. Native Am. Stud., Univ. Calif., Unpubl. electronic file

Vega Sosa C, ed. 1994. *Códices y Documentos sobre México: Primer Simposio*. Mexico, D.F.: Inst. Nac. Antropol. Hist.

von Nagy CL. 1997. Some comments on the Madrid deer-hunting almanacs. See Bricker & Vail 1997, pp. 27–71

Wald RF. 2004. The languages of the Dresden Codex: legacy of the Classic Maya. In *The Linguistics of Maya Writing*, ed. S Wichmann, pp. 27–58. Salt Lake City: Univ. Utah Press (Orig. circulated as an unpublished ms. in 1994)

Whittaker G. 1986. The Mexican names of three Venus gods in the Dresden Codex. *Mexicon* 8:56–60

Willson RW. 1924. *Astronomical Notes on the Maya Codices*. Pap. Peabody Mus. Archaeol. Ethnol., Vol. 6, No. 3. Cambridge, MA: Harvard Univ.

Wulfing B. 1994. The structure of the eclipse almanac on 12b–18b of the Madrid Codex. See Vega Sosa 1994, pp. 17–35

Zimmermann G. 1956. *Die Hieroglyphen der Maya-Handschriften*. Hamburg: Cram, de Gruyter

Persistent Hunger: Perspectives on Vulnerability, Famine, and Food Security in Sub-Saharan Africa

Mamadou Baro and Tara F. Deubel

Department of Anthropology, and the Bureau of Applied Research in Anthropology, University of Arizona, Tucson, Arizona 85721; email: baro@email.arizona.edu, deubel@email.arizona.edu

Annu. Rev. Anthropol. 2006. 35:521–38

The *Annual Review of Anthropology* is online at anthro.annualreviews.org

This article's doi: 10.1146/annurev.anthro.35.081705.123224

Copyright © 2006 by Annual Reviews. All rights reserved

0084-6570/06/1021-0521$20.00

Key Words

malnutrition, poverty, natural disasters, conflicts, Sahel, political inequalities

Abstract

This review examines the persistence of chronic hunger in Sub-Saharan Africa in the twenty-first century and reviews dominant famine theories, concepts of vulnerability, and household livelihood security and responses to recent food crises in the region. The authors argue that famine occurrences are linked to historical and contemporary socioeconomic processes that have increased over time the vulnerability of African households to hunger and reduced their resilience to environmental and economic shocks, political conflict, and the rapid spread of HIV/AIDS. Approaches to famine need to move away from the "emergency relief" framework to better address the underlying conditions that make food shortages endemic. Future food security for Africa requires an integrated long-term response to household vulnerability on the part of African governments, civil society, and international partners by incorporating new technologies, local expertise, and active involvement of African communities living with the realities of recurrent famine.

INTRODUCTION

Famines and food shortages have recurred throughout human history owing to a variety of interrelated causes, including environmental crises and natural disasters, economic, social, and political inequalities, and violent conflicts. In the twenty-first century, however, the percentage of the world's population facing acute and chronic hunger is decreasing on every continent except Africa (Brown 2001). Sub-Saharan Africa is the only region of the world in which chronic food insecurity and threats of famine remain endemic for most of the population and the number of malnourished people is steadily increasing (Devereux & Maxwell 2001, Rukuni 2002). By 2010, an estimated 32% of Sub-Saharan Africa's total population of 400–500 million will suffer from malnutrition, compared with 4%–12% in other developing countries (Steyn & Walker 2000). Improving food security thus remains a central concern for African development and requires concerted effort on the part of African governments and international donors.

Although the imperative is clear to better address Sub-Saharan Africa's ongoing food crises, the international community and regional governments still lack consensus on how to define and respond to famine adequately. Drawing on multidisciplinary approaches, this chapter reviews dominant theories and conceptual frameworks for the study of vulnerability, food security, and famine in Sub-Saharan Africa; lessons learned from hunger prevention and relief programs; and perspectives on the future of hunger in the region, especially in the context of the HIV/AIDS pandemic's increasingly deleterious impacts. We demonstrate that Sub-Saharan Africans are not passive, powerless victims of famine and food insecurity. We argue that famines and food shortages are linked to persistent vulnerabilities, which are often the result of historical and contemporary processes that limit the options and opportunities of households.

A CONCEPTUAL FRAMEWORK FOR FAMINE, FOOD SECURITY, AND VULNERABILITY

In their discussion of famine in Ethiopia, Webb & von Braun (1994) define famine as "a catastrophic disruption of society as manifested in a cumulative failure of production, distribution and consumption systems" (p. 35). The principal consequences of famine are a concentrated decline of food consumption resulting in chronic weight losses for individuals and sharp increases in excess mortality, massive social disruption, and long-term resource depletion. Although famine has long been considered a discrete event triggered by external causes and amenable to technical solutions, researchers and scholars have recently challenged this view, arguing that famine must be understood as a long-term socioeconomic process that accelerates destitution of a society's most vulnerable groups to the point where their livelihood systems become untenable (Walker 1989, p. 6).

The negative effects of famine in Sub-Saharan Africa have been magnified by an upsurge of complex emergency situations rooted in structural vulnerabilities that limit equitable access to resources (Vogel & Smith 2002). High death tolls from famines are increasingly correlated with the presence of violent conflicts and the concentration of populations in refugee camps where disease epidemics are a common cause of mortality (de Waal 1998). Over the past two decades, 28 African countries have experienced violent conflicts along with their debilitating effects on livelihoods, food production, and access (Devereux & Maxwell 2001).[1] **Table 1** presents an overview of selected African famines during the twentieth century and their primary causes, of which nearly half involve conflict situations.

---

[1]In a study of 38 countries that experienced conflicts between 1961 and 2000, Teodosijevic (2003) determined that per capita agricultural and food production are 10% lower during a conflict and in the 5 years following it than in the 5 years prior to the conflict (Pingali et al. 2005).

Table 1 Selected twentieth-century African famines. Source: Devereux & Maxwell 2001, p. 118

Location	Years	Causal triggers	Estimated mortality
Nigeria (Hausaland)	1902–1908	Drought	5000
Tanzania (south)	1906–1907	Conflict	37,500
West Africa (Sahel)	1913–1914	Drought	125,000
Tanzania (central)	1917–1919	Conflict and drought	30,000
Zimbabwe	1922	Drought	47
Tanzania	1929	Drought	500
Rwanda	1943–1944	Conflict and drought	300,000
Malawi (Nyasaland)	1949	Drought	200
Ethiopia (Tigray)	1957–1958	Drought and locusts	250,000
Ethiopia (Wollo)	1966	Drought	50,000
Nigeria (Biafra)	1968–1970	Conflict	1,000,000
West Africa (Sahel)	1969–1974	Drought	101,000
Ethiopia (Tigray and Wollo)	1972–1974	Drought	350,000
Somalia	1974–1975	Drought	20,000
Uganda (Karamoja)	1980–1981	Conflict and drought	30,000
Mozambique	1982–1985	Conflict and drought	100,000
Ethiopia	1983–1985	Drought	800,000
Sudan (Darfur, Kordofan)	1984–1985	Conflict	250,000
Sudan (south)	1988	Conflict	250,000
Somalia	1991–1993	Conflict and drought	400,000
Sudan (Bahr el Ghazal)	1998	Conflict and drought	70,000

Review of Famine Theories

Theories of famine have shifted from an emphasis on environmental and demographic causes to economic and sociopolitical causes. Early work on famine was heavily influenced by Malthus who proposed that famine followed excessive population growth and served to keep carrying capacity in check by reducing populations to a level consistent with food production. Contrary to Malthus's predictions, however, famines have not limited population growth to any significant extent over history (Devereux 2001 a,b). Largely because of Malthus's influence, "the criterion of famine became a measurable increase in the death rate of an aggregation of individuals, diagnosed by medical professionals as being due to starvation and causally related to a measurable decrease in the availability of food" (de Waal 1989, pp. 17–18). This emphasis on famine as a "technical malfunction" requiring the intervention of experts (e.g., demographers, medical specialists, and agronomists or economists) has long dominated the field and obscured the social processes underlying food crises. The assumed linkage among famine, starvation, and mass mortality in both popular conceptions and technical definitions stems directly from the debate started by Malthus more than two centuries ago. Yet as more nuanced analyses have recently demonstrated, famine can occur in varying degrees of severity well before critical food shortages become evident. For example, villagers in Sudan distinguish a "famine that kills" from a range of other food crises experienced at the household level that may cause hunger and destitution but not necessarily lead to death (de Waal 2004).

SEN'S ENTITLEMENT APPROACH

The groundbreaking work of Amartya Sen in *Poverty and Famines* (1981) introduced a new paradigm in famine studies by rejecting

Malthusian notions of food availability decline (FAD) per head and insisting on the salience of market forces and the role of the state in determining individual entitlements to food. According to Sen, starvation occurs when a person does not have access to enough food, often despite the availability of food for those who can afford it. Famines invariably affect populations in different ways depending on a household's ability to acquire food during crisis times. For instance, at the height of the 1972–1974 famine in Ethiopia, there was no significant reduction in overall food output, and people succumbed to starvation while food prices remained fairly stable. Similarly, during the Sahel famine of the mid-1970s, a survey by the Food and Agricultural Organization determined that the most-affected countries—Mali, Mauritania, and Niger—all produced enough grain even during the worst year (1973) to feed their populations, if the grain had been equally distributed.

In Sen's (1989, 1999) framework, vulnerability to famine is directly related to a household's level of entitlements. He defines entitlements as "a key set of alternative commodity bundles that a person can command in society using the totality of rights and opportunities that he or she faces" (p. 8). Entitlement relations are based on four different types of ownership: production, trade, labor, and inheritance or transfer. Through a combination of these means, individuals gain access to food directly or to the ability to acquire (purchase) it indirectly. Market functioning is central to a household's ability to access food, and starvation can occur even when food is readily available at local markets if a household lacks the appropriate entitlements. Famine is thus characterized by a collapse of entitlements for certain segments of society and the failure of the state to protect those entitlements. Sen's theoretical contributions revolutionized famine policy by shifting the debate from issues of availability to emphasizing the ability of individuals to obtain access to and control over food resources (Webb & von Braun 1994).

REVISING SEN: FAMINE AS A POLITICALLY DRIVEN PROCESS

Although Sen's work remains central in famine research and development studies more generally, several critics have cogently argued that Sen's overemphasis on economic market-based causation neglects the salience of politics, historical processes, and social disruption in creating conditions of vulnerability and famine (de Waal 1990, Duffield 1998, Edkins 2001, Hendrie 1997, Keen 1994, Rangasami 1985). In Sen's analysis, market forces replaced previous nonhuman actors (i.e., supernatural or natural explanations that considered famine an act of God or nature) and defined famine as an economic rather than a natural disaster (Keen 1994). Further shifting the focus of the debate, we should now examine the role of political agency in provoking and sustaining acute and chronic food insecurity, especially among disenfranchised and war-torn populations involved in complex humanitarian emergencies.[2]

In his reassessment of Sen's entitlement theory, de Waal (1990) points out that Sen fails to explain two central phenomena witnessed in famines: (*a*) Many people choose not to consume food rather than sell their vital assets, and (*b*) most famine mortality is caused by the outbreak of disease and widespread epidemics rather than simple undernutrition. In de Waal's integrated model of famine, a natural disaster or economic crisis precipitates famine, causing a loss of entitlements to staple foods and a threat to long-term socioeconomic stability. In this situation, people resort to a variety of coping strategies for temporary solutions, but the strategies often lead to impoverishment and social disruption. When coping strategies completely break down, social collapse ensues and results

---

[2]A humanitarian emergency is defined as "a situation affecting large civilian populations and usually involving a combination of conflict, food insecurities, and population displacement resulting in significant excess mortality or morbidity" (Kaiser et al. 2003, p. 129).

in health crises and excess mortality. Social collapse at this level is usually accompanied by violence, which renders food and medical relief less effective and quickly turns entitlement loss into destitution. In de Waal's view, famine is not limited to the standard notion of mass starvation unto death, but can also be considered "a more virulent form of poverty that leads to death" (p. 486).

Keen's (1994) case study of famine and relief efforts in southwest Sudan, one of the first to incorporate a theoretical conception of power into famine analyses, urges that famine be approached with a critical eye toward those who benefit from its misfortune. He asserts that famine does not merely reflect a failure of markets or policy; it is an indicator of success for particular groups of local, national, and international actors, especially in arenas of violent conflict and war, such as Sudan. Yet "famine discourse" tends to focus exclusively on the plight of the victims, ignoring the motives of its instigators and beneficiaries and what they gain by fostering and maintaining long-term famine conditions. Endorsing a liberal conception of the state as a protector of the public interest, Sen (1989) insists on the role of public policy in protecting entitlements. However, Keen counter-argues that states and powerful groups may actively promote famine and obstruct relief, especially when obstruction becomes a military strategy and weapon of war.

Drawing on a Foucaultian notion of the knowledge-power in discourse, Hendrie (1997) argues that the common discursive representation of famine as a "disaster event" effaces culpability and detaches the occurrence of famine "from its embeddedness within a set of historically specific and locally based economic and political processes" (p. 63). She closely examines how power is exercised in the context of international relief operations using a case study of refugees in Tigray, Ethiopia, who migrated to eastern Sudan in late 1984 following famine there. The range of technologies used to measure and control famine situations includes anthropomet-

ric measurements, early warning indicators, and the creation of universalized "vulnerable groups" who lose their individual identities to homogenization. Using Foucault's example of the institutionalization of madness, Hendrie notes that famine has been removed from the everyday social sphere and relocated into an expert realm of regulation and control that are exerted by powerful humanitarian institutions. Her work highlights the need to incorporate local discourses on famine in scientific research to understand better the particular contexts in which famines occur and to improve the planning and on-the-ground implementation of hunger relief programs. This need is significant because insiders' and outsiders' perceptions often differ significantly; insiders view famine as a problem of poverty and an intensification of ongoing processes rather than as an unusual or extraordinary circumstance.

Taking a more radical stance, Edkins (2001) advocates replacing the term famine with "mass starvation" in an effort to assign responsibility and demand accountability for the occurrence of famine, while linking it discursively with the genocides and mass killings. Edkins argues the dominant framework that regards famine as a failure that can be redressed by scientific or technical solutions limits many of the present ways of defining and theorizing famine. In her view, more emphasis should be placed on assigning responsibility for the persistence of hunger.

Defining Food Security

Large-scale problems of famine in Sub-Saharan Africa cannot be addressed without first improving the underlying food security status of populations at the national, regional, and household levels (Park et al. 1993). The earliest definition of food security emerged from the World Food Conference of 1975 and focused on "the availability at all times of adequate world supplies of basic foodstuffs to sustain a steady expansion of food consumption" (Maxwell & Watkins 2003). By 1986 this had shifted to an emphasis on food access, as shown by the World Bank's definition of food security as "access by all people at all times to the food required for them to lead a healthy and productive life" (von Braun et al. 1999, p. 34). The four key elements that jointly comprise food security are the availability of food resources, access to those resources, sufficient consumption of food, and appropriate utilization in a sanitary and nutritious manner (Hussein 2002). Without all four elements, food security cannot be assured.

Food insecurity thus has multiple causes, and it is rooted in "combinations of political instability, environmental marginality and economic powerlessness" (Vogel & Smith 2002, p. 316). It is no longer viewed as the result of agriculture's failure to produce sufficient food, but rather as the consequence of the failure of livelihood systems to guarantee access to sufficient food at the household level (Devereux & Maxwell 2001). Food insecurity may occur as an acute or chronic problem, enduring for varying time periods and differing in degrees of severity. A population suffering from chronic food insecurity is more vulnerable to full-blown famine, and small fluctuations can lead to emergencies (Herdt 2004). Factors such as volatile price swings, limited government capacity to provide food and agricultural support, and the politicization of land ownership create conditions in which people have little resistance to disruptions of normal activities by drought, poor harvests, economic crises, and price inflation that may quickly create conditions for famine.

Because food insecurity is a multidimensional phenomenon, it is difficult to measure, and measurement requires examination of a combination of related indicators (Frankenberger & Coyle 1993). Some of the proxy indicators commonly used in food security assessments include agricultural production, livestock holdings, landholdings, multiple income sources that typically generate varied amounts of income, daily food consumption in terms of quantity and diversity, local food prices, anthropometric measurements of children under five (to assess wasting and stunting), and the degree to which households rely on coping strategies, such as wild plant consumption, seasonal migration and wage labor, and asset liquidation.

Several major shifts in food security studies and policies have occurred since the 1970s. First, the unit of analysis has moved from the global/national level to the local/household level. Second, the scope of analysis has shifted from a "food first" approach to an emphasis on the performance and sustainability of household livelihoods. Third, subjective perceptions of food security among local populations now complement objectively measurable indicators of food security (Devereux & Maxwell 2001). By combining quantitative and qualitative indicators, food security studies have thus improved in accuracy and validity. For example, food security assessments have begun to rely on local knowledge of household vulnerability by asking local populations to rank the vulnerability status of individual households and communities (Woodson 1997).

Participation by individuals, transparency in the management of resources, and vulnerability reduction must figure among the primary goals to fight against famine and hunger in Sub-Saharan Africa.

INCORPORATING VULNERABILITY AND THE HOUSEHOLD LIVELIHOOD SECURITY FRAMEWORK

In terms of chronic poverty and vulnerability, Africa remains the world's most disadvantaged continent. The 2000–2001 World Development Report states that nearly half (40%) of the total Sub-Saharan population of ~500 million people lives below the international poverty line of one dollar per day (Devereux & Maxwell 2001). By 2020 the population is projected to increase by 70%, accompanied by a 30% rise in child malnutrition (Pinstrup-Andersen et al. 1999). The gross national product has fallen ~1% annually in the past two decades across the continent (Gaile & Ferguson 1996), and Africa's share of world agricultural exports has decreased from 10% to 4% since 1960 (Devereux & Maxwell 2001).

While the broad term vulnerability has been often used to mean vulnerability to poverty or risk, it has sometimes been treated as a cause and/or symptom of poverty. Vulnerability frameworks arose from the realization that the underlying vulnerability status of a population is a more important determinant of the extent and duration of a crisis than the discrete environmental hazards that may trigger the crisis (Prowse 2003). For instance, the relationship between drought and famine is strongest in places where the resource base is poor, poverty is endemic, and public capacity for prevention is weak. Although coordinated, rapid government intervention prevented drought from leading to famine in Zimbabwe, countries such as Sudan and Ethiopia are highly susceptible to drought-induced famine owing to political and economic systems weakened by repeated crises over time (von Braun et al. 1999).

In the Sahel, persistent vulnerability characterizes the relationship of the population to a continuous record of droughts and food shortages (Finan & Langworthy 1997). Simplistic portrayals of food shortages and hunger in the Sahel do little to reveal the underlying causes of a crisis. Famines and droughts in that region of Africa can be viewed within a framework of structural vulnerability defined as a function of exposure to stress and the limited ability to recover from negative impacts. The multidimensionality of vulnerability requires not only a focus on environmental factors such as limited rainfall, but also a consideration of social inequalities (e.g., power differences among classes and ethnic groups) and struggles over land and other natural resources (Blaikie 1985). Vulnerability is a socially constructed phenomenon influenced by institutional and environmental dynamics. An adequate vulnerability framework not only provides an understanding of the current crisis

situation, but also allows an analysis of future risk scenarios (Nelson 2005).

Although the concept of vulnerability is a powerful one, it must be made useful for policy makers. This idea implies that local variations in vulnerability must be presented to policy makers in a comprehensible and functional manner.

Vulnerability can be analyzed on various levels, including individual, community, regional, and national levels. It can be further separated into external factors that comprise the particular risks and shocks experienced by a population and the internal aspects that relate to a population's increasing inability to cope with those shocks (Chambers 1989). During the 1990s vulnerability analysis became a domain of expertise in its own right with the rise of vulnerability assessment studies and mapping. Vulnerability mapping uses a geographic information systems (GIS) framework for organizing data layers that includes secondary data on water sources, rainfall, and basic physical and social infrastructure. With this basic data set, the framework uses a community sampling process and a participatory research approach to involve local populations in the actual definition and mapping of their own vulnerability (Nelson 2005).

The main gaps that still need to be addressed in vulnerability studies include the multiple scales of analysis that create problems in aggregating data, the absence of objective criteria against which to compare a zero state of no vulnerability, and the complicated nature of dynamic systems that involve different combinations of variables over time and space (Webb & Harinarayan 1999). Vulnerability mapping tends to be descriptive. It is important to add an analysis of causality within the framework.

A household's capacity to absorb and recover from famines (or other shocks) can be analyzed instructively from a livelihood perspective (Ellis & Mdoe 2003). Livelihoods are the means by which the household as a unit and its individual members make a living and

GIS: geographic information systems

pursue their goals. They encompass the existing capabilities and assets as well as the sustainability types of socioeconomic activities pursued (Chambers & Conway 1992, Ellis 2000). Households and livelihoods represent the private dimension of vulnerability. Ideally, households operate in ways that minimize risk and that increase the ability to manage negative shocks (Nelson 2005).

The Household Livelihood Security Approach

The Household Livelihood Security (HHLS) framework grew out of a food security perspective but is based on the observation that food is not the only basic need. Other needs such as political participation, education, shelter, and meeting social obligations are as important as food. A livelihood "comprises the capabilities, assets (stores, resources, claims, and access) and activities required for a means of living; a livelihood that is sustainable can cope with and recover from stress and shocks, maintain or enhance its capabilities and assets, and provide sustainable livelihood opportunities for the next generation" (Frankenberger 2003).

Household livelihood security, then, refers to adequate and sustainable access to income and resources to meet basic needs (including food, potable water, health facilities, educational opportunities, housing, involvement in policymaking, and time for community participation and social integration). Livelihoods include a range of on-farm and off-farm activities that together provide a variety of procurement strategies to make a living. Thus, each household can have several possible sources of entitlement, which constitute its livelihood. These entitlements are based on the household's endowments and its position in the legal, political, and social fabric of society. The risk of livelihood failure determines the level of vulnerability of a household to income, food, health, and nutritional insecurity. The greater the share of resources devoted to the acquisition of food and health service,

the higher the vulnerability of the household to food and nutritional insecurity. Therefore, livelihoods are secure when households have secure ownership of, or access to, resources (both tangible and intangible) and income-earning activities, including reserves and assets, to offset risks, ease shocks, and meet contingencies. Households have secure livelihoods when they can acquire, protect, develop, utilize, exchange, and benefit from assets and resources (Frankenberger 2003).

Two major challenges of incorporating HHLS into food security analysis are integrating local livelihoods data into central databases at the national level and financing the costs of scaling up the methods employed at the local level (Hussein 2002).

HOUSEHOLD COPING STRATEGIES

In the 1980s several scholars began looking systematically at the range of coping strategies employed by African households in food crisis periods (Corbett 1988, de Waal 1989, Rahmato 1991, Watts 1983). Normally, coping strategies differ from everyday livelihood strategies; however, in regions that face repeated shocks, coping strategies may come to be integrated into the routine set of daily livelihood activities. As coping strategies are blended with "normal" activities, people become more sensitive to shocks and less resilient (Davies 1993). Roncoli et al. (2001) point out that although coping strategies may serve the short-term purpose of responding to a crisis, the same strategies may require substantial trade-offs, increase risk, and constrain long-term responses and adaptation.

One of the underlying assumptions in earlier famine studies was that households would react to crises by seeking first to ensure food consumption. Studies conducted in Sudan, Nigeria, and Burkina Faso, among other countries, revealed that although coping strategies vary according to context, several common trends emerge across rural villages of Sub-Saharan Africa, and households confronted by risks to their food entitlements seek to minimize long-term impacts in similar ways. In his detailed ethnographic study of the effects of the 1973–1974 famine in northern Nigeria, Watts (1983) noted that households tend to hold onto key assets as long as possible and do not resort to mass migration until all other options have been exhausted. In times of crisis, households often prioritize safeguarding their present assets or purchasing new ones instead of acting to maintain or increase levels of food consumption (Corbett 1988). For example, during the 1984–1985 famine in Darfur, Sudan, people spent as little as 10% of their incomes on food, utilizing most of their money instead to preserve household assets (de Waal 1990). Furthermore, when assets must be disposed of, there is an observed hierarchy in which assets that take the form of self-insurance (e.g., jewelry) are liquidated well before productive assets (e.g., livestock, land, or tools). Accordingly, the sale of productive assets can be considered a clear distress signal that indicates a lack of other options.

The stages of coping strategies begin with insurance mechanisms, followed by the disposal of productive assets, and finally, destitution, usually accompanied by forced migration (Corbett 1988). Rationing food consumption is a common response that starts well before disposal of key assets. Rising levels of malnutrition should thus be interpreted not as failure of strategies adopted but as one of their costs. "Famines and food crises may be seen by household decision makers primarily as a threat to the long-term economic security of the households, rather than simply in terms of an increased risk of malnutrition, disease or mortality" (p. 1108). In this view, famine conditions are created when a majority of households are forced to prioritize the maintenance of current food consumption levels over their future capacity to ensure income generation.

Inter-household transfers and loans increase in the early stages of response to food shortages. Because coping strategies follow a distinct pattern, the timing of relief plays a critical role in determining the effectiveness of these strategies.

Niger's 2004–2005 Food Crisis

Images of malnourished Nigerien children televised around the world in 2005 caught the international community's attention. However, a careful examination of the historical record suggests that the food crisis experienced in Niger in 2005 was not a transitory emergency but a permanent feature of mounting vulnerability. Growing population pressures, land degradation, climate change, reduced income-generating opportunities, and a complexity of other factors, including the low status of women, are working together to make Niger the poorest country in the world. Chronic malnutrition levels of 40% are recorded in many areas of Niger, and it is estimated that 40% of the rural population cannot satisfy its minimal calorie intake requirements. Food production and arable land per capita are declining. Niger is becoming increasingly dependent on food aid and imports. Since the 1980s, Niger has increasingly become unable to feed itself. Even in a good rainfall year such as 2005, rural families who can produce enough food to feed themselves year round are rare. Most families produce enough food to cover their needs for no more than six months. Diets are generally deficient in protein, calories, and essential vitamins and minerals. In addition, the decline of pastoral and agricultural resources is also leading to an increased number of conflicts between farmers and herders. The traditional coping mechanisms of both groups are no longer as viable as they once were in dealing with drought and food shortages (Bernus 1980, Mortimore 1991).

The scarcity of farmland has forced Niger's agrarian population to revert to survival strategies incompatible with sustainable natural resource management. Niger's heavy reliance on increasingly scarce wood as the main source of household energy is a major cause of natural resource degradation. Land scarcity is forcing many farmers onto lands traditionally reserved for pastoralists. This results in lower yields and increased conflicts with pastoralists.

The food crisis experienced in Niger in 2005 was not a transitory emergency but a permanent characteristic of the rising struggle for survival in Niger. Annual rainfall data for the past 30 years shows that 1973, 1975, 1981, 1983, 1987, 1993, 2002, and 2004 were the worst rainfall years. However, 2004 was far from being the driest year for Niger in the past 30 years. So what made 2004 stand out in the media? Where were the media in 2002, 1993, . . . 1973? Medecins sans Frontières were the first to report the high rates of malnutrition in Niger in 2005. However, the child malnutrition rates reported in 2005 were similar to previous years (CARE-BARA 1997).

One lesson from the recent food crisis in Niger concerns the tardiness with which assistance was mobilized despite repeated warnings since the poor harvest of 2004. High market prices, poor management of the national cereal reserves, and locust infestations in some areas have aggravated the food shortage situation.

Effective and sustainable ways to deal with famine and food shortages in Niger must address the underlying causes of increased vulnerability for most households in the country. Among those underlying causes, one must figure the low status of women in Niger's male-dominated society. In addition, food crisis prevention should be an integrated component of emergency relief assistance. However, one major challenge is to have donors ready and willing to fund crisis prevention and alternatives to famine relief interventions rather than fund emergencies that never end.

THE FUTURE OF FOOD SECURITY IN SUB-SAHARAN AFRICA: TOWARD A RIGHTS-BASED APPROACH

Food Security as a Human Right

The International Covenant on Economic, Social, and Cultural Rights adopted by the United Nations in 1966 formalized the right to food as a basic human right, which had been cited in the 1948 Declaration of Human Rights. The Rome Declaration on World Food Security in 1996 reaffirmed the "right of everyone to have adequate access to safe and nutritious food . . . and be free from hunger" (FAO 1996, p. 631). However, despite these declarations, no international mechanisms have been devised to uphold this right formally. The 1996 World Food Summit brought together leaders of 185 countries to develop actions to end world hunger. Food insecurity and vulnerability mapping systems were created at this summit to monitor global and national efforts to reach food security goals. Another tool recently devised to link human rights standards with humanitarian interventions is the The Sphere Project (Oxfam 2000), which is the first attempt to develop globally applicable minimum standards of humanitarian response (Young & Way 2004).

A rights-based approach to food security emerges from a more general human rights framework that affirms the basic rights of all people irrespective of race, culture, religion and gender. The approach implicates a wide range of local, nongovernmental, and international actors in defining policy and actions to reduce hunger. It can refocus attention on several important aspects of food security, including the responsibility of international institutions and states to guarantee human rights, the agency of food-insecure groups to claim their legal rights, and the ways of incorporating rights-based indicators into food security measurement (Hussein 2002).

Impacts of HIV/AIDS on Food Security

The most significant change in livelihood security and the nature of famine over the past decade in Sub-Saharan Africa has been the rapidly growing impact of HIV/AIDS (de Waal 2004). The AIDS epidemic has affected Sub-Saharan Africa more than any other region of the world, and the highest global rates of HIV infection and AIDS-related deaths are in Africa, especially southern Africa (de Waal & Whiteside 2003). In addition, AIDS claims a high proportion of lives of the most productive adult household members, leaving behind children and senior household members who have difficulty replacing the lost labor force (Kadiyala & Gillespie 2003).

In an analysis of the recent food crisis in southern Africa, De Waal & Whiteside (2003) argue that HIV/AIDS has created a new category of highly vulnerable households owing to the presence of illness or AIDS-related deaths. The rising threat of HIV/AIDS to African livelihoods is the root cause of a new variant of famine in which African households face increasing vulnerability to food shortages and diminished possibilities of recovery. Elevated rates of adult morbidity and mortality caused by AIDS drastically reduce the household labor force, skills, and assets. The burden of caring for sick individuals further decreases the productive capacity of the household and increases dependency ratios within households. Because AIDS increases inter- and intrahousehold inequality, it is also a significant factor in making Africans more susceptible to the effects of famine (de Waal & Whiteside 2003).

In addition, the relationship between HIV and malnutrition creates a vicious cycle. HIV-infected individuals have a greater need for proper nutrition and caloric intake and are more vulnerable to food crises. Food insecurity also raises risk of exposure to initial HIV infection by increasing the likelihood that people will engage in high-risk behaviors, such as seasonal migration. HIV and malnutrition compound their effects reciprocally in an afflicted individual: As increased morbidity makes dietary intake requirements higher, the individual has greater nutritional deficiency, which further suppresses the immune system and hastens the progression of the disease (Gillespie & Kadiyala 2004, Hendriks 2005). Whereas other household members may choose to reduce caloric intake in the

early stages of a crisis, as a strategy to preserve their livelihoods in the long run, HIV-positive individuals face severe health repercussions in this situation. HIV sufferers have greater nutritional needs (Haddad & Gillespie 2001); therefore reducing overall food consumption is not a viable strategy (O'Donnell 2004). Fortified, high-energy foods developed in the 1990s have been used successfully by nutrition specialists in patient-specific treatments, including those for HIV patients. Nevertheless, these food supplements do not reduce the necessity of expanding access to antiretroviral drugs or other medical treatments for HIV/AIDS patients (Webb 2003).

The realities of the HIV/AIDS pandemic in Africa must be more fully integrated into famine, food security, and vulnerability studies and interventions. Gillespie & Kadiyala (2004) advocate adopting an HIV/AIDS lens in all development and humanitarian programming, using a framework similar to the household livelihood security framework described above, which would more fully integrate the changing needs of communities affected by HIV/AIDS into the discourse and practice of aid.

FAMINE PREVENTION AND RESPONSE STRATEGIES

The idea of early warning systems can be traced to the Indian Famine Codes established in the colonial era to provide a systematic assessment of risk of famine in India. During the 1970s, the combination of falling food stocks worldwide and an increase in droughts affecting India and Africa renewed interest in early warning systems (Webb & Harinarayan 1999). Contemporary famine early warning systems (FEWS) use remote-sensing data from satellites that detect levels of chlorophyll production in plants as an indicator of food production. Together with economic data on prices and quantities of foods available in local markets, these data provide indications of national and regional food needs, which are used in policy decisions

FEWS: famine early warning systems

WFP: World Food Program

(Gaile & Ferguson 1996). These systems are often conceived and funded by the international community to prevent massive disasters. They are not designed to address localized small-scale vulnerabilities. The fact that food crises occur in Sub-Saharan Africa on a regular basis is evidence of the limitations of the existing warning systems.

Howe & Devereux (2004) have argued for the need to develop a multilevel, graduated definition of famine based on intensity and magnitude measures to complement traditional early-warning systems in a comprehensive humanitarian information system (Maxwell & Watkins 2003). Currently there are no generally accepted criteria of which rates indicate the onset of a famine, and this lack of consensus contributes to delays in intervention and lack of accountability on the part of various stakeholders. The establishment of such criteria would allow for more effective and proportionate responses and greater accountability of food crises. In this proposed universal system, famine intensity would measure the severity of a crisis in terms of anthropometric and mortality indicators and food security descriptors, whereas famine magnitude would assess the aggregate impact of the crisis in affected populations according to excess mortality rates. Such scales would establish standardized criteria for identifying the onset of famines worldwide and would serve as a useful tool for stakeholders engaged in famine prevention and relief.

GEOGRAPHIC INFORMATION SYSTEMS

Geographic information systems (GIS) are playing an increasingly important role in food security. A GIS stores and links cartographic map features with geographically referenced, spatio-temporal data on socioeconomic and other kinds of conditions. GIS methods have been most widely used in the developing world for public health and epidemiology, especially for tracking cases of tuberculosis and malaria, and have become standard tools in humanitarian emergencies (Park & Baro 2003). GIS is especially useful as a component of rapid assessments to identify the magnitude and locations of a crisis and the resources needed for relief operations. GIS has greatly improved ways of presenting and analyzing epidemiological data and spatio-temporal information that has implications for programmatic planning and logistics, resource allocation, and monitoring and evaluation of humanitarian emergencies (Kaiser et al. 2003, p. 137). Further integration of GIS methods in prevention and relief efforts will enable improvements in famine early warning systems, assessments, monitoring and evaluation.

Improving the Aid Encounter: The Role of International Organizations, Government, and Civil Society

Since the mid-1970s with the onset of a world food crisis, the international community has created several structures to monitor, prevent, and respond to global food crises, including the World Food Program (WFP), a branch of the United Nations responsible for obtaining and moving large quantities of food in response to emergencies, global FEWS, and expanded agricultural programs in foreign universities funded by USAID and other bilateral aid programs (Herdt 2004). Traditionally, famine relief in Africa has taken the form of multilateral food aid brokered by large international organizations such as WFP, national governments, and nongovernmental and community-based organizations. Food aid can be essential not only in replacing lost assets but also in lessening the economic threat of famines by helping to preserve existing assets (de Waal 1990). One of the biggest problems associated with food aid has been the inadequacy of African transportation infrastructures for ensuring reliable and equitable food delivery. In recent food crises in Sudan and Ethiopia, for example, food relief piled up in capital cities and intermediate points owing to a lack of available and reliable transportation to distribute food to remote rural areas (Gaile & Ferguson 1996). Also, the high potential for diversion of food aid can be attributed to corruption at various levels. Government corruption and inefficiency are major obstructions to food aid distribution (Lee 2004). Even in the best-case scenario when food aid successfully arrives at its destination, its trajectory commonly ends in a site conveniently located along a main paved road axis for ease of unloading and storage. Because of these logistical constraints, remote villages are rarely served directly by traditional food aid programs.

For more than half a century, millions of people affected by famine have been fed by American humanitarian groups provided with food by the U.S. government. To save money, Congress is considering spending a quarter of the food-aid budget on purchases of food from other countries, although current law requires such purchases to be from American farmers. This change risks cutting out the U.S. middlemen who make significant profits from the food-aid business. Indeed, the funds going to middlemen are as great as those going to farmers. Most major charities have also been tied into this system of contractual obligations and quid pro quo arrangements, and they doubt that there will be as much congressional support for aid if it does not also benefit U.S. farmers (Thurow & Kilman 2005).

[Whereas] parts of Africa are routinely wracked by hunger, some countries often produce surpluses of wheat and corn. In 2003, for instance, the United States sent ~100,000 tons of American-grown grain to Uganda at a cost of $57 million to feed people in the country's north. At the same time, Ugandan farmers elsewhere were producing surplus crops their government could not afford to buy and transport. John Magnay, chief executive of Uganda Grain Traders Ltd., estimates that the United States could have purchased more than twice as much grain if it had bought it locally. He calculates that USAID spent $447 per ton for U.S.

corn delivered to his country. The cost for Ugandan corn was $180 per ton. (Thurow & Kilman 2005, p. A1)

There is no doubt that U.S. farmers and shippers are able to benefit from the bilateral food programs, but is that benefit more important than finding creative and more efficient ways to save lives and protect livelihoods?

Cash transfer programs are gaining more advocates in the African context and are likely to continue expanding in the future. Cash transfers offer several benefits over food aid, especially by significantly decreasing the overhead and transportation costs of delivery, increasing local cash flows, stimulating market growth, and allowing beneficiaries more autonomy to prioritize household needs and to choose how to spend aid in local markets. Critics of cash programs have aired concerns that cash transfers have a higher potential for corruption, are difficult to monitor, and could lead to rapid price increase because of an influx of cash in local markets. In 2005, in Niger, the British Red Cross initiated the first large-scale pilot cash-assistance program in the Tanout region of northeastern Niger to benefit 5700 households in 90 of the most vulnerable villages in Tanout. Each household received a lump sum of $240 to meet household food and livestock needs in response to last year's widespread food shortages and livestock loss. Global positioning satellite points were established for each household for long-term monitoring purposes. The project was well received by local communities who cited the advantages of controlling their own use of the aid. Today, this innovative project is viewed as one of the best success stories during the recent food crisis in Niger.

Recent critics of aid programs have pointed out that donors often remain "trapped in an eternal present" (Keen 1994, p. 215) with little understanding of the historical context or future implications of famines or famine relief operations. In addition, agencies have tended to separate short-term relief efforts from longer-term development initiatives, thereby constructing a false dichotomy between two points that coexist on the same continuum. Famine prevention needs to be more fully integrated into long-term development programs rather than waiting until a crisis erupts. Humanitarian relief should ideally aim to preserve livelihoods, and relief should be linked to longer-term development programs (Pingali et al. 2005). In addition, both emergency and sustainable development interventions should be better tailored to the needs of heterogeneous groups with different income and livelihood strategies and geographic locations (Webb & von Braun 1994).

A Needed Focus on Exit Strategies

An exit strategy for an emergency food program is a specific plan describing how the program will withdraw from a region or population while assuring that the achievement of development goals is not jeopardized and that further progress toward these goals will continue after the program ends. "Exit" refers to the withdrawal of externally provided resources, whether material goods, human resources, or technical assistance, from the operational area. The goal of an exit strategy is to assure the sustainability of the program's impacts and activities.

Any emergency response to a famine or food crisis must be accompanied by appropriate exits from these same emergencies. Knowing how to end an emergency response must be as important as knowing when to begin one.

Disasters or crises often extend beyond national boundaries. In these settings, one must consider the broader regional context. A primary example of cross-border crisis is conflict. For example, one cause of the complex emergency in Côte d'Ivoire, and a critical component of the response, is massive displacement both internally and in neighboring countries.

A second example of a shock that requires a regional approach is HIV/AIDS, a long-wave emergency often exacerbated by other shocks. One common coping strategy for populations facing long-term poverty, conflict, or detrimental changes in the policy or macroeconomic situation is cross-border migration. This is particularly problematic in a region with high rates of HIV/AIDS, such as southern Africa.

Emergency responses in the face of recurrent shocks can be programmed more strategically by undertaking activities that reduce households' exposure to risk and increase their resilience to shocks before they occur. Emergency response is put into a broader framework of risk management and can be effectively linked to safety nets and development activities. We must establish a holistic conceptual framework that focuses on short- and long-term vulnerability. The primary emphasis should be on the risks and resiliencies of households and communities. Such a conceptual framework not only identifies the types of information that need to be collected in assessments, but also identifies the types of interventions appropriate for saving lives in the short term and enhancing livelihoods in the long term. The key to this framework is to illustrate that artificial divisions between emergency programming and development programming are inappropriate. By focusing on vulnerability these distinctions are no longer relevant.

Although often problematic and inadequate, the work of international aid organizations has been indispensable in relieving some of Africa's greatest food crises in recent decades. Alleviating famine, however, should not fall exclusively within the purview of international organizations. African governments must play a major role in improving national-level responses before relying on external sources of aid. Sen (1999) proposed that famines have never occurred in functioning electoral democracies and that democracy is the best guarantee against famine. This statement has been challenged by the occurrence of famines in democratic regimes in India (Bihar Famine) and Sudan

(1986–1989 famine) that ensued despite the presence of democratic governments with competitive elections and a free press (Myhrvold-Hanssen 2003). Although Sen insists on the importance of a free press and active political opposition in preventing famine, one must consider the constraints posed by illiteracy on the ultimate power of the press. Africa has the lowest literacy rates in the world, and this factor limits the ability of the population to react to early warnings issued by the press.

Nevertheless, Sen's link between famine and governance remains a crucial consideration in the future of hunger relief. Famines are not likely to cease without improving government accountability and strengthening civil society. Good governance must include efficient and accountable use of resources, transparent and nondiscriminatory distribution of resources, participatory planning, and control of resources at a decentralized, local level (Webb & von Braun 1994). Good governance also requires the presence of a strong and active civil society, and this is another area in which capacity building is needed. Education is another essential component in reducing food insecurity. Studies of child malnutrition have shown that improvement in women's education is the single most important factor in reducing child malnutrition, associated with a 43% decline in malnutrition (Smith & Haddad 2000). More emphasis on ensuring basic literacy and access to education and health care throughout Africa is an important long-term investment in future food security.

In conclusion, an important paradigm shift is underway in the field of famine and food security studies. Famine is now explained less in terms of an anomalous disaster event and more commonly as a process rooted in long-term social, economic, and political inequalities and sharply exacerbated by the incidence of violent conflict and war. More research on the household-level impacts of famine and contextual knowledge in crisis situations is necessary to understand better the nature, scale, and history of crises and the evolution of different aspects of food security as conditions change during crises (Flores et al. 2005). This type of local knowledge is essential to assess the needs, most effective responses, and role of social actors. Anthropological methods are well suited to play a key role in addressing these knowledge gaps. Anthropologists have added valuable perspectives in famine and food security studies, including the addition of long-term ethnographic studies, integration of qualitative data and local forms of knowledge, and a greater emphasis on the socio-political dimensions of food crises that address power relations.

Future food security for Africa depends on good governance, sound economic growth policies, and active preparedness (Webb & von Braun 1994). Until the underlying issues of political accountability and economic disparity are adequately addressed, in the context of African governance and civil society, by international humanitarian interventions and local development planning, the persistence of hunger will continue to plague most African nations well into the twenty-first century.

ACKNOWLEDGMENTS

The authors gratefully acknowledge the assistance and comments of the following individuals: at the University of Arizona, Professors Jane Hill and Thomas K. Park in the Department of Anthropology; Professor Timothy Finan, Drexel Woodson, and Don Nelson at the Bureau of Applied Research in Anthropology; graduate students Micah Boyer, Lauren Carruth, Allison Davis, Karyn Fox, Aminata Niang, John Mazzeo, Stefanie Herrmann, and Colin T. West in the Department of Anthropology; Timothy Frankenberger and Clara Hagens at TANGO International; Alex de Waal at Justice Africa; Director Steven Loyston and staff from the International Federation of Red Cross and Red Crescent operations in Niger; and Paul Jenkins and Paul Anticoni from the British Red Cross in London. The views expressed in this review are solely those of the authors.

LITERATURE CITED

Bernus E. 1980. Famines et sécheresses chez les Touaregs Sahéliens. *Africa* 50(1):1–7

Berry L, Downing TE. 1993. Drought and famine in Africa, 1981–86: a comparison of impacts and responses in six countries. See Field 1993a, pp. 35–58

Blaikie PM, ed. 1994. *At Risk: Natural Hazards, People's Vulnerability, and Disasters*. New York/London: Routledge

Brown L. 2001. Eradicating hunger: a growing challenge. In *State of the World 2001*. New York: Worldwatch Inst., Norton

CARE-BARA. 1997. *Evaluation de la Sécurité des Conditions de Vie dans le Département de Maradi au Niger*. Atlanta: CARE International

Chambers R. 1989. *Farmer First: Farmer Innovation and Agricultural Research*. London: Intermed. Technol.

Chambers R, Conway G. 1992. *Sustainable rural livelihoods: practical concepts for the 21st century*. Discussion Pap. 296, Inst. Dev. Stud., Univ. of Sussex

Corbett J. 1988. Famine and household coping strategies. *World Dev.* 16(9):1099–112

Davies S. 1993. Are coping strategies a cop out? *IDS Bull.*

de Waal A. 1989. *Famines That Kill*. Oxford: Clarendon Press

de Waal A. 1990. A re-assessment of entitlement theory in the light of the recent famines in Africa. *Dev. Change* 21:469–90

de Waal A. 1998. *Famine Crimes: Politics and the Disaster Relief Industry in Africa*. Bloomington: Indiana Univ. Press

de Waal A. 2004. *Famine that Kills: Darfur, Sudan 1984–1985*. New York: Oxford Univ. Press

de Waal A, Whiteside A. 2003. New variant famine: AIDS and food crisis in Southern Africa. *Lancet* 362:1234–37

Devereux S. 2001a. Livelihood insecurity and social protection: a re-emerging issue in rural development. *Dev. Policy Rev.* 19(4):507–19

Devereux S. 2001b. Sen's entitlement approach: critiques and counter-critiques. *Oxford Dev. Stud.* 29(3):245–63

Devereux S, Maxwell S. 2001. *Food Security in Sub-Saharan Africa*. London: ITDG

Duffield JS. 1998. *World Power Forsaken: Political Culture: Political Culture, International Institutions, and German Security Policy After Unification*. Stanford, CA: Stanford Univ. Press

Edkins J. 2001. *Whose Hunger? Concepts of Famine, Practices of Aid*. Minneapolis: Univ. Minn. Press

Ellis F. 2000. *Rural Livelihoods and Diversity in Developing Countries*. Oxford: Oxford Univ. Press

Ellis F, Mdoe N. 2003. Livelihoods and rural poverty reduction in Tanzania. *World Dev.* 31:1367–84

Finan T, Langworthy M. 1997. *Waiting for Rain: Agriculture and Ecological Imbalance in Cape Verde*. Boulder, CO: Lynne Rienner

Flores M, Khwaja Y, White P. 2005. Food security in protracted crises: building more effective policy frameworks. *Disasters* 29(Supp. 1):S25–51

Food and Agriculture Organisation of the United Nations (FAO). 1996. Commitment 3. Rome declaration on world food security and world food summit plan of action. *Report of the World Food Summit*. Rome: FAO

Frankenberger T. 2003. *Managing Risks, Improving Livelihoods: Program Guidelines for Conditions of Chronic Vulnerability*. Tucson: Tango Int. 2nd ed.

Frankenberger T, Coyle PE. 1993. Integrating household food security into Farming Systems Research Extension. *J. Farm. Syst. Res. Extension*

Gaile GL, Ferguson A. 1996. Success in African social development: some positive indications. *Third World Q.* 17(3):557–72

Gillespie S, Kadiyala S. 2004. *HIV/AIDS and Hunger*. Ithaca, NY: Int. Food Policy Res. Inst.

Haddad L, Gillespie S. 2001. Effective food and nutrition policy responses to HIV/AIDS: what we know and what we need to know. *J. Int. Dev.* 13:487–511

Hendriks SL. 2005. The challenges facing empirical estimation of household food (in)security in South Africa. *Dev. South. Afr.* 22(1):103–23

Hendrie B. 1997. Knowledge and power: a critique of an international relief operation. *Disasters* 21(1):57–76

Herdt RW. 2004. Food shortages and international agriculture programs. *Crit. Rev. Plant Sci.* 23(6):505–17

Howe P, Devereux S. 2004. Famine intensity and magnitude scales: a proposal for an instrumental definition of famine. *Disasters* 28(4):353–72

Hussein K. 2002. Food security: rights, livelihoods and the world summit—five years later. *Soc. Policy Admin.* 36(6):626–47

Kadiyala S, Gillespie S. 2003. *Rethinking food aid to fight AIDS food consumption and nutrition division*. Discussion Pap. 159.

Kaiser R, Spiegel PB, Henderson AK, Gerber ML. 2003. The application of geographic information systems and global positioning systems in humanitarian emergencies: lessons learned, programme implications and future research. *Disasters* 27(2):127–40

Keen D. 1994. *The Benefits of Famine: The Political Economy of Famine and Relief in Southwestern Sudan, 1983–1989*. Princeton, NJ: Princeton Univ. Press

Lee H. 2004. Fasting for food: Ethiopia's years of famine. *Harvard Int. Rev.* 26

Maxwell D, Watkins B. 2003. Humanitarian information systems and emergencies in the Greater Horn of Africa: logical components and logical linkages. *Disasters* 27:72

Mortimore M. 1991. *Adapting to Drought: Farmers, Famines and Desertification in West Africa*. New York: Cambridge Univ. Press

Myhrvold-Hanssen TL. 2003. *Democracy, News Media, and Famine Prevention: Amartya Sen and The Bihar Famine of 1966–67*. Oxford: Oxford Univ. Press

Nelson D. 2005. *The public and private sides of persistent vulnerability to drought: an applied model for public planning in Ceará, Brazil*. PhD thesis, Tucson: Univ. Ariz. Press

O'Donnell M. 2004. *Food Security, Livelihoods and HIV/AIDS: A Guide to the Linkages, Measurement and Programming Implications*. London: Save the Children

Oxfam. 2000. *The Sphere Project: Humanitarian Charter and Minimum Standards in Disaster Response*. Oxford: Oxfam

Park T, Mamadou B. 2003. The Six Cities Project: developing a methodology of surveying densely populated areas using social science assisted and diachronic remote sensing based classification of habitation. *J. Polit. Ecol.* 10:1–23

Park TK, Baro M, Ngaido T. 1993. Crisis of nationalism in mauritania. In *Risk and Tenure in Arid Lands: The Political Ecology of Development in the Senegal River Basin*, ed. TK Park, pp. 87–121. Tucson: Univ. Ariz. Press

Pingali P, Alinovi L, Sutton J. 2005. Food security in complex emergencies: enhancing food system resilience. *Disasters* 29(Suppl. 1):S5–24

Pinstrup-Andersen P, Pandya-Lorch, Rosegrant MW. 1999. *The World Food Situation: Recent Developments, Emerging Issues and Long Term Prospects.* Washington, DC: Int. Food Policy Res. Inst.

Prowse M. 2003. *Towards a clearer understanding of the relation between vulnerability and chronic poverty.* CPRC Work. Pap. No. 24. Chronic Poverty Res. Cent. (CD)

Rahmato D. 1991. *Famine and Survival Strategies: A Case from Northeast Ethiopia.* Uppsala, Sweden: Nordiska Afrikainstitutet

Rangasami A. 1985. Failure of exchange: entitlements theory of famine: a response. *Econ. Polit. Weekly* 20

Roncoli C, Ingram K, Kirshen P. 2001. The costs and risks of coping with drought: livelihood impacts and farmers' responses in Burkina Faso. *Climate Res.* 19:119–32

Rukuni M. 2002. Africa: addressing growing threats to food security. *Am. Soc. Nutr. Sci.* 132:S3443–48

Sen A. 1981. *Poverty and Famines: An Essay on Entitlement and Deprivation.* Oxford, UK: Clarendon

Sen A. 1989. *Inequality Reexamined.* Oxford: Oxford Univ. Press

Sen A. 1999. *Development as Freedom.* Oxford, UK: Oxford Univ. Press

Smith LC, Haddad L. 2000. *Overcoming child malnutrition in developing countries: Past Achievements and Future Choices. Food Agriculture and the Environment.* Discussion Pap. 30. Washington, DC: Int. Food Policy Res. Inst.

Steyn NP, Walker ARP. 2000. Nutritional status and food security in Sub-Saharan Africa: predictions for 2020. *Asia Pac. J. Clin. Nutr.* 1:1–6

Thurow R, Kilman S. 2005. Meal ticket: farmers, charities join forces to block famine-relief revamp; Bush administration wants to purchase African food; lobby says buy American; proposal is stuck in Congress. *Wall Street J.* Oct. 26, p. A1

Vogel C, Smith J. 2002. The politics of scarcity: conceptualising the current food security crisis in Southern Africa. *South Afr. J. Sci.* 98:315–17

von Braun J, Teklu T, Webb P. 1999. *Famine in Africa: Causes, Responses and Prevention.* Baltimore, MD: Johns Hopkins Univ.

Walker P. 1989. *Famine Early Warning Systems: Victims and Destitution.* London: Earthscan

Watts M. 1983. *Silent Violence: Food, Famine and Peasantry in Northern Nigeria.* Berkeley: Univ. Calif. Press

Webb P, Harinarayan A. 1999. The measure of uncertainty: the nature of vulnerability and its relationship to malnutrition. *Disasters* 23(4):292–305

Webb P, Harinarayan A. 2003. Can famine relief meet health and hunger goals simultaneously? *Lancet* 362:40–41

Webb P, von Braun J. 1994. *Famine and Food Security in Ethiopia: Lessons for Africa.* New York: Wiley

Woodson DG. 1997. Lamanjay, food security, sécurité alimentaire: a lesson in communication from BARA's mixed methods approach to baseline research in Haiti, 1994–1996. *Cult. Agric.* 19(3):108–22

Young H, Way SA. 2004. Linking rights and standards: the process of developing "rights-based" minimum standards on food security, nutrition and food aid. *Disasters* 28(2):142–59

Subject Index

See also Biodiversity conservation

Consumption
  globalization of food and, 37–48
    food-based corporations, 38, 40–42, 46–48
    food futures, 46–48
    global governance of, 38, 42–43, 46–48
    hunger and, 37, 47–48
    impact on consumption, 41
    international trade and, 39
    labor relations and, 39
    production systems, 40–41
  See also Food
Convention on Biological Diversity (CBD), 319
Creolization, 433–48
Critical discourse analysis (ecocriticism)
  environmental discourses and, 457, 470–71
Cultural diversity
  globalization and, 153–54, 167
Cultural ecology, 79
Cultural evolution
  cultural primatology and, 171–86
    cultural anthropology and, 180–83
    cultural traits working model, 183–86
    cultural transmission theory, 176
    Japanese foundations, 172
    social learning and, 171–72, 174–76
    traditions and, 171, 176–80
  See also Cultural primatology; Culture
Cultural knowledge
  biodiversity and, 317–19, 321–30
  wine connoisseurship and, 481–93
Cultural primatology, 171–86
  cultural anthropology and, 180–83
  "cultural panthropology" and, 172–74
  cultural traits working model, 183–86
    behavioral patterns, 183–86
    external variables, 183–86
    psychological attributes, 183–86
  cultural transmission theory, 176
  Japanese foundation work, 172
  social learning and, 171–72, 174–76
    mechanisms of, 174–76
    socioecology of animal, 176–80
  traditions and, 171, 176–80
  See also Cultural evolution; Culture
Culture
  classes of definitions, 172
  cultural primatology and, 171–86
  social learning and, 173
    cultural primatology and, 171–86
    cultural traits working model, 183–86
    mechanisms of, 174–76

socioecology of animal, 176–80
  See also Cultural evolution; Cultural
    primatology
Customary law (jus cogens) and, 101–2

D

de Waal A
  integrated model of famine, 524–26
Diamond JD
  overshoot, degradation, and collapse studies,
    60, 63–66, 69–72
Diaspora
  food and memory and, 367

E

Early Homo
  See Homo (early)
Early states
  See Southeast Asia (first millennium)
Easter Island, 64–67, 69–71
Ecolinguistics
  See Environmental discourses
Ecological systems theory, 81
Ecology
  anthropological ecology of practice, 80–81
  anthropological systems ecology, 79–80
  cultural ecology, 79
  ecological systems theory, 81
  environmental history, 80
  historical ecology, 75–91
  landscape ecology, 80
  political ecology, 80
  See also Historical ecology
Ecotourism
  protected areas and, 262–63
Edkins J
  assigning responsibility for persistent hunger,
    525
Environment
  obesogenic, 337–38, 348–51
  protected areas, 251–65
    conflict and, 260
    displacement and, 257–60
    distribution of marine and terrestrial,
      254–55
    ecotourism and, 262–63
    gender practices and, 260–61
    generification of external world and, 256
    global growth of, 253
    globalization and, 253, 265
    NGOs and management of, 252, 255–57

dietary change and adaptive versatility,
209–22
diet models, 213, 219–22
environmental dynamics and, 211–12
fossil evidence, 210–11
paleontological evidence, 215–19
See also *Homo* (early)
Feminism
archaeology and, 1, 5–6, 11
Finance, 15, 17–18, 25–29
deregulation, 18
fictions of, 15, 25–29
materiality and, 25–29
financialization of world economy, 26
quantification, 25–29
effects of, 26
humanism vs., 26
risk and, 18
social studies of, 17
See also Money
Finland
ethnography of, 153–67
archives, 159–65
emphasis on cultural features, 163
necessity of comparison, 153, 159–61
Finnishness, 157–59
language in relationship, 157–59
Finno-Ugric studies, 153, 157–67
languages, 157–67
folklore, 153, 160–67
asking broad questions in a comparative
way, 161, 165
fairy tales and, 165
Finnish and Comparative Folklore
Research, 160
Finnish method of folklore studies, 162
Folklore Archives of the Finnish Literature
Society, 161–62
motifs, 162
rune singers, 164
inventing, 155–57
Christianity and, 156, 160
discovery and conquest and, 156–57
Novgorod, 156
unity and diversity, 157
Kalevala, 161, 165
mythology, 160, 164–65
comparative method and quest for origins,
160
folk religion and, 165
shamanism and, 165
nationalism and, 153, 155, 165

problem of native anthropology, 165–66
recent research trends, 164–65
old materials answering new questions, 165
from texts to performance, 164–65
rune singers, 164
Suomen Kansan Vanhat Runot, 162
Finnish and Comparative Folklore Research, 160
Finnish method of folklore studies, 162
Folklore, 153, 160–67
Finno-Ugric cultures
asking broad questions in a comparative
way, 161, 165
comparative method and quest for origins,
160
Finnish and Comparative Folklore
Research, 160
Finnish method of folklore studies, 162
Folklore Archives of the Finnish Literature
Society, 161–62
motifs, 162
rune singers and, 164
Food, 37–48, 337–39, 348–51, 361–74, 521–35
as commodities, 38–40, 46–48
globalization of, 38–40
international trade and, 39
labor relations and, 39
nation-based agrarian structures and, 39
cultural construct of, 364
defining, 364
food-based corporations, 38, 40–42, 46–48
impact on consumption, 41
nutrition and, 41
production systems, 40–41
food futures, 46–48
gender and, 44, 46, 349, 370–71
global governance of, 38, 42–43, 46–48
Food and Agriculture Organization (FAO),
42, 47
General Agreement on Tariffs and Trade
(GATT), 42
International Monetary Fund (IMF), 42
local exchange and trading systems
(LETS), 43
United Nations, 42
World Bank, 42
World Trade Organization (WTO), 42–43
globalization of, 37–48
gender and, 44, 46
global imaginary and, 43–45
migration and, 45
history and, 361
hunger and, 37, 47–48, 521–35

identity and, 361, 366
invented traditions and, 361, 368–70
labor and, 39
  "feminization" of, 39
memory and, 361–74
  agents of memory, 370–71
  defining, 363–64
  diaspora and, 367
  gender and, 370–71
  as a marker of transformations, 371–72
  nationalism and, 368–70
  nostalgia and, 361, 367–68
  rituals of remembering and forgetting, 372
  sensuality and, 361, 365–66
obesity and, 337–39, 348–51
policymaking and, 47–48
security, 37, 47–48, 337–39, 348–51
sustainability and, 47–48
See also Agriculture; Famine; Food security;
  Globalization; Governance
Food and Agriculture Organization (FAO), 42, 47
Food security, 37, 47–48, 333–35, 348–51, 521–35
defining, 525–26
  four key elements, 526
family early warning systems (FEWS) and, 531
geographical information systems (GIS) and,
  532
Household Livelihood Security Framework
  (HHLS) and, 528
human rights–based approach, 530–31
measurement of, 526
obesity and, 337–39, 348–51
Sub-Saharan Africa and, 521–35
See also Famine

G
Gender
alcohol and, 229, 235–37
food and memory and, 370–71
globalization and, 44, 46
labor and, 39
obesity and, 341–42, 349–51
  body image and, 350–51
  fertility and, 341–41
social practices and
  protected areas and changes in, 260–61
General Agreement on Tariffs and Trade (GATT),
  42
General Agreement on Trade and Services
  (GATS), 103
Geographical information systems (GIS)

food security and, 532
Globalization, 37–48, 153–54, 167, 295–309
conservation and, 253, 265
cultural diversity and, 153–54, 167
food and, 37–48
  food-based corporations, 38, 40–42, 46–48
  food futures, 46–48
  global governance of, 38, 42–43, 46–48
  hunger and, 37, 47–48
  impact on consumption, 41
  international trade and, 39
  labor relations and, 39
  nation-based agrarian structures and, 39
  politics and, 37, 47–48
  production systems, 40–41
international law and, 99–111
  anthropology of, 106–11
  customary law (jus cogens) and, 101–2
  development of, 102–4
  environmental issues, 99–100
  human rights and, 99–102, 104–11
  indigenous rights and, 99, 104–7
  international human rights law, 109
  international peace and security, 99–100,
    106–7, 110–11
  international tribunals and transitional
    justice, 110–11
  knowledge practices and, 108
  law of the sea, 99–100
  regulation of global commons, 99–100
  sovereignty and, 99–100
  terrorism and, 105
obesity and, 337–41, 348–51
sovereignty and
  reevaluation of, 295–309
  violence and, 296
sustainability and, 47–48
See also Agriculture; Food; Governance;
  International law
Governmentality
sovereignty and, 295, 302–6
Governance
global food, 42–48
  Food and Agriculture Organization (FAO),
    42
  food politics and, 37
  General Agreement on Tariffs and Trade
    (GATT), 42
  International Monetary Fund (IMF), 42
  local exchange and trading systems
    (LETS), 43
  policymaking and, 47–48

Inter-American Court of Human Rights (2001), 107

Peruvian Truth and Reconciliation Commission, 106

U.N. Sub-Commission on the Prevention of Discrimination and Protection of Minorities, 104

U.N. Working Group on Indigenous Populations, 104–5

inequality and, 105–6

international human rights law, 109

human rights as a social practice, 109

state retreat and legal failure and, 109

international indigenism and, 192

United Nations and, 104

U.N. High Commission on Human Rights, 106

U.N. Human Rights Commission, 104

Universal Declaration of Human Rights (UDHR), 102, 105

World War II and, 104

Hunger

globalization of food and, 37, 47–48

Sub-Saharan Africa and, 521–35

See also Famine; Food security; Sub-Saharan Africa

I

Indigenous people, 191–203, 317–30

biodiversity conservation and, 317–30

cultural knowledge and, 317–19, 321–30

indigenous memory and, 317–19, 324–30

landscape, 317, 319, 327–28

local knowledge and, 317–19, 321–30

memory work, 328–30

milieu of, 328

place, 317, 319, 326–30

repatriation of germplasm, 320

resilience, 320

sensory embodiment, 317, 321–30

collaboration and, 191, 200–1

community and state and, 199–200

community-based natural resource management (CBNRM) and, 200

conservation and, 191, 196–99

integrated conservation and developmental projects (ICDPs), 198–99

definitions, 192

displacement of

protected areas and, 256–62

environmental politics and, 191–203

ethics and, 191, 201–3

indigeneity, 191, 193

critique of, 193–95

importance of place, 194

modernity and, 191, 193, 203

plasticity of, 194–95

indigenous knowledge, 191, 195–96

intellectual property rights and, 196

indigenous rights movements, 191–92, 201

violence and, 191, 201

international indigenism, 192–93

identity politics and, 192

Kayapó, 197, 199, 202–3

See also Biodiversity conservation

Inequality

human rights and, 105–6

political

hunger in Sub-Saharan Africa and, 521, 523–27

Institutional failure

food insecurity and, 523–27

resource management and, 117–30

common-pool resources and, 119–20

communal action dilemmas and, 119–20

finding solutions to, 128–30

government management and, 117–18, 123–26

local community management and, 117–18, 127–28

private property governance and, 117–18, 120–23

property rights and, 119–20

resource sustainability and, 117, 119–30

Insurgents, 295, 297, 305–8

Integrated conservation and developmental projects (ICDPs), 198–99

International Cooperative Biodiversity Group, 196

International Criminal Court, 110

International law, 99–111

anthropology of, 106–11

customary law (*jus cogens*) and, 101–2

development of, 102–4

Agreement on Trade-Related Aspects of International Property Rights (TRIPS), 103

European Union, 103

General Agreement on Trade and Services (GATS), 103

International Monetary Fund, 103

lex mercatoria, 103

North American Free Trade Agreement (NAFTA), 103

as distinct from other ecologies, 79–81
hard-core postulates of, 75–76
Herodotus and, 78
human-mediated disturbance, 75–79,
81–85
species invasion, 82, 87–90
history of, 77, 87–90
interaction with temporal dimension, 77,
87–90
species diversity, 75, 77, 81–91
transformation, 75, 79–91
Amazonia and, 85–87
See also Historical ecology; Southeast Asia
(first millennium)
Landscape ecology, 80
Language
creolization and, 433–48
Linguistics
Mayan, 279–90
Literacy, 135, 140–45
Local exchange and trading systems (LETS), 43
Longue durée, 78, 79

M

Malnutrition, 521–35
See also Famine; Food security; Hunger
Malthus TR, 59–60, 67–68, 72, 523, 524
Material culture, 135–45
alcohol and, 229–42
meaning and, 138–40, 145
texts and, 135–45
Maya, 61, 64, 68, 71
Maya codices, 497–512
astronomical and calendrical studies, 500–2,
508
commentaries, 502–3
deities, 500
future research trends, 511–12
hieroglyphic texts, 499–500
iconographic studies, 502–3
linguistic and textual analysis, 506–7
Maya–highland Mexican connections, 510–11
online resources, 511–12
provenience and dating, 503–6
Maya writing
epigraphy of, 279–90
historical linguistics and, 279–90
Mayan languages, 279–90
Classic period, 279–90
Memory
defining, 363–64

food and, 361–74
agents of memory, 370–71
diaspora and, 367
gender and, 370–71
as a marker of transformations, 371–72
nationalism and, 368–70
nostalgia and, 361, 367–68
rituals of remembering and forgetting,
372
sensuality and, 361, 365–66
Mesopotamia, 61–63, 68, 71
Norse Greenland, 63
Roman Empire and deforestation, 63, 69
Migration
globalization of food and, 45
Mimesis, 319, 324
Minoan and Mycenaean collapses, 63, 68–69
Modernity, 191, 193, 203
indigeneity and, 191, 193
Money, 15–30
abstraction and, 15, 19–23, 27
Bretton Woods agreements, 18, 25, 26
commensuration, 15, 19–23
deregulation, 18
fictions of finance and, 15, 25–29
humanism vs. quantification, 25
materiality and, 25–29
financialization of world economy, 26
folk theory, 17, 24
general purpose vs. special purpose, 20–22
gold standard, 18
local exchange and trading systems, 19
markets and, 27
materiality of, 27
monetary metaphors, 16
political entities and, 27
quantification, 15, 19, 23–25
effects of, 26
humanism vs., 26
number and, 23–25
See also Finance
Mythologies, 160, 164–65
Finno-Ugric cultures
comparative method and quest for origins,
160
folk religion and, 165
shamanism and, 165

N

Nationalism
ethnography and, 153, 155, 165

food and memory and, 368–70

Native anthropology
    problem of, 165–66

Natural disasters
    food security and, 521–25

Nongovernmental organizations (NGOs), 101, 107, 111, 252, 255–57
    management of protected areas and, 252, 255–57

Norse Greenland, 63

O

Oaxaca, Mexico, 7–9
    Zapotec
        cosmos, 8
        state, 7–8
        texts, 8
Obesity, 337–51
    cultural, behavioral, and economic effects, 348–51
        body image norms, 350–51
        costs of "good" vs. "bad" foods, 349
        decline in home cooking, 349
        fast food, 349
        low levels of physical activity, 349–50
        portion size blindness, 348
        recreational snacking, 348–49
        sedentization, 348
    environment and, 337–38, 348–51
    evolution, 337–39, 341–43
        fertility and, 341–42
        social feeding and, 343
    food security and, 337–39, 348–51
    genetics, 337–39, 343–44, 350–51
    measures of, 339–40
    neurophysiology, 337, 344–48
    nutrition transition, 337–39
    population trends, 337–41, 348–51
    socioeconomic status and, 337–39, 349–51
Obesogenic environments, 337–38, 348–51
Oenology, 481–93
Overshoot and collapse, 59–72
    archaeology of, 59, 67–72
    defined, 60
    studies in, 61–71
        Anasazi, 64–65, 69, 71
        Cahokia, 63, 69, 71
        Easter Island, 64–67, 69–71
        Harappan Civilization, 63
        Maya, 61, 64, 68, 71

Mesopotamia, 61–63, 68, 71
Minoan and Mycenaean collapses, 63, 68–69
Norse Greenland, 63
Roman Empire and deforestation, 63, 69

P

Place
    biodiversity conservation and, 317, 319, 326–30
    indigeneity and, 194
    protected, 257–60
    See also Biodiversity conservation; Protected areas
Political correctness, 10–12, 167
    cultural diversity and, 167
Political ecology, 80
Politics
    alcohol and, 229, 232, 237
    environmental, 191–203
    famine and, 523–27
    globalization of food and, 37, 47–48
    identity politics, 192
Postcolonialism
    alcohol and, 229
    sovereignty and, 295, 297–309
Postmodernism, 1, 2, 5, 9, 11–12
Poverty
    hunger and famine and, 521, 523–30
Power
    sovereignty and, 295–302
Property rights
    resource management and, 119–23
    See also Resource management
Protected areas, 251–65
    commodification and, 262–63
        trophy species and, 263
    conflict and, 257–60
    displacement and, 257–60
    distribution of marine and terrestrial, 254–55
    ecotourism and, 262–63
    gender practices and, 260–61
    generification of external world and, 256
    global growth of, 253
    globalization and, 253, 265
    NGOs and management of, 252, 255–57
    separation from culture, 256–57
    social practices and, 260–63
    use rights and, 257–60
    as virtualism, 251, 253–56

Cumulative Indexes

Contributing Authors, Volumes 27–35

Good I, 30:209–26
Goodenough WH, 32:1–12
Graham E, 27:25–62
Gravlee CC, 34:231–52
Greely HT, 27:473–502
Gremillion H, 34:13–32
Grine FE, 35:209–28
Gupta D, 34:409–27
Guyer JI, 33:499–523

H

Haeri N, 29:61–87
Hammer MF, 31:303–21
Hanks WF, 34:67–83
Hansen KT, 33:369–92
Hansen TB, 35:295–315
Harding S, 28:285–310
Harpending HC, 27:153–69
Harrell S, 30:139–61
Hayashida FM, 34:43–65
Hayes MG, 29:217–42
Hefner RW, 27:83–104
Hill K, 28:397–430; 34:639–65
Hogle LF, 34:695–716
Holtzman JD, 35:361–78
Houston SD, 33:223–50
Hurtado AM, 34:639–65
Hutchinson JF, 30:85–108

I

Igoe J, 35:251–77

J

Jablonski NG, 33:585–623
Jackson JE, 34:549–73
James P, 34:639–65
Johns T, 28:27–50
Johnstone B, 29:405–24
Jones D, 28:553–75
Joyce RA, 34:139–58

K

Kane S, 30:457–79
Kaplan H, 28:397–430
Kaufman SR, 34:317–41
Keyes CF, 31:233–55
King SR, 30:505–26

Kohl PL, 27:223–46
Koo KS, 33:297–317
Korbin JE, 32:431–46
Kulick D, 29:243–85
Kuzawa CW, 27:247–71
Kyratzis A, 33:625–49

L

Lamb Z, 34:619–38
Lambourne CA, 34:639–65
Lansing JS, 32:183–204
LaRoche CJ, 34:575–98
Lederman R, 27:427–49
Lemon A, 31:497–524
Leonard WR, 34:121–38; 451–71
Leone MP, 34:575–98
Lindenbaum S, 30:363–85;
   33:475–98
Little PE, 28:253–84
Lofink H, 35:337–60
Lomnitz C, 34:105–20
Lovejoy CO, 32:85–109

M

Maffi L, 34:599–617
Mahon M, 29:467–92
Manaster Ramer A, 27:451–72
Maskovsky J, 32:315–38
Mason T, 30:457–79
Mathur S, 29:89–106
Maurer B, 35:15–36
Mazzarella W, 33:345–67
McCollum MA, 32:85–109
McDade T, 27:247–71
McDade TW, 34:495–521
McGrew WC, 27:301–28
McHenry HM, 29:125–46
Meindl RS, 27:375–99
Mencher JP, 29:107–24
Mendoza-Denton N, 28:375–95
Merlan F, 34:473–94
Merry SE, 35:99–116
Meskell L, 31:279–301
Meyer B, 33:447–74
Michael L, 31:121–45
Michalove PA, 27:451–72
Mills MB, 32:41–62
Mintz SW, 31:99–119
Monaghan L, 31:69–97

Moore SF, 34:1–11
Moran K, 30:505–26
Moreland J, 35:135–51
Morgan LM, 34:317–41
Morgen S, 32:315–38
Mufwene SS, 33:201–22
Mühlhäusler P, 35:457–79
Mullin MH, 28:201–24
Mullings L, 34:667–93

N

Nazarea VD, 35:317–35
Nguyen V-K, 32:447–74
Nuckolls JB, 28:225–52

O

Okongwu AF, 29:107–24
O'Rourke DH, 29:217–42
Orser CE Jr, 27:63–82
Ortiz S, 31:395–417
Oths KS, 34:231–52

P

Paley J, 31:469–96
Palmié S, 35:433–56
Panter-Brick C, 31:147–71
Parker R, 30:163–79
Patterson TC, 28:155–74
Peace A, 35:457–79
Peirano MGS, 27:105–28
Peregrine PN, 30:1–18
Perry SE, 35:171–90
Peschard K, 32:447–74
Peterson LC, 31:449–67
Phillips L, 35:37–57
Poole D, 34:159–79
Povinelli EA, 30:319–34

R

Redmond EM, 33:173–99
Reed SA, 27:503–32
Reischer E, 33:297–317
Reisigl M, 28:175–99
Relethford JH, 27:1–23
Renfrew C, 34:343–61
Reno PL, 32:85–109
Reyes-García V, 34:121–38

Rhodes LA, 30:65–83
Richards M, 32:135–62
Robb JE, 27:329–46
Robbins J, 33:117–43
Rodman PS, 28:311–39
Rogers SC, 30:481–504
Rosenman BA, 32:85–109
Ross CF, 29:147–94
Rubertone PE, 29:425–46
Ruff C, 31:211–32
Russell KF, 27:375–99

S

Sahlins M, 28:i–xxiii
Sapolsky RM, 33:393–418
Scheinsohn V, 32:339–61
Schell LM, 32:111–34
Scheyd GJ, 34:523–48
Schildkrout E, 33:319–44
Schoenemann PT,
    35:379–406
Schoepf BG, 30:335–61
Schurr TG, 33:551–83
Scoones I, 28:479–507
Segato RL, 27:129–51
Senghas RJ, 31:69–97
Sharp LA, 29:287–328
Shepherd N, 31:189–209
Sherry ST, 27:153–69
Sherzer J, 31:121–45
Shukla S, 30:551–72
Siikala J, 35:153–70
Silk JB, 31:21–44
Silverman EK, 33:419–45
Silverstein M, 27:401–26;
    35:481–96
Silverstein PA, 34:363–84

Simons A, 28:73–108
Smart A, 32:263–85
Smart J, 32:263–85
Smedley A, 30:xvii–xxxii
Smith EA, 29:493–524
Smith ME, 33:73–102
Snodgrass JJ, 34:451–71
Sorensen MV, 34:451–71
Spencer CS, 33:173–99
Spencer J, 29:1–24
Spindler GD, 29:xv–xxxviii
Stahl AB, 33:145–72
Stanish C, 30:41–64
Stark MT, 35:407–32
Steedly MM, 28:431–54
Stepputat F, 35:295–315
Stewart K, 28:285–310
Stocks A, 34:85–104
Stokes M, 33:47–72
Strathern M, 33:1–19
Strong PT, 34:253–68
Stronza A, 30:261–83
Swisher CC, 33:271–96

T

Tainter JA, 35:59–74
Taylor JS, 34:741–56
Teaford MF, 35:209–28
Threlkeld B, 34:619–38
Tomasello M, 28:509–29
Trinkaus E, 34:207–30

U

Ulijaszek SJ, 35:337–60
Ungar PS, 35:209–28

V

Vadez V, 34:121–38
Vail G, 35:497–519
van der Veer P, 31:173–87
Van Esterik P, 31:257–78
Van Wolputte S,
    33:251–69
Vigil JD, 32:225–42
Voland E, 27:347–74

W

Walker PL, 30:573–96
Walsh M, 34:293–315
Warren KB, 34:549–73
Watkins J, 34:429–49
Weiss KM, 27:273–300
Wells JCK, 31:323–38
West P, 35:251–77
Wichmann S, 35:279–94
Wilson ML, 32:363–92
Wilson SM, 31:449–67
Wishnie M, 29:493–524
Wodak R, 28:175–99
Wolfe TC, 29:195–216
Wrangham RW,
    32:363–92

Y

Yelvington KA, 30:227–60
Yon DA, 32:411–29

Z

Zegura SL, 31:303–21
Ziegler TE, 31:45–67

Chapter Titles, Volumes 27–35

Sociocultural Anthropology

History, Theory, and Methods

Economics, Ecology, Technology, and Development

ANNUAL REVIEWS
Intelligent Synthesis of the Scientific Literature

Annual Reviews – Your Starting Point for Research Online
http://arjournals.annualreviews.org

- Over 900 Annual Reviews volumes—more than 25,000 critical, authoritative review articles in 32 disciplines spanning the Biomedical, Physical, and Social sciences— available online, including all Annual Reviews back volumes, dating to 1932

- Current individual subscriptions include seamless online access to full-text articles, PDFs, Reviews in Advance (as much as 6 months ahead of print publication), bibliographies, and other supplementary material in the current volume and the prior 4 years' volumes

- All articles are fully supplemented, searchable, and downloadable — see http://anthro.annualreviews.org

- Access links to the reviewed references (when available online)

- Site features include customized alerting services, citation tracking, and saved searches

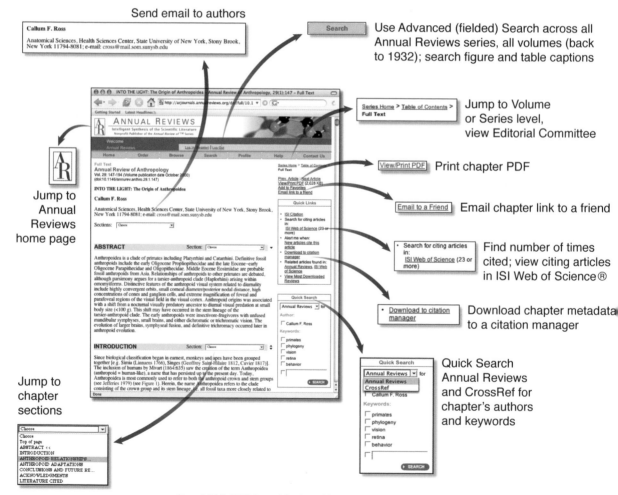

Copyright ® 2006 Annual Reviews, Nonprofit Publisher of the *Annual Review of* Series